The Handbook of Speech Perception

Blackwell Handbooks in Linguistics

This outstanding multi-volume series covers all the major subdisciplines within linguistics today and, when complete, will offer a comprehensive survey of linguistics as a whole.

Already published:

The Handbook of Child Language
Edited by Paul Fletcher and Brian MacWhinney

The Handbook of Phonological Theory
Edited by John A. Goldsmith

The Handbook of Contemporary Semantic Theory
Edited by Shalom Lappin

The Handbook of Sociolinguistics
Edited by Florian Coulmas

The Handbook of Phonetic Sciences
Edited by William J. Hardcastle and John Laver

The Handbook of Morphology
Edited by Andrew Spencer and Arnold Zwicky

The Handbook of Japanese Linguistics
Edited by Natsuko Tsujimura

The Handbook of Linguistics
Edited by Mark Aronoff and Janie Rees-Miller

The Handbook of Contemporary Syntactic Theory
Edited by Mark Baltin and Chris Collins

The Handbook of Discourse Analysis
Edited by Deborah Schiffrin, Deborah Tannen, and Heidi E. Hamilton

The Handbook of Language Variation and Change
Edited by J. K. Chambers, Peter Trudgill, and Natalie Schilling-Estes

The Handbook of Historical Linguistics
Edited by Brian D. Joseph and Richard D. Janda

The Handbook of Language and Gender
Edited by Janet Holmes and Miriam Meyerhoff

The Handbook of Second Language Acquisition
Edited by Catherine Doughty and Michael H. Long

The Handbook of Bilingualism
Edited by Tej K. Bhatia and William C. Ritchie

The Handbook of Pragmatics
Edited by Laurence R. Horn and Gregory Ward

The Handbook of Applied Linguistics
Edited by Alan Davies and Catherine Elder

The Handbook of Speech Perception
Edited by David B. Pisoni and Robert E. Remez

The Handbook of Speech Perception

Edited by

David B. Pisoni and Robert E. Remez

BLACKWELL PUBLISHING
350 Main Street, Malden, MA 02148-5020, USA
9600 Garsington Road, Oxford OX4 2DQ, UK
550 Swanston Street, Carlton, Victoria 3053, Australia

First published 2005 by Blackwell Publishing Ltd

3 2006

Library of Congress Cataloging-in-Publication Data

The handbook of speech perception / edited by David B. Pisoni and Robert E. Remez.
p. cm. — (Blackwell handbooks in linguistics)
Includes bibliographical references and index.
ISBN 0-631-22927-2 (hardback : alk. paper)
1. Speech perception. I. Pisoni, David B. II. Remez, Robert E. III. Series.

P37.5.S68H36 2005
401′.9—dc22

2004016173

ISBN-13: 978-0-631-22927-8 (hardback : alk. paper)

A catalogue record for this title is available from the British Library.

Set in 10/12pt Palatino
by Graphicraft Ltd, Hong Kong

The publisher's policy is to use permanent paper from mills that operate a sustainable forestry policy, and which has been manufactured from pulp processed using acid-free and elementary chlorine-free practices. Furthermore, the publisher ensures that the text paper and cover board used have met acceptable environmental accreditation standards.

For further information on
Blackwell Publishing, visit our website:
www.blackwellpublishing.com

Contents

Contributors

Edward T. Auer, Jr., House Ear Institute. Email: eauer@hei.org

William Badecker, Johns Hopkins University. Email: badecker@jhu.edu

Gregory F. Ball, Johns Hopkins University. Email: gball@jhu.edu

Lynne E. Bernstein, House Ear Institute. Email: lbernstein@hei.org

Z. S. Bond, Ohio University. Email: zbond1@ohiou.edu

Cynthia G. Clopper, Indiana University. Email: cclopper@indiana.edu

Anne C. Cutler, Max Planck Institute for Psycholinguistics. Email: anne.cutler@mpi.nl

Guy O. Dove, University of Louisville. Email: Guy.dove@louisville.edu

Edward Flemming, Stanford University. Email: flemming@csli.stanford.edu

Alexandra P. Fonaryova Key, University of Louisville. Email: Alexandra.key@louisville.edu

Carol A. Fowler, Haskins Laboratories. Email: cfowler@haskins.yale.edu

Bruno Galantucci, Haskins Laboratories. Email: Bruno.galantucci@haskins.yale.edu

Timothy Q. Gentner, University of Chicago. Email: t-gentner@uchicago.edu

Bruce R. Gerratt, University of California – Los Angeles. Email: bgerratt@ucla.edu

Derek M. Houston, Indiana University School of Medicine. Email: dmhousto@indiana.edu

Keith A. Johnson, Ohio State University. Email: kjohnson@ling.ohio-state.edu

Jody Kreiman, University of California – Los Angeles. Email: jkreiman@ucla.edu

Paul A. Luce, The State University of New York – Buffalo. Email: luce@buffalo.edu

Mandy J. Maguire, University of Louisville. Email: Mandy.maguire@louisville.edu

Conor T. McLennan, The State University of New York – Buffalo. Email: mclennan@buffalo.edu

Dennis L. Molfese, University of Louisville. Email: dlmolfese@mac.com

Victoria J. Molfese, University of Louisville. Email: tori@louisville.edu

Lynne C. Nygaard, Emory University. Email: lnygaar@emory.edu

David B. Pisoni, Indiana University. Email: Pisoni@indiana.edu

Lawrence J. Raphael, Adelphi University. Email: raphael@adelphi.edu

Robert E. Remez, Barnard College. Email: remez@columbia.edu

Lawrence D. Rosenblum, University of California – Riverside. Email: larry.rosenblum@verizon.net

James R. Sawusch, University at Buffalo. Email: jsawusch@acsu.buffalo.edu

Núria Sebastián-Gallés, Parc Cientific de Barcelona- Hospital de Sant Joan de Déu. Email: nsebastian@ub.edu

Mitchell S. Sommers, Washington University. Email: Msommers@artsci.wustl.edu

Kenneth N. Stevens, Massachusetts Institute of Technology. Email: stevens@speech.mit.edu

Rosalie M. Uchanski, CID at Washington University School of Medicine. Email: UchanskiR@ent.wustl.edu

Jacqueline Vaissière, Laboratoire de Phonetique et de Phonologique. Email: jacqueline.vaissiere@univ-paris3.fr

Diana Vanlancker-Sidtis, New York University. Email: Diana.vanlancker@nyu.edu

Amanda C. Walley, University of Alabama – Birmingham. Email: awalley@uab.edu

Susan Ellis Weismer, University of Wisconsin – Madison. Email: ellisweismer@facstaff.wisc.edu

Preface

Historically, the study of audition has lagged behind the study of vision, partly, no doubt, because seeing is our first sense, hearing our second. But beyond this, and perhaps more importantly, instruments for acoustic control and analysis demand a more advanced technology than their optic counterparts: having a sustained natural source of light, but not of sound, we had lenses and prisms long before we had sound generators and oscilloscopes. For speech, moreover, early work revealed that its key perceptual dimensions are not those of the waveform as it impinges on the ear (amplitude, time), but those of its time-varying Fourier transform, as it might appear at the output of the cochlea (frequency, amplitude, time). So it was only with the invention of instruments for analysis and synthesis of running speech that the systematic study of speech perception could begin: the sound spectrograph of R. K. Potter and his colleagues at Bell Telephone Laboratories in New Jersey during World War II, the Pattern Playback of Franklin Cooper at Haskins Laboratories in New York, a few years later. With these devices and their successors, speech research could finally address the first task of all perceptual study: definition of the stimulus, that is, of the physical conditions under which perception occurs.

Yet a reader unfamiliar with the byways of modern cognitive psychology who chances on this volume may be surprised that speech perception, as a distinct field of study, even exists. Is the topic not subsumed under general auditory perception? Is speech not one of many complex acoustic signals to which we are exposed, and do we not, after all, simply hear it? It is, of course, and we do. But due partly to the peculiar structure of the speech signal and the way it is produced, partly to the peculiar equivalence relation between speaker and hearer, we also do very much more.

To get a sense of how odd speech is, consider writing and reading. Speech is unique among systems of animal communication in being amenable to transduction into an alternative perceptuomotor modality. The more or less continuously varying acoustic signal of an utterance in any spoken language can be transcribed as a visual string of discrete alphabetic symbols, and can then be reproduced from that string by a reader. How we effect the transforms from analog signal to discrete message, and back again, and the nature of the percept that mediates these transforms are central problems of speech research.

Notice that without the alphabet as a means of notation, linguistics itself, as a field of study, would not exist. But the alphabet is not merely a convenient means of representing language; it is also the primary objective evidence for our intuition that we speak (and language achieves its productivity) by combining a few dozen discrete phonetic elements to form an infinite variety of words and sentences. Thus, the alphabet, recent though it is in human history, is not a secondary, purely cultural aspect of language. The inventors of the alphabet brought into consciousness previously unexploited segmental properties of speech and language, much as, say, the inventors of the bicycle discovered previously unexploited cyclic properties of human locomotion. The biological nature and evolutionary origins of the discrete phonetic categories represented by the alphabet are among many questions on which the study of speech perception may throw light.

To perceive speech is not merely to recognize the holistic auditory patterns of isolated words or phrases, as a bonobo or some other clever animal might do; it is to parse words from a spoken stream, and segments from a spoken word, at a rate of several scores of words per minute. Notice that this is not a matter of picking up information about an objective environment, about banging doors, passing cars, or even crying infants; it is a matter of hearers recognizing sound patterns coded by a conspecific speaker into an acoustic signal according to the rules of a natural language. Speech perception, unlike general auditory perception, is intrinsically and ineradicably intersubjective, mediated by the shared code of speaker and hearer.

Curiously, however, the discrete linguistic events that we hear (segments, syllables, words) cannot be reliably traced in either an oscillogram or a spectrogram. In a general way, their absence has been understood for many years as due to their manner of production: extensive temporal and spectral overlap, even across word boundaries, among the gestures that form neighboring phonetic segments. Yet how a hearer separates the more or less continuous flow into discrete elements is still far from understood. The lack of an adequate perceptual model of the process may be one reason why automatic speech recognition, despite half a century of research, is still well below human levels of performance.

The ear's natural ease with the dynamic spectrotemporal patterns of speech contrasts with the eye's difficulties: oscillograms are impossible, spectrograms formidably hard, to read – unless one already knows what they say. On the other hand, the eye's ease with the static linear string of alphabetic symbols contrasts with the ear's difficulties: the ear has limited powers of temporal resolution, and no one has ever devised an acoustic alphabet more efficient than Morse code, for which professional rates of perception are less than a tenth of either normal speech or normal reading. Thus, properties of speech that lend themselves to hearing (exactly what they are, we still do not know) are obstacles to the eye, while properties of writing that lend themselves to sight are obstacles to the ear.

Beyond the immediate sensory qualities of speech, a transcript omits much else that is essential to the full message. Most obvious is prosody, the systematic variations in pitch, loudness, duration, tempo, and rhythm across words, phrases, and sentences that convey a speaker's intentions, attitudes, and feelings. What a transcript leaves out, readers put back in, as best they can. Some readers are so good at this that they become professional actors.

Certain prosodic qualities may be peculiar to a speaker's dialect or idiolect, of which the peculiar segmental properties are also omitted from a standard transcript. What role, if any, these and other indexical properties (specifying a speaker's sex, age, social status, person, and so on) may play in the perception of linguistic structure remains to be seen. I note only that, despite their unbounded diversity within a given language, all dialects and idiolects converge on a single phonology and writing system. Moreover, and remarkably, all normal speakers of a language can, in principle if not in fact, understand language through the artificial medium of print as quickly and efficiently as through the natural medium of speech.

Alphabetic writing and reading have no independent biological base; they are, at least in origin, parasitic on spoken language. I have dwelt on them here because the human capacity for literacy throws the biological oddity of speech into relief. Speech production and perception, writing and reading, form an intricate biocultural nexus at the heart of modern western culture. Thanks to over 50 years of research, superbly reviewed in all its diversity in this substantial handbook, speech perception offers the student and researcher a ready path into this nexus.

Michael Studdert-Kennedy
Haskins Laboratories
New Haven, Connecticut

To

Alvin M. Liberman

and

Peter W. Jusczyk

Introduction

The major goal of *The Handbook of Speech Perception* is to present the research and theory that has guided our understanding of human speech perception. Over the last three decades, enormous theoretical and technical changes have occurred in perceptual research on speech. From its origins in psychophysical assessments of basic phonetic attributes in telecommunication systems, the research agenda has broadened in scope considerably over the years to encompass multisensory speech perception, speech perception with sensory prostheses, speech perception across the life span, speech perception in neuropathological disorders, as well as the study of the perception of linguistic, paralinguistic, and indexical attributes of speech. Growth in these diverse areas has spurred theoretical developments reflecting a variety of perspectives for explaining and modeling speech perception in its various manifestations. *The Handbook of Speech Perception* was conceived to provide a timely forum for the research community by presenting a collection of technical and theoretical accomplishments and challenges across the field of research.

The scope of the topics encompassed here matches the interdisciplinary nature of the research community that studies speech perception. This includes several neighboring fields: audiology, speech and hearing sciences, behavioral neuroscience, cognitive science, computer science and electrical engineering, linguistics, physiology and biophysics, and experimental psychology. We estimate that the chapters are accessible to non-specialists while also engaging to specialists. While *The Handbook of Speech Perception* takes a place among the many excellent companion volumes in the Blackwell series on language and linguistics, the topics collected here are motivated by the specific concerns of the perception of spoken language, and therefore it is unique in the series.

The 27 chapters are organized into six sections. Each chapter provides an informed and critical introduction to the topic under consideration by including: (1) a synthesis of current research and debate; (2) a narrative comprising clear examples and findings from the research literature and the author's own research program; and (3) a look toward the future in terms of anticipated developments in the field.

In Part I, "Sensing Speech," five chapters cover a wide range of foundational issues in the field. James Sawusch provides a technical summary of current techniques for the analysis and synthesis of speech; Robert Remez discusses several theoretical problems about the perceptual organization of speech and how it differs from other auditory signals; Lawrence Rosenblum presents empirical and theoretical arguments for the primacy of multimodal speech perception; Lynne Bernstein discusses the neural substrates of speech perception; Dennis Molfese et al. describe recent electrophysiological findings on speech perception and language development.

In Part II, "Perception of Linguistic Properties," seven chapters survey the major areas of the field of human speech perception. Kenneth Stevens describes the role of linguistic features in speech perception and lexical access; Edward Flemming discusses the relations between speech perception and phonological contrast within an optimality theoretic framework; Lawrence Raphael provides a detailed summary of the major acoustic cues to segmental phonetic perception; Rosalie Uchanski describes the rapidly growing literature on the perception of clear speech; Jacqueline Vaissière provides an extensive review and interpretation of the contribution of intonation to speech perception; Anne Cutler describes the role of lexical stress in speech perception; and Zinny Bond discusses perceptual functions from the perspective of mishearing, or slips of the ear.

The four chapters in Part III focus on the "Perception of Indexical Properties" of speech. Cynthia Clopper and David Pisoni describe recent findings on the perception of dialect variation; Jody Kreiman, Diana Van Lancker-Sidtis and Bruce Gerratt present a summary and theoretical framework on the perception of voice quality; Keith Johnson discusses talker normalization in speech perception; and Lynne Nygaard reviews research on the integration of linguistic and non-linguistic properties of speech.

Part IV is concerned with "Speech Perception by Special Listeners." Derek Houston offers a perspective on the development of speech perception in infancy; Amanda Walley provides an extensive review of speech perception in childhood; Mitchell Sommers describes recent findings on age-related changes in speech perception and spoken word recognition; David Pisoni reviews findings on the speech perception of deaf children with cochlear implants; William Badecker discusses speech perception following brain injury; Núria Sebastián-Gallés considers speech perception across languages; and Susan Ellis-Weismer examines the recent literature on speech perception in children with specific language impairment.

Part V presents two chapters on "Recognition of Spoken Words." Paul Luce and Conor McLennan discuss the challenges of phonetic variation in word recognition; Edward Auer and Paul Luce examine the conceptualization of probabilistic phonotactics in word recognition.

The final section, Part VI, contains two chapters that present quite different "Theoretical Perspectives" on speech perception. Carol Fowler and Bruno Galantucci discuss the relation between speech perception and speech production while Timothy Gentner and Gregory Ball present a neuroethological perspective on the perception of vocal communication signals.

There are many decisions that face an editor in composing an ideal handbook, one that can be useful for the student and researcher alike. Early in our discussions, we understood that we would not be creating a comprehensive review of method and theory in research on speech perception. For one reason, technical methods and technical problems evolve rapidly as researchers explore one or another opportunity. For another, the *Annual Reviews* already exist and can satisfactorily offer a snapshot of a field at a particular instant. Aiming higher, we asked each of the contributors to produce a lively essay expressing a point of view to introduce the reader to the major issues and findings in the field. The result is a broad-ranging and authoritative collection that articulates a perspective on exactly those critical questions that are likely to move a rapidly changing field of research.

The advent of a handbook can be viewed as a sign of growth and maturity of a discipline. *The Handbook of Speech Perception* brings the diverse field of speech perception together for the researcher who, while focusing on a specific aspect of speech perception, might desire a clearer understanding of the aims, methods, and prospects for advances across the field. In addition to the critical survey of developments across a wide range of research on human speech perception, we also imagine the *Handbook* facilitating the development of multi-disciplinary research on speech perception.

We cannot conclude without acknowledging the many individuals on whose creativity, knowledge, and cooperation this endeavor depended, namely, the authors whose essays compose *The Handbook of Speech Perception*. A venture of this scope cannot succeed without the conscientious care of a publisher to protect the project, and we have received the benefit of this attention from Blackwell's Tami Kaplan and Sarah Coleman; thanks also to our copy-editor, Anna Oxbury. The skill and resourcefulness of Luis Hernandez was critical to the production of the work, and we are grateful for his timely good deeds on our behalf. And, for her extraordinary versatility and assiduousness in steering the authors and the editors to the finish line, we offer our sincere thanks to Darla Sallee. We also wish to acknowledge the valuable contributions of Cynthia Clopper and Susannah Levi who helped with the final proof of the entire book.

David B. Pisoni and Robert E. Remez
Bloomington and New York

Part I Sensing Speech

1 Acoustic Analysis and Synthesis of Speech

JAMES R. SAWUSCH

1.1 Overview

The speech signal is the end point for speaking and the starting point for listening. While descriptions of language and language processes use terms like word, phrase, syllable, intonation, and phoneme, it is important to remember that these are explanatory constructs and not observable events. The observable events are the movements of the articulators and the resulting sound. Consequently, understanding the nature of speech sounds is critical to understanding both the mental processes of production and perception. It is also important to be able to create sounds that have particular acoustic qualities for studies of perception. The focus in this chapter is speech analysis and synthesis as an aid to understanding the processes of speech perception. In analysis, we seek to characterize the energy at each frequency at each point in time and whether the signal is periodic or aperiodic. These qualities are related to the processes and structures of articulation and may be exploited by the listener in perception. In synthesis, we seek to reproduce speech from a small set of values (parameters) that describe the desired articulatory or acoustic qualities of the signal. Our starting point will be the nature of the articulatory system and a characterization of how sound is produced and modified in speech.

1.2 The Speech Signal

In overview, the production of speech sounds involves an air source that passes through the vocal folds. The folds are either held open or vibrate. The "sound" (air flow) is then modified as it passes through the vocal tract. A representation of the human vocal tract, in cross-section, is shown in Figure 1.1(a). The net effect of this chain of events is the speech signal. This characterization of speech production is known as the source-filter model (see Fant, 1960) and is shown schematically in panels b, c, d, and e in Figure 1.1.

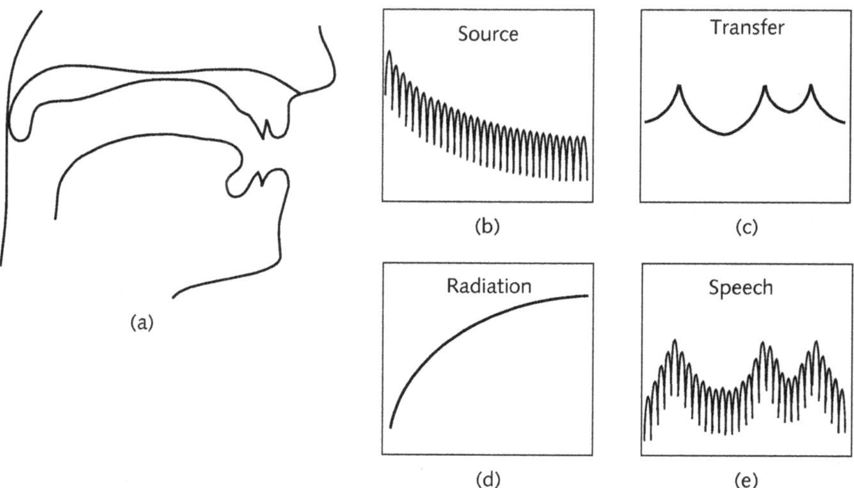

Figure 1.1 Source-filter characterization of speech production with cross-section of vocal tract.

1.2.1 *Source-filter*

As the air stream from the lungs passes through the larynx, it can set the vocal folds vibrating. The rate at which the vocal folds vibrate is determined by their size and the muscle tension placed on them. Adult males generally have longer and more massive vocal folds than children, and adult females are intermediate. Like the strings on a piano, longer, more massive vocal folds produce a lower rate of vibration. Listeners hear this as a lower pitch voice. When the vocal folds are vibrating, we refer to the resulting speech signal as voiced. However, it is also possible for the talker to pass air through the larynx without causing the vocal folds to vibrate. In this case, the resulting speech signal is voiceless. A schematic representation of the spectrum (energy at different frequencies) of voicing is shown in Figure 1.1(b). There is energy at the fundamental frequency (the rate of vocal fold vibration) and at integer multiples of the fundamental (the harmonics).

The air stream then enters the vocal tract. One very simplified way to describe the vocal tract is as a series of tubes. In fluent speech, the talker moves the tongue, lips and jaw from one configuration to another to produce the sounds of speech. At any one point in time, the position of the tongue, lips, and jaw can be approximated as a series of one or more tubes of different lengths and uniform cross-sectional areas. This is shown schematically in Figure 1.1(a) where the tongue, lips, and jaw position are appropriate for the vowel /æ/ as in "bat." The effect of the vocal tract on the air stream passing through it is to pass some frequencies and attenuate others. Every tube has a natural or resonant frequency, set by the length of the tube. Again, like a piano, the long tube (string) has a lower resonant frequency and the short tube (string) has a higher resonant frequency. The resonance characteristics of the vocal tract for the vowel /æ/ are shown schematically in Figure 1.1(c). The peaks in panel (c) represent the resonant frequencies. The

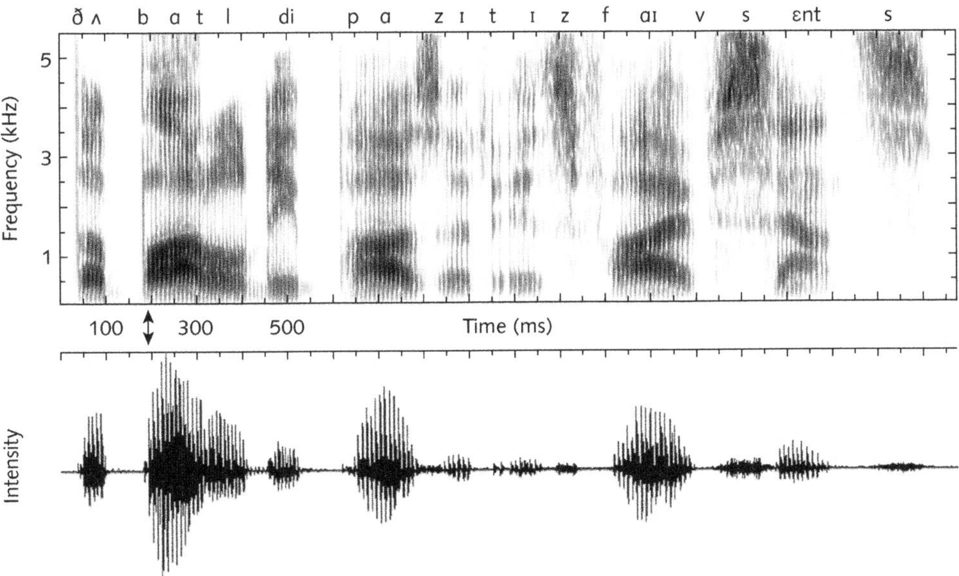

Figure 1.2 Wide-band spectrogram (top) and waveform (bottom) of "The bottle deposit is five cents."

vocal tract thus shapes the air stream and the resulting sound represents the combined effects of the larynx (source) and the vocal tract (filter).

Finally, the sound radiates out of the vocal tract (the effect of which is shown in panel d) and results in the sound spectrum shown in panel (e). The sounds of speech are the result of a source (voiced or voiceless) that is passed through a filter (the vocal tract). The complex nature of the speech signal is due to the dynamic nature of the speech production process. The movement of the tongue, lips, and jaw means that the frequency composition of speech changes as the shape of the vocal tract changes. The bottom part of Figure 1.2 shows an example: the speech signal for the sentence "The bottle deposit is five cents." The vertical scale is in units of pressure while the horizontal scale displays time.

1.2.2 *The digital domain*

Before proceeding, a few words are in order about the process of recording and converting the sound signal into a digital form. A microphone converts pressure in air to a voltage (the electrical equivalent). This is still a continuous, analog signal. Since most modern speech analysis and synthesis is done by computer, we need to convert the signal into a digital form that has sufficient fidelity to preserve the details of the signal that listeners use in speech recognition. This is accomplished by a process of sampling. At regular time intervals, the voltage of the signal is converted to a numerical (digital) form using an analog-to-digital converter. The two key aspects or parameters of this process are the sampling rate and the precision of the conversion (resolution).

The upper limit for human hearing is approximately 20 kHz. So, for high fidelity, the sampling rate needs to represent frequencies up through 20 kHz. To represent a frequency, we need a minimum of two values: one for the increase in pressure and one for the decrease in pressure. Without at least two values, we cannot capture and represent the change over time that corresponds to that frequency. Thus, our sampling rate has to be at least twice the highest frequency that we wish to represent. For human hearing, this means that our sampling rate must be at least twice 20 kHz. With a sampling rate of 44.1 kHz (used for compact disk recordings), we can capture and represent frequencies in the range of human hearing. While musical instruments produce harmonics at high frequencies, there are few acoustic qualities that are correlated with linguistic structure in human speech above 10 kHz. Most of the acoustic information that signals linguistic properties in voiced speech occurs below 5 kHz. Consequently, a sampling rate near 20 kHz is quite adequate for speech and most speech research related to perception uses sampling rates in the 10 kHz to 20 kHz range.

The second key parameter is the precision of the conversion between analog and digital formats. Again, using our CD example, each point in time is represented by a 16-bit number. This provides a range of numbers from -2^{15} to 2^{15} or −32,768 to 32,767 for representing the sound pressure at each point in time. This is sufficient to represent most of the dynamic range of human hearing and can faithfully represent and reproduce loud and soft sounds in the same recording. While the range of intensity in speech is not as large as in music, a 16-bit representation is a good choice to preserve the details of the signal such as the change from a soft /f/ or /θ/ to a vowel such as /ɑɪ/ (e.g. "five" in Figure 1.2).

One final note. When converting an analog signal such as speech into digital form, frequencies higher than one-half the sampling rate need to be removed (filtered) before the conversion to digital form. This is because these frequencies cannot be accurately represented. Unless the signal is filtered before sampling, these frequencies will appear in the resulting digital waveform as distortion at low frequencies (referred to as "aliasing"). Typically, a low-pass filter is used to remove the frequencies above one-half the sampling rate.

1.3 Acoustic Analysis

1.3.1 Fourier analysis

The starting point for speech analysis on a computer is the Fourier transform. Jean Baptiste Joseph Fourier (1768–1830) proposed that any periodic signal can be represented as the sum of a set of sinusoids (pure tones) with particular amplitudes and phases. The Discrete Fourier Transform (DFT) represents a mathematical means of determining the amplitudes and phases of a set of sinusoids that represent the frequency composition of a sound. Put another way, the DFT converts a function (the sound) in the time domain (change in pressure over time) to a function in the frequency domain (the spectrum) which represents the intensity at each frequency. Figure 1.3 shows a brief part of the acoustic signal from Figure 1.2 on the bottom and the corresponding power spectrum for this part of the signal on the top. If we take repeated short samples of the signal and

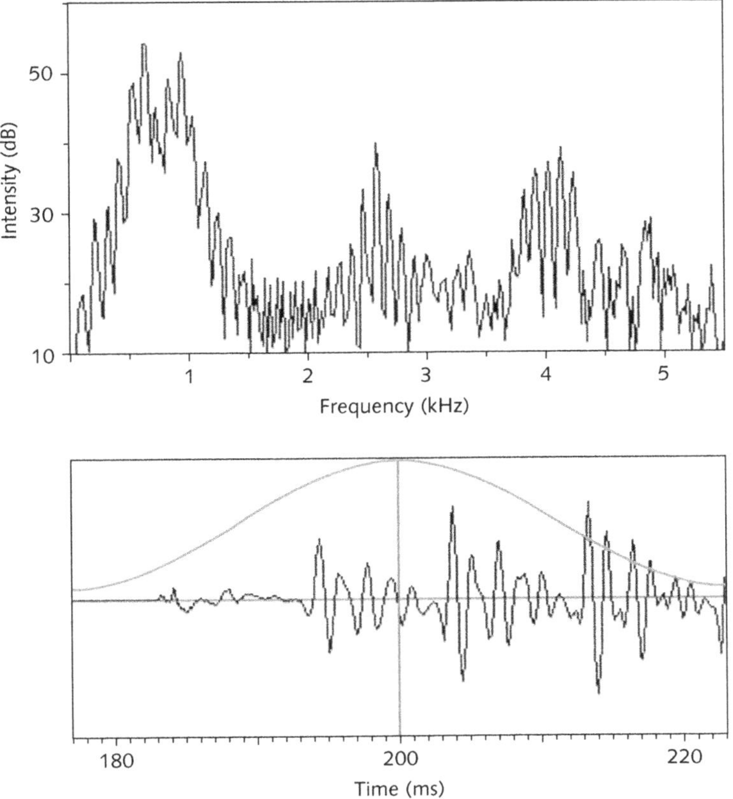

Figure 1.3 Spectral cross section at the release of the consonant /b/ in "bottle" in Figure 1.2.

convert each into a spectrum, we can display the information in the form shown in the top half of Figure 1.2. This is called a sound spectrogram. Time is on the horizontal axis and frequency is on the vertical axis. The darkness in the graph represents intensity with white representing low intensity and black high intensity at that frequency and time. The dark concentrations of energy over time in Figure 1.2 are called formants and these represent the natural resonances of the vocal tract. The lowest frequency formant is termed the first formant (F1), the next is the second formant (F2), and so forth.

This brief description hides a wealth of important details about speech (see Childers, 2000; Flanagan, 1972; Oppenheim & Schafer, 1975). Some of these details are important, so we will expand on them. The first is that this particular analysis was done after the signal had been pre-emphasized. Pre-emphasis has the effect of tilting the spectrum so that the high frequencies are more intense. This process makes the higher frequency formants show up more clearly in the spectrogram. The second important detail is the duration of the acoustic signal that is transformed into a spectral representation. We will focus on durations that are appropriate for examining the acoustic consequences of articulation. There is a trade-off between the length of the signal and the frequency resolution in the spectrum. Time and frequency are reciprocals since frequency is change over time. If a long signal is examined, then we can get a very detailed picture in the frequency domain. That is, we achieve good frequency resolution. If the sample comes from a part of the speech sound where the articulators were moving rapidly, then the frequency composition of the sound would also be changing. However, because we are analyzing this part of the sound as a single entity, the rapid changes will be smeared over time and our detailed resolution spectrum will show the average intensity at each frequency during this time interval. The detailed frequency resolution comes at the cost of low temporal resolution. Figure 1.3 shows a relatively long stretch of our sentence (46.3 ms), centered at 200 ms, which is near the onset of the stop consonant /b/. The individual harmonics in the spectrum are resolved quite well. However, any rapid changes in the spectrum such as formant frequency transitions or the details of a release burst have been lost. A spectrum computed with a long temporal window such as this one is referred to as a narrow-band spectrum because it captures a detailed frequency resolution of the signal.

Figure 1.4 shows the same part of the sound as Figure 1.3. Here, a much shorter segment of 5.8 ms centered at the same point in time as in the previous

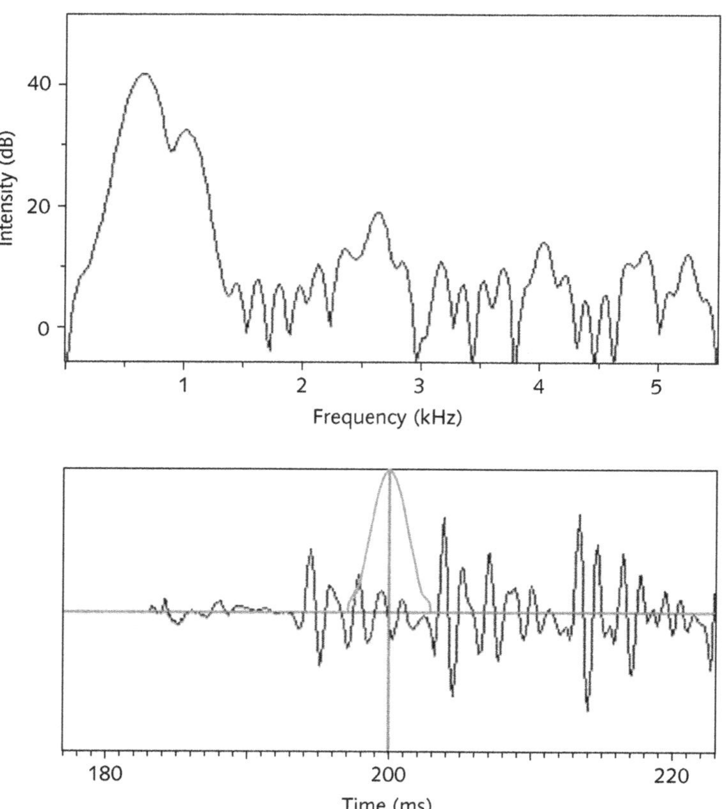

Figure 1.4 Spectral cross section at the release of the consonant /b/ in "bottle" in Figure 1.2.

example has been selected. Because the duration of the sound segment is relatively short, the frequency resolution in the spectrum will be relatively coarse. This can be seen in the top panel of Figure 1.4. The individual harmonics of the spectrum are no longer resolved here. Only broad peaks representing multiple harmonics are present. However, if this 5.8 ms part of the signal were compared to the 5.8 ms before and the 5.8 ms after, we could determine the nature of any changes in the spectrum that would correspond to rapid movements of the speech articulators. This computation with a short temporal window is referred to as a wide-band spectrum. In Figure 1.2 the location of the spectral sections shown in Figures 1.3 and 1.4 is marked by the arrow at 200 ms. Both spectral sections represent the onset of voicing in the consonant /b/. The speech sound at this point contains a release burst followed by rapid formant transitions. These temporal changes are preserved in the wide-band spectrogram and spectral section (Figures 1.2 and 1.4). A narrow-band spectrogram of the sound would partly or completely obscure these rapid spectrum changes.

Our next issue is illustrated by the bell-shaped curve superimposed on the sound in the bottom panels in both Figures 1.3 and 1.4. This curve is referred to as a window function and represents the portion of the sound that will be transformed into the spectrum. The purpose of a window function is to determine which part of the sound will be transformed. In addition to the length of the window, which we have just described, there are also different shaped windows. The bell shaped curve in Figure 1.4 is called a Hamming window. The amplitude of the sound is adjusted at each point to reflect the height of the window function relative to the horizontal axis. The result is that the part of the sound at the center of the window is treated at its full original amplitude and sounds near the edge of the window are attenuated to near zero. A window that tapers at the beginning and end reduces distortion in the spectrum. A fuller treatment of this can be found in Saito and Nakata (1985; also Oppenheim & Schafer, 1975).

The last step is to repeat this process for the entire utterance: select a short portion of the sound, impose the window function, and process with the FFT. This procedure results in a spectrum like those shown in Figures 1.3 and 1.4 for each point in time. To ensure that our analysis does not miss any of the information in the signal, this is usually done so that successive segments of the sound overlap. In order to display the frequency information over time, the height on the graph in Figure 1.4 is represented on a black (intense) to white (quiet) scale and each of our samples represents the information for one point in time in Figure 1.2. The sound spectrogram shown in Figure 1.2 is based on a series of short (5.8 ms) time windows such as those in Figure 1.4 and is a wide-band spectrogram. In this display, the resonant frequencies of the vocal tract show up as the dark concentrations of energy over time. These are referred to as formants.

The fundamental frequency (F0) or voice pitch does not show up as a concentration of energy in this display. Rather, the fundamental appears as the alternating light and dark vertical striations that are seen most clearly in the vowels such as the /ɑ/ of the word "bottle" in Figure 1.2. In order to understand why F0 appears this way, look at the bottom panel of Figure 1.4. Here, the 5.8 ms window is shown superimposed upon the first vocal pulse of the consonant /b/. The 5.8 ms segment is shorter in duration than one vocal pulse (which is approximately 10 ms). The overall amplitude of the signal in the window will change with the precise positioning of the window on the waveform. When the window is positioned over a more intense part of the waveform, the resulting spectrum will have more energy and this appears as a darker vertical band. When the window is positioned over a portion of the waveform with less energy, the resulting spectrum will have less energy overall and a lighter vertical band will appear in the spectrogram. Since the intensity of the sound rises and falls with each vocal pulse, the alternating light and dark areas of the spectrogram recur at regular intervals corresponding to the fundamental frequency (rate of vocal fold vibration). Since the resolution in frequency is inversely proportional to the resolution in time (as described above), the short temporal window used in the wide-band spectrogram of Figure 1.2 does not resolve the individual harmonics of the male talker's voice. Since the individual harmonics are not resolved, F0 does not appear as a separate horizontal dark band. The narrow-band spectrum of Figure 1.3 does resolve the individual harmonics.

The description thus far illustrates the choices that must be made in any speech analysis: sampling rate, window type, window duration. These factors determine the frequency and temporal resolution of the spectrum. Even with careful choices for these alternatives, the spectrogram has some limits. First, since our analysis is of the combined effects of the source and the filtering of the vocal tract, the concentrations of energy that we have called formants are not necessarily the same as the resonant frequencies of the vocal tract. From the standpoint of investigating the acoustic structure of speech and its implications for speech perception and production, this can be a problem. The question is one of what information we need from the sound. If it is the information available to the listener, then the spectrogram is a good first order approximation. A more detailed approximation would be based on an understanding of the workings of the ear and the neural representation of sound. However, if we need to measure the resonant frequencies of the vocal tract, then the spectrogram is limited because the spectrum represents the source as modified by the vocal tract rather than the vocal tract itself. A further complication is that an estimate of the bandwidth of the formants is sometimes also desired and is not easily measured from the spectrogram or a cross-sectional spectrum. The bandwidths of formants are useful in formant synthesizers (discussed later).

What is needed is a method of separating the influences of the source (excitation) from the filter (vocal tract). There are two widely used approaches that attempt to do this: Linear Predictive Coding and cepstral analysis. We will examine Linear Predictive Coding because of its widespread use in extracting formant frequencies and bandwidths for formant synthesis. For a treatment of cepstral analysis, the reader should see Deller, Hansen, and Proakis (1993, ch. 6) or Wakita (1996).

1.3.2 *Linear Predictive Coding*

In Linear Predictive Coding (LPC), the speech waveform is modeled (predicted) based on a source function and a transfer function. This approach treats human speech production as a source exciting or driving a set of resonators. However, the analogy is not quite exact. The glottal source in human voiced speech is more complex than the impulse excitation that is built into LPC so the transfer function in LPC does contain influences of the glottis (see Atal & Hanauer, 1971). In spite of this caveat, LPC does produce a smoothed spectrum that can be used for estimating formant frequencies and bandwidths. In turn, this information can be used to remove the influence of the transfer function (vocal tract) from the speech signal in a process known as inverse filtering. This allows researchers to examine the nature of the source (see Klatt & Klatt, 1990; Price, 1989 for examples). The variant of LPC that is described here is known as the all-pole model (Markel & Gray, 1976). The transfer function can be thought of as a set of resonators or tubes. This neglects any influence of zeros (anti-resonators) where energy in the source is effectively damped or canceled by the transfer function. In human speech there are zeros in the transfer function for certain classes of speech sounds, such as nasals. In all-pole LPC, the effects of zeros are modeled by using additional poles (resonators). We will return to this limitation of LPC later.

Mathematically, LPC models the sound. Each sample in the waveform is predicted based on a linear combination of a set of immediately preceding samples. The first step in LPC is to determine the coefficients of the equation that yields the best prediction of the next sample of the waveform based on the set of previous sample points. This represents the transfer function in the time domain. Using an FFT, the time domain function is converted to the frequency domain. Figure 1.5 shows the resulting LPC spectrum for an 11.4 ms part of the waveform that is centered at the same point in the sound as the wide-band spectrum of Figure 1.4. The LPC shows a smoothed spectrum that makes it easier to measure formant frequencies and bandwidths. In Figure 1.5, the formant frequencies for the first five formants are shown by the dashed vertical lines through the peaks in the LPC spectrum. The formant bandwidth for F5 is shown as the distance (in frequency) between points that are 3 dB below the peak (center frequency of the formant) on either side of the peak. The mathematics for estimating the peak and the bandwidth are fairly straightforward (see Markel & Gray, 1976) and widely used in software for speech analysis.

This brief overview hides a wealth of important details about LPC analysis. For example, the analysis can be done asynchronously to the speech signal or pitch synchronously with one analysis frame per vocal pulse. The order of the LPC can be adjusted depending upon the source characteristics of the portion of the waveform with more coefficients used for voiced parts of the signal and fewer for voiceless parts. A fuller description of these choices and others is necessary to understanding the limits and uses of LPC, but it is beyond the bounds of this chapter. A good starting point for the adventurous (and mathematically inclined) reader is Markel and Gray (1976) or Deller et al. (1993). Childers (2000) provides a good technical overview with software to illustrate the process.

The LPC can be used to measure formant frequencies and bandwidths because it makes assumptions about the nature of the speech signal: Speech can be modeled accurately using an all-pole model excited by an impulse. Then, we separate the transfer function from the impulse source. This results in a temporal signal that has less influence of the source (glottis) and more clearly reflects the influence of the vocal tract than the original sound. Thus, the peaks in the spectrum of the predicted function are a reasonable approximation to the resonant frequencies of the vocal tract. In performing an LPC analysis, as in the basic spectral analysis, a sample of the waveform of a particular size is chosen and a windowing function

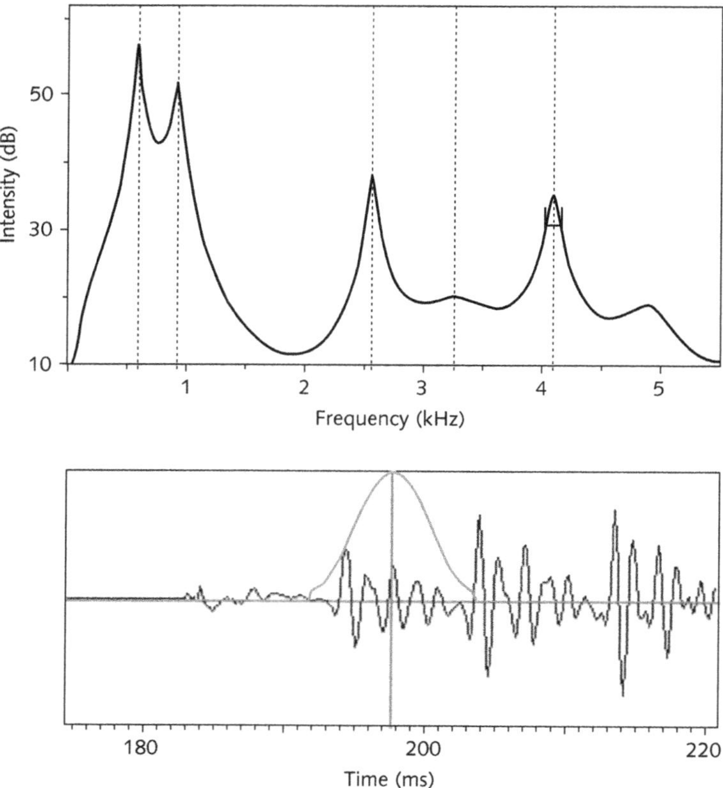

Figure 1.5 LPC spectrum showing the frequencies of the first five formants and the bandwidth of the fifth formant at the release of the consonant /b/ in "bottle."

such as the Hamming window is imposed upon the speech segment. Also, like the basic spectral analysis, the speech signal is typically pre-emphasized to tilt the spectrum upward with increasing frequency. This increases the intensity of the higher frequency energy in the signal and leads to a more accurate estimation of the higher frequency formants.

One additional parameter must be chosen: the order of the LPC. The researcher must choose the number of poles to use in the model. Using too few poles will result in a formant being missed or having two closely spaced formants merged in the analysis. Using too many may result in spurious peaks in the estimated spectrum. The choice of the number of poles is reducible to the sampling rate of the sound (which determines the upper frequency limit of the spectrum) and the length of the talker's vocal tract. For a male talker, Markel and Gray suggest that a good rule of thumb is the sampling rate in kHz plus 4 or 5. With a sampling rate of 10 kHz, 14 or 15 would be appropriate as the LPC order. The LPC spectrum in Figure 1.5 uses 14 poles with a sampling rate of 11,050 Hz. With an adult female, the vocal tract is shorter and the order of the LPC can be slightly less because fewer formants are present in the spectrum (see Atal & Hanauer, 1971 or Markel & Gray, 1976).

Since LPC is often used to measure formant frequencies over entire syllables, words, or phrases, it is convenient to have an automated method for making the measurement. Markel and Gray (1976; see also McCandless, 1974 or Childers, 2000 for a summary and software) provide a thorough treatment of this process. There are a number of potential problems that any user of automated formant tracking should be aware of. Before describing these, we should note some basics of how automated formant tracking works. The starting point is the "raw" data of the peaks and their bandwidths from each LPC spectral section (see Figure 1.5). In addition, we need an assessment of the source of the speech signal as voiced or not. These data can then be converted to formant tracks using a set of constraints. The first constraint is to define a frequency region for each formant and starting values. Furthermore, this region and starting values should be scaled for the vocal tract length of the talker. For a male voice, the search for F1 could be confined to the frequency region of 220 Hz to 900 Hz with a starting value in the area of 450–500 Hz. Similarly, bounds and starting values for F2, F3, F4, and F5 can be established.

Second, we use a continuity constraint. The value for any particular formant at one point in time is likely to be similar to the time before and the time after. The formants do change in frequency over time, but these changes tend to be smooth even when they are fairly rapid. The third constraint is a bandwidth constraint. During voiced speech, the formants tend to be reasonably well defined as peaks in the LPC spectrum. A very broad peak (with wide bandwidth) is not likely to be one of the formants. Using these constraints, peaks can be assigned to formants. The usual starting point is to assign the lowest frequency peak to the first formant, the next peak to the second formant, and so forth. If the second formant is not found in a particular spectral section (see below), these constraints will keep the peak corresponding to the third formant from being inadvertently assigned to the second formant. In addition, a value can be assigned to any missing formants based on the idea that changes between points in time will be smooth. That is, we can fill in missing values by interpolating between points in time with known values.

1.3.3 *Potential problems in speech analysis*

There are a number of problems that may be encountered in attempting to measure the formants in speech. The first is very simple. Sometimes a formant is not evident in the speech signal. To understand how this can happen, we need to go back to the source-filter model of production. In voiced speech, the source is a harmonic spectrum consisting of a fundamental and its harmonics. This source spectrum passes through the vocal tract, which acts as a set of resonators. Those parts of the source spectrum that are a good match to the resonant frequencies pass through while other harmonics are attenuated. Peaks in the resulting spectrum will be good estimates of the vocal tract resonances to the extent that harmonics of the fundamental were reasonably close to the vocal tract resonant frequencies in production.

With a low fundamental frequency, the harmonics are closely spaced. In this case, as shown for the vowel /ɑ/ on the top in Figure 1.6(a), it is reasonably

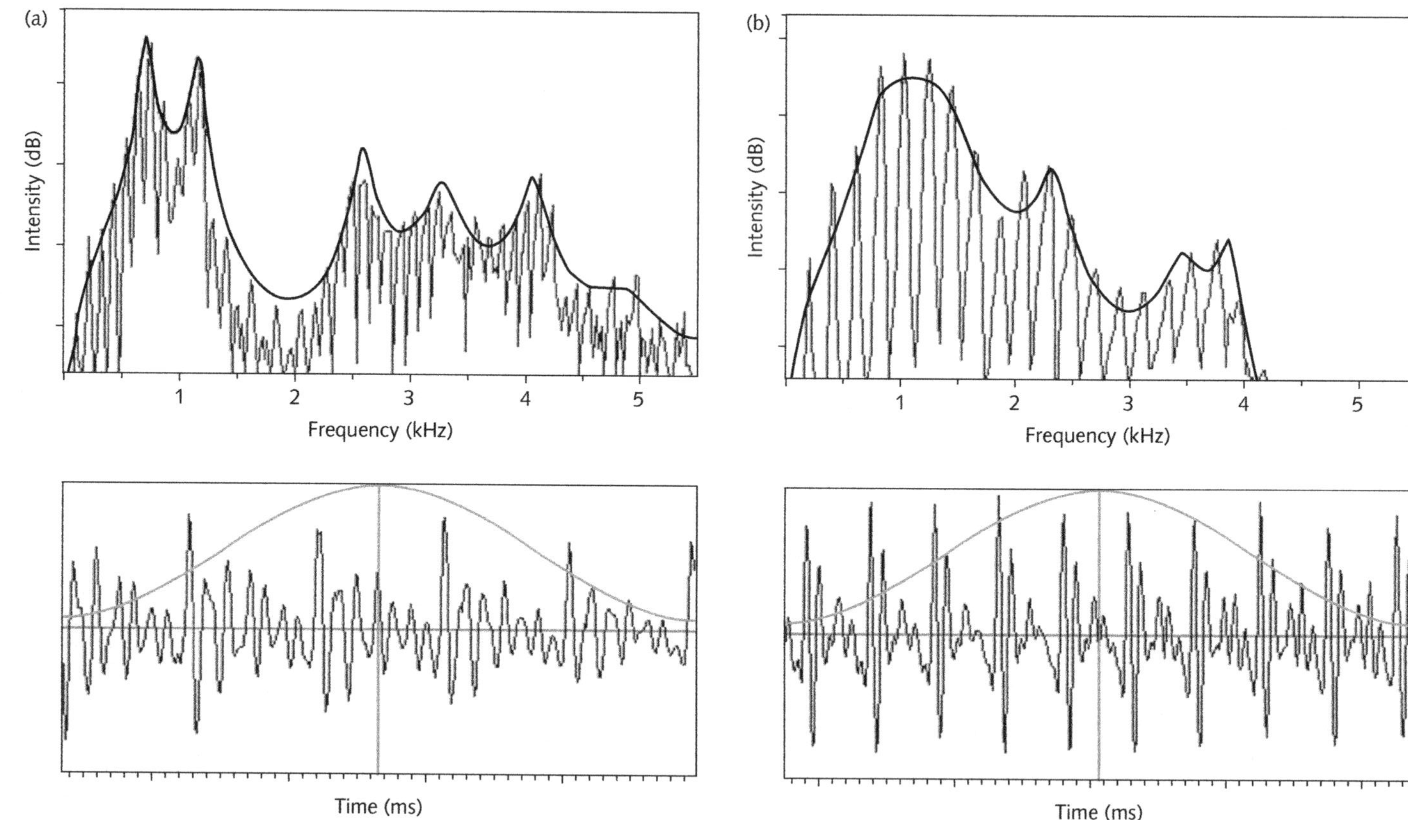

Figure 1.6 Narrow-band spectral sections and LPC of the vowel /ɑ/ spoken by a male (a) and female (b).

likely that at least one harmonic will be close to each formant (resonance) so that the peaks in the spectrum will correspond to the formants. With a higher fundamental frequency, as shown on the bottom in Figure 1.6(b) for a female voice with the same vowel, the harmonics are more widely spaced. If a vocal tract resonance falls between harmonics, then the resulting sound may not have sufficient energy at the resonant frequency to produce a peak in the spectrum. If two formants are close in frequency, then all of the harmonics near the two formants may be similar in intensity. As the fundamental gets higher, these problems get worse. Since the average female fundamental is nearly twice that of the average male, these problems are more pronounced for female speech. The average fundamental frequency for a child is even higher and it can be difficult to find either F1 or F2 in any particular spectral section in a child's voice. Using LPC for the analysis will not avoid this problem. The signal does not contain the spectral peak so there is no resonator (pole) to model.

This problem is shown in the narrow band spectrum and LPC (smooth curve) in Figure 1.6(b). The average F0 in this portion of the vowel /ɑ/, spoken by a female, is 220 Hz. There should be two formants (F1 and F2) in the vicinity of 1100 Hz. Only a single, broad peak can be found in the spectrum and LPC. The solution is to move to spectral sections at other points in time. Since F0 and the formants change over time, it should be possible to find each of the formants in some frames and then, as described above, use continuity constraints to estimate the missing values. In the case of the sound in Figure 1.6(b), moving to an earlier or later part of the sound reveals a first formant frequency above 900 Hz and a second formant below 1300 Hz. Of course, if the parts of the speech signal where the values are missing correspond to speech sounds with rapid changes in articulation, this estimation process will miss the rapid changes and can be inaccurate.

A second area that needs special attention is the measurement of nasals. When the velum is lowered during speech, air is allowed to flow into the nasal tract in addition to the vocal tract. This produces additional resonances and antiresonances. The nasal resonances show up as peaks in the spectrum and the antiresonances show up as troughs (regions of very low energy) in the spectrum. If automated formant tracking is used with LPC analysis, it is possible that a nasal resonance will be misidentified as a formant. There are automated procedures for dealing with this (see Childers, 2000 for a summary). However, hand correction based on an inspection of the spectrum may be necessary. If precise estimation of the location of the nasal zeros is needed, as would be the case in attempting to precisely synthesize a particular talker's utterances, then once again hand inspection of the spectrum is usually necessary.

1.3.4 *Other forms of analysis*

The human auditory system performs the same task of converting changes in air pressure into a frequency representation that we have been discussing. However, there are a number of critical differences between the sound spectrogram or LPC and human hearing. If our goal is to represent the sound information in a manner that reflects human perception then these differences are very important. Perhaps the most important difference is in the frequency scale. All of the spectral sections and spectrograms that have been presented use a linear frequency scale. The distance between adjacent points on this scale is a constant. This is not the case in human hearing. At low frequencies, in the range up to about 500 Hz, the relation between physical differences in frequency and perceived differences in pitch is roughly linear. Above that point, it is approximately logarithmic. That is, the human scale is compressed. Another way of describing this is that at low frequencies, humans have good frequency resolution. Above about 500 Hz, the frequency resolution diminishes as frequency increases. However, the corresponding temporal resolution increases. This relation between frequency and frequency resolution is found in studies of masking that investigate which frequencies in a sound (the mask) make it difficult to perceive some aspect of a second sound (the target) (see Moore, 1988; Patterson & Moore, 1986). This results in an estimate of human frequency resolution that is usually called the critical band.

A first step in approximating the information in human hearing is to "re-filter" a simple spectral analysis into a representation based on critical bands. The spectral information from an FFT is band-pass filtered using a filter bank where the width of the filter is fixed up to about 500 Hz and above 500 Hz is proportional to the center frequency of the filter. The precise bandwidths can be derived from critical band or critical ratio scales that reflect the results of masking experiments. This approach produces a spectral representation (frequency scale) that more closely reflects human perception. However, since it is based on a conversion of a linear analysis, the resulting information does not accurately capture the details of human temporal sensitivity. In some circumstances, this may be sufficient. Forrest, Weismer, Milenkovic, and Dougall (1988), Kewley-Port (1983), Klatt (1982), and Sawusch and Gagnon (1995) have all used this type of representation in attempts at modeling aspects of human speech perception. An alternative that accomplishes the same goal is exemplified in the work of Syrdal and Gopal (1986). They converted the formant frequencies for a set of vowels to a Bark scale (Zwicker & Terhardt, 1980). The Bark scale is similar to using critical bands and approximates human hearing more closely than a simple linear frequency scale.

A second step is to model, more closely, the analysis of sound provided by the peripheral auditory system. In this case, both the temporal and the spectral properties of the system are important. Seneff (1988) and Shamma (1988) have described basic analyses that mimic human processing and the relevance of this for human speech recognition. Patterson, Allerhand, and Giguère (1995) described a model of the peripheral coding of sound that is consistent with both perceptual data from masking studies and neurophysiological data from single-cell recordings in animals. The behavior of their model is like a hybrid of narrow- and wide-band spectrograms. At low frequencies, individual harmonics in the spectrum are resolved as in a narrow-band spectrogram. At higher frequencies, harmonics are not resolved. However, information about the fundamental is preserved in the temporal pattern of the information, much as it is in a wide-band spectrogram.

As an example of differences between human hearing and the spectrogram, consider the vowel /i/. The second and third formants are typically high in frequency and close to one another (Peterson & Barney, 1952). Chistovich has proposed that the second and third formants in this frequency region are not resolved separately in human perception. In place of the separate F2 and F3 formants, Chistovich and Lublinskaya (1979) proposed that a single spectral peak representing the merging of F2 and F3 is used in human perception. Another way of saying this is that the qualities that can be measured in the sound spectrum are not necessarily the cues used by a listener in recognizing the sounds of speech. To the extent that the representation of sound by the peripheral auditory system and a sound spectrogram or LPC are different, researchers must use a form of measurement appropriate to their goals. While an LPC analysis is appropriate for determining a set of values to use with a speech synthesizer (see below), it may not be appropriate and may even be misleading when used to model human perceptual processes (Klatt, 1982).

1.4 Speech Synthesis

In early research on speech perception, synthetic speech was generated with hardware synthesizers such as the Pattern Playback (Cooper, Liberman, & Borst, 1951), the parallel resonance synthesizer system at Haskins Laboratories (Scott, Grace, & Mattingly, 1966), and the OVE (Liljencrants, 1968). Klatt (1980; Klatt & Klatt, 1990) provided a description of a computer software implementation of a formant synthesizer. This synthesizer has been widely used in speech research. The focus here will be on the use of Klatt's software-based approach because of its flexibility.

1.4.1 Cascade/parallel formant synthesis

The Klatt (1980) software synthesizer is a cascade/parallel design. The cascade branch acts as a set of resonators in series. This means that the F2 resonator acts upon the source after it has already been modified by the F1 resonator. This basic design was originally described by Fant (1960) and is also embodied in the OVE synthesizer (Liljencrants, 1968). To specify each formant, a center frequency, bandwidth, and amplitude are needed. However, because of the cascaded design, only the formant frequencies and bandwidths are free to vary. The formant amplitudes are determined from the individual formant frequencies, their bandwidths, and formant interactions. In the cascade branch of the Klatt synthesizer, the user controls the frequency and bandwidth of the formants and the amplitudes are set automatically. In addition to the formant resonators, two additional resonators are present in the cascade section: a nasal pole and a nasal zero. These are used to produce a pole (formant) and a zero (anti-formant or trough in the spectrum) for nasal consonants and vowels. The driving source for the cascade branch can be either a periodic, voiced source or an aperiodic source (aspiration).

The parallel branch of the synthesizer is used to synthesize fricatives, affricates, and plosive bursts associated with stop consonants. It can also be used with the voiced source to achieve more control of the details of the sound. In the parallel branch the formant resonators act independently of one another and their effects on the source are summed to produce the output. Consequently, the frequency, bandwidth, and amplitude for each resonator (formant) must all be specified. Holmes (1983) has argued that this type of parallel configuration is actually preferred over the cascade configuration because of the ability to copy the details of specific voices and produce natural sounding synthetic speech.

The parallel configuration is preferred for the synthesis of fricatives because of interactions that take place when a narrow constriction is present in the vocal tract. For example, in producing an /ʃ/, the tongue is raised and a narrow opening is present between the tongue and the palate. As air moves through this narrow opening, it produces turbulence. The "noise" of this turbulence is then shaped by the part of the vocal tract following the constriction (see Stevens, 1999, pp. 175–9). There are also zeros in the spectra of fricatives (see Fant, 1960; Klatt, 1980; Stevens, 1999 for details). The solution to modeling the acoustic structure of fricatives is to control the amplitude as well as the bandwidth and frequency of each resonator independently (in parallel). This allows the synthesizer to approximate the complex spectra of fricatives at the additional cost of precisely controlling amplitude parameters for all of the formants.

In the Klatt (1980) synthesizer, the voice source was designed to mimic a male voice. Klatt and Klatt (1990) describe a modified version of the Klatt (1980) synthesizer whose major changes involve modifications in the voicing source. A revised model of voicing with more flexible control of the details of the glottal wave shape and degree of breathiness was implemented. These changes allow synthesis of a reasonably high quality female voice. Using the available parameters of the earlier synthesizer and scaling the fundamental frequency and formant parameters to reflect a female voice resulted in a voice that sounded more like a scaled male voice than like a female voice. The problem is that the female voice is not simply a scaled male voice (see Henton, 1999 for review). Klatt and Klatt (1990), in their review of research on acoustic measurements of male and female voices, noted that one consistent finding was that the open quotient for females was larger than for males. The open quotient is the percentage of a pitch period during which the vocal folds are open. Klatt and Klatt summarize the data as showing a 50% open quotient for males and a 60% quotient for females (see also Price, 1989). The appearance of breathiness in female voices was much less consistent and was also found for male speech. Finally, the incidence of creaky voice, in which the fundamental frequency drops to a lower than normal value and the open period is shorter than normal, seems to be more common in males (see also Henton, 1999).

The Klatt and Klatt synthesizer includes control parameters for the open quotient (OQ) and the tilt of the spectrum (attenuation of high frequencies relative to low, see Cranen & Schroeter, 1996 for an articulatory rationale). By adjusting OQ, tilt, and the degree of aspiration (AH) it is possible to synthesize a large range of natural sounding voices, including female and breathy speech. Klatt and Klatt also describe the results of a detailed synthesis experiment in which various acoustic parameters related to breathiness in a voice were varied. However, in spite of the improvements in speech synthesis, both Klatt (1987) and Henton (1999) have noted that we are still a substantial way from routine speech synthesis, by rule, of natural sounding female speech.

1.4.2 *Synthetic speech in perceptual experiments*

Since the early studies of speech perception using the Pattern Playback at Haskins Laboratories (e.g., Delattre, Liberman, & Cooper, 1955), synthetic speech has been

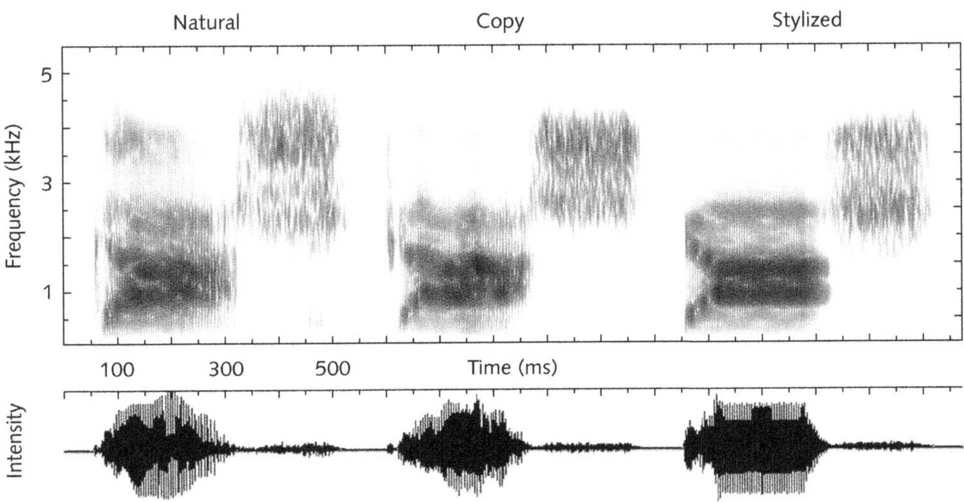

Figure 1.7 Wide-band spectrograms of /gaʃ/ ("gosh") spoken by a female (left), copy synthesis (center), and stylized synthesis (right).

used extensively to study the relationship between attributes of the sound, such as formant frequencies, and listeners' perception. From these studies we have learned a great deal about speech perception and speech cues (see Raphael, this volume). The synthetic stimuli used in experiments have ranged from highly stylized "cartoons," in which only one or two attributes of the signal are varied, to highly natural sounding tokens based on copy synthesis that have been used to explore the factors that underlie the perception of naturalness and voice quality. Figure 1.7 contains sound spectrograms of one natural and two synthetic versions of the word /gaʃ/ ("gosh") in a female voice. On the right is a highly stylized, but intelligible, version. It contains no release burst at the onset of /g/, the vowel is steady-state with no change in the formants over time, there are no formant transitions into the fricative /ʃ/, and a constant F0 (monotone) has been used. The syllable in the center is the result of copy synthesis. The F0, formant frequencies, and bandwidths of the natural syllable (on the left) were tracked and then hand edited. Both synthetic utterances were generated with the Klatt and Klatt (1990) synthesizer in cascade mode.

At times it has seemed as though our view of what constitute the cues that drive perception was conditioned by the technology for measuring the speech signal. Early research focused on formant frequencies and led to the description of a set of acoustic cues for perception. The mapping between speech cues and percept was found to be complex (see Liberman, Cooper, Shankweiler, & Studdert-Kennedy, 1967 for a review) and has led many investigators to conclude that there is no invariant, one-to-one mapping between acoustic attributes and perception. However, this has also led some investigators to question whether the focus on formant frequencies in perception is a mistake (e.g. Blandon, 1982). As investigators have examined the speech signal in other ways, alternative descriptions of the relevant information for perception have been proposed (Forrest et al., 1988;

Stevens & Blumstein, 1978; Zahorian & Jagharghi, 1993). As an example, Stevens and Blumstein (1978) and Forrest et al. (1988) both proposed that the shape of the short-term spectrum determined perception (for stops and voiceless obstruents respectively). While the details of their proposals differ, the emphasis was clearly on a description of the signal that did not emphasize formants and their frequencies. Furthermore, the shape of the short-term spectrum is generally correlated with the frequency and intensity of the formants. Thus, these alternative proposals do not deny that the formants carry information relevant to perception. Rather, the debate is over the best way to characterize the information in the speech spectrum that is exploited by the listener in perception.

The key to evaluating these alternative proposals again lies in the use of the techniques of analysis and synthesis described here. As an example, Lahiri, Gewirth, and Blumstein (1984) proposed that change in the shape of the short-term spectrum, from release to the onset of voicing, was the basis for perception of bilabial and alveolar places of articulation in stops. They gave a detailed, computational description of the means for determining the change in shape of the short-term spectrum. They also showed that their description accurately classified natural stops in multiple languages. A thorough test of this proposal requires that synthetic stimuli be generated that are classified differently by different theories. For example, a /bɑ/ can be generated based on copy synthesis of the syllables of a talker. Then, the formant bandwidths and amplitudes (but not the formant frequencies) can be modified so that the change over time from release to the onset of voicing matches the description of Lahiri et al. for a /d/ rather than a /b/. This new syllable has the formant tracks for one place of articulation but the short-term spectrum for another place of articulation. Dorman and Loizou (1996) and Richardson (1992) generated stimuli like these and presented them to listeners. Listeners' responses generally followed the movement of the formants rather than the description proposed by Lahiri et al.

1.4.3 *Challenges in speech synthesis*

One of the challenges in speech synthesis has already been noted: synthesizing natural sounding female (or child) speech. Careful copy synthesis can produce very natural sounding speech for different voices. The challenge for the future is to codify the "art" of copy synthesis so that it can be automated and expressed as a set of rules. As Klatt (1987) noted over a decade ago and is still the case (see Henton, 1999), the quality of speech synthesized by rule is high in intelligibility but still not natural sounding. Natural sounding synthesis by rule would be very useful in studies of spoken language processing because it would offer a stimulus with more control than available in natural speech. One obstacle to natural sounding synthesis by rule may lie in the approach to synthesis. Copy synthesis involves tailoring the control parameters for a synthesizer to mimic the details of a particular talker's utterances. In doing this, the synthetic utterance contains both multiple acoustic correlates to phonetic distinctions and acoustic correlates to a talker's voice. It may be that for synthetic speech to really sound natural it will also have to sound like a particular talker. As listeners, humans have extensive experience with many voices. Naturalness, for a listener, may depend upon similarity to an actual voice or voices. The perception of naturalness may also interact with intelligibility and phonetic perception. The acoustic correlates to phonetic distinctions vary, in their details, across talkers. Listeners, in turn, use acoustic cues to both talker voice and phonetic quality in making phonetic judgments (e.g. Mullennix & Pisoni, 1990).

A related issue is whether the acoustic qualities in a synthetic stimulus are processed by a listener is the same way that the listener would process natural speech. As an example, speaking rate and the durations of speech segments influence perception (see Miller, 1981). These effects are readily found with synthetic syllables. However, would they be found with natural speech? Put another way, are the effects of speaking rate due to the degraded or ambiguous nature of the synthetic syllables used in perceptual experiments? This issue was raised by Shinn, Blumstein, and Jongman (1985) with respect to the synthetic stimuli often used in speaking rate experiments. Miller and Wayland (1993) and Newman and Sawusch (1996) have both shown that influences of speaking rate also occur for high quality speech syllables including edited natural speech. The key issue here is the redundant nature of the acoustic structure of natural speech. When synthetic stimuli are used listeners may use the available acoustic-phonetic information in a manner differently than they would process the same phonetic distinction with natural speech. The only resolution to this question is to compare the effects observed with synthetic stimuli to those found with natural speech.

ACKNOWLEDGMENT

The preparation of this chapter was supported, in part, by NIDCD grant R01-DC00219 to the University at Buffalo.

REFERENCES

Atal, B. S. & Hanauer, S. L. (1971). Speech analysis and synthesis by linear prediction of the speech wave. *Journal of the Acoustical Society of America*, 50, 637–55.

Blandon, A. (1982). Arguments against formants in the auditory representation of speech. In R. Carlson & B. Granström (eds.), *The Representation of Speech in the Peripheral Auditory System* (pp. 95–102). New York: Elsevier Biomedical Press.

Childers, D. G. (2000). *Speech Processing and Synthesis Toolboxes*. New York: John Wiley & Sons.

Chistovich, L. A. & Lublinskaya, V. V. (1979). The "center of gravity" effect in vowel spectra and critical distance between the formants: Psychophysical study of perception of vowel-like stimuli. *Hearing Research*, 1, 185–95.

Cooper, F. S., Liberman, A. M., & Borst, J. M. (1951). The interconversion of audible and visible patterns as a basis for research in the perception of speech. *Proceedings of the National Academy of Science*, 37, 318–25.

Cranen, B. & Schroeter, J. (1996). Physiologically motivated modeling of the voice source in articulatory analysis/synthesis. *Speech Communication*, 19, 1–19.

Delattre, P., Liberman, A. M., & Cooper, F. S. (1955). Acoustic loci and transitional cues for consonants. *Journal of the Acoustical Society of America*, 27, 769–74.

Deller, J. R. Jr., Hansen, J. H. L., & Proakis, J. G. (1993). *Discrete-Time Processing of Speech Signals*. New York: Macmillan.

Dorman, M. F. & Loizou, P. C. (1996). Relative spectral change and formant transitions as cues to labial and alveolar place of articulation. *Journal of the Acoustical Society of America*, 100, 3825–30.

Fant, C. G. M. (1960). *Acoustic Theory of Speech Production*. The Hague: Mouton.

Flanagan, J. L. (1972). *Speech Analysis Synthesis and Perception*. New York: Springer-Verlag.

Forrest, K., Weismer, G., Milenkovic, P., & Dougall, R. N. (1988). Statistical analysis of word-initial voiceless obstruents. Preliminary data. *Journal of the Acoustical Society of America*, 84, 115–23.

Henton, C. (1999). Where is female synthetic speech? *Journal of the International Phonetic Association*, 29, 51–61.

Holmes, J. N. (1983). Formant synthesizers: Cascade or parallel? *Speech Communication*, 2, 251–73.

Karlsson, I. (1991). Female voices in speech synthesis. *Journal of Phonetics*, 19, 111–20.

Kewley-Port, D. (1983). Time-varying features as correlates of place of articulation in stop consonants. *Journal of the Acoustical Society of America*, 73, 322–35.

Klatt, D. H. (1980). Software for a cascade/parallel formant synthesizer. *Journal of the Acoustical Society of America*, 67, 971–95.

Klatt, D. H. (1982). Speech processing strategies based on auditory models. In R. Carlson & B. Granstrom (eds.), *The Representation of Speech in the Peripheral Auditory System* (pp. 181–96). New York: Elsevier Biomedical Press.

Klatt, D. H. (1987). Review of test-to-speech conversion in English. *Journal of the Acoustical Society of America*, 82, 737–93.

Klatt, D. H. & Klatt, L. C. (1990). Analysis, synthesis, and perception of voice quality variations among female and male talkers. *Journal of the Acoustical Society of America*, 87, 820–57.

Lahiri, A., Gewirth, L., & Blumstein, S. E. (1984). A reconsideration of acoustic invariance for place of articulation in diffuse stop consonants: Evidence from a cross-language study. *Journal of the Acoustical Society of America*, 76, 391–404.

Liberman, A. M., Cooper, F. S., Shankweiler, D. P., & Studdert-Kennedy, M. (1967). Perception of the speech code. *Psychological Review*, 74, 431–61.

Liljencrants, J. (1968). The OVE-III speech synthesizer. *IEEE Transactions on Audio and Electroacoustics*, AU-16, 137–40.

Markel, J. D. & Gray, A. H. Jr. (1976). *Linear Prediction of Speech*. New York: Springer-Verlag.

McCandless, S. S. (1974). An algorithm for automatic formant extraction using linear prediction spectra. *IEEE Transactions on Acoustics, Speech, and Signal Processing*, 22, 135–41.

Miller, J. L. (1981). Effects of speaking rate on segmental distinctions. In P. D. Eimas & J. L. Miller (eds.), *Perspectives on the Study of Speech* (pp. 39–74). Hillsdale, NJ: Lawrence Erlbaum.

Miller, J. L. & Wayland, S. C. (1993). Limits in the limitations of context-conditioned effects in the perception of [b] and [w]. *Perception & Psychophysics*, 54, 205–10.

Moore, B. C. J. (1988). Dynamic aspects of auditory masking. In G. M. Edelma, W. E. Gall, & W. M. Cowan (eds.), *Auditory Function: Neurobiological Bases of Hearing* (pp. 585–607). New York: John Wiley & Sons.

Mullennix, J. W. & Pisoni, D. B. (1990). Stimulus variability and processing dependencies in speech perception. *Perception & Psychophysics*, 47, 379–90.

Newman, R. S. & Sawusch, J. R. (1996). Perceptual normalization for speaking rate: Effects of temporal distance. *Perception & Psychophysics*, 58, 540–60.

Oppenheim, A. V. & Schafer, R. W. (1975). *Digital Signal Processing*. Englewood Cliffs, NJ: Prentice-Hall.

Patterson, R. D., Allerhand, M. H., & Giguère, C. (1995). Time-domain modeling of peripheral auditory processing: A modular architecture and a software platform. *Journal of the Acoustical Society of America*, 98, 1890–4.

Patterson, R. D. & Moore, B. C. J. (1986). Auditory filters and excitation patterns as representations of frequency resolution. In B. C. J. Moore (ed.), *Frequency Selectivity in Hearing* (pp. 123–77). London: Academic Press.

Peterson, G. & Barney, H. (1952). Control methods used in a study of the vowels. *Journal of the Acoustical Society of America*, 24, 175–84.

Price, P. J. (1989). Male and female voice source characteristics: Inverse filtering results. *Speech Communication*, 8, 261–77.

Richardson, K. H. (1992). An analysis of invariance in English stop consonants (Doctoral dissertation, State University of New York at Buffalo, 1991). *Dissertation Abstracts International*, 53-B, 1633.

Saito, S. & Nakata, K. (1985). *Fundamentals of Speech Signal Processing*. New York: Academic Press.

Sawusch, J. R. & Gagnon, D. A. (1995). Auditory coding, cues, and coherence in phonetic perception. *Journal of Experimental Psychology: Human Perception and Performance*, 21, 635–52.

Scott, R. S., Grace, D. A., & Mattingly, I. G. (1966). A computer-controlled on-line speech synthesizer system. In *Digest of Technical Papers: International Communication Conference* (pp. 104–5) New York: Lewis Winner.

Seneff, S. (1988). A joint synchrony/mean-rate model of auditory speech processing. *Journal of Phonetics*, 16, 55–76.

Shamma, S. (1988). The acoustic features of speech sounds in a model of auditory processing: vowels and voiceless fricatives. *Journal of Phonetics*, 16, 77–91.

Shinn, P. C., Blumstein, S. E., & Jongman, A. (1985). Limitations of context conditioned effects in the perception of [b] and [w]. *Perception & Psychophysics*, 38, 397–407.

Stevens, K. N. (1999). *Acoustic Phonetics*. Cambridge, MA: MIT Press.

Stevens, K. N. & Blumstein, S. E. (1978). Invariant cues for place of articulation in stop consonants. *Journal of the Acoustical Society of America*, 64, 1358–68.

Syrdal, A. K. & Gopal, H. S. (1986). A perceptual model of vowel recognition based on the auditory representation of American English vowels. *Journal of the Acoustical Society of America*, 79, 1086–1100.

Wakita, H. J. (1996). Instrumentation for the study of speech acoustics. In N. J. Lass (ed.), *Principles of Experimental Phonetics* (pp. 469–94). St. Louis, MO: Mosby.

Zahorian, S. A. & Jagharghi, A. J. (1993). Spectral shape versus formants as acoustic correlates for vowels. *Journal of the Acoustical Society of America*, 94, 1966–82.

Zwicker, E. & Terhardt, E. (1980). Analytical expressions for critical-band rate and critical bandwidth as a function of frequency. *Journal of the Acoustical Society of America*, 68, 1523–5.

2 Perceptual Organization of Speech

ROBERT E. REMEZ

How does a perceiver resolve the linguistic properties of an utterance? This question has motivated many investigations within the study of speech perception and a great variety of explanations. In a retrospective summary 15 years ago, Klatt (1989) reviewed a large sample of theoretical descriptions of the perceiver's ability to project the sensory effects of speech, exhibiting inexhaustible variety, into a finite and small number of linguistically defined attributes, whether features, phones, phonemes, syllables, or words. Although he noted many distinctions among the accounts, with few exceptions they exhibited a common feature. Each presumed that perception begins with a speech signal, well-composed and fit to analyze. This common premise shared by otherwise divergent explanations of perception obliges the models to admit severe and unintended constraints on their applicability. To exist within the limits set by this simplifying assumption, the models are restricted to a domain in which speech is the only sound; moreover, only a single talker ever speaks at once. Although this designation is easily met in laboratory samples, it is safe to say that it is rare *in vivo*. Moreover, in their exclusive devotion to the perception of speech the models are tacitly modular (Fodor, 1983), whether or not they acknowledge it.

Despite the consequences of this dedication of perceptual models to speech and speech alone, there has been a plausible and convenient way to persist in invoking the simplifying assumption. This fundamental premise survives intact if a preliminary process of perceptual organization finds a speech signal, follows its patterned variation amid the effects of other sound sources, and delivers it whole and ready to analyze for linguistic properties. The indifference to the conditions imposed by the common perspective reflects an apparent consensus that perceptual organization of speech is simple, automatic, and accomplished by generic means. However, despite the rapidly established perceptual coherence of the constituents of a speech signal, the perceptual organization of speech cannot be reduced to the available and well-established principles of auditory perceptual organization.

2.1 Perceptual Organization and the Gestalt Legacy

2.1.1 *A generic auditory model of organization*

The dominant contemporary account of auditory perceptual organization is Auditory Scene Analysis (Bregman, 1990). This theory of the resolution of auditory sensation into streams, each issuing from a distinct source, developed empirically in the past 30 years, though its intellectual roots run deep. The Gestalt psychologist Wertheimer (1923/1938) established the basic premises of the account in a legendary article, the contents of which are roughly known to all students of introductory psychology. In visible and audible examples, Wertheimer described the coalescence of elementary figures into groups and contours, arguing that sensory experience is organized in patterns, and is not registered as a mere spatter of individual receptor states. By considering a series of hypothetical cases, and without knowing the sensory physiology that would not be described for decades (Mountcastle, 1998), he justified organizing principles of *similarity, proximity, closure, symmetry, common fate, continuity, set,* and *habit*. Hindsight suggests that Wertheimer framed the problem astutely, given our contemporary understanding of the functions of the sensory periphery that integrate the action of visual and auditory receptors (Hochberg, 1974).

Setting the indefinitely elastic principle of habit aside, the simple Gestalt-derived criteria of grouping are arguably reducible to two functions: (1) to compose an inventory of sensory elements; and (2) to create contours or groups on the principle that like binds to like. Whether groups occur due to the spectral composition of auditory elements, their common on- or offset, proximity in frequency, symmetry of rate of change in an auditory dimension, harmonic relationship, or the interpolation of brief gaps, and so on, each is readily understood as a case in which similarity among a set of auditory sensory elements promotes grouping. A group composed according to these functions forms a sensory contour or perceptual stream. It is a small but necessary extrapolation to assert that an auditory contour consists of elements originating from a single source of sound, and therefore that perceptual organization parses sensory experience into concurrent streams each issuing from a different sound producing event (Bregman & Pinker, 1978).

In a series of ongoing experiments, researchers adopted Wertheimer's auditory conjectures, and calibrated the resolution of auditory streams by virtue of the principles and their corollaries. For example, Bregman and Campbell (1971) reported that auditory streams formed when a sequence of 100 ms tones differing in frequency was presented to listeners. According to a procedure that has become standard, the series of brief tones was presented repetitively to listeners, who were asked to report the order of tones in the series. Instead of hearing a sequence of high and low pitches, though, listeners grouped tones into two streams each composed of similar elements, one of high pitch and another of low (see Figure 2.1). Critically, the perception of the order of elements was veridical within streams, but perception of the intercalation order across the streams was erroneous. In another example, Bregman, Ahad, and Van Loon (2001) reported

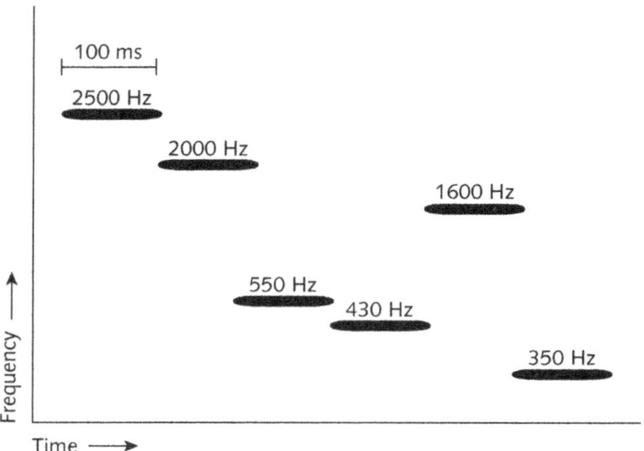

Figure 2.1 This sequence of tones presented to listeners by Bregman & Campbell (1971) was reported as two segregated streams, one of high and another of low tones. Critically, the intercalation of the high and low streams (that is, the sequence: high, high, low, low, high, low) was poorly resolved.

that a sequence of 65 ms bursts of band-limited noise were grouped together or split into separate perceptual streams as a function of the similarity in center frequency of the noise bursts. A sizable literature of empirical tests of this kind spans 40 years, and calibrates the sensory conditions of grouping by one or another variant of similarity. A compilation of the literature is offered by Bregman (1990), and the theoretical yield of this research is summarized by Darwin (1997).

Typically, studies of auditory perceptual organization have reported that listeners are sensitive to quite subtle properties in the formation of auditory groups. It is useful to consider an exemplary case, for the detailed findings of auditory amalgamation and segregation define the characteristics of the model and ultimately determine its applicability to speech. In a study of concurrent grouping of harmonically related tones by virtue of coincident onset, a variant of similarity in a temporal dimension, Dannenbring and Bregman (1978) reported that synchronized tones were grouped together, but a discrepancy as brief as 35 ms in lead or lag in one component was sufficient to disrupt coherence with other sensory constituents, and to split it into a separate stream. There are many similar cases documenting the exquisite sensitivity of the auditory sensory channel in segregating streams on the basis of slight departures from similarity: in *frequency* (Bregman & Campbell, 1971), in *frequency change* (Bregman & Doehring, 1984), in *fundamental frequency* (Steiger & Bregman, 1982), in *common modulation* (Bregman, Abramson, Doehring, & Darwin, 1985), in *spectrum* (Dannenbring & Bregman, 1976; Warren, Obusek, Farmer, & Warren, 1969), due to brief *interruptions* (Miller & Licklider, 1950), in *common onset/offset* (Bregman & Pinker, 1978), in *frequency continuity* (Bregman & Dannenbring, 1973, 1977), in *melody* and *meter* (Jones & Boltz, 1989); these are reviewed by Bregman (1990) and by Remez, Rubin, Berns, Pardo, and Lang (1994).

2.1.2 Gestalt principles of organization applied to speech

Because explanations of speech perception have depended on an unspecified account of perceptual organization, it has been natural to take Auditory Scene Analysis as a theory of first resort for understanding the perceptual solution to the cocktail party problem (Cherry, 1953), specifically, of attending to a single stream of speech amid other sound sources. However, this premise was largely unsupported by direct evidence. The crucial empirical cases that had formed the model had rarely included natural sources of sound, neither the instruments of the orchestra (though, see Iverson, 1995) which are well modeled physically (Rossing, 1990), nor ordinary mechanical sources (Gaver, 1993), nor the sounds of speech, with several provocative exceptions. It is instructive to consider some of the cases in which tests of perceptual organization using speech sounds appeared to confirm the applicability to speech of the general auditory account of perceptual organization.

In one case establishing grouping by similarity, a repeating series of syllables of the form CV–V–CV–V was observed to split into distinct streams of like syllables, one of CVs and another of Vs, much as Gestalt principles propose (Lackner & Goldstein, 1974). Critically, this perceptual organization precluded the perceptual resolution of the relative order of the syllables across streams, analogous to the index of grouping used by Bregman and Campbell (1971). In another case calibrating grouping by continuity, a series of vowels formed a single perceptual stream only when formant frequency transitions leading into and out of the vowel nuclei were present (Dorman, Cutting, & Raphael, 1975). Without smooth transitions, the spectral discontinuity at the juncture between successive steady-state vowels exceeded the tolerance for grouping by closure – that is, the interpolation of gaps – and the perceptual coherence of the vowel series was lost. In another case examining organization by the common fate, or similarity in change of a set of elements, a harmonic component of a steady-state vowel close to the center frequency of a formant was advanced or delayed in onset relative to the rest of the harmonics composing the synthetic vowel (Darwin & Sutherland, 1984). At a lead or lag of 32 ms, consistent with findings deriving from arbitrary patterns, the offset harmonic segregated into a different stream than the synchronous harmonics composing the vowel. In consequence, when the leading or lagging harmonic split, the height of the vowel was perceived to be different, as if the perceptual estimate of the center frequency of the first formant had depended on the grouping. In each of these instances, the findings with speech sounds were well explained by the precedents of prior tests using arbitrary patterns of sound created with oscillators and noise generators.

These outcomes should have seemed too good to be true. It was as if an account defined largely through tests of ideal notions of the resolution of similarity in simple auditory sequences proved to be adequate to accommodate the diverse acoustic constituents and spectral patterns of natural sound. With hindsight, we can see that accepting this conclusion does require one credulous assumption: namely, that tests using arbitrary trains of syllables, meticulously phased harmonic components, and sustained steady-state vowels adequately express the ordinary complexity of speech, and the perceiver's ordinary sensitivity. In short, a sufficient test of organization by the generic principles of Auditory Scene Analysis is obliged to incorporate the kind of variability that has defined the technical description of speech perception. And a closer approximation to the conditions of ordinary listening must motivate the empirical tests. By satisfying these constraints, a set of functions rather different from the generic auditory model can be seen at work in the perceptual organization of speech.

2.2 The Plausibility of the Generic Account of Perceptual Organization

2.2.1 *A brief review of the acoustic properties of speech*

One challenge of perceptual organization facing a listener is simple to state: To find and follow a speech stream. This would be an easy matter were the acoustic constituents of a speech signal or their auditory sensory correlates unique to speech; or if the speech signal were more or less stationary in its spectrum; or if the acoustic elements and the auditory impressions they evoke were similar, moment by moment. None of these is true, however, which inherently undermines the plausibility of any attempt to formalize perceptual organization of speech as a task of determining successive or simultaneous similarities in auditory experience. First, none of the multitude of naturally produced vocal sounds composing a speech signal is unique to speech. Arguably, the physical models of speech production succeed so well because they exploit an analogy between vocal sound and acoustic resonance (Fant, 1960; Stevens & House, 1961). Second, one signature aspect of speech is the presence of multiple acoustic maxima and minima in the spectrum, and the variation over time in the frequencies at which the acoustic energy is concentrated (Stevens & Blumstein, 1981). This frequency variation of the formant centers is interrupted at stop closures, creating an acoustic spectrum that is both nonstationary and discontinuous. Third, the complex pattern of articulation by which talkers produce consonant holds and approximations creates heterogeneous acoustic effects consisting of hisses, whistles, clicks, buzzes, and hums (Stevens, 1998). The resulting acoustic pattern of speech consists of a nonstationary, discontinuous series of periodic and aperiodic elements none of which in detail is unique to a vocal source.

The diversity of acoustic constituents of speech is readily resolved as a coherent stream, perceptually, though the means by which this occurs challenges the potential of the generic auditory account. Although some computational implementations of Gestalt grouping have disentangled spoken sources of simple nonstationary spectra (Parsons, 1976; Summerfield, 1992), these have occurred for a signal free of discontinuities, as occurs in the production of sustained, slowly changing vowels. Slow and sustained change in the spectrum, though, is hardly typical of ordinary speech which is characterized by consonant closures that impose rapid spectral changes and episodes of silence of varying duration. To resolve a signal despite silent discontinuities requires grouping by closure to extrapolate across brief silent gaps. To invoke generic auditory properties in providing this function would oppose present evidence, though. For example, in an empirical attempt to discover the standard for grouping by closure (Neff, Jesteadt & Brown, 1982) the temporal threshold for gap detection was found to diverge from the tolerance of discontinuity in grouping. It is unlikely, then, that a generic mechanism of extrapolation across gaps is responsible for the establishment of perceptual continuity, whether in auditory form or in the perception of speech.

Evidence from tests of auditory form suggest that harmonic relations – that is, sharing a fundamental frequency – and amplitude comodulation – that is, pulsing at a common rate – promote grouping albeit weakly (Bregman, Levitan, & Liao, 1990), and these two characteristics are manifest by oral and nasal resonances and by voiced frication. This might be the likeliest principle to explain the coherence of voiced speech by generic auditory means, for an appeal to similarity in frequency variation among the formants is unlikely to explain their coherence. Indeed, the pattern of frequency variation of the first formant typically differs from that of the second and neither the first nor second resembles the third, due to the different articulatory causes of each (Fant, 1960). To greatly simplify a complex relation, the center frequency of the first formant often varies with the opening and closing of the jaw, while the frequency of the second formant varies with the advancement and retraction of the tongue, and the frequency of the third formant alternates in its articulatory correlate. Accordingly, different patterns of frequency variation are observed in each resonance due to the relative independence of the control of these articulators (see Figure 2.2). Even were generic auditory functions to bind the comodulated formants into a single stream, without additional principles of perceptual organization, a generic Gestalt-derived parsing mechanism that aims to compose perceptual streams of similar auditory elements would fail; indeed, it would fracture the acoustically diverse components of a single speech signal into streams of similar elements, one of hisses, another of buzzes, a third of clicks, and so on, deriving an incoherent profusion of streams despite the common origin of the acoustic elements in phonologically governed sound production (Darwin & Gardner, 1986; Lackner & Goldstein, 1974; Remez et al., 1994). Apart from this consideration, in principle, a small empirical literature exists on which to base an adequate account of the perceptual organization of speech.

2.2.2 *A few clues*

There is a passage in Schubert's Symphony No. 8 in B minor (D. 759, the "Unfinished," measures 13–26 of the first movement) in which the parts played by oboe and clarinet, a unison melody, fuse so thoroughly that no trace of oboe or clarinet quality remains. This instance in which two sources of sound are treated perceptually as one led Broadbent and Ladefoged (1957) to attempt a study that offered a clue about the nature of perceptual organization of speech. Beginning with a synthetic sentence composed of two formants, they created two single formant patterns, one of the first formant and the other of the second, each excited at the

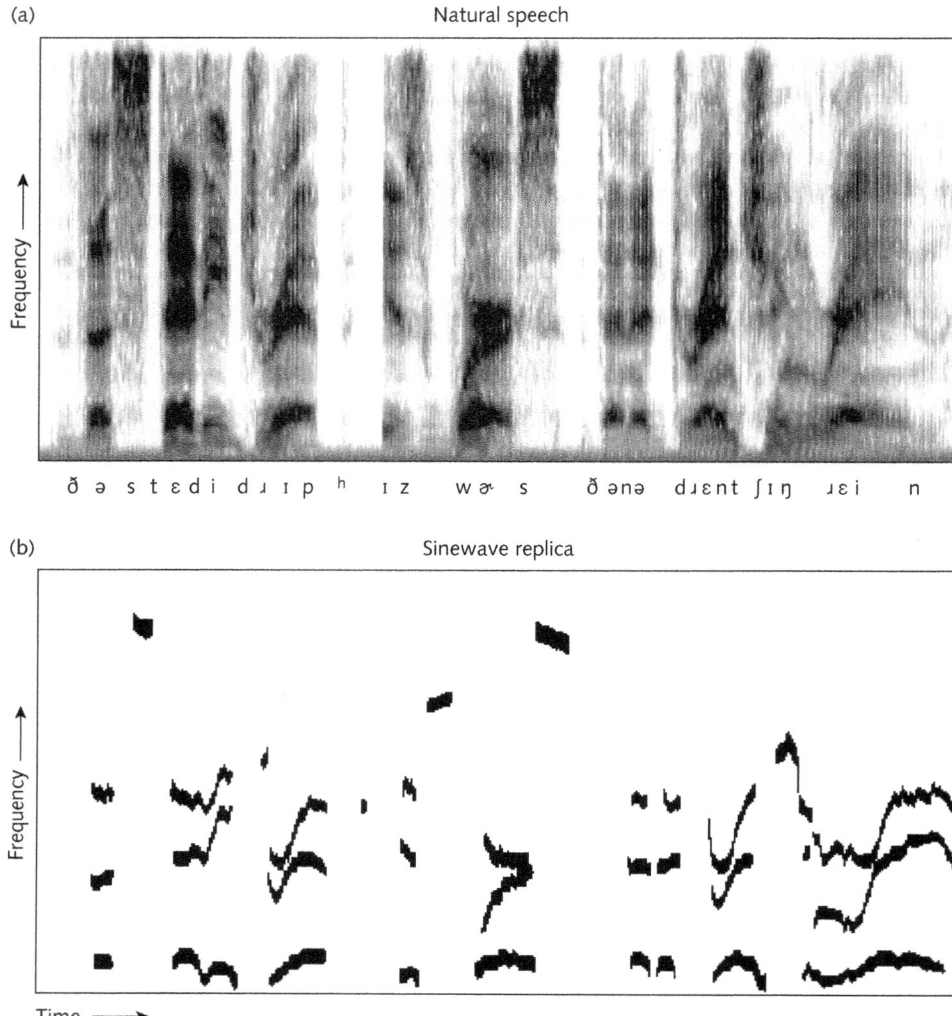

Figure 2.2 A comparison of natural and sinewave versions of the sentence, "The steady drip is worse than a drenching rain." (a) natural speech; (b) sinewave replica.

same fundamental frequency. Concurrently, the two formants evoked an impression of an English sentence; singly, each evoked an impression of an unintelligible buzz.

In one test condition, the formants were presented dichotically, in analogy to an oboe and a clarinet playing in unison. This resulted in perception of a single voice speaking the sentence, as if two spatially distinct sources had combined. Despite the dissimilarities in spatial locus of the components, this outcome is consistent with a generic auditory account of organization on grounds of harmonicity and amplitude comodulation. However, when each formant was rung on a different fundamental, subjects no longer reported a single voice, as if fusion failed to occur because neither harmonicity nor amplitude comodulation existed to oppose the spatial dissimilarity of the components. It is remarkable, nonetheless, that in view of these multiple lapses of similarity, subjects accurately reported the sentence, "What did you say before that?" although in this condition it seemed to be spoken by two talkers, one at each ear, each speaking at a different pitch. In other words, listeners reported divergent perceptual states: (1) the splitting of the auditory streams due to dissimilar pitch; and, (2) the combining of auditory streams to form speech. Although a generic Gestalt-derived account can explain a portion of the results, it cannot explain the combination of spatially and spectrally dissimilar formant patterns to compose a single speech stream.

In fine detail, research on perception in a speech mode also broached this topic, though indirectly. This line of research aimed to calibrate the difference in the resolution of auditory form and phonetic form of speech, thereby to identify psychoacoustic and psychophysical characteristics unique to speech perception. By opposing acoustic patterns evoking speech perception with nonspeech control patterns, the perceptual effect of variation in an acoustic correlate of a phonetic contrast was compared to the corresponding effect of the same acoustic property removed from the phonetically adequate context. For instance, Mattingly, Liberman, Syrdal, and Halwes (1971) examined the discriminability of a second formant frequency transition as an isolated acoustic pattern and within a synthetic syllable in which its variation was correlated with the perception of the *place of articulation* of a stop consonant. A finding of different psychophysical effect, roughly, Weber's law for auditory form and categorical perception for phonetic form, was taken as the signature of each perceptual mode. In a variant of the method specifically pertinent to the description of perceptual organization, Rand (1974) separated the second formant frequency transition, the correlate of the place contrast, from the remainder of a synthetic syllable and arrayed the acoustic components dichotically. In consequence, the critical second formant frequency transition presented to one ear was resolved as an auditory form while it also contributed to the phonetic contrast it evoked in apparent combination with the formant pattern presented to the other ear. In other words, with no change in the acoustic conditions, a listener could resolve the properties of the auditory form of the formant frequency transition or the phonetic contrast it evoked. The dichotic presentation permitted two perceptual organizations of the same element concurrently, due to the spatial and temporal disparity that blocked fusion on generic auditory principles, and due to the phonetic potential of the fused components. This phenomenon of concurrent auditory and phonetic effects of a single acoustic element was described as *duplex perception* (Liberman, Isenberg, & Rakerd, 1981; Nygaard, 1993; Whalen & Liberman, 1996) and it has been described as an effect of a peremptory aspect of phonetic organization and analysis.[1] No matter how the evidence ultimately adjudicates the psychophysical claims, it is instructive to note that the generic auditory functions of perceptual organization only succeed in rationalizing the split of the dichotic components into separate streams, and fail to provide a principle by which the combination of elements occurs.

2.2.3 Organization by coordinate variation

A classic understanding of the perception of speech derives from study of the acoustic correlates of phonetic contrasts and the physical and articulatory means by which they are produced (reviewed by Raphael, this volume; also, see Fant, 1960; Liberman, Ingemann, Lisker, Delattre, & Cooper, 1959; Stevens & House, 1961). In addition to calibrating the perceptual response to natural samples of speech, researchers also used acoustic signals produced synthetically in detailed psychoacoustic studies of phonetic identification and differentiation. In typical terminal analog speech synthesis, the short-term spectra characteristic of the natural samples are preserved, lending the synthesis a combination of natural vocal timbre and intelligibility (Sawusch, this volume). Acoustic analysis of speech and synthesis that allows parametric variation of speech acoustics have been important for understanding the normative aspects of perception, that is, the relation between the typical or likely auditory form of speech sounds encountered by listeners and the perceptual analysis of phonetic properties (Diehl, Molis, & Castleman, 2001; Lindblom, 1996; Massaro, 1994; Stevens, 1998).

However, a focus on natural samples and on synthetic idealizations of natural speech discounts the adaptability and versatility of speech perception, and draws attention from the properties of speech that are relevant to understanding perceptual organization. Because grossly distorted speech remains intelligible (for example, Licklider, 1946; Miller, 1946) when many of the typical acoustic correlates are absent, it is difficult to sustain the hypothesis that finding and following a speech stream crucially depends on meticulous registration of the brief and numerous acoustic correlates of phonetic contrasts described in classic studies. But, if the natural acoustic products of vocalization do not determine the perceptual organization and analysis of speech, what does?

An alternative to this conceptualization was prompted by the empirical use of a technique that combines digital analysis of speech spectra and digital synthesis of time-varying sinusoids (Remez, Rubin, Pisoni, & Carrell, 1981). This research has revealed the perceptual effectiveness of acoustic patterns that exhibit the gross spectrotemporal characteristics of speech without incorporating the fine acoustic structure of vocally produced sound. Perceptual research with these acoustic materials (and their relatives – noise band vocoded speech: Shannon, Zeng, Kamath, Wygonski, & Ekelid, 1995; acoustic chimeras: Smith, Delgutte, & Oxenham, 2002; see, also, Remez, Yang, Piorkowski, Wissig, Batchelder, & Nam, 2002) has permitted an estimate of a listener's sensitivity to the time-varying patterns of speech spectra independent of the sensory elements that compose them.

The premise of sinewave replication is simple, though in practice it is as laborious as other forms of copy synthesis. Three or four tones, each approximating the center frequency and amplitude of an oral, nasal, or fricative resonance, are created to imitate the coarse grain attributes of a speech sample. Lacking the momentary aperiodicities, harmonic spectra, broadband formants, and regular pulsing of natural and most synthetic speech, a sinewave replica of an utterance differs acoustically and qualitatively from speech while remaining intelligible. A spectrogram of a sinewave sentence is shown in the bottom panel of Figure 2.2;

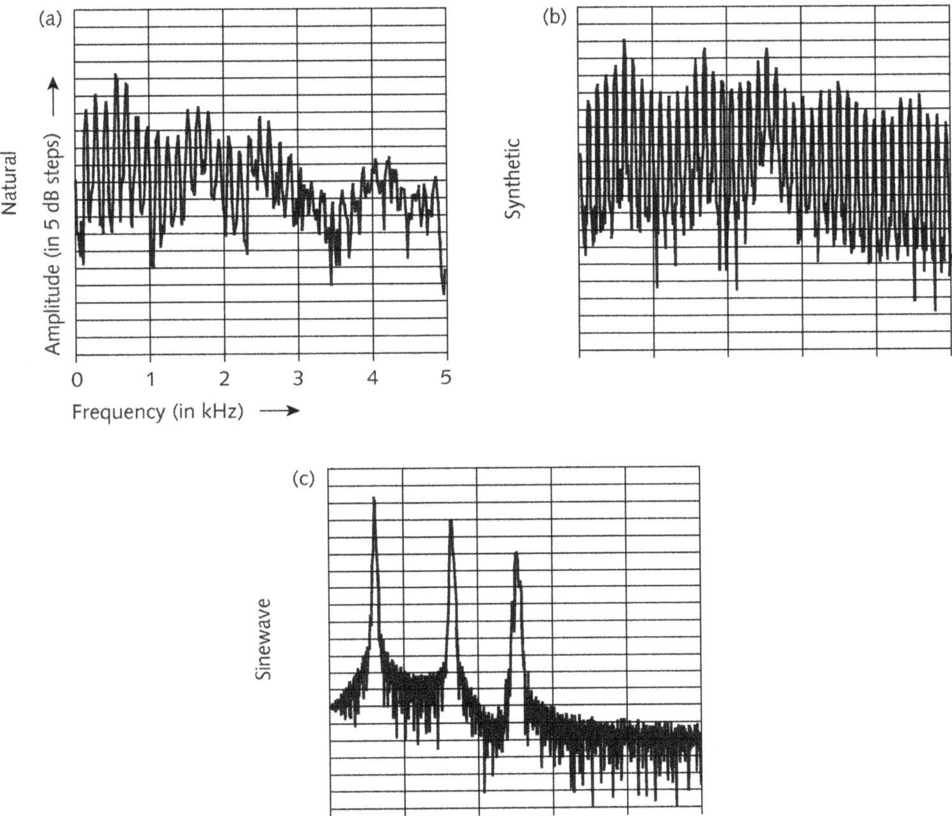

Figure 2.3 A comparison of the short-term spectrum of (a) natural speech; (b) terminal analog synthetic speech; and (c) sinewave replica. Note the broadband resonances and harmonic spectra in natural and synthetic speech, in contrast to the sparse, nonharmonic spectrum of the three tones.

a comparison of short-term spectra of natural speech and both synthetic and sinewave imitations is shown in Figure 2.3.

It is significant that three or four tones reproducing a natural formant pattern evoke an experience in a naive listener of several concurrent whistles changing in pitch and loudness, and do not automatically elicit an impression of speech. In other words, the immediate experience of the listener is accurately predicted by a generic auditory account, because acoustic elements that change frequency at different rates to different extents, onsetting and offsetting at different moments in different frequency ranges, are dissimilar along many dimensions that specify separate perceptual streams according to Gestalt principles. However, once instructed that the tones compose synthetic speech, a listener readily reports linguistic properties as if hearing the original natural utterance on which the sinewave replica was modeled. To be precise, intelligibility of sinewave speech is variable, and performance under different listening and instructional conditions has varied between 50% and 85% correct (Liebenthal, Binder, Piorkowski, & Remez, 2003; Remez et al., 1994). Within this range of performance levels, these acoustic conditions pose a crucial test of a Gestalt-derived account of perceptual organization, for a perceiver must integrate the tones in order to compose a single coherent speech stream, thereby resolving the linguistic properties of the signal. Several tests support this claim of true integration preliminary to analysis.

In direct assessments, the intelligibility of sinewave replicas of speech exceeded intelligibility predicted from the presentation of individual tones (Remez, Rubin, Nygaard, & Howell, 1987; Remez et al., 1981; Remez et al., 1994). This superadditive performance is evidence of integration, and it persisted even when the tones came from separate spatial sources, violating similarity in location (Remez et al., 1994; cf. Broadbent & Ladefoged, 1957). In combining the individual tones into a single time-varying coherent stream, however, this complex organization necessary for phonetic analysis does not exclude an auditory organization as independently resolvable streams of tones (Remez & Rubin, 1984, 1993). In fact, the perceiver's resolution of the pitch contour associated with the frequency pattern of tonal constituents is acute whether or not the fusion of the tones supporting phonetic perception occurs (Remez, Pardo, Piorkowski, & Rubin, 2001). On this evidence rests the claim that sinewave replicas are *bistable*, exhibiting two simultaneous and exclusive organizations.

Even if the processes by which these states occurred were strictly parallel, the bistable occurrence of auditory and phonetic perceptual organization is not amenable to further simplification. A sinewave replica of speech allows two organizations, much as the celebrated cases of visual bistability do: the duck-rabbit figure, Woodworth's equivocal staircase, Rubin's vase, and Necker's cube. Unlike the visual cases of alternating stability, the bistability that occurs in the perception of sinewave speech is simultaneous. A conservative description of these findings is that an organization of the auditory properties of sinewave signals occurs according to Gestalt-derived principles that promote integration or segregation; and, that phonetic perceptual analysis is incompatible with that organization. However, the concurrent variation of the tones satisfies a non-Gestalt principle of coordinate auditory variation despite local dissimilarities, and these promote integration of the components into a single stream. This organization is susceptible to phonetic analysis.

2.3 The Perceptual Organization of Speech

2.3.1 Characteristics of the perceptual coherence of speech

While much remains to discover about perceptual organization dependent on complex coordinate variation, research on the psychoacoustics and perception of speech from a variety of laboratories permits a rough sketch of the parameters. The portrait of perceptual organization offered here gathers evidence from different research programs that aimed to address a range of perceptual questions, for there is no unified attempt at present to understand the organization of perceptual streams that approach the complexity of speech. Overall, these results expose the perceptual organization of speech as fast, unlearned, nonsymbolic, keyed to complex patterns of sensory variation, indifferent to auditory quality, and requiring attention whether elicited or exerted.

The evidence that perceptual organization of speech is *fast* rests on long-established findings that the auditory trace of speech fades rapidly. Although estimates vary with the task used to calibrate the durability of unelaborated auditory sensation, all of the measures reflect the urgency with which the fading trace is recoded into a more stable phonetic form (Howell & Darwin, 1977; Pisoni & Tash, 1974). It is unlikely that much of the auditory form of speech persists beyond a tenth of a second, and it has decayed beyond access by 400 ms. The sensory integration required for perceptual organization is tied to this pace. Contrary to this notion of perceptual organization as exceedingly rapid, an extended version of Auditory Scene Analysis (Bregman, 1990) proposes a resort to a cognitive mechanism occurring well after primitive grouping takes place, to function as a supplement to the Gestalt-based mechanism. Such knowledge-based mechanisms are also featured as a method to resolve difficult grouping in recent artifactual approaches to perceptual organization (for example, Cooke & Ellis, 2001). However, the formal or practical advantages that this method achieves come at a clear cost, namely, to reject boundary conditions that subscribe to the natural auditory limits of perceptual organization.

The propensity to organize an auditory pattern by virtue of complex coordinate variation is apparently *unlearned*, or nearly so. In tests with infant listeners, 14-week-old subjects exhibited the pattern of adult sensitivity to dichotically arrayed components of synthetic syllables (Eimas & Miller, 1992; cf. Whalen & Liberman, 1987). In this case, the pattern of perceptual effects evident in infants was contingent on the integration of sensory elements despite detailed failures of auditory similarity on which Gestalt grouping depends. Perhaps it is an exaggeration to claim that this organizational function is strictly unlearned, for even the youngest subject in the sample had been encountering airborne sound for three months, and undeniably had an opportunity to refine its sensitivity through learning. However, the development of sensitivity to complex auditory patterns cannot plausibly result from a history of meticulous trial and error in listeners of such tender age, nor is it likely to reflect specific knowledge of the auditory effects that typify American English phonetic expression. It is far likelier that this sensitivity represents the emergence of an organizational component of listening that must be present for speech perception to develop, and 14-week-olds still have several months ahead of them before the phonetic properties of speech become conspicuous (Houston, this volume; Jusczyk, 1997).

Research on sinewave replicas of speech has shown that the perceptual organization of speech is *nonsymbolic* and *keyed to patterns of sensory variation*. The evidence is provided by tests (Remez et al., 1994; Remez, 2001) that used tone analogs of sentences in which a sinewave replicating the second formant was presented to one ear while tone analogs of the first, third, and fricative formants were presented to the other ear. In such conditions, much as Broadbent and

Ladefoged had found, perceptual fusion readily occurs despite the violation of spatial dissimilarity and the absence of other attributes to promote Gestalt-based grouping. To sharpen the test, an intrusive tone was presented in the same ear with the tone analogs of the first, third, and fricative tones. This single tone presented by itself does not evoke phonetic impressions, and is perceived as an auditory form without symbolic properties: it merely changes in pitch and loudness without phonetic properties. In order to resolve the speech stream under such conditions, a listener must reject the intrusive tone, despite its spatial similarity to the first, third, and fricative tones of the sentence, and appropriate the tone analog of the second formant to form the speech stream despite its spatial displacement from the tones with which it combines. Control tests established that a tone analog of the second formant fails to evoke an impression of phonetic properties. Performance of listeners in a transcription task, a rough estimate of phonetic coherence, was good if the intrusive tone did not vary in a speechlike manner. That is, an intrusive tone of constant frequency or of arbitrary frequency variation had no effect on the perceptual organization of speech. When the intrusive tone exhibited the pattern of a temporally reversed second formant – exhibiting the tempo and range of frequency variation appropriate for a second formant, without supplying the proper variation that would combine with other tones to form an intelligible stream – performance suffered. It was as if the criterion for integration of a tone was specific to its speechlike variation under conditions in which it was nonetheless unintelligible.

Since the advent of the telephone, it has been obvious that a listener's ability to find and follow a speech stream is *indifferent to auditory quality*. The lack of spectral fidelity in early forms of speech technology made speech sound phony, literally, yet it was readily recognized that this lapse of natural quality did not compromise the usefulness of speech as a communication channel (Fletcher, 1929). This fact indicates clearly that the functions of perceptual organization hardly aim to collect aspects of sensory stimulation that have the precise auditory quality of natural speech. Indeed, Liberman and Cooper (1972) argued that early synthesis techniques evoked phonetic perception because the perceiver cheerfully forgave departures from natural quality that were often extreme. In techniques such as speech chimeras (Smith et al., 2002) and sinewave replication, the acoustic properties of intelligible signals lie beyond the productive capability of a human vocal tract, and the impossibility of such spectra as vocal sound does not evidently block the perceptual organization of the sound as speech. The variation of a spectral envelope can be taken by listeners to be speechlike despite acoustic details that give rise to impressions of gross unnaturalness. Findings of this sort contribute a powerful argument against psychoacoustic explanations of speech perception generally, and perceptual organization specifically.

Ordinary subjective experience of speech suggests that perceptual organization is automatic, for speech seems to pop right out of a nearby commotion. Despite this impression that perceptual organization of speech is unbidden, findings with sinewave replicas of utterances show that the perceptual organization of speech *requires attention*, and is not an automatic consequence of a class of sensory effects. This feature differs from the automatically engaged process proposed in strict modular terms by Liberman and Mattingly (1985). With sinewave signals, most subjects fail to resolve the phonetic properties of sinewave words and sentences unless they are asked specifically to listen for speech (Remez et al., 1981; cf. Liebenthal et al., 2003), indicating that the auditory forms alone do not evoke speech perception. Critically, a listener who is asked to attend to arbitrary tone patterns as if listening to speech fails to report phonetic impressions, indicating that signal structure as well as phonetic attention are required for the organization and analysis of speech. The prospect that generic auditory perceptual organization is similar to speech perception in requiring attention has been raised in recent studies of arbitrary patterns (Carlyon, Cusack, Foxton, & Robertson, 2001). Of course, a natural vocal signal exhibits the phenomenal quality of speech, and this is evidently sufficient to elicit a productive form of attention for perceptual organization to ensue.

2.3.2 *Generic auditory organization and speech perception*

The intelligibility of sinewave replicas of utterances, of noise-band vocoded speech, and of speech chimeras reveals that a perceiver can find and follow a speech signal lacking the multiple detailed similarities among acoustic and auditory constituents on which Gestalt-based generic functions operate. These findings show that perceptual organization of speech can occur solely by virtue of attention to the complex coordinate variation of an acoustic pattern. Of course, the use of such exotic acoustic signals for the proof creates some uncertainty that ordinary speech perception is satisfactorily characterized by tests using these acoustic oddities. An argument of Remez et al. (1994) for considering these tests to be a useful index of the perception of commonplace speech signals begins by noting that phonetic perception of sinewave replicas of utterances depends on a simple instruction to listen to the tones as speech. Because the disposition to hear sinewave words and sentences appears readily, without arduous or lengthy training, this prompt adaptation to phonetic organization and analysis suggests that the ordinary cognitive resources of speech perception are operating for sinewave speech. Although some form of short-term perceptual learning might be involved, the swiftness of the appearance of adequate perceptual function is evidence that any special induction to accommodate sinewave signals is a marginal component of perception.

Despite all, natural speech consists of large stretches of glottal pulsing, which create amplitude comodulation over time and harmonic relations among concurrent portions of the spectrum. This has led to a reasonable proposal (Barker & Cooke, 1999) that generic auditory grouping functions, although not necessary for the perceptual organization of speech, contribute to perceptual organization when speech spectra satisfy the Gestalt criteria. A critical empirical test was provided by Carrell and Opie (1992) and in detail it offers an index of the plausibility of the claim. In the test, the intelligibility of sinewave sentences was compared in two acoustic conditions: (1) three-tone time varying sinusoids; and (2) three-tone time varying sinusoids on which a regular amplitude pulse was imposed. Although the tone patterns in the first condition were not susceptible to Gestalt-based grouping, because they failed to exhibit similarity in each of the relevant dimensions that we have discussed, the pulsed tone patterns in the second condition exhibited amplitude comodulation and harmonicity in its complex spectra (Bregman et al., 1990). All other things being equal, the perceptual organization attributable to complex coordinate variation should have been reinforced by perceptual organization attributable to similarity that triggers generic auditory grouping. Indeed, Carrell and Opie found that pulsed sentences were more intelligible than smoothly varying sinusoids, as if the spectral components once bound more securely were more successfully analyzed.

The assertion offered by Barker and Cooke (1999) about this phenomenon is that generic auditory functions can reinforce the grouping of speech signals, although the evidence on close examination does not yet warrant an endorsement of a hybrid model of perceptual organization. Carrell and Opie (1992) had used a range of pulse rates and conditions in their study, and reported that the intelligibility gain attributable to pulsing a sinewave sentence was restricted to a pulse rate in the range of 50–100 Hz. No benefit of pulsing was observed for a pulse rate of 200 Hz. While this topic certainly merits additional study, the available evidence supports a conclusion that a hybrid model of perceptual organization is restricted to speech signals produced by low bass voices, and whatever benefit is seen for such speech does not extend to tenors, to say nothing of altos and sopranos. Most generously, we might conclude that the relation of primitive Gestalt-based generic auditory grouping and the more abstract organization by sensitivity to coordinate variation cannot be defined without stronger evidence, and that it is premature to conclude that the Gestalt set plays a prominent or even a secondary role in the perceptual organization of speech.

2.4 Implications of Perceptual Organization for Theories of Speech Perception

2.4.1 *The nature of speech cues*

What causes the perception of speech? A classic answer takes a linguistically significant contrast – voicing, for instance – and provides an inventory of acoustic correlates of a careful articulation of the contrast (for example, Lisker, 1978). A perceptual account that reverses the method would depict a meticulous listener collecting individual acoustic correlates as they land and assembling them in a stream, thereby to tally the strength with which a constellation of cues indicates the likely occurrence of a linguistic constituent. Klatt's (1989) retrospective survey of perceptual accounts describes many approaches that treat the acoustic signal as a straightforward composite of acoustic correlates. The function of perceptual organization, usually omitted in such accounts, establishes the perceiver's compliance with the acoustic products of a specific source of sound, and in the case of speech, it is the function that finds and tracks the acoustic products of vocalization. However, it is clear from evidence of several sorts – tolerance of distortion, effectiveness of impossible signals, forgiveness of departures from natural timbre – that the organizational component of perception which yields a speech stream fit to analyze cannot collect acoustic cues piecemeal, as this simple view describes. The functions of perceptual organization act, instead, as if attuned to a complex form of regular if unpredictable spectrotemporal variation within which the specific acoustic and auditory elements matter far less than the overall configuration they compose.

The evolving portrait of speech perception that includes organization and analysis recasts the cue as the property of perception that gives speech its phenomenality, though not its phonetic effect. If the transformation of natural speech to chimera, to noise-band vocoded signal, and to sinewave replica is phonetically conservative, preserving the fine details of subphonemic variation while varying to the extremes of timbre or auditory quality, then it is apparent that the competent listener derives phonetic impressions from the properties that these different kinds of signal share, and derives qualitative impressions from their unique attributes. The shared attribute, for want of a more precise description, is a complex modulation of spectrum envelopes, although the basis for the similar effect of the infinitely sharp peaks of sinewave speech and the far coarser spectra of chimerical and noise-band vocoded speech has still to be explained. None of these manifests the cues present in natural speech despite the success of listeners in understanding the message. The conclusion supported by these findings is clear: phonetic perception does not require speech cues. Instead, the organizational component of speech perception operates on a spectrotemporal grain that is requisite both for finding and following a speech signal and for analyzing its linguistic properties. The speech cues that seemed formerly to bear the burden of stimulating phonetic analyzers into action appear in hindsight to provide little more than auditory quality subordinate to the phonetic stream.

An additional source of evidence is encountered in the phenomenal experience of perceivers who listen to speech via electrocochlear prostheses (Goh, Pisoni, Kirk, & Remez, 2001). Intelligibility of speech perceived via a cochlear implant is often excellent, rivaling that of normal hearing, and recent studies with infant and juvenile subjects (Svirsky, Robbins, Kirk, Pisoni, & Miyamoto, 2000) suggest that this form of sensory substitution is effective even at the earliest stages of language development (see Pisoni, this volume). The mechanism of acoustic transduction at the auditory periphery is anomalous, it goes without saying, and the phenomenal experience of listeners using this appliance to initiate neural activity differs hugely from ordinary auditory experience of natural speech. Despite the absence of veridical perceptual experience of the raw qualities of natural speech, electrocochlear prostheses are effective in the self-regulation of speech production by their users, and are effective perceptually despite the abject deficit in delivering speech cues. What brings about the perception of speech, then? Without the acoustic moments, there is no stream of speech, but the stream itself plays a causal role beyond that which has been attributed to momentary cues since the beginning of technical study of speech.

2.4.2 *A constraint on normative descriptions of speech perception*

The application of powerful statistical techniques to problems in cognitive psychology has engendered a variety of normative, incidence based accounts of perception. Since the 1980s, a technology of parallel computation based loosely on an idealization of the neuron has driven the creation of a proliferation of devices that perform intelligent acts. The exact modeling of neurophysiology is rare in this enterprise, though probabilistic models attired as neural nets enjoy a hopeful if unearned appearance of naturalness that older, algorithmic explanations of cognitive processes unquestionably lack. Used as a theory of human cognitive function, it is more truthful to say that neural nets characterize the human actor as an office full of clerks at an insurance company, endlessly tallying the incidence of different states in one domain (perhaps age and zip code, or the bitmap of the momentary auditory effect of a noise burst in the spectrum) and associating them (perhaps, in a nonlinear projection) with those in another domain (perhaps, the risk of major surgery, or the place of articulation of a consonant).

In the perception of speech and language, the ability of perceivers to differentiate levels of linguistic structure has been attributed to a sensitivity to inhomogeneities in distributions of specific instances of sounds, words, and phrases. Although a dispute has taken shape about the exact dimensions of the domain within which sensitivity to distributions can be useful (for instance, Peña, Bonatti, Nespor, & Mehler, 2002; *contra* Seidenberg, MacDonald, & Saffran, 2002), there is confident agreement that a distributional analysis of a stream of speech is performed in order to derive a linguistic phonetic segmental sequence. Indeed, this is claimed as one key component of language acquisition in early childhood (Saffran, Aslin, & Newport, 1996). The presumption of this assertion obliges a listener to establish and maintain in memory a distribution of auditory tokens projectable into phonetic types. This is surely false. The rapid decay of an auditory trace of speech leaves it uniquely unfit for functions lasting longer than 100 ms, and for this reason it is simply implausible that stable perceptual categories rest on durable representations of auditory exemplars of speech samples. Moreover, the notion of perceptual organization presented in this essay argues that a speech stream is not usefully represented as a series of individual cues, neither for purposes of perceptual organization nor analysis. Indeed, in order to determine that a particular acoustic moment is a cue in fact, a perceptual function already sensitive to coordinate variation must apply. Whether or not a person other than a researcher compiling entries in the *Dictionary of American Regional English* can become sensitive to distributions of linguistic properties as such, it is exceedingly unlikely that the perceptual resolution of linguistic properties in utterances is much influenced by representations of the statistical properties of speech sounds. Indeed, the clerks are free to tally what they will, but perception must act first to provide the instances.

2.4.3 Multisensory perceptual organization

Fifty years ago, Sumby and Pollack (1954) conducted a pioneering study of the perception of speech presented in noise in which listeners could also see the talkers whose words they aimed to recognize. The point of the study was to calibrate the level at which the speech signal would become so faint in the noise that to sustain adequate performance attention would switch from an inaudible acoustic signal to the visible face of the talker. In fact, the visual channel contributed to intelligibility at all levels of performance, indicating that the perception of speech is ineluctably multisensory. But, how does the perceiver determine the audible and visible composition of a speech stream? This problem (reviewed by Bernstein, this volume, and by Rosenblum, this volume) is a general form of the listener's specific problem of perceptual organization, understood as a function that follows the speechlike coordinate variation of a sensory sample of an utterance. To assign auditory effects to the proper source, the perceptual organization of speech must capture the complex sound pattern of a phonologically governed vocal source, sensing the spectrotemporal variation that transcends the simple similarities on which the Gestalt-derived principles rest. It is obvious that Gestalt principles couched in auditory dimensions would fail to merge auditory attributes with visual attributes. Because auditory and visual dimensions are simply incommensurate, it is not obvious that any notion of similarity would hold the key to audio-visual combination. The single property that the two senses share, localization in azimuth and range, is violated freely without harming audiovisual combination, and therefore cannot be requisite for multisensory perceptual organization.

The phenomenon of multimodal perceptual organization confounds straightforward explanation in yet another instructive way. Audiovisual speech perception can be fine under conditions in which the audible and visible components are useless separately for conveying the linguistic properties of the message (Rosen, Fourcin, & Moore, 1981). In addition, neither spatial alignment nor temporal alignment of the audible and visible components must be veridical for multimodal perceptual organization to deliver a coherent stream fit to analyze (see Bertelson, Vroomen, & de Gelder, 1997; Conrey & Pisoni, 2003; Munhall, Gribble, Sacco, & Ward, 1996). Under such discrepant conditions, audiovisual integration occurs despite the perceiver's evident awareness of the spatial and temporal misalignment, indicating a divergence in the perceptual organization of events and the perception of speech. In consequence, it is difficult to conceive of an account of such phenomena by means of perceptual organization based on tests of similar sensory details applied separately in each modality. Instead, it is tempting to speculate that an account of perceptual organization of speech can ultimately be characterized in dimensions that are removed from any specific sensory modality, yet is expressed in parameters appropriate to the sensory samples available at any moment.

2.5 Conclusion

Perceptual organization is the critical function by which a listener resolves the sensory samples into streams specific to worldly objects and events. In the perceptual organization of speech, the auditory correlates of speech are resolved into a coherent stream fit to analyze for its linguistic and indexical properties. Although many contemporary accounts of speech perception are silent about perceptual organization, it is unlikely that the generic auditory functions of perceptual grouping provide adequate means to find and follow the complex properties of speech. It is possible to propose a rough outline of an adequate account of the perceptual organization of speech by drawing on relevant findings from different research projects spanning a variety of aims. The evidence from these projects suggests that the critical organizational functions that operate for speech are: fast, unlearned, nonsymbolic, keyed to complex patterns of coordinate sensory variation, indifferent to sensory quality, and requiring attention whether elicited or exerted. Research on other sources of complex natural sound has the potential to reveal whether these functions are unique to speech or are drawn from a common stock of resources of unimodal and multimodal perceptual organization.

ACKNOWLEDGMENTS

In conducting some of the research described here and in composing this essay, the author is grateful for the sympathetic understanding of: Peter Bailey, Robert Krauss, Jennifer Pardo, Rebecca Piorkowski, David Pisoni, Philip Rubin, Ann Senghas, Michael Studdert-Kennedy, and Stephanie Wissig. This work is supported by a grant to Barnard College from the National Institute on Deafness and Other Communication Disorders (DC00308).

NOTE

1 It is notable that the literature on duplex perception contains meager direct evidence that the auditory and phonetic properties of the duplex acoustic test items are available simultaneously. The empirical evaluation of auditory and phonetic form employed sequential measures, sometimes separated by a week, that assessed the perception of auditory form in one test and phonetic form in another. Evidence is provided that phonetic perception is distinct from a generic auditory process, but the literature is silent on the criteria of perceptual organization required for phonetic analysis.

REFERENCES

Barker, J. & Cooke, M. (1999). Is the sine-wave cocktail party worth attending? *Speech Communication*, 27, 159–74.

Bertelson, P., Vroomen, J., & de Gelder, B. (1997). Auditory-visual interaction in voice localization and in bimodal speech recognition: The effects of desynchronization. In C. Benoît & R. Campbell (eds.), *Proceedings of the Workshop on Audio-visual Speech Processing: Cognitive and Computational Approaches* (pp. 97–100). Rhodes, Greece: ESCA.

Bregman, A. S. (1990). *Auditory Scene Analysis*. Cambridge, MA: MIT Press.

Bregman, A. S. & Campbell, J. (1971). Primary auditory stream segregation and perception of order in rapid sequence of tones. *Journal of Experimental Psychology*, 89, 244–9.

Bregman, A. S. & Dannenbring, G. L. (1973). The effect of continuity on auditory stream segregation. *Perception & Psychophysics*, 13, 308–12.

Bregman, A. S. & Dannenbring, G. L. (1977). Auditory continuity and amplitude edges. *Canadian Journal of Psychology*, 31, 151–8.

Bregman, A. S. & Doehring, P. (1984). Fusion of simultaneous tonal glides: The role of parallelness and simple frequency relations. *Perception & Psychophysics*, 36, 251–6.

Bregman, A. S. & Pinker, S. (1978). Auditory streaming and the building of timbre. *Canadian Journal of Psychology*, 32, 19–31.

Bregman, A. S., Abramson, J., Doehring, P., & Darwin, C. J. (1985). Spectral integration based on common amplitude modulation. *Perception & Psychophysics*, 37, 483–93.

Bregman, A. S., Ahad, P. A., & Van Loon, C. (2001). Stream segregation of narrow-band noise bursts. *Perception & Psychophysics*, 63, 790–7.

Bregman, A. S., Levitan, R., & Liao, C. (1990). Fusion of auditory components: Effects of the frequency of amplitude modulation. *Perception & Psychophysics*, 47, 68–73.

Broadbent, D. E. & Ladefoged, P. (1957). On the fusion of sounds reaching different sense organs. *Journal of the Acoustical Society of America*, 29, 708–10.

Carlyon, R. P., Cusack, R., Foxton, J. M., & Robertson, I. H. (2001). Effects of attention and unilateral neglect on auditory stream segregation. *Journal of Experimental Psychology: Human Perception and Performance*, 27, 115–27.

Carrell, T. D. & Opie, J. M., (1992). The effect of amplitude comodulation on auditory object formation in sentence perception. *Perception & Psychophysics*, 52, 437–45.

Cherry, E. (1953). Some experiments on the recognition of speech, with one and two ears. *Journal of the Acoustical Society of America*, 25, 975–9.

Conrey, B. L. & Pisoni, D. B. (2003). Audiovisual asynchrony detection for speech and nonspeech signals. *Proceedings of Audio Visual Speech Processing 2003*, 25–30.

Cooke, M. & Ellis, D. P. W. (2001). The auditory organization of speech and other sources in listeners and computational models. *Speech Communication*, 35, 141–77.

Dannenbring, G. L. & Bregman, A. S. (1976). Stream segregation and the illusion of overlap. *Journal of Experimental Psychology: Human Perception and Performance*, 2, 544–55.

Dannenbring, G. L. & Bregman, A. S. (1978). Streaming vs. fusion of sinusoidal components of complex tones. *Perception & Psychophysics*, 24, 369–76.

Darwin, C. J. (1997). Auditory grouping. *Trends in Cognitive Sciences*, 1, 327–33.

Darwin, C. J. & Gardner, R. B. (1986). Mistuning a harmonic of a vowel: Grouping and phase effects on vowel quality. *Journal of the Acoustical Society of America*, 79, 838–44.

Darwin, C. J. & Sutherland, N. S. (1984). Grouping frequency components of vowels: When is harmonic not a harmonic? *The Quarterly Journal of Experimental Psychology*, 36A, 193–208.

Diehl, R. L., Molis, M. R., & Castleman, W. A. (2001). Adaptive design of sound systems. In E. Hume and K. Johnson (eds.), *The Role of Speech Perception in Phonology* (pp. 123–39). San Diego: Academic Press.

Dorman, M. F., Cutting, J. E., & Raphael, L. J. (1975). Perception of temporal order in vowel sequences with and without formant transitions. *Journal of Experimental Psychology: Human Perception and Performance*, 104, 121–9.

Eimas, P. & Miller, J. (1992). Organization in the perception of speech by young infants. *Psychological Science*, 3, 340–5.

Fant, C. G. M. (1960). *The Acoustic Theory of Speech Production*. The Hague: Mouton.

Fletcher, H. (1929). *Speech and Hearing*. New York: D. Van Nostrand.

Fodor, J. A. (1983). *The Modularity of Mind*. Cambridge, MA: MIT Press.

Gaver, W. W. (1993). What in the world do we hear? An ecological approach to auditory event perception. *Ecological Psychology*, 5, 285–313.

Goh, W. D., Pisoni, D. B., Kirk, K. I., & Remez, R. E. (2001). Audio-visual perception of sinewave speech in an adult cochlear implant user: A case study. *Ear & Hearing*, 22, 412–19.

Hochberg, J. (1974). Organization and the Gestalt tradition. In E. C. Carterette & M. P. Friedman (eds.), *Handbook of*

Perception, Vol. I: Historical and Philosophical Roots of Perception (pp. 179–210). New York: Academic Press.

Howell, P. & Darwin, C. J. (1977). Some properties of auditory memory for rapid formant transitions. *Memory & Cognition*, 5, 700–8.

Iverson, P. (1995). Auditory stream segregation by musical timbre: Effects of static and dynamic acoustic attributes. *Journal of Experimental Psychology: Human Perception and Performance*, 21, 751–63.

Jones, M. R. & Boltz, M. (1989). Dynamic attending and responses to time. *Psychological Review*, 96, 459–91.

Jusczyk, P. W. (1997). *The Discovery of Spoken Language*. Cambridge, MA: MIT Press.

Klatt, D. H. (1989). Review of selected models of speech perception. In W. Marslen-Wilson (ed.), *Lexical Representation and Process* (pp. 169–226). Cambridge, MA: MIT Press.

Lackner, J. R. & Goldstein, L. M. (1974). Primary auditory stream segregation of repeated consonant-vowel sequences. *Journal of Acoustical Society of America*, 56, 1651–2.

Liberman, A. M., Ingemann, F., Lisker, L., Delattre, P., & Cooper, F. S. (1959). Minimal rules for synthesizing speech. *Journal of the Acoustical Society of America*, 31, 1490–9.

Liberman, A. M., Isenberg, D., & Rakerd, B. (1981). Duplex perception of cues for stop consonants: Evidence for a phonetic mode. *Perception & Psychophysics*, 30, 133–43.

Liberman, A. M. & Mattingly, I. G. (1985). The motor theory of speech perception revised. *Cognition*, 21, 1–36.

Liberman, A. M. & Cooper, F. S. (1972). In search of the acoustic cues. In A. Valdman (ed.), *Papers in Linguistics and Phonetics to the Memory of Pierre Delattre* (pp. 329–38). The Hague: Mouton.

Licklider, J. C. R. (1946). Effects of amplitude distortion upon the intelligibility of speech. *Journal of the Acoustical Society of America*, 18, 429–34.

Liebenthal, E., Binder, J. R., Piorkowski, R. L., & Remez, R. E. (2003). Short-term reorganization of auditory analysis induced by phonetic experience. *Journal of Cognitive Neuroscience*, 15, 549–58.

Lindblom, B. (1996). Role of articulation in speech perception: Clues from production. *Journal of the Acoustical Society of America*, 99, 1683–92.

Lisker, L. (1978). Rapid vs. rabid: A catalog of acoustic features that may cue the distinction. *Haskins Laboratories Status Report on Speech Perception*. New Haven, CT: Haskins Laboratories, SR-54, 127–32.

Massaro, D. W. (1994). Psychological aspects of speech perception: Implications for research and theory. In M. A. Gernsbacher (ed.), *Handbook of Psycholinguistics* (pp. 219–63). San Diego: Academic Press.

Mattingly, I. G., Liberman, A. M., Syrdal, A. K., & Halwes, T. G. (1971). Discrimination in speech and nonspeech modes. *Cognitive Psychology*, 2, 131–57.

Miller, G. A. (1946). Intelligibility of speech: Effects of distortion. In *Transmission and Reception of Sounds Under Combat Conditions* (pp. 86–108). Washington, DC: National Defense Research Committee.

Miller, G. A. & Licklider, J. C. R. (1950). The intelligibility of interrupted speech. *Journal of the Acoustical Society of America*, 22, 167–73.

Mountcastle, V. B. (1998). *Perceptual Neuroscience*. Cambridge, MA: Harvard University Press.

Munhall, K. G., Gribble, P., Sacco, L., & Ward, M. (1996). Temporal constraints on the McGurk effect. *Perception & Psychophysics*, 58, 351–62.

Neff, D. L., Jesteadt, W., & Brown, E. L. (1982). The relation between gap discrimination and auditory stream segregation. *Perception & Psychophysics*, 31, 493–501.

Nygaard, L. C. (1993). Phonetic coherence in duplex perception: Effects of acoustic differences and lexical status. *Journal of Experimental Psychology*, 19, 268–86.

Parsons, T. W. (1976). Separation of speech from interfering speech by means of harmonic selection. *Journal of the Acoustical Society of America*, 60, 911–18.

Peña, M., Bonatti, L. L., Nespor, M., & Mehler, J. (2002). Signal-driven computations in speech processing. *Science*, 298, 604–7.

Pisoni, D. B. & Tash, J. (1974). Reaction times to comparisons within and across phonetic categories. *Perception & Psychophysics*, 15, 285–90.

Rand, T. C. (1974). Dichotic release from masking for speech. *Journal of the Acoustical Society of America*, 55, 678–80.

Remez, R. E. (2001). The interplay of phonology and perception considered from the perspective of perceptual organization. In E. Hume & K. Johnson (eds.), *The Role of Speech Perception in Phonology* (pp. 27–52). San Diego: Academic Press.

Remez, R. E. & Rubin, P. E. (1984). On the perception of intonation from sinusoidal sentences. *Perception & Psychophysics*, 35, 429–40.

Remez, R. E. & Rubin, P. E. (1993). On the intonation of sinusoidal sentences: Contour and pitch height. *Journal of the Acoustical Society of America*, 94, 1983–8.

Remez, R. E., Pardo, J. S., Piorkowski, R. L., & Rubin, P. E. (2001). On the bistability of sine wave analogues of speech. *Psychological Science*, 12, 24–9.

Remez, R. E., Rubin, P. E., Berns, S. M., Pardo, J. S., & Lang, J. M. (1994). On the perceptual organization of speech. *Psychological Review*, 101, 129–56.

Remez, R. E., Rubin, P. E., Nygaard, L. C., & Howell, W. A. (1987). Perceptual normalization of vowels produced by sinusoidal voices. *Journal of Experimental Psychology: Human Perception and Performance*, 13, 41–60.

Remez, R. E., Rubin, P. E., Pisoni, D. B., & Carrell, T. D. (1981). Speech perception without traditional speech cues. *Science*, 212, 947–50.

Remez, R. E., Yang, C. Y., Piorkowski, R. L., Wissig, S., Batchelder, A., & Nam, H. (2002). The effect of variation in naturalness on phonetic perception identification. *Journal of the Acoustical Society of America*, 111, 2432.

Rosen, S. M., Fourcin, A. J., & Moore, B. C. J. (1981). Voice pitch as an aid to lipreading. *Nature*, 291, 150–2.

Rossing, T. D. (1990). *The Science of Sound*. Reading, MA: Addison-Wesley.

Saffran, J. R., Aslin, R. N., & Newport, E. L. (1996). Statistical learning by 8-month-old infants. *Science*, 274, 1926–8.

Seidenberg, M. S., MacDonald, M. C., & Saffran, J. R. (2002). Does grammar start where statistics stop? *Science*, 298, 553–4.

Shannon, R. V., Zeng, F., Kamath, V., Wygonski, J., & Ekelid, M. (1995). Speech recognition with primarily temporal cues. *Science*, 270, 303–4.

Smith, Z. M., Delgutte, B., & Oxenham, A. J. (2002). Chimaeric sounds reveal dichotomies in auditory perception. *Nature*, 416, 87–90.

Steiger, H. & Bregman, A. S. (1982). Competition among auditory streaming, dichotic fusion, and diotic fusion. *Perception & Psychophysics*, 32, 153–62.

Stevens, K. N. (1998). *Acoustic Phonetics*. Cambridge, MA: MIT Press.

Stevens, K. N. & Blumstein, S. E. (1981). The search for invariant acoustic correlates of phonetic features. In P. D. Eimas & J. L. Miller (eds.), *Perspectives on the Study of Speech* (pp. 1–38). Hillsdale, NJ: Lawrence Erlbaum.

Stevens, K. N. & House, A. S. (1961). An acoustical theory of vowel production and some of its implications. *Journal of Speech & Hearing Research*, 4, 303–20.

Sumby, W. H. & Pollack, I. (1954). Visual contribution to speech intelligibility in noise. *Journal of the Acoustical Society of America*, 26, 212–15.

Summerfield, Q. (1992). Roles of harmonicity and coherent frequency modulation in auditory grouping. In M. E. H. Schouten (ed.), *The Auditory Processing of Speech: From Sounds to Words* (pp. 157–66). Berlin: Mouton de Gruyter.

Svirsky, M. A., Robbins, A. M., Kirk, K. I., Pisoni, D. B., & Miyamoto, R. T. (2000). Language development in profoundly deaf children with cochlear implants. *Psychological Science*, 11, 153–8.

Warren, R. M., Obusek, C. J., Farmer, R. M., & Warren, R. P. (1969). Auditory sequence: Confusion of patterns other than speech or music. *Science*, 164, 586–7.

Wertheimer, M. (1923). Unsuchungen zur Lehre von der Gestalt, II, *Psychologische Forschung* (pp. 301–50). [Translated as, "Laws of organization in perceptual forms," in W. D. Ellis (ed.) (1938). *A Sourcebook of Gestalt Psychology* (pp. 71–88). London: Routledge & Kegan Paul.]

Whalen, D. H. & Liberman, A. M. (1987). Speech perception takes precedence over nonspeech perception. *Science*, 237, 169–71.

Whalen, D. H. & Liberman, A. M. (1996). Limits on phonetic integration in duplex perception. *Perception & Psychophysics*, 58, 857–70.

3 Primacy of Multimodal Speech Perception

LAWRENCE D. ROSENBLUM

It is becoming increasingly clear that human speech is a multimodal function, usually apprehended by visual (lipreading) as well as auditory (hearing) means, with even haptic apprehension a possibility. Our impression that speech perception is primarily an auditory function might be based more on technological artifacts (telephone and radios) than any privileged nature of auditory speech perception. This is not to argue that hearing speech is not usually the easiest way to comprehend spoken language, or that languages have not evolved to take advantage of auditory sensitivities. Rather, nearly 50 years of research on multimodal speech has revealed a ubiquity and automaticity of the function which forces a rethinking of the information, operations, and neurophysiology of speech perception.

In this chapter, we propose that multimodal speech is the *primary* mode of speech perception: it is not a function piggybacked on auditory speech. This primacy of multimodal speech implies that the operations, neurophysiology, information, and evolution of speech perception are based on primitives which are not tied to any single modality (see also Fowler, 1986; Liberman & Mattingly, 1985). From this theoretical perspective, sensory modality is largely invisible to the speech perception function and the relevant information for phonetic resolution is modality-neutral. Support for this perspective will come from evidence for: (1) the ubiquity and automaticity of multimodal speech; (2) extremely early speech integration; (3) the neurophysiological primacy of multimodal speech; and (4) modality-neutral speech information. Some speculations on the multimodal basis of the evolution of spoken language will also be presented. Throughout this chapter, we will argue that this theoretical approach to speech fits well with recent evidence on multimodal primacy of *general* (nonspeech) perception.

3.1 The Ubiquity and Automaticity of Multimodal Speech

Multimodal speech is used in many everyday contexts.[1] The importance of visual speech perception (lipreading) for listeners with hearing impairments is well known and has been extensively documented in the literature. Research shows that visual speech can be particularly useful for enhancing the degraded speech provided by cochlear implant devices (e.g., Geers & Brenner, 1994; Kaiser et al., 2003; Lachs, Pisoni, & Kirk, 2001; and see Grant & Seitz, 2000). However, visual speech also facilitates comprehension for listeners with good hearing. For most of us, visual speech enhances auditory speech when it is degraded by background noise or by a heavy foreign accent (MacLeod & Summerfield, 1990; Reisberg, McLean, & Goldfield, 1987; Sumby & Pollack, 1954). Visual speech can even enhance clear auditory speech that conveys particularly complicated content (Arnold & Hill, 2001; Reisberg et al., 1987). It is also known that visual speech helps with an infant's language development (for a review, see Mills, 1987). In fact, visually impaired, but normal hearing infants are often delayed in acquiring the phonetic distinctions that are difficult to hear but easy to see (e.g., /m/ vs. /n/).

Perhaps the most phenomenally compelling demonstrations of multimodal speech are known as McGurk effects (McGurk & MacDonald, 1976). These effects involve discrepant audible and visible utterances (syllables; words), that are dubbed so as to seem synchronously produced. The resultant percepts are "heard" as speech segments that are strongly influenced by the visual component. Classic examples of McGurk effects involve cases in which the visual component overrides the audio component (e.g., visual /va/ dubbed to audio /ba/ is "heard" as "va"), or the visual segment fuses with the audio segment to produce a compromised perceived segment (e.g., visual /ga/ dubbed to audio /ba/ is "heard" as "da").[2]

McGurk effects are often cited by researchers and theorists as evidence for the automaticity of multimodal speech integration. For example, McGurk effects are observed regardless of whether observers are aware of the dubbing procedure; whether the audio and visual components are spatially separate (Bertelson et al., 1994); or even if observers are unaware that they are seeing a face (Rosenblum & Saldaña, 1996). McGurk effects have been reported in observers with various native language backgrounds (e.g., Massaro et al., 1993; Sekiyama & Tohkura, 1991; 1993), as well as with 5-month-old infants (e.g., Burnham & Dodd, 1996; Rosenblum, Schmuckler, & Johnson, 1997). Finally, McGurk effects happen when the influencing information comes from touching, rather than seeing an articulating face (Fowler & Dekle, 1991), suggesting that multimodal speech integration can occur even when perceivers have virtually no experience with the influencing information.

Observations of the ubiquity and automaticity of audiovisual speech have had important influences on theories of speech perception. For example, visual speech research has played a critical role in the current debate over the objects of speech (phonetic) perception (e.g., Diehl & Kluender, 1989; Fowler & Rosenblum, 1991). This theoretical controversy concerns whether the perceptual primitives of speech are auditory or gestural in nature.[3] Theories such as the motor theory (Liberman & Mattingly, 1985; Liberman & Whalen, 2000) and direct/ecological approaches to speech perception (Fowler, 1986; Fowler & Rosenblum, 1991) have maintained that the primitives of the speech perception function are gestural and are not contained in any surface dimensions of the energy media (acoustics; optics) through which they are conveyed. Alternatively, auditory-based theories (e.g., Diehl & Kluender, 1989; Massaro, 1987; Stevens, 1989) propose that the perceptual primitives for speech perception take an auditory form. From this perspective, speech perception closely follows the surface acoustic changes of the speech signal, with little reference to any of the underlying gestural parameters involved in the signals' production.

The importance of visual speech findings to the perceptual primitives debate should be clear. To the degree that visual speech can be shown to be an integral part of the speech perception function, gestural theories are supported (Fowler & Rosenblum, 1991; Liberman & Mattingly, 1985). Thus, the motor and ecological theories have both discussed the automaticity with which visual speech is integrated in, for example, the McGurk effect as supportive of gestural primitives.

Proponents of auditory theories, on the other hand, interpret McGurk-type findings as revealing little more than the strength with which experience can link visual speech information onto associated auditory primitives (e.g., Diehl & Kluender, 1989; Kluender, 1994; Massaro, 1987). Motor and ecological theorists have countered these experiential explanations by citing findings of multimodal speech integration across various native language populations (e.g., Massaro et al., 1993); in pre-linguistic infants (e.g., Rosenblum et al., 1997); and in contexts where integration is induced via a modality (touch) with which subjects have had no speech experience (Fowler & Dekle, 1991). The perceptual primitives question continues to be an important issue in the speech perception literature, and visual speech research continues to play a pivotal role in this debate.

The issue of perceptual primitives bears heavily on the arguments addressed in this chapter. In proposing that speech is inherently multimodal, I will be taking a position contrary to strict auditory theories of speech perception. At the same time, arguments for the importance of multimodal speech do not preclude perspectives which assume modality-specific perceptual primitives (e.g., Bernstein, Auer, & Moore, 2004; Massaro, 1987). As an example, Bernstein and her colleagues (Bernstein, this volume; Bernstein et al., 2004) have argued for a speech function which carries out separate and simultaneous modality-specific analyses of auditory and visual inputs. In contrast, we argue that even at the earliest stages of perceptual analysis, the speech function is relatively unconcerned with modality, and that speech information is composed of modality-neutral dimensions. In this sense, our approach will be closely aligned with a gestural perspective.

The next section will continue to build the argument for multimodal speech primacy by showing that speech integration occurs very early in the process, possibly at the stage of information extraction.

3.2 Multimodal Speech is Integrated at the Earliest Observable Stage

One of the most studied issues in multimodal speech research concerns the stage in the process where information from the separate sensory modalities is integrated. Theories on this issue have ranged from proposing that integration occurs at: (1) the informational input (Green, 1998; Rosenblum & Gordon, 2001); (2) before feature extraction (Summerfield, 1987); (3) after feature extraction (Massaro, 1987); and (4) after segment, or even word recognition (Bernstein et al., 2004). Most of this literature has been discussed thoroughly in review chapters of

Quentin Summerfield (1987) and Kerry Green (1998) and will not be reiterated in detail here (see also Schwartz, Robert-Ribes, & Escudier, 1998). However, much of the research reviewed in these chapters supports multimodal speech primacy, and is worth addressing briefly.

In their chapters, both Summerfield (1987) and Green (1998) offer compelling arguments that multimodal speech is integrated at an early stage of the process, at least before the stage of phonetic categorization. Summerfield (1987) argues that the speech perception system takes in all auditorily and visually-specified linguistic dimensions, integrates them, and then performs phonetic categorization. To support his argument, he cites evidence from Green and Miller (1985) showing that visually perceived rate of articulation can influence perception of the auditory voice onset time (VOT) feature in ways similar to the influences of auditorily conveyed speaking rate (e.g., Diehl, Souther, & Convis, 1980). In showing a cross-modal effect at the featural level, this research provides support for the proposal that integration occurs pre-categorically.

Green (1998) comes to similar conclusions. He discusses evidence from his own laboratory that cross-modal influences work at a featural level. Using a McGurk paradigm, Green found that visible influences on audible place of articulation can influence the interpretation of other auditory feature dimensions such as voice onset time (Green & Kuhl, 1989). Green and his colleagues (Green & Gerdman, 1995; Green & Norrix, 2001) also showed that visually influenced coarticulatory information can affect perception of adjacent segments in the same way as auditory information and that a coarticulatory context established solely in one modality can influence segments in the other modality. All of these influences occur similarly to the influences induced by unimodal auditory changes in articulatory place cues. Potentially then, the extraction of speech features can be influenced by articulatory states which are conveyed from within or across modalities implicating a very early stage of cross-modal integration.

To summarize, much of the research on multimodal speech perception has shown evidence for integration at a point before segments are phonetically categorized, possibly even before phonetic features are extracted. Considered in another way, the research shows evidence that audiovisual speech is integrated at one of the earliest possible stages that can be observed using behaviorally-based perceptual methodologies.[4] Evidence for extremely early integration is consistent with a speech function that is relatively unconcerned with modality. Later, we argue that recent neuropsychological research supports similar conclusions.

Beyond the issue of *where* in the process integration occurs, both Summerfield and Green have speculated on *what* form or metric the information takes at the point of integration (see also Schwartz et al., 1998; as well as Bernstein et al., 2004). Both theorists argue that integration is best construed in terms of modality-neutral, gestural primitives (see also Rosenblum & Saldaña, 1996; Studdert-Kennedy, 1989). This metric would be based on properties of articulatory dynamics rather than on dimensions of either the auditory or visual streams themselves. In his chapter, Summerfield (1987) concluded that a modality-independent, gestural metric was most feasible in light of the evidence existent at the time, as well as considerations of parsimony: a modality-independent metric would obviate the extra step of translating the auditory and/or visual information into a unifiable form. Green (1998) concurs with Summerfield's conclusions and argues that a gestural/articulatory metric would best explain his findings that cross-modal featural influences occur in a way closely analogous to influences existent within unimodal auditory speech (see also Schwartz et al., 1998). Summerfield's proposal of a modality-independent gestural metric provides the foundation for the thesis of modality-neutral speech information to be discussed in a later section.

It should be mentioned that the evidence for the automaticity and early integration of multimodal speech fits well with findings on multimodal perception outside the domain of speech (for reviews, see Shimojo & Shams, 2001; Stoffregen & Bardy, 2001; but see Remez et al., 1998). It has long been known that visual information can influence fundamental auditory judgments including location (e.g., Bermant & Welch, 1976; Radeau & Bertelson, 1974) and event identity (Saldaña & Rosenblum, 1994), as well as induce auditory aftereffects (Kitagawa & Ichihara, 2002). Vision can also bias basic vestibular, tactile, and kinesthetic judgments (e.g., Clark & Graybiel, 1966; Kinney & Luria, 1970; Lee, 1976; Mergner & Rosemeier, 1998). Other well-known examples of intersensory influence show that auditory information can influence vision in terms of location (Bertelson & Radeau, 1981), duration (Walker & Scott, 1981), and perception of the number of visual events (O'Leary & Rhodes, 1984; Shams, Kamitami, & Shimojo, 2000). There is also a sizable literature showing that subject response time and accuracy in many contexts can be enhanced by multimodal vs. unimodal input (e.g., Stein et al., 1996; Vroomen & de Gelder, 2000; Welch & Warren, 1986).

The primacy of nonspeech multimodal integration is also evident in the human development literature. Young infants seem to be highly sensitive to audiovisual correspondences of object location, synchrony, approaching (vs. receding) sound-emitting objects, and emoting human faces (Bahrick & Pickens, 1994; Marks, 1978; Meltzoff & Moore, 1977, 1983; Walker, 1982; Walker-Andrews & Lennon, 1985).

In summary, the predominance of cross-modal influences now reported in the literature suggest that true unimodal perception – perception unaffected by more than one modality – is rare (e.g., Stoffregen & Bardy, 2001). Regardless, the findings supporting the primacy and early integration of multimodal speech concur with findings outside the speech domain. Next, we will see similar evidence in the neurophysiological literature.

3.3 Neurophysiological Primacy of Multimodal Speech

The primacy of multimodal speech suggests that speech perception is sensitive to multimodal dimensions at a very early stage. Recent findings in the neurophysiology of speech support early integration, as well as a speech mechanism that is relatively unconcerned with modality (Calvert et al., 1999; MacSweeney et al., 2000; but see Bernstein et al., 2002).

Much of the early neuropsychological research relevant to multimodal speech produced ambiguous results. For example, Campbell and her colleagues examined whether visual speech perception displays a left hemisphere (LH) advantage in a way consistent with lateralization of auditory speech (e.g., Rinne et al., 1999; Shankweiler & Studdert-Kennedy, 1975). Potentially, evidence for similar laterality of auditory and visual speech could be supportive of early integration and a common mechanism. Initially, Campbell (1986) reported a right hemisphere (RH) advantage for matching photographs of mouth shapes to heard speech segments. However, subsequent research using more realistic stimuli revealed that patients with LH lesions had greater difficulty in lipreading, suggesting some LH involvement in the function (Campbell, Landis, & Regard, 1986; Campbell, 1992). Complicating matters more, lateralization of visual speech might occur differently in the context of audiovisual integration. Using a McGurk paradigm, Baynes, Funnell, and Fowler (1994), as well as Diesch (1995), found evidence of bilateral hemisphere involvement in perceiving the visual speech component. In both of these studies, laterality depended on methodological specifics such as the type of integrated syllable, the visual location of the response word, and the hand used by subjects to indicate a response. However, in a more recent set of studies, Smeele et al. (Smeele, 1996; Smeele et al., 1998) found more consistent evidence for a LH advantage for lipreading syllables from an articulating face.

Certainly, solid conclusions from the laterality research would be premature. It could turn out that visual and audiovisual speech perception, like so many other functions, are partially lateralized (e.g., Ellis, 1989; Hellige, 1993). Regardless, the extant laterality results leave open the possibility that multimodal speech integration occurs early and a common mechanism might be used for auditory and visual speech. In fact, stronger evidence for this possibility has emerged from neural imaging research.

Sams et al. (1991) used a mismatched negativity technique to show that changes in visual speech information can change *auditory cortex* activity during audiovisual integration (see also Mottonen et al., 2002). A similar pattern of results was recently observed by Callan et al. (2001) using EEG measurements and a speech in noise methodology. These findings provide neurophysiological support for an early speech perception mechanism (at auditory cortex) that is sensitive to multimodal information.

Even more compelling evidence for early multimodal speech sensitivity has emerged from recent fMRI research. In a series of studies, Calvert, MacSweeney, and their colleagues (Calvert et al., 1997; MacSweeney et al., 2000; MacSweeney et al., 2002; see also Calvert, 2001) report evidence that a *silent lipreading* task can induce primary auditory cortex (PAC) activity similar to that induced by auditory speech. Generally this activation occurs in the LH, including the tip of Heschl's gyrus at the junction of primary and secondary auditory cortex. Follow-up studies revealed that this PAC activity is not related to the background noise emitted by the fMRI apparatus and cannot be induced with nonspeech facial contortions ("gurns") (MacSweeney et al., 2000). These findings suggest that in an important way, modality is relatively unimportant to the speech perception mechanism, even at the level of auditory cortex.

However, this fMRI research has not been without controversy. Recently, Bernstein and her colleagues (2002) questioned the exact cortical location of activation from lipread stimuli in the Calvert et al. (1997) studies. They argue that based on the activation levels reported by Calvert et al., it is questionable that PAC itself was responsive to visual speech. When conducting their own fMRI experiments, Bernstein et al. failed to find PAC activity from lipreading that was similar to that induced by a pulse tone auditory control stimulus. There were a number of methodological differences between the Calvert et al. and Bernstein et al. studies that could account for the diverging results. These differences include the nature of the speech material, the participants, the analyses, as well as the criteria established for true cortical activity. Clearly, more research is needed to clarify these important findings using fMRI techniques.

Before leaving the topic of neurophysiology, it should be mentioned that the accumulating if somewhat controversial evidence for the neurophysiological primacy of multimodal speech fits well with recent findings outside the speech perception literature (e.g., Shimojo & Shams, 2001). There is growing evidence for numerous brain regions and neuronal sites that are specifically tuned to multimodal input (Meredith, 2002; Stein & Meredith, 1993). Moreover, brain regions once thought to be sensitive to unimodal input are now known to be modulated by input from other modalities (Eimer, 2001; Laurienti et al., 2002; Macaluso, Frith, & Driver, 2000; Shams et al., 2001). Further evidence for neurophysiological multimodal primacy is also found in research on neuroplasticity and neurodevelopment in animals and humans (Buechel et al., 1998; Cohen et al., 1997; Rauschecker & Korte, 1993; Sadato et al., 1996). In sum, there is much emerging neurophysiological data to support a conceptualization of neural architecture in which the sensory brain is organized around multimodal input (but see Bernstein et al., 2004; Mesulam, 1998). Certainly, this fits well with the fMRI findings of Calvert, MacSweeney, and colleagues (Calvert et al., 1997; MacSweeney et al., 2000; Calvert, 2001) that auditory cortex is sensitive to lipread speech. These emerging neurophysiological findings are also consistent with the behavioral research on the perception of speech and nonspeech discussed in the previous section.

3.4 Modality-Neutral Speech Information

Thus far, we have considered evidence from both behavioral and neurophysiological studies showing that multimodal speech information is integrated very early in both the cognitive and neural architecture. However, another explanation for this seemingly immediate integration can be offered. It is possible that as far as the speech perception function is concerned, the sensory streams are never actually separate. The suggestion is that in an important way, modality is invisible to the speech perception function, and that the relevant sensory information is best interpreted as neutral with regard to input modality. This general idea of modality-neutral information is not new and has been discussed both in and out of the speech literature for many years (Gibson, 1966, 1979; Stein & Meredith, 1993; Stoffregen & Bardy, 2001; Summerfield, 1987). The novelty in the current argument lies with: (1) its explicit implications for multimodal speech integration; (2) its increased cogency based on accumulating evidence for the primacy of multimodal speech; and (3) its connection to the emerging neurophysiological and behavioral literatures on *nonspeech* multimodal perception.

The proposal of modality-neutral speech information follows directly from Summerfield's suggestion of modality-independent information (see also Kuhl & Meltzoff, 1984). Briefly stated, speech information is considered to be composed of higher-order, time-varying patterns of energy (light, sound) whose more abstract nature allows for a common form in multiple energy arrays. Furthermore, these cross-modal patterns are gesturally-based so as to inform about articulatory dynamics and support gestural perceptual primitives. This is not to argue that all speech information is available equally in all modalities. Rather, all relevant speech information regardless through which modality it is best available takes a form that is defined by higher-order gestural structure, and not by superficial dimensions of sensory physiology. This renders the job of a specific sense organ to sample the higher-order structure as it exists in the energy range to which the organ is sensitive. Moreover, for modality-neutral information, "cross-modal" integration is not something that occurs within the perceiver, but instead occurs in – *and as a property of* – the information itself (see Rosenblum, 2002; Rosenblum & Gordon, 2001).[5]

We argue that the evidence discussed in this chapter for a primacy of multimodal speech warrants a serious consideration of modality-neutral speech information. For example, the findings of Green and colleagues that cross-modal influences work at the featural level suggests that the relevant features are actually modality-neutral and articulatory. Furthermore, evidence of sensitivity to visual speech in auditory cortex could be interpreted as auditory cortex sensitivity to modality-neutral primitives.

The implications of modality-neutral information are theoretically significant. Most obviously, the thesis calls for new descriptions of speech information based on higher-order, gestural primitives which are not constrained to specific modalities (e.g., Browman & Goldstein, 1985). Certainly, this perspective echoes arguments proffered by the motor and ecological approaches described earlier (Fowler & Rosenblum, 1991; Liberman & Mattingly, 1985). Other implications of modality-neutral speech information include a different understanding of the sensory systems, as well as implications for the form of information at the point of integration. As Summerfield argued, modality-independent/neutral information would not require the extra step of transforming acoustic parameters and visible features into a common usable metric. Some examples of modality-neutral speech information of both specific and broad types will be considered next.

3.4.1 *Specific examples of modality-neutral speech information*

In his influential essay, Summerfield (1987) speculated on ways in which auditory and visual speech information could be described in a modality-independent form. When a speaker articulates a syllable /ma/ repeatedly with a regular frequency, its audio and visual information take on a common form. In the acoustic structure, this repetitive gesture can influence both overall amplitude and formant structure with a rate specific to the articulatory rate. For the optical structure, the gesture involves visible lip and (possibly) jaw opening trajectories which would structure light in a way again specific to the articulatory rate. While the details of the structured energy are different across sensory modalities, the higher-order information for *frequency of oscillation* could be considered modality-independent. Summerfield also considers modality-neutral descriptions of the information for articulatory quantal changes (e.g., changes from a state where articulators are not making contact to a state where they are), as well as for changes in articulatory direction. He provides examples of analogous kinematic patterns in the optic and acoustic signals for both classes of changes. To the extent a sensory mechanism is sensitive to these patterns, it is sensitive to modality-neutral information.

Since Summerfield's initial conjectures about modality-neutral speech primitives, supportive evidence has grown along both specific and broad lines. For example, evidence for informational commonalities across audio and visual speech has come from research examining correlations between these dimensions. Research by Vatikiotis-Bateson and his colleagues (Munhall & Vatikiotis-Bateson, 1998; Yehia, Rubin, & Vatikiotis-Bateson, 1998) has revealed strikingly close correspondences between visible speech kinematics and the associated acoustic signals. Their experiments involve 3D kinematic tracking of facial and interior articulatory movements, as well as analyses of the corresponding acoustic signal. The analyses reported by Vatikiotis-Bateson et al. show impressively high correlations between visible facial kinematics and acoustic dimensions such as RMS amplitude and spectral composition. In fact, the estimation of speech acoustics from facial kinematics is better than the estimation from internal vocal tract measures. The authors interpret their results as evidence that visible speech kinematics directly reflects the time course and amplitude of vocal tract opening and closing. Because these parameters are also instantiated in the corresponding acoustics, they can be considered modality-neutral. Interestingly, when applied to a noise source, the acoustic RMS amplitude and spectral parameters estimated from facial kinematics can produce a relatively intelligible auditory speech signal (Yehia et al., 1998).

The research of Vatikiotis-Bateson and his colleagues is also noteworthy in revealing surprising visibility of articulatory dimensions usually considered invisible. Kinematic analyses show that visible gestures usually associated with the lips are actually spread to more remote positions on the face and that much of the kinematics of the tongue are reflected in the more visible movements of the jaw. Their analyses also show that even changes in intraoral air pressure, usually considered inaccessible in visual speech, are reflected in visible displacement of landmarks on the surface of the skin. Certainly, evidence for greater detail available in visible speech does not, in and of itself, provide direct support for perceptual effectiveness of modality-neutral speech information. Still, the more articulatory detail that is available visibly and auditorily, the more feasible a modality-neutral description becomes.

The Vatikiotis-Bateson et al. research can be seen as a start at formalizing some of the speculations offered by Summerfield (1987) on modality-independent speech information. In the next sections, additional evidence for informational commonalities in the *general* nature of auditory and visual speech will be considered. It will be argued that multimodal speech possesses an *informational similitude*: i.e., the salient *general* properties of speech information are observed to be similar across modalities.

3.4.2 *Informational similitude in auditory and visual speech: Time-varying dimensions*

Historically, most descriptions of visible speech information have taken the form of pictorial information for static articulatory positions (e.g., Braida, 1991;

Massaro & Cohen, 1990; Montgomery & Jackson, 1983; for a review, see Rosenblum & Saldaña, 1998). As an example, Montgomery and Jackson (1983) defined visual vowel information in a scaling space representing the degree of lip spreading and rounding as well as peak tongue height. However, more recent research in our lab and others has shown that, as for auditory speech, the time-varying dynamic dimensions of visual speech are critically informative (e.g., Rosenblum & Saldaña, 1998).

First, research on both auditory and visual modalities has shown that isolated time-varying aspects of the signals can provide useful speech information. In auditory speech research, signals which do not involve the traditional cues of formants, transitions, and noise bursts can still be understood as speech (Remez et al., 1981; see also Shannon et al., 1995). These auditory signals are composed of a small set of sine-waves synthesized to track the frequency and amplitude of the center formant frequencies of an utterance as they change over time. This sinewave speech can be understood well enough for listeners to transcribe sentences and can induce perceptual effects characteristic of natural speech stimuli (Remez et al., 1987; Williams, Verbrugge, & Studdert-Kennedy, 1983). Because sinewave speech essentially isolates the time-varying linguistically significant parameters of the signal, it demonstrates the perceptual salience of these dimensions (Remez et al., 1998).

With regard to visual speech, work in our laboratory has shown that isolated time-varying *visual* information for articulation is also perceptually salient (e.g., Rosenblum, Johnson, & Saldaña, 1996; Rosenblum & Saldaña, 1996; Rosenblum & Saldaña, 1998). For these demonstrations, a point-light technique was implemented in which small illuminated dots are affixed to a darkened face. The face is then filmed speaking in the dark so that only the dots and their movements are visible in the resultant stimuli. Research has shown that while these visual images contain no standard facial features, they do provide visual speech information to the degree that they can enhance auditory speech in noise and integrate with auditory speech in a McGurk-effect paradigm (Rosenblum et al., 1996; Rosenblum & Saldaña, 1996). Thus, isolated time-varying articulatory information conveyed either visually or auditorily supports speech perception. In this sense, time-varying information for speech can be considered a modality-neutral property that encodes linguistically significant information.

Not only are the dynamic dimensions of speech useful for audio and visual speech, there is research in both domains showing greater relative salience of time-varying over static speech information. In auditory speech, it has been shown that the portions of the signal that are least changing (vowel nuclei; consonantal burst targets) are less informative than portions that are more dynamic and influenced by coarticulation (Blumstein, Isaacs, & Mertus, 1982; Strange, Jenkins, & Johnson, 1983; Strange et al., 1976). For instance, much of the vowel nucleus of a CVC syllable can be deleted without hindering vowel identification (Jenkins, Strange, & Edman, 1983; Strange et al., 1983). These "silent-center syllables" were created by extracting up to 60% of the vowel nucleus and replacing it with silence. Research shows that silent-center syllables are recognized as easily as intact syllables and that the extracted portion of the syllable, which should contain the most "canonical" portions of the vowel, are relatively less informative (Strange et al., 1983).

Recent research in our laboratory has shown analogous findings for visual speech (Yakel, 2000; Yakel et al., in preparation). We asked normal hearing observers to lipread a face articulating nine different vowels in a /bVb/ syllable context. The syllables were modified in ways similar to those made on the auditory syllables used in the Strange et al. (1983) study. Visual "blank-center" syllables analogous to silent-center syllables were created by extracting out roughly 50–60% of the vowel nucleus of the visual speech stimuli. These extracted portions were replaced with black video frames. Also included in the identification tests were the extracted centers themselves, as well as the original intact syllables. Importantly, the extracted center stimuli actually included the most extreme visible vowel articulatory positions of the utterances, thereby containing the information usually considered closest to the "canonical" visible vowel. Despite the presence of this information, our results showed that the extracted center stimuli were *not* as identifiable as the blank-center stimuli, which were as easily identified as the original intact syllables. A follow-up experiment revealed that the lower performance observed with the extracted-center syllables was not related to the fact that they were composed of fewer visible frames than either the control or blank-center stimuli (Yakel, 2000; Yakel et al., in preparation).

These results suggest that, as for auditory speech, the most salient parts of visible vowels lie at the more coarticulated portions of the syllables. We believe that this is a useful finding for two reasons. First, as stated, most descriptions of visible speech information have comprised sequences of static articulatory positions (e.g., Braida, 1991; Massaro & Cohen, 1990; Montgomery & Jackson, 1983). Clearly, our findings showing that the coarticulated/dynamic portions of visible vowels are more informative than the extreme "canonical" articulatory positions challenge this static interpretation of visible speech information. Our results bolster the point-light speech findings in showing that not only is time-varying information useful, it might in fact be the most salient dimension in lipreading CVC syllables.

Second, and more germane to the current chapter, finding evidence for greater salience in the more coarticulated portions of the visual speech signal suggests an informational similitude across visual and auditory speech. Finding greater cross-modal salience for time-varying dimensions provides additional support for the interpretation of these dimensions as modality-neutral. Moreover, evidence for a common informational form across modalities supports a speech perception mechanism that is sensitive to underlying gestural primitives instantiated in any modality. In the next section, we will examine another general property common to both auditory and visual speech which could act as modality-neutral information.

3.4.3 *Informational similitude in auditory and visual speech: Indexical dimensions of speech*

Another class of informational properties salient in both auditory and visual speech is the dimension of the speaker. Over the last 15 years, auditory speech perception research has revealed that the indexical properties of an utterance (those associated with specific speakers) play an important role in phonetic recovery (for a review see this volume: Johnson; Kreiman et al.; Nygaard). There is now substantial evidence that speaker-specific information can facilitate speech perception in the contexts of single vs. multiple speaker lists (Mullennix, Pisoni, & Martin, 1989; Sommers, Nygaard, & Pisoni, 1994), word naming and identification in noise (Nygaard, Sommers, & Pisoni, 1994; Nygaard & Pisoni, 1998), recognition memory (Bradlow, Nygaard, & Pisoni, 1999; Palmeri, Goldinger, & Pisoni, 1993), implicit memory (Church & Schacter, 1994; Goldinger, 1992, 1998), and form-based priming (Saldaña & Rosenblum, 1994).

There is also evidence that phonetic properties of the speech signal can be used for speaker recognition. Remez and his colleagues (1997) conducted sinewave speech re-synthesis to isolate the phonetic dimensions of individual speakers' natural sentences. They argue that sinewave speech retains phonetic dimensions which also include speaker-specific, idiolectic properties (e.g., coarticulatory assimilation; rhythmic style). Remez et al. found that listeners could recognize familiar speakers from these stimuli in both matching and identification contexts. They conclude that common speaker-specific phonetic information can be used for both speech and speaker recovery and that this use of the same articulatory information could (partly) underlie the contingencies observed between the two functions (Remez et al., 1997).

The observed relations between auditory speech perception and the indexical properties of speech have had important implications for theories of speech. Specifically, these research findings have provided new and important evidence against the long-held view that the speech function involves a "stripping-away" of non-phonetic properties of the signal (e.g., Pisoni, 1997). It has become clear that not only are indexical dimensions of the speech signal relevant to phonetic perception, they are often facilitative (Pisoni, 1997).

Analogous conclusions are now being drawn about *visual* speech perception. Evidence is mounting that speaker information can influence recovery of visual speech. For example, familiarity with a speaker's articulation can facilitate speed and accuracy in recognizing visible vowels (Schweinberger & Soukup, 1998). Relatedly, lipreading sentences is easier from a single speaker list than a multiple speaker list (Yakel, Rosenblum, & Fortier, 2000), suggesting that the short-term familiarity with a speaker's articulatory movements/gestures available in an hour-long experimental session can facilitate visual speech perception. Furthermore, memory for audiovisually presented words can be influenced by visual attributes of a speaker (Sheffert & Fowler, 1995). Also, even the robust McGurk effect can be influenced by prior familiarity with a speaker's face (Walker, Bruce, & O'Malley, 1995; but see Green et al., 1991; Rosenblum & Yakel, 2001).

Another class of evidence for the link between visible speech and speaker perception has involved showing common informational influences across the functions. This research has shown that image manipulations known to especially disrupt face perception can also disrupt visual speech (see Rosenblum, Yakel, & Green, 2000, for a review). For example, it has long been known that inverting the image of a face makes it disproportionately harder to recognize, relative to inverting non-face images (see Valentine & Bruce, 1988 for a review). Relatedly, an upright face context facilitates perception of facial image distortions (e.g., inverted eyes and mouth) relative to an inverted face context (see Bartlett & Searcy, 1993 for a review). Audiovisual speech researchers have recently found analogous image influences on visual speech perception. Thus, speaker face image inversion (Bertelson et al., 1994; Green, 1994; Jordan & Bevan, 1997; Massaro & Cohen, 1996) as well upright facial distortions (inverted mouths) (Rosenblum, Yakel, & Green, 2000) can disrupt visual and audiovisual speech perception. Potentially, the disruptive influences of these face image manipulations have a similar basis for both visual speech and face perception (e.g., influences of configural/holistic information).

Not only can upright facial context information bear on both functions, it seems that articulatory kinematics can also be used for both visual speech and speaker recognition. We have recently implemented our point-light technique to show that isolated visible speech can be used to identify speakers (Rosenblum et al., 2002; Rosenblum, Smith, & Niehus, in preparation). These experiments were designed to follow the auditory speaker recognition experiments of Remez and colleagues (Remez et al., 1997). Recall that Remez et al. isolated the phonetic properties of speakers' sentences using sinewave resynthesis techniques and found that listeners could recognize familiar speakers from these stimuli in both matching and identification contexts. Remez et al. suggested that there is speaker-specific idiolectic style information available in the isolated phonetics retained in the sinewave speech.

In our visual analogue to the Remez et al. work, we isolated visual speech information using the point-light technique. Because the point-light technique isolates the time-varying aspects of visible speech, the technique also serves to eliminate the "pictorial" information usually associated with face recognition (facial features and configurations, face shape, skin tone, hairline, etc.) (see also Bassili, 1978; Berry, 1990, 1991; Bruce & Valentine, 1988). We reasoned that if visible phonetic characteristics could provide idiolectal information in a way analogous to the sinewave stimuli of Remez et al., then observers should be able to recognize speakers from articulating point-light faces.

Our tests involved two sets of experiments. In the first set, subjects were asked to match an unfamiliar fully-illuminated articulating face to one of two point-light images based on speaker identity (2AFC procedure). We found that subjects could make these matches at better than chance levels for nine of ten of the speakers tested. A number of control conditions established that subjects' matching ability was not based on any static frame information available in the point-light stimuli and that appropriately ordered and timed visible articulatory movements were needed for successful matching (Rosenblum et al., 2002).

The second set of experiments tested whether the information available from point-light speakers would allow a set of friends to recognize each other without the benefit of seeing a fully-illuminated face on each trial (Rosenblum et al., in preparation). For these purposes, seven graduate students who had at least two years of regular contact with one another were videotaped speaking under point-light conditions. These point-light stimuli were then presented to the graduate students who were asked to recognize their friends from the point-light stimuli under both matching (2AFC; written name to face) and single presentation conditions (Remez et al., 1997). We found that under both conditions, subjects were able to recognize five of their seven friends at better than chance levels. A control condition established that observers' success at this task was not based on any static/pictorial information retained in the point-light stimuli.

We are presently examining the informational basis for these judgments using response confusion data and kinematic analyses of the visible articulations (Rosenblum et al., in preparation). What has been revealed so far is that speaker recognition does *not* seem to be based on utterance properties such as overall duration or speaker gender (see also Remez et al., 1997; Fellowes, Remez, & Rubin, 1997). Potentially, as in the Remez et al. studies, our subjects are able to recognize point-light speakers from idiolectic information (coarticulatory assimilation; rhythmicity) available in the visible gestures (see also Lachs, 1999, 2002).

We believe the results of the point-light speaker identification experiments are of theoretical importance for three reasons. First, they add to the growing literature that time-varying face information can facilitate face recognition in degraded image conditions (Christie & Bruce, 1998; Knight & Johnston, 1997; Lander, Christie, & Bruce, 1999). Second, our results suggest that common articulatory information can be used for both visual speech and face perception which is contrary to traditional accounts of the informational basis of these functions (e.g., mouth shapes for lipreading; facial features, configurations for face perception). In fact, finding common information for visual speech and speaker perception challenges "modular" accounts of both functions (e.g., Bruce & Valentine, 1988; Fodor, 1983; Liberman & Mattingly, 1985). Finally, our point-light speaker findings are important because they are closely analogous to the auditory speech perception results of Remez and his colleagues (1997). Results in both domains suggest an informational connection between speech and speaker properties, providing a further example of informational similitude across auditory and visual speech (see also Lachs, 1999, 2002; Lachs & Pisoni, 2004, in press).

To date, the explanations of how speaker information influences speech recovery for both auditory and visual speech have focused on modality-specific information. For auditory speech perception, explanations have concentrated on mechanisms which link the separate representation systems for phonological and voice information (Church & Schacter, 1994), or the use of common phonetic information, where "phonetic" pertains to the *acoustic consequences* of articulatory effects which relate to a specific utterance (Remez et al., 1997). For visual speech perception, explanations of speech-speaker contingencies have focused on the use of common visual information including visible facial features (Yakel et al., 2000), visible face configural dimensions (Jordan & Bevan, 1997; Rosenblum et al., 2000), and common visible articulatory style (Lachs & Pisoni, 2004, in press; Rosenblum et al., 2002).

While the current explanations of speech-speaker contingencies have focused on modality-specific information, it could be that the basis of the contingencies in both modalities is related to the use of information that takes the form of *modality-neutral, articulatory-gestural* properties. Potentially, the perceptual primitives which provide the link between speech and speaker are the idiolectic articulatory dimensions available across auditory and visual modalities. If so, then an explanation for why the contingencies are observed cross-modally is that the speech perception mechanism is sensitive to the gestural contingencies available in multiple modalities and exploits this information. In this way, the informational contingencies can be considered modality-neutral. If this interpretation is correct, an interesting prediction follows. If speaker-informing idiolectic information is modality-neutral, then *cross-modal* speaker matching should be possible using articulatory information. In other words, observers should be able to match heard voices to seen speakers based on speaker-specific information conveyed in both modalities: i.e., observers should be able to "hear a face."

In fact, recent findings from three independent laboratories report evidence that perceivers are able to match voices to silent speaking faces. First, projects by both Kamachi et al. (2003) and Lachs (1999, 2002) used a 2AFC procedure to test if subjects could match a voice to one of two fully-illuminated faces, or match a face to one of two voices based on speaker identity. Both sets of researchers found that subjects performed these tasks at better than chance levels. Next, research by both Lachs and Pisoni (2004, in press) and our own laboratory (Rosenblum & Nichols, 2000; Rosenblum et al., under review) tested voice-to-face matching using point-light speaker stimuli. Because point-light techniques isolate visual speech information, this method provided a more rigorous test of whether matching could be accomplished using visible idiolectic properties. (The earlier fully-illuminated face-to-voice matching demonstrations by Lachs and Kamachi et al. might have been accomplished using non-speech properties such as attractiveness, confidence, or ethnicity.) Both projects revealed voice-to-point-light speaker cross-modal matching performance at levels significantly above chance. Furthermore, our project involved a number of control conditions which established that subjects' matching performance was not based on static frame information available in the point-light stimuli. These conditions also demonstrated that appropriately ordered and timed visible articulatory movements were needed for successful cross-modal speaker matching (Rosenblum et al., 2002).

Finally, research by Lachs and Pisoni (2004, in press) as well as work in our own laboratory (Smith & Rosenblum, 2003) has tested voice-to-face matching conditions in which the stimuli of both modalities were reduced to time-varying idiolectic dimensions. In both projects, sinewave speech resynthesis (Remez et al., 1997) was carried out on the auditory component of the stimuli and subjects were asked to match these sinewave sentences to point-light sentences from the same speaker. Both projects reveal preliminary results that subjects can match sinewave voices to point-light faces for many speakers at better than chance levels. We are currently conducting follow-up experiments to determine if matching performance is based on the movement aspects of the point-light stimuli. If the sinewave speech to point-light speaker matching results stand, then additional support for the salience of modality-neutral idiolectic speaker information will be obtained.

In summary, recent findings from several research groups have revealed commonalities across auditory and visual speech information. These commonalities take the form of specific correspondences between visible and auditory signals previously considered only loosely related (Munhall & Vatikiotis-Bateson, 1998; Yehia et al., 1998). These correspondences demonstrate the existence of modality-neutral properties, similar in form to those first hypothesized by Summerfield (1987). At a broader level, informational similitude has been observed as a common salience of time-varying and indexical dimensions across modalities. This similitude could reflect a speech perception function sensitive to modality-neutral gestural information instantiated across signals. Certainly, many more examples of modality-neutral information will need to be uncovered, at more specific levels (e.g., Browman & Goldstein, 1985). Still, even these initial examples have important implications for theoretical accounts of speech perception. As argued, the existence of modality-neutral information supports a speech mechanism relatively unconcerned with modality (e.g., Calvert et al., 1997) as well as an integrative function operating at the level of the information extraction (e.g., Green, 1998). In these ways, this research fits well with the previous evidence for the primacy of multimodal speech perception. In the final section, some speculations on the evolutionary implications of multimodal speech primacy will be addressed.

3.5 Visible Speech and the Evolution of Spoken Language: Speculations and Predictions

If the primary mode of speech perception is multimodal, then there should be evidence for the influence of multimodal speech on the evolution of spoken language, as well as the phonological inventories of extant languages. While very little has been written on these issues (but see Burnham, 1998), a survey of recent literature invites some speculations.

Two currently influential theories of language evolution assume some critical role of visuofacial information. In MacNeilage's (1998) frame/content theory of language evolution, the "frame" of spoken language production is constructed from components of ingestive mastication. MacNeilage proposes that the oscillatory nature of mandibular movements during mastication provided the evolutionary support for the cyclical nature of syllabic speech. A critical step between mastication and spoken language, according to MacNeilage, was the assignment of ingestive gestures with communicative potential. MacNeilage suggests that this assignment could easily arise from the oscillatory *visuofacial* communication known to be used by many non-human primates (e.g., teethchattering, lipsmacks, tonguesmacks). Later, the communicative relevance of these visuofacial gestures could have been generalized to accompanying rudimentary vocal oscillations. Moreover, these visible facial gestures could support the mimetic capacity often considered to be precursory to language (Donald, 1991). In these ways, the communicative aspects of visuofacial gestures could have played a pivotal role in the evolution of spoken language in providing the link between ingestive and communicative articulatory movements (MacNeilage, 1998).

Other theorists have proposed that much of the evolution of language actually occurred in a visual medium (e.g., Armstrong, Stokoe, & Wilcox, 1994; Corballis, 2002; Hewes, 1992). From this perspective, the first true language was likely gestural in nature, not spoken, and these gestures were composed of both manual and facial articulations. An example of this class of theories has been proposed in a recent book by Corballis (2002). As evidence, Corballis discusses the continued use of a gestural language for the great apes, as well as evidence that Broca's area was enlarged long before the vocal tract was ready for speech. With regard to visuofacial gestures, Corballis considers them to be a critical link from manual to audible gestures and he speculates that language likely evolved from being primarily manual, to facial and manual, and then ultimately to facial and vocal. Ultimately, the vocal aspects of language took on greater importance for several reasons including its usefulness in the dark and over greater distances, as well as its ability to free the hands. However, Corballis argues that gesture has not been supplanted by vocal speech, but instead, "... clearly lurks behind the surface of speech, as though ready to come to the rescue when speech fails" (2002, p. 192). He cites the McGurk effect as evidence that gestural/visuofacial influences are still evident in modern speech.

To summarize, visuofacial gestures likely provided an important link between a visually-based communication system and one which made greater use of audible language. Potentially then, the language facility evolved to make use of gestures of all types, whether auditorily or visually conveyed. In this sense, the importance of visible gestures could provide the evolutionary basis for a speech perception mechanism sensitive to multimodal information. If so, then an interesting prediction follows. If the primacy of multimodal speech has an evolutionary basis, then it should have a traceable phylogeny. Potentially, primates should show evidence for audiovisual integration of "speech" in much the same way as pre-linguistic infants (Rosenblum et al., 1997). In fact, there is recent evidence for primate sensitivity to audiovisual *correspondences* in conspecific vocal calls. Recently, Ghazanfar and Logothetis (2003) used a preferential looking paradigm and found that rhesus monkeys looked longer at a video of a monkey face which matched either the "coo" or "alarm" calls presented auditorily. While this experiment shows primate sensitivity to cross-modal correspondence, it does not demonstrate cross-modal *integration*, as such. To examine audiovisual integration in primates, we have initiated a new research project to test the McGurk effect in rhesus macaques. Evidence for a McGurk effect in primates would provide further support of an evolutionary basis for multimodal speech primacy, as well as evidence against experiential accounts of the effect (e.g., Diehl & Kluender, 1989; Massaro, 1987).

Another prediction regarding the evolution of language follows from the primacy of multimodal speech. To the degree that language evolved to be both heard and seen, there should be evidence for some influence of visual speech on the phonological inventories of modern languages. Most discussions of constraints on phonological inventories have addressed the influences of auditory distinctiveness (e.g., Diehl & Kluender, 1989; Flemming, this volume; Ohala, 1984, 1996) and articulatory stability (e.g., Clements, 1985; Fowler, 1996). However, it could be that with the variance remaining from these other influences, visual speech plays a role in shaping the phonological inventories of spoken language.

In fact, there is evidence that languages display a phonetic complementarity between heard and seen speech such that linguistic distinctions that are harder to hear, are easier to see and vice versa (e.g., the /m/-/n/ distinction mentioned above) (Summerfield, 1987; Walden, Prosek, & Worthington, 1975). Certainly, this complementarity is partly related to the acoustical properties of vocal tract anatomy (C. A. Fowler, 1994, personal communication). Thus, while it is easier to see consonants produced towards the front of the mouth, any closure of the frontal cavity will likely produce a less distinct acoustic signal than when the frontal cavity is open. Still, it is an open question whether phonological inventories do select for segments that are *either* easy to hear or see. If visual speech does constrain phonological inventories, the world's languages should include relatively few phonetic segments that are both difficult to hear *and see*.

These speculations on the evolution of language and the composition and development of phonological inventories follow from the assumption that speech evolved to be heard and seen. This is not to ignore the predominance of auditory influences on spoken language evolution (cf. Fowler, 1989, 1996). However, it follows from the primacy of multimodal speech that some influence of the gestural information available through primarily visual means should be evident in these domains.

3.6 Conclusions

In this essay, we have argued that the primary mode of speech perception is multimodal. Support for the primacy of multimodal speech perception was provided by evidence for its ubiquity and automaticity, as well as behavioral and neurophysiological findings of early sensitivity to multimodal speech. It was further proposed that the appropriate conceptualization of speech information is in terms of modality-neutral properties that are higher-order and gesturally-based. Evidence for modality-neutral information was provided by the close correspondences between auditory and visual speech signals, as well as more general informational similitude across modalities. Finally, speculations were offered about multimodal influences on the evolution of language.

Throughout the essay, parallels have been drawn between findings on multimodal speech perception and findings on nonspeech multimodal perception. The behavioral and neurophysiological research literature on nonspeech perception supports a general sensory architecture organized around multimodal input. In this sense, speech seems fully consistent with nonspeech perception in displaying multimodal primacy. In fact, surveying the recent nonspeech multimodal literature reveals that speech research is cited as providing prototypical examples of multimodal primacy (e.g., McGurk effects; visual speech activation of auditory cortex). This fact is partly a consequence of the vast research supporting gestural primitives of speech perception (e.g., Fowler, 1986; Fowler & Rosenblum, 1991; Liberman & Mattingly, 1985). Ironically, it may be that part of the legacy of the motor theory – a "speech is special" theory – will be to inspire new research directions that uncover modality-neutral, distal event primitives for *nonspeech* perception.

Beyond evidence for multimodal speech primacy, we also offered a few predictions derived from the approach. These predictions included: (1) successful cross-modal matching based on isolated idiolectic information; (2) a traceable phylogeny of multimodal speech as evidenced in a McGurk effect in primates; and (3) evidence that visible speech can have some influence on phonological inventories. Several other predictions can be derived from the multimodal primacy/modality-neutral information account. For example, we would anticipate evidence of cross-modal priming and transfer of training to the speech of specific speakers; and that intrastimulus modality switching would have a relatively negligible interfering effect on speech perception. These and other predictions can be used to assess the proposal that sensory modality is relatively invisible to the speech function and speech information is best construed as modality-neutral.

ACKNOWLEDGMENTS

Preparation of this chapter was supported by NSF Grant BCS-0111949 awarded to the author. The author wishes to thank Edward Auer, Lynne Bernstein, Michael Gordon, and Nicolas Smith for helpful discussions.

NOTES

1 This chapter will concentrate on *audiovisual* examples of multimodal speech perception. There is also a sizable literature on vibrotactile aid devices that shows effective integration of tactile and visual speech information (for reviews see Kishon-Rabin et al., 1996; Reed et al., 1993). Audiovisual multimodal speech is emphasized in the current chapter because of its relevance to everyday communication as well as its theoretical importance in the general speech perception literature.

2 Examples of McGurk effects are available on the internet (e.g., Gordon & Rosenblum, 2001), and can be produced with readily available video editing software, or even demonstrated live in the classroom with no equipment (Cobb & Lewis, 2001).

3 The gestural and auditory theories are not the only approaches to the perceptual objects issue. For example, Remez (1986, 1989) has argued that the true perceptual objects of speech are the actual events and objects to which the speaker refers. From this perspective, the gestures and auditory components are both part of the linguistic informational medium which indirectly conveys the speaker's referents. This approach has a number of theoretically significant implications including the fact that speech, in involving an indirect apprehension of the message referents, is necessarily different from perception of nonspeech events. Furthermore, evidence against auditory primitives, including the multimodal effects discussed here, are equally as supportive of linguistic perceptual objects as they are of gestural perceptual objects. In the current chapter, the gestural vs. auditory perceptual object perspectives are emphasized simply because of their historical prominence in the audiovisual speech literature.

4 There is evidence that McGurk-type visual influences do not affect auditory adaptation (Roberts & Summerfield, 1981; Saldaña & Rosenblum, 1994). This finding has been interpreted by Bernstein et al. (2004) as evidence that integration occurs at a later stage than claimed by, for example, Green (1998). However, other theorists have interpreted these results as simply reflecting low-level auditory mechanisms such as adaptation in the auditory nerve (A. M. Liberman, 1993, personal communication; Schwartz et al., 1998).

5 This explanation of integration via modality-neutral information addresses instances for which information is congruent across modalities. Certainly, this constitutes the vast majority of natural cases. However, modality-neutral explanations of integrating discrepant cross-modal information (e.g., McGurk effects), have been formulated and can be found in papers by Stoffregen and Bardy (2001), and Rosenblum and Gordon (2001).

REFERENCES

Armstrong, D., Stokoe, W. C., & Wilcox, S. (1994). *Gesture and the Nature of Language*. Cambridge: Cambridge University Press.

Arnold, P. & Hill, F. (2001). Bisensory augmentation: A speechreading advantage when speech is clearly audible and intact. *British Journal of Psychology*, 92, 339–55.

Bahrick, L. E. & Pickens, J. N. (1994). Amodal relations: The basis for intermodal perception and learning in infancy. In D. J. Lewkowicz & R. Lickliter (eds.), *The Development of Intersensory Perception: Comparative Perspectives* (pp. 205–32). Hillsdale, NJ: Lawrence Erlbaum.

Bartlett, J. C. & Searcy, J. (1993). Inversion and configuration of faces. *Cognitive Psychology*, 25, 281–316.

Bassili, J. N. (1978). Facial motion in the perception of faces and of emotional expression. *Journal of Experimental Psychology: Human Perception and Performance*, 4, 373–9.

Baynes, K., Funnell, M. G., & Fowler, C. A. (1994). Hemispheric contributions to the integration of visual and auditory information in speech perception. *Perception & Psychophysics*, 55, 633–41.

Bermant, R. I. & Welch, R. B. (1976). Effect of degree of separation of visual-auditory stimulus and eye position upon spatial interaction of vision and audition. *Perceptual & Motor Skills*, 43, 487–93.

Bernstein, L. E., Auer, E. T., Moore, J. K., Ponton, C., Don, M., & Singh, M. (2002). Visual speech perception without primary auditory cortex activation. *NeuroReport*, 13, 311–15.

Bernstein, L. E., Auer, E. T., & Moore, J. K. (2004). Modality-specific perception of auditory and visual speech. In G. A. Calvert, C. Spence, & B. E. Stein (eds.), *The Handbook of Multisensory Processing* (pp. 203–23). Cambridge, MA: MIT Press.

Berry, D. S. (1990). What can a moving face tell us? *Journal of Personality and Social Psychology*, 58, 1004–14.

Berry, D. S. (1991). Child and adult sensitivity to gender information in patterns of facial motion. *Ecological Psychology*, 3, 349–66.

Bertelson, P. & Radeau, M. (1981). Cross-modal bias and perceptual fusion with auditory-visual spatial discordance. *Perception & Psychophysics*, 29, 578–84.

Bertelson, P., Vroomen, J., Wiegeraad, G., & de Gelder, B. (1994). Exploring the relation between McGurk interference and ventriloquism. *Proceedings of the 1994 International Conference on Spoken Language Processing (ICSLP94)*, 2, 559–62.

Blumstein, S., Isaacs, E., & Mertus, J. (1982). The role of gross spectral shape as a perceptual cue to place of articulation in initial stop consonants. *Journal of the Acoustical Society of America*, 72, 43–50.

Bradlow, A. R., Nygaard, L. C., & Pisoni, D. B. (1999). Effects of talker, rate, and amplitude variation on recognition memory for spoken words. *Perception & Psychophysics*, 61, 206–19.

Braida, L. D. (1991). Crossmodal integration in the identification of consonant segments. *Quarterly Journal of Experimental Psychology*, 43, 647–77.

Browman, C. P. & Goldstein, L. M. (1985). Dynamic modeling of phonetic structure. In V. A. Fromkin (ed.), *Phonetic Linguistics: Essays in Honor of Peter Ladefoged* (pp. 35–53). New York: Academic Press.

Bruce, V. & Valentine, T. (1988). When a nod's as good as a wink: The role of dynamic information in facial recognition. In M. M. Gruneberg, P. E. Morris, & R. N. Sykes (eds.), *Practical Aspects of Memory: Current Research and Issues, Vol. 1: Memory in Everyday Life* (pp. 169–74). New York: John Wiley & Sons.

Buechel, C., Price, C., Frackowiak, R. S. J., & Friston, K. (1998) Different activation patterns in the visual cortex of late and congenitally blind subjects. *Brain*, 121, 409–19.

Burnham, D. (1998). Language specificity in the development of auditory-visual speech perception. In R. Campbell, B. Dodd, & D. Burnham (eds.), *Hearing by Eye II: The Psychology of Speechreading and Audiovisual Speech* (pp. 27–60). Hove, UK: Psychology Press.

Burnham, D. & Dodd, B. (1996). Auditory-visual speech perception as a direct process: The McGurk effect in infants and across languages. In D. Stork & M. Hennecke (eds.), *Speechreading by Humans and Machines* (pp. 103–14). Berlin: Springer-Verlag.

Callan, D. E., Callan, A. M., Kroos, C., & Vatikiotis-Bateson, E. (2001). Multimodal contribution to speech perception revealed by independent component analysis: A single-sweep EEG case study. *Cognitive Brain Research*, 10, 349–53.

Calvert, G. A. (2001). Crossmodal processing in the human brain: Insights from functional neuroimaging studies. *Cerebral Cortex*, 1, 1110–23.

Calvert, G. A., Brammer, M. J., Bullmore, E. T., Campbell, R., Iversen, S. D., & David, A. S. (1999). Response amplification in sensory-specific cortices during crossmodal binding. *NeuroReport*, 10, 2619–23.

Calvert, G. A., Bullmore, E. T., Brammer, M. J., Campbell, R., Iversen, S. D., Woodruff, P., McGuire, P., Williams, S., & David, A. S. (1997). Silent lipreading activates the auditory cortex. *Science*, 276, 593–6.

Campbell, R. (1986). The lateralization of lip-read sounds: A first look. *Brain and Cognition*, 5, 1–21.

Campbell, R. (1992). The neuropsychology of lipreading. *Philisophical Transcriptions of the Royal Society of London*, 335, 39–45.

Campbell, R. (1998). Everyday speechreading: Understanding seen speech in action. *Scandinavian Journal of Psychology*, 39, 163–7.

Campbell, R. T., Landis, T., & Regard, M. (1986). Face recognition and lip-reading: A neurological dissociation. *Brain*, 109, 509–21.

Christie, F. & Bruce, V. (1998). The role of dynamic information in the recognition of unfamiliar faces. *Memory & Cognition*, 26, 780–90.

Church, B. A. & Schacter, D. L. (1994). Perceptual specificity of auditory priming: Implicit memory for voice intonation and fundamental frequency. *Journal of Experimental Psychology: Learning, Memory, and Cognition*, 20, 521–33.

Clark, B. & Graybiel, A. (1966). Influence of contact cues on the perception of the oculogravic illusion. *US Navy Aerospace Medical Institute & National Aeronautics & Space Administration Joint Report.*

Clements, G. N. (1985). The geometry of phonological features. *Phonological Yearbook*, 2, 225–52.

Cobb, V. & Lewis, C. C. (2001). *Perk Up Your Ears: Discovering Your Sense of Hearing*. New York: Millbrook Press.

Cohen, L. G., Celnik, P., Pascual-Leone, A., Faiz, L., Corwell, B., Honda, M., Sadato, H., Gerloff, C., Catala, M. D., & Hallett, M. (1997). Functional relevance of crossmodal plasticity in the blind. *Nature*, 389, 180–2.

Corballis, M. C. (2002). *From Hand to Mouth: The Origins of Language.* Princeton: Princeton University Press.

Diehl, R. L. & Kluender, K. R. (1989). On the objects of speech perception. *Ecological Psychology*, 1, 121–44.

Diehl, R. L., Souther, A. F., & Convis, C. L. (1980). Conditions on rate normalization in speech perception. *Perception & Psychophysics*, 27, 435–43.

Diesch, E. (1995). Left and right hemifield advantages of fusions and combinations in audiovisual speech perception. *Quarterly Journal of Experimental Psychology: Human Experimental Psychology*, 48, 320–33.

Donald, M. (1991). *Origins of the Modern Mind: Three Stages in the Evolution of Culture and Cognition*. Cambridge, MA: Harvard University Press.

Eimer, M. (2001). Crossmodal links in spatial attention between vision, audition, and touch: Evidence from event-related brain potentials. *Neuropsychologia*, 39, 1292–1303.

Ellis, H. D. (1989). Processes underlying face recognition. In R. Bruyer (ed.), *Neuropsychology of Face Perception and Facial Expression* (pp. 1–27). Hillsdale, NJ: Lawrence Erlbaum.

Fellowes, J. M., Remez, R. E., & Rubin, P. E. (1997). Perceiving the sex and identity of a talker without natural vocal timbre. *Perception & Psychophysics*, 59, 839–49.

Fodor, J. (1983). *The Modularity of Mind.* Cambridge, MA: MIT Press.

Fowler, C. A. (1986). An event approach to the study of speech perception from a direct-realist perspective. *Journal of Phonetics*, 14, 3–28.

Fowler, C. A. (1989). Real objects of speech perception: A commentary on Diehl and Kluender. *Ecological Psychology*, 1, 145–60.

Fowler, C. A. (1996). Listeners do hear sounds, not tongues. *Journal of the Acoustical Society of America*, 99, 1730–41.

Fowler, C. A. & Dekle, D. J. (1991). Listening with eye and hand: Cross-modal contributions to speech perception. *Journal of Experimental Psychology: Human Perception and Performance*, 17, 816–28.

Fowler, C. A. & Rosenblum, L. D. (1991). Perception of the phonetic gesture. In I. G. Mattingly & M. Studdert-Kennedy (eds.), *Modularity and the Motor Theory of Speech Perception* (pp. 33–59). Hillsdale, NJ: Lawrence Erlbaum.

Geers, A. & Brenner, C. (1994). Speech perception results: Audition and lipreading enhancement. *Volta Review*, 96, 97–108.

Ghanzafar, A. A. & Logothetis, N. K. (2003). Facial expressions linked to monkey calls. *Nature*, 423, 937–8.

Gibson, J. J. (1966). *The Senses Considered as Perceptual Systems.* Boston, MA: Houghton Mifflin.

Gibson, J. J. (1979). *The Ecological Approach to Visual Perception.* Boston, MA: Houghton-Mifflin.

Goldinger, S. D. (1992). Words and voices: Implicit and explicit memory for spoken words. *Research on Speech Perception Technical Report No. 7.* Bloomington, IN: Speech Research Laboratory, Indiana University.

Goldinger, S. D. (1998). Echoes of echoes? An episodic theory of lexical access. *Psychological Review*, 105, 251–79.

Gordon, M. S. & Rosenblum, L. D. (2001). Audiovisual Speech Web-Lab: An internet teaching and research laboratory. *Behavioral Research Methods, Instruments, & Computers*, 33, 267–9.

Grant, K. W. & Seitz, P.-F. (2000). The use of visible speech cues for improving auditory detection of spoken sentences. *Journal of the Acoustical Society of America*, 108, 1197–1208.

Green, K. P. (1994). The influence of an inverted face on the McGurk effect. Poster presented at the Spring, 1994, meeting of the Acoustical Society of America, Cambridge, MA. *Journal of the Acoustical Society of America*, 95, 3014 (abstract).

Green, K. P. (1998). The use of auditory and visual information during phonetic processing: Implications for theories of speech perception. In R. Campbell & B. Dodd (eds.), *Hearing by Eye II: Advances in the Psychology of Speechreading and Audiovisual Speech* (pp. 3–25). Hove, UK: Psychology Press.

Green, K. P. & Gerdman, A. (1995). Cross-modal discrepancies in coarticulation and the integration of speech information: The McGurk effect with mismatched vowels. *Journal of Experimental Psychology: Human Perception and Performance*, 21, 1409–26.

Green, K. P. & Kuhl, P. K. (1989). The role of visual information in the processing of place and manner features in speech perception. *Perception & Psychophysics*, 45, 34–42.

Green, K. P. & Miller, J. L. (1985). On the role of visual rate information in phonetic perception. *Perception & Psychophysics*, 38, 269–76.

Green, K. P. & Norrix, L. (2001). The perception of /r/ and /l/ in a stop cluster: Evidence of cross-modal context effects. *Journal of Experimental Psychology: Human Perception and Performance*, 27, 166–77.

Green, K. P., Kuhl, P. K., Meltzoff, A. M., & Stevens, E. B. (1991). Integrating speech information across talkers, gender, and sensory modality: Female faces and male voices in the McGurk effect. *Perception & Psychophysics*, 50, 524–36.

Hellige, J. B. (1993). *Hemispheric Asymmetry: What's Right and What's Left*. Cambridge, MA: Harvard University Press.

Hewes, G. W. (1992). Primate communication and the gestural origin of language. *Current Anthropology*, 33, 65–84.

Jenkins, J. J., Strange, W., & Edman, T. R. (1983). Identification of vowels in "vowelless" syllables. *Perception & Psychophysics*, 34, 441–50.

Jordan, T. R. & Bevan, K. (1997). Seeing and hearing rotated faces: Influences of facial orientation on visual and audio-visual speech recognition. *Journal of Experimental Psychology: Human Perception and Performance*, 23, 388–403.

Kaiser, A. R., Kirk, K. I., Lachs, L., & Pisoni, D. B. (2003). Talker and lexical effects on audiovisual word recognition by adults with cochlear implants. *Journal of Speech, Language, & Hearing Research*, 46, 390–404.

Kamachi, M., Harold, H., Karen, L., & Vatikiotis-Bateson, E. (2003). Putting the face to the voice: Matching identity across modality. *Current Biology*, 13, 1709–14.

Kinney, J. A. & Luria, S. M. (1970). Conflicting visual and tactual-kinesthetic stimulation. *Perception & Psychophysics*, 8, 189–92.

Kishon-Rabin, L., Boothroyd, A., & Hanin, L. (1996). Speechreading enhancement: A comparison of spatial-tactile display of voice fundamental frequency (F0) with auditory F0. *Journal of the Acoustical Society of America*, 100, 593–602.

Kitagawa, N. & Ichihara, S. (2002). Hearing visual motion in depth. *Nature*, 416, 172–4.

Kluender, K. R. (1994). Speech perception as a tractable problem in cognitive science. In M. A. Gernsbacher (ed.), *Handbook of Psycholinguistics* (pp. 173–217). San Diego, CA: Academic Press.

Knight, B. & Johnston, A. (1997). The role of movement in face recognition. *Visual Cognition*, 4, 265–73.

Kuhl, P. K. & Meltzoff, A. N. (1984). The intermodal representation of speech in infants. *Infant Behavior and Development*, 7, 361–81.

Lachs, L. (1999). A voice is a face is a voice: Cross-modal source identification of indexical information in speech. *Research on Spoken Language Processing Progress Report No. 23*, Indiana University, pp. 241–58.

Lachs, L. (2002). Vocal tract kinematics and crossmodal speech information. *Research on Spoken Language Processing Technical Report No. 10*. Bloomington, IN: Speech Research Laboratory, Indiana University.

Lachs, L. & Pisoni, D. B. (2004). Crossmodal source information and spoken word recognition. *Journal of Experimental Psychology: Human Perception and Performance*, 30, 378–96.

Lachs, L. & Pisoni, D. B. (In press). Crossmodal source identification in speech perception. *Ecological Psychology*.

Lachs, L., Pisoni D. B., & Kirk, K. I. (2001). Use of audiovisual information in speech perception by prelingually deaf children with cochlear implants: A first report. *Ear and Hearing*, 22, 236–51.

Lander, K., Christie, F., & Bruce, V. (1999). The role of movement in the recognition of famous faces. *Memory & Cognition*, 27, 974–85.

Laurienti, P. J., Burdette, J. H., Wallace, M. T., Yen, Y. F., Field, A. S., & Stein, B. E. (2002). Deactivitation of sensory-specific cortex by cross-modal stimuli. *Journal of Cognitive Neuroscience*, 14, 420–9.

Lee, D. N. (1976). A theory of visual control of braking based on information about time-to-collision. *Perception*, 5, 437–59.

Liberman, A. M. & Mattingly, I. G. (1985). The motor theory of speech perception revised. *Cognition*, 21, 1–36.

Liberman A. M. & Whalen D. H. (2000). On the relation of speech to language. *Trends In Cognitive Science*, 4, 187–96.

Macaluso, E., Frith, C. D., & Driver, J. (2000). Modulation of human visual cortex by crossmodal spatial attention. *Science*, 289, 1206–8.

MacLeod, A. & Summerfield, Q. (1990). A procedure for measuring auditory and audio-visual speech reception thresholds for sentences in noise: Rationale, evaluation, and recommendations for use. *British Journal of Audiology*, 24, 29–43.

MacNeilage, P. F. (1998). The frame/content theory of evolution of speech production. *Behavioral & Brain Sciences*, 21, 499–546.

MacSweeney, M., Amaro, E., Calvert, G. A., & Campbell, R. (2000). Silent speechreading in the absence of scanner noise: An event-related fMRI study. *NeuroReport*, 11, 1729–33.

MacSweeney, M., Calvert, G. A., Campbell, R., et al. (2002). Speechreading circuits in people born deaf. *Neuropsychologia*, 40, 801–7.

Marks, L. (1978). *The Unity of the Senses*. New York: Academic Press.

Massaro, D. W. (1987). Speech perception by ear and eye. In B. Dodd & R. Campbell (eds.), *Hearing by Eye: The Psychology of Lip-Reading* (pp. 53–83). Hillsdale, NJ: Lawrence Erlbaum.

Massaro, D. W. & Cohen, M. M. (1990). Perception of synthesized audible and visible speech. *Psychological Science*, 1, 55–63.

Massaro, D. W. & Cohen, M. M. (1996). Perceiving speech from inverted faces. *Perception & Psychophysics*, 58, 1047–65.

Massaro, D. W., Cohen, M. M., Gesi, A., Heredia, R., & Tsuzaki, M. (1993). Bimodal speech perception: An examination across languages. *Journal of Phonetics*, 21, 445–78.

McGurk, H. & MacDonald, J. W. (1976). Hearing lips and seeing voices. *Nature*, 264, 746–8.

Meltzoff, A. N. & Moore, M. K. (1977). Imitation of facial and manual gestures by human neonates. *Science*, 198, 75–8.

Meltzoff, A. N. & Moore, M. K. (1983). The origins of imitation in infancy: Paradigm, phenomena, and theories. *Advances in Infancy Research*, 2, 265–301.

Meredith, M. A. (2002). On the neuronal basis for multisensory convergence: a brief overview. *Cognitive Brain Research*, 14, 31–40.

Mergner, T. & Rosemeier, T. (1998). Interaction of vestibular, somatosensory and visual signals for postural control and motion perception under terrestrial and microgravity conditions – a conceptual model. *Brain Research Reviews*, 28, 118–35.

Mesulam, M. M. (1998). From sensation to cognition. *Brain*, 121, 1013–52.

Mills, A. E. (1987). The development of phonology in the blind child. In B. Dodd & R. Campbell (eds.), *Hearing by Eye: The Psychology of Lip Reading* (pp. 145–62). Hillsdale, NJ: Lawrence Erlbaum.

Montgomery, A. A. & Jackson, P. L. (1983). Physical characteristics of the lips underlying vowel lipreading performance. *Journal of the Acoustical Society of America*, 73, 2134–44.

Mottonen, R., Krause, C. M., Tiippana, K., & Sams, M. (2002). Processing of changes in visual speech in the human auditory cortex. *Cognitive Brain Research*, 13, 417–25.

Mullennix, J. W., Pisoni, D. B., & Martin, C. S. (1989). Some effects of talker variability on spoken word recognition. *Journal of the Acoustical Society of America*, 92, 1085–99.

Munhall, K. G. & Vatikiotis-Bateson, E. (1998). The moving face during speech communication. In R. Campbell, B. Dodd, & D. Burnham (eds.), *Hearing by Eye II: The Psychology of Speechreading and Audiovisual Speech* (pp. 123–39). Hove, UK: Psychology Press.

Nygaard, L. C. & Pisoni, D. B. (1998). Talker-specific learning in speech perception. *Perception & Psychophysics*, 60, 355–76.

Nygaard, L. C., Sommers, M. S., & Pisoni, D. B. (1994). Speech perception as a talker-contingent process. *Psychological Science*, 5, 42–6.

Ohala, J. J. (1984). An ethological perspective on common cross-language utilization of F0 of voice. *Phonetica*, 41, 1–16.

Ohala, J. J. (1996). Speech perception is hearing sounds, not tongues. *Journal of the Acoustical Society of America*, 99, 1718–25.

O'Leary, A. & Rhodes, G. (1984). Cross-modal effects on visual and auditory object perception. *Perception & Psychophysics*, 35, 565–9.

Palmeri, T. J., Goldinger, S. D., & Pisoni, D. B. (1993). Episodic encoding of voice attributes and recognition memory for spoken words. *Journal of Experimental Psychology: Learning, Memory, and Cognition*, 19, 309–28.

Pisoni, D. B. (1997). Some thoughts on "normalization" in speech perception. In K. Johnson & J. Mullennix (eds.), *Talker Variability in Speech Processing* (pp. 9–32). San Diego, CA: Academic Press.

Radeau, M. & Bertelson, P. (1974). The after-effects of ventriloquism. *Quarterly Journal of Experimental Psychology*, 26, 63–71.

Rauschecker, J. P. & Korte, M. (1993). Auditory compensation for early blindness in cat cerebral cortex. *Journal of Neuroscience*, 13, 4538–48.

Reed, C. M., Delhorne, L. A., & Durlach, N. I. (1993). Historical overview in tactile aid research. In A. Risberg, S. Felicetti, & K.-E. Spens (eds.), *Proceedings of the Second International Conference on Tactile Aids, Hearing Aids, and Cochlear Implants*. Edsbruck, Sweden: Akademitryck AB.

Reisberg, D., McLean, J., & Goldfield, A. (1987). Easy to hear but hard to understand: A lip-reading advantage with intact auditory stimuli. In B. Dodd & R. Campbell (eds), *Hearing by Eye: The Psychology of Lip Reading* (pp. 97–113). Hillsdale, NJ: Lawrence Erlbaum.

Remez, R. E. (1986). Realism, language, and another barrier. *Journal of Phonetics*, 14, 89–97.

Remez, R. E. (1989). When the objects of perception are spoken. *Ecological Psychology*, 1, 161–80.

Remez, R. E., Fellowes, J. M., Pisoni, D. B., Goh, W. D., & Rubin, P. E. (1998). Multimodal perceptual organization of speech: Evidence from tone analogs of spoken utterances. *Speech Communication*, 26, 65–73.

Remez, R. E., Fellowes, J. M., & Rubin, P. E. (1997). Talker identification based on phonetic information. *Journal of Experimental Psychology: Human Perception & Performance*, 23(3), 651–66.

Remez, R. E., Rubin, P. E., Nygaard, L. C., & Howell, W. A. (1987). Perceptual normalization of vowels produced by sinusoidal voices. *Journal of Experimental Psychology: Human Perception & Performance*, 13(1), 40–61.

Remez, R., Rubin, P., Pisoni, D., & Carrell, T. (1981). Speech perception without traditional speech cues. *Science*, 212, 947–50.

Rinne, T., Alho, K., Alku, P., Holi, M., Sinkkonen, J., Virtanen, J., Bertrand, O., & Naeaetaenen, R. (1999). Analysis of speech sounds is left-hemisphere predominant at 100–150 ms after sound onset. *NeuroReport*, 10; 1113–17.

Roberts, M. & Summerfield, Q. (1981). Audiovisual presentation demonstrates that selective adaptation in speech perception is purely auditory. *Perception & Psychophysics*, 30, 309–14.

Rosenblum, L. D. (2002). The perceptual basis of audiovisual speech integration. *Proceedings of the 7th International Conference on Spoken Language Processing* (ICSLP), 1461–4.

Rosenblum, L. D. & Gordon, M. S. (2001). The generality of specificity: Some lessons from audiovisual speech. *Behavioral & Brain Sciences*, 24, 239–40.

Rosenblum, L. D. & Nichols, S. (2000). Recognizing speakers from visual speech information. Talk presented at the 41st meeting of the Psychonomics Society, New Orleans, LA, November 19.

Rosenblum, L. D. & Saldaña, H. M. (1996). An audiovisual test of kinematic primitives for visual speech perception. *Journal of Experimental Psychology: Human Perception and Performance*, 22, 318–31.

Rosenblum, L. D. & Saldaña, H. M. (1998). Time-varying information for visual speech perception. In R. Campbell, B. Dodd, & D. Burnham (eds.), *Hearing by Eye II: The Psychology of Speechreading and Audiovisual Speech* (pp. 61–81). Hove, UK: Psychology Press.

Rosenblum, L. D. & Yakel, D. A. (2001). The McGurk effect from single and mixed speaker stimuli. *Acoustic Research Letters Online*, 2, 67–72.

Rosenblum, L. D., Johnson, J. A., & Saldaña, H. M. (1996). Visual kinematic information for embellishing speech in noise. *Journal of Speech & Hearing Research*, 39, 1159–70.

Rosenblum, L. D., Schmuckler, M. A., & Johnson, J. A. (1997). The McGurk effect in infants. *Perception & Psychophysics*, 59, 347–57.

Rosenblum, L. D., Smith, N. M., Nichols, S., Lee, J., & Hale, S. (under review). Hearing a face: Cross-modal speaker matching using isolated visible speech. *Perception & Psychophysics.*

Rosenblum, L. D., Smith, N. M., & Niehus, R. P. (in preparation). Look who's talking: Identifying friends from visible articulation. *Psychological Science.*

Rosenblum, L. D., Yakel, D. A., Baseer, N., Panchal, A., Nordarse, B. C., & Niehus, R. P. (2002). Visual speech information for face recognition. *Perception & Psychophysics*, 64, 220–9.

Rosenblum, L. D., Yakel, D. A., & Green, K. G. (2000). Face and mouth inversion effects on visual and audiovisual speech perception. *Journal of Experimental Psychology: Human Perception and Performance*, 26, 806–19.

Sadato, N., Pascual-Leone, A., Grafman, J., Ibanez, V., Deiber, M. P., Dold, G., & Hallett, M. (1996). Activation of the primary visual cortex by Braille reading in blind subjects. *Nature*, 380, 526–8.

Saldaña, H. M. & Rosenblum, L. D. (1994). Voice information in auditory form-based priming. *Journal of the Acoustical Society of America*, 95, 2870.

Sams, M., Aulanko, R., Hamalainen, M., Hari, R., Lounasmaa, O. V., Lu, S.-T., & Simola, J. (1991). Seeing speech: visual information from lip movements modifies activity in the human auditory cortex. *Neuroscience Letters*, 127, 141–5.

Schwartz, J. L., Robert-Ribes, J., & Esculier, P. (1998). Ten years after Summerfield: A taxonomy of models for audiovisual fusion in speech perception. In R. Campbell, B. Dodd, & D. Burnham (eds.), *Hearing by Eye II: The Psychology of Speechreading and Audiovisual Speech* (pp. 85–108). Hove, UK: Psychology Press.

Schweinberger, S. R. & Soukup, G. R. (1998). Asymmetric relationships among perceptions of facial identity, emotion, and facial speech. *Journal of Experimental Psychology: Human Perception and Performance*, 24, 1748–65.

Sekiyama, K. & Tohkura, Y. (1991). McGurk effect in non-English listeners: Few visual effects for Japanese subjects hearing Japanese syllables of high auditory intelligibility. *Journal of the Acoustical Society of America*, 90, 1797–1805.

Sekiyama, K. & Tokhura, Y. (1993). Inter-language differences in the influence of visual cues in speech perception. *Journal of Phonetics*, 21, 427–44.

Shams, L., Kamitani, Y., & Shimojo, S. (2000). Illusions: What you see is what you hear. *Nature*, 408, 788.

Shams, L., Kamitani, Y., Thompson, S., & Shimojo, S. (2001). Sound alters visual evoked potentials in humans. *NeuroReport*, 12, 3849–52.

Shankweiler, D. & Studdert-Kennedy, M. (1975). A continuum of lateralization for speech perception. *Brain and Language*, 2, 212–25.

Shannon, R. V., Zeng, F.-G., Kamath, V., Wygonski, J., & Ekelid, M. (1995). Speech recognition with primarily temporal cues. *Science*, 270, 303–4.

Sheffert, S. M. & Fowler, C. A. (1995). The effects of voice and visible speaker change on memory for spoken words. *Journal of Memory and Language*, 34, 665–85.

Shimojo, S. & Shams, L. (2001). Sensory modalities are not separate modalities: Plasticity and interactions. *Current Opinion in Neurobiology*, 11, 505–9.

Smeele, P. M. T. (1996). Psychology of human speechreading. In D. Stork (ed.), *Speechreading by Man and Machine: Models, Systems, and Applications* (pp. 3–15). 1995 NATO ASI workshop, Chateau de Bonas, France: Springer Verlag.

Smeele, P. M. T., Massaro, D. W., Cohen, M. M., & Sittig, A. C. (1998). Laterality in visual speech perception. *Journal of Experimental Psychology: Human Perception and Performance*, 24, 1232–42.

Smith, N. M. & Rosenblum, L. D. (2003). Idiolectic information for cross-modal speaker recognition. *Abstracts of the Psychonomic Society*, 8, 14.

Sommers, M. S., Nygaard, L. C., & Pisoni, D. B. (1994). Stimulus variability and spoken word recognition I: Effects of variability in speaking rate and overall amplitude. *Journal of the Acoustical Society of America*, 96, 1314–24.

Stein, B. E. & Meredith, M. A. (1993). *The Merging of the Senses*. Cambridge, MA: MIT Press.

Stein, B. E., London, N., Wilkinson, L. K., & Price, D. D. (1996). Enhancement of perceived visual intensity by auditory stimuli: A psychophysical analysis. *Journal of Cognitive Neuroscience*, 8, 497–506.

Stevens, K. N. (1989). On the quantal nature of speech. *Journal of Phonetics*, 17, 3–45.

Stoffregen, T. A. & Bardy, B. G. (2001). On specification and the senses. *Behavioral & Brain Sciences*, 24, 195–261.

Strange, W., Jenkins, J. J., & Johnson, T. L. (1983). Dynamic specification of coarticulated vowels. *Journal of the Acoustical Society of America*, 74, 695–705.

Strange, W., Verbrugge, R. R., Shankweiler, D. P., & Edman, T. R. (1976). Consonant environment specifies vowel identity. *Journal of the Acoustical Society of America*, 60, 213–24.

Studdert-Kennedy, M. (1989). Cues to what? A comment on Diehl and Kluender "On the objects of speech perception." *Ecological Psychology*, 1, 181–93.

Sumby, W. H. & Pollack, I. (1954). Visual contribution to speech intelligibility in noise. *Journal of the Acoustical Society of America*, 26, 212–15.

Summerfield, Q. (1987). Some preliminaries to a comprehensive account of audio-visual speech perception. In B. Dodd & R. Campbell (eds.), *Hearing by Eye: The Psychology of Lip Reading* (pp. 53–83). Hillsdale, NJ: Lawrence Erlbaum.

Valentine, T. & Bruce, V. (1988). Mental rotation of faces. *Memory & Cognition*, 16, 556–66.

Vroomen, J. & de Gelder, B. (2000). Sound enhances visual perception: Cross-modal effects of auditory organization on vision. *Journal of Experimental Psychology: Human Perception and Performance*, 26, 1583–90.

Walden, B. E., Prosek, R. A., & Worthington, D. W. (1975). Auditory and audiovisual feature transmission in hearing-impaired adults. *Journal of Speech & Hearing Research*, 18, 272–80.

Walker, A. S. (1982). Intermodal perception of expression behaviors by human infants. *Journal of Experimental Child Psychology*, 33, 514–35.

Walker, J. T. & Scott, K. J. (1981). Auditory-visual conflicts in the perceived duration of lights, tones, and gaps. *Journal of Experimental Psychology: Human Perception and Performance*, 7, 1327–39.

Walker, S., Bruce, V., & O'Malley, C. (1995). Facial identity and facial speech processing: Familiar faces and voices in the McGurk effect.

Perception & Psychophysics, 57, 1124–33.

Walker-Andrews, A. S. & Lennon, E. M. (1985). Auditory-visual perception of changing distance by human infants. *Child Development*, 56, 544–8.

Welch, R. B. & Warren, D. H. (1986). Intersensory interactions. In K. R. Boff, L. Kaufman, & J. P. Thomas (eds.), *Handbook of Perception and Human Performance. Vol. 1: Sensory Processes and Perception* (pp. 25.1–25.36). New York: John Wiley & Sons.

Williams, D. R., Verbrugge, R. R., & Studdert-Kennedy, M. (1983). Judging sine wave stimuli as speech and nonspeech. *Journal of the Acoustical Society of America*, 74, S66.

Yakel, D. A. (2000). Effects of time-varying information on vowel identification accuracy in visual speech perception. Doctoral dissertation, University of California, Riverside.

Yakel, D. A., Rosenblum, L. D., & Fortier, M. A. (2000). Effects of talker variability on speechreading. *Perception & Psychophysics*, 62, 1405–12.

Yakel, D. A., Rosenblum, L. D., Smith, N., & Burns, D. (in preparation). Salience of time varying information for visual speech perception. To be submitted to *Perception & Psychophysics*.

Yehia, H. C., Rubin, P. E., & Vatikiotis-Bateson, E. (1998). Quantitative association of vocal-tract and facial behavior. *Speech Communication*, 26, 23–43.

4 Phonetic Processing by the Speech Perceiving Brain

LYNNE E. BERNSTEIN

As a consequence of developments in non-invasive methods for studying brain function, the underlying neural mechanisms of speech perception are being localized spatially and temporally. Theoretical issues that until recently were addressed almost solely with behavioral evidence can now be addressed in relation to functional neuroanatomy and neurophysiology in healthy behaving humans. Some of the recent findings were not anticipated by the behaviorally-based theories. This should not be surprising, as the brain mechanisms responsible for processing speech are complex and non-linear: the expectation that behavioral evidence could adequately predict functional neuroanatomy and neurophysiology would be overly optimistic (Friston et al., 1996; Picton et al., 2000).

This chapter focuses on two central theoretical issues concerning phonetic processing. The first is whether the phonetic attributes of speech stimuli are processed by a cortical system exclusively specialized for speech. The second is whether audiovisual speech processing relies on early neuronal convergence of phonetic information. The findings discussed here support the following views: First, not all of the cortical areas that process speech are specialized for speech stimuli. Second, extensive unisensory processing precedes the binding of auditory and visual speech representations. Thus, a single phonetic processing area that is independent of sensory modality appears not to have been implemented in the speech perceiving brain.

4.1 Speech Processing along the Bottom-Up Cortical Pathways

Whether speech is processed by a specialized neural system, as opposed to a general purpose auditory system, is the subject of a longstanding debate in the speech perception literature. Liberman and Whalen (2000) reviewed the issue and framed it elegantly, opposing what they called *horizontal* versus *vertical* theories of speech perception. The former generally posit that speech stimuli are first processed by general auditory mechanisms and then are passed on to linguistic ones. The latter posit that:

> the biological roots of language run deep, penetrating even the level of speech and to the primary motor and perceptual processes that are engaged there. Seen from that perspective, speech is a constituent of a vertically organized system, specialized from top to bottom for linguistic communication. (p. 187)

Top to bottom is not a neuroanatomically precise description. In translating the phrase into neuroanatomical terms, a sensible assumption would be that *top to bottom* is relevant to cortical-level neural processing, not to the periphery (the ear and the eye), nor to the subcortical structures that intervene between the periphery and the cortex. From the ear to the auditory cortex, the speech signal is processed subcortically by the brainstem and thalamus. However, the processing at subcortical stages is most likely general to all auditory stimuli (Scott & Johnsrude, 2003). Likewise, specialization for visual speech perception (if such exists) is unlikely prior the level of the cerebral cortex.

4.1.1 *The primary areas*

Hearing and vision each have their own obligatory primary entry levels into cortex. The primary areas are counted as the first cortical synaptic levels. For hearing, this is the primary auditory cortex (Kaas & Hackett, 2000), also referred to as *core*, and *Brodmann area (BA) 41* (Brodmann, 1909). For vision, the primary visual cortex is V1 (Felleman & Van Essen, 1991) or BA 17 (see Figure 4.1; note that BA 41 is actually approximately in the transaxial plane but is shown externally in the figure).

Early levels of cortical processing are conventionally thought to be the first three levels of the bottom-up cortical synaptic hierarchy. In general for the auditory and visual systems, the primary unisensory cortical sensory areas project to unisensory association areas at the next and higher synaptic levels, and those areas project to other unisensory association areas at yet higher levels of the cortical synaptic hierarchy (Felleman & Van Essen, 1991; Kaas & Hackett, 2000; Mesulam, 1998). But, it should be noted, processing is not strictly serial: cortical areas become concurrently active as processing proceeds temporally (e.g., Eggermont & Ponton, 2002).

Speech information enters the auditory and visual cortical processing pathways at the same locations as nonspeech information. Primary sensory areas comprise finely tuned neurons that process elementary stimulus properties, whereas higher levels represent information with coarsely tuned neurons that are more specialized, depending on the stimulus type (Mesulam, 1998). For hearing, the primary areas process the elementary features that include pitch, temporal properties, and intensity (Eggermont & Ponton, 2002). The primary areas of the visual system process the elementary features including color, form, motion, size, and depth (Bartels & Zeki, 1998).

Studies of auditory processing using intracortical recordings in humans (Steinschneider et al., 1999) and functional brain imaging (with either functional magnetic resonance imaging (fMRI) or position emission tomography (PET)) support the generalization that speech is not preferentially processed by the primary auditory cortex (Binder et al., 2000; Celsis et al., 1999; Huckins et al., 1998; Scott &

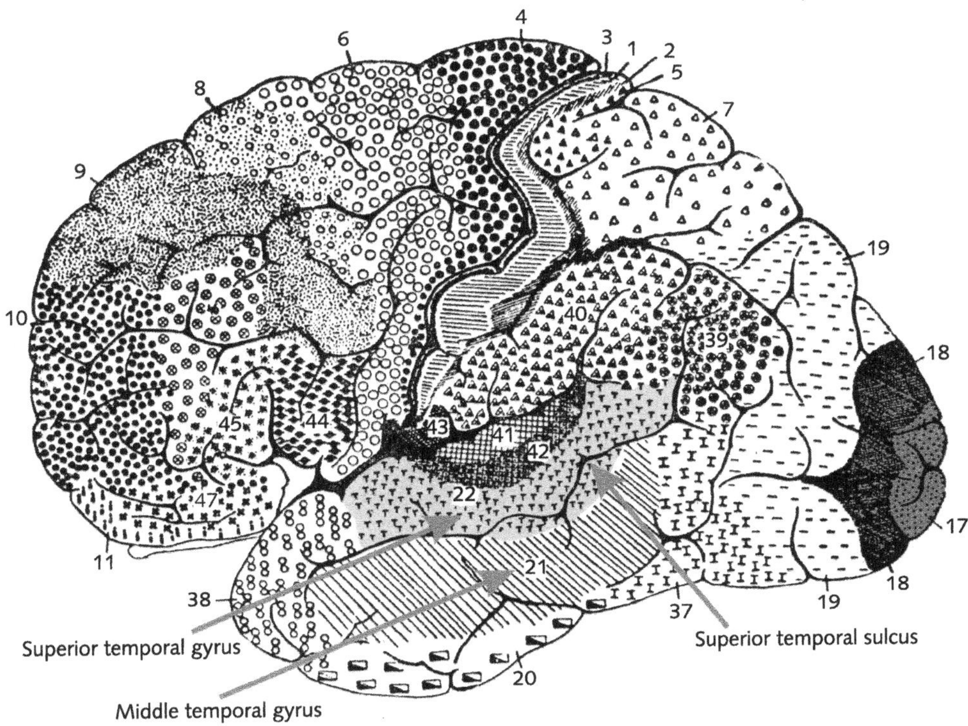

Figure 4.1 Brodmann (1909) areas of the human brain and anatomical labels.

Johnsrude, 2003; Scott et al., 2000). The primary visual area, V1, has not been studied specifically with regard to the distinction between speech and nonspeech stimuli, but there is no expectation that it would perform processing specific to speech features, just as it is not specialized for other complex visual stimuli (Mesulam, 1998).

4.1.2 *The early unisensory association areas*

Various animal and human studies confirm that the bottom-up flow of all auditory and visual stimulus information, including speech, is from the primary cortical areas to unisensory association areas (Bartels & Zeki, 1998; Felleman & Van Essen, 1991; Kaas & Hackett, 2000; Mesulam, 1998). The second auditory level, the first association area, designated BA 42 (see Figure 4.1), is considered to be homologous to the monkey auditory belt area, which neuronal tracer studies show receives its input from the auditory core (Hackett, Stepniewska, & Kaas, 1998). This level has been shown to be insensitive to speech versus nonspeech contrasts in humans (e.g., Belin et al., 2000; Binder et al., 2000; Eggermont & Ponton, 2002; Liégeois-Chauvel et al., 1999; Scott & Johnsrude, 2003; Wise et al., 2001).

At the third synaptic level, the primary auditory cortex and belt are surrounded by a more extensive parabelt area, designated 22 by Brodmann (1909) (Figure 4.1), and it extends onto the lateral surface of the superior temporal gyrus. Intracortical recordings in humans of evoked potentials during pre-surgical studies of epilepsy patients have shown transcortical passage of activation, which confirms that this area is hierarchically connected to the previous synaptic levels (Howard et al., 2000; Liégeois-Chauvel et al., 1994). Recent monkey studies focused on the belt and parabelt have revealed that the parabelt is also subdivided and participates in several different hierarchically organized pathways (e.g., Kaas & Hackett, 2000) that likely have different functions.

A current theory is that one auditory pathway is more concerned with category identification and the other more with location (Belin & Zattore, 2000; Kaas & Hackett, 2000; Rauschecker & Tian, 2000; Scott & Johnsrude, 2003). This possibility follows earlier work that identified *what* and *where* pathways in the visual system (Ungerleider & Haxby, 1994). Even so, although the early levels may be segregated into different paths, there is not apparently identification of specific objects at early levels. It is a general finding that the second and perhaps the third cortical synaptic levels are not specialized for any particular categories of stimulation such as speech, faces, or other objects (e.g., Binder et al., 2000; Halgren et al., 1999; Mesulam, 1998).

4.1.3 *Functional evidence concerning speech processing at early areas*

The results from functional brain imaging studies (fMRI and PET) are consistent with the view that the first three levels of the auditory cortex do not process phonetic stimulus attributes preferentially (Benson et al., 2001; Celsis et al., 1999; Scott et al., 2000). For example, Binder et al. (2000) presented unstructured noise, frequency-modulated (FM) tones, reversed speech, pseudowords, and words. FM tones activated the belt and parabelt areas more than did noise, but these areas were not differentially activated by speech versus FM tones.

Two types of cortical electrical data, intracortical (invasive) and scalp-recorded (non-invasive) activity, have been used to study early auditory speech processing. For example, Steinschneider et al. (1999) revealed in humans, using intracortical recordings, that voice onset time (VOT) is extremely well-represented in the primary auditory cortex and belt areas. Syllables with short VOTs produced a large electrical response, time-locked to the consonant onset, followed by a low amplitude component time-locked to voicing onset. In contrast, responses evoked by syllables with longer VOTs contained prominent components time-locked to both stimulus onset and voicing onset.

Intracortical recordings are relatively rare. Scalp-recorded event-related potentials (ERPs) obtained using electrophysiological and evoked magnetoencephalographic field (MEG) recordings afford neurophysiological measures of brain activity with high temporal resolution (< 1 ms) and, with currently evolving techniques, moderately good spatial resolution (< 10 mm). These measures are thought to mostly reflect excitatory post-synaptic potentials arising from large populations of pyramidal cells oriented in a common direction (Creutzfeldt, Watanabe, & Lux 1966; Mitzdorf, 1986; Vaughan & Arezzo, 1988).

Analyses of ERP data suggest that the origins of auditory evoked activity can be modeled successfully by dipole sources (mathematical representations of the

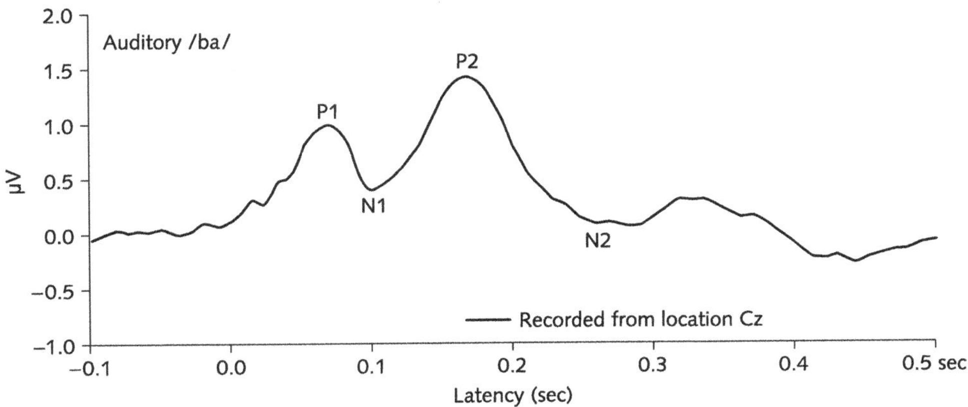

Figure 4.2 Illustration of an event-related potential to an acoustic /ba/ stimulus recorded from the scalp at the vertex location.

cortical generators) placed in the temporal lobe of each hemisphere. Positive and negative peaks in the ERP waveforms, labeled P1 (positive peak latency approximately 50 ms) and N1 (negative peak latency of approximately 100 ms) (see Figure 4.2) are represented in tangentially-oriented dipoles (i.e., sources oriented tangentially to the lateral cortical surface). That is, the P1 and N1 peaks appear to represent activity arising from the primary auditory cortex (BA 41) and the unisensory auditory association areas (belt and parabelt areas (BA 42/22)) (e.g., Knight et al., 1988; Ponton et al., 1993; Scherg & Von Cramon, 1985, 1986). These ERPs are considered to be obligatory responses to auditory system stimulation; that is, they occur in response to almost all forms of auditory stimulation, including clicks, noise or tone bursts, or speech sounds. In addition, they are obtained without requiring conscious attention to the stimuli.

While the latency and amplitude of the P1 and N1 peaks to auditory stimuli are most affected by the physical characteristics of the stimulus (e.g., duration and loudness), the later peaks (P2 – peak latency of approximately 175 ms – and N2 – peak latency about 225 ms) are more affected by factors such as arousal and attention (Näätänen & Picton, 1987), suggesting that auditory ERPs of latencies earlier than approximately 100 ms are generated at early levels of the cortical pathway. Specifically, the N1 component appears to be generated by the lemniscal pathway, which projects from the central nucleus of the inferior colliculus to the ventral division of the medial geniculate nucleus, and terminates in the primary auditory cortex, a pathway that appears to represent stimulus attributes (Ponton & Eggermont, 2001). Therefore, if there were very early specialization for speech features, it would be predicted to be reflected in the N1. Results from scalp-recorded electrophysiology studies support the prediction that N1 is not sensitive to the same contrasts observed in behavioral studies of phonetic perception.

For example, Sharma and Dorman (1999) showed with scalp-recorded ERPs that when VOT was short (/da/ stimulus), only a single distinct electrical peak component at around 100 ms (labeled N1) was obtained. For longer VOTs (/ta/ stimulus), two distinct N1 components were obtained. In addition, the discontinuity between the single component peak and the double peak coincided with the perceptual /da/-/ta/ boundary of the stimulus continuum. However, Sharma, Marsh, and Dorman (2000) in a subsequent study showed that the N1 is unlikely to be a correlate of phonetic perception. Two stimulus continua were investigated, /ba/-/pa/ and /ga/-/ka/. Perceptually, the latter results in a longer VOT boundary than the former. A single N1 peak was obtained for both continua when the VOT was < 30 ms, and a double N1 peak was obtained for both when the VOT was > 40 ms. The VOT that elicited the double N1 peak for the /ga/-/ka/ continuum occurred at 20 ms shorter VOT than required for perceptual identification of /ka/. Sharma and Dorman (2000) reported that N1 responses for a continuum from pre-voiced to voiced bilabial stops were the same for Hindi- and English-speaking listeners, even though voicing categories in the two languages do not coincide in the critical values of VOT.

Thus, the findings suggest that the responses, at around 100 ms latency and earlier, are not specialized for speech in terms of the differential coding of the phonetic properties used within language. That the scalp-recorded N1 peak has been localized independently to the auditory parabelt areas (see Eggermont & Ponton, 2002, for a review of the cortical generator sites for the early and middle auditory evoked potentials) is consistent with the conclusion that at the first two or three synaptic levels of the cortex, speech stimuli do not receive specialized neural processing, although sensitivity to speech signal characteristics is present.

4.1.4 Early visual areas

Studies of the visual pathways show that the earliest unisensory association areas are not tuned to specific visual categories (Mesulam, 1998). Specific categories such as faces and objects are not preferentially processed by early visual primary or association areas such as V1 (BA 17), V2 (BA 18), V4 (BA 19), and V5/MT (middle temporal/BA 37). For example, V5/MT is specialized for motion (Watson et al., 1993), and V4 might be specialized for color (Zeki, 2001), each at the second synaptic levels (Felleman & Van Essen, 1991). Early visual areas such as V1 and V5 are activated by visual speech stimuli (Bernstein et al., 2003; Calvert et al., 1999; Campbell et al., 2001; Ludman et al., 2000; Paulesu et al., in press), as would be expected given their role in the coding of all elementary stimulus properties. But there is not any evidence to date that these early areas are differentially sensitive to speech.

4.1.5 Phonetic processing at higher synaptic levels

The most convincing evidence for speech-specific processing has been obtained for cortical areas beyond the first three bottom-up synaptic levels. However, the evidence has not produced consensus concerning the organization of phonetic processing at the higher levels. For example, the superior temporal sulcus (which separates the superior temporal gyrus and the middle temporal gyrus, Figure 4.1), at the fourth synaptic level (Kaas & Hackett, 2000), has been shown to prefer speech to FM tones and noise (Binder et al., 2000). But the upper bank of the superior temporal sulcus has also been shown to be selective for human vocal versus non-vocal sounds, even when the vocal sounds did not contain speech (Belin et al., 2000). Spectrally inverted speech activates the left posterior superior temporal sulcus, according to Scott et al. (2000). But increasing intelligibility of speech has been shown to be associated with increasingly anterior regions along the superior temporal sulcus (Scott et al., 2000).

Binder et al. (2000) have proposed a somewhat different organization, with sensitivity to phonetic information attributed to cortex dorsal to the primary auditory cortex. However, Binder et al. (2000, Figure 9), summarizing results for the contrast between speech and nonspeech, suggest that the superior temporal sulcus is active and possibly responsible for representing temporal and spectral feature combinations. They also reported evidence that the more anterior and inferior temporal areas were more strongly activated by words than non-words, at least partly consistent with the results on anterior activity reported by Scott et al. (2000). The distinction between the posterior and anterior areas sensitive to phonetic stimuli likely results from differences in function. For example, the posterior area might be associated with the ability to repeat and represent lexical forms, whereas the anterior area might be associated with word representations and associative knowledge (cf., Hickok & Poeppel, 2000; Scott et al., 2000; Wise et al., 2001).

Unisensory visual association areas include the fusiform, inferior temporal, and middle temporal gyri. The area defined as the lateral occipital complex, located on the lateral bank of the fusiform gyrus extending ventrally and dorsally, appears to have a strong role in processing information about object shape or structure, independent of the particular visual cues to structure, and not to be differentially activated by types of visual objects (Grill-Spector, Kourtzi, & Kanwisher, 2001). At the fourth synaptic level, differential activations are observed due to complex objects versus faces (Büchel, Price, & Friston, 1998; Halgren et al., 1999; Nobre, Allison, & McCarthy, 1994; Puce et al., 1996). Face processing at this level seems to be concerned with faces as a general category, their detection and perception, but not with recognizing specific faces nor facial expressions (Tong et al., 2000). It is not known whether or not there are many category-specific areas in the visual pathway (Grill-Spector et al., 2001).

Bernstein, Auer, and Moore (2004) have speculated that visual speech is processed as a special category by the visual system. Alternatively, perhaps, this status obtains only in individuals who are proficient lipreaders (Bernstein, Demorest, & Tucker, 2000). Research on higher level vision has not resolved whether even the so-called *fusiform face area* is specialized for faces *per se* or is particularly sensitive to over-learned categories of stimulation.

Of relevance to speech, which is a dynamic visual stimulus, are studies that have investigated faces in motion. In Puce et al. (1998), a number of studies involving movements by face areas are compared. Moving eyes and mouths (nonspeech) activated a bilateral region centered in the superior temporal sulcus, 2.2–3.0 cm posterior to a region reported for lipreading in Calvert et al. (1997; see also, Bernstein et al., 2002), and 0.5–1.5 cm anterior and inferior to a region activated by hand and body movement (Bonda et al., 1996). Thus, comparison across studies seems to support specialization for phonetic versus non-phonetic visual speech processing several synaptic levels along the bottom-up visual speech pathway. But, alternatively, errors of localization during the processing and interpretation of the BOLD (blood oxygen level dependent) signal obtained during fMRI could lead to incorrect attribution of areas specialized for visual phonetic processing. Additional studies are needed that directly compare speech and nonspeech visual stimuli, controlling for a wide range of different visual stimulus properties.

4.1.6 *Conclusions about phonetic processing specialization*

We now return to whether "speech is a constituent of a vertically organized system specialized from top to bottom for linguistic communication" (Liberman & Whalen, 2000, p. 187). While speech is evidently part of a vertically organized system, that system does not appear to be specialized for speech at all of its levels. The pure vertical view can be saved, perhaps, by re-defining "top to bottom" beginning at a later – perhaps third or fourth – cortical level. But that maneuver does not seem consistent with the spirit of vertical theories.

On the other hand, the findings about the cortical synaptic hierarchy are also not support for the horizontalist or *auditorist* view. According to Trout (2001), "Auditorism is committed to the view that many of the distinctive achievements of speech perception . . . require *only* general auditory mechanisms, and that the auditory periphery supplies sufficient sensitivity for the analysis of the incoming speech signal" (p. 524, emphasis added).

The neural findings suggest that speech perception *does* require general purpose mechanisms, both auditory and visual, and that the periphery (ear and eye), as well as subcortical structures, *must* supply sufficient sensitivity for the information in the speech signal to be preserved for processing at higher cortical levels. But evidence for early elementary processing, and even processing similarities across species (cf., Eggermont, 2001), does not constitute evidence for the sufficiency of general purpose auditory mechanisms for phonetic perception. The findings suggest that there are higher level cortical areas that are sensitive to phonetic stimulus forms. Thus, what might be called *pure* horizontal or vertical theories do not seem to have been implemented in the human cerebral cortex. Earlier processing appears to be responsible for elementary auditory attributes and later processing appears to be more sensitive to phonetic information. Furthermore, the auditory and visual pathways appear to become more specialized at approximately the same rate from one synaptic level to the next in the bottom-up cortical pathway.

Alternatively, Bartels and Zeki (1998) have suggested that a specialized system can be defined as the direct and indirect pathways (including feedback) to the specialized areas along with those specialized areas. For example, the specialized system for processing visual motion could be regarded as the earlier visual areas V1 followed by V2 that are not specialized for motion. Furthermore, they propose that nodes or areas within a system can independently contribute to conscious perception, as, for example, when visual form is perceived from motion, but the motion of the forms is itself also perceived. Similarly, in the case of auditory speech perception, early auditory areas are shared among specialized systems such as phonetic and voice processing systems (Belin et al., 2000), allowing the listener to perceive both the message and the qualities of the talker's voice. Specialized systems thus can, and must, share less specialized cortical areas. This is a direct consequence of the hierarchical and parallel architecture of the bottom-up cortical pathways (Mesulam, 1998; Rauschecker, 1998; Zeki, 1998).

4.2 Audiovisual Speech Processing

The second main issue here is whether audiovisual (AV) phonetic processing relies on early convergence. Early phonetic convergence is taken here to imply involvement of multisensory cells at early levels of the bottom-up synaptic hierarchy that are specialized for processing both auditory and visual phonetic information. A quintessential example of neural convergence studied by Stein and colleagues (Meredith, 2002; Stein, 1998; Stein & Meredith, 1993) is the multisensory neurons in the (anaesthetized) cat superior colliculus, a subcortical structure concerned with detection and localization of events in extra-personal space. These neurons respond to more than one of auditory, visual, and somatosensory stimulation, and do so – under certain stimulus conditions – more vigorously than would be predicted by summing their unisensory responses. Meredith (2002) points out, however, that for the mammalian brain, "relatively little is known about the nature of multisensory convergence onto individual neurons and the functional architecture underlying multisensory convergence" (p. 33).[1] Convergence could alternatively involve neural networks that represent stimulus information, independent of the sensory input system. In either case, beyond the convergence process, the stimulus would be represented amodally.

4.2.1 *AV speech perception*

Early AV phonetic convergence has intuitive appeal, because the phonetic effects of AV processing are rarely consciously noted during everyday communication. Speech researchers themselves paid hardly any attention to AV speech perception (cf., Sumby & Pollack, 1954), until McGurk and MacDonald (1976) published their study in which mismatched auditory and visual syllables were presented. An example of the so-called *McGurk effect* is when an auditory /ba/ is dubbed to a visual /ga/, and listeners report hearing /da/. Numerous studies have replicated the McGurk effect (e.g., Green & Kuhl, 1989; Green & Norrix, 2001; Massaro, 1987; Massaro, Cohen, & Smeele, 1996; Munhall & Tohkura, 1998; Munhall et al., 1996; Saldaña & Rosenblum, 1994; Sekiyama, 1997; Walker, Bruce, & O'Malley, 1995).

The typical description or explanation of McGurk effects, expressed at the level of sub-segmental phonetic features, is consistent with a theoretical early convergence mechanism (Fowler, 2004; Green, 1998; Massaro, 1989, 1999; Schwartz, Robert-Ribes, & Escudier, 1998; Summerfield, 1987; cf., Braida, 1991). McGurk perceptual effects appear to emerge from a process that eliminates the original sensory stamp from the phonetic information, producing a transformed auditory impression. That the neural processing mechanism results in an amodal representation has seemed "uncontroversial" to some theorists (Schwartz et al., 1998).

What has been debated is the form that the amodal representation might take. Rosenblum (2002), for example, states that, "the informational metric taken at the point of speech integration is best construed as an articulation based, modality-independent form" (p. 1461) Massaro (1987) has proposed an integration process that involves independent analysis of modality specific sub-segmental features that are evaluated against abstract phoneme representations. That is, segmental representations are the abstract (hence modality-independent) products of combining features. The possibility that auditory and visual representations might bind after modality specific processing of larger patterns – beyond the level of phonetic features – has been explicitly rejected by some theorists (Summerfield, 1987; Braida, 1991).

Indeed, several types of additional behavioral evidence are consistent with early AV phonetic integration, including the following: (1) Gender incongruency between auditory and visual stimuli does not abolish the McGurk effect (Green et al., 1991); (2) Selective attention to one modality or the other does not abolish it (Massaro, 1987); (3) Explicit knowledge about incongruity between auditory and visual stimuli does not abolish it (Summerfield & McGrath, 1984); and (4) Phonetic goodness judgments can be affected by visual speech (Brancazio, Miller, & Pare, 2000). All of these effects imply that AV processing is not penetrated by high level cognition and is, therefore, an early process.

However, behavioral evidence that does not seem consistent with early AV processing also exists: (1) Large stimulus onset asynchronies between auditory and visual syllables do not abolish the McGurk effect (± 0.267 ms, Massaro et al., 1996; 180 ms, Munhall et al., 1996); (2) Reductions in the strength of the McGurk effect occur for familiar versus unfamiliar talkers (Walker et al., 1995); (3) McGurk effect strength varies across language or culture (Sekiyama & Tohkura, 1993); (4) Reductions in McGurk effect strength can be obtained as the result of training (Massaro, 1987); and (5) Visual stimuli do not selectively adapt auditory speech continua (Saldaña & Rosenblum, 1994).

AV effects involving long stimulus onset asynchronies suggest that processing latencies need not be early. Effects due to talker familiarity and culture or language suggest a role for high level cognition. Training effects could be due to changes in perception and/or attention, as well as higher-level, post-perceptual strategies. The demonstration that a visual phonetic stimulus does not selectively adapt an auditory phonetic continuum has been interpreted as evidence that auditory and visual phonetic processes do not interact early (Bernstein et al., 2004).

4.2.2 *Evidence for early convergence from fMRI*

As reviewed above, processing that is specifically phonetic seems to be initiated no earlier than the fourth bottom-up synaptic level of the cerebral cortex (Benson et al., 2001; Binder et al., 2000; Celsis et al., 1999; Scott & Johnsrude, 2003; Scott et al., 2000). If AV phonetic processing relies on convergence of phonetic representations, that should occur no earlier than unisensory phonetic processing.

Calvert, Campbell, and Brammer (2000) obtained response patterns to AV versus auditory-only and visual-only speech using fMRI. Congruent AV speech resulted in superadditive activation levels in the posterior ventral bank of the superior temporal sulcus relative to the sum of activation in response to auditory-alone and visual-alone speech. Incongruent AV speech produced responses lower in activation than the sum of the responses to the unisensory stimuli. This pattern was interpreted as indicative of convergence, possibly of the type observed for multisensory neurons in the superior colliculus (Stein & Meredith, 1993). Calvert et al. concluded that "these data clearly support the hypothesis that crossmodal binding of sensory inputs in man can be achieved by convergence onto multisensory cells localised [*sic*] in heteromodal cortex" (p. 655).

That conclusion is not inevitable. The superior temporal sulcus is an extremely complex and large multimodal area. It responds not only to speech but also to nonspeech motions of mouths and eyes (Puce et al., 1998). It is activated by spoken and written words (Binder et al., 2000; Fiez et al., 1996). It is activated in deaf adults viewing fingerspelling (Auer, Bernstein, & Singh, 2001). Raij, Uutela, and Hari (2000) showed that the left posterior superior temporal sulcus was activated in response to combinations of spoken and written letters of the Finnish alphabet.

In addition, the BOLD response is an indirect measure of neural activity. As a result, fMRI spatial resolution is not fine enough to obtain data on individual neurons, as is done for recordings made in animal models (Meredith, 2002). Thus, the effects reported by Calvert et al. (2000) could be due to co-mingled unisensory neurons (Meredith, 2002; Zeki, 2001). Also, fMRI temporal resolution is on the order of seconds, yet convergence based on early bottom-up phonetic processing would be predicted to occur within approximately 150 ms, in order to be consistent with the dynamics of bottom-up stimulus processing through the first several synaptic levels (Foxe & Simpson, 2002; Krolak-Salmon et al., 2001; Steinschneider et al., 1999; Yvert et al., 2001). Thus, it is not possible to know with fMRI the detailed temporal dynamics of AV processing. Another consideration is that fMRI at the strengths used with humans does not resolve the activity at different cortical layers. The consequence here is that activity in a particular area cannot be unambiguously attributed to either feedforward or feedback units.

4.2.3 *Neuroanatomical problems with convergence*

Convergence is also problematic given longstanding results from neuroanatomy. Classical monkey studies failed to show direct early connections between the auditory core and V1 (Jones & Powell, 1970). Mesulam (1998) summarizing the literature states that "One of the most important principles in the organization of the primate cerebral cortex is the absence of interconnections linking unimodal areas that serve different sensory functions" (p. 1023). Furthermore, this seems to be true also at the level of early unisensory association areas. According to Mesulam:

> This is particularly interesting since many of these unimodal association areas receive monosynaptic feedback from heteromodal cortices which are responsive to auditory and visual stimuli. The sensory-petal (or feedback) projections from heteromodal cortices therefore appear to display a highly selective arrangement that actively protects the fidelity of sensory tuning during the first four synaptic levels of sensory-fugal [feedforward] processing. (p. 1023)

Even at the second through fourth synaptic levels, processing should be protected from contamination by phonetic information of another input system. If this principle holds, and if phonetic processing is initiated at the fourth synaptic level, AV interaction follows unisensory phonetic processing.

However, very recent results of scalp-recorded electrophysiological studies in humans have implied that there could be auditory inputs to early visual areas (Giard & Peronnet, 1999; Molholm et al., 2002). Also, Falchier et al. (2002) showed in monkeys, using tracers injected into V1, that there was a small proportion of connections from auditory cortex to the visual periphery area of V1. There were virtually no connections to the central visual cortex. However, these auditory projections were suggested to play a role in spatial localization or event detection. Thus, this animal model does not directly support the existence of early AV phonetic convergence in humans. At present, knowledge about cortical architecture remains incomplete, and connections between early areas of sensory cortices might be found that have some functional role in AV phonetic processing. Strong evidence should be required, however, to overturn the classical conclusions about the protection against contamination of information by an alternate sensory system as articulated by Mesulam (1994, 1998). To overturn the classical view for speech requires showing that any early transcortical connections actually involve phonetic processing and not merely detection, localization, or response modulation.

4.2.4 *Theoretical arguments against convergence*

Outside of speech perception, convergence has been considered deficient as a potential mechanism for perceiving complex, non-invariant stimuli. Mesulam (1994, 1998) has pointed out that, in principle: (1) If a convergent cortical area were needed to represent all of the information relevant to a complex percept, then the brain (or an omniscient homunculus) would have to solve the problem of directing all of the needed information to that location for re-representation; and (2) Convergence of the type in (1) would lead to contamination of the original perceptual information.[2]

Mesulam (1998) suggests, as an alternative, areas that act as binding sites for sensory-specific representations, perhaps, by creating look-up tables or links. Mesulam employs the term *convergence* in the sense of multiple unisensory pathways feeding into the same area. But he specifically rejects the notion that complex, non-invariant information converges onto the same representation from two different sensory systems. Even at higher synaptic levels, he questions the possibility of convergence onto a common format.

Singer (1998) points out that while convergence on particular sets of neurons in a feedforward architecture is useful for rapid processing of frequently encountered stereotyped combinations of stimulus attributes, convergence is very costly in terms of the number of neurons needed and is not well-suited to dealing with varying and diverse stimulus properties. Singer proposes that the brain solves the binding problem by creating functionally coherent, dynamically created assemblies that as a whole represent particular stimulus content. These dynamic units are thought to be brought about through widespread neuronal synchronization.

Zeki (1998) points out that anatomical studies of the visual system show that there are no cortical areas to which visual pathways uniquely project (see Felleman & Van Essen, 1991), and which act as integrators of all the different visual sources (Bartels & Zeki, 1998). Moutoussis and Zeki (1997) have commented on the charm of convergence:

> To all of us, intuitively much of the most appealing solution [to the binding problem] was an anatomical convergence, a strategy by which the results of operations performed in all the specialized visual areas would be relayed to one area or a set of areas – which would then act as the master integrator and, perhaps, even perceptive areas. Apart from the logical difficulty of who would then perceive the image provided by the master area(s) . . . there is a more practical difficulty – the failure to observe an area or a set of areas that receive outputs from all the antecedent visual areas. Thus the convergent anatomical strategy is not the brain's chosen method of bringing this integration about. (pp. 1412–13)

4.2.5 *Convergence to overcome the diverse qualia of auditory and visual speech*

Nevertheless, convergence for AV speech stimuli might seem justified because of the diverse qualia of auditory and visual stimuli that seem to argue for a transformation into a common amodal format. However, researchers have noted that the biomechanical speech articulation processes that produce acoustic signals also produce optical signals. This commonality of origin has justified studies of the relationship between acoustic and optical speech signals (Jiang et al., 2002; Yehia, Kuratate, & Vatikiotis-Bateson, 1999; Yehia, Rubin, & Vatikiotis-Bateson, 1998). These studies have shown that there are consistent relationships between optical and acoustic phonetic measures.

Bernstein et al. (2004) proposed that binding of auditory and visual speech information could be accomplished by cortical networks that have learned the predictable correspondence between auditory and visual information, without re-representing the information in an amodal format. They demonstrated, using methods from multilinear regression (Jiang et al., 2002) applied to acoustic and optical speech signals, that correspondence between acoustic and optical speech signals could be established without conversion to a common metric (see also Yehia et al., 1998).

For example, Jiang et al. (2002) showed that a linear relationship could be computed between acoustic features and 3-dimensional optical measures. This demonstration was performed on a large number of nonsense syllables and several sentences spoken by four talkers. Good predictions were obtained from acoustic features to 3-dimensional optical data and vice versa. The systematic correspondence between optical and acoustic phonetic stimulus patterns could be learned by a speech perceiving brain, which would not be required to re-represent acoustic and optical patterns in terms of an amodal format. The binding problem for AV speech could be solved, perhaps, by synchrony among sensory-specific distributed representations.

4.3 General Conclusions

Phonetic perception has now taken its place as a central topic in cognitive neuroscience. Admittedly, these are early times in studying the speech perceiving brain, but the findings that have begun to emerge clearly challenge previously held views on the two issues presented here. The first main issue concerned the theoretical dichotomy between horizontal and vertical theories of speech perception (Liberman & Whalen, 2000), which motivated much debate; but the speech perceiving brain appears to be organized along neither dimension exclusively. The second main issue concerned AV speech processing research, which was seen to belong within the general area of research on neural binding mechanisms, a fact that is well-recognized within cognitive neuroscience (Calvert, 2001; Molholm et al., 2002; Mottonen et al., 2002; Raij et al., 2000). Although little is known about the neural mechanisms of AV phonetic binding, the behaviorally based accounts of early phonetic convergence seem unlikely on anatomical grounds; and theoretical considerations argue generally against neuronal convergence for binding complex non-invariant representations.

ACKNOWLEDGMENTS

The author expresses thanks to Edward T. Auer, Jr. for his comments on the chapter and his assistance with Figure 4.1. This chapter was written with support of the National Science Foundation. The views expressed here are those of the author and do not necessarily represent those of the National Science Foundation.

NOTES

1 Bernstein et al. (2004) presented a review of the literature on the neural connections involving the superior colliculus in the monkey. Their review concluded that superior colliculus AV convergence is unlikely to be the support for the binding of AV phonetic information in humans. That is, subcortical AV convergence seems an unlikely mechanism for AV phonetic convergence at the cortical level.

2 Of course, results from McGurk experiments seem to show contamination. But it should be noted that Sekiyama and Tohkura (1991) have shown that the McGurk effect is significantly weaker in Japanese relative to American perceivers. At the same time, critically, the Japanese results indicate separable sensitivity to visual speech information. They state

> When the stimuli . . . were composed of conflicting auditory and visual syllables, the Japanese subjects often reported incompatibility between what they heard and what they saw, instead of showing the McGurk effect . . . This implies that the visual information is processed to the extent that the audiovisual discrepancy is detected most of the time. It suggests that, for

> clear speech, the Japanese use a type of processing in which visual information is not integrated with the auditory information even when they extract some lip-read information from the face of the talker. (p. 76)

These findings suggest that sensory-specific representations are maintained by Japanese perceivers, and that AV integration of the McGurk type is therefore not obligatory nor necessarily early.

REFERENCES

Auer, E. T., Jr., Bernstein, L. E., & Singh, M. (2001). Comparing cortical activity during the perception of two forms of biological motion for language communication. In D. W. Massaro, J. Light, & K. Geraci (eds.), *Proceedings of Audio Visual Speech Perception 2001* (pp. 40–4).

Bartels, A. & Zeki, S. (1998). The theory of multistage integration in the visual brain. *Proceedings of the Royal Society of London*, Series B: Biological Sciences, 265, 2327–32.

Belin, P. & Zattore, R. J. (2000). "What," "where" and "how" in auditory cortex. *Nature Neuroscience*, 3, 965–6.

Belin, P., Zatorre, R. J., Lafaille, P., Ahad, P., & Pike, B. (2000). Voice-selective areas in human auditory cortex, *Nature*, 403, 309–12.

Benson, R. R., Whalen, D. H., Richardson, M., Swainson, B., Clark, V. P., Lai, S., & Liberman, A. M. (2001). Parametrically dissociating speech and nonspeech perception in the brain using fMRI. *Brain and Language*, 78, 364–96.

Bernstein, L. E., Auer, E. T., Jr., Moore, J. K., Ponton, C. W., Don, M., & Singh, M. (2002). Visual speech perception without primary auditory cortex activation. *NeuroReport*, 13, 311–15.

Bernstein, L. E., Auer, E. T., Jr., Zhou, Y., & Singh, M. (2003). Cortical specialization for visual speech versus non-speech face movements in color video and point lights. Cognitive Neuroscience Society, March 30–April 1.

Bernstein, L. E., Auer, E. T., Jr., & Moore, J. K. (2004). Audiovisual speech binding: convergence or association? In G. A. Calvert, C. Spence, & B. E. Stein (eds.), *Handbook of Multisensory Processing* (pp. 203–23). Cambridge, MA: MIT Press.

Bernstein, L. E., Demorest, M. E., & Tucker, P. E. (2000). Speech perception without hearing. *Perception & Psychophysics*, 62, 233–52.

Binder, J. R., Frost, J. A., Hammeke, T. A., Bellgowan, P. S., Springer, J. A., Kaufman, J. N., & Possing, E. T. (2000). Human temporal lobe activation by speech and nonspeech sounds. *Cerebral Cortex*, 10, 512–28.

Bonda, E., Petrides, M., Ostry, D., & Evans, A. (1996). Specific involvement of human parietal systems and the amygdala in the perception of biological motion. *Journal of Neuroscience*, 16, 3737–44.

Braida, L. D. (1991). Crossmodal integration in the identification of consonant segments. *Quarterly Journal of Experimental Psychology: Human Experimental Psychology*, 43A, 647–77.

Brancazio, L., Miller, J. L., & Pare, M. A. (2000). Visual influences on internal structure of phonetic categories. *Journal of the Acoustical Society of America*, 108, 2481.

Brodmann, K. (1909). *Vergleichende Lokalisatinslehre der Grosshirnrinde in ihren Prinzipien dargestellt auf Grund des Zellenbaues*. Leipzig: J. A. Barth.

Büchel, C., Price, C., & Friston, K. (1998). A multimodal language region in the ventral visual pathway. *Nature*, 394, 274–77.

Calvert, G. A. (2001). Crossmodal processing in the human brain: insights from functional neuroimaging studies. *Cerebral Cortex*, 11, 1110–23.

Calvert, G. A., Brammer, M. J., Bullmore, E. T., Campbell, R., Iversen, S. D., & David, A. S. (1999). Response amplification in sensory-specific cortices during crossmodal binding. *NeuroReport*, 10, 2619–23.

Calvert, G. A., Bullmore, E. T., Brammer, M. J., Campbell, R., Williams, S. C., McGuire, P. K., Woodruff, P. W., Iversen, S. D., & David, A. S. (1997). Activation of auditory cortex during silent lipreading. *Science*, 276, 593–6.

Calvert, G. A., Campbell, R., & Brammer, M. J. (2000). Evidence from functional magnetic resonance imaging of crossmodal binding in the human heteromodal cortex. *Current Biology*, 10, 649–57.

Campbell, R., MacSweeney, M., Surguladze, S., Calvert, G., McGuire, P., Suckling, J., Brammer, M. J., & David, A. S. (2001). Cortical substrates for the perception of face actions: an fMRI study of the specificity of activation for seen speech and for meaningless lower-face acts (gurning). *Cognitive Brain Research*, 12, 233–43.

Celsis, P., Boulanouar, K., Doyon, B., Ranjeva, J. P., Berry, I., Nespoulous, J. L., & Chollet, F. (1999). Differential fMRI responses in the left posterior superior temporal gyrus and left supramarginal gyrus to habituation and change detection in syllables and tones. *NeuroImage*, 9, 135–44.

Creutzfeldt, O. D., Watanabe, S., & Lux, H. D. (1966). Relations between EEG phenomena and potentials of single cortical cells. I: Evoked responses after thalamic and epicortical stimulation. *Electroencephalography and Clinical Neurophysiology*, 20, 1–18.

Eggermont, J. J. (2001). Between sound and perception: reviewing the search for a neural code. *Hearing Research*, 157, 1–42.

Eggermont, J. J. & Ponton, C. W. (2002). The neurophysiology of auditory perception: from single units to evoked potentials. *Audiology & Neuro-otology*, 7, 71–99.

Falchier, A., Clavagnier, S., Barone, P., & Kennedy, H. (2002). Anatomical evidence of multimodal integration in primate striate cortex. *Journal of Neuroscience*, 22, 5749–59.

Felleman, D. J. & Van Essen, D. C. (1991). Distributed hierarchical processing in the primate cerebral cortex. *Cerebral Cortex*, 1, 1–47.

Fiez, J. A., Raichle, M. E., Balota, D. A., Tallal, P., & Petersen, S. E. (1996). PET activation of posterior temporal regions during auditory word presentation and verb generation. *Cerebral Cortex*, 6, 1–10.

Fowler, C. (2004). Speech as a supramodal or amodal phenomenon. In G. Calvert, C. Spence, & B. E. Stein (eds.), *Handbook of Multisensory Processes* (pp. 189–201). Cambridge, MA: MIT Press.

Foxe, J. J. & Simpson, G. V. (2002). Flow of activation from V1 to frontal cortex in humans: A framework for defining "early" visual processing. *Experimental Brain Research*, 142, 139–50.

Friston, K. J., Price, C. J., Fletcher, P., Moore, C., Frackowiak, R. S., & Dolan, R. J. (1996). The trouble with cognitive subtraction. *NeuroImage*, 4, 97–104.

Giard, M. H. & Peronnet, F. (1999). Auditory-visual integration during multimodal object recognition in humans: A behavioral and electrophysiological study. *Journal of Cognitive Neuroscience*, 11, 473–90.

Green, K. P. (1998). The use of auditory and visual information during phonetic processing: Implications for theories of speech perception. In R. Campbell, B. Dodd, & D. Burnham (eds.), *Hearing by Eye II: Advances in the Psychology of Speechreading and Auditory-visual Speech* (pp. 3–25). Hove, UK: Psychology Press.

Green, K. P. & Kuhl, P. K. (1989). The role of visual information in the processing of place and manner features in speech perception. *Perception & Psychophysics*, 45, 34–42.

Green, K. P. & Norrix, L. W. (2001). Perception of /r/ and /l/ in a stop cluster: Evidence of cross-modal context effects. *Journal of Experimental Psychology: Human Perception and Performance*, 27, 166–77.

Green, K. P., Kuhl, P. K., Meltzoff, A. N., & Stevens, E. B. (1991). Integrating speech information across talkers, gender, and sensory modality: Female faces and male voices in the McGurk effect. *Perception & Psychophysics*, 50, 524–36.

Grill-Spector, K., Kourtzi, Z., & Kanwisher, N. (2001). The lateral occipital complex and its role in object recognition. *Vision Research*, 41, 1409–22.

Hackett, T. A., Stepniewska, I., & Kaas, J. H. (1998). Subdivisions of auditory cortex and ipsilateral cortical connections of the parabelt auditory cortex in macaque monkeys. *Journal of Comparative Neurology*, 394, 475–95.

Halgren, E., Dale, A. M., Sereno, M. I., Tootell, R. B., Marinkovic, K., & Rosen, B. R. (1999). Location of human face-selective cortex with respect to retinotopic areas. *Human Brain Mapping*, 7, 29–37.

Hickok, G. & Poeppel, D. (2000). Towards a functional neuroanatomy of speech perception. *Trends in Cognitive Sciences*, 4, 131–8.

Howard, M. A., Volkov, I. O., Mirsky, R., Garell, P. C., Noh, M. D., Granner, M., Damasio, H., Steinschneider, M., Reale, R. A., Hind, J. E., & Brugge, J. F. (2000). Auditory cortex on the human posterior superior temporal gyrus. *Journal of Comparative Neurology*, 416, 79–92.

Huckins, S. C., Turner, C. W., Doherty, K. A., Fonte, M. M., & Szeverenyi, N. M. (1998). Functional magnetic resonance imaging measures of blood flow patterns in the human auditory cortex in response to sound. *Journal of Speech, Language, and Hearing Research*, 41, 538–48.

Jiang, J., Alwan, A., Keating, P., Auer, E. T., Jr., & Bernstein, L. E. (2002). On the relationship between face movements, tongue movements, and speech acoustics. *EURASIP Journal on Applied Signal Processing: Special issue on Joint Audio-Visual Speech Processing*, 2002, 1174–88.

Jones, E. G. & Powell, T. P. (1970). An anatomical study of converging sensory pathways within the cerebral cortex of the monkey. *Brain*, 93, 793–820.

Kaas, J. H. & Hackett, T. A. (2000). Subdivisions of auditory cortex and processing streams in primates. *Proceedings of the National Academy of Sciences of the United States of America*, 97, 11793–9.

Knight, R. T., Scabini, D., Woods, D. L., & Clayworth, C. (1988). The effects of lesions of superior temporal gyrus and inferior parietal lobe on temporal and vertex components of the human AEP. *Electroencephalography and Clinical Neurophysiology*, 70, 499–509.

Krolak-Salmon, P., Henaff, M. A., Tallon-Baudry, C., Yvert, B., Fischer, C., Vighetto, A., Betrand, O., & Mauguiere, F. (2001). How fast can the human lateral geniculate nucleus and visual striate cortex see? *Society for Neuroscience Abstracts*, 27, 913.

Liberman, A. M. & Whalen, D. H. (2000). On the relation of speech to language. *Trends in Cognitive Sciences*, 4, 187–96.

Liégeois-Chauvel, C., de Graaf, J. B., Laguitton, V., & Chauvel, P. (1999). Specialization of left auditory cortex for speech perception in man depends on temporal coding. *Cerebral Cortex*, 9, 484–96.

Liégeois-Chauvel, C., Musolino, A., Badier, J. M., Marquis, P., & Chauvel, P. (1994). Evoked potentials recorded from the auditory cortex in man: Evaluation and topography of the middle latency components. *Electroencephalography and Clinical Neurophysiology*, 92, 204–14.

Ludman, C. N., Summerfield, A. Q., Hall, D., Elliott, M., Foster, J., Hykin, J. L., Bowtell, R., & Morris, P. G. (2000). Lip-reading ability and patterns of cortical activation studied using fMRI. *British Journal of Audiology*, 34, 225–30.

Massaro, D. W. (1987). *Speech Perception by Ear and Eye: A Paradigm for Psychological Inquiry*. Hillsdale, NJ: Lawrence Erlbaum.

Massaro, D. W. (1989). Multiple book review of *Speech Perception by Ear And Eye: A Paradigm for Psychological Inquiry. Behavioral and Brain Sciences*, 12, 741–54.

Massaro, D. W. (1999). Speechreading: Illusion or window into pattern recognition. *Trends in Cognitive Sciences*, 3, 310–17.

Massaro, D. W., Cohen, M. M., & Smeele, P. M. (1996). Perception of asynchronous and conflicting visual and auditory speech. *Journal of the Acoustical Society of America*, 100, 1777–86.

McGurk, H. & MacDonald, J. (1976). Hearing lips and seeing voices. *Nature*, 264, 746–8.

Meredith, M. A. (2002). On the neuronal basis for multisensory convergence: a brief overview. *Cognitive Brain Research*, 14, 31–40.

Mesulam, M. M. (1994). Neurocognitive networks and selectively distributed processing. *Revue Neurologique*, 150, 564–9.

Mesulam, M. M. (1998). From sensation to cognition. *Brain*, 121, 1013–52.

Mitzdorf, U. (1986). The physiological causes of VEP: Current source density analysis of electrically and visually evoked potential. In R. Q. Cracco & I. Bodis-Wollner (eds.), *Evoked Potentials* (pp. 141–54). New York: Alan R. Liss Inc.

Molholm, S., Ritter, W., Murray, M. M., Javitt, D. C., Schroeder, C. E., & Foxe, J. J. (2002). Multisensory auditory-visual interactions during early sensory processing in humans: A high-density electrical mapping study. *Cognitive Brain Research*, 14, 115–28.

Mottonen, R., Krause, C. M., Tiippana, K., & Sams, M. (2002). Processing of changes in visual speech in the human auditory cortex. *Cognitive Brain Research*, 13, 417–25.

Moutoussis, K. & Zeki, S. (1997). A direct demonstration of perceptual asynchrony in vision. *Proceedings of the Royal Society of London*, Series B: Biological Sciences, 264, 393–9.

Munhall, K. G. & Tohkura, Y. (1998). Audiovisual gating and the time course of speech perception. *Journal of the Acoustical Society of America*, 104, 530–9.

Munhall, K. G., Gribble, P., Sacco, L., & Ward, M. (1996). Temporal constraints on the McGurk effect. *Perception & Psychophysics*, 58, 351–62.

Näätänen, R. & Picton, T. (1987). The N1 wave of the human electric and magnetic response to sound: A review and an analysis of the component structure. *Psychophysiology*, 24, 375–425.

Nobre, A. C., Allison, T., & McCarthy, G. (1994). Word recognition in the human inferior temporal lobe. *Nature*, 372, 260–3.

Paulesu, E., Perani, D., Blasi, V., Silani, G., Borghese, N. A., De Giovanni, U., Sensolo, S., & Fazio, F. (in press). A functional-anatomical model for lipreading. *Journal of Cognitive Neuroscience*.

Picton, T. W., Bentin, S., Berg, P., Donchin, E., Hillyard, S. A., Johnson, R., Jr., Miller, G. A., Ritter, W., Ruchkin, D. S., Rugg, M. D., & Taylor, M. J. (2000). Guidelines for using human event-related potentials to study cognition: Recording standards and publication criteria. *Psychophysiology*, 37, 127–52.

Ponton, C. W. & Eggermont, J. J. (2001). Of kittens and kids: Altered cortical maturation following profound deafness and cochlear implant use. *Audiology & Neuro-otology*, 6, 363–80.

Ponton, C. W., Don, M., Waring, M. D., Eggermont, J. J., & Masuda, A. (1993). Spatio-temporal source modeling of evoked potentials to acoustic and cochlear implant stimulation. *Electroencephalography and Clinical Neurophysiology*, 88, 478–93.

Puce, A., Allison, T., Asgari, M., Gore, J. C., & McCarthy, G. (1996). Differential sensitivity of human visual cortex to faces, letterstrings, and textures: A functional magnetic resonance imaging study. *Journal of Neuroscience*, 16, 5205–15.

Puce, A., Allison, T., Bentin, S., Gore, J. C., & McCarthy, G. (1998). Temporal cortex activation in humans viewing eye and mouth movements. *Journal of Neuroscience*, 18, 2188–99.

Raij, T., Uutela, K., & Hari, R. (2000). Audiovisual integration of letters in the human brain. *Neuron*, 28, 617–25.

Rauschecker, J. P. (1998). Cortical processing of complex sounds. *Current Opinion in Neurobiology*, 8, 516–21.

Rauschecker, J. P. & Tian, B. (2000). Mechanisms and streams for processing of "what" and "where" in auditory cortex. *Proceedings of the National Academy of Sciences of the United States of America*, 97, 11800–6.

Rosenblum, L. D. (2002). The perceptual basis for audiovisual speech integration. *Proceedings of the 7th International Conference on Spoken Language Processing*, September 16–20, Denver, CO.

Saldaña, H. M. & Rosenblum, L. D. (1994). Selective adaptation in speech perception using a compelling audiovisual adaptor. *Journal of the Acoustical Society of America*, 95, 3658–61.

Scherg, M. & Von Cramon, D. (1985). Two bilateral sources of the late AEP as identified by a spatio-temporal dipole model. *Electroencephalography and Clinical Neurophysiology*, 62, 32–44.

Scherg, M. & Von Cramon, D. (1986). Evoked dipole source potentials of the human auditory cortex. *Electroencephalography and Clinical Neurophysiology*, 65, 344–60.

Schwartz, J.-L., Robert-Ribes, J., & Escudier, P. (1998). Ten years after Summerfield: A taxonomy of models for audio-visual fusion in speech perception. In R. Campbell, B. Dodd, & D. Burnham (eds.), *Hearing by Eye II: The Psychology of Speechreading and Auditory-visual Speech* (pp. 85–108). Hove, UK: Psychology Press.

Scott, S. K. & Johnsrude, I. S. (2003). The neuroanatomical and functional organization of speech perception. *Trends in Neurosciences*, 26, 100–7.

Scott, S. K., Blank, C. C., Rosen, S., & Wise, R. J. (2000). Identification of a pathway for intelligible speech in the left temporal lobe. *Brain*, 123, 2400–6.

Sekiyama, K. (1997). Cultural and linguistic factors in audiovisual speech processing: The McGurk effect in Chinese subjects. *Perception & Psychophysics*, 59, 73–80.

Sekiyama, K. & Tohkura, Y. (1991). McGurk effect in non-English listeners: Few visual effects for Japanese subjects hearing Japanese syllables of high auditory intelligibility. *Journal of the Acoustical Society of America*, 90, 1797–1805.

Sekiyama, K. & Tohkura, Y. (1993). Inter-language differences in the influence of visual cues in speech perception. *Journal of Phonetics*, 21, 427–44.

Sharma, A. & Dorman, M. F. (1999). Cortical auditory evoked potential correlates of categorical perception of voice-onset time. *Journal of the Acoustical Society of America*, 106, 1078–83.

Sharma, A. & Dorman, M. F. (2000). Neurophysiologic correlates of cross-language phonetic perception. *Journal of the Acoustical Society of America*, 107, 2697–703.

Sharma, A., Marsh, C. M., & Dorman, M. F. (2000). Relationship between N1 evoked potential morphology and the perception of voicing. *Journal of the Acoustical Society of America*, 108, 3030–5.

Singer, W. (1998). Consciousness and the structure of neuronal representations. *Philosophical Transactions of the Royal Society of London*, Series B: Biological Sciences, 353, 1829–40.

Stein, B. E. (1998). Neural mechanisms for synthesizing sensory information and producing adaptive behaviors. *Experimental Brain Research*, 123, 124–35.

Stein, B. E. & Meredith, M. A. (1993). *The Merging of the Senses*. Cambridge, MA: MIT Press.

Steinschneider, M., Volkov, I. O., Noh, M. D., Garell, P. C., & Howard, M. A., 3rd (1999). Temporal encoding of the voice onset time phonetic parameter by field potentials recorded directly from human auditory cortex. *Journal of Neurophysiology*, 82, 2346–57.

Sumby, W. H. & Pollack, I. (1954). Visual contribution to speech intelligibility in noise. *Journal of the Acoustical Society of America*, 26, 212–15.

Summerfield, Q. (1987). Some preliminaries to a comprehensive account of audio-visual speech perception. In B. Dodd & R. Campbell (eds.), *Hearing by Eye: The Psychology of Lip-Reading* (pp. 3–52). Hove, UK: Psychology Press.

Summerfield, Q. & McGrath, M. (1984). Detection and resolution of audio-visual incompatibility in the perception of vowels. *Quarterly Journal of Experimental Psychology: Human Experimental Psychology*, 36, 51–74.

Tong, F., Nakayama, K., Moscovitch, M., Weinrib, O., & Kanwisher, N. (2000). Response properties of the human fusiform face area. *Cognitive Neuropsychology*, 17, 257–79.

Trout, J. D. (2001). The biological basis of speech: What to infer from talking to the animals. *Psychological Review*, 108, 523–49.

Ungerleider, L. G. & Haxby, J. V. (1994). "What" and "where" in the human brain. *Current Opinion in Neurobiology*, 4, 157–65.

Vaughan, H. & Arezzo, J. (1988). The neural basis of event-related potentials. In T. W. Picton (ed.), *Human Event-Related Potentials* (pp. 45–96). Amsterdam: Elsevier Science Publishers.

Walker, S., Bruce, V., & O'Malley, C. (1995). Facial identity and facial speech processing: Familiar faces and voices in the McGurk effect. *Perception & Psychophysics*, 57, 1124–33.

Watson, J. D., Myers, R., Frackowiak, R. S., Hajnal, J. V., Woods, R. P., Mazziotta, J. C., Shipp, S., & Zeki, S. (1993). Area V5 of the human brain: Evidence from a combined study using positron emission tomography and magnetic resonance imaging. *Cerebral Cortex*, 3, 79–94.

Wise, R. J., Scott, S. K., Blank, S. C., Mummery, C. J., Murphy, K., & Warburton, E. A. (2001). Separate neural subsystems within "Wernicke's area." *Brain*, 124, 83–95.

Yehia, H., Kuratate, T., & Vatikiotis-Bateson, E. (1999). Using speech acoustics to drive facial motion. *Proceedings of the International Congress of Phonetic Sciences* (ICPhS 1999) (pp. 631–4). San Francisco, CA: IPA.

Yehia, H., Rubin, P., & Vatikiotis-Bateson, E. (1998). Quantitative association of vocal-tract and facial behavior. *Speech Communication*, 26, 23–43.

Yvert, B., Crouzeix, A., Bertrand, O., Seither-Preisler, A., & Pantev, C. (2001). Multiple supratemporal sources of magnetic and electric auditory evoked middle latency components in humans. *Cerebral Cortex*, 11, 411–23.

Zeki, S. (1998). Parallel processing, asynchronous perception, and a distributed system of consciousness in vision. *Neuroscientist*, 4, 365–72.

Zeki, S. (2001). Localization and globalization in conscious vision. *Annual Review of Neuroscience*, 24, 57–86.

5 Event-Related Evoked Potentials (ERPs) in Speech Perception

DENNIS L. MOLFESE, ALEXANDRA P. FONARYOVA KEY, MANDY J. MAGUIRE, GUY O. DOVE, AND VICTORIA J. MOLFESE

5.1 What Are Event-Related Potentials?

The event-related potential (ERP) is a synchronized portion of the ongoing EEG pattern. Evoked potential waveforms reflect changes in brain activity over time during stimulus processing (Rockstroh et al., 1982). Such changes are reflected in the amplitude (μV height of the wave at different points) or in the latency (time lapsed in milliseconds – ms – since stimulus onset) of certain peaks within the ERP. The ERP differs from the more traditional EEG measure because it reflects a portion of the ongoing EEG activity that is *time-locked* to the onset of a specific event (the stimulus) occurring outside the individual in the environment or internally as a cognitive process. This time-locked feature is the real strength of the ERP and represents a major advantage over the traditional EEG measures. ERPs allow direct correlations between brain measures and behavior that reflect processing in time at the millisecond level.

One common approach to characterizing the ERP is to identify in sequence the positive and negative peaks (i.e., the points at which portions of the ERP wave reaches the most positive and negative peak values) following stimulus onset. Thus, this labeling system identifies the order in which the peaks occur while at the same time indicating their polarity (see Figure 5.1). For example, "N1" refers to the first negative going peak in the waveform while "N2" refers to the second negative occurring peak, and so forth. Likewise, "P1" refers to the first positive deflection or peak in the ERP waveform while "P2" refers to the second peak, etc. An alternate and more recent scheme for naming ERP components is to label the positive and negative peaks by their latency (usually defined as the time from stimulus onset). Thus, the "N200" in this scheme refers to the negative peak that occurs 200 ms following stimulus onset. Generally, variations in latency and amplitude of these peaks are interpreted to reflect speed of processing (latency) or extent of processing (amplitude). In general, shorter latencies indicate

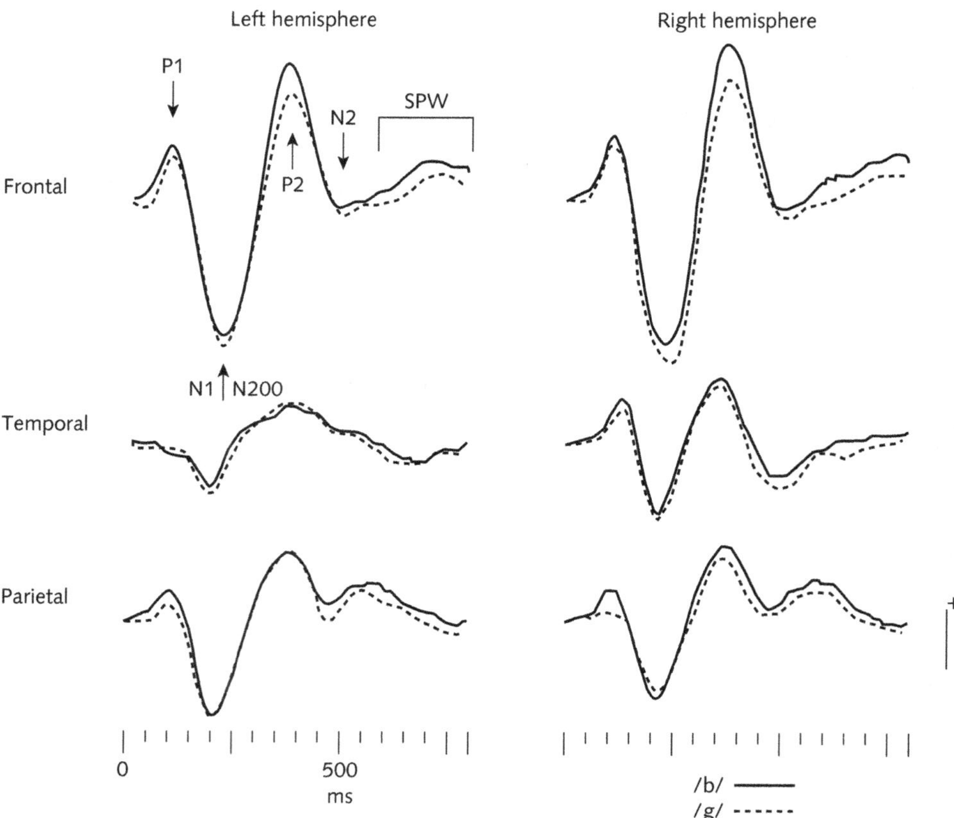

Figure 5.1 Group averaged auditory ERPs recorded from the left and right frontal, temporal, and parietal electrode sites of a group of 100 3-year-old children listening to a series of consonant-vowel syllables in which place of articulation varied from /b/ (solid line) to /g/ (dashed line). Arrows mark traditional peak regions where analyses are focused. "N" and "P" indicate "Negative" and "Positive" peaks, respectively. Numerals indicate the sequence in which the peaks occur. Peaks can also be designated by latency in ms from stimulus onset so that N1 also is identified as N200. Calibration is 2.5 μV with positive up. Duration is 800 ms from stimulus onset.

more rapid processing while larger amplitudes suggest increased processing activity.

The ERP is generally believed to reflect post-synaptic (dendritic) potentials (Allison et al., 1986). Even so, the information recorded at the scalp cannot capture all of the generated electrical activity for several reasons: (1) the distance from the cortical regions generating the signal to the scalp may be too great relative to the signal's strength; (2) variations in brain matter (e.g., neurons, glial cells, fiber tracts, cerebral spinal fluid, bone, muscle) can reduce signal strength or change current paths; or (3) the orientation of cortical columns generating the signal may not project the current directly to the scalp under an electrode, thereby making it difficult to trace the ERP to its origins within the brain. Nevertheless, as the data presented here show, consistent results have been obtained using this methodology across studies and participant groups that enable ERP data to be interpreted meaningfully with regard to several broad neurophysiological, developmental, and psychological issues. These findings have contributed to recent models of cognitive development.

5.2 ERPs Index Speech Perception

Initial attempts to investigate ERP correlates of speech perception focused on the more general question of whether there are differences in the brain responses evoked by speech signals compared to nonspeech sounds (Cohn, 1971; Friedman et al., 1975; Galambos et al., 1975; Jaramillo et al., 2001; Kayser et al., 1998; Molfese, Freeman, & Palermo, 1975; Morrell & Salamy, 1971; Neville, 1974). However, as Molfese (1978b) noted, speech sounds differ from nonspeech sounds on many acoustical dimensions (e.g., fundamental frequency, formant structure and duration, number of formants, frequency transitions, and rise, decay times, etc.), making it difficult to determine whether ERP differences are due to the specific linguistic properties of the speech stimuli, the usual dimension under study, or to some other aspects of the multiple acoustic differences that separate these two classes of stimuli. Consequently, the present chapter will focus on the perception of speech stimuli.

Researchers investigating the neural correlates of speech perception have utilized one of three procedures: habituation (Dorman, 1974), mismatch negativity (MMN) (Kraus et al., 1993b), and equal probability (Molfese, Freeman, & Palermo, 1975; Molfese & Molfese, 1979a). The habituation paradigm involves repeating one stimulus at a fixed interval (e.g., 1 s) for some number of trials and then presenting a new stimulus. Usually, after only a few repetitions the amplitude of the ERP decreases and the latency may shift. The occurrence of a new stimulus produces a "rebound" effect in which the ERP amplitude and latencies are restored. The MMN paradigm involves the presentation of two different stimuli. One occurs more frequently (70% of trials) while the second occurs less frequently (30% of trials). Both stimuli are intermixed in a block of trials. These stimuli are usually presented while subjects attend to another task. Analyses focus on the appearance of a large negative slow wave occurring between 150 and 350 ms in response to the infrequently occurring stimulus. An illustration of the MMN is presented in Figure 5.2 in which the arrow identifies the region of the MMN difference effect during a task comparing responses to tones of different frequencies. In the equal probability task, stimuli occur equally often but are randomly ordered relative to each other. In this case, attention to the stimulus usually results in larger amplitude ERPs with shorter latencies. Analyses may focus on several peaks in the ERP rather than a single peak as in the case of MMN. The present chapter focuses on ERP studies of speech perception involving voice onset time (VOT), place of articulation, and vowels. A further section reviews the use of ERP measures for predicting later emerging language-related skills.

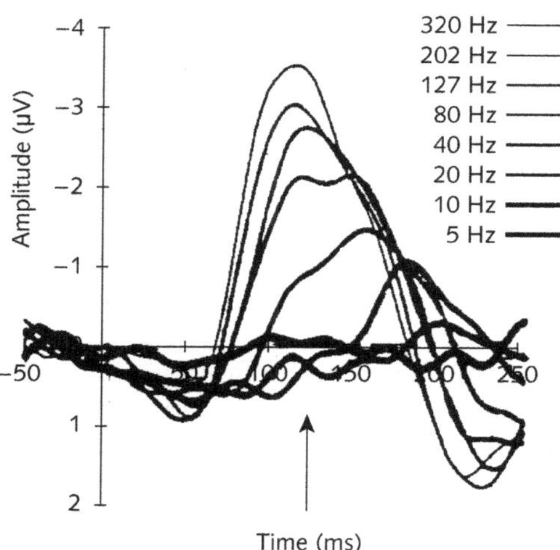

Figure 5.2 MMN to tones varying in frequency. Group averaged difference waves calculated by subtracting ERPs to the standard (frequent) tone from ERPs to deviant (infrequent) tones.

5.3 Voice Onset Time

VOT is the temporal interval between the beginning of laryngeal pulsing and the onset of consonant release. Numerous studies have shown that VOT is an important perceptual cue for the distinction between voiced and voiceless forms of stop consonants such as /b/ and /p/ (Lieberman et al., 1967). As reviewed elsewhere in this volume (see Raphael), adult listeners differentiate a variety of speech sounds by the phonetic labels attached to them, readily discriminating between consonants from different phonetic categories, such as (/ba/ and /pa/), while they perform at chance levels when asked to discriminate between two different /ba/ sounds that differ acoustically to the same extent as the /ba–pa/ difference (Lisker & Abramson, 1970). This pattern of successful discrimination for speech sounds representing different phonetic categories along with chance levels of discrimination for same-category contrasts is referred to as "categorical perception" (Harnard, 1987). Studies with infants (Eimas et al., 1971), children (Streeter, 1976), and adult listeners (Lisker & Abramson, 1970) have demonstrated categorical perception for a wide range of segmental phonetic contrasts such as voicing /ba, pa, ga, ka/ and place of articulation /ba, da, ga/.

5.3.1 *Adult VOT: ERP studies*

Dorman (1974) conducted the first ERP study of English VOT perception with adults using a habituation paradigm in which a speech token from within one phonetic category was repeated for a series of trials, after which a second token was introduced from either the same category or a different category. Auditory ERPs were recorded from the Cz lead (a position located at the central top of the head, and midway between the left and right ears, Jasper, 1958) of 50 adults, who were divided into five groups of 10 subjects. Computer synthesized speech sounds with different VOT characteristics, 250 ms in durations, were presented at fixed inter-stimulus intervals. The ERP N1–P2 peak-to-peak amplitude (the N1 range was 75–125 ms and the P2 range was 175–225 ms) were measured. The only amplitude effects noted were for the ERPs elicited by the stimuli from a different phonetic category than the habituating stimuli. Based on these results, Dorman (1974) concluded that ERPs can indicate the categorical perception of voicing cues.

In a follow-up study, Molfese (1978b) reported that ERPs reflected categorical discrimination of VOT when consonants from two different voicing categories were presented with equal probability of occurrence. He recorded ERPs from the left and right temporal regions of 16 adults during a phoneme identification task. Adults listened to randomly ordered sequences of synthesized bilabial stop consonants with VOT values of +0 ms, +20 ms, +40 ms, and +60 ms. After a brief delay, the adults pressed a series of keys to identify the speech sound. Two regions of the ERP (one component centered on 135 ms and a second occurring between 300 and 500 ms following stimulus onset) changed systematically when the speech sounds were from different phonetic categories but not when the sounds were from the same category. Electrophysiological studies employing similar stimuli with a variety of different populations have replicated this finding with infants (Molfese & Molfese, 1979b), children (Molfese & Hess, 1978; Molfese & Molfese, 1988), and adults (Molfese, 1980a; Segalowitz & Cohen, 1989). Surprisingly, however, in all studies in which this categorical discrimination effect was observed, it occurred over the *right* temporal region. This findings goes against the common belief that the left temporal region of the brain should be most responsive to speech and language stimuli.

5.3.2 Child VOT: ERP studies

Molfese and Hess (1978) recorded ERPs from the left and right temporal scalp regions of 12 preschool-age children (mean age = 4 years, 5 months) in response to randomly ordered series of synthesized consonant-vowel syllables in which the initial velar stop consonant sounds varied in VOT from +0 ms, to +20 ms, to +40 ms, to +60 ms. Analyses, like Molfese (1978b), also indicated a categorical-like discrimination effect whereby one late-occurring portion of the waveform (peak latency = 444 ms) changed systematically in response to consonants from different phonetic categories but did not respond differentially to consonants from within the same phonetic category. As in the case of Molfese (1978b), this effect occurred over the right hemisphere (RH). Unlike the adult study by Molfese, however, electrodes placed over both hemispheres detected a second portion of the auditory ERP that occurred earlier in the waveform than this RH effect and also discriminated the voiced from the voiceless consonants in a categorical-like manner (peak latencies = 198 and 342 ms). Similar results were reported by Molfese and Molfese (1988) with three-year old children.

5.3.3 *Infant VOT: ERP studies*

The ERP work with adults and children was later extended to include newborn and older infants. This step offered the opportunity to identify both the abilities that are present early in development and to chart changes in speech discrimination abilities during the early stages of language acquisition. Molfese and Molfese (1979a) presented the four consonant-vowel syllables used by Molfese (1978b) to 16 infants between 2 and 5 months of age (mean = 3 months, 25 days). ERPs were again recorded from the left and right temporal locations. Analyses identified one component of the auditory ERP recorded from over the RH approximately 920 ms following stimulus onset that discriminated between the different speech sounds in a categorical manner. As in the case of Molfese and Hess (1978), a second portion of the auditory ERP that was present over both hemispheres also discriminated between the consonant sounds in a categorical-like manner. The major portion of this component occurred 528 ms following stimulus onset. These results paralleled the findings of Molfese and Hess in revealing two portions of the auditory ERP that discriminated between speech sounds, a bilateral component that occurred earlier in the waveform, followed by a RH lateralized component that occurred later in time and that also discriminated between the sounds categorically. A final portion of the ERP waveform was found to differ between the two hemispheres across all of the different stimuli.

A recent study by Pang et al. (1998) using the MMN paradigm failed to find a RH effect. They investigated discrimination abilities for voiced and voiceless consonants in 8-month-old infants (n = 15). Natural speech /da/ was the standard stimulus (probability of 0.8) and /ta/ was the contrasting syllable (probability of 0.2). ERPs were recorded from frontal, central, temporal, and parietal leads in each hemisphere and at midline, referred to as Cz during data collection and later referenced to the average reference. The results identified a mismatch response at 200–300 ms over the left central region and at 200–350 ms over the left temporal area. Although Pang et al. argued that the discrepant findings could be due to the differences in reference points, or changes in developmental organization of the brain, it is important to note that Pang et al. did not analyze any of the ERP wave after 350 ms, while Molfese and Molfese (1979a) found that their RH effect occurred approximately 600 ms later.

A second experiment described by Molfese and Molfese (1979a) failed to observe any such bilateral or RH lateralized effects with 16 full-term newborn infants (8 female) less than 48 hours after birth. However, Simos and Molfese (1997) subsequently found ERPs recorded from newborns that discriminated between but not within phonetic-like categories when presented with nonspeech auditory stimuli that were modeled after the temporal delays for VOT.

These results indicated that infants displayed sensitivity to differences between phoneme categories. Differences in ERPs to variations in VOT were present over several cortical areas, some involving only left hemisphere (LH) or RH and some being common to both hemispheres. ERPs recorded in a listener perhaps as early as 2 months of age discriminate between speech tokens from different phonetic categories. This effect continues into the child and adult years.

5.3.4 *Speech vs. nonspeech processing of temporal-order information*

Pisoni (1977) reported that speech perception makes use of certain auditory processing mechanisms. He presented adult listeners with a series of two-tone nonspeech stimuli that varied in the onset of one tone relative to a second tone and found that they discriminated between tokens at temporal delays approximating those at the perceptual boundaries for speech sounds differing in VOT. In a follow-up study, Molfese (1980a) investigated whether the laterality effects noted for the VOT stimuli also occurred for the Tone Onset Time (TOT) sounds. If RH and bilateral category-like effects occurred for nonspeech stimuli containing comparable temporal delays to VOT, such effects might also be due to the temporal nature of the acoustic cues rather than to their "speech" quality.

Molfese (1980a) recorded ERPs from 16 adults to the TOT sounds used by Pisoni (1977) with onsets of 0, +20, +40, and +60 ms. An early ERP response at 145 ms over both hemispheres and a second component centered at 330 ms over RH electrode sites categorically discriminated the +0 and +20 ms TOT sounds from the +40 and +60 ms sounds. In a study of three-year-old children, Molfese and Molfese (1988) replicated the effects reported by Molfese (1980a) for both TOT and VOT stimuli. Both stimulus sets produced identical RH responses, reinforcing the conclusion that ERPs are indeed the result of responses to temporal structure rather than to some general "speech" quality per se.

5.3.5 *Hemisphere mechanisms involved in processing VOT*

Although RH discrimination of the VOT cue seems paradoxical in light of arguments that language processes are carried out primarily by the LH, results from lesion studies have addressed this concern. First, clinical studies of VOT involving stroke patients provide converging evidence that VOT is discriminated, if not exclusively, then at least in part, by a RH component (for a review of this literature, see Molfese, Molfese, & Parsons, 1983). For example, Miceli et al. (1978) found that a left-brain-damaged aphasic group made fewest errors with stimuli differing in voicing compared to errors in place of articulation contrasts. Blumstein, Baker, and Goodglass (1977) also found fewer errors for voicing contrasts than for place of articulation contrasts with LH-damaged Wernicke aphasics. Additionally, Perecman and Kellar (1981), based on their own findings that LH-damaged patients continue to match sounds on the basis of voicing but not place, speculated that either hemisphere could process voicing contrasts but that the place of articulation cue was more likely to be processed by only the LH. Second, the electrophysiological studies of Molfese and his colleagues point to several regions of the brain that appear responsive to voicing contrasts including the RH.

Three general findings have emerged from our ERP research on the perception of VOT. First, ERPs systematically vary in response to differences in the temporal delays common to voiced and voiceless stop consonants. Second, from at least 2 months of age, the infant's brain appears to distinguish voiced from voiceless stop consonants in a categorical manner. In fact, even from birth it appears that infants are highly sensitive to the temporal differences that separate voiced from voiceless consonants in English (Simos & Molfese, 1997). Third, categorical discrimination across different age groups appears to be mediated by multiple processing mechanisms within the brain. This processing is initially reflected in the region of the first large negative ERP component (N100) that engages the auditory cortex within both hemispheres to discriminate voiced from voiceless consonant sounds. Subsequently, a temporally disparate response occurs approximately 300 ms later in adults and children (and up to 500 ms later in infants) that appears to arise from brain processes within the right temporal lobe to make a similar discrimination along phonetic category boundaries. The early emergence of these processes in development suggests that the auditory mechanisms upon which phonetic perception depends must be sensitive to these basic acoustic properties early in life. Subsequently, as the brain develops and the complex interactions occur with emerging cognitive functions and environmental interactions, the linguistic functions incorporate and utilize these basic acoustic attributes as the foundation for developing later phonetic skills.

5.4 Place of Articulation

Numerous studies with infants, children, and adults have also investigated the ERP correlates of acoustic and phonetic cues important for the perception of American English consonant place of articulation in stop consonants (Molfese, 1978a, 1980b; Molfese, Buhrke, & Wang, 1985; Molfese, Linnville et al., 1985; Molfese & Molfese, 1979b, 1980, 1985; Molfese & Schmidt, 1983). As in the case of VOT, ERP studies of place of articulation cues identified both lateralized and bilateral hemisphere responses that discriminated between the different consonant sounds. Some important differences were found, however, both in the development of ERP responses to place of articulation cues and in the character of the lateralized brain responses that distinguished the perception of these cues from VOT.

5.4.1 Adult place of articulation: ERP studies

Wood, Goff, and Day (1971) published the first ERP study on the perception of place of articulation contrasts. They compared the ERPs recorded in two identification tasks. In one task, listeners indicated whether a /ba/ or /da/ syllable was heard. In the second task, the listeners indicated whether they heard a /ba/-low syllable with an initial fundamental frequency of 104 Hz or whether a /ba/-high syllable with an initial fundamental frequency of 140 Hz was heard. Wood et al. reported that ERPs over the LH varied only during the phonetic identification task (see also Lawson & Galliard, 1981; Wood, 1975). However, Grabow et al. (1980) failed to replicate these results, possibly because Wood et al. did not control for baseline shifts in the background EEG.

In a related study, Molfese (1978a) recorded ERP responses from the left and right temporal regions of ten adults in response to randomly ordered series of consonant-vowel syllables that varied in consonant place of articulation, bandwidth, and phonetic transition quality. Changes in the place of articulation cue signaled either the consonant /b/ or /g/. Bandwidth was manipulated in two sets of stimuli: nonspeech sounds contained analogs of formants composed of sinewaves 1 Hz in bandwidth, whereas a set of speech sounds contained formants with speechlike bandwidths of 60, 90, and 120 Hz for formants 1 through 3. The phonetic transition quality cue was also manipulated. One stimulus set contained formant transitions that normally characterize human speech patterns while the second set contained formant transitions atypical for consonant sounds in the initial consonant position in human speech.

Two intervals of the auditory ERP that peaked at 70 and 300 ms following stimulus onset discriminated consonant phonetic transition quality and place of articulation only over the LH temporal electrode site. As in the case of Molfese (1978b), who also used only a single LH temporal site, no bilateral place of articulation discrimination was observed. Similar LH place of articulation discrimination effects have since been found by Molfese (1980b) and Molfese & Schmidt (1983), with the exception that for auditory ERP data collected from more electrode recording sites over each hemisphere consistent discrimination of the place of articulation cues were noted for both hemispheres (bilateral effects). In another study employing natural and synthetic speech stimuli, Gelfer (1987) replicated the lateralized and bilateral effects as well as the latencies of the ERP effects reported earlier by Molfese and Schmidt (1983).

Several general findings from the adult studies of the perception of place of articulation are notable. When multiple electrode sites are employed, bilateral stimulus discrimination effects are found. Furthermore, these bilateral effects invariably occur early in the waveform and prior to the onset of a lateralized place of articulation discrimination response. This temporal sequence between bilateral and lateralized effects was also found in the VOT discrimination studies reviewed earlier. In addition to stimulus-related hemisphere effects, portions of the ERPs were found to vary between hemispheres that are unrelated to stimulus, task, or subject features. Apparently, during the discrimination process both hemispheres initially discriminate between place of articulation and VOT at the same time, approximately 100 ms following stimulus onset. Shortly afterwards, at approximately 300 ms following stimulus onset, a second independent process in the LH discriminates between differences in the place of articulation cue, while the RH at approximately 400 ms discriminates the VOT cue. Finally, throughout this time course and afterwards there are brief periods of activity during which the two hemispheres are responding quite differently, which may be unrelated to the auditory or phonetic discrimination of the stimuli.

Such temporal difference in response to nearly identical stimulus information suggests different types of neural processing operations as information moves through the nervous system and is utilized at different levels by the language and cognitive systems. This conclusion receives additional support when one considers the ERP components that reflect such changes. Variations in the initial large negative peak (i.e., N100 in adults) similar over both hemispheres are generally believed to reflect sensory input into the temporal lobes that supports initial primary auditory processing and some initial higher levels of processing. In contrast, later occurring ERP components such as the P300 and the following

N400 in adults that respond asymmetrically to the speech contrasts generally reflect activation of a variety of temporal and frontal lobe functions associated with more complex information processing. Given this scenario, it seems reasonable to hypothesize that both hemispheres are initially engaged in processing the acoustic signal as it first arrives from the auditory periphery. The later lateralized processing might then reflect more advanced linguistic and cognitive processes that utilize this acoustic information. The finding that the perception of some speech cues may have a biological substrate in the temporal lobes (and more specifically in the primary auditory projection areas within the temporal lobe – Heschl's gyrus) that supports initial processing and discrimination could facilitate both the selection of such cues (VOT) as language relevant and aid in the processing of that information (Kuhl, 1999; Kuhl & Miller, 1975; Kuhl & Padden, 1982).

5.4.2 *Place of articulation in children: ERP studies*

Relatively few ERP studies have been conducted on the perception of place of articulation in children. Generally, these studies have found that ERPs are able to detect perceptual differences between consonant sounds varying in place of articulation as well as small variations within a phoneme category. Kraus et al. (1993a) compared ERPs elicited by synthesized speech stimuli in 16 school-aged children (7–11 years) and 10 adults. They intermixed fewer repetitions of /da/ and /ga/ that contained different onset frequencies for the second and third formant transitions into repetitions of the standard (more frequent) /ga/. MMN discriminated between consonant sounds, and was larger in children than in adults.

In another study, Kraus et al. (1993b) used ERPs to reveal the perceptual discrimination of speech sounds that children or adults cannot discriminate using standard behavioral paradigms. MMN was recorded from the Fz electrode placed on the scalp of ten children, aged 7–11 years, and a group of adults while they listened to synthesized speech variants of the voice stop consonant /da/ that occurred 15% of the time within a group of standard /da/ presentations. Both adults and children displayed a MMN effect for the deviant stimuli, indicating that they were able to discriminate between speech variations that occurred within a consonant category that could not be distinguished behaviorally.

5.4.3 *Place of articulation in infants: ERP studies*

Several studies have also been carried out to assess infants' ability to discriminate speech sounds differing in place of articulation. The paradigms of choice included equiprobable presentation (Molfese & Molfese, 1979b) and MMN (Dehaene-Lambertz & Dehaene, 1994). The results indicate that newborns are sensitive to place of articulation in stop consonants. This distinction is present at birth as well as later in the infancy period.

Molfese and Molfese (1979b) conducted the earliest research investigating ERP correlates of place of articulation perception in infants. Unlike the earlier findings for VOT, place of articulation discrimination in speech sounds was clearly present from birth. In this study, ERPs were recorded from the left and right temporal regions (T3 and T4) of 16 full-term newborn human infants within two days of birth. Infants were presented series of consonant-vowel syllables that differed in the second formant transition (F2, which signaled the place of articulation information), and formant bandwidth. As with adults, one auditory ERP component that appeared only over the LH recording site discriminated between the two consonant sounds when they contained normal speech formant characteristics (peak latency = 192 ms). A second region of the auditory ERP varied systematically over both hemispheres and also discriminated between the two speechlike consonant sounds (peak latency = 630 ms). Finally, the ERPs differed between hemispheres at approximately 288 ms following stimulus onset. This hemisphere difference occurred across all stimuli.

In a replication and extension, Molfese and Molfese (1985) presented a series of consonant-vowel syllables that varied in place of articulation and formant structure to 16 newborn infants. Two different consonant sounds, /b/ and /g/, combined with three different vowel sounds were presented using both speech or nonspeech formant structures. ERPs were again recorded from the left and right temporal regions (T3, T4). As in the case of Molfese and Molfese (1979b), analyses identified two regions of the auditory ERP that discriminated place of articulation contrasts. One region, with a peak latency of 168 ms, was detected only over the LH site and discriminated between the two different consonant sounds. Dehaene also noted LH responses in 2- to 4-month-old infants (Dehaene-Lambertz & Dehaene, 1994; Dehaene-Lambertz, 2000). Molfese and Molfese (1985) also reported that a second region with a peak latency of 664 ms discriminated this place of articulation difference and was detected by electrodes placed over both hemispheres.

In research with older infants, Dehaene-Lambertz and Dehaene (1994) examined discrimination of consonants varying in the place of articulation in 16 infants aged 2 to 3 months. ERPs were obtained using a 58-electrode net in response to simple CV syllables /ba/ and /ga/. The trials included four repetitions of the same syllable followed by the fifth repetition of the same stimulus (standard) or a different stimulus (deviant). The results indicated that infants discriminated between the two types of trials around 390 ms after the critical stimulus onset. Further, ERPs were larger over LH parietal areas as compared to the RH.

In another study, Dehaene-Lambertz (2000) used a similar paradigm to examine the perception of speech and nonspeech stimuli in 16 infants of 4 months of age. Stimuli included variations in place of articulation produced by male and female speakers. ERPs obtained using a 64-channel net indicated that /ba/ was discriminated from /ga/ between 320 and 400 ms over bilateral frontal and left temporal regions. Male vs. female voices elicited different responses over frontal, central, and occipital regions. Additional voice-related effects were present in 400–480 ms intervals at frontal and left occipital areas in both hemispheres. Further, the LH generated large amplitudes for all stimulus types, leading the authors to conclude that the LH has an advantage for processing speech information. Thus, across all studies, ERPs successfully discriminated between place of articulation differences. These effects appeared primarily but not exclusively over LH electrode sites.

5.4.4 *Lateralized and bilateral brain responses*

The relationship between lateralized and bilateral responses, although consistent across studies, remains unclear. There is some support for an ontogenetic as well as phylogenetic role in the development of the bilateral response after the lateralized responses (Molfese, Laughlin et al., 1986; Molfese, Molfese et al., 2002). There also appear to be consistent patterns of brain responses to speech cues from infancy into adulthood. For example, Molfese and Molfese (1980) noted the presence of only LH lateralized responses in 11 preterm infants born on average 35.9 weeks post-conception. Stimuli identical to those employed in Molfese (1978a) with adults were presented to these infants while ERPs were recorded from the LH (T3) and RH (T4) temporal regions. As found with the full-term infants (Molfese & Molfese, 1979a), a portion of the auditory ERP recorded over the LH discriminated between speech stimuli containing different consonant transition cues. Another auditory ERP component responded differently to speech versus nonspeech formant structures.

Interestingly, the lateralized effect noted for these infants for the place of articulation cue occurred before that for the bilateral effect, a finding opposite to that noted for adults. However, the reversal of the temporal relationship between the bilateral and lateralized responses appears to be a legitimate one, given that virtually identical results were found by Molfese and Molfese (1985) and Molfese and Molfese (1979b) with different populations of infants and different place of articulation stimulus sets. This temporal pattern of initial lateralized responses followed by bilateral responses is opposite to that noted previously for both VOT and place of articulation cues for adults as well as that found for infants exposed to changes in the VOT/temporal cue. These ERP differences suggest that different neural mechanisms support the perception and discrimination of VOT and place of articulation.

Data from nonhuman studies offer some additional insight into the role that these bilateral and lateralized responses play in the perception of speech cues and their ultimate contribution to language processing. Two separate studies with one-year-old infant rhesus monkeys, one investigating place of articulation perception (Molfese, Laughlin et al., 1986), and a second studying VOT (Morse et al., 1987), found left and right lateralized categorical discrimination responses, respectively, but no bilateral responses. A VOT discrimination study with two breeds of dogs, 2-month-old collies and beagles, also noted a RH lateralized categorical discrimination response but no bilateral responses (Adams, Molfese, & Betz, 1987). Given the absence of the bilateral response in nonhuman primates and other mammals, it is conceivable that the bilateral response differentiates humans from other mammals in the discrimination of speech contrasts, not, as usually argued, the uniquely lateralized LH mechanisms in the human brain (Lenneberg, 1967, p. 67).

5.5 Vowel Perception

ERP correlates of vowel perception also have been studied across the life span, more often using the MMN paradigm and less frequently the equal probability paradigm. Vowel sounds generally reflect articulation during a steady-state mode where vocal tract dimensions are maintained for some time period before changes occur as transitions are made to other vowel or consonant sounds.

In general, ERP studies of vowel perception support several conclusions: (1) perception appears to occur early in speech processing, but is not localized to one specific scalp region, producing different ERP scalp distributions than either VOT or place of articulation cues (Molfese & Erwin, 1981); (2) no single localized brain region subserves vowel detection, a point that fits with the notion that vowels are determined by complex relational acoustic cues (Lieberman & Blumstein, 1988); (3) between and within category perception occurs in early vowel processing, suggesting that the pre-attentive discrimination processes responsible for MMN are sensitive to both acoustic and phonetic properties (Aaltonen et al., 1987; Näätanen et al., 1997); (4) unlike findings from VOT and place of articulation, no hemisphere effects were found to interact with vowel identification (Molfese & Erwin, 1981), a finding consistent with behavioral studies (Blumstein et al., 1977); (5) MMN latencies decrease with age; (6) MMN amplitude for vowel sounds appears larger (Csépe, 1995) or of equal size (Csépe, 1995) in infants (Cheour et al., 1997) or children compared to adults; (7) variations in MMN amplitude do not map directly onto changes in other ERP components, suggesting that different cortical and cognitive mechanisms produce variations in MMN vs. N2 and N4 components (see Pang & Taylor, 2000).

5.6 Use of ERPs in Speech Perception to Predict Language Outcomes

A number of electrophysiological studies conducted over the past three decades have been successful in predicting later language development based on neonatal evoked response potential to speech sounds. If outcomes can be predicted from tests conducted early in development, the opportunity for initiating interventions could be pushed back to a much earlier developmental period thereby allowing clinicians more time to intervene with the affected child. Such early interventions could conceivably offer the opportunity to intervene and mitigate or even eliminate a disorder before it could seriously impact the child's development. Initial studies that restricted analyses of the visually elicited ERP to a light flash to a single early peak in the brainwave (usually the latency of the N1 component at approximately 146 ms) reported some success in short-term prediction, but failed to find a long-term relationship after 12 months of age (Butler & Engel, 1969; Engel & Fay, 1972; Engel & Henderson, 1973; Henderson & Engel, 1974; Jensen & Engel, 1971).

Despite the failure of early attempts, more recent findings suggest that relationships might in fact exist (Molfese, 1989, 2000; Molfese & Molfese, 1985, 1997; Molfese & Searock, 1986). This difference in success between studies reflects a number of differences in methodology and experimental design. First, while the relationship of the photic flashes used by earlier investigators to subsequent language skills is not known, some data are available suggesting that speech perception is directly related to language development. Since predictors of successful performance are generally better if they measure predicted skills, the inclusion of more language relevant materials as the evoking stimuli logically should increase the predictive accuracy for later language skills. Second, the frequency range of the evoked potential studied by current investigators includes a lower range of frequencies (below 2 Hz) than those employed by earlier investigators. Given that approximately 95% of the brainwave frequencies characterizing the evoked potentials of very young infants are concentrated below 2 Hz, such a strategy utilizes a much higher percentage of the neonate's brainwave activity, thereby increasing the likelihood of identifying relevant components related to later language skills. Third, more recent investigations analyze longer portions of the ERP waveform while previous researchers confined their analysis to a single peak of short duration in the waveform. Molfese & Molfese (1997) have argued that if all data collected are analyzed instead of only a small subset, the likelihood of identifying a relationship between early brain responses and later development should be improved. Considered together, these differences in measures and stimuli across studies could be responsible for the improved success of more recent studies in different laboratories using auditory ERPs recorded at birth to predict later cognitive and language functioning.

In a series of studies, Molfese and Molfese (1979a, 1985, 1988, 1997) first isolated and identified lateralized components of the ERP that are related to long-term language outcomes. In fact, other theoreticians historically speculated that the absence of hemispheric or lateralized differences in a child indicates that the child is at risk for certain cognitive or language disabilities (Travis, 1931). Three decades later Lenneberg (1967) proposed that lateralization is a biological sign of language. Such views advanced the notion that hemisphere differences in the perception of speech sounds are predictive of later language development. In sharp contrast to this view, Molfese and Molfese (1985) argued that predictions concerning later performance are enhanced only when specific speech perception processing capacities are lateralized. Hemisphere differences per se were not expected to predict later language outcomes.

Molfese and Molfese (1985) first established the validity of a variety of speech perception factors as predictors of long-term outcomes in language development from ERP measures taken shortly after birth. They recorded ERPs in response to different consonant and vowel contrasts from 16 infants using electrodes placed over the left and right temporal areas (T3 and T4) at birth and again at six-month intervals until the child's third birthday. Information was also obtained for a variety of prenatal and perinatal factors, IQ and language measures, and a range of SES and parental factors.

Analyses indicated that ERPs recorded at birth identified children who performed better or worse on language tasks by 3 years of age. Two ERP components were identified. An initial negative peak (N1) that occurred between 88 and 240 ms over LH electrodes reliably discriminated children whose McCarthy Verbal Index scores were above 50 (the High group) from those with lower scores (i.e., the Low group). The Low group failed to display such lateralized discrimination for either the speech or the nonspeech sounds. A second component of the ERP with a late negative peak latency of 664 ms also discriminated High from Low groups. Unlike the earlier component, however, the second component occurred across both hemispheres and, consequently, reflected bilateral activity. While the second component discriminated speech from nonspeech stimuli, its ability to discriminate between specific consonant sounds depended on which vowel followed the consonant. Hemispheric differences alone did not discriminate between infants who later developed better or poorer language skills. Furthermore, given that the ERP components discriminating between the two groups were sensitive to different speech and nonspeech contrasts, it appears that the ERPs reflected the infants' sensitivity to specific language-related cues rather than the overall readiness of the brain to respond to any general stimulus in its environment.

In additional analyses, Molfese and Molfese (1986) applied a stepwise multiple regression model in which Peabody Picture Vocabulary Test (PPVT) and McCarthy Verbal Index scores served as dependent variables while the ERP components obtained at birth that best discriminated the different consonant sounds from Molfese and Molfese (1985) were used as the independent variables. This model accounted for 78% of the total variance in predicting McCarthy scores from the brain responses, whereas 69% of the variance was accounted for in predicting PPVT scores (Molfese, 1989). Clearly, a strong relation exists between early ERP discrimination of speech sounds and later language skills. Interestingly, the inclusion of perinatal measures and Brazelton scores improved the amount of variance by less than 3%, reinforcing the proposal that brain responses are more robust than behavior in predicting developmental outcomes.

Molfese and Searock (1986) extended the predictive relationship between early ERP activity and emerging language skills at 3 years to include discrimination of vowel sounds. Infants who discriminated between more vowel sounds at 1 year of age performed better on language tasks at 3 years. Thus, ERPs at birth as well as at 1 year successfully predict language performance at 3 years. Molfese (1989) replicated these findings using a different sample of infants, different electrode placements, and different statistical approaches. ERPs were recorded at birth from frontal, temporal, and parietal scalp areas over the LH and RH of 30 infants in response to the speech syllables /bi/ and /gi/ and their nonspeech analogues. Discriminant function procedures used the ERP components identified by Molfese and Molfese (1985) to successfully classify 68.6% of the HIGH group performers and 69.7% of the LOW group. Thus, predictors identified in one sample of infants were successfully used to correctly classify a second group of infants in terms of their later language skills.

More recently, Molfese and Molfese (1997) reported that the relationship between early neonatal ERPs and later language performance measures continues into the elementary school years. ERPs were recorded from 71 full term, newborn infants, in response to nine consonant-vowel syllables that combined each of the initial consonants, /b, d, g/ with a following vowel, either /a, i, u/. Electrode sites and recording procedures were identical to Molfese (1989). Although there were no differences between groups in prenatal, perinatal, and SES measures, analyses indicated high accuracy ranging from 89% to 97% in classifying children's performance on Stanford-Binet verbal scores at 5 years of age based on their neonatal ERPs to speech.

A subsequent study by Molfese (2000) reported that neonatal ERPs can predict reading skills up to 8 years later. Auditory ERPs were recorded from LH and RH frontal, temporal, and parietal scalp regions of these 48 children during the newborn period to /bi/ and /gi/ and nonspeech homologues of these sounds. All of the children were also tested within two weeks of their eighth birthday using a variety of language and cognitive measures. By 8 years of age this group included 17 dyslexics, 7 poor readers, and 24 controls matched on the basis of IQ, reading scores, and SES factors (Wechsler, 1991, WISC-3; Wilkinson, 1993, WRAT). The peak latencies and amplitudes from the ERP regions earlier identified by Molfese and Molfese (1985) were the dependent measures in a discriminant function analysis used to classify the children's reading performance at 8 years. In general, results indicated faster latencies for the control children in comparison to the dyslexic and poor reading groups as well as larger N1 amplitudes for the control infants while the N2 amplitudes were larger in the dyslexic and poor reading groups. The poor reading group also generated a larger P2 amplitude response. Analyses correctly classified 81.3% of the children at 8 years of age. These data extend findings previously reporting strong relationships in reading and language between neonatal speech discrimination and verbal performance measures at 3 and 5 years, indicating a strong relationship between infants' ability to discriminate speech sounds and later language and reading performance (Guttorm et al., submitted; Lyytinen et al., 2003).

5.6.1 *Why are ERPs predictive of language development?*

The obvious question arising from these results is why any measure, behavioral or brain, should discriminate developmental outcomes over a large age range with such high precision. Are human accomplishments predetermined from birth? Are genetic factors so potent that they all but force certain developmental outcomes despite the influence of environmental factors? Molfese and Molfese (1997) suggested that these data reflect the state of an underlying perceptual mechanism upon which some aspects of later developing and emerging verbal and cognitive processes are based. As a result of genetic and gestational factors, the prenatal organism develops a set of perceptual abilities that are highly responsive to environmental variations. For most individuals, these perceptual abilities readily enable us to discriminate stimuli within our environment in quite similar ways. For others, however, aspects of these perceptual skills may not respond to environmental elements in the same way. It is these fundamental differences in perceptual skills that set the stage for early detection of responses that influence later language development outcomes.

Numerous studies from other laboratories also support this interpretation. For example, Kraus et al. (1996) tested 90 control (6–15 years) and 91 learning disabled children (LD). The latter group was diagnosed clinically as LD, Attention Deficit Disordered, or both. All had normal IQ scores greater than 85, although the normal children differed from those with LD on listening comprehension, visual processing speed, reading, spelling, and word auditory memory. Kraus et al. presented two sets of synthesized consonant-vowel syllables. MMN results indicated more robust MMN responses for the able perceivers while the poor perceivers did not generate such clear responses. Kraus et al. concluded that an auditory processing deficit contributed to these formant frequency discrimination difficulties in these children.

Using a different paradigm, Kraus et al. found that children who differed in language related skills also generated different ERP responses. Similar results were published by a number of investigators using the MMN paradigm and a variety of speech sound contrasts (Cheour et al., 1997; Kraus et al., 1996).

The argument that developmentally early differences in the perceptual substrate underlying speech perception and spoken language processing play a role in later language development is developed further using VOT as an example. As noted earlier, VOT is a perceptual cue utilized to discriminate voiced from voiceless stop consonants. American English speakers display a perceptual boundary that allows them to normally discriminate voiced stop consonants (e.g., /b, d, g/) from voiceless stop consonants (e.g., /p, t, k/) (Liberman et al., 1967; Stevens & Klatt, 1974). The discrimination and identification of consonant sounds varying in voicing suggests that this cue is perceptually based and utilizes the temporal lag between the release of the occlusion of the vocal tract and the onset of laryngeal pulsing (i.e., vocal fold vibration). Even 1-month-old infants discriminate voiced from voiceless stop consonants in ways that are fundamentally similar to those of adult language users (Eimas et al., 1971). This ability to discriminate between speech sounds with certain temporal delays is not limited to humans (Kuhl & Miller, 1975; Morse, 1976).

However, what happens if auditory sensitivity to an acoustic boundary such as VOT is shifted away from the usual category boundary for a native American English-speaking child? A shift of only +20 ms results in the infant hearing only one consonant sound across a range heard by most listeners as two different speech sounds. The voiced and voiceless bilabial stop consonants produced by the parent would be heard as the same consonant. The infant whose perceptual boundary had shifted from +30 ms to +50 ms would only hear the word "big," instead of the words "big" and "pig." As a consequence, the child's language environment appears less differentiated phonetically and the infant's ability to map from sound differences (/b/ vs. /p/) to word meaning differences ("big" vs. "pig") is impaired. Since half of the consonant sounds in American English are voiced, the potential exists that the infant would experience other voiced vs. voiceless confusions as well. An even more difficult scenario is one where the acoustic boundary is shifted only +10 ms, thereby impairing the perception of some consonant sounds (and consequently word perception) but not others, making it more difficult to diagnose. Such shifts could differentially affect different consonant sounds in the same word depending on coarticulated information, further confusing the child.

All of these factors could make the task of mapping from phonetic contrasts to word meaning a much more formidable one (see Houston, this volume). In the meantime, infants with normally developed auditory systems can accurately discriminate relevant phonetic cues to readily hear phonetic contrasts between words (e.g., "big" and "pig") in their language environment and go on to develop different semantic links to characterize these different sounding words. Since the task for normally hearing infants is not as formidable because of their ability to hear the voicing differences, these infants can use their resources to advance in other cognitive areas. This gives them an advantage over infants with possible auditory resolution problems who continue to try sorting out what they perceive as auditory ambiguities. Added to these tasks facing phonetically impaired infants and young children are the influences of the early sensory and linguistic environment that can vary in its adequacy for meeting cognitive and language needs. Parents and other caretakers may differ in the time and expertise needed to stimulate linguistic development or promote academic-related skills through the provision of materials and provide a physical environment that is enriching (Hart & Risley, 1995; Molfese & Thompson, 1985; Molfese, DiLalla, & Bunce, 1997). A less stimulating language-learning environment may provide fewer opportunities to acquire additional cues to help the child recognize that they do not perceive their environment correctly, thereby making their disability even more difficult to overcome.

5.7 Summary and Conclusions

Over the past three decades neuroscientists have used a variety of electrophysiological techniques and a number of different experimental paradigms to investigate the role of the brain in speech perception. The rich behavioral work on the perception of speech cues certainly facilitated this development, providing a solid theoretical and methodological framework for such investigations. As discussed in this chapter, the ERP has proved to be a reliable neurobiological correlate of speech perception across the life span, permitting comparisons between infants, children, and adults. Over this period of time, the research questions have matured from the initial questions regarding whether ERP measures could simply discriminate speech from nonspeech sounds to investigating parallels between findings from ERP and the behavioral literature regarding the perception of specific speech cues. Methodological advances including the use of MMN and equal probability approaches further advanced the study of the neural processing of speech cues, adding to our understanding of speech perception and spoken language understanding. The convergence of ERP findings on speech perception across populations and paradigms has been exceptional. As other methodologies develop for the study of real-time brain processing such as high-density array ERP techniques (Molfese, Molfese et al., 2002) and these techniques are merged with techniques that identify functional brain areas involved in speech perception and language processes, new and exciting vistas will emerge.

As the last millennium drew to a close, investigators began to address questions regarding the consequence of speech perception processes that appeared so early in development. Clearly, some of the phonological skills that are important for analyzing sound patterns in spoken words are present at or near birth and others develop in infancy. Young infants discriminate between speech sounds that contain phonetic contrasts characteristic of their language environments and also display sensitivity to phonetic contrasts that are characteristic of other languages (Eilers, Wilson, & Moore, 1977; Eimas et al., 1971; Molfese & Molfese, 1979a; Molfese, 2000). This sensitivity changes in later infancy toward increased attention to speech contrasts unique to the infant's language environment, a change that appears to facilitate language acquisition. Preschool children develop the ability to segment spoken monosyllabic words into onsets and rimes and are able to play nursery rhyme games (Vellutino & Scanlon, 1987). Children also learn to segment polysyllabic words into syllables as they approach kindergarten age and monosyllabic words into phonemes around first grade (Liberman et al., 1967). Over the past decade, numerous findings have emerged suggesting that phonological processing skills are fundamental to language development and the acquisition of reading (Brady, 1991; Catts et al., 1999; Wagner, Torgesen, & Rashotte, 1994). Other studies have uncovered links between neural measures of speech sound discrimination in infancy and later language related outcomes. With these findings on the neural correlates of speech perception and new behavioral methods for assessment and intervention, future generations could realize enormous benefits from the elimination of deficits such as reading and learning disabilities.

ACKNOWLEDGMENTS

This work was supported in part by grants from the National Institute of Child Health and Human Development (R01-HD17860), and the US Department of Education (R215K000023, R215R990011).

REFERENCES

Aaltonen, O., Niemi, P., Nyrke, T., & Tuhkanen, M. (1987). Event-related brain potentials and the perception of a phonetic continuum. *Biological Psychology*, 24, 197–207.

Adams, C., Molfese, D. L., & Betz, J. C. (1987). Electrophysiological correlates of categorical speech perception for voicing contrasts in dogs. *Developmental Neuropsychology*, 3, 175–89.

Allison, T., Wood, C. C., & McCarthy, G. M. (1986). The central nervous system. In M. G. H. Coles, E. Donchin, & S. W. Porges (eds.), *Psychophysiology: Systems, Processes, and Applications* (pp. 5–25). New York: Guilford.

Blumstein, S., Baker, E., & Goodglass, H. (1977). Phonological factors in auditory comprehension in aphasia. *Neuropsychologia*, 15, 19–30.

Brady, S. (1991). The role of working memory in reading disability. In S. A. Brady & D. P. Shankweiler (eds.), *Phonological Processes in Literacy: A tribute to Isabelle Y. Liberman* (pp. 129–61). Hillsdale, NJ: Lawrence Erlbaum.

Butler, B. & Engel, R. (1969). Mental and motor scores at 8 months in relation to neonatal photic responses. *Developmental Medicine and Child Neurology*, 11, 77–82.

Catts, H., Fey, M., Zhang, X., & Tomblin, J. (1999). Language basis of reading and reading disabilities: Evidence from a longitudinal investigation. *Scientific Study of Reading*, 3, 331–61.

Cheour, M. et al. (1997). The mismatch negativity to changes in speech sounds at the age of 3 months. *Developmental Neuropsychology*, 13, 167–74.

Cohn, R. (1971). Differential cerebral processing of noise and verbal stimuli. *Science*, 172, 599–601.

Csépe, V. (1995). On the origin and development of the mismatch negativity. *Ear and Hearing*, 16, 91–104.

Dehaene-Lambertz, G. (2000). Cerebral specialization for speech and non-speech stimuli in infants. *Journal of Cognitive Neuroscience*, 12, 449–60.

Dehaene-Lambertz, G. & Dehaene, S. (1994). Speed and cerebral correlates of syllable discrimination in infants. *Nature*, 370, 292–5.

Dorman, M. F. (1974). Auditory evoked potential correlates of speech sound discrimination. *Perception & Psychophysics*, 15, 215–20.

Eilers, R., Wilson, W., & Moore, J. (1977). Developmental changes in speech discrimination in infants. *Journal of Speech & Hearing Research*, 20, 766–80.

Eimas, P., Siqueland, E., Jusczyk, P., & Vigorito, J. (1971). Speech perception in infants. *Science*, 171, 303–6.

Engel, R. & Fay, W. (1972). Visual evoked responses at birth, verbal scores at three years, and IQ at four years. *Developmental Medicine and Child Neurology*, 14, 283–9.

Engel, R. & Henderson, N. (1973). Visual evoked responses and IQ scores at school age. *Developmental Medicine and Child Neurology*, 15, 136–45.

Friedman, D., Simson, R., Ritter, W., & Rapin, I. (1975). Cortical evoked potentials elicited by real speech words and human sounds. *Journal of Electroencephalography and Clinical Neurophysiology*, 38, 13–19.

Galambos, R., Benson, P., Smith, T. S., Schulman-Galambos, C., & Osier, H. (1975). On hemispheric differences in evoked potentials to speech stimuli. *Journal of Electroencephalography and Clinical Neurophysiology*, 39, 279–83.

Gelfer, M. (1987). An AER study of stop-consonant discrimination. *Perception & Psychophysics*, 42, 318–27.

Grabow, J., Aronson, A., Offord, K., Rose, D., & Greene, K. (1980). Hemispheric potentials evoked by speech sounds during discrimination tasks. *Journal of Electroencephalography and Clinical Neurophysiology*, 49, 48–58.

Guttorm, T. K., Leppänen, P. H. T., Eklund, K. M., Poikkeus, A.-M., Lyytinen, P., & Lyytinen, H. (submitted). Brain responses to changes in vowel duration measured at birth predict later language skills in children with familial risk for dyslexia.

Harnard, S. (ed.) (1987). *Categorical Perception: The Groundwork of Cognition.* New York: Cambridge University Press.

Hart, B. & Risley, T. R. (1995). *Meaningful Differences.* Baltimore: Paul H. Brookes Publishing Co.

Henderson, N. & Engel, R. (1974). Neonatal visual evoked potentials as predictors of psychoeducational testing at age seven. *Developmental Psychology*, 10, 269–76.

Jaramillo, M., Ilvonen, T., Kujala, T., Alku, P., Tervaniemi, M., & Alho, K. (2001). Are different kinds of acoustic features processed differently for speech and non-speech sounds. *Cognitive Brain Research*, 12, 459–66.

Jasper, H. H. (1958). The ten-twenty electrode system of the International Federation of Societies for Electroencephalography: Appendix to report of the committee on methods of clinical examination in electroencephalography. *Journal of Electroencephalography and Clinical Neurophysiology*, 10, 371–5.

Jensen, D. R. & Engel, R. (1971). Statistical procedures for relating dichotomous responses to maturation and EEG measurements. *Electroencephalography and Clinical Neurophysiology*, 30, 437–43.

Kayser, J., Tenke, C., & Bruder, G. (1998). Dissociation of brain ERP topographies for tonal and phonetic oddball tasks. *Psychophysiology*, 35, 576–90.

Kraus, N., McGee, T., Carrell, T., Shama, A., Micoo, A., & Nicol, T. (1993a). Speech-evoked cortical potentials in children. *Journal of the American Academy of Audiology*, 4(4), 238–48.

Kraus, N., McGee, T. J., Micco, A., Sharma, A., Carrell, T. D., & Nicol, T. G. (1993b). Mismatch negativity in school-age children to speech stimuli that are just perceptually different. *Electroencephalography and Clinical Neurophysiology*, 88, 123–30.

Kraus, N., McGee, T. J., Carrell, T. D., Zecker, S. G., Nicol, T. G., & Koch, D. B. (1996). Auditory neurophysiologic responses and discrimination deficits in children with learning problems. *Science*, 273, 971–3.

Kuhl, P. K. (1999). Speech, language, and the brain: Innate preparation for learning. In M. Konishi & M. Hauser (eds.), *Neural Mechanisms of Communication* (pp. 419–50). Cambridge, MA: MIT Press.

Kuhl, P. K. & Miller, J. D. (1975). Speech perception by the chinchilla: Voiced-voiceless distinction in alveolar plosive consonants. *Science*, 190, 69–72.

Kuhl, P. K. & Padden, D. M. (1982). Enhanced discriminability at the phonetic boundaries for the voicing feature in macaques. *Perception & Psychophysics*, 32, 542–50.

Lawson, E. A. & Gailliard, A. W. K. (1981). Mismatch negativity in a phonetic discrimination task. *Biological Psychology*, 13, 281–8.

Lenneberg, E. (1967). *Biological Foundations of Language*. New York: John Wiley & Sons.

Liberman, A., Cooper, F., Shankweiler, D., & Studdert-Kennedy, M. (1967). Perception of the speech code. *Psychological Review*, 74, 431–61.

Lieberman, P. & Blumstein, S. (1988). *Speech Physiology, Speech Perception, and Acoustic Phonetics*. Cambridge: Cambridge University Press.

Lisker, L. & Abramson, A. S. (1970). The voicing dimension: Some experiments in comparative phonetics. In: *Proceedings of the 6th International Congress of Phonetic Sciences* (pp. 563–7). Prague: Academia.

Lyytinen, H., Leppänen, P. H. T., Richardson, U., & Guttorm, T. K. (2003). Brain functions and speech perception in infants at risk for dyslexia. In V. Csépe (ed.), *Dyslexia: Different Brain, Different Behaviour* (pp. 113–52), Neuropsychology and Cognition Series. Dordrecht: Kluwer.

Miceli, G., Caltagirone, C., Gianotti, G., & Payer-Rigo, P. (1978). Discrimination of voice versus place contrasts in aphasia. *Brain and Language*, 6, 47–51.

Molfese, D. L. (1978a). Left and right hemispheric involvement in speech perception: Electrophysiological correlates. *Perception & Psychophysics*, 23, 237–43.

Molfese, D. L. (1978b). Neuroelectrical correlates of categorical speech perception in adults. *Brain and Language*, 5, 25–35.

Molfese, D. L. (1980a). Hemispheric specialization for temporal information: Implications for the processing of voicing cues during speech perception. *Brain and Language*, 11, 285–99.

Molfese, D. L. (1980b). The phoneme and the engram: Electrophysiological evidence for the acoustic invariant in stop consonants. *Brain and Language*, 10, 372–6.

Molfese, D. L. (1989). The use of auditory evoked responses recorded from newborns to predict later language skills. In N. Paul (ed.), *Research in Infant Assessment* (pp. 68–81). White Plains: March of Dimes.

Molfese, D. L. (2000). Predicting dyslexia at 8 years using neonatal brain responses. *Brain and Language*, 72, 238–45.

Molfese, D. L. & Erwin, R. J. (1981). Intrahemispheric differentiation of vowels: Principal component analysis of auditory evoked responses to computer synthesized vowel sounds. *Brain and Language*, 13, 333–44.

Molfese, D. L. & Hess, T. M. (1978). Speech perception in nursery school age children: Sex and hemispheric differences. *Journal of Experimental Child Psychology*, 26, 71–84.

Molfese, D. L. & Molfese, V. J. (1979a). Hemisphere and stimulus differences as reflected in the cortical responses of newborn infants to speech stimuli. *Developmental Psychology*, 15, 505–11.

Molfese, D. L. & Molfese, V. J. (1979b). Infant speech perception: Learned or innate? In H. Whitaker & H. Whitaker (eds.), *Advances in Neurolinguistics: Vol. 4* (pp. 225–40). New York: Academic Press.

Molfese, D. L. & Molfese, V. J. (1980). Cortical responses of preterm infants to phonetic and nonphonetic speech stimuli. *Developmental Psychology*, 16, 574–81.

Molfese, D. L. & Molfese, V. J. (1985). Electrophysiological indices of auditory discrimination in newborn infants: The bases for predicting later language development. *Infant Behavior and Development*, 8, 197–211.

Molfese, D. L. & Molfese, V. J. (1986). Psychophysical indices of early cognitive processes and their relationship to language. In J. E. Obrzut & G. W. Hynd (eds.), *Child Neuropsychology, Vol. 1: Theory and research* (pp. 95–116). New York: Academic Press.

Molfese, D. L. & Molfese, V. J. (1988). Right hemisphere responses from preschool children to temporal cues contained in speech and nonspeech materials: Electrophysiological correlates. *Brain and Language*, 33, 245–59.

Molfese, D. L. & Molfese, V. J. (1997). Discrimination of language skills at five years of age using event related potentials recorded at birth. *Developmental Neuropsychology*, 13, 135–56.

Molfese, D. L. & Schmidt, A. L. (1983). An auditory evoked potential study of consonant perception. *Brain and Language*, 18, 57–70.

Molfese, D. L. & Searock, K. (1986). The use of auditory evoked responses at one year of age to predict language skills at 3 years. *Australian Journal of Communication Disorders*, 14, 35–46.

Molfese, V. J. & Thompson, B. (1985). Optimality versus complications: Assessing predictive values of perinatal scales. *Child Development*, 56, 810–23.

Molfese, D. L., Buhrke, R. A., & Wang, S. L. (1985). The right hemisphere and temporal processing of consonant transition durations: Electrophysiological correlates. *Brain and Language*, 26, 49–62.

Molfese, V. J., DiLalla, L., & Bunce, D. (1997). Prediction of the intelligence test scores of 3- to 8-year old children by home environment, socioeconomic status, and biomedical risks. *Merill-Palmer Quarterly*, 43, 219–34.

Molfese, D. L., Freeman, R., & Palermo, D. (1975). The ontogeny of lateralization for speech and nonspeech stimuli. *Brain and Language*, 2, 356–68.

Molfese, D. L., Laughlin, N. K., Morse, P. A., Linnville, S., Wetzel, F., & Erwin, R. (1986). Neuroelectrical correlates of categorical perception for place of articulation in normal and lead-treated rhesus macaques. *Journal of Clinical and Experimental Neuropsychology*, 8, 680–96.

Molfese, D. L., Linnville, S. E., Wetzel, W. F., & Licht, D. (1985). Electrophysiological correlates of handedness and speech perception contrasts. *Neuropsychologia*, 23, 77–86.

Molfese, D. L., Molfese, V., Modglin, A., Kelly, S., & Terrell, S. (2002). Reading and cognitive abilities: Longitudinal studies of brain and behavior changes in young children. *Annals of Dyslexia*, 52, 99–119.

Molfese, V. J., Molfese, D. L., & Parsons, C. (1983). Hemispheric involvement in phonological perception. In S. Segalowitz (ed.), *Language Functions and Brain Organization* (pp. 29–49). New York: Academic Press.

Morrell, L. K. & Salamy, J. G. (1971). Hemispheric asymmetry of electrocortical responses to speech stimuli. *Science*, 174, 164–6.

Morse, P. A. (1976). Speech perception in the human infant and rhesus monkey. *Annals of the New York Academy of Sciences*, 280, 694–707.

Morse, P. A., Molfese, D. L., Laughlin, N. K., Linnville, S., & Wetzel, F. (1987). Categorical perception for voicing contrast in normal and lead-treated macaques: Electrophysiological indices. *Brain and Language*, 30, 630–80.

Näätanen, R. et al. (1997). Language-specific phoneme representations revealed by electric and magnetic brain responses. *Nature*, 385, 432–4.

Neville, H. (1974). Electrographic correlates of lateral asymmetry in the processing of verbal and nonverbal auditory stimuli. *Journal of Psycholinguistic Research*, 3, 151–63.

Pang, E. W. & Taylor, M. J. (2000). Tracking the development of the N1 from age 3 to adulthood: An examination of speech and non-speech stimuli. *Clinical Neurophysiology*, 11, 388–97.

Pang, E., Edmonds, G., Desjardins, R., Khan, S., Trainor, L., & Taylor, M. (1998). Mismatch negativity to speech stimuli in 8-month-old infants and adults. *International Journal of Psychophysiology*, 29, 227–36.

Perecman, E. & Kellar, L. (1981). The effect of voice and place among aphasic, nonaphasic right-damaged and normal subjects on a metalinguistic task. *Brain and Language*, 12, 213–23.

Pisoni, D. B. (1977). Identification and discrimination of the relative onset time of two component tones: Implications for voicing perception in stops. *Journal of the Acoustical Society of America*, 61, 1352–61.

Rockstroh, B., Elbert, T., Birbaumer, N., & Lutzenberger, W. (1982). *Slow Brain Potentials and Behavior*. Baltimore: Urban-Schwarzenberg.

Segalowitz, S. & Cohen, H. (1989). Right hemisphere EEG sensitivity to speech. *Brain and Language*, 37, 220–31.

Simos, P. G. & Molfese, D. L. (1997). Electrophysiological responses from a temporal order continuum in the newborn infant. *Neuropsychologia*, 35, 89–98.

Stevens, K. N. & Klatt, D. H. (1974). Role of formant transitions in the voiced-voiceless distinction for stops. *Journal of the Acoustical Society of America*, 55, 653–9.

Streeter, L. A. (1976). Language perception of two-month-old infants shows effects of both innate mechanisms and experience. *Nature*, 259, 39–41.

Travis, L. (1931) *Speech Pathology*. New York: Appleton-Century.

Vellutino, F. & Scanlon, D. (1987). Phonological coding: Phonological awareness, and reading ability: Evidence from a longitudinal and experimental study. *Merrill-Palmer Quarterly*, 33, 321–63.

Wagner, R., Torgesen, J., & Rashotte, C. (1994). Development of reading-related phonological processing abilities: New evidence of bidirectional causality from a latent variable longitudinal study. *Developmental Psychology*, 30, 73–87.

Wechsler, D. (1991). *Wechsler Intelligence Scales for Children*. New York: The Psychological Corporation.

Wilkinson, G. S. (1993). *Wide Range Achievement Test*. Wilmington, DE: Wide Range.

Wood, C. A. (1975). Auditory and phonetic levels of processing in speech perception: Neurophysiological information processing analysis. *Journal of Experimental Psychology: Human Perception and Performance*, 104, 3–20.

Wood, C. A., Goff, W., & Day, R. (1971). Auditory evoked potentials during speech perception. *Science*, 173, 1248–51.

Part II Perception of Linguistic Properties

6 Features in Speech Perception and Lexical Access

KENNETH N. STEVENS

6.1 Introduction

In the model of human speech perception to be described in this chapter, our concern is with the process by which human listeners are able to extract word sequences from running speech. It is assumed that there is a lexicon in which some representation of words in the language is stored. There is an initial processing of the speech signal by the peripheral auditory system – processing that is the same whether the signal is speech or nonspeech sounds. This initial peripheral transformation is followed by a type of processing that is specific to speech and language. This speech-specific processing provides sufficient information about the phonetic categories to permit access to the lexicon, resulting in a postulated word sequence. In this chapter, the focus is primarily on the parts of this sequence that are specifically related to the aspect of lexical access that is derived from processing of the acoustic signal, and not on the use of syntax and semantics in this process.

We assume that words are represented in the memory of speakers and listeners in terms of sequences of segments, each of which consists of a bundle of binary distinctive features (Jakobson, 1928). There is a universal set of such features. In any given language there is a subset of these features that are distinctive in the sense that changing the value of one such feature in a segment in a word can potentially create a different word. A pair of words that differ only in one feature in any one of the segments is called a minimal pair. Examples are the pairs *pat/bat*, *bait/bet*, and *pat/pad*, where the feature that generates the minimal pair is in the initial consonant, the vowel, and the final consonant, respectively. The mental representation of a word also consists of a specification of its syllable structure and, in the case of words with more than one syllable, the assignment of stress. The lexicon contains a variety of other information that is not of concern here, such as syntactic and semantic features.

In this chapter, evidence for a universal set of distinctive features is reviewed, and some of the features that are used distinctively in English are listed, together with the defining articulatory and acoustic correlates of these features. The representation of words in terms of segments (or bundles of features) and syllable structure is illustrated. Examples of the spectrographic representations for some words and word sequences in English are given. Some of these examples show variability in the acoustic patterns for words spoken casually. Variability in the acoustic manifestation of some features is shown to arise from the introduction of articulatory gestures to enhance the perceptual contrast for the features and from overlap of gestures from adjacent segments. Finally, a model of the process of identification of words in running speech is proposed. In this model, listeners retrieve the underlying distinctive features based on the extraction of acoustic cues related to the overlapping articulatory gestures that are implemented by the speaker. Contact is then made with the lexicon, which is represented by the same features.

6.2 Evidence for Distinctive Features

We take the view that the universal features in terms of which words are represented in memory have their origin in the physical properties of the human speech production system as a generator of sounds and the properties of the perceptual system as a receiver of these sounds (Stevens, 1972, 1989). The structures that are controlled by speakers, and the states of these structures when they produce speech, appear at first glance to be capable of being varied through a continuous range, although there are endpoints in these movements as the structures come in contact with fixed surfaces or as the displacements reach the ends of their ranges. However, for various reasons to be discussed, the acoustic and perceptual consequences of these movements can exhibit categorical effects. That is, as an articulatory structure is displaced through a range of positions or configurations, the relation between the resulting acoustic properties and the articulatory displacement is either discontinuous or shows a maximum or minimum. Within a particular region of articulatory space, the acoustic properties are relatively insensitive to articulatory changes, whereas when the articulation strays outside of this region there are abrupt changes in the acoustic properties. Corresponding to these acoustic changes there are distinctive changes in the perception of the sound. Thus the articulatory system for generating speech can be regarded as a generator of sounds that lead to categorical acoustic and perceptual properties.

We review next some examples of the features, showing the quantal nature of the articulatory/acoustic/perceptual relations that define them. (See also Stevens, 1972, 1989.)

1 When a sufficiently narrow constriction is produced in the airway by an articulator in the oral cavity, and if the velopharyngeal port is closed, there is a significant increase in pressure in the vocal tract behind this constriction. There are two acoustic consequences of this action: (a) a rather abrupt reduction in amplitude of vocal-fold vibration or a cessation of vibration because of the reduced transglottal pressure, and (b) generation of turbulence noise in the vicinity of the constriction, either continuous noise (if the constriction remains narrow) or a burst of noise (if the oral closure is complete, and is subsequently released). This articulatory action defines the feature [−sonorant] for consonants.
2 In the case of segments that are [−sonorant], continued vocal-fold vibration may be either facilitated or inhibited depending on the stiffness or slackness

of the vocal folds. This articulatory action is the basis for the feature [stiff vocal folds] (Halle & Stevens, 1971; Stevens, 1977; Titze, 1992).

3 Also for [–sonorant] consonants, a clear distinction can be made, acoustically and perceptually, between those consonants produced with a complete closure and abrupt amplitude decrease and increase at the times of closure and release ([–continuant]) and those produced with a continuing narrow constriction and continuous turbulence noise ([+continuant]).

4 Within the class of [+continuant] consonants, the articulator producing the constriction can be shaped to produce an air jet that impinges on an obstacle (such as the lower incisors) somewhat downstream from the constriction, resulting in a noise source that is effective in creating strong excitation of the natural frequencies of the acoustic cavity anterior to the constriction. The resulting sound output has a substantially greater amplitude than the contrasting articulation for which there is no such obstacle with an impinging air jet or the obstacle is close to the constriction (Stevens, 1998). The feature defined by these articulatory actions is [strident].

5 In the case of consonants, the constriction that forms the consonant can be the lips, the tongue blade, or the tongue body, and the position and shape of each of these articulators can be manipulated. A consequence of these various places of articulation is that there are distinctive shapes and lengths of the acoustic cavity anterior to the constriction. These front-cavity shapes result in particular natural frequencies being excited by the acoustic sources due to turbulence in the air stream. Examples are the fricative consonants /s/ and /ʃ/, both of which are produced with the tongue blade. With a more anterior placement (for /s/) the front-cavity resonance is usually in the range of F4 to F6 (i.e., the fourth to the sixth natural frequencies of the vocal tract), whereas for the more posterior placement, the natural frequency of the anterior portion of the vocal tract is F3 (Fant, 1960; Stevens, 1998). These two placements, then, give acoustic and perceptual results that are distinctively different. The feature in this case is [+anterior] for /s/ and [–anterior] for /ʃ/.

6 Vowels are normally produced with a source at the glottis, and with the tongue body shaped to create a single passage from glottis to lips that has no side branches. Different vowels are generated by manipulating the tongue body in the front-back direction or in the high-low direction. The natural frequencies of the vocal tract (particularly F1 and F2) change in consistent ways as the tongue body is displaced. In the case of front-back movement, the frequency of F2 is the principal acoustic correlate, with F2 being high when the tongue body is fronted and low when the tongue body is backed. For front vowels F2 is normally constrained to be above the second natural frequency of the subglottal system, thus avoiding generating a vowel for which the F2 prominence is perturbed by acoustic coupling to the subglottal resonance. For similar reasons, F2 is normally constrained to be below the frequency of this subglottal resonance for back vowels (Stevens, 1998). In the case of front vowels, which have the higher value of F2, and are therefore closer to F3, listener responses to this F2–F3 combination are qualitatively different from the responses when F2 is lower (Carlson, Granstrom, & Fant, 1970; Chistovich & Lublinskaya, 1979; Syrdal & Gopal, 1986). Thus there is both acoustic and perceptual motivation for the feature [back] for vowels.

These examples illustrate some of the articulatory/acoustic/perceptual relations that underlie the various distinctive features that form a universal set. Many other examples could be given. Acoustic and perceptual properties of the type listed here form the basis for a set of categories or features in terms of which the sounds of language are organized. In the examples given above, each distinctive feature is grounded in a particular acoustical/perceptual consequence. Similar "defining" attributes are assumed to exist for all of the universal set of distinctive features. When some features are implemented in running speech, however, additional articulatory and acoustic attributes may be introduced in certain contexts through action of articulators other than the defining ones. These actions appear to be introduced in order to enhance the perceptual contrast carried by the basic or defining gestures. This concept of enhancing gestures is discussed further in Sections 6.5 and 6.6. In Section 6.6 it is also noted that the defining gestures and their acoustic correlates for the features of a segment may be weakened or even obliterated due to overlap of gestures from adjacent segments or to prosodic influences.

Indirect evidence for the role of distinctive features in speech perception comes from experiments that examine consonant confusions made by listeners when they identify the consonants in consonant-vowel syllables in noise and with band-pass filtering (Miller & Nicely, 1955). The results of these experiments show that the patterns of confusions are organized along featural lines. In the presence of noise and certain types of band-pass filtering, some features are poorly identified while others are robust. Miller and Nicely suggest that the perception of any one feature is somewhat independent of the perception of the other features, as though separate channels are involved in the perception of the different features.

The distinctive features also play a fundamental role in the phonological rules that are part of the knowledge possessed by speakers of a language. The discovery that speech sounds are complexes of features can be credited to the Russian linguists R. Jakobson and N. Trubetzkoy (see Jakobson, 1928). The first attempt to provide a connection between these features and acoustic theories of speech production was made in 1952 by Jakobson, Fant, and Halle. Chomsky and Halle (1968) proposed a revision of the inventory of distinctive features some years later. Chomsky and Halle also compiled a number of rules involving distinctive features – rules that capture phonological patterns observed in English.

6.3 Inventories of Features

The distinctive features appear to be of two kinds: articulator-free features and articulator-bound features (Halle, 1992). Features in either set have their origin in particular articulatory actions that give rise to basic acoustic and perceptual attributes. In the case of articulator-free features, the articulatory actions are classified in terms of the type of constriction or narrowing that is produced in the vocal tract, without specifying which articulator is creating the constriction. Examples are the features [sonorant], [continuant], and [strident] for consonants, discussed above. Articulator-bound features, on the other hand, specify which articulator forms the constriction, how that articulator is shaped or positioned, and the actions of other articulators which do not themselves create the constriction but which

Table 6.1 Articulator-free features for some consonants in English

	t, d	*s, z*	*θ, ð*	*n*
continuant	–	+	+	–
sonorant	–	–	–	+
strident		+	–	

influence the acoustic pattern that emerges when the constriction is formed. The features [anterior] and [back] discussed above are examples of articulator-bound features.

Thus for the initial consonant in the word *mat*, the fact that no pressure is built up in the oral cavity is expressed by an articulator-free feature ([+sonorant] in this case). The fact that this closure is made by the lips is captured by the feature [+lips]. Over the time interval within this closure, and also extending beyond this lip closure, a velopharyngeal opening is created, providing evidence for the feature [+nasal] which is included in the bundle of features for /m/. The velopharyngeal opening gesture, however, is not a direct cause of the action that a complete closure was made in the oral cavity, although it influences the acoustic properties in the vicinity of the labial closure and release. As another example, an articulator-free feature for the initial consonant in the word *zoo* is [+continuant], and the articulator that forms the narrowing in the oral cavity is identified by the feature [+tongue blade]. The state of the vocal folds, described here by [–stiff vocal folds] is not involved in forming the type of constriction that is mandated by [+continuant], but it has an influence on certain acoustic properties near the fricative closure and release.

The basic articulator-free features can be described simply as [vowel], [consonant], and [glide], with further subdivision of [+consonant] segments into the features [continuant], [sonorant], and [strident], which classify consonants as stops, strident fricatives, nonstrident fricatives, and sonorant consonants. Examples of this classification are shown in Table 6.1. The feature [strident] is only distinctive for [+continuant] segments, and [sonorant] is distinctive only for [–continuant] segments. It is suggested that the defining acoustic correlate for vowels is a maximum in the low-frequency spectrum amplitude; for glides there is a minimum in low-frequency amplitude without a spectrum discontinuity; and for consonants there is an abrupt spectrum discontinuity at the time the constriction for the consonant is formed and again at the time it is released. This discontinuity takes different forms depending on the features [continuant], [sonorant], and [strident]. Thus the presence of a vowel, a glide, or a consonant is specified in the signal by acoustic landmarks. The occurrence of a maximum or minimum in low-frequency amplitude is a landmark that signals the presence of a vowel or a glide, and an acoustic measure of abruptness in amplitude change in different frequency bands is a landmark indicating the presence of a consonant closure or release.

For an articulator-bound feature, the defining articulatory correlate identifies which articulator produces the action, together with the state or positioning of that

Table 6.2 Listing of articulator-free features, articulators, and articulator-bound features for some consonants in English

	b	*d*	*g*	*p*	*f*	*s*	*z*	*ʃ*	*m*	*l*
continuant	−	−	−	−	+	+	+	+	−	−
sonorant	−	−	−	−					+	+
strident						+	+	+		
lips	+			+	+				+	
tongue blade		+				+	+	+		+
tongue body			+							
round	−			−	−				−	
anterior		+				+	+	−		+
lateral									−	+
high			+							
low			−							
back			+							
nasal									+	−
stiff vocal folds	−	−	−	+	+	+	−	+		

articulator. The acoustic pattern that results from this action is manifested in the speech signal in the general vicinity of the acoustic landmark that is generated from the articulator-free features for the segment.

In the case of the consonants, there are two kinds of articulator-bound features, as noted above: features specifying the active or primary articulator that forms the constriction and the acoustic discontinuity, and features specifying actions of other articulators that influence or modulate the acoustic properties in the vicinity of the landmarks. A listing of the articulator-free and articulator-bound features for some consonants in English is given in Table 6.2. The first three features in the table are the articulator-free features. The next three features identify the articulator that produces the constriction for the consonant. The features [anterior] and [lateral] apply only to tongue-blade consonants, and specify how the tongue blade is to be positioned and shaped. The tongue-body features [high], [low], and [back] apply only to velar consonants, for which the articulator forming the constriction is the tongue body. (Velar consonants are always [+high] and [+back] in English.) The feature [nasal] applies to sonorant consonants. And the feature [stiff vocal folds] (for [−sonorant] consonants) indicates whether or not a consonant is voiced. These last two features specify the actions of articulators that are not the primary articulators for consonants.

Features for some vowels and glides in English are listed in Table 6.3. The features specifying tongue-body position are [high], [low], and [back]. Each of these features has a defining acoustic correlate that describes the formant pattern in the vicinity of the vowel landmark in terms of the relations of the formant frequencies to each other and to a pattern that is speaker-dependent. Additional features that modulate these basic tongue-body features are [round], which specifies lip

Table 6.3 Listing of the features for some vowels and glides in English

	i	*ɛ*	*æ*	*a*	*ʌ*	*u*	*w*	*j*	*h*	*aj*
high	+	−	−	−	−	+	+	+		−+
low	−	−	+	+	−	−	−	−		+−
back	−	−	−	+	+	+	+	−		+−
round				−	−	+	+			
tense	+	−			−	+	+	+		+
spread glottis							−	−	+	

rounding, and [tense], which specifies the articulatory state in the pharyngeal region. Articulator-bound features for glides include tongue-body features (in the case of /w/ and /j/), and [spread glottis] for /h/.

6.4 Lexical Representation

It is proposed that a speaker/listener for a language is equipped with a lexicon of words, each of which is represented in memory as a sequence of bundles of distinctive features. Examples of this representation for the words *sudden* and *help* are shown in Table 6.4. At the top of the table a representation of the syllable structure for each word is displayed (cf. Clements & Keyser, 1983). Each syllable is represented by a tree with σ (for syllable) at the top node, the syllable onset (o) on the left branch and the rime (r) at the right branch. The rime can be further divided into syllable nucleus and coda. When a speaker plans an utterance, it is assumed that at some stage in the planning process there is a representation of the utterance in terms of sequences of lexical items of the type illustrated in Table 6.4, together with the syllable structure and other prosodic markers of prominence and of phrase boundaries.

Two features identified as [stressed] and [reducible] are included in the representation of syllabic nuclei. These features indicate whether a syllable is lexically stressed and also mark syllables that can potentially be reduced. A full set of features is specified for vowels marked as [reducible]. When a vowel is reduced, however, these features are not contrastive. It can happen that a normally reduced vowel can be spoken with emphasis, in which case the features for the vowel need to be specified. Also, a normally reduced vowel can become stressed when certain affixes are applied to the word and the underlying vowel features come to the surface. An example is the second vowel in the words *photograph* (reduced) and *photography* (stressed).

The matrix of features for a given word has many blanks or unspecified values. There are a number of cases where, in a given language, a particular feature is redundant, in the sense that its value as + or − is predictable from the other features. For example, a [+continuant] consonant in English is redundantly [−sonorant]. Or, a vowel that is [−back] does not have to be specified for the feature [round]. If the articulator-free features are known, the number of articulator-bound features

Table 6.4 Lexical representations for the words *sudden* and *help* (The syllable structure of each word is schematized at the top: σ = syllable, o = onset, r = rime)

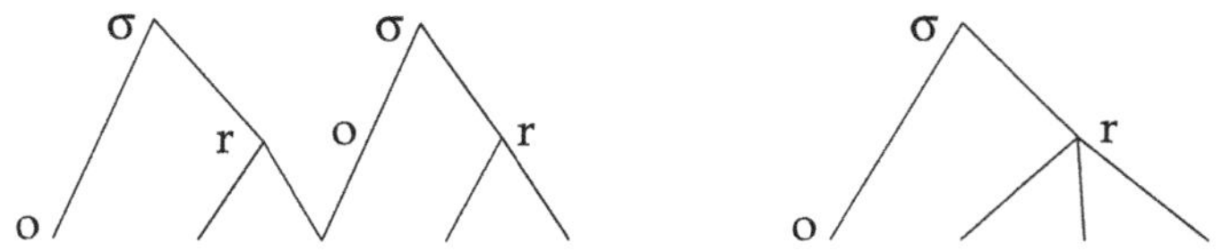

	s	*ʌ*	*d*	*ə*	*n*		*h*	*ɛ*	*l*	*p*
vowel		+		+				+		
glide							+			
consonant	+		+		+				+	+
stressed		+		−				+		
reducible		−		+				−		
continuant	+		−		−				−	−
sonorant			−		+				+	−
strident	+									
lips										+
tongue blade	+		+		+				+	
tongue body										
round										−
anterior	+		+		+				+	
lateral									+	
high		−		−				−		
low		−		−				−		
back		+		+				−		
tense		−						−		
spread glottis							+			
nasal					+					
stiff vocal folds	+		−							+

that are required in order to identify a segment within a word is, on average, about three.

6.5 Some Simple Examples of Acoustic/Articulatory/Featural Relations

Examples of how some features are represented in the sound are displayed as spectrograms in Figure 6.1. In the utterance *a mat* in Figure 6.1(a), the two vowels are produced with a mouth opening greater than that used to produce the adjacent

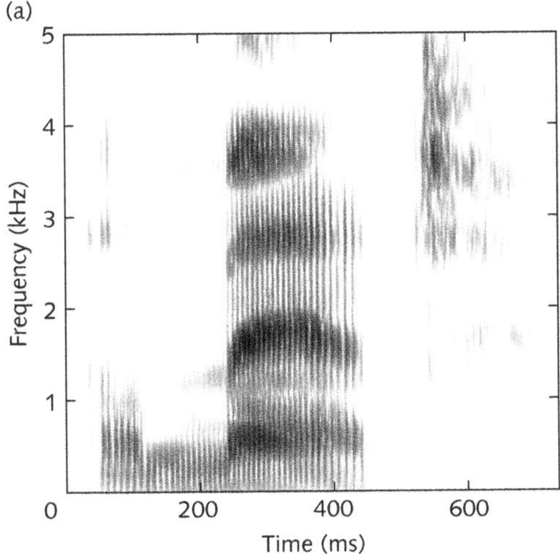

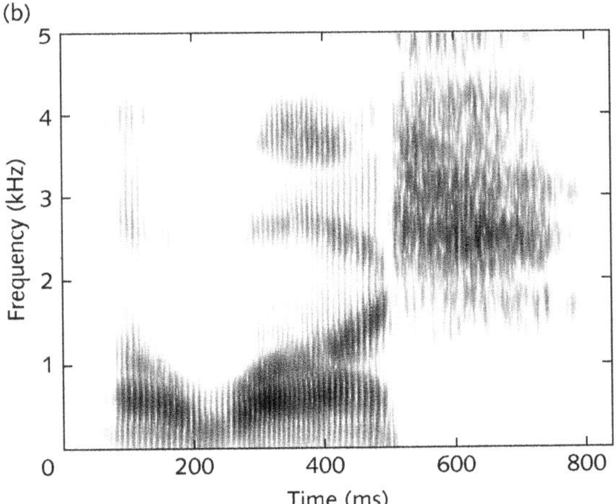

Figure 6.1 Spectrograms of (a) *a mat* and (b) *a wash* produced by a female speaker. These spectrograms illustrate some basic landmarks for vowels, stop, nasal, and fricative consonants, and a glide, together with some articulator-bound features.

consonants, and the acoustic cue for the feature [+vowel] is a peak in amplitude in the first-formant range. The closure and release for the consonant /m/ appear as acoustic discontinuities at about 100 and 220 ms. At these discontinuities, there is continuation of glottal vibration with no change in amplitude, indicating the articulator-free feature [+sonorant]. The articulator-bound feature [+nasal] is cued by the spectrum shape of the nasal murmur on the "murmur" sides of the discontinuities and by some nasalization of the vowels immediately before the closure consonant landmark and immediately following the release landmark. (The nasalization of the vowels is not well represented in the spectrogram.) The articulator-bound feature [+lips] is signaled by the formant transitions (particularly those for F2 and F3) in the vowels immediately preceding and following the two consonant landmarks and by the nature of the discontinuities in the spectrum, particularly in the F2 frequency range.

The first two formant frequencies in the vicinity of the maximum in low-frequency amplitude for the vowel in *mat* (i.e., the vowel landmark), at about 300 ms, show that F2 and F3 are at about 1800 Hz and 2700 Hz. The difference between F3 and F2 is within the 3 to 3.5 bark spacing proposed by Chistovich and Lublinskaya (1979) as a threshold for perceptual assessment of two-formant stimuli, indicating a vowel that is [–back]. The first formant at about 650 Hz is more than 3 bark above the fundamental frequency of about 160 Hz – a cue for a vowel that is [+low] (Traunmüller, 1981).

The spectrogram of *a wash* in Figure 6.1(b) shows the minimum amplitude indicative of a glide landmark at about 230 ms, with a low F2 signaling the feature [+back]. The high F1 and low F2 near the vowel landmark, at about 380 ms, are cues for the features [+low, +back]. A consonant landmark can also be seen at about 500 ms, and the discontinuity shows continuous strong frication noise at high frequencies, evidence for the feature [+strident]. In English, only strident fricatives are [+tongue blade], and the predominance of frication noise in the F3 region, at about 2500 Hz, is a cue for [–anterior].

6.6 Sources of Variability in Acoustic Correlates of Features

In the simple examples of consonants and vowels in monosyllabic words just described, the process of estimating the various articulator-free and articulator-bound features for the vowel and for the syllable-initial consonant is relatively straightforward. The acoustic landmarks are well-defined and the acoustic cues for the various features can be easily extracted based on knowledge of the defining articulatory and acoustic/perceptual correlates of the features. Several additional factors must be taken into account when a wider variety of words is used and when the words occur in running speech. These factors can introduce modifications in the way the features are represented in the acoustic signal. That is, even though the existence of a feature is based on a particular defining articulatory action with a corresponding primary acoustic correlate, in certain contexts it is possible that this defining acoustic property may be weakened or obliterated. The factors that cause these changes include the influence of prosody, the introduction of enhancing gestures, and the effects of gestural overlap.

First, the segments and the words can occur in various prosodic environments, and the set of acoustic cues that are needed to identify the various features for a segment depend on the prosodic context in which the segment occurs. Among the prosodic characteristics are the effects of beginnings and endings of phrases, position of a segment within a syllable, syllable stress within a word, and prominence of a syllable within a phrase. For example, at the end of a phrase there may be a pause, and the glottis may become more spread, leading to a reduced high-frequency amplitude for a vowel and to the lack of an acoustic landmark corresponding to the release of a final consonant. Or, a syllable-final nasal consonant may show a more extensive region of nasalization in the preceding vowel than the nasalization interval in a vowel that follows a syllable-initial nasal consonant. Other evidence for syllable position comes from phonotactic constraints. For example, glides are always syllable-initial, and a consonant that follows a [−tense] vowel is always in the coda of the syllable. Placing reduced prominence on some syllables can cause significant changes in the acoustic representation of the features for the segments in and adjacent to the syllables. These modifications are generally a consequence of overlap of articulatory gestures within the reduced syllable with gestures from adjacent syllables. Some examples of the influence of such overlap in reduced syllables are given below in the discussion of gestural overlap.

Secondly, in certain segmental and prosodic environments speakers of a language introduce articulatory gestures in addition to the defining gestures for a feature. These additional gestures are added to enhance the perceptual saliency of the feature in environments where the perceptual contrast for the feature may be at risk. The enhancing gestures may not only strengthen the primary acoustic correlate for the feature, but also introduce new acoustic cues that contribute to identification of the feature. Some examples of enhancement are described in Bilcher, Diehl, and Cohen (1990), Keyser and Stevens (2001), Kingston and Diehl (1995), and Kluender, Diehl, and Wright (1988). Two such examples in English (from Keyser & Stevens) are: (1) the acoustic manifestation of the feature [+stiff vocal folds] in a stop consonant in pretonic position is enhanced by spreading the glottis, leading to an interval of aspiration immediately following the consonant release; and (2) an alveolar [−sonorant] consonant is produced with a tongue-body position that is somewhat fronted, to provide transitions of the second formant that are perceptually distinct from those of labial and velar consonants. The fronting of the tongue body to produce an alveolar stop consonant is shown in the spectrogram of the word *dote*, in Figure 6.2(a). Evidence for the fronting is the relatively high frequency of the second formant F2, and, to some extent, F3. This action enhances the distinction with the minimally contrasting words *boat* and *goat*, in Figures 6.2(b) and 6.2(c). The formant movements (particularly of F2) are quite different for the labial and velar consonants.

A third source of variability is caused by overlap in the articulatory gestures associated with adjacent segments, and this overlap can lead to weakening and sometimes extinguishing of cues for some features (Browman & Goldstein, 1992). One example of gestural overlap occurs in a sequence of two stop consonants, as in the sequence /pt/ in the words *top tag*. The closure for /t/ often precedes the labial release for /p/, and consequently there is no acoustic landmark for the /p/ release or for the /t/ closure. The articulator-bound features for these two consonants must be deduced based on acoustic cues in the vicinity of the closure landmark for /p/ and the release landmark for /t/. Spectrograms of two spoken versions of *top tag* are shown in Figure 6.3. In one version (Figure 6.3a) there is no acoustic evidence for the /p/ release or the /t/ closure, whereas for the other (Figure 6.3b), the noise burst appears to reflect both the /p/ release (a brief transient) and the frication caused by the tongue-blade closure. Both versions are identified by listeners as the same consonant sequence.

Another example of gestural overlap occurs in the final syllable of the word *sudden*. The final three segments of this word are represented in the lexicon by feature bundles for /dən/, where the vowel is reduced. In casual speech, the

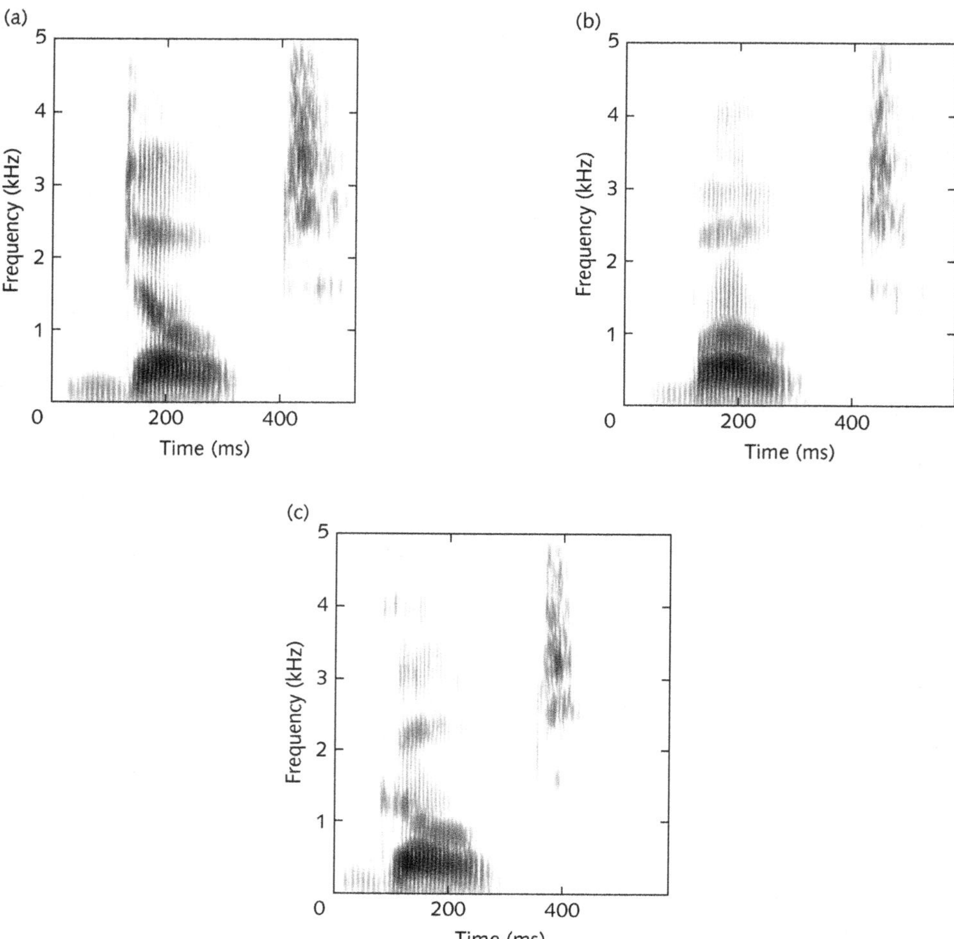

Figure 6.2 Spectrograms of the words (a) *dote,* (b) *boat,* and (c) *goat* produced by a male speaker. The relatively high frequency of F2 near the /d/ release in (a) is evidence for a fronted tongue-body position for this alveolar consonant. This F2 transition enhances the distinction between the alveolar /d/ and the labial and velar in (b) and (c).

nasalization and the tongue-blade gesture for /n/ may extend back through the vowel, leaving, in effect, a syllabic nasal. Since the place of articulation for /d/ is the same as for /n/, the gesture at the end of /d/ is simply an opening of the velopharyngeal port, thereby causing an abrupt decrease in the intraoral pressure, and the tongue-blade closure continues through the stop consonant and the nasal murmur. Two versions of the word *sudden* are shown in Figure 6.4. The version in Figure 6.4(a) shows no evidence of an acoustic landmark for the /n/ closure, since the tongue blade remains in a closed alveolar position from the /d/ closure through the rest of the word. The abrupt amplitude increase at about 400 ms is due to the velopharyngeal opening gesture. The other version (Figure 6.4b) is

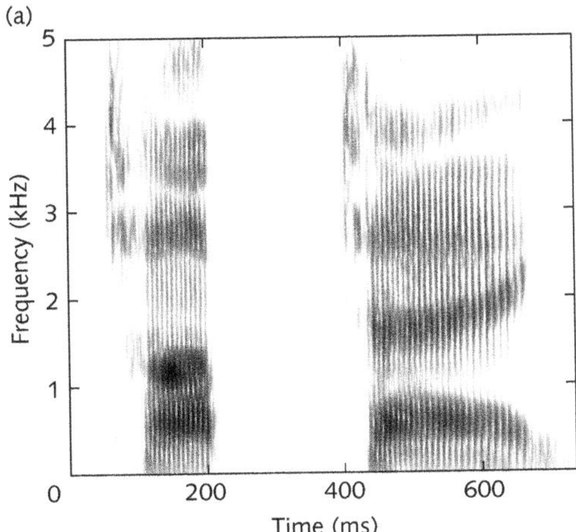

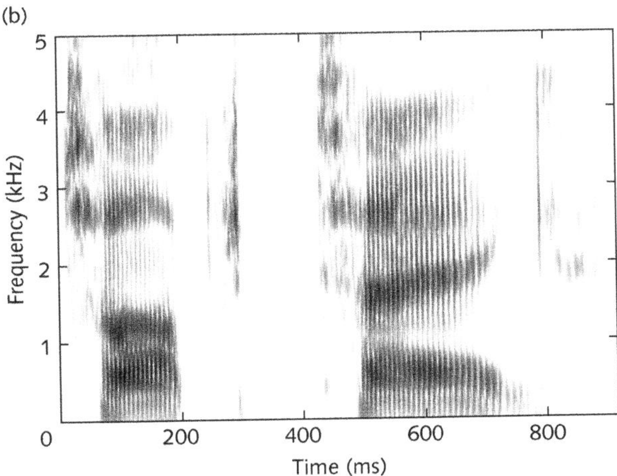

Figure 6.3 Spectrograms of two versions of *top tag* produced by a male speaker: (a) casually spoken version, in which the /p/ release and /t/ closure are not evident acoustically; (b) carefully spoken version in which these events can be seen in the spectrogram between about 240 and 300 ms.

produced with a release of /d/ into the schwa vowel /ə/, followed by the closing gesture for /n/. Again these two somewhat different acoustic patterns are identified as the same word by speakers of English; both versions of this word are represented in the lexicon by the same pattern of features, as shown in Table 6.4.

Gestural overlap can also occur in vowel sequences, particularly when a reduced syllable follows a syllable that is more prominent. Thus, for example, in a sequence like *saw a dog*, it can happen that the tongue-body gestures for the two-vowel sequence overlap so that there is not a separate amplitude prominence for each vowel. The tongue-body height has a continuous movement with only one peak

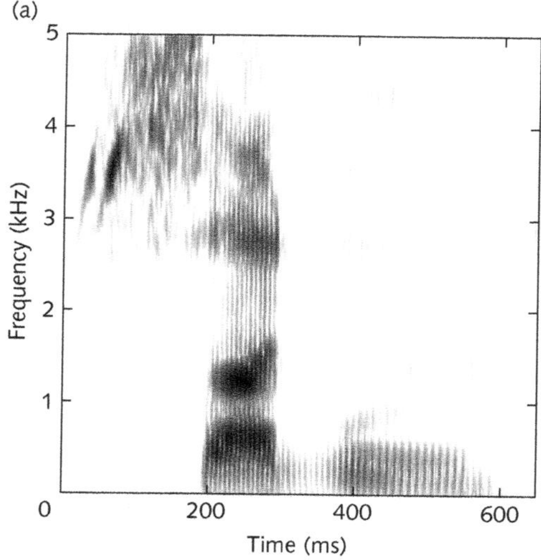

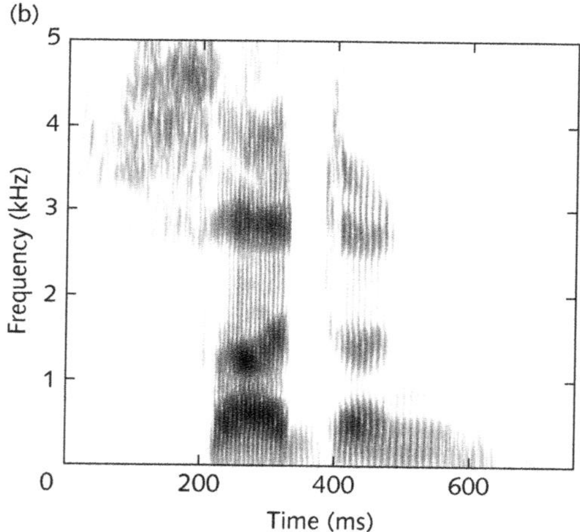

Figure 6.4 Spectrograms of the word *sudden* produced in a casual manner in (a) and a clearer manner in (b), produced by a male speaker. In (a) the /ən/ sequence is produced as syllabic nasal, whereas in (b) there is clear evidence for a vowel and a landmark at the time of /n/ closure, at about 480 ms.

or maximum in mouth opening, leading to just one peak in the first-formant frequency and hence only a single vowel landmark. An utterance of this sequence of words produced in this way is shown in Figure 6.5(a). There is no evidence of a separate peak or landmark in the low-frequency amplitude or in F1 for the reduced vowel. However, the movement of the formants (particularly F2) preceding the closure for /d/ provides a cue for a gesture toward a reduced vowel. A different version of the same sequence, spoken more clearly by the same speaker, is shown in the spectrogram of Figure 6.5(b). In this case the word boundary is

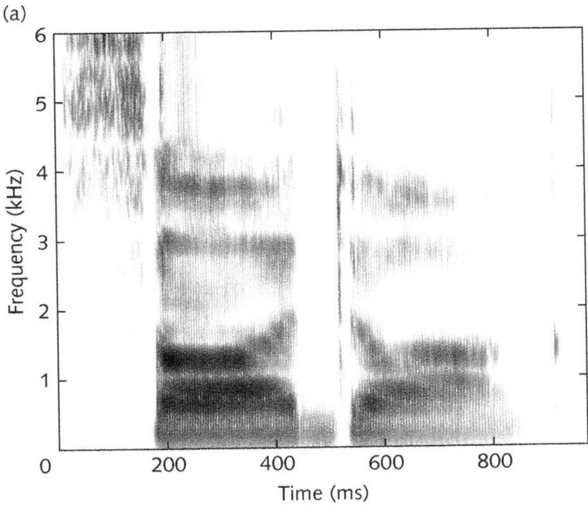

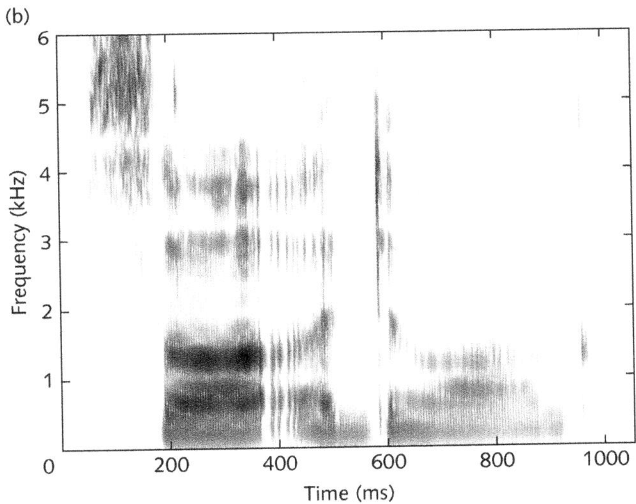

Figure 6.5 (a) Spectrogram of the utterance *saw a dog* produced in a casual manner. There is no separate amplitude peak for the weak vowel /ə/. (b) Spectrogram of the same utterance produced in a more careful way. The vowel /ə/ is separated from /ɑ/ with glottalization, indicating a word boundary. In both utterances, indirect evidence for /ə/ appears in the time course of the F2 transition immediately preceding the /d/ closure. Female speaker.

marked by glottalization, together with a reduction in low-frequency amplitude between the two vowels. Once again, however, both versions are interpreted by speakers as the same sequence of words.

As a further example of overlap, consider the consonant sequence in *batman*. A version of this word spoken in a casual way is contrasted with a more carefully

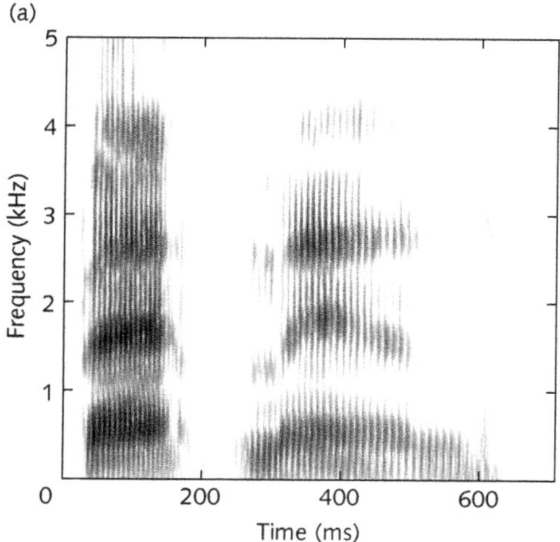

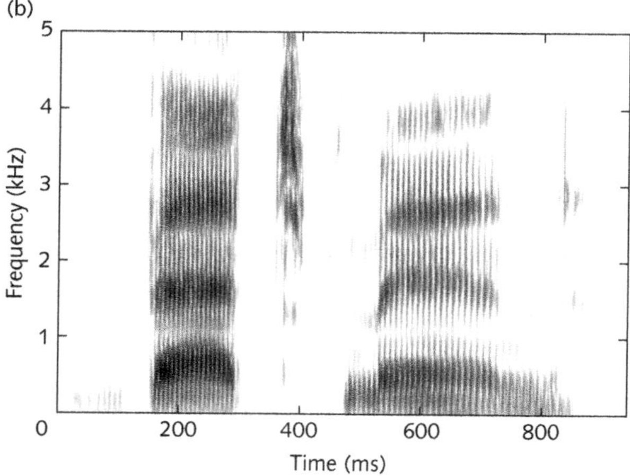

Figure 6.6 Spectrogram of two utterances of the word *batman* produced by a male speaker. The utterance (a) was produced more casually than (b). The more carefully produced utterance (b) shows a noise burst for /t/ whereas for the more casually produced version the first vowel is terminated with glottalization and an apparent labial closure, as evidenced by a falling F2.

spoken version of the same word in Figure 6.6. In the more casual version in Figure 6.6(a) there is no evidence of a /t/ release. And, in fact, at the end of the vowel there is even evidence that the labial closure for /m/ is anticipated in a brief interval of apparent glottalization just as the vowel is terminating. Some glottalization is apparent at the end of the vowel; this is an enhancement for the feature [+stiff vocal folds]. The movements of F2 and F3 up to a time just preceding the onset of glottalization are those which might be expected from a fronting tongue-body gesture, i.e., the gesture that is used to enhance the distinction between the alveolar consonant and other places of stop-consonant articulation.

In the clear version of *batman* in Figure 6.6(b), the /t/ release is apparent, as are the F2 and F3 transitions for the tongue-body fronting gesture. In spite of the differences in the two acoustic patterns, both are clearly identified by listeners as the same word. As in the examples just described, the distinctive features in terms of which the lexical item for *batman* is specified are the same for both versions of the word. The different instantiations of the word arise because the gestures used to implement the features may overlap more in one version than in the other, and the glottal gesture used to enhance the voicelessness of /t/ is implemented in one version but not in the other.

A similar influence of overlap occurs in the casually spoken word *help*, for which the lexical representation in terms of features is given in Table 6.4. Frequently, speakers produce the /l/ without touching the tongue blade against the hard palate. However, acoustic evidence for the lateral feature comes from the tongue-backing gesture for /l/, which is manifested in the offglide from the preceding vowel. This tongue-backing movement is regarded as an enhancing gesture for the feature [lateral], particularly in syllable-final position. Thus we again have a situation where a primary defining gesture, in this case the raised tongue-blade gesture to make contact with the palate, is obliterated, but an enhancing gesture (in this case the tongue-backing) remains to implement the feature. A clearly articulated version of the word *help* would show evidence of tongue-blade contact as an abrupt acoustic discontinuity at the end of the vowel.

All of these influences are sources of variability in the acoustic manifestation of the features. Although there is a defining articulatory gesture for each feature, together with a primary acoustic correlate for the feature, a language can introduce enhancing gestures when the feature is in a particular environment. These enhancing gestures can strengthen the primary acoustic cues and can also introduce new cues for the feature. Furthermore, gestural overlap can lead to the obliteration or modification of the acoustic landmarks that are the primary acoustic correlates of the articulator-free features. In such cases, a landmark or a set of landmarks may identify a region of the signal in which acoustic evidence for adjacent segments may reside simultaneously. In some cases the primary cues for articulator-bound features may be obliterated through gestural overlap, and the cues that emerge from the enhancing process may be the only cues that remain (Keyser & Stevens, under review). Any model of speech perception for running speech must account for the modifications that may be introduced by prosodic factors, by the introduction of enhancing gestures, and by gestural overlap. For each of the pairs of utterances illustrated in Figures 6.3 to 6.6, the lexical representation in terms of features is the same. A listener must be able to extract these underlying features through processing of the signal in spite of the significant acoustic differences between the different versions.

For all of the examples of overlap described above, the surface acoustic representation of an utterance with and without significant overlap is quite different, at least as viewed on the spectrograms. Yet, in spite of this surface variability, listeners give an invariant response when asked to identify the words. It is noted, however, that for each of the comparison pairs some of the articulatory gestures that create the two patterns are essentially the same, except for changes in the timing of the gestures. It is as though the listeners are sensitive to aspects of the acoustic pattern that provide information about these gestures, and ignore certain timing changes, even though these timing changes produce significant modifications in the surface spectral patterns. When a listener is in a mode of interpreting a speech pattern, he/she is selective in attending to particular aspects of this pattern. The acoustic cues that are used to identify the underlying distinctive features are cues that provide evidence for the gestures that produced the acoustic pattern. This view that a listener focuses on acoustic cues that provide evidence for articulatory gestures suggests a close link between the perceptually relevant aspects of the acoustic pattern for a distinctive feature in speech and the articulatory gestures that give rise to this pattern. The potential role of articulatory gestures as a route to uncovering the segmental units of speech has elements of the direct-realist theory and the motor theory of speech perception advanced by Fowler (1986) and by Liberman and Mattingly (1985), respectively.

6.7 Acoustic Landmarks and their Relation to Segments

As has been noted above, there are three basic types of landmarks: (1) landmarks normally produced when the mouth is maximally open during a vowel, generally leading to a maximum in the frequency of the first formant and a maximum in the amplitude of the F1 spectrum prominence; (2) landmarks caused by a narrowing in the vocal tract, with a minimum in low-frequency amplitude and a smooth change in low-frequency amplitude and in the first formant frequency into (and/or out of) an adjacent vowel; and (3) abrupt changes in amplitude and spectrum caused by the formation or closure of a consonantal constriction produced by an oral articulator. In general, the occurrence of the first type of landmark is a signal that a vowel segment is produced, and the occurrence of the second type of landmark is evidence that a glide segment is produced. A consonant is always produced with both a closing and a releasing gesture, and, unless there are overlap effects, each of these two gestures is manifested in the signal as an abrupt discontinuity. Due to overlap, it often occurs that only one landmark indicating the presence of a consonant segment can be observed in the signal, as observed in Figure 6.3.

Abrupt amplitude changes other than those produced by a constricting or releasing gesture of an oral articulator can, however, occur. One possible source of such a discontinuity is the opening or closing of the velopharyngeal port without involvement of release or closure of an oral articulator, as in the words *number* or *sudden* (cf. Figure 6.4a). A discontinuity can also result from an opening of the glottis, as at the voicing onset in an aspirated stop consonant (e.g., *pat*) or from glottalization, as in some versions of the /t/ in *batman* (cf. Figure 6.6a). A rapid amplitude onset or decay can also occur in utterance-initial or utterance-final position, usually due to control of respiration.

In running speech, there are often sequences in which there is no landmark that provides direct evidence for an underlying segment. Two examples have been given above: the word *sudden* with a vowel-like landmark but no abrupt landmark resulting from an underlying /ən/ sequence, and the sequence *saw a dog*, with no separate landmark for the reduced vowel. Another example could occur in the casually spoken utterance *I'm done with it*, where the glide landmark for

/w/ is observed but there is no tongue-blade closure for /n/, and hence no abrupt landmark. In these and other similar cases, evidence for the additional segment must be derived from analysis of acoustic parameters in the regions between the existing landmarks. Thus in *sudden* the nasal murmur for the syllabic /n/ shows the presence of an underlying nasal consonant; in *saw a dog*, the formant trajectories between the /ɑ/ vowel landmark and the /d/ closure provide evidence for an underlying /ə/; and in *done with*, nasalization in the first vowel and in the glide is a cue for an underlying sequence /nw/.

In these examples where there is an apparent abrupt acoustic landmark that is not produced by action of an oral articulator, or where an underlying segment fails to surface as an acoustic landmark, additional acoustic information beyond that arising from amplitude changes is required to uncover the presence of the segments and their articulator-free features. This acoustic information comes from analysis of changes in the spectrum, particularly from the frequencies of spectrum prominences in the sound.

Abrupt acoustic discontinuities that are not associated directly with the release or closure of a consonant can also provide cues for articulator-bound features or for syllable or word boundaries. For example, time of onset of voicing for a pretonic voiceless stop consonant provides evidence for the feature [+stiff vocal folds], the acoustic mark for velopharyngeal closure in *number* indicates a nasal-stop sequence with the same place of articulation, and, in Figure 6.5(b), the incidence of glottalization can mark a word boundary in the sequence *saw a*.

6.8 Toward a Feature-Based Model of Speech Perception

The above review of the speech production process provides a background for specifying the requirements of a model that proposes how listeners extract information from the speech signal and use this information to access the words in running speech. Based on acoustic evidence in the signal, the listener must be able to identify the sequence of words that underlie this acoustic pattern in spite of the potentially significant variability in the acoustic patterns for the words, as described above. The task of the listener can be described by a series of steps as schematized in Figure 6.7. The output of this model is a sequence of words that are represented in memory in the manner shown in Table 6.4, together with other prosodic markers.

The proposed model assumes that two kinds of operations are potentially involved in uncovering the sequence of words intended by the speaker. One is a direct analysis path in which the acoustic signal is interpreted in terms of feature bundles. This segment/feature pattern is then used to access words in the lexicon, which is also stored in terms of sequences of feature bundles. Other kinds of information, including syntactic and semantic knowledge and visual cues from the speaker's face, can contribute to this decision. The second set of operations is a synthesis and comparison path in which hypothesized word sequences are the inputs to an internal synthesis of landmarks and parameters that could be generated by these sequences. This synthesized pattern is compared with landmarks and parameters derived from the signal, and the selected word sequence is the

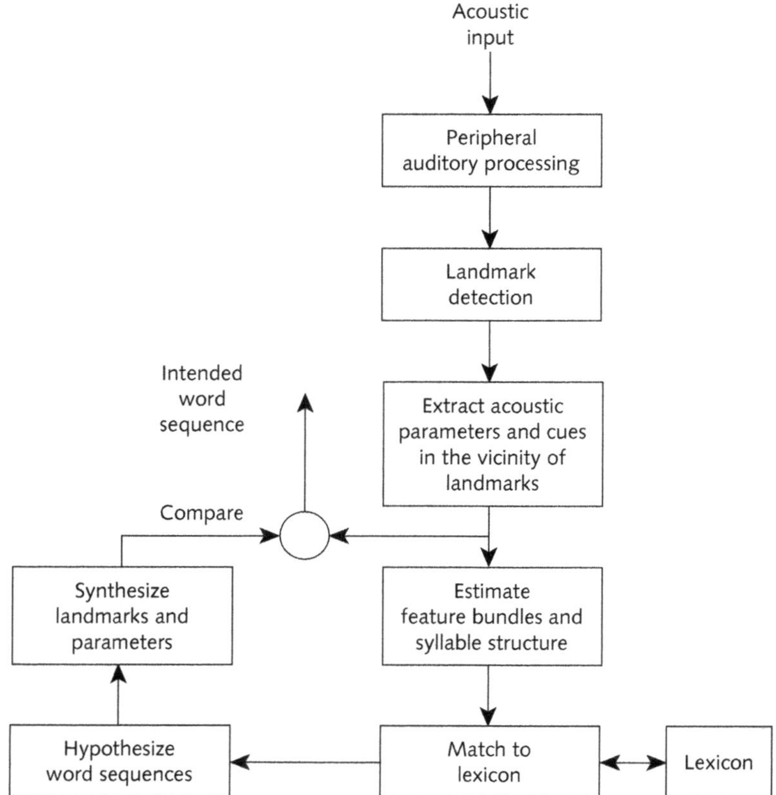

Figure 6.7 Block diagram of a model of human lexical access. The input at the top is the acoustic speech signal for an utterance produced by a speaker. The output is the sequence of words intended by the speaker. The model consists of a direct analysis path in which arrays of feature bundles are estimated and are matched to the lexicon to obtain hypothesized word sequences, and a synthesis path that determines whether a hypothesized word sequence could produce an acoustic pattern that matches the pattern derived from the acoustic signal.

one yielding the best match (Stevens & Halle, 1967). In this chapter, we focus primarily on the direct or "bottom-up" processing of the signal. The "analysis-by-synthesis" aspect is discussed briefly in Section 6.8.6. The types of processing that are involved in the bottom-up and top-down paths are quite different. In the bottom-up path, the acoustic analysis leads to hypotheses concerning the bundles of distinctive features underlying an utterance, and require a matching of estimated feature bundles with stored feature bundles in the lexicon. The top-down path begins with hypothesized words specified by feature bundles and generates articulatory patterns and resulting acoustic parameters that are compared with parameters derived from the signal.

There are at least two reasons why both a "bottom-up" and a "top-down" path are hypothesized in this model of human lexical access (but see also Norris,

McQueen, & Cutler, 2000). The bottom-up path estimates the distinctive features based on local analysis of the signal; contextual information on adjacent segments or phrase boundaries may not be available to contribute to estimation of the features. Consequently, some features may be estimated only with low confidence. When one or more words are hypothesized after lexical matching, then top-down analysis is initiated. In this case the context in which each feature occurs is known, and consequently information is available to synthesize a more precise acoustic pattern to match against the signal-derived pattern. Another motivation for top-down analysis arises in running speech where, at a particular point in a sentence, knowledge of the syntax and of the topic of the sentence suggests only a limited number of possible words. A decision among these words could be made solely through top-down processing without resorting to decisions based on a detailed bottom-up analysis. The primary focus in the following sections is the bottom-up analysis.

6.8.1 *Peripheral auditory processing*

The initial step at the top of Figure 6.7 is processing by the peripheral auditory system. It is assumed that this first processing step is a general auditory transformation that is the same whether the signal is speech or nonspeech. At the level of the cochlea, the auditory nerve, and later stages in the auditory system, the sound wave is transformed into mechanical action and then patterns of electrical activity. There are spectral and temporal representations in the auditory nerve, and spectral peaks are evident as synchrony in firings (Sachs & Young, 1980; Seneff, 1988; Shamma, 1985). Abruptness in changes in amplitude and in spectrum are enhanced (cf. Delgutte & Kiang, 1984a, 1984b) relative to their representations in terms of simple measures based on simple Fourier transforms. Some aspects of this peripheral auditory processing enhance acoustic attributes that are relevant to identifying distinctive features at later stages in the model.

6.8.2 *Landmark identification*

The second step is to identify acoustic landmarks that provide evidence for the presence of vowel, glide, and consonant segments. These landmarks are of various kinds, and they are derived by examining patterns of change in amplitude in different frequency bands. Peaks in amplitude in low-frequency bands in the region of the first-formant frequency identify times when vowels are being produced, and hence mark syllabic nuclei (Howitt, 2000). At times when there is a narrowing or releasing of a constriction in the oral cavity for a consonant, particular types of abrupt changes occur in these amplitudes in bands over a range of frequencies. These discontinuities, then, represent acoustic landmarks that can identify consonantal closing or releasing gestures (Liu, 1996). The type of acoustic discontinuity contains cues for the articulator-free features [sonorant], [continuant], and [strident]. That is, the consonant can be classified as a sonorant, as an obstruent stop consonant, or as a fricative consonant, with the fricative further classified as strident or nonstrident. Minima in low-frequency bands but without discontinuities are potential cues for glides (Espy-Wilson, 1992; Sun, 1996). This landmark-detection stage, then, leads to an initial estimation of the presence of syllabic nuclei and of the articulator-free features for the segments or feature bundles that are in the vicinity of these syllabic nuclei.

In this model of human speech perception, the detection of landmarks is largely an auditory process based on maxima and minima in amplitude or abruptnesses of amplitude changes in different frequency ranges. However, the interpretation of these landmarks as indicators of the presence of phonological segments and as cues for classification of these segments in terms of articulator-free features is clearly a process that is specific to speech and language.

6.8.3 *Extraction of acoustic parameters and cues for features*

The landmarks provide a starting point for the acoustic analysis in the third processing step of the model. In this step, several acoustic parameters are extracted in regions around the landmarks, and, in the case of abrupt consonantal landmarks, descriptors that specify in more detail the nature of the acoustic discontinuity are derived (see also Stevens, 2002). The selection of parameters to extract is motivated by the need to provide information about the articulatory gestures that generated the speech pattern, and, in particular, the gestures that gave rise to the acoustic landmarks. It is assumed that there is a universal set of such parameters, and that most of these parameters are utilized in any given language. How information is extracted from these parameters to provide cues that help to identify distinctive features for segments in a given language, however, is expected to be highly dependent on the language, particularly the features that are distinctive in that language.

Tracking of the time course of the parameters around the landmarks has three purposes. Although most of the acoustic landmarks provide direct evidence for the presence of vowel, glide, or consonant segments, some segments may not surface as simple acoustic landmarks, and some landmarks may not be reliable indicators of phonological segments. Thus one purpose of the more detailed analysis is to provide additional acoustic cues that can be used to refine the estimates of the presence of segments and their articulator-free features – estimates that do not emerge from the initial landmark-finding process. The amplitude changes in different frequency bands, on which the landmarks are based, are now supplemented by additional acoustic data that relate to changes in the spectrum shape, particularly the changes in the frequencies of spectral prominences. The second purpose of this stage in the analysis is to use these parameters for estimating sets of acoustic cues that help in identifying the articulator-bound features for the segments. And a third purpose is to identify, where possible, the syllable affiliation of each segment, i.e., to determine the syllable structure of the type represented in Table 6.4.

The parameters that are tracked in the vicinity of a given landmark depend on the type of landmark – whether it is a vowel or glide landmark, a landmark for a fricative consonant adjacent to a vowel (and whether or not the consonant is strident), a landmark for a stop consonant adjacent to a vowel, a landmark for a sonorant consonant adjacent to a vowel, or a landmark that arises from a consonant-consonant sequence. In all cases, however, the acoustic parameters that are extracted must provide evidence for two kinds of articulatory actions: (1) relevant aspects of the shape of the vocal tract above the glottis, including its variation with time, locations of constrictions, and time course of the velopharyngeal opening, and (2) the presence or absence of glottal vibration, the fundamental frequency, and the glottal configuration. The parameters that are used to infer the vocal-tract shape are indicators of the frequencies and amplitudes of spectral prominences – prominences that arise from the natural frequencies or resonances of the vocal tract. The parameters that provide information about the acoustic sources specify spectrum shapes or periodicities that arise from mechanical or aerodynamic processes rather than from acoustic resonances.

With regard to the landmark-refining aspect, estimation of the parameters can have two functions. First, interpretation of the parameters can establish whether the landmarks determined in the second step are indeed landmarks that specify the presence of a vowel, a glide, or a closure or release for a consonant, and second, they can establish whether a vowel, glide, or consonant segment should be added to the segment sequence determined by landmarks. In the first case, further analysis could show that some apparent landmarks are not the result of a vocalic nucleus or the result of the creation or release of a consonantal constriction in the oral cavity. For example, an abrupt landmark might be a consequence of prosodic events such as glottalization at the onset of a vowel-initial word (as in Figure 6.5b) or an abrupt onset following a pause. In the second case, a landmark may be missing because of overlap of gestures in production of the utterance (as for the utterance of *sudden* in Figure 6.4a or *saw a dog* in Figure 6.5a), and acoustic information other than that provided by the pattern of amplitude changes in auditory-based frequency bands must be tapped. This information comes from a more detailed examination of additional parameters in the speech signal.

We now review the inventory of acoustic parameters or descriptors that might be examined in the vicinity of landmarks, either to refine the estimates of articulator-free features or as a basis for deriving cues that identify the articulator-bound features and the syllable affiliations for the segments. In particular, we look at acoustic parameters or descriptors in the vicinity of landmarks that have been identified in the second stage of the model.

We review first the parameters that can provide relevant information in the vicinity of a vowel or glide landmark or, more generally, in the region that is centered on a vowel landmark and is between two consonantal or abrupt landmarks. In such a region, it is assumed that the vocal tract has no major constriction at which turbulence noise is generated, and there is an acoustic source in the vicinity of the glottis. The interpretation of the parameters for the purpose of identifying the features of the segments depends on whether the evidence is in the vicinity of the vowel landmark or is in the vowel region near the consonant landmark. The parameters include time variation of formant frequencies, amplitudes of spectrum prominences corresponding to formants, evidence for nasalization (Chen, 1997), fundamental frequency, aspects of the spectrum shape of the vowel after accounting for the influence of the formants (Hanson, 1997), and measures of the amount of aspiration noise present in the sound. These parameters provide evidence for tongue-body movements, velopharyngeal opening, vocal-fold stiffness, and glottal spreading or constricting. Examination of these parameters is also carried out in the vicinity of glide landmarks.

At an abrupt landmark where there is an acoustic dislocation or discontinuity with a vowel on one side of this discontinuity, there are three kinds of measures that can potentially provide evidence for the features and the syllable affiliation of the consonant that produced the discontinuity. One is the time variation of some acoustic parameters on the vowel side of the landmark, indicating articulatory movements (including nasalization) and changes in laryngeal state during the time when the consonant constriction has been released (or, if the vowel portion precedes the landmark, the time just before the consonant constriction is formed). The second type of measure is the time variation of acoustic parameters on the constricted side of the landmark. And a third kind of descriptor is the change in certain acoustic measures across the landmark. When a landmark is produced by an obstruent consonant adjacent to a vowel, the parameters on the obstruent side of the landmark include the time variation of the frication noise throughout the interval and amplitudes of spectrum prominences in the frequency regions of each of the formants in the frication noise. The parameters should also show whether glottal pulses are present, the frequency of these pulses, and the amplitude of the pulses at low frequencies. When a landmark is produced by a sonorant consonant (i.e., a nasal or liquid consonant), the parameters include changes in amplitudes of formant prominences across the landmark and measures of spectrum shape within the consonant region.

In the vicinity of each landmark (or places in the signal where segments are postulated even though no landmark is present) a set of acoustic cues is derived from the parameters that have been extracted. These cues can be sampled values of parameters at particular points in time, changes of parameters over specified time intervals, or values of one sampled parameter in relation to another. The cues are attached to or associated with the segments (and their articulator-free features) that have been inferred from the acoustic landmarks, as modified or refined in the manner described above. If a listener can see the speaker, visual information about the movements of lips, jaw, and other aspects of the face also provide cues for some of the features.

As an example, we consider a possible set of cues for place of articulation in the vicinity of a landmark at the release of a stop consonant. These cues include measures of the movement of the formants (particularly F2 and F3) in the following vowel region, the spectrum amplitude of the frication noise burst in one frequency region relative to another, the duration of the frication noise burst, and the spectrum amplitude of the noise burst in a particular frequency region relative to the spectrum amplitude of the adjacent vowel in the same frequency region. These cues provide evidence for one or more of the following articulatory actions: the length of the acoustic cavity anterior to the consonant constriction, the shape and rate of movement of the active articulator that forms the constriction, and the movement of the tongue body and mandible preceding or following the consonant release. All of these cues, then, indicate some aspect of articulation that permits a listener to determine whether the stop consonant is produced by the lips, the tongue blade, or the tongue body. (See, for example, Delattre, Liberman, & Cooper, 1955; Liberman, Delattre, & Cooper, 1952; Liberman et al., 1954; Stevens, Manuel, & Matthies, 1999; Sussman, McCaffrey, & Matthews, 1991.) For these cues, there is evidence from perceptual experiments that each contributes to identification of the feature by listeners. While some of the cues provide direct information about the defining articulatory gesture for the consonant place (e.g., the front-cavity resonance), others may give evidence for an enhancing gesture (e.g., tongue-body movement for a tongue-blade consonant).

The parameters and the cues derived from the parameters also provide information about the syllable structure and other prosodic aspects of an utterance. Articulatory and acoustic evidence for the syllable affiliation of consonants in running speech appears in a variety of forms (cf. Krakow, 1999). For example, in a vowel preceding a nasal consonant in English, nasalization in the vowel extends over a longer time interval when the consonant is a postvocalic component of the syllable (e.g., *seen Alice*) than when it is prevocalic for the next syllable (e.g., *see Nellie*) (Krakow, 1993). A stop consonant that is aspirated is almost always a syllable-initial consonant. There are also acoustic cues for word boundaries as well as syllable affiliation. For example, glottalization preceding a vowel is often evidence that the vowel is word-initial (e.g., *saw apples*) (Dilley, Shattuck-Hufnagel, & Ostendorf, 1996), and, of course, the presence of a pause usually indicates a word-initial (postpausal) or a word-final (prepausal) segment. Evidence for a reduced vowel often surfaces as a shortened vowel duration, a reduced amplitude, and an increased spectrum tilt in the vowel (Stevens, 1994) as a consequence of a spread glottal configuration.

6.8.4 Estimating the distinctive feature bundles and syllable structure

There may be several acoustic cues for an articulator-bound feature, some arising from basic feature-defining gestures for the feature and others from enhancing gestures. The particular combination of cues for a feature often depends on other features for the same segment. For example, some of the cues for place of articulation for the release landmark of a syllable-initial stop consonant, for which there is a release burst, may be different from those for a nasal consonant, where there is no noise burst but an abrupt increase in amplitude in certain parts of the spectrum. At the landmark for a closure for a stop consonant there is usually no noise burst, and hence some of the available cues for place of articulation are different from the cues near the consonant release. Likewise, the features of an adjacent segment can influence the weighting of cues for a feature. As an example, the combination of cues for stop-consonant place of articulation may depend on whether the following vowel is [−back] or [+back] (Delattre et al., 1955; Stevens et al., 1999; Sussman et al., 1991). And, as has been noted, the prosody, including the syllable affiliation of a consonant, can influence the way in which a particular feature is implemented. Furthermore, if an utterance is heard in the presence of noise, some of the cues may be masked, and only a subset may then be available to identify a feature.

In effect, then, each feature for a segment is identified by a module for that feature, as schematized in Figure 6.8. The principal input to the module is a set of acoustic cues that potentially contribute to identification of the feature. The module also has several other inputs. One is the time of the landmark around which the

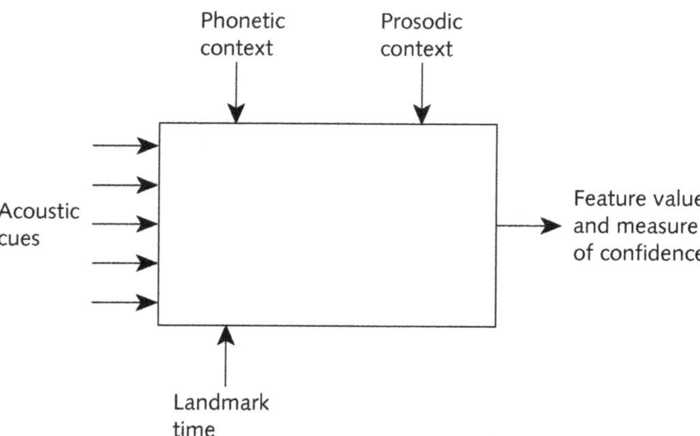

Figure 6.8 Schematic representation of a module for estimating an articulator-bound feature.

cues are to be determined. Other inputs identify other relevant features in the same segment (i.e., based on the same landmark), features of relevant adjacent segments, syllable position, and prosodic environments (such as a phrase-final segment). Still another input (not shown in the figure) is a representation of the noise or other environmental factors that can have an influence on the robustness of the acoustic cues. The output of the module is the value of the estimated feature for the landmark, together with a measure of the confidence of the estimate. There is an array of such modules, together with a module for estimating the syllable position for each segment.

In the case of a module that estimates the feature values for place of articulation for consonants, for example, some of the acoustic cues at the input are of the type described in Section 6.8.3 for syllable-initial stop consonants. Additional cues may be added to this list to include cues that may be needed in estimating place of articulation for nasal and fricative consonants. For a given landmark, the selection of combinations of cues for estimating place-of-articulation features will depend on information from other modules concerning the voicing feature for the segment, the values of the feature [sonorant] and [continuant], the syllable affiliation of the segment, certain features of the adjacent vowel, etc. There must be protocols for communicating these pieces of information between modules. Thus the acoustic cues for a given feature are not entirely independent of the context of other features. If two consonant landmarks occur in sequence, then the modules that are involved in estimating the features based on cues in the vicinity of one of these landmarks must make reference to cues from the adjacent landmark and to the time between landmarks to determine whether the two landmarks represent the closure and release for the same consonant. In this case, the cues from both landmarks should be combined to estimate the features for the consonant.

The output of this fourth step in the model of Figure 6.7 is a sequence of bundles of distinctive features. The array of distinctive features for a given segment or bundle must be constrained so that it captures the relevant contrasts for the segment in the language. That is, there are only particular combinations of features that can occur in a language, and any hypothesized bundle of features can consist of only these combinations. For example, in English there is only one possible feature bundle that contains the feature [+spread glottis], i.e., the segment /h/. Or, the feature combination [+continuant, +back] is not a valid combination for a consonant in English. There may be some lack of confidence in identifying some of the features, particularly if noise or some other environmental condition is present, and each feature may be assigned a confidence rating at this stage. Also, at this stage, analysis of the acoustic signal will provide some additional information concerning the syllable structure, possible word boundaries, phrase boundaries, and syllable prominence. Some of this information is used to assist in estimating the features.

6.8.5 Accessing the lexicon

Contact with the lexicon occurs in the final stage of the bottom-up process. This contact is made by finding sequences of words that provide a match to the hypothesized feature bundles and syllable structure. In running speech, other information may be available to the listener in addition to that derived from analysis of the acoustic signal. This information includes visual cues derived from observation of the speaker's face, and syntactic and semantic evidence derived from the context. Cues of this type could greatly aid in the search for words in the lexicon, particularly in the presence of noise. In this chapter, however, we limit our discussion to lexical access based on the estimated feature bundles, on segmental information in the immediate context of the segments, and on estimates of the syllable affiliation of each segment.

Several strategies could be followed in this process of accessing a sequence of lexical items that matches the information on feature bundles and syllable structure derived from the signal. (See, for example, Tyler & Frauenfelder, 1987, and other chapters in this volume for a discussion of proposed strategies.) One approach is to proceed from left to right; that is, to establish first a cohort of words for which the initial segment matches the initial signal-derived feature bundle, then to reduce this cohort based on the feature bundle for the second segment, and so on, until a cohort of words from the lexicon is determined. Another possible strategy is to begin with the segment for which the signal-based features have been extracted with the highest confidence, and then move successively to segments for which the confidence in estimation of the features is lower. Or, one might begin by matching vocalic nuclei and then moving to other segments within each syllable.

It is possible, of course, that not every feature is needed to identify a word, because a change in the value of one or more features may not correspond to a word in the language. Or, a sequence of feature bundles and syllable structures estimated from the signal may not correspond to a word or a sequence of words in the lexicon. In this case, confidence ratings for the features must be used to eliminate feature values that are estimated with low confidence.

It is noted that up to this stage at which words and word sequences are hypothesized, there is no point at which a phoneme is identified as an autonomous unit. The word sequences are derived by identifying distinctive features and organizing them into bundles, and the phoneme is not a unit in this process. Conscious identification of a phoneme as a unit can only occur after the word in which the phoneme appears is recognized (Norris et al., 2000).

6.8.6 *Verifying hypothesized words: Analysis by synthesis*

Whatever strategy is followed as the lexical search is pursued, the result of the matching is a set of cohorts of words or word sequences. As shown in Figure 6.7, each sequence can then be examined through "analysis by synthesis" to determine the most likely candidate sequence (Stevens & Halle, 1967). For a given hypothesized word, the sequence of gestures that produces this word is internally synthesized, and the acoustic pattern corresponding to this group of gestures is estimated. In terms of the proposed model, this acoustic pattern is expressed in terms of a set of acoustic landmarks and parameters of the type described in Sections 6.8.2 and 6.8.3. The articulatory synthesis is performed internally, and the internally synthesized patterns are then compared with the acoustic patterns measured in the signal. The hypothesized word or word sequence that gives the closest match to the measured acoustic pattern is then selected as the "best" sequence. In the internal synthesis of the acoustic parameters for a given segment, the context in which each feature occurs is available, and this context may permit better estimates of the acoustic parameters to be made than would be possible if the context were not known. In the initial "bottom up" analysis leading to estimates of the features, this contextual information may not be available, particularly if it is information that is present in the signal after the time of the relevant landmark, and consequently some of the features may not be estimated with confidence. If it is assumed that a listener is able to carry out both the direct bottom-up analysis and the top-down synthesis, then the listener must be endowed with tools for performing acoustic-to-articulatory-to-feature transformation in the bottom-up process (as in modules like Figure 6.8) and feature-to-articulatory-to-acoustic transformation in the top-down process. Although the distinctive features are universal, and are based on defining gestures and acoustic attributes, the enhancing gestures for particular features in particular contexts may be language-dependent. Consequently the learning of these transformations must have a language-specific component.

The details of these issues of lexical search strategies and internal synthesis and matching are only touched on here, and are beyond the scope of this chapter. Other chapters in this volume address these issues.

REFERENCES

Bilcher, D. L., Diehl, R. L., & Cohen, L. B. (1990). Effects of syllable duration on the perception of the Mandarin Tone 2/Tone 3 distinction: Evidence of auditory enhancement. *Journal of Phonetics*, 18, 37–49.

Browman, C. P. & Goldstein, L. (1992). Articulatory phonology: An overview. *Phonetica*, 49, 155–80.

Carlson, R., Granstrom, B., & Fant, G. (1970). Some studies concerning perception of isolated vowels. *Speech Transmission Laboratory Quarterly Progress and Status Report*, 2–3, Royal Institute of Technology, Stockholm, 19–35.

Chen, M. Y. (1997). Acoustic correlates of English and French nasalized vowels. *Journal of the Acoustical Society of America*, 102, 2360–70.

Chistovich, L. A. & Lublinskaya, V. V. (1979). The "center of gravity" effect in vowel spectra and critical distance between the formants: Psychoacoustical study of the perception of vowel-like stimuli. *Hearing Research*, 1, 185–95.

Chomsky, N. & Halle, M. (1968). *The Sound Pattern of English*. New York: Harper & Row.

Clements, G. N. & Keyser, S. J. (1983). *CV Phonology: A Generative Theory of the Syllable*. Cambridge, MA: MIT Press.

Delattre, P. C., Liberman, A. M., & Cooper, F. S. (1955). Acoustic loci and transitional cues for consonants. *Journal of the Acoustical Society of America*, 27, 769–73.

Delgutte, B. & Kiang, N. Y. S. (1984a). Speech coding in the auditory nerve I: Vowel-like sounds. *Journal of the Acoustical Society of America*, 75, 866–78.

Delgutte, B. & Kiang, N. Y. S. (1984b). Speech coding in the auditory nerve IV: Sounds with consonant-like dynamic characteristics. *Journal of the Acoustical Society of America*, 75, 897–907.

Dilley, L., Shattuck-Hufnagel, S., & Ostendorf, M. (1996). Glottalization of word-initial vowels as a function of prosodic structure. *Journal of Phonetics*, 24, 423–44.

Espy-Wilson, C. Y. (1992). Acoustic measures for linguistic features distinguishing the semivowels /w j r l/ in American English. *Journal of the Acoustical Society of America*, 92, 736–57.

Fant, G. (1960). *Acoustic Theory of Speech Production*. The Hague: Mouton.

Fowler, C. A. (1986). An event approach to the study of speech perception from a direct-realist perspective. *Journal of Phonetics*, 14, 3–28.

Halle, M. (1992). Features. In W. Bright (ed.), *Oxford International Encyclopedia of Linguistics* (pp. 207–12). New York: Oxford University Press.

Halle, M. & Stevens, K. N. (1971). A note on laryngeal features. *Research Laboratory of Electronics, Report No. 101* (pp. 198–213). Cambridge, MA: Massachusetts Institute of Technology.

Hanson, H. M. (1997). Glottal characteristics of female speakers: Acoustic correlates. *Journal of the Acoustical Society of America*, 101, 466–81.

Howitt, A. W. (2000). Automatic syllable detection for vowel landmarks. PhD thesis, Massachusetts Institute of Technology, Cambridge MA.

Jakobson, R. (1928). Quelles sont les méthodes les mieux appropriées à un exposé complet et pratique de la grammaire d'une langue quelconque? *Actes du Premier Congrès International des Linguistes*, (Leiden, 1930) (pp. 33–6). Reprinted 1962 in *Selected Writings I* (pp. 3–6), The Hague: Mouton.

Jakobson, R., Fant, C. G. M., & Halle, M. (1952). Preliminaries to speech analysis: the distinctive features and their correlates. *MIT Acoustics Laboratory Technical Report 13*. Reprinted 1967, Cambridge, MA: MIT Press.

Keyser, S. J. & Stevens, K. N. (2001). Enhancement revisited. In M. Kenstowicz (ed.), *Ken Hale: A Life in Language* (pp. 271–91). Cambridge MA: MIT Press.

Keyser, S. J. & Stevens, K. N. (under review). Enhancement and overlap in the speech chain. *Language*.

Kingston, J. & Diehl, R. (1995). Intermediate properties in the perception of distinctive feature values. In B. Connell & A. Arvaniti (eds.), *Papers in Laboratory Phonology IV* (pp. 7–27). Cambridge: Cambridge University Press.

Kluender, K. R., Diehl, R. L., & Wright, B. A. (1988). Vowel-length differences before voiced and voiceless consonants: An auditory explanation. *Journal of Phonetics*, 16, 153–69.

Krakow, R. A. (1993). Nonsegmental influences on velum movement patterns: Syllables, sentences, stress, and speaking rate. In M. K. Huffman & R. A. Krakow (eds.), *Phonetics and Phonology V: Nasals, Nasalization, and the Velum* (pp. 87–116). San Diego: Academic Press.

Krakow, R. A. (1999). Physiological organization of syllables: A review. *Journal of Phonetics*, 27, 23–54.

Liberman, A. M. & Mattingly, I. G. (1985). The motor theory of speech perception revised. *Cognition*, 21, 1–36.

Liberman, A. M., Delattre, P. C., & Cooper, F. S. (1952). The role of selected stimulus-variables in the perception of the unvoiced stop consonants. *American Journal of Psychology*, 65, 497–516.

Liberman, A. M., Delattre, P. C., Cooper, F. S., & Gerstman, L. J. (1954). The role of consonant-vowel transitions in the perception of the stop and nasal consonants. *Psychological Monographs: General and Applied*, 68(8), 1–13.

Liu, S. A. (1996). Landmark detection for distinctive feature-based speech recognition. *Journal of the Acoustical Society of America*, 100, 3417–30.

Miller, G. A. & Nicely, P. E. (1955). An analysis of perceptual confusions among some English consonants. *Journal of the Acoustical Society of America*, 27, 339–52.

Norris, D., McQueen, J. M., & Cutler, A. (2000). Merging information in speech recognition: Feedback is never necessary. *Journal of Behavioral and Brain Sciences*, 23, 299–325.

Sachs, M. B. & Young, E. D. (1980). Encoding of steady-state vowels in the auditory nerve: Representation in terms of discharge rate. *Journal of the Acoustical Society of America*, 66, 470–9.

Seneff, S. (1988). A joint synchrony/mean rate model of auditory speech processing. *Journal of Phonetics*, 16, 55–76.

Shamma, S. A. (1985). Speech processing in the auditory system I: The representation of speech sounds in the responses of the auditory nerve. *Journal of the Acoustical Society of America*, 78, 1612–21.

Stevens, K. N. (1972). The quantal nature of speech: Evidence from articulatory-acoustic data. In P. B. Denes & E. E. David, Jr. (eds.), *Human Communication: A Unified View* (pp. 51–66). New York: McGraw-Hill.

Stevens, K. N. (1977). Physics of laryngeal behavior and larynx modes. *Phonetica*, 34, 264–79.

Stevens, K. N. (1989). On the quantal nature of speech. *Journal of Phonetics*, 17, 3–46.

Stevens, K. N. (1994). Prosodic influences on glottal waveform: Preliminary data. *Proceedings of the International Symposium on Prosody* (pp. 53–64), Yokohama, Japan.

Stevens, K. N. (1998). *Acoustic Phonetics*. Cambridge, MA: MIT Press.

Stevens, K. N. (2002). Toward a model for lexical access based on acoustic landmarks and distinctive features. *Journal of the Acoustical Society of America*, 111, 1872–91.

Stevens, K. N. & Halle, M. (1967). Remarks on analysis by synthesis and distinctive features. In W. Wathen-Dunn (ed.), *Models for the Perception of Speech and Visual Form* (pp. 88–102). Cambridge, MA: MIT Press.

Stevens, K. N., Manuel, S. Y., & Matthies, M. (1999). Revisiting place of articulation measures for stop consonants: Implications for models of consonant production. *Proceedings of the International Congress of Phonetics Sciences 2* (pp. 1117–20), San Francisco, CA.

Sun, W. (1996). Analysis and interpretation of glide characteristics in pursuit of an algorithm for recognition. SM thesis, Massachusetts Institute of Technology, Cambridge, MA.

Sussman, H. M., McCaffrey, H. A., & Matthews, S. A. (1991). An investigation of locus equations as a source of relational invariance for stop place categorization. *Journal of the Acoustical Society of America*, 90, 1309–25.

Syrdal, A. K. & Gopal, H. S. (1986). A perceptual model of vowel recognition based on the auditory representation of American English vowels. *Journal of the Acoustical Society of America*, 79, 1086–100.

Titze, I. R. (1992). Phonation threshold pressure: A missing link in glottal aerodynamics. *Journal of the Acoustical Society of America*, 91, 2926–35.

Traunmüller, H. (1981). Perceptual dimension of openness in vowels. *Journal of the Acoustical Society of America*, 69, 1465–75.

Tyler, L. K. & Frauenfelder, U. H. (1987). The process of spoken word recognition: An introduction. In U. H. Frauenfelder & L. K. Tyler (eds.), *Spoken Word Recognition* (pp. 1–20). Cambridge, MA: MIT Press.

7 Speech Perception and Phonological Contrast

EDWARD FLEMMING

7.1 Introduction

The idea that the nature of speech perception plays a role in shaping phonology is not new. There is a substantial literature that proposes and tests perceptual explanations for phonological patterns, e.g., Liljencrants and Lindblom (1972), Lindblom (1986), Ohala (1981, 1990, 1993). Most of this research addresses general tendencies in phonological patterning, e.g., the cross-linguistic tendency for front vowels to be unrounded, which leaves the problem of going from the general to the particular: particular languages may violate the general tendencies, as in the case of a language with front rounded vowels. Recently phonologists have begun to tackle this problem, incorporating principles that invoke properties of human speech perception into models that derive generalizations about phonological systems, but also allow for analyses of individual languages. This area of research has proven very productive, and there is now substantial evidence for the importance of perceptual considerations in phonological theory, but there is little agreement on the proper formalization of the influence of speech perception on phonology. This issue is the organizing theme of the chapter.[1]

A key element in the development of this research has been Optimality Theory (OT, Prince & Smolensky, 1993), which offers a framework for constructing analyses of individual languages out of constraints expressing general preferences of the kind identified in the works cited above. In OT terms, the central question addressed here is: What is the form of the constraints imposed on phonology by speech perception? We will review the main types of evidence that have been used to argue for perceptual constraints in phonology to clarify exactly what kind of constraints they motivate. In the process, we will also examine the kinds of experimental evidence that have been adduced in formulating analyses.

7.2 Dispersion and Enhancement

The most direct evidence for perceptual constraints in phonology comes from generalizations about inventories of phonological contrasts. Phonetic descriptions distinguish hundreds of sound types, but a typical language has only about 30

Figure 7.1 Two common vowel inventories.

contrasting sounds (Maddieson, 1984). These inventories of contrasting sounds are far from being a random sample of the set of attested speech sounds, rather the observed inventories are subject to many restrictions, some of which can be explained in terms of perceptual constraints.

One well-established example involves preferences for particular vowel qualities. There is a strong cross-linguistic preference for vowels to be front unrounded or back rounded unless they are low vowels, as in the common vowel inventories illustrated in Figure 7.1 (low vowels are typically described as central or back and unrounded). In Maddieson's (1984) survey of a genetically diverse sample of languages, 94% of front vowels are unrounded and 93.5% of back vowels are rounded. Where a language does have front rounded, central, or back unrounded vowels, these appear in addition to front unrounded and back rounded vowels.

It is hard to imagine any articulatory basis for this relationship between backness and rounding. The tongue and lips are articulatorily relatively independent, so it would appear to be as easy to round the lips with the tongue body forward as with it retracted. On the other hand there is a straightforward perceptual account of the covariation of backness and rounding. The primary perceptual dimensions of vowel quality correspond well to the frequencies of the first two formants (Delattre et al., 1952; Plomp, 1975, Shepard, 1972). Front and back vowels are differentiated primarily by the frequency of the second formant (F2), with front vowels having a high F2 and back vowels having a low F2. Lip-rounding generally lowers F2, so the ordering of front and back, rounded and unrounded vowels, and central vowels in terms of F2 is shown in Figure 7.2. Thus the maximally distinct F2 contrast is between front unrounded and back rounded vowels (Liljencrants & Lindblom, 1972; Stevens, Keyser, & Kawasaki, 1986). Maximally distinct contrasts are preferred because they are less likely to be confused by listeners.

The general preference for maximally distinct contrasts follows from the functionalist hypothesis that phonological systems are well adapted for communication. Efficient communication depends on fast, accurate perception of speech sounds, and listeners are faster and more accurate in identifying the category to which a stimulus belongs if the stimulus is more distinct from contrasting categories (e.g., Ashby, Boynton, & Lee, 1994; Kellogg, 1931; Pisoni & Tash, 1974; Podgorny & Garner, 1979). We will see that the principle of maximization of distinctiveness is the key perceptual constraint on phonology.

Evidence for this principle has been discussed under a variety of labels. Lindblom and Engstrand (1989) refer to the tendency to maximize the perceptual distinctiveness of contrasting speech sounds as "dispersion," invoking the notion

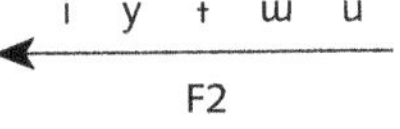

Figure 7.2 The ordering of vowel qualities on the F2 dimension.

of separation in perceptual space. Similar phenomena have been discussed by Stevens et al. (1986) under the rubric of "enhancement." They observe that distinctive features are often accompanied by "redundant" features that "strengthen the acoustic representation of distinctive features and contribute additional properties which help the listener to perceive the distinction" (p. 426). The relationship between [back] and [round] in vowels is treated as one of enhancement: [round] enhances distinctive [back]. So enhancement essentially involves combining feature differences so as to maximize the perceptual distinctiveness of contrasts. Consequently instances of enhancement also provide evidence for maximization of distinctiveness. Other work providing evidence for dispersion/enhancement includes Diehl (1991), Flemming (2002, pp. 53–6), and Ohala (1985, pp. 225ff). We will review two further cases here to illustrate the range of phenomena involved.

Another example discussed by Stevens et al. (1986) is the enhancement of frication contrasts. Fricatives are distinguished from other sound types by the presence of significant turbulence noise, generated by forcing a jet of air through a narrow constriction. The distinctiveness of this manner contrast can thus be enhanced by increasing the intensity of turbulence noise in the fricative. This is achieved by directing the jet of air against an obstacle downstream, as in the coronal sibilant [s], where a jet of air is directed against the upper teeth (Shadle, 1991; Stevens et al., 1986, p. 439). The greater distinctness of such sibilant fricatives from non-fricatives can explain their cross-linguistic prevalence: in Maddieson's (1984) survey, 83% of languages have some kind of [s], and if a language has only one fricative it is usually an [s] sound (84%).

Maximization of the distinctiveness of contrasts between sibilants has been argued to explain an otherwise puzzling observation about the realization of post-alveolar fricatives: in English and French, the post-alveolar fricative [ʃ] is accompanied by lip protrusion (Ladefoged & Maddieson, 1996, p. 148). There is no articulatory basis for this pattern, but it plausibly serves to make post-alveolar [ʃ] more distinct from the anterior sibilant [s]. These sounds are differentiated by the frequency of the first peak in the noise spectrum. This peak is at the resonant frequency of the cavity in front of the constriction, and so is lower in post-alveolar fricatives, since they have a larger front cavity than dentals and alveolars. Protruding the lips increases this difference by further enlarging the front cavity (Ladefoged & Maddieson, 1996, p. 149). Polish provides an interesting variant of this pattern. There are three contrasting sibilants, dental [s̪], alveopalatal [ɕ], and retroflex (apical post-alveolar) [ʂ], and the retroflex is produced with lip protrusion (Puppel, Nawrocka-Fisiak, & Krassowska, 1977, p. 157). This is the expected pattern given the goal of maximizing distinctiveness because the retroflex has the lowest front cavity resonance due to the space below the tongue blade. Lowering this resonance further by protruding the lips makes the retroflex more distinct from the other sibilants (Flemming, 2002, pp. 55ff).

7.2.1 *Phonological analyses of dispersion effects*

There have been two basic approaches to the analysis of dispersion effects: (1) analyses that incorporate a preference for maximally distinct contrasts into phonological theory, and (2) analyses that employ standard markedness constraints. The latter approach is in a sense the default option, since it employs only the standard apparatus of phonological theory (as outlined in the next section), but we will see that dispersion effects provide strong evidence for the distinctiveness constraints posited in the former approach, although these constraints are of a novel type.

We will first provide a brief overview of Optimality Theory (OT, Prince & Smolensky, 1993) and its suitability as a framework for formalizing the influence of speech perception on phonology. Then we will turn to the particular proposals for formalizing perceptual constraints.[2] Although the discussion will focus on analyses formulated in OT, the issues raised are relevant to any analysis of these phenomena.

7.2.2 *Optimality Theory*

In its basic form, an OT grammar maps input underlying forms onto their surface realizations. For example, in Russian obstruents are devoiced in word-final position, so the morpheme /sad/ 'garden' is pronounced [sat] (the underlying voiced final stop surfaces when a vowel-initial suffix is added, as in the dative singular [sadu]). In OT, the mapping between input and output is divided into two components: a mapping from an input form to a set of candidate outputs, and an evaluation function which selects the best member of the candidate set as the actual output. The optimality of candidate outputs is determined by reference to a ranked set of constraints.

Standard OT posits two basic types of constraints: constraints that evaluate the well-formedness of the candidate outputs – markedness constraints – and constraints that require the output to be as similar to the input as possible – faithfulness constraints. These two types of constraints are liable to conflict – satisfying markedness constraints often requires altering the input, which necessarily violates some faithfulness constraint. For example, a simple-minded analysis of the Russian facts above posits a markedness constraint forbidding word-final voiced obstruents, *FINALVOICEDOBSTRUENT. The fully faithful realization of [sad] violates this constraint, but devoicing the final stop, as in [sat] violates the faithfulness constraint IDENT[VOICE] which requires that voicing specifications of input segments should be unchanged in the output.

Conflicts between constraints are resolved by reference to a ranking of the constraints: the higher ranked constraint prevails. So in Russian, *FINALVOICED-OBSTRUENT must outrank IDENT[VOICE] (written: *FINALVOICEDOBSTRUENT $\gg$ IDENT[VOICE]) since the voicing of an input stop is changed in order to satisfy the former constraint. If this ranking were reversed the candidate [sad] would win.

OT analyses are typically illustrated using tableaux, as in example (1). The input form is shown in the top left cell while the candidate outputs are listed below it in the first column. The constraints are listed in the top row, with higher-ranked constraints on the left. If a candidate violates a constraint, a mark (*) is placed at the intersection of the constraint column and the candidate row. In (1), candidate (a), [sad] violates *FINALVOICEDOBSTRUENT, so a mark is placed under that constraint in row (a). Candidate (b), [sat], satisfies this constraint, so [sad] is eliminated (indicated by the exclamation point after the mark), and [sat] is the optimal output (indicated by the "pointing hand" in the first column). Note that it is not necessary to satisfy all the constraints in order to be the optimal candidate – candidate (b), [sat], is optimal although it violates IDENT[VOICE]. Indeed, since constraints frequently conflict, it is not usually possible to satisfy them all.

(1)

	/sad/	*FINALVOICEDOBS	IDENT[VOICE]
a.	sad	*!	
b.	☞ sat		*

One of the key strengths of OT is the way in which it relates the analysis of the typology of languages to the analyses of individual languages. The two are connected by the hypothesis that all phonological grammars are constructed from the same set of constraints, but differ in the ranking of those constraints. Typological universals can then be derived from the nature of the universal set of constraints, while the patterns of individual languages are hypothesized to derive from particular rankings of these constraints.

This provides a suitable framework for formalizing the preference for distinct contrasts because any such preference is a universal tendency which may be violated to a greater or lesser extent as a result of conflicting constraints. For example, languages like French and German have front rounded vowels in addition to front unrounded and back rounded vowels. That is, these languages eschew maximally distinct F2 contrasts in favor of distinguishing more contrastive vowels. Conversely, grounding constraints in basic considerations of communicative efficiency, and the nature of human speech perception provides a basis for the universality of those constraints: if a constraint is based on universal properties of communication and perception, it is unsurprising that it is operative in all languages.

7.2.3 *The constraints that motivate dispersion*

Two kinds of constraints have been proposed in the analysis of dispersion phenomena: basic segmental markedness constraints, and constraints on the distinctiveness of contrasts. A basic markedness constraint in OT prohibits some representational structure, such as a syllable without an onset, or a segment which has the feature combination [–sonorant, +voice]. A number of researchers have suggested that constraints of this form can be motivated by perceptual considerations (e.g., Côté, 2000; Hume, 1998). Certainly, the most common analysis of the preference for peripheral vowels (i.e., front unrounded and back rounded vowels) has been to propose constraints against other types of vowels, as in (2) (e.g., Calabrese, 1988).[3]

(2) *[–back, +round]
*[+back, –round]

Ranking these constraints above faithfulness to [back] or [round] yields a language without non-peripheral vowels because inputs containing these vowels will not be realized faithfully (3–4).[4]

(3)

	/y/	*[−back, +round]	*[+back, −round]	IDENT[round]
a.	☞ i			*
b.	y	*!		

(4)

	/ɯ/	*[−back, +round]	*[+back, −round]	IDENT[round]
a.	☞ u			*
b.	ɯ		*!	

Although these constraints can derive languages in which back and round co-vary appropriately, they do not follow directly from the perceptual considerations behind Liljencrants and Lindblom's (1972) analysis. It was suggested that in order to facilitate speech perception, contrasting sounds should be maximally distinct. This explanation implies a dispreference for F2 contrasts involving non-peripheral vowels because they are less distinct than contrasts between front unrounded and back rounded vowels. The constraints in (2) do not mention contrasts – they simply prohibit front rounded, central, and back unrounded vowels. Liljencrants and Lindblom's proposal is implemented more directly by constraints that penalize less distinct contrasts (distinctiveness constraints), e.g., a constraint ranking along the lines shown in (5), where *X-Y means that words should not be minimally differentiated by the contrast between sounds X and Y (more general formulations are discussed below).

(5) *y-ɯ ≫ *i-ɯ, *y-u ≫ *i-u

The crucial difference between these two proposals is that the analysis based on distinctiveness constraints predicts that non-peripheral vowels should be unproblematic as long as they do not enter into front-back (F2) contrasts, whereas the constraints in (2) ban these sound types regardless of what they contrast with. For example, a back unrounded vowel presents no particular perceptual difficulties if the listener knows that it is the only vowel that can appear in the context. It does not violate *i-ɯ or any other distinctiveness constraint because there is no contrast, but it would violate *[+back, −round].

In general, the reasoning outlined above motivates constraints based on the distinctiveness of contrasts between sounds, not on the sounds themselves. Basic markedness constraints as in (2) apply to individual sounds, not contrasts, and so cannot be motivated in this way. More importantly, there is empirical evidence that phonology is in fact subject to constraints on the distinctiveness of contrasts: the markedness of a sound depends on the contrasts that it enters into. These constraints are novel in that they evaluate the difference between contrasting forms, whereas standard markedness constraints evaluate individual phonological forms.

Before evaluating this evidence, it is useful to place distinctiveness constraints in the context of a specific model. The most developed proposal is the dispersion theory of contrast (Flemming, 1996, 2002, 2004; Ní Chiosáin & Padgett, 2001), which builds on ideas from Lindblom's Theory of Adaptive Dispersion (Lindblom, 1986; Lindblom & Engstrand, 1989). In this model, the preference to maximize the distinctiveness of contrasts is opposed by two other goals: maximization of the number of contrasts permitted in any given context, and minimization of articulatory effort. Increasing the number of contrasting sounds makes more efficient communication possible by increasing the information content of each sound, since it allows a single segment to differentiate more words. This goal conflicts with maximizing distinctiveness because fitting more contrasts into the finite space of possible speech sounds implies that the sounds must be closer together. Avoiding effortful articulations further restricts the possibilities for realizing distinct contrasts, so this principle also conflicts with maximization of distinctiveness.[5] Thus selecting a set of contrasts that best satisfies these three goals involves finding an optimal balance between them (cf. Lindblom, 1986). This optimization is modeled within the framework of OT.

The preference to maximize the distinctiveness of contrasts is implemented in terms of a ranked set of constraints requiring a specified minimum perceptual distance between contrasting forms (6). For example, the constraint MINDIST = 2 requires a minimum perceptual distance of 2 steps on the relevant scale for two phonemes to be contrastive. Sounds are represented as located in a multidimensional perceptual space where closer sounds are more confusable. For example, (7) shows the assumed location of high vowels on the dimension corresponding to F2 frequency, measured in arbitrary units. Assuming for simplicity that these vowels differ on this dimension only, it can be seen that the contrast [i-u] involves a distance of 4, and thus satisfies all the MINDIST constraints in (6), while [i-y] involves a distance of only 1, and thus violates MINDIST = 2 and all lower-ranked constraints. In other words, the less distinct a contrast is, the greater the violation.

(6) MINDIST = 1 ≫ MINDIST = 2 ≫ . . . ≫ MINDIST = 4

(7) F2:

5	4	3	2	1
i	y	ɨ	ɯ	u

The preference to maximize the number of contrasts is implemented as a constraint, MAXIMIZE CONTRASTS, which is satisfied by the largest inventory of contrasts. A constraint of this type is needed to moderate the effects of distinctiveness constraints, which would otherwise always result in the selection of a few maximally distinct sounds. As suggested above, maintaining more contrasts is valuable because it allows each segment to differentiate more words. MAXIMIZE CONTRASTS is a positive constraint in that it assigns positive marks corresponding to the number of contrasting sounds permitted in the context under evaluation, rather than assigning violation marks like a standard markedness constraint. Evaluation of this constraint is indicated in (8) by using one check mark (✓) for each contrasting sound category in the candidate inventory, so candidate (a) [i-u] receives two check marks, because there are two contrasting vowels, while candidate (d) [i-ɨ-u] receives three check marks. More check marks indicate a better candidate.

The conflict between these two types of constraints is illustrated in (8–9) with the simple example of selecting a set of contrasting high vowels. The balance between maximizing distinctiveness and maximizing the number of contrasts is determined by position of MAXIMIZE CONTRASTS in the hierarchy of MINDIST constraints. In (8), MINDIST = 3 outranks MAXIMIZE CONTRASTS, so the largest inventory, (d), is eliminated, because it does not satisfy MINDIST = 3. The most distinct inventory (a), containing front unrounded and back rounded vowels, best satisfies the MINDIST constraints, and hence is the winner. Contrasts involving back unrounded vowels (b), or front rounded vowels (c) are less distinct, and therefore lose to candidate (a).

(8)

		MINDIST = 2	MINDIST = 3	MAXIMIZE CONTRASTS	MINDIST = 4
a.	☞ i-u			✓✓	
b.	i-ɯ			✓✓	*!
c.	y-u			✓✓	*!
d.	i-ɨ-u		*!	✓✓✓	**

In (9), MAXIMIZE CONTRASTS ranks above MINDIST = 3 – i.e., the number of contrasts is more important. So the winning candidate is (d) which fits in three contrasting vowels while satisfying the higher-ranked constraint MINDIST = 2.

(9)

		MINDIST = 2	MAXIMIZE CONTRASTS	MINDIST = 3	MINDIST = 4
a.	i-u		✓✓!		
b.	i-ɯ		✓✓!		*
c.	y-u		✓✓!		*
d.	☞ i-ɨ-u		✓✓✓	*	**

Effort minimization is assumed to play a negligible role in the selection of F2 contrasts in most contexts,[6] but in other cases it may play a role in explaining why languages do not avail themselves of maximally distinct contrasts.

Another consequence of effort minimization is that difficult articulations should only be employed in order to realize more distinct contrasts, so where contrasts are neutralized, considerations of effort minimization are likely to be dominant. This leads to the prediction that preferred vowel qualities should depend on contrastive status: in F2 contrasts, front unrounded and back rounded vowels are preferred (8), but if all vowel F2 contrasts are neutralized, backness and rounding of vowels should be governed by effort minimization. On the other hand, the basic markedness constraints in (2) are insensitive to contrastive status, and consequently predict that peripheral vowels should be preferred in all circumstances.

Flemming (2004) discusses two test cases in which all F2 contrasts are neutralized: "vertical" vowel inventories, and fully neutralizing vowel reduction in unstressed syllables, as in English reduction to schwa. Both cases conform to the predictions of the dispersion-theoretic analysis: backness and rounding of vowels assimilate to adjacent consonants, often yielding central or centralized vowel qualities which would be highly marked in F2 contrasts, but are favored by effort minimization.

The best-known examples of "vertical" vowel inventories, lacking F2 contrasts, are found in Northwest Caucasian languages such as Kabardian and Shapsug (Colarusso, 1988, 1992; Kuipers, 1960; Smeets, 1984). These languages are often described as having only central vowels, but this is a claim about the underlying vowel inventory posited as part of a derivational analysis, not an observation about the surface vowels. On the surface, these languages have a system of five normal length vowels [i, e, a, o, u] (Kuipers, 1960, pp. 23ff; Smeets, 1984, p. 123), and a "vertical" system of two extra short vowels, which can be transcribed broadly as [ɨ, ə].[7] However, the precise backness and rounding of these vowels depends on context. They are realized as a smooth transition between the lip and tongue positions of the preceding and following consonants, deviating only to realize the required vowel height (Colarusso, 1988, p. 307). An unrelated vertical vowel language, Marshallese, is similar (Bender, 1968; Choi, 1992). The transitional vowel qualities result from assimilation in backness and rounding to preceding and following consonants, which is plausibly the least effort production strategy. The resulting vowel qualities are often central, back unrounded, front rounded, or short diphthongs involving these qualities – all vowel types which would be highly marked in the presence of F2 contrasts. There are no vertical vowel inventories containing the peripheral vowels that are predicted by the basic markedness constraints in (2) – i.e., there are no inventories such as [i, e, a] or [u, o, a].[8]

Neutralization of F2 contrasts is also observed in languages such as English where all vowel quality distinctions are neutralized to a schwa vowel in some unstressed syllables. This process is also found in Southern Italian dialects (Maiden, 1995) and Dutch (Booij, 1995). Phonetic studies of schwa in Dutch (van Bergem, 1994) and English (Kondo, 1994) indicate that this vowel is comparable to a vertical vowel in that F2 is an almost linear interpolation between values determined by the preceding and following contexts. Again, schwa is a marked vowel where there are quality contrasts – it is often excluded from those positions – but it is the unmarked vowel where all quality contrasts are neutralized. Basic markedness constraints predict that markedness should not depend on contrastive status, so we should expect one of the peripheral vowels, [i, u] or [a], to be the sole vowel in neutralization contexts.

Distinctiveness constraints and basic markedness constraints are also differentiated by predictions concerning enhancement. Distinctiveness constraints predict that enhancement should only apply to contrasts, since enhancement is analyzed as a consequence of constraints on the distinctiveness of contrasts. This is inherent in Stevens et al.'s (1986) conception of enhancement, but it is not predicted by analyses in terms of basic markedness constraints, because the latter are insensitive to contrast. Evidence on this point comes from enhancement of stop voicing contrasts (Flemming, 2004). Stevens et al. (1986, p. 439) argue that pre-nasalization can serve as an enhancement of stop voicing. One of the cues that distinguishes voiced stops from voiceless stops is the presence of voicing during the closure, as opposed to the silence of a voiceless stop closure (Stevens & Blumstein, 1981), so the distinctiveness of this contrast can be increased by increasing the intensity of voicing. This can be achieved by lowering the velum during the early part of the stop closure, yielding a pre-nasalized stop. It is generally difficult to sustain voicing during a stop because air pressure builds up behind the closure, and when oral pressure approaches subglottal pressure, airflow through the glottis ceases, and voicing ceases (Ohala, 1983; Westbury & Keating, 1986). Lowering the velum during the stop closure allows air to be vented through the nose, slowing the build up of oral pressure, and thus facilitating voicing. In addition, voicing during an oral stop is radiated only through the neck and face, resulting in a low intensity acoustic signal, whereas lowering the velum allows sound to be radiated from the nose, resulting in greater intensity.

Pre-nasalization serves as an enhancement of stop voicing contrasts in Mixtec (Iverson & Salmons, 1996), Southern Barasano (Smith & Smith, 1971), Guaraní (Gregores & Suárez, 1967), and a variety of other languages discussed by Herbert (1986, pp. 16ff) – that is, voiceless stops are contrasted with pre-nasalized stops rather than plain voiced stops. But voiced stops are never enhanced by prenasalization where they do not contrast with voiceless stops. Non-contrastive voiced stops can arise through intervocalic voicing, a pattern where voiced stops are found between vowels ([ada], not *[ata], but only voiceless stops occur elsewhere ([ta], not *[da]). However, we do not find intervocalic prenasalization of stops (i.e., prenasalized stops between vowels, but only voiceless stops elsewhere).[9]

These generalizations are very difficult to account for with simple markedness constraints. The existence of languages which have pre-nasalized stops but not plain voiced stops shows that some markedness constraint must favor prenasalized stops over voiced stops, e.g., PRENASALIZE "voiced stops should be prenasalized." Then a language with voiceless stops and prenasalized stops (like Mixtec) would be derived by ranking this constraint above faithfulness to [nasal] (10) so any voiced stops in the input are replaced by prenasalized stops.

(10) PRENASALIZE ≫ IDENT[nasal]

However, this ranking derives prenasalization of voiced stops even where voicing is not contrastive. For example, if intervocalic voicing of stops follows from ranking a constraint against voiceless stops occurring between vowels (*VTV) above faithfulness to voicing (11), then this ranking can be combined with the prenasalization ranking in (10) to derive the unattested pattern of intervocalic prenasalization, as shown in (12).

(11) *VTV ≫ IDENT[voice]

(12)

	/ata/	*VTV	PRENASALIZE	IDENT [nasal]	IDENT [voice]
a.	ata	*!			
b.	ada		*!		*
c.	☞ a^{n}da			*	*

This consequence is avoided if the constraint PRENASALIZE is replaced by constraints favouring maximally distinct voicing contrasts, e.g., *T-D ≫ *T-^{N}D (where T, D, and ^{N}D represent voiceless, voiced, and prenasalized stops, respectively). These distinctiveness constraints only apply to contrasts, so prenasalization of voiced stops is correctly predicted to occur only where there are voicing contrasts. Elsewhere voiced stops are preferred over prenasalized stops because voiced stops are simpler to articulate.

These, and other examples discussed in Flemming (2004), indicate that phonology includes distinctiveness constraints, as we would expect if considerations of ease of perception influence phonology. Basic markedness constraints do not follow from perceptual considerations and cannot account for dispersion effects because dispersion applies only to contrasts while basic markedness constraints are indifferent to the contrastive status of a sound.

7.3 Licensing by Cue

A second source of evidence for perceptual constraints is the typology of contextual neutralization. Contextual neutralization is a pattern of distribution in which a contrast is permitted in some environments, but is suspended in others. For example, stop voicing contrasts may be permitted before sonorants ([**b**a] vs. [**p**a], [**b**la] vs. [**p**la]), but not before obstruents ([a**p**ta], *[a**b**ta]). In a situation like this, the voicing contrast is said to be *neutralized* before obstruents.

Steriade (1995, 1999) observes that different types of contrast have different characteristic environments of neutralization. For example, the following are well-attested patterns of distribution for three types of contrasts, following Steriade (1999):[10]

(13) a. Obstruent voicing contrasts are permitted only before sonorants (e.g., German, Lithuanian, Russian, Sanskrit).

b. Major place contrasts (labial vs. coronal vs. dorsal) are permitted only before vowels (e.g., Japanese, Luganda, Selayarese).

c. Retroflexion contrasts (retroflex vs. apical alveolar) are permitted only after vowels (e.g., Gooniyandi, Miriwung, Walmatjari).

Steriade argues that the general characterization of these diverse contexts of neutralization makes crucial reference to perceptual distinctiveness: in each case, the contrasts are neutralized first in environments where "the *cues* to the relevant contrast would be diminished or obtainable only at the cost of additional articulatory maneuvers" (Steriade, 1997, p. 1). Contrasts differ in their distribution of cues so they are subject to different patterns of neutralization. This is dubbed the "Licensing by Cue" hypothesis – the presence of a contrast in a particular environment is licensed by the availability of perceptual cues to that contrast.

For example, the distribution of obstruent voicing contrasts (13a) is analyzed in these terms by Steriade (1997). One of the primary cues to obstruent voicing distinctions is Voice Onset Time (VOT), the lag between the release of the obstruent constriction and the onset of voicing (Lisker & Abramson, 1970). Steriade observes that this cue is generally only available where a voiced sonorant follows, and so is absent before obstruents, and in word-final position before pause. Voicing contrasts in these environments can only be realized by cues such as voicing during the consonant constriction, consonant duration, and duration of the preceding vowel, which are hypothesized to be weaker cues than VOT. So according to this analysis, languages like Russian and German disallow voicing contrasts in precisely the environments where a key cue to the contrast, VOT, is unavailable. Given the importance of VOT as a cue to obstruent voicing, it is very plausible that voicing is less confusable before sonorants than before obstruents or word-finally, but there is surprisingly little direct evidence on this point. Studies of voicing perception generally have not directly compared perception of voicing in different contexts.

Similar factors have been argued to explain restrictions on the distribution of major place contrasts (labial vs. coronal vs. dorsal). These contrasts preferentially occur where there is a following vowel, or, failing that, a following approximant. A number of studies have shown that major place distinctions are less confusable in pre-vocalic position than in pre-consonantal or pre-pausal position (Redford & Diehl, 1999; Wright, 2001). Fujimura, Macchi, and Streeter (1978) and Ohala (1990) have also shown that release cues to major place contrasts dominate over closure cues in stimuli that have been edited so that these cues conflict. This difference in distinctiveness appears to have multiple causes. The greater distinctiveness of pre-vocalic stops may be attributed to the presence of the release burst which provides cues to place, in addition to the formant transition cues that are also available in post-vocalic position (Dorman, Studdert-Kennedy, & Raphael, 1977). Consonant clusters are often articulatorily overlapped so the constriction of a second consonant is formed before the constriction of the first consonant is released. Where the second consonant is an obstruent, this results in the loss or attenuation of the release burst of the first consonant (Henderson & Repp, 1982).

Another factor that has been suggested to contribute to the greater distinctiveness of pre-vocalic place contrasts is the nature of the peripheral auditory system (Wright, 1996, 2001). Auditory nerve fibers respond most strongly to rapid rises from low intensity within their frequency band, and the transition from a consonant to a vowel often involves rapid onsets of this kind, especially where the consonant is an obstruent (Delgutte & Kiang, 1984; Greenberg, 1995). This effectively amplifies release formant transitions and stop bursts. As noted by Ohala (1990, pp. 261ff), experiments by Fujimura et al. (1978) support an auditory-perceptual basis for the greater distinctiveness of onset consonants: they found that in stimuli with conflicting cues to place, release cues dominated closure cues, even when the stimuli were played backwards – i.e., the release cues were reversed closure transitions. However, Redford and Diehl (1999) also found that the formant transitions of onsets were more distinctly articulated than word-final consonants, so production differences may play a role in explaining the observed difference in distinctiveness.

The patterns of distribution of obstruent voicing and major place contrasts are broadly similar in that both preferentially occur before sonorants, but there are differences of detail, some of which follow from differences in the nature of the cues to these two types of contrast. When obstruent voicing contrasts are permitted before sonorant consonants, they are allowed before all sonorants, whereas major place contrasts are usually subject to further restrictions. For example, many languages, including English, do not allow coronal stops before coronal laterals, although labials and velars contrast in this environment: *plan, clan, *tlan* (Kawasaki, 1982, p. 14).

The insensitivity of voicing contrasts to the nature of a following sonorant is expected, given that the primary cue to voicing is VOT. The realization of VOT depends only on the presence of a voiced sonorant of sufficient duration; place of articulation, nasality, and laterality make little difference. On the other hand, primary cues to stop place contrasts are the release burst and formant transitions. Approximants and vowels allow the realization of both, but simply realizing a burst and formant transitions is not adequate to support contrast: the burst and/or formant transitions must be distinct for contrasting places of articulation. The distinctiveness of these cues can be affected by coarticulation with the following vowel or approximant.

Kawasaki (1982, pp. 157ff) and Flemming (2002, pp. 132ff) argue that these factors underlie the restrictions on coronal stops before laterals. That is, coarticulation effects make the burst and formant transitions of coronals insufficiently distinct from velars in this context. The lateral constrains the position of the tongue tip and body, so the formant transitions in coronal-lateral and velar-lateral clusters are very similar, while a labial is generally distinguished by a lower F2 due to lip constriction (Kawasaki, 1982, pp. 67ff; Olive, Greenwood, & Coleman, 1993, p. 284). The coronal and velar closures are at or behind the location of the lateral constriction, so in both cases frication noise is generated at this lateral constriction at release, resulting in acoustically similar bursts.

A more striking example of how distribution of contrasts differs depending on the nature of the cues involved comes from the comparison between major place contrasts and retroflexion contrasts (Steriade, 1995, 2001). The contrast between retroflex and apical alveolar consonants is found in many Australian and Dravidian languages. It is commonly restricted to positions following a vowel, so it is neutralized word-initially and following consonants (Steriade, 1995). This is in sharp distinction from most other place contrasts, which, as we have seen, occur preferentially *before* vowels. Steriade argues that this difference follows from differences in the distribution of cues to these types of contrasts. Retroflexes are distinguished from apical alveolars by a low third formant at closure (Stevens & Blumstein, 1975). However, the tongue tip moves forward during the closure of a retroflex and is released at the alveolar ridge, so these sounds are articulatorily and acoustically very similar at release (Anderson, 1997; Butcher, 1995; Dave, 1977; Spajić, Ladefoged, & Bhaskararao, 1994). Closure transitions are only available where the consonant is preceded by a vowel, hence this cue is missing in other environments, making the contrast less distinct (Anderson, 1997). So the retroflexion contrast differs from other place contrasts in that it is realized most distinctly on a preceding vowel rather than a following vowel, but given this difference we can see that all place contrasts are liable to neutralize in environments where it would be difficult to make them distinct.

It should be noted that the patterns of distribution described for major place and obstruent voicing contrasts have often been analyzed as involving neutralization of contrasts in the coda of syllables (e.g., Ito, 1989; Vennemann, 1972). Steriade (1997, 1999) and Côté (2000) present detailed arguments in favor of the "Licensing by Cue" analysis. In the present context, the important weaknesses of a coda-neutralization account are that it does not extend to retroflexion contrasts, which are neutralized in word-initial and post-consonantal onsets, but are permitted in codas and intervocalic onsets, and that it cannot relate the patterns of distribution to the nature of the features involved.

While the analyses sketched above indicate that considerations of distinctiveness play a central role in accounting for the distribution of contrasts, it is clear that other constraints are important also. For example, stop bursts will only be absent before obstruents if some constraint requires the stop closure to overlap with the following consonant. One general phenomenon that implicates additional constraints is word-final neutralization. For example, in German, obstruent voicing is neutralized preceding obstruents and in word-final position. For words spoken in isolation, these are both environments in which VOT cues are unavailable, because there is no following sonorant, but in phrase-medial position, a word-final obstruent might be followed by a sonorant, allowing the realization of VOT differences. If contrast is governed strictly by the availability of cues, the voicing contrast should be permitted in this context, but in German, and many similar languages, voicing is neutralized in word-final position, regardless of phrasal context. So the analysis in terms of licensing by cue must be supplemented by additional constraints relating to morphosyntactic structure. Steriade (1997) analyzes this pattern as resulting from generalization of the citation form of words. That is, there is a general preference to give words a uniform pronunciation in all contexts, and this is modeled on the pronunciation of the word spoken in isolation. This analysis is formalized in terms of Output-Output Correspondence constraints (Benua, 1997; Kenstowicz, 1997; Steriade, 2000). A comparable distinction between word-internal and cross-word sequences must be made in syllabification-based analyses in order to block syllabification of a word-final consonant as an onset to a following vowel-initial word.

7.3.1 *Formalizing Licensing by Cue*

Steriade (1997, 1999) formalizes the Licensing by Cue hypothesis in terms of constraints on the distinctiveness of contrasts. Although the specifics are rather different from dispersion theory, the general conception is very similar, so the same constraints motivated above in the analysis of enhancement can be used to analyze patterns of contextual neutralization (Flemming, 2002, pp. 40ff).[11]

7.3.1.1 *Distinctiveness constraints*

In the case of obstruent voicing, we will assume that there is a perceptual dimension corresponding to VOT, which takes a value of 0 for voiced and 1 for voiceless obstruents.[12] Languages that restrict voicing contrasts to pre-sonorant positions require a VOT difference for the contrast to be adequately distinct. In other words, MINDIST = VOT:1 ranks above MAXIMIZE CONTRASTS. This sets a threshold for minimum distinctiveness that can be met in pre-sonorant position, so a voicing contrast is permitted in that environment (14).

(14)

	_V	MINDIST = VOT:1	MAXIMIZE CONTRASTS	*[+voice, −son]
a.	☞ dV-tV		✓✓	*
b.	dV		✓!	*
c.	tV		✓!	

Pre-pausally, no VOT difference is possible, and a difference in closure voicing alone is insufficient, so a voicing contrast is not permitted (15, # indicates a word boundary). Given that there is no contrast, obstruents are realized with the least-effort laryngeal state. In pre-pausal position, this is voiceless, given the difficulties involved in maintaining vocal fold vibration during an obstruent (cf. Section 7.2.3). This preference is formalized as a constraint against voiced obstruents, *[+voice, −sonorant].

(15)

	V_#	MINDIST = VOT:1	MAXIMIZE CONTRASTS	*[+voice, −son]
a.	Vd#-Vt#	*!	✓✓	*
b.	Vd#		✓	*!
c.	☞ Vt#		✓	

Voicing contrasts are also neutralized before obstruents, because VOT differences cannot be realized in this position either (17). However, in this case, the neutralized stop is voiced, assimilating to the following obstruent (in this case [g]). A plausible analysis of this pattern is that it is especially difficult to initiate voicing during an obstruent – due to hysteresis effects it is easier to maintain voicing from a sonorant into a following obstruent than it is to initiate voicing during an obstruent following a voiceless sound (Westbury & Keating, 1986). Thus we can posit the constraint in (16), named *TD for brevity, universally ranked above *[+voice, −son].

(16) *TD: *[−voice][+voice, −sonorant]

This constraint forces assimilation in obstruent sequences, as shown in the following tableau:

(17)

	V_gV	MINDIST = VOT:1	MAXIMIZE CONTRASTS	*TD	*[+voice, −son]
a.	VdgV-VtgV	*!	✓✓	*	*
b.	☞ VdgV		✓		*
c.	VtgV		✓	*!	

Languages with broader distribution of obstruent voicing rank MAXIMIZE CONTRASTS above MINDIST = VOT:1, tolerating less distinct contrasts in order to realize more contrasts. But no language will prefer less distinct contrasts over more distinct contrasts of a similar type.

Neutralization of retroflexion is analyzed along similar lines: a MINDIST constraint requiring an F3 difference is ranked above MAXIMIZE CONTRASTS, so the contrast is neutralized where it is not possible to realize this cue.

7.3.1.2 *Faithfulness constraints*

An alternative approach to formulating the perceptual constraints that account for these generalizations about the distribution of contrasts makes use of faithfulness constraints (Boersma, 1998; Jun, 1995; Steriade, 1995, 2001). This is a natural move since faithfulness constraints play a central role in the regulation of contrasts in standard OT. Essentially, a faithfulness constraint like IDENT F, where F is a feature, favours preserving underlying differences – if the input contains [+F], the output should contain [+F], if the input contains [–F], the output should contain [–F]. So if IDENT F is satisfied, an underlying difference between [+F] and [–F] is preserved on the surface, and the language has a contrast in F.

Perceptual factors are introduced by distinguishing IDENT F constraints for different contexts, then ranking them according to the distinctiveness of an F contrast in that context. For example, we might posit the ranking of IDENT[voice] constraints in (18).

(18) IDENT[voice]/ _ [+son] ≫ IDENT[voice]/ _ # ≫ IDENT[voice]/ _ [−son]

The distribution of voicing contrasts is then determined by the position of a constraint against voiced obstruents, *[+voice, –son]. For example, the ranking in (19) derives neutralization everywhere except before sonorants (the German pattern).[13] If *[+voice, –son] is ranked lower, then the contrast is permitted in more positions, but again contrasts are permitted first in more distinct environments. These constraints predict that neutralization always yields voiceless obstruents, so an additional constraint, such as *TD, is required to derive assimilation to following obstruents.

(19) IDENT[voi]/ _ [+son] ≫ ***[+voice, −son]** ≫ IDENT[voi]/ _ # ≫ IDENT[voi]/ _ [−son]

This approach works elegantly in simple cases, but it has some limitations that make it incapable of providing a comprehensive account of perceptual effects. The fundamental limitation of faithfulness constraints is that they can only block change between input and output, they cannot motivate change. This is problematic because there are various phenomena that have been argued to be perceptually motivated which crucially involve unfaithfulness to input forms, including the dispersion phenomena discussed in Section 2. For example, a language with only the peripheral vowels [i, e, a, o, u] must unfaithfully map non-peripheral input vowels such as [y, ɯ] onto one of these vowels. Ranking IDENT[round] low in the constraint hierarchy, for example, makes it relatively acceptable to realize [y, ɯ] as [i] and [u] respectively, but it does not favor these realizations. Unfaithful mappings can only be motivated by markedness constraints, and as we have seen above, the markedness constraints that best account for this pattern are distinctiveness constraints implementing a preference for maximally distinct F2 contrasts. The same applies to other cases of dispersion and enhancement. For example, enhancement of voicing contrasts by pre-nasalizing voiced stops (Section 7.2.3) implies unfaithful realization of input voiced stops as pre-nasalized stops, which must be motivated by a markedness constraint.

More generally, perceptually-ranked featural faithfulness constraints can only account for patterns of neutralization, but arguably neutralization is just one way of avoiding an otherwise indistinct contrast. That is, an indistinct contrast may be avoided by giving up the contrast (neutralization), or by making the contrast more distinct (enhancement). We have seen that distinctiveness constraints can be used to derive both patterns, but perceptually-ranked faithfulness constraints can only derive neutralization.

This limitation applies not only to the analysis of segment-internal enhancements of the kind just discussed, but also to modification of the environment of a contrast (cf. Côté, 2000, pp. 175ff; Hume & Johnson, 2001, pp. 8ff). For example, it has been suggested that vowel epenthesis is often motivated by the need to make consonant contrasts more distinct (e.g., Côté, 2000; Wright, 1996, p. 40). One such pattern is epenthesis into clusters of three consonants, exemplified from Yawelmani Yokuts (Kisseberth, 1970; Newman, 1944) in (20). Similar patterns are observed in Cairene Arabic (Broselow, 1976) and Lenakel (Lynch, 1978).

(20)	/paʔt + mi/	→	[paʔitmi]	'having fought'
cf.	/paʔt + al/	→	[paʔtal]	'might fight'
	/lihm + mi/	→	[lihimmi]	'having run'
cf.	/lihm + al/	→	[lihmal]	'might run'

Côté (2000) analyzes this pattern in terms of the markedness constraint C↔V: "A consonant is adjacent to a vowel" – that is, epenthesis applies to ensure that every consonant is adjacent to a vowel, which is not the case in a triconsonantal cluster. Formally, epenthesis is derived by ranking C↔V above DEPV, the faithfulness constraint that is violated by inserting a vowel[14] (see Kager, 1998, pp. 107ff; for a similar analysis based on syllabification constraints).

As Côté (2000) argues, it is perceptually desirable for consonants to be adjacent to a vowel because many consonantal contrasts are best realized in this position.

As noted above, formant transitions are important place cues that are best realized on a vowel. The contrast between presence and absence of a consonant is also more distinct adjacent to a vowel because the change in constriction between consonant and vowel results in salient spectral discontinuities (Liu, 1996; Ohala, 1980; Stevens, 1998, pp. 245ff). The nature of the spectral change, e.g. the rate and magnitude of change in different frequency bands, may also provide cues to consonant manner (Liu, 1996; Stevens, 1985).[15]

This analysis cannot be implemented in terms of perceptually-ranked faithfulness constraints. Ranking constraints against consonant deletion (MaxC) according to the strength of the cues to the presence of a consonant can only allow deletion of poorly-cued consonants, it cannot motivate epenthesis to improve the cues to a consonant. The unfaithful insertion of a vowel can only be motivated by a markedness constraint violated by triconsonantal clusters, such as C↔V.

Perceptually-ranked faithfulness constraints favor perceptually minimal changes between input and output. This arrangement predicts that indistinct contrasts are more likely to be lost because they can be neutralized by perceptually minimal changes, but it does not implement a general preference for distinct contrasts, and so cannot account for the observed range of perceptually motivated phenomena. However, there is evidence that perceptually minimal change between input and output is preferred in alternations (i.e., contextual variation in the realization of morphemes) (Steriade, forthcoming), so perceptual ranking of faithfulness constraints may be motivated on independent grounds.

7.3.1.3 Sound change via misperception

The limitations of perceptually-ranked faithfulness constraints are shared by some theories that locate perceptual constraints in the process of sound change rather than in synchronic grammars (e.g., Blevins & Garrett, 1998; Ohala, 1990). According to these accounts, indistinct contrasts appear to be dispreferred in languages because they are more likely to be lost over time through misperception on the part of language users. For example, Ohala (1990) argues that consonants often assimilate in place to a following consonant (e.g. anka > aŋka) because the unassimilated cluster is easily misperceived as the assimilated cluster. This is related to the observation above that post-vocalic major place contrasts are relatively indistinct, but according to Ohala this pattern results from "'innocent' misapprehension" on the part of listeners, so no dispreference for indistinct contrasts needs to be encoded in grammars.

Sound change through misperception, like perceptually-ranked faithfulness constraints, can only hope to account for neutralization, not dispersion or enhancement. For example, at least some cases in which stop voicing contrasts are enhanced by prenasalization of voiced stops (Section 7.2.3) seem to have arisen via a sound change from earlier voiced stops to prenasalized stops (Herbert, 1986, pp. 16ff). This change cannot be attributed to misperception, rather prenasalization seems to be a strategy that speakers have hit upon to make stop voicing contrasts more distinct, so a preference for distinct contrasts is necessary to account for this pattern. In general, a mechanism of sound change via misperception only predicts that less distinct contrasts are more likely to be lost, it cannot account for cases in which speakers appear to take measures to increase the distinctiveness of contrasts – i.e., dispersion and enhancement phenomena (cf. Steriade, 2001, pp. 233ff for a similar argument).

Relating sound change directly to patterns of misperception also incorrectly predicts some unattested sound changes. For example, a study of vowel confusions in French (Robert-Ribes et al., 1998) found that [i] is confused with [y] much more frequently than it is confused with [u]. This difference in distinctiveness is expected, and is hypothesized to lie behind the cross-linguistic preference for contrasts like [i-u] over front rounding contrasts like [i-y]. An "innocent misapprehension" model might attribute this preference to the greater tendency for [i-y] contrasts to be lost through misperception. However, the study found that [i] is misidentified as [y] at about the same rate as the converse misidentification of [y] as [i]. So if sound changes arise from misperception, we would expect a change [i] > [y] to be as likely as [y] > [i], but while the latter change is well attested (e.g., in Old English (Lass & Anderson 1975, pp. 286ff) and Greek (Newton, 1972, p. 19)), unconditioned rounding of front vowels is unattested. Significantly, unrounding front vowels increases the distinctiveness of front-back contrasts, while the unattested change would reduce distinctiveness without any compensatory benefits.

7.3.1.4 Basic markedness constraints

A final approach to formalizing the perceptual constraints responsible for contextual neutralization is to use basic markedness constraints. For example, in the analysis of voicing neutralization reviewed above, Steriade (1997) proposes a distinctiveness constraint against obstruent voicing contrasts appearing where there is no following sonorant. The closest equivalent basic markedness constraint would be a constraint requiring voiced obstruents to be followed by sonorants (cf. Lombardi, 1995, 1999). Constraints of this kind are widely used in the analysis of contextual neutralization (McCarthy, 2002, p. 87), but usually without appealing to any perceptual motivation. However, some researchers have used basic markedness constraints to formalize perceptually motivated constraints (e.g., Côté, 2000; Hume, 1998).

We saw in Section 7.2.3 that basic markedness constraints are inadequate for the analysis of dispersion effects, and are difficult to motivate on perceptual grounds because perceptual considerations disfavour indistinct contrasts, not individual sounds. Similar difficulties face the use of basic markedness constraints in the analysis of Licensing by Cue effects. A basic constraint on obstruent voicing must ban [+voice] or [–voice] rather than the contrast between them. This is not only perceptually unmotivated, it leads to empirical difficulties. For example, it is common for the result of neutralization to be phonetically distinct from either of the sounds that occur in positions of contrast (cf., Trubetzkoy, 1939, pp. 71–3). This is the case in the neutralization of retroflexion contrasts, for example. Butcher (1995) studied several Australian languages that contrast retroflex and apical alveolar consonants, and found that neutralization of this contrast in word-initial position yields an intermediate consonant, generally post-alveolar (unlike apical alveolars), but apical rather than sub-laminal (the contrastive retroflexes are sub-laminal). This intermediate status is reflected in uncertainty among Australianists as to the appropriate transcription for these sounds (Butcher, 1995; Steriade, 1995).

If the distinction between retroflexes and apical alveolars is treated as binary (e.g. [+/−anterior]), then formulating a constraint against either retroflexes or apical alveolars in word initial position predicts that the other articulation should be favored in neutralization, which is not accurate, since an intermediate articulation is actually observed. If we make a three-way distinction between apical alveolars, retroflexes, and an intermediate articulation, then it is possible to formulate constraints against either extreme appearing in word-initial position, but it would also be necessary to prevent the intermediate place from surfacing in environments of contrast. These problems are avoided if we recognize that it is the *contrast* between retroflexes and apical alveolars that is problematic in word-initial position. In the absence of contrast, the intermediate apical is preferred as less effortful than a sub-laminal retroflex, but more distinct from laminal coronals than an apical alveolar.

7.4 Conclusions

The evidence reviewed here leads to the conclusions that (1) speech perception does play a role in shaping phonological patterns, and (2) the relevant constraints are constraints on the distinctiveness of contrasts.

We have examined two types of phonological patterns that have been related to the perceptual properties of speech sounds: dispersion/enhancement and contextual neutralization. Both phenomena can be analyzed in terms of a preference for more distinct contrasts and the converse dispreference for indistinct contrasts. Dispersion of contrastive sounds in perceptual space is a direct consequence of maximization of distinctiveness, while enhancement phenomena simply reflect the fact that greater distinctiveness is often achieved by covarying physiologically unrelated articulations such as tongue body backness and lip rounding. Contextual neutralization also follows from the preference for distinct contrasts given the fact that the distinctiveness of a contrast type varies according to context. For example, obstruent voicing contrasts are more distinct before a sonorant than in other environments, so some languages only allow voicing contrasts before sonorants, neutralizing the contrast elsewhere.

Thus, the two patterns are fundamentally similar: a language with front unrounded and back rounded vowels avoids the less distinct contrasts between front rounded and back rounded vowels, and a language that only allows obstruent voicing contrasts before sonorants avoids the less distinct contrasts involving obstruent voicing in other contexts. Alternative analyses in terms of basic markedness constraints, perceptually-ranked faithfulness constraints, or sound change through misperception are more conservative in that they operate with the basic types of markedness and faithfulness constraints most widely used in OT phonology, but they cannot provide adequate accounts of the full range of perceptually-based phonological phenomena.

NOTES

1 I would like to thank David Pisoni, Robert E. Remez, and Donca Steriade for helpful comments on this chapter.

2 For more detailed introductions to OT, see Kager (1998) and McCarthy (2002).

3 It is common to specify central vowels as [+back, −round], in which cases these constraints are sufficient. If central vowels are distinguished from back unrounded vowels, a constraint against this class of vowels is required also.

4 The dotted line between the top two constraints in (3–4) indicates that the relative ranking of these constraints cannot be determined – that is, either ranking yields the desired result.

5 Articulatory effort is not necessarily equivalent to energy expenditure. Although this is usually assumed to be an important component of articulatory effort (e.g., Kirchner, 1998; Lindblom, 1983; Nelson, 1983), there may also be costs associated with precision, for example. The aspect of effort that is most relevant in the examples discussed here relates to the smoothness of movements – movements are hypothesized to be more difficult if they involve abrupt changes in direction. It has been observed that humans generally employ smooth trajectories in speech production (Perkell, 1997, p. 357) and in arm movements (e.g., Flash & Hogan, 1985; Uno, Kawato, & Suzuki, 1989). This preference has been attributed to minimization of energy expenditure (Nelson, 1983), but it has also been analyzed in terms of minimizing error in the face of noise internal to the motor control system (Harris & Wolpert, 1998).

6 Effort becomes a more significant factor where vowel duration is very short, and in the environment of consonants that place strong constraints on F2, such as palatalized and velarized consonants (Flemming, forthcoming).

7 Kuipers actually transcribes the Kabardian high vowel as [ə], the mid-vowel as [a], and the "long" low vowel as [ā], and Colarusso (1988) follows him in this. However, their descriptions, Colarusso's phonetic transcriptions, and acoustic data in Choi (1991) all indicate that the vowels are actually high and mid, respectively.

8 It might be suggested that vertical vowels are phonologically unspecified for [back] and [round] rather than being specified for the marked vowel qualities described here (Choi, 1992). However, such unspecified vowels only occur in the absence of F2 contrasts, so this would imply an even more dramatic change from a preference for peripheral vowels in F2 contrasts to a preference for otherwise unattested unspecified vowels where there is no contrast.

9 See Kingston and Diehl (1994) for a related argument that voicing-dependent perturbations of F_0 adjacent to stops are active enhancements of stop voicing contrasts, so these effects are reduced or absent where there is no voicing contrast.

10 References: German, Lithuanian, Russian, Sanskrit: Steriade (1997), Japanese: Ito (1989), Luganda: Tucker (1962), Selayarese: Mithun and Basri (1986), Gooniyandi: McGregor (1990), Miriwung: Hamilton (1996), Walmatjari: Hudson and Richards (1969).

11 Steriade proposes constraints of the form *αvoice/C that penalize obstruent voicing contrasts in a particular context, C. These constraints are ranked according to the richness of cues to voicing available in that context. These constraints are replaced here by

MINDIST constraints that refer directly to the cues that differentiate contrasting obstruents. This allows for variability in the cues realized in a given context, depending on the production strategy adopted (cf. Koontz-Garboden, 2002; Steriade, 1997).

12 In fact there are two basic types of obstruent "voicing" contrasts: fully voiced vs. voiceless unaspirated, and voiceless unaspirated vs. aspirated, so a more general analysis requires three levels of VOT (Flemming, 2002).

13 This analysis is structurally very similar to the one proposed in Lombardi (1995), but Lombardi employs a faithfulness constraint specific to pre-sonorant onsets.

14 DEPV must also be outranked by MAXC, the offending consonant is deleted rather than being rescued by vowel epenthesis. Deletion in triconsonantal clusters is observed in a number of languages, e.g., Korean (Kim & Shibatani, 1976).

15 It should be noted that these kinds of considerations properly motivate constraints requiring consonant *contrasts* to be realized adjacent to vowels (i.e., distinctiveness constraints), as discussed at length in Section 7.2.3. The limitations of basic markedness constraints are addressed further in Section 7.1.4.

REFERENCES

Anderson, V. (1997). The perception of coronals in Western Arrernte. *Proceedings of Eurospeech 1997: Fifth Conference on Speech Communication and Technology*, 1, 389–92.

Ashby, F. G., Boynton, G., & Lee, W. W. (1994). Categorization response time with multidimensional stimuli. *Perception & Psychophysics*, 55, 11–27.

Bender, B. W. (1968). Marshallese phonology. *Oceanic Linguistics*, 7, 16–35.

Benua, L. (1997). Transderivational identity. PhD dissertation, University of Massachusetts, Amherst.

Blevins, J. & Garrett, A. (1998). The origins of consonant-vowel metathesis. *Language*, 74, 508–56.

Boersma, P. (1998). Functional phonology. PhD dissertation, University of Amsterdam.

Booij, G. (1995). *The Phonology of Dutch*. Oxford: Oxford University Press.

Broselow, E. I. (1976). The phonology of Egyptian Arabic. PhD dissertation, University of Massachusetts, Amherst.

Butcher, A. (1995). The phonetics of neutralization: The case of Australian coronals. In J. W. Lewis (ed.), *Studies in General and English Phonetics: Essays in Honour of Professor J. D. O'Connor* (pp. 10–38). New York: Routledge.

Calabrese, A. (1988). Towards a theory of phonological alphabets. PhD dissertation, MIT.

Choi, J. D. (1991). An acoustic study of Kabardian vowels. *Journal of the International Phonetic Association*, 21, 1–12.

Choi, J. D. (1992). Phonetic underspecification and target interpolation: An acoustic study of Marshallese vowel allophony (*UCLA Working Papers in Phonetics* 82). PhD dissertation, University of California, Los Angeles.

Colarusso, J. (1988). *The Northwest Caucasian Languages: A Phonological Survey*. New York: Garland.

Colarusso, J. (1992). *A Grammar of the Kabardian Language*. Calgary: University of Calgary Press.

Côté, M.-H. (2000). Consonant cluster phonotactics: A perceptual approach. PhD dissertation, MIT (distributed as *MIT Dissertations in Linguistics*).

Dave, R. (1977). Retroflex and dental consonants in Gujarati. A palatographic and acoustic study. *Annual Report of the Institute of Phonetics, University of Copenhagen*, 11, 27–156.

Delattre, P. C., Liberman, A. M., Cooper, F. S., & Gerstman, L. J. (1952). An experimental study of the acoustic determinants of vowel color: Observations on one- and two-formant vowels synthesized from spectrographic patterns. *Word*, 8, 195–210.

Delgutte, B. & Kiang, N. Y. S. (1984). Speech coding in the auditory nerve IV: Sounds with consonant-like dynamic characteristics. *Journal of the Acoustical Society of America*, 75, 897–907.

Diehl, R. L. (1991). The role of phonetics in the study of language. *Phonetica*, 48, 120–34.

Dorman, M. F., Studdert-Kennedy, M., & Raphael, L. J. (1977). Stop-consonant recognition: Release bursts and formant transitions as functionally equivalent, context-dependent cues. *Perception & Psychophysics*, 22, 109–22.

Flash, T. & Hogan, N. (1985). The coordination of arm movements: An experimentally confirmed mathematical model. *Journal of Neuroscience*, 5, 1688–703.

Flemming, E. (1996). Evidence for constraints on contrast: The dispersion theory of contrast. *UCLA Working Papers in Phonology*, 1 (ed. C.-S. K. Hsu), 86–106.

Flemming, E. (2002). *Auditory Representations in Phonology*. New York: Routledge.

Flemming, E. (2004). Contrast and perceptual distinctiveness. In B. Hayes, R. Kirchner, & D. Steriade (eds.), *The Phonetic Bases of Markedness* (pp. 232–76). Cambridge: Cambridge University Press.

Fujimura, O., Macchi, M., & Streeter, L. A. (1978). Perception of stop consonants with conflicting transitional cues: A cross-linguistic study. *Language and Speech*, 21, 337–46.

Greenberg, S. (1995). Auditory processing of speech. In N. J. Lass (ed.), *Principles of Experimental Phonetics*. St Louis: Mosby.

Gregores, E. & Suárez, J. A. (1967). *A Description of Colloquial Guaraní*. The Hague: Mouton.

Hamilton, P. (1996). Constraints and markedness in the phonotactics of Australian aboriginal language. PhD dissertation, University of Toronto.

Harris, C. M. & Wolpert, D. M. (1998). Signal-dependent noise determines motor planning. *Nature*, 394, 780–4.

Henderson, J. B. & Repp, B. H. (1982). Is a stop consonant released when followed by another stop consonant? *Phonetica*, 39, 71–82.

Herbert, R. K. (1986). *Language Universals, Markedness Theory and Natural Phonetic Processes*. Berlin: Mouton de Gruyter.

Hudson, J. & Richards, E. (1969). The phonology of Walmatjari. *Oceanic Linguistics*, 8, 171–89.

Hume, E. (1998). The role of perceptibility in consonant/consonant metathesis. *Proceedings of the West Coast Conference on Formal Linguistics*, 17, 293–307.

Hume, E. & Johnson, K. (2001). A model of the interplay of speech perception and phonology. In E. Hume & K. Johnson (eds.), *The Role of Speech Perception in Phonology* (pp. 3–26). New York: Academic Press.

Ito, J. (1989). A prosodic theory of epenthesis. *Natural Language and Linguistic Theory*, 7, 217–59.

Iverson, G. K. & Salmons, J. C. (1996). Mixtec prenasalization as hypervoicing. *International Journal of American Linguistics*, 62, 165–75.

Jun, J. (1995). Perceptual and articulatory factors in place assimilation: An optimality-theoretic approach. PhD dissertation, UCLA.

Kager, R. (1998). *Optimality Theory*. Cambridge: Cambridge University Press.

Kawasaki, H. (1982). An acoustical basis for universal constraints on sound sequences. PhD dissertation, University of California, Berkeley.

Kellogg, W. N. (1931). The time of judgment in psychometric measures. *American Journal of Psychology*, 43, 65–86.

Kenstowicz, M. (1997). Base identity and uniform exponence: Alternatives to cyclicity. In J. Durand & B. Laks (eds.), *Current Trends in Phonology: Models and Methods* (pp. 363–93). Salford: University of Salford.

Kim, K.-O. and Shibatani, M. (1976). Syllabification phenomena in Korean. *Language Research*, 12, 91–8.

Kingston, J. & Diehl, R. L. (1994). Phonetic knowledge. *Language*, 70, 419–54.

Kirchner, R. (1998). An effort-based approach to consonant lenition. PhD dissertation, UCLA.

Kisseberth, C. (1970). On the functional unity of phonological rules. *Linguistic Inquiry*, 1, 291–306.

Kondo, Y. (1994). Targetless schwa: is that how we get the impression of stress timing in English? *Proceedings of the Edinburgh Linguistics Department Conference 1994*, 63–76.

Koontz-Garboden, A. (2002). Voicing contrasts in medial stop clusters. Unpublished manuscript, Stanford.

Kuipers, A. H. (1960). *Phoneme and Morpheme in Kabardian (Eastern Adyghe)*. Janua Linguarum, series minor, 8. The Hague: Mouton.

Ladefoged, P. & Maddieson, I. (1996). *The Sounds of the World's Languages*. Oxford: Blackwell.

Lass, R. & Anderson, J. M. (1975). *Old English Phonology*. Cambridge: Cambridge University Press.

Liljencrants, J. & Lindblom, B. (1972). Numerical simulation of vowel quality systems: The role of perceptual contrast. *Language*, 48, 839–62.

Lindblom, B. (1983). Economy of speech gestures. In P. F. MacNeilage (ed.), *The Production of Speech* (pp. 217–46). New York: Springer-Verlag.

Lindblom, B. (1986). Phonetic universals in vowel systems. In J. J. Ohala & J. J. Jaeger (eds.), *Experimental Phonology*. New York: Academic Press.

Lindblom, B. & Engstrand, O. (1989). In what sense is speech quantal? *Journal of Phonetics*, 17, 107–21.

Lisker, L. & Abramson, A. S. (1970). The voicing dimension: Some experiments in comparative phonetics. *Proceedings of the 6th International Congress of Phonetic Sciences* (pp. 563–7). Prague: Academia.

Liu, S. (1996). Landmark detection for distinctive feature-based speech recognition. *Journal of the Acoustical Society of America*, 100, 3417–30.

Lombardi, L. (1995). Laryngeal neutralization and syllable wellformedness. *Natural Language and Linguistic Theory*, 13, 39–74.

Lombardi, L. (1999). Positional faithfulness and voicing assimilation in Optimality Theory. *Natural Language and Linguistic Theory*, 17, 267–302.

Lynch, J. (1978). *A Grammar of Lenakel*. Pacific Linguistics, Series B, 55. Australian National University, Canberra.

Maddieson, I. (1984). *Patterns of Sounds*. Cambridge: Cambridge University Press.

Maiden, M. (1995). Vowel systems. In M. Maiden & M. Parry (eds.), *The Dialects of Italy* (pp. 7–14). London: Routledge.

McCarthy, J. J. (2002). *A Thematic Guide to Optimality Theory*. Cambridge: Cambridge University Press.

McGregor, W. (1990). *A Functional Grammar of Gooniyandi*. Amsterdam: John Benjamins.

Mithun, M. & Basri, H. (1986). The phonology of Selayarese. *Oceanic Linguistics*, 25, 210–54.

Nelson, W. L. (1983). Physical principles for economies of skilled movement. *Biological Cybernetics*, 46, 135–47.

Newman, S. (1944). *The Yokuts Language of California*. The Viking Fund Publications in Anthropology 2, New York: The Viking Fund.

Newton, B. (1972). *The Generative Interpretation of Dialect: A Study of Modern Greek Phonology*. Cambridge: Cambridge University Press.

Ní Chiosáin, M. & Padgett, J. (2001). Markedness, segment realization, and locality in spreading. In L. Lombardi (ed.), *Segmental Phonology in Optimality Theory* (pp. 118–56). Cambridge: Cambridge University Press.

Ohala, J. J. (1980). The application of phonological universals in speech pathology. In N. Lass (ed.), *Speech and Language: Advances in Basic Research and Practice, III* (pp. 75–97). New York: Academic Press.

Ohala, J. J. (1981). The listener as a source of sound change. *Papers from the Parasession on Language and Behavior*, Chicago Linguistics Society, 178–203.

Ohala, J. J. (1983). The origin of sound patterns in vocal tract constraints. In P. F. MacNeilage (ed.), *The Production of Speech* (pp. 189–216). New York: Springer.

Ohala, J. J. (1985). Around *Flat*. In V. Fromkin (ed.), *Phonetic Linguistics: Essays in Honor of Peter Ladefoged* (pp. 223–42). New York: Academic Press.

Ohala, J. J. (1990). The phonetics and phonology of aspects of assimilation. In J. Kingston & M. E. Beckman (eds.), *Papers In Laboratory Phonology I: Between the Grammar and Physics of Speech* (pp. 258–75). Cambridge: Cambridge University Press.

Ohala, J. J. (1993). The perceptual basis of some sound patterns. In D. A. Connell & A. Arvaniti (eds.), *Papers in Laboratory Phonology IV: Phonology and Phonetic Evidence* (pp. 87–94). Cambridge: Cambridge University Press.

Olive, J. P., Greenwood, A., & Coleman, J. (1993). *Acoustics of American English Speech: A Dynamic Approach*. New York: Springer-Verlag.

Perkell, J. S. (1997). Articulatory processes. In W. J. Hardcastle & J. Laver (eds.), *The Handbook of Phonetic Sciences* (pp. 333–70). Oxford: Blackwell.

Pisoni, D. B. & Tash, J. (1974). Reaction times to comparisons within and across phonetic categories. *Perception & Psychophysics*, 15, 285–90.

Plomp, R. (1975). Auditory analysis and timbre perception. In G. Fant & M. Tatham (eds.), *Auditory Analysis and Perception of Speech* (pp. 7–22). New York: Academic Press.

Podgorny, P. & Garner, W. R. (1979). Reaction time as a measure of inter- and intraobject visual similarity: Letters of the alphabet. *Perception & Psychophysics*, 26, 37–52.

Prince, A. & Smolensky, P. (1993) *Optimality Theory: Constraint Interaction in Generative Grammar*. Report no. RuCCS-TR-2, Rutgers University Center for Cognitive Science, New Brunswick, NJ.

Puppel, S., Nawrocka-Fisiak, J., & Krassowska, H. (1977). *A Handbook of Polish Pronunciation for English Learners*. Warsaw: Panstwowe Wydawnictwo Naukowe.

Redford, M. A. & Diehl, R. L. (1999). The relative perceptual distinctiveness of initial and final consonants in CVC syllables. *Journal of the Acoustical Society of America*, 106, 1555–65.

Robert-Ribes, J., Schwartz, J.-L., Lallouache, T., & Escudier, P. (1998). Complementarity and synergy in bimodal speech: Auditory, visual, and audio-visual identification of French oral vowels in noise. *Journal of the Acoustical Society of America*, 103, 3677–89.

Shadle, C. (1991). The effects of geometry on the source mechanisms of consonants. *Journal of Phonetics*, 19, 409–24.

Shepard, R. N. (1972). Psychological representation of speech sounds. In E. David & P. Denes (eds.), *Human Communication: A Unified View* (pp. 67–113). New York: McGraw-Hill.

Smeets, R. (1984). *Studies in West Circassian Phonology and Morphology*. Leiden: Hakuchi Press.

Smith, R. & Smith, C. (1971). Southern Barasano phonemics. *Linguistics*, 75, 80–5.

Spajić, S., Ladefoged, P., & Bhaskararao, P. (1994). The rhotics of Toda. *UCLA Working Papers in Phonetics*, 87, 35–66.

Steriade, D. (1995). Neutralization and the expression of contrast. Unpublished manuscript, UCLA.

Steriade, D. (1997). Phonetics in phonology: The case of laryngeal neutralization. *UCLA Working Papers in Linguistics*, 3, 25–146.

Steriade, D. (1999). Alternatives to syllable-based accounts of consonantal phonotactics. In O. Fujimura, B. D. Joseph, & B. Palek (eds.), *Proceedings of Linguistics and Phonetics 1998: Item Order in Language and Speech* (pp. 205–45). Prague: Karolinum Press.

Steriade, D. (2000). Paradigm uniformity and the phonetics-phonology boundary. In M. Broe & J. Pierrehumbert (eds.), *Papers in Laboratory Phonology 5: Acquisition and the Lexicon* (pp. 313–34). Cambridge: Cambridge University Press.

Steriade, D. (2001). Directional asymmetries in place assimilation. In E. Hume & K. Johnson (eds.), *The Role of Speech Perception in Phonology* (pp. 219–50). New York: Academic Press.

Steriade, D. (forthcoming). The phonology of perceptibility effects: The P-map and its consequences for constraint organization. In K. Hanson & S. Inkelas (eds.), *The Nature of the Word: Essays in Honor of Paul Kiparsky*. Cambridge, MA: MIT Press.

Stevens, K. N. (1985). Evidence for the role of acoustic boundaries in the perception of speech sounds. In V. A. Fromkin (ed.), *Phonetic Linguistics: Essays in Honor of Peter Ladefoged* (pp. 243–55). New York: Academic Press.

Stevens, K. N. (1998). *Acoustic Phonetics*. Cambridge, MA: MIT Press.

Stevens, K. N. & Blumstein, S. E. (1975). Quantal aspects of consonant production and perception: A study of retroflex consonants. *Journal of Phonetics*, 3, 215–33.

Stevens, K. N. & Blumstein, S. E. (1981). The search for invariant acoustic correlates of phonetic features. In P. D. Eimas & J. L. Miller (eds.), *Perspectives on the Study of Speech* (pp. 1–38). Hillsdale, NJ: Lawrence Erlbaum.

Stevens, K. N., Keyser, S. J., & Kawasaki, H. (1986). Toward a phonetic and phonological theory of redundant features. In J. S. Perkell & D. H. Klatt (eds.), *Invariance and Variability in Speech Processes* (pp. 426–49). Hillsdale, NJ: Lawrence Erlbaum.

Trubetzkoy, N. S. (1939). *Grundzüge de Phonologie*. Travaux du Cercle Linguistique de Prague, 7.

Tucker, A. N. (1962). The syllable in Luganda: A prosodic approach. *Journal of African Languages*, 1, 122–66.

Uno, Y., Kawato, M., & Suzuki, R. (1989). Formation and control of optimal trajectories in human multijoint arm movement: Minimum torque-change model. *Biological Cybernetics*, 61, 89–101.

van Bergem, D. R. (1994). A model of coarticulatory effects on the schwa. *Speech Communication*, 14, 143–62.

Vennemann, T. (1972). The theory of syllabic phonology. *Linguistiche Berichte*, 19, 1–18.

Westbury, J. & Keating, P. A. (1986). On the naturalness of stop consonant voicing. *Journal of Linguistics*, 22, 145–66.

Wright, R. (1996). Consonant clusters and cue preservation in Tsou. PhD dissertation, UCLA.

Wright, R. (2001). Perceptual cues in contrast maintenance. In E. Hume & K. Johnson (eds.), *The Role of Speech Perception in Phonology* (pp. 251–77). New York: Academic Press.

8 Acoustic Cues to the Perception of Segmental Phonemes

LAWRENCE J. RAPHAEL

8.1 Introduction

This paper reviews some of what is known – and, by default, some of what is not known – about the acoustic cues to the perception of segmental phonemes of human language. "Perception" in this context refers only to human responses to acoustic stimuli. It does not refer to algorithmic and other analyses of the acoustic signal that are used to sort phonemes into categories, although such analyses may be discussed when they have served as the basis for constructing experimental stimuli to test human perception.

The major focus in this paper will be on the identity of the acoustic cues, that is, what they are, rather than on how they may be processed. This distinction is not an easy one to make. Indeed, in some instances it is not possible to maintain it. There are several reasons for this, including the fact that multiple cues to a percept may function as part of an integrative process and often enter into trading relationships with one another. Then, too, the research claiming primacy for one speech cue or another is often driven by theoretical concerns that implicate processing as evidence. Although discussion of the relative importance of speech cues continues, as it has for the past half century, more recent research has tended to recognize that primacy may shift from one cue to another because of such factors as phonetic context, speaker, and the linguistic experience of listeners. Consequently, a common theme throughout much of what follows is that several cues to the perception of a particular speech sound are often available to listeners and that listeners are capable of using some or all of them.

The organization of this description of acoustic cues follows a rationale that is dictated, in general, by speech articulation: It begins with the stop consonants (the sounds with the greatest articulatory constrictions/obstructions to airflow), and proceeds through the fricatives (and affricates), nasals, semivowels, and vowels/diphthongs (the sounds usually described has having the most open, unobstructed articulations).

The reader will notice that the lion's share of space has been devoted to the stop consonants and the vowels. This is merely a reflection of the fact that these sounds have attracted more attention – and more controversy – from and among speech scientists than any other classes of sounds.

8.2 The Acoustic Cues: Consonants

8.2.1 Acoustic cues to the stop consonants

8.2.1.1 Manner

The acoustic cues to the stop manner of articulation were first established mainly by using spectrograms as the basis for creating synthetic speech stimuli. One of the most noticeable acoustic features associated with stops in spectrograms is the vertical spike marking the release, and it was a synthetic approximation to this spike that was first used in the initial perceptual studies of stops by Liberman and his colleagues at Haskins Laboratories (Cooper et al., 1952; Liberman, Delattre, & Cooper, 1952). The experimenters observed that "stops as a class could be approximated satisfactorily by representing the sounds as vertical bars . . ." (Liberman et al., 1952, p. 500). Indeed, it is clear that in the earliest stages of research, the experimenters equated stop manner with stop release and its acoustic man-ifestation and recognized its presence in the acoustic signal as a cue.

When copying spectrographic features as synthetic patterns, experimenters soon noticed the vowel formant transitions following the release of initial stops. They discovered that voiced stop + vowel syllables could be successfully synthesized without the presence of a burst (at least before vowels with a relatively high F1) as long as the frequency of the first formant transition was rising (Cooper et al., 1952; Liberman et al., 1954). Thus, a rising first formant joined the inventory of stop manner cues. In order to synthesize voiceless stops, however, the experimenters found that they had to reduce the extent of the F1 transition. That they could reduce this cue and still obtain stop percepts was a function of the CV syllables they were creating. That is, the (relative) silence that accompanies stop closure and the rapid increase in signal intensity following release were both represented in the synthetic stimuli. When the experimenters synthesized nasal + vowel syllables, the nasal resonances replaced the silence and the rise in the F1 transition was completely eliminated. This confirmed the initial hypothesis that the rising F1 transition did, indeed, have cue value for stop manner.

The importance of the relative silence of the closure interval as a cue to stop perception was not established experimentally for several years (Bastian, 1962; Bastian, Eimas, & Liberman, 1961; Dorman, Raphael, & Liberman, 1979; Raphael & Dorman, 1980). This was done by inserting a short interval of silence between the frication of [s] and the onset of the formant transitions for [l] in the word *slit*, which caused listeners to hear it as *split*.

The salience of the silent interval as a cue to stop manner has been exploited by many subsequent studies focusing on such matters as perceptual coherence, trading relationships between and among cues, and the relationship of speech production to speech perception (Best, Morrongiello, & Robson, 1981; Dorman et al., 1979; Fitch et al., 1980; Hodgson & Miller, 1996; Nittrouer & Crowther, 2001; Summerfield & Bailey, 1977; Summerfield et al., 1981).

8.2.1.2 Place

The acoustic cues to the place of articulation of stop consonants were first established in the 1950s. Early work from Haskins Laboratories using synthetic stimuli identified the contributions of burst "frequency," and the transitions of the second and third formants following stop release (and preceding stop closure) (Harris et al., 1958; Liberman et al., 1952; Liberman et al., 1954).

It should be understood that the earliest perceptual study of burst frequency, which employed stimuli synthesized on the pattern playback, included schematic stop bursts that were of uniform and limited bandwidth (600 Hz) and duration (15 ms). Some examples of the stimuli are shown in Figure 8.1. The synthetic vowels that followed the bursts were steady-state and of uniform duration (300 ms). The early findings of the experiment were most notable for the observation that the perception of the stop bursts was, to a certain extent, context-dependent. That is, although high-frequency bursts (above 3000 Hz) and very low-frequency bursts

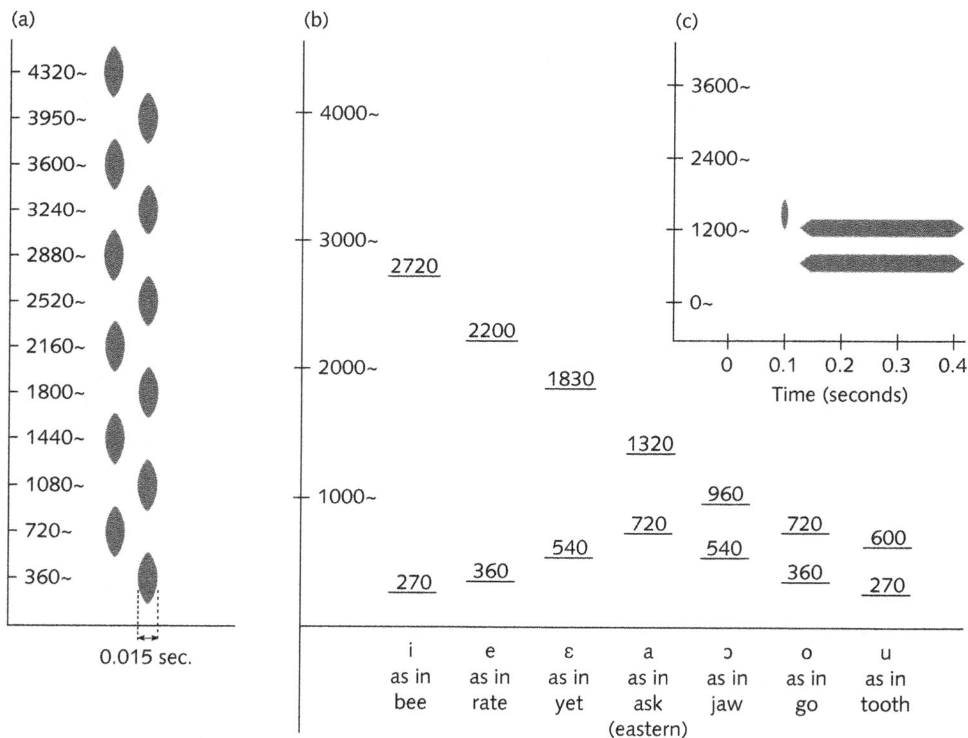

Figure 8.1 Synthetic stimuli used by Liberman, Delattre, & Cooper (1952) to determine the effect of combining stop bursts of different frequencies with two-formant vowels. (a) shows the frequencies of the synthetic bursts; (b) shows the frequencies of the vowel formants that were combined with each of the various bursts; (c) shows one of the synthetic syllables.

Source: A. M. Liberman, P. C. Delattre, & F. S. Cooper (1952). The role of selected stimulus variables in the perception of the unvoiced stop consonants. *American Journal of Psychology*, 65, 497–516. Reprinted with the permission of the *American Journal of Psychology*.

(360 Hz) were perceived consistently as /t/ and /p/, respectively, a mid-frequency burst (1440 Hz) was perceived as /p/ before /i/ and /u/, but as /k/ before /a/ (see also Schatz, 1954).

Lacking evidence of an invariant cue to place of articulation in the stop burst, experimenters turned their attention to the formant transitions, especially the transitions of the second formant (F2), between stops and the vowels that followed them (Liberman et al., 1954). They constructed an experimental continuum of synthetic two-formant CV stimuli in which the starting frequency of the second formant of the vowels [i, e, ɛ, a, ɔ, o, u] was varied in equal 120 Hz steps from 480 Hz below, 720 Hz above the steady-state F2 of the following vowel. The stimuli contained no release-bursts. Examples of these stimuli are shown in Figure 8.2.

In general, listeners reported hearing labial stops when the F2 transitions were rising in frequency, alveolar stops when the transitions were flat or slightly falling, and velar stops when the transitions were steeply falling. This generality, however, was not free from contextual effects. The direction and amount of frequency change of F2 were largely determined by the nature of the following vowel. Before front

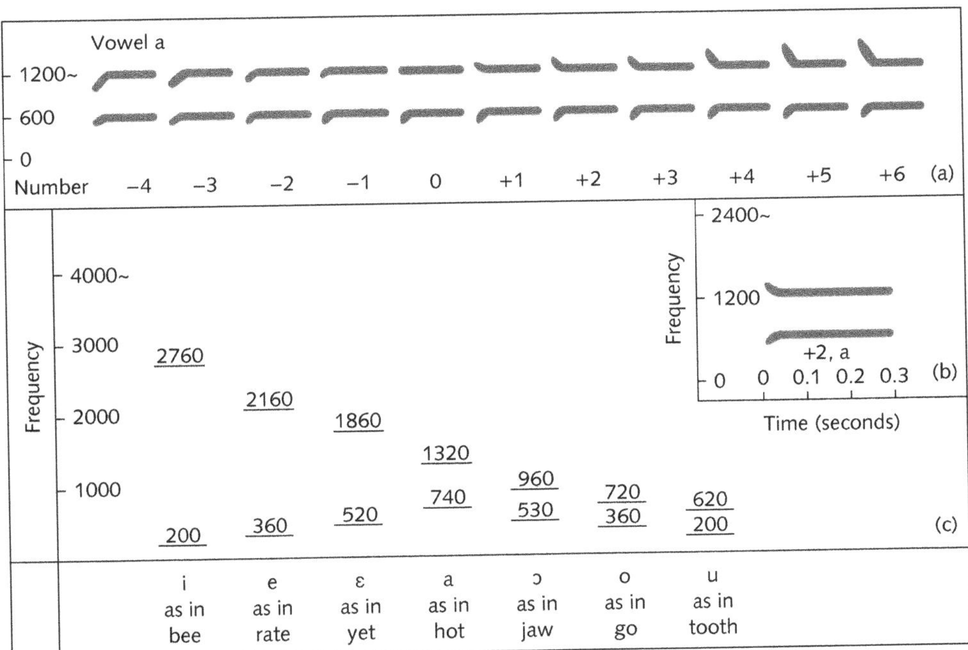

Figure 8.2 Two-formant synthetic patterns used by Liberman et al. (1954) to study the effect of varying the F2 transition on the identification of place of articulation for the voiced stops. (a) shows the vowel /a/ with a full range of transitions. (b) shows a single pattern. (c) shows the two-formant patterns for various vowels which were combined with the range of transitions shown in (a).

Source: A. M. Liberman, P. C. Delattre, F. S. Cooper, & L. J. Gerstman (1954). The role of consonant-vowel transitions in the perception of the stop and nasal consonants. *Psychological Monographs*, 68(8) (Whole No. 379). Reprinted with permission of *Psychological Monographs: General and Applied* and the American Psychological Association.

vowels with high second formant frequencies, the transitions were neither flat nor slightly falling, but rose in frequency. Moreover, the amount of frequency change, even when its direction fell within the scope of the general description, displayed considerable variability from one vowel context to another.

The effort to find an explanation for the unitary percepts that were cued by variable formant transitions led to the development of the concept of the locus (Delattre, Liberman, & Cooper, 1955). Using the Pattern Playback, Delattre et al. first synthesized two-formant CV patterns with steady-state second formants. They determined the F2 frequencies that cued the strongest stop percepts for each place of articulation. Next, using a uniform F1, they created an experimental continuum in which the F2 transitions varied from steeply rising to steeply falling. Examples of the stimuli are shown in Figure 8.3. Delattre et al. found that when the transitions all pointed to a particular point (the locus) on the frequency scale (the frequency of one of the three steady-state formants used earlier), listeners consistently identified the same place of articulation. Listeners did so, however, only if the onset frequencies of the F2 transitions were located at some point intermediate to the frequencies of the locus and the following steady-state second formants. When the F2 transitions originated at the locus frequency, listener's responses to the stimuli varied across all three places of stop articulation.

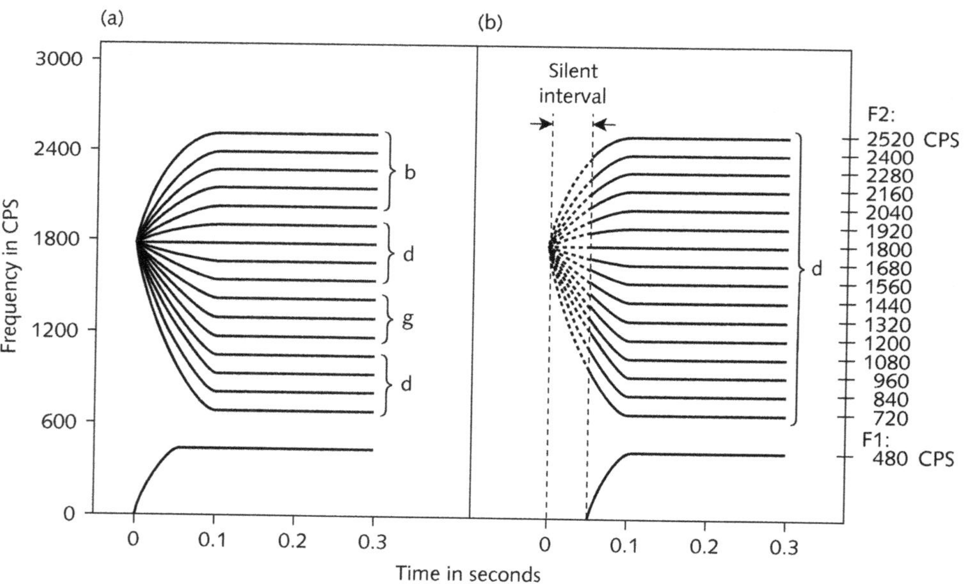

Figure 8.3 Synthetic stimuli used by Delattre, Liberman, & Cooper (1955) to determine the locus of the alveolar stop /d/. (a) shows the varyingly perceived identity of two-formant patterns with a rising F1 and with F2 originating at 1,800 Hz. When the onset of the formant transitons was delayed by 50 ms, as in (b), all the patterns were heard as /d/.

Source: P. C. Delattre, A. M. Liberman, & F. S. Cooper (1955). Acoustic loci and transitional cues for consonants. *Journal of the Acoustical Society of America*, 27, 769–73. Reprinted with permission from the *Journal of the Acoustical Society of America*.

The concept of the locus as a solution to the problem of a lack of invariance between percept and acoustic signal set the stage for many of the theoretically-driven debates of the following decades concerning the perception of place of articulation in stop consonants. These debates have focused on two major issues. The first is whether or not there are invariant acoustic cues in the speech signal; the second is concerned with the relative importance of dynamic vs. static cues. Neither of these issues has been resolved to date.

In a response to two studies by Cole and Scott (1974a, 1974b) that proposed invariant properties for stop bursts, Dorman, Studdert-Kennedy, and Raphael (1977) cross-spliced bursts and vowels produced by two speakers in a wide variety of vocalic contexts. Dorman et al. concluded that bursts and transitions were functionally equivalent cues that varied in relative effectiveness depending on context and that, in most instances, speakers used all the available cues when categorizing sounds.

The averaged short-term spectrum following stop release emerged as another possible invariant feature for stop place identification from a series of studies using synthetic speech (Blumstein & Stevens, 1979, 1980; Stevens & Blumstein, 1978). The results of the perceptual experiments led Blumstein and Stevens to the conclusion that the gross shape of the spectrum within a 10–20 ms interval following the release of a syllable-initial voiced stop contains invariant and sufficient information for the identification of place of articulation (see Figure 8.4).

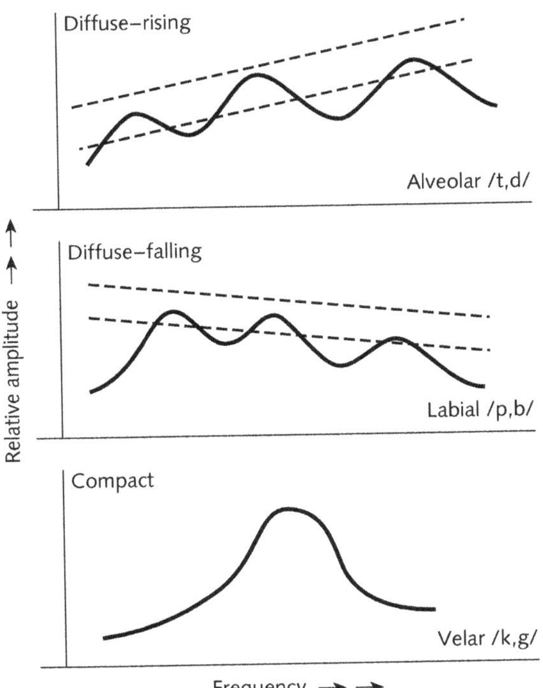

Figure 8.4 Stevens and Blumstein's (1978) averaged short-term spectra, displaying distinctive and invariant patterns that distinguish stop place of articulation.

Blumstein and Stevens (1980) also suggested that the acoustic invariance they found in the gross shape of the onset spectrum could lead to a "simple and direct model of speech perception at the segmental level" (p. 661), which would be applicable both to adults and to infants as they acquire speech and language. Support for their proposal concerning children (if not infants) was provided by Ohde et al. (1995) who partially replicated Blumstein and Stevens' (1980) study, using the same synthesis parameters. Testing groups of adults and children of 5, 6, 7, 9, and 11 years of age, they also found that the short-term average spectrum following stop release contained sufficient information for place identification for adults and children and that neither group relied on formant transitions to categorize stimuli.

A study by Lahiri, Gewirth, and Blumstein (1984) took a revisionist stance with regard to the invariant property and cue value of gross spectral shape after determining that gross spectral shape was not a successful classifier of stop place for /b/ and /d/ in Malayalam, French, and English. The authors proposed an alternative invariant property, the "change in the distribution of spectral energy from the burst onset to the onset of voicing" (p. 391), which was successfully used to classify the stops in all three languages. Using synthetic speech, they tested the perceptual efficacy of this property by creating "conflicting-cue stimuli" in which the frequency characteristics of the formant transitions for a given place of articulation remained unchanged while the formant amplitudes were adjusted at the onsets of either the burst or phonation to reflect a different place of articulation. Lahiri et al. reported that listeners labeled the stops on the basis of the adjusted amplitude characteristics of the formants (rather than on the information contained in the formant transitions).

A recent replication of the Lahiri et al. (1984) study by Dorman and Loizou (1996), using natural speech, produced sharply conflicting results. Listeners were reported to have classified the place of articulation of the labial and alveolar stops on the basis of the formant transitions. Dorman and Loizou cautioned against assuming that a metric that can be used to classify sounds will be effective as a perceptual cue in natural speech, which contains cues that may be absent from synthetic stimuli.

This caution is also implied in a perceptual study of locus equations by Fruchter and Sussman (1997) They take the position that locus equations are not specifiers of place of articulation for stops, although they are a "partially distinctive cue" (p. 2998) that is important in some, but not all, vowel contexts. The locus equations that they tested were derived from acoustic analyses of natural speech CVCs in which F2 onset frequencies are plotted against F2 frequencies at the midpoint of the following vowel (Sussman, McCaffrey, & Matthews, 1991). The 1997 study, which was preceded by several that did not directly test perception (Sussman et al, 1991; Sussman, Fruchter, & Cable, 1995; Sussman, Hoemeke, & Ahmed, 1993), used burstless, synthetic CV stimuli in which the frequencies of the second formant onsets and the steady-state formants of the following vowels varied in a fashion analogous to the stimuli used by Liberman et al. (1954). In addition, and unlike the earlier (1954) study, three sets of F3 onset frequencies, each appropriate to one of the three places of articulation, were used for each of the ten vowel contexts. The results of the perceptual experiment led Fruchter and Sussman to conclude that "F2 onset and F2 vowel, in combination, are significant cues for the perception of stop consonant place of articulation" (p. 3007).

It is important to note that although the term "locus equation(s)" is redolent of the "acoustic locus" (Delattre et al., 1955), it does not refer to a specific point on the frequency scale that has no instantiation in the acoustic signal. Similarly, although the acoustic information from which a locus equation is derived occurs in much the same time period as the averaged short-term spectra (Blumstein & Stevens, 1979, 1980; Stevens & Blumstein, 1978) and the change in the distribution of spectral energy from the burst onset to the onset of voicing (Lahiri et al., 1984), the locus equation is not an average, does not incorporate frequency information from the burst, and is not proposed as a strictly invariant cue (Fruchter & Sussman, 1997, p. 2998).

The results of the studies described in this section indicate that, although the potential cues to the perception of stop place of articulation are generally well known, their relative importance varies according to context, making it impossible to establish primacy. There seems to be a consensus that listeners can and do rely on whatever cues are available. Given the fact that place information is supplied by many components of the acoustic signal and that many or most of these components are simultaneously available, we might suppose that listeners rely on those acoustic cues which are most salient in a particular context, or which resolve the ambiguity resulting from the context-conditioned weakening of other cues. The search for a single invariant cue will, no doubt, continue. Those proposed so far, even if they are, in fact, invariant, have shown some of the same sensitivity to context that the patently variable cues show. And, of course, the explanatory value of an invariant cue that does not convey information unambiguously in a particular context would be seriously compromised.

8.2.1.3 Voicing

Research into the identification of the acoustic cues to the phonological opposition of cognate pairs of stops has a pedigree almost as long as that of place-cue research. The acoustic cues to "voicing" distinctions, like those to place identification, are numerous and vary from context to context. The relevant context in this case, however, is determined more by position within a syllable or di-syllable and by syllabic prominence than by the identities of the neighboring vowels. That is, the importance and settings of voicing cues for stops are closely related to whether (1) the stop initiates a syllable, terminates a syllable, or occurs intervocalically, and (2) whether the syllable precedes a heavily stressed vowel or a weakly stressed vowel.

Descriptions of the bases for the voicing opposition are often somewhat obscure because the terms "voiced" and "voiceless" are indiscriminately used in both the phonetic and phonological domains. In the former, they are often intended to mean, respectively, "phonated" and "unphonated" or to indicate the presence or absence of a periodic source.

In the latter, they are simply category labels which can describe oppositions that are cued by the presence or absence of phonation and/or aspiration – or by combinations of these with other cues of greater or lesser importance.

English is typical of languages that use both phonation and aspiration to differentiate stop voicing categories, depending on context. For instance, in syllable-initial position before a heavily stressed vowel, English /p, t, k/ are usually described as voiceless and aspirated, whereas /b, d, g/ are described as voiced and unaspirated. Early tape-cutting experiments investigated the perception of pre-vocalic stops preceded by /s/ (as in *spill, still, skill*) that are often described as voiceless and unaspirated (Lotz et al., 1960; Reeds & Wang, 1961). When the /s/-frication was deleted, English-speaking listeners reported hearing words initiated by "voiced" stops (*bill, dill, gill*), not voiceless stops (*pill, till, kill*). The experimenters concluded that, in the edited stimuli, "aspiration is a more dominant cue than voicing in the perceptual separation of these two classes of consonants." Speakers of other languages (e.g., Spanish, Hungarian) did not perceive the edited stimuli as did the English speakers. Rather, they classed them as "voiceless."

The differences in perception between speakers of different languages reflect differences in the constituents of the phonological units of each language. In English, in absolute initial position, both /p, t, k/ and /b, d, g/ are usually voiceless (i.e., phonation does not occur during the closure period and release of the stop). Listeners must therefore rely on the presence vs. absence of aspiration to cue the "voicing" class of the stop. Since /p, t, k/ are unaspirated when preceded by /s/, they are identified as /b, d, g/ when the preceding /s/ is deleted. In contrast, phonation does occur during the closure for Spanish and Hungarian /b, d, g/, but not for /p, t, k/, when they occur in initial position. Because neither class of sounds is aspirated, listeners must rely on the presence vs. absence of phonation to cue the "voicing" class of a stop.

The relationship between phonation and aspiration was captured in a series of studies that proposed the acoustic measure of voice onset time (VOT) as a means of categorizing stop consonant cognates and which tested VOT continua perceptually (Lisker & Abramson, 1964, 1967, 1970). These studies built on an earlier experiment carried out by Liberman, Delattre, and Cooper (1958) in which they found that synthetic stimuli were perceived as /b, d, g/ or as /p, t, k/ depending on the duration and starting frequency of the first formant transition. When closure voicing and a full rising first formant were present, listeners perceived voiced stops. When the closure voicing was eliminated and as the F1 transition was "cut back" (which delayed its onset and increased its onset frequency), listeners' perceptions shifted to /p, t, k/, even when the F2 and F3 transitions were excited by a harmonic source. The experimenters also presented evidence that the delay in F1 onset, without a change in onset frequency, was sufficient to cue the voicing distinction.

The VOT measure is the temporal difference (in ms) between the onset of phonation and transient noise burst of stop release. VOT values are negative when phonation precedes stop release (voicing lead) and positive when phonation onset occurs after stop release (voicing lag) (Lisker & Abramson, 1964).

After constructing a synthetic continuum of VOT stimuli ranging from –150 ms to +150 ms for use in perceptual experiments, Lisker and Abramson found that speakers of English, Spanish and Thai divided the continuum into stop categories appropriate to their languages (Lisker & Abramson, 1970). Speakers of English differentiated stops with short voicing lag from those with long voicing lag. Speakers of Spanish, which like English, is a two-category language with regard to voicing distinctions, differentiated stops with voicing lead from those with short lag. The speakers of Thai differentiated three categories, corresponding to the three-way voicing opposition of their language: voicing lead vs. short lag vs. long lag.

It should be understood that synthetic VOT continua usually consist of stimuli that undergo a series of changes that make them quite different from other continua in which there may be only a single independent variable. The stimuli in VOT continua may contain many of the acoustic results of varying the temporal relationship between supra-glottal events and glottal states. Thus, stimuli may differ from each other not only with regard to the timing of phonation onset, but also with regard to the presence and duration of aspiration, the extent of F1 frequency change, the duration of the attenuation of the F1 transition, and other associated features, many of which have minor but measureable cue value. VOT stimuli are, therefore, best thought of as a complex of acoustic cues, rather than as a single acoustic cue. Figure 8.5 illustrates a set of synthetic stimuli differing in VOT.

Although the role of F0 perturbation in cueing the voiced-voiceless distinction is generally considered secondary, its effects are measurable in experimental conditions. F0 has been found to be level or to rise after the release of voiced stops and to fall following the release of a voiceless stop (Lehiste & Peterson, 1961; Ohde, 1984). Experimenters have found that they could affect listeners' perceptions using stimuli in which VOT is either ambiguous (Abramson & Lisker, 1965; Whalen et al., 1990) or not ambiguous (Whalen et al., 1993).

Researchers have proposed a number of acoustic cues to the phonological voicing oppositions of stops in syllable-final position. As in the case of the cues to place of articulation, the salience of each proposed cue varies with context, and

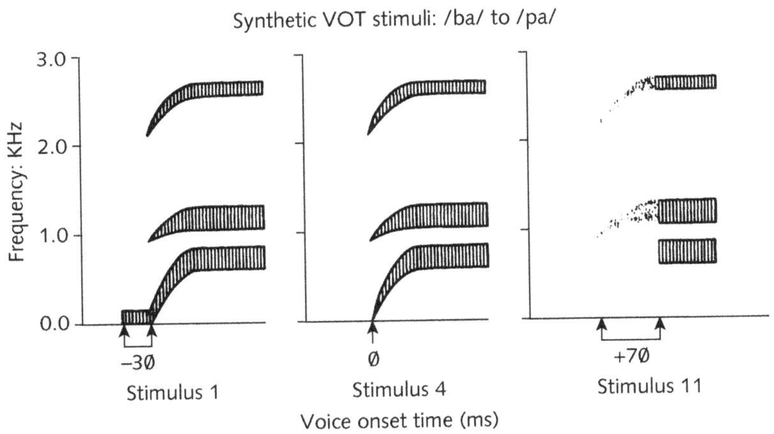

Figure 8.5 Three schematic stimuli from an 11-step synthetic VOT continuum showing the effect of varying the timing of voicing onset relative to release. Stimulus 1, with a VOT value of −30 ms contains closure voicing, a full rising F1 transition, and periodically excited transitions in F2 and F3. Stimulus 4, with a zero onset VOT, is identical to stimulus 1, except for the absence of closure voicing. Stimulus 11, with a VOT value of +70 ms contains an attenuated F1 transition and aperiodically excited transitions in F2 and F3.

combinations of cues may also serve to disambiguate percepts that are conveyed by cues that are, individually, weak in a particular context. The presence vs. absence of phonation during syllable-final stop closure, as one might expect, can carry considerable weight in many contexts (Hillenbrand et al., 1984; Hogan & Rozsypal, 1980; Lisker, 1981; Parker, 1974; Raphael, 1981).

The status of preceding vowel duration and vocalic nuclei in general as a perceptual cue has been the focus of many studies, some of which have employed natural speech stimuli, others synthetic stimuli, and some a mixture of both. The bulk of the available data have been gathered for English, where the durational differences between vowels and vocalic nuclei preceding voiced vs. voiceless stops are unusually large compared to many other languages. The results of several studies in which preceding vowel duration was varied found it to be a sufficient cue to the voicing distinction (Krause, 1982; O'Kane, 1978; Raphael, 1972; Raphael, Dorman, & Liberman, 1980; Raphael et al., 1975). In contrast, other studies have challenged the sufficiency of vowel duration (Hogan & Rozsypal, 1980; Revoile et al., 1982; Wardrip-Fruin, 1982) and have proposed alternative cues, either as supplements to vowel duration or as primary cues.

Several studies have suggested that the offset characteristics of vowels (especially the F1 transition) preceding final stop consonants are important to the perception of the voicing (Parker, 1974; Walsh & Parker, 1981, 1983; Walsh, Parker, & Miller, 1987). Although O'Kane (1978), in an experiment using natural CVC stimuli, found "no empirical support" for Parker's (1974) claims and held that vowel duration was the major cue, Revoile et al. (1982) edited the waveforms of vowels in natural CVC syllables, eliminating vowel duration differences before voiced and voiceless stops. They found that exchanging formant transitions between voiced and voiceless consonants caused listeners to identify voicing class according to the original context of the transitions. Fischer and Ohde (1990), using synthetic CVC stimuli, investigated the cue values of vowel duration, frequency of F1 transition offset, and rate of F1 change. They found that both vowel duration and the frequency of F1 offset affected listeners' perception of voicing class. The relative salience of the cues appeared to be dependent on the frequency of the F1 steady-state: transition offset was more salient when the F1 of the preceding vowel was high; vowel duration was more salient when F1 was low.

Crowther and Mann (1992) used synthetic CVC stimuli to investigate the effectiveness of vocalic duration and F1 offset frequency as cues to final stop voicing in speakers of English, Japanese, and Mandarin. The native English speakers were most responsive to differences in vocalic duration compared to the Japanese and, especially, to the Mandarin speakers. F1 offset frequency produced smaller perceptual effects.

The release-burst of final stops has been investigated in a number of studies, and, for once, there seems to be general agreement that the presence of a burst contributes to the perception of a voiceless stop (Malécot, 1958; Wang, 1959; Wolf, 1978). Both Wang and Malécot found that replacing the releases of final /p, t, k/ with those of /b, d, g/ tended to shift listeners' perceptions to the voiced stops; they attributed this result to the fact that there was a considerable amount of phonation during the closures of the voiceless stops.

The durational difference between voiced (shorter) and voiceless (longer) stop closures has been proposed as a perceptual cue, especially for medial (intervocalic) stops (see below), because the difference is more marked than in final position, where the cue is less salient when stops are released (Raphael, 1981). Port (1981) and Port and Dalby (1982) proposed that there is constant ratio of closure duration to vowel duration that provides important information about stop voicing. Barry (1979), however, maintains that the ratio is not constant and is conditioned by distribution within utterances and other cues to voicing (see also Massaro & Cohen, 1983; Repp & Williams, 1985).

The bulk of the perceptual studies reported here (as well as many others not reported) have used isolated CVC syllables as stimuli. It is, of course, true that stops occur far more frequently followed and/or preceded by other sounds than in absolute initial or final position (i.e., preceded or followed by silence) (Pickett, Bunnell, & Revoile, 1995). Although a few studies have investigated stop voicing in contexts that are at least slightly more extended than isolated CVCs (e.g., Raphael, 1981; Repp & Williams, 1985), there are studies of intervocalic stops that provide information about a context that differs from the "standard" CVC.

The speech cue that is, perhaps, most often remarked on is the closure duration of intervocalic stops. Using natural speech utterances of minimal pairs such as *rupee–ruby* and *rapid–rabid*, Lisker (1957a, 1981) varied the duration of the closure interval for intervocalic stops in post-stress position from 40 to 150 ms. He found that shorter durations (around 60 ms) cued voiceless percepts, whereas longer durations (around 130 ms) cued voiced percepts. It is, however, the case that all phonation occurring during the closure intervals of the originally voiced stops was deleted from the test stimuli. With closure phonation present, voiceless percepts are unlikely to be elicited even at the longer values of closure duration. More recently, Cazals and Palis (1991) obtained results similar to Lisker's for the part of their study dealing with normal subjects.

The multiplicity of cues to voicing in stops and their variable effectiveness, depending on context, is similar to the case for cues to place and manner of articulation. Once again, it seems reasonable to assume that listeners can avail themselves of the presence of multiple cues to a percept and use as much of the information in the speech signal as they need to make a decision about voicing class.

8.2.2 *Acoustic cues to the fricative and affricate consonants*

8.2.2.1 *Manner*

Having considered stops, we will now turn our attention to fricatives and affricates. Fricatives are formed by sending the airstream through a narrow constriction which causes it to become turbulent, generating an aperiodic source of sound. The aperiodicity, or frication, is the defining manner cue to fricatives. The frication of fricatives is often of relatively greater duration than other aperiodic segments found in the acoustic signal for speech (e.g., stop bursts, aspiration following stop release), although identification is possible from noise segments as short as 30–50 ms (Gerstman, 1957; Jongman, 1989).

Affricates are sequences of stops and fricatives that listeners integrate perceptually into a single phonological entity. The sequence of acoustic segments generated by the stop + fricative sequence thus contains cues for both stops and fricatives. That is, there is a period of relative silence as a result of the complete occlusion of the vocal tract, followed by a transient burst noise that is contiguous with a period of frication generated as the articulators move into position for the fricative element of the sound. Affricates are, in fact, distinguished from fricatives by the presence of a silent closure interval and by the fact that the period of frication is shorter in duration than the frication of fricatives. The fricative-affricate distinction is also marked by a difference in rise time. The stop occlusion of the affricate causes an increase in intraoral pressure which underlies the rapid rise time that serves as a cue to affricate manner. The fricatives, in contrast, have a more gradual onset of energy (a longer rise time) that serves as a manner cue. These manner cues have been shown to participate in a trading relationship (Dorman et al., 1979; Dorman, Raphael, & Eisenberg, 1980).

8.2.2.2 Place

The cues to fricative place of articulation derive from two sources. The first, which occurs within the time course of the sounds themselves is the spectrum of the fricative noise. The so-called "grooved" (lingua-alveolar and post-alveolar) fricatives (/s, z, ʃ, ʒ/) can be distinguished from the "slit" (labio- and lingua-dental) fricatives /θ, ð, f, v/ on the basis of a concentration of high-frequency energy for the former and a more even spread of frequency throughout the spectrum for the latter (Harris, 1958). Intensity differences also cue the distinction between the anteriorly and posteriorly articulated fricatives. The relatively higher intensity of /s, z, ʃ, ʒ/ results from the presence of a significant resonating cavity in front of the constrictions that are formed to produce them; the absence of such a resonating cavity for /θ, ð, f, v/ causes their intensities to be relatively lower. In addition, the spectrum of the most intense portion of frication for the lingua-alveolar grooved fricatives /s, z/ distinguishes them perceptually from the post-alveolar grooved fricatives /ʃ, ʒ/: The lingua-alveolars are cued by aperiodic energy with a lower border around 4–5 kHz, whereas the post-alveolars are cued by frication that extends as low as 2–3 kHz (Heinz & Stevens, 1961).

The second source of cues to fricative place of articulation resides, as in the case of the stops, in the formant transitions (especially those of the second formant) that precede and/or follow the fricative noise. The transitions associated with the lingua-alveolars and alveolar-palatals are not as critical for place identification (as those of the labio- and lingua-dentals) because of the difference in the spectra of the fricative noise. They have, however, been shown to determine the identification of place when the spectrum of fricative noise is ambiguous between /s, z/ and /ʃ, ʒ/ (Mann & Repp, 1980; Whalen, 1981). Because the noise spectra of the labio- and lingua-dental fricatives are quite similar to each other (and of relatively low intensity), the associated formant transitions are more critical in disambiguating them (Harris, 1958), although even these transitions often do not enable listeners to make highly accurate identifications.

Once again, we note that affricate place of articulation is cued by a combination of the acoustic features that contribute to stop and fricative place identification. Because English has only two affricates, both post-alveolar, the cues to place of articulation are not as important as they are in languages with affricates at two or more places of articulation: When English-speaking listeners perceive stop-plus-fricative sequences as typical affricates, they are constrained to identify place of articulation as post-alveolar.

8.2.2.3 *Voicing*

The primary acoustic cue to the voicing distinction for syllable-initial and intervocalic fricatives and affricates is the presence vs. absence of phonation during the duration of frication. A cue related to the phonatory contrast resides in the differences between the greater intensity of frication in /θ, f, s, ʃ/ as opposed to /v, ð, z, ʒ/. Presumably, the abducted vocal folds during the production of the voiceless fricatives allow a greater volume of air to pass through the glottis into the oral constriction. The interruptions to or restriction of glottal air flow in the case of the voiced fricatives reduce the volume of air flow and thus the intensity of the turbulent source at the point of constriction.

For fricatives occurring in syllable-final position, durational cues can assume greater importance, especially in a language (such as in English) in which final fricatives can be partially or wholly unphonated (devoiced). An inverse relationship exists between the duration of frication of a final fricative and the duration of the vocalic segment that precedes it. That is, the difference between vocalic durations (long before voiced fricatives; short before voiceless fricatives) is much the same as in the case of vocalic segments preceding voiced and voiceless stops, and the durations of syllable-final voiceless fricatives are greater than those of their voiced cognates in the same context. Perceptual experiments using synthetic speech and hybrid synthetic-natural speech stimuli in monosyllables have indicated that the vowel duration, the duration of fricative noise, and the ratio between them can cue the voicing distinction (Denes, 1955; Raphael, 1972), although the salience of preceding vowel duration as a cue in connected speech (outside of pre-pausal position) has raised some question concerning its cue value (Stevens et al., 1992).

The voicing distinction between the affricates is cued by a combination of the acoustic features that cue the voicing oppositions between voiced and voiceless stops and fricatives, the particular cues involved varying with context.

8.2.3 *Acoustic cues to the nasal consonants*

8.2.3.1 *Manner*

The production of nasal sounds requires a lowered velum and an occluded oral cavity. The nasal resonance generated by such an articulation accounts for the primary cue to nasal manner: a low-frequency (below 500 Hz) nasal formant or "murmur" (Fujimura, 1962). Because of the occluded oral cavity and the extension of the vocal tract into a nasal side-branch that is a highly damped resonator, nasal consonants are characterized by anti-resonances that render the sounds comparatively weak, and this weakness itself contributes to the impression of nasality. The relatively sluggish movements of the velum are likely to insure the spread of the nasal murmur to surrounding segments, which also cues the perception of nasal manner (Ali et al., 1971).

8.2.3.2 Place

The occluded oral cavity in nasal production attenuates the oral resonances that distinguish /m/ from /n/ from /ŋ/. Thus, although each nasal has a distinctive spectrum, the acoustic properties varying with nasal place contrasts are not particularly prominent. This fact, coupled with similarity of the (relatively highly damped) nasal murmur for all the sounds makes it difficult for listeners to distinguish among them. Listeners must therefore rely on the formant transitions into and out of the nasal articulation to aid in identification (Kurowski & Blumstein, 1984; Malécot, 1956; Repp, 1986). There seems to be a general consensus among speech researchers that the formant transitions take precedence over the nasal spectrum as cues to place.

8.2.4 Acoustic cues to the semivowel consonants

8.2.4.1 Manner

The semivowels are often subdivided into two classes: glides (/w, j/) and liquids (/r, l/). They do, however, have enough articulatory-acoustic features in common to justify a common label. As that label suggests, the sounds bear a strong relationship to vowels with regard to a *relatively* unconstricted articulation and a prominent formant structure. In particular, the similarity is even stronger between semivowels and diphthongs because of the articulatory movements and the changes in formant frequencies that the movements generate in both classes of sounds (Liberman et al., 1956). Furthermore, the movements of the articulators and the formants are internal to the segments themselves and not, as in the case of most other consonants, found in neighboring segments.

The vocalic nature of the semivowels and their similarity to diphthongs has led investigators to identify the cues to semivowel manner in terms of contrasts with diphthongs. One such contrast resides in the brief, steady-state segment (30–50 ms) that initiates semivowels in prevocalic position but which is not found at diphthong onset. (O'Connor et al., 1957). A second contrast concerns the rate of formant frequency change, which is faster for semivowels than for diphthongs but not as fast as the formant transitions preceding or following stops (Liberman et al., 1956).

8.2.4.2 Place

The specific changes in formant frequency that cue place of articulation for semivowels are often described in relation to the vowel each most closely resembles. For instance, the steady-state onset of /w/ is similar in formant structure to the vowel /u/, whereas the analogous portion of /j/ resembles /i/. The F1 and F2 transitions for prevocalic /w/, then, will rise, given their low frequencies compared to almost all other vowels. For prevocalic /j/, F1 will rise, but F2 and F3 will fall. Formant movements appear to cue the perception of semivowel glides only in pre-vocalic and intervocalic context for speakers of English, a language in which glides are not distributed as perceptual entities in pre-consonantal or pre-pausal contexts.

The semivowel liquids, /r/ and /l/, on the other hand, can occur before consonants and silence, as well as in pre- and intervocalic positions. The formant structures of their steady-state segments resemble those of a central vowel such as /ɝ/. The cue which distinguishes them from each other resides in the third formant which changes in frequency into or out of an /r/-segment, but which remains relatively stable and becomes somewhat attenuated in the environment of /l/ (Lisker, 1957b; O'Connor et al., 1957).

8.3 The Acoustic Cues: Vowels

There has never been any serious doubt that formants are the primary cues to the perception of vowels. Researchers were aware from spectrographic analysis that formant frequencies varied from vowel to vowel for a given speaker (Peterson & Barney, 1952). Attempts to synthesize identifiable vowels using only the two lowest steady-state formants (of relatively great duration: 250–300 ms) were very successful (Delattre et al., 1952). Nonetheless, the authors realized that other information, such as the third and higher formants and/or F0, might also contribute to the identification of vowels. Because they used stimuli comprising only F1 and F2, and because those stimuli were synthesized at a monotone (120 Hz) F0, they could not reach firm conclusions concerning the cue value of those components.

Spectrographic evidence, however, provided information that raised critical questions about the perception of vowels. Some of that information and the questions it led to were:

1. Formant frequencies for the same vowel are highly variable, being dependent on vocal tract size (Peterson & Barney, 1952) and context (including rate of speech, lexical and sentence stress placement). *Given this variability, how do listeners manage to recognize different sets of formant frequencies as the same vowel?*
2. The acoustic structure of vowels contains more information than just the frequencies of F1 and F2. F3 and higher formants and F0 are also present when speakers utter vowels. *Even if speakers rely primarily on F1 and F2 to identify vowels, does the other acoustic information within the vowel contribute to vowel recognition, and does it help to explain the ability of listeners to identify different formant patterns as the same vowel?*
3. In connected speech, vowel context extends beyond the formant patterns that characterize vowels, including not only neighboring consonants within the same syllable, but also vowels and consonants in neighboring syllables. *Do these extended contexts contribute to listeners' identification of vowels?*
4. In connected speech most vowels, especially those that are weakly stressed and/or intrinsically short, are briefer (often much briefer) in duration than 250–300 ms, the duration used by Delattre et al. (1952) in their study of vowel perception. The range of durational variation is also conditioned by the tempo of articulation. *Given the variability of vowel duration and of the tempo of context that co-varies with duration, do listeners identify vowels on the basis of duration, and can they identify shorter vowels as well as longer ones?*

5 In connected speech, formant frequencies are rarely steady-state for very long (if at all) as they were in the 1952 study by Delattre et al. *Given the continuously variable nature of vowel formant frequencies, can listeners identify vowels as accurately when their formant structure is changing as when their formant structure is stable?*

An answer often given to the first question, concerning listeners' ability to recognize different formant patterns as the same vowel, is that listeners are able to "normalize" the various patterns of formant frequency. Normalization schemes based on acoustic information wholly contained within the vowel are often characterized as "intrinsic" (Neary, 1989). That is, they attempt to provide answers to the second question asked above concerning the use of information other than F1 and F2 in vowel identification.

We can divide the studies of intrinsic normalization into two groups. The first group comprises those studies that present models based on statistical evidence showing that the inclusion of certain acoustic features aside from the lowest two formant frequencies, or that a different treatment of formant information, reduces the amount of overlap among the vowels in simple F1/F2 plots (e.g., Peterson & Barney, 1952). Overlap reduction has been attained by using the ratios between adjacent formants and between F1 and F0 using various scaling techniques (e.g., logarithmic, Bark, mel) as well as absolute formant frequency values in Hertz (Hillenbrand & Gayvert, 1993; Miller, 1989; Syrdal, 1985; Syrdal & Gopal, 1986). Modeling techniques that rely on formant ratios have a long pedigree, Lloyd's (1890, 1896) work being the first reported instance (cf. Halberstam, 1998; Miller, 1989).

The second group of intrinsic normalization studies, more relevant to our concern here with the perception of speech cues, reports data from perceptual experiments in which acoustic features intrinsic to the vowel are systematically manipulated. Varying F0 and F3, Fujisaki and Kawashima (1968) obtained boundary shifts in perception between synthesized /o/ and /a/ and between /e/ and /u/ (see also Hirihara & Kato, 1992 for boundary shifts conditioned by F0 changes). Lehiste and Meltzer (1973) and Ryalls and Lieberman (1982) varied the F1–F0 ratio and obtained changes in correct identifications of vowels. Traunmüller (1981) observed that perception of one-formant synthetic vowel height/openness was primarily conditioned by the F1–F0 relationship rather than by the frequency of F1 alone (but see Hoemeke & Diehl, 1994; and Fahey, Diehl, & Traunmüller, 1996, for qualifications of this finding). Ainsworth (1975) and Neary (1989), found that doubling F0 caused increases in perceived values of F1 and F2 in synthetic stimuli. Neary (1989) also varied the frequency of F3 and found that it had a smaller effect on perception than the changes in F0.

A study of the relative effects of F0 and of formant energy higher than F2 on the perception of synthetic "phonated" and "whispered" vowels was conducted by Nusbaum and Morin (1992). Their results, like those of Neary (1989), indicated that although F0 and formants above F2 contribute to vowel identification, F0 is the more important cue. More recently, Halberstam (1998) partially replicated and extended Nusbaum and Morin's (1992) study using natural speech stimuli. The whispered stimuli were found to have the expected elevated formant frequencies compared to the phonated vowels (Eklund & Traunmüller, 1997; Kallail & Emanuel, 1984; Peterson, 1961). Results confirmed the effects for F0 and

(and formants above F2) found in previous studies, but also indicated that the higher formants were more salient as cues to whispered than to phonated vowels.

The experimental literature, then, contains a great deal of evidence supporting the idea that acoustic information internal to the vowel, other than F1 and F2, contributes to vowel identification and so may aid in the normalization process. But what of information that is extraneous to the vowel, the extended contexts mentioned in question (3) above? Normalization schemes based on acoustic information found in the extended context are often characterized as "extrinsic" (Neary, 1989).

The extrinsic normalization process was first formulated by Joos (1948), who proposed that hearing a small sample of vowels by a given speaker will enable the listener to estimate the dimensions of the F1/F2 space of that speaker and so estimate the location of any vowel produced within the space. That vocalic context in preceding syllables can affect listeners' perception of a vowel in a target syllable was demonstrated by Ladefoged and Broadbent (1957). They synthesized the sentence "Please say what this word is" followed by a target /bVt/ syllable that contained one of four vowels. The identification of the vowel in the target syllable varied depending on the formant frequencies used in the preceding sentence. Other studies have demonstrated similar effects of precursor vowels (Ainsworth, 1975; Dechovitz, 1977; Neary, 1989).

The effectiveness of precursor vowels as "cues" to vowel perception is supported by the fact that vowels are identified more accurately in blocked-speaker conditions than in mixed-speaker conditions (Assman, Neary, & Hogan, 1982; Macchi, 1980; Strange et al., 1976). It should be noted, however, that mixed-speaker conditions can result in high rates of correct identification (Assman et al., 1982; Macchi, 1980). The fourth question (above) concerns vowel duration, an acoustic feature that is not extrinsic to the vowel. Leaving the aside the obvious case of vowel systems which contain phonologically opposed long (geminate) and short versions of the same vowels, we might ask if the difference between intrinsically long and and instrinsically short vowels in a language such as English (Peterson & Lehiste, 1960) contributes to identification.

Gay (1970) found that synthetic stimuli with the same amount of change in second formant frequency were perceived as monophthongs at short durations but as diphthongs at long durations. The effect of a carrier sentence was investigated by Verbrugge and Shankweiler (1977). Using natural speech stimuli, they found that the vowels in rapidly articulated /pVp/ syllables were perceived less accurately when they were heard in a carrier sentence spoken at a slow rate than when presented in the original, rapidly spoken carrier sentences or in isolation.

Johnson and Strange (1982) constructed natural speech stimuli using a carrier sentence spoken at a fast and at a slower (normal) rate, into which a /tVt/ syllable was embedded. They presented listeners with the original sentences, the excised /tVt/ syllables, and hybrid stimuli consisting of the rapid version of the carrier sentence followed by either the fast or the slow version of the /tVt/ syllable. They found that listeners made more identification errors for the intrinsically long vowels when they were preceded by the rapid version of the carrier sentence than by the slower carrier sentence or than when they were presented in isolation.

Using natural speech /bVb/ stimuli, Strange, Jenkins, and Johnson (1983) created "silent center" stimuli by deleting the central portions of the vowels.

Listeners heard the silent center syllables and the excised centers of the vowels at their original durations and at durations that were fixed within each (silent center, isolated center) condition. Manipulating the durational information evoked higher error rates for the identification of isolated vowel centers. Error rates increased only minimally as the result of manipulating the durations of the silent center stimuli.

The results of the well-known "silent center" experiments of Strange and Jenkins (Jenkins, Strange, & Edman, 1983; Strange et al., 1983; Strange, 1989) provide an answer to the fifth question asked above: Listeners are able to identify vowels quite accurately using only the cues contained in the formant transitions to and from the central portion of the vowel. Strange (1999) points out that "in some cases, listeners identified the vowels in Silent-Center syllables as well as they did the vowels in the original unmodified syllables" (p. 164).

Although it is clear that listeners can identify vowels that are produced in isolation with relatively steady-state formants, that they can also do so using only the dynamic information found in formant transitions should not be surprising. Isolated vowels are rarely heard outside of speech laboratories and courses in phonetics and linguistics. Most of the time, by far, listeners have to perceive vowels spoken in the context of running speech, where, as we have said, steady-state formants are rarely, if ever, found. It is reasonable to assume that if listeners could not use such dynamic information, they would have great difficulty in perceiving vowels accurately, at least as they are heard in the usual forms of social communication.

8.4 Concluding Remarks

Over the past half century the concept of the speech cue has evolved in disparate ways. We have seen how experimenters initally assumed a rather simple relationship between speech cues and phonetic percepts, one in which a single acoustic feature would invariably elicit a particular phonetic response from listeners. As experimenters gathered more data, often with the aid of increasingly sophisticated technology, this simple view of the speech cue was abandoned. It became evident that the acoustic signal was replete with numerous redundant features arising from the complex articulatory activity that generates speech sounds, and that listeners are able to use those acoustic features that are consistently associated with a particular phonetic entity in order to identify it. Lisker's (1986) study that identified 16 cues to the opposition of /b/-/p/ in intervocalic context is only one illustration of the extensive redundancy to be found in the acoustic speech signal. Thus the "speech cue" became a "constellation" of cues, each of which, if varied, could affect the location of the boundaries between phonetic/phonological categories.

In some instances a single speech cue among many has been assigned general primacy, but in many others primacy has been found to vary, shifting among the constituent cues depending on the phonetic context(s) in which a particular sound occurs. The notion of primacy has been further weakened by the realization that trading relations exist among cues to the same phonetic percept.

Although the simplest sort of invariant relationship between cue and percept is not to be found, many researchers have refused to abandon invariance as an explanatory principle, raising it, instead, to a more abstract level by identifying invariant features derived from temporally integrated analyses of acoustic properties. The auditory response to these properties has been proposed as the basis for the identification of phonetic segments.

More recently, researchers have begun to use the statistical analysis of the acoustic properties of the speech signal in an attempt to predict the performance of listeners on perceptual tasks. Early work focused on explanations of listener identification of isolated vowels and syllables (Neary, 2003). Other research has explored the speed that infants learn the phonetic properties of unfamiliar languages (Kuhl, 2003; Morgan, White, & Kirk, 2003).

It remains to be seen if researchers can specifiy the distributional properties of the speech signal that must underlie the predictive power of these statistical models, especially if they are to be applied to extended samples of speech that comprise many segments. Whatever the outcome, it would appear that the notion of the speech cue is undergoing yet another transformation, one that removes it from the constraints of invariance, but which also may be less reliant on the responses of listeners to experimental manipulation of specific properties of the acoustic structure of the speech signal.

REFERENCES

Abramson, A. S. & Lisker, L. (1965). Voice onset time in stop consonants: Acoustic analysis and synthesis. *Proceedings of the Fifth International Congress on Acoustics*, Liege, A51.

Ali, L., Gallagher, T., Goldstein, J., & Daniloff, R. (1971). Perception of coarticulated nasality. *Journal of the Acoustical Society of America*, 49, 538–40.

Ainsworth, W. A. (1975). Intrinsic and extrinsic factors in vowel judgments. In G. Fant & M. Tatham (eds.), *Auditory Analysis and Perception of Speech* (pp. 103–13). London: Academic Press.

Assman, P. F., Nearey, T. M., & Hogan, J. T. (1982). Vowel identification: Orthographic, perceptual, and acoustic aspects. *Journal of the Acoustical Society of America*, 71, 675–989.

Barry, W. J. (1979). Complex encoding in word-final voiced and voiceless stops. *Phonetica*, 36, 361–72.

Bastian, J. (1962). Silent intervals as closure cues in the perception of stops. *Haskins Laboratories, Speech Research and Instrumentation*, 9, Appendix F.

Bastian, J., Eimas, P., & Liberman, A. (1961). Identification and discrimination of phonemic contrast induced by silent interval. *Journal of the Acoustical Society of America*, 33, 842(A).

Best, C. T., Morrongiello, B. A., & Robson, B. (1981). Perceptual equivalence of acoustic cues in speech and nonspeech perception. *Perception & Psychophysics*, 29, 199–211.

Blumstein, S. E. & Stevens, K. N. (1979). Acoustic invariance in speech production: Evidence from measurements of the spectral characteristics of stop consonants. *Journal of the Acoustical Society of America*, 66, 1001–17.

Blumstein, S. E. & Stevens, K. N. (1980). Perceptual invariance and onset spectra for stop consonants in different vowel environments. *Journal of the Acoustical Society of America*, 67, 648–62.

Cazals, Y. & Palis, L. (1991). Effect of silence duration in intervocalic velar plosive on voicing perception for normal and hearing-impaired speakers. *Journal of the Acoustical Society of America*, 89, 2916–21.

Cole, R. A. & Scott, B. (1974a). The phantom in the phoneme: Invariant cues for stop consonants. *Perception & Psychophysics*, 15, 101–7.

Cole, R. A. & Scott, B. (1974b). Toward a theory of speech perception. *Psychological Review*, 81, 348–74.

Cooper, F. S., Delattre, P. C., Liberman, A. M., Borst, J. M., & Gerstman, L. J. (1952). Some experiments on the perception of synthetic speech sounds. *Journal of the Acoustical Society of America*, 24, 507–606.

Crowther, C. S. & Mann, V. (1992). Native language factors affecting use of vocalic cues to final consonant voicing in English. *Journal of the Acoustical Society of America*, 92, 711–22.

Dechovitz, D. (1977). Information conveyed by vowels: A confirmation. *Haskins Laboratories Status Reports on Speech Research*, SR 51/52, 213–19.

Delattre, P. C., Liberman, A. M., & Cooper, F. S. (1955). Acoustic loci and transitional cues for consonants. *Journal of the Acoustical Society of America*, 27, 769–73.

Delattre, P. C., Liberman, A. M., Cooper, F. S., & Gerstman, L. J. (1952). An experimental study of the acoustic determinants of vowel color: observations on one- and two- formant vowels synthesized from spectrographic patterns. *Word*, 8, 195–210.

Denes, P. (1955). Effect of duration on perception of voicing. *Journal of the Acoustical Society of America*, 27, 761–4.

Dorman, M. F. & Loizou, P. C. (1996). Relative spectral change and formant transitions as cues to labial and alveolar place of articulation. *Journal of the Acoustical Society of America*, 100, 3825–30.

Dorman, M. F., Raphael, L. J., & Eisenberg, D. (1980). Acoustic cues for a fricative-affricate contrast in word-final position. *Journal of Phonetics*, 8, 397–405.

Dorman, M. F., Raphael, L. J., & Liberman, A. M. (1979). Some experiments on the sound of silence in phonetic perception. *Journal of the Acoustical Society of America*, 65, 1518–32.

Dorman, M. F., Studdert-Kennedy, M., & Raphael, L. J. (1977). Stop consonant recognition: Release bursts and formant transitions as functionally equivalent, context-dependent cues. *Perception & Psychophysics*, 22, 109–22.

Eklund, I. & Traunmüller, H. (1997). Comparative study of male and female whispered and phonated versions of the long vowels of Swedish. *Phonetica*, 54, 1–21.

Fahey, R. P., Diehl, R. L., & Traunmüller, H. (1996). Perception of back vowels: Effects of varying F1-F0 Bark distance. *Journal of the Acoustical Society of America*, 99, 2350–7.

Fischer, R. M. & Ohde, R. N. (1990). Spectral and durational properties of front vowels as cues to final stop-consonant voicing. *Journal of the Acoustical Society of America*, 88, 1250–9.

Fitch, H., Halwes, T., Erickson, D., & Liberman, A. M. (1980). Perceptual equivalence of two acoustic cues for stop-consonant manner. *Perception & Psychophysics*, 27, 343–50.

Fruchter, D. & Sussman, H. M. (1997). The perceptual relevance of locus equations. *Journal of the Acoustical Society of America*, 102, 2997–3008.

Fujimura, O. (1962). Analysis of nasal consonants. *Journal of the Acoustical Society of America*, 34, 1865–75.

Fujisaki, H. & Kawashima, T. (1968). The roles of pitch and higher formants in the perception of vowels. *IEEE Audio Electroacoustics*, AU-16 1, 73–7.

Gay, T. (1970). A perceptual study of American English diphthongs. *Language and Speech*, 13, 65–88.

Gerstman, L. J. (1957). Perceptual dimensions for the friction portions of certain speech sounds. Unpublished doctoral dissertation, New York University.

Halberstam, B. (1998). Vowel normalization: The role of fundamental frequency and upper formants. Unpublished doctoral dissertation, City University of New York.

Harris, K. S. (1958). Cues for the discrimination of American English fricatives in spoken syllables. *Language and Speech*, 1, 1–7.

Harris, K. S., Hoffman, H. S., Liberman, A. M., Delattre, P. C., & Cooper, F. S. (1958). Effect of third-formant transitions on the perception of the voiced stop consonants. *Journal of the Acoustical Society of America*, 30, 122–6.

Heinz, J. M. & Stevens, K. N. (1961). On the properties of the voiceless fricative consonants. *Journal of the Acoustical Society of America*, 33, 589–96.

Hillenbrand, J. & Gayvert, R. T. (1993). Vowel classification based on fundamental frequency and formant frequencies. *Journal of Speech & Hearing Research*, 36, 694–700.

Hillenbrand, J., Ingrisano, D. R., Smith, B. L., & Flege, J. E. (1984). Perception of the voiced-voiceless contrast in syllable-final stops. *Journal of the Acoustical Society of America*, 76, 18–26.

Hirihara, T. & Kato, H. (1992). The effect of F0 on vowel identification. In Y. Tohkura, E. Vatikiotis-Bateson, & Y. Sagisaka (eds.), *Speech Perception, Production and Linguistic Structure* (pp. 88–111). Burke, VA: IOS Press.

Hodgson, P. & Miller, J. L. (1996). Internal structure of phonetic categories: Evidence for within-category trading relations. *Journal of the Acoustical Society of America*, 100, 565–76.

Hoemeke, K. A. & Diehl, R. L. (1994). Perception of vowel height: The role of F1-F0 distance. *Journal of the Acoustical Society of America*, 96, 661–74.

Hogan, J. T. & Rozsypal, A. J. (1980). Evaluation of vowel duration as a cue for the voicing distinction in the following word-final consonant. *Journal of the Acoustical Society of America*, 67, 1764–71.

Jenkins, J. J., Strange, W., & Edman, T. R. (1983). Identification of vowels in "vowelless" syllables. *Perception & Psychophysics*, 34, 441–50.

Johnson, T. L. & Strange, W. (1982). Perceptual constancy of vowels in rapid speech. *Journal of the Acoustical Society of America*, 72, 1761–70.

Jongman, A. (1989). Duration of fricative noise required for identification of English fricatives. *Journal of the Acoustical Society of America*, 85, 1718–25.

Joos, M. (1948). Acoustic phonetics. *Language*, 24, supplement 2.

Kallail, K. J. & Emanuel, F. W. (1984). An acoustic comparison of isolated whispered and phonated vowel samples produced by adult male subjects. *Journal of Phonetics*, 12, 175–86.

Krause, S. E. (1982). Vowel duration as a perceptual cue to postvocalic consonant voicing in young children and adults. *Journal of the Acoustical Society of America*, 71, 990–5.

Kuhl, P. K. (2003). Early language acquisition: Statistical learning and social learning. *Journal of the Acoustical Society of America*, 114, 2445(A).

Kurowski, K. & Blumstein, S. E. (1984). Perceptual integration of the murmur and formant transitions for place of articulation in nasal consonants. *Journal of the Acoustical Society of America*, 76, 383–90.

Ladefoged, P. & Broadbent, D. E. (1957). Information conveyed by vowels. *Journal of the Acoustical Society of America*, 29, 98–104.

Lahiri, A., Gewirth, L., & Blumstein, S. E. (1984). A reconsideration of acoustic invariance for place of articulation in diffuse stop consonants: Evidence from a cross-language study. *Journal of the Acoustical Society of America*, 76, 391–404.

Lehiste, I. & Meltzer, D. (1973). Vowel and speaker identification in natural and synthetic speech. *Language and Speech*, 16, 356–64.

Lehiste, I. & Peterson, G. E. (1961). Some basic considerations in the analysis of intonation. *Journal of the Acoustical Society of America*, 33, 419–23.

Liberman, A. M., Delattre, P. C., & Cooper, F. S. (1952). The role of selected stimulus variables in the perception of the unvoiced stop consonants. *American Journal of Psychology*, 65, 497–516.

Liberman, A. M., Delattre, P. C., & Cooper, F. S. (1958). Some cues for the distinction between voiced and voiceless stops in initial position. *Language and Speech*, 1, 153–67.

Liberman, A. M., Delattre, P. C., Cooper, F. S., & Gerstman, L. J. (1954). The role of consonant-vowel transitions in the perception of the stop and nasal consonants. *Psychological Monographs*, 68(8) (Whole No. 379).

Liberman, A. M., Delattre, P. C., Gerstman, L. J., & Cooper, F. S. (1956). Tempo of frequency change as a cue for distinguishing classes of speech sounds. *Journal of Experimental Psychology*, 52, 127–37.

Lisker, L. (1957a). Closure duration and the intervocalic voiced-voiceless distinction in English. *Language*, 33, 42–9.

Lisker, L. (1957b). Minimal cues for separating /w, r, l, y/ in intervocalic position. *Word*, 13, 257–67.

Lisker, L. (1981). On generalizing the *Rapid-Rabid* distinction based on silent gap duration. *Haskins Laboratories Status Reports on Speech Research*, SR-54, 127–32.

Lisker, L. (1986). "Voicing" in English: A catalogue of acoustic features signaling /b/ versus /p/ in trochees. *Language and Speech*, 29, 3–11.

Lisker, L. & Abramson, A. S. (1964). A cross-language study of voicing in initial stops: Acoustic measurements. *Word*, 20, 384–422.

Lisker, L. & Abramson, A. S. (1967). Some effects of context on voice onset time in English stops. *Language and Speech*, 10, 1–28.

Lisker, L. & Abramson, A. S. (1970). The voicing dimension: Some experiments in comparative phonetics. *Proceedings of the Sixth International Congress of Phonetic Sciences, Prague, 1967* (pp. 563–7). Prague: Academia Publishing House of the Czechoslovak Academy of Sciences.

Lloyd, R. J. (1890). *Some Researches into the Nature of Vowel-Sound*. Edinburgh: Turner & Dunnet.

Lloyd, R. J. (1896). The genesis of vowels. *Transactions of the Royal Society of Edinburgh*, 1896, 972–3.

Lotz, J., Abramson, A. S., Gerstman, L. J., Ingemann, F., & Nemser, W. J. (1960). The perception of stops by speakers of English, Spanish, Hungarian, and Thai: A tape-cutting experiment. *Language and Speech*, 3, 71–6.

Macchi, M. J. (1980). Identification of vowels spoken in isolation versus vowels spoken in consonantal context. *Journal of the Acoustical Society of America*, 68, 1636–42.

Malécot, A. (1956). Acoustic cues for nasal consonants: An experimental study involving a tape-splicing technique. *Language*, 32, 274–84.

Malécot, A. (1958). The role of releases in the identification of released final stops. *Language*, 34, 370–80.

Mann, V. A. & Repp, B. H. (1980). Influence of vocalic context on perception of the /ʃ/-/s/ distinction. *Perception & Psychophysics*, 28, 213–28.

Massaro, D. W. & Cohen, M. M. (1983). Consonant/vowel ratio: An improbable cue in speech. *Perception & Psychophysics*, 33, 501–5.

Miller, J. D. (1989). Auditory-perceptual interpretation of the vowel. *Journal of the Acoustical Society of America*, 85, 2114–33.

Morgan, J. L., White, K. S., & Kirk, C. (2003). Distributional and statistical bases of allophonic groupings. *Journal of the Acoustical Society of America*, 114, 2445(A).

Nearey, T. M. (1989). Static, dynamic, and relational properties in vowel perception. *Journal of the Acoustical Society of America*, 85, 2088–113.

Nearey, T. M. (2003). Explicit pattern recognition models for speech perception. *Journal of the Acoustical Society of America*, 114, 2445(A).

Nittrouer, S. & Crowther, C. S. (2001). Coherence in children's speech perception. *Journal of the Acoustical Society of America*, 110, 2129–40.

Nusbaum, H. C. & Morin, T. M. (1992). Paying attention to differences among talkers. In Y. Tohkura, E. Vatikiotis-Bateson, & Y. Sagisaka (eds.), *Speech Perception, Production and Linguistic Structure* (pp. 113–23). Burke, VA: IOS Press.

O'Connor, J. D., Gerstman, L. J., Liberman, A. M., Delattre, P. C., & Cooper, F. S. (1957). Acoustic cues for the perception of initial /w, j, r, l/ in English. *Word*, 13, 25–43.

Ohde, R. N. (1984). Fundamental frequency as an acoustic correlate of stop consonant voicing. *Journal of the Acoustical Society of America*, 75, 224–30.

Ohde, R. N., Haley, K. L., Vorperian, H. K., & McMahon, C. W. (1995). A developmental study of the perception of onset spectra for stop consonants in different vowel environments. *Journal of the Acoustical Society of America*, 64, 3800–12.

O'Kane, D. (1978). Manner of vowel termination as a perceptual cue to the voicing of postvocalic stop consonants. *Journal of Phonetics*, 6, 311–18.

Parker, F. (1974). The coarticulation of vowels and stop consonants. *Journal of Phonetics*, 2, 211–21.

Peterson, G. (1961). Parameters of vowel quality. *Journal of Speech & Hearing Research*, 4, 10–29.

Peterson, G. & Barney, H. (1952). Control methods used in a study of vowels. *Journal of the Acoustical Society of America*, 24, 175–84.

Peterson, G. & Lehiste, I. (1960). Duration of syllable nuclei in English. *Journal of the Acoustical Society of America*, 32, 693–703.

Pickett, J. M., Bunnell, H. T., & Revoile, S. G. (1995). Phonetics of intervocalic consonant perception: Retrospect and prospect. *Phonetica*, 52, 1–40.

Port, R. F. (1981). Linguistic timing factors in combination. *Journal of the Acoustical Society of America*, 69, 262–74.

Port, R. F. & Dalby, J. (1982). Consonant/vowel ratio as cue for voicing in English. *Perception & Psychophysics*, 32, 141–52.

Raphael, L. J. (1972). Preceding vowel duration as a cue to the perception of the voicing characteristic of word-final consonants in American English. *Journal of the Acoustical Society of America*, 51, 1296–1303.

Raphael, L. J. (1981). Durations and contexts as cues to word-final cognate opposition in English. *Phonetica*, 38, 126–47.

Raphael, L. J. & Dorman, M. F. (1980). Silence as a cue to the perception of syllable-initial and syllable-final stop consonants. *Journal of Phonetics*, 8, 269–75.

Raphael, L. J., Dorman, M. F., Freeman, F., & Tobin, C. (1975). Vowel and nasal duration as cues to voicing in word-final stop consonants: Spectrographic and perceptual studies. *Journal of Speech & Hearing Research*, 18, 389–400.

Raphael, L. J., Dorman, M. F., & Liberman, A. M. (1980). On defining the vowel duration that cues voicing in final position. *Language and Speech*, 23, 297–308.

Reeds, J. A. & Wang, W.-S. Y. (1961). The perception of stops after s. *Phonetica*, 6, 78–81.

Repp, B. H. (1986). Perception of the [m] – [n] distinction in CV syllables. *Journal of the Acoustical Society of America*, 72, 1987–99.

Repp, B. H. & Williams, D. R. (1985). Influence of following context on perception of the voiced-voiceless distinction in syllable-final stop consonants. *Journal of the Acoustical Society of America*, 78, 445–57.

Revoile, S., Pickett, J. M., Holden, L. D., & Talkin, D. (1982). Acoustic cues to final stop voicing for impaired- and normal-hearing listeners. *Journal of the Acoustical Society of America*, 72, 1145–54.

Ryalls, J. H. & Lieberman, P. (1982). Fundamental frequency and vowel perception. *Journal of the Acoustical Society of America*, 72, 1631–4.

Schatz, C. D. (1954). The role of context in the perception of stops. *Language*, 30, 47–56.

Stevens, K. N. & Blumstein, S. E. (1978). Invariant cues for place of articulation in stop consonants. *Journal of the Acoustical Society of America*, 64, 1358–68.

Stevens, K. N., Blumstein, S. E., Glicksman, L., Burton, M., &

Kurowski, K. (1992). Acoustic and perceptual characteristics of voicing in fricatives and fricative clusters. *Journal of the Acoustical Society of America*, 91, 2979–3000.

Strange. W. (1989). Dynamic specification of coarticulated vowels spoken in sentence context. *Journal of the Acoustical Society of America*, 85, 2135–53.

Strange, W. (1999). Perception of Vowels. In J. M. Pickett (ed.), *The Acoustics of Speech Communication* (pp. 153–65). Boston: Allyn & Bacon.

Strange, W., Jenkins, J. J., & Johnson, T. L. (1983). Dynamic specification of coarticulated vowels. *Journal of the Acoustical Society of America*, 74, 695–705.

Strange, W., Verbrugge, R. R., Shankweiler, D. P., & Edman, T. R. (1976). Consonant environment specifies vowel identity. *Journal of the Acoustical Society of America*, 60, 213–24.

Summerfield, Q. & Bailey, P. (1977). On the dissociation of spectral and temporal cues for stop consonant manner. *Journal of the Acoustical Society of America*, 61, S-46(A).

Summerfield, Q., Bailey, P. J., Seton, J., & Dorman, M. F. (1981). Fricative envelope parameters and silent intervals in distinguishing "slit" and "split." *Phonetica*, 38, 181–92.

Sussman, H. M., Fruchter, D., & Cable, A. (1995). Locus equations derived from compensatory articulation. *Journal of the Acoustical Society of America*, 97, 3112–24.

Sussman, H. M., Hoemeke, K. A., & Ahmed, F. S. (1993). A cross-linguistic investigation of locus equations as a phonetic descriptor for place of articulation. *Journal of the Acoustical Society of America*, 94, 1256–68.

Sussman, H. M., McCaffrey, H. A., & Matthews, S. A. (1991). Investigation of locus equations as a source of relational invariance for stop place categorization. *Journal of the Acoustical Society of America*, 90, 1309–25.

Syrdal, A. K. (1985). Aspects of a model of the auditory representation of American English vowels. *Speech Communication*, 4, 121–35.

Syrdal, A. K. & Gopal, H. (1986). A perceptual model of vowel recognition based on the auditory representation of American English vowels. *Journal of the Acoustical Society of America*, 79, 1086–100.

Traunmüller, H. (1981). Perceptual dimension of openness in vowels. *Journal of the Acoustical Society of America*, 69, 1465–75.

Verbrugge, R. R. & Shankweiler, D. P. (1977). Prosodic information for vowel identity. *Haskins Laboratory Status Report on Speech Research*, SR 51/52, 27–35.

Walsh, T. & Parker, F. (1981). Vowel termination as a cue to voicing in post-vocalic stops. *Journal of Phonetics*, 9, 105–8.

Walsh, T. & Parker, F. (1983). Vowel length and vowel transition cues to [+/− voice] in post-vocalic stops. *Journal of Phonetics*, 11, 407–12.

Walsh, T., Parker, F., & Miller, C. J. (1987). The contribution of F1 decline to the perception of [+/− voice]. *Journal of Phonetics*, 15, 101–3.

Wang, W. S.-Y. (1959). Transition and release as perceptual cues for final plosives. *Journal of Speech & Hearing Research*, 2, 66–73.

Wardrip-Fruin, C. A. (1982). On the status of phonetic categories: Preceding vowel duration as a cue to voicing in final stop consonants. *Journal of the Acoustical Society of America*, 71, 187–95.

Whalen, D. H. (1981). Effects of vocalic formant transitions and vowel quality on the English [s] – [š] boundary. *Journal of the Acoustical Society of America*, 69, 275–82.

Whalen, D. H., Abramson, A. S., Lisker, L., & Mody, M. (1990). Gradient effects of fundamental frequency on stop consonant voicing judgments. *Phonetica*, 47, 36–49.

Whalen, D. H., Abramson, A. S., Lisker, L., & Mody, M. (1993). F0 gives voicing information even with unambiguous voice onset times. *Journal of the Acoustical Society of America*, 93, 2152–9.

Wolf, C. G. (1978). Voicing cues in English final stops. *Journal of Phonetics*, 6, 299–309.

9 Clear Speech

ROSALIE M. UCHANSKI

> A voice said, "Thank you," so softly, that only the purest articulation made the words intelligible.
>
> From *The Maltese Falcon*, by Dashiell Hammett

9.1 Introduction

Throughout a typical day the speech produced by an individual varies greatly. The details of utterances depend on the environment, the physical and emotional state of the talker, and the composition of the audience. For instance, vocal level might increase in the presence of noticeable ambient noise or when the distance between talker and listener is lengthened. Speech produced in a large auditorium or hall is likely to be produced more slowly than in a small enclosure. Under emotional stress or the influence of alcohol, the fundamental frequency of speech is likely to be higher in contrast to relaxed speech. The variety of vocabulary and the complexity of syntax are adjusted in speech directed to a child, and speech directed to an infant exhibits large vocal pitch variations. And, when talking to a hearing-impaired listener an individual will typically aim to speak clearly. It is this final style of speech, clear speech, that is the topic of this chapter.

In the first section, we define clear speech. Then, the benefits of clear speech are discussed. This discussion includes the size of the clear speech benefit, the types of listeners who benefit, the ability of talkers to speak clearly, the environments in which clear speech is beneficial, and the modalities in which clear speech is beneficial. In the subsequent section, the physical characteristics of clear speech will be described, and the relations between these physical characteristics and the clear speech benefit will be presented. Finally, applications of and future directions for clear speech research will be discussed.

9.2 What is "Clear Speech"?

From a practical viewpoint, clear speech is a speaking style often adopted by talkers when speaking in difficult communication situations, e.g., when speaking in a very noisy or reverberant environment, or when talking to a hearing-impaired person. A clear speaking style may also be elicited by explicit instructions to a talker to produce highly enunciated speech. Clear speech is just one in a large class of speaking styles from which talkers choose, consciously or unconsciously, as the situation warrants. Though not an exhaustive list, this large class of speaking styles includes infant-directed speech (also called "motherese" or "parentese," e.g., Fernald et al., 1989; Kuhl et al., 1997), speech produced in noise (called Lombard speech; e.g., Bond, Moore, & Gable, 1989; Letowski, Frank, & Caravella, 1993; Pisoni et al., 1985; Summers et al., 1988), shouted speech (Rostolland, 1982), speech produced during simultaneous communication (Schiavetti et al., 1996; Schiavetti et al., 1998), speech produced while under stress or a cognitive workload (Lively et al., 1993; Tolkmitt & Scherer, 1986), and speech produced during human-computer error resolution (Oviatt, MacEachern, & Levow, 1998).

The idea of speaking clearly or enunciating with additional effort is certainly not a new one. Over the years, speaking clearly has been of interest, for example, in the theater, radio broadcasting, and military and aircraft communication (e.g., Birmingham & Krapp, 1922; Miller, 1946). And certainly other terms have been used to describe the speaking style we now call clear speech, terms such as "good diction" or "distinct enunciation." In some past research the primary goal was to train talkers to become clearer when speaking, and a secondary goal was to identify factors influencing a talker's clarity, factors such as the type of instructions given and the clarity of speech in the models used for imitation (Snidecor, Mallory, & Hearsey, 1944; Tolhurst, 1957). In other research the aim was to identify particular talkers who would be best suited for communications operations, as in the military (Miller, 1946). That is, rather than train an individual talker to adopt a clear speaking style, the goal was to identify the clearest or most intelligible talkers amongst a group of talkers. In this chapter, we will focus primarily on the perceptual and acoustic changes that occur when an individual talker changes from a conversational to a clear speaking style, i.e., *intra*-talker differences. However, discussion of *inter*-talker differences will also be presented in regards to both acoustic and intelligibility measures (e.g., Bond & Moore, 1994; Bradlow, Torretta, & Pisoni 1996; Gagné et al., 1994).

How do we know clear speech when we hear it? And, how is clear speech described quantitatively? Descriptions of clear speech are usually made by comparing some aspect of clear speech to samples of conversational or plain speech. Implicitly, the terms "conversational" or "plain" speech mean the type of speech produced under casual or typical circumstances when no special speaking effort or instruction is made. Thus, for whatever measure chosen (perceptual, acoustic, or articulatory), clear speech is described *relative to* the same measures found for conversational speech. We use this comparison-based method of describing clear speech and other speaking styles because our current knowledge of speech acoustics and speech perception is inadequate to classify accurately any given speech sample as "motherese" or "clear" or "produced under stress" (e.g., Slaney & McRoberts, 2003). Similarly, our current knowledge of speech acoustics and speech perception is inadequate to predict accurately the intelligibility of a given speech sample solely from its acoustic signal properties. Consequently, we use human listening experiments to determine the intelligibility of a specific speech sample or recording.

Finally, our discussion of clear speech will be limited to the physical and perceptual characteristics associated with a change in speaking style from conversational to clear when saying the same syllables or sequences of words. Thus, other strategies that could make a speech message more easily understood, such as using a simpler syntax, using a simpler vocabulary, and inserting optional relative pronouns, will not be considered here (e.g., Imaizumi, Hayashi, & Deguchi, 1993; Valian & Wales, 1976). For further details about these other strategies as they apply to aural rehabilitation, see Erber (1993) and Tye-Murray (1998). In addition, our discussion of clear speech will not include changes in speech clarity within the course of sentences and phrases due to factors such as semantic variation, predictability of subsequent words, and the number of previous references to a particular item or person. More information on these changes in speech clarity can be found, for example, in Aylett (2000a, 2000b), Hunnicutt (1985), and van Bergem (1988).

9.3 Benefits of Clear Speech

9.3.1 *Perceptual*

In this section, we examine whether there is a perceptual benefit to a clear speaking style. And if so, then who benefits? Is age or hearing status of the listener important? Is there a benefit in typical listening environments? Does language experience matter? Does modality matter? The studies presented initially examine the perceptual benefit of listeners through audition alone. Later in this section visual and audio-visual benefits are reported. Researchers of the early studies did not dismiss the visual system in the context of clear speech. Historically, however, the motivation for the earliest studies of clear speech was to develop new signal processing schemes for possible incorporation into hearing aids. Hence, the initial interest was in the possible benefit of clear speech afforded through the auditory system alone.

9.3.1.1 *Listeners, environments, and language experience*

It might seem intuitively obvious or just common sense that if a talker makes a concerted effort to speak more clearly then his/her effort should be beneficial to listeners, especially if the listeners have a hearing impairment. That is, a talker's clear speech should be easier for a hearing-impaired person to understand than a talker's conversational speech. However, not until 1985 was evidence available to support this belief (Picheny, Durlach, & Braida, 1985). In an earlier study, normal hearing listeners in a noise background, not hearing-impaired listeners, were employed (Chen, 1980). However, the substantial clear speech advantage found for the identification of CV syllables in Chen's study was promising enough to warrant further investigation with hearing-impaired listeners and sentence-length materials. In the landmark study by Picheny et al., three male talkers were instructed to produce hundreds of nonsense sentences (syntactically correct sentences with nonsensical semantics) using both conversational and clear speaking styles. After normalization of their overall rms-level, these sentences were presented to five listeners with varying degrees of hearing loss, ranging from mild to severe and from flat to steeply sloping. The age of these listeners ranged from 24 to 64 years, with a mean of 52 years. The sentences were presented in quiet to the listeners using two different frequency-gain characteristics (i.e., two simulated hearing-aid systems), and at three intensity levels. Overall, the findings were robust. Picheny et al. (1985) reported that clear speech was more intelligible than conversational speech by 17 percentage points and that this result was roughly independent of listener, presentation level, and frequency-gain characteristic.

Table 9.1 provides a summary of clear speech studies and lists the size of the clear speech advantage (advantage = intelligibility score for clear speech – intelligibility score for conversational speech) in each study. Since Picheny's study, clearly spoken sentences have been shown to benefit young normal-hearing listeners in noise (Bradlow & Bent, 2002; Gagné et al., 1995; Krause & Braida, 2002; Payton, Uchanski, & Braida, 1994; Uchanski et al., 1996), in reverberation (Payton et al., 1994), and in environments with noise and reverberation combined (Payton et al., 1994). And, for elderly listeners, clear speech has been found beneficial for those with normal hearing and with moderate hearing loss when listening in a noise background (Helfer, 1998). Elderly listeners with mild-to-moderate presbyacusic losses listening in noise also benefit from clear speech (Schum, 1996).[1]

For listeners with more severe hearing loss, a benefit from clear speech has been confirmed in two subsequent studies (Payton et al., 1994; Uchanski et al., 1996), and has been extended beyond the quiet listening environment reported originally by Picheny at al. (1985). These listeners with more severe hearing loss also benefit from clear speech when listening in noise, in reverberation, and in combinations of noise and reverberation (Payton et al., 1994). Thus, for listeners with either normal or impaired hearing, there is a significant perceptual advantage to listening to clear speech as compared to conversational speech. Besides the demonstrated clear speech intelligibility advantage found for normal-hearing and impaired-hearing listeners, the results from several studies indicate that the more degrading the acoustic environment, the greater the clear speech advantage (Payton et al., 1994; Bradlow & Bent, 2002). For example, for hearing-impaired listeners, clear speech advantages were 15 and 29 percentage points, respectively, for rooms with reverberation times (RT) of 0.18 and 0.6 seconds (Payton et al., 1994).

A recent study by Ferguson and Kewley-Port (2002), however, calls into question the generally robust intelligibility advantage of clear speech. For young normal hearing adults (YNH), vowels in clearly spoken words by one male talker had higher identification scores than vowels in conversationally spoken words (at –10 dB SNR). However, for elderly hearing-impaired listeners (EHI) there was essentially no difference in vowel identification for the clear and conversational words (–3 dB SNR), and results were highly vowel-dependent.[2] Curiously, for sentence-length materials, this same talker's clear speech had an intelligibility advantage of 19 percentage points when presented to EHI listeners (+3 dB SNR). We do not know whether the absence of a clear speech advantage for isolated words for EHI listeners would hold for other talkers' recordings and for other speech materials.

Table 9.1 Summary of clear speech studies

Study	*Clear speech advantage (pct pts)*	*Listeners*	*Hearing aid?*	*Modality*	*Auditory environment*	*Language: speech materials*	*Talker(s)*	*Talkers: trained or experienced?*
Chen (1980)	10, 12, 15, 15, 7	NH [young adult]	n/a	A	WN [8, −4 dB, −10 dB, −15 dB, −21 dB]	Amer Engl: CVs	adult: 3 M	Yes
Picheny et al. (1985)	17	HI [24–64 yrs]	OMCL, ORTHO	A	quiet	Amer Engl: nonsense sentences	adult: 3 M	Yes
Gagné et al. (1994)	7	NH [young adult]	n/a	A	HI-simul (HELOS)	Canad Engl: words [open-set]	adult: 10 F	No
"	3	"	"	V	n/a	Canad Engl: words [closed-set]	"	"
"	4	"	"	AV	HI-simul (HELOS)	Canad Engl: words [open-set]	"	"
Payton et al. (1994)	16	HI [50–59 yrs]	OMCL	A	quiet	Amer Engl: nonsense sentences	adult: 1 M	Yes
"	15, 29	"	"	A	reverb [.18 s, .6 s]	"	"	"
"	28, 34	"	"	A	SSN [9.5 dB, 5.3 dB]	"	"	"
"	34	"	"	A	SSN [9.5 dB] + reverb [.18 s]	"	"	"
"	16	NH [young adult]	n/a	A	HI-simul WN	"	"	"
"	15, 20	"	"	A	reverb [.18 s, .6 s] + HI-simul (WN)	"	"	"
"	20, 18, 28	"	"	A	SSN [9.5 dB, 5.3 dB, 0 dB] + HI-simul (WN)	"	"	"
"	28	"	"	A	SSN + reverb + HI-simul WN	"	"	"
Gagné et al. (1995)	14	NH [young adult]	n/a	A	WN [0 dB]	Canad Engl: sentences	adult: 6 F	No
"	8	"	"	V	n/a	"	"	"
"	11	"	"	AV	WN [−7 dB]	"	"	"
Schum (1996)	22 RAUs	mild to moder presb [elderly, 60–77 yrs]	unaided	A	CN [+3 dB]	Amer Engl: sentences	adult: 6 F, 4 M	No
"	17 RAUs	"	"	A	"	"	elderly: 6 F, 4 M	"
Uchanski et al. (1996)	15	HI [aged 28–60]	OMCL	A	quiet	Amer Engl: nonsense sentences	adult: 3 M	Yes
"	16	NH [young adult]	n/a	A	WN [−4 dB]	"	"	"
Helfer (1997)	14	NH [young adult]	n/a	A	MB [+2 dB]	Amer Engl: nonsense sentences	adult: 1 F	No
"	15, 19, 20	"	"	AV	MB [+2 dB, 0 dB, −2 dB]	"	"	"
Helfer (1998)	15	NH to moder presb [elderly, 61–88 yrs]	unaided	A	MB [+3 dB]	Amer Engl: nonsense sentences	adult: 1 F	No
"	11	"	"	AV	"	"	"	"

(*cont'd* on p. 212)

Table 9.1 *(cont'd)*

Study	*Clear speech advantage (pct pts)*	*Listeners*	*Hearing aid?*	*Modality*	*Auditory environment*	*Language: speech materials*	*Talker(s)*	*Talkers: trained or experienced?*
Krause (2001)	16*	NH [young adult]	n/a	A	SSN [−1.8 dB]	Amer Engl: nonsense sentences	adult: 3 F, 1 M	Yes
"	6* (ns)	HI [40–65 yrs]	NAL	A	quiet	"	"	"
Bradlow & Bent (2002)	14, 19 RAUs	NH [young adult]	n/a	A	WN [−4 dB, −8 dB]	Amer Engl: rev BKB sentences	adult: 1 F, 1 M	No
"	6, 4 RAUs	non-native speaking NH [young adult]	"	A	"	"	"	"
Ferguson & Kewley-Port (2002)	15	NH [young adult]	n/a	A	MB [−10 dB]	Amer Engl: 10 /bVd/	adult: 1 M	No
"	−1	HI [elderly]	simul linear HA	A	MB [−3 dB]	"	"	"
"	19	HI [elderly]	"	A	MB [+3 dB]	Amer Engl: CID sentences	"	"
Gagné et al. (2002)	13	NH [young adult]	n/a	A	WN [−7 dB]	Canad French: CV's, VCV's	young: 6 F	No
"	10	"	"	V	n/a	"	"	"
"	7	"	"	AV	WN [−14 dB]	"	"	"
Krause & Braida (2002)	18	NH [young adult]	n/a	A	SSN [−1.8 dB]	Amer Engl: nonsense sentences	adult: 4 F, 1 M	Yes
"	14*	"	"	A	"	"	"	"
"	12**	"	"	A	"	"	"	"
Bradlow et al. (2003)	6, 13 RAUs	NH [school-age children]	n/a	A	WN [−4 dB, −8 dB]	Amer Engl: rev BKB sentences	adult: 1 F, 1 M	No
"	6, 12 RAUs	NH LD [school-age children]	"	A	"	"	"	"

Key:
Clear speech advantage = clear score − conv score
Listeners: HI = hearing-impaired, NH = normal-hearing, LD = learning-disabled
Modality: A = auditory, V = visual, AV = audio-visual
Auditory environment: WN = white or broadband noise, MB = multitalker babble, SSN = speech-shaped noise, CN = cafeteria noise; dB SNR; reverb (reverberation time in sec)
n/a = not applicable
ns = not statistically significant

* for clear/norm and conv/norm speaking styles, i.e., both styles have speaking rates of roughly 180 wpm
** for clear/slow and conv/slow speaking styles, i.e., both styles have speaking rates of roughly 100 wpm

The previously mentioned results have all been obtained with listeners who were native English-speaking adults with normal English language abilities. Even the aforementioned hearing-impaired adults fit this description as they were all post-lingually deafened. Bradlow and Bent (2002) examined the benefit of speaking clearly for a group of young adult listeners who have normal hearing but are not native English listeners. They found that a clear speaking style was still beneficial but that the size of the overall intelligibility advantage was substantially smaller for non-native listeners than for the native listeners. Their results indicate that the perceptual benefit of a clear speaking style is contingent on extensive experience with the sound structure of the test language.

Another study examined the benefit of clear speech for normal-hearing listeners with less-than-mature language experience, namely, school-age children (Bradlow, Kraus, & Hayes, 2003). Bradlow, Kraus, and Hayes presented clear and conversationally-spoken sentences to learning-disabled children and children with no history of learning or attention problems. Both listener groups had higher keyword-correct scores for clear speech than for conversational speech. Since these speech materials and listening conditions were the same as those used in the Bradlow and Bent (2002) study, a comparison can also be made between children and adults who both listened in their native language. The result, a larger intelligibility benefit from clear speech for adults than for school-age children, is consistent with the idea that as experience with a language increases the intelligibility advantage of clear speech also increases. And, consistent with earlier studies, the advantage for clear speech over conversational speech was greater in the poorer listening situation (lower SNR) than in the easier listening situation for the normal-hearing school-age children.

9.3.1.2 Modalities

All the previously mentioned experiments presented speech through *audition* alone. Some researchers, however, have examined the benefit of clear speech when presented *audio-visually* (Gagné et al., 1994; Gagné et al., 1995; Gagné, Rochette, & Charest, 2002; Helfer, 1997; Helfer, 1998) and *visually* (Gagné et al., 1994; Gagné et al., 1995; Gagné et al., 2002). In the earlier study by Helfer (1997), 30 normal-hearing young adults were presented conversational and clear sentences, in a noise background, both auditorily (A) and audio-visually (AV). For both modality conditions (A and AV), using a +2 dB SNR, clear speech was more intelligible than conversational speech (by 14 and 15 percentage points, respectively). In the more recent study by Helfer (1998), older adults served as listeners, and speech was presented both auditorily and audio-visually in a background of noise. The listeners' hearing abilities ranged from normal to moderate presbyacusic. Again, clear speech was found to be significantly more intelligible than conversational speech in both the A and AV conditions, by 15 and 11 percentage points, respectively. Since Helfer found no relation between degree of hearing loss and clear speech benefit, she concluded that clear speech helps many elderly listeners, regardless of mild hearing loss, and even when the talker's face is visible.

One group of researchers (Gagné et al., 1994; Gagné et al., 1995; Gagné et al., 2002) has examined the benefit of clear speech auditorily, audio-visually, and visually. Interpretation of the results from the two earlier studies is confounded by the use of different tasks in different modality conditions, and of different listeners for the different modality conditions. However, the design of Gagné's most recent study (Gagné et al., 2002) avoids these earlier problems through the use of multiple talkers, multiple tokens, multiple listeners, and nonsense syllables. Speech materials were 18 CVs and 18 VCVs spoken both conversationally and clearly in Canadian French. Averaged across all six talkers, clear speech was more intelligible than conversational speech in all three modality conditions with 13, 10, and 7 percentage point advantages for the A, V, and AV conditions, respectively. There were significant interactions between talker and modality as individual talkers displayed different patterns of clear speech effects across perceptual modalities.

Though, in general, clear speech provides a perceptual benefit in all three modality conditions (A, V, and AV), as yet, no investigation of the integration process of clear speech across the A and V modalities has been made. In some related research on multimodal speech perception, Munhall et al. (1996) found that multimodal integration, as measured by the McGurk effect, also holds for clear speech. However, since modeling of the integration process itself (e.g., using the techniques of Braida, 1991) has not been done for clear speech stimuli, it remains to be seen whether clear speech has an effect on integration ability separate from its beneficial effect on perception in each individual modality.

9.3.1.3 *Talkers and training*

Just as there is considerable variability in the intelligibility of conversational (or typical) speech produced by many talkers (Bond & Moore, 1994; Bradlow et al., 1996; Cox, Alexander, & Gilmore, 1987; Hood & Poole, 1980), one might also expect there to be considerable variability in the ability of talkers to produce a more intelligible clear speaking style. And, one might expect training and/or instructions to have an effect on this ability. While no clear speech study has been designed explicitly to examine talker variability or the effects of talker training, many clear speech studies have reported results relevant to this issue.

In each of the studies with more than one talker, there has been a significant effect of talker on the clear speech advantage. For example, in Picheny et al.'s study (1985), three male talkers, with experience in public speaking (e.g., debate club) or talking with hearing-impaired people, were employed. The clear speech advantages for these three talkers ranged from 9 to 22 percentage points, but the effect of talker differences accounted for only about 7% of the total variance in the data. The 20 talkers of Schum's study (1996) yielded clear speech advantages that ranged from roughly 2 to 45 Rationalized Arcsine Units (Studebaker, 1985). And, in each of the three studies by Gagné et al. (with 10, 6, and 6 talkers, respectively (1994, 1995, 2002)), there was also a significant talker effect. Since talker variability is significant, a handful of talkers, at a minimum, should be employed in clear speech studies.

Currently, no one knows whether any particular talker characteristic (gender, age, size, etc.) is related to his/her ability to produce clear speech. The study by Schum (1996) is the only one to examine the effect of any talker characteristic on the ability to produce clear speech, in this case, age. In Schum's study, ten young and ten elderly talkers were used. The talkers did not have any formal speaking training and did not have a hearing loss. Though the average clear speech advantage was larger for the young (22 Rationalized Arcsine Units) than for the elderly talkers (17 Rationalized Arcsine Units), these are not statistically different as both talker groups exhibited a wide range of clear speech advantages.

The effects of training on the production of clear speech have not been examined explicitly in recent years. During WWII a study was carried out on different methods of training talkers for military telephone operators (Snidecor et al., 1944). A method called "Mass Drill" was found to be most effective as it resulted in talkers using louder speech and good loudness control. For applications with hearing-impaired listeners in which level may be normalized or controlled, training focused on speech intensity is largely irrelevant. Though different methods of training have not been tested for their effectiveness in producing clear speech, the amount of training has been explored. Many of the studies of clear speech have found a significant improvement in the intelligibility of a talker's clear speech when compared to his/her conversational speech – even with very minimal training in the form of simple instructions (Bradlow & Bent, 2002; Bradlow et al., 2003; Ferguson & Kewley-Port, 2002; Gagné et al., 1994; Gagné et al., 1995; Gagné et al., 2002; Helfer, 1997; Helfer, 1998). Example instructions are "speak as though you are talking to a hearing-impaired person . . . imagine you are communicating in a noisy environment . . . take care to enunciate each word carefully." Schum states explicitly that if talkers asked for further details, such as whether to speak louder, slower, or more dramatically, they were told to do whatever they felt was necessary in order to be better understood. With one exception (the single talker in the Ferguson & Kewley-Port study), the talkers employed in these studies with simple instructions were able to produce a clear speaking style as demonstrated by their significantly higher intelligibility scores for various kinds of listeners.

The other clear speech studies (Krause & Braida 2002; Payton et al., 1994; Picheny et al., 1985; Uchanski et al., 1996) used talkers with somewhat more training. The three earlier studies used speech samples from the same three male talkers, who had been chosen for their previous experience in public speaking and/or speaking to hearing-impaired people. The study by Krause and Braida (2002) employed a different set of talkers, and by design, differed in the talker training and speech-elicitation procedures. The primary goal of this study was to elicit clear speech at normal speaking rates through careful talker selection, training and monitoring. From an initial group of 15 talkers, 5 were selected for further training and speech recording, based primarily on the size of their associated change in speaking rate when speaking clearly. For subsequent speech training and recording, both speaking rate and clarity were regulated in an interactive human-listening arrangement similar to that used in Chen's study (1980).[3] Talkers were encouraged to experiment with different speaking strategies and were allowed to practice as much as they desired.

The talkers in Krause and Braida's study (2002) did produce typical clear speech when speaking rate was not regulated. That is, clear speech was produced at a speaking rate slower than that of conversational speech. More importantly, these talkers were also able to produce a clear style of speech *without* a substantial change in speaking rate. The intelligibility of these speech materials was tested with normal-hearing listeners in a background of speech-shaped noise. As found in many previous studies, clear speech at typical slow rates ("clear/slow") was more intelligible than typical conversational speech ("conversational/normal-speaking-rate" or "conv/norm"). In this study the clear speech advantage was 18 percentage points ("clear/slow" vs. "conv/norm"). At normal speaking rates (~180 wpm), "clear/norm" was found to be more intelligible than "conv/norm" by 14 percentage points. And, finally, "clear/slow" had an advantage of 12 percentage points over "conv/slow" (that is, both speaking styles at ~100 wpm). When these same speaking styles were presented to three hearing-impaired listeners, there was a smaller (and not statistically significant) advantage of 6 percentage points for clear/norm over conv/norm speech (Krause, 2001). At this time, the reason for this discrepancy in benefit for normal-hearing and hearing-impaired listeners is not understood.

9.3.2 *Physiological*

In addition to the well-documented perceptual benefit of clear speech found from listening experiments, Cunningham et al. (2001, 2002) have examined the physiological benefits of clear speech for human and animal listeners. In these experiments, conversational-like and clear-like synthetic VCV syllables were presented to subjects (human and guinea pig) in quiet and in noise. Clear-like syllables had enhanced stop-burst levels and lengthened intervocalic stop-gaps. In general, neural responses were greater (larger in amplitude) for the clear-like stimuli than for the conversational-like stimuli, especially for stimuli presented in a noise background.

9.3.3 *Summary*

Roughly speaking, how big is the clear speech benefit? Using data from Miller, Heise, & Lichten (1951), a change in speech perception scores can be converted into an equivalent improvement in SNR. Using the steepest portion[4] of the words-correct vs. SNR curve in Figure 3 of Miller et al. (1951), the typical clear speech advantage of 15 percentage points corresponds roughly to a +5 dB improvement in SNR. This +5 dB improvement in SNR for words in nonsense sentences represents an intermediate value between +4.3 dB for words in meaningful sentences and +6 dB for isolated words. Any noise-reduction algorithm would probably be considered quite successful if it increased the effective SNR by as much as 5 dB.

As shown in Table 9.1, clear speech provides a fairly robust and pervasive intelligibility benefit although the amount of benefit is not the same for all listeners, listening situations, modalities, talkers, and speech materials. In general, many different types of listeners benefit from clear speech: those with impaired hearing with a range of severity of hearing loss, people with normal hearing listening in noise and/or reverberation, school-age children, young adults, the elderly, native-language listeners, non-native listeners, and learning-disabled school-age children. Clear speech is beneficial in different environments such as noise, reverberation, and a combination of noise and reverberation. In fact, the intelligibility advantage of clear speech over conversational speech tends to increase as the listening environment degrades. Thus, clear speech can provide significant perceptual benefit especially when it is needed most. Also, in general, there is a benefit to a clear speaking style in all three speech "listening" modalities (A, V, and AV). Clear speech can be produced by non-professional talkers via simple instructions, and by talkers who are young or old. With some additional training, experienced talkers could also produce a form of clear speech that did not necessitate a significant change in speaking rate. And, finally, a clear speech advantage has been found in more than one language.

9.4 Physical Characteristics of Clear Speech and Their Relation to Intelligibility

Some common ideas and assumptions about how to produce clear speech are: (1) articulate all phonemes precisely and accurately, (2) slow one's speech rate just a bit, (3) pause slightly between phrases and thoughts, and (4) modestly increase vocal volume. Or, as recently stated so succinctly, "Don't talk so fast and pronounce your sounds better" (Ross, 2000). But what, exactly, do talkers do differently when they change from a conversational to a clear speaking style? What are measurable, physical differences between conversational and clear speech? How is a clear speaking style like, or unlike, other speaking styles such as slow speech, infant-directed speech and loud speech? And, ultimately, can we identify precisely which physical changes are responsible for the associated intelligibility improvement from conversational to clear speech? These are some questions addressed in this section. A multitude of physical characteristics of clear speech will be presented, and related results from other speaking styles will be discussed. More importantly, the relation, if any, of this characteristic to speech intelligibility will be examined, including any relevant results from research on inter-talker intelligibility.

Although clear speech provides a benefit through both the auditory and visual senses, this section will focus exclusively on the acoustic properties of clear speech. Currently, physical characteristics of visible clear speech have not been reported. Several acoustic analyses of clear speech are based on the nonsense sentences produced by the three male talkers employed in Picheny et al.'s (1985) initial perceptual study (Payton & Braida, 1999; Picheny, Durlach, & Braida, 1986; Uchanski, 1988). Other acoustic analyses of clear speech from other talkers include studies by Bradlow et al. (2003), Chen (1980), Cutler and Butterfield (1990), Krause and Braida (2002, 2003), and Matthies et al. (2001). The studies by Krause and Braida (2002, 2003), however, not only employed different talkers but also included a form of clear speech called "clear/norm," which was produced with careful regulation of speaking rate (i.e., near normal speaking rates of ~180 wpm). The acoustic analyses in these reports are based on nonsense sentences produced by five talkers (four female, one male), or in some cases, based on only two of these five talkers. Unless stated otherwise, "clear" will refer to clear speech produced without any constraint in speaking rate. In the studies by Krause and Braida, this style is called "clear/slow" because this unconstrained clear speaking style typically has a *slower* speaking rate (~100 wpm) than that found for plain, conversational speech. Analogously, in this review, conversational speech is synonymous with "conv/norm" since unconstrained conversational speech is typically produced with a relatively normal speaking rate (~180 wpm). To illustrate these speaking styles, spectrograms of clear/slow, clear/norm and conv/norm speech are shown in Figures 9.1 and 9.2. In Figure 9.1 are spectrograms of a sentence spoken both conversationally (aka conv/norm) and clearly (aka clear/slow). In Figure 9.2 are spectrograms of another sentence spoken in both the conversational (conv/norm) and clear/norm speaking styles.

9.4.1 Global characteristics

9.4.1.1 Intensity

Clear speech is produced at levels 5 to 8 dB greater than those of conversational speech (Picheny et al., 1986). An increase in intensity is also found in other speaking styles, such as when speech is produced in noise (Bond et al., 1989; Clark, Lubker, & Hunnicutt, 1988; Summers et al., 1988) or when shouted (Rostolland, 1982). However, since overall rms levels of clear and conversational speech were equated in the listening experiments reported previously, an overall level difference, while notable, cannot be a contributing factor to the higher intelligibility of clear speech.

9.4.1.2 Speaking rate

Picheny et al. (1986) reported speaking rates of 160 to 205 wpm for conversational speech and 90 to 100 wpm for clear speech. From subsequent analyses, Picheny et al. determined that the slower speaking rate for the clear/slow speaking style was attributable to increases in the occurrence and average duration of pauses, and to increases in the duration of many sound segments. Similar results have been reported by other researchers. Bradlow et al. (2003) found overall sentence duration increases of 51% and 116% for their one male and one female talker, respectively, to accompany the change in speaking style from conversational to clear. More importantly, Krause and Braida (2002) reported recently on the existence of a form of clear speech, called clear/norm, with speaking rates of 144 to 200 wpm (average, 174 wpm) for their five talkers. These speaking rates are comparable to the conversational speaking rates of these same talkers which range from 140 to 204 wpm (average, 179 wpm). Other speaking styles, such as speech produced in noise and speech produced under a cognitive workload, also exhibit longer word durations or equivalently lower speaking rates (Junqua, 1993; Lively et al., 1993; Summers et al., 1988). However, a slowing down in speaking rate is not found consistently in the studies of speech produced in noise. For example, Letowski et al. (1993) report no difference in speaking rate between Lombard speech and speech produced in quiet.

Several studies have addressed the possible effect of speaking rate on the high intelligibility of clear speech. Two studies evaluated artificial manipulations of the speaking rate of conversational and clear speech, using uniform time-scaling (Picheny, Durlach, & Braida, 1989) and non-uniform time-scaling (Uchanski et al., 1996). Unfortunately, the results of these two studies were equivocal. Other

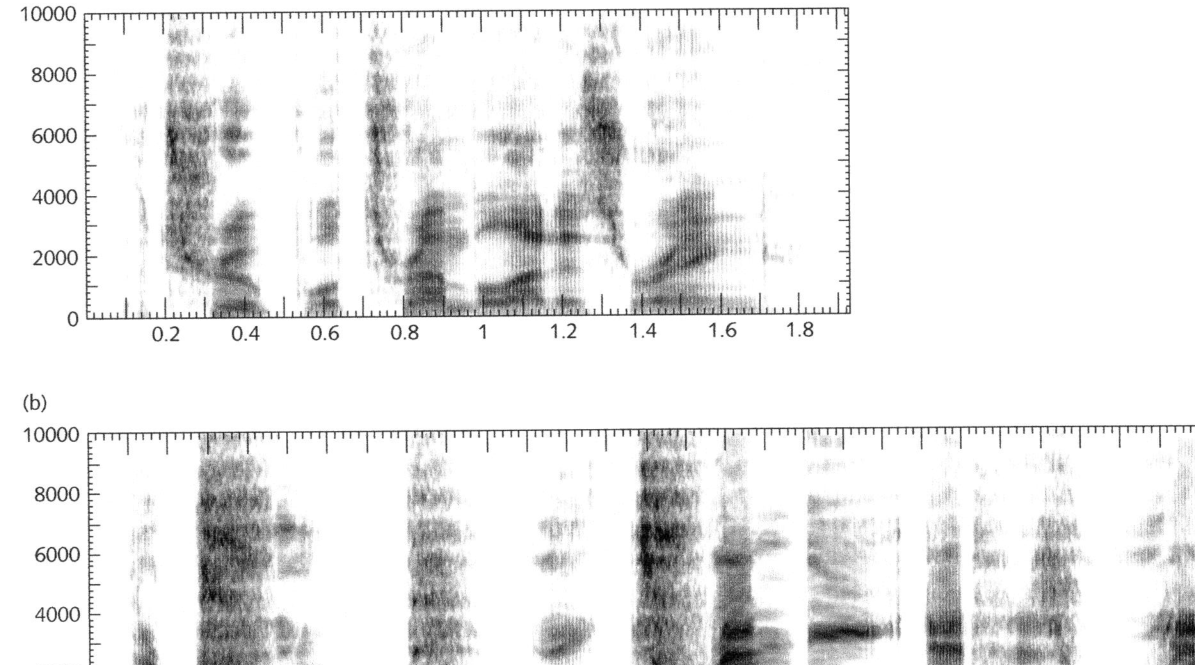

Figure 9.1 Spectrograms of the sentence "The troop will tremble at his ring," spoken by a male talker in both a conversational (aka conv/norm) (a) and clear (aka clear/slow) (b) speaking style.

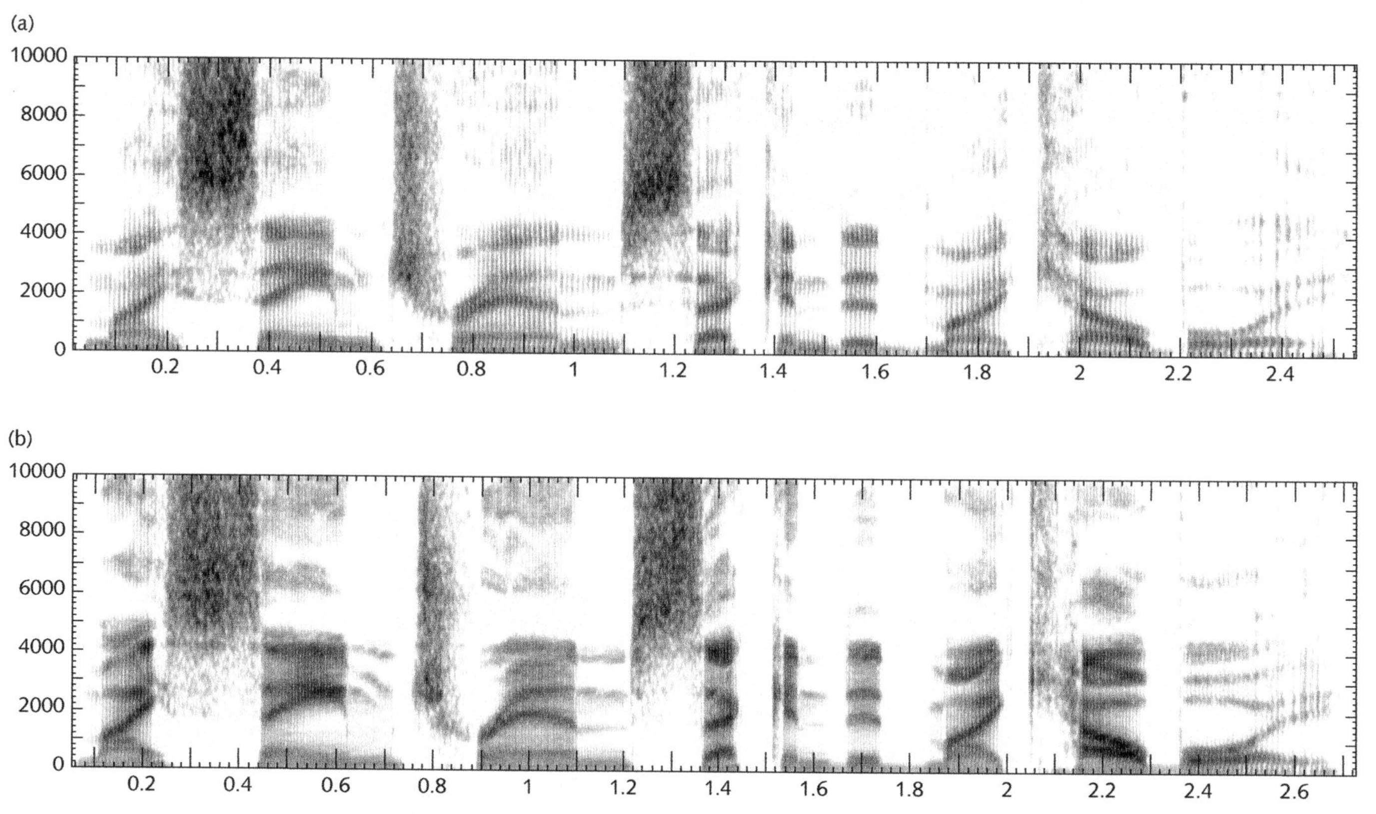

Figure 9.2 Spectrograms of the sentence "My sane trend seconded my cowboy," spoken by a male talker (a different talker than the one shown in Figure 9.1) in both a conversational (aka conv/norm) (a) and clear/norm (b) speaking style.

studies, though, have generally found that time-expansion has little or no beneficial effect on the intelligibility of speech (Nejime & Moore, 1998; Schmitt, 1983; Schon, 1970). Also, results from studies of inter-talker intelligibility are mixed with respect to the possible contribution of speaking rate. Cox et al. (1987, 6 talkers) and Bradlow et al. (1996, 20 talkers) found no correlation between speaking rate and intelligibility while Bond and Moore (1994, 3 talkers) and Hazan and Markham (2004, 45 talkers) did find a correlation between speaking rate (or equivalently, word duration) and intelligibility.

In addition to evaluating the effect on intelligibility of artificially changing speaking rate, some researchers have investigated the possibility of naturally maintaining a conversational speaking rate while simultaneously increasing speech clarity. Tolhurst (1957) and Uchanski et al. (1996) failed in their attempt to have talkers produce clear or "precise" speech at normal speaking rates. In contrast, a recent demonstration of the existence of naturally-produced clear speech at normal speaking rates (~180 wpm) (Krause & Braida, 2002) seems to indicate that clear speech need not be slow. However, since only a small and not-significant advantage was found for clear/norm speech over conv/norm speech for three hearing-impaired listeners, it is still possible that for some listeners speaking rate is a contributing factor to the high intelligibility of clear speech.

9.4.1.3 Pauses

Picheny et al. (1986) reported an increase in the number of occurrences of pauses and the average duration of pauses for clear speech. In this study a pause was defined as any silent interval between words, greater than 10 ms, excluding silent intervals preceding word-initial plosives. Analogous pause analyses by Krause and Braida (2003) and Bradlow et al. (2003) confirm the results of Picheny, i.e., there are more and longer pauses in clear than in conversational speech. However, Krause and Braida's analysis of clear/norm speech found almost exactly the same pause distributions for both clear/norm and conv/norm speech. Specifically, for 50 sentences, conv/norm speech had 318 pauses total with an average duration of 42 ms and clear/norm speech had 339 pauses total with an average duration of 49 ms. These statistics contrast with the 632 pauses with an average duration of 130 ms found for clear/slow speech. Cutler and Butterfield's (1990) analysis of conversational and clear speech found more pauses in clear speech, and that the pauses were inserted especially before words starting with weak syllables. They hypothesized that such pauses could serve as acoustic cues to the more difficult word boundaries for spoken English, but no intelligibility evaluation was included in their study. This idea is consistent with the pause occurrences found in infant-directed speech (Fernald et al., 1989) and speech from teachers talking to deaf children (Imaizumi et al., 1993), in which pauses are inserted especially before phrase boundaries.

The relation between pause occurrence and speech intelligibility is not certain. Artificial insertion of pauses in conversational speech has not produced an increase in intelligibility (Uchanski et al., 1996). Analyses of the natural occurrence of pauses from clear/slow speech indicate a correlation between pauses occurrence and intelligibility (Bradlow et al., 2003; Picheny et al., 1986). Pause data from clear/norm speech, however, which show little difference in pause occurrence between clear/norm and conv/norm speech, cast doubt on a contributing role of pauses to the high intelligibility of clear/norm speech.

9.4.1.4 *Fundamental frequency*

Compared to conversational speech, clear speech often has a higher F0 and a larger range in F0, suggesting larger amounts of laryngeal tension. This acoustic difference is easily apparent in the spectrograms of Figures 9.1 and 9.2. In Bradlow et al.'s (2003) study of clear speech, average F0 was increased by 1.1 and 5.4 semitones, and F0 range was increased by 6.2 and 5.8 semitones, respectively, for the one male and one female talker. However, changes in F0 are not consistent across the talkers in the studies by Picheny et al. (1986) and Krause and Braida (2003). Increases in average F0 and F0 range are also found for speech produced in noise (Bond et al., 1989; Clark et al., 1988; Summers et al., 1988), for infant-directed speech (Fernald et al., 1989; Grieser & Kuhl, 1988), and for speech produced with an increase in the distance from the listener (Lienard & Benedetto 1999). However, except for the study by Summers et al. (1988) in which speech produced in noise exhibited a small but significant intelligibility advantage, none of the other studies include a perceptual evaluation of the speech.

It seems unlikely that a simple increase in average F0 contributes to the high intelligibility of clear speech. In fact, in most studies of inter-talker intelligibility and acoustic characteristics, average F0 is uncorrelated with intelligibility (Bond & Moore, 1994; Bradlow et al., 1996;[5] Hazan & Markham, 2004; Miller, 1946). An artificial increase in both average F0 and F0 range of conv/norm speech (in a simple manner that may differ from natural variations) did not increase intelligibility (Krause, 2001). Perhaps the naturally-produced increase in average F0 is an irrelevant by-product of an increased vocal effort that serves to increase the relative intensities of higher frequency components in the speech spectrum.

9.4.1.5 *Long-term speech spectrum (LTSS), spectral tilt, center of gravity*

Though these measures – long-term speech spectra, spectral tilt, and spectral center of gravity – are related, across-study comparisons are difficult. Researchers have used different spectral analysis systems (with varying numbers and bandwidths of filters), different speech materials, different talkers, and different bandwidths of the speech signal. In Picheny et al.'s study (1986), long-term rms spectra of conversational and clear speech are only slightly different from each other, with all talkers showing a tendency for higher spectrum levels in clear speech at higher frequencies. In Krause and Braida's (2003) study, the speech of four of the five talkers analyzed show more intense frequency components in the region around 1000 Hz and above, for clear/norm speech compared to conv/norm speech. A change in spectral tilt or slope of the long-term speech spectrum is also found for Lombard speech (e.g., Junqua, 1993; Pittman & Wiley, 2001; Summers et al., 1988; Tartter, Gomes, & Litwin, 1993), speech produced under cognitive stress (Lively et al., 1993), and speech produced at an increased distance from the listener (Lienard & Benedetto, 1999). For these other speaking styles, again, spectral components at higher frequencies have higher levels than those found in conversational speech.

While it is possible that differences in spectral tilt (or an equivalent measure) contribute to increased intelligibility, this has not been tested explicitly – for the long-term signal. However, since many of the studies of clear speech with hearing-impaired listeners used simulated hearing-aid systems with a gain (National Acoustics Laboratory, Octaves-most-comfortable-level) which would have included some suitable sort of high-frequency emphasis, it is doubtful that an additional simple high-frequency emphasis would increase the intelligibility of conversational speech. Also, not all speaking styles that show an increase in spectral tilt (or high frequency energy) are associated with an increase in intelligibility. Speech produced under a cognitive workload has increased high frequency energy but shows no increase in intelligibility (Lively et al., 1993). Finally, we do not know exactly which speech sounds are responsible for the change in spectral tilt – and we do not know how much of this change in spectral tilt is due to glottal source changes vs. supra-glottal changes.

9.4.1.6 *Temporal envelope modulations*

Using techniques originally developed for the calculation of the Speech Transmission Index (Houtgast & Steeneken, 1973), the modulation spectra were computed for various speaking styles. The modulation spectra of clear/slow speech have higher peaks in the 1–3 Hz region than those found for conv/norm speech (Krause & Braida, 2003; Payton & Braida, 1999), which presumably reflects the substantial difference in speaking rate between these two speaking styles. However, some differences remain even in the comparison of clear/norm with conv/norm speech (which have roughly similar speaking rates), particularly in the 2–4 Hz region of the 1000 Hz analysis band and especially for one talker (Krause & Braida, 2003). To test the hypothesis that the strong components in the 2–4 Hz region contribute to the high intelligibility of clear/norm speech, Krause (2001) modified these modulation frequencies (in several octave bands) of conv/norm speech and tested its effect on intelligibility. For both normal-hearing listeners in noise and hearing-impaired listeners, the artificially-introduced increase in the modulation depth of low frequency components (< 3–4 Hz) in the speech envelope did not increase intelligibility.

9.4.2 *Phonological characteristics*

The occurrences of various phonological phenomena in conv/norm, clear and clear/norm speech have been measured in various studies. Roughly, there are fewer instances of vowel modification/reduction to a schwa (Lindblom, 1990; Moon & Lindblom, 1994; Picheny et al., 1986), fewer instances of burst elimination (Bradlow et al., 2003; Picheny et al., 1986), fewer instances of alveolar flapping (Bradlow et al., 2003; Picheny et al., 1986), and more instances of sound insertions in clear speech than in conv/norm speech (Picheny et al., 1986). For some of these measures, the number of possible instances is very small, and hence the reliability of these data is questionable. In addition, we do not know if the phonological differences between clear and conversational speech contribute to the high intelligibility of clear speech since no experiments have been performed in which these phenomena are manipulated either naturally or artificially. In the comparisons of clear/norm to conv/norm speech, there are no significant differences in the occurrence of phonological phenomena (Krause & Braida, 2003). Hence, these phenomena probably do not contribute much to the high intelligibility of clear/norm speech.

9.4.3 Acoustic/phonetic characteristics

9.4.3.1 General: Short-term spectra and duration

In the study by Krause and Braida (2003), short-term spectra for individual speech sounds and sound classes were computed for each talker – for clear/norm and conv/norm speech. For consonants, no consistent differences were noted. This result differs from the earlier findings of Picheny et al. (1986) in which spectra for /s/ and /t/ exhibited an increase in the frequency of the maximum spectral peak and an increase in the intensity of the spectral peak. However, for vowel sounds, the short-term spectra exhibit higher spectral prominences in clear/norm than in conv/norm speech. Krause (2001) increased the amplitudes of the second and third formants of voiced portions of conv/norm speech to examine their effect on intelligibility. The intelligibility of formant-enhanced speech compared to unprocessed conv/norm speech was significantly higher for normal-hearing listeners in noise but was the same for hearing-impaired listeners.

Clear speech produced without a constraint on speaking rate generally has increased durations of speech segments, though not by the same amount or by the same percentage for all speech sounds (Bradlow et al., 2003; Ferguson & Kewley-Port, 2002; Picheny et al., 1986). Bradlow (2003) reports vowel lengthening in clear speech for both English and Spanish relative to their durations in conversational speech, though the amount of lengthening is less for Spanish. In a comparison of clear/norm speech to conv/norm speech, only a small number of segments show a statistically significant difference in duration (Krause & Braida, 2003). And, as mentioned previously in regards to speaking rate, most studies in which duration of a word or CV-syllable has been manipulated artificially have shown little effect of durational changes on speech perception, e.g., Gordon-Salant (1986) and Montgomery and Edge (1988).

9.4.3.2 Vowel properties

In clear speech, the formant frequencies of vowels generally span a larger space (F1 vs. F2) than do the formants of conversationally spoken vowels (Bradlow, 2003; Chen, 1980; Ferguson & Kewley-Port, 2002; Krause & Braida, 2003; Moon & Lindblom, 1994; Picheny et al., 1986). Bradlow (2003) found similar amounts of vowel expansion in clear speech for both English and Spanish vowels. However, Krause and Braida (2003) found a less consistent trend in their comparison of formants of clear/norm vs. conv/norm speech, in that only the tense vowels of one talker showed a larger vowel space. An expanded vowel space is also found in infant-directed speech in multiple languages (English, Russian, and Swedish: Kuhl et al., 1997). And, for synthetic speech, an expanded vowel space is associated with preferred vowel targets (Johnson, Flemming, & Wright, 1993). For other speaking styles, though, there is a general tendency for F_1 to increase while there is relatively little effect on F_2 (Bond et al., 1989; Lienard & Benedetto, 1999; Summers et al., 1988). This result, found for speech produced in noise and speech produced with an increasing distance from the listener, differs from that of clear speech in which both F_1 and F_2 can be affected.

Other measurements of clearly spoken vowels have also been made. Very briefly, clear speech often has increased rates of F_2 transitions (Moon & Lindblom, 1994), longer durations of formant transitions (Chen, 1980), and narrower formant bandwidths (Krause & Braida, 2003). However, these results are not always consistent across the vowels examined or across all vowel classes.

The relation between vowel properties and intelligibility is still largely unknown. For example, no intelligibility experiments were reported for either infant-directed speech or synthetic hyper-articulated speech to examine the effect of an increased vowel-space. In studies of inter-talker intelligibility, some researchers find a correlation between vowel space or vowel dispersion and intelligibility (Bond & Moore, 1994; Bradlow et al., 1996) while others do not (Hazan & Markham, 2004; Hazan & Simpson, 2000). A tighter clustering of vowel formants, though associated with higher intelligibility in Chen (1980), has not been found to correlate with intelligibility in subsequent clear speech analyses or in the study of inter-talker intelligibility by Bradlow et al. (1996). And, it seems that simple relations will not suffice. In Moon and Lindblom's (1994) study, both tense and lax vowels had higher F_2 values in clear speech than in citation-style speech, yet only tense vowels were found to be more intelligible (Moon, 1995).

9.4.3.3 *Consonant properties: Voice-onset-time (VOT) and consonant-vowel ratio*

Picheny et al. (1986) reported longer VOTs in clear speech for unvoiced plosives for all three talkers, as did Chen (1980). Krause and Braida's (2003) examination of the clear/norm speech of two talkers found that only one talker exhibited longer VOTs for unvoiced plosives. In fact, the other talker produced unvoiced plosives in clear/norm speech with VOTs shorter than those in conv/norm speech.

For some other speaking styles, there is no reported change in VOT (for speech produced in noise vs. quiet, Clark et al., 1988; and for plain slow, German speech, Hertrich & Ackermann, 1995). However, for speech produced with simultaneous communication (a combination of speech and manually coded English often used in classrooms for the education of deaf children), a small increase in VOT for unvoiced plosives is found (Schiavetti et al., 1996). Unfortunately, the intelligibility of speech was not evaluated for any of these other speaking styles. In a study of inter-talker intelligibility (with three talkers), no relation was found between ΔVOT (VOT for unvoiced plosive minus VOT for voiced plosive) and intelligibility (Bond & Moore, 1994). Yet Krause and Braida (2003) report that the talker with the longer VOTs for unvoiced plosives also exhibits the greater intelligibility advantage for clear/norm speech relative to conv/norm speech. So, there is a possibility that lengthened VOTs, especially for unvoiced plosives, contribute to the high intelligibility of clear/norm speech. Though based on disordered speech, this possibility is consistent with the significant correlations found between ΔVOT and the intelligibility of speech produced by deaf talkers (Metz et al., 1985; Monsen, 1978).

Picheny et al. (1986) reported an increase in relative power (measured re: peak sentence level) for clearly spoken consonants compared to their conversationally spoken counterparts (with some increases as large as 15 dB). The biggest increases were found for unvoiced sounds, which is consistent with Chen (1980). In Bradlow et al.'s (2003) study of clear speech, moderate increases in consonant-vowel ratio of 1.3 dB and 1.8 dB for their one male and one female talker, respectively, are reported. However, Krause and Braida (2003) did not find any significant increase in consonant-vowel ratio for clear/norm relative to conv/norm speech, except for the affricate sounds (2–3 dB larger consonant-vowel ratio). And, unlike Picheny's results, Krause and Braida did not find an increase in consonant power in clear/norm compared to conv/norm speech.

Much attention in the literature has been directed at the role that consonant-vowel ratio has on consonant identification and intelligibility (e.g., Gordon-Salant, 1986; Montgomery & Edge, 1988; Revoile et al., 1987). Results from more recent studies, by Sammeth et al. (1999), Kennedy et al. (1998), and Freyman and Nerbonne (1989), highlight two important points, namely (1) audibility of the consonant sound, and (2) that an artificially-introduced constant increase in consonant-vowel ratio may not be optimal for all consonant classes or for all listeners. In addition, intelligibility improvements found for nonsense syllables or words do not always extend to sentence-length materials (Hazan & Simpson, 1998). Also, in three studies of inter-talker intelligibility that examined consonant-vowel ratio, no correlation between consonant-vowel ratio and intelligibility was found (Freyman & Nerbonne, 1989; Hazan & Markham, 2004; Hazan & Simpson, 2000).

9.4.4 *Articulatory and glottal characteristics*

In a study of articulatory movements using electromyographic signals from lip muscles, Wohlert and Hammen (2000) state that clear speech involves a "re-organization" of motor control relative to other speaking styles. Matthies et al. (2001) report that the peak velocities of lip movements are greater for clear speech than for conversational speech for /iCu/ syllables. These studies demonstrate that the production of clear speech requires more effort and expends more energy than does the production of conversational speech.

Cummings and Clements (1995) estimated glottal waveforms for eleven different speaking styles, including clear speech. They describe the glottal waveform of clear speech roughly as a combination of the glottal waveforms of Lombard speech and slow speech. Unfortunately, the relation between the glottal waveform and the glottal spectrum for clear speech was not discussed, especially regarding any possible effects on the amplitudes of higher harmonics in the glottal spectrum.

9.4.5 *Summary*

First, the physical characteristics of clear speech indicate that it is a distinct speaking style. Though clear speech shares many acoustic characteristics with other speaking styles, such as Lombard speech, clear speech differs from these speaking styles in several ways. For example, changes in the frequency of F_1, lengthening of VOTs for unvoiced plosives, and parameters of the glottal waveform are all different for clear speech than for speech produced in noise. Second, there is a multitude of differences between clear and conversational speech – and a somewhat smaller number of differences between clear/norm and conv/norm speech. Third, the physical characteristics of clear speech are consistent with clear speech perceptual data in that talker variability is significant. Note, however, this result is not exclusive to studies of clear speech. For Lombard speech, for example, there is also much inter-talker variability as well as inconsistencies in both acoustic and perceptual results across various studies.

Unfortunately, we still cannot answer several basic questions such as (1) which properties of clear speech are responsible for its increased intelligibility? and (2) is all clear speech alike? Partly, this ignorance is due to the relatively small numbers of talkers in the clear speech studies, the variability in the acoustic data especially across talkers, and to the extremely laborious efforts required for many of the acoustic/phonetic analyses. However, this ignorance is also a reflection of our lack of knowledge about the exact relations between the acoustic characteristics of speech and the perception of speech in general. We would like to assume that the same acoustic or physical characteristics that distinguish clear from conversational speech *within a talker* would also distinguish the most intelligible from the least intelligible talker *amongst a group of talkers*. The problem of identifying the acoustic properties that relate directly to intelligibility is unsolved for clear speech as it is also unsolved for different talkers of conversational speech (Bradlow et al., 1996) and for disordered speech (Monsen, 1978; Weismer & Martin, 1992).

Once identified, it is likely that such relations will not be simple. And, the generality of any resulting relations to other speaking styles or types of speech should be made cautiously. For example, for many speaking styles (clear speech, Lombard, etc.), longer duration, higher F0, and increased intensity are associated with an intelligibility increase. However, similar acoustic differences exist between the speech produced by adult cochlear implant users, pre- and post-implant, and yet the intelligibility change is in the opposite direction. That is, speech of deaf adults pre-implantation exhibits longer duration, higher F0, and higher intensity than speech produced post-implantation and is *less* intelligible (Gould et al., 2001).

Also, in studying the relations between acoustic characteristics and intelligibility, the communication situation and the listener cannot be ignored. Results from Ferguson and Kewley-Port (2002) and Krause and Braida (2003), in particular, indicate there may be a complex interaction between a talker's clear speech characteristics, and the listener or the listening situation. In the former study, though the speech stimuli were the same and were obtained from one talker, two listener groups differed drastically in their clear speech benefit. In the latter study, two talkers exhibited clear speech advantages for normal hearing listeners in a noise background for their clear/norm speaking style. However, the two talkers' clear/norm speech differed in their intelligibility advantage in other listening situations – even for the same types of listeners.

9.5 Applications and Future Directions

9.5.1 Applications

Clear speech is a distinct speaking style that is more intelligible than conversational speech for many types of listeners, in many listening situations, across all three modality conditions (A, V, and AV). Despite our current inability to identify the specific characteristics of clear speech that contribute to its high intelligibility, clear speech has a contributing role in aural rehabilitation, education, and basic speech research.

In the field of aural rehabilitation, clear speaking styles are routinely encouraged (Oticon, 1997; Schum, 1997). The results of Helfer (1997, 1998), Schum (1996) and others demonstrate that adopting a clear speaking style is generally beneficial to a listener, regardless of age, regardless of hearing loss (over the range of normal to mildly impaired), and regardless of whether visual cues are present. Older and younger listeners, with and without impaired hearing, and the communication partners of these people should know that speaking clearly *and* facing the listener will *both* make communication easier when a difficult situation arises. And, no special talker training is required.

Clear speech may be useful in education too. If teachers adopt a clear speaking style, then normal-hearing children in noisy classrooms (Crandell & Smaldino, 1999) and children with learning disabilities (Bradlow et al., 2003) should benefit perceptually. Also, the use of cue-enhanced speech stimuli, based on clear speech characteristics, seems to improve the perception of speech contrasts for listeners with learning or language disabilities (e.g., Tallal et al., 1996; Cunningham et al., 2001) and possibly for second language learners (Hazan & Simpson, 2000).

Finally, though much of clear speech research has been directed towards clinical goals, especially towards understanding and providing benefit to hearing-impaired listeners, linguists and other speech scientists use clear speech in their research. Lindblom (1990) cites the existence of clear speech as supporting evidence for the proposal that talkers can vary their articulation along a hypo- to hyper- (H&H) continuum in response to the communication situation. A clear speaking style in response to degraded ambient conditions also supports the Dual-Process Theory of the Role of Hearing in Speech Production (Perkell et al., 2000).

9.5.2 Future research

"Clearly," many unknowns remain regarding clear speech. Foremost, some new perceptual studies are warranted for both clear (clear/slow) and clear/norm speech.[6] In particular, a deeper examination of the potential benefits of these speaking styles for hearing-impaired listeners is needed to address possible interactions between benefit and age of the listener, severity of hearing loss of the listener, hearing aid, and talker. It is worth knowing, for example, whether a clear speaking style benefits moderate-to-severely hearing-impaired listeners *while* using their own hearing aid (such as a state-of-the-art wideband compression hearing aid). There may be unknown effects and interactions of wideband compression on clear vs. conversational speaking styles. Also, it is especially important to document the advantage, if any, of clear/norm speech over conv/norm speech for hearing-impaired listeners before much more effort is expended on the examination of clear/norm speech and the manipulation of conv/norm speech to be like clear/norm speech. Finally, besides additional perceptual studies, other areas for further research include the development of new methods to describe and quantify talker variability both perceptually and acoustically, for both conversation and clear speaking styles, the exploration of new methods to describe speech characteristics, such as a recently proposed estimate of consonant reduction (van Son & Pols, 1999), the characterization of sub- vs. supra-glottal effects in the production of clear speech (Alku, Vintturi, & Vilkman, 2002), and the search for more efficient methods of determining the intelligibility of clear and conversational speaking styles from individual talkers (Howell & Bonnett, 1997; Miller, 1946).

ACKNOWLEDGMENTS

The author wishes to express her heartfelt thanks to Karen L. Payton, Jean C. Krause, and Louis D. Braida for the use of the waveforms illustrated in the spectrograms. The author owes an additional thank you to Louis D. Braida for noticing the quotation from Dashiell Hammett's book. Special thanks also to Ann Bradlow for sharing her thoughts and pre-prints.

NOTES

1 It is possible that not all elderly listeners will benefit from a clear speaking style. Since clear speech is typically spoken at a slower speaking rate, slower clear speech might be beneficial only for listeners with good working memories (Small, Andersen, & Kempler, 1997). That is, a loss in working memory may counteract the benefit of slow clear speech that has been found for many elderly listeners.

2 In another study, using clearly spoken vowels from eight female talkers, vowel identification was also found to be highly vowel-dependent with the largest benefit for the vowels /a/ and /i/. (See DeMerit, 1997.)

3 There is some evidence that talker clarity is dependent on the presence of a listener (Charles-Luce, 1997).

4 To give a conservative estimate of an equivalent improvement in SNR.

5 After the talkers were separated by gender.

6 And it will be important to use a variety of speech materials. The results of Ferguson and Kewley-Port (2002) and Hazan and Simpson (1998) demonstrate that the same style of speech can yield very different perceptual results for syllables than for sentences.

REFERENCES

Alku, P., Vintturi, J., & Vilkman, E. (2002). Measuring the effect of fundamental frequency raising as a strategy for increasing vocal intensity in soft, normal and loud phonation. *Speech Communication*, 38, 321–34.

Aylett, M. (2000a). Modelling clarity change in spontaneous speech. In R. J. Baddeley, P. J. B. Hancock, & P. Foldiak (eds.), *Information Theory and the Brain* (pp. 204–20). Cambridge: Cambridge University Press.

Aylett, M. (2000b). Stochastic Suprasegmentals: Relationships between redundancy, prosodic structure and care of articulation in spontaneous speech. *Proceedings of ICSLP* (pp. 646–9). Beijing.

Birmingham, A. I. & Krapp, G. P. (1922). *First Lessons in Speech Improvement*. New York, Charles Scribner's Sons.

Bond, Z. S. & Moore, T. J. (1994). A note on the acoustic-phonetic characteristics of inadvertently clear speech. *Speech Communication*, 14, 325–37.

Bond, Z. S., Moore, T. J., & Gable, B. (1989). Acoustic phonetic characteristics of speech produced in noise and while wearing an oxygen mask. *Journal of the Acoustical Society of America*, 85, 907–12.

Bradlow, A. R. (2003). Confluent talker- and listener-related forces in clear speech production. In C. Gussenhoven & N. Warner (eds.), *Laboratory Phonology, 7* (pp. 241–73). Berlin & New York: Mouton de Gruyter.

Bradlow, A. R. & Bent, T. (2002). The clear speech effect for non-native listeners. *Journal of the Acoustical Society of America*, 112, 272–84.

Bradlow, A. R., Kraus, N., & Hayes, E. (2003). Speaking clearly for learning-impaired children: Sentence perception in noise. *Journal of Speech, Language and Hearing Research*, 46, 80–97.

Bradlow, A. R., Torretta, G. M., & Pisoni, D. B. (1996). Intelligibility of normal speech I: Global and fine-grained acoustic-phonetic talker characteristics. *Speech Communication*, 20, 255–72.

Braida, L. D. (1991). Crossmodal integration in the identification of consonant segments. *Quarterly Journal of Experimental Psychology Section A: Human Experimental Psychology*, 43, 647–77.

Charles-Luce, J. (1997). Cognitive factors involved in preserving a phonemic contrast. *Language and Speech*, 40, 229–48.

Chen, F. R. (1980). Acoustic characteristics and intelligibility of clear and conversational speech at the segmental level. Unpublished master's thesis, MIT, Cambridge, MA.

Clark, J. E., Lubker, J. F., & Hunnicutt, S. (1988). Some preliminary evidence for phonetic adjustment strategies in communication difficulty. In R. Steele & T. Threadgold (eds.), *Language Topics: Essays in Honour of Michael Halliday* (pp. 161–80). Amsterdam: John Benjamins.

Cox, R. M., Alexander, G. C., & Gilmore, C. (1987). Intelligibility of average talkers in typical listening environments. *Journal of the Acoustical Society of America*, 81, 1598–1608.

Crandell, C. C. & Smaldino, J. J. (1999). Improving classroom acoustics: Utilizing hearing-assistive technology and communication strategies in the educational setting. *Volta Review*, 101, 47–62.

Cummings, K. E. & Clements, M. A. (1995). Analysis of the glottal excitation of emotionally styled and stressed speech. *Journal of the Acoustical Society of America*, 98, 88–98.

Cunningham, J., Nicol, T., Zecker, S. G., Bradlow, A., & Kraus, N. (2001). Neurobiologic responses to speech in noise in children with learning problems: Deficits and strategies for improvement. *Clinical Neurophysiology*, 112, 758–67.

Cunningham, J., Nicol, T., King, C., Zecker, S. G., & Kraus, N. (2002). Effects of noise and cue enhancement on neural responses to speech in auditory midbrain, thalamus and cortex. *Hearing Research*, 169, 97–111.

Cutler, A. & Butterfield, S. (1990). Durational cues to word boundaries in clear speech. *Speech Communication*, 9, 485–95.

DeMerit, J. (1997). Acoustic and perceptual effects of clear speech on duration-dependent vowel contrasts. Unpublished doctoral thesis. University of Wisconsin, Madison.

Erber, N. P. (1993). *Communication and Adult Hearing Loss*. Melbourne: Clavis Publishing.

Ferguson, S. H. & Kewley-Port, D. (2002). Vowel intelligibility in clear and conversational speech for normal-hearing and hearing-impaired listeners. *Journal of the Acoustical Society of America*, 112, 259–71.

Fernald, A., Taeschner, T., Dunn, J., Papousek, M., De Boysson-Bardies, B., & Fukui, I. (1989). A cross-language study of prosodic modifications in mothers' and fathers' speech to preverbal infants. *Journal of Child Language*, 16, 47–501.

Freyman, R. L. & Nerbonne, G. P. (1989). The importance of consonant-vowel intensity ratio in the intelligibility of voiceless consonants. *Journal of Speech & Hearing Research*, 32, 524–35.

Gagné, J.-P., Masterson, V., Munhall, K. G., Bilida, N., & Querengesser, C. (1994). Across talker variability in audtiory, visual, and audiovisual speech intelligibility for conversational and clear speech. *Journal of the Academy of Rehabilitative Audiology*, 27, 135–58.

Gagné, J. P., Querengesser, C., Folkeard, P., Munhall, K. G., & Zandipour, M. (1995). Auditory, visual, and audiovisual speech intelligibility for sentence-length stimuli: An investigation of conversational and clear speech. *The Volta Review*, 97, 33–51.

Gagné, J.-P., Rochette, A.-J., & Charest, M. (2002). Auditory, visual and audiovisual clear speech. *Speech Communication*, 37, 213–30.

Gordon-Salant, S. (1986). Recognition of natural and time/intensity altered CVs by young and elderly subjects with normal hearing. *Journal of the Acoustical Society of America*, 80, 1599–1607.

Gould, J., Lane, H., Vick, J., Perkell, J. S., Matthies, M. L., & Zandipour, M. (2001). Changes in speech intelligibility of postlingually deaf adults after cochlear implantation. *Ear and Hearing*, 22, 453–60.

Grieser, D. L. & Kuhl, P. K. (1988). Maternal speech to infants in a tonal language: Support for universal prosodic features in motherese. *Developmental Psychology*, 24, 14–20.

Hazan, V. & Markham, D. (2004). Acoustic-phonetic correlates of talker intelligibility in adults and children. *Journal of the Acoustical Society of America*, 116, 3108–18.

Hazan, V. & Simpson, A. (1998). The effect of cue-enhancement on the intelligibility of nonsense word and sentence materials presented in noise. *Speech Communication*, 24, 211–26.

Hazan, V. & Simpson, A. (2000). The effect of cue-enhancement on consonant intelligibility in noise: Speaker and listener effects. *Language and Speech*, 43, 273–94.

Helfer, K. S. (1997). Auditory and auditory-visual perception of clear and conversational speech. *Journal of Speech, Language and Hearing Research*, 40, 432–43.

Helfer, K. S. (1998). Auditory and auditory-visual recognition of clear and conversational speech by older adults. *Journal of the American Academy of Audiology*, 9, 234–42.

Hertrich, I. & Ackermann, H. (1995). Coarticulation in slow speech: Durational and spectral analysis. *Language and Speech*, 38, 159–87.

Hood, J. D. & Poole, J. P. (1980). Influence of the speaker and other factors affecting speech intelligibility. *Audiology*, 19, 434–55.

Houtgast, T. & Steeneken, H. J. M. (1973). The modulation transfer function in room acoustics as a predictor of speech intelligibility. *Acustica*, 28, 66–73.

Howell, P. & Bonnett, C. (1997). Speaking clearly for the hearing impaired: Intelligibility differences between clear and less clear speakers. *European Journal of Disorders of Communication*, 32, 89–97.

Hunnicutt, S. (1985). Intelligibility versus redundancy: Conditions of dependency. *Language and Speech*, 28, 47–56.

Imaizumi, S., Hayashi, A., & Deguchi, T. (1993). Planning in speech production: Listener adaptive characteristics. *Japan Journal of Logopedics and Phoniatrics*, 34, 394–401.

Johnson, K., Flemming, E., & Wright, R. (1993). The hyperspace effect: Phonetic targets are hyperarticulated. *Language*, 69, 505–28.

Junqua, J.-C. (1993). The Lombard reflex and its role on human listeners and automatic speech recognizers. *Journal of the Acoustical Society of America*, 93, 510–24.

Kennedy, E., Levitt, H., Neuman, A. C., & Weiss, M. (1998). Consonant-vowel intensity ratios for maximizing consonant recognition by hearing-impaired listeners. *Journal of the Acoustical Society of America*, 103, 1098–1114.

Krause, J. C. (2001). Properties of naturally produced clear speech at normal rates and implications for intelligibility enhancement. Unpublished doctoral thesis, MIT, Cambridge, MA.

Krause, J. C. & Braida, L. D. (2002). Investigating alternative forms of clear speech: The effects of speaking rate and speaking mode on intelligibility. *Journal of the Acoustical Society of America*, 112, 2165–72.

Krause, J. C. & Braida, L. D. (2003). Acoustic properties of naturally produced clear speech at normal speaking rates. *Journal of the Acoustical Society of America*, 115, 362–78.

Kuhl, P. K. et al. (1997). Cross-language analysis of phonetic units in language addressed to infants. *Science*, 277, 684–6.

Letowski, T., Frank, T., & Caravella, J. (1993). Acoustical properties of speech produced in noise presented through supraaural earphones. *Ear and Hearing*, 14, 332–8.

Lienard, J.-S. & D. Benedetto, M.-G. (1999). Effect of vocal effort on spectral properties of vowels. *Journal of the Acoustical Society of America*, 106, 411–22.

Lindblom, B. (1990). Explaining phonetic variation: A sketch of the H&H Theory. In W. J. Hardcastle & A. Marchal (eds.), *Speech Production and Speech Modelling* (pp. 403–39). The Netherlands: Kluwer Academic Publishers.

Lively, S. E., Pisoni, D. B., Summers, W. V., & Bernacki, R. H. (1993). Effects of cognitive workload on speech production: Acoustic analyses and perceptual consequences. *Journal of the Acoustical Society of America*, 93, 2962–73.

Matthies, M., Perrier, P., Perkell, J. S., & Zandipour, M. (2001). Variation in anticipatory coarticulation with changes in clarity and rate. *Journal of Speech, Language and Hearing Research*, 44, 340–53.

Metz, D. E., Samar, V. J., Schiavetti, N., Sitler, R. W., & Whitehead, R. L. (1985). Acoustic dimensions of hearing-impaired speakers' intelligibility. *Journal of Speech & Hearing Research*, 28, 345–55.

Miller, G. A. (1946). Transmission and reception of sounds under combat conditions: Selecting and training personnel. *Combat Instrumentation* (pp. 208–15). Washington, DC: Office of Scientific Research and Development: National Defense Research Committee.

Miller, G. A., Heise, G. A., & Lichten, W. (1951). The intelligibility of speech as a function of the context of the test materials. *Journal of Experimental Psychology*, 41, 329–35.

Monsen, R. B. (1978). Toward measuring how well hearing-impaired children speak. *Journal of Speech & Hearing Research*, 21, 197–219.

Montgomery, A. A. & Edge, R. A. (1988). Evaluation of two speech enhancement techniques to improve intelligibility for hearing-impaired adults. *Journal of Speech & Hearing Research*, 31, 386–93.

Moon, S.-J. (1995). Formant patterns of clear speech and their implications for phonetic invariance. *Linguistics in the Morning Calm*, 3, 411–22.

Moon, S.-J. & Lindblom, B. (1994). Interaction between duration, context, and speaking style in English stressed vowels. *Journal of the Acoustical Society of America*, 96, 40–55.

Munhall, K. G., Gribble, P., Sacco, L., & Ward, M. (1996). Temporal constraints on the McGurk effect. *Perception & Psychophysics*, 58, 351–62.

Nejime, Y. & Moore, B. C. J. (1998). Evaluation of the effect of speech-rate slowing on speech intelligibility in noise using a simulation of cochlear hearing loss. *Journal of the Acoustical Society of America*, 103, 572–6.

Oticon (1997). *Your Way to Better Communication: Clear Speech*. Oticon, Report 906 35 110.

Oviatt, S., MacEachern, M., & Levow, G.-A. (1998). Predicting hyperarticulate speech during human-computer error resolution. *Speech Communication*, 24, 87–110.

Payton, K. L. & Braida, L. D. (1999). A method to determine the speech transmission index from speech waveforms. *Journal of the Acoustical Society of America*, 106, 3637–48.

Payton, K. L., Uchanski, R. M., & Braida, L. D. (1994). Intelligibility of conversational and clear speech in noise and reverberation for listeners with normal and impaired hearing. *Journal of the Acoustical Society of America*, 95, 1581–92.

Perkell, J. S. et al. (2000). A theory of speech motor control and supporting data from speakers with normal hearing and with profound hearing loss. *Journal of Phonetics*, 28, 233–72.

Picheny, M. A., Durlach, N. I., & Braida, L. D. (1985). Speaking clearly for the hard of hearing I: Intelligibility differences between clear and conversational speech. *Journal of Speech & Hearing Research*, 28, 96–103.

Picheny, M. A., Durlach, N. I., & Braida, L. D. (1986). Speaking clearly for the hard of hearing II: Acoustic characteristics of clear and conversational speech. *Journal of Speech & Hearing Research*, 29, 434–46.

Picheny, M. A., Durlach, N. I., & Braida, L. D. (1989). Speaking clearly for the hard of hearing III: An attempt to determine the contribution of speaking rate to differences in intelligibility between clear and conversational speech. *Journal of Speech & Hearing Research*, 32, 600–3.

Pisoni, D. B., Bernacki, R. H., Nusbaum, H. C., & Yuchtman, M. (1985). Some acoustic-phonetic correlates of speech produced in noise. In *Proceedings of 1985 International Conference on Acoustics, Speech, and Signal Processing* (pp. 1581–4).

Pittman, A. L. & Wiley, T. L. (2001). Recognition of speech produced in noise. *Journal of Speech, Language and Hearing Research*, 44, 487–96.

Revoile, S. G., Holden-Pitt, L., Edward, D., Pickett, J. M., & Brandt, F. (1987). Speech-cue enhancement for the hearing impaired: Amplification of burst/murmur cues for improved perception of final stop voicing. *Journal of Rehabilitation Research and Development*, 24, 207–16.

Ross, M. (2000). Talking to a person who is hard of hearing. Accessed from http://www.therubins.com on December 16, 2001.

Rostolland, D. (1982). Acoustic features of shouted voice. *Acustica*, 50, 118–25.

Sammeth, C. A., Dorman, M. F., & Stearns, C. J. (1999). The role of consonant-vowel amplitude ratio in the recognition of voiceless stop consonants by listeners with hearing impairment. *Journal of Speech, Language and Hearing Research*, 42, 42–55.

Schiavetti, N., Whitehead, R. L., Metz, D. E., Whitehead, B., & Mignerey, M. (1996). Voice onset time in speech produced during simultaneous communication. *Journal of Speech & Hearing Research*, 39, 565–72.

Schiavetti, N., Whitehead, R. L., Whitehead, B., & Metz, D. E. (1998). Effect of fingerspelling task on temporal characteristics and perceived naturalness of speech in simultaneous communication. *Journal of Speech, Language and Hearing Research*, 41, 5–17.

Schmitt, J. F. (1983). The effects of time compression and time expansion on passage comprehension by elderly listeners. *Journal of Speech & Hearing Research*, 26, 373–7.

Schon, T. D. (1970). The effects on speech intelligibility of time-compression and -expansion on normal-hearing, hard of hearing, and aged males. *Journal of Auditory Research*, 10, 263–8.

Schum, D. J. (1996). Intelligibility of clear and conversational speech of young and elderly talkers. *Journal of the American Academy of Audiology*, 7, 212–18.

Schum, D. J. (1997). Beyond hearing aids: Clear speech training as an intervention strategy. *The Hearing Journal*, 50, 36–40.

Slaney, M. & McRoberts, G. (2003). BabyEars: A recognition system for affective vocalizations. *Speech Communication*, 39, 367–84.

Small, J. A., Andersen, E. S., & Kempler, D. (1997). Effects of working memory capacity on understanding rate-altered speech. *Aging Neuropsychology and Cognition*, 4, 126–39.

Snidecor, J. C., Mallory, L. A., & Hearsey, E. L. (1944). *Methods of Training Telephone Talkers for Increased Intelligibility*. New York: The Psychological Corporation.

Studebaker, G. A. (1985). A "Rationalized" arcsine transform. *Journal of Speech & Hearing Research*, 28, 455–62.

Summers, W. V., Pisoni, D. B., Bernacki, R. H., Pedlow, R. I., & Stokes, M. A. (1988). Effects of noise on speech production: Acoustic and perceptual analyses. *Journal of the Acoustical Society of America*, 84, 917–28.

Tallal, P. et al. (1996). Language comprehension in language-learning impaired children improved with acoustically modified speech. *Science*, 271, 81–4.

Tartter, V. C., Gomes, H., & Litwin, E. (1993). Some acoustic effects of listening to noise on speech production. *Journal of the Acoustical Society of America*, 94, 2437–40.

Tolhurst, G. C. (1957). Effects of duration and articulation changes on intelligibility, word reception and listener preference. *Journal of Speech and Hearing Disorders*, 22, 328–34.

Tolkmitt, F. J. & Scherer, K. R. (1986). Effect of experimentally induced stress on vocal parameters. *Journal of Experimental Psychology: Human Perception and Performance*, 12, 302–13.

Tye-Murray, N. (1998). *Foundations of Aural Rehabilitation: Children, Adults and Their Family Members*. San Diego: Singular Publishing Group.

Uchanski, R. M. (1988). Spectral and temporal contributions to speech clarity for hearing impaired listeners. Unpublished doctoral thesis, MIT, Cambridge: MA.

Uchanski, R. M., Choi, S. S., Braida, L. D., Reed, C. M., & Durlach, N. I. (1996). Speaking clearly for the hard of hearing IV: Further studies of the role of speaking rate. *Journal of Speech & Hearing Research*, 39, 494–509.

Valian, V. V. & Wales, R. J. (1976). What's what: Talkers help listeners hear and understand by clarifying syntactic relations. *Cognition*, 4, 115–76.

van Bergem, D. R. (1988). Acoustic vowel reduction as a function of sentence accent, word stress, and word class. *Speech Communication*, 12, 1–23.

van Son, R. J. J. H. & Pols, L. C. W. (1999). An acoustic description of consonant reduction. *Speech Communication*, 28, 125–40.

Weismer, G. & Martin, R. E. (1992). Acoustic and perceptual approaches to the study of intelligibility. In R. D. Kent (ed.), *Intelligibility in Speech Disorders* (pp. 67–118). Vol. 1 in the 7-vol. series Studies in Speech Pathology and Clinical Linguistics (series eds., R. D. Kent & M. J. Ball). Amsterdam: John Benjamins.

Wohlert, A. B. & Hammen, V. L. (2000). Lip muscle activity related to speech rate and loudness. *Journal of Speech, Language and Hearing Research*, 43, 1229–39.

10 Perception of Intonation

JACQUELINE VAISSIÈRE

10.1 Introduction

All primates vocalize on an expiratory airflow and they make use of the oscillation of the vocal folds to generate sounds. The acoustic correlate of the rate of vibration is the fundamental frequency (F0) of voice; its perceptual correlate is pitch. By manipulating the stiffness and length of the vocal folds, elevating or lowering the larynx, and changing the subglottal pressure, humans can vary the periodicity of vocal fold vibration and control the temporal course of the modulation, F0 range, F0 height, the size and direction of F0 movements, the shape of the glottal-pulse waveform, their rate of change, and their timing relative to the articulatory maneuvers for the realization of phonemes. All human languages exploit F0 modulation in a controlled way to convey meaning, i.e., intonation. As a first approximation, intonation is the use of F0 variation for conveying information at levels higher than the word, i.e., the phrase, the utterance, the paragraph, and discourse as a whole. F0 modulation contributes to the perception of the syntactic structure of a sentence (it has a demarcative function), its modality (it has a modal function), informational structuring (focus marking and topic delimitation), speaker attitudes and emotions, and the dialog situation (the speaker's communicative intention, and his or her intention to give or to keep turn). This chapter provides an overview of the role of intonation in speech perception, with special focus on the perception of intonation contours.

In recent years, the intonational aspects of speech have become an important area of study in phonetics, phonology, and speech science. The current interest in research on intonation has been encouraged by several factors. First, there has been tremendous technical progress in the last decade. There is now wide access to inexpensive speech analysis and synthesis software, real-time F0 detection, large database facilities, video techniques for multimodal analysis, as well as neuro-imaging techniques. Furthermore, the hope of drawing on intonation to improve automatic speech synthesis of texts, speech recognition, and human–machine dialog systems, as well as language identification and speaker recognition, attracts many engineers. Second, the last two decades have witnessed a conceptual advance in the formal representation of pitch contours, and phonologists have been strongly encouraged to study intonation. Finally, the shift of interest from the purely

Table 10.1 Some of the multiple functions of intonation

Syntactic	*Segmentation of continuous speech into syntactic units of different size:* Prosodic words, syntagma, propositions, utterances, paragraphs
Informational	*Segmentation of continuous speech into informational units:* Theme/rheme, given/new, focus/parenthesis
Interactive	*Regulation of the speaker–listener interaction:* Attraction of attention and arousal, turn-taking/holding, topic end/continuation
Modal	*Communicative intent:* Assertion/question/order, etc.
Attitudinal	*Attitudes of the speaker toward what he says:* Doubt, disbelief, etc. *Attitudes of the speaker toward the listener:* Politeness, irony, etc.
Emotional	*Speaker's arousal:* Joy, anger, etc.
Other	*Characteristics of the speaker:* Identity, sex, age, physiological state, regional varieties, stylistic variations, sociocultural background, etc. *Prosodic continuity, intelligibility, lexical access, memory and recall*

syntactic aspects of language to the speech communication process as a whole has established the relevance of prosody in real-life situations and focused greater interest on the role of intonation in interaction. Many, if not all, of the communicative functions of intonation are not observable in laboratory speech, but surface in interactive, spontaneous speech. The perceptual (central and peripheral) and cognitive (innate and acquired) principles underlying the processing of intonation are not known, however. Despite conceptual advances, there is as yet no comprehensive model of intonation perception which includes the interaction between the various often conflicting functions of intonation.

The goal of this chapter is threefold. First, we present a number of facts which explain why there is as yet no complete theory concerning the perception of intonation, and why intonation is such a complex process to study and understand. Second, we review the findings that have nonetheless been made on the syntactical, informational, interactive, modal, attitudinal, and emotional aspects of intonation (see Table 10.1). The contribution of F0 contours to speaker identity (sex, age, socio-cultural background, regional accent, Gussenhoven & Rietveld, 1998; Grabe et al., 2000), to source separation (Brokx & Nooteboom, 1982; Darwin, 1975), and attention focusing (Cohen, Douaire, & Elsabbagh, 2001), to intelligibility of speech (Swerts & Geluykens, 1993) and to acceleration of lexical access are not considered here, nor is the tactile perception of intonation (Auer, Bernstein, & Coulter, 1998), the perception of subjective pauses (Duez, 1993), the neural basis of intonation (Gandour et al., 2003), the processing of intonation by hearing-impaired subjects (Grant, 1987), and the effect of age (Most & Frank, 1994) or the contribution of intonation to the perception of a foreign accent (Van Els & DeObt, 1987) and the development of the comprehension of intonation patterns during language acquisition (Moore, Harris, & Patriquin, 1993). Third, we propose several tentative components of a psychophonetic code that seem to account for a number of striking cross-linguistic similarities in the perception of intonational features across languages. Some suggestions for further research will be presented in the conclusion.

10.2 Why Is Intonation Difficult to Study?

10.2.1 Lack of a clear definition of intonation

There is currently no universally accepted definition of intonation. The term may be strictly restricted to the perceived F0 pattern, or include the perception of other prosodic parameters fulfilling the same functions: pauses, relative loudness, voice quality, duration, and segmental phenomena related to varying strengthening of the speech organs. Furthermore, there is no broad consensus as to the *object* and *aim* of intonational studies. Pierrehumbert suggests "that it is just the grammatical intonation distinctions which are properly of interest for linguists" (1980, p. 60), whereas other researchers emphasize that "the grammatical functions of intonation are secondary to the emotional one" (Bolinger, 1986, p. 260; see also Fonagy, 1983). Intonation is "a symptom of how we feel about what we say and how you feel when you say it" (Bolinger, 1989, p. 1). In this chapter, all the major functions of intonation will be considered because they interact in everyday speech communication situations.

There is also no general agreement on how to represent intonation. Should one focus on pitch levels, pitch movements, or configurations? Phonologists generally prefer a pitch-level approach with only two levels (as in Pierrehumbert, 1980), while phoneticians generally favor more levels (four to six or more), or expandable/compressible ranges or sloping grids of (near) parallel lines rather than levels. We do not tackle the problem of the representation of pitch contours, because it is a matter of too much controversy (Ladd, 1996).

10.2.2 Approaches to intonation and its perception

There are many theoretical approaches to the study of intonation, reflecting deep theoretical and representational differences. First, for those researchers committed to a strictly linear system, the symbolic representation of intonation and the number of prosodic units play the primary role. In Pierrehumbert's model for American English, intonation is essentially considered as the sum of atomistic local events: pitch accents, phrase accents, and boundary tones (Pierrehumbert, 1980). Second, the adherents of a superpositional representation of intonation suggest that the final F0 contour is best reconstructed as the sum of superimposed global baselines, semi-global phrase components, and local word accent commands. Öhman and Fujisaki give physiological motivation for such a superimposition (Fujisaki & Sudo, 1971; Öhman, 1967). Third, for the advocates of a morphological or pragmatic approach, function plays a key role. All the cues, whether pragmatic particles, or intonational, syntactic, facial and gestural cues, that fulfill the same function in a given language are to be described together: functional equivalence is a major concern (Danes, 1960; Rossi, 1999; Uldall, 1964). Fourth, the listener-oriented approach at IPO (Institute for Perception Research at Eindhoven) assumes that F0 contours should be described in terms of a number of perceptually relevant F0 patterns. Various F0 contours may be "perceptually equivalent," i.e., variants of the same F0 pattern (Cohen & t'Hart, 1967; t'Hart, Collier, & Cohen, 1990). Finally, linear and superpositional approaches to intonation converge in their effort toward a compositional interpretation of intonational meanings (see Section 10.3). More and more researchers consider it necessary to attempt to study intonational phenomena under several aspects (phonetic, phonological, physiological, functional, perceptual, and neuronal).

10.2.3 Multiple cues, cue trading, and cross-linguistic functional equivalence

Intonational cues can surface as temporally short-ranged local cues, such as juncture tone; as semi-global cues, such as resetting of the baseline, concerning a part of the utterance; and as global cues, such as manipulation of declination tendency, pitch range, pitch register, and rate of speech over an entire utterance. Pitch accent and tone languages display more semi-global and global cues than languages with strong lexical stress (English), which favor more local cues mainly anchored relative to the lexically stressed syllable. Local cues may however be used in tonal and pitch-accent languages: the final tone in tone languages may undergo change due to intonation; in Serbo-Croatian, lexical contrasts are neutralized by intonation in sentence initial and final position (Lehiste, 1970, p. 101) (see Hirst & Di Cristo, 1998, for a survey on intonation in 20 languages).

All the parameters of speech melody, local and global, are perceived in an integrated way. Several properties of the pitch contour guide the interpretation of an utterance as a question or a statement (Gosy & Terken, 1994) and combine additively in producing finality judgments (Swerts, Bouwhuis, & Collier, 1994; for affect, see Ladd et al., 1985). Fonagy proposed the hypothesis that the melody of sentences for which the listeners give multiple meanings (in free choice tests) is produced by the effective superimposition of several everyday simple intonation patterns and they should be considered as complex: the complex intonation pattern expresses simultaneously the messages conveyed usually by two or more simple intonation patterns. He found that the complex melodies were reproduced in a much less consistent way by French and Hungarian speakers than simple melodies (Fonagy & Fonagy, 1987).

Other parameters than pitch, such as pause duration, intensity, and voice quality, may help to signal a prosodic contrast. The effects of duration and pitch contour seem to be additive in phrasing (Streeter, 1978). More phonetic cues create a perception of stronger boundaries (De Pijper & Sanderman, 1994; see also Swerts,

1997). Intonation is a perceptually more important factor than pause duration for the clarification of the topical make-up of a text (Swerts & Geluykens, 1993). For native speakers of English listening to Czech or Slovakian, F0 fall is a relatively more important cue to the perceptual segmentation of speech than is pause duration (Henderson & Nelms, 1980). The presence of a pre-focal hesitation pause strengthens the interpretation of a focal peak delay as signaling question intonation (House, 2003).

All the cues seem to form coherent wholes: young infants (aged 9 months) react differently to normal (coincident) phrase boundaries and non-coincident boundaries (strings segmented within the predicate phrase) (Jusczyk et al., 1992). There is also evidence of trading relations between parameters (Nooteboom, Brokx, & De Rooij, 1978; see Pisoni & Luce, 1987a; Repp, 1982, on trading relationships and context effect in speech perception). Cues form a context-dependent hierarchy. In post-focus position, the range of F0 is smaller (see examples in Figure 10.4) and temporal cues may take over the leading role for phrasing (French), and for stress marking (Swedish) (and laryngealization for stress marking in Serbo-Croatian, Lehiste, 1970, p. 101). Peak F0 height and slope also trade in determining the category boundary between contrastive and non-contrastive focus in English (Bartels & Kingston, 1994); a delayed peak often substitutes for a higher peak (House, 2003). There is little evidence of cue trading for children, for whom duration has a strong influence on identification of the phrasal units, whereas pitch has only a slight influence (Beach, Katz, & Skowronski, 1996). The weight of each acoustic parameter depends on the position of the syllable in the word (McClean & Tiffany, 1973) and of the word in the prosodic contours (Nakatani & Schaffer, 1978).

Several cues may be functionally equivalent cross-linguistically. In mora-based Japanese, for example, duration is constrained at the phonological level, and F0 at the lexical level. I suggest that (1) a semi-global resetting of the baseline at the beginning of each new prosodic phrase (Fujisaki & Sudo, 1971) in Japanese may be considered as a kind of substitute for phrase-final lengthening as a phrase boundary marker; (2) the final topic-marker "wa" may be considered as a substitute for a continuation rise; and (3) the expansion of the local F0 range is functionally equivalent to the displacement of phrase accent in English for the expression of focus. As a consequence, the description of intonation in a language cannot be done without considering whether or not other acoustic cues and other linguistic means fulfill similar functions.

10.2.4 Non-applicability of well-established research methods

The well-established experimental methods developed in psychoacoustics do not actually apply in the field of intonation. F0 perception in speech includes not only a psychoacoustic level but also higher-level cognitive and linguistic processing (Pisoni & Luce, 1987b). While higher-order linguistic decisions may determine auditory shape in some cases, the reverse can also be true (Studdert-Kennedy & Hadding-Koch, 1973).

Traditional linguistic paradigms, such as the criteria of phonological distinctiveness and semantic differentiation, which have proved their validity in the discovery of phonemes, fail in the study of intonation. When the listener is asked to identify the same stimulus pattern as yes-no question, echo question, call for confirmation, alternative question, rhetorical question, disbelieving question, a question to oneself, an all-or-none decision is hardly possible.

One may reasonably consider intonational meaning as involving both all-or-none contrasts on the one hand and dimensions of gradiency within categories on the other (Ainsworth & Lindsay, 1986; Ladd & Morton, 1997). Differences in F0 range are commonly assumed to have continuous rather than categorical effects on affective judgments. The coexistence of both discrete and continuous dimensions of intonation makes perceptual experiments difficult to carry out and interpret.

How does one decide what is a linguistic function of intonation and what is not? In a given language, morpho-syntactic mechanisms, such as a modal particle, word order, and expressions such as "I strongly believe that . . ." may be entirely replaceable by intonation and intonation may be a reinforcing cue. In some languages, intonation may be the only means available for expressing yes-no questions or some attitudes. Intonation may be the only factor used to resolve certain syntactic ambiguities, but ambiguities are rare in everyday speech.

Furthermore, intonation has no self-evident perceptual units. A semantic unit such as a word tends to be acoustically marked by a lexically prominent syllable even in tone languages. Two or more words may be prosodically grouped into a single phrase, which is variously called *intermediate phrase, phonological phrase, "groupe rythmique," "groupe mineur,"* "sense-group," *"buntetsu"* (in Japanese). This low-level grouping is generally achieved by superimposing the prosodic characteristics of a single word onto a sequence of several words. Two sense-groups may also be further grouped into a larger intonational group, or *"groupe majeur"* or *intonational phrase.* The end of an utterance non-final intonational group is typically marked by some kind of F0 raising and pre-boundary lengthening. Intonational phrases are then grouped into a prosodic (or phonological) utterance, typically ending in an F0 fall and low F0 value, low intensity, and final lengthening. Utterances are also grouped into prosodic paragraphs (or *topic units*), with raised F0 values at the beginning, and lowest F0 values at the end. The various units are marked by both a strength hierarchy of stress and varying strength of boundaries (see Shattuck-Hufnagel & Turk, 1996 for a summary of English facts). It is difficult to find acoustically well-defined units: there are large inter-style, inter-rate, inter-speaker variations, and the final prosodic organization is also determined by the size of the constituents. Implementing five levels of boundary strength gives synthetic speech higher quality than rule sets with fewer levels (Sanderman & Collier, 1996b).

10.2.5 *The lack of standardized methods*

A large number of experimental methods have been used to study the perception of intonation and the role of intonation in speech perception.[1] Synthetic speech allows a researcher to systematically change one parameter at a time, such as F0, which represents a clear advantage over natural speech production for evaluating the contribution of each individual parameter. Intonational focusing, however, always involves an action of the respiratory muscles. Such an increase has several "natural" acoustic consequences (unless compensatory adjustments are made at the glottal level): higher intensity, higher F0, less steep spectral slope, stronger release of the obstruents, longer VOT, etc. Isolated F0 manipulation using synthetic speech stimuli therefore may be inappropriate for studying the perception of focus in everyday speech. Furthermore, the F0-manipulated versions retain much of their original characteristics: the accompanying cues may substitute for F0 features.

10.2.6 Effect of phonetic context and discourse context on the perception of intonation

The intonational features are perceived relationally according to context.

10.2.6.1 Intrinsic and cointrinsic context

First, perception of the F0 features of a vowel is by no means independent from its loudness and duration, its phonetic quality, the voicing quality of the subsequent consonant (see Lehiste, 1970 for an exhaustive review), the melodic context (Hadding-Koch & Studdert-Kennedy, 1964), the timing of the F0 movement relatively to the onset of the vowel (House, 1990), and the time course of intensity (Rossi, 1978; see also Fonagy, 2000, pp. 137–48). Such results call for a configurational approach to F0 contour perception, or at least for a combination of atomistic cues and holistic patterns.

10.2.6.2 The discourse context

Second, there is often little agreement between the speaker's intention and the listener's interpretation when utterances are heard out of context in Danish, Dutch, French, and Swedish (Beun, 1990; Fonagy & Bérard, 1972; Hadding-Koch, 1961; Uldall, 1964). In their judgments of speakers' intentions, like sarcasm, adults rely heavily on global context as well as intonation, but children are less attuned to contextual information (Capelli, Nakagawa, & Madden, 1990). As a consequence of the influence of the pragmatic context, it is not possible to draw any permanent link between form and function. The perceived meaning of prosodic signals should be treated as a pragmatic implicature or a pragmatic inference (Wichmann, 2002).

10.2.7 Perception of intonation as a language-specific process and non-language-specific process

Tonal languages use F0 primarily to signal lexical contrasts. In Japanese, a pitch-accent language, the word tonal patterns are the most straightforward component of the *shape* of the F0 contour. In stress languages, such as English, the need to realize the lexical stresses strongly constrains F0. In French, F0, duration and intensity are tightly linked to word boundaries and intonation (especially its demarcative function) and are the main determinants of the *shape* of the F0 contour. There are highly language-specific characteristics, "semantic," "systemic," "realizational," and "phonotactic" distinctions in intonational structure across languages (Ladd, 1996), but all types of languages, tonal, pitch-accent, stress, and boundary languages, use intonation and share intonational features.

The perception of intonational phenomena and the linguistic significance of F0 patterns depend on the listener's cultural and linguistic background. It is generally hypothesized that the perceptual mapping between the acoustic signal and intonational categories is sensitive to the abstract structural properties of individual phonological systems. Every single perceptual experiment on speech-like stimuli involving listeners whose native languages differed shows differences in the identification and discrimination of basic intonational elements such as word stress (Berinstein, 1979; Watanabe, 1988), prominence, modalities (Makarova, 2001), attitudes and perceived emotion (Abelin & Allwood, 2000; Kim, Curtis, & Carmichael, 2001).

The same cues are generally used but their hierarchy may be different. In the perception of prominence in speech and nonspeech signals, amplitude cues override duration cues for English-speaking listeners, whereas native Estonian listeners are more responsive to duration cues (Lehiste & Fox, 1992). French informants do not classify a syllable as accented when it has a falling pitch movement, whereas Swedish and Dutch listeners do. Also, the location of the onset of the pitch movement seems to have much less weight in French than in Dutch or Swedish for detecting accentuation (Beaugendre, House, & Hermes, 1997). When Japanese and Russian subjects were asked to identify two-syllable re-synthesized stimuli with modified rising-falling contours as exclamations, interrogatives, or declaratives, the perception of stimuli as declarative was similar for both groups of subjects, while the perception of stimuli as interrogative and exclamatory was in some cases significantly different (Makarova, 2001).

10.3 Cross-Linguistic Similarities in Intonational Meanings and Underlying Psychophonetic Code

Despite differences obtained in perception experiments involving native speakers of different languages, the literature on a large number of related and unrelated languages points to several universal tendencies in perception between intonational form and intonational meaning. It seems natural to attempt to explain similarities in the interpretation of intonational contours by identifying features shared by human speakers (the present proposal follows up on Vaissière, 1995, and Gussenhoven, 2002). Figure 10.1 illustrates five elements of a proposed hypothetical psychophonetic code. The elements will be described below.

10.3.1 Psychoacoustic rhythms, initial strengthening, and final lengthening

The first part relates to basic psychoacoustic rhythmic tendencies. The similarities in the way of segmenting speech (demarcative function) in languages are

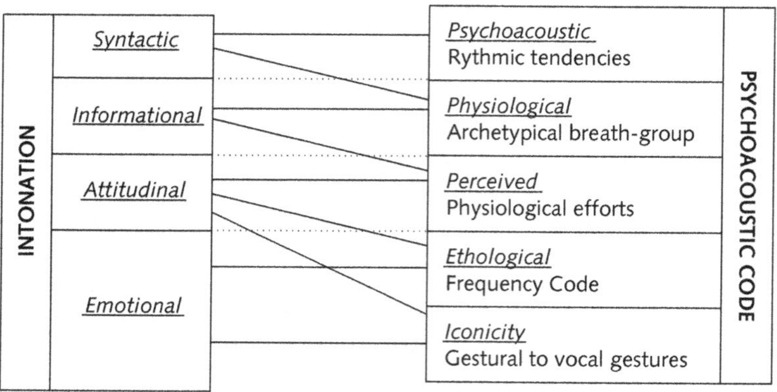

Figure 10.1 Some of the multiple functions of intonation.

Figure 10.2 Basic rhythmic unit composed of two (left) or three (right) elements. Filled circles and rectangles indicate perceived extra-loudness and final lengthening, respectively. Parentheses refer to the way listeners will most likely chunk the continuum.

tentatively explained by the inference of two non-linguistic rhythmic principles which associate lengthening with the notion of end (and relaxation) and strengthening with the notion of beginning.

10.3.2 *The two basic rhythmic tendencies (Fraisse, 1956)*

Through psychoacoustic experiments using nonspeech stimuli, Fraisse (1956) distinguished two types of rhythmic organization: "*rythmitisation intensive,*" sensitive to strengthening of the initial element, and "*rythmitisation temporelle,*" building on the lengthening of the final element or pauses. Figure 10.2 illustrates the repetition of a hypothesized basic rhythmic unit, where the two basic rhythms are combined, with initial extra loudness and final lengthening.

10.3.3 *Final lengthening as boundary marker*

The two types of rhythm seem to be reflected in a large set of phenomena linked to segmentation, at the word and phrase level (see also Allen, 1975). First, the basic tendencies are reflected in the manner languages mark word stress. The word-accent seems to come from intonation in exactly the same way that word-boundary phenomena come from utterance-boundary phenomena. Intonation becomes grammaticalized as a word stress when the suprasegmental features of pitch, duration, and intensity that would have characterized a word in isolation (where it gets prominent intonation) are encoded along with the word, and thus seem to function in words in context (Hyman, 1977). As a general tendency, initial stress (or early stress, as in English) in a word tends to be marked by extra loudness, and late stress (French, Italian, Spanish) by extra lengthening.[2] Even when they do not receive primary or secondary stress, word-initial consonants and syllables tend to be produced with greater strengthening, and word-final rhyme is lengthened, at least in European languages.

Second, the basic rhythmic tendencies seem to have been phonologized in boundary marking. Final lengthening and a decrease in speech rate convey relaxation and ending. Speakers tend to lengthen the final element in the unit: the final syllable in a word, the final stressed syllable (and the final syllable) in a phrase, the final phrase in an utterance, and the final utterance in a paragraph. English listeners expect the duration of the pre-boundary syllable to reflect the rank of the phonological boundary, whether or not it coincides with an intonation contour boundary (Gussenhoven & Rietveld, 1992; Streeter, 1978). When asked to judge the duration of pairs of vowels of equal duration, and with level F0 patterns, 68% of listeners judge the first syllable to be longer (Lehiste, 1975).

The tendency to isochrony has been observed in a number of languages (but not all): the average duration of syllables (words) in longer words (phrases) tends to be shorter than in shorter words (phrases), due to compression. It has two major consequences. First, shortening of syllables in long units and lengthening in short units contribute to perceptual integration into units. Preferred vowel duration depends on the number of following syllables in the word. Second, isochronous intervals facilitate attention by guiding expectations as to when the next stressed syllable is likely to occur (Lehiste, 1980; see Cutler, this volume; also Cutler, Dahan, & van Donselaar, 1997).

Interstress intervals tend to be perceived as more isochronous than they are acoustically. Disruption of the expected pattern is used to convey crucial information about syntactic structure: interstress interval lengthening is interpreted by listeners as indicating the presence of an underlying juncture.

Third, the two types of rhythm often coexist in languages. French uses mainly final lengthening for marking different degrees of syntactic boundaries, and initial strengthening (more extreme articulatory movements, with raised intensity and F0) for informational structuring. In contrast, English makes greater use of "intensive rhythmitization," by marking lexical stresses, but also uses final lengthening as a boundary marker (see Vaissière, 1991 and 2002 for the notion of dominant and regressive rhythms, and differences between English and French, respectively).

Fourth, most of the studies that compare the effects of F0 and duration show the importance of duration (in particular interstress lengthening) over F0 in the perception of phrase boundaries (Lehiste, Olive, & Streeter, 1976; Price et al., 1991). In their production, children (age 5–7) use duration and not intonation to mark phrase boundaries in spontaneous speech (Verma et al., 1994).

10.3.4 *Breath-group and perceived effort*

The structural and continuity markers which have a cross-linguistic validity are interpreted as deviations from a physiologically-based F0 archetypal pattern (Lieberman, 1967). The same global archetypal F0 pattern seems to be cross-linguistically used for statements in a large number of languages (Bolinger, 1989). Deviations from that archetypical pattern carry meanings.

10.3.5 *The archetypal breath-group and higher-level segmentation*

10.3.5.1 *Physiological aspects*

Speech is superimposed on expiration. The basic F0 and intensity shape corresponding to phonation in a single expiration is a sharp rise followed by a fall, a pattern shared by non-human primates and infant cry (Lieberman, 1967). Between two successive breath-groups, there is inhalation and subsequent resetting of subglottal pressure and F0 values. Humans use sophisticated breath control mechanisms, generally taking in more air when they intend to say more, which raises subglottal pressure and F0. Increasing muscular effort is required to maintain constant subglottal pressure as the volume of air in the lungs decreases; the unmarked F0 and intensity pattern is declining, which seems to indicate that speakers do not fully compensate for decreasing lung volume over the course of the utterance (Collier, 1975; for a summary of physiological explanations, see Vaissière, 1983). Figure 10.3(a) gives a schematic representation of the F0 pattern associated with the unmarked breath-group (used for neutral statements). The F0 contour oscillates between two "abstract" declination lines, the baseline, connecting F0 valleys, and the plateau connecting F0 peaks. F0 range tends to decrease from the beginning of the sentence to the end. The plateau declines more rapidly than the baseline.

10.3.5.2 *Linguistic use of the characteristics of the archetypal pattern*

F0 fluctuations within unmarked declarative utterances help delimit successive sense-groups or phrases. Figure 10.3(b) represents typical F0 curves in declarative sentences (composed here of four and three prosodic phrases, for French and English, respectively; in the figure, each prosodic phrase comprises a single prosodic word). Each language seems to put emphasis on one aspect of the archetypal F0 pattern and English infants show very early preference for the predominant stress patterns of English words (Jusczyk, Cutler, & Redanz, 1993). For example, in French, the slowly rising portion ending by final lengthening is perceptually dominant. It contrasts with English, where a rapidly falling contour is associated with the word-stressed syllable (Figure 10.3b) and the perception of stresses dominates. Danish favors the low F0 value, aligning it with the word-stressed syllable; in Japanese, what is mainly perceived is a contrast between successive stretches of baseline and plateau: an F0 jump to the baseline on the word's second

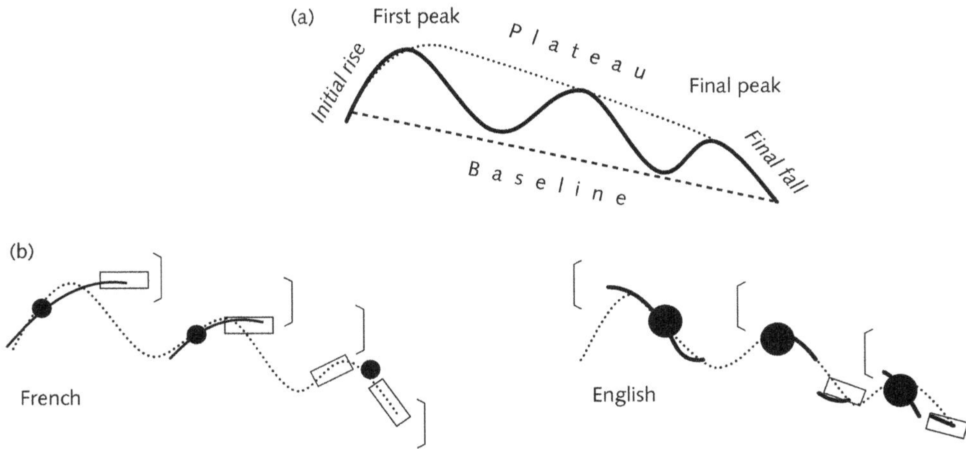

Figure 10.3 (a) The basic archetypal pattern found in many languages. The curve corresponds to the natural course of F0 and intensity. (b) Highly abstract typical F0 contour in French (left) and English (right) declaratives. Filled black points and rectangles represent extra loudness and word-final lengthening, respectively. Bracketing indicates perceived boundaries.

mora is followed by a F0 plateau continuing until the word-accented syllable, and a low F0 value associated with the syllable (if any) following the accented one.

From this vantage point, we suggest that in each language, the statistically most frequent way of combining F0, duration, intensity and segmental characteristics (entailing a particular repartition of effort along the word syllables) becomes a prototype. Some of the impressionistic loudness and duration characteristics are represented in Figure 10.3.

The same basic components of the archetypal intonation pattern are used to contribute to the hierarchical organization of discourse, by marking beginnings and ends. Initial rise – final fall in F0 summons up the notion of a complete unit, such as a definite statement. Initial F0 rise is linked to the notion of beginning. In discourse, suppressing the initial F0 peak suggests to the listener that the utterance elaborates on the previous utterance(s) (Nakajima & Allen, 1993). Final fall in F0 or lowered F0 contour and low intensity (and decreasing rate, as seen above) suggest finality, i.e., the end of a phrase (Streeter, 1978), an utterance, a paragraph (Lehiste, 1975), a topic unit in spontaneous discourse (Geluykens & Swerts, 1994), or a turn (Schaffer, 1984). A fall is judged to convey an impression of finality only if it restores the pitch to the level of the lower declination line (Collier, 1984). When topic and turn terminations interfere with each other in discourse, speakers avoid using low tones at the end of a topic, reserving them to signal turn finality. Listeners can reliably discriminate between turn-final and non-turn-final topic units (Geluykens & Swerts, 1994).

Continuing declination line is associated with the notion of integration, continuity, and preplanning. The rate of declination actually observed exceeds the rate of decline predicted by physiology, suggesting that declination has essentially been phonologized (Vaissière, 1995). Linguistically controlled declination, as in downstep and downdrift phenomena, indicates integration. F0 fall-rise pattern at clause and phrase boundaries is associated with the notion of end-and-beginning, that is, of disjuncture between phrases, clauses, sentences (Lea, 1980), and syllables (Ainsworth, 1986).

10.3.5.3 Linguistic use of the characteristics of the deviations of the archetypal pattern

While prosodic word profiles differ greatly from one language to the next, they seem to be "deformed" by intonation in rather similar ways. Final rising F0 and final non-low value are frequently associated with the notions of non-assertiveness, incompleteness, continuity. Raised tone seems to indicate points of "interest" within utterances and also to indicate that more is to follow, as in questions (Bolinger, 1964). "Yes-no" questions in Swedish display a terminal rise and an overall higher F0 than statements. Other Swedish utterances in which the speaker wants to draw the listener's special attention also display an overall high F0 and a terminal rise: in listening tests the labels "question," "surprise," "interest" have been found to be interchangeable (Hadding-Koch, 1961, pp. 126ff). An accent-lending rise followed by level pitch seems to indicate turn-keeping in Dutch, while accent-lending rise followed by a second rise is ambiguous between turn-keeping and turn-yielding (Caspers, 1998; for a review of recent research, Hirschberg & Swerts, 1998). When a language differentiates between question and continuation, higher F0, less steep declination and/or steeper rise are associated with question marking.

Declination slope over the entire utterance carries meanings. More F0 declination than expected and higher articulation rate influence the listener's perception of a "spontaneous" over a "read" speaking style (Laan, 1997), probably suggesting to the listener lack of preplanning. The most steeply falling intonation contours are identified as being declarative, the least falling ones as being interrogative, and contours in the middle of the continuum as being nonfinal (Thorsen, 1980). As a first approximation, the topline is very sensitive to pragmatic factors, and the baseline to syntactic factors.

Non-continuity in the declination along the utterance and its partial F0 (and intensity) reset, with or without actual breathing-in and/or pausing, is frequently interpreted by the listener as marking a new phrase (Streeter, 1978), an intonational clause, or topic. The amount of reset reflects the hierarchical structure: the higher the reset, the deeper the node. A lack of reset is used as a continuation mark: the unit is perceptually integrated with the preceding unit.

The same principles seem to hold for units larger and smaller than the utterance (for the notion of recursivity, see Vaissière, 1995). Utterance-highest F0 peaks decline from the beginning of a paragraph (or of a topic) to its end (Lehiste, 1975). In French, in an isolated word, a peak located at the word beginning, on the penultimate, or at the very end of the word indicates an answer, a doubt, and a question, respectively. Early F0 peak in the stressed syllable corresponds to established fact, medial and late peaks are perceived as implying a new fact (for German, Kohler, 1991; for Dutch, Caspers, 1999).

Concerning the perception of declination: the second accented syllable in a phrase should have lower pitch than the first one to be perceived as having equally strong stress. Listeners seem to normalize their perception of the overall contour in terms of expected declination (Pierrehumbert, 1979) in complex ways (Gussenhoven et al., 1997; Terken, 1994).

10.3.6 *Perceived expiratory effort and the expression of focus and arousal*

The next element playing a role in the perception of intonation is the effort code (see also Gussenhoven, 2002). As is well known, loudness judgments on speech are more closely related to the degree of vocal effort in speech production than to the speech signal's surface acoustic properties, such as intensity or F0. The listener perceives the amount of global effort made by the speaker and it seems advisable to separate the various types of perceived effort by taking physiology into account (for a first application to French with four physiologically-determined types of stress, see Vaissière, 2001).

Different degrees of strengthening of the supraglottal speech organs (the tongue, the lips, and the velum) mainly affect *timbre*. Supraglottal tensing results in higher position of the velum, longer and larger closure for obstruents, and more precise articulation. Initial stress in French should be considered as "supraglottal" stress and corresponds to a localized hyperarticulation. Supraglottal strengthening may spread to the glottal level, but it need not be the case.

Laryngeal effort affects F0 contours, voice quality (i.e., the shape of the glottal-pulse waveform and spectral balance), and glottal resistance. Pitch-accent languages may be said to have a laryngeal stress. Spectral balance turned out to be a reliable cue in the differentiation between initial- and final-stressed words in Dutch, just behind duration, with the overall intensity and phonemic quality as the poorest cues (Sluijter & Van Heuven, 1997). Some attitudes and modalities are expressed solely by laryngeal maneuvers. F0 features, as well as voice quality, play the key role here.

Sudden extra activity of the respiratory muscles, mainly affecting subglottal pressure, leads directly to an increase in the speed of glottal opening, in amplitude of vocal folds displacement, and in intensity, and indirectly to F0 raising and segmental changes through aerodynamic changes (e.g., VOT). Occurrences of nuclear stress, sentence stress, and emphatic stress have always been found to correlate well with a burst of intercostal activity, increased subglottal pressure and increased loudness (Ladefoged, Draper, & Whitteridge, 1958, for English; Benguerel, 1973, for French), but not always with both intensity and pitch excursion. Expiratory stress (or flow-induced stress) seems to be perceived as focus and emphasis. F0 contour and height seem to be by-products of the local increase in subglottal pressure.

Sustained expiratory effort leads to increased F0 range and lack of declination, and expresses involvement and arousal. Happiness and surprise are associated with large pitch variation, high pitch level and ascending scales. Music and speech seem to share similar interpretation (Collier & Hubbard, 2001).

Disturbance of the respiratory system is frequently found in states of anxiety; the increase in respiration rate leads to increased subglottal pressure and higher F0 (Williams & Stevens, 1972). Listeners' stereotype of psychological stress includes

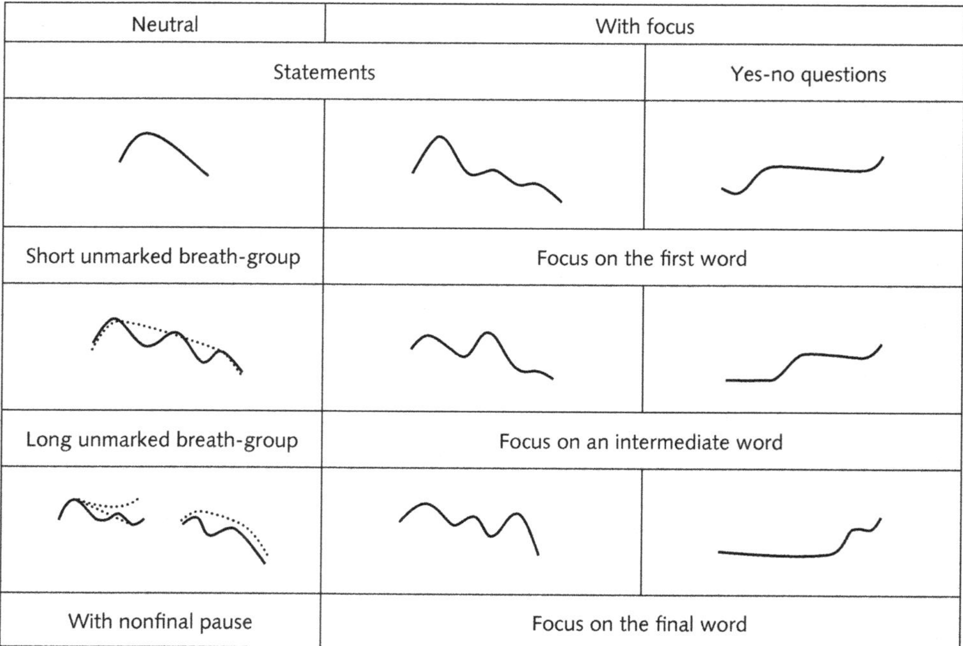

Neutral
With focus
Statements
Yes-no questions
Short unmarked breath-group
Focus on the first word
Long unmarked breath-group
Focus on an intermediate word
With nonfinal pause
Focus on the final word

Figure 10.4 Typical F0 contours in neutral statement (left) of different length, and the deformations they often undergo to mark modalities and focus.

elevated pitch and amplitude levels, as well as their increased variability (Streeter, MacDonald, & Galotti, 1983).

Focusing allows listeners to speed up the comprehension of words that convey new information, whereas given information is processed faster if it is not accented (Terken & Nooteboom, 1987). In a question-answering task, appropriately phrased utterances (quite predictably) produced faster reaction times (Sanderman & Collier, 1996a).

Figure 10.4 illustrates the typical F0 pattern in statements and in questions, with narrow focus on the initial, medial, and final word (this figure would be valid for French, Japanese, English, Danish, and Chinese). The excess of physiological effort at one point in the utterance seems to be done at the expense of surrounding parts, particularly the following part. The long-range effects of the realization of focus call again for a multiparametric and holistic approach to intonation in many languages.

Pitch, duration, and intensity have been found to be relevant to the intonational-perceptual marking of focus (Batliner, 1991). Depending on language, speaker, and style, acoustic cues include (1) a displacement of sentence stress onto the focused word; (2) a further strengthening and lengthening of the lexically stressed syllable, hand in hand with the shortening and reduction of non-focused words; (3) an increase in the magnitude of the underlying tonal movement, leading to a substantial pitch range expansion and top line modifications, followed by post-focal pitch range reduction; (4) a sharp F0 fall between the emphasized word and the following word in the phrase, followed by a relatively flat and low F0 contour on post-focal words; (5) a supplementary focal tone, as in Swedish; or (6) other "tonal" change. It has been proposed that the distinction between contrastive and non-contrastive focus in English can be conveyed by the difference between a *L + H** (*rise* on the stressed syllable) vs. *H** (*high* on the stressed syllable) pitch accent (Pierrehumbert & Hirschberg, 1990).

10.4 Iconicity and the Frequency Code

10.4.1 *Expressive settings, facial gestures, and intonation*

Universals in intonational meaning may draw on an archaic genetic code where the motivation of the signs originates; this appears to be especially salient in the expression of affect (Bolinger, 1989). Expressive intonation often goes hand in hand with deviations superimposed on the (ideal) neutral phonatory and articulatory setting of the entire utterance. Tenderness is expressed by melodicity (intrasyllabic regularity of vocal fold vibration), relaxed vocal folds, breathiness as well as smooth articulatory transitions, and labialization. When two fundamental frequency curves differed only in their angularity (in suddenness of change of direction), the French sentences with a more angular fundamental frequency curve were rated as being significantly more aggressive than their smoother counterparts (Fonagy et al., 1979). Smallness is suggested by high F0 as well as palatalization (a fronted position of the tongue mainly raises F2 frequency). The expression of disgust includes glottalization and pharyngealization. F0 irregularities, forceful innervation of the glottal muscles, narrow constriction of the glottal space as well as retracted lips and tongue retraction characterize anger and hostility (see Fonagy, 2000, drawing on tomographic and cineradiographic studies).

Intentions can often be recovered not only from vocal (especially intonation) gesture and settings, but also from facial gestures, the nominal content of the message then being redundant (Bolinger, 1989). In making judgments about intonation patterns, much of the listener's attention is directed to visual inspection of the upper part of the talker's face, which may play a greater role than words (Lansing & McConkie, 1999). Raised eyebrows often go hand in hand with an F0 rise in the expression of surprise, and labialization with tenderness (see Fonagy, 2000 for a review). Loudness judgments were also found to be affected significantly by visual information even when subjects were instructed to base their judgments only on what they hear and not what they see (Rosenblum & Fowler, 1991).

There seem to be large cross-linguistic similarities in phonatory and articulatory deviations and facial gestures for the expression of attitudes and emotion. This is the basis for proposing the Iconicity Code, a gestural-to-lingual code. Iconicity involves ethology, and the development of more or less elaborate intonational "*signifiés*" from instinctive "*signifiants*" or signs that originally expressed uncontrolled primary emotion. These primitive signs were then conventionalized and integrated into the linguistic code; but there remains a resemblance between the spoken forms and the things they stand for. Motivation dominates in the expression of emotion, while the expression of attitude is more conventionalized; the expression of moods is part of the grammar. It is indeed a general observation that the least motivated intonation phenomena (the most arbitrary) are least recognized cross-linguistically. In foreign languages, it may be easier to recognize and render emotions than to distinguish a question from a statement. We refer to Fonagy (2000) for a thorough account of these issues (see also Bolinger, 1989).

According to Fonagy, Bolinger and others, speech melody could be conceived in terms of virtual bodily gesturing. First, the degree of general excitement and tension (arousal) is reflected in the degree of tension of the vocal folds: higher pitch means greater excitement. Low F0 (and a slower speaking rate) characterize passive emotion and detachment, whereas high F0 and more rapid speech characterize active emotion. Second, melodicity characterizes *agreeable* emotion, and lack of melodicity disagreeable emotion (Fonagy, 1981).[3] Third, vocal gesturing is in proportion to expression and content: the pitch range is proportional to the degree of involvement. In synthetic speech experiments, small pitch variation is found to be associated with disgust, anger, fear, boredom, and large pitch variation with happiness, pleasantness, activity, surprise (Bolinger, 1989; Hirschberg & Ward, 1992; Scherer, 1994), and benevolence (Brown, Strong, & Rencher, 1973, see also Fonagy, 1983).

10.4.2 The frequency code

The well-known frequency code (Bolinger, 1989; Morton, 1994; Ohala, 1984) is another aspect of the iconicity principle; it is the one best documented in the literature, and while there is no firm evidence for it, there seems to be no clear counter-example, and it tends to be accepted. First, by the laws of acoustics, a larger vocal tract has lower formant frequencies. Second, a slower rate of vibration of the vocal folds is physiologically related to larger vocal folds, and so to a larger sound source (i.e., vocalizer). Nonhuman terrestrial vertebrates use similar sounds in similar ways; it is often hypothesized that the fundamental, unifying principle of vocalizations used in hostile or friendly, appeasing contexts is that they convey an impression of the size of the vocalizer (Morton, 1994). Third, a majority of women have a posterior glottal chink: thus, female voices tend to have a breathier voice quality than male voices.

Speakers can control up to a certain extent mean formant frequencies, F0, and degrees of breathiness in their voice. The natural links seem to provide an explanation for the cross-linguistic observation that high formant frequencies, high F0, and breathiness are all associated with the same primary meaning of small vocalizer, conveying secondary meanings such as subordinate, submissive, non-threatening, desirous of the receiver's goodwill, polite, lack of threat by the subject, more femininity, hesitation, uncertainty, or surprise. The association of greater pitch range with incredulity can be accounted for by the previously noted tendency of listeners to associate larger pitch ranges with greater degree of speaker involvement; conversely, the association of smaller pitch ranges with uncertainty can be explained as a consequence of the perception of less speaker involvement (Hirschberg & Ward, 1992; Ward & Hirschberg, 1988). Also, the lower the degree of certainty, the higher the mean F0 value will be (Bolinger, 1989). Speech directed to infants typically exhibits a larger pitch range and higher average pitch, probably to empathize with the infant's smallness or to attract and sustain its attention. The intonation at the end of a sentence has a great impact on politeness judgments and speech rate plays an important role: raised F0 is heard as more polite (Ito, 2002; Ofuka et al., 2000). Lower formants, lower F0, and the creaky quality of the voice conveys the primary meaning of large vocalizer, with the secondary meanings dominant, aggressive, threatening, definitive, more authoritative (see also Bolinger, 1964).

10.5 Discussion and Conclusions

The first part of the chapter considered the difficulties that researchers face when they approach the study of intonation: lack of clear definitions, non-applicability of otherwise standardized experimental methods used in psychoacoustics and laboratory phonology, the effects of phonetic and melodic context and the speaker's native language on the perception of intonational phenomena. As a consequence, it appears that the results obtained in one context cannot be extended and generalized to other prosodic contexts in any simple straightforward way (Verhoeven, 1994). In the second part, we attempted to put together a number of non-linguistic facts to explain cross-linguistic similarities in the interpretation of intonational phenomena: psychoacoustic rhythmic tendencies, physiological considerations, and an ethological iconicity code.

Our goal in this chapter has been to show that intonation plays many different roles in speech perception. The studies on the use of prosody in parsing suggest a supporting, rather than a leading role for prosody in the grouping of words into constituents (Cutler, 1997). Not all phonetically similar sentences can be disambiguated by listeners on the basis of prosodic differences alone (see Price et al., 1991) and ambiguous sentences are very rare in every day conversation. In utterances in which prosody and syntax conflict, the localization of the click by listeners was determined by the syntactic structure assigned to the sentence, and not by prosody (Fodor & Bever, 1965). When presented with recordings of ambiguous constituent structures, listeners generally ignore prosodic features when other linguistic cues (semantic and pragmatic) are available (Berkovits, 1980). Syntax and semantics provide much stronger topic cues than intonation (Schaffer, 1984). In contrast, the affective functions of intonation are generally not redundant with the linguistic properties of an utterance. Under some circumstances, the way we say things may be much more important that what we say. Intonation offers effective shortcuts or heuristics: a simple word like "yes," "oui," "da" may express approbation, confirmation, doubt, impatience, joy, anger, irony, evidence, or tenderness. Listeners have no difficulties in differentiating all these to recover the speaker's intended message, although many of the differences are so subtle that they are hard to identify and measure acoustically.

Intonational studies are in vogue at the present time. Intonation is an extremely lively field of research, but still much has to be done. First, perception rather than acoustics has strong claims to being the best starting-point for the study of intonation, a phenomenon that involves multiple acoustic cues. Only listening tests can provide reliable behavioral data on perceptual equivalence, on the one hand, and functional equivalence within one language or cross-linguistically on the other hand. It does not seem reasonable to build intonational models from intuition and acoustic analysis alone, without appropriate perceptual testing with human listeners.

Second, at this point in time, we need to develop uncontroversial universal methods for describing intonation. Prosodic transcriptions should include several sharply distinguished levels (one must be perceptual, another acoustic, and another interpretative). At the highest level of description, transcription should capture the interpretation of the sentence by the listener, its syntactic structure, its mode, and its informational structure as well as the attitude perceived. An intermediate level should include local intonational phenomena: the perceived strength of boundaries between words, jumps and glides in pitch, and local stresses, among others. Parallel listening experiments on music and nonsense speech materials may help.

Third, intonational studies should include as many parameters as possible, including physiological ones. F0 contour has been privileged in past research (see Pierrehumbert, 1980, pp. 11–12; t'Hart et al., 1990); but it is not the only speech cue that listeners use in perception. Limits of perceptibility of pitch phenomena may change depending on accompanying cues and on the physiological interpretation of the deviations by the listener. It should be borne in mind that without appropriate tools, most research concentrates on an incomplete inventory of parameters, such as mean F0 and duration values (Murray & Arnott, 1993, for emotion). For example, in Moba, an African tone language, glottal stop and vowel shortening mark assertion, while breathiness and vowel lengthening mark interrogation (Rialland, 1985). The role of intensity needs wider empirical attention: the fact that intensity downtrend may not parallel F0 downtrend has been largely unexplored. Intonation and prosody in general can barely be considered independently from segmental characteristics (glottalization, initial strengthening, etc.). Also, multimodal analysis of speech including body and facial gestures seems very promising for future studies in the perception of intonation, starting out from laboratory materials, and moving on toward a study of intonation in spontaneous speech in real-life situations. It is likely that continuing interest in emotions and attitudes in speech will show the limitations inherent in a "Tone and Break Indices" description restricted to pitch levels.

Fourth, great care should be taken to ensure that experimental stimuli presented to the listeners have physiological plausibility. Ways of obtaining physiological data (e.g., subglottal pressure, EMG) are often invasive, but glottographic and fibroscopic data are rather easy to obtain. Listeners interpret stimuli differently using very subtle nuances. In particular, perceptual experiments are needed to test whether the listener can distinguish between loudness from different physiological origins, an increase in respiratory effort resulting in increasing intensity and/or F0, or to laryngeal maneuvers (see the chapter on loudness in Lehiste, 1970), since, at least in French, they assume a different function (Vaissière, 2001).

Fifth, statistical knowledge on the use of the different intonational patterns within and across languages, dialects, styles, and speakers is an indispensable component of any study of the perception of intonation. Within a given language, statistics are necessary for establishing the most common intonational pattern the listeners are exposed to and for building probabilistic models of the auditory processing of intonational cues by both infant and adult listeners. Enormous amounts of speech are necessary to obtain stable statistical evidence on factor combinations in the study of the interaction between layers of meaning, in particular the interplay between discourse structure and grammatical and informational structure: systematic perceptual experiments with synthesized stimuli are a necessary complement. An intonational pattern, although rarely observed, may be easily interpreted by listeners.

Statistical knowledge should be derived from both databases of spontaneous speech and from different kinds of well-controlled material: the syntactic role of intonation stands out in isolated sentences; in a text, the information structure becomes apparent; in dialog, it is interaction which will attract the researcher's attention. None of these functions should be considered as more or less important than any other: they all coexist in everyday conversation and listeners as well as students of intonation will have to cope with these basic facts.

Sixth, more cross-linguistic, cross-dialectal, and cross-stylistic studies on differences in perception and production of intonation in infants, children, and adults are needed. More research on the developmental aspects of intonation in different cultures is needed: newborns are more sensitive to such prosodic phenomena and phonotactic characteristics than previously believed. No firm conclusion about the universality of any part of intonational phenomena can be drawn until more languages have been studied. For the time being, we mainly rely on the lack of counter-evidence. Perceptual tests involving listeners of different languages are extremely important. Nonetheless, great care should be taken in designing the task: while it seems a very natural task for a native of English, Dutch, or German to decide which syllable in a word is more "stressed," it is very awkward and unnatural for a native of French: a French word carries often more than one stress (supralexically determined); the coexisting (supralexical) stresses correspond to different physiological maneuvers in French, have different acoustic correlates, and therefore cannot be ranked; the notion of lexical "stress" does not correspond to physiological or psychological reality (Vaissière, 2001). Cross-linguistic studies should involve linguists who master the phonological (segmental and prosodic) systems of their respective languages.

Seventh, the interaction between the different types of intonation within specific languages requires more detailed exploration. At present, very few studies venture into the field of multiple-parameter interactions between structural and affective aspects of intonation (see, however, Pell, 2001). Thorough investigations must be conducted to test out the elements of the psychophonetic code and their possible interactions.

A fundamental assumption that runs throughout the present chapter is that language-specific properties of intonation can only be understood within the larger context of universal principles. Studies are necessary to explore the psychophonetic code and reveal the basic common denominators. Collaboration between specialists of various domains becomes essential: psychoacousticians, psycholinguists, physiologists, developmental scientists, and others. If one takes a narrow view of studies on intonation and its perception, it has to be acknowledged that most of the literature in this field actually consists of case studies. There is a long way to go before firm and solid conclusions can be reached. From what has been said about language-specificity, it is a natural conclusion that successful experiments in speech perception will have to use listeners whose native languages differ greatly to avoid unwarranted conclusions; investigations that confine themselves only to the languages of Europe are limited in scope from the outset. Languages from Africa and Asia that possess widely varied tonal systems should by all means be included. This appears as a major challenge for future research on the perception of intonation.

Of all dimensions of speech, intonation is clearly the most difficult to study. Young children and even dogs know how to decode much of intonational meaning, and yet no existing speech synthesis system can be said to be able to correctly reproduce natural attitudinal and emotional nuances carried by intonation. The problem of how intonation works is still very far from being solved. One has to remember Bolinger's word to the wise: intonation is a half-tamed savage (Bolinger, 1978, p. 475). If, as seems to be the case, the complexity of intonation is typical of human complexity, then there is still a long way to go before the perception of intonation yields all of its secrets.

ACKNOWLEDGMENTS

Un grand merci to Ilse Lehiste and Ivan Fonagy for their careful reading and suggestions. Many thanks to Alexis Michaux, Klaus Kohler, Cécile Fougeron, and Shinji Maeda for their useful suggestions on former versions of this chapter.

NOTES

1 Due to the lack of a standardized research methodology, a large array of experimental methods are used in the study of the specific role of intonation in speech perception:

(i) For the construction of experimental stimuli, manipulation can be done by building a corpus of semantically unpredictable sentences. Speakers or actors are asked to vary phrasing, accentuation, modalities, social attitudes, or emotions on one and the same sentence, to hum the utterances, or to mimic them by using reiterant speech and nonsense syllables (Liberman & Streeter, 1978). Cross-splicing allows us to move part of an utterance into a new context. Degradation and delexicalization of stimuli are done by band-pass filtering, rotating speech, spectral scrambling, noise addition, time-compression, or using laryngographic recordings (content-filtered speech). There are now extensive possibilities for well-controlled manipulation by computer of one prosodic parameter at a time, and copying an intonation contour from one utterance onto another.

(ii) The listener may also be asked to perform a wide range of behavioral tasks: to discriminate stimuli; to estimate the perceptual distance between two contours; to assess the excursion size of a pitch movement in a comparison test; to perform by computer perceptual close-copy stylization of F0 contours (in the IPO style); to shadow the utterance; to transcribe prosodically the utterance (taken in or out of context), with or without access to the actual F0 curves; to localize clicks in sentences where intonation has been manipulated; to formulate judgments of prosodic appropriateness, felicity, and naturalness on anomalous, ill-formed, cross-spliced prosodic contours, or to give a pragmatic interpretation. Reaction times may be measured in all cases.

(iii) One of the main difficulties in carrying out research on intonation is inferring the level of listening used by the listeners. At the lowest, most concrete, psychoacoustic level, the naïve ear can be trained to perform an analytic transcription of each successive syllable (as high, mid, low, rising, flat, or falling, etc.). As the size of the window analysis increases, the listener can locate intersyllabic discontinuous tone-steps (jumps), and intersyllabic distances. When it encompasses one or several words, she or he may detect (lexical) stresses and pitch accent, narrow focus, estimate the strength of the perceived boundary between the successive words, and derive the local syntactic structure (right or left branched phrase). When the subject listens to the whole utterance in a broad fashion, she or he is able to recognize the speaker's communicative intention from the linearized speech signal (t'Hart & Collier, 1975): (a) the structural aspects of the utterance (its syntactic phrasing and its informational structure), (b) its modalities, (c) its affective aspects (social attitudes and emotion), and (4) discursive aspects (turn-taking and change of topics). An important reminder is that in modifying one parameter only, experiments leave all the other traits of the original utterance unchanged, and some traits may entertain a trading relationship with F0. The listeners may also be disturbed by the lack of the usual accompanying cues.

2 For a number of reasons linked to perception (and higher sensitivity to durational difference on the penultimate (Lehiste, 1979) and/or the necessity of a tail for F0 contrasts (Bolinger, 1978), the penultimate syllable is a favored position for stress (after the initial and final position) (see also Hyman, 1977).

3 Note that contrasts in melodicity are just suppressed in synthesized F0.

REFERENCES

Abelin, Å. & Allwood, J. (2000). Cross-linguistic interpretation of emotional prosody. ISCA Workshop on Speech and Emotion: A conceptual framework for research. Belfast, http://www.qub.ac.uk/en/isca/proceedings.

Ainsworth, W. A. (1986). Pitch change as a cue to syllabification. *Journal of Phonetics*, 14(2), 257–64.

Ainsworth, W. A. & Lindsay, D. (1986). Perception of pitch movement on tonic syllables in British English. *Journal of the Acoustical Society of America*, 79(2), 472–80.

Allen, G. D. (1975). Speech rhythm: Its relation to performance universals and articulatory timing. *Journal of Phonetics*, 3, 75–86.

Auer, E., Bernstein, L., & Coulter, D. (1998). Temporal and spatio-temporal vibrotactile displays for voice fundamental frequency: An initial evaluation of a new vibrotactile speech perception aid with normal-hearing and hearing-impaired individuals. *Journal of the Acoustical Society of America*, 104(4), 2477–89.

Bartels, C. & Kingston, J. (1994). Salient pitch cues in the perception of contrastive focus. *Journal of the Acoustical Society of America*, 95(5), 2973.

Batliner, A. (1991). Deciding upon the relevancy of intonational features for the marking of focus: A statistical approach. *Journal of Semantics*, 8(3), 171–89.

Beach, C. M., Katz, W. F., & Skowronski, A. (1996). Children's processing of prosodic cues for phrasal interpretation. *Journal of the Acoustical Society of America*, 99(2), 1148–60.

Beaugendre, F., House, D., & Hermes, D. J. (1997). Accentuation boundaries in Dutch, French and Swedish. In A. Botinis, G. Kouroupetroglou, & G. Carayiannis (eds.), *Proceedings of the European Speech Communication Association Workshop on Intonation: Theory, Models and Applications* (pp. 43–6). Athens, Greece.

Benguerel, P. (1973). Corrélats physiologiques de l'accent en francais [Acoustic correlates of word lexical stress]. *Phonetica*, 27(1), 21–35.

Berinstein, A. E. (1979). Cross-linguistic study on the perception and production of stress, *UCLA Working Papers in Phonetics*, 47, 1–59. Los Angeles.

Berkovits, R. (1980). Perception of intonation in native and non-native speakers of English. *Language and Speech*, 23(3), 271–80.

Beun, R. J. (1990). The recognition of Dutch declarative questions. *Journal of Pragmatics*, 14(1), 39–56.

Bolinger, D. L. (1964). Intonation as a universal. *Proceedings of the 9th International Congress on Linguistics* (pp. 833–48). The Hague: Mouton.

Bolinger, D. L. (1978). Intonation across languages. In J. H. Greenberg (ed.), *Universals of Human Language, vol. II: Phonology* (pp. 471–524). Palo Alto: Stanford University Press.

Bolinger, D. L. (1986). *Intonation and Its Parts: Melody in Spoken English.* Stanford: Stanford University Press.

Bolinger, D. L. (1989). *Intonation and Its Use: Melody in Grammar and Discourse.* Stanford: Stanford University Press.

Brokx, J. P. L. & Nooteboom, S. G. (1982). Intonation and the perceptual separation of simultaneous voices. *Journal of Phonetics*, 10(1), 23–36.

Brown, B. L., Strong, W. J., & Rencher, A. C. (1973). Perceptions of personality from speech: Effects of manipulations of acoustical parameters. *Journal of the Acoustical Society of America*, 54(1), 29–35.

Capelli, C. A., Nakagawa, N., & Madden, C. M. (1990). How children understand sarcasm: The role of context and intonation. *Child Development*, 61(6), 1824–41.

Caspers, J. (1998). Who's next? The melodic marking of question versus continuation in Dutch. *Language and Speech*, 41(3–4), 375–98.

Caspers, J. (1999). An experimental investigation of meaning differences between the "early" and the "late" accent-lending fall in Dutch. *Linguistics in the Netherlands*, 16, 27–39.

Cohen, A. & t'Hart, J. (1967). On the anatomy of intonation. *Lingua*, 19, 177–92.

Cohen, H., Douaire, J., & Elsabbagh, M. (2001). The role of prosody in discourse processing. *Brain Cognition*, 46(1–2), 73–82.

Collier, R. (1975). Physiological correlates of intonation patterns. *Journal of the Acoustical Society of America*, 58(1), 249–55.

Collier, R. (1984). Some physiological and perceptual constraints on tonal systems. In B. Butterworth, B. Connie, & O. Dahl (eds.), *Explanations for Language Universals* (pp. 237–48). Berlin, New York, Amsterdam: Mouton.

Collier, W. & Hubbard, T. (2001). Musical scales and evaluations of happiness and awkwardness: Effects of pitch, direction, and scale mode. *American Journal of Psychology*, 114(3), 355–75.

Cutler, A. (1997). Prosody and the structure of message. In Y. Sagisaka, N. Campbell, & N. Higuchi (eds.), *Computing Prosody: Computational Models for Processing Spontaneous Speech* (pp. 63–6). New York: Springer Verlag.

Cutler, A., Dahan, D., & Donselaar, W. van (1997). Prosody in the comprehension of spoken language: A literature review. *Language and Speech*, 40(2), 141–201.

Danes, F. (1960). Sentence intonation from a functional point of view. *Word*, 16(1), 34–54.

Darwin, C. (1975). On the dynamic use of prosody in speech perception. In A. Cohen & S. G. Nooteboom (eds.), *Structure and Process in Speech Perception* (pp. 178–95). Berlin: Springer Verlag.

De Pijper, J. R. & Sanderman, A. A. (1994). On the perceptual strength of prosodic boundaries and its relation to suprasegmental cues. *Journal of the Acoustical Society of America*, 96(4), 2037–48.

Duez, D. (1993). Acoustic correlates of subjective pauses. *Journal of Psycholinguistic Research*, 22(1), 21–39.

Fodor, J. A. & Bever, T. G. (1965). The pscyhological reality of linguistic segments. *Journal of Verbal Learniing and Verbal Behavior*, 4, 414–20.

Fonagy, I. (1981). Emotions, voice and music: Research aspects on singing. J. Sundberg, Stockholm, publication no. 33 of the Royal Swedish Academy of Music, 51–79.

Fonagy, I. (1983). *La vive voix: essais de psycho-phonétique* [Living speech: essays on psychophonetics]. Paris: Payot.

Fonagy, I. (2000). *Languages within Languages: An Evolutive Approach*. Amsterdam, Philadelphia: John Benjamins.

Fonagy, I. & Bérard, E. (1972). "Il est huit heures": Contribution à l'analyse sémantique de la vive voix ["It's eight o'clock": contribution to the semantic analysis of spoken language]. *Phonetica*, 26, 157–92.

Fonagy, I. & Fonagy, J. (1987). Analysis of complex (integrated) melodic patterns. In R. Channon & L. Shockey (eds.), *In Honor of Ilse Lehiste* (pp. 75–97). Dordrecht, Holland: Foris.

Fonagy, I., Fonagy, J., & Sap, J. (1979). A la recherche de traits pertinents prosodiques du français parisien: Hypothèses et synthèses. *Phonetica*, 36, 1–20.

Fraisse, P. (1956). *Les structures rythmiques*. Louvain: Publications Universitaires.

Fujisaki, H. & Sudo, H. (1971). A generative model for the prosody of connected speech in Japanese. *Annual Report of Engineering Research Institute, Tokyo*, 30, 75–80.

Gandour, J., Wong, D., Dzemidzic, M., Lowe, M., Tong, Y., & Li, X. (2003). A cross-linguistic fMRI study of perception of intonation and emotion in Chinese. *Human Brain Mapping*, 18, 149–57.

Geluykens, R. & Swerts, M. (1994). Prosodic cues to discourse boundaries in experimental dialogues. *Speech Communication*, 15(1–2), 69–77.

Gosy, M. & Terken, J. (1994). Question marking in Hungarian: Timing and height of pitch peaks. *Journal of Phonetics*, 22(3), 269–81.

Grabe, E., Post, B., Nolan, F., & Farrar, K. (2000). Pitch accent realization in four varieties of British English. *Journal of Phonetics*, 28(2), 161–85.

Grant, K. W. (1987). Identification of intonation contours by normally hearing and profoundly hearing-impaired listeners. *Journal of the Acoustical Society of America*, 62(4), 1172–8.

Gussenhoven, C. (2002). Intonation and interpretation: Phonetics and phonology. *Proceedings of the Speech Prosody 2002 Conference* (pp. 47–57). Aix-en-Provence, France.

Gussenhoven, C. & Rietveld, A. C. M. (1992). Intonation contours, prosodic structure and preboundary lengthening. *Journal of Phonetics*, 20(3), 283–303.

Gussenhoven, C. & Rietveld, T. (1998). On the speaker-dependence of the perceived prominence of F0 peaks. *Journal of Phonetics*, 26(4), 371–80.

Gussenhoven, C., Repp, B. H., Rietveld, A., Rump, H. H., & Terken, J. (1997). The perceptual prominence of fundamental frequency peaks. *Journal of the Acoustical Society of America*, 102(5), 3009–22.

Hadding-Koch, K. (1961). Acoustic-phonetic studies in the intonation of Southern Swedish. *Travaux de l'Institut de Phonétique de Lund III*. Lund: C. W. P. Gleerup.

Hadding-Koch, K. & Studdert-Kennedy, M. (1964). An experimental study of some intonation contours. *Phonetica*, 11, 175–85.

Henderson, A. I. & Nelms, S. (1980). Relative salience of intonation fall and pause as cues to the perceptual segmentation of speech in an unfamiliar language. *Journal of Psycholinguistic Research*, 9(2), 147–59.

Hirschberg, J. & Swerts, M. (eds.) (1998). Prosody and conversation. *Language and Speech* (special issue), 41(3–4).

Hirschberg, J. & Ward, G. (1992). The influence of pitch, range, duration, amplitude and spectral features on the interpretation of the rise-fall-rise pattern intonation contour in English. *Journal of Phonetics*, 20, 241–51.

Hirst, D. & Di Cristo, A. (1998). *Intonation Systems: A Survey of Twenty Languages*. Cambridge: Cambridge University Press.

House, D. (1990). *Tonal Perception in Speech*. Lund, Sweden: Lund University Press.

House, D. (2003). Perceiving question intonation: The role of pre-focal pause and delayed focal peak. *Proceedings of the International Congress of Phonetic Science* (pp. 755–8). Barcelona.

Hyman, L. (1977). On the nature of linguistic stress. In L. Hyman (ed.), *Studies in Stress and Accent*. University of Southern California, Southern California Occasional Papers in Linguistics, 4, 37–82.

Ito, M. (2002). Japanese politeness and suprasegmentals: A study based on natural speech materials. *Speech Prosody 2002* (pp. 415–18), Aix-en-Provence, France.

Jusczyk, P., Hirsh Pasek, K., Nelson, D. G. K., Kennedy, L. J., Woodward, A., & Piwoz, J. (1992). Perception of acoustic correlates of major phrasal units by young infants. *Cognitive Psychology*, 24(2), 252–93.

Jusczyk, P. W., Cutler, A., & Redanz, N. J. (1993). Infants' preference for the predominant stress patterns of English words. *Child Development*, 64(3), 675–87.

Kim, S., Curtis, E., & Carmichael, L. (2001). Emphatic Koreans and neutral Americans? *Journal of the Acoustical Society of America*, 109(5), 2474–5.

Kohler, K. (1991). Prosody in speech synthesis: The interplay between basic research and TSS application. *Journal of Phonetics*, 19, 121–38.

Laan, G. P. M. (1997). The contribution of intonation, segmental durations, and spectral features to the perception of a spontaneous and a read speaking style. *Speech Communication*, 22(1), 43–65.

Ladd, D. R. (1996). *Intonational Phonology*. Cambridge: Cambridge University Press.

Ladd, D. R. & Morton, R. (1997). The perception of intonational emphasis: Continuous or categorical? *Journal of Phonetics*, 25(3), 313–42.

Ladd, D. R., Silverman, K., Tolkmitt, F., Bergmann, G., & Scherer, K. R. (1985). Evidence for the independent function of intonation contour type, voice quality, and F0 range in signaling speaker affect. *Journal of the Acoustical Society of America*, 78(2), 435–44.

Ladefoged, P., Draper, M., & Whitteridge, D. (1958). Syllables and stress. *Miscellanea Phonetica*, 3, 1–14.

Lansing, C. & McConkie, G. (1999). Attention to facial regions in segmental and prosodic visual speech perception tasks. *Journal of Speech Language and Hearing Research*, 42(3), 529–39.

Lea, W. (1980). Prosodic aids to speech recognition. In W. Lea (ed.), *Trends in Speech Recognition* (pp. 166–205). Englewood Cliffs, NJ: Prentice-Hall.

Lehiste, I. (1970). *Suprasegmentals.* Cambridge: Cambridge University Press.

Lehiste, I. (1975). The phonetic structure of paragraphs. In A. Cohen & S. G. Nooteboom (eds.), *Structure and Process in Speech Perception* (pp. 195–206). Berlin: Springer Verlag.

Lehiste, I. (1979). The perception of duration within sequences of four intervals. *Journal of Phonetics*, 7, 313–16.

Lehiste, I. (1980). Phonetic manifestation of syntactic structure in English. *Annual Bulletin, Research Institute of Logopedics and Phoniatrics*, 14, 1–27.

Lehiste, I. & Fox, R. A. (1992). Perception of prominence by Estonian and English listeners. *Language and Speech*, 35(4), 419–34.

Lehiste, I., Olive, J., & Streeter, L. A. (1976). Role of duration in disambiguating syntactically ambiguous sentences. *Journal of the Acoustical Society of America*, 60(5), 1199–202.

Liberman, M. Y. & Streeter, L. A. (1978). Use of nonsense-syllable mimicry in the study of prosodic phenomena. *Journal of the Acoustical Society of America*, 63, 231–3.

Lieberman, P. (1967). *Intonation, Perception and Language.* Cambridge, MA: MIT Press.

Makarova, V. (2001). Perceptual correlates of sentence-type intonation in Russian and Japanese. *Journal of Phonetics*, 29(2), 137–54.

McClean, M. D. & Tiffany, W. R. (1973). The acoustic parameters of stress in relation to syllable position, speech loudness and rate. *Language and Speech*, 16(3), 283–90.

Moore, C., Harris, L., & Patriquin, M. (1993). Lexical and prosodic cues in the comprehension of relative certainty. *Journal of Child Language*, 20, 153–67.

Morton, E. S. (1994). Sound symbolism and its role in non-human vertebrate communication. In L. Hinton, J. Nichols, & J. Ohala (eds.), *Sound Symbolism* (pp. 348–65). Cambridge: Cambridge University Press.

Most, T. & Frank, Y. (1994). The effects of age and hearing loss on tasks of perception and production of intonation. *Volta Review*, 96(2), 137–49.

Murray, J. R. & Arnott, J. L. (1993). Towards the simulation of emotion in synthetic speech: A review of the literature on human vocal emotion. *Journal of the Acoustical Society of America*, 93(2), 1097–108.

Nakajima, S. & Allen, J. F. (1993). A study on prosody and discourse structure in cooperative dialogues. *Phonetica*, 50, 197–210.

Nakatani, L. H. & Schaffer, J. A. (1978). Hearing "words" without words: Prosodic cues for word perception. *Journal of the Acoustical Society of America*, 63(1), 234–45.

Nooteboom, S. G., Brokx, J. P. L., & De Rooij, J. J. (1978). Contributions of prosody to speech perception. In W. J. M. Levelt & G. B. Flores d'Arcais (eds.), *Studies in the Perception of Language* (pp. 75–107). New York: John Wiley & Sons.

Ofuka, E., McKeown, J. D., Waterman, M. G., & Roach, P. J. (2000). Prosodic cues for rated politeness in Japanese speech. *Speech Communication*, 32(3), 199–217.

Ohala, J. J. (1984). An ethological perspective on common cross-language utilization of F0 of voice. *Phonetica*, 41(1), 1–16.

Öhman, S. E. G. (1967). Word and sentence intonation: A quantitative model. *Quarterly Progress and Status Report* (pp. 20–54). Stockholm, Speech Translation Laboratory.

Pell, M. (2001). Influence of emotion and focus location on prosody in matched statements and questions. *Journal of the Acoustical Society of America*, 109(4), 1668–80.

Pierrehumbert, J. (1979). The perception of fundamental frequency declination. *Journal of the Acoustical Society of America*, 66, 363–9.

Pierrehumbert, J. (1980). The phonology and phonetics of English intonation.

Cambridge, MA: MIT, distributed by Indiana University Linguistic Club.

Pierrehumbert, J. & Hirschberg, J. (1990). The meaning of intonation in the interpretation of discourse. In P. Cohen, J. Morgan, & M. Pollack (eds.), *Intentions in Communication* (pp. 271–311). Cambridge, MA: MIT Press.

Pisoni, D. B. & Luce, P. A. (1987a). Trading relations, acoustic cue integration, and context effect in speech perception. In M. E. H. Schouten (ed.), *The Psychophysics of Speech Perception* (pp. 155–72). Dordrecht, Boston, Lancaster: Martinus Nijhoff.

Pisoni, D. B. & Luce, P. A. (1987b). Acoustic-phonetic representations in word recognition. *Cognition*, 25(1–2), 21–52.

Price, P. J., Ostendorf, M., Shattuck-Hufnagel, S., & Fong, G. (1991). The use of prosody in syntactic disambiguation. *Journal of the Acoustical Society of America*, 90, 2956–70.

Repp, B. H. (1982). Phonetic trading relations and context effects: New experimental evidence for a speech mode of perception. *Psychological Bulletin*, 92(1), 81–110.

Rialland, A. (1985). Le fini/infini ou l'affirmation/l'interrogation en moba (langue voltaïque parlée au Nord-togo) [Finite/infinite or declarative/ interrogative in Moba (Altaïc language spoken in North Togo]. *Studies in African Linguistics*, supplement 9, 258–61.

Rosenblum, L. & Fowler, C. (1991). Audiovisual investigation of the loudness-effort effect for speech and nonspeech events. *Journal of Experimental Psychology: Human Perception and Performance*, 17(4), 976–85.

Rossi, M. (1978). Interactions of intensity glides and frequency glissandos. *Language and Speech*, 21(4), 384–96.

Rossi, M. (1999). *L'intonation, le système du français: description et modélisation* [Intonation, the French system: description and modelization]. Paris: Orphrys.

Sanderman, A. A. & Collier, R. (1996a). Good prosody facilitates comprehension. *Journal of the Acoustical Society of America*, 100(4), 2823.

Sanderman, A. A. & Collier, R. (1996b). Prosodic rules for the implementation of phrase boundaries in synthetic speech. *Journal of the Acoustical Society of America*, 100(5), 3390–7.

Schaffer, D. B. (1984). The role of intonation as a cue to topic management in conversation. *Journal of Phonetics*, 12(4), 327–44.

Scherer, K. (1994). Vocal affect expression: A review and a model for future research. *Psychological Bulletin*, 92(2), 143–65.

Shattuck-Hufnagel, S. & Turk, A. E. (1996). A prosody tutorial for investigators of auditory sentence processing. *Journal of Psycholinguistic Research*, 25(2), 193–247.

Sluijter, A. & Van Heuven, V. (1997). Spectral balance as an acoustic correlate of linguistic stress. *Journal of the Acoustical Society of America*, 100(4), 2471–85.

Streeter, L. A. (1978). Acoustic determinants of phrase boundary perception. *Journal of the Acoustical Society of America*, 64–6, 1582–92.

Streeter, L. A., MacDonald, N. H., & Galotti, K. M. (1983). Acoustic and perceptual indicators of emotional stress. *Journal of the Acoustical Society of America*, 73(4), 1354–361.

Studdert-Kennedy, M. & Hadding-Koch, K. (1973). Auditory and linguistic processes in the perception of intonation contours. *Language and Speech*, 16(4), 239–313.

Swerts, M. (1997). Prosodic features at discourse boundaries of different strength. *Journal of the Acoustical Society of America*, 101(1), 514–21.

Swerts, M. & Geluykens, R. (1993). The prosody of information units in spontaneous monologue. *Phonetica*, 50, 189–96.

Swerts, M., Bouwhuis, D. G., & Collier, R. (1994). Melodic cues to the perceived "finality" of utterances. *Journal of the*

Acoustical Society of America, 96(4), 2064–75.

Terken, J. (1994). Fundamental frequency and perceived prominence of accented syllables. *Journal of the Acoustical Society of America*, 95(6), 3662–5.

Terken, J. & Nooteboom, S. G. (1987). Opposite effects of accentuation and deaccentuation on verification latencies for given and new information. *Language and Cognitive Processes*, 2(3/4), 145–63.

t'Hart, J. & Collier, R. (1975). Integrating different levels of intonation analysis. *Journal of Phonetics*, 3, 235–55.

t'Hart, J., Collier, R., & Cohen, A. (1990). *A Perceptual Study of Intonation*. Cambridge: Cambridge University Press.

Thorsen, N. (1980). A study of the perception of sentence intonation: Evidence from Danish. *Journal of the Acoustical Society of America*, 67, 1014–30.

Uldall, E. T. (1964). Dimensions of meaning in intonation. In D. Abercrombie, D. B. Fry, P. A. D. MacCarthy, N. C. Scott, & J. L. M. Trim (eds.), *In Honour of Daniel Jones* (pp. 271–9). London: Longman.

Vaissière, J. (1983). Language-independent prosodic features. In A. Cutler & D. R. Ladd (eds.), *Prosody: Models and Measurements* (pp. 53–66). Berlin: Springer-Verlag.

Vaissière, J. (1991). Rhythm, accentuation and final lengthening in French. In. J. Sundberg, R. Carlson, & L. Nord, (eds.), *Music, Language, Speech and Brain* (pp. 108–20), Wenner-Gren International Symposium Series. London: Macmillan Press.

Vaissière, J. (1995). Phonetic explanations for cross-linguistic similarities. *Phonetica*, 52, 123–30.

Vaissière, J. (2001). Changements de sons et changements prosodiques: du latin au français [Sound changes and prosodic changes: from Latin to Modern French]. *Parole*, 15/16, 53–88.

Vaissière, J. (2002). Cross-linguistic prosodic transcription: French versus English. In N. B. Volskaya, N. D. Svetozarova, & P. A. Skrelin (eds.), *Problemy i metody eksperimental'no-foneticheskih issledovanij: In honour of the 70th anniversary of Prof. L. V. Bondarko* (pp. 147–64). St Petersburg: St Petersburg State University.

Van Els, T. J. M. & DeObt, K. (1987). The role of intonation in foreign accent. *Modern Language Journal*, 71(2), 147–55.

Verhoeven, J. (1994). The discrimination of pitch alignment in Dutch. *Journal of Phonetics*, 22, 65–85.

Verma, S., Mannering, A. M., Kornell, B. M., Katz, W. F., & Beach, C. (1994). Prosodic cues for phrasal boundaries in productions by children and adults. *Journal of the Acoustical Society of America*, 96(5), 3308.

Ward, G. & Hirschberg, J. (1988). Intonation and propositional attitude: The pragmatics of L*+H L H%. *Proceedings of the Eastern States Conference on Linguistics (ESCOL)*, 5, 512–22.

Watanabe, K. (1988). Sentence stress perception by Japanese students. *Journal of Phonetics*, 16(2), 181–6.

Wichmann, A. (2002). Attitudinal intonation and the inferential process. *Speech Prosody 2002* (pp. 11–5). Aix-en-Provence. http://www.lpl.univ-aix.fr/sp2002/pdf/wichmann.pdf.

Williams, C. E. & Stevens, K. N. (1972). Emotion and speech: Some acoustical correlates. *Journal of the Acoustical Society of America*, 52(2), 1238–50.

11 Lexical Stress

ANNE CUTLER

Stress is accentuation of syllables within words, or of words within sentences. This chapter deals with the first of these phenomena: lexical, or word stress. In lexical-stress languages, the syllables of any polysyllabic word are not created equal. Some syllables may serve as the locus of accentual prominence; others may not. Perceptually, this results in a distinction in salience between the syllables within a word. Thus *syllable* has initial stress: *SYLlable*. *Syllabic* is stressed on the second syllable: *sylLABic* (upper case denotes a stressed syllable).

Although the term *stress* is properly an abstraction, speech perception deals with physical realities, and so, as Section 11.1 describes, research on stress perception has largely been concerned with the acoustic characteristics of stressed versus unstressed syllables, and how listeners exploit the acoustic information to make decisions about where stress occurs. Differences across languages in the realization and function of stress have important perceptual consequences; this issue is considered in Section 11.2. Only in some languages is stress a potential contributor to spoken-word recognition; the empirical evidence on this question is surveyed in Section 11.3.

11.1 Acoustic Realization and Perceptual Apprehension of Stress

11.1.1 The scope of this survey

Like speech perception research in general, research on the perception of stress came of age when it became possible not only to measure the acoustic properties of speech signals, but to manipulate them. This was in the middle of the twentieth century.

The research described in this section concerns word stress in free-stress languages, although the manifestation of stress in free- versus fixed-stress languages has not always been kept apart in the literature (Section 11.2, below, will address this distinction). Also it has not always been the case that word stress has been kept apart from phrase and sentence stress, especially in earlier literature; however, prominence within the utterance more properly belongs in the domain of intonation research (see Vaissière, this volume).

In words, stressed syllables very often differ from unstressed syllables in nature – phonological systems assign stress to heavier syllables but not to lighter syllables, for instance. But stressed syllables also differ from unstressed syllables in their acoustic realization. Figure 11.1 shows spectrograms of the utterance *say the word pervert again*, spoken by a male speaker of American English. In the top spectrogram the verb reading (*perVERT*) is shown, in the bottom spectrogram the noun reading (*PERvert*); although the syllables have the same segmental structure in each reading, the acoustic realization is clearly different.

Speech perception research paid great attention to acoustic realization. The measurements and manipulations concerned the suprasegmental parameters of speech: that is, those dimensions within which any speech signal must be realized (Lehiste, 1970), but which in principle can vary independently while the segmental identity of a syllable remains constant. In practice this involved three acoustic dimensions: the durational patterning of the utterance, the fundamental frequency (F0) of the voice, and the signal amplitude. Perceptually these correspond to utterance timing, pitch, and loudness.

11.1.2 *Multiply determined stress judgments*

Fry (1955, 1958) conducted a systematic study of word stress in English minimal noun/verb pairs such as *OBject – obJECT*. Fry measured the duration and peak amplitude of each vowel, and found almost non-overlapping distributions for the stressed versus unstressed versions of comparable syllables, with the stressed syllables being longer and with higher amplitude than the unstressed. He then synthesized versions of the same words, varying these two parameters independently in 5 steps each, and varying F0 in 16 steps. Listeners' judgments of which syllable bore stress in the resulting synthetic words showed more effect of the durational manipulation than of the amplitude manipulation; change in F0 had an all-or-none effect, such that a syllable with a noticeably higher peak F0, or a clear F0 movement, was always judged to be stressed. The function of stressed syllables in stress languages is to serve as possible locations for accentual prominence within utterance intonation contours, and this result suggests that listeners are highly sensitive to where intonational prominence is realized; wherever this occurs, the location is judged to be a stressed syllable. Fry (1958) thus cautiously concluded that this F0 effect may be strongest for stress perception, with the effect of duration also being significant, but that of amplitude negligible. However, he also pointed out that vowel quality needed to be investigated, and he undertook this task in a subsequent study (Fry, 1965), in which shifts of the vowel formant ratios (e.g., for *object*, stepwise from [ɒ] to [ə] in the first syllable or from [ɛ] to [ɪ] in the second) were compared to durational and amplitude manipulations. The suprasegmental factors here proved more closely related to stress judgments than this type of vowel change.

If subjective impressions suggested that stressed syllables were louder than unstressed, this impression was quickly disconfirmed even by some of the earliest studies. Mol and Uhlenbeck (1956) reversed the amplitude relationship of stressed

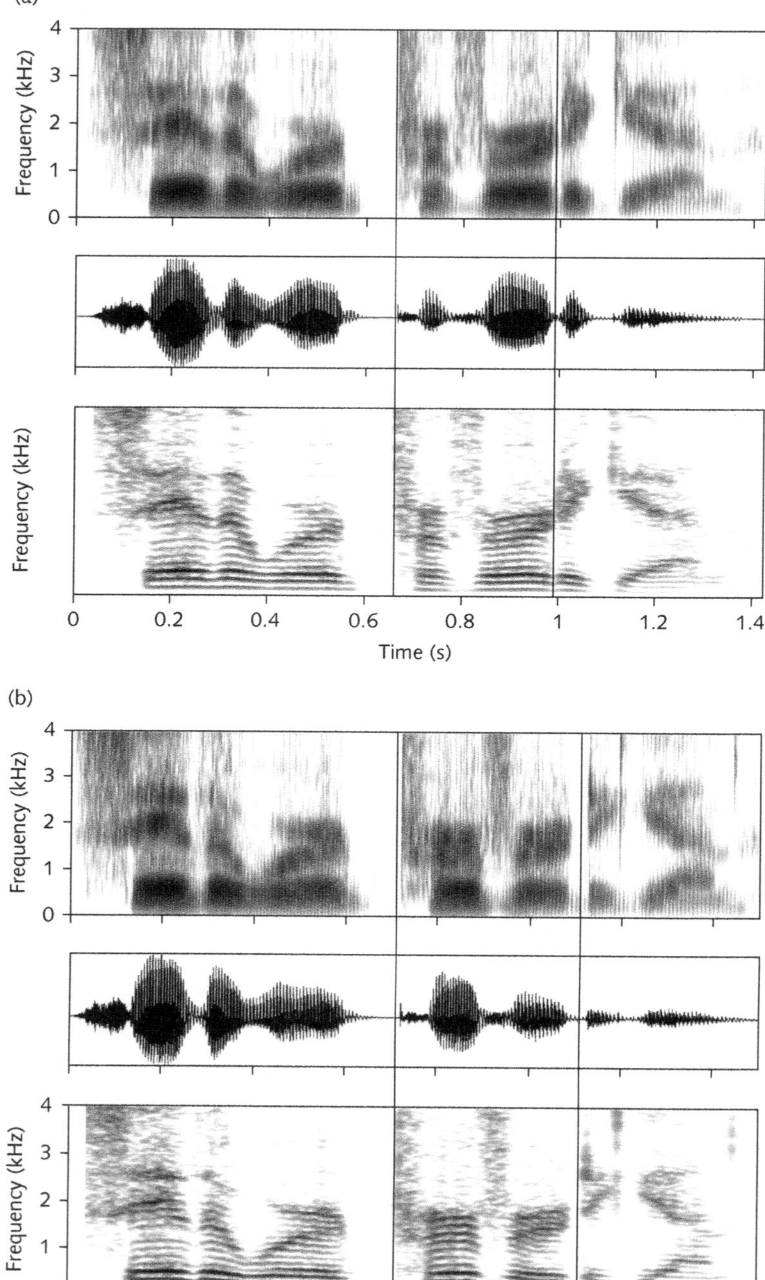

Figure 11.1 Sound spectrograms of the words perVERT (a) and PERvert (b), in the carrier sentence "Say the word . . . again," spoken by a male speaker of American English. Each figure consists of three display panels: above, a broad-band spectrogram; in the middle, a waveform display; and below, a narrow-band spectrogram. Vertical lines indicate onset and offset of pervert. The figure is modeled on a figure presented by Lehiste and Peterson (1959, p. 434).

versus unstressed syllables while leaving other parameters unchanged, and found that the reversal did not affect perceived stress; Bolinger (1958) added amplitude to pitch accents realized in synthesized sentences, and found that listeners' naturalness judgments if anything favored accents with less added amplitude. Ladefoged, Draper, and Whitteridge, introducing their pioneering 1958 electromyographic study of speech muscle activity, reported that "it is generally agreed" that stress has no single acoustic correlate (p. 9).

This was also the conclusion of studies by Lehiste and Peterson (1959), and Lieberman (1960). Lehiste and Peterson (on whose work Figure 11.1 is based) further drew attention to the non-independence of the acoustic parameters measured in stress studies and segmental factors – consonants and, especially, vowels can differ in intrinsic duration, amplitude, and pitch. Lieberman's study aimed to derive an algorithm for determining which of two syllables is stressed. Measurements of the three acoustic parameters in over 700 tokens of bisyllables (25 minimal pairs, produced in context by 16 speakers) showed that greater duration, higher average F0 and amplitude measures (higher peak, higher integral of amplitude across the syllable, and greater amplitude ratio of one syllable to the other in a word) were all strongly correlated with stress. Where one measure was not in the predicted direction, there was almost always a trade-off because other correlates of stress were present (in no fewer than 97% of cases). Lieberman concluded that no single acoustic cue to stress is necessarily important, but that all cues may be evaluated together.

11.1.3 *In search of a unitary underlying factor*

Should there be, no matter how complex the realization, some unitary underlying factor distinguishing stressed from unstressed syllables? The concept of articulatory effort figures in this role in many early studies (e.g. Fonagy, 1958, 1966; Ladefoged et al., 1958; Lehiste & Peterson, 1959; Van Katwijk, 1974). The latter two papers propose an explicitly perceptual account: "perception of linguistic stress is based upon judgements of the physiological effort involved in producing vowels" (Lehiste & Peterson, 1959, p. 428); "the perceptual effect [is] a pitch contour which could have been produced with an increment of subglottal pressure" (Van Katwijk, 1974, p. 66).

How could a notion like articulatory effort be tested? Lindblom (1963) considered that his measurements of Swedish vowel formant frequencies, which suggested invariant vowel targets attained to a greater or lesser extent as a function only of vowel duration, implied that vowel reduction should not be explained in terms of lesser articulatory effort: only timing patterns determined whether or not a vowel would be reduced. Van Katwijk's (1974) measurements of subglottal pressure found little evidence of stress-related pressure increase.

Harder still to assess was the proposal that listener judgments of stress depended on perceived effort. However a relevant contribution was made in the work of Isačenko and Schädlich (1966; followed up by Bleakley, 1973); in German utterances, stressed syllables could be signaled by any F0 obtrusion from the overall contour, so that a stressed syllable could be either higher or lower in pitch than its neighbors. Listeners rated both types of obtrusion as stress, which argued against commitment to greater perceived articulatory effort, and instead confirmed sensitivity to location of intonational prominence. Morton and Jassem (1965) found a similar result with English listeners judging synthesized nonsense bisyllables.

11.1.4 *Reducing the complexity?*

As the technology for manipulating speech signals improved, the complexity underlying stress perception was further confirmed. Nakatani and Aston (1978) used linear predictive coding techniques to manipulate orthogonally the natural duration, amplitude, and F0 attributes of bisyllables with initial or final stress, and found, as had others before them, that all exercised effects on stress judgments, although the effect of amplitude variation was weakest. In general, the effects were additive, except that durational variation lost its effect in sentence-final position, and F0 lost its effect when the word in question was deaccented in the intonation contour because it followed a contrastive accent (for comparable findings see Huss, 1975, 1978). Nakatani and Aston also reported speaker differences in the realization of stress contrasts (see also Howell, 1993). Other studies showed that differences between stressed and unstressed syllables in the three standard acoustic parameters were maintained across speech rates (Gay, 1978; McClean & Tiffany, 1973), while experiments in languages with fixed-position stress, or in languages with other phonological effects interacting with the stress system, further complicated the picture (see Section 11.2 below).

Attempts were made to develop perceptual measures that might facilitate greater comparability across studies. Gussenhoven and Blom (1978) proposed a "language-neutral test" based on paired judgments of perceived contrast between isolated vowels. Taylor and Wales (1987) proposed a contrast ratio:

$$(\text{stressed} - \text{unstressed})/(\text{stressed} + \text{unstressed})$$

which, they reported, for the three standard acoustic dimensions predicted judgments of perceived stress far more effectively than other ratios (such as the most commonly used subtraction ratio, i.e., the simple difference in any of the parameters between stressed and unstressed syllables, or the ratio stressed/unstressed, i.e., the division of one set of values by the other).

More recent research has tried to disentangle the complexity and multiple determination of stress perception by considering potential confounds. For instance, might stress judgments be complicated by the possibility that word stress placement can shift (so that English *thirteen* is stressed on the second syllable in *the number thirteen*, but on the first in *thirteen numbers*)? However, the undoubted shift in perceptual prominence in many such contrasting phrases does not result from a simple reversal of relative placement of a word's syllables on acoustic dimensions (see, e.g., Cooper & Eady, 1986; Shattuck-Hufnagel, Ostendorf, & Ross, 1994; Van Heuven, 1987). Likewise, measurements revealed little support for the notion of durational compensation within stress groups in English, such that segments of syllables might be longer in, say, a two-syllable foot (*save it*) than in a four-syllable foot (*savoring it*); segment durations are longer in syllables with primary stress than in syllables with secondary stress, and longer in turn in the latter than in unstressed syllables, such that syllable duration can be fully predicted given knowledge of the segments and stress pattern of the word (Crystal & House, 1988, 1990).

11.1.5 Summary

Research on stress perception continues both within and outside the speech perception literature. For example, it has long been of interest to speech engineers whether the use of stress-related information in the signal could improve the performance of automatic speech recognizers (see, e.g., Lea, 1977; Marshall & Nye, 1983; Waibel, 1988, for English; van Kuijk & Boves, 1999, for Dutch), and some successful implementations have been reported (e.g., Kiriakos & O'Shaughnessy, 1989; Sholicar & Fallside, 1988).

Over nearly 50 years, however, perceptual studies have elaborated but not fundamentally altered the early claims concerning the suprasegmental dimensions involved. Syllables are perceived to be stressed if they exhibit F0 excursion (Fry, 1958), whereby the timing of the F0 movement within the syllable can be crucial for determining stress perception (Thorsen, 1982, for Danish), and some types of F0 movement may require more excursion than others (Hermes & Rump, 1994, for Dutch F0 rise versus rise-fall). Greater syllable duration is likewise associated with perceived stress (Fry, 1955). These two factors are the most strongly related and the least controversial.

More controversial is the common finding that amplitude manipulations only weakly affect stress perception (despite psychoacoustic research showing that quite small changes in this dimension are indeed perceptible; Sorin, 1981). Turk and Sawusch (1996) found listeners' perception of duration and amplitude variation to be non-orthogonal; importantly, they observed effects of irrelevant durational variation on judgments of loudness to be greater than effects of amplitude variation on judgments of relative length. This, they argued, provided a rationale for why prominence judgments should be based on duration, or on duration and amplitude together, but not on the latter alone.

Beckman (1986) proposed that a measure of total amplitude (across a syllable) could capture effects on stress judgments, but as pointed out by Sluijter, van Heuven, and Pacilly (1997), such a measure is inevitably confounded with syllable duration. An indirect amplitude effect may however exist, in the factor which Sluijter and van Heuven (1996) termed spectral balance; stressed vowels have more energy in the higher frequency regions of the spectrum than unstressed vowels do. A linear discriminant analysis of their measurement data suggested that the most reliable correlate of the presence of stress was durational lengthening, with this spectral balance effect next in importance; overall amplitude had the usual weak impact on the analysis. A perceptual study of the spectral balance effect by Sluijter et al. (1997) showed that manipulations of this factor had a moderate effect when speech was presented to listeners over headphones, but a greatly increased effect when the speech was presented via loudspeakers! Sluijter et al. concluded that spectral balance directly reflects articulatory effort, in rehabilitation of the claim that perceived loudness is the most reliable cue to stress.

Campbell and Beckman (1997), however, failed to replicate the acoustic effect in English; they found spectral differences as a function of focal accent, but not as a function of lexical stress in the absence of accentual variation; this would therefore rule out analogous perceptual effects in English. On this issue, the last word may not yet be spoken.

11.2 Language-Specificity of Stress and Its Perceptual Consequences

11.2.1 Stress in phonological systems

The empirical evidence summarized in Section 11.1 was taken exclusively from studies of West Germanic languages. The evidence is similar across languages because the stress systems of these closely related languages are, although not identical, quite similar (see Figure 11.2). However, Germanic languages do not serve as a yardstick for languages across the world. First, stress characterizes the word-level phonology of only a subset of the world's languages. Second, there is considerable variation in word stress patterning even within stress languages, most obviously in the contrast between freely varying (as in the Germanic languages) and fixed-stress placement. Fixed-stress systems are considered in more detail below.

Little acoustic and perceptual evidence exists for non-Germanic free-stress languages. Measurements of segmentally matched stressed and unstressed syllables in Arabic by de Jong and Zawaydeh (1999) revealed duration and F0 correlates "remarkably like" the results reported for English (p. 20). In Spanish, stress is perceived if cued by F0 and duration or by F0 and amplitude, but not by any one cue alone (Llisterri et al., 2003); syllable weight and lexical analogy also affect stress perception (Face, 2000, 2003). Williams' (1985) experiments on synthesized Welsh minimal stress pairs found strong effects of duration on listeners' stress judgments, but inconsistent effects of F0. In Thai (a tone language), stress is signaled effectively by duration alone (Potisuk, Gandour, & Harper, 1996). It should be noted that some forms of English can also show other patterning than that described in Section 11.1. For instance, in Indian English (Bansal, 1966) and Welsh English (Williams, 1985) F0 movement can be decoupled from stress; in each case this can induce stress misperceptions by speakers of other varieties of English, who may for instance be led by F0 peaks or movements on unstressed syllables to judge those syllables as stressed.

In general, stress realization (and its perceptual reflection) will be dependent on other features of a language's phonological system. As Potisuk et al. (1996) point out, F0 does not vary as a function of stress in Thai because of its preemption by the tone system. Shen (1993) also observed that prominence in Mandarin is signaled by means other than F0. And just as tone preempts F0, so quantity distinctions in the segmental system render durational variation less useful for other purposes such as signaling stress. Berinstein (1979) found that speakers of Mayan languages with fixed final stress could learn to use duration variation as a position-independent cue to stress judgment, producing similar performance to

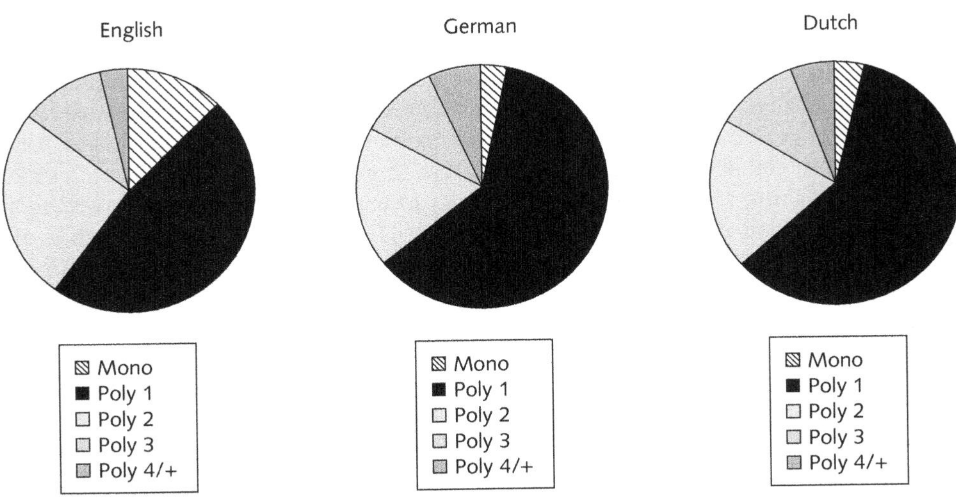

Figure 11.2 Distribution of lexical stress placement in three closely related languages: English, German, Dutch (from the CELEX lexical database; Baayen, Piepenbrock, & Van Rijn, 1993); monosyllabic words (Mono) versus polysyllabic words with stress on the first (Poly 1), second (Poly 2), third (Poly 3) or fourth or later syllable (Poly 4/+). The proportion of polysyllabic words is higher in the latter two languages; this is because the criteria for lemma inclusion admit many compounds in German and Dutch which are listed as separated lemmas in English. The tendency to word-initial stress in all three languages can be appreciated further when statistics for secondary stress are added. In English, secondary stress occurs on the initial syllable of about one-third of words with primary stress on the second syllable (7.7% in 25.2%), and most words with primary stress on the third (10.7% in 10.9%) or later syllable (2.3% in 3.6%). For German and Dutch, the values are similar: German 15.4% in 19%, 6.2% in 10.1%, and 3.5% in 6.8%; Dutch 12.7% in 20.1%, 8.1% in 10.5%, and 4% in 5.6%. Together, monosyllabic words and words with primary or secondary stress on the first syllable comprise 81% of the English lexicon and 89% of the German and Dutch lexicons.

speakers of English, but only if their language did not have vowel quantity distinctions – i.e., only if their language had not already preempted durational variation as a cue to something other than stress.

11.2.2 *Culminative vs. demarcative functions of stress*

Lexical stress variation has the word as its domain. In each word, only one syllable bears primary stress (although a few languages may not conform to this generalization; see Hyman, 1977, for further discussion). Thus stress is sometimes termed culminative within the word.

The single primary stress constraint does not rule out further distinctions among syllables which do not bear primary stress. Phonological accounts of the metrical structure of stress languages can encompass fine-grained distinctions of prominence within utterances (see Van der Hulst, 1999, for descriptions of the metrical structure of a range of European languages). Thus in English *PRESident*, primary stress falls on the initial syllable, whereas it falls on the third syllable in *presiDENtial*. But the remaining three syllables of *presiDENtial* are not all unstressed; the first syllable is said to bear secondary stress. The vowel in the initial syllable is not reduced, whereas those in the second and final syllables are likely to be; however, the possibility of vowel reduction is not a prerequisite for a contrast between secondary and lesser stress (consider Spanish *presidente*, which exhibits the same relative salience across its four syllables as English *presidential*, although Spanish has no vowel reduction). It is an empirical issue whether distinguishing between syllables with primary versus secondary stress (for example, in *presi-* from English *president* versus *presidential*) is perceptually necessary; this will be considered further in section 11.3 below.

The culminative function of stress may be contrasted with the so-called demarcative function, a term applying to stress which falls always at a particular position within the word. Again, one syllable within a polysyllabic word is the location of this fixed stress. The term demarcative refers to the potential for fixed-position stress to function as a marker of word boundaries (perhaps especially in languages with fixed word-initial stress, such as Finnish, Hungarian, Czech). Note, however, that fixed placement of stress of course implies that stress is not contrastive, i.e., cannot distinguish one word from another.

These properties are potentially important in perception. If stress can distinguish between words, listeners may use cues to stress in identifying spoken words; but if stress cannot help in this way, there is no reason for listeners to use it in word recognition. Similarly, if stress can signal word boundaries, listeners may use stress cues for segmenting continuous speech into words; but if stress were to have no systematic relation to position within the word, it could not be of use in segmentation.

11.2.3 Free stress and segmentation

Most research on the role of stress in the segmentation of speech has in fact been conducted in free-stress languages: notably in English and Dutch. Although both these languages are classified as having free stress, the place where stress will fall is not arbitrary, but is determined by considerations of syllable weight; morphological factors then conspire to place the designated stress-bearing syllable more often than not, as Figure 11.2 showed, in word-initial position. In typical conversational speech in English, the tendency to word-initial stress is even stronger than in the lexicon (Cutler & Carter, 1987). Listeners' behavior shows effects of this regularity; nonwords with initial stress can be repeated more rapidly, and attract higher word-likeness ratings, than nonwords with final stress (Vitevitch et al., 1997). The distributional asymmetry, combined with listener sensitivity to the pattern, opens the way for stress to be useful in segmentation in these languages, too.

Indeed, a substantial body of evidence from both English and Dutch indicates that listeners do treat stressed syllables as probable word onsets. Missegmentations of speech are more likely to involve stressed syllables being erroneously taken for word-initial and unstressed syllables being erroneously taken for word-internal than the reverse pattern, both in English (Cutler & Butterfield, 1992) and Dutch

(Vroomen, Van Zon, & De Gelder, 1996). Thus *a must to avoid* heard as *a muscular boy* is a natural error – the stressed last syllable is taken as a new word, while the unstressed two syllables preceding it are taken as internal to another word. Similarly, English listeners find word-spotting – detecting a real word in a spoken nonsense sequence – difficult if the word is spread over two strong syllables (e.g., *risk* in [rɪskib]) but easier if it is spread over a strong followed by a weak, unstressed syllable (e.g., *risk* in [rɪskəb]) (Cutler & Norris, 1988; see Quené & Koster, 1998, and Vroomen et al., 1996, for analogous evidence from Dutch). The difficulty in the former case is explained as resulting from division of the sequence at the onset of the second strong syllable on the strategy that any such syllable (with primary or secondary stress) is likely to be a new word; consequently, detection of *risk* in [rɪskib] requires that its component phonemes be reassembled, while no such delay affects detection of *risk* in [rɪskəb]. These findings suggest that listeners use distributional consistencies of stress placement to segment speech even in languages in which stress is not strictly demarcative. So far, however, similar studies of segmentation in fixed-stress languages are not available.

11.2.4 *Fixed stress discriminability*

In fact, there are reasons for caution with the superficially appealing notion of a demarcative role for stress cues in listening. One relevant consideration is that the acoustic realization of stress in fixed-stress languages is "weak" (Dogil, 1999; Rigault, 1970) in comparison to stress in free-stress languages. Early measurements of Hungarian (fixed initial stress) by Fonagy (1966) found the unstressed final syllables of bisyllabic words to be both longer and louder than the stressed initial syllables. Janota (1967) reported that F0 did not serve as a perceptual cue to stress in synthesized nonwords for Czech listeners (fixed initial stress); Rigault (1970) found in both Czech and French (fixed accent on final syllable of rhythmic groups) an absence of systematicity in stress realization. For Polish (fixed penultimate stress), Jassem (1962, cited in Morton & Jassem, 1965 and in Dogil, 1999) found no effective acoustic correlate of stress other than in F0. Dogil (1999) observed that Jassem's study was confounded with intonational variation, and conducted measurements of the same Polish words in different intonational frames; he found no consistent acoustic correlates of stress at all, and also no consistent reflections of putative rhythmic stresses in this language. Dogil proposed that in Polish, word stress has no other expression than as the abstract feature marking positions with which intonational movement may be associated. In contrast to lexical-stress languages, then, fixed-stress languages may not distinguish stressed from unstressed syllables at all in the absence of intonational realization of the abstract difference.

Another consideration is that although fixed stress is sometimes located at a word boundary, this is not always so (as in Polish, where stress is on the penultimate syllable). Given that the process of spoken-word recognition involves continuous exploitation of incoming acoustic information (see Frauenfelder & Floccia, 1998, for a review), fixed stress other than at a word edge will involve additional processing complexity. A third consideration is that fixed stress may affect all words irrespective of word class, or may be sensitive to grammatical factors.

This last consideration motivated investigations by Dupoux and Peperkamp (2002; Peperkamp & Dupoux, 2002), who aim ultimately to explain the acquisition of word prosody by infants. Dupoux and Peperkamp suggest that overall listener sensitivity to stress cues in adulthood will depend on the function of stress in their native language; in general, languages without lexically contrastive stress will not require that listeners develop sensitivity to stress information in speech. However, such non-contrastive languages differ in how accessible the rules for prosodic prominence are to an infant. In some languages (e.g., Finnish, French), prominence is unaffected by grammatical factors; infants should be able to learn early that stress plays no useful contrastive role and can be ignored. In other languages (e.g., Hungarian, Polish), prominence rules affect lexical words and grammatical (function) words differently; this pattern should be harder to learn, with the result that some sensitivity to stress contrasts may develop. Initial studies by Dupoux et al. (1997) and Dupoux, Peperkamp, and Sebastián-Gallés (2001) showed that speakers of French have great difficulty processing stress contrasts in nonsense materials, e.g., deciding whether a token *bopeLO* should be matched with an earlier token of *bopeLO* or *boPElo*. The same contrasts are easy for speakers of Spanish, which does distinguish words via stress. Dupoux and Peperkamp then tested Finnish speakers, whose performance indeed resembled that of French speakers, and speakers of Hungarian and Polish, whose performance fell between the French/Finnish and the Spanish levels.

11.2.5 Fixed stress and segmentation

Dupoux and Peperkamp's (2002) work suggests that fixed-stress languages cannot be treated as a unitary class. With regard to lexical segmentation, the available evidence on fixed-stress languages still falls far short of that on free-stress languages. In Indonesian (with phrase-final accent) listeners do not show evidence of using stress placement for segmentation (van Zanten & van Heuven, 1998). However, some studies on French and on Finnish (fixed initial stress) have provided evidence consistent with use of demarcation cues by listeners. In French, the accent-bearing right boundary of a rhythmic group is always also the right boundary of a word; Dahan (1996) found that listeners detect target syllables located at a rhythmic group boundary more rapidly than the same syllables elsewhere in an utterance. In Finnish, a word-spotting study by Suomi, McQueen, and Cutler (1997) showed that vowel harmony (which is a word-level phenomenon) can be used by listeners in segmentation; indirect evidence on stress processing can be deduced from their control experiment, in which excised embedded words from the word-spotting materials were recognized no less rapidly if taken from a preceding context (e.g., *palo* from *kupalo*) than from a following context (e.g., *palo* from *paloku*). Although the former type could be considered not to have been uttered with canonical stress, no deleterious effects of this on word recognition were observed. Vroomen, Tuomainen, and De Gelder (1998) replicated the Suomi et al. finding but showed that even stronger than vowel harmony was the effect on segmentation exercised by clearly marked word-initial stress. In a further experiment, Vroomen et al. showed that Finnish listeners were sensitive to vowel harmony and to stress (operationalized as higher F0) in learning the "words" of an artificial language, while Dutch listeners were sensitive only to the stress cue and French listeners were sensitive to neither cue.

These results are difficult to account for in the light of Dupoux and Peperkamp's (2002) finding that stress contrasts were overlooked by both French and Finnish listeners. However, it should be noted that the type of segmentation task used by Dahan (1996) does not directly tap word processing. Further, Vroomen et al. (1998) do not report how stress was realized in their word-spotting materials, but it is possible that as in their artificial language study, a clear F0 correlate was available. As Finnish has fixed initial stress, the initial syllable is the designated location for the realization of intonational prominence, but in the absence of such higher-level effects, Finnish stressed syllables are in fact not distinct in F0 from unstressed syllables (Suomi, Toivanen, & Ylitalo, 2003). The principal acoustic correlate of Finnish word stress is segmental lengthening within a word's initial two morae, even when the second mora is also the second syllable (Suomi & Ylitalo, 2004). The confound observed by Dogil (1999) in Jassem's (1962) work may thus also apply to Vroomen et al.'s study: listeners may have been able to use information relevant not to the lexical but to the intonational structure of the utterance (see Vaissière, this volume, for evidence on intonation perception).

11.2.6 *The contrastive potential of stress*

The putative contrastive function of stress must be considered in the light of the undeniable rarity of minimal word pairs which differ in stress alone (such as, for example, *trusty* and *trustee* in English). Free-stress languages make remarkably little use of the contrastive possibilities which stress in principle offers them. But there are other ways in which stress may be useful in word recognition. Statistical analyses by Altmann and Carter (1989) established that the amount of information conveyed by phonetic segments in English is highest for vowels in stressed syllables. Further, stressed syllables are acoustically reliable: they are more readily identified than unstressed syllables when excised from a context (Lieberman, 1963), and speech distortions are more likely to be detected in stressed than in unstressed syllables (Bond & Garnes, 1980; Browman, 1978; Cole & Jakimik, 1980; Cole, Jakimik, & Cooper, 1978). In gated presentation of spontaneously spoken – but not of read – sentences, stressed syllables are recognized earlier than unstressed syllables (McAllister, 1991). Also in spontaneous speech, word-initial target phonemes are detected more rapidly on lexically stressed than unstressed syllables (Mehta & Cutler, 1988). Note that acoustic differences between stressed and unstressed syllables are relatively large in spontaneous speech. With laboratory-read materials, however, such differences do not always arise; Mattys and Samuel (2000) found that phoneme detection was in general faster in words with initial stress, irrespective of whether the target phoneme occurred in the stressed syllable or elsewhere in the word.

Models of spoken-word recognition agree that continuous evaluation of speech input results in simultaneous activation of multiple candidate word forms which at any moment are supported by the input; eventual recognition proceeds on the basis of further input information but also via a process of competition between the activated words (Frauenfelder & Floccia, 1998). Within this presumably universal framework, the input information constraining activation will be necessarily language-specific. Like segmental contrasts, the relevant suprasegmental contrasts will differ across languages. If listeners do take account of stress, it can certainly help to reduce the number of word candidates. Van Heuven & Hagman's (1988) analyses of the Dutch vocabulary established that words could on average be identified after 80% of their phonemes (counting from word onset) had been considered; when stress information was included, however, a forward search was successful given only 66% of the phonemes. Wingfield, Goodglass, and Lindfield (1997) found that stress was relevant in determining the number of potential English word candidates from which listeners' recognition of gated words could be predicted. Section 11.3 considers empirical evidence for whether stress correlates in fact do constrain spoken word recognition.

11.3 Stress in the Recognition of Spoken Words

11.3.1 Lexical activation

The acoustic information in the signal which varies as a function of stress could play an early constraining role in lexical activation in the following way: as speech input activates word candidates, only those candidates which match the structure signaled by the input in stress as well as in segmental structure would become active. Words with non-matching stress or mismatching segments would not come into consideration.

Note that this means that stress information could play a substantial role in lexical activation even in languages where the number of word pairs distinguished by suprasegmental stress cues alone is vanishingly small. Word candidates may be activated by partial information as words are spoken; an utterance of *bottle* may temporarily cause activation of *bother, botch,* and *botany* among other words (Allopenna, Magnuson, & Tanenhaus, 1998; Zwitserlood, 1989). A word-initial syllable consisting of a given string of phonetic segments may be differently stressed in different words even though the words do not form a minimal stress pair. Although this is more likely in stress languages without vowel reduction, it also happens in English and similar languages. Thus *music* begins with stressed *mu-* while *museum* begins with unstressed *mu-*; *ad-* has primary stress in *admiral* but secondary stress in *admiration*. If stress cues distinguish these syllables for the purposes of lexical activation, then *mu-* is not the same syllable in *music* and *museum*, and the utterance of one will not activate, even temporarily, the other.

The same opposition can of course occur with non-initial portions of words – compare *-day* in *today* or *Tuesday*, or *-cide* in *decide* or *suicide* – and this difference may play a crucial role in listening situations in which initial portions of a word have for some reason not been heard. But the role of stress information in constraining lexical activation via distinctions in word-initial sequences is potentially even more significant.

Evidence from studies of the effect of segmental mismatch on lexical activation suggests that as incoming phonetic information matches one of two competitors but not the other, the losing competitor suffers inhibition (Vitevitch & Luce, 1998). Listeners exploit distinctive information rapidly to favor a matched competitor, which is thus enabled to compete more effectively and actually cause significant reduction in activation of its mismatched rival. The effects of a stress mismatch and a segmental mismatch were directly compared by Soto-Faraco, Sebastián-Gallés, and Cutler (2001). In their study, native speakers of Castilian Spanish heard spoken sentences (of a non-constraining type such as *He did not know how to write the word . . .*) ending with a word fragment which fully matched one of two potential words and differed from the other in just a single phoneme or in stress pattern. For instance, the fragment *prinCI-* (stressed on the second syllable) matches the first two syllables of the Spanish word *prinCIpio* (beginning) and differs only in stress from the first two syllables of the Spanish word *PRINcipe* (prince). Likewise, the fragment *sardi-* matches *sardina* (sardine) but mismatches *sardana* (a type of dance) in a single vowel, and the fragment *bofe-* fully matches *bofeton* (smack) but mismatches *boletin* (bulletin) in a single consonant. At the offset of the word fragment listeners saw a string of letters on a screen and were asked to decide whether this string was a real word. Their responses were significantly faster to a visually presented word after matching fragments (e.g., to SARDINA after *sardi-*, to PRINCIPIO after *prinCI-*, etc.) than after control fragments (e.g., *manti-*); responses after fragments which minimally mismatched and favored another word (e.g., to SARDINA after *sarda-*, to PRINCIPIO after *PRINci-*, etc.) were, crucially, significantly slower than responses after control fragments. The three types of mismatch information (vocalic, consonantal, stress) each produced the same pattern of inhibition in Soto-Faraco et al.'s experiment.

Donselaar, Koster, and Cutler (2005) replicated the stress comparison from Soto-Faraco et al.'s fragment priming study in Dutch, presenting fragments like *octo-* which matched one of either *OCtopus* or *okTOber* and mismatched the other only in stress placement. They too found that responses preceded by a matching prime were significantly facilitated, while responses preceded by a mismatching prime were slowed, in comparison to responses after the control prime. Again, listeners used the stress information to speed the victory of one of two competitors for lexical recognition. By comparison, a similar study by Cutler and Donselaar (2001) found that fragments like *MUzee* which mismatched *muSEum* in stress did not cause facilitation of the matched word, but also did not cause inhibition; no Dutch word begins *MUzee* so there is no competitor to inhibit the mismatched word. Words such as *museum* are thus activated only when their initial portions are appropriately stressed. This was shown directly by another of Cutler and Donselaar's (2001) experiments, using the word-spotting task, in which listeners monitor short nonsense strings for the presence of any embedded real word. McQueen, Norris, and Cutler (1994) had shown that this task could reveal competition effects; the English word *mess* was detected more rapidly in the nonsense context *neMES* (which activates no competitor) than in *doMES* (which activates *doMEStic*, competition from which slows the recognition of *mess*). Cutler and Donselaar replicated this result in Dutch: *zee* 'sea' was detected more rapidly in *luZEE* (activating no competitor) than in *muZEE* (activating *museum*). In *MUzee*, however, the detection of *zee* was not significantly slowed, suggesting that *museum* had not been activated.

A single-syllable fragment (e.g., the first syllable of *octopus* or *oktober*) produced significant facilitation if it matched, but did not produce inhibition if it mismatched, i.e., was taken from a word with the contrasting stress pattern (Donselaar et al.,

2005); the same pattern appeared in a fragment priming study in German by Friedrich (2002). Friedrich, Kotz, and Gunter (2001) presented fragments of varying length, but did not use target pairs contrasting in onset stress such as *octopus-oktober*, so that (as in Donselaar et al.'s study with *museum*) no competition and hence no inhibition was involved; however, these authors found that facilitation did not significantly increase with increasing fragment size. The difference in inhibition due to the constraint in the competition process exercised by two syllables versus one is presumably a function of number of remaining potential competitors; after two syllables the competitor set will be smaller. In either case, cues to stress in the realization of word-initial portions are clearly used by listeners.

This series of studies on Spanish, Dutch, and German has brought the investigation of cues to stress into the currently accepted activation-competition framework of spoken-word recognition theory. Friedrich (2002) also measured evoked response potentials (ERPs), and found evidence for a difference in these measures between prime-target pairs which matched versus mismatched in F0 correlates of stress. It is to be expected that the coming years will see more studies of this issue using electrophysiological and brain imaging techniques. What is remarkable is that although, overall, most research on the perception of stress has been conducted on English, directly comparable experiments to those just described in Spanish, Dutch, and German have not been done in English. In fact there is good reason for this: directly analogous experiments are actually impossible. This is because of the strong tendency in English for any unstressed syllable adjacent to a stressed syllable to contain a reduced vowel. Thus there are effectively no such pairs in English as *octopus/oktober* in Dutch; the second syllable of English *octopus*, for instance, is reduced and hence has a different vowel than English *October*.

This does not however rule out partially comparable experiments. One possibility in English is to compare pairs in which the stress placement contrast does not involve primary stress on the first syllable versus primary stress on the second syllable, but another placement contrast. In fact Soto-Faraco et al.'s (2001) stress experiment included some pairs contrasting primary stress on second versus third syllables (e.g., *coMEdia* 'comedy' versus *comeDOR* 'dining room'), and so did Donselaar et al.'s (2005) Dutch fragment priming experiment (e.g., *dyNAmo* 'dynamo' versus *dynaMIET* 'dynamite'). These are again not possible to match exactly with English examples; but a first- vs. third-syllable contrast in primary stress can be achieved. There are in fact many English pairs in which the second syllable is reduced in both, but primary stress is either on the first or the third syllable – e.g., *admiral* versus *admiration*. In such pairs a fragment comprising only the first two syllables (e.g., *admi-*) would in one case have primary stress plus a weak syllable, in the other secondary stress plus a weak syllable.

Cooper, Cutler, and Wales (2002) carried out a fragment priming study using such English word pairs, and found clear evidence that English listeners too can make use of cues to stress in recognizing spoken words: *admi-* with primary stress on the first syllable activated ADMIRAL to a greater extent than ADMIRATION, while *admi-* with secondary stress on the first syllable activated ADMIRATION to a greater extent than ADMIRAL. Single-syllable fragments (e.g., *mus-* from *music* or *museum*) also produced facilitation when stress cues matched. Cooper et al. found, however, no evidence of inhibition from stress-mismatching primes, either with one- or two-syllable fragments; they argued that stress cues contribute less to resolution of inter-word competition in English than segmental information does, and in particular less than the wider range of stress contrasts contributes in Spanish and Dutch.

However, their results do show that English listeners can exploit suprasegmental stress cues in word recognition if they are given the opportunity. Cooper et al.'s conclusion thus modifies an earlier conclusion by Cutler (1986), reached on the basis of a priming study using not fragments but minimal stress pairs: for example *FORbear* versus *forBEAR*, or *trusty* versus *trustee*. Such pairs are rare but a few do exist in English. The task used was cross-modal priming of associated words: listeners were presented with sentences which were neutral until the occurrence of the critical pair, e.g.: *The person that she was hurrying to see was the trusty/trustee . . .*, and made lexical decisions about words presented visually at offset of the critical word in the sentence. Whichever member of the stress pair had been heard, listeners' responses to associates of both members of the pair were facilitated in comparison to control words. Cutler argued that the undoubted suprasegmental differences between, for instance, *FORbear* and *forBEAR* were ineffective in constraining lexical activation, so that for English listeners *forbear* was effectively a homophone. L. Slowiaczek (personal communication) reached the same conclusion on the basis of the finding that phrase-stress and compound-stress realizations of sequences such as *green house* primed associates related to both. The findings of Cooper et al. (2002) suggest, however, that the proposed inutility of stress cues in the initial stages of lexical activation does not extend to all types of stress contrast in English. Note that a cross-modal priming study in Dutch, planned as a direct replication of Cutler's (1986) experiment, failed to find significant priming at all by initially-stressed members of minimal stress pairs (*VOORnaam* 'firstname'), and inconsistent results for finally-stressed tokens (*voorNAAM* 'respectable') (Jongenburger & van Heuven, 1995a; Jongenburger, 1996), despite the other clear evidence for the use of stress cues in activation in Dutch; studies of minimal pairs may thus not provide the best window on the exploitation of stress information.

11.3.2 Lexical selection

Other types of word recognition studies, using tasks which do not tap into the early activation and competition stages, also show that listeners exploit stress cues in distinguishing between spoken words. Connine, Clifton, and Cutler (1987), for example, asked listeners to categorize an ambiguous consonant (varying along a continuum between [d] and [t]) in either *DIgress-TIgress* (in which *tigress* is a real word) or *diGRESS-tiGRESS* (in which *digress* is a real word). Listeners' responses showed effects of stress-determined lexical status, in that /t/ was reported more often for the *DIgress-TIgress* continuum, but /d/ more often for the *diGRESS-tiGRESS* continuum. The listeners clearly could use the stress information in the signal, and in their stored representations of these words, to resolve the phonetic ambiguity. However, this does not entail that knowing stress patterns in advance can facilitate access to the stored representations of words. Cutler and Clifton (1984) examined the effects of providing such information in a word recognition task, by comparing recognition of the same words in a blocked-presentation condition (all items presented were bisyllabic and initially stressed, for example) versus a mixed condition. They found that neither visual nor auditory lexical decision was speeded by prior specification of stress pattern.

Another way in which stress can play a role in word recognition is via canonical correlations between stress pattern and word class (e.g., initial stress for bisyllabic nouns in English, final stress for bisyllabic verbs; see Sereno, 1986, for the relevant statistics). Words which can be either nouns or verbs (such as *rescue* or *control*) show slight prosodic differences consistent with the canonical patterns when read in their two word class realizations (Sereno & Jongman, 1995). Listeners know and can use this; in studies by Kelly and colleagues (Cassidy & Kelly, 1991; Kelly, 1988, 1992; Kelly & Bock, 1988), subjects who were asked to use bisyllabic nonwords in a sentence as if they were words treated initially-stressed nonwords as nouns and finally-stressed nonwords as verbs. Further, when asked to use verbs as nonce-nouns subjects chose verbs with initial stress, while for nouns acting as nonce-verbs they chose nouns with final stress. This is analogous to knowledge of other stress regularities which has been demonstrated in production studies (see Colombo, 1991, for a review).

However, canonical patterning again does not directly speed spoken-word recognition, so that, for instance, whether or not a bisyllabic word conforms to the dominant noun/verb pattern does not affect how rapidly its grammatical category is judged – *cigar* is perceived as a noun just as rapidly as *apple*, and *borrow* is perceived as a verb as rapidly as *arrive* (Cutler & Clifton, 1984). Arciuli and Cupples (2002) replicated this result. Davis and Kelly (1997) also found no significant difference in the same classification task for native English speakers, but interestingly nonnative speakers of English – whose responses were of course much slower than those of the native speakers – did show a response advantage in their study for words which conformed to the canonical stress pattern for nouns and verbs respectively.

Gating is a task in which words are presented in fragments of increasing size; the dependent variable is how large a fragment is needed for listeners to recognize the word. Jongenburger and van Heuven (1995b; see also Jongenburger, 1996), using Dutch minimal pairs such as *voornaam* in sentence context, found that listeners' word guesses only displayed correct stress judgments for the initial syllable of the target word once the whole of that initial syllable and part of the following vowel were available. This result suggests again that minimal stress pairs may not exhibit the strongest possible effects of stress information on word activation, since it contrasts with another gating study (Van Heuven, 1988), in which listeners could correctly assign just the first syllable of a word, in sentence context, to one of two words in which it was respectively stressed versus unstressed (e.g., *si-* to *SIlo* versus *siGAAR*).

For English, Lindfield, Wingfield, and Goodglass (1999) conducted a gating study in which the presentation of word-initial fragments was contrasted with a condition in which the same fragments were presented along with additional information about how long the target word was, or how many syllables it had and what the stress pattern was. Recognition of the target occurred earlier in the latter condition. Arciuli and Cupples (2003) found however that adding low-pass filtered versions of the remainder of a gated word did not lead to earlier recognition compared with the gated fragment alone.

Related to gating studies are experiments in which listeners are presented with parts of words and asked to select (usually in a two-way forced choice) the source word. In Dutch, van Heuven (1988), Jongenburger (1996), and Cutler and Donselaar (2001) found that listeners could correctly select between two Dutch words with a segmentally identical but stress-differentiated initial syllable (e.g., *ORgel* and *orKEST*, or a minimal pair such as *VOORnaam-voorNAAM*) when presented with only the first syllable; Cutler and Donselaar found that the second syllables of minimal stress pairs (e.g., *-naam*) could also be accurately judged.

The high proportion of correct responses in the Dutch studies (for example, 85% for first and 80% for second syllables in Cutler and Donselaar's experiment) was not equaled in a similar study in English by Mattys (2000), though here too listeners performed above chance with both two-syllable and one-syllable word-initial fragments (on average 62% and 54% correct, respectively). Similarly, Cooper et al. (2002) found that English listeners correctly assigned 59% of initial syllables to source words such as *music* versus *museum*. Remarkably, however, Dutch listeners outperformed the native speakers in the same experiment, scoring 72% correct assignments. As discussed in section 11.3.1, the contribution of stress information in resolving lexical competition may be greater in some other languages than in English, and this difference may allow some proficient non-native users of English to exploit English stress cues more effectively than native speakers do.

11.3.3 *Lexical mismatch*

Other evidence that English listeners do not make maximal use of stress information in speech comes from studies of the perception of mis-stressed words. Small, Simon, and Goldberg (1988) found that mis-stressing did not inhibit word recognition if it effectively created the target word's stress pair (e.g., *INsert* pronounced as *inSERT* or vice versa), though recognition was significantly inhibited if the mis-stressing created a nonword (e.g., *chemist* pronounced *cheMIST*, or *polite* pronounced *POlite*). Similarly, Bond and Small (1983) found that word recognition in shadowing was achieved despite mis-stressing as long as the mis-stressing did not result in an alteration of vowel quality; Slowiaczek (1990) found the same for word identification in noise. Cutler and Clifton (1984) found that shifting stress without altering vowel quality had a much smaller adverse effect on recognition than stress shifts which changed full vowels to reduced or vice versa.

In contrast, Dutch experiments on the perception of mis-stressed words (using gating: van Heuven, 1985; van Leyden & van Heuven, 1996; or a semantic judgment task: Cutler & Koster, 2000; Koster & Cutler, 1997) have shown that mis-stressing harms word recognition in that language, and at least in Koster and Cutler's (1997) study the effects of mis-stressing were of similar magnitude to the effects of segmental mispronunciation. Mis-stressing of finally-stressed Dutch words (*PIloot* instead of *piLOOT*) is more harmful than mis-stressing of initially-stressed words (*viRUS* instead of *VIrus*) both in gating (van Heuven, 1985; van Leyden & van Heuven, 1996) and in a semantic decision task (Koster & Cutler, 1997).

In German, the same result appeared when ERPs were recorded as listeners made decisions about correctly stressed versus mis-stressed words (Friedrich, 2002): *KAnal* instead of *kaNAL* produced a deviant electrophysiological response, while *kaNU* instead of *KAnu* did not.

The suggestion from these cross-linguistic comparisons is that mis-stressing is more harmful in other stress languages than in English. In English, deviant stress sometimes seems to have no effect at all. Thus, Slowiaczek (1991) presented listeners with a sentence context and a stress pattern and asked them to judge a target word for acceptability; she found that the stress pattern information was often ignored, in that listeners responded "yes" to words which were semantically acceptable in the context but did not have the target stress pattern.

A cross-splicing study by Fear, Cutler, and Butterfield (1995) suggested that listeners pay more attention to the distinction between full and reduced vowels than to stress distinctions among full syllables. Listeners in this study heard tokens of words such as *audience, auditorium, audition, addition*, in which the initial vowels had been exchanged between words; they rated cross-splicings among any of the first three of these as insignificantly different from the original, unspliced tokens. Lower ratings were received only by cross-splicings involving an exchange between the initial vowel of *addition* (which is reduced) and the initial vowel of any of the other three words. Especially the vowels in stressed syllables seem to be important to listeners. Bond (1981) compared the disruptive effects on word recognition of several types of segmental distortion; most disruptive was distortion of vowels in stressed syllables. The number of features involved in disruption of a stressed vowel is irrelevant; any replacement of such a vowel is harmful (Small & Squibb, 1989). Likewise, mispronunciations in stressed syllables inhibit phantom word recognitions resulting from the combination of dichotically presented input (Mattys & Samuel, 1997).

11.4 Conclusion

Unsurprisingly, given the distribution of psycholinguistic laboratories across the world, a majority of the research concerning the use of stress information in spoken-word recognition has been carried out in English. However, the role of lexical stress in word recognition may not be the same in English and in other free-stress languages. The evidence certainly suggests that stress cues play a role in the initial activation of lexical forms in those languages where it contributes significant information to word identification; Dutch, German, and Spanish all appear to be included in this category. English is less clearly a good member of the category; English listeners can use stress information in activation if given the opportunity, but the opportunity in fact arises less often in word discrimination in English than in the other languages studied. Furthermore, several experimental demonstrations of better use of English stress information by nonnative than by native speakers now exist. Thus the language in which most psycholinguistic research (on any topic) is conducted unfortunately turns out to be rather unrepresentative in the role its word prosody plays in word recognition.

Recommendations for future research are therefore obvious. More laboratory investigations of the role of stress in word recognition in other languages with lexical stress are needed. The application of new techniques to study lexical processing on line is also recommended. But it is not only in spoken-word recognition that the predominance of research on English has skewed the picture of lexical stress perception. The fact that most early studies were carried out in a language with free stress, i.e., in which stress can fall at different positions in different words, also determined expectations in later research. Stress is certainly the same across all stress languages in that it always refers to a distinction between those syllables which may express accentual prominence and those which may not; but its manifestations are different in free- versus fixed-stress languages. In English and similar languages, stressed syllables and unstressed syllables differ acoustically, and much research effort focused on the perceptual consequences of this. But in fixed-stress languages, as Section 11.2 described, such intrinsic acoustic differences between stressed and unstressed syllables are not necessarily to be expected. There are at least as many fixed- as free-stress languages in the world (Goedemans, 2003). In fixed-stress languages, too, far more perceptual research is needed. In all cases, effects due to intrinsic characteristics of stressed versus unstressed syllables must be distinguished from effects which arise from differences in the applicability of intonational prominence.

ACKNOWLEDGMENTS

The material in Section 11.3 was in large part covered in the review article of Cutler, Dahan, and Donselaar (1997), and I thank Delphine Dahan and Wilma van Donselaar once again for their collaboration on that project. Thanks also to Lalita Murty for valuable research for Section 11.1, Roel Smits, Ethan Cox, and Dennis Pasveer for assistance with constructing the figures, and Bob Ladd for helpful comments on the text.

REFERENCES

Allopenna, P. D., Magnuson, J. S., & Tanenhaus, M. K. (1998). Tracking the time course of spoken word recognition using eye movements: Evidence for continuous mapping models. *Journal of Memory and Language*, 38, 419–39.

Altmann, G. T. M. & Carter, D. M. (1989). Lexical stress and lexical discriminability: Stressed syllables are more informative, but why? *Computer Speech and Language*, 3, 265–75.

Arciuli, J. & Cupples, L. (2002). The effects of lexical stress in visual and auditory word recognition. *Proceedings of the Ninth Australian International Conference on Speech Science & Technology*. Melbourne.

Arciuli, J. & Cupples, L. (2003). Stress typicality effects in native and non-native speakers of English. *Proceedings of the 15th International Congress of Phonetic Sciences* (pp. 2051–4). Barcelona.

Baayen, R. H., Piepenbrock, R., & van Rijn, H. (1993). *The CELEX lexical database* (CD-ROM). Philadelphia: Linguistic Data Consortium, University of Pennsylvania.

Bansal, R. K. (1966). The intelligibility of Indian English. PhD thesis, London University.

Beckman, M. E. (1986). *Stress and Non-Stress Accent*. Dordrecht: Foris.

Berinstein, A. E. (1979). A crosslinguistic study on the perception and production of stress. *UCLA Working Papers in Phonetics*, 47.

Bleakley, D. (1973). The effect of fundamental frequency variations on the perception of stress in German. *Phonetica*, 28, 42–59.

Bolinger, D. L. (1958). On intensity as a qualitative improvement of pitch accent. *Lingua*, 7, 175–82.

Bond, Z. S. (1981). Listening to elliptic speech: Pay attention to stressed vowels. *Journal of Phonetics*, 9, 89–96.

Bond, Z. S. & Garnes, S. (1980). Misperceptions of fluent speech. In R. Cole (ed.), *Perception and Production of Fluent Speech* (pp. 115–32). Hillsdale, NJ: Lawrence Erlbaum.

Bond, Z. S. & Small, L. H. (1983). Voicing, vowel and stress mispronunciations in continuous speech. *Perception & Psychophysics*, 34, 470–4.

Browman, C. P. (1978). Tip of the tongue and slip of the ear: Implications for language processing. *UCLA Working Papers in Phonetics*, 42.

Campbell, N. & Beckman, M. E. (1997). Stress, prominence and spectral tilt. In A. Botinis, G. Kouroupetroglou, & G. Carayiannis (eds.), *Intonation: Theory, Models and Applications (Proceedings of a European Speech Communication Association Workshop, September 18–20, 1997)* (pp. 67–70). Athens: ESCA and University of Athens Department of Informatics.

Cassidy, K. W. & Kelly, M. H. (1991). Phonological information for grammatical category assignments. *Journal of Memory and Language*, 30, 348–69.

Cole, R. A. & Jakimik, J. (1980). How are syllables used to recognize words? *Journal of the Acoustical Society of America*, 67, 965–70.

Cole, R. A., Jakimik, J., & Cooper, W. E. (1978). Perceptibility of phonetic features in fluent speech. *Journal of the Acoustical Society of America*, 64, 44–56.

Colombo, L. (1991). The role of lexical stress in word recognition and pronunciation. *Psychological Research*, 53, 71–9.

Connine, C. M., Clifton, C. E., & Cutler, A. (1987). Effects of lexical stress on phonetic categorization. *Phonetica*, 44, 133–46.

Cooper, N., Cutler, A., & Wales, R. (2002). Constraints of lexical stress on lexical access in English: Evidence from native and nonnative listeners. *Language and Speech*, 45, 207–28.

Cooper, W. E. & Eady, S. J. (1986). Metrical phonology in speech production. *Journal of Memory and Language*, 25, 369–84.

Crystal, T. H. & House, A. S. (1988). Segmental duration in connected-speech signals: Syllabic stress. *Journal of the Acoustical Society of America*, 4, 1574–85.

Crystal, T. H. & House, A. S. (1990). Articulation rate and the duration of syllables and stress groups in connected speech. *Journal of the Acoustical Society of America*, 88, 101–12.

Cutler, A. (1986). *Forbear* is a homophone: Lexical prosody does not constrain lexical access. *Language and Speech*, 29, 201–20.

Cutler, A. & Butterfield, S. (1992). Rhythmic cues to speech segmentation: Evidence from juncture misperception. *Journal of Memory and Language*, 31, 218–36.

Cutler, A. & Carter, D. M. (1987). The predominance of strong initial syllables in the English vocabulary. *Computer Speech and Language*, 2, 133–42.

Cutler, A. & Clifton, C. E. (1984). The use of prosodic information in word recognition. In H. Bouma & D. G. Bouwhuis (eds.), *Attention and Performance X: Control of Language Processes* (pp. 183–96). Hillsdale, NJ: Lawrence Erlbaum.

Cutler, A. & Donselaar, W. van (2001). *Voornaam* is not a homophone: Lexical prosody and lexical access in Dutch. *Language and Speech*, 44, 171–95.

Cutler, A. & Koster, M. (2000). Stress and lexical activation in Dutch. *Proceedings of* the Sixth International Conference on Spoken Language Processing, vol. 1 (pp. 593–6). Beijing.

Cutler, A. & Norris, D. G. (1988). The role of strong syllables in segmentation for lexical access. *Journal of Experimental Psychology: Human Perception and Performance*, 14, 113–21.

Cutler, A., Dahan, D., & Donselaar, W. van (1997). Prosody in the comprehension of spoken language: A literature review. *Language and Speech*, 40, 141–201.

Dahan, D. (1996). The role of rhythmic groups in the segmentation of continuous French speech. *Proceedings of the Fourth International Conference on Spoken Language Processing* (pp. 1185–8). Philadelphia.

Davis, S. M. & Kelly, M. H. (1997). Knowledge of the English noun-verb stress difference by native and nonnative speakers. *Journal of Memory and Language*, 36, 445–60.

de Jong, K. & Zawaydeh, B. A. (1999). Stress, duration, and intonation in Arabic word-level prosody. *Journal of Phonetics*, 27, 3–22.

Dogil, G. (1999). The phonetic manifestation of word stress in Lithuanian, Polish and German and Spanish. In H. van der Hulst (ed.), *Word Prosodic Systems in the Languages of Europe* (pp. 273–311). Berlin/New York: Mouton de Gruyter.

Donselaar, W. van, Koster, M., & Cutler, A. (2005). Exploring the role of lexical stress in lexical recognition. *Quarterly Journal of Experimental Psychology*, 58A.

Dupoux, E. & Peperkamp, S. (2002). Fossil markers of language development: Phonological "deafnesses" in adult speech processing. In J. Durand & B. Laks (eds.), *Phonetics, Phonology, and Cognition* (pp. 168–90). Oxford: Oxford University Press.

Dupoux, E., Pallier, C., Sebastián-Gallés, N., & Mehler, J. (1997). A destressing "deafness" in French. *Journal of Memory and Language*, 36, 406–21.

Dupoux, E., Peperkamp, S., & Sebastián-Gallés, N. (2001). A robust method to study stress "deafness." *Journal of the Acoustical Society of America*, 110, 1606–18.

Face, T. L. (2000). The role of syllable weight in the perception of Spanish stress. In H. Campos, E. Herburger, A. Morales-Front, & T. J. Walsh (eds.), *Hispanic Linguistics at the Turn of the Millennium* (pp. 1–13). Somerville, MA: Cascadilla Press.

Face, T. L. (2003). Degrees of phonetic similarity and analogically-driven stress perception in Spanish. *Proceedings of the 15th International Congress of Phonetic Sciences* (pp. 1723–6). Barcelona.

Fear, B. D., Cutler, A., & Butterfield, S. (1995). The strong/weak syllable distinction in English. *Journal of the Acoustical Society of America*, 97, 1893–1904.

Fonagy, I. (1958). Elektrophysiologische Beiträge zur Akzentfrage [Electrophysiological contributions on accent]. *Phonetica*, 2, 12–58.

Fonagy, I. (1966). Electrophysiological and acoustic correlates of stress and stress perception. *Journal of Speech & Hearing Research*, 9, 231–44.

Frauenfelder, U. H. & Floccia, C. (1998). The recognition of spoken words. In A. D. Friederici (ed.), *Language Comprehension: A Biological Perspective* (pp. 1–40). Berlin: Springer Verlag.

Friedrich, C. K. (2002). Prosody and spoken word recognition: Behavioral and ERP correlates. PhD thesis. University of Leipzig.

Friedrich, C. K., Kotz, S. A., & Gunter, T. C. (2001). Event-related evidence of word fragment priming: New correlate for language processing? *Psychophysiology*, 38 (supplement 1), 42.

Fry, D. B. (1955). Duration and intensity as physical correlates of linguistic stress. *Journal of the Acoustical Society of America*, 27, 765–8.

Fry, D. B. (1958). Experiments in the perception of stress. *Language and Speech*, 1, 126–52.

Fry, D. B. (1965). The dependence of stress judgments on vowel formant structure. *Proceedings of the Fifth International Congress of Phonetic Sciences* (pp. 306–11). Basel/New York: Karger.

Gay, T. (1978). Physiological and acoustic correlates of perceived stress. *Language and Speech*, 21, 347–53.

Goedemans, R. (2003). A typology of stress systems. Unpublished manuscript, Leiden University.

Gussenhoven, C. & Blom, J. G. (1978). Perception of prominence by Dutch listeners. *Phonetica*, 35, 216–30.

Hermes, D. J. & Rump, H. H. (1994). Perception of prominence in speech intonation induced by rising and falling pitch movements. *Journal of the Acoustical Society of America*, 96, 83–92.

Howell, P. (1993). Cue trading in the production and perception of vowel stress. *Journal of the Acoustical Society of America*, 94, 2063–73.

Huss, V. (1975). Neutralisierung englischer Akzentunterschiede in der Nachkontur [Neutralization of post-nuclear accent contrasts in English]. *Phonetica*, 32, 278–91.

Huss, V. (1978). English word stress in the post-nuclear position. *Phonetica*, 35, 86–105.

Hyman, L. (1977). On the nature of linguistic stress. In L. Hyman (ed.), *Studies in Stress and Accent* (pp. 37–81). Southern California Occasional Papers in Linguistics, SCOPIL 4. Los Angeles: University of Southern California.

Isačenko, A. V. & Schädlich, H.-J. (1966). Untersuchungen über die deutsche Satzintonation [Studies on German sentence intonation]. In *Studia Grammatica VII* (pp. 7–67). Berlin: Akademie-Verlag.

Janota, P. (1967). An experiment concerning the perception of stress by Czech listeners. *Acta Univ. Carolinae, Philologica Phonetica Pragensia*, 6, 45–68.

Jassem, W. (1962). Akcent jezyka polskiego [Accent in the Polish language]. *Prace Jezykoznawcze*, 31 (Wroclaw).

Jongenburger, W. (1996). *The Role of Lexical Stress During Spoken-Word Processing*. PhD thesis, University of Leiden. The Hague: Holland Academic Graphics.

Jongenburger, W. & van Heuven, V. J. (1995a). The role of linguistic stress in the time course of word recognition in stress-accent languages. *Proceedings of the Fourth European Conference on Speech Communication and Technology* (pp. 1695–98). Madrid.

Jongenburger, W. & van Heuven, V. J. (1995b). The role of lexical stress in the recognition of spoken words: prelexical or postlexical? *Proceedings of the Thirteenth International Congress of Phonetic Sciences* (pp. 368–71). Stockholm.

Kelly, M. H. (1988). Phonological biases in grammatical category shifts. *Journal of Memory and Language*, 27, 343–58.

Kelly, M. H. (1992). Using sound to solve syntactic problems: The role of phonology in grammatical category assignments. *Psychological Review*, 99, 349–64.

Kelly, M. H. & Bock, J. K. (1988). Stress in time. *Journal of Experimental Psychology: Human Perception and Performance*, 14, 389–403.

Kiriakos, B. & O'Shaughnessy, D. (1989). Lexical stress detection in isolated English words. *Speech Communication*, 8, 113–24.

Koster, M. & Cutler, A. (1997). Segmental and suprasegmental contributions to spoken-word recognition in Dutch. *Proceedings of EUROSPEECH 97* (pp. 2167–70). Rhodes.

Ladefoged, P., Draper, M. H., & Whitteridge, D. (1958). Syllables and stress. In *Miscellanea Phonetica III* (pp. 1–14). London: International Phonetic Association, University College.

Lea, W. A. (1977). Acoustic correlates of stress and juncture. In L. M. Hyman (ed.), *Studies in Stress and Accent* (pp. 83–119). Southern California Occasional Papers in Linguistics, SCOPIL 4. Los Angeles: University of Southern California.

Lehiste, I. (1970). *Suprasegmentals*. Cambridge, MA: MIT Press.

Lehiste, I. & Peterson, G. (1959). Vowel amplitude and phonemic stress in American English. *Journal of the Acoustical Society of America*, 31, 428–35.

Lieberman, P. (1960). Some acoustic correlates of word stress in American English. *Journal of the Acoustical Society of America*, 33, 451–4.

Lieberman, P. (1963). Some effects of semantic and grammatical context on the production and perception of speech. *Language and Speech*, 6, 172–87.

Lindblom, B. (1963). Spectrographic study of vowel reduction. *Journal of the Acoustical Society of America*, 35, 1773–81.

Lindfield, K. C., Wingfield, A., & Goodglass, H. (1999). The role of prosody in the mental lexicon. *Brain and Language*, 68, 312–17.

Llisterri, J., Machuca, M., de la Mota, C., Riera, M., & Rios, A. (2003). The perception of lexical stress in Spanish. *Proceedings of the 15th International Congress of Phonetic Sciences* (pp. 2023–6). Barcelona.

Marshall, C. W. & Nye, P. W. (1983). Stress and vowel duration effects on syllable recognition. *Journal of the Acoustical Society of America*, 74, 433–43.

Mattys, S. L. (2000). The perception of primary and secondary stress in English. *Perception & Psychophysics*, 62, 253–65.

Mattys, S. L. & Samuel, A. G. (1997). How lexical stress affects speech segmentation and interactivity: Evidence from the migration paradigm. *Journal of Memory and Language*, 36, 87–116.

Mattys, S. L. & Samuel, A. G. (2000). Implications of stress pattern differences in spoken word recognition. *Journal of Memory and Language*, 42, 571–96.

McAllister, J. (1991). The processing of lexically stressed syllables in read and spontaneous speech. *Language and Speech*, 34, 1–26.

McClean, M. D. & Tiffany, W. R. (1973). The acoustic parameters of stress in relation to syllable position, speech loudness and rate. *Language and Speech*, 16, 283–90.

McQueen, J. M., Norris, D. G., & Cutler, A. (1994). Competition in spoken word recognition: Spotting words in other words. *Journal of Experimental Psychology: Learning, Memory and Cognition*, 20, 621–38.

Mehta, G. & Cutler, A. (1988). Detection of target phonemes in spontaneous and read speech. *Language and Speech*, 31, 135–56.

Mol, H. G. & Uhlenbeck, G. M. (1956). The linguistic relevance of intensity in stress. *Lingua*, 5, 205–13.

Morton, J. & Jassem, W. (1965). Acoustic correlates of stress. *Language and Speech*, 8, 159–81.

Nakatani, L. H. & Aston, C. H. (1978). Perceiving stress patterns of words in sentences. *Journal of the Acoustical Society of America*, 63 (supplement 1), S55(A).

Peperkamp, S. & Dupoux, E. (2002). A typological study of stress "deafness." In C. Gussenhoven & N. L. Warner (eds.), *Papers in Laboratory Phonology VII* (pp. 203–40). Berlin: de Gruyter.

Potisuk, S., Gandour, J., & Harper, M. P. (1996). Acoustic correlates of stress in Thai. *Phonetica*, 53, 200–20.

Quené, H. & Koster, M. L. (1998). Metrical segmentation in Dutch: Vowel quality or stress? *Language and Speech*, 41, 185–202.

Rigault, A. (1970). L'accent dans deux langues à accent fixe: Le français et le Tchèque [Stress in two fixed-stress languages: French and Czech]. *Studia Phonetica*, 3, 1–12.

Sereno, J. A. (1986). Stress pattern differentiation of form class in English. *Journal of the Acoustical Society of America*, 79, S36.

Sereno, J. A. & Jongman, A. (1995). Acoustic correlates of grammatical class. *Language and Speech*, 38, 57–76.

Shattuck-Hufnagel, S., Ostendorf, M., & Ross, K. (1994). Stress shift and early pitch accent placement in lexical items in American English. *Journal of Phonetics*, 22, 357–88.

Shen, X. S. (1993). Relative duration as a perceptual cue to stress in Mandarin. *Language and Speech*, 36, 415–33.

Sholicar, J. R. & Fallside, F. (1988). A prosodically and lexically constrained approach to continuous speech recognition. *Proceedings of the Second Australian International Conference on Speech Science and Technology* (pp. 106–11). Sydney.

Slowiaczek, L. M. (1990). Effects of lexical stress in auditory word recognition. *Language and Speech*, 33, 47–68.

Slowiaczek, L. M. (1991). Stress and context in auditory word recognition. *Journal of Psycholinguistic Research*, 20, 465–81.

Sluijter, A. M. C. & van Heuven, V. J. (1996). Spectral balance as an acoustic correlate of linguistic stress. *Journal of the Acoustical Society of America*, 100, 2471–85.

Sluijter, A. M. C., van Heuven, V. J., & Pacilly, J. J. A. (1997). Spectral balance as a cue in the perception of linguistic stress. *Journal of the Acoustical Society of America*, 101, 503–13.

Small, L. H. & Squibb, K. D. (1989). Stressed vowel perception in word recognition. *Perceptual and Motor Skills*, 68, 179–85.

Small, L. H., Simon, S. D., & Goldberg, J. S. (1988). Lexical stress and lexical access: Homographs versus nonhomographs. *Perception & Psychophysics*, 44, 272–80.

Sorin, C. (1981). Functions, roles and treatments of intensity in speech. *Journal of Phonetics*, 9, 359–74.

Soto-Faraco, S., Sebastián-Gallés, N., & Cutler, A. (2001). Segmental and suprasegmental mismatch in lexical access. *Journal of Memory and Language*, 45, 412–32.

Suomi, K. & Ylitalo, R. (2004). On durational correlates of word stress in Finnish. *Journal of Phonetics*, 32, 35–63.

Suomi, K., McQueen, J. M., & Cutler, A. (1997). Vowel harmony and speech segmentation in Finnish. *Journal of Memory and Language*, 36, 422–44.

Suomi, K., Toivanen, J., & Ylitalo, R. (2003). Durational and tonal correlates of accent in Finnish. *Journal of Phonetics*, 31, 113–38.

Taylor, S. & Wales, R. (1987). Primitive mechanisms of accent perception. *Journal of Phonetics*, 15, 235–46.

Thorsen, N. (1982). On the variability in F0 patterning and the function of F0 timing in languages where pitch cues stress. *Phonetica*, 39, 302–16.

Turk, A. E. & Sawusch, J. R. (1996). The processing of duration and intensity cues to prominence. *Journal of the Acoustical Society of America*, 99, 3782–9.

van der Hulst, H. G. (1999). Word accent. In H. van der Hulst (ed.), *Word Prosodic Systems in the Languages of Europe* (pp. 3–116). Berlin/New York: Mouton de Gruyter.

van Heuven, V. J. (1985). Perception of stress pattern and word recognition: Recognition of Dutch words with incorrect stress position. *Journal of the Acoustical Society of America*, 78, S21.

van Heuven, V. J. (1987). Stress patterns in Dutch (compound) adjectives: Acoustic measurements and perception data. *Phonetica*, 44, 1–12.

van Heuven, V. J. (1988). Effects of stress and accent on the human recognition of word fragments in spoken context: Gating and shadowing. *Proceedings of Speech '88*, 7th FASE symposium (pp. 811–18). Edinburgh.

van Heuven, V. J. & Hagman, P. J. (1988). Lexical statistics and spoken word recognition in Dutch. In P. Coopmans & A. Hulk (eds.), *Linguistics in the Netherlands 1988* (pp. 59–68). Dordrecht: Foris.

van Katwijk, A. (1974). *Accentuation in Dutch: An Experimental Linguistic Study*. Assen: Van Gorcum.

van Kuijk, D. & Boves, L. (1999). Acoustic characteristics of lexical stress in continuous telephone speech. *Speech Communication*, 27, 95–111.

van Leyden, K. & van Heuven, V. J. (1996). Lexical stress and spoken word recognition: Dutch vs. English. In C. Cremers & M. den Dikken (eds.),

Linguistics in the Netherlands 1996 (pp. 159–70). Amsterdam: John Benjamins.

van Zanten, E. A. & van Heuven, V. J. (1998). Word stress in Indonesian: Its communicative relevance. *Journal of the Humanities and Social Sciences of Southeast Asia and Oceania* [Bijdragen tot de Taal-, Land- en Volkenkunde], 154, 129–47.

Vitevitch, M. S. & Luce, P. A. (1998). When words compete: Levels of processing in spoken word recognition. *Psychological Science*, 9, 325–9.

Vitevitch, M. S., Luce, P. A., Charles-Luce, J., & Kemmerer, D. (1997). Phonotactics and syllable stress: Implications for the processing of spoken nonsense words. *Language and Speech*, 40, 47–62.

Vroomen, J., Tuomainen, J., & De Gelder, B. (1998). The roles of word stress and vowel harmony in speech segmentation. *Journal of Memory and Language*, 38, 133–49.

Vroomen, J., van Zon, M., & de Gelder, B. (1996). Cues to speech segmentation: Evidence from juncture misperceptions and word spotting. *Memory & Cognition*, 24, 744–55.

Waibel, A. (1988). *Prosody and Speech Recognition*. London: Pitman.

Williams, B. (1985). Pitch and duration in Welsh stress perception: The implications for intonation. *Journal of Phonetics*, 13, 381–406.

Wingfield, A., Goodglass, H., & Lindfield, K. C. (1997). Word recognition from acoustic onsets and acoustic offsets: Effects of cohort size and syllabic stress. *Applied Psycholinguistics*, 18, 85–100.

Zwitserlood, P. (1989). The locus of the effects of sentential-semantic context in spoken-word processing. *Cognition*, 32, 25–64.

12 Slips of the Ear

Z. S. BOND

> The study of speech production and analysis . . . asks how the person's mental representations enter into articulation and perception.
>
> Chomsky (1996, p. 23)

12.1 Introduction

In everyday conversation, speakers employ various reductions and simplifications of their utterances, so that what they say departs in significant ways from the clarity norms found in formal speech or laboratory recordings. Both listeners and speakers are sometimes engaged in other tasks while carrying on a conversation, distracted, or preoccupied with their own ideas, so listeners vary in the amount of attention they pay to speech. Not surprisingly, sometimes listeners fail to understand what a speaker has said. Instead, a listener perceives, clearly and distinctly, something that does not correspond to the speaker's intended utterance. The following is a typical example. At a doctoral dissertation defense, a member of the audience heard the candidate say "chicken dance," a phrase that had absolutely no connection with the dissertation topic of early literacy. Then she saw a proper name on a graphic: Schikedanz. The listener suspected that something was wrong from the inappropriateness of what she had heard and recovered the speaker's intended utterance from subsequent information.

Over the past years, I have collected approximately 1,000 examples of slips of the ear taking place in everyday casual conversation. For a few of the misperceptions, I was a participant in a conversation as either a speaker or a listener. Interested friends, students, and colleagues have contributed the majority. I have described this data set in *Slips of the Ear: Errors in the Perception of Casual Conversation* (1999a). All my examples are from English as spoken in the United States and Canada. Many of the examples reported here appeared in the original publication.

Investigations of speech errors have a long history. Though slips of the tongue have received the most attention, slips of the ear have been described from a linguistic or psycholinguistic point of view since the seminal work of Meringer (1908) and Meringer and Mayer (1895). Meringer and Mayer included 47 German misperceptions in their corpus. They observed that stressed vowels tend to be perceived correctly whereas consonants are misperceived more frequently. Celce-Murcia (1980) analyzed these misperceptions as well as her own collection and noted that many misperceptions showed grammatical coherence coupled with a lack of appropriateness to the conversation or situation. Celce-Murcia suggested that dialect differences might be one cause of misperceptions. Labov (1994) has found that more than a quarter of the misperceptions in his collection are directly traceable to dialect differences and observed that nasal and liquid consonants promote misperceptions by obscuring vowel quality.

Slips of the ear can also be found in popular collections, where they are sometimes known as "mondegreens," a relatively obscure term coined to honor the misperception of a line from a ballad:

They hae slain the Earl of Murray
And laid him on the green → And Lady Mondegreen

Because children's misperceptions or misunderstandings tend to be humorous, they are particularly common in these popular collections. Often the misunderstandings concern material learned by rote. Some examples have become apocryphal, for example "One Nation and a Vegetable" and "I lead the pigeons to the flat" as misunderstandings of the Pledge of Allegiance, and "Jose, can you see?" from the *Star Spangled Banner*. There are popular collections of mysterious ailments such as "very close veins" and "fire balls of the uterus" and of song lyrics such as "There's a can of fish all over the world," "Don't cry for me, Marge and Tina," and "Row, row, row your boat . . . Life's a butter dream" (see Edwards, 1995).

Misperceptions and misunderstandings have also been consciously created in humorous writing, from Gilbert and Sullivan operettas to cartoons. In the *Pirates of Penzance*, the hero is mistakenly apprenticed as a pirate, instead of a pilot, because his nursemaid misunderstood her instructions. In the cartoon strip *The Family Circus*, the children talk about the windshield whappers and the Umpire State building. Whether some reported misperceptions are created or spontaneous is unclear. Circulated by e-mail, husband's note to his wife: Someone from the Guyna College called. They said Pabst beer is normal.

Both spontaneous and artfully created misperceptions provide language-based humor, in that many have a wild appropriateness. Spontaneous misperceptions do something more. Slips of the ear or misperceptions and misunderstandings provide a unique window into the ways listeners use linguistic knowledge in understanding speech. They show that listeners use the phonetics, phonology, lexicon, and syntax of their language in understanding speech.

12.2 Phonetic Knowledge

Although the majority of slips of the ear show a relatively complex relationship between the speaker's utterance and the listener's misperception, in a portion of errors a listener misperceives a single segment. That is, the speaker's utterance and the listener's perception differ in only one segment. It is logical to assume that phonetic information which is rarely misperceived provides reliable information, whereas phonetic information which is frequently misperceived is less reliable. Misperceptions of single segments involve consonants much more frequently than vowels.

12.2.1 *Vowel misperceptions*

All collectors of slips of the ear have observed that simple stressed vowel misperceptions are exceedingly rare. In my collection, only 5% of the misperceptions involved stressed vowels as the only error. Although errors in which a stressed vowel is replaced by a very different vowel, such as

It's like a math problem → mouth problem

do occur, they are highly unusual, first, in that the misperceived vowel is not in a phonetic environment which affects vowel quality and, second, in that the phonetic distance between the target and the misperception is considerable. More commonly, vowel misperceptions occur in consonantal environments which affect vowel quality, such as the liquids /r, l/ and the nasals, as Labov (1994) has observed. Misperceptions primarily involve vowel height; other perceptual dimensions are misperceived much less frequently. The following are examples of typical stressed vowel errors:

Alan → Ellen
Wendy will come → windy
Cherri and me → cheery and me

Experimental data support the resilience of stressed vowels to misperception. In examining the role of consonants vs. vowels in the perception of fluent speech, Cole et al. (2001) report that listeners identify about twice as many words accurately when they have vowel information available as when they have consonant information available. Similarly, Neel, Bradlow, and Pisoni (1996/7) found more consonant than vowel misidentifications in spoken sentences. When listeners are given incorrect vowel information, they find it much more disruptive than incorrect consonant information. Bond and Small (1983) asked listeners to shadow passages which contained mispronounced consonants and mispronounced stressed vowels. Listeners had little difficulty recovering intended words when they contained mispronounced consonants but they recovered only 15% of the words containing mispronounced vowels.

Pisoni (1981) has argued that stressed syllables provide "an island of reliability," that is, reliable phonetic information which listeners use to interpret the stream of speech. Altman and Carter (1989) also argue for the informational value of stressed syllables. Grosjean and Gee (1987) and Cutler and her colleagues (Butterfield & Cutler, 1988; Cutler & Butterfield, 1992; Cutler & Norris, 1988) have proposed that stressed syllables provide reliable information for segmenting the continuous speech stream. Only when a task requires strategic responses do listeners prefer consonant information over vowel information (see Van Ooijen, 1996).

Even though stressed vowels seem to provide reliable phonetic information, occasionally the stress pattern of target words is misperceived, and this is always accompanied by phonetic restructuring of some sort. For example:

giving an award → giving an oral
roll up the back window → patrol the back window
I'm in the political science department → pickle science department

Misperceptions of unstressed vowels are more common than misperceptions of stressed vowels, suggesting that the status of unstressed vowels in speech is relatively fluid. The quality of vowels in unstressed syllables may be misperceived or unstressed syllables may be perceptually lost or added.

Misinterpretations of the intended quality of unstressed vowels may occur in content words, as in:

Grammar Workshop → grandma workshop

More commonly, vowel quality misperceptions occur in function words, as in:

Attacks in the ear → a tax on the ear
They took footprints when you're born → in the dorm

Errors of this type may be less perceptual than grammatical, because listeners frequently tend to report hearing function words which are appropriate to the form of an utterance.

When unstressed vowels are added or lost, the shape of the target word changes, because adding or omitting unstressed vowels necessarily changes the number of syllables. For example:

evolution of tense systems → intense systems
Dec writer [a printer popular in the 1980s] → decorator
You can spend a mint eating → a minute

In the first slip, the listener heard a spurious initial syllable; in the second, the listener failed to detect a word boundary and altered the phonological shape of the word by reporting a spurious medial syllable. In the third misperception, the listener added a syllable at the end of the target word.

The reverse type of misperception, loss of unstressed vowels as part of the loss of unstressed syllables, is approximately equally common. For example:

My coffee cup refilled → my coffee cup fell
Accidents → actions
I teach speech science → speech signs

The first example shows some phonological restructuring as well as loss of an initial syllable. In spite of the phonological restructuring, the verb maintains past tense, though the verb form becomes irregular. In the second example, a medial syllable is lost. In the third example, a syllabic nasal loses its syllabicity.

Slips of the ear typically lose or add only one syllable. Although perceptual errors affecting more than one syllable occur, they are relatively rare without considerable concomitant restructuring of the target utterance.

12.2.2 Consonant misperceptions

Slips of the ear affecting consonants are much more plentiful than vowel slips, whether as misperceptions of single segments or as parts of errors involving a more extensive mismatch between a target utterance and its misperception. Consonants may be lost or added, or one consonant may be substituted for another.

Consonants are lost at any position within a word, the two examples below showing consonant loss in initial and final position.

When their condition → air condition
The only poor meet → the only poor me

Final consonants are lost much more frequently than initial consonants, undoubtedly because they tend to receive weak and indistinct articulation.

Spurious consonant perceptions can be seen in the two examples:

else → elfs
Tapas bars → topless bars

Though these particular errors do not have any obvious phonetic motivation, a number of consonant additions were associated with word boundary misassignments. For example, the spurious consonant in:

Slip of the ear → slip of the year

may have resulted when the listener interpreted the final segment of the article as a word-initial glide, distributing a single segment over two words.

Consonants may be substituted for each other relatively freely. Table 12.1 shows the variety of possible misperceptions of one target consonant, the voiceless alveolar stop /t/. Examples of misperceptions of a resonant, the bilabial nasal /m/ are given in Table 12.2.

In consonant substitutions, basic manner of articulation categories tend to be maintained in that resonants are most commonly misperceived as resonants and obstruents as obstruents. Consonant misperceptions involving substitutions tend to be more common in word-initial position than elsewhere, in a ratio of two to one.

Even though many of the contributors to the collection of slips of the ear speak other languages or are familiar with them, English misperceptions are almost invariably built out of the inventory of English segments. In the data set, there is only one exception:

Patwin → paʔwin

Table 12.1 Misperceptions of /t/

Misperceived as another stop:
great → grape
at least this part of it → park
training for great books → grade books

Misperceived as a fricative:
Tagalog → Thagalog
She had on a trench suit → a French suit

Misperceived as an affricate:
I'll bet that'll be a teary program → cheery program

Misperceived as a resonant:
booty → boolie
Fifth Street → fifth string

Table 12.2 Misperceptions of /m/

Misperceived as a stop:
I'm getting married this Friday → buried
Ma'am → Pam

Misperceived as another resonant:
I'm trying to find some matches → latches
Key lime pie → key line pie

The alveolar stop of the target utterance may very well have been produced as an allophonic glottal stop. The listener, an anthropological linguist, did not compensate for the phonological reduction and reported perceiving a glottal stop with which she was familiar from her work with other languages.

12.2.3 *Segment order*

Sometimes slips of the ear resulted in a change in the order of segments or of syllables in the intended utterance. These errors suggest that listeners take advantage of global information distributed in the target utterance.

There was only one example of misordering of adjacent segments, the type of misordering traditionally termed metathesis:

They're all Appalachian whites → Appalachian waste

Misorderings of segments within a syllable were more common, as in:

Falstaff → Flagstaff
I can ink it in → I can nick it in
Do lions have manes? → have names

Misorderings also crossed syllable boundaries, as in

Acton Road → Atkin Road

and even word boundaries:

I'm making boats → taking notes
Spun toffee → fun stocking
Friar Tuck pizza → Kentucky Fried pizza

In investigations of slips of the tongue, a generalization with almost no exceptions is that segments retain their position within syllable onsets and rhymes. That generalization does not hold for slips of the ear.

Misorderings seem to involve considerable restructuring of the phonology of the target utterance, so the details provided by any one example are certainly not definitive. Nevertheless, the overall impression is that listeners take advantage of information which is not sequential. Whether listeners operate within a fixed time window or are simply opportunistic is not clear. They treat the phonetic information which specifies words as if it were a braid, in which cues for individual segments overlap (see Mattys, 1997).

12.3 Phonological Knowledge

Listeners use knowledge of the phonology of their language in understanding casual conversation, as shown by misperceptions which seem to result from listener attempts to deal with phonological reductions and language varieties. Listeners also show sensitivity to phonotactics, the permissible shape of words.

12.3.1 Phonological reduction

In casual speech, listeners hear various kinds of pronunciations which differ from the shape words have in their canonical form. Most of the time, these reductions provide no difficulty for listeners because they report reduced forms as intended by speakers. Sometimes listeners make an error by treating the phonetic stream literally, rather than recovering the intended utterance. At other times, they treat an utterance as if it had undergone phonological reduction, even when it has not. Both of the misperceptions

find me → fine me
in harmony with the text → test

probably represent accurate responses to words in which consonant clusters have been reduced, a literal interpretation of the phonetic material. In the same way, in the misperception traitor → trader

the listener was presented with a flap, the typical realization of intervocalic alveolar stop, /t/ (see Patterson & Connine, 2001). The listener recovered a homophonous word with the flap as a realization of intervocalic /d/. In the misperception

I tripped on a tent pole → tadpole

the listener probably failed to detect the nasalized vowel which would provide the only cue for the nasal consonant.

The reverse of these errors, treating an utterance as if it has undergone reduction, indicates that listeners use phonological knowledge in recovering the intended utterances. In the misperceptions:

Mrs Winner → Winter
Fine sunny weather → fine Sunday weather
The Old Creek Inn was deserted → creek end

the listeners recover spurious consonants, consonants which could have been omitted in a reduced pronunciation. Similarly, in the misperception

You can weld with it – braze → braids

the listener recovered a consonant which could have been omitted in producing a consonant cluster.

Although there is considerable debate about the nature of the mechanisms responsible for dealing with reduced forms, experimental evidence also supports the idea that listeners compensate for specific kinds of phonological reductions. Marslen-Wilson and colleagues (Gaskell & Marslen-Wilson, 1997; Marslen-Wilson, Nix, & Gaskell, 1995) used words which had assimilated place of articulation, such as "leam" for "lean" in "lean meat." Listener perceptual interpretations were sensitive to possible assimilations from context. Based on statistical differences in the occurrence of flaps, Patterson and Connine (2001) suggest that some words may be represented in the mental lexicon as reduced forms, requiring no perceptual compensation. Gow (2003) has made a similar suggestion about words which have undergone place of articulation assimilations.

12.3.2 *Phonological well-formedness*

Almost invariably, listener misperceptions were phonologically well-formed. There is only one counter-example in the data set, a misperception by a child:

The men are out lumbering in the forests → are out tlumbering

The child misperception served as a target in another misperception. The speaker was describing slips of the ear to an adult colleague and mentioned that one example had violated English phonotactic constraints. In spite of the introduction which might have been expected to prepare the listener for what was to come, he "corrected" the sequence to something more acceptable in English:

tlumbering → klumbering

A similar example involved a proper name. The listener adjusted the non-English syllable onset to fit English phonotactics:

Sruti → Trudy

In the misperception

a fancy seductive letter → a fancy structive letter

the listener probably failed to detect a short unstressed vowel in the first syllable; he reported the voiced /d/ as voiceless, as is appropriate in English syllable onsets even when he perceived a nonword. Typically, listeners tend to perceptually assimilate non-native words and segments to their native language, a process which is sometimes known by the curious name, the Law of Hobson Jobson.

12.3.3 *Language varieties*

When listeners hear speech produced in a different dialect or with a foreign accent, their misperceptions can take two forms, just as in the case of phonological reductions. Listeners can perceive the phonetic detail veridically and recover something other than the intended utterance or they can compensate inappropriately for the dialect or accent characteristics of the speaker.

In the misperception

Kings → kangs

the listener reported hearing a nonword when presented with the nasalized vowel produced by the speaker from the South. Similarly, in the misperception

That's a special → spatial

the listener failed to compensate for the tensing of lax vowels characteristic of speech in southeast Ohio.

Veridical perception of phonetic detail leading to an error in recovering the intended utterance can also result from foreign accent. For example, a speaker with a noticeable Eastern European accent produced a flap for the English rhotic, as would be appropriate in her native language. The listener treated the flap as a reduction of an English alveolar stop:

barrel → bottle

Listeners may also misperceive in attempting to compensate for speaker characteristics, using expectations about the phonology of various dialects. One vowel misperception seems to have resulted from attempting to compensate for dialect differences:

Wattsville → Whitesville

The speaker from South Carolina gave the name of a town, and the listener from Ohio corrected for the monophthongal vowel he believed the Southern speaker was employing. Similarly, in the misperception

It's Lawson → Larson

the Ohio listener corrected for the supposed r-less pronunciation of a speaker from the East Coast of the United States.

12.4 Lexical Knowledge

Listeners report their misperceptions in words and claim that they hear words, because words are the consciously available result of the perceptual process. Their errors suggest strategies which they employ in partitioning the stream of speech and finding discrete items in the mental lexicon.

12.4.1 *Nonwords*

Because slips of the ear occasionally result in the perception of nonwords, phonological sequences which do not map onto any existing lexical item, it seems that one way in which listeners access the mental lexicon is through a phonological code.

Undoubtedly, there are multiple reasons for misperceptions leading to nonwords. In the case of proper names or specialized vocabulary, listeners may simply not have sufficient knowledge to recover the intended utterance. Two misperceptions of this kind might be:

The anechoic chamber → the ambionic chamber
The mining of Haiphong harbor → Haithong harbor

Some perceptions of nonwords resulted from a failure to compensate for the dialect of the speaker. The misperception mentioned above

Kings → kangs

is an example. Another example of the same type is:

Call Star Fire → /sta fa/

The listener was told to call Star Fire, the name of a gas station, by a speaker using an r-less dialect. The listener perceived the phonetic material accurately, but could not find an appropriate proper name in her lexicon, and did not have sufficient knowledge about the dialect of the speaker to make an appropriate compensation.

Sometimes common words were misperceived as well, without any obvious motivation in the linguistic or non-linguistic environment. For example:

The article → the yarticle
Sitter problems → sinter
Paula played with Tom → polyp laden /θam/

It is interesting to note that the listeners' perceptions did not default to the nearest existing lexical items but instead the listeners heard nonwords.

12.4.2 Word boundaries

Because casual speech is a continuous stream, listeners have to segment the stream in some way in order to find phonological sequences to compare with words in their mental lexicon. Slips of the ear involving word boundaries suggest that listeners employ stressed syllables as aids in segmentation.

In the simplest case of word boundary errors, all properties of the target utterance correspond with the perceived utterance except for the presence of word boundaries. A classic error of this type is:

acute back pain → a cute back pain

The listener perceived the phonological material accurately but misanalyzed the speaker's utterance, interpreting the initial unstressed syllable as an article. Listeners may fail to detect word boundaries, insert spurious word boundaries, or shift the location of a word boundary.

In all cases of word boundary loss which do not involve radical phonological restructuring of some sort, the environment for the loss is a stressed syllable followed by an unstressed syllable, as in the following:

We're going to pour him into the car → purim into the car
Chris De Pino → Christofino
He works in an herb and spice shop → an urban spice shop

Many perceptions of spurious word boundaries were also associated with stressed vowels. In these cases, phonetic information was analyzed as if word boundaries preceded stressed syllables. For example:

attacks in the ear → a tax on the ear
Americana → a Mary Canna
At the parasession → at the Paris session

Because other phonetic cues to word boundary location are available, there are also exceptions to the tendency to add word boundaries before stressed vowels. One student misanalyzed a Japanese surname as including a given name, placing the spurious word boundary after the first syllable:

Yoshimura → Yo Shimura

Shifted word boundaries typically involved misassigning a consonant from word-initial to word-final position, or the reverse, as in:

I need a loose crew → loose screw
We could give them an ice bucket → a nice bucket
Dix [Dixon] Ward → Dick Sward

The typical errors in word boundary placement indicate that listeners employ expectations about the structure of their language. As Cutler and Carter (1987) have documented, the great majority of English nouns begin with a stressed syllable. Listeners use this expectation about the structure of English and partition the continuous speech stream employing stressed syllables.

12.4.3 *Content words and function words*

Sometimes listeners seem to be extremely inattentive to phonetic information in the speech signal and report a content word only vaguely related to the speaker's utterance. These substitutions are curious because the misperceptions seem to come from a semantic domain appropriate to the target.

Athens → Akron
pathology → psychology
Stockholm → Scotland
sounds interesting → sounds intriguing

It is possible that when errors such as these occur, a listener is functioning in a discourse mode, aware of little more than the gist of the conversation, paying almost no attention to the phonetic details of what the speaker is saying. Voss (1984) has reported some similar examples.

Because function words tend to be unstressed in ordinary conversation, they are often misperceived or adjusted to fit the utterance. Listeners misperceive function words sometimes in the context of other misperceptions, sometimes not:

Did you put the food out for him → for them
When were you here → Why were you here?
I think I see a place → his face

In the first two examples, the listeners misidentified a function word. In the third example, the listener misperceived a content word as well as a function word.

Function words may result from misperceptions of word boundaries. The listeners heard spurious word boundaries and interpreted unassigned phonological material as appropriate function words.

Jefferson Starship → Jeffers and starship
You swallowed a watermelon → You smiled at a watermelon
I've been doing research → a search

Sometimes, listeners also reinterpret or adjust function words to be appropriate to a misperceived utterance, either reporting a spurious word or not reporting any trace of one. In the slip of the ear

hypnotic age regression → hypnotic aid to regression

the listener probably misperceived "age" as "aid" and then added a preposition as required. In the reverse type of error, the listener loses a function word:

change for a dollar → exchange a dollar

The word "exchange" does not require a preposition, so the preposition is simply absent in the reported perception.

12.4.4 *Morphology*

Perceptual errors related to morphology primarily involved inflectional rather than derivational affixes, most commonly the plural suffix. In these misperceptions, either a morphologically simple word was interpreted as a plural, or the reverse, a plural word was interpreted as monomorphemic. In these misperceptions, the target utterance contains phonetic material which can be interpreted as a plural, either in the word itself or in the initial consonant of the following word.

Her niece was in the hospital → her knees
on an island with a moat surrounding it → with moats surrounding it

In the reverse error, a fricative representing a plural was interpreted as part of the stem:

matches → mattress

Some plural forms did not have phonological support in the target utterance but rather appeared by conforming the perception to fit grammatical requirements. For example, in the misperception:

It'll be a confusing weekend → You're confusing weekends

the listener may have misinterpreted the beginning of the utterance and supplied the appropriate plural form. Similarly, in

It will be done next year → in six years

the listener supplied a plural form appropriate to the numeral.

In other errors involving the perception of inflectional morphology, listeners displayed a strong tendency to interpret morphologically complex forms as monomorphemic. In these errors, phonological material was sometimes reinterpreted; at other times, phonological material was simply lost. Some examples are given in Table 12.3.

Table 12.3 Errors in the perception of morphology

A monomorphemic word is interpreted as a possessive:
A loose end in this problem → a leaf's end

A possessive is interpreted as part of the stem:
Olga's son → the sun
Skipper's treat → trick or treat

A monomorphemic word is interpreted as a verb:
I was through on a bus → I was thrown off a bus

A verbal suffix is interpreted as part of the stem:
Citrus craving → citrus gravy
This friend of ours who visited → is an idiot

Some evidence that morphemes have an independent status in the lexicon is provided by errors in which the stem is misperceived but retains its morphological affixes. For example, in the misperception

Bloomfield's personality was warped here → Whorfed here

the listener retained the same verb tense suffix in the misperception even when the target was misinterpreted as a proper noun, forming a nonce form.

In comparison with misperceptions of inflectional morphology, errors involving derivational morphology were rare. The few examples appear to be phonological in nature rather than involving any specific morphological structure. For example:

Felicity conditions → ballistic conditions
He hasn't heard of any viable reasons → buyable reasons

Although there is some evidence that morphological affixes have an independent status as elements of the lexicon, most of the errors affecting morphology in some way appear to be primarily phonological, that is, based on misperceptions of phonological information. All things being equal, morphologically complex words are analyzed as mono-morphemic rather than the reverse, and morphological suffixes are adjusted to fit grammatical requirements (see Bond, 1999b, for further discussion).

12.5 Syntax

Most slips of the ear are local, typically affecting words or short phrases. When slips of the ear involve relatively longer stretches of speech, the misperceptions can show considerable divergence from the target utterances. Short slips do not provide much information about syntax, while long but radically restructured slips make it difficult to determine exactly what was misperceived.

12.5.1 *Well-formed and ill-formed utterances*

Most slips of the ear produced syntactically well-formed utterances in that the erroneously perceived portions did not create syntactic deviance. On occasion, misperceptions created utterances which listeners were unable to parse. In the misperception

has knocked real dents → has not real dents

the listener misinterpreted the verb "knocked" as the negative "not" and indicated incomprehension before the speaker could complete his utterance. This misperception suggests that listeners almost immediately attempt to map what they hear onto syntactic structures.

Even though listeners seem to expect well-formed utterances, a portion of misperceptions were ungrammatical to various degrees. Some showed minor deviations from well-formedness, such as missing articles:

I just got back from Denison → from dentist
Wouldn't she look good with a ring in her nose → oregano nose

Other slips departed further from well-formedness. Probably the most syntactically deviant misperception was:

We offered six → we Alfred six

in which a verb was misinterpreted as a proper name without any adjustments of the remainder of the phrase. Apparently, although listeners expect syntactic well-formedness, syntactic structure does not constrain interpretation of utterances to the same degree that phonological structure does.

12.5.2 *Constituents*

As a minimum, sentence understanding requires that listeners locate constituents and assign structural relationships. Consequently, we would expect that misperceived utterances preserve the integrity of constituents. The misperception data support the idea that constituents function as perceptual units.

First, misperceptions which involve misordering of segments were almost always located within constituents. In the total collection of misperceptions, there were only four apparent counter-examples, errors in the order of segments which seem to cross constituent boundaries in some way:

I have to eat too → I have eighty-two
She wants to be a teacher → She wants me to teach her
without your mother along → without your mother-in-law
my three-ninety class → my three-D night class

All four of these misperceptions also involve considerable phonological restructuring of the target utterance.

Second, word boundary misperceptions seem to be restricted to constituents. There was only one word boundary misperception which clearly crossed a major constituent boundary. The slip took place in the context of a riddle:

What goes "zzub, zzub, zzub"?
A bee flying backwards → A beef lying backwards

Perhaps the listener was prepared to suspend normal expectations when faced with a very odd question.

Major syntactic constituents are typically produced with a unified intonation contour and with the constituent boundaries phonetically characterized in some way (see, e.g., Gussenhoven & Jacobs, 1998, for phonological descriptions). Very few word boundary misperceptions crossed intonational contours. The few examples involve direct address, such as:

I know what happened to our ice, Andy → to high Sandy

or an explanation:

Sonic, the hedgehog → son of the hedgehog

Even misperceptions which restructured the phonology and lexicon quite radically seem to maintain the overall phrasing of the target utterance. For example,

I wasn't getting anywhere with all those vowel adjustments → with all those bottles of aspirin
How've you been? → Got a minute?

It seems likely that the phonological structure of constituents provides a framework or scaffolding which guides listener perception. Phrases defined by intonation seem to serve as units of segmentation with which listeners begin syntactic analysis.

12.5.3 *Argument structure and function*

Even though constituents seem to be resistant to misperception, their function and internal structure can be misanalyzed in many different ways. There seem to be two primary causes of syntactic misanalyses, often operating jointly. Listeners recover a word which is phonetically similar to the target but has a different part of speech or they mislocate word boundaries.

A misperception which leads to an incorrect part of speech assignment to a word can have consequences at any level of syntactic analysis. When the listener recovered a verb instead of an interrogative, she interpreted the speaker's question as a command:

Where are your jeans? → Wear your jeans

changing the function of the utterance. A student wished her classmate good luck, using a phrase from the movie *Star Wars*. The listener reinterpreted the auxiliary and following noun phrase as a noun:

May the Force be with you → metaphors be with you

A verb was interpreted as a homophonous noun with an adjustment of the function word:

I'm going to try to get it towed → to get a toad

In the reverse part of speech assignment, a noun was interpreted as a verb:

structure, style and usage → instruct your style and usage

In

I'm going to go downstairs and do some laminating → lemon eating

a noun was interpreted as a verb with a direct object.

Quite often, listeners adjust or "edit" portions of utterances so that they have the appropriate lexical items for well-formedness. In the misperception:

Missed the news → must 'a [have] snoozed

the listener interpreted the word "missed" as the near homophone "must" and the remainder of the utterance as the continuation of the verb phrase. In

John's nose is on crooked → John knows his own cooking

the noun "nose" was interpreted as the homophonous verb "knows" and the remainder of the utterance was interpreted as the required argument. Swinney (1979) and Tannenhaus, Leiman, and Seidenberg (1979) have reported that the same phenomenon, recovering homophones regardless of their part of speech, can be observed in experimental situations.

Misperceptions of word boundaries affected the perceived syntactic structure of phrases. For example, conjoined nouns or noun phrases were interpreted as a single noun phrase:

cinema and photography → cinnamon photography
a purse and a billfold → a personal billfold

The reverse error, interpreting a noun phrase as a conjoint, also occurred but more rarely:

Jefferson Starship → Jeffers and starship

Apparently, almost any kind of phrase or clause may be misanalyzed. For example, a prepositional phrase was interpreted as a modifier in:

a plate of lasagna → potato lasagna

A relative clause was interpreted as a predicate in:

This friend of ours who visited → This friend of ours is an idiot

No one syntactic property or characteristic of target utterances was invariably perceived correctly, thus serving to provide reliable syntactic information. Neither the purpose of the utterance as a whole nor the structure of any of its parts survived misperceptions reliably. Overall phrasing and rhythm, however, tended to be preserved.

12.6 Semantics and Pragmatics

Listeners do not appear to be constrained by semantic plausibility or contextual appropriateness. There are numerous misperceptions which involve radical changes in phonology and syntax, completely lacking in semantic appropriateness. Some examples:

After the rubber boat had been wrecked in the squall → After the rubber boot had been erected in the squirrel
I'm going to go back to bed until the news → I'm going to go back to bed and crush the noodles
I seem to be thirsty → I sing through my green Thursday
A linguini is a noodle → a lean Wheatie
My interactive Pooh → Mayan rack of Pooh

Languages allow speakers to say novel and unexpected things. Listeners, in turn, are willing to entertain novel and unexpected utterances.

12.7 Summary and Theoretical Implications

Phonetic errors show that stressed vowels resist misperception in comparison with consonants. The status of unstressed vowels is much more fluid because they are fragile, readily lost or added and, particularly in function words, changed to make the word fit grammatical requirements. The fundamental manner of articulation feature, obstruent vs. resonant, is somewhat more resistant to misperception, in that resonants tend to be perceived as resonants and obstruents tend to be perceived as obstruents. Misperceptions are not equally likely in all positions in a word: consonant substitutions tend to occur word-initially; consonant loss tends to affect final consonants. Finally, listeners take advantage of phonetic information wherever it is available, sometimes making errors about the order of segments.

Listener misperceptions suggest that in speech perception they act in accordance with knowledge of the phonology of their language. Listeners expect utterances to be phonologically well formed, and they "correct" consonant sequences which do not correspond to English phonotactic constraints. Listener misperceptions which result from compensating for phonological reductions suggest that listeners act as if phonological knowledge guided their interpretations of reduced speech. In the same way, listeners appear to have expectations about the phonological characteristics of dialects and sometimes use these in understanding speakers from other dialect areas.

The lexical representations which listeners employ involve a phonological code, as indicated by the perceptual occurrence of nonwords. Listeners seem to employ stressed syllables to locate word boundaries, showing knowledge of the statistical structure of their language. They are not particularly attentive to function words, adding or modifying them as needed by the structure of phrases or sentences.

Listener misanalyses of syntactic structure appear to be related to misplaced word boundaries and misassigned part of speech roles. That is, listeners recover a homophonous or nearly homophonous word from a different lexical category than the word in the target utterance. No one syntactic property resists misperception. However, phrases defined by intonation contours seem to be resistant to error and perhaps provide a framework or scaffolding for syntactic interpretation. Listeners are open to extremely implausible utterances, not at all constrained by semantic or pragmatic appropriateness. It may be that the perception of an odd or unusual utterance leads listeners to question what they have heard and to detect a perceptual error, a slip of the ear.

I should end with a note of caution. Slips of the ear are not directly observable. Rather, slips of the ear become available through listener reports. Because slips have been collected from spontaneous, casual conversations, the speakers' target utterances are also not available. Rather, the data set for slips of the ear consists of speakers' intentions and listener reports of their perceptions.

These difficulties are not unique to perceptual errors but rather characterize most investigations based on observations of fleeting actions. Though any one slip may be misreported by a listener or depend on an undetected error by a speaker, when many slips share characteristics, we may be reasonably sure that they represent real perceptual processes. In addition, "the analysis of naturally occurring errors forces us to consider behavior that is not constrained by the artificiality of the experimental laboratory" (Norman, 1981, p. 13). By examining complex activities in natural settings, we develop a clear understanding of what our theoretical constructs should be able to account for.

Listeners are faced with a phonetic stream, what Sapir (1921) calls the "rumble of speech" (p. 56); it is rapid and inconsistent, full of assimilations, deletions and many other kinds of reductions. Most of the time, listeners untangle the rumble of speech and recover listener intentions. They do this by applying strategies based on their extensive knowledge of the structure of their language.

ACKNOWLEDGMENTS

My thanks to Scott Jarvis, Emilia Marks, and Verna Stockmal for providing helpful comments on an earlier version of this paper.

REFERENCES

Altman, G. & Carter, D. (1989). Lexical stress and lexical discriminability: Stressed syllables are more informative, but why? *Computer Speech and Language*, 3, 265–75.

Bond, Z. S. (1999a). *Slips of the Ear: Errors in the Perception of Casual Conversation*. San Diego, CA: Academic Press.

Bond, Z. S. (1999b). Morphological errors in casual conversation. *Brain and Language*, 68, 144–50.

Bond, Z. S. & Small, L. H. (1983). Voicing, vowel, and stress mispronunciations in continuous speech. *Perception & Psychophysics*, 34, 470–4.

Butterfield, S. & Cutler, A. (1988). Segmentation errors by human listeners: Evidence for a prosodic segmentation strategy. *Proceedings of Speech '88* (pp. 827–33). Edinburgh.

Celce-Murcia, M. (1980). On Meringer's corpus of "slips of the ear." In V. A. Fromkin (ed.), *Errors of Linguistic Performance: Slips of the Tongue, Ear, Pen and Hand* (pp. 199–211). New York: Academic Press.

Chomsky, N. (1996). Language and thought: Some reflections on venerable themes. In *Powers and Prospects: Reflections on Human Nature and the Social Order* (pp. 1–30). Boston: South End Press.

Cole, R. A., Massaro, D. W., Yan, Y., Mak, B., & Fanty, M. (2001). The role of vowels versus consonants to word recognition in fluent speech. URL: http://mambo.ucsc.edu/psl/dwm.

Cutler, A. & Butterfield, S. (1992). Rhythmic cues to speech segmentation: Evidence from juncture misperception. *Journal of Memory & Language*, 31, 218–36.

Cutler, A. & Carter, D. M. (1987). The predominance of strong initial syllables in the English vocabulary. *Computer Speech and Language*, 2, 133–42.

Cutler, A. & Norris, D. (1988). The role of strong syllables in segmentation for lexical access. *Journal of Experimental Psychology: Human Perception and Performance*, 14, 113–21.

Edwards, G. (1995). *'Scuse Me while I Kiss this Guy and other Misheard Lyrics*. New York: Simon & Schuster.

Gaskell, M. G. & Marslen-Wilson, W. (1997). Integrating form and meaning: A distributed model of speech perception. *Language and Cognitive Processes*, 12, 613–56.

Gow, D. W. (2003). Feature parsing: Feature cue mapping in spoken word recognition. *Perception & Psychophysics*, 65, 475–90.

Grosjean, F. & Gee, J. P. (1987). Prosodic structure and spoken word recognition. *Cognition*, 25, 135–55.

Gussenhoven, C. & Jakobs, H. (1998). *Understanding Phonology*. London: Arnold.

Labov, W. (1994). *Principles of Linguistic Change: Internal Fctors*. Oxford: Blackwell.

Marslen-Wilson, W., Nix, A., & Gaskell, G. (1995). Phonological variation in lexical access: Abstractness, inference and English place assimilation. *Language and Cognitive Processes*, 10, 285–308.

Mattys, S. L. (1997). The use of time during lexical processing and segmentation: A review. *Psychonomic Bulletin & Review*, 4, 310–29.

Meringer, R. (1908). *Aus dem Leben der Sprache: Versprechen, Kindersprache Nachahmungstrieb* [From the life of language: Mis-speaking, child language, the imitative instinct]. Berlin: B. Behr.

Meringer, R. & Mayer, K. (1895). *Versprechen und Verlesen* [Mis-speaking and mis-reading]. Stuttgart: G. J. Goschensche Verlagshandlung.

Neel, A. T., Bradlow, A. R., & Pisoni, D. B. (1996/7). Intelligibility of normal speech: II. Analysis of transcription errors. *Research on Speech Perception, Progress Report No. 21* (pp. 421–37). Bloomington: Indiana University.

Norman, D. A. (1981). Categorization of action slips. *Psychological Review*, 88, 1–15.

Patterson, D. & Connine, C. M. (2001). A corpus analysis of variant frequency in American English flap production. Paper presented at Acoustical Society of America, June.

Pisoni, D. B. (1981). Some current theoretical issues in speech perception. *Cognition*, 10, 249–59.

Sapir, E. (1921). *Language*. New York: Harcourt Brace.

Swinney, D. A. (1979). Lexical access during sentence comprehension: (Re)consideration of context effects. *Journal of Verbal Learning and Verbal Behavior*, 18, 645–59.

Tannenhaus, M. K., Leiman, J. M., & Seidenberg, M. S. (1979). Evidence for multiple stages in the processing of ambiguous words in syntactic context. *Journal of Verbal Learning and Verbal Behaviour*, 18, 427–41.

Van Ooijen, B. (1996). Vowel mutability and lexical selection in English: Evidence from a word reconstruction task. *Memory & Cognition*, 25, 573–83.

Voss, B. (1984). *Slips of the Ear: Investigations into the Speech Perception Behaviour of German Speakers of English.* Tubingen, Germany: Gunter Narr Verlag.

Part III Perception of Indexical Properties

13 Perception of Dialect Variation

CYNTHIA G. CLOPPER AND
DAVID B. PISONI

13.1 Introduction

Variability in speech comes in many forms: within-speaker variability, cross-speaker variability, segment realization variability, and word environment variability as well as numerous others (Klatt, 1989). The traditional approach to the study of speech perception and spoken language processing has been to ignore these important sources of phonetic variability and to rely on abstract phonemic descriptions that are immune to variability across utterances, talkers, and contexts. A different approach, however, is to recognize that these sources of variability are natural consequences of language variation and investigate how variation and variability are processed in speech perception. This second alternative espouses the notion that variation in speech matters and that listeners can and do encode details of the indexical properties of the speech signal as a routine part of the normal speech perception process (Pisoni, 1993, 1997).

Fifty years ago, Peterson and Barney (1952) recorded 33 men, 28 women, and 15 children reading two lists of 10 [hVd] syllables. They took first and second formant frequency measurements for each of the vowels produced by each of the talkers. A scatterplot of the F1 values by the F2 values for each talker revealed a vowel space containing large overlapping ellipses for each of the 10 vowels. In their discussion of these findings, Peterson and Barney pointed out the continuous nature of the vowel space; there were no obvious breaks in the data as one moves from one vowel category to another in the F1 × F2 plane. In addition, they noted that the distribution of tokens for a single vowel represents the enormous variability with which any given vowel is produced across different talkers.

More recently, Hillenbrand et al. (1995) and Hagiwara (1997) have replicated Peterson and Barney's (1952) findings with respect to individual talker variation in terms of [hVd] formant frequency measures. Both of these studies also found large differences in mean formant values across their talkers compared to the formant values in the Peterson and Barney study. In particular, Hillenbrand et al. found a dramatic shift in the low vowels of their talkers, reflecting the Northern Cities Vowel Shift that has taken place in the last 50 years in urban areas in the northern United States. Hagiwara, on the other hand, found a dramatic shift in the back vowels, reflecting the southern California trend of back vowel fronting.

These two newer sets of measurements suggest that researchers who are interested in studying human speech perception will need to consider not only the effects of talker variability on vowel formants in production, but also the impact of regional dialect variation on vowel production and the implications of these differences for spoken language processing tasks.

While this acoustic-phonetic research in the speech sciences was being carried out in the laboratory, sociolinguists were engaged in conducting extensive research on vowel systems in the United States. Labov, Ash, and Boberg (in press) recorded 700 individuals across North America as part of their telephone survey (TELSUR) project. Based on an acoustic analysis of the vowels contained in the utterances, they have mapped the major and minor regional dialects of American English. The resulting atlas provides quantitative evidence for the major vowel shift phenomena that are currently taking place in North American English, including the Northern Cities Shift, the Southern shift, the low-back merger found in the west and upper midwest areas, and Canadian raising. In addition, Thomas (2001) used the individual vowel spaces of nearly 200 talkers in various locations around the country and of several ethnic backgrounds as the basis for his description of vocalic variation in North American English, including detailed discussions of the vowel systems of communities in Ohio, North Carolina, and Texas, as well as African American, Mexican American, and Native American varieties. Finally, many other researchers working in sociolinguistics and dialect geography have conducted small-scale studies of the vowel systems of regions from Maine to California. The combined results of these research efforts provide mounting evidence of an enormous amount of variation in speech production as a result of regional and ethnic status.

Despite the obvious close relationship between speech perception research and sociolinguistic research on variation in speech production, speech perception researchers and sociolinguists have been working in almost complete isolation from one another. Speech researchers are typically interested in discovering ways to understand and model how humans perceive, process, and encode spoken language and are faced with questions about acoustic-phonetic invariance in the speech signal and the role of different types of variability in language processing. In addition, theoretical linguists have also been working under the assumption that language can be modeled as an idealized symbolic system with relatively fixed underlying abstract phonological representations. Variation at the phonetic level has not been considered relevant to understanding, modeling, or describing language under this symbolic view. Until recently, variation in speech was treated as a source of noise; that is, as a set of attributes that were irrelevant to the underlying representations on which symbolic processes operated. As such, phonetic differences between talkers were treated as an undesirable set of attributes that needed to be reduced or eliminated in order to reveal the true underlying linguistic properties of the message (Pisoni, 1997).

In contrast to the typical psycholinguistic approach, sociolinguists have described natural variation as it occurs on social, regional, and ethnic levels and they have been faced with questions about the social implications of variability such as stereotypes, prejudice, and language attitudes as they impact the classroom and the workplace. Until recently, however, the question of how variation in language is perceived, processed, and encoded by listeners in order to allow them to make social judgments based on speech samples had been largely ignored by both speech researchers and sociolinguists. In this chapter, we describe some of the progress that has been made over the last 15 years in addressing the relationship between speech perception and dialect variation, as well as the implications of this research for studies of human speech perception, speech recognition and synthesis technologies, and linguistic theory.

13.2 Where Speech Perception and Sociolinguistics Intersect

Researchers working in the fields of sociolinguistics and speech perception have provided large amounts of evidence to support the notion that linguistic variation between talkers due to regional and ethnic differences is real and robust and is an important property of spoken language. We know less about what naïve listeners know about these sources of variation. While sociolinguists have spent much of their time documenting the linguistic variation that exists (Labov et al., in press), speech perception researchers have devoted their time and effort to reducing or eliminating these natural sources of variability or simply ignoring them entirely (Johnson & Mullennix, 1996).

There are a handful of research methodologies, however, that have been used to investigate the question of what naïve listeners know about ethnic and regional linguistic variation. Some of these experimental methodologies stem from the social psychology literature, such as attitude judgments and the matched-guise technique (Lambert et al., 1960; Preston, 1989). Others have been developed in the field of perceptual dialectology, such as map-drawing tasks (Preston, 1986). Still others stem from the forensic linguistics literature, such as accent imitation and caricature (Markham, 1999). Finally, more recently several researchers have employed experimental methods developed in cognitive psychology to explore the perception of variation in discrimination, matching, identification, and categorization tasks (e.g., Clopper & Pisoni, 2004a, c; Preston, 1993; Williams, Garrett, & Coupland, 1999).

13.2.1 *Map-drawing tasks*

One of the more unique methodologies employed by sociolinguistic researchers interested in the mental representations of dialect variation is the map-drawing task designed by Preston (1986). In this task, naïve participants are given a map of the United States (or Brazil or Japan) and are asked to draw and label the areas where they think "people speak differently." The results of these studies have shown that the cognitive maps that these participants have of dialect variation do not correspond to the dialect maps that are drawn by sociolinguists and dialect geographers. In fact, while most undergraduates in the United States will identify some portion of the country as "South" and most can reliably identify New York City as having its own unique accent, composite maps of groups of participants invariably have one or more regions that are not labeled at all. That is, unlike experienced dialectologists, naïve participants in these studies believe that some regions of the United States are accent-free. Preston (1986) had adults in Indiana, Hawaii, New York, and Michigan complete this map-drawing task. He found that where the participants were from had a substantial effect on how they drew the maps. In particular, his participants tended to label more dialect regions in close geographic proximity to themselves than farther away. These findings suggest that naïve listeners are, in fact, sensitive to the variation in speech that they hear through personal experience with and exposure to people from areas surrounding their hometown or state.

More recently, Tamasi (2003) used a variation on the map-drawing task to elicit mental representations of dialect from participants in Georgia and New Jersey. In her study, Tamasi gave naïve adults a stack of index cards with the state names written on them and asked the participants to sort the cards into piles based on how people speak in each state. Like Preston (1986), she found that naïve participants reliably identify salient regional varieties of American English, such as Southern and Northeastern varieties.

While the map-drawing and card-sorting tasks reveal something about the mental representations that naïve listeners have about dialect variation, the experimental methodologies rely on judgments made from knowledge and experiences stored in memory that may be highly biased and unreliable. The underlying assumption of Preston's (1986) map-drawing research is that the participants have full-formed mental representations of what they think the speech of a certain region sounds like. The results of these studies are unable to provide an understanding of speech perception or dialect perception, however, because they are based on measures of memory, not direct measures of perception. In order to address issues of speech perception and dialect variation, researchers need to obtain some kind of direct behavioral response to actual samples of spoken language. For example, participants could be given a map of the United States and, after listening to a short sample of speech, asked to indicate on the map all of the places that the talker might be from. Such a perceptual categorization task would reveal not only the participants' perception of the speech sample under study, but also would provide information about how the participants mentally represent dialect regions, because they would be indicating on their map all of the places where they believe people talk in the same way as the speaker who produced the sampled item. Using these kinds of procedures, measures of perceptual similarity and the underlying similarity spaces could be obtained.

13.2.2 *Attitude judgments*

In other research, Preston (1989) asked his participants to make judgments about the "correctness," "pleasantness," and intelligibility of the English spoken in each of the 50 states. In general, he found that although participants rated their own speech as most intelligible and most pleasant, they made their correctness ratings based on what seems to be a set of perceived notions about where Standard American English is spoken. Specifically, western and northern states were typically identified as having the most "correct" English by all participants, regardless of where they were from. Similarly, southern states were identified as having the least "correct" English, even by participants from southern Indiana, who speak a variety of southern American English. These findings reflect what Preston calls "linguistic insecurity." Participants who are linguistically secure with respect to the variety of English that they speak are more likely to label their own variety as "correct" than participants who are linguistically insecure.

Like the map-drawing task described above, however, these attitude judgments rely on participant reports that are based on mental representations of language in long-term memory and there is no evidence to suggest that the participants necessarily have personal experience with or first-hand knowledge of the varieties of English that they label as least pleasant or most correct. These attitude judgments could instead be highly biased and based on social stereotypes found in the media or perceived norms taught in the classroom by prescriptive grammarians.

13.2.3 *Matched-guise technique*

Another research methodology that has been used in studies of language attitudes, particularly with respect to ethnic and racial varieties, is the matched-guise technique (Lambert et al., 1960). In a matched-guise experiment, listeners hear utterances read by a single talker who assumes multiple guises (e.g., dialects, varieties, or languages). Listeners are asked to rate the talker on subjective scales such as intelligence, friendliness, and socioeconomic status. By using a single talker to produce the speech samples, variation in quality that can safely be attributed to anatomy is arguably controlled, although differences in quality that are functional, not anatomical, are not controlled in this method. Under such circumstances, researchers can be more confident that their results reflect attitudes toward phonological properties of language varieties and not to inherent differences in voice quality between talkers of different varieties. Studies of this kind have found that nonstandard language varieties are rated lower than standard varieties on scales related to "intelligence" by all listeners, revealing a general tendency to relate linguistic standardness with intelligence. However, it is also often the case that speakers of nonstandard varieties will rate those varieties more highly on scales related to "friendliness," showing solidarity with speakers of the same variety (Linn & Pichè, 1982; Luhman, 1990). These types of ratings studies suggest that listeners can and do make a number of attitudinal judgments about a talker based on his or her speech and that, in many cases, these judgments correspond to social stereotypes or prejudices often associated with the group that is represented by a certain language variety.

In these sociolinguistic and social psychology studies, there is no way to separate the attitude judgments made by the listeners from their ability to recognize the dialect of the speaker. The analysis of results collected using the matched-guise technique often assumes that the listeners first identified the racial, ethnic, or regional accent of the talker before making their attitudinal response. However, listeners in these tasks are rarely if ever asked to identify where the speaker is from before (or after) making their ratings. It therefore seems premature to conclude from these studies that listeners think that speakers of Appalachian English, for example, are friendly and unintelligent when in fact the only conclusion that can be drawn is that when the talker is speaking in an Appalachian English guise, the listeners rate him or her as being friendly and unintelligent

(Luhman, 1990). In addition, the issue of native-like pronunciation in all of the guises used in this kind of study is often overlooked. The crucial assumption made in this research is that the talker is equally competent in all of the guises he or she uses. It is difficult to know to what extent the talker truly controls each dialect and to what extent the characteristic or stereotyped features of each dialect are merely caricatured.

13.2.4 *Speech caricatures*

The imitation or caricaturization task is a similar method that has been used in the forensic linguistics literature. In one study, Markham (1999) asked eight native speakers of Swedish to read a prepared passage and an unfamiliar passage using a number of different regional accents. He then asked linguistically-trained judges to listen to each of the passages and identify the accent as well as rate the reading on its naturalness and purity. Markham found that some talkers were indeed able to convincingly imitate some accents, even for native listeners of that accent. These results suggest that in some cases, listeners are able to perceive and represent the variation in the language around them, as well as accurately reproduce the phonological characteristics of non-native varieties. By including both a prepared passage and a sight-reading passage, Markham was able to elicit several levels of proficiency in dialect imitation.

An instructive follow-up and extension to this study would be to play the speech samples to untrained native listeners of the different varieties represented and ask them to identify where the talkers were from and then rate the nativeness or naturalness of the productions. This kind of study would permit a more detailed examination of what the naïve listener knows about his or her own language variety, as well as provide another measure of the talkers' abilities to imitate and reproduce non-native varieties.

13.2.5 *Vowel matching*

One experimental technique that does assess naïve listeners' perception of variation in production is the vowel-matching task used by Niedzielski (1999) in her study of the perception of the Northern Cities Shift in Detroit English. In this task, listeners heard sentence-length utterances and were asked to select one of six synthesized vowel tokens that they thought matched the vowel in a target word in each sentence. Half of the listeners were told that the talker was from Detroit (as she actually was) and half of the listeners were told that the talker was from neighboring Canada. Niedzielski found that listeners who were told that the talker was from Canada most often selected the synthetic token that matched the actual vowel as the "best match." However, the listeners who were told that the talker was from Detroit most often selected the synthetic token that corresponded to a canonical (i.e., unshifted) vowel as the "best match." These results suggest that vowel perception is not absolute and invariant but is mediated by "knowledge" about the talker, such as where the listener believes the talker is from (see also Ladefoged & Broadbent, 1957).

Based on these data, Niedzielski (1999) concluded that Detroiters perceive themselves as speaking "standard" English, but that they perceive Canadians as speaking "with an accent" and this affected their perception of the vowels that they heard. One problem with this interpretation, however, lies in the design of the task. The listeners in Niedzielski's study were told to select the "best match" from six synthesized vowel tokens as part of a project on improving speech synthesis. The listeners who were told that the talker was from Detroit may have selected canonical vowels because they wanted to be "helpful" to the experimenter by selecting the "best" vowels and not the "best match" vowels. In addition, although synthesized speech can be useful in tasks like this in which a range of tokens that are carefully controlled for formant values is necessary, even high-quality synthetic speech produced by rule is a degraded signal and is consistently less natural than real speech samples obtained from real human talkers. Research relying on behavioral responses to synthetic speech should therefore be supplemented with converging evidence from studies involving natural speech.

Using a number of different methodologies from a variety of subfields of linguistics and psychology, several researchers have begun to collect evidence to support the proposal that people can and do perceive and encode the variability in the speech they hear around them. Map-drawing, attitude judgment, and matched-guise tasks can provide researchers with valuable information about how listeners conceptualize the varieties of their native language. Caricature studies provide additional information about the salient properties of a given language variety and provide some insight into how well people can translate the knowledge they gain about linguistic variability through perception to production. Phonological studies of linguistic variation provide researchers with a more formal basis for discussing what naïve listeners do and do not know about variation through thorough linguistic description. Finally, vowel-matching tasks and other similar experimental paradigms in cognitive psychology allow researchers to investigate perception of variation at lower levels of representation than the other kinds of tasks because, in ideal situations, these methodologies do not require the listeners to make more complex attitude judgments about the talkers.

The questions that remain to be investigated in dialect perception are related to how listeners actually use information in the speech signal to identify where a talker is from. These kinds of questions can be explored using a wide variety of experimental techniques developed in cognitive psychology, cognitive science, speech perception, and spoken word recognition research. Numerous experimental paradigms are available in the field of speech perception that allow dialect researchers to investigate the perception of variation. For example, studies of dialect recognition or categorization based on actual speech samples can provide new insights concerning the sources of stimulus information about language variation that are actually encoded in memory. Perceptual learning paradigms can be used to examine the role of short-term linguistic experience in dialect identification, categorization, and discrimination. There has been some progress in this direction over the last few years. The application of new experimental methods to the study of the perception of linguistic variation has already provided further insights into dialect perception and complements the earlier research using more traditional sociolinguistic and social psychological methods.

13.3 Dialect Categorization

Dialect categorization studies are quite limited in the literature, but several researchers have developed methodologies to determine whether listeners can identify where a talker is from based only on a short speech sample. These perceptual studies employ traditional identification or categorization methodologies developed in the fields of cognitive psychology and psycholinguistics for studying speech perception and spoken word recognition (Grosjean & Frauenfelder, 1997). Listeners are presented with short segments of speech spoken by a number of talkers and are simply asked to identify where they think the talker is from using either a closed-set categorization task or an identification task (e.g., Clopper & Pisoni, 2004c; Preston, 1993; Williams et al., 1999). While these kinds of studies cannot answer questions about how the listeners use their knowledge of variation to make judgments about the talkers, they can provide new information about how listeners use their knowledge of variation to determine where the talker is from. In combination with acoustic analyses of the speech signal and/or synthetic manipulation of the speech to highlight certain features, these kinds of studies can also be used to answer basic questions about which acoustic properties of the speech signal are perceptually most salient to listeners in identifying a talker's dialect. By studying and identifying the acoustic cues used in dialect categorization, we can better determine what kinds of information about dialect variation are encoded, stored, and represented by the naïve listener based on his or her everyday experiences with linguistic variation in the environment.

Recently, Purnell, Idsardi, and Baugh (1999) conducted an implicit dialect identification experiment using the matched-guise technique. A single male talker using three racial guises (African American Vernacular English, Chicano English, and Standard American English) left answering machine messages for landlords in five neighborhoods in the San Francisco area. The researchers measured dialect identification by examining the relationship between the number of returned phone calls leading to appointments with a landlord from each neighborhood and the minority population living in each neighborhood. They found that the number of appointments for the Standard American English guise remained relatively constant across all five neighborhoods. However, the number of appointments for the African American Vernacular English and the Chicano English guises declined as the population of minorities in the neighborhood became smaller. Purnell et al. concluded that the landlords could identify the dialect, and therefore race, of the talker from just a brief sample of speech left on an answering machine.

Baugh (2000) has described the behavior of the landlords in this study as "linguistic profiling" and has appeared on National Public Radio to discuss the findings of his study. While the issues related to racial identification are important, the design of the original study itself was fundamentally flawed in several ways. The first problem has to do with the use of the matched-guise technique itself. As mentioned above, there are serious concerns about the ability of a single talker to accurately produce utterances natively in multiple guises. The talker in the Purnell et al. (1999) study may not have had equally good control of all three guises. Second, the authors acknowledge that the dialects they used were "broadly" defined, but it is well known in the linguistic literature that phonetic and phonological variation among white speakers is much more regionally based than variation among African American speakers (Wolfram & Schilling-Estes, 1998). Therefore, it is possible that similar results could have been obtained using a northern white guise, a southern white guise, and a New York City white guise. A relationship then might become apparent between perceived socioeconomic status and number of appointments made by the landlords that also corresponds to the mean socioeconomic status of a given neighborhood. While the results of Baugh's research do seem to show that some people use their perception of dialect in making decisions in everyday life, the experiment by Purnell et al. itself did not control for the well-known and well-documented relationship between dialect and socioeconomic status (Labov, 2001).

In a more direct study of dialect identification, Preston (1993) asked naïve adult listeners from Michigan and Indiana to identify nine male talkers on a north–south continuum between Dothan, Alabama and Saginaw, Michigan. The talkers were all middle-aged males and the speech samples were short utterances taken from longer narratives. The listeners heard each talker only once and were asked to identify which of the nine cities they thought the talker was from. While listeners were quite poor at identifying exactly where each talker was from, they were able to distinguish between north and south. The major boundary for the two groups of listeners was slightly different, suggesting that dialect identification is only partly based on where the listener is from.

More recently, Preston (2002) suggested that the difference in the location of the north-south boundary for the two listener groups could be related to differences in what they were listening for. In particular, his other studies have shown that Michiganders pride themselves on having the most "correct" English in the United States, while Hoosiers pride themselves on sounding "pleasant." Preston suggested that one possible explanation for the difference in perceived boundary in the identification task is that the Michiganders were making their identifications based on "correctness," while the Hoosiers were making their identifications based on "pleasantness."

One weakness of Preston's (1993) study is that the listeners heard each talker only once and had to assign one talker to each city. Listeners therefore had to make their first response without reference to any context other than their own speech. They could make the remaining responses by comparing the voice on that trial with all of the voices they had heard previously. It is well-known in social and cognitive psychology that behavioral responses to stimuli require reference and comparison to a standard, either internal or external. If a benchmark is not provided by the experimenter, then the participant must rely on his or her own internal standard which may shift over the course of the experiment (Helson, 1948).

In order to reduce the effects of shifts in participants' standards for comparison, an alternative might be to provide listeners with all nine talkers and the option to listen to each one as many times as they want and in any order that they want so that the listeners could each create their own continuum of the nine talkers, without being restricted to a single repetition of each talker presented in random order. Despite this methodological problem, Preston's (1993) dialect identification study provides some additional evidence that naïve listeners can distinguish northern talkers from southern talkers. His research also gives some insight into what listeners might be doing in making these judgments, but we still do not know what specific acoustic properties of the speech signal listeners are basing their "correctness" or "pleasantness" judgments on.

One of the first studies that explicitly investigated dialect categorization was conducted by Williams et al. (1999) on varieties of English spoken in Wales. They recorded two adolescent males from each of six regions in Wales and two speakers of Received Pronunciation (RP) telling personal narratives. The authors then played short segments of these narratives back to different groups of adolescent boys from each of the six regions and asked them to categorize each talker into one of eight categories (the six regions of Wales, RP, or "don't know"). No feedback was provided about the accuracy of their responses.

Overall, the listeners were able to correctly categorize the talkers with about 30% accuracy. Williams et al. (1999) also looked at the performance of each group of listeners on the two talkers from their own region and found that performance on same-dialect talkers was not much better than categorization performance overall. The average performance was about 45% correct on talkers from the same region as the listeners. While the talkers were selected from a larger set of recordings based on phonological criteria established by the authors, they did find a significant difference in how well the two talkers from any given region were identified by the listeners (from the same region or from a different region). The authors suggested that this difference may be due to the availability of more salient phonological cues in some narratives or to the content of the narratives themselves as revealing something about the region in which the talker lived.

Van Bezooijen and her colleagues (Van Bezooijen & Gooskens, 1999; Van Bezooijen & Ytsma, 1999) have conducted similar dialect categorization research in the Netherlands and the United Kingdom. In the Netherlands, Van Bezooijen and Gooskens asked native Dutch listeners to identify the province of origin of three male talkers from each of four regional varieties of Dutch in a forced-choice categorization task using speech samples taken from interviews with an experimenter. The listeners were able to accurately categorize 40% of the male talkers. Van Bezooijen and Ytsma found similar results with female Dutch talkers using read speech passages. In the United Kingdom, Van Bezooijen and Gooskens reported that native British English listeners could identify the area of origin of male British English talkers with 52% accuracy. These studies used mainly spontaneous speech samples as stimuli with the expectation of revealing the "true" dialect of the talkers. However, the lack of segmental and contextual control of the stimulus materials themselves does not allow us to consider what the perceptual differences between the talkers should be attributed to.

More recent work by Clopper and Pisoni (2004c) has also focused on the question of dialect categorization. In one set of studies, we considered the question of how well listeners could identify where talkers were from and what acoustic-phonetic properties of the speech signal the listeners might be using to categorize the talkers. We selected sentence-length utterances from 11 male talkers in their twenties from each of six dialect regions in the United States from the TIMIT Acoustic-Phonetic Continuous Speech Corpus (Zue, Seneff, & Glass, 1990). Participants listened to the sentences and were then asked to categorize each talker into one of the six geographic regions using a touchscreen display of the continental

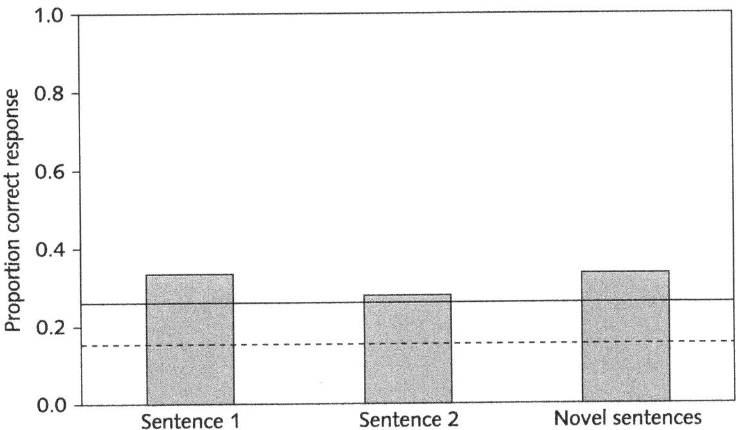

Figure 13.1 Proportion correct responses in each phase of the dialect categorization task. Chance performance (17%) is indicated by the dashed line. Performance statistically above chance (25%) is indicated by the solid line.
Source: Replotted from C. G. Clopper & D. B. Pisoni (2004). Some acoustic cues for the perceptual categorization of American English regional dialects. *Journal of Phonetics*, 32, 111–40.

United States. No feedback was provided. In the first two phases of the experiment, listeners heard each of the talkers reading the same sentence. In the final phase, listeners heard each of the talkers reading a different novel sentence.

Like Williams et al. (1999), we found that our listeners were only about 30% accurate in categorizing the talkers in a six-alternative forced-choice categorization task. Figure 13.1 shows the overall performance of the listeners in each of the three phases of the experiment. A clustering analysis on the confusion matrices of their responses revealed that listeners were not randomly guessing in doing this task, but instead that they were making broad distinctions between New England, Southern, and Western talkers. As an example, the clustering solution for the sentence, "She had your dark suit in greasy wash water all year" is shown in Figure 13.2. In this representation of perceptual similarity, perceptual distance is represented by the lengths of the vertical branches. These three perceptual clusters roughly correspond to the three major regional dialects of American English that Labov and his colleagues have discussed in the phonological variation literature (Labov, 1998). While overall performance was just above chance in terms of categorization accuracy, the results of the clustering analysis suggest that the listeners were responding in a systematic fashion and made categorization judgments based on three broader dialect clusters than those presented as response alternatives.

All but one of the dialect categorization studies described so far have used only male talkers. However, sociolinguists have argued that women tend to be more conservative in their speech, often using fewer stigmatized forms (Labov, 1990). Speech stimuli recorded from male talkers might therefore be expected to reveal more regional or substratal forms. However, sociolinguists have also shown that women tend to be ahead of men in language changes in progress, regardless of whether the changes are above or below the level of conscious social awareness

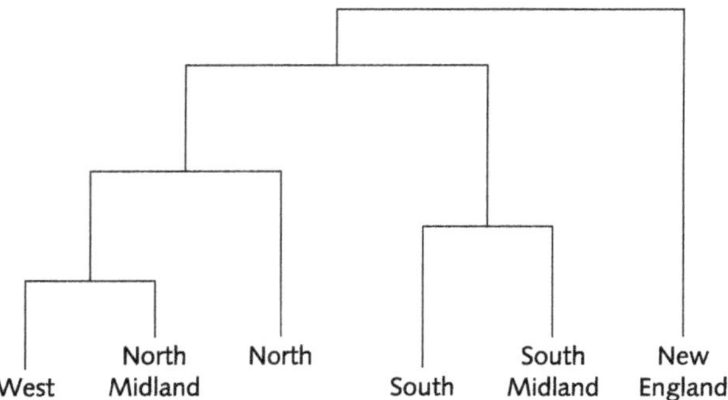

Figure 13.2 Clustering solution for the sentence, "She had your dark suit in greasy wash water all year." Perceptual distance is represented by the length of the vertical branches.

Source: Replotted from C. G. Clopper & D. B. Pisoni (2004). Some acoustic cues for the perceptual categorization of American English regional dialects. *Journal of Phonetics*, 32, 111–40.

(Labov, 1990; Milroy & Milroy, 1993). Speech stimuli recorded from female talkers might therefore be expected to reveal current changes in progress. Recently, Clopper, Conrey, and Pisoni (in press) replicated the earlier categorization and perceptual clustering results with a set of female talkers and with a set of mixed male and female talkers. Their results demonstrate that dialect categorization performance is robust across gender and presentation condition.

The stimulus materials used in the initial categorization study by Clopper and Pisoni (2004c) were also subjected to an acoustic analysis. Acoustic measures of the sentences confirmed that the talkers could be differentiated in terms of their dialect based on a number of reliable, well-defined acoustic-phonetic properties. A logistic regression analysis revealed seven acoustic-phonetic cues that were good predictors of dialect affiliation for our talkers. A similar regression analysis of the results of the categorization study with the measures obtained from the acoustic analysis revealed that these listeners were attending to only four of the seven available cues in the speech signal. These listeners were also attending to an additional 12 cues that were not good predictors of the dialect affiliation of these talkers. The four overlapping cues revealed listeners' sensitivity to stereotypes (New England r-lessness and North /oʊ/ pronunciation) and to prominent but less stereotyped variations (New England /æ/ backing and South Midland /u/ fronting). Taken together, the results of the categorization study and the acoustic analysis suggest that listeners can broadly categorize talkers by dialect region and that they are able to make use of several reliable and robust acoustic cues in the speech signal to do so.

In a follow-up to our earlier dialect categorization study, we investigated the effects of the residential history of the listener on dialect categorization performance (Clopper & Pisoni, 2004a). In several previous studies, Preston (1989, 1993) has shown that participants from different parts of the country perform differently on his map-drawing and attitude judgment tasks. In our study, we asked two groups of young adults to carry out the same six-alternative dialect categorization task described above. The first group ("homebodies") consisted of listeners who

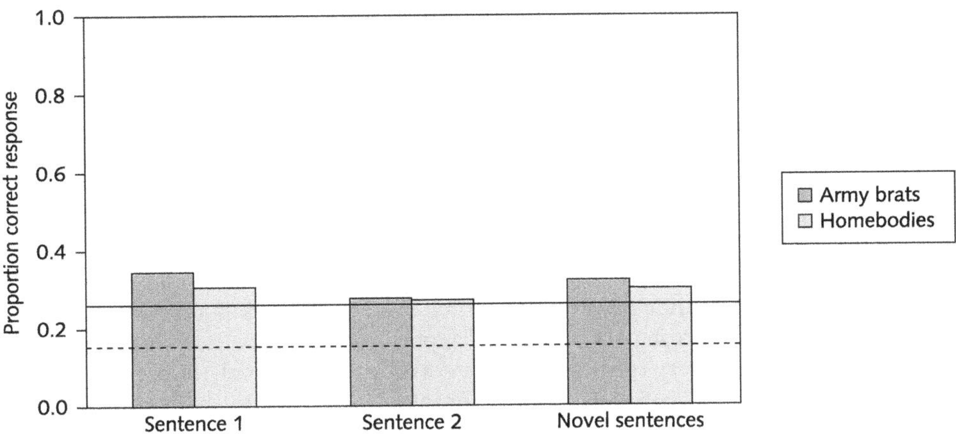

Figure 13.3 Proportion correct responses in each phase of the dialect categorization task for the "army brat" listener group and the "homebodies" listener group. Chance performance (17%) is indicated by the dashed line. Performance statistically above chance (25%) is indicated by the solid line.
Source: Replotted from C. G. Clopper & D. B. Pisoni (2004). Homebodies and army brats: some effects of early linguistic experience and residential history on dialect categorization. *Language Variation and Change*, 16, 31–48.

had lived exclusively in Indiana. The second group ("army brats") consisted of listeners who had lived in at least three different states (including Indiana). We hypothesized that the listeners in the "army brat" group would perform better on the categorization task than the "homebodies" because through their real-life experiences living in a number of different places they would have been exposed to more variation than listeners who had lived in only one state.

The categorization results confirmed our prediction. The listeners in the "army brat" group performed better overall than the listeners in the "homebody" group. Figure 13.3 shows the proportion correct performance in each of the three phases for each of the listener groups. The clustering analysis on the data in this experiment also revealed differences in the underlying perceptual similarity spaces of the dialects for the two listener groups, although the overall finding for both groups reflected the basic three-cluster structure (New England, South, West) found in the first experiment. These results replicate and extend Preston's (1989, 1993) earlier findings using the map-drawing task which showed that personal experience with linguistic variation is an important contributing factor that affects how well people can identify where talkers are from based on their speech.

The perceptual similarity results obtained from the confusion data from our initial six-alternative forced-choice categorization experiment were also confirmed by an auditory free classification task (Clopper & Pisoni, 2003). Naïve listeners were presented with the male talkers used in our previous experiments (Clopper & Pisoni, 2004a, c) and were asked to group them by dialect. They were allowed to make as many groups with as many talkers in each group as they wanted. In addition, they could listen to each talker as many times as they wanted. The resulting data were submitted to a hierarchical clustering analysis and the same three main clusters were obtained: New England, South, and West. These new results confirm that naïve listeners can make broad distinctions between the major varieties of American English, even in an unconstrained free classification task without any training or feedback.

13.3.1 *Perceptual learning of dialect variation*

Training and perceptual learning studies are often used in the field of cognitive psychology to ensure that poor performance on a given task is not due merely to the participants' unfamiliarity with the experimental procedures and to determine how much participants can improve and at what level their performance will asymptote (Green & Swets, 1966). Therefore, in order to determine whether or not personal experience in a laboratory setting would produce improvements in categorization performance, we conducted a set of short-term perceptual learning studies in which listeners were asked to learn to categorize a subset of the talkers used in the previous categorization tasks and then to generalize to new talkers (Clopper & Pisoni, in press).

One group of listeners was trained to identify a single talker from each of the six regions (the "one-talker" group). A second group of listeners was trained to identify three talkers from each of the regions (the "three-talker" group). Training consisted of three phases in which both groups of listeners heard sentences and were asked to categorize the talker by dialect. In the first two phases, the talkers all produced the same sentence. In the third phase of training, every talker read a different, novel sentence. Feedback was given after every trial to aid in learning. Following the three training phases, the listeners participated in a test phase using the same talkers as in the training phases but without feedback to ensure that they had learned which talkers were from where. Finally, the last phase of the experiment was the generalization phase in which the listeners heard novel sentences produced by new talkers and were asked to categorize them without feedback. In both the test and generalization phases, the talkers all produced different, novel sentences. Because the sentences were different across the different phases of the experiment, listeners had to rely on properties related to dialect and not individual sentences or talkers.

Categorization performance results are shown in Figure 13.4 for each of the five phases of the experiment for each of the two groups of listeners. While the one-talker group performed better in the training phases of the experiment, the three-talker group performed better in the final generalization phase. This "cross-over effect" suggests that while exposure to greater variation in training may produce more difficult initial learning in the training phases, these conditions produce better generalization to new talkers at final test. Despite the fact that the training sessions for both groups were relatively short in comparison to other types of language-based perceptual learning experiments, listeners in the three-talker group were better able to categorize new talkers than listeners in the one-talker group. These results on perceptual learning of dialect variation suggest that even when explicit instructions are not given about how to do the task, listeners know what to listen for and can extract information out of the acoustic

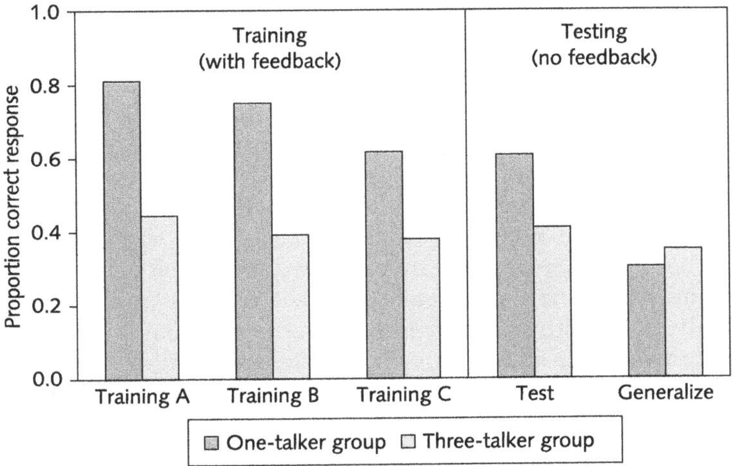

Figure 13.4 Proportion correct responses in each phase of the perceptual learning experiment for each of the listener groups.
Source: Replotted from C. G. Clopper & D. B. Pisoni (in press). Effects of talker variability on perceptual learning of dialects. *Language and Speech*.

signal that helps them in identifying the dialect of other unfamiliar talkers with very little exposure to the stimuli.

The dialect categorization studies discussed above have a variety of goals with respect to the theoretical issues they wish to address. The matched-guise task focused on the judgments and decisions participants made based on their perception of the ethnicity of the talker (Purnell et al., 1999). The dialect categorization studies focused on how listeners made judgments about where a talker was from and what acoustic-phonetic properties of the speech signal the listeners were using to make such identifications (Clopper et al., in press; Clopper & Pisoni, 2004a, c; Preston, 1993; Williams et al., 1999). Finally, the perceptual learning study examined the role that experience and learning have on dialect categorization abilities in naïve listeners (Clopper & Pisoni, in press). Despite these disparate goals, however, there is one general theoretical conclusion that the results of all of the studies lead to that cannot be ignored: phonetic variation attributable to dialect differences between talkers is well-resolved perceptually. Naïve listeners can make reliable judgments about where an unfamiliar talker is from without explicit instructions about what to listen for. This perceptual ability suggests that listeners retain a memory of the varieties of their native language and these representations develop naturally through a person's experience with and exposure to his community and the world at large. Specifically, recent findings from our lab have shown that greater personal experience with and exposure to multiple dialects lead to better performance on the dialect categorization task. Experience both in real life and in the laboratory contributes to the information that listeners encode about the variation that they hear in the language around them.

13.4 Looking Forward

The relatively small literature investigating the relationship between dialect variation and speech perception in the laboratory means that there is still much to be done before we can fully understand how dialect variation is perceived, encoded, and represented in memory by naïve listeners. The little research that has been done on these problems suggests that experimental methodologies such as categorization paradigms and perceptual learning tasks from cognitive psychology and new methodologies developed by perceptual dialectologists such as map-drawing tasks and the elicitation of dialect characteristics, combined with acoustic-phonetic analyses can provide converging information that will help us begin to answer fundamental questions about how listeners identify the dialect of a talker and how they use this information in a range of speech perception and spoken language processing tasks.

13.4.1 Methodological extensions

Several possibilities for extensions to the basic methodology of the dialect identification and categorization tasks are appropriate given the findings described in this chapter. First, the relatively poor performance of the listeners in the categorization tasks, their apparent ability to make only broad categorical distinctions, and Preston's (1986, 1989) findings that naïve participants do not have cognitive maps that correspond to linguists' maps of dialect variation all suggest that in conducting future categorization studies we might want to reconsider the response format and alternatives that we provide for our listeners. Perhaps fewer response alternatives, representing broader categories (e.g., North, South, and West) would result in better performance because they more directly reflect how listeners perceive and represent linguistic variation. Another alternative to the multiple choice tasks used in the studies discussed above would be a simple binary forced-choice discrimination task in which listeners have to indicate whether or not the talker has the same dialect as they do (e.g., "sounds like me" or "does not sound like me").

Second, all of the results described in this chapter have relied on accuracy data obtained from behavioral tasks. However, another common dependent measure used by psychologists interested in speech perception and spoken language processing is response latency. By modifying the methodology slightly to force listeners to respond under time pressure, researchers could easily obtain response latency data that may provide some additional insights into the underlying process of how listeners make their decisions. Are some varieties easier (faster) to identify than others? Are some listeners faster to respond than others? Do listeners respond faster to talkers from their own region than to talkers from other regions? These are all interesting and important research questions that have not been investigated previously and should provide further evidence about the role of dialect variation in language processing, perception, and encoding.

The perceptual learning study discussed here also represents merely the tip of the iceberg of possible laboratory-based training methodologies that could be employed to investigate how listeners learn what to attend to. The single study that has been conducted so far involved only short-term perceptual learning in a single test session of less than one hour and short-term retention with the generalization phase immediately following the last training phase. While a small amount of improvement was observed for the group trained on multiple talkers over the group trained on only one talker, neither group performed much above the levels of untrained listeners in our other experiments. It would be of some interest to determine at what level of performance the listeners would asymptote, if the training were continued over a number of sessions or over a number of weeks. Similarly, it would be of some interest to find out how long listeners would be able to retain the new dialect information they had learned in the training sessions. Would the listeners exposed to more talkers still perform better on novel talkers after one day or one week? The effects of dialect variability on long-term memory and retention have not been studied at all despite their importance for the development of language attitudes and social categories. These are all interesting and theoretically important questions about perceptual learning of dialect variation in speech.

13.4.2 *Listener populations*

Another similarity between all of the categorization studies discussed above is that the talkers and listeners were all young to middle-aged normal-hearing adults. It would be useful to extend this research to other populations such as infants, children, older adults, non-native speakers, and hearing-impaired adults and children to investigate the effects of age, language background, and hearing impairment on dialect categorization. In particular, studies with infants and children would allow us to determine at what age the abilities to discriminate and categorize dialects arise. Given some of the recent findings in the infant and child speech perception literature, we might expect this ability to arise quite early in development. For example, Houston and Jusczyk (2000) found that 10.5-month-old infants could discriminate the linguistic content of the speech signal from the indexical properties of the talker better than 7.5-month-olds. And, Spence, Rollins, and Jerger (2002) have shown that 3-, 4-, and 5-year-olds can use indexical information to identify cartoon characters by their voice. These findings suggest that indexical properties of speech, such as dialect variation, are encoded in speech perception early in development and that children quickly learn to separate these talker-specific properties from the linguistic meaning.

Nathan and her colleagues (Nathan & Wells, 2001; Nathan, Wells, & Donlan, 1998) have recently explored the role of dialect variation in spoken language processing by children with language delays. In particular, they assessed speech intelligibility by linguistically normal and delayed children in two dialect conditions: their own London dialect and an unfamiliar Glaswegian dialect. The language-delayed children showed greater impairment with the unfamiliar dialect than the typically developing children. These results suggest that language delays span a wide range of linguistic abilities, including those related to processing indexical information in the speech signal. Additional research is needed to determine the time-course of development of sociolinguistic competence in both normally-developing and language-delayed children.

Dialect categorization studies with older adults could provide additional knowledge about the role of linguistic experience in dialect categorization. One prediction is that older adults might perform better than younger adults because they have had more time to come into contact with more variation over their lifetime. In their study of dialect categorization in Wales, Williams et al. (1999) used two populations of listeners, adolescents and schoolteachers. Although the authors did not report any statistical comparisons of performance differences between the two groups, the schoolteachers performed better (52% correct) than the adolescents (30% correct). Williams et al. concluded from these results that linguistic experience comes with age and that the difference in categorization between the two populations could be attributed to the greater overall experience of the teachers with linguistic variation. If performance continues to increase with age and experience, we might expect to find better categorization performance for older adults than for the college-aged listeners used in most of the studies discussed above.

When it comes to dialect categorization by non-native listeners, there are several reasons to predict that these listeners would perform more poorly on a categorization task than native listeners. First, non-native listeners typically have less experience with and exposure to the variation in the target language. Second, they are less sensitive to the variation in a second language than native speakers, particularly with respect to phonetic variation within a single phonological category. However, Bradlow and Pisoni (1999) found that non-native listeners were not more susceptible to talker variability effects in word recognition than native listeners, suggesting that some kinds of indexical variability have the same effects on all listeners. In addition, Bradlow and Bent (2003) reported that non-native listeners perform better than native listeners on speech intelligibility tasks involving non-native speech samples. Dialect categorization research using non-native listeners would be an important contribution to our understanding of how linguistic variation is perceived and in what ways second language perception is constrained by language background.

Research using hearing-impaired populations would provide evidence for the robustness of variation in cases where the speech signal is degraded. A case study conducted in our lab of a post-lingually deafened adult cochlear implant user on the six-alternative categorization task without training or feedback revealed performance that was within one standard deviation of the performance of normal-hearing listeners (Clopper & Pisoni, 2004b). These results suggest that at least some of the information that is encoded by normal-hearing listeners in this perceptual task is available to and encoded by cochlear implant users. However, research on both adult and pediatric cochlear implant users has shown that they perform more slowly and less accurately on talker discrimination tasks than their normal-hearing peers, suggesting that indexical information in speech is not perceived and encoded in the same way for the two populations (Cleary, 2002; Kirk et al., 2002). More research on these clinical populations would provide further insights into the kinds of information that are available to and encoded by listeners in making categorization judgments about language variation.

13.4.3 Other measures of speech perception

Another approach to the study of the perception of dialect variation that has barely been examined is measuring the perceptual similarity spaces of different listeners. The clustering analyses that we conducted based on the confusion matrices from our dialect categorization studies reflect just one method of determining the perceptual similarity of the dialects we studied. Our results suggested that the perceptual similarity between dialects is based in part on the phonological similarity of the dialects, but it also might be influenced by the stereotyped uniqueness of a given variety. In particular, New England and South were often the most distinct dialects for our listeners and these two dialects are both associated with a number of stereotyped features. The use of other methodologies from the cognitive psychology literature such as paired comparisons, free classification, and similarity ratings tasks should provide converging evidence for the similarities between dialects and between talkers within a given dialect as they are perceived by naïve listeners.

In addition, electrophysiological and neuroimaging approaches to the study of the perception of dialect variation have barely been explored. Recently, Conrey (2001) reported the results of a vowel merger perception experiment in which she recorded reaction times in a cross-modal semantic priming task. She found that the behavioral reaction times in her study correlated with prior electrophysiological research on semantic priming. This correlation suggests that electrophysiological measures of the perception of vowel mergers might also reveal interesting results that would provide further insights into the perception of dialect variation. In addition, fMRI research has revealed some cortical differences in activities showing how linguistic form and linguistic content are processed (Ni et al., 2000) and between first and second language processing in bilinguals (Kim et al., 1997). Future fMRI research on the processing of indexical variation in speech and the role of linguistic experience with dialect variation in language processing should provide new fundamental neurobiological knowledge about how variation and variability are perceived, processed, and encoded by the human listener.

13.5 Implications for Speech Research, Speech Technology, and Theoretical Linguistics

There are many important theoretical reasons to gain a better understanding of dialect variation and perception. In terms of human speech perception, the more we know about how variation and variability are perceived, the better we will be able to understand and model spoken language processing. Most current models of speech perception assume that variation is stripped off early in a process of normalization so that the meaningful symbolic content of the signal can be recognized (Pisoni, 1997). This assumption is central to all of the traditional abstractionist views of speech and language as symbolic systems, in which the variation is treated as irrelevant noise. However, in order to fully understand the process of human speech perception, we need to learn more about how the major sources of variability are perceived and encoded along with the linguistic message of the utterance (see Klatt, 1989). Researchers have only recently begun to moderate the traditional symbolic view of language and to investigate the contributions of linguistic variability in human speech perception. For example, in addition to the recent findings of the "army brat" study reported above, there is also an extensive literature on the role of talker variability and talker-specific information in speech perception that suggests that indexical properties of speech are perceived and encoded by listeners in laboratory-based linguistic tasks (e.g., Mullennix, Pisoni, & Martin, 1989; Nygaard, Sommers, & Pisoni, 1994). Dialect variation is clearly one of the indexical properties that is perceived and encoded in everyday language situations and its impact on speech perception deserves further investigation.

The implications for automatic speech recognition (ASR) systems with respect to variation and variability are perhaps even more striking. The variation that exists in a single language is simply enormous and is constantly changing as the language changes. Humans are able to adapt quickly and easily to new talkers and linguistic changes, but ASR systems are still severely limited with respect to variation and change and current systems require large amounts of training before they can accurately recognize speech. Ideally, ASR systems would be able to recognize not only a large number of lexical items, but also a large number of talkers and a large number of languages. However, most of the currently available commercial speech recognition systems are limited to only a few talkers (e.g., personal computer speech-to-text software) or have limited vocabularies within a specialized semantic domain (e.g., interactive automated flight information programs). One of the new areas of research in ASR systems is the "speech graffiti" project at Carnegie Mellon whose goal is to develop a universal speech interface that is much more flexible than standard touchtone phone menu systems, but more rigid than a true natural language interface (Rosenfeld, Olsen, & Rudnicky, 2000). The idea behind the project is to build a human–machine speech interface that will be useful for an unlimited number of talkers across multiple domains, such as movie or apartment listings and flight information. The more we know about variability and variation in speech and how it is processed and encoded by human listeners, the more we will be able to apply our knowledge of human speech perception to building truly robust ASR systems in the future.

Like ASR systems, speech synthesis technology has typically been limited to a small number of default synthetic voices and a limited vocabulary domain. The most natural synthetic speech can be built from the concatenation of resynthesized speech units smaller than the word, but larger than diphones. However, these systems are usually highly constrained in vocabulary. Successful speech synthesis of large vocabularies typically involves the concatenation of diphone strings, but the result is less natural speech (Black, 2002). Researchers at the University of Edinburgh in Scotland have been working to create a speech synthesizer using diphone concatenation that can produce speech in a number of different dialects of English, including Irish, Scottish, British, and American English varieties (Fitt & Isard, 1999). In addition to issues of prosody and sentence focus which remain problematic for speech synthesis programs (Wightman et al., 2000), "natural" speech synthesis must also be able to replicate and reproduce important human features of speaking style such as register shifts and dialect variation, given the importance of such factors in human communication and interaction (Giles & Bourhis, 1976). As we learn more about what parts of the acoustic signal are important and linguistically significant for human listeners in identifying where someone is from, we will be better equipped to design synthesis systems that exhibit the appropriate characteristics of a given dialect.

Research on the perception of dialect variation also has some important implications for the field of theoretical linguistics. Like many speech perception researchers, theoretical linguists typically assume that each lexical item specifies one underlying phonemic input that is transformed through serial derivation or parallel candidate selection into a phonetic output. Generative phonologists typically assume a one-to-one mapping between idealized symbolic phonemic forms in the mental lexicon and phonetic outputs in production. However, results of the studies on dialect caricatures discussed above suggest that naïve listeners have multiple mappings between underlying and surface forms, both productively and conceptually. In the sociolinguistics literature, variable rule analysis has been adopted by many researchers to account for variable phonetic outputs given a single underlying form in a single talker (Labov, 1969). However, acknowledging and accounting for the possibility of a one-to-many relationship between phonemic representations and phonetic forms in production has yet to occur in the mainstream generative paradigm. The research discussed in this chapter, however, demonstrates that phonological variation is an important property of human speech perception and any model of phonology would be seriously remiss in overlooking these physically and psychologically real aspects of human language performance.

The exemplar approach to theoretical phonology may be able to account for the perception of linguistic variation. As Clopper and Pisoni (2004a, in press) demonstrated, experience with linguistic variation has an effect on performance in explicit tests of dialect categorization. Given that experience is a central theme of exemplar models, we might expect that this approach would produce a psychologically plausible model of the perception of variation. In addition, Pierrehumbert (2001, 2002) and Bybee (2001) have recently developed models within the exemplar framework to account for phonological and morphological change. The intrinsic link between diachronic language change and synchronic linguistic variation also suggests that similar models may be able to account for the mechanisms behind regional, social, and ethnic variation.

Finally, cognitive scientists have recently begun to embrace the notion of "embodiment" and to explore the relation between cognition and human interaction with the world (Clark, 2001; Núñez & Freeman, 1999). Recent work in the fields of speech perception and sociolinguistics crucially reveals that language is more complex than a simple symbolic system and that the perception of speech involves not only extraction of the linguistic meaning of the utterance, but also a number of other processes including identification of the indexical properties of the talker. Language as a cognitive and neurobiological process is therefore embedded in our physical and social interactions with the environment. Any psychologically real model of human language processing must begin to account for the variability inherent in actual language use.

Researchers in social psychology, sociolinguistics, forensic linguistics, psycholinguistics, and cognitive psychology have all contributed to the rapidly growing literature on the relationship between regional, social, and ethnic language variation and speech perception. The results of these diverse studies reveal that naïve listeners are aware of linguistic variation to the extent that they can imitate it, use it to identify where people are from and to make judgments about social characteristics of the talkers. The implications of these findings are widespread as well, including issues related to models of human speech perception, speech perception in clinical populations, language development, speech recognition and speech synthesis technologies, neural biology and behavior, cognition and language, and theoretical linguistics. There is much work still to be done in the area of dialect perception in the future and there is a need for multi-disciplinary discussion of the results of these studies and their implications for our understanding of human language.

ACKNOWLEDGMENTS

This work was supported by the NIH NIDCD R01 Research Grant DC00111 and the NIH NIDCD T32 Training Grant DC00012 to Indiana University. We would also like to acknowledge the valuable advice that we received on various aspects of this project from Kenneth de Jong, Caitlin Dillon, Luis Hernandez, and Robert Nosofsky, as well as the assistance of Jeffrey Reynolds and Adam Tierney with data collection.

REFERENCES

Baugh, J. (2000). Racial identity by speech. *American Speech*, 75, 362–4.

Black, A. W. (2002). Text-to-speech synthesis. Paper presented at the 143rd Meeting of the Acoustical Society of America, Short Course on Speech Technology and Conversational Systems. Pittsburgh, Pennsylvania, June 1–2.

Bradlow, A. R. & Bent, T. (2003). Listener adaptation to foreign-accented speech. Paper presented at the International Congress of Phonetic Sciences. Barcelona, Spain, August 3–9.

Bradlow, A. R. & Pisoni, D. B. (1999). Recognition of spoken words by native and non-native listeners: Talker-, listener-, and item-related factors. *Journal of the Acoustical Society of America*, 106, 2074–85.

Bybee, J. (2001). *Phonology and Language Use*. Cambridge: Cambridge University Press.

Clark, A. (2001). *Mindware*. New York: Oxford University Press.

Cleary, M. (2002). Perception of talker similarity by normal-hearing children and hearing-impaired children with cochlear implants. Poster presented at the 143rd Meeting of the Acoustical Society of America. Pittsburgh, Pennsylvania, June 3–7.

Clopper, C. G. & Pisoni, D. B. (2003). Free classification of regional varieties of American English. Poster presented at New Ways of Analyzing Variation 32. Philadelphia, Pennsylvania, October 9–12.

Clopper, C. G. & Pisoni, D. B. (2004a). Homebodies and army brats: Some effects of early linguistic experience and residential history on dialect categorization. *Language Variation and Change*, 16, 31–48.

Clopper, C. G. & Pisoni, D. B. (2004b). Perceptual dialect categorization by an adult cochlear implant user: A case study. Paper presented at the 8th International Cochlear Implant Conference. Indianapolis, Indiana, May 10–13.

Clopper, C. G. & Pisoni, D. B. (2004c). Some acoustic cues for the perceptual categorization of American English regional dialects. *Journal of Phonetics*, 32, 111–40.

Clopper, C. G. & Pisoni, D. B. (in press). Effects of talker variability on perceptual learning of dialects. *Language and Speech*.

Clopper, C. G., Conrey, B. L., & Pisoni, D. B. (in press). Effects of talker gender on dialect categorization. *Journal of Language and Social Psychology*.

Conrey, B. (2001). Effects of dialect on merger perception. Poster presented at New Ways of Analyzing Variation 30. Raleigh, North Carolina, October 11–13.

Fitt, S. & Isard, S. (1999). Synthesis of regional English using a keyword lexicon. *Proceedings of Eurospeech 1999*, 823–6.

Giles, H. & Bourhis, R. Y. (1976). Methodological issues in dialect perception: Some social psychological perspectives. *Anthropological Linguistics*, 18, 294–304.

Green, D. M. & Swets, J. A. (1966). *Signal Detection Theory and Psychophysics*. New York: John Wiley & Sons.

Grosjean, F. & Frauenfelder, U. H. (1997). *A Guide to Spoken Word Recognition Paradigms*. Hove, UK: Psychology Press.

Hagiwara, R. (1997). Dialect variation and formant frequency: The American English vowels revisited. *Journal of the Acoustical Society of America*, 102, 655–8.

Helson, H. (1948). Adaptation-level as a basis for a quantitative theory of frames of reference. *Psychological Review*, 55, 297–313.

Hillenbrand, J., Getty, L. A., Clark, M. J., & Wheeler, K. (1995). Acoustic characteristics of American English vowels. *Journal of the Acoustical Society of America*, 97, 3099–111.

Houston, D. M. & Jusczyk, P. W. (2000). The role of talker-specific information in word segmentation by infants. *Journal of Experimental Psychology: Human Perception and Performance*, 26, 1570–82.

Johnson, K. & Mullennix, J. W. (eds.) (1996). *Talker Variability in Speech Processing*. San Diego: Academic Press.

Kim, K. H. S., Relkin, N. R., Lee, K.-M., & Hirsch, J. (1997). Distinct cortical areas associated with native and second languages. *Nature*, 388, 171–4.

Kirk, K. I., Houston, D. M., Pisoni, D. B., Sprunger, A. B., & Kim-Lee, Y. (2002). Talker discrimination and spoken word recognition by adults with cochlear implants. Poster presented at the 25th Mid-Winter Meeting of the Association for Research in Otolaryngology. St Petersburg, Florida, January 26–31.

Klatt, D. H. (1989). Review of selected models of speech perception. In W. Marslen-Wilson (ed.), *Lexical Representation and Process* (pp. 169–226). Cambridge, MA: MIT Press.

Labov, W. (1969). Contraction, deletion, and inherent variability of the English copula. *Language*, 45, 715–62.

Labov, W. (1990). The intersection of sex and social class in the course of linguistic change. *Language Variation and Change*, 2, 205–54.

Labov, W. (1998). The three English dialects. In M. D. Linn (ed.), *Handbook of Dialects and Language Variation* (pp. 39–81). San Diego: Academic Press.

Labov, W. (2001). *Principles of Linguistic Change: Social Factors*. Malden, MA: Blackwell.

Labov, W., Ash, S., & Boberg, C. (in press). *Atlas of North American English*. Berlin: Mouton de Gruyter.

Ladefoged, P. & Broadbent, D. E. (1957). Information conveyed by vowels. *Journal of the Acoustical Society of America*, 29, 98–104.

Lambert, W., Hodgson, E. R., Gardner, R. C., & Fillenbaum, S. (1960). Evaluation reactions to spoken languages. *Journal of Abnormal and Social Psychology*, 60, 44–51.

Linn, M. D. & Pichè, G. (1982). Black and white adolescent and preadolescent attitudes toward Black English. *Research in the Teaching of English*, 16, 53–69.

Luhman, R. (1990). Appalachian English stereotypes: Language attitudes in Kentucky. *Language in Society*, 19, 331–48.

Markham, D. (1999). Listeners and disguised voices: The imitation and perception of dialectal accent. *Forensic Linguistics*, 6, 289–99.

Milroy, J. & Milroy, L. (1993). Mechanisms of change in urban dialects: The role of class, social network and gender. *International Journal of Applied Linguistics*, 3, 57–77.

Mullennix, J. W., Pisoni, D. B., & Martin, C. S. (1989). Some effects of talker variability on spoken word recognition. *Journal of the Acoustical Society of America*, 85, 365–78.

Nathan, L. & Wells, B. (2001). Can children with speech difficulties process an unfamiliar accent? *Applied Psycholinguistics*, 22, 343–61.

Nathan, L., Wells, B., & Donlan, C. (1998). Children's comprehension of unfamiliar regional accents: A preliminary investigation. *Journal of Child Language*, 25, 343–65.

Ni, W., Constable, R. T., Mencl, W. E., Pugh, K. R., Fulbright, R. K., Shaywitz, S. E., Shaywitz, B. A., Gore, J. C., & Shankweiler, D. (2000). An event-related neuroimaging study distinguishing form and content in sentence processing. *Journal of Cognitive Neuroscience*, 12, 120–33.

Niedzielski, N. (1999). The effect of social information on the perception of sociolinguistic variables. *Journal of Language and Social Psychology*, 18, 62–85.

Núñez, R. & Freeman, W. J. (eds.) (1999). *Reclaiming Cognition: The Primacy of Action, Intention, and Emotion*. Bowling Green, OH: Imprint Academic.

Nygaard, L. C., Sommers, M. S., & Pisoni, D. B. (1994). Speech perception as a talker-contingent process. *Psychological Science*, 5, 42–6.

Peterson, G. E. & Barney, H. L. (1952). Control methods used in a study of the vowels. *Journal of the Acoustical Society of America*, 24, 175–84.

Pierrehumbert, J. B. (2001). Exemplar dynamics: Word frequency, lenition and contrast. In J. Bybee & P. Hopper (eds.), *Frequency Effects and Emergent Grammar* (pp. 137–58). Amsterdam: John Benjamins.

Pierrehumbert, J. B. (2002). Word-specific phonetics. In C. Gussenhoven & N. Warner (eds.), *Laboratory Phonology 7* (pp. 101–40). Berlin: Mouton de Gruyter.

Pisoni, D. B. (1993). Long-term memory in speech perception: Some new findings on talker variability, speaking rate, and perceptual learning. *Speech Communication*, 13, 109–25.

Pisoni, D. B. (1997). Some thoughts on "normalization" in speech perception. In K. Johnson & J. W. Mullennix (eds.), *Talker Variability in Speech Processing* (pp. 9–32). San Diego: Academic Press.

Preston, D. R. (1986). Five visions of America. *Language in Society*, 15, 221–40.

Preston, D. R. (1989). *Perceptual Dialectology: Nonlinguists' Views of Areal Linguistics*. Providence, RI: Foris.

Preston, D. R. (1993). Folk dialectology. In D. R. Preston (ed.), *American Dialect Research* (pp. 333–78). Philadelphia: John Benjamins.

Preston, D. R. (2002). The social interface in the perception and production of Japanese vowel devoicing: It's not just your brain that's connected to your ear. Paper presented at the 9th Biennial Rice University Symposium on Linguistics: Speech Perception in Context. Houston, Texas, March 13–16.

Purnell, T., Idsardi, W., & Baugh, J. (1999). Perceptual and phonetic experiments on American English dialect identification. *Journal of Language and Social Psychology*, 18, 10–30.

Rosenfeld, R., Olsen, D., & Rudnicky, A. (2000). A universal human–machine speech interface. *Technical Report CMU-CS-00-114*. Pittsburgh, PA: School of Computer Science, Carnegie Mellon University.

Spence, M. J., Rollins, P. R., & Jerger, S. (2002). Children's recognition of cartoon voices. *Journal of Speech, Language, and Hearing Research*, 45, 214–22.

Tamasi, S. L. (2003). Cognitive patterns of linguistic perceptions. Doctoral dissertation, University of Georgia, Athens.

Thomas, E. R. (2001). *An Acoustic Analysis of Vowel Variation in New World English.* Durham, NC: Duke University Press.

Van Bezooijen, R. & Gooskens, C. (1999). Identification of language varieties: The contribution of different linguistic levels. *Journal of Language and Social Psychology*, 18, 31–48.

Van Bezooijen, R. & Ytsma, J. (1999). Accents of Dutch: Personality impression, divergence, and identifiability. *Belgian Journal of Linguistics*, 13, 105–29.

Wightman, C. W., Syrdal, A. K., Stemmer, G., Conkie, A., & Beutnagel, M. (2000). Perceptually based automatic prosody labeling and prosodically enriched unit selection improve concatenative text-to-speech synthesis. *Proceedings of the International Conference on Spoken Language Processing*, 2, 71–4.

Williams, A., Garrett, P., & Coupland, N. (1999). Dialect recognition. In D. R. Preston (ed.), *Handbook of Perceptual Dialectology* (pp. 345–58). Philadelphia: John Benjamins.

Wolfram, W. & Schilling-Estes, N. (1998). *American English.* Malden, MA: Blackwell.

Zue, V., Seneff, S., & Glass, J. (1990). Speech database development at MIT: TIMIT and beyond. *Speech Communication*, 9, 351–6.

14 Perception of Voice Quality

JODY KREIMAN, DIANA VANLANCKER-SIDTIS, AND BRUCE R. GERRATT

14.1 Why Should We Care about Voice Quality?

The speaking voice naturally conveys information about the speaking individual. Talkers may sound elderly, or bored, or distracted. Listeners may discern that a speaker is inebriated, or physically ill, or telling an exciting secret. By their voices, adult speakers almost always reveal whether they are male or female, and in addition their voices may suggest a particular geographical background, psychological state, and personality. Known voices are often easily recognized, and it is common to rapidly form a distinct impression from the voice of someone we do not know. The impressions listeners gain from voices are not necessarily accurate; indeed, everyone has known the surprise of meeting a telephone acquaintance who clashes with a mental picture formed earlier. Despite these occasional mismatches, voice quality is a primary means by which speakers project their identity – their "physical, psychological, and social characteristics" (Laver, 1980, p. 2) – to the world. Patients with a voice disorder sometimes complain that the disordered voice does not convey who they are. In some cases, patients dislike the image they portray so much that they avoid speaking, resulting in significant social and work-related difficulties. Voice quality problems may also interfere with speech intelligibility, creating a major handicap in verbal communication (Kempler & Van Lancker, 2002).

Table 14.1 summarizes the many judgments that listeners make when listening to a voice. These human abilities arise from a long evolutionary process, and many animal species use vocal quality to signal or perceive size, threat, and kin relationships (Cheney & Seyfarth, 1980; Rendall, Rodman, & Edmond, 1996). Human infants' ability to recognize voices is in place at birth (DeCasper & Fifer, 1980). Voice conveys much of the emotion and attitude communicated by speech (Banse & Scherer, 1996; Breitenstein, Van Lancker, & Daum, 2001; Ellgring & Scherer, 1996; Van Lancker & Pachana, 1998; Williams & Stevens, 1972). Alterations in voice quality relative to the speaker's normal vocal delivery may signal irony or sarcasm (Van Lancker, Canter, & Terbeek, 1981). Faster rate and higher pitch increase the perceived "competence" of a speaker (Brown, Strong, & Rencher, 1974). Listeners may also judge the speaker's sexual preference (Linville, 1998), status as native or non-native speaker (Piske, MacKay, & Flege, 2001), and a myriad of personality

Table 14.1 Judgments listeners make from voice

Spoken message
Physical characteristics of the speaker
Age
Appearance (height, weight, attractiveness)
Dental and oral/nasal status
Health status, fatigue
Identity
Intoxication
Race, ethnicity
Sex
Sexual orientation
Smoker/non smoker
Psychological characteristics of the speaker
Arousal (relaxed, hurried)
Competence
Emotional status/mood
Intelligence
Personality
Psychiatric status
Stress
Truthfulness
Social characteristics of the speaker
Education
Occupation
Regional origin
Role in conversational setting
Social status

factors (Scherer, 1979) based on voice quality cues. Vocal cues also indicate order of turn-taking in conversation (Schegloff, 1998; Wells & Macfarlane, 1998), and resolve sentential ambiguities (Kjelgaard, Titone, & Wingfield, 1999; Schafer et al., 2000).

The measurement of vocal quality thus plays an important role in a broad range of disciplines, and topics related to the perception and measurement of voice quality have wide-reaching implications. As a result, scholars from many different disciplines have studied voice production and perception. Table 14.2 lists some of these disciplines, with a sample of their associated research questions. These topics encompass much of human existence, and indicate how central voice quality is to that existence.

Early linguistic theorists (e.g., Denes & Pinson, 1993; Sapir, 1926–7) were also interested in voice quality, but treated voice as an accidental, nonlinguistic feature of performance individuated by the particular speaker and context. Such

Table 14.2 Disciplines incorporating the study of voice quality

Discipline	Some typical research questions
Acoustics	How can reliable and meaningful acoustic measures of unstable voice signals be derived?
Animal behavior	How do non-human animals recognize kin? What social information is communicated by voice?
Biology	How has the vocal tract evolved? What is the biological significance of vocalization?
Computer science, signal processing, electrical engineering	How can voice signals be transmitted efficiently? How can voices be synthesized convincingly? How can accuracy of computer voice recognizers be improved?
Forensic science, law enforcement	How reliable is "earwitness" testimony? How can the identity of the speaker in a recording be verified? Can truthfulness be judged from voice?
Linguistics, phonetics	How does voice quality affect the meaning of a spoken message? How do speakers and listeners produce and perceive differences in voice quality?
Medicine:	
Dentistry	How does tooth loss affect vocalization?
Developmental biology	How and when do infants learn to recognize their mothers or other people? What social cues are conveyed using voice information?
Gerontology	How does voice quality change with aging? What changes are normal, and which signal disease?
Neurology	How do neurological disorders affect voice quality? Can neurological disorders be detected in the human voice? What information conveyed in voice is disrupted by brain damage?
Obstetrics	How do babies learn to recognize their mothers' voices in utero? What other voice information are they using?
Otolaryngology	How is voice produced? How can different aspects of voice be quantified? How can voice disorders be detected and treated? How can effects of treatment be documented?
Pediatrics	How do babies bond with mothers? How do children learn to recognize voice identity and vocally transmitted social and psychological cues?
Physiology	How do the vocal organs function? How is phonation controlled?

Table 14.2 *(cont'd)*

Surgery	How do surgical interventions in the vocal tract affect the ability to vocalize? Can surgical intervention treat transgendered voices?
Music:	
Singing	How does singing voice differ from speaking voice? What makes a good singing voice good? How can different aspects of singing voice be quantified?
Vocal coaching	How do trained voices differ from untrained voices? How can vocal disorders be avoided?
Physics	How and why do laryngeal tissues vibrate? How do changes in patterns of vibration correspond to changes in sound?
Psychology:	
Cognitive psychology	How does voice quality affect spoken word recognition? How do speakers recognize voices? What cues in voice signal affective and attitudinal meanings?
Clinical psychology	Can depression or psychopathology be reliably detected in the human voice? Can personality or emotional state be judged from voice?
Neuropsychology	What brain mechanisms are involved in the perception and production of voice? How are familiar and unfamiliar voices perceived? How are mood, motivation, and emotion related to vocal cues in brain organization?
Psychophysics	How do listeners respond to complex auditory signals? What acoustic voice features are perceptually important, and under what circumstances? How do features interact to determine what listeners hear?
Social psychology	How do voices signal social relationships? How does voice information direct conversational turn-taking? How are nonliteral and sarcastic meanings communicated by voice?
Speech science	How are normal voice and speech produced? What measurements of normal function are appropriate? How are pitch and loudness controlled? How do different parts of the production mechanism interact? How do respiration and articulation interact with voice?
Speech pathology	How does vocal pathology affect voice quality? How can voice disorders be prevented and treated behaviorally? How can voices be rehabilitated? How can treatment efficacy be assessed?

nonlinguistic aspects of speech were viewed as carrying extralinguistic information about the speaker, but were not considered part of the system of language per se. In this view, speaker-specific information in spoken messages was extraneous material that had to be stripped away or perceptually normalized to reach the underlying linguistic message projected by the talker. This assumption has been superceded by evidence that voice quality cues interact significantly with linguistic events to determine meaning (e.g., Goldinger, Pisoni, & Logan, 1991; Mullennix, Pisoni, & Martin, 1989), even in languages without phonemic voice quality contrasts. These interactions take many forms. Recent studies suggest that word prosody is represented in the mental lexicon, and that it is utilized by listeners in perceiving speech (Lindfield, Wingfield, & Goodglass, 1999). Grammatical contrasts can be conveyed by voice quality (Crystal, 1969; Cutler, Dahan, & van Donselaar, 1997; Kjelgaard et al., 1999; Ladd, 1996; Raczaszek et al., 1999; Schafer et al., 2000). In a given speech sample, speakers' attitudes – contempt, doubt, enthusiasm – toward the accompanying verbal content, toward themselves, or toward the listener may be revealed in paralinguistic cues, thereby affecting the overall meaning of the message. Two powerful resources of intonation are irony and sarcasm, which may actually cause the message to communicate a meaning opposite to the apparent lexical content. A propositional statement transmitted by someone who appears, by voice, to be lying, differs in truth value, impact, importance, and viability from the same message carried by a sincere-sounding voice. (Conversely, sociopaths aim to project sincerity, however falsely, by speaking more quietly than controls (Louth et al., 1998).) Experimental data also showed that tape-recorded statements incidentally spoken in a male voice were rated as more important than the same statements spoken in a female voice (Geiselman & Bellezza, 1977). Finally, substantial evidence indicates that learned familiarity with a talker's voice facilitates deciphering the spoken message itself (e.g., Nygaard & Pisoni, 1998; see Luce & McLennan, this volume).

Thus, it appears that voice characteristics serve important functions that have previously been treated as purely linguistic. It follows that the traditional theoretical separation between linguistic and paralinguistic aspects of the vocal signal cannot be strictly maintained. Measuring vocal quality is therefore important for understanding speech perception as well as many other aspects of human and animal behavior.

14.2 What Is Voice? The Definitional Dilemma

Although a clear definition of voice is a prerequisite to its study, the broad range of functions subserved by voice has made it difficult to provide a single, useful, all-purpose definition. As Sundberg (1987) noted, everyone knows what voice is until they try to pin it down, and several senses of the term are in common use.

Definitions of voice fall into two general classes. Voice can be very narrowly defined as "sound produced by vibration of the vocal folds," excluding the effects of vocal tract resonances, vocal tract excitation from turbulent noise, and everything else that occurs during speech production. This definition corresponds approximately to the linguistic voicing feature, referring to the vibrational state of the vocal folds during production of vowels and voiced consonants. Authors in this tradition typically distinguish voice from speech, consistent with Sapir's distinction above.

Anatomical constraints make it difficult to study voice as narrowly defined. Some authors have used the output of a laryngograph as an approximation to the laryngeal source (e.g., Abberton & Fourcin, 1978), and experiments with excised larynges (e.g., Berry, Montequin, & Tayama, 2001) allow direct access to laryngeal vibrations. However, most authors adopt the practical expedient of controlling for the effects of the vocal tract on voice by restricting voice samples to steady state vowels (usually /a/). This practice allows experimenters to study natural-sounding phonation, while holding non-laryngeal factors constant. This approach is the most common implementation of narrow definitions of voice, and we will use this meaning ourselves in what follows.

Voice can also be defined very broadly as essentially synonymous with speech. Besides details of phonatory quality, listeners collate a very large amount of acoustic-auditory material when they gather paralinguistic information from the ongoing speech of individual talkers. Articulatory details, pitch and amplitude variations, and temporal patterning all contribute to how a speaker "sounds" (Banse & Scherer, 1996). Broad definitions of voice aim to reflect this fact, and generally portray voice as the result of a complex sequence of cognitive, physiological, and acoustic events, the familiar "speech chain" (Denes & Pinson, 1993). Sound is produced by the coordinated action of the respiratory system, vocal folds, tongue, jaw, lips, and soft palate. These actions produce an acoustic signal, which travels to the ears of the listener and back to the speaker in the form of feedback. The auditory percept (a stretch of speech) is first peripheral, within mechanisms and physiology of the ear, followed by neurological activation of the eighth cranial nerve and the auditory pathway to the receiving areas in the brain. As increasingly complex cognitive processes are invoked, the stretch of speech under analysis may be described in terms of a number of complex messages (Table 14.1). In some perspectives, everything subsumed in this depiction of speech is coterminous with the broader notion of voice, sometimes referred to as a "voice pattern" to distinguish it from the narrower notion of voice as vocal fold vibration. The information voice patterns convey (more or less successfully) about affect, attitude, psychological state, pragmatics, grammatical function, sociological status, and personal identity emerges from this complex enfolding of phonatory, phonetic, and temporal detail.

Precisely which stage in this chain of events receives focus depends on the interest of the practitioner or experimenter, or on the task faced by the listener. For example, surgeons typically approach voice in terms of physiological function, with secondary concern for the exact perceived quality that results from phonation. A typical physiologically-oriented definition characterizes voice as "sounds generated by the voice organ . . . by means of an air stream from the lungs, modified first by the vibrating vocal folds, and then by the rest of the larynx, and the pharynx, the mouth, and sometimes also the nasal cavities" (Sundberg, 1987, p. 3). Engineers are often interested in the acoustic waveform that correlates with vocal sound, and therefore define voice in terms of acoustic attributes. In diametric contrast, psychologists are not especially interested in how the voice is physically produced, but instead define voice in terms of what a listener hears. Speech scientists and animal biologists may focus on either aspect.

Defining voice quality is equally problematic. The overall quality (or timbre) of a sound is traditionally defined as "that attribute of auditory sensation in terms of which a listener can judge that two sounds similarly presented and having the same loudness and pitch are dissimilar" (ANSI, 1960, p. 45; cf. Helmholtz, 1885). By this definition, quality is multidimensional, including the spectral envelope and its changes in time, fluctuations of amplitude and fundamental frequency, and the extent to which the signal is periodic or aperiodic (Plomp, 1976). This large number of degrees of freedom makes it difficult to operationalize the concept of quality, particularly across tasks. According to the ANSI definition, quality is a perceptual response in the psychophysical task of determining that two sounds are dissimilar, and it is unclear how this definition might generalize to other common, seemingly-related tasks like speaker recognition or evaluation of a single stimulus. Evidence also suggests that quality may not be independent of frequency and amplitude (Krumhansl & Iverson, 1992; Melara & Marks, 1990), as the ANSI definition seemingly requires. Finally, this definition is essentially negative: it states that quality is not pitch and loudness, but does not indicate what it does include (Plomp, 1976). Such complications have led to frequent criticism of the ANSI definition, which some claim amounts to no definition at all (see, e.g., Bregman, 1990, for review).

Chagrin about this situation has led some voice researchers to adopt definitions of quality that simply echo the narrow or broad definitions of voice described above, so that voice quality is characterized in physiological terms. Consistent with narrow definitions of voice, quality may be defined as the perceptual impression created by the vibration of the vocal folds. More broadly, voice quality may be considered the perceived result of coordinated action of the respiratory system, vocal folds, tongue, jaw, lips, and soft palate. For example, Abercrombie viewed voice quality as "those characteristics which are present more or less all the time that a person is talking: it is a quasi-permanent quality running through all the sound that issues from his mouth" (1967, p. 91). Similarly, Laver referred to voice quality as "a cumulative abstraction over a period of time of a speaker-characterizing quality, which is gathered from the momentary and spasmodic fluctuations of short-term articulations used by the speaker for linguistic and paralinguistic communication" (1980, p. 1).

Such definitions do very little to specify listeners' contributions to quality, which are essential to defining what is after all a perceptual phenomenon. For example, the perceptual importance of different aspects of a voice depends on context, attention, a listener's background, and other factors (Gerratt et al., 1993; Kreiman et al., 1992), and is affected by the listening task (Gerratt & Kreiman, 2001; Gerratt et al., 1993). Thus, the measured response to a given voice signal is not necessarily constant across listeners or occasions.

Some of the difficulty that arises when contemplating the nature of quality may be due to the fact that quality is often treated as analogous to pitch and loudness, the two other perceptual attributes of sound specified in the ANSI definition. Authors often discuss *the* pitch or *the* loudness of a signal, presumably because these factors can be scaled unidimensionally, from low to high or faint to strong (Plomp, 1976). In fact, some authors even treat pitch and fundamental frequency (F0), or loudness and intensity, as synonymous in informal writing. However, quality is multidimensional. It cannot be successfully scaled unidimensionally, and it does not possess a unique acoustic determinant. Given this fact, the perceptual effect created by a voice signal will always depend on factors like task demands, and listener attention will vary across the multiple facets of the signal, so that some are more important than others from occasion to occasion. For this reason, a single perceived quality may not consistently result from a given signal, relative to the listener. In contrast, pitch and loudness do not ordinarily vary in this way, because of their unidimensional nature.

The strength of the ANSI definition is that it treats sound quality as the result of a perceptual process rather than as a fixed quantity, and highlights the importance of both listeners and signals in determining quality. Listeners usually listen to voices in order to gather information about the environment, and the information they attend to varies with their purpose and with the information available from a particular utterance. Considered in this light, the ANSI definition has distinct advantages; in fact, its limitations can be reduced by broadening the definition to include different tasks, rather than narrowing its focus to include only a small set of specific acoustic variables. Voice quality may best be thought of as an interaction between a listener and a signal, such that the listener takes advantage of whatever acoustic information is available to achieve a particular perceptual goal. Which aspects of the signal are important will depend on the task, the characteristics of the stimuli, the listener's background, perceptual habits, and so on. Given the many kinds of information listeners extract from voice signals, it is not surprising that these characteristics vary from task to task, voice to voice, and listener to listener.

Studies of familiar voice recognition (Remez, Fellowes, & Rubin, 1997; van Dommelen, 1990) highlight the importance of signal/listener interactions in voice perception. Specific articulatory information is key to identifying some individual voices, but not relevant to others (Van Lancker, Kreiman, & Wickens, 1985), such that three conditions of signal alteration (backwards, rate changed to slower or faster speech) affected the recognizability of individual voices differently. Perceptual processing of voice quality differs qualitatively depending on whether the listener is familiar or unfamiliar with the voice (see Kreiman, 1997, for review). Listeners' perceptual strategies can thus be expected to vary depending on the differential familiarity of the voices. Listeners' attention to different cues to voice identity also depends on the total voice pattern in which the cue operates (Van Lancker, Kreiman, & Emmorey, 1985; Van Lancker et al., 1985), so that the importance of a single cue varies across voices as well as listeners. Definitions of quality that focus on aspects of production or on the signal cannot account for such effects. Voice quality is the result of perceptual processes, and must be defined in terms of both signals and listeners.

14.3 Measuring Vocal Quality

Given the difficulties inherent in defining voice and vocal quality, it is not surprising that considerable confusion also surrounds quality measurement. By its nature, quality is perceptual: it is the psychological impression created by a physical stimulus, and thus depends on both the listener and the voice, as discussed above. However, the psychoacoustic study of complex multidimensional auditory signals is in its infancy (e.g., Melara & Marks, 1990; see Yost et al., 1989, for review), and little research has examined the perceptual processes listeners apply to voice signals. Research has focused instead on defining static descriptive labels for voices. In this approach, vocal quality is treated as if it can be decomposed into a set of specific qualities, whose presence or absence characterize a speaker's voice.

The most common approach to the problem of specifying voice quality is simply to create a long list of terms to describe listeners' impressions. Listeners then assess quality by indicating the extent to which a voice possesses each feature. (Alternatively, listeners may simply mark the features that are relevant to the case at hand.) Terms in such lists tend to be rather mixed in their level of description, and may describe voices visually (e.g., brilliant, dark), kinesthetically (strained, tight), physically (heavy, thin, pointed), aesthetically (pleasing, faulty), with reference to anatomy (pectoral, nasal), and so on (e.g., Orlikoff, 1999).

These dimensional approaches to measuring voice quality depend on descriptive traditions rather than theory, and have changed very little in nearly two thousand years. Table 14.3 includes three lists of features for voices, one venerable (Julius Pollux, second century AD; cited by Austin, 1806) and two modern (Gelfer, 1988; Moore, 1964, cited by Pannbacker, 1984). A few differences exist among these lists. For example, the oldest list includes terms related to the personality and emotional state of the speaker (confused, doleful), and terms related to articulation and rhetorical ability (articulate, distinct), reflecting the importance of rhetoric in Roman culture (see Gray, 1943, or Laver, 1981, for review). More modern compendia include terms like "breathy" and "nasal" that are commonly used in the study of vocal pathology. However, similarities among the lists are striking. Although alignment of terms across lists is approximate, only 8 of 40 terms lack at least one close counterpart in the other lists, mostly due to the loss of terms for articulation or emotion (persuasive, doleful, articulate) in the modern vocabulary for voice, as noted above.

Redundancies and ambiguities abound in such lists of terms, which tend to be exhaustive rather than efficient. To address this problem, some researchers have applied factor analysis to reduce large lists of overlapping features to small non-redundant sets. In such studies, listeners evaluate each of a set of voices on a number of rating scales like those in Table 14.3. Two general approaches have been used in voice quality research. In the first (Holmgren, 1967), voice samples (spoken passages of text) are rated on a relatively small set of semantic differential scales that have been selected to represent an a priori underlying set of factors. Because no standard factors or dimensions have been established for voice quality, such studies have adopted factors (e.g., potency, evaluation, activity) and scales (e.g., sweet/sour, strong/weak, hot/cold; Osgood, Suci, & Tannenbaum, 1957) that are theoretically related, but not obviously applicable to voice quality. Alternatively, investigators have asked listeners to rate voice samples (again, spoken sentences or passages of text) on large sets of voice quality scales that do not derive from an a priori factor structure (Fagel, van Herpt, & Boves, 1983; Voiers, 1964). Such exploratory studies attempt to ensure that all possible perceptual factors are represented in the derived factors by oversampling the semantic space for voice quality.

In either case, statistical analysis of listeners' ratings produces a small number of orthogonal factors that capture as much of the variance in the underlying

Table 14.3 Venerable and modern labels for voice quality

After Julius Pollux, second century AD[a]	*Moore, 1964*[b]	*Gelfer, 1988*
High (*altam*)	–	High
Powerful (*excelsam*)	Ringing	Strong, intense, loud
Clear (*claram*)	Clear, light, white	Clear
Extensive (*latam*)	Rich	Full
Deep (*gravam*)	Deep	Resonant, low
Brilliant (*splendidam*)	Bright, brilliant	Bright, vibrant
Pure (*mundatam*)	–	–
Smooth (*suavam*)	Cool, smooth, velvety	Smooth
Sweet (*dulcem*)	–	–
Attractive (*illecebrosam*)	Pleasing	Pleasant
Melodious, cultivated (*exquisitam*)	Mellow	Mellow, musical
Persuasive (*persuasibilem*)	–	–
Engaging, tractable (*pellacem, tractabilem*)	Open, warm	Easy, relaxed
Flexible (*flexilem*)	–	Well-modulated
Executive (*volubilem*)	–	Efficient
Sonorous, harmonious (*stridulam*)	Chesty, golden, harmonious, orotund, round, pectoral	Balanced, open
Distinct (*manifestam*)	–	–
Perspicuous, articulate (*perspicuam*)	–	–
Obscure (*nigram*)	Dark, gutteral, throaty	Husky, gutteral, throaty
Dull (*fuscam*)	Dead, dull, heavy	Dull, heavy, thick
Unpleasing (*injucundam*)	–	Unpleasant
Small, feeble (*exilem, pusillam*)	Breathy	Breathy, soft, babyish
Thin (*angustam*)	Constricted, heady, pinched, reedy, shallow, thin	Thin
Faint (*difficilem auditu, molestam*)	Whispery	Weak
Hollow, indistinct (*subsurdam, obscuram*)	Covered, hollow	Muffled
Confused (*confusam*)	–	–
Discordant (*absonam*)	Blatany, whiney	Strident, whining
Unharmonious, uncultivated (*inconcinnam, neglectam*)	Coarse, crude	Coarse, gruff
Unattractive, unmanageable (*intractabilem*)	–	Shaky

(*cont'd* on p. 348)

Table 14.3 (*cont'd*)

After Julius Pollux, second century AD[a]	*Moore, 1964*[b]	*Gelfer, 1988*
Uninteresting (*inpersuasibilem*)	Blanched, flat	–
Rigid (*rigidam*)	Hard, tight	Monotonous, constricted, flat
Harsh (*asperam*)	Harsh, strident, twangy	Harsh, gravelly
Cracked (*distractam*)	Pingy, raspy	Strained, raspy, grating, creaky
Doleful (*tristem*)	–	–
Unsound, hoarse (*infirmam, raucam*)	Faulty, hoarse, poor, raucous, rough	Hoarse, rough, labored, noisy
Brassy (*aeneam*)	Buzzy, clangy, metallic	Metallic
Shrill, sharp (*acutam*)	Cutting, hooty, piercing, pointed, sharp, shrill	Shrill, sharp
–	Nasal	Nasal
–	Denasal	Denasal
–	Toothy	–

[a] Cited in Austin, 1806.
[b] Cited in Pannbacker, 1984.

ratings as possible. Each original scale is given a weight on each factor, so that scales that are strongly related to the factor receive large weights, and scales that are weakly related to the factor receive low weights. Factors are then given summary labels based on the scales that they comprise. For example, a factor with large weights on scales like "fast," "agitated," "tense," "busy," and "exciting" might be labeled "animation" (Voiers, 1964), while one with large weights on scales like "vivacious," "expressive," "melodious," "cheerful," "beautiful," "rich," and "active" might be labeled "melodiousness" (Fagel et al., 1983).

Voice feature schemes derived from factor analysis do have obvious advantages over large lists of terms. Such protocols typically include three to six factors (Table 14.4), and thus are manageable for listeners and investigators alike. In theory, factors are independent of one another, reducing concerns about redundancies or overlap across scales, while at the same time they capture much of the information in the scalar ratings, so economy is achieved with minimal loss of information. Finally, this approach preserves the descriptive tradition of quality assessment, because factors are defined in terms of the underlying scales. Thus, factor analytic approaches bring the impression of scientific rigor to the familiar descriptive approach of quality assessment.

Many limitations to such approaches are also apparent. First, results of factor analytic studies depend on the input scales and stimuli. That is, a factor will not emerge unless that factor is represented in the set of rating scales and is also perceptually relevant for the specific voices and utterances studied. Studies often employ restricted populations of speakers, small sets of voices, and short stimuli; for example, the well-known GRBAS[1] protocol was developed from the results of

Table 14.4 Factor analytic studies of normal voice quality

Speakers	*Stimuli*	*Listeners*	*Input scales*	*Derived factors*	*Reference*
5 male, 5 female	spoken passage	235	35 7-point bipolar	5 factors: melodiousness articulation quality voice quality pitch tempo	Fagel et al. (1983)
16 male	sentences	32	49 7-point bipolar	4 factors: clarity roughness magnitude animation	Voiers (1964)
10 male	spoken passage	20	12 scales representing 4 underlying factors	2 factors: (1) slow/fast, resting/busy, intense/mild, simple/complex; (2) clean/dirty, beautiful/ugly	Holmgren (1967)

factor analyses that used five steady-state vowels produced by only 16 speakers (Isshiki et al., 1969; see Hirano, 1981, for review). Such restrictions can significantly limit the extent to which results can be generalized to the full spectrum of vocal qualities, and results of factor analyses may vary substantially from study to study. The validity of the factors as perceptual features also depends on the validity of the underlying scales, which has never been established. Thus, even a large-scale factor analysis (or multiple analyses) will not necessarily result in a valid or reliable rating instrument for voice quality. Idiosyncrasies in labeling the factors may also obscure differences among studies. For example, in studies of pathological voice quality Isshiki et al. (1969) found a "breathiness" factor that loaded highly on the scales dry, hard, excited, pointed, cold, choked, rough, cloudy, sharp, poor, and bad, while a "breathiness" factor reported by Hammarberg et al. (1980) corresponded to the scales breathy, wheezing, lack of timbre, moments of aphonia, husky, and not creaky. Finally, Voiers (1964) reported perceptual factors related to reliable constant listener biases and interactions between specific voices and listeners, in addition to factors related only to the target voices. Emergence of such factors suggests that an adequate perceptual model cannot be framed solely in terms of the stimuli, but must also account separately for differences among listeners. Overall, it thus appears that factor analysis has not convincingly identified scales for vocal quality that are independent and valid.

Dependence on underlying descriptive terminology can be avoided by deriving perceptual features for voices through multidimensional scaling (MDS), rather than factor analysis. In MDS listeners assess the similarity of the experimental voice stimuli directly, without reference to scales for specific qualities. The analysis produces an n-dimensional perceptual space from these similarity ratings, such that distances between voices in the space are proportional to the rated similarities (more similar = closer together). Dimensions in this space are then interpreted, usually by examining correlations between rated and/or measured characteristics of the input stimuli and stimulus coordinates or clustering of stimuli in the space. Through this process, exploratory MDS can reveal how overall vocal quality (as it determines similarities between voices) relates to scales for particular qualities. Discovery of a dimension that is highly associated with some specific quality provides evidence for the "psychological reality" of that particular quality as an important vocal feature.

Studies applying MDS to study normal vocal quality are listed in Table 14.5. As with factor analysis, results have varied substantially from study to study. Some of these differences can be attributed to differences in study design. Note that three of these eleven studies used vowels as stimuli, while the rest used longer, more complex speech samples, which yield additional information and address questions about the broader definition of voice quality. Dimensions associated with stimulus duration or pitch variability typically emerge when sentence stimuli are employed, rather than steady-state vowels. Differences have also been reported in the perceptual features derived for male and female voices (Murry & Singh, 1980; Singh & Murry, 1978). However, variability in solutions has emerged due to factors other than stimulus characteristics. In particular, variability in the perceptual dimensions that emerge from studies of fixed sets of stimuli indicate that listeners differ both as individuals and as groups in the perceptual strategies they apply to voices (Gelfer, 1993; cf. Kreiman, Gerratt, & Precoda, 1990, or Kreiman et al., 1992, who studied pathological voice quality). Thus, it does not appear that any specific features are always important for characterizing the quality of all voices under all circumstances.

Scaling solutions may also leave large amounts of variance unaccounted for, and published reports may explain less than half of the variance in the underlying similarity judgments, even for simple vowel stimuli (Murry & Singh, 1980; Murry, Singh, & Sargent, 1977). This may occur because of the limited resolution of MDS: The number of extractable dimensions depends on the number of stimuli studied, which generally equals 20 or less (although additional perceptual features may also be derived from clustering of stimuli in the space). It is possible that more dimensions (providing more explanatory power) exist in the data than can be extracted due to the small numbers of voices involved. Alternatively, large amounts of variance may remain unexplained because the dimensional model of quality implied by MDS and factor analytic studies is not a good description of how quality is perceived.

A study of pathological voice quality (Kreiman & Gerratt, 1996) supports the latter explanation. In that study, listeners judged the similarity of all possible pairs of vowel productions obtained from very large sets of speakers (80 males and 80 females) representing a variety of diagnoses and ranging in quality from nearly normal to severely disordered. In this study, use of vowel stimuli limited the

Table 14.5 Multidimensional scaling studies of normal voice quality

Speakers	*Stimuli*	*Listeners*	*Derived dimensions*	*Reference*
8 male	Vowels	6	4 dimensions: F0 glottal source spectrum jitter formant frequencies	Matsumoto et al., 1973
9 male	Phrase	15	3 dimensions: F0 intensity intonation pattern	Carterette and Barnebey, 1975
20 male	Word	11	4 dimensions: F0 utterance duration speaker's age "superior" vs. "inferior" voice quality	Walden et al., 1978
10 male, 10 female	Sentence	10	3 dimensions: speaker sex pitch (male voices only) utterance duration (female voices only)	Singh and Murry, 1978
20 male	Vowel	10	4 dimensions: pitch formant frequencies (2 dimensions) perceived nasality	Murry and Singh, 1980
20 female	Vowel	10	4 dimensions: pitch perceived breathiness formant frequencies perceived effort	Murry and Singh, 1980
20 male	Passage	10	4 dimensions: pitch and effort perceived hoarseness formant frequencies 1 uninterpreted dimension	Murry and Singh, 1980

(*cont'd* on p. 352)

Table 14.5 *(cont'd)*

Speakers	*Stimuli*	*Listeners*	*Derived dimensions*	*Reference*
20 female	Passage	10	4 dimensions: perceived effort and nasality pitch utterance duration 1 uninterpreted dimension	Murry and Singh, 1980
10 male	Sentence	24	4 dimensions: perceived masculinity perceived creakiness perceived variability perceived mood	Kreiman and Papcun (1991)
20 female	Sentence	20 speech-language pathologists	5 dimensions: pitch loudness perceived age perceived variability voice quality	Gelfer, 1993
20 female	Sentence	20 untrained	2 dimensions: pitch and resonant quality variability, age, and rate	Gelfer, 1993

information available to listeners, consistent with the narrow definition of voice, so that the perceptual task was somewhat simpler than with connected speech stimuli. Despite this simplification, multidimensional scaling solutions for male and female voices each accounted for less than half of the variance in the underlying data, and revealed two-dimensional solutions in which the most severely pathological voices were separated from voices with milder pathology. Separate analyses of the data from individual listeners accounted for more variance (56–83%). However, stimuli did not disperse in these perceptual spaces along continuous scale-like linear dimensions, but instead clustered together in groups that lacked subjective unifying percepts. Different voices clustered together for each listener; in fact, no two voices ever occurred in the same cluster for all listeners, suggesting that listeners lacked a common notion of what constitutes similarity with respect to voice quality, even when quality is narrowly defined. If listeners lack a common perceptual space for voice quality in its most restricted sense, then a single set of perceptual features for voice quality more broadly defined is not likely to be discoverable.

Note that all MDS studies of voice to date have been exploratory, in that experimenters used sets of heterogeneous voices to discover the perceptual dimensions of vocal quality. In principle, experimenters could also structure a stimulus set according to some hypothesized perceptual model and then use

MDS experimentally to determine whether listeners can actually recover the input dimensions. Such applications have not appeared in studies of vocal quality (see, e.g., Shepard, 1972, for classic examples of experimental MDS analyses examining the perceptual validity of linguistic distinctive features). An experimental approach could also be used to provide evidence for the perceptual importance of different instrumental measures of voice, as a step toward validation of such measures. Such studies also remain for future research.

In the absence of empirical evidence for the validity of particular descriptors or dimensions, it is unclear why some should be included, and others excluded, in a descriptive framework for vocal quality. Further, each traditional descriptive label is holistic and independent, and labels do not combine to form a decomposed, permutable set. This makes it difficult to understand precisely how qualities differ from one another, or how seemingly similar qualities are related. Finally, in this tradition it is often unclear how quality relates to other parts of the speech chain. In particular, there is no formal theoretical linkage between a given quality and the physiological configuration that produced it (although terms like "nasal" may imply that such a linkage exists).

The phonetic/articulatory features for voice quality proposed by Laver (1980, 2000; Ball, Esling, & Dickson, 2000) were designed in response to these limitations. In this approach, voice quality, as mentioned above, is characterized as "quasi-permanent" and derived cumulatively throughout an individual's vocal sound production (Abercrombie, 1967, p. 91). It is then described in terms of the global long-term physiological configuration that (hypothetically) underlies the overall sound of a speaker's voice. Laryngeal and supralaryngeal aspects of voice are both specified, and are assumed to be auditorily separable. The specific features are derived from phonetic theory, and include laryngeal raising and lowering, lip rounding and spreading, jaw position (open, closed), tongue tip and body position (raised, lowered, advanced, retracted), pharyngeal constriction or expansion, velum position, and glottal state (modal voice, falsetto, whisper, creak, breathiness, harshness) (see Laver, 1980, 2000, for more details). This model of voice quality was originally developed to describe normal voices (Laver, 1980), but has been adapted as a clinical voice evaluation protocol called "vocal profile analysis" that is widely used in Britain (Laver et al., 1981; Wirz & Mackenzie Beck, 1995).

Vocal profile analysis is analytic, consistent with phonetic models of speech production, and nearly exhaustive in the physiological domain. Because quasi-independent features (or "settings") can combine in different ways, the system can be used to describe a broad range of voice qualities in a single framework, rather than applying vague terms whose relationships to each other are unclear. Thus, for example, "hoarse" voice might appear in this system as "deep, (loud), harsh/ventricular, whispery voice," or "gruff" voice might become "deep, harsh, whispery, creaky voice" (Laver, 1968). The primary limitation of this system is the fact that it models perception in terms of speech production processes without established or documented reference to a listener. That is, by describing voice quality in detailed terms of the supposed underlying physiological configuration, profile analysis indicates where perceptual information about quality *might* be. However, it does not indicate which of the many aspects specified are meaningful, or, indeed, perceptible to listeners, how listeners actually use different features to assess quality, whether (or when, or why) some features might be more important than others, or how dimensions interact perceptually. The assumption that listeners are able to separate different features auditorily is also questionable, particularly given recent evidence that listeners have difficulty isolating individual dimensions of complex voice patterns (Fry, 1968; Kreiman & Gerratt, 2000a).

14.4 Limitations of Traditional Quality Assessment Protocols

The results reviewed above indicate that the validity of dimensional and featural protocols for assessing voice quality remains highly questionable. These protocols model voice quality solely in terms of the voice itself, although couching many of the descriptive labels in perceptual terms. They also assume an ideal and fixed listener. Most of these approaches imply that voice quality can reasonably be represented as a list or grouping of descriptors or dimensions – that there is a list of attributes that listeners can and do attend to, and that the same set adequately describes all voices. Whether quality is broadly or narrowly construed, such frameworks imply a well-defined perceptual space for voice quality, applicable to all voices and true for all listeners, which listeners all exploit in essentially the same way.

However, substantial evidence and theoretical considerations contradict these requirements. A well-defined, theoretically motivated set of features for voice has not emerged, despite many years' research; and listeners apparently exploit vocal signals in unique ways. Data thus suggest that a common perceptual space for voices cannot be defined, so efforts to specify a perceptually valid set of scales for voice quality are unlikely to succeed.

A further difficulty with dimensional protocols is their unreliability as measurement tools. Most studies of listener reliability have focused on pathological voices, due to the importance of scalar ratings in clinical assessments of voice quality (e.g., Gerratt et al., 1991). Across studies, scales, and statistics, average interrater reliability has ranged from extremely low ($r^2 = 0.04$) to extremely high (100% of ratings within +/− one scale value) (see Kreiman et al., 1993, for review). Analyses of the reliability with which listeners judge individual voices indicate that listeners almost never agree in their ratings of a single voice. Even using the simplest of phonated stimuli, the likelihood that two raters would agree in their ratings of moderately pathological voices on various 7-point scales averaged 0.21 (where chance is 0.14); further, more than 60% (and as much as 78%) of the variance in voice quality ratings was attributable to factors other than differences among voices in the quality being rated (Kreiman & Gerratt, 1998). The voice profile analysis system is also less than perfectly reliable. Wirz and Mackenzie Beck (1995) reported that the majority of 242 listeners who completed a three-day training course in the system's use rated voices within one scale value of a target score for 52–65% of items in a post-test. Studies of rating reliability for normal voices are less common, but not more encouraging. For example, Gelfer (1988) asked listeners to rate 20 normal female voices (speaking sentences) on 16 different quality scales. Kendall's coefficient of concordance for these data ranged from 0.14 to 0.69 across scales, with values averaging 0.33 overall.

In summary, despite a long history of research, significant difficulties continue to plague traditional approaches to vocal quality measurement. Such approaches suffer from possibly irresolvable issues of rating reliability and validity. It is not clear what if any features characterize quality, or how traditional descriptors or dimensions relate to overall quality (broadly or narrowly construed) or to each other. More modern articulatory distinctive-feature approaches are analytical and motivated by phonetic theory, but while they enumerate articulatory possibilities, they do not accommodate listeners' behavior. Featural systems in general suffer from this limitation, because they model quality as if it inheres in voices, without also accounting for such listener-dependent factors as attention, experience, and response bias.

Given the difficulties, both theoretical and operational, inherent in measuring voice quality, some authors (particularly those studying pathological voices) have argued that perceptual measures of voice should be replaced with instrumental measures (see, e.g., Orlikoff, 1999, for review). In contrast to perceptual measures, instrumental measures of acoustic, aerodynamic, or physiological events promise precision, reliability, and replicability. Considerations like these have motivated several measurement systems for voice, including the Dysphonia Severity Index (Wuyts et al., 2000) and the Hoarseness Diagram (Frohlich et al., 2000). However, because vocal quality is the perceptual response to a stimulus, development of instrumental protocols for measuring quality ultimately depends on our ability to define quality in a way that accounts for perceptual factors that introduce variability in listeners' judgments. Although it might be possible to devise objective methods to quantify specific quality dimensions, it is more difficult to set up general rules specifying which dimensions are selected and how they combine to produce a final evaluative judgment (Bodden, 1997). Further, no comprehensive theory exists describing the relationships between physiology, acoustics, and vocal quality, so it is difficult to establish which instrumental measures ought to correspond to perceptually meaningful differences in vocal quality, or why such associations should exist. Existing research has been limited largely to correlational studies, which have produced highly variable results that are difficult to interpret. (See Kreiman & Gerratt, 2000b, for extended discussion.)

14.5 Alternatives to Dimensional and Featural Measurement Systems for Voice Quality

Finding valid and reliable alternatives to traditional voice quality scaling methods requires hypotheses about the sources of listener disagreements, so that psychophysical techniques can be developed to determine the sources of such variability, and ultimately control them. Previous studies of pathological voices (Gerratt et al., 1993; Kreiman & Gerratt, 2000a) suggest that traditional perceptual scaling methods are best understood as a kind of matching task, in which external stimuli (the voices) are compared to stored mental representations that serve as internal standards for the various rating scales. These idiosyncratic internal standards appear to vary with listeners' previous experience with voices (Kreiman et al., 1990; Verdonck-de Leeuw, 1998) and with the context in which a judgment is made (Gerratt et al., 1993; cf. Gescheider & Hughson, 1991), and vary substantially across listeners as well as within a given listener (Gerratt et al., 1993; Kreiman et al., 1993). Listeners may invoke one or more of a set of standards or templates to provide the internal matching vehicle. Severity of vocal pathology, difficulty isolating individual dimensions in complex perceptual contexts, task demands, and experiential factors can also influence perceptual measures of voice (de Krom, 1994; Kreiman & Gerratt, 2000a). These factors add uncontrolled variability to scalar ratings of vocal quality, and contribute to listener disagreements.

A protocol that does not rely on internal standards, and that makes it easier for listeners to focus their attention appropriately and consistently, would eliminate many of these sources of listener disagreement. One such approach (Gerratt & Kreiman, 2001) applies speech synthesis in a method-of-adjustment task. This allows listeners to vary acoustic parameters to create an acceptable auditory match to a voice stimulus. When a listener chooses a match to a test stimulus, the synthesis settings parametrically represent the listener's perception of voice quality. Because listeners directly compare each synthetic token they create to the target voice, they need not refer to internal standards, which may be varying and incomplete, for particular voice qualities. Further, listeners can manipulate acoustic parameters and hear the result of their manipulations immediately. Such manipulations bring the particular acoustic dimension to the foreground, helping listeners focus their attention consistently. In theory, then, this method should improve agreement among listeners in their assessments of voice quality relative to traditional rating scale techniques, because it controls the major sources of variance in quality judgments.

This method of quality measurement also provides other practical advantages. First, quality is measured in acoustic terms, so that the relationship between acoustic parameters and what a listener hears is established directly, rather than correlationally. Thus, measuring quality with synthesis can experimentally establish the perceptual relevance of different acoustic attributes of voice. Mappings between acoustics and quality also mean that hypotheses can be tested about the perceptual relationships between different signals, because quality is measured parametrically. The perceptual importance of different parameters can also be evaluated in naturally occurring complex multivariate contexts. (See Kreiman & Gerratt, 2003, for an example of this kind of application.)

Finally, note that this approach to quality measurement follows directly from the ANSI standard definition of sound quality, in that it measures quality psychophysically as those aspects of the signal that allow a listener to determine that two sounds of equal pitch and loudness are different. In this method, listeners also create a direct mapping between the acoustic signal and a perceptual response, thus modeling quality as a process, not as a fixed entity. These characteristics suggest that the method should provide measures of quality that are valid as well as reliable.

In a preliminary assessment of this method (Gerratt & Kreiman, 2001), listeners were asked to adjust the noise-to-signal ratio for 12 pathological voices so that the resulting synthetic stimuli matched the natural voices as closely as possible. In a separate experiment, listeners judged the noisiness of the same stimuli using a traditional 100 mm visual-analog rating scale whose two ends were labeled "no noise" and "extremely noisy." In the synthesizer task, only 3 out of 120 listener responses differed from those of other listeners by more than a difference limen, for an agreement rate of 97.5%. In contrast, the average likelihood of agreement between two listeners in traditional noisiness ratings equaled 22%. These results indicate that listeners given a method-of-adjustment task can in fact agree in their perceptual assessments of pathological voice quality, and that tools can be devised to measure quality perception reliably.

Apart from the small number of studies using this method, a few additional limitations to this approach should also be noted. First, studies applying this technique have all focused on pathological voice quality. In theory, this approach should apply equally to normal voices, but that work has not been done. How this approach might apply to voice quality as broadly conceived is another large question. The available technology limits stimuli to vowels at present, which restricts the extent to which results can be generalized to the broad spectrum of tasks involving voice quality (Table 14.1).

14.6 Conclusions

The appropriate method for measuring what listeners hear when they listen to voices remains an unresolved issue, and providing accurate, replicable, valid measures of vocal quality presents significant challenges. In our view, this problem is more likely to be resolved by developing methods that can assess the interactions between listeners and signals, rather than treating quality solely as a function of the voice signals themselves. Although voice quality is a psychoacoustic phenomenon, understanding of voice quality has not received the benefit of classic psychophysical research methods. Pitch and loudness can often be treated as if they were functions of the signal, because measures of frequency and intensity are fairly well correlated with listeners' perceptual judgments. However, this simplification is inappropriate in the case of quality, because quality is multidimensional and listeners are flexible and variable. This is the case even when the definition of voice is constrained to refer only to laryngeal aspects of sound production. The complexities multiply with broader definitions of voice and voice quality.

Issues of quality measurement have implications beyond the study of quality itself. Once the relationship between a signal and a percept is understood, it may be possible to determine which physiological parameters create perceptually meaningful changes in phonation. At present, it is not possible to determine which aspects of vocal physiology are perceptually important, in part because the relationship between perception and acoustics (which links production to perception in the "speech chain") is poorly understood. Correlations between acoustic measures of voice and many kinds of listener judgments remain hard to interpret (Scherer, 1986). Some progress has been made in understanding the acoustic determinants of perceived affect, voice identity, and perception of physiological characteristics like age and sex, but much remains to be understood. Better methods of quality assessment have important implications for understanding aspects of normal voice perception (age, gender, identity, etc.) that are based in physiology, extending them to the impact of habitual speech patterns on listeners' perceptions. An improved understanding of the issues surrounding measurement of vocal quality is a first step toward these broader goals.

ACKNOWLEDGEMENT

This research was supported in part by grant DC01797 from the National Institute on Deafness and Other Communicative Disorders.

NOTE

1 Grade (i.e., severity of deviation), Roughness, Breathiness, Asthenicity (or weakness), and Strain.

REFERENCES

Abberton, E. & Fourcin, A. J. (1978). Intonation and speaker identification. *Language and Speech*, 21, 305–18.

Abercrombie, D. (1967). *Elements of General Phonetics*. Chicago: Aldine.

ANSI (1960). Acoustical terminology. ANSI S1.1.12.9. New York: American National Standards Institute.

Austin, G. (1806). *Chironomia*. London: Cadell and Davies. Reprinted by Southern Illinois University Press, Carbondale, IL, 1966.

Ball, M. J., Esling, J., & Dickson, C. (2000). The transcription of voice quality. In R. D. Kent & M. J. Ball (eds.), *Voice Quality Measurement* (pp. 49–58). San Diego: Singular Publishing Group.

Banse, R. & Scherer, K. R. (1996). Acoustic profiles in vocal emotion expression. *Journal of Personality and Social Psychology*, 70, 614–36.

Berry, D. A., Montequin, D. W., & Tayama, N. (2001). High-speed digital imaging of the medial surface of the vocal folds. *Journal of the Acoustical Society of America*, 110, 2539–47.

Bodden, M. (1997). Instrumentation for sound quality evaluation. *Acustica*, 83, 775–83.

Bregman, A. S. (1990). *Auditory Scene Analysis*. Cambridge, MA: MIT Press.

Breitenstein, C., Van Lancker, D., & Daum, I. (2001). The contribution of speech rate and pitch variation to the perception of vocal emotions in a German and an American sample. *Cognition and Emotion*, 15, 57–79.

Brown, B. L., Strong, W. J., & Rencher, A. E. (1974). 54 voices from 2: The effects of simultaneous manipulations of rate, mean fundamental frequency, and variance of fundamental frequency on ratings of personality from speech. *Journal of the Acoustical Society of America*, 55, 313–18.

Carterette, E. C. & Barnebey, A. (1975). Recognition memory for voices. In A. Cohen & S. G. Nooteboom (eds.), *Structure and Process in Speech Perception* (pp. 246–65). New York: Springer.

Cheney, D. L. & Seyfarth, R. M. (1980). Vocal recognition in free ranging Vervet monkeys. *Animal Behavior*, 28, 362–7.

Crystal, D. (1969). *Prosodic Systems and Intonation in English*. Cambridge: Cambridge University Press.

Cutler, A., Dahan, D., & van Donselaar, W. (1997). Prosody in the comprehension of spoken language: A literature review. *Language and Speech*, 40, 141–201.

DeCasper, A. J. & Fifer, W. P. (1980). Of human bonding: Newborns prefer their mother's voice. *Science*, 208, 1174–6.

de Krom, G. (1994). Consistency and reliability of voice quality ratings for different types of speech fragments.

Journal of Speech & Hearing Research, 37, 985–1000.

Denes, P. B. & Pinson, E. N. (1993). *The Speech Chain: The Physics and Biology of Spoken Language* (2nd edition). New York: W. H. Freeman.

Ellgring, H. & Scherer, K. R. (1996). Vocal indicators of mood change in depression. *Journal of Nonverbal Behavior*, 20, 83–110.

Fagel, W. P. F., van Herpt, L. W. A., & Boves, L. (1983). Analysis of the perceptual qualities of Dutch speakers' voice and pronunciation. *Speech Communication*, 2, 315–26.

Frohlich, M., Michaelis, D., Strube, H. W., & Kruse, E. (2000). Acoustic voice analysis by means of the hoarseness diagram. *Journal of Speech, Language, and Hearing Research*, 43, 706–20.

Fry, D. B. (1968). Prosodic phenomena. In B. Malmberg (ed.), *Manual of Phonetics* (pp. 365–410). Amsterdam: North Holland.

Geiselman, R. E. & Bellezza, F. S. (1977). Incidental retention of speaker's voice. *Memory & Cognition*, 5, 658–65.

Gelfer, M. P. (1988). Perceptual attributes of voice: Development and use of rating scales. *Journal of Voice*, 2, 320–6.

Gelfer, M. P. (1993). A multidimensional scaling study of voice quality in females. *Phonetica*, 50, 15–27.

Gerratt, B. R. & Kreiman, J. (2001). Measuring vocal quality with speech synthesis. *Journal of the Acoustical Society of America*, 110, 2560–2566.

Gerratt, B. R., Kreiman, J., Antonanzas-Barroso, N., & Berke, G. S. (1993). Comparing internal and external standards in voice quality judgments. *Journal of Speech & Hearing Research*, 36, 14–20.

Gerratt, B. R., Till, J., Rosenbek, J. C., Wertz, R. T., & Boysen, A. E. (1991). Use and perceived value of perceptual and instrumental measures in dysarthria management. In C. A. Moore, K. M. Yorkston, & D. R. Beukelman (eds.), *Dysarthria and Apraxia of Speech* (pp. 77–93). Baltimore: Brookes.

Gescheider, G. A. & Hughson, B. A. (1991). Stimulus context and absolute magnitude estimation: A study of individual differences. *Perception & Psychophysics*, 50, 45–57.

Goldinger, S. D., Pisoni, D. B., & Logan, J. S. (1991). On the nature of talker variability effects on recall of spoken word lists. *Journal of Experimental Psychology: Learning, Memory, and Cognition*, 17, 152–62.

Gray, G. W. (1943). The "voice qualities" in the history of elocution. *Quarterly Journal of Speech*, 29, 475–80.

Hammarberg, B., Fritzell, B., Gauffin, J., Sundberg, J., & Wedin, L. (1980). Perceptual and acoustic correlates of abnormal voice qualities. *Acta Otolaryngologica (Stockholm)*, 90, 441–51.

Helmholtz, H. (1885[1954]). *On the Sensations of Tone*. New York: Dover Publications.

Hirano, M. (1981). *Clinical Examination of Voice*. New York: Springer.

Holmgren, G. L. (1967). Physical and psychological correlates of speaker recognition. *Journal of Speech & Hearing Research*, 10, 57–66.

Isshiki, N., Okamura, H., Tanabe, M., & Morimoto, M. (1969). Differential diagnosis of hoarseness. *Folia Phoniatrica*, 21, 9–19.

Kempler, D. & Van Lancker, D. (2002). The effect of speech task on intelligibility in dysarthria: Case study of Parkinson's disease. *Brain and Language*, 80, 449–64.

Kjelgaard, M. M., Titone, D. A., & Wingfield, A. (1999). The influence of prosodic structure on the interpretation of temporary syntactic ambiguity by young and elderly listeners. *Experimental Aging Research*, 25, 187–207.

Kreiman, J. (1997). Listening to voices: Theory and practice in voice perception research. In K. Johnson & J. W. Mullennix, *Talker Variability in Speech Processing* (pp. 85–108). New York: Academic Press.

Kreiman, J. & Gerratt, B. R. (1996). The perceptual structure of pathologic voice quality. *Journal of the Acoustical Society of America*, 100, 1787–95.

Kreiman, J. & Gerratt, B. R. (1998). Validity of rating scale measures of voice quality. *Journal of the Acoustical Society of America*, 104, 1598–608.

Kreiman, J. & Gerratt, B. R. (2000a). Sources of listener disagreement in voice quality assessment. *Journal of the Acoustical Society of America*, 108, 1867–79.

Kreiman, J. & Gerratt, B. R. (2000b). Measuring vocal quality. In R. D. Kent & M. J. Ball (eds.), *Voice Quality Measurement* (pp. 73–102). San Diego: Singular Publishing Group.

Kreiman, J. & Gerratt, B. R. (2003). Jitter, shimmer, and noise in pathological voice quality perception. In *Proceedings of VOQUAL 2003* (pp. 57–61). Geneva: ISCA.

Kreiman, J. & Papcun, G. (1991). Comparing discrimination and recognition of unfamiliar voices. *Speech Communication*, 10, 265–75.

Kreiman, J., Gerratt, B. R., Kempster, G. B., Erman, A., & Berke, G. S. (1993). Perceptual evaluation of voice quality: Review, tutorial, and a framework for future research. *Journal of Speech & Hearing Research*, 36, 21–40.

Kreiman, J., Gerratt, B. R., & Precoda, K. (1990). Listener experience and perception of voice quality. *Journal of Speech & Hearing Research*, 33, 103–15.

Kreiman, J., Gerratt, B. R., Precoda, K., & Berke, G. S. (1992). Individual differences in voice quality perception. *Journal of Speech & Hearing Research*, 35, 512–20.

Krumhansl, C. L. & Iverson, P. (1992). Perceptual interactions between musical pitch and timbre. *Journal of Experimental Psychology: Human Perception and Performance*, 18, 739–51.

Ladd, D. R. (1996). *Intonational Phonology*. Cambridge: Cambridge University Press.

Laver, J. (1968). Voice quality and indexical information. *British Journal of Disorders of Communication*, 3, 43–54. Reprinted in J. Laver (ed.), *The Gift of Speech* (pp. 147–61). Edinburgh: Edinburgh University Press, 1991.

Laver, J. (1980). *The Phonetic Description of Voice Quality*. Cambridge: Cambridge University Press.

Laver, J. (1981). The analysis of vocal quality: From the classical period to the 20th century. In R. Asher & E. Henderson (eds.), *Toward a History of Phonetics* (pp. 79–99). Edinburgh: Edinburgh University Press. Reprinted in J. Laver (ed.), *The Gift of Speech* (pp. 350–71). Edinburgh: Edinburgh University Press, 1991.

Laver, J. (2000). Phonetic evaluation of voice quality. In R. D. Kent & M. J. Ball (eds.), *Voice Quality Measurement* (pp. 37–48). San Diego: Singular Publishing Group.

Laver, J., Wirz, S., Mackenzie, J., & Hiller, S. M. (1981). A perceptual protocol for the analysis of vocal profiles. *Edinburgh University Department of Linguistics Work in Progress*, 14, 139–55. Reprinted in J. Laver (ed.), *The Gift of Speech* (pp. 265–80). Edinburgh: Edinburgh University Press, 1991.

Lindfield, K. C., Wingfield, A., & Goodglass, H. (1999). The role of prosody in the mental lexicon. *Brain and Language*, 68, 312–17.

Linville, S. E. (1998). Acoustic correlates of perceived versus actual sexual orientation in men's speech. *Folia Phoniatrica et Logopaedica*, 50, 35–48.

Louth, S. M., Williamson, S., Alpert, M., Pouget, E. R., & Hare, R. D. (1998). Acoustic distinctions in the speech of male psychopaths. *Journal of Psycholinguistic Research*, 27, 375–84.

Matsumoto, H., Hiki, S., Sone, T., & Nimura, T. (1973). Multidimensional representation of personal quality of vowels and its acoustical correlates. *IEEE Transactions on Audio and Electroacoustics*, AU-21, 428–36.

Melara, R. D. & Marks, L. E. (1990). Interaction among auditory dimensions: Timbre, pitch, and loudness. *Perception & Psychophysics*, 48, 169–78.

Moore, P. (1964). *Organic Voice Disorders*. Englewood Cliffs, NJ: Prentice-Hall.

Mullennix, J., Pisoni, D. B., & Martin, C. S. (1989). Some effects of talker variability on spoken word recognition. *Journal of the Acoustical Society of America*, 85, 365–78.

Murry, T. & Singh, S. (1980). Multidimensional analysis of male and female voices. *Journal of the Acoustical Society of America*, 68, 1294–300.

Murry, T., Singh, S., & Sargent, M. (1977). Multidimensional classification of abnormal voice qualities. *Journal of the Acoustical Society of America*, 61, 1630–5.

Nygaard, L. C. & Pisoni, D. B. (1998). Talker-specific learning in speech perception. *Perception & Psychophysics*, 60, 355–76.

Orlikoff, R. (1999). The perceived role of voice perception in clinical practice. *Phonoscope*, 2, 87–106.

Osgood, C. E., Suci, G. J., & Tannenbaum, P. H. (1957). *The Measurement of Meaning*. Urbana, IL: University of Illinois Press.

Pannbacker, M. (1984). Classification systems of voice disorders: A review of the literature. *Language, Speech, and Hearing Services in Schools*, 15, 169–74.

Piske, T., MacKay, I., & Flege, J. E. (2001). Factors affecting degree of foreign accent in an L2: A review. *Journal of Phonetics*, 29, 191–215.

Plomp, R. (1976). *Aspects of Tone Sensation*. London: Academic Press.

Pollux, J. (1706). *Onomasticon*. Amsterdam edition.

Raczaszek, J., Tuller, B., Shapiro, L. P., Case, P., & Kelso, S. (1999). Categorization of ambiguous sentences as a function of a changing prosodic parameter: A dynamical approach. *Journal of Psycholinguistic Research*, 28, 367–93.

Remez, R. E., Fellowes, J. M., & Rubin, P. E. (1997). Talker identification based on phonetic information. *Journal of Experimental Psychology: Human Perception and Performance*, 23, 651–66.

Rendall, D., Rodman, P. S., & Edmond, R. E. (1996). Vocal recognition of individuals and kin in free-ranging rhesus monkeys. *Animal Behavior*, 51, 1007–15.

Sapir, E. (1926–7). Speech as a personality trait. *American Journal of Sociology*, 32, 892–905.

Schafer, A. J., Speer, S. R., Warren, P., & White, S. D. (2000). Intonational disambiguation in sentence production and comprehension. *Journal of Psycholinguistic Research*, 29, 169–82.

Schegloff, E. A. (1998). Reflections on studying prosody in talk-in-interaction. *Language and Speech*, 41, 235–63.

Scherer, K. R. (1979). Personality markers in speech. In H. Giles (ed.), *Social Markers in Speech* (pp. 147–201). Cambridge: Cambridge University Press.

Scherer, K. R. (1986). Vocal affect expression: A review and a model for future research. *Psychological Bulletin*, 99, 145–65.

Shepard, R. N. (1972). Psychological representation of speech sounds. In E. E. David, Jr. & P. B. Denes (eds.), *Human Communication: A Unified View* (pp. 67–113). New York: McGraw-Hill.

Singh, S. & Murry, T. (1978). Multidimensional classification of normal voice qualities. *Journal of the Acoustical Society of America*, 64, 81–7.

Sundberg, J. (1987). *The Science of the Singing Voice*. DeKalb, IL: Northern Illinois University Press.

van Dommelen, W. A. (1990). Acoustic parameters in human speaker recognition. *Language and Speech*, 33, 259–72.

Van Lancker, D. & Pachana, N. (1998). The influence of emotion on language and communication disorders. In B. Stemmer & H. A. Whitaker (eds.), *The Handbook of Neurolinguistics* (pp. 302–13). San Diego: Academic Press.

Van Lancker, D., Canter, G. J., & Terbeek, D. (1981). Disambiguation of ditropic sentences: Acoustic and phonetic correlates. *Journal of Speech & Hearing Research*, 24, 330–5.

Van Lancker, D., Kreiman, J., & Emmorey, K. (1985). Familiar voice recognition: Patterns and parameters. Part I: Recognition of backwards voices. *Journal of Phonetics*, 13, 19–38.

Van Lancker, D., Kreiman, J., & Wickens, T. (1985). Familiar voice recognition: Parameters and patterns.

Part II: Recognition of rate-altered voices. *Journal of Phonetics*, 13, 39–52.

Verdonck-de Leeuw, I. M. (1998). Perceptual analysis of voice quality: Trained and naive raters, and self-ratings. In G. de Krom (ed.), *Proceedings of Voicedata98 Symposium on Databases in Voice Quality Research and Education* (pp. 12–15). Utrecht: Utrecht Institute of Linguistics.

Voiers, W. D. (1964). Perceptual bases of speaker identity. *Journal of the Acoustical Society of America*, 36, 1065–73.

Walden, B. E., Montgomery, A. A., Gibeily, G. J., Prosek, R. A., & Schwartz, D. M. (1978). Correlates of psychological dimensions in talker similarity. *Journal of Speech & Hearing Research*, 21, 265–75.

Wells, B. & Macfarlane, S. (1998). Prosody as an interactional resource: Turn-projection and overlap. *Language and Speech*, 41, 265–94.

Williams, C. E. & Stevens, K. N. (1972). Emotion and speech: Some acoustical correlates. *Journal of the Acoustical Society of America*, 52, 1238–50.

Wirz, S. & Mackenzie Beck, J. (1995). Assessment of voice quality: The Vocal Profiles Analysis Scheme. In S. Wirz (ed.), *Perceptual Approaches to Communication Disorders* (pp. 39–55). London: Whurr Publishers.

Wuyts, F. L., de Bodt, M. S., Molenberghs, G., Remacle, M., Heylen, L., Millet, B., van Lierde, K., Raes, J., & van de Heyning, P. H. (2000). The dysphonia severity index: An objective measure of vocal quality based on a multiparameter approach. *Journal of Speech, Language, and Hearing Research*, 43, 796–809.

Yost, W. A., Braida, L., Hartmann, W. W., Kidd, G. D., Jr., Kruskal, J., Pastore, R., Sachs, M. B., Sorkin, R. D., & Warren, R. M. (1989). *Classification of Complex Nonspeech Sounds.* Washington, DC: National Academy Press.

15 Speaker Normalization in Speech Perception

KEITH JOHNSON

Acoustic-phonetic analysis of speech, made practical by the advent of the speech spectrograph (Koenig, Dunn, & Lacy, 1946), prompted a number of foundational questions regarding the perception of speech because spectrograms showed that speech is highly variable both within and between talkers. Among early researchers, Liberman et al. (1967) focused on within-talker variation in the acoustic cues for stop place of articulation, while others focused on between-talker variation in the acoustic cues for vowels. "Speaker normalization" refers to this second line of research centering on the fact that phonologically identical utterances show a great deal of acoustic variation across talkers, and that listeners are able to recognize words spoken by different talkers despite this variation. In defining speaker normalization in this way, we assume that phonological identity occurs when utterances are identified by listeners as instances of the same linguistic object (word or phoneme). For example, the word "cat" spoken by a man and a woman might be identified as "cat" by listeners although spectrograms will show that the man and woman have quite different vowel formant frequencies (Figure 15.1).

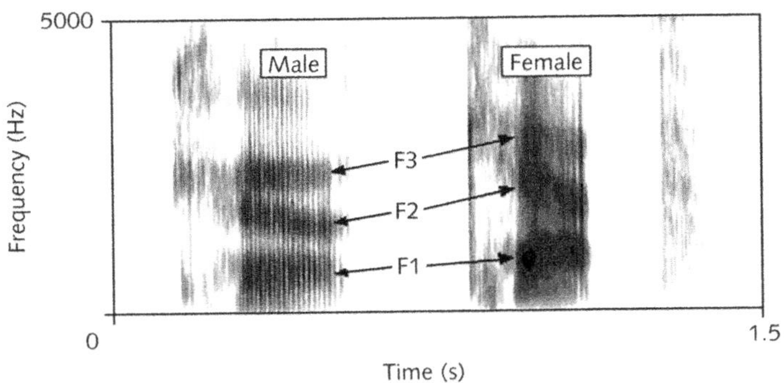

Figure 15.1 Spectrograms of a man and a woman saying "cat." The three lowest vowel formants (vocal tract resonant frequencies) are marked as F1, F2, and F3.

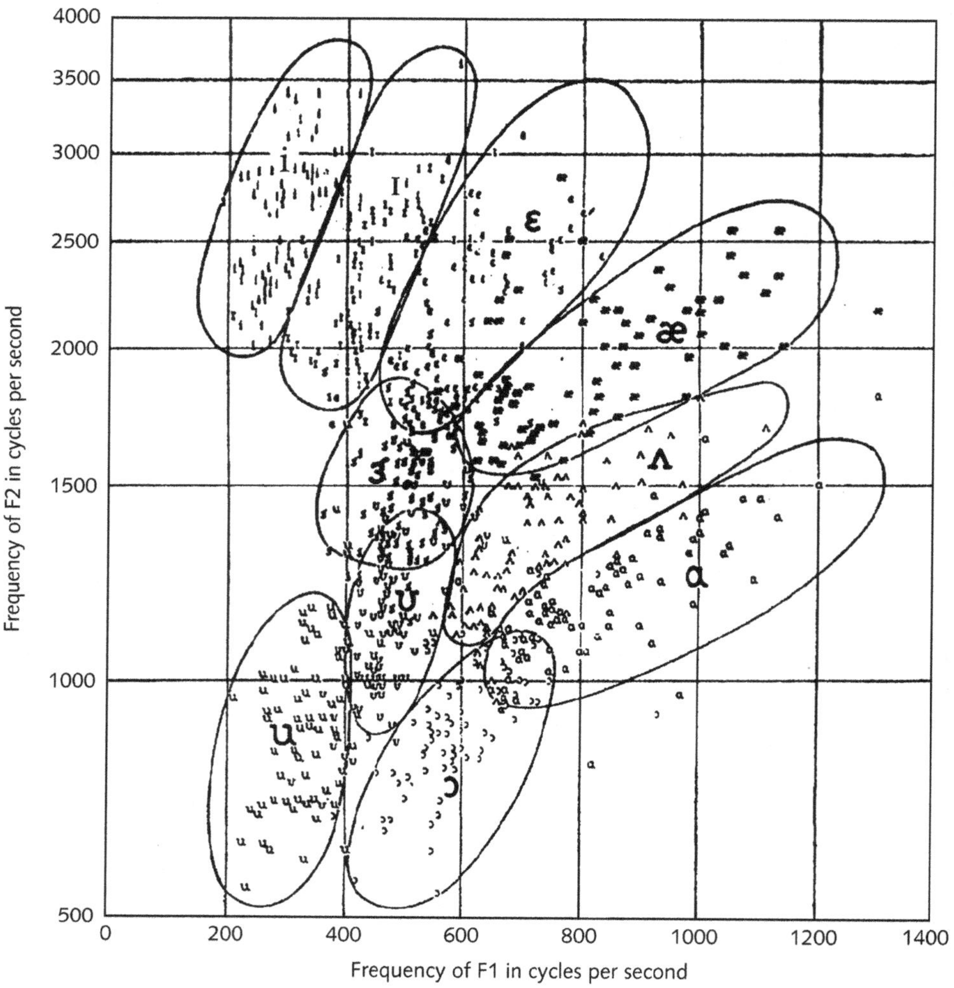

Figure 15.2 Scatter plot of first and second formant frequency values of American English vowels (From Peterson & Barney, 1952).

The most dramatic demonstration of between-speaker acoustic vowel variation is the well-known study reported by Peterson and Barney (1952). Figure 15.2 shows their plot of the first two vowel formant frequencies (F1 and F2) of vowels produced by men, women, and children. All of the vowels represented in the figure were correctly identified by listeners. This figure – one of the most frequently reprinted in all of phonetics – has prompted decades of research, and serves as a starting point for this contribution.

Speaker normalization research prompted by between-talker vowel formant variation seeks to explain how listeners can correctly identify vowels when the main acoustic cues for vowel identity (F1 and F2) are ambiguous.

15.1 Perceiving Vowels in Isolated Syllables

15.1.1 *Formants in vowel perception*

The importance of vowel formants (resonant frequencies of the vocal tract) in cueing vowel sounds has been known for over a century. For example, Helmholtz (1885) synthesized vowel sounds with resonators having frequencies that matched the vowel formant frequencies. The role of vowel formants in vowel perception was also demonstrated by Fry et al. (1962) using a continuum of synthetic vowels.

A debate pitting "formant-based" theories of vowel perception, in which auditory preprocessing is assumed to code vowels in terms of formant frequencies, against "whole spectrum" theories of vowel perception, in which a neural spectrogram serves as input to perception, suggests that the perceptual importance of vowel formants may result from the fact that the resonant frequencies of the vocal tract are the primary determinants of the spectral shape of vowels (see Rosner & Pickering, 1994, pp. 152–6). What is clear though is that in numerous studies using multidimensional scaling to empirically discover the dimensions of the perceptual vowel space (Fox, 1982, 1983; Mohr & Wang, 1968; Pols, van der Kamp, & Plomp, 1969; Rakerd & Verbrugge, 1985; Shepard, 1972; Terbeek & Harshman, 1972), the first two perceptual dimensions always correspond to the frequencies of F1 and F2. However, the perceptual value of F1 and F2 are modulated by other acoustic properties of vowels.

15.1.2 *Perceptual influence of F0*

Miller (1953) doubled the fundamental frequency of vocal fold vibration (F0) of two-formant vowels (from 120 Hz to 240 Hz) and found vowel category boundary shifts for most of the vowels of English. Fujisaki and Kawashima (1968) also studied the role of F0 in vowel perception and found F1 boundary shifts of 100 Hz to 200 Hz for F0 shifts of 200 Hz. Slawson (1968) estimated that an octave change in F0 produced a perceived change in F1 and F2 of about 10 to 12%.

Listeners are also strongly affected by mismatched F0. Lehiste and Meltzer (1973) found lower vowel perception accuracy when they put children's high F0 with male vowel formants, and (to a lesser extent) when they put a low male F0 with children's vowel formants. Gottfried and Chew (1986) found that listener vowel identification performance was less accurate when vowels were produced by a countertenor at a much higher F0 than is typical for a male voice.

Johnson (1990b) found that the F0 effect was sensitive to mode of presentation. If tokens having different F0 were randomly mixed, so that listeners couldn't predict the upcoming F0, the F0 vowel boundary shift was observed, but when stimuli were presented blocked by F0, the boundary shift was substantially reduced.

15.1.3 *Perceptual influence of higher formants*

It has also been reported that the boundaries between vowel categories are sensitive to the frequencies of a vowel's higher formants (F3–F5), though this effect seems to be much weaker than that of F0. Fujisaki and Kawashima (1968) demonstrated an F3 effect with two different vowel continua. An F3 shift of 1500 Hz produced a vowel category boundary shift of 200 Hz in the F1–F2 space for a /u/–/e/ continuum, but a boundary shift of only 50 Hz in an /o/–/a/ continuum. Slawson (1968) found very small effects of shifting F3 in six different vowel continua. Nearey (1989) found a small shift in the mid-point of the /ʊ/ vowel region (comparable to a boundary shift) when the frequencies of F3–F5 were raised by 30%, but this effect only occured for one of the two sets of stimuli tested. Johnson (1989) also found an F3 boundary shift, but attributed it to spectral integration (Chistovich, Sheikin, & Lublinskaja, 1979) of F2 and F3 because the F3 frequency manipulation only influenced the perception of front vowels (when F2 and F3 are within 3 Bark of each other) and not back vowels which have a larger frequency separation of F2 and F3. This gives higher formant perceptual "normalization" a different basis than is normally assumed (see the literature on effective F2 (abbreviated F2′), starting with Carlson, Granström, & Fant, 1970, as summarized in Rosner & Pickering, 1994).

15.2 Formant Ratio Theories

Potter and Steinberg (1950) stated that in vowel perception "a certain spatial pattern of stimulation on the basilar membrane may be identified as a given sound regardless of position along the membrane" (p. 812). This is the basic idea of formant ratio theories – vowels are relative patterns, not absolute formant frequencies. The importance of formants and the effects of F0 and F3 in vowel perception support the formant ratio approach.

Miller (1989) traced formant ratio theories of vowel normalization from Lloyd (1890a, 1890b, 1891, 1892), noting that "statements of the formant-ratio theory appear in the literature every few years since Lloyd's work . . . and, interestingly, the authors usually seem to be unaware of prior descriptions of the notion" (p. 2115). An explanation for this may be that most formant ratio theories seem to be inspired by an analogy between vowels and musical chords. For example, Potter and Steinberg (1950) in discussing their idea that vowels are a pattern of stimulation on the basilar membrane drew the analogy: "Musical chords, for example, are identified in this manner. Thus, the ear can identify a chord as a major triad, irrespective of its pitch position" (p. 812). They proposed that principles of Gestalt psychology permit the constancy of a visual object regardless of the exact location of the image on the retina, and must also be at work in audition to permit the constancy of patterns of stimulation on the basilar membrane. Traunmüller (1981, 1984) also concluded that "perception of phonetic quality" can be "seen as a process of tonotopic Gestalt recognition" (1984, p. 49).

Sussman (1986; Sussman et al., 1998) suggested a neuronal circuit, the "combination-sensitive neuron" that could accomplish this. His vowel normalization and representation model is shown in Figure 15.3. Combination-sensitive neurons combine information from two formants at the point labelled (1) in the graph and then from three formants at point (2). Circuits comparable to this have been found in the auditory systems of a number of species (see Sussman et al., 1998, for a listing with references).[1] Though Sussman demurred regarding

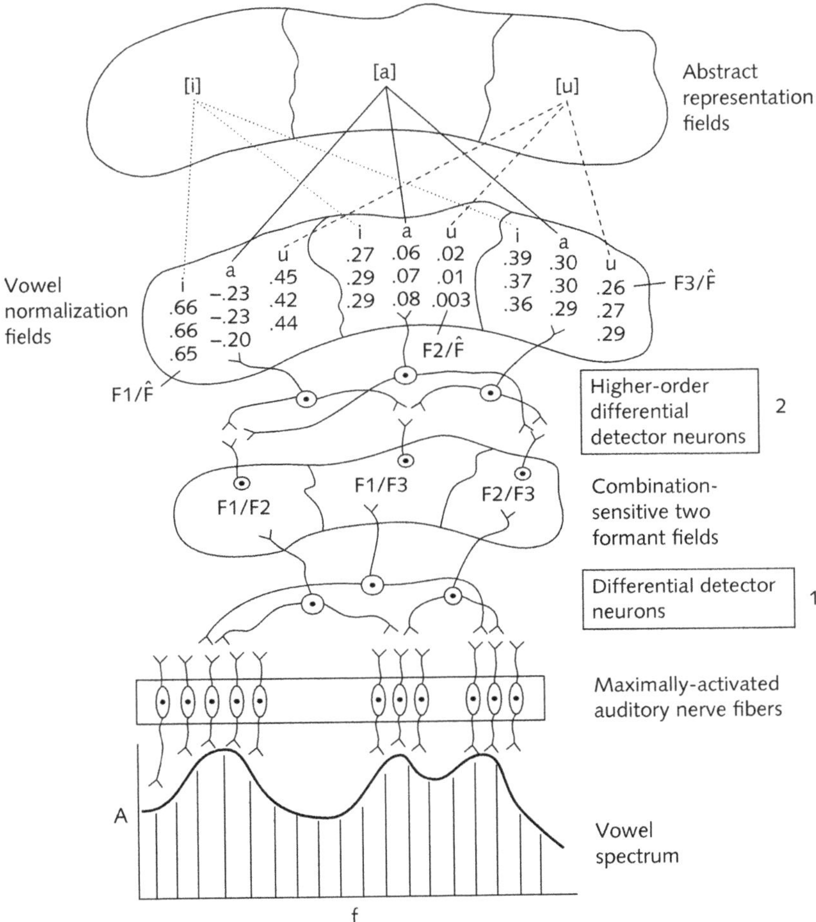

Figure 15.3 Sussman's (1986) vowel normalization/representation model, making use of combination-sensitive neurons to code relations among formant frequencies. Formant ratio data for men, women and children are shown in the "vowel normalization fields."

"the specific arithmetic processing" to be implemented by combination-sensitive neurons, in his simulations he used the natural log of the ratios F1/F*, F2/F*, F3/F* where F* is the geometric mean of all of the formants. Bladon, Henton, and Pickering (1984) implemented a whole spectrum matching model of vowel perception that shares something of the spirit of Potter and Steinberg's and Sussman's approach to the formant ratio hypothesis. Though Bladon et al. didn't propose a neural mechanism like Sussman's, they did demonstrate that one way to concieve of matching "spatial patterns of stimulation on the basilar membrane" is to calculate auditory vowel spectra and then slide the spectra from female talkers down into the range occupied by male talkers.

Table 15.1 Formulations of the formant ratio hypothesis

Peterson (1961)	log(Fn) – log(F1), n = 2, 3, 4
Sussman (1986)	log(Fn/F*), n = 1, 2, 3, F* = (F1 + F2 + F3)/3
Syrdal & Gopal (1986)	Bark(F1) – Bark(F0), Bark(F2) – Bark(F1), Bark(F3) – Bark(F2)
Miller (1989)	log(F1/SR), log(F2/F1), log(F3/F2)

15.2.1 *Forms of the formant ratio hypothesis*

A number of analytical statements of formant ratio normalization have been given. This section briefly presents them with a focus on their similarities.

Note in comparing the formulations in Table 15.1 that log(x) – log(y) = log(x/y). Thus, Peterson (1961) and Miller (1989) have one dimension in common: log(F2/F1) = log(F2) – log(F1). Note also that the Bark scale is a non-linear scale similar to the log scale. Thus, Miller and Syrdal & Gopal (1986) have almost the same dimensions – one difference being that Syrdal and Gopal enter F0 directly, while Miller's formula reduces the influence of F0 fluctuation by using a "sensory reference" (SR) derived from the geometric mean of F0 over an interval of time. It is interesting that F3 and F0 have equal status in Syrdal & Gopal and Miller, and that F0 is not included in the formant ratios of Peterson or Sussman (1986). This seems to run counter to the fact that the effect of F0 on perception is much larger and more consistent than the effect of F3 and the higher formants. In fact, there are a number of other perceptual effects that suggest that formant ratio theories are inadequate.

15.3 From Auditory Gestalts to Vocal Tract Actions

15.3.1 *Beyond formants*

As important as formant frequencies are in vowel perception, it has also been demonstrated that listeners use "secondary" cues. Lehiste and Peterson (1961) showed that American English vowels differ in terms of duration and formant frequency movement trajectories – tense vowels are longer than lax vowels, low vowels are longer than high vowels, and formant trajectories differ for vowels that are otherwise close in the F1/F2 space. For example, /e/ is more narrowly transcribed [eᴵ] while /ɛ/ tends more to [ɛᵊ]. The perceptual importance of these acoustic characteristics of American English vowels has been demonstrated in studies on the perception of synthetic steady-state vowels and on the perception of "silent-center" vowels. Lehiste and Meltzer (1973) showed that listeners are not very successful in correctly identifying fixed duration vowels synthesized with steady-state formant frequencies (51% correct with ten vowel categories). They were much better at identifying the original isolated vowel recordings – though with mixed lists containing tokens from men, women, and children the identification rate even in this task was quite low (79% correct) (see also Ainsworth, 1970). Nearey and Assmann (1986) spliced small chunks out of vowels near the beginning of the vowel segment (the "nucleus") and near the end (the "glide") and found that correct identification was higher when the chunks were played in the order nucleus-glide than when either chunk was presented alone or when they were played in the order glide-nucleus. Hillenbrand and Nearey (1999) presented an extensive study of vowel identification that confirms the conclusions of these earlier studies. Flat-formant vowels (vowels synthesized with only steady-state formant frequencies, but having the duration of the original utterance) were correctly identified 74% of the time, while vowels synthesized with the original formant frequency trajectories were correctly identified 89% of the time.

The point in citing these studies is to counter the tendency (sometimes stated explicitly) to think of formant ratio vowel representations as points in a normalized vowel space. Miller's (1989) description of vowels as trajectories through normalized space is much more in keeping with the data reviewed in this section. However, even with these richer vowel representations, formant ratio theories fail to account for perceptual speaker normalization.

15.3.2 *Whispered vowels*

Rosner & Pickering (1994) note that formant ratio models of vowel perception that necessarily include F0 (e.g., Miller, 1989; Syrdal & Gopal, 1986; and Traunmüller, 1981) have no explanation for the fact that listeners can identify whispered vowels. It should be noted, though, that whispered vowels are not identified as accurately as normally phonated vowels. Eklund and Traunmüller (1997) found error rates of 4.5% for voiced vowels and 12% for whispered vowels. In whisper the vocal tract resonances (particularly F1) shift up in frequency with the glottis open (introducing tracheal resonances and zeros), and X-ray studies show that vowel articulations also change in whispered speech (Sovijärvi, 1938). So it is not surprising that whispered vowels are harder to identify, but the fact remains that models that require F0 in the representation of vowels fail to account for the perception of whispered vowels.

15.3.3 *Beyond vowels*

Though the focus of speaker normalization research has been on vowel perception, listeners are also sensitive to talker differences in the perception of consonants and prosody. Schwartz (1968) found in an acoustic study that fricatives produced by men and women have, on average, different spectral shapes (fricatives produced by women had slightly higher spectral center of gravity), and May (1976) found that when a continuum from [s] to [ʃ] was spliced to [ɑ] produced by a male or a female voice, the [s]-[ʃ] boundary was at a higher spectral center of gravity for the female voice. This was taken to mean that listeners "normalized" the fricative based on the contextual information provided by the vowel. This finding has been replicated a number of times (e.g., Johnson, 1991; Mann & Repp, 1980; Strand & Johnson, 1996).

Leather (1983) found speaker normalization effects with Mandarin Chinese tones. The pitch range of a context utterance influenced the perception of test tones spanning a range of F0 values. This type of tone normalization effect has also been reported by Fox and Qi (1990) and by Moore (1996).

15.3.4 *Scatter reduction*

Normalization algorithms such as formant ratio recoding are evaluated according to how well they reduce within-category scatter and between-category vowel overlap. The goal is to devise a cognitively plausible algorithm that is able to separate the overlapping clusters of vowels in the Peterson and Barney (1952) figure, for example, and so classify the vowels about as accurately as Peterson and Barney's listeners did. When it comes to scatter reduction, though, no algorithm has been shown to work better than simple statistical standarization of formant values (Disner, 1980; Lobanov, 1971; Nearey, 1978).[2] The problem with this kind of method, from the perspective of cognitive plausibility, is that in order to recode a talker's formants into speaker-specific z-scores ($z = (x - \bar{x})/sd$) the algorithm has to have a full listing of formant frequency measurements of vowels produced by the talker. It does not seem plausible to suppose that listeners could have enough information from an unfamiliar talker to be able to perform this kind of normalization.

Despite this, most of the practically useful vowel normalization algorithms require that summary statistics be derived over a full set of vowels for each talker. As we have seen, Lobanov's (1971) method requires the mean and standard deviation of F1 and F2. Nearey's (1978) constant log interval normalization uses the mean of the log values of the talkers' F1 and F2. Gerstman's (1968) range normalization technique (which is less successful than formant standardization or log interval coding) requires that the minimum and maximum values of F1 and F2 be found. Bladon et al. (1984) used a single value to normalize vowels – a boolean to indicate whether the talker is male or female. If the vowel was produced by a woman the auditory spectrum was shifted down by about 1 Bark. The spectra of vowels produced by men were not shifted. In this approach 1 Bark is about the magnitude of the average frequency difference between the formants of vowels produced by men and of those produced by women (see Figures 15.5 and 15.6 below).

The main point of these observations is to note that it has proven useful in the practical quantitative normalization of vowel formant data to express formant frequencies relative to a representation of the talker. In Lobanov's method the talker representation has four dimensions μ_{F1}, μ_{F2}, σ_{F1}, and σ_{F2}. In Nearey's most successful version of the constant log interval method the speaker is represented as μ_{logF1} and μ_{logF2}. For Bladon et al. the boolean shift factor is a kind of talker representation – men are represented as 0 and women are represented as 1. In considering these normalization algorithms as possible models of human perceptual speaker normalization, it is interesting to note that a perceptual frame of reference perhaps analogous to these statistical acoustic representations is used by listeners. We turn now to some evidence supporting this view.

15.3.5 *Context influences perception*

One of the cleverest and most influential studies of vowel perception was the one reported by Ladefoged and Broadbent (1957). Like Peterson and Barney's (1952) study, Ladefoged and Broadbent's results have had a lasting impact on the theory of speech perception. They found that vowels judged in the context of a precursor carrier phrase with the vowel formant frequencies shifted up were identified differently than when the precursor phrase had relatively low vowel formants. In effect, the test vowels were identified as if the precursor phrase provided a coordinate system within which to judge them. This "extrinsic" context effect has been demonstrated in numerous subsequent studies (Ainsworth, 1974; Dechovitz, 1977; Nearey, 1978, 1989). Remez et al. (1987) found that the context formant range effect also occurs in the perception of sinewave analogs of speech. Johnson (1990a) found a variant of the effect in which the F0 range of the carrier phrase was varied instead of the vowel formant frequency range. The effect of carrier phrase F0 range was comparable to the vowel formant frequency range effect noted by Ladefoged and Broadbent.

The impact of context on vowel perception suggests that listeners use a cognitive "frame of reference" that is in some sense a representation of the talker who produced the speech. If something like this actually happens in speech perception, it would be reasonable to expect to find evidence that listeners take a little time to adapt to a new talker and exhibit processing difficulties such as misperceptions and/or slowed responses before talker adaptation has been completed. These expectations have been borne out in a number of studies over the years.

15.3.6 *Talker normalization is an active process*

Creelman (1957) found that word recognition accuracy in noise decreases when the identity of the talker is unpredictable from trial to trial. In this study and many later ones, talker identity was kept predictable by presenting stimuli in "single-talker" lists, while in the unpredictable talker condition the stimuli were presented in "mixed-talker" lists. Summerfield and Haggard (1973) found that word recognition reaction times were slower in mixed-talker lists than in single-talker lists. Verbrugge et al. (1976) found that vowel identification was more accurate in single-talker lists (9.5% errors) than in mixed-talker lists (17% errors). Mullennix, Pisoni, and Martin (1989) tested word recognition speed and accuracy in mixed and single-talker lists and also investigated interactions with word frequency and lexical density. They suggested that speaker adaptation is an active process and that talker voice information is not automatically "removed" from the speech signal by a normalizing recoding of the signal, otherwise the talker variability manipulation would not have had an effect.

Kakehi (1992) described experiments done earlier by Kato and Kakehi (1988) that investigated listener adaptation to talker voice. They found a very interesting effect of adaptation (as indicated by increased syllable recognition accuracy in noise) over the course of five successive stimuli. Accuracy increased monotonically from 70% correct on the first stimulus produced by a talker, to 76% correct on the fifth stimulus. After the fifth stimulus, no further increase in recognition accuracy was observed. This study calibrates the amount of information needed to adapt to a new talker for isolated nonsense syllables (letter names, basically). Nusbaum and Morin (1992) used a speeded phoneme monitoring task to evaluate the effect of talker uncertainty in a mixed-talker list. They found that listeners were slower to report the presence of target syllables in mixed-talker lists. This was taken to indicate that speaker normalization is an active adaptation process that demands cognitive resources.

15.3.7 Talker normalization is subject to expectations

Magnuson and Nusbaum (1994) compared "1-voice" instructions with "2-voice" instructions in a mixed-talker monitoring task where the two synthetic voices were only slightly different in F0. Listeners were told either that the tokens were produced by two talkers or one. In the 2-voice instruction condition, they found the typical advantage for blocked-talker presentation versus the mixed-talker presentation, but this effect disappeared in the 1-voice instruction condition. A perceptual effect of instructions was also found in another study by Johnson, Strand, and D'Imperio (1999). In one experiment, listeners were presented synthetic tokens on a "hood" [hʊd]–"HUD" [hʌd] continuum with an androgynous voice. One group of listeners was told that the talker was female and the other group was told that the talker was male. The category boundaries were different as a function of instructions in the same direction as found when F0 or visual gender was used to cue talker differences.

Eklund and Traunmüller (1997) found evidence of a connection between talker perception and vowel perception, this time in a study of whispered speech. When listeners misidentified the sex of the talker their vowel identification error rate was 25%, but when they correctly identified the sex of the speaker the vowel error rate was only 5%. This suggests that talker perception and vowel perception are interconnected with each other, as the studies using experimenter-suggested talker expectations seems to show.

15.3.8 Audio-visual interactions in normalization

Several studies have shown that listeners process speech differently in audio-visual presentation depending on the visual gender of the talker (Johnson et al., 1999; Schwippert & Benoit, 1997; Strand & Johnson, 1996; Walker, Bruce, & O'Malley, 1995). Auditory/visual perceptual integration is more likely to occur when the gender of the visually presented face matches the gender of the auditorily presented word. Strand and Johnson, and Johnson et al. also found that fricative and vowel identification boundaries can be shifted by visual gender in much the way that they can be shifted by F0, or other auditory cues for talker gender. Walker et al. found a very interesting interaction between auditory/visual integration and listener familiarity with the talker.

Taken together, these phenomena suggest that listeners perceive speech relative to an internal representation of the person talking. The earliest and most straightforward proposal was that the "talker" frame of reference (or perceptual coordinate system) for speech perception is the vocal tract of the talker.

15.4 Vocal Tract Normalization

Whereas formant ratio theories view normalization as a function of the auditory Gestalt encoding of vowels, vocal tract normalization theories consider that listeners perceptually evaluate vowels on a talker-specific coordinate system – most simply, by reference to the perceived length of the talker's vocal tract. The normalization mechanism in this approach is thus a kind of predictive analysis-by-synthesis mental model of the vocal tract.

Here is Martin Joos' (1948) account of vocal tract normalization.

> On first meeting a person, the listener hears a few vowel phones, and on the basis of this small but apparently sufficient evidence he swiftly constructs a fairly complete vowel pattern to serve as a background (coordinate system) upon which he correctly locates new phones as fast as he hears them . . . On first meeting a person, one hears him say "How do you do?" The very first vowel phone heard is a sample of the noise this speaker makes when his articulation is (in my dialect) low central; the last one is a sample of the noise he makes with his highest and backest articulation; and in the middle (spelling "y") there is a sample of sound belonging to palatal articulation, offering evidence about his higher and fronter vowels. Now these samples of sound as sound are already sufficient to establish the acoustic vowel pattern: the pattern's corners are now located, and the other phones can be assumed to be spaced relative to them as they generally are spaced in this dialect. (p. 61)

The fact that perceived vowel quality is influenced by the formant frequencies of context vowels (Ladefoged & Broadbent, 1957) suggests that something like Joos' "coordinate system" is involved in vowel perception. And evidence that speaker normalization is an active process open to visual information about the talker, and other information that can be used to specify the talker's vocal tract size, fits with the idea that listeners are constructing a perceptual frame of reference. Additionally, the analysis-by-synthesis mechanism is general enough to be extended to account for perceptual normalization in the perception of consonants and tones.

Besides extrinsic cues such as the range of formant frequency values in the immediately preceding speech context, some vowel internal cues carry information about the talker's vocal tract. For example, though F0 is not causally linked to vocal tract length (as Nearey, 1989, memorably noted with his imitations of the cartoon character Popeye, whose vocal tract was long though his vocal pitch was high, and the American television personality Julia Child, whose low pitch voice belied her short vocal tract), there is a presumptive correlational relationship so that F0 may serve as a rough vocal tract length cue which could play a role in establishing the vocal tract normalization "coordinate system." The frequency of the third formant is causally linked to vocal tract length and was used explicitly by Nordström and Lindblom (1975) in a vowel normalization algorithm. They first calculated the length of the vocal tract for a particular speaker from the frequency of F3 in low vowels and then rescaled the other vowel formants produced by this speaker to a standard speaker-independent vocal tract length.

15.4.1 *How much context is needed?*

Verbrugge et al. (1976) noted that single syllables presented in mixed-talker lists are identified very accurately (95% correct in Peterson & Barney's 1952, study), and concluded that "there is clearly a great deal of information within a single syllable which specifies the identity of its vowel nucleus" (p. 203). They conducted experiments comparing vowel identification in a mixed-talker list, with or without a set of three context syllables. In each condition, there was a slight but statistically unreliable increase in vowel identification accuracy with the addition of precursor vowels – whether they were point vowels or not. However, they also noted that vowel identification performance in a single-talker list was much better than in a mixed-talker list. This suggests that limited context like a set of three nonsense vowel sounds does not provide much talker information beyond that already available in an isolated syllable and that this initial short-term adaptation to talker is different from vowel identification performance based on more extended familiarity with the talker.

This difference in performance for stimuli presented with point vowels as the immediate context in a vowel identification experiment and stimuli presented in a single-talker list is not predicted by the vocal tract normalization theory. However, the different patterns of results in Verbrugge et al. (1976) and Kato and Kakehi (1988) casts doubt on any conclusions we might draw from either study. Further exploration of the time-course of talker adaptation is needed.

15.4.2 *Uniform scaling, non-uniform scaling, and vocal tract perception*

Nordström and Lindblom's (1975) uniform scaling approach to vowel normalization used a single scale factor (hence "uniform" scaling) to shift vowel formant measurements into a talker-independent coordinate system.[3] For the F-scaling factor they used the ratio (k) of the speaker's vocal tract length, to a reference vocal tract length (l_{AV}/l_{ref}). They estimated l_{AV} from the average F3 value found in low vowels, and Fant (1975) showed that k can be estimated as an F3 ratio:

$$k = \mathrm{F3}_{AV}/\mathrm{F3}_{ref}$$

Though uniform scaling reduces talker differences quite a bit, it had been recognized for some time (Fant, 1966) that no uniform scaling method can capture systematic, cross-linguistic patterns that have been observed in male/female vowel formant differences. In dealing with these male/female differences, Fant (1966) used separate scale factors for the F1, F2, and F3 of each vowel in order to relate male and female measurements. This gives 30 scale factors per talker for a system with ten vowels.

The non-uniformity of male/female formant differences means that a normalization routine like Nearey's (1978) one-parameter version of the constant log interval method or Bladon, Henton, and Pickering's (1984) one-parameter spectral shift method are unlikely to succeed in equating male and female vowels. Both of these succeed better than Fant's (1966) uniform scaling of formant values in Hz because their nonlinear scales absorb some variation due to the fact that male and female vowel formants differ as a function of formant frequency – approximating each other somewhat closely at low formant frequencies and differing quite a lot at higher frequencies. Nonetheless, uniform normalization, based on the implicit assumption that vocal tract length is the only difference between men and women, neglects the effects of other important differences in vocal tract geometry. For example, men tend to have a proportionally longer pharynx than women, and thus lower back-cavity resonance frequencies.

Non-uniform normalization, utilizing different scale factors for different formants (including multiparameter models like Lobanov, 1971, and Nearey, 1978) provides more complex representations of the talker – reflecting presumably, for the moment, differences in vocal tract geometry beyond vocal tract length. Model studies of typical vocal tract differences between men and women have attempted to derive Fant's (1966) non-uniform scaling factors from anatomical differences between men and women (Goldstein, 1980; Nordström, 1977; Traunmüller, 1984).

Rather than simply rescale formant frequencies based on an estimate of vocal tract length, or characterize the talker in terms of acoustic formant scale factors, McGowan (1997; McGowan & Cushing, 1999) attempted to recover a detailed characterization of vocal tract geometry from the acoustic signal. One difficulty with this more literal approach to vocal tract normalization is that indeterminacies in the extraction of acoustic parameters are magnified during vocal tract simulation. This coupled with a degree of vocal tract underspecification (such that virtually identical acoustic values can be produced by substantially different vocal tracts, Atal et al., 1978) puts speech gesture recovery, as a practical normalization strategy, out of reach at this time. Whether listeners veridically recover the talker's vocal tract for use in perceptual speaker normalization is another question.

The presence of individual differences in speech production (Johnson, Ladefoged, & Lindau, 1993) also complicates matters for vocal tract normalization. Though normalization research has usually focused on male/female differences in vocal tract size and shape, vocal tracts – even within genders – come in lots of different sizes and shapes. Johnson et al.'s results suggest that talkers apparently adopt different (possibly arbitrarily different) articulatory strategies to produce the "same" sounds. Thus, accurate recovery of the talker's articulatory gestures would not completely succeed in "normalizing" speech.

15.5 Talkers or Vocal Tracts?

We turn now to a discussion of talkers, starting with consideration of the articulatory origins of gender differences in speech, followed by a discussion of the role of the perceived identity of the talker in speech perception. As noted above, talkers may differ from each other at the level of their articulatory habits of speech. This in itself would suggest that perception may not be able to depend on vocal tract normalization to "remove" talker differences by removing vocal tract differences. However, because so much of the normalization literature focuses on the differences between men's and women's speech, we will start by asking a prickly question.

15.5.1 Do men's and women's voices differ only by anatomy?

Vocal tract normalization theory assumes that speakers differ from each other in vocal tract anatomy, but that when this source of difference is factored out all speakers of a language have the same phonetic targets. Traunmüller (1984) presented results supporting this idea from simulations of differences between male and female formant frequencies. In his simulations, Traunmüller modeled male/female differences in pharynx length and resting tongue position (assuming that the descent of the larynx lowers the resting position of the tongue). Possible gender difference in resting tongue position had not been considered in previous studies (Goldstein, 1980; Nordström, 1977) and Traunmüller offered no data to support the crucial assumption. Nonetheless, his simulated male/female formant ratios closely match the average ratios reported by Fant (1966, 1975). Rosner and Pickering (1994) accepted Traunmüller's conclusion that "it is not necessary to postulate sex-specific vowel articulations in order to explain the [non-uniform formant scaling] data" (Traunmüller, 1984, p. 55).

However, it has been noted by several researchers (Chan, 1997; Henton, 1992; Meditch, 1975) that men and women differ from each other at most levels of linguistic structure. Gender differences in speech production patterns have also been frequently noted (e.g., Byrd, 1994). Because dialect variation is often cued by phonetic differences, it seems reasonable to expect that male and female phonological "dialects" may exist in most languages.

Some researchers posit an ethological basis for some male/female differences (Ohala, 1984), while others suggest that male/female differences may be an aid to communication (Diehl et al., 1996). Whatever the cause for behavioral gender differences in speech, there is reason to believe that anatomical differences are not the exclusive source of the differences between men's and women's vowel spaces. The evidence suggests that talkers differ from each other in other ways that can not be predicted from vocal tract anatomy differences alone, and thus that the "coordinate system" used by listeners in speech perception is probably related to talker differences that extend beyond vocal tract differences.

15.5.2 Acquisition of gender differences

Data from studies of gender differentiation in children show that listeners can correctly identify the sex of prepubescent boys and girls on the basis of short recorded speech samples. Results from these studies are summarized in Table 15.2. These data have been taken to suggest that boys and girls learn to speak differently before their vocal tract geometries diverge at puberty (but see below). Acoustic analysis of the stimuli used in the Sachs, Lieberman, and Erickson (1973),

Table 15.2 Results of studies in which listeners were asked to identify the sex of children on the basis of short recorded speech samples. The data listed under males and females are the percent correct gender identification scores for boys and girls

	% correct		*Age*	*Speech segment duration*
	Boys	*Girls*		
Sachs et al. (1973)	86%	75%	4–14 years	3 seconds
Meditch (1975)	85%	74%	3–5 years	2 minutes
Bennett & Weinburg (1979)				
phonated vowels	68%	63%	6–7 years	1 second
whispered vowels	67%	65%	6–7 years	1 second
sentence (monotone)	81%	63%	6–7 years	3 seconds
sentence (normal)	71%	69%	6–7 years	3 seconds
Ingrisano et al. (1980)	70%		4.5 years	3 seconds
Perry et al. (2001)				
blocked by age	67%	62%	4 years	CVC syllables
	74%	56%	8 years	
	82%	56%	12 years	
	99%	95%	16 years	

Bennett and Weinburg (1979), and Perry, Ohde, and Ashmead (2001) studies indicate that listeners' responses were based primarily on the frequencies of the vowel formants, particularly F2, rather than F0, the most salient cue for adult gender.

Figure 15.4 shows children's average vowel formant data from the extensive study by Lee, Potamianos, and Narayanan (1999), together with data from 4-, 8-, 12-, and 16-year-olds from Perry et al. (2001). Data not shown in the figure for 8-year-olds from Bennett (1981), for 11-year-olds from White (1999), for 11-, 12-, and 13-year-olds and adults from Eguchi and Hirsh (1969), and for 9-year-olds and adults from Most, Amir, and Tobin (2000) show the same trends. Boys and girls show small, consistent (and when tested, significant) differences in their vowel formant frequencies well before the onset of puberty. After the age of about 13 years boys and girls begin to differ more substantially.

Bennett (1981, p. 238) found a relationship between measures of gross body size and children's formant frequencies which suggested that "the larger overall size of male children also results in a larger vocal tract." Perry et al. (2001) quantified the extent to which gender differences in children's vowel formants can be predicted from age and body size. In their regression analysis, age and body size measurements account for most of the variance in children's measured formant frequencies (82–87% of the variance), but gender as a separate predictive factor also accounts for a significant proportion of the variance of each formant. Gender accounted for 5% of additional variance of F1 and F3 and 9% of

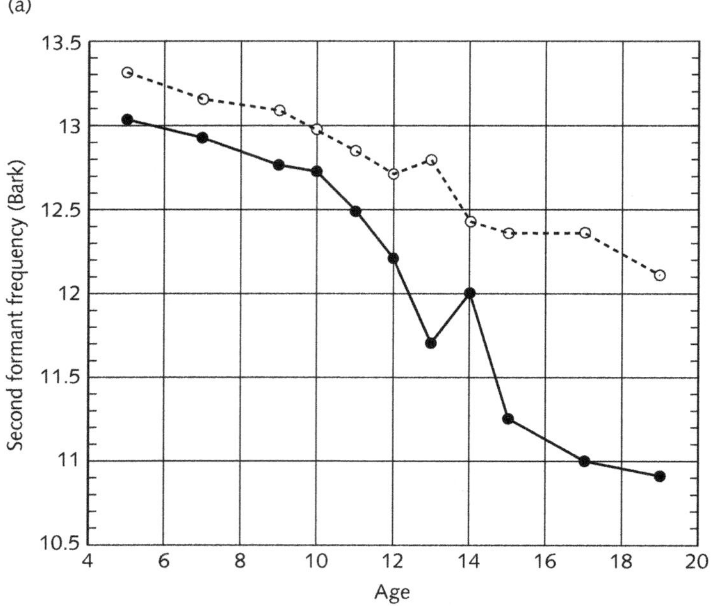

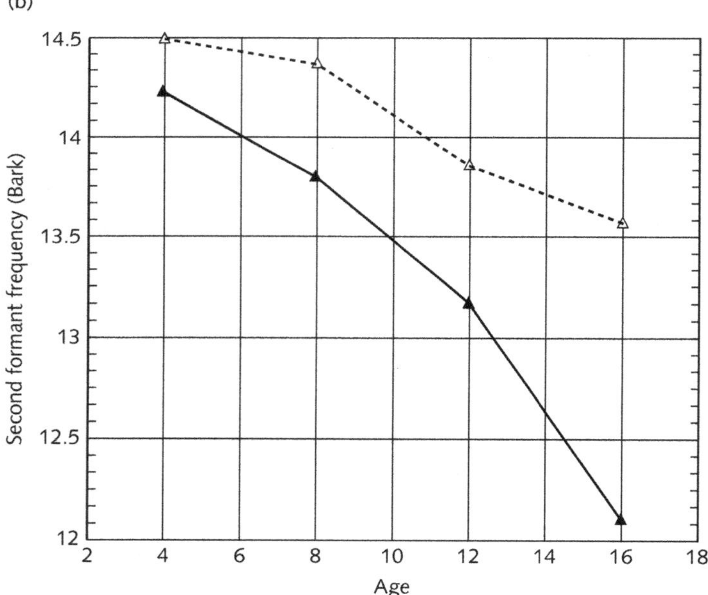

Figure 15.4 Average frequencies of the second vowel formant (in Bark), for children ranging from 5 to 17 years old. Data plotted in panel (a) are from Lee et al. (1999) and data plotted in panel (b) are from Perry et al. (2001). Filled symbols and solid lines plot the male formant frequencies and open symbols and dashed lines plot the female formant frequencies.

additional F2 variance. It is interesting that the largest gender effect was observed for F2 – the formant that has the largest range of speaker controllable variation. The authors of all of these studies on sex differentiation in children's speech conclude much as White (1999, p. 579) did that, "males and females may well adopt gender-specific articulatory behaviors from childhood to further enhance sex distinctions."

15.5.3 *Cross-linguistic gender differences*

Bladon, Henton, and Pickering (1984) compared the amount of spectral shift needed to normalize male and female spectra for speakers of different languages. They found that the difference between men and women varied from language to language. Cross-linguistic variation in how male and female talkers differ from each other might indicate that cultural factors are involved in defining and shaping male or female speech – and thus that anatomy does not completely determine the vowel formant frequencies.

Figure 15.5 shows the gender difference for F1, F2, and F3, for 26 different groups of speakers. This dataset, which was drawn from a number of published reports, includes data for many unrelated languages, as opposed to the generally western-language bias of previous cross-linguistic comparisons. For Figure 15.5, the male/female formant frequency differences for five vowels [i, e, a, o, u] in each language were averaged. If the language has fewer than five vowel qualities the

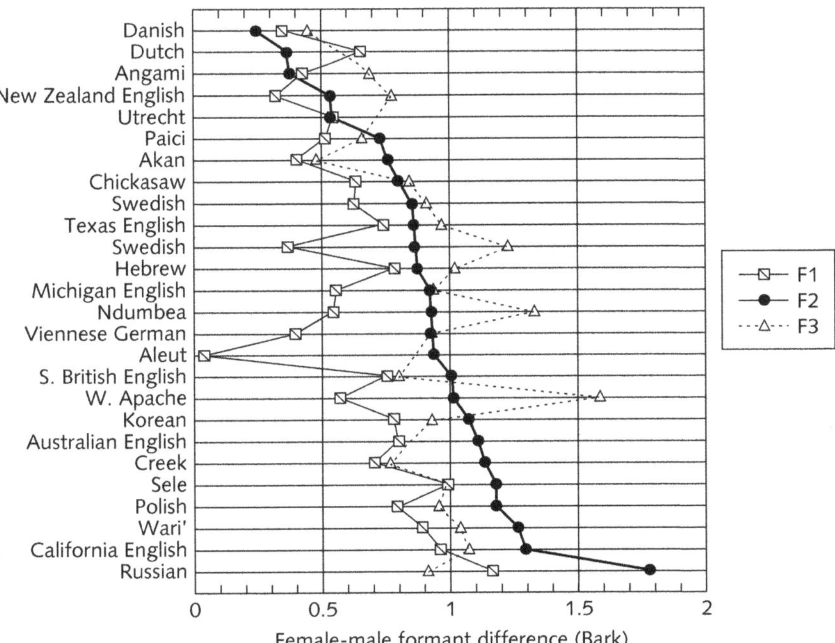

Figure 15.5 The difference between men's and women's average formant frequencies for 26 groups of speakers.

average was over the three or 4 vowels in the language. Only long vowels were sampled if the language distinguishes between long and short vowels. The languages were sorted from smallest gender difference for F2 (Danish) to largest F2 difference (Russian), and as the figure shows, the first and third formants show the same general trend as F2, though the ordering would be somewhat different if we sorted by F1 or F3 differences.

As the figure shows, men and women have quite similar vowel formants in some languages like Danish with less than half of a Bark difference between men and women for F1, F2, and F3, while other languages show formant frequency differences that are more than double this, like Russian.

Figure 15.6 shows the formant frequency differences between men and women as a function of the women's formant frequencies for the raw data that went into Figure 15.5. (The F by DF space was suggested by Simpson, 2001.) The horizontal axis shows the vowel formant frequency for women's vowels, and the vertical axis shows the formant frequency difference between men and women. Three clusters of points, for F1, F2, and F3, are shown against Traunmüller's (1984) model predictions plotted with filled symbols. Traunmüller's gender differences predictions match the average cross-linguistic pattern for this sample of 26 studies quite well, indicating that vocal tract geometry differences may account for the

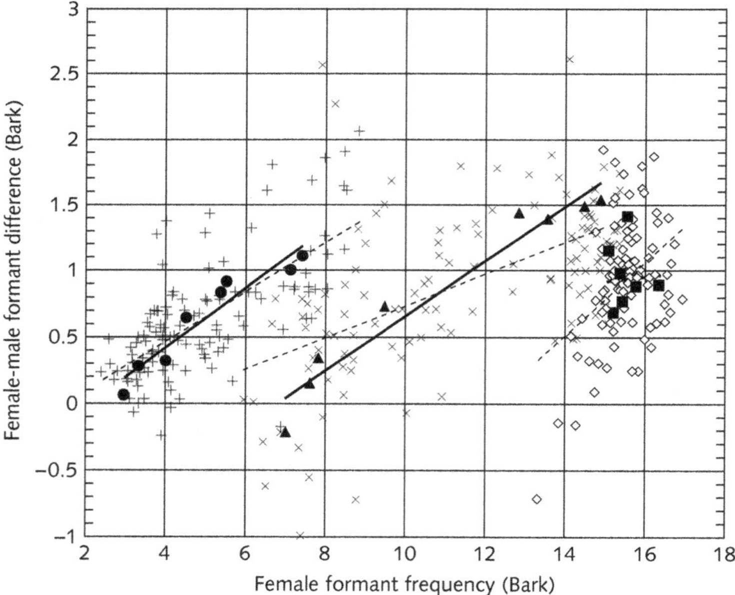

Figure 15.6 The F by DF space for 26 groups of male and female adult speakers. Male/female formant differences are plotted as a function of female formant frequency. F1 values from the cross-linguistic data set are plotted with plus signs, F2 data are plotted with x, and F3 is plotted with diamonds. The solid symbols plot the predicted F by DF relationships from Traunmüller's (1984) simulations of male-female "anatomy-only" formant differences. The solid regression lines are fit to Traunmüller's predictions, and the dashed regression lines fit the cross-linguistic data.

general pattern of the data, but the data are not tightly clustered around the predicted values. Overall only 30% of the variance is accounted for by the vocal tract differences model.

Traunmüller's (1984) model of male/female vocal tract differences was based on anatomy studies of particular speakers, so the unexplained variance in Figure 15.6 needs to be partialled between variance due to specific talker's vocal tract (vs. average male or female geometry) and remaining gender differences in habits of articulation attributable to gender "dialect" differences specific to particular speech communities.

These explorations into gender differences in vowel production by children and across cultures suggest that talkers choose different styles of speaking as social, dialectal gender markers. Thus, a speaker normalization that removes vocal tract differences will fail to account for the linguistic categorical similarity of vowels that are different due to different habits of articulation (for individuals or gender "dialect" differences). Numerous studies indicate that talker-specific characteristics interact with spoken language processing. What is more, if listeners were not able to sense the aspects of phonetic production that vary due to the idiosyncrasies of talkers, then they would be unable to control their own expression of these free subphonemic contrasts.

15.5.4 *Familiarity with the talker affects recognition*

Interactions between talker identity and spoken language processing have been found in studies where prior familiarity with the talker influences processing. For example, Lightfoot (1989) trained listeners to recognize talkers and found that listeners remembered words presented in a serial recall list better when they were spoken in a familiar voice. Walker et al. (1995) took advantage of listeners' natural familiarity with talkers (by using colleagues as talkers and listeners) and found that audio/visual integration in the "McGurk effect" was modulated by familiarity. When the face and voice came from different talkers, the audio and visual streams were not integrated for listeners who were familiar with the talkers. Nygaard and Pisoni (1998) using a talker learning paradigm like Lightfoot's found that learning a talker from sentences does not lead to better word recognition performance, but learning a talker from words leads to better word recognition performance and learning talkers from sentences leads to better sentence processing performance. This is a quite important finding because it suggests that the talker information being learned is not simply related to static vocal tract geometry, but instead must have something to do with how people say things in the particular instances heard – reflecting their habits of articulation.

15.5.5 *Sociophonetic effects in spoken language processing*

We saw in Section 15.3.7 that listener expectations can influence speech perception. We discussed that data under the heading "From auditory gestalts to vocal tract actions" because it could be assumed that the effect of listener expectations is limited to relating the incoming speech to a particular vocal tract representation. However, further evidence suggests that listeners' expectations are related to social stereotypes rather than veridical vocal tract parameters. In sociophonetics it has been demonstrated through "matched-guise" experiments that listeners are likely to attribute personality traits to people on the basis of their speech patterns. Recently, this approach has been extended to speech perception. Rubin (1992) found that speech intelligibility is reduced when American college-age listeners associate a voice with an Asian-looking face. He presented the same recorded lectures with a picture of an Asian lecturer or a Caucasian lecturer, and found lower listening comprehension scores for listeners who saw the Asian lecturer. Niedzielski (1997) found that the perceived nationality of a talker ("Canadian" or "American") influenced vowel perception. She used a vowel-matching procedure and told one group of listeners that the speaker was from Ontario, Canada and another group of listeners that the speaker was a native of Detroit. In matching synthetic vowel tokens to naturally produced words, listeners chose vowel tokens that exhibited Canadian raising (the pronunciation of the English /a^{u}/ diphthong as [ʌ^{u}]) if the talker was identified as a "Canadian," but choose non-raised variants as vowel matches if the talker was identified as an "American." What is especially telling about this result is that the speaker (a Detroit native) actually pronounced the words with Canadian raising, so these Detroit listeners ended up giving non-veridical answers in their matching responses to the "American" speaker. In both of these studies, listeners' socially-based expectations, regarding the talker's group membership, influenced perception. Similar perceptual effects for socially-based expectations have also been observed for gender in speech perception.

Strand (2000) found that gender stereotypicality influences auditory word recognition. She measured stereotypicality implicitly as the convergence of a multidimensional scaling analysis of the perceptual space for a group of talkers and a speeded gender classification task. The main result of Strand's study is that auditory word naming was slower when the talker was a nonstereotypical male or female than when the talker was stereotypical. Interestingly, the male "non-stereotypical" talker in this study had an unusually low fundamental frequency – so he was nonstereotypical by sounding somewhat "hypermale" rather than being a bit androgynous.

15.5.6 *Exemplar effects in word recognition*

Acoustic-phonetic details of utterances seem to be a part of the listener's long-term representation of speech. This has been demonstrated in tests of recognition memory and more importantly in tests of auditory word recognition. Palmeri, Goldinger, and Pisoni (1993) using a continuous recognition memory task, found that spoken words were more accurately recognized as "old" when they were repeated in the same voice than if they were repeated by a different talker. Church and Schacter (1994) found effects of voice, affect, and pitch range in an implicit memory task. Word recognition performance was better when primes (presented in a study list) and targets (presented in a test list) matched on these dimensions. These findings indicate that fine phonetic details, such as those associated with talker differences, remain as a part of the listener's memory of words. Goldinger (1996, 1997) also tested for the influence of talker-specific information in recognition memory for words. He found that talker repetition affected recognition memory with a one-day gap between study and test. More significantly, he also found repetition effects in perceptual identification. Previously heard items were identified more accurately even at the longest interval tested – one week between exposure and test. The long retention of talker-specific acoustic detail in this study is not consistent with abstractionist models of speaker normalization like the formant ratio and vocal tract normalization theories but is support for episodic/exemplar coding models.

15.6 Talker Normalization

Exemplar-based memory models (a common approach to the study of categorization and memory in cognitive psychology) offer an advance over vocal tract normalization theory in accounting for speaker normalization in speech perception. In this approach, cognitive *categories* are represented as collections of the stored cognitive representations of experienced *instances* of the category, rather than as normalized abstract representations from which category-internal structure has been removed (Hintzman, 1986; Kruschke, 1992; Nosofsky, 1986, 1988).

Instance-based, or exemplar-based models exhibit behavior that is very much like the generalization behavior of prototype theories (Hintzman, 1986). The main difference is that generalization in an instance-based system takes place during retrieval/activation of the category rather than during category storage/creation. Thus, on-line category adaptation, such as talker adaptation, is possible.

In exemplar-based "speaker normalization" the frame of reference, or coordinate system, is a set of "experienced" exemplars rather than a vocal tract (Johnson, 1997a, 1997b). Rather than warp the input signal to match a fixed internal template, the internal representation adapts according to the "perceived identity of the talker" (Johnson, 1990a), as exemplars appropriate for the talker are activated and inappropriate exemplars are deactivated forming a base activation rate (Nosofsky, 1988). In this system talker cues of all kinds can be involved in tuning the activated set of exemplars – visual representation, prior expectations, recognition of a specific known voice, and acoustic cues (F0 as a gender cue, but also formant range).

Additionally, exemplar models offer an adaptation mechanism that accounts for all kinds of variation that influences listeners including dialect variation, and the impact of unusual acoustic environments such as reverberation. Some surprising findings in the literature can be explained when perception is considered to be based on an exemplar-based memory system: for example, Nygaard and Pisoni's (1998) odd finding that talker learning is mode specific – talker representations learned from isolated words were not helpful to listeners in a sentence processing task; Eklund and Traunmüller's (1997) finding that talker and word misperceptions are correlated – listeners were more likely to misperceive the message if the gender of the talker had been misperceived; Strand's (2000) finding that nonstereotypical voices were processed more slowly than stereotypical voices. These results are difficult to account for in traditional abstractionist views of speech perception, but have a fairly straightforward explanation in exemplar-based models.

There are however some findings in the literature that seem to pose problems for exemplar-based models. For example, Nygaard, Sommers, and Pisoni (1994) found that familiarity with a talker's voice resulted in improved word recognition for novel stimuli not used in training listeners to become familiar with the talker. If, as might be expected from an exemplar-based model, the listeners' knowledge of the talkers was based solely upon the exemplars presented during training, then the word recognition gain should have been limited to performance with those particular exemplars.

In summary, research on the talker normalization problem indicates that the listener's perceptual representations of linguistic categories are richly structured, with information about talker identity retained in linguistic representations. One promising theoretical approach that captures the rich internal structure of linguistic categories, while also accounting for processes of generalization, is to model linguistic categories as collections of experienced instances rather than seeing speech perception as a process of mapping highly variable inputs onto invariant abstract representations.

NOTES

1 Sussman's figure leaves out the fact that central auditory cortex has a tonotopic organization, and thus supports absolute frequency coding as well as the relative coding provided by combination-sensitive neurons.
2 Hindle (1978) describes a six parameter regression model attributed to Sankoff, Shorrock, and McKay (see Hindle, 1978) which reduces scatter to such an extent that known sociolinguistic variability is removed from the normalized vowel space.
3 Actually, as with many other studies, they chose a "standard male" vowel space as the reference.

REFERENCES

Ainsworth, W. A. (1970). Perception of synthesized isolated vowels and h_d words as a function of fundamental frequency. *Journal of the Acoustical Society of America*, 49, 1323–4.

Ainsworth, W. A. (1974). The influence of precursive sequences on the perception of synthesized vowels. *Language and Speech*, 17, 103–9.

Assmann, P. F., Nearey, T. M. & Hogan, J. T. (1982). Vowel identification: Orthographic, perceptual, and acoustic aspects. *Journal of the Acoustical Society of America*, 71, 975–89.

Atal, B. S., Chang, J. J., Mathews, M. V., & Tukey, J. W. (1978). Inversion of articulatory-to-acoustic transformation of the vocal tract by a computer-sorting technique. *Journal of the Acoustical Society of America*, 63, 1535–55.

Bennett, S. (1981). Vowel formant frequency characteristics of preadolescent males and females. *Journal of the Acoustical Society of America*, 69, 231–8.

Bennett, S. & Weinberg, B. (1979). Sexual characteristics of preadolescent children's voices. *Journal of the Acoustical Society of America*, 65, 179–89.

Bladon, R. A., Henton, C. G., & Pickering, J. B. (1984). Towards an auditory theory of speaker normalization. *Language Communication*, 4, 59–69.

Byrd, D. (1994). Relations of sex and dialect to reduction. *Speech Communication*, 15, 39–54.

Carlson, R., Granström, B., & Fant, G. (1970). Some studies concerning perception of isolated vowels. *Speech Transmission Laboratory Quarterly Progress and Status Report 2–3/1970*, 19–35.

Chan, M. K. M. (1997). Gender differences in the Chinese language: A preliminary report. In H. Lin (ed.), *Proceedings of the Ninth North American Conference on Chinese Linguistics* (NACCL-9, May, vol. 2, pp. 35–52). Los Angeles: GSIL Publications, University of Southern California.

Chistovich, L. A., Sheikin, R. L., & Lublinskaja, V. V. (1979). "Centres of gravity" and spectral peaks as the determinants of vowel quality. In B. Lindblom & S. Öhman (eds.), *Frontiers of Speech Communication Research* (pp. 143–57). New York: Academic Press.

Church, B. A. & Schacter, D. L. (1994). Perceptual specificity of auditory priming – implicit memory for voice, intonation, and fundamental-frequency. *Journal of Experimental Psychology: Learning, Memory, and Cognition*, 20, 521–33.

Creelman, C. D. (1957). Case of the unknown talker. *Journal of the Acoustical Society of America*, 29, 655.

Dechovitz, D. (1977). Information conveyed by vowels: A confirmation. *Haskins Laboratory Status Report on Speech Research*, SR-53/54, 213–19.

Diehl, R. L., Lindblom, B., Hoemeke, K. A., & Fahey, R. P. (1996). On explaining certain male-female differences in the phonetic realization of vowel categories. *Journal of Phonetics*, 24, 187–208.

Disner, S. F. (1980). Evaluation of vowel normalization procedures. *Journal of the Acoustical Society of America*, 67, 253–61.

Eguchi, S. & Hirsh, I. J. (1969). Development of speech sounds in children. *Acta Otolaryngologica*, Supplementum 257, 1–51.

Eklund, I. & Traunmüller, H. (1997). Comparative study of male and female whispered and phonated versions of the long vowels of Swedish. *Phonetica*, 54, 1–21.

Fant, G. (1966). A note on vocal tract size factors and non-uniform F-pattern scalings. *Speech Transmission Laboratory Quarterly Progress and Status Report*, 4, 22–30.

Fant, G. (1975). Non-uniform vowel normalization. *Speech Transmission Laboratory Quarterly Progress and Status Report*, 2–3, 1–19.

Fox, R. A. (1982). Individual variation in the perception of vowels: Implications for a perception-production link. *Phonetica*, 39, 1–22.

Fox, R. A. (1983). Perceptual structure of monophthongs and diphthongs in English. *Language and Speech*, 26, 21–60.

Fox, R. & Qi, Y. Y. (1990). Context effects in the perception of lexical tone. *Journal of Chinese Linguistics*, 18, 261–83.

Fry, D. B., Abramson, A. S., Eimas, P. D., & Liberman, A. M. (1962). The identification and discrimination of synthetic vowels. *Language and Speech*, 5, 171–89.

Fujisaki, H. & Kawashima, T. (1968). The roles of pitch and higher formants in the perception of vowels. *IEEE Transactions on Audio and Electroacoustics*, AU-16, 73–7.

Gerstman, L. J. (1968). Classification of self-normalized vowels. *IEEE Transactions on Audio and Electroacoustics*, AU-16, 78–80.

Goldinger, S. D. (1996). Words and voices: Episodic traces in spoken word identification and recognition memory. *Journal of Experimental Psychology: Learning, Memory, and Cognition*, 22, 1166–83.

Goldinger, S. D. (1997). Words and voices: Perception and production in an episodic lexicon. In K. Johnson & J. W. Mullennix (eds.), *Talker Variability in Speech Processing* (pp. 33–66). San Diego: Academic Press.

Goldstein, U. (1980). An articulatory model for the vocal tracts of growing children. Unpublished PhD Dissertation, MIT.

Gottfried, T. L. & Chew, S. L. (1986). Intelligibility of vowels sung by a countertenor. *Journal of the Acoustical Society of America*, 79, 124–30.

Helmholtz, H. L. F. (1885). *On the Sensations of Tone* (translated by A. J. Ellis) (2nd edition). New York: Longman.

Henton, C. (1992). The abnormality of male speech. In G. Wolf (ed.), *New Departures in Linguistics* (pp. 27–55). New York: Garland.

Hillenbrand, J. M. & Nearey, T. M. (1999). Identification of resynthesized /hVd/ utterances: Effects of formant contour. *Journal of the Acoustical Society of America*, 105, 3509–23.

Hindle, D. (1978). Approaches to vowel normalization in the study of natural speech. In D. Sankoff (ed.), *Language Variation: Models and Methods* (pp. 161–71). New York: Academic Press.

Hintzman, D. L. (1986). "Schema abstraction" in a multiple-trace memory model. *Psychological Review*, 93, 411–28.

Ingrisano, D., Weismer, G., and Schuckers, G. H. (1980). Sex identification of preschool children's voices. *Folia Phoniatrica*, 32, 61–9.

Johnson, K. (1989). Higher formant normalization results from auditory integration of F2 and F3. *Perception & Psychophysics*, 46, 174–80.

Johnson, K. (1990a). The role of perceived speaker identity in F0 normalization of vowels. *Journal of the Acoustical Society of America*, 88, 642–54.

Johnson, K. (1990b). Contrast and normalization in vowel perception. *Journal of Phonetics*, 18, 229–54.

Johnson, K. (1991). Differential effects of speaker and vowel variability on fricative perception. *Language and Speech*, 34, 265–79.

Johnson, K. (1997a). Speech perception without speaker normalization: An exemplar model. In K. Johnson & J. W. Mullennix (eds.), *Talker Variability in Speech Processing* (pp. 145–66). San Diego: Academic Press.

Johnson, K. (1997b). The auditory/perceptual basis for speech segmentation. *Ohio State University Working Papers in Linguistics*, 50, 101–13.

Johnson, K., Ladefoged, P., & Lindau, M. (1993). Individual differences in vowel production. *Journal of the Acoustical Society of America*, 94, 701–14.

Johnson, K., Strand, E. A., & D'Imperio, M. (1999). Auditory-visual integration of talker gender in vowel perception. *Journal of Phonetics*, 27, 359–84.

Joos, M. A. (1948). Acoustic phonetics. *Language*, 24, supplement 2, 1–136.

Kakehi, K. (1992). Adaptability to differences between talkers in Japanese monosyllabic perception. In Y. Tohkura, E. Vatikiotis-Bateson, & Y. Sagisaka (eds.), *Speech Perception, Speech Production, and Linguistic Structure* (pp. 135–42). Tokyo: OHM.

Kato, K. & Kakehi, K. (1988). Listener adaptability to individual speaker differences in monosyllabic speech perception. *Journal of the Acoustical Society of Japan*, 44, 180–6.

Koenig, W., Dunn, H. K., & Lacy, L. Y. (1946). The sound spectrograph. *Journal of the Acoustical Society of America*, 18, 19–49.

Kruschke, J. K. (1992). ALCOVE: An exemplar-based connectionist model of category learning. *Psychological Review*, 99, 22–44.

Ladefoged, P. & Broadbent, D. E. (1957). Information conveyed by vowels. *Journal of the Acoustical Society of America*, 29, 98–104.

Leather, J. (1983). Speaker normalization in the perception of lexical tone. *Journal of Phonetics*, 11, 373–82.

Lee, S., Potamianos, A., & Narayanan, S. (1999). Acoustics of children's speech: Developmental changes of temporal and spectral parameters. *Journal of the Acoustical Society of America*, 105, 1455–68.

Lehiste, I. & Meltzer, D. (1973). Vowel and speaker identification in natural and synthetic speech. *Language and Speech*, 16, 356–64.

Lehiste, I. & Peterson, G. E. (1961). Transitions, glides, and diphthongs. *Journal of the Acoustical Society of America*, 33, 268–77.

Liberman, A. M., Cooper, F. S., Shankweiler, D., & Studdert-Kennedy, M. (1967). Perception of the speech code. *Psychological Review*, 74, 431–61.

Lightfoot, N. (1989). Effects of talker familiarity on serial recall of spoken word lists. *Research on Speech Perception Progress Report* (Bloomington: Indiana University, Department of Psychology) 15, 419–43.

Lindau, M. E. (1975). Features for vowels. Unpublished PhD Dissertation, UCLA.

Lloyd, R. J. (1890a). *Some Researches into the Nature of Vowel-Sound*. Liverpool, UK: Turner & Dunnett.

Lloyd, R. J. (1890b). Speech sounds: Their nature and causation (I). *Phonetische Studien*, 3, 251–78.

Lloyd, R. J. (1891). Speech sounds: Their nature and causation (II–IV). *Phonetische Studien*, 4, 37–67, 183–214, 275–306.

Lloyd, R. J. (1892). Speech sounds: Their nature and causation (V–VII). *Phonetische Studien*, 5, 1–32, 129–41, 263–71.

Lobanov, B. M. (1971). Classification of Russian vowels spoken by different speakers. *Journal of the Acoustical Society of America*, 49, 606–8.

Magnuson, J. S. & Nusbaum, H. C. (1994). Some acoustic and non-acoustic conditions that produce talker normalization. *Proceedings of the 1994 Spring Meeting of the Acoustical Society of Japan* (pp. 637–8).

Mann, V. A. & Repp, B. H. (1980). Influence of vocalic context on perception of the [ʃ]–[s] distinction. *Perception & Psychophyics*, 23, 213–28.

May, J. (1976). Vocal tract normalization for /s/ and /ʃ/. *Haskins Laboratories Status Report on Speech Research*, SR-48, 67–73.

McGowan, R. S. (1997). Vocal tract normalization for articulatory recovery and adaptation. In K. Johnson & J. W. Mullennix (eds.), *Talker Variability in Speech Processing* (pp. 211–26). San Diego: Academic Press.

McGowan R. S. & Cushing S. (1999). Vocal tract normalization for midsagittal articulatory recovery with analysis-by-synthesis. *Journal of the Acoustical Society of America*, 106, 1090–105.

Meditch, A. (1975). The development of sex-specific speech patterns in young children. *Anthropological Linguistics*, 17, 421–33.

Miller, J. D. (1989). Auditory-perceptual interpretation of the vowel. *Journal of the Acoustical Society of America*, 85, 2114–34.

Miller, R. L. (1953). Auditory tests with synthetic vowels. *Journal of the Acoustical Society of America*, 25, 114–21.

Mohr, B. & Wang, W. (1968). Perceptual distances and the specification of phonological features. *Phonetica*, 18, 31–45.

Moore, C. (1996). Speaker and rate normalization in the perception of lexical tone by Mandarin and English listeners. PhD Dissertation, Cornell University, Ithaca, NY.

Most, T., Amir, O., & Tobin, Y. (2000). The Hebrew vowel system: Raw and normalized acoustic data. *Language and Speech*, 43, 295–308.

Mullennix, J. W., Pisoni, D. B., & Martin, C. S. (1989). Some effects of talker variability on spoken word recognition. *Journal of the Acoustical Society of America*, 85, 365–78.

Nearey, T. M. (1978). Phonetic feature systems for vowels. Indiana University Linguistics Club, Bloomington, IN.

Nearey, T. M. (1989). Static, dynamic, and relational properties in vowel perception. *Journal of the Acoustical Society of America*, 85, 2088–113.

Nearey, T. M. & Assmann, P. F. (1986). Modeling the role of inherent spectral change in vowel identification. *Journal of the Acoustical Society of America*, 80, 1297–1308.

Niedzielski, N. A. (1997). The effect of social information on the phonetic perception of sociolinguistic variables. PhD Dissertation, UC Santa Barbara.

Nordström, P.-E. (1977). Female and infant vocal tracts simulated from male area functions. *Journal of Phonetics*, 5, 81–92.

Nordström, P.-E. & Lindblom, B. (1975). A normalization procedure for vowel formant data. *Proceedings of the 8th International Congress of Phonetic Sciences*, Leeds, UK.

Nosofsky, R. M. (1986). Attention, similarity, and the identification-categorization relationship. *Journal of Experimental Psychology: General*, 115, 39–57.

Nosofsky, R. M. (1988). Exemplar-based accounts of relations between classification, recognition, and typicality. *Journal of Experimental Psychology: Learning, Memory, and Cognition*, 14, 700–8.

Nusbaum, H. C. & Morin, T. M. (1992). Paying attention to differences among talkers. In Y. Tohkura, Y. Sagisaka, & E. Vatikiotis-Bateson (eds.), *Speech Perception, Speech Production, and Linguistic Structure* (pp. 113–34). Tokyo: OHM.

Nygaard, L. C. & Pisoni, D. B. (1998). Talker-specific learning in speech perception. *Perception & Psychophysics*, 60, 355–76.

Nygaard, L. C., Sommers, M. S., & Pisoni, D. B. (1994). Speech perception as a talker-contingent process. *Psychological Science*, 5, 42–5.

Ohala, J. J. (1984). An ethological perspective on common cross-language utilization of F0 of voice. *Phonetica*, 41, 1–16.

Palmeri, T. J., Goldinger, S. D., & Pisoni, D. B. (1993). Episodic encoding of voice attributes and recognition memory for spoken words. *Journal of Experimental Psychology: Learning, Memory, and Cognition*, 19, 309–28.

Perry, T. L., Ohde, R. N., & Ashmead, D. H. (2001). The acoustic bases for gender identification from children's voices. *Journal of the Acoustical Society of America*, 109, 2988–98.

Peterson, G. E. (1961). Parameters of vowel quality. *Journal of Speech & Hearing Research*, 4, 10–29.

Peterson, G. E. & Barney, H. L. (1952). Control methods used in the study of vowels. *Journal of the Acoustical Society of America*, 24, 175–84.

Pols, L. C. W., van der Kamp, L. J. T., & Plomp, R. (1969). Perceptual and physical space of vowel sounds. *Journal of the Acoustical Society of America*, 46, 458–67.

Potter, R. & Steinberg, J. (1950). Toward the specification of speech. *Journal of the Acoustical Society of America*, 22, 807–20.

Rakerd, B. & Verbrugge, R. R. (1985). Linguistic and acoustic correlates of the perceptual structure found in an individual differences scaling study of vowels. *Journal of the Acoustical Society of America*, 77, 296–301.

Remez, R. E., Rubin, P. E., Nygaard, L. C., & Howell, W. A. (1987). Perceptual normalization of vowels produced by sinusoidal voices. *Journal of Experimental Psychology: Human Perception and Performance*, 13, 40–61.

Rosner, B. S. & Pickering, J. B. (1994). *Vowel Perception and Production*. Oxford: Oxford University Press.

Rubin, D. L. (1992). Non-language factors affecting undergraduates' judgements of non-native English-speaking teaching assistants. *Research in Higher Education*, 33, 4.

Sachs, J., Lieberman, P., & Erickson, D. (1973). Anatomical and cultural determinants of male and female speech. In R. W. Shuy & R. W. Fasold (eds.), *Language Attitudes: Current Trends and Prospects* (pp. 74–84). Washington, DC: Georgetown University Press.

Schwartz, M. F. (1968). Identification of speaker sex from isolated voiceless fricatives. *Journal of the Acoustical Society of America*, 43, 1178–9.

Schwippert, C. & Benoit, C. (1997). Audiovisual intelligibility of an androgynous speaker. In C. Benoit &

R. Campbell (eds.), *Proceedings of the ESCA Workshop on Audiovisual Speech Processing (AVSP'97): Cognitive and Computational Approaches* (pp. 81–4). Rhodes, Greece.

Shepard, R. N. (1972). Psychological representation of speech sounds. In P. B. Denes & E. E. David (eds.), *Human Communication: A Unified View* (pp. 76–113). New York: McGraw-Hill.

Simpson, A. P. (2001). Dynamic consequences of differences in male and female vocal tract dimensions. *Journal of the Acoustical Society of America*, 109, 2153–64.

Slawson, A. W. (1968). Vowel quality and musical timbre as functions of spectrum envelope and fundamental frequency. *Journal of the Acoustical Society of America*, 43, 87–101.

Sovijärvi, A. (1938). Die gehaltenen, geflüsterten und gesungenen Vokale und Nasale der finnischen Sprache. *Annales Academiae Scientiarum, Fennicae*, Helsinki B64, 2.

Strand, E. A. (2000). Gender stereotype effects in speech processing. PhD Dissertation. Ohio State University.

Strand, E. A. & Johnson, K. (1996). Gradient and visual speaker normalization in the perception of fricatives. In D. Gibbon (ed.), *Natural Language Processing and Speech Technology: Results of the 3rd KONVENS Conference, Bielefeld* (pp. 14–26). Berlin: Mouton de Gruyter.

Summerfield, Q. & Haggard, M. P. (1973). Vocal tract normalization as demonstrated by reaction times. *Report of Speech Research in Progress*, 2, 1–12, The Queen's University of Belfast, Ireland.

Sussman, H. M. (1986). A neuronal model of vowel normalization and representation. *Brain and Language*, 28, 12–23.

Sussman, H. M., Fruchter, D., Hilbert, J., & Sirosh, J. (1998). Linear correlates in the speech signal: The orderly output constraint. *Behavioral and Brain Sciences*, 21, 241–99.

Syrdal, A. K. & Gopal, H. S. (1986). A perceptual model of vowel recognition based on the auditory representation of American English vowels. *Journal of the Acoustical Society of America*, 79, 1086–100.

Terbeek, D. & Harshman, R. (1972). Is vowel perception non-Euclidian? *Journal of the Acoustical Society of America*, 51, 81.

Traunmüller, H. (1981). Perceptual dimension of openness in vowels. *Journal of the Acoustical Society of America*, 69, 1465–75.

Traunmüller, H. (1984). Articulatory and perceptual factors controlling the age- and sex-conditioned variability in formant frequencies of vowels. *Speech Communication*, 3, 49–61.

Verbrugge, R. R., Strange, W., Shankweiler, D. P., & Edman, T. R. (1976). What information enables a listener to map a talker's vowel space? *Journal of the Acoustical Society of America*, 60, 198–212.

Walker, S., Bruce, V., & O'Malley, C. (1995). Facial identity and facial speech processing: Familiar faces and voices in the McGurk effect. *Perception & Psychophysics*, 57, 1124–33.

White, P. (1999). Formant frequency analysis of children's spoken and sung vowels using sweeping fundamental frequency production. *Journal of Voice*, 13, 570–82.

16 Perceptual Integration of Linguistic and Nonlinguistic Properties of Speech

LYNNE C. NYGAARD

Imagine speaking with someone who has an unusual or unfamiliar dialect. At first, we may have difficulty understanding what is being said, but given time, we slowly become accustomed to the particular way in which the talker shapes his or her speech sounds. This example illustrates that speech not only contains the linguistic content of an intended utterance, such as the syllables, words, and phrases of speech, but also a multitude of talker-specific characteristics such as emotional tone of voice, cues to talker identity, dialect, and accent. Although these characteristics are informative, they also introduce an enormous amount of variability into the acoustic realization of spoken language.

One of the consequences of this variation is that during speech communication, speakers produce an acoustic signal that contains multiple layers of information. From the complex phonological structure of speech to the infinite variability introduced by individual talkers' voice and style, the speech signal codes the talker's intended message at both linguistic and nonlinguistic levels. This layering implies that the listener must somehow disentangle attributes of the signal related to linguistic structure from attributes related to tone of voice or talker identity, for instance, in order to correctly recover both *what* the speaker has said and *how* the speaker said it. In order to accomplish this separation of linguistic structure from surface form, it has been assumed that these two types of information must be acoustically, perceptually, and/or representationally distinct (e.g., Jackson & Morton, 1984; McClelland & Elman, 1986; Studdert-Kennedy, 1976).

The purpose of this chapter is to discuss the relationship between linguistic and nonlinguistic information in spoken language processing. I first focus on the importance of surface characteristics in the representation and processing of spoken language and then I review research examining the role this information plays in speech perception and spoken word recognition. In this chapter, I question the traditional theoretical distinction between linguistic and nonlinguistic information in the speech signal and examine evidence for an alternative proposal that linguistic and nonlinguistic properties are integrally related components of the same acoustic speech signal and, consequently, the speech perceptual process. I propose, as have others (e.g., Goldinger, 1998; Jusczyk, 1993; Pisoni, 1993, 1997), that theoretical accounts of spoken language processing will need to include a role for the representation and processing of the "surface form" of spoken language.

16.1 Variation as a Source of Noise

The majority of research on speech perception and spoken language processing has focused on the complex relationship between acoustic properties of speech and underlying phonological and lexical correlates. Researchers have often assumed an idealized context-free world of representation in which abstract units are organized and processed according to purely linguistic properties (Halle, 1985; see Tenpenny, 1995). On the one hand, researchers have investigated how abstract linguistic units are extracted from the highly variable speech signal (Green et al., 1991; Joos, 1948; Ladefoged & Broadbent, 1957; Pisoni, 1997; Summerfield & Haggard, 1973). On the other hand, a separate body of research has examined how various surface characteristics are perceived and identified (Scherer et al., 1991; Van Lancker, Kreiman, & Emmorey, 1985; Van Lancker, Kreiman, & Wickens, 1985). This empirical and theoretical separation of the perception of linguistic and nonlinguistic properties of speech implies a process in which variants of a particular type of linguistic unit are normalized to arrive at an abstract, prototypical representation (Joos, 1948; Krulee, Tondo, & Wightman, 1983). Subsequent linguistic analysis is further assumed to be isolated from the analysis of the variability stripped away at an earlier stage of processing (Liberman & Mattingly, 1985, 1989).

Recently, however, variation in the speech signal and its influence on linguistic processing has begun to be explicitly investigated. Variability due to the idiosyncratic characteristics of a talker's voice, for example, has been shown to affect the time course and accuracy of spoken word recognition. Mullennix, Pisoni, and Martin (1989), for example, found that lists of words in which the talker's voice varied from item to item were more difficult to identify in noise than low variability lists in which all words were presented in a single talker's voice. Other surface characteristics such as speaking rate have also been found to influence perceptual processing (Sommers, Nygaard, & Pisoni, 1994). These studies suggest that variation in the nonlinguistic aspects of speech is time and resource demanding and influences the processing of the linguistic aspects of speech.

In addition to studies that demonstrate the processing consequences of high variability materials, a complementary body of work suggests that surface form characteristics are retained in memory along with linguistic content (Bradlow, Nygaard, & Pisoni, 1999; Goldinger, Pisoni, & Logan, 1991; Martin et al., 1989; Nygaard, Burt, & Queen, 2000; Nygaard, Sommers, & Pisoni, 1995). Palmeri, Goldinger, and Pisoni (1993) found that in a continuous recognition memory experiment, listeners were better able to recognize words that were repeated in the same as opposed to a different voice. Voice characteristics were retained along with linguistic content. Numerous other studies have found evidence for the retention of talker's voice and, to a certain extent, other types of surface form, in both explicit memory (Craik & Kirsner, 1974; Geiselman, 1979; Geiselman & Bellezza, 1976, 1977; Geiselman & Crawley, 1983) and implicit memory (Church & Schacter, 1994; Cole, Coltheart, & Allard, 1974; Goldinger, 1996; Nygaard &

Pisoni, 1998; Schacter & Church, 1992) for spoken words. These findings, taken together with evidence for the influence on perceptual processing of variation in word form, point to the conclusion that surface form is not discarded during the processing of spoken language, but rather retained and used.

Although evidence suggests that variation is time and resource demanding during linguistic processing and that surface characteristics are retained in memory along with linguistic content, less clear is the exact relationship between linguistic content and surface form. One possibility is that these two sources of information are integrally related, each aspect of the speech signal influencing the processing of the other. Certainly, evidence suggests that variability is informative and contributes to our understanding of a talker's intended utterance. Further, variation in the shape and structure of linguistic units, at least in part, carries informative nonlinguistic information. Finally, research suggests that the interpretation of linguistic content is fundamentally altered by the surface characteristics in which the linguistic form is uttered, indicating that the semantic content of surface form is integrated early on in processing with linguistic content.

Based on research demonstrating the dependence of the perception of speech on surface characteristics, the two sources of information appear not to be separately processed but rather are part and parcel of the same fundamental acoustic-phonetic dimensions and, consequently, of related perceptual analyses. The next sections review these findings.

16.2 Variability as a Source of Information

Much of the variation in the way speech is produced stems from characteristics of particular talkers. Aspects of a talker's voice convey information about the talker's identity (Monsen & Engebretson, 1977; Peterson & Barney, 1952; Van Lancker, Kreiman, & Emmorey, 1985; Van Lancker, Kreiman, & Wickens, 1985), emotional state (Frick, 1985; Murray & Arnott, 1993; Scherer et al., 1991), region of origin (Labov, 1972; see Clopper & Pisoni, this volume), health, and age of a particular talker. These idiosyncratic characteristics introduce variation in the speech signal, but also importantly, bring an enormous amount of information into the communicative context. Just as there is a layering of information in linguistic structure, surface form contains information that ranges from clearly linguistic (e.g., lexical stress) to less clearly linguistic (e.g., emotional tone of voice). Nevertheless, differences in the way in which an utterance is pronounced provide information about the speaker and the message he or she is intending to convey.

One clearly linguistic aspect of spoken language consists of certain properties of speech that are suprasegmental. These are aspects of speech that span or overlay several smaller linguistic units such as phonetic segments. Suprasegmental characteristics are crucially important in determining word meaning, lexical access, word and sentence parsing, and syntactic interpretation. Cutler (1994; this volume) has found that lexical stress and prosody help listeners segment the continuous speech stream and may initiate and facilitate lexical access and word recognition. Early in development, infants use prosodic information provided by adults not only to engage in emotional communication (Walker-Andrews &

Dickson, 1997), but also to segment the speech stream as well as to initiate lexical access (Jusczyk, Cutler, & Redanz, 1993). Kjelgaard and Speer (1999) have found that sentential prosody disambiguates syntactic structure in spoken sentences. Prosodic contours provide reliable information about syntactic breaks in utterances (Kjelgaard & Speer, 1999), signal phrasal and sentential boundaries (Speer, Crowder, & Thomas, 1993), and certainly determine utterance type (e.g., question, command, statement) (Cooper, Eady, & Mueller, 1985). Clearly, these aspects of spoken language are linguistic in nature, providing lexical and syntactic information.

Other aspects of spoken language have traditionally been considered nonlinguistic. Characteristics of the speech signal such as talker identity, emotional tone of voice, accent, and dialect are all considered to be processed and identified separately from the recovery of linguistic content. These characteristics of speech are informative, however, and are readily identified and used to gauge characteristics of the speaker and communicative setting. For example, listeners in a variety of situations will monitor their conversational partners' vocal style and modify their own speech production to match or mismatch (Namy, Nygaard, & Sauerteig, 2002). If their vocal characteristics match, listeners and speakers endorse positive attributes of one another. Mismatching characteristics appear to socially distance conversational partners from one another and may send a message of individual identity (Shepard, Giles, & Le Poire, 2001).

One particularly salient type of surface form is emotional tone of voice. Listeners readily identify the emotional state of a conversational partner from their speech. A large body of research has investigated what properties of the speech signal carry emotional information and how listeners use that information to correctly recognize emotional prosody (Frick, 1985; Murray & Arnott, 1993; Scherer et al., 1991). Individuals who demonstrate difficulties with perception and identification of emotional tone have been shown to have difficulty in social situations (Nowicki & Carton, 1997). These findings suggest that in everyday conversation emotional prosody is crucially informative. However, little research has examined the way in which emotion is incorporated into linguistic processing and analysis.

The findings on the perception of nonlinguistic aspects of spoken language suggest that these properties are readily identified, represented, informative, and extremely important for spoken communication. Yet, the relationship of these attributes with respect to linguistic processing has received relatively less attention in research on spoken language. In the next section, I review some classic and more recent research suggesting that the identity or form of linguistic units changes systematically with particular types of surface form and that these changes have consequences for the perception of speech.

16.3 Acoustic and Perceptual Consequences of Informative Variation

Different sources of variation result in acoustic consequences that are measurable and perceptible. These sources not only overlay acoustic dimensions of the speech signal but also reshape and change the phonological form of an utterance. Although listeners are able to classify segments into phonemic classes despite

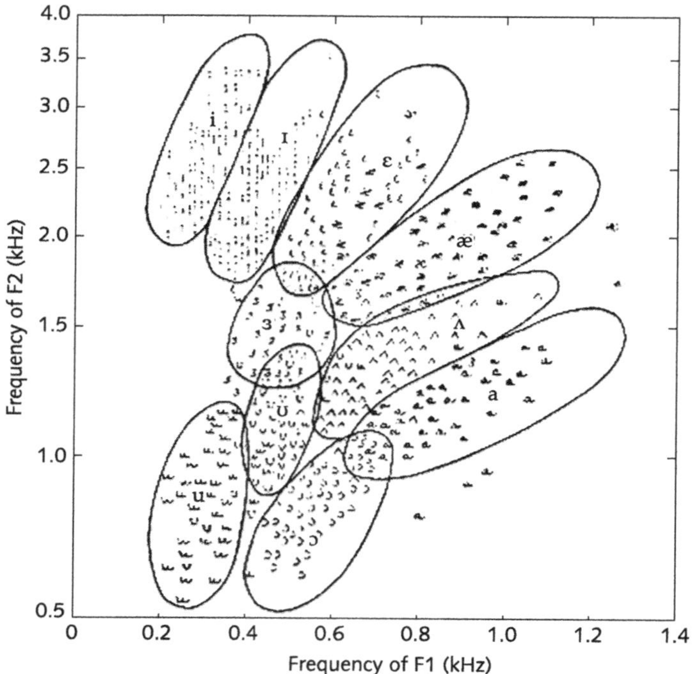

Figure 16.1 First formant frequency plotted as a function of second formant frequency for multiple vowels from multiple talkers (Adapted from Peterson & Barney, 1952).

a range of phonetic variations, these variations turn out to be informative, as reviewed above. One classic example of this phenomenon is the change that a talker's voice imposes on vowel acoustic structure. Peterson and Barney (1952) measured vowel formant frequencies for a variety of different vowels and a number of different talkers, including men, women, and children. They found, as shown in Figure 16.1, that the center frequencies of the first two formants of particular vowels overlapped across speakers. A particular intended vowel of one individual overlapped acoustically with the values for a different vowel produced by a different speaker (e.g., one person's *bet* might be another person's *bit*). Particulars of the size and shape of each talker's vocal tract changed the acoustic structure of their vowels. This classic example of talker variability suggests that properties of the signal that carry phonemic weight also carry talker identity.

It should be noted that not only do vowels differ in absolute acoustic shape depending on speaker, but listeners are also sensitive to these changes. Listeners can identify individuals from their voices and use talker information to make linguistic decisions. Ladefoged and Broadbent (1957) presented listeners with synthetic sentences in which the formant frequencies were either shifted up or down in frequency to mimic different talkers' voices. Listeners identified the last word of carrier phrases as either *bit*, *bet*, *bat*, or *but* and these synthesized tokens did not change. They found that listeners changed their judgments of vowel identity based on the properties of the carrier phrase. The same token (i.e., *bet*) was judged to contain one vowel following one carrier phrase and another vowel following another carrier phrase. Listeners appeared to be taking into account the properties of different "talkers'" speech and changing their phonemic classifications accordingly.

Another aspect of spoken language that causes significant changes in the structure of the speech signal is speaking rate. Several researchers have documented the changes in formant transition, vowel, overall syllable, and sentential context duration that accompany changes in the articulation rate of a talker (e.g., Miller, Grosjean, & Lomanto, 1984). A large body of research suggests that listeners take into account the speaking rate of an utterance in order to determine the identity of linguistic units (Miller & Liberman, 1979; Miller & Volaitis, 1989; Summerfield, 1981; Volaitis & Miller, 1992). Miller and Liberman (1979), for example, found that the duration of the vowel in a CV syllable altered the categorization boundary of a *ba-wa* continuum. Listeners identified the stop-liquid distinction in the context of the perceived speaking rate of the syllable. Speaking rate changes the acoustic realization of particular linguistic units and listeners seem to compensate for this alteration by adjusting their perceptual and phonemic boundaries.

Although talker and rate have been most extensively studied, a number of other factors have been shown to influence the acoustic structure of linguistic units. Bradlow, Torretta, and Pisoni (1996) have found that individual talkers' vocal styles impose fine-grained phonetic changes in the speech signal and these changes may have consequences for intelligibility. Recently, Local (2002) has shown that even discourse elements such as turn-taking rules can influence the acoustic realization of phoneme-sized units. He has also shown that the effects of preceding and following phonetic context, syntactic structure, as well as pragmatic or discourse constraints can be far-reaching in terms of the extent of the speech signal that is influenced. These effects extend well beyond the traditional phoneme-sized unit and suggest that linguistic units are flexible, changing depending on a variety of factors.

Other aspects of a speaker's productions such as articulation effort (Moon & Lindblom, 1994), speaking style (Uchanski et al., 1996; Uchanski, this volume), and articulatory precision for given versus new information (Lindblom, 1990), all have profound effects on the acoustic speech signal introducing variation that is both informative and systematic. For example, Wouters and Macon (2002a) found that spectral dynamics of vowels depend not only on vowel duration but also on prosodic factors. Clearly, in addition to classic research on the talker and speaking rate variation, a new body of work is classifying the acoustic-phonetic effects of a variety of other types of articulatory changes. Although there is less work to date, for example, on the degree to which listeners attend to and use prosodic cues in the speech signal for information about discourse level rules, it is clear that these changes exist, are fairly systematic, and could potentially provide information to the listener. These studies do often show that these changes influence intelligibility and naturalness. For example, Wouters and Macon (2002b) found that speech synthesized with fine-grained variation was judged more natural and intelligible by listeners suggesting that these changes do influence linguistic processing.

Many questions remain, however, about how all these factors ultimately influence listeners' perception of speech and what type of processing and representation could underlie both the extraction of the linguistic content of speech and a sensitivity to the informative variation inherent in a talker's speech production.

16.4 Dependence of Linguistic Processing on Surface Form

Although many aspects of a talker's speech production influence the structure of linguistic units and may be informative to listeners, the aspect of speech that has received the most attention is change due to individual characteristics of a talker's voice. An enormous number of characteristics of a talker can fundamentally change the acoustic realization of speech. A large body of research has been devoted to determining what aspects of a talker's vocal tract anatomy result in changes to the speech signal (Joos, 1948; Monsen & Engebretson, 1977; Peterson & Barney, 1952). In addition, researchers have examined how listeners identify particular talker's voices (Bachorowski & Owren, 1999; Van Lancker, Kreiman, & Emmorey, 1985; Van Lancker, Kreiman, & Wickens, 1985); what makes some speakers more or less distinctive or intelligible than others (Bradlow et al., 1996); what personality characteristics are associated with particular talker attributes (Brown & Bradshaw, 1985); how soon in development infants can identify voices (Mehler et al., 1978); and under what conditions talkers are easier or harder to identify (Read & Craik, 1995). In general, acoustic attributes of the speech signal associated with talker identity are multidimensional in nature. Speakers may have different characteristic fundamental frequencies, formant spacing, breathiness, relative segment durations, overall speaking rate and vocal effort, to name but a few.

Traditionally, the perception of talker identity has been considered separately from the perception of the linguistic content of speech. As mentioned previously, a body of work has investigated the changes to linguistic structure due to individual differences in talkers' voices and speaking styles. However, much of this work assumes a perceptual process that normalizes differences due to talkers' voice to arrive at canonical linguistic symbols that in turn underlie subsequent linguistic processing (Brown & Carr, 1993; Jackson & Morton, 1984; Joos, 1948; Shankweiler, Strange, & Verbrugge, 1977). An alternative view suggests that variation is not discarded during speech perception and spoken word recognition, but is retained and used (Goldinger, 1998; Pisoni, 1993, 1997). That is, talker information, at least, may not be processed independently of linguistic content (Nygaard & Pisoni, 1998). Although listeners certainly need to extract linguistic units that are consistent across speakers, the speech perceptual process does not seem to be independent from the processing of talker characteristics (Nygaard, Sommers, & Pisoni, 1994). Given that linguistic structure changes as a result of characteristics of a talker's voice, it follows that these two aspects of spoken language might be linked in processing.

16.4.1 *Intelligibility*

One finding that suggests such a link stems from studies investigating the intelligibility of speech containing different sources of variation. Speakers differ in intelligibility and certainly, dialect and accent significantly impact listeners' ability to extract the linguistic content of speech. Nygaard and Queen (2000), for example, asked listeners to learn the voices of ten talkers, five male and five female. After learning, they found that talkers varied considerably in intelligibility with both individual differences (between talker) and group differences (between sex) in how well listeners could extract the linguistic content of speech. Bradlow et al. (1996) report similar findings. In their experiment, listeners were simply asked to transcribe sentence-length utterances produced by 20 different talkers (ten male and ten female). Bradlow et al. found that talkers varied with respect to intelligibility. Individual differences in talkers' voices affected the ease and accuracy with which listeners were able to transcribe the sentences.

Nygaard and Queen (2002) have shown that accented speech is significantly less intelligible than speech produced by talkers from one's own dialect or accent group. Numerous other studies along with our everyday experience demonstrate this finding as well (Bradlow & Pisoni, 1999; Clopper & Pisoni, this volume; Irwin, 1977; Lane, 1963; Van Wijngaarden, Steeneken, & Houtgast, 2002). The changes imposed on the speech signal by an individual's native phonological system significantly influence listeners' ability to extract linguistic content. Dialect differences, as well, involve changes at multiple levels of linguistic structure from syntactic construction, prosodic or intonational contours, lexical inventory, and phonological realization.

The impact of talker variation from individual and group differences on intelligibility provides indirect evidence that linguistic processing depends on the amount of change or variation that is introduced into the speech signal. This variation is not only present in irrelevant acoustic dimensions which overlay linguistic structure but is also present in the range of production types of particular linguistic structures or units.

16.4.2 *Talker identification*

Evidence for the dependence of the perception of talker identity on type of linguistic materials also suggests that the two types of information are linked. Goggin et al. (1991) evaluated talker identification performance in a foreign versus native language. In one experiment, native English-speaking listeners identified bilingual talkers from their voices when speaking either English or German. Goggin et al. found that listeners were better able to identify talkers when the talkers were speaking the listeners' native language than when speaking a foreign language. This finding suggests that individual talkers shape the speech signal in systematic ways. Listeners need to know the linguistic content of an utterance in order to attribute variation to a particular talker's voice. That talker identification depends on knowledge of linguistic structure once again suggests that these two properties of speech are carried along overlapping dimensions of the acoustic speech signal.

Mullennix and Pisoni (1990) directly tested the degree to which talker and phonetic information are integrally related. In a Garner (1974) speeded classification task, listeners either classified initial phonemes or classified speakers according to gender. They found that irrelevant (to the classification) variation in talker's voice slowed response times to initial phonemes. Likewise, irrelevant variation in initial phoneme slowed response times to gender classification. Interestingly, Green, Tomiak, and Kuhl (1997) reported similar findings with speaking rate and initial phoneme classification in a speeded classification task. These results provide evidence that talker, rate, and phonetic content are all integrally related, rather than separable, dimensions of the speech signal.

Remez, Fellowes, & Rubin (1997) investigated whether time-varying phonetic information was sufficient to support the perception of talker identity. In their experiment, listeners identified talkers' voices from sinewave analogs of speech. Sinewave speech consists of three time-varying sinusoids that track the center frequencies of the first three formants of a natural utterance. These signals preserve the time-varying information in speech without the short-term acoustic attributes that have been traditionally endorsed as cues to phonetic identity. In previous research, Remez et al. (1981) have shown that sinewave speech supports phonetic perception. Listeners were presented with sinewave analogs of sentence-length utterances. When unaware of the linguistic nature of these stimuli, listeners reported hearing buzzes, whistles, or science fiction sounds. When informed that these stimuli were speech, listeners successfully transcribed the sinewave utterances.

When listeners are cued to the linguistic content of sinewave speech, Remez et al. (1987) have subsequently demonstrated that listeners take into account properties of sinewave speech that signal differences in talker's voice to judge phonetic content. In a task similar to Ladefoged and Broadbent (1957), Remez et al. (1987) found that sinewave precursor phrases shifted up or down in frequency altered listeners' judgments of vowel identity. Thus, even in sinewave analogs of speech that presumably preserve only time-varying phonetic information, listeners take into account the concomitant talker variation in order to judge linguistic content.

In their experiment on talker identity, Remez et al. (1997) asked listeners to identify familiar voices from sinewave analogs of speech. The listeners and talkers were taken from a group of co-workers at Haskins Laboratories who were highly familiar with one another's voices. Remez et al. found that listeners were able to identify voices from sinewave analogs. In addition, they found that measures of voice similarity were comparable for natural tokens of the utterances and for matching sinewave analogs. That the perceptual judgments of sinewave speech matched those of the natural utterances suggests that processes underlying the perception of talker identity were fundamentally similar. That is, the information in the natural acoustic speech signal that allowed listeners to identify talkers was also present in the sinewave analogs of those talkers' voices. Given that sinewave speech arguably preserves only time-varying phonological information, the acoustic information for talker identity may be inherent in different talkers' time-varying phonetic information.

16.4.3 *Talker familiarity*

Additional research examining the relationship between the processing of linguistic and nonlinguistic properties of speech has investigated the role of talker familiarity on spoken language processing. Nygaard, Sommers, and Pisoni (1994; Nygaard & Pisoni, 1998) examined whether familiarity with a set of talkers' voices would influence the extraction of the linguistic content of speech. Nygaard et al. asked listeners to learn to identify a set of ten talkers' voices from single word utterances. On each of nine days of training, listeners were familiarized with each talker's voice (five male and five female) and learned to associate a common name with each talker's voice. After talker training, one group of listeners transcribed words mixed with noise produced by the talkers that they had learned during training. Another group of listeners transcribed utterances produced by a new set of talkers that they had not learned during training.

The results revealed that listeners who were familiar with the set of talkers' voices had more accurate transcription performance than listeners who were unfamiliar with that set of talkers' voices. Listeners were better able to extract the linguistic content of speech produced by familiar talkers. Interestingly, the results revealed large individual listener differences. Listeners differed significantly in their ability to learn voices from single word utterances and those listeners who were poor at learning the talkers' voices also did not show improvement in extracting linguistic content from the learned talkers' speech. These findings suggest that attention to and familiarity with talker-specific characteristics of the speech signal significantly influence the processing of the linguistic content of speech. Perceptual learning on an aspect of speech that has been assumed to be irrelevant with respect to linguistic processing was shown to influence a task involving linguistic analysis.

In another study, Bradlow and Pisoni (1999) also found that familiarity and experience with particular speaking styles of particular talkers influenced recognition of spoken words. Listeners in their experiment were presented with lists of words produced at different speaking rates (slow, medium, and fast) by different talkers (ten male and ten female). The lists contained "easy" and "hard" words in order to examine the interaction of talker and speaking rate with lexical difficulty. "Easy" words are high-frequency words with few, low-frequency neighbors. "Hard" words are low-frequency words with many, high-frequency neighbors. Previous research has shown that "easy" words are identified faster and more accurately than "hard" words, suggesting that the degree to which words overlap in phonological similarity influences spoken word recognition (Luce & Pisoni, 1998).

In Bradlow and Pisoni's study, listeners heard each list produced by one talker at one speaking rate and transcribed each word on the list. Transcription performance was evaluated for each speaking rate and talker as well as a function of experience with each speaker and rate (i.e., first versus fourth quartile performance). Bradlow and Pisoni found that transcription performance improved as a function of experience and improved more for the "hard" than for the "easy" words. Listeners appeared to learn particular characteristics of individual talkers incidentally, and implicitly determined the range and variation of particular talkers' utterances. Talker familiarity, in turn, significantly influenced how well listeners extracted the linguistic content of speech.

Yonan and Sommers (2000) replicated the role of talker familiarity in linguistic analysis with older individuals. Yonan and Sommers investigated whether older individuals would benefit from familiarity with a talker's voice as do younger listeners. They also examined whether explicit training with and attention to talkers' voices was required to show a benefit of familiarity. They found that just as with younger listeners, older listeners, despite an impaired ability to explicitly identify talkers' voices, derived the same or more benefit in linguistic processing from implicit memory of a talker's voice. In addition, Yonan and Sommers found that listeners who were exposed to voices incidentally while doing a semantic judgment task demonstrated the same benefit in linguistic processing as listeners who had been explicitly asked to attend to the talkers' voices. The authors argued that their findings suggest that implicit memory systems may underlie the influence of talker familiarity on linguistic analysis. Certainly, explicit attention to attributes of a talker's voice during familiarization is not necessary. Listeners may routinely encode both linguistic and talker information when simply listening to speech in day-to-day conversation. Perceptual learning of voices may be an automatic product of the processing and representation of linguistic structure.

16.4.4 *Learning native and non-native contrasts*

Another area of research that supports the view that variation is represented and used during spoken language processing are studies on the learning of non-native contrasts. Consistent with the view that linguistic units are abstract representations, researchers initially hypothesized that prototypical, idealized synthetic stimuli would provide language learners with the key information needed to distinguish among linguistic units. By preserving acoustic-phonetic information thought to be crucial to differences between particular contrasts, while at the same time removing seemingly irrelevant variation in talker's voice and phonetic context, researchers such as Strange and Dittmann (1984) investigated whether non-native listeners would be able to attend to and learn non-native contrasts. Strange and Dittmann found, however, that listeners were largely unsuccessful at learning non-native contrasts from synthetic stimuli.

Lively, Logan, and Pisoni (1993; Lively et al., 1994; Logan, Lively, & Pisoni, 1991) introduced non-native contrasts to listeners through training with high variability lists. In several experiments, Japanese listeners received explicit training on the /r/-/l/ contrast. Listeners identified contrasting pairs of words such as *rock* vs. *lock* produced by several different speakers. In addition, the /r/-/l/ contrast occurred in various phonetic contexts. Lively et al. found that listeners were successful at learning the /r/-/l/ contrast from their high variability materials. Listeners were better able to identify the /r/-/l/ contrast overall and were better able to generalize learning to novel utterances. The variation in productions of given linguistic units appeared to be retained in representations of spoken language and was used by non-native listeners to classify novel instances of the same phonemic contrast.

In a developmental study, Houston and Jusczyk (2000) found that 7.5-month-old infants familiarized with isolated words produced by one speaker did not necessarily segment and recognize those words embedded in fluent passages if the speaker changed from familiarization to test. Infants were familiarized with isolated words produced by talkers that were either similar (same gender) or dissimilar (different gender) to the talkers used at test. Infants familiarized with talkers with similar acoustic characteristics oriented longer to passages that contained the familiarized words than to passages without those words. Infants familiarized with talkers with dissimilar acoustic characteristics (i.e., frequency) did not orient significantly longer to the passages containing previously familiarized words. Slightly older infants (10.5-month-olds) oriented longer to passages containing familiarized words regardless of the perceptual and/or acoustic dissimilarities between talkers. These findings suggest that at least initially infants' representations of spoken words include talker-specific information and that that talker information influences word recognition. Subsequent research (as cited in Houston & Jusczyk, 2000) found that after a one-day delay, even 10.5-month-olds had difficulty generalizing to new talkers. Houston and Jusczyk suggest that infants' generalization abilities may be based on shifts in weighting phonetic versus talker information, rather than an increased ability to normalize or discard talker-specific characteristics.

Taken together with findings from adult memory for spoken language, talker identification, intelligibility, and talker learning, these findings suggest a representational system that preserves talker-specific characteristics. Listeners appear to represent details of the surface form of spoken language and familiarity with surface form influences the recovery of linguistic intent. Further, surface form may be an integral aspect of phonetic structure in particular, and linguistic structure in general, in the sense that these two aspects of spoken language may not be disentangled perceptually and/or representationally. Linguistic and nonlinguistic information in the speech signal may not be of a fundamentally different nature, but rather may reflect integral aspects of the same perceptual processing and representational system.

16.5 Links between Meaning of Surface Form and Linguistic Content

Although a growing body of research has examined whether nonlinguistic characteristics are retained in memory for spoken language and used during language processing, relatively less attention has been paid to the question of how the informative aspects of surface form are integrated with the processing of linguistic content. Does the *way* in which something is said influence a listener's analysis of *what* is being said? At what point in linguistic processing are the meaningful aspects of surface form integrated with the content of speech? The traditional view has been that the processing of nonlinguistic information occurs separately from the processing of linguistic content. If this assumption is correct, then any integration would necessarily have to occur at a relatively late stage of processing, once lexical and syntactic processing are complete. However, if this assumption is incorrect, and the processing of nonlinguistic information is integrally related to the processing of linguistic information, then surface characteristics should influence linguistic processing at relatively early stages. To date, only a small handful of studies have examined the ways in which the meaningful aspects of surface form might alter or influence lexical, syntactic, or semantic processing.

One domain that may contain the most promise in addressing these questions involves the perception of emotional speech. Emotion can be conveyed and is readily identifiable both through the content of words and through emotional prosody. Speakers can describe feelings using explicit emotion terms, such as *sad*, *happy*, or *disgusted*, as well as with words that have emotional connotations, such as *wedding*, *funeral*, or *cancer* (Vakoch & Wurm, 1997; Wurm & Vakoch, 2000). Emotional words and phrases can, in addition, be produced in an emotional tone of voice and listeners are adept at recognizing and identifying emotional tone of voice (Frick, 1985; Pittam & Scherer, 1993). Because emotional prosody is a type of surface characteristic that carries clear meaning, its hypothesized influence on the processing of emotional words and sentences would be relatively straightforward.

In order to investigate the influence of tone of voice on linguistic analysis, Kitayama and Howard (1994) presented listeners with sentence-length utterances that were produced with congruent or incongruent emotional prosody. They found that emotional tone of voice influenced the interpretation of sentence-length utterances in an emotion-congruent manner. For example, listeners were more likely to interpret sentences as having a sad meaning if produced in a sad tone of voice. In turn, sentence meaning influenced the interpretation of emotional prosody. Judgments of tone of voice changed depending on sentence content. This finding was one of the first to suggest that linguistic processing is not carried out independently of the processing of emotional tone of voice (see also, Joanette, Goulet, & Hannequin, 1990; Kitayama, 1990, 1991, 1996).

In a similar study, Nygaard and Lunders (2002) investigated whether emotional tone of voice would influence the selection and interpretation of word meaning. Because context has been found to exert the most influence when linguistic information alone is ambiguous, we sought to determine if emotional tone of voice would influence the selection of word meaning in lexically ambiguous emotional homophones (see also Halberstadt, Niedenthal, & Kushner, 1995). Emotional homophones were selected that had one emotional meaning, either happy or sad, and one neutral meaning (e.g., *die/dye*, *bridal/bridle*). In addition, each meaning mapped onto a distinct spelling. We presented listeners with emotional homophones, along with filler words with happy, neutral, and sad meanings, in either a happy, neutral, or sad tone of voice. Separate groups of listeners independently rated tone of voice in a forced choice identification task and items not reliably identified as the intended tone of voice were replaced. In addition, acoustic analysis of duration, fundamental frequency (F0), F0 variabilitiy, and relative amplitude revealed significant differences along these acoustic dimensions among the three tones of voice. Transcription performance was then examined to determine if emotional tone of voice would influence which meaning of the homophone was selected.

Figure 16.2 illustrates our findings. Listeners were more likely to select the emotional meaning of a homophone when tone of voice was congruent with that meaning. When emotional tone of voice was incongruent with the emotional meaning, listeners more often transcribed the neutral spelling of each homophone. Emotional tone of voice influenced the selection of word meaning in this task. Listeners selected the spelling and presumably the meaning that matched the tone of voice in which each word was presented.

We also found that this congruency effect was larger when tone of voice was blocked as opposed to when tone of voice varied from item to item. This finding suggests that tone of voice set up an expectancy or perceptual set above and

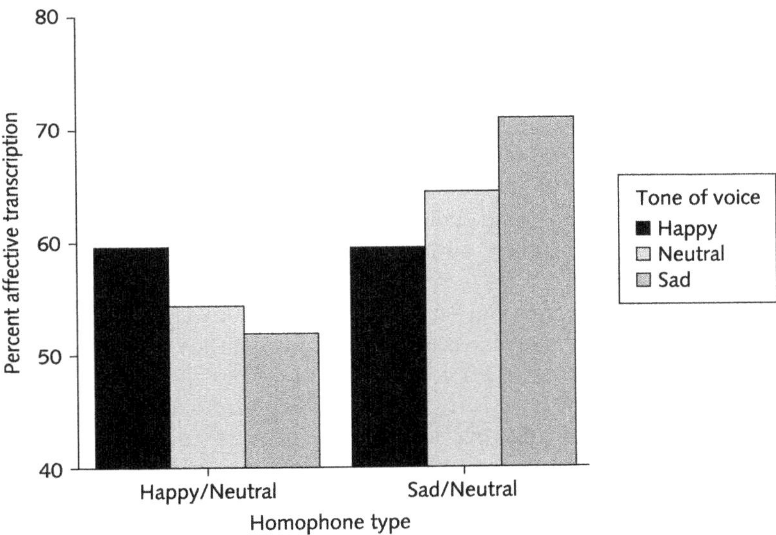

Figure 16.2 Percent correct transcription performance is plotted as a function of homophone types for happy, neutral, and sad tone of voice (Adapted from Nygaard & Lunders, 2002).

beyond the local influence of the tone of voice of each word and its corresponding effect on the selected meaning for that word. Both findings, the influence of tone of voice and the larger effect size when tone of voice was blocked, are consistent with the hypothesis that emotional tone of voice can influence the lexical processing of spoken words. Nygaard and Lunders (2002) suggested that one way in which this could occur was if tone of voice operated in a manner analogous to sentential context. Certainly, it is clear that the ongoing interpretation of sentential context can influence or bias which meaning of a homophone will be differentially activated and accessed. Our results provide evidence that tone of voice may act as another kind of constraint on how lexical meaning is selected.

Although Nygaard and Lunders' (2002) results suggest that tone of voice can influence lexical selection, it remains unclear as to whether emotional prosody can influence the time course of lexical activation and competition. Few studies have examined this question directly, however, there is some evidence that emotional tone of voice may operate relatively early in the processing of spoken words. In addition, tone of voice may influence lexical processing in both an emotion-independent and emotion-congruent fashion, suggesting both a general arousal and a specific semantic component to the influence.

Wurm et al. (2001) investigated the effects of emotional tone of voice on lexical decision times. They presented listeners with emotion words and nonwords at the end of semantically neutral carrier phrases. In one experiment, tone of voice was blocked so that all stimuli were presented in a single tone of voice. In another experiment, tone of voice varied so that the emotional prosody of each carrier phrase and target word/nonword changed from trial to trial. Wurm et al. found that emotional tone of voice influenced lexical decision times, but only when tone of voice was blocked. Target words in the blocked condition that were embedded in a carrier phrase that had a congruent tone of voice were responded to faster than were target words produced in an incongruent tone of voice. Tone of voice had little effect on reaction times in the condition in which tone of voice varied from trial to trial. Wurm et al. concluded that tone of voice set up a general expectancy that in turn influenced the processing of spoken words. At the very least, these findings suggest that emotional tone of voice is not completely independent of linguistic processing. In fact, emotional tone appears to affect the time course of lexical decisions.

Nygaard and Queen (2002) found that emotional tone of voice also influenced naming responses. Naming tasks ask listeners to repeat or shadow spoken words as quickly as possible and are assumed to tap into a relatively early stage of lexical processing (Lively, Pisoni, & Goldinger, 1994). Nygaard and Queen (2002) presented lists of happy, sad, and neutral words produced in congruent, incongruent, or neutral tones of voice. We found that emotional words produced in a congruent tone of voice were responded to more quickly than words presented in an incongruent tone of voice. We also found that words produced with emotional prosody, whether congruent or incongruent, were named more quickly than words produced in a neutral tone of voice. Finally, unlike Wurm et al. (2001), we found that the congruency effect, faster responses when tone of voice and word meaning matched, occurred both for single words blocked by tone of voice and for single word lists in which tone of voice varied from trial to trial.

It should be noted that other experiments have failed to find an effect of emotional tone of voice on linguistic processing. Wurm and Vakoch (1996) found little influence of tone of voice on lexical decision times for emotional words. Listeners did not seem to integrate emotional prosody with emotional meaning and Wurm and Vakoch found no congruence or incongruence effect. In the Wurm et al. (2001) study mentioned earlier, emotional tone of voice was only shown to influence lexical decision times when words were embedded in carrier phrases and when tone of voice was blocked. Although Nygaard and Lunders (2002) and Nygaard and Queen (2002) both demonstrated effects of emotional tone of voice on lexical selection and word naming latencies, effect sizes were larger for stimuli presented in a blocked format in which tone of voice did not vary from trial to trial. When tone of voice did vary, effect sizes were reduced.

A recent study conducted by Kitayama and Ishii (2002) suggests that effect sizes may vary depending on the emphasis that a particular culture places on emotional tone of voice as a source of information in spoken communication. Using a Stroop-like interference task, Kitayama and Ishii found that emotional tone of voice influenced judgments of emotional meaning for Japanese but not for English speakers. Conversely, emotional meaning influenced judgments of emotional tone of voice for English but not Japanese speakers. These findings suggest that the degree to which, and manner in which, emotional tone of voice and emotional meaning are integrated can vary as a function of culture and linguistic experience.

Although much more research needs to be done on these problems, it appears that emotional tone of voice may be integrated with meaningful aspects of spoken words relatively early in linguistic processing. These findings suggest that tone of voice influences linguistic processing in a meaningful way well before linguistic analysis is complete. Evidence that other surface characteristics affect linguistic comprehension in a meaningful way is even scarcer. However, Kunihira (1971) found that native English speakers were above chance at determining the meaning of Japanese antonym pairs if they were provided with natural prosody. He presented monolingual English speakers with antonyms in Japanese and listeners were asked to choose the meaning of the antonym (forced choice) when the words were written, produced in a monotone voice, or produced with more natural prosody. Listeners were at chance determining meaning when words were written or monotone, but significantly above chance in the natural prosody condition.

Similarly, Sasso, Namy, and Nygaard (in preparation) have found that adult listeners can determine the meaning of a dimensional adjective such as hot, cold, tall, or short, from prosodic information alone. Three female talkers were taught the meaning of novel words (i.e., *blicket*) and then asked to produce the novel words with infant-directed intonation that was congruent with the newly learned meaning. The talkers were told that the novel word utterances were going to be embedded in a subsequent novel word-learning task in which listeners would be asked to determine the meaning of the word (by pointing to a matching picture) based on prosodic characteristics.

Figure 16.3 illustrates the results of this study. When listeners were presented with these utterances in a word-learning task, they successfully disambiguated the dimensional adjectives from their prosodic cues alone. Our finding suggests that adult speakers, when asked, can produce prosodic cues that vary with respect to word meaning. In turn, adult listeners can use those cues to determine word meaning, at least for the dimensional adjectives, such as hot/cold, tall/short, big/little, and happy/sad, that were used in this experiment.

Although these studies on emotion are preliminary, they point to a perceptual-processing system in which informative surface characteristics are used relatively early in linguistic analysis to constrain or color the semantic meaning of a particular word. Certainly, we know that linguistic devices such as irony, sarcasm, and humor often employ mismatches between the semantic content of an utterance and the way in which it is actually said. The research reviewed here provides initial evidence that properties of speech that have been traditionally considered nonlinguistic in nature may serve a distinctly linguistic function even at the level of speech perception and spoken word recognition.

16.6 Theoretical Overview

Although the evidence reviewed points to the close interdependence of linguistic and nonlinguistic processing, the question remains as to what sort of linguistic representations might underlie these effects. One proposal is that linguistic representations may be rich, perceptual entities that include the range of utterance types or variation that a listener encounters. Rather than extracting abstract, idealized, canonical symbolic linguistic representations, listeners encode and represent the surface form or perceptual characteristics of spoken language along with the more abstract linguistic structure. Goldinger (1998, see also Jusczyk, 1993, 1997) has proposed that spoken words are represented in the lexicon as collections of detailed exemplars that include the surface form of spoken language.

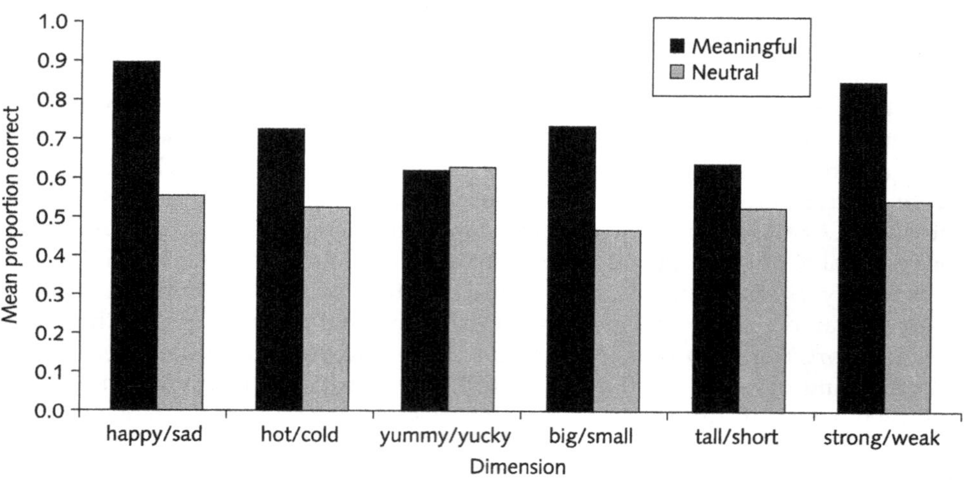

Figure 16.3 Mean proportion correct meaning selection for the six dimensional adjective pairs produced with meaningful or neutral prosody (Adapted from Sasso et al. in preparation).

Each time a listener encounters a particular phonological form, surface characteristics such as talker's voice would be included in the representation of that word. When listeners are asked to process a spoken word, the item is compared with all previously encountered exemplars. The degree to which a to-be-identified word is similar to previously stored exemplars determines how quickly and accurately it will be identified. On this view, our perception of speech rests on our history of contact with particular linguistic instantiations.

Exemplar-based models account for many of the findings reviewed above (see also Johnson, this volume). For example, the role of variability in learning non-native contrasts is well explained with an exemplar-based approach. As non-native listeners collect examplars of particular linguistic segments, the degree to which the range of variation in surface form is included across examplars will determine how well listeners will generalize to new instances. When a new instance of a word/contrast is encountered, if a listener has a range of instantiations represented, the likelihood that the new instance will be similar to an existing examplar would be quite high. The same rationale applies to the talker familiarity effect. As listeners become accustomed to or learn a particular talker's voice, they accumulate exemplars specific to that particular talker (see Johnson, this volume). When a word produced by that talker is to be identified, the wealth of similar exemplars that are simultaneously accessed are large, leading to more accurate and presumably faster identification.

Similarly, the initial acquisition of linguistic representations by infants may be tied to clusters of exemplars that have specific surface form characteristics (i.e., female voice). At early stages in the language acquisition process, infants are conservative about generalizing to utterances produced by new speakers with characteristics outside the realm of their representational experience. As infants begin to accumulate a wider range of exemplars with more varied talker characteristics, they begin to recognize words they know, produced by speakers with unfamiliar surface form characteristics (see Houston, this volume). For adult speakers, encountering an individual with an unfamiliar dialect or accent results in the same phenomenon. The unfamiliar surface characteristics of accented speech do not necessarily map onto the range of variation already represented. Over time, as listeners become accustomed to the distinct way a non-native speaker's phonological system restructures their productions, they are better able to extract the linguistic content of the accented speech.

Although Goldinger's (1998) model of lexical representation suggests that perceptual or surface characteristics of spoken words are encoded and retained in memory and influence the time course of word recognition, it is not clear whether these attributes must be preserved in a truly integrated representation. A representation that simply preserves the co-occurrence of these attributes with linguistic form would seem to be consistent with Goldinger's view. For example, an exemplar could consist of a re-description and separation of linguistic and nonlinguistic form with both aspects of the speech signal preserved as different aspects of the exemplar. Findings illustrating the interdependence of surface and linguistic structure, however, suggest that disentangling what counts as purely linguistic and what counts as purely nonlinguistic is difficult to determine both for speech researchers and for the listener. The dependence of talker identification on familiarity with language-specific linguistic form (Goggin et al., 1991) as well as listeners' ability to identify talkers from sinewave speech (Remez et al., 1997) suggest that the properties that support one type of identification process also support the other types of identification process. Information that is used for talker identification, for example, may be the same as is used for phonological processing. These findings along with other research suggesting that familiarity with a talker's voice facilitates the recovery of linguistic content are consistent with a view of lexical representation in which linguistic and nonlinguistic properties of speech are preserved in integrated, perceptually based representations.

Given that lexical representations appear to include some detailed aspects of surface characteristics, how do these properties then influence the processing of the semantic content of spoken language? Assuming that emotional tone of voice, for example, does influence the time course of lexical processing and selection of word meaning in an emotion-congruent fashion, then how do existing models, including exemplar models, of language processing account for this effect? Any model must account for the integration of emotional tone of voice fairly early during language processing and must account for the findings that the influence of tone of voice may not be as strong as the influence of linguistic or sentential context. Nygaard and Lunders (2002) speculate that emotional tone of voice may act like sentential context as one powerful constraint on the selection of word meaning. That is, listeners may derive emotional meaning from prosodic characteristics and then use that interpretation to constrain or bias lexical access and spoken word recognition. Tone of voice or prosody in general might not influence processing to the same extent as sentential context because these properties may not be as reliable or informative as the ongoing semantic representation of an utterance's linguistic structure.

An alternative account, consistent with exemplar-based models, states that the reason emotional words are processed more quickly comes as a by-product of the co-occurrence of particular emotional tones with particular semantic content and perhaps phonological form. Sad words, for example, may most often be produced in a sad tone of voice. Both properties, linguistic and nonlinguistic, would be included in lexical representations. When words with congruent tone of voice and semantic content are encountered, many similar exemplars would be accessed and consequently speed and/or bias processing. When words with incongruent tone of voice are encountered, far fewer exemplars would be in memory and lexical processing would be consequently slowed.

At this point, however, few process models have been extended to incorporate the range of effects that variation in surface form might have on linguistic processing. Evidence suggests that models of speech and language processing will in the future need to include a role for the representation and influence of nonlinguistic characteristics in spoken word recognition and perhaps in other aspects of sentence and discourse processing. Converging evidence from a variety of sources points to a linguistic representation system that necessarily includes nonlinguistic properties of speech. Further, these nonlinguistic characteristics are often indistinguishable from and may be isomorphic with linguistic structure. Lexical representation, and perhaps linguistic representations in general, may be perceptually based, incorporating the rich, highly-detailed information that is crucially important for successful spoken communication.

REFERENCES

Bachorowski, J-A. & Owren, M. J. (1999). Acoustic correlates of talker sex and individual talker identity are present in a short vowel segment produced in running speech. *Journal of the Acoustical Society of America*, 106, 1054–63.

Bradlow, A. R., Nygaard, L. C., & Pisoni, D. B. (1999). Effects of talker, rate, and amplitude variation on recognition memory for spoken words. *Perception & Psychophysics*, 61, 206–19.

Bradlow, A. R. & Pisoni, D. B. (1999). Recognition of spoken words by native and non-native listeners: Talker-, listener-, and item-related factors. *Journal of the Acoustical Society of America*, 106, 2074–85.

Bradlow, A. R., Torretta, G. M., & Pisoni, D. B. (1996). Intelligibility of normal speech I: Global and fine-grained acoustic-phonetic talker characteristics. *Speech Communication*, 20, 255–72.

Brown, B. & Bradshaw, J. (1985). Towards a social psychology of voice variations. In H. Giles & R. St Clair (eds.), *Recent Advances In Language, Communication and Social Psychology* (144–81). London: Lawrence Erlbaum.

Brown, J. & Carr, T. (1993). Limits on perceptual abstraction in reading: Asymmetric transfer between surface forms differing in typicality. *Journal of Experimental Psychology: Learning, Memory, and Cognition*, 19, 1277–96.

Church, B. A. & Schacter, D. L. (1994). Perceptual specificity of auditory priming: Implicit memory for voice intonation and fundamental frequency. *Journal of Experimental Psychology: Learning, Memory, and Cognition*, 20, 521–33.

Cole, R. A., Coltheart, M., & Allard, F. (1974). Memory of a speaker's voice: Reaction time to same- or different-voiced letters. *Quarterly Journal of Experimental Psychology*, 26, 1–7.

Cooper, W. E., Eady, S. J., & Mueller, P. R. (1985). Acoustical aspects of contrastive stress in question-answer contexts. *Journal of the Acoustical Society of America*, 77, 2142–56.

Craik, F. I. M. & Kirsner, K. (1974). The effect of speaker's voice on word recognition. *Quarterly Journal of Experimental Psychology*, 26, 274–84.

Cutler, A. (1994). The perception of rhythm in language. *Cognition*, 50, 79–81.

Frick, R. W. (1985). Communicating emotion: The role of prosodic features. *Psychological Bulletin*, 97, 412–29.

Garner, W. R. (1974). *The Processing Of Information and Structure*. Potomac, MD: Lawrence Erlbaum.

Geiselman, R. E. (1979). Inhibition of the automatic storage of speaker's voice. *Memory & Cognition*, 7, 201–4.

Geiselman, R. E. & Bellezza, F. S. (1976). Long-term memory for speaker's voice and source location. *Memory & Cognition*, 4, 483–9.

Geiselman, R. E. & Bellezza, F. S. (1977). Incidental retention of speaker's voice. *Memory & Cognition*, 5, 658–65.

Geiselman, R. E. & Crawley, J. M. (1983). Incidental processing of speaker characteristics: Voice as connotative information. *Journal of Verbal Learning and Verbal Behavior*, 22, 15–23.

Goggin, J. P., Thompson, C. P., Strube, G., & Simental, L. R. (1991). The role of language familiarity in voice identification. *Memory & Cognition*, 19, 448–58.

Goldinger, S. D. (1996). Words and voices: Episodic traces in spoken word identification and recognition memory. *Journal of Experimental Psychology: Learning, Memory, and Cognition*, 22, 1166–83.

Goldinger, S. D. (1998). Echoes of echoes? An episodic theory of lexical access. *Psychological Review*, 105, 251–79.

Goldinger, S. D., Pisoni, D. B., & Logan, D. B. (1991). The nature of talker variability effects on recall of spoken word lists. *Journal of Experimental Psychology: Learning, Memory, and Cognition*, 17, 152–62.

Green, K. P., Kuhl, P., Meltzoff, A., & Stevens, E. (1991). Integrating speech information across talkers, gender, and sensory modality: Female faces and male voices in the McGurk effect. *Perception & Psychophysics*, 50, 524–36.

Green, K. P., Tomiak, G. R., & Kuhl, P. K. (1997). The encoding of rate and talker information during phonetic perception. *Perception & Psychophysics*, 59, 675–92.

Halberstadt, J. B., Niedenthal, P. M., & Kushner, J. (1995). Resolution of lexical ambiguity by emotional state. *Psychological Science*, 6, 278–82.

Halle, M. (1985). Speculation about the representation of words in memory. In V. Fromkin (ed.), *Phonetic Linguistics* (pp. 101–14). New York: Academic Press.

Houston, D. M. & Jusczyk, P. W. (2000). The role of talker-specific information in word segmentation by infants. *Journal of Experimental Psychology: Human Perception and Performance*, 26, 1570–82.

Irwin, D. H. (1977). The intelligibility of English speech to non-native English speakers. *Language and Speech*, 20, 308–16.

Jackson, A. & Morton, J. (1984). Facilitation of auditory word recognition. *Memory & Cognition*, 12, 568–74.

Joanette, Y., Goulet, P., & Hannequin, D. (1990). *Right Hemisphere and Verbal Communication*. New York: Springer-Verlag.

Joos, M. A. (1948). Acoustic phonetics. *Language*, 24, supplement 2, 1–136.

Jusczyk, P. W. (1993). From language-general to language-specific capacities: The WRAPSA model of how speech perception develops. *Journal of Phonetics*, 21, 3–28.

Jusczyk, P. W. (1997). *The Discovery of Spoken Language*. Cambridge, MA: MIT Press.

Jusczyk, P. W., Cutler, A., & Redanz, N. J. (1993). Infants' preference for the predominant stress patterns of English words. *Child Development*, 64, 675–87.

Kitayama, S. (1990). Interaction between affect and cognition in word perception. *Journal of Personality and Social Psychology*, 58, 209–17.

Kitayama, S. (1991). Impairment of perception by positive and negative affect. *Cognition and Emotion*, 5, 255–74.

Kitayama, S. (1996). Remembrance of emotional speech: Improvement and impairment of incidental verbal memory by emotional voice. *Journal of Experimental Social Psychology*, 32, 289–308.

Kitayama, S. & Howard, S. (1994). Affective regulation of perception and comprehension: Amplification and semantic priming. In P. M. Niedenthal & S. Kitayama (eds.), *The Heart's Eye: Emotional Influences in Perception and Attention* (pp. 41–65). New York: Academic Press.

Kitayama, S. & Ishii, K. (2002). Word and voice: Spontaneous attention to emotional utterances in two languages. *Cognition and Emotion*, 16, 29–59.

Kjelgaard, M. M. & Speer, S. R. (1999). Prosodic facilitation and interference in the resolution of temporary syntactic closure ambiguity. *Journal of Memory and Language*, 40, 153–94.

Krulee, G., Tondo, D., & Wightman, F. (1983). Speech perception as a multilevel processing system. *Journal of Psycholinguistic Research*, 12, 531–54.

Kunihira, S. (1971). Effects of the expressive voice on phonetic symbolism. *Journal of Verbal Learning and Verbal Behavior*, 10, 427–9.

Labov, W. (1972). *Sociolinguistic Patterns*. Philadelphia: University of Pennsylvania Press.

Ladefoged, P. & Broadbent, D. E. (1957). Information conveyed by vowels. *Journal of the Acoustical Society of America*, 29, 948–104.

Lane, H. (1963). Foreign accent and distortion. *Journal of the Acoustical Society of America*, 35, 451–3.

Liberman, A. M. & Mattingly, I. G. (1985). The motor theory of speech perception revised. *Cognition*, 21, 1–36.

Liberman, A. M. & Mattingly, I. G. (1989). A specialization for speech perception. *Science*, 243, 489–94.

Lindblom, B. (1990). Explaining phonetic variation: A sketch of the H&H theory. In W. Hardcastle & A. Marchal (eds.), *Speech Production and Speech Modeling* (pp. 403–39). Dordrecht: Kluwer Academic.

Lively, S. E., Logan, J. E., & Pisoni, D. B. (1993). Training Japanese listeners to identify English /r/ and /l/. II: The role of phonetic environment and talker variability in learning new perceptual categories. *Journal of the Acoustical Society of America*, 94, 1242–55.

Lively, S. E., Pisoni, D. B., & Goldinger, S. D. (1994). Spoken word recognition: Research and theory. In M. A. Gernsbacher (ed.), *Handbook of Psycholinguistics* (pp. 265–301). San Diego, CA: Academic Press.

Lively, S. E., Pisoni, D. B., Yamada, R. A., Tohkura, Y., & Yamada, T. (1994). Training Japanese listeners to identify English /r/ and /l/. III: Long-term retention of new phonetic categories. *Journal of the Acoustical Society of America*, 96, 2076–87.

Local, J. (2002). Variable domains and variable relevance: Interpreting phonetic exponents. Paper presented at the ISCA International Tutorial and Research Workshop on Temporal Integration in the Perception of Speech, Aix-en-Provence, France.

Logan, J. S., Lively, S. E., & Pisoni, D. B. (1991). Training Japanese listeners to identify English /r/ and /l/: A first report. *Journal of the Acoustical Society of America*, 89, 874–86.

Luce, P. A. & Pisoni, D. B. (1998). Recognizing spoken words: The neighborhood activation model. *Ear and Hearing*, 19, 1–36.

Martin, C. S., Mullennix, J. W., Pisoni, D. B., & Summers, W. V. (1989). Effects of talker variability on recall of spoken word lists. *Journal of Experimental Psychology: Learning, Memory, and Cognition*, 15, 676–81.

McClelland, J. L. & Elman, J. L. (1986). The TRACE model of speech perception. *Cognitive Psychology*, 18, 1–86.

Mehler, J., Bertoncini, J., Barriere, M., & Jassik-Gerschenfeld, D. (1978). Infant recognition of mother's voice. *Perception*, 7, 491–7.

Miller, J. L., Grosjean, F., & Lomanto, C. (1984). Articulation rate and its variability in spontaneous speech: A reanalysis and some implications. *Phonetica*, 41, 215–25.

Miller, J. L. & Liberman, A. M. (1979). Some effects of later occurring information on the perception of stop consonant and semivowel. *Perception & Psychophysics*, 25, 457–65.

Miller, J. L. & Volaitis, L. E. (1989). Effect of speaking rate on the perceptual structure of a phonetic category. *Perception & Psychophysics*, 46, 505–12.

Monsen, R. B. & Engebretson, A. M. (1977). Study of variations in the male and female glottal wave. *Journal of the Acoustical Society of America*, 62, 981–93.

Moon, S.-J. & Lindblom, B. (1994). Interaction between duration, context, and speaking style in English stressed vowels. *Journal of the Acoustical Society of America*, 96, 40–55.

Mullennix, J. & Pisoni, D. B. (1990). Stimulus variability and processing dependencies in speech perception. *Perception & Psychophysics*, 47, 379–90.

Mullennix, J., Pisoni, D. B., & Martin, C. S. (1989). Some effects of talker variability on spoken word recognition. *Journal of the Acoustical Society of America*, 85, 365–78.

Murray, I. R. & Arnott, J. L. (1993). Toward the simulation of emotion in synthetic speech: A review of the literature on human vocal emotion. *Journal of the Acoustical Society of America*, 93, 1097–108.

Namy, L. L., Nygaard, L. C., & Sauerteig, D. (2002). Perceptual and social determinants of sex differences in vocal accommodation. *Journal of Language and Social Psychology*, 21, 422–32.

Nowicki, S., Jr. & Carton, E. (1997). The relation of nonverbal processing ability of faces and voices and children's feelings of depression and competence. *Journal of Genetic Psychology*, 158, 357–63.

Nygaard, L. C., Burt, S. A., & Queen, J. S. (2000). Surface form typicality and asymmetric transfer in episodic memory for spoken words. *Journal of Experimental Psychology: Learning, Memory, and Cognition*, 26, 1228–44,

Nygaard, L. C. & Lunders, E. R. (2002). Resolution of lexical ambiguity by emotional tone of voice. *Memory & Cognition*, 30, 583–93.

Nygaard, L. C. & Pisoni, D. B. (1998). Talker-specific perceptual learning in speech perception. *Perception & Psychophysics*, 60, 355–76.

Nygaard, L. C. & Queen, J. S. (1998). Emotional tone of voice influences spoken word recognition. Paper presented at the 39th Annual Meeting of the Psychonomic Society, Dallas, TX.

Nygaard, L. C. & Queen, J. S. (2000). The role of sentential prosody in learning voices. Paper presented at the 139th meeting of the Acoustical Society of America, Atlanta, GA.

Nygaard, L. C. & Queen, J. S. (2002). Factors influencing the effects of accentedness on spoken word recognition. Paper presented at the 43rd Annual Meeting of the Psychonomic Society, Kansas City, Missouri.

Nygaard, L. C., Sommers, M. S., & Pisoni, D. B. (1994). Speech perception as a talker-contingent process. *Psychological Science*, 5, 42–6.

Nygaard, L. C., Sommers, M. S., & Pisoni, D. B. (1995). Effects of stimulus variability on perception and representation of spoken words in memory. *Perception & Psychophysics*, 57, 989–1001.

Palmeri, T. J., Goldinger, S. D., & Pisoni, D. B. (1993). Episodic encoding of voice attributes and recognition memory for spoken words. *Journal of Experimental Psychology: Learning, Memory, and Cognition*, 19, 309–28.

Peterson, G. E. & Barney, H. L. (1952). Control methods used in a study of the vowels. *Journal of the Acoustical Society of America*, 24, 175–84.

Pisoni, D. B. (1993). Long-term memory in speech perception: Some new findings on talker variability, speaking rate, and perceptual learning. *Speech Communication*, 13, 109–25.

Pisoni, D. B. (1997). Some thoughts on "normalization" in speech perception. In K. Johnson & J. W. Mullennix (eds.), *Talker Variability in Speech Processing* (pp. 9–32). San Diego: Academic Press.

Pittam, J. & Scherer, K. R. (1993). Vocal expression and communication of emotion. In M. Lewis & J. M. Haviland (eds.), *Handbook of Emotions* (pp. 185–97). New York: Guilford Press.

Read, D. & Craik, F. I. M. (1995). Earwitness identification: Some influences on voice recognition. *Journal of Experimental Psychology: Applied*, 1, 6–18.

Remez, R. E., Fellowes, J. M., & Rubin, P. E. (1997). Talker identification based on phonetic information. *Journal of Experimental Psychology: Human Perception and Performance*, 23, 651–66.

Remez, R. E., Rubin, P. E., Nygaard, L. C., & Howell, W. A. (1987). Perceptual normalization of vowels produced by sinusoidal voices. *Journal of Experimental Psychology: Human Perception and Performance*, 13, 40–61.

Remez, R. E., Rubin, P. E., Pisoni, D. B., & Carrell, T. D. (1981). Speech perception without traditional speech cues. *Science*, 212, 947–50.

Sasso, D., Namy, L. L., & Nygaard, L. C. (in preparation). The role of prosody in word learning. Manuscript in preparation.

Schacter, D. L. & Church, B. (1992). Auditory priming: Implicit and explicit memory for words and voices. *Journal of Experimental Psychology: Learning, Memory, and Cognition*, 18, 915–30.

Scherer, K. R., Banse, R., Wallbott, H. G., & Goldbeck, T. (1991). Vocal cues in emotion encoding and decoding. *Motivation and Emotion*, 15, 123–48.

Shankweiler, D. P., Strange, W., & Verbrugge, R. R. (1977). Speech and the problem of perceptual constancy. In R. Shaw & J. Bransford (eds.), *Perceiving, Acting, and Knowing: Toward an Ecological Psychology* (pp. 315–45). Hillsdale, NJ: Lawrence Erlbaum.

Shepard, C. A., Giles, H., & Le Poire, B. A. (2001). Communication accommodation theory 25. In W. P. Robinson & H. Giles (eds.), *The New Handbook of Language and Social Psychology* (pp. 33–56). New York: John Wiley & Sons.

Sommers, M. S., Nygaard, L. C., & Pisoni, D. B. (1994). Stimulus variability and spoken word recognition: I. Effects of variability in speaking rate and overall amplitude. *Journal of the Acoustical Society of America*, 96, 1314–24.

Speer, S. R., Crowder, R. G., & Thomas, L. M. (1993). Prosodic structure and sentence recognition. *Journal of Memory and Language*, 32, 336–58.

Strange, W. & Dittmann, S. (1984). Effects of discrimination training on the perception of /r-l/ by Japanese adults learning English. *Perception & Psychophysics*, 36, 131–45.

Studdert-Kennedy, M. (1976). Speech perception. In N. J. Lass (ed.), *Contemporary Issues in Experimental Phonetics* (pp. 243–93). New York: Academic Press.

Summerfield, Q. (1981). On articulatory rate and perceptual constancy in phonetic perception. *Journal of Experimental Psychology: Human Perception and Performance*, 7, 1074–95.

Summerfield, Q. & Haggard, M. P. (1973). Vocal tract normalization as demonstrated by reaction times. *Report of Speech Research in Progress*, 2(2), 12–23. Queens University of Belfast, Ireland.

Tenpenny, P. L. (1995). Abstractionist versus episodic theories of repetition priming and word identification. *Psychonomic Bulletin & Review*, 2, 339–63.

Uchanski, R. M., Choi, S. S., Braida, L. D., & Reed, C. M. (1996). Speaking clearly for the hard of hearing IV: Further studies of the role of speaking rate. *Journal of Speech & Hearing Research*, 39, 494–509.

Vakoch, D. A. & Wurm, L. H. (1997). Emotional connotation in speech perception: Semantic associations in the general lexicon. *Cognition and Emotion*, 11, 337–49.

Van Lancker, D., Kreiman, J., & Emmorey, K. (1985). Familiar voice recognition: Patterns and parameters. Part I. Recognition of backward voices. *Journal of Phonetics*, 13, 19–38.

Van Lancker, D., Kreiman, J., & Wickens, T. (1985). Familiar voice recognition: Patterns and parameters. Part II: Recognition of rate-altered voices. *Journal of Phonetics*, 13, 39–52.

Van Wijngaarden, S. J., Steeneken, H. J. M., & Houtgast, T. (2002). Quantifying the intelligibility of speech in noise for non-native listeners. *Journal of the Acoustical Society of America*, 111, 1906–16.

Volaitis, L. E. & Miller, J. L. (1992). Phonetic prototypes: Influences of place of articulation and speaking rate on the internal structure of voicing categories. *Journal of the Acoustical Society of America*, 92, 723–35.

Walker-Andrews, A. S. & Dickson, L. R. (1997). Infants' understanding of affect. In S. Hala, (ed.), *The Development of Social Cognition: Studies in Developmental Psychology* (pp. 161–86). East Sussex, UK: Psychology Press.

Wouters, J. & Macon, M. W. (2002a). Effects of prosodic factors on spectral dynamics. I. Analysis. *Journal of the Acoustical Society of America*, 111, 417–27.

Wouters, J. & Macon, M. W. (2002b). Effects of prosodic factors on spectral dynamics. II. Synthesis. *Journal of the Acoustical Society of America*, 111, 428–38.

Wurm, L. H. & Vakoch, D. A. (1996). Dimensions of speech perception: Semantic associations in the affective lexicon. *Cognition and Emotion*, 10, 409–23.

Wurm, L. H. & Vakoch, D. A. (2000). The adaptive value of lexical connotation in speech perception. *Cognition and Emotion*, 14, 177–91.

Wurm, L. H., Vakoch, D. A., Strasser, M. R., Calin-Jageman, R., & Ross, S. E. (2001). Speech perception and vocal expression of emotion. *Cognition and Emotion*, 15, 831–52.

Yonan, C. A. & Sommers, M. S. (2000). The effects of talker familiarity on spoken word identification in younger and older listeners. *Psychology and Aging*, 15, 88–99.

Part IV Speech Perception by Special Listeners

17 Speech Perception in Infants

DEREK M. HOUSTON

The initial speech perception skills that infants acquire during the first few months of life put them in a position to learn words, to develop a grammar, and to draw from a wide range of nonlinguistic sources of information in the speech signal (e.g., affect, indexical properties). The primary focus of this chapter is on some of the early speech perception skills that are relevant for learning words: speech discrimination, segmentation of words from fluent speech, and construction of lexical representations of the sound patterns of words. We will then turn to some recent findings on the speech perception skills of hearing-impaired infants and discuss the relevance of this new research direction for future investigations of infant speech perception.

17.1 Infant Speech Discrimination

17.1.1 *Early speech discrimination abilities: A simplified version*

Recognizing spoken words involves identifying sequences of segments and features from acoustic-phonetic properties in the speech signal. Because different words are often highly similar phonetically (e.g., *bat* and *pat*), a great deal of perceptual precision is required for language learners to identify a word and not confuse it with phonetically similar words. Hence, a fundamental building block of spoken word recognition is the ability to discriminate between phonemes in words.

More than 30 years ago, Peter Eimas and his colleagues discovered that young infants are sensitive to subtle differences between segmental phonemes in English (Eimas, 1974; Eimas & Miller, 1980b; Eimas et al., 1971). Using the High Amplitude Sucking procedure (HAS), Eimas et al. (1971) tested 1- and 4-month-olds' ability to discriminate synthetic versions of the CV syllables [ba] and [pa]. The stimuli were synthesized such that they differed only with respect to *voicing*, which is primarily determined by voice onset time (VOT) – the amount of time between the initial burst (caused by release of the lips from closed position) and the onset of voicing. English-speaking adults almost invariably perceive syllable-initial bilabial obstruents as [b] when the VOT is less than 25 and as [p] when the VOT is greater than 25 ms. (Abramson & Lisker, 1967; Liberman et al., 1961; Lisker & Abramson, 1964). Eimas et al. showed that infants could discriminate differences between stimuli whose VOTs differed by 20 ms when the pairs of stimuli came from different adult phonemic categories (e.g., VOTs of 20 and 40 ms) but not when they fell into the same category (e.g., VOTs of –20 and 0 ms or 60 and 80 ms). Their findings suggested that infants as young as 1 month of age could discriminate the [b]–[p] contrast "categorically." That is, the performance of infants was similar to the performance of adults in the sensitivity to linguistic attributes.

Following Eimas et al.'s (1971) pioneering study, numerous investigators have demonstrated that infants 6 months of age or younger are sensitive to other consonantal contrasts involving *place of articulation* (Bertoncini et al., 1987; Eimas, 1974; Eimas & Miller, 1980b; Holmberg, Morgan, & Kuhl, 1977; Jusczyk, Copan, & Thompson, 1978; Levitt et al., 1988; Moffitt, 1971; Morse, 1972) and *manner of articulation* (Eimas, 1975a; Eimas & Miller, 1980a, 1980b; Hillenbrand, Minifie, & Edwards, 1979; Miller & Eimas, 1983). As in Eimas et al. (1971), these investigations also demonstrated that infants discriminate consonant contrasts categorically (Eimas, 1974, 1975a; Eimas & Miller, 1980a, 1980b).

Findings on infants' discrimination of vowels differ somewhat from their discrimination of consonants. Unlike consonants, adults discriminate steady-state vowels in a continuous rather than a categorical manner (Fry et al., 1962; Pisoni, 1973; Stevens et al., 1969). Swoboda, Morse, and Leavitt (1976) discovered that 2-month-olds not only discriminated [i] and [ê] but they also discriminated vowel sounds that fell within the same vowel category but differed with respect to formant frequencies, suggesting that infants, like adults, also perceive vowels in a continuous manner.

The early investigations of infant speech perception demonstrated that during the first six months of life, well before the beginning of linguistic communication, infants are able to discriminate some speech sounds categorically. These findings led some researchers to conclude that infants' categorical perception of speech was part of a biological endowment for language (Eimas et al., 1971). These initial research findings have also led to the view that infants are born with the ability to discriminate any phonetic contrasts that can potentially be linguistically relevant in the world's languages (Eimas, Miller, & Jusczyk, 1987; Werker & Pegg, 1992). Indeed, Nittrouer (2001) has recently cautioned against presenting an overly simplified view of infant speech perception in which infants are equipped with a universal speech discrimination system that is able to discriminate all of the world's phonetic contrasts and that with experience and exposure to language infants either lose the abilities to perceive differences or learn to ignore the contrasts that are not linguistically relevant in the ambient language (see Aslin, Werker, & Morgan (2002) for a critique of her claims that developmental scientists have presented an overly simplified interpretation of infant speech perception and Nittrouer (2002) for a reply).

Evidence for the existence of a universal speech discrimination system comes from several studies showing that infants can distinguish some phonetic contrasts that are not relevant in their linguistic environment. In one study, Trehub

(1976) found that English-learning 1- to 4-month-olds discriminated the vowel contrast [pa]–[pã] and the consonantal contrast [řa]–[za], which are not linguistically distinctive in English. Unlike infants, English-speaking adults often confused the [řa]–[za] contrast, suggesting that linguistic experience produces a loss of sensitivity to non-native contrasts.

To explore the time course of sensitivity to non-native speech contrasts, other researchers have also investigated infants' sensitivities to selected non-native contrasts across different ages. For example, Werker and Tees (1984) tested English-learning 6- to 8-, 8- to 10-, and 10- to 12-month-olds on English, Hindi, and Nthlakapmx (a Native Canadian language) consonant contrasts. They found that while almost all of the 6- to 8-month-olds discriminated all of the segmental consonantal contrasts, only about half of the 8- to 10-month-olds and almost none of the 10- to 12-month-olds discriminated the non-native contrasts.

Other investigations found similar shifts of consonant discrimination abilities between 6 and 12 months: English-learners' sensitivity to other Hindi contrasts (Werker & Lalonde, 1988) and to some Zulu contrasts (Best, 1991) and Japanese-learners' sensitivity to the English [r]–[l] distinction (Tsushima et al., 1994). Taken together, these findings suggest that sometime during the second half of the first year of life, infants' attention to segmental phonetic contrasts in speech becomes finely tuned to those phonetic distinctions that constitute linguistically significant differences in the ambient language-learning environment.

17.1.2 *Early speech perception skills revisited*

A major accomplishment of the first 30 years of research on infant speech perception was the demonstration that infants are not born into a booming, buzzing confusion. Rather, infants exhibit some organization in their perceptual skills even during the first few months of life. However, a more careful look at the perceptual findings reveals several complications to the initial simplistic view that infants are born with a biologically endowed universal speech perception system that is equipped to deal with all possible sounds in any language and that over time they lose the ability to discriminate the contrasts that are not linguistically relevant (see Aslin & Pisoni, 1980).

First of all, it does not appear that infants are able to discriminate all vowel contrasts. Investigators have found that infants are sensitive to some vowel contrasts (Kuhl, 1983; Polka & Werker, 1994; Trehub, 1973) but not others (Lacerda & Sundberg, 2001). For example, Trehub (1973) found that English-learning 1- to 4-month-olds can distinguish [a]–[i] and [i]–[u] contrasts. On the other hand, Lacerda (1993) found that Swedish-learning 6- to 12-month-olds could discriminate between [a] and [ʌ] but not between [a] and [ɑ].

With respect to consonant discrimination, several investigations have revealed patterns of infant speech discrimination performance that are inconsistent with the idea of a universal discrimination device for all of the world's languages. For example, Lasky, Syrdal-Lasky, and Klein (1975) tested Spanish-learning 4.5- to 6-month-olds on three different VOT contrasts. They found that the Spanish-learning infants were able to discriminate a pair of speech sounds that was irrelevant for Spanish but relevant for English, similar to results obtained with

English-learning infants (Eimas et al., 1971). However, the Spanish-learning infants did not discriminate a contrast that is distinctive in Spanish. Lasky et al. (1975) concluded that their findings were consistent with Eimas' (1975b) proposal that infants are born with some innate phonetic feature detectors. However, because the infants in their study did not discriminate the Spanish contrast, the findings are inconsistent with the idea that infants are able to discriminate all potentially relevant contrasts.

Finally, a recent study provides some counterevidence to the hypothesis that infants maintain perceptual sensitivity to linguistically relevant contrasts and then lose sensitivity to contrasts that are not linguistically relevant. Polka, Colantonio, and Sundara (2001) tested 6- to 8-month-olds, 10- to 12-month-olds, and adults from French- and English-speaking backgrounds on a phonetic contrast that is linguistically relevant only for English – the [d]–[ð] contrast. They found no significant differences in discrimination ability between French- and English-learning infants at both ages. However, English-speaking adults discriminated the contrasts better than French-speaking adults and better than any of the groups of infants they tested. Moreover, the discrimination of the French-speaking adults did not differ from any of the groups of infants. Polka et al.'s findings suggest that exposure to English facilitates discrimination of the [d]–[ð] contrast rather than maintaining that discrimination, and that sensitivity to the [d]–[ð] contrast is not lost when learning a language in which that contrast is not linguistically relevant (Polka et al., 2001).

Based on the findings that infants are not born with adult-like speech discrimination abilities (e.g., Lasky et al., 1975), Aslin and Pisoni (1980) proposed that infants come pre-wired with general auditory processing skills that are then modified selectively by experience and activities in the language-learning environment. Some direct evidence to support their proposal comes from a recent study by Maye, Werker, and Gerken (2002). They presented 6- and 8-month-old infants with eight unaspirated alveolar stops that differed with respect to VOT to form a continuum from [da] to [ta]. Some infants were familiarized with more tokens in the middle of the VOT ranges (unimodal distribution condition) while others heard more tokens from the endpoints of the stimulus continuum (bimodal distribution condition). Infants were then tested to assess their ability to discriminate the two endpoints. Maye et al. (2002) found that only infants in the bimodal distribution condition showed discrimination of the endpoints. These findings suggest that infants can become sensitive to the distribution of sounds presented to them over a short period of time in the laboratory, and that variation in the frequency of occurrence of the input stimuli affects the development of their perceptual categories.

There is also evidence in the literature that the distribution of sounds in the input also affects infants' vowel perception. Grieser and Kuhl (1989) found that English-learning 6-month-olds generalize (i.e., fail to discriminate) variations of the English vowel [i] more to a prototypical version of the vowel [i] than to an atypical version of [i]. Kuhl refers to this effect as the "perceptual magnet effect" (Kuhl, 1991, 1993). She argues that infants' perceptual systems are selectively shaped by the variations of vowels that occur in the ambient language, such that the variations within a vowel category are perceived as more similar to the prototypical version of that vowel category than to less typical variations of equal acoustic similarity. In a demonstration of the effect of language experience on vowel categories, Kuhl et al. (1992) tested American and Swedish infants on the American vowel [i] and the Swedish vowel [y] and found that infants showed a perceptual magnet effect for a vowel in their native language but not for a vowel in the other language. In contrast, Polka and Bohn (1996) found that English and German 6- to 8-month-olds and 10- to 12-month-olds discriminated German contrasts (i.e., [dut]–[dyt]) and English contrasts (i.e., [dɛt]–[dæt]) equally well and showed no evidence for a perceptual magnet effect. Furthermore, infants displayed asymmetric discrimination patterns for the contrasts (e.g., poorer discrimination from [dut] to [dyt] than vice versa), which led Polka and Bohn to conclude that some vowels (i.e., those in the extreme corners of the F1/F2 vowel space) appear to serve as universal perceptual attractors. These latter findings raise the possibility that infants' perception of vowels may be influenced by a combination of both innate perceptual biases and the experienced distribution of vowels in the input.

Overall, the recent findings support the hypothesis that input affects infants' perception of both consonants and vowels. However, the final perceptual system may be more influenced by what is linguistically relevant than the inventory of sounds in the ambient language (Best, McRoberts, & Goodell, 2001). Often, listeners are exposed to variants just as often in a language where they are irrelevant than when they make meaningful distinctions. For example, MacKain (1982) reviewed Lisker and Abramson's (1967) analyses of English-speakers' VOTs of stop consonants when they produced words in isolation and in sentences. MacKain pointed out that pre-voiced stop consonants were produced frequently by English speakers in addition to voiced and voiceless stops, even though the difference between pre-voiced and voiced is not linguistically contrastive in English (MacKain, 1982). Thus, mere exposure to different phonetic properties is not enough to allow infants to form phonological categories.

As an alternative to the idea that the perceptual system is shaped primarily by exposure to phonetic features in the ambient language (Aslin & Pisoni, 1980; Eimas, 1975a), Best (1994) proposed that speech discrimination skills are ultimately shaped by sensitivity to phonetic properties that function contrastively to distinguish words in the native language. According to Best's Perceptual Assimilation Model (PAM), listeners categorize novel speech events by their similarity to native categories (Best, 1994; Best, McRoberts, & Sithole, 1988). PAM predicts that non-native contrasts in which both sounds fall in different native categories or in which one sound falls in one category and the other does not fall in any native category will be discriminated by listeners of all ages. In contrast, non-native sounds that fall within a single native category should be discriminated only by younger infants who have not yet formed native phonological categories that would assimilate the sounds into a single category.

Consistent with the predictions of PAM, Best and her colleagues have observed a developmental pattern in which listeners' discrimination skills become increasingly more influenced by their native-language categories. They found that younger infants, 6- to 8-month-olds, are able to discriminate contrasts that fall within a single category in the native language (Best et al., 1995) as well as contrasts that fall in different categories (Best, 1991) and non-assimilable contrasts, which fall outside any category in the ambient language (e.g., Zulu clicks for

English-learning infants) (Best et al., 1988). In contrast to the younger infants, Best found that 10- to 12-month-olds discriminate the non-assimilable contrasts but not contrasts that fall within a single category (Best et al., 1995). These findings are consistent with other studies in which infants display a decline in their ability to discriminate segmental contrasts that are not linguistically relevant in their native language (e.g., Werker & Tees, 1984; but see Polka et al., 2001, for differing results), suggesting that infants' discrimination abilities change as infants acquire knowledge of the characteristics of their phonological system.

However, Best also observed that a child's phonological system is not fully developed by 12 months of age. Infants who were 10 to 12 months of age showed less consistent discrimination than 6- to 8-month-olds for some non-native contrasts in which the two sounds fell into different native categories (Best, 1991). Best suggests that infants may attend to lower-order phonetic properties (i.e., simple articulatory gestures) in the ambient language to form native categories, whereas more mature listeners may form phonological categories by attending to higher-order coordinative structures (i.e., combinations of articulatory gestures) during the word-learning process (Best, 1994). In other words, infants' perceptual systems may change gradually over time as they detect phonetic properties in the input and as they learn which changes in coordinated phonetic structures serve to differentiate words in their language.

17.1.3 Conclusions regarding speech discrimination

Taken together, the evidence suggests that infants begin life with at least some general auditory processing biases and then exposure to the ambient language influences the development of their perceptual system. Some of the evidence suggests that during the first year of life, and before infants have developed a vocabulary, phonetic properties of the ambient language affect their perception of phonetic segments (Best, 1991; Best et al., 1988; Grieser & Kuhl, 1989; Kuhl et al., 1992; Werker & Tees, 1984) and that infants can show short-term sensitivities to distributional information (Maye et al., 2002). However, even after substantial exposure to the sounds of the native language, infants' discrimination abilities are not adult-like at the end of the first year of life (Best, 1991; Polka et al., 2001). It is likely that word learning plays an important role in shaping the mature speech perception system to what is linguistically contrastive in the native language (Best, 1994; Best et al., 2001).

While there has been enormous progress made in understanding infants' speech discrimination abilities in the last 30 years since Eimas et al.'s (1971) initial experiment, there are numerous issues that must be addressed. While young infants have impressive discrimination skills, some studies have failed to demonstrate discrimination of particular contrasts (Lasky et al., 1975). However, it should be noted that the evidence against the idea of universal perceptual abilities is based on negative results (Aslin et al., 2002). It is possible that new, more sensitive ways of measuring speech discrimination skills, such as event-related potentials (Dehaene-Lambertz & Dehaene, 1994), will reveal that infants are in fact able, at some level, to discriminate all contrasts that are potentially linguistically relevant for the world's languages. Such findings would force infant researchers to revisit the earlier proposal that infants are innately sensitive to all potentially relevant phonetic contrasts.

What do these discrimination skills tell us about infants' language acquisition? Of course, infants must be able to differentiate sounds if they are to recognize the words they hear. However, to recognize spoken words they must also encode and store the sound patterns of words in memory. Studies of infant speech discrimination may reveal something about their representations of the sound patterns of words. For example, in habituation studies, it is possible that infants form a representation of the syllable with which they are habituated and then recognize that it differs from another stimulus. But at what level do they form these representations? And do these representations persist in long-term memory?

Our understanding of infants' auditory processing may be enhanced by physiological investigations of auditory development. In a recent study, Moore (2002) investigated the maturation of the human auditory cortex in postmortem brain tissue from the 16th week of gestation to 27 years of age. She found that infants do not form neural projections from the thalamus to the primary auditory cortex until around 4.5 months of age and argues that cortical processing of auditory information does not begin until then. Thus, the nature of the lexical representations that young infants form may be very different from what they form later on in life. Moreover, the relation between auditory-perceptual discrimination skills and language development may be constrained by the development of connections between the auditory system and other neurological structures in the cortex (Moore, 2002).

Findings on the effects of language experience on speech discrimination suggest that infants may be sensitive to the distribution of sounds in their language-learning environment. However, this observation begs the question of how infants extract the distributional information that would be helpful for discrimination in the first place. MacKain (1982) raised several specific issues in addressing the assumption that early language experience affects speech discrimination. One issue was the idea that infants are exposed to different sets of contrasts in different languages. In order to have access to contrasts, rather than sounds, infants must have some way of knowing that speech segments vary along underlying perceptual continua. To do that, infants must extract and represent detailed segmental information as opposed to syllabic or other high-order information. And they must extract this information from exposure to natural continuous speech where there is an enormous amount of other varying phonetic information and differences between phones become blurred (Lisker & Abramson, 1967). How infants deal with these challenges and how they acquire knowledge about the distributional information from the ambient language is still an important issue for future research in infant speech perception.

The evidence that speech discrimination is affected by the distribution of the input may reveal a general mechanism that may be important for language acquisition – sensitivity to distributional information in sequential patterns. Sensitivity to distributional information may be very important for segmenting words from fluent speech, which is the topic we turn to next.

17.2 Infant Speech Segmentation

Words are not usually uttered in isolation, even to infants. Indeed, about 90–95% of utterances addressed to infants (excluding vocatives, fillers, and social expressions) are in the form of fluent speech (van de Weijer, 1998). Very rarely do abstract nouns, verbs, or prepositions occur in isolation, and some function words, such as "of," virtually never do (van de Weijer, 1998). Even when caregivers are explicitly encouraged to teach their infants words, they only present the words in isolated contexts about 20% of the time (Woodward & Aslin, 1990). Thus, language learners must possess or rapidly develop the ability to segment words from fluent speech.

A growing body of evidence suggests that infants are able to segment words from fluent speech well before they are able to produce words. In a seminal study, Jusczyk and Aslin (1995) adapted the headturn preference procedure (HPP) to explore infants' ability to segment and recognize words from fluent speech. In their version of the HPP, which is displayed in Figure 17.1, infants were seated on a caregiver's lap in a three-sided booth. At the beginning of each trial, infants' attention was directed to the center of the booth with a blinking light. Subsequently, the center light went off and, randomly, either the left or right side light started blinking. When the infant oriented to the side light, the experimenter

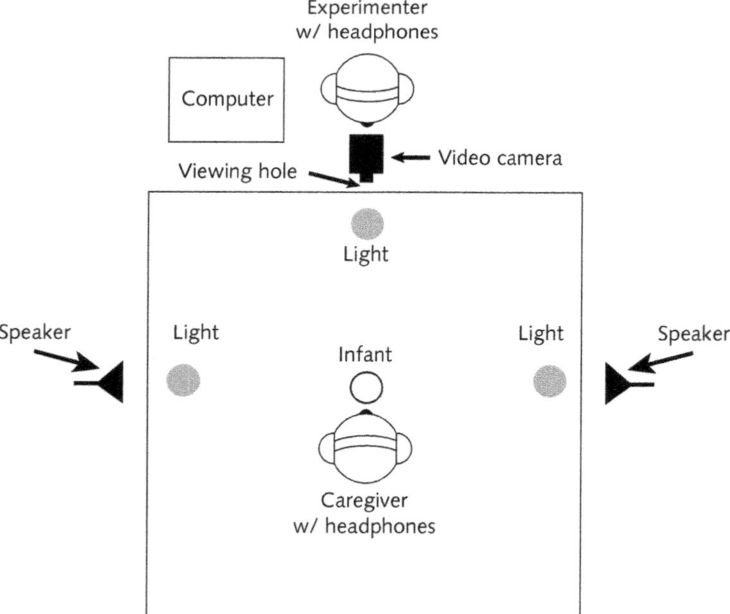

Figure 17.1 The Headturn Preference Procedure as implemented originally by Jusczyk and Aslin (1995) and subsequently by Jusczyk and colleagues. Infants are seated on a caregiver's lap, and their looks to the lights are recorded into a computer by the experimenter observing through a viewing hole. Both the experimenter and the caregiver wear earplugs and listen to loud masking music over headphones.

initiated the onset of the speech stimulus, which was presented through a loudspeaker behind the blinking light. The blinking light and speech continued until the infant looked away for 2 seconds or more.

In Jusczyk and Aslin's (1995) original study, infants were first presented with words in isolation during a familiarization phase, either *cup* and *dog* or *bike* and *feet*. During a test phase, four passages of connected speech were presented in random order, each containing one of the four target words one time in each of six sentences. Jusczyk and Aslin found that 7.5-month-olds, but not 6-month-olds, showed significantly longer looking times to the blinking light when presented with the passages containing the familiarized words than when presented with control passages. These findings suggest that by 8 months of age, infants can segment words from fluent speech and that the lexical representations they form from isolated versions of words are generalizable to words spoken in fluent speech. This is an impressive accomplishment for an infant.

Since Jusczyk and Aslin's (1995) study, several investigators have explored the possible cues that infants might use to segment words from fluent speech. There are several sources of information in speech that infants may use to help them in the segmentation process. For example, information about prosody may be important in early speech segmentation because infants are sensitive to prosodic patterns in speech from a very early age. Within the first two months of life, infants display preferences for the prosodic patterns of their native language (Mehler et al., 1988), and are able to discriminate foreign languages that differ rhythmically (Dehaene-Lambertz & Houston, 1998; Nazzi, Bertoncini, & Mehler, 1998). Because infants display an early sensitivity to prosodic patterns in speech, it is possible that prosody may play an important role in the earliest stages of segmentation.

Infants begin to show preference for the prosodic properties of words in their native language between 6 and 9 months of age. For example, Jusczyk, Friederici et al. (1993) found that 6-month-old English-learning infants listen significantly longer to English than to Norwegian words, which differ markedly in their prosodic characteristics. Furthermore, other evidence shows that English-learning infants become sensitive to some of the rhythmic properties of English words by 9 months. For example, one characteristic of English stress is that most content words in English conversational speech (about 90%) begin with a strong syllable, defined as a syllable with an unreduced vowel (Cutler & Carter, 1987). Jusczyk, Cutler, and Redanz (1993) found that English-learning 9-month-olds, but not 6-month-olds, listen longer to lists of bisyllabic words with the predominant stress pattern of English, strong/weak (e.g., "pliant," "donor"), than to weak/strong words (e.g., "abut," "condone"). These findings indicate that between 6 and 9 months of age infants develop sensitivity to language-specific prosodic properties that are useful in segmenting words from fluent speech.

Sensitivity to the predominant stress pattern of English words appears to influence infants' segmentation of speech as well. For instance, Echols, Crowhurst, and Childers (1997) found that English-learning 9-month-olds were better able to recognize strong/weak than weak/strong bisyllables contained within longer sequences of strong/weak/strong syllables. Similarly, Morgan and Saffran (1995) found that 9-month-olds were more likely to treat strong/weak bisyllables as cohesive units than weak/strong bisyllables. Finally, Jusczyk, Houston, and

Newsome (1999) demonstrated that English-learning 7.5-month-olds segment strong/weak but not weak/strong English words from the context of fluent speech. These findings suggest that infants raised in an English-speaking environment are more likely to expect and possibly listen for words that conform to a strong/weak than a weak/strong stress pattern.[1] As a further test of this hypothesis, Jusczyk et al. (1999) tested English-learning infants' segmentation of strong/weak units that crossed word boundaries. They found that when 7.5-month-olds were presented with passages in which weak/strong target words were always followed by the same function word (e.g., *guitar is*), the infants segmented strong/weak units across word boundaries (e.g., *taris*). Moreover, in a cross-linguistic investigation of two rhythmically similar languages, English and Dutch, 9-month-old English-learning infants segmented strong/weak Dutch words from Dutch fluent speech as did Dutch infants (Houston et al., 2000). These findings suggest that infants apply a rhythmic-based segmentation strategy to a foreign language that has similar rhythmic properties.

In a more recent study, the role of stress in infants' segmentation was explored by testing 7.5-month-olds' ability to segment three-syllable words from fluent speech (Houston, Santelmann, & Jusczyk, 2004). Infants were able to segment words from fluent speech in which the primary stress fell on the initial syllables (e.g., *cantaloupe*) but not words in which the primary stress fell on the final syllables (e.g., *jamboree*). For the stress-final words, infants displayed segmentation of only the final syllables (e.g., *ree*). These findings suggest that degree of stress contributes to infants' ability to locate word onsets in fluent speech. Overall, these recent investigations suggest that infants' sensitivity to prosodic information in speech, especially syllable stress, plays an important role in segmenting words from fluent speech.

Another potential source of information that can be used to segment words from fluent speech is based on the transitional probabilities of syllables. Listeners may implicitly or explicitly notice regularities in the co-occurrence of syllables to infer potential word boundaries. For example, if syllables x (e.g., /ba/) and y (e.g., /tl/) occur much more often together than apart, listeners may infer that $x + y$ (e.g., "bottle") forms a cohesive unit. Likewise, $x + y$ may be perceived as more cohesive if the pattern occurs across a variety of contexts (e.g., "big bottle," "yellow bottle," "fill the bottle with milk") than if the context is fixed. In fact, Goodsitt, Morgan, and Kuhl (1993) found that 7-month-olds were more likely to treat bisyllables as cohesive units if they were previously presented in a variable context than if the context was fixed.

Similarly, in an influential study on statistical learning, Saffran, Aslin, and Newport (1996) presented 8-month-olds with a sequence of 12 synthetic CV syllables in which each two-syllable sequence they heard had either a 1.00 or .33 probability of occurring together. For example, in one case, /da/ was always followed by /ro/, which was always followed by /pi/. However, /da/ was preceded by three different syllables and /pi/ was followed by three different syllables. After a two-minute exposure to the sequence of syllables, 8-month-olds showed significant looking time differences between 1.00 probability sequences (e.g., /da/ro/pi/) and .33 probability sequences (e.g., /pi/go/la/ or /tu/da/ro/), suggesting that they treat the 1.00 probability sequences as cohesive perceptual units. A follow-up investigation by Aslin, Saffran and Newport (1998) provided additional evidence that infants specifically used transitional probabilities as opposed to the higher overall frequency of the 1.00 probability sequences than the .33 probability sequences (but see Perruchet & Vinter, 1998) for an explanation of the results based on basic properties of memory and associative learning rather than on learning transitional probabilities).

Recent investigations have pitted stress cues and transitional probabilities against each other to determine which source of information infants rely on as the primary cue in speech segmentation. Two independent investigations, using Saffran et al.'s (1996) paradigm found that 8- to 9-month-olds relied more on stress cues than transitional probabilities (Johnson & Jusczyk, 2001; Thiessen & Saffran, 2003). In contrast to the older infants, Thiessen and Saffran (2003) found that younger infants (6.5 to 7 months of age) showed more sensitivity to transitional probabilities in segmenting words from fluent speech. However, whether the same pattern of findings would also be observed in infants' segmentation of natural speech has yet to be investigated.

These recent findings suggest that infants are sensitive to transitional probabilities at a very young age, at least in the context of Saffran et al.'s (1996) experimental procedure, which used synthesized syllables presented at a constant rate. These findings also raise the interesting possibility that young infants may use transitional probabilities as an initial method for segmenting words from natural fluent speech. In order to know if and when infants use transitional probabilities of syllables to segment words from natural speech, several factors must be considered, such as the nature of the stimulus input and infants' perceptual and memory capacities.

With respect to the stimulus input to infants, spoken English contains thousands of unique syllables and each one varies in its acoustic properties depending on its surrounding phonetic context and the idiosyncrasies of each talker's pronunciation. At the present time, very little is known about the frequency of word recurrence or the transitional probabilities of syllables in recurring words (but see Brent & Siskind, 2001, and van de Weijer, 1998, for some analyses of input to infants). Gathering this information would be an important initial step for understanding the contribution that transitional probabilities of syllables make in segmenting words from fluent speech.

Another important step would be to assess infants' potential skills for making use of transitional probabilities of syllables for segmentation. For example, it is critical to know more about the nature of the representations they construct for syllables. Do infants encode the same syllable [bi] in the words *beetle*, *baby*, and *bee* or are they encoded as different syllables due to differences in amounts of stress, sentential contexts, and talkers' pronunciations? Also, what are infants' processing and memory capacities for syllables and how do they constrain infants' computation of transitional probabilities? Do infants compute transitional probabilities of all syllables or only of acoustically salient syllables in the input? If infants encode only a subset of syllables, how does this affect their computation of the transitional probabilities? Investigating these issues would be fruitful for determining the role that transitional probabilities of syllables have in infants' segmentation of words from fluent speech.

It is possible that specific properties in the speech signal may constrain and direct infants' computation of transitional probabilities. For example, stressed syllables may mark places where infants compute transitional probabilities of syllables. Certainly, the findings of Jusczyk, Houston, and Newsome (1999) and Houston et al. (2004) suggest this. In both studies, infants picked up on the co-occurrences of syllables only when they were headed by stressed syllables. However, when stress fell at the ends of words, the infants did not show any evidence of using transitional probabilities to segment words from fluent speech, suggesting that syllable stress may constrain infants' computation of transitional probabilities. Thus, learning that stressed syllables mark word onsets might be a good first-pass strategy for segmenting words from fluent speech.

How might infants learn that words begin with stressed syllables? Jusczyk, Houston, & Newsome (1999) suggested that infants may pick up that information from the words that they hear in isolation. Indeed, Brent and Siskind (2001) recently reported that infants do hear some words in isolation and that these words tend to be repeated often. From this subset of words, infants may pick up some general properties of English words. Another possibility is that infants' early sensitivity to rhythmic properties of the native language may allow them to discover the canonical stress pattern of words in that language (Nazzi, Jusczyk, & Johnson, 2000).

Segmenting the speech stream at stressed syllables may serve as a good initial strategy for infants to locate some words in natural speech. Also, by chunking fluent speech into smaller units, infants would position themselves to discover other sources of information useful for word segmentation, such as phonotactic and allophonic cues. For example, extracting a word like *taste* from fluent speech exposes two allophonic variants of /t/, the initial aspirated /t/ and the second unreleased stop. By analyzing such chunks, English-learning infants may correctly infer that [t^h] usually marks a word onset. Similarly, attention to the fact that some sequences occur relatively more often within words (e.g. [ft]) while others occur more often between words (e.g. [vt]) could also provide potential word segmentation cues. Indeed, there is evidence that infants are sensitive to phonotactic information by 9 months of age (Friederici & Wessels, 1993; Jusczyk, Luce, & Charles-Luce, 1994).

Recently, several investigators have explored whether infants use phonotactic and allophonic information to segment words. Jusczyk, Hohne, and Bauman (1999) found that 10.5-month-old, but not 9-month-old, English-learners are sensitive to allophonic cues to word boundaries. In particular, 10.5-month-olds were able to use allophonic information to distinguish between "nitrates" and "night rates" in fluent speech contexts. Similarly, Mattys et al. (1999) demonstrated that 9-month-olds are sensitive to how phonotactic patterns typically align with word boundaries. Moreover, Mattys and Jusczyk (2001) found that 9-month-olds were better able to segment words when good phonotactic cues to word boundaries were present than when such cues were absent. These findings suggest that infants use segmental allophonic information to extract words from fluent speech. It is possible that this emerges from an initial stress-based segmentation strategy in which infants chunk continuous speech into smaller, more analyzable units (Jusczyk, 1997).

17.2.1 *Future directions in infant segmentation*

Several other sources of acoustic-phonetic information might also play a role in word segmentation. In a recent study, Johnson (2003) investigated 8-month-olds' sensitivity to subphonemic information in speech (i.e., allophonic and co-articulatory information). Infants were presented with sentences containing sequences that were produced either as cohesive units (e.g., *catalogue*) or as three-word phrases (e.g., *cat a log*). Johnson (2003) found that 8-month-olds segmented the trisyllabic words as cohesive units only when the sentences contained the words produced as cohesive units. However, when infants were presented with sentences containing three-word idioms that were produced as fixed phrases (e.g., *piece of cake*), infants segmented these from fluent speech as cohesive units. These findings suggest that infants' segmentation of words from fluent speech may be influenced by very subtle phonetic information in the speech signal.

These studies reveal much about how infants segment words from fluent speech. However, this research has focused almost exclusively on nouns. Nouns have different phonological properties than words of other grammatical categories (Kelly, 1992), and these phonological properties may have an impact on segmentation. Morgan, Allopenna, and Shi (1996) suggested that infants may distinguish content words and function words in fluent speech by attending to acoustic-phonetic cues, such as stress and vowel characteristics, that differentiate them. However, there has been very little research on other types of words. One notable exception is a recent study by Höhle and Weissenborn (2003) who investigated German-learning infants' segmentation of function words from fluent speech. They found that 8-month-olds but not 6.5-month-olds were able to segment words of this lexical class from fluent speech.

Another notable exception is Nazzi et al.'s (2003) recent investigation of infants' segmentation of verbs from fluent speech. They tested 10.5-, 13.5-, and 16.5-month-olds on their segmentation of weak/strong and strong/weak verbs. In English, nouns more often have a strong/weak pattern than a weak/strong pattern, whereas verbs display the opposite. Recall that Jusczyk, Houston, and Newsome (1999) found that 7.5-month-olds were able to segment strong/weak nouns from fluent speech, but segmentation of weak/strong nouns from fluent speech was not observed until 10.5 months of age. Nazzi et al. (2003) found that infants did not segment verbs from fluent speech until 13.5 months of age. One possible reason for differences in infants' segmentation of nouns and verbs may be due to differences in acoustic properties of nouns and verbs in fluent speech. Nazzi et al. (2003) performed acoustic analyses on the two sets of stimuli and found differences in pitch accent between the target nouns and target verbs presented in the test passages.

It is also possible that infants may use other sources of information to segment verbs from fluent speech. By 13.5 months of age, infants may be able to produce and understand the meaning of some nouns and social expressions. Thus, they may be using some lexical and syntactic knowledge in addition to phonological information to segment verbs and other classes of words from fluent speech. Clearly, much more work is needed to understand how infants segment all classes of words from fluent speech.

17.3 Infants' Representations of the Sound Patterns of Words

To build a vocabulary, infants must not only discriminate differences between the sound patterns of words and segment them from fluent speech, they must also encode and store the words in memory for later recognition. Also, infants must cope with variability of the acoustic-phonetic forms of words. To satisfy all these demands, lexical representations must be sufficiently detailed that the listener can recognize precisely which words are uttered, but, at the same time, the representations must be robust to variability associated with individual differences of vocal qualities and articulation.

Thus, two important questions to ask regarding word recognition are: How closely must a phonetic sequence match a stored sequence to be recognized as a familiar item? And, do infants recognize words based solely on linguistically relevant properties or do other, indexical, properties also play a role in recognizing words as familiar?

As part of their original study of speech segmentation, Jusczyk and Aslin (1995) explored how detailed infants' representations were for the words they segmented from fluent speech. They assessed how detailed 7.5-month-olds' representations were by first familiarizing them with nonwords that differed from the real target words used in their previous experiments by only the place of articulation of the first phoneme (i.e., *tup*, *zeet*, *gike*, and *bawg* rather than *cup*, *feet*, *bike*, and *dog*) and then testing them on passages of fluent speech that contained the real words. In contrast to when infants were familiarized and tested with the real words, infants did not orient significantly longer to the passages containing the corresponding target words after familiarization with the nonwords. Tincoff and Jusczyk (1996) obtained similar results when they changed the final phonemes of the target words. Their findings suggest that 7.5-month-old infants form precise representations of words that are generalizable to new instances of the same word but not overgeneralized to phonetically similar, but not equivalent, nonwords.

Another source of variability in the acoustic realization of words are the changes associated with articulatory and voice characteristics of different talkers. Can infants cope with talker variability? The findings of Jusczyk and Aslin (1995) suggest that infants are sensitive to acoustic information that is relevant to segmental contrasts in language and have precise word representations. However, in most of the earlier infant word recognition research, the stimuli typically consisted of recordings from a single talker. Given that infants are also sensitive to the indexical properties of speech, it is possible that they may encode both indexical and phonological properties when forming word representations. If this is correct, then infants might have some difficulty recognizing words produced by different talkers, different accents, or different affective voice qualities.

To explore the effect of talker variability on infant word recognition, Houston and Jusczyk (2000) tested infants' abilities to recognize words produced by different talkers. Using the HPP, infants were familiarized with two isolated words (*cup* and *dog*, or *bike* and *feet*) produced by one talker and presented with passages produced by a different talker during the test phase. Houston and Jusczyk (2000) found that 7.5-month-olds recognized the familiarized words in passages when the familiarization talker and the test talker were of the same sex but not when they were of different sexes. The findings suggest that, at this age, infants recognize the similarity between words only when they are relatively similar phonetically and indexically.

To be able to learn the meanings of words, infants must also form representations of the sound patterns of words that are not only robust to talker differences; the representations must also persist in long-term memory. In a subsequent study, Houston and Jusczyk (2003) investigated the nature of infants' long-term memory for spoken words. It is possible that the fine acoustic details associated with talker-specific information decay with time leaving only the linguistically relevant information. The investigation employed the same procedure as Jusczyk and Aslin (1995) except that the familiarization and test phases were separated by a one-day delay.

The pattern of results was the same as in Jusczyk and Aslin (1995). Infants oriented significantly longer to the passages containing the familiarized words than to the control passages when the words and passages were produced by the same talker but not when they were produced by different talkers of the same sex. These findings suggest that talker-specific information serves as an important cue for retrieving spoken words from memory. To test this hypothesis further, Houston and Jusczyk (2003) familiarized 7.5-month-olds with words from one talker, and then tested them on the following day with two passages (one with the familiar word and one with a control word) from the same talker and two passages from a different talker of the same sex (also one familiar and one control). Infants displayed recognition for the familiar voice and for the familiarized words produced by the familiar talker and for those produced by the novel talker, in contrast to the results found in the previous experiment. Evidently, the presence of the familiar talker during testing helped the infants recall the words from memory such that they were then able to recognize them by the novel talker. These findings suggest that talker-specific information in speech persists in memory and can facilitate the recall of words from long-term memory.

While infants may have some difficulty coping with talker variability at 7.5 months of age, infants seem to make substantial progress dealing with talker variability by the end of their first year of life. For example, Houston and Jusczyk (2000) also tested 10.5-month-olds' ability to recognize words in passages after familiarization with words produced by a talker of the opposite sex. In contrast to the 7.5-month-olds, 10.5-month-olds demonstrated recognition of the familiarized words in this condition. These findings suggest that during the first year of life, infants make significant progress recognizing words produced by different talkers.

How do infants learn to cope with talker variability in speech? Houston (1999) investigated the possibility that exposure to talker variability may contribute to infants' ability to form robust representations that are generalizable across different talkers. In a series of experiments, infants were first familiarized with two words produced by four talkers and then were presented with passages containing these words produced by a fifth talker. The perceptual similarity of the familiarization talkers to each other and the average perceptual similarity between the test talker and the familiarization talkers were manipulated across four experiments.[2] A schematic of the talkers' perceptual similarity space in each experiment is displayed in Figure 17.2.

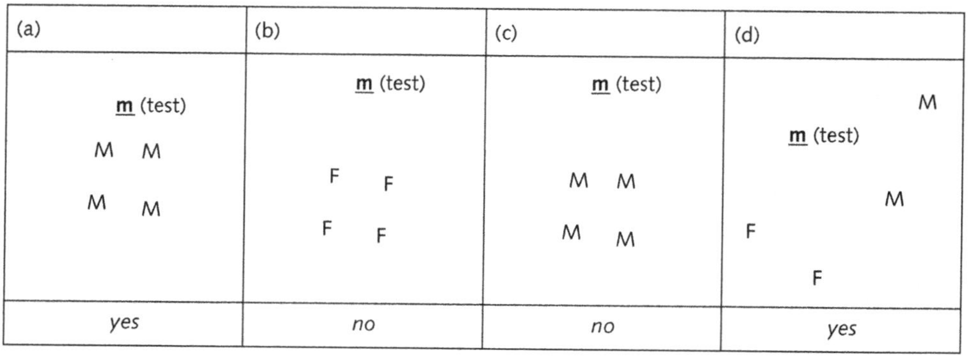

(a)	(b)	(c)	(d)
m (test) M M M M	m (test) F F F F	m (test) M M M M	M m (test) M F F
yes	*no*	*no*	*yes*

Figure 17.2 A schematic of talker-variability conditions and findings from Houston (1999). Each panel displays a sample condition from one of four experiments. The talkers who produced the words used in the familiarization phases are represented as Ms (male talkers) and Fs (female talkers). The talker who produced the test passages is represented as m (the test passages were produced by a male talker in each of these sample conditions). Approximate perceptual similarity of the familiarization talkers to each other and their perceptual similarity to the test talkers are represented by distance. At the bottom of each panel, yes or no indicates whether or not infants demonstrated recognition of the familiarized words in the test passages in that experiment.

The results were similar to Houston and Jusczyk (2000). When infants were familiarized and tested with words and passages produced by perceptually similar talkers who were all of the same sex, infants recognized the familiarized words in passages produced by a novel talker (Figure 17.2a). Houston (1999) also tested infants in conditions where the test talker was relatively different from the familiarization talkers. In these conditions infants did not display recognition of the familiarized words in the test passages, whether they were produced by a talker of the opposite sex (Figure 17.2b) or of the same sex (Figure 17.2c).

Houston (1999) hypothesized that the perceptual similarity of the familiarization talkers to each other induced infants to form representations that were not generalizable to a relatively dissimilar talker and that infants' word representations may be more generalizable if encoded from relatively dissimilar talkers. To assess this possibility, infants were familiarized with words produced by talkers who were relatively dissimilar to each other, and then tested with passages produced by another relatively dissimilar talker (Figure 17.2d). Importantly, the average perceptual distance between the test talker and the familiarization talkers was similar to the experiments in which the infants failed to show recognition of the familiarized words in the passages. In contrast to the previous two experiments, infants in the final experiment did show evidence of recognition of the familiarized words in the passages. These findings suggest that infants' representations of the sound patterns of words become more robust and generalizable when they are familiarized with words in which the distribution of talkers is relatively large with respect to the perceptual similarity space they are drawn from (see also Singh, 2002).

Children's understanding of the meaning of content words (i.e., nouns, verbs, spatial prepositions) is enhanced as they encounter words in multiple sentential contexts and in a range of real-life contexts where the sound pattern of words can be linked to their referents (Carey, 1982). Thus, being able to store words in long-term memory and recognize the equivalence of the sound patterns of words produced by different talkers is an important developmental prerequisite for acquiring a vocabulary. Indeed, Hollich (2002) recently found that when 24-month-olds were exposed to novel words produced by multiple talkers, they were more easily able to associate those words to novel objects than if they were exposed to the novel words produced by a single talker. These findings suggest that forming generalizable phonological word representations is important for word learning.

If infants' representations of words become more generalizable with respect to talker-specific information, do their representations also become more generalizable or even overgeneralized with respect to linguistically relevant information? Several recent investigations have provided evidence that infants' representations of speech sounds may shift from being highly detailed to overgeneralized by the end of the first year of life. For example, Hallé and Boysson-Bardies (1996) investigated 11-month-olds' representations of familiar words. Using the HPP, they presented infants with lists of familiar words, familiar words altered by one phoneme, and rare words. Infants showed a preference for altered familiar words over rare words but no preference for unaltered versus altered familiar words. The authors interpreted their findings as evidence that 11-month-olds form mental representations of familiar words but that these representations are more holistic than adults' representations.

There are several possible reasons why younger children may have relatively more holistic representations for the sound patterns of words than older children or adults. One reason may be that in the process of word learning, infants focus on forming a link between semantic and phonetic information and thus they have fewer processing resources dedicated to encoding fine phonetic details in the speech signal.

Recently, Werker and her colleagues have reported evidence in support of this view. Stager and Werker (1997) investigated 14-month-olds' ability to associate novel words to novel objects using a modified Visual Habituation Switch design (Werker et al., 1998). They found that 14-month-olds could learn the associations between the novel words and novel objects when the novel words were phonetically dissimilar (*lif* and *neem*) but not when they were very similar (*bih* and *dih*). However, the 14-month-olds were able to discriminate *bih* and *dih* under a speech discrimination condition that did not encourage them to link novel words to novel objects.

More recently, Werker et al. (2002) found that, unlike the 14-month-olds, 17- and 20-month-olds were able to form word-object associations with the phonetically similar *bih* and *dih* nonwords. Werker and colleagues concluded that when infants begin to learn words, their attention focuses on building sound-meaning associations and less on encoding fine-grained phonetic differences between similar words. This latter developmental shift from more holistic perception at 11 to 14 months of age to more detailed analysis at 17 to 20 months of age corresponds with emerging word learning skills. For example, starting around 18 months, many young children begin to produce on average about one new word per day

(Fenson et al., 1994). It is possible that infants are able to learn the meanings of words more rapidly as they develop more mature perceptual capacities to form detailed phonological representations of words.

Another reason why infants' lexical representations may be more holistic than adults' is because of the relatively small size of children's lexicons. Charles-Luce and Luce (1990, 1995) analyzed productive vocabularies of young children and found that their lexicons contained fewer phonetically similar words than would be predicted by their vocabulary size. They argued that children are able to employ a holistic, less fine-tuned approach to word learning because of the similarity structure of words in their lexicons. Children do not need to encode their first words in much detail because they do not have many other words in their lexicons that could cause confusion. As children acquire more words and their lexicons begin to increase in size, their lexical representations become more fine-grained, which helps to avoid falsely recognizing phonetically similar words (Charles-Luce & Luce, 1990, 1995; Jusczyk, 1986; Walley, 1993; Walley, Smith, & Jusczyk, 1986).

The idea that phonological neighborhoods are relatively sparsely populated in children's lexicons has been challenged by some investigators (Coady & Aslin, 2003; Dollaghan, 1994). To investigate phonological neighborhoods in children, Coady and Aslin examined lexical corpora of two children aged 2 years, 3 months to 3 years, 6 months. Similar to the findings of Charles-Luce and Luce, they found that the children had sparser neighborhoods than adults. However, further analyses of these two children revealed that they tended to acquire new words from denser than average neighborhoods, counter to the notion that children learn words that are not confusable with other words. Moreover, when Coady and Aslin computed neighborhood density using a ratio count (percentage of lexicon that neighbors each word) rather than a raw count (number of words that neighbor each word), their results indicated that children have denser neighborhoods than adults. These findings are evidence against the idea that children's representations are necessarily less detailed than adults'.

Consistent with these latter findings on young children, some recent evidence suggests that fine phonetic details are retained in infants' word representations, even at 14 to 24 months of age (Bailey & Plunkett, 2002; Swingley & Aslin, 2000, 2002). In one study, Swingley and Aslin (2002) measured infants' preferential looking to a target object (e.g., a baby) versus a distractor object (e.g., a dog) when the target word was named aloud. The investigators found that 14-month-olds showed a greater preference for the target object when the target word was produced accurately (e.g., "Look at the baby") than when it was mispronounced (e.g., "Look at the vaby") but that infants' looking preference to the target object was significantly above chance in both conditions. The authors concluded that infants encode fine acoustic-phonetic details in speech, as shown by the better performance in the exact match condition, but that a close lexical neighbor (e.g., vaby) may also activate lexical representations.

In a follow-up study, Swingley (2003) replicated the previous findings using words where the mispronounced segment occurred word-medially. He also compared infants' recognition of words that came from dense and sparse neighborhoods and found that infants were no more or less susceptible to mispronunciations for words coming from sparse neighborhoods than words coming from dense neighborhoods (but see Hollich, Jusczyk, & Luce, 2002, for evidence that neighborhood density affects infants' learning associations between novel words and novel objects). Taken together, these recent findings suggest that infants retain details of words but that similar sounding words can activate representations of the real words. Also, increasing lexicon size does not seem to pressure word representations into becoming phonetically more detailed.

The results of all of these studies suggest that infants across a wide range of ages encode phonetic details of words. However, the way infants form lexical representations may depend on the distribution of the input they are exposed to early in life. For example, Maye et al. (2002) found that infants' categories of sounds could be influenced by whether there was a monomodal or bimodal distribution of syllables. Likewise, Houston (1999) found that infants could generalize their representations of words when they were exposed to exemplars produced by a variety of different talkers. The way infants make use of fine phonetic detail in speech may also depend on the nature of the task. During word learning, forming semantic categories may influence the organization of the representations. For example, in Stager and Werker's (1997) study, infants may have accepted *bih* as the name of *dih*, not because they were unable to detect the difference but because they were at a developmental stage where they were flexible to the possibility that a semantic category, in this case a novel object, could organize exemplars together as disparate as *bih* and *dih*.

17.3.1 Jusczyk's WRAPSA model of the developing lexicon

The proposal that infants encode both phonetic and indexical details of the sound patterns of words in their mental lexicons is consistent with an exemplar view of word representation (Goldinger, 1996, 1998; Johnson, 1997; Jusczyk, 1993, 1997). Peter Jusczyk's Word Recognition and Phonetic Structure Acquisition (WRAPSA) model (Jusczyk, 1993, 1997) adopts an exemplar approach to describe the developing lexicon. The WRAPSA model postulates that at the first level of infant speech perception auditory analyzers pick up auditory input and provide a description of the spectral and temporal features present in the acoustic signal. After exposure to speech, a weighting scheme is developed that gives prominence to features that are important for understanding the particular language the infant is acquiring. Once the input is recoded and weighted, potential word candidates are extracted from fluent speech and then are stored as representations in the mental lexicon. The WRAPSA model proposes that during infancy, many new instances of a word may not be recognized as similar to any stored exemplars because relatively few exemplars have been encoded. Moreover, acoustically different instances of the same word may initially be treated as distinct words until infants' mental lexicon becomes larger and enriched with more exemplars that listeners use to extract both linguistic and talker-specific information.

The exemplar view of the mental lexicon can be contrasted with more traditional abstractionist views of speech perception and word recognition that assert that representations of spoken words contain only idealized phonological information (Liberman & Mattingly, 1985). For example, Sussman (1984, 1986) posits that specialized neural assemblies in the brain are dedicated to extracting the linguistic information from speech and ignoring the indexical properties in the signal. However, numerous investigations over the last 15 years have shown that listeners encode talker-specific information and that these sources of variability affect word identification (Goldinger, 1996; Mullennix, Pisoni, & Martin, 1989; Nygaard, Sommers, & Pisoni, 1994; Sommers, Nygaard, & Pisoni, 1994), word recognition (Bradlow, Nygaard, & Pisoni, 1999; Craik & Kirsner, 1974; Palmeri, Goldinger, & Pisoni, 1993), and serial recall of words (Goldinger, Pisoni, & Logan, 1991; Martin et al., 1989). And there is also new evidence that talker variability affects word recognition in young infants (Houston, 1999; Houston & Jusczyk, 2000, 2003).

It should be noted that along with the exemplar view of word representations, there are other approaches to speech perception that are compatible with the notion that listeners' representations contain talker-specific as well as linguistically relevant information (see Best, 1994; Church & Schacter, 1994; Fowler, 1986; Remez, Fellowes, & Rubin, 1997). Also, there are several other more general approaches to categorization that incorporate an important role for stimulus variability. For example, Ashby's decision-bound model (Ashby & Perrin, 1988; Maddox & Ashby, 1993) asserts that representation boundaries are influenced by the distribution of instances in psychological space. These types of categorization models differ from exemplar models because they assume that representational spaces within particular decision bounds are associated with particular abstract concepts. To date, a decision-bound model has not been formulated to specifically address speech perception or word learning in infants. If one were proposed, it might provide a potentially useful alternative to an exemplar view.

In exemplar models, the organization of individual exemplars is flexible and categorization will change depending on what dimensions are being attended to. For example, in Johnson's (1997) model of talker recognition, exemplars are directly connected to properties that are important to listeners, such as voice quality and linguistic value (see Johnson, this volume). These properties serve as labels that organize the sets of exemplars according to which properties are selectively attended to by the listener (Nosofsky, 1988). It is possible that listeners from infancy through adulthood encode both linguistic and nonlinguistic details in the representations of spoken words. Exactly when infants exhibit more holistic versus detailed representations may depend on the distribution of the exemplars that they are actually exposed to and the nature of the processing task used to assess their performance.

17.4 Speech Perception in Deaf Infants Who Receive Cochlear Implants

A cochlear implant is an auditory prosthesis with internal and external components. The external part consists of a microphone that picks up sound, a signal processor that converts sound into electric impulses, and a transmitter that is magnetically attached to the internal device to which it transmits the electric impulses via radio waves. The impulses are sent to an array of electrodes, which are surgically inserted into the cochlea. The electrodes stimulate the auditory nerves, providing auditory information to the brain. The auditory information that listeners receive from cochlear implants is impoverished in comparison to acoustic hearing using normal auditory mechanisms. However, technological advances in cochlear implantation have allowed a growing number of people who are profoundly deaf to perceive sound, understand speech, and develop spoken language (see Svirsky et al., 2000; Pisoni, this volume).

From a theoretical perspective, it is of interest to compare language development of normally-hearing infants to infants who are initially deprived of auditory input and then receive exposure to sound at a later age via a cochlear implant. Do these children follow a similar but delayed developmental path to normal-hearing infants, even though their early auditory experience was radically different? If not, how does the initial absence of auditory information affect the development of spoken language? Some language development researchers have hypothesized that there is a "sensitive period" in which the capacity to learn languages declines because of decreasing neural plasticity (Lenneberg, 1967; Newport, 1990). These important theoretical issues in neural and behavioral development can be explored for the first time in a pediatric population by investigating the speech perception and language skills of hearing-impaired infants who are deprived of auditory input during the early part of the sensitive period and then receive a cochlear implant to provide them access to sound.

The work discussed so far in this chapter provides only a small sample of an enormous amount of evidence that infants are born with impressive speech perception capacities and learn a great deal about the organization of speech sounds during the first year of life (Jusczyk, 1997). Presumably, these early speech perception skills lay the foundation for children's ability to learn words and acquire knowledge about syntactic structures as well as the ability to perceive affective information in speech. However, very little is known about the effects that a delay in developing early speech perception skills might have on acquiring spoken language. This issue is especially important for the growing population of young children who are born congenitally deaf and then gain access to speech via cochlear implants.

There are good reasons to suspect that there will be consequences to the perceptual system as a result of auditory deprivation early in life. A body of evidence in neural development already exists showing that a period of auditory deprivation affects auditory development at several different levels: degeneration of spiral ganglion cells in the cochlea (Leake & Hradek, 1988; Rebscher, Snyder, & Leake, 2001), re-organization of the sensory cortices (Neville & Bruer, 2001; Rauschecker & Korte, 1993), and impaired development of neural pathways connecting the auditory cortex to other cortices (Kral et al., 2000; Ponton & Eggermont, 2001). Thus, the language development of deaf infants with cochlear implants may be affected not only by the quality of the auditory information they receive through their cochlear implants but also by the fact that, until receiving a cochlear implant, their neural development has occurred during a period of auditory deprivation.

My colleagues and I have begun investigating the speech perception and language skills of deaf infants after cochlear implantation. In one study, a modified version of the Visual Habituation procedure was used to assess infants' attention to speech and measure their speech discrimination skills after implantation in comparison to normal-hearing controls (Houston, Pisoni et al., 2003). Infants were presented with contrasting speech sounds that differed on gross-level attributes – for example, a continuous ("ahhh") versus discontinuous ("hop hop hop") speech pattern. This kind of gross-level pattern contrast is among the first that hearing-impaired children are tested on for detection and discrimination in clinical measures of speech perception (Moog & Geers, 1990). During a habituation phase, infants were presented with a red-and-white checkerboard pattern in the center of a TV monitor. On half of the trials, the visual display was accompanied by a repeating speech sound ("sound trials"). The other half of the trials consisted of the checkerboard pattern with no sound ("silent trials"). After the infants reached a habituation criterion to both types of trials, they were presented with one "old trial" containing the original speech sound and one "novel trial" using a novel speech sound, both paired with the same checkerboard pattern.

Within a couple of months after implantation, these deaf infants looked significantly longer to the novel trial than to the old trial, suggesting that, like normal-hearing infants, they were able to reliably discriminate the speech sounds. However, in contrast to normal-hearing infants, deaf infants with cochlear implants did not show an overall preference for the sound trials over the silent trials during the habituation period, suggesting that the presence of the sounds did not sustain their attention to the checkerboard pattern the same way it did with normal-hearing infants.

Less attention to speech after implantation may have cascading effects on the acquisition of other speech perception skills. To acquire knowledge about the organization of sounds in the ambient language and to become sensitive to language-specific properties, infants must attend to speech in their environment. It is possible that if infants who use cochlear implants pay less attention to speech than normal-hearing infants, they may be slower in learning language-specific properties of the target language, even if they are able to hear them through their cochlear implants. And, because sensitivity to language-specific properties is important for speech segmentation, infants with cochlear implants might also have compounded difficulty segmenting words from fluent speech, which may, in turn, lead to more difficulty learning words and developing a lexicon. It is important to investigate these speech perception skills in deaf infants who use cochlear implants to see if their acquisition is simply delayed by the onset of access to sound or is also atypical because of factors such as attention to speech. Moreover, this program of clinical research can provide valuable new insights into the role of attention in the development of speech perception skills.

Attention to speech may also affect infants' ability to associate speech sounds to objects – an important skill for novel word learning. In a recent study, we investigated association of speech sounds to visual events in deaf infants at several intervals after cochlear implantation (Houston, Ying et al., 2003). Using the Preferential Looking Paradigm the speech sounds used in Houston, Pisoni, et al. (2003) were paired with visual events that shared intersensory redundancy with the speech sounds and presented to infants on a TV monitor during a *training phase*. For example, "hop hop hop" was paired with a toy kangaroo hopping and "ahhh" was paired with a toy airplane moving across a table. Recent

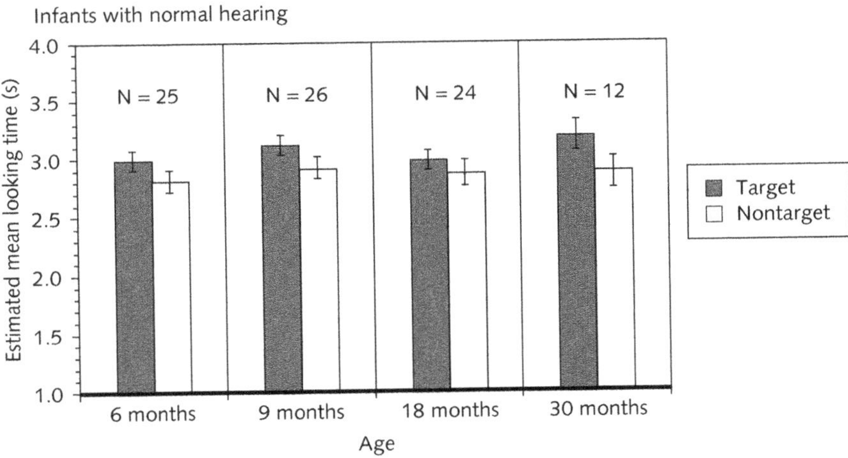

Figure 17.3 Estimated mean looking times (and standard error) for the infants with normal hearing.
Source: D. M. Houston, E. Ying, D. B. Pisoni, & K. I. Kirk (2003). Development of pre word-learning skills in infants with cochlear implants. *The Volta Review*, 103 (monograph) (4), 303–26.

studies of typical developing infants with normal hearing have shown that intersensory redundancies, such as temporal synchrony, can facilitate the ability to learn arbitrary pairings between speech sounds and objects (Gogate & Bahrick, 1998). These pairings were used so that early development of infants' ability to associate speech sounds to visual objects after cochlear implantation could be detected. Normal-hearing infants from 6 to 30 months of age were also tested for comparison.

During the *test phase*, infants were presented with both visual events and with one of the two speech sounds, alternating across trials in a semi-random order. Videotape recordings of the infants' looking patterns were analyzed to determine their looking times to the visual event that the speech sound was originally paired with ("target") and their looking times to the other visual event ("nontarget"). The normal-hearing infants' mean looking times to the target and nontarget are presented in Figure 17.3. The mean looking times of the deaf infants at each post-cochlear implantation interval are displayed in Figure 17.4 – on the left for infants implanted before 15 months of age (earlier implanted deaf infants) and on the right for infants implanted between 16 and 25 months of age (later implanted deaf infants). Normal-hearing infants and earlier implanted infants looked longer to the target visual events than to the nontarget visual events, suggesting that they were able to learn the sound-object pairings (Houston, Ying, et al., 2003). In contrast, later implanted infants failed to show this pattern, even after one year of experience with their cochlear implants. These findings suggest that early implantation may facilitate the use of intersensory perception in learning arbitrary associations between speech sounds and objects.

These two studies of deaf infants demonstrate how procedures commonly used in developmental science may be useful for investigating speech perception and

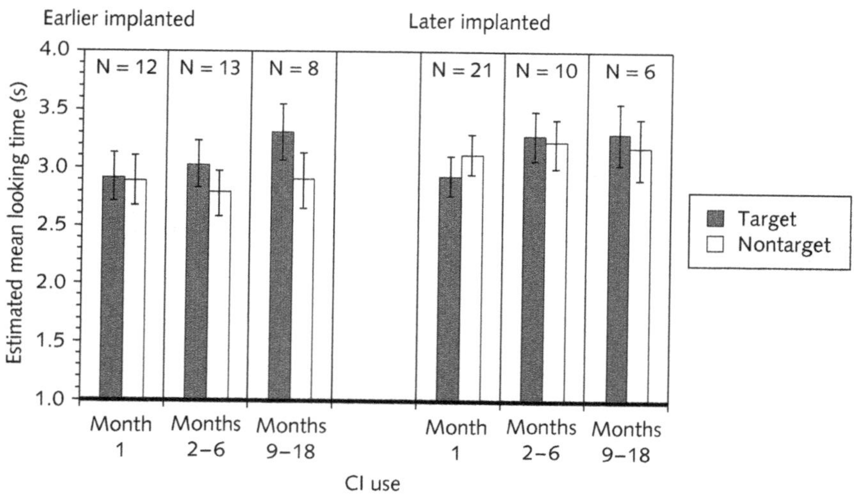

Figure 17.4 Estimated mean looking times (and standard error) for infants who use cochlear implants. Bars on the left represent infants with very early implantation. Bars on the right represent infants with later implantation.
Source: D. M. Houston, E. Ying, D. B. Pisoni, & K. I. Kirk (2003). Development of pre word-learning skills in infants with cochlear implants. *The Volta Review*, 103 (monograph) (4), 303–26.

language in a population of infants that are following an atypical path of auditory and speech perception development. Deaf infants with cochlear implants are a unique clinical population who have initially experienced periods of complete or nearly complete auditory deprivation and then receive access to sound after cochlear implantation. Research on these infants and other populations of hearing-impaired infants (e.g., those who use conventional amplification) can inform us about the importance of early sensory experience in developing speech perception skills and spoken language.

17.5 Conclusions

Research on infant speech perception provides new knowledge about how basic speech perception processes support word learning. Also, this work provides a roadmap and a range of techniques for evaluating the progress of atypical populations. In turn, atypical populations can provide important information about language development in general. One way to assess the role particular auditory or perceptual abilities have in language acquisition is to study how language develops when the acquisition of these abilities is delayed or follows an atypical path. For example, how does a period of early auditory deprivation affect intersensory perception? And how might atypical development of intersensory perception then affect word learning? Continued research with normal and clinical populations will inform us about how speech perception leads to word learning and language development and provide more informed techniques for facilitating the word learning and language development of atypical populations.

ACKNOWLEDGMENTS

Preparation of this chapter was facilitated by a Research Grant from NIDCD (DC006235) and support from the Philip F. Holton Fund. I would like to thank David Pisoni, Robert Remez, Thierry Nazzi, George Hollich, Tonya Bergeson, and David Horn for helpful comments on previous versions of this chapter; Joshua Goergen for assistance in estimating the number of syllables in English; and Carrie Hansel for assistance in preparing figures.

NOTES

1 These findings led Jusczyk, Houston, and Newsome (1999) to characterize English-learning infants as following a Metrical Segmentation Strategy (MSS). Cutler and colleagues had proposed that English-speaking adults rely on the MSS as a first-pass strategy in segmenting words from fluent speech (Cutler, 1990; Cutler & Butterfield, 1992; Cutler et al., 1994; Cutler & Norris, 1988). The MSS derives from the discovery that the vast majority of words in English begin with a strong syllable (Cutler & Carter, 1987) and from evidence that adult English listeners are apt to treat strong syllables as word onsets (Cutler & Butterfield, 1991; Cutler & Norris, 1988; McQueen, Norris, & Cutler, 1994).

2 The perceptual similarity of the talkers was defined as their distance from each other on a multidimensional scaling solution derived from similarity judgments from adult listeners (see Houston, 2003).

REFERENCES

Abramson, A. S. & Lisker, L. (1967). Discriminability along the voice continuum: Cross language tests. Paper presented at the Proceedings of the Sixth International Congress of Phonetic Sciences, Prague.

Ashby, F. G. & Perrin, N. A. (1988). Toward a unified theory of similarity and recognition. *Psychological Review*, 95(1), 124–50.

Aslin, R. N. & Pisoni, D. B. (1980). Some developmental processes in speech perception. In G. H. Yeni-Komshian, J. F. Kavanagh, & C. A. Ferguson (eds.), *Child Phonology* (vol. 2, pp. 67–96). New York: Academic Press.

Aslin, R. N., Saffran, J. R., & Newport, E. L. (1998). Computation of conditional probability statistics by 8-month-old infants. *Psychological Science*, 9, 321–4.

Aslin, R. N., Werker, J. F., & Morgan, J. L. (2002). Innate phonetic boundaries revisited (L). *Journal of the Acoustical Society of America*, 112(4), 1257–60.

Bailey, T. M. & Plunkett, K. (2002). Phonological specificity in early words. *Cognitive Development*, 17, 1265–1282.

Bertoncini, J., Bijeljac-Babic, R., Blumstein, S. E., & Mehler, J. (1987). Discrimination in neonates of very short CV's. *Journal of the Acoustical Society of America*, 82(1), 31–7.

Best, C. T. (1991). Phonetic influences on the peception of non-native speech contrasts by 6–8 and 10–12 month olds. Paper presented at the Biennial meeting of the Society for Research in Child Development, Seattle, WA.

Best, C. T. (1994). Learning to perceive the sound patterns of English. In C. Rovee-Collier & L. P. Lipsitt (eds.), *Advances in Infancy Research* (vol. 9, pp. 217–304). Norwood, NJ: Ablex.

Best, C. T., McRoberts, G. W., & Goodell, E. (2001). Discrimination of non-native consonant contrasts varying in perceptual assimilation to the listener's native phonological system. *Journal of the Acoustical Society of America*, 109(2), 775–94.

Best, C. T., McRoberts, G. W., Lafleur, R., & Silver-Isenstadt, J. (1995). Divergent developmental patterns for infants' perception of two nonnative consonant contrasts. *Infant Behavior and Development*, 18, 339–50.

Best, C. T., McRoberts, G. W., & Sithole, N. M. (1988). Examination of the perceptual re-organization for speech contrasts: Zulu click discrimination by English-speaking adults and infants. *Journal of Experimental Psychology: Human Perception and Performance*, 14, 345–60.

Bradlow, A. R., Nygaard, L. C., & Pisoni, D. B. (1999). Effects of talker, rate, and amplitude variation on recognition memory for spoken words. *Perception & Psychophysics*, 61, 206–19.

Brent, M. R. & Siskind, J. M. (2001). The role of exposure to isolated words in early vocabulary development. *Cognition*, 81, B33–B44.

Carey, S. (1982). Semantic development: The state of the art. In E. Wanner & L. R. Gleitman (eds.), *Language Acquisition: The State of the Art* (pp. 347–89). Cambridge: Cambridge University Press.

Charles-Luce, J. & Luce, P. A. (1990). Similarity neighborhoods of words in young children's lexicons. *Journal of Child Language*, 17, 205–15.

Charles-Luce, J. & Luce, P. (1995). An examination of similarity neighborhoods in young children's receptive vocabularies. *Journal of Child Language*, 22, 727–35.

Church, B. A. & Schacter, D. L. (1994). Perceptual specificity of auditory priming: Implicit memory for voice intonation and fundamental frequency. *Journal of Experimental Psychology: Learning, Memory, and Cognition*, 20, 521–33.

Coady, J. A. & Aslin, R. N. (2003). Phonological neighbourhoods in the developing lexicon. *Journal of Child Language*, 30, 441–69.

Craik, F. I. M. & Kirsner, K. (1974). The effect of speaker's voice on word recognition. *Quarterly Journal of Experimental Psychology*, 26, 274–84.

Cutler, A. (1990). Exploiting prosodic probabilities in speech segmentation. In T. M. A. Gerry (ed.), *Cognitive Models of Speech Processing: Psycholinguistic and Computational Perspectives* (pp. 105–21). ACL-MIT Press series in natural language processing. Cambridge, MA: MIT Press.

Cutler, A. & Butterfield, S. (1991). Word boundary cues in clear speech: A supplementary report. *Speech Communication*, 10(4), 335–53.

Cutler, A. & Butterfield, S. (1992). Rhythmic cues to speech segmentation: Evidence from juncture misperception. *Journal of Memory and Language*, 31, 218–36.

Cutler, A. & Carter, D. M. (1987). The predominance of strong initial syllables in the English vocabulary. *Computer Speech and Language*, 2, 133–42.

Cutler, A., McQueen, J., Baayen, H., & Drexler, H. (1994). Words within words in a real-speech corpus. Paper presented at the Fifth Australian International Conference on Speech Science and Technology, Perth.

Cutler, A. & Norris, D. (1988). The role of strong syllables in segmentation for lexical access. *Journal of Experimental Psychology: Human Perception and Performance*, 14(1), 113–21.

Dehaene-Lambertz, G. & Dehaene, S. (1994). Speed and cerebral correlates of syllable discrimination in infants. *Nature*, 370, 292–5.

Dehaene-Lambertz, G. & Houston, D. (1998). Faster orientation latencies toward native language in two-month-old infants. *Language and Speech*, 41, 21–43.

Dollaghan, C. A. (1994). Children's phonological neighborhoods: Half empty or half full? *Journal of Child Language*, 21, 257–73.

Echols, C. H., Crowhurst, M. J., & Childers, J. (1997). Perception of rhythmic units in speech by infants and adults. *Journal of Memory and Language*, 36, 202–25.

Eimas, P. D. (1974). Auditory and linguistic processing of cues for place of articulation by infants. *Perception & Psychophysics*, 16, 513–21.

Eimas, P. D. (1975a). Auditory and phonetic coding of the cues for speech: Discrimination of the [r-l] distinction by young infants. *Perception & Psychophysics*, 18, 341–7.

Eimas, P. D. (1975b). Speech perception in early infancy. In L. B. Cohen & P. Salapatek (eds.), *Infant Perception: From Sensation to Cognition* (vol. 2, pp. 193–231). New York: Academic Press.

Eimas, P. D. & Miller, J. L. (1980a). Contextual effects in infant speech perception. *Science*, 209, 1140–1.

Eimas, P. D. & Miller, J. L. (1980b). Discrimination of the information for manner of articulation. *Infant Behavior and Development*, 3, 367–75.

Eimas, P. D., Miller, J. L., & Jusczyk, P. W. (1987). On infant speech perception and the acquisition of language. In S. Harnad (ed.), *Categorical Perception* (pp. 161–95). New York: Cambridge University Press.

Eimas, P. D., Siqueland, E. R., Jusczyk, P., & Vigorito, J. (1971). Speech perception in infants. *Science*, 171(968), 303–6.

Fenson, L., Dale, P., Reznick, S., Bates, E., Thal, D., & Pethick, S. (1994). Variability in early communicative development. *Monographs of the Society for Research in Child Development*, 59 (serial number 242).

Fowler, C. A. (1986). An event approach to the study of speech perception from a direct-realist perspective. *Journal of Phonetics*, 14, 3–28.

Friederici, A. D. & Wessels, J. M. I. (1993). Phonotactic knowledge and its use in infant speech perception. *Perception & Psychophysics*, 54, 287–95.

Fry, D. B., Abramson, A. S., Eimas, P. D., & Liberman, A. M. (1962). The identification and discrimination of synthetic vowels. *Language and Speech*, 5, 171–89.

Gogate, L. J. & Bahrick, L. E. (1998). Intersensory redundancy facilitates learning of arbitrary relations between vowel sounds and objects in seven-month-old infants. *Journal of Experimental Child Psychology*, 69, 133–49.

Goldinger, S. D. (1996). Words and voices: Episodic traces in spoken word identification and recognition memory. *Journal of Experimental Psychology: Learning, Memory, and Cognition*, 22, 1166–83.

Goldinger, S. D. (1998). Echoes of echoes? An episodic theory of lexical access. *Psychological Review*, 105(2), 251–79.

Goldinger, S. D., Pisoni, D. B., & Logan, J. S. (1991). On the nature of talker variability effects on recall of spoken word lists. *Journal of Experimental Psychology: Learning, Memory, and Cognition*, 17(1), 152–62.

Goodsitt, J. V., Morgan, J. L., & Kuhl, P. K. (1993). Perceptual strategies in prelingual speech segmentation. *Journal of Child Language*, 20, 229–52.

Grieser, D. & Kuhl, P. K. (1989). The categorization of speech by infants: Support for speech-sound prototypes. *Developmental Psychology*, 25, 577–88.

Hallé, P. A. & Boysson-Bardies, B. de. (1996). The format of representation of recognized words in infants' early receptive lexicon. *Infant Behavior and Development*, 19, 463–81.

Hillenbrand, J. M., Minifie, F. D., & Edwards, T. J. (1979). Tempo of spectrum change as a cue in speech sound discrimination by infants. *Journal of Speech & Hearing Research*, 22, 147–65.

Höhle, B. & Weissenborn, J. (2003). German-learning infants' ability to detect unstressed closed-class elements in continuous speech. *Developmental Science*, 6(2), 122–7.

Hollich, G. (2002). Talker variation and word learning. Paper presented at the Acoustical Society of America, Pittsburgh, PA, June.

Hollich, G., Jusczyk, P. W., & Luce, P. A. (2002). Lexical neighborhood effects in 17-month-old word learning. *Proceedings of the 26th Annual Boston University Conference on Language Development* (pp. 314–23). Boston, MA: Cascadilla Press.

Holmberg, T. L., Morgan, K. A., & Kuhl, P. K. (1977). Speech perception in early infancy: Discrimination of fricative consonants. Paper presented at the Meeting of the Acoustical Society of America, Miami Beach, FL.

Houston, D. M. (1999). The role of talker variability in infant word representations. Doctoral dissertation, The Johns Hopkins University, Baltimore, MD.

Houston, D. M. & Jusczyk, P. W. (2000). The role of talker-specific information in word segmentation by infants. *Journal of Experimental Psychology: Human Perception and Performance*, 26(5), 1570–82.

Houston, D. M. & Jusczyk, P. W. (2003). Infants' long-term memory for the sound patterns of words and voices. *Journal of Experimental Psychology: Human Perception and Performance*, 29, 1143–54.

Houston, D. M., Jusczyk, P. W., Kuijpers, C., Coolen, R., & Cutler, A. (2000). Cross-language word segmentation by 9-month-olds. *Psychonomic Bulletin & Review*, 7, 504–9.

Houston, D. M., Pisoni, D. B., Kirk, K. I., Ying, E., & Miyamoto, R. T. (2003). Speech perception skills of deaf infants following cochlear implantation: A first report. *International Journal of Pediatric Otorhinolaryngology*, 67, 479–95.

Houston, D. M., Santelmann, L., & Jusczyk, P. W. (2004). English-learning infants' segmentation of trisyllabic words from fluent speech. *Language and Cognitive Processes*, 19(1), 97–136.

Houston, D. M., Ying, E., Pisoni, D. B., & Kirk, K. I. (2003). Development of pre word-learning skills in infants with cochlear implants. *The Volta Review*, 103 (monograph) (4), 303–26.

Johnson, E. K. (2003). Word segmentation during infancy: The role of subphonemic cues to word boundaries. Unpublished doctoral dissertation, The Johns Hopkins University, Baltimore, MD.

Johnson, K. (1997). Speech perception without speaker normalization: An exemplar model. In K. Johnson & J. W. Mullennix (eds.), *Talker Variability in Speech Processing* (pp. 145–65). San Diego, CA: Academic Press.

Johnson, E. K. & Jusczyk, P. W. (2001). Word segmentation by 8-month-olds: When speech cues count more than statistics. *Journal of Memory and Language*, 44, 548–67.

Jusczyk, P. W. (1986). Toward a model of the development of speech perception. In J. S. Perkell & D. H. Klatt (eds.), *Invariance and Variability in Speech Processes* (pp. 1–35). Hillsdale, NJ: Lawrence Erlbaum.

Jusczyk, P. W. (1993). From general to language specific capacities: The WRAPSA Model of how speech perception develops. *Journal of Phonetics*, 21, 3–28.

Jusczyk, P. W. (1997). *The Discovery of Spoken Language*. Cambridge, MA: MIT Press.

Jusczyk, P. W. & Aslin, R. N. (1995). Infants' detection of the sound patterns of words in fluent speech. *Cognitive Psychology*, 29(1), 1–23.

Jusczyk, P. W., Copan, H., & Thompson, E. (1978). Perception by 2-month-old infants of glide contrasts in multisyllabic utterances. *Perception & Psychophysics*, 24, 515–20.

Jusczyk, P. W., Cutler, A., & Redanz, N. J. (1993). Infants' preference for the predominant stress patterns of English words. *Child Development*, 64, 675–87.

Jusczyk, P. W., Friederici, A. D., Wessels, J., Svenkerud, V. Y., & Jusczyk, A. M. (1993). Infants' sensitivity to the sound patterns of native language words. *Journal of Memory and Language*, 32, 402–20.

Jusczyk, P. W., Hohne, E. A., & Bauman, A. (1999). Infants' sensitivity to allophonic cues for word segmentation. *Perception & Psychophysics*, 61, 1465–76.

Jusczyk, P. W., Houston, D. M., & Newsome, M. (1999). The beginnings of word segmentation in English-learning infants. *Cognitive Psychology*, 39, 159–207.

Jusczyk, P. W., Luce, P. A., & Charles-Luce, J. (1994). Infants' sensitivity to phonotactic patterns in the native language. *Journal of Memory and Language*, 33, 630–45.

Kelly, M. H. (1992). Using sound to solve syntactic problems: The role of phonology in grammatical category assignments. *Psychological Review*, 99, 349–64.

Kral, A., Hartmann, R., Tillein, J., Held, S., & Klinke, R. (2000). Congenital auditory deprivation reduces synaptic activity within the auditory cortex in a layer-specific manner. *Cerebral Cortex*, 10, 714–26.

Kuhl, P. K. (1983). Perception of auditory equivalence classes for speech in early infancy. *Infant Behavior and Development*, 6, 263–85.

Kuhl, P. K. (1991). Human adults and human infants show a "perceptual magnet effect" for the prototypes of speech categories, monkeys do not. *Perception & Psychophysics*, 50, 93–107.

Kuhl, P. K. (1993). Innate predispositions and the effects of experience in speech perception: The native language magnet theory. In B. D. Boysson-Bardies, S. D. Schonen, P. Jusczyk, P. McNeilage, & J. Morton (eds.), *Developmental Neurocognition: Speech and Face Processing in the First Year of Life* (pp. 259–74). Dordrecht: Kluwer.

Kuhl, P. K., Williams, K. A., Lacerda, F., Stevens, K. N., & Lindblom, B. (1992). Linguistic experiences alter phonetic perception in infants by 6 months of age. *Science*, 255, 606–8.

Lacerda, F. (1993). Sonority contrasts dominate young infants' vowel perception, *PERILUS XVII* (pp. 55–63). Stockholm University.

Lacerda, F. & Sundberg, U. (2001). Auditory and articulatory biases influence the initial stages of the language acquisition process. In F. Lacerda, C. v. Hofsten, & M. Heimann (eds.), *Emerging Cognitive Abilities in Early Infancy* (pp. 91–110). Mahwah, NJ: Lawrence Erlbaum.

Lasky, R. E., Syrdal-Lasky, A., & Klein, R. E. (1975). VOT discrimination by four to six and a half month old infants from Spanish environments. *Journal of Experimental Child Psychology*, 20, 215–25.

Leake, P. A. & Hradek, G. T. (1988). Cochlear pathology of long term neomycin induced deafness in cats. *Hearing Research*, 33, 11–34.

Lenneberg, E. (1967). *Biological Foundations of Language*. New York: John Wiley & Sons.

Levitt, A., Jusczyk, P. W., Murray, J., & Carden, G. (1988). Context effects in two-month-old infants' perception of labiodental/interdental fricative contrasts. *Journal of Experimental Psychology: Human Perception and Performance*, 14(3), 361–8.

Liberman, A. M. & Mattingly, I. G. (1985). The motor theory of speech perception revised. *Cognition*, 21, 1–36.

Liberman, A. M., Harris, K. S., Eimas, P. D., Lisker, L., & Bastian, J. (1961). An effect of learning on speech perception: The discrimination of durations of silence with and without phonetic significance. *Language and Speech*, 54, 175–95.

Lisker, L. & Abramson, A. S. (1964). A cross language study of voicing in initial stops: Acoustical measurements. *Word*, 20, 384–422.

Lisker, L. & Abramson, A. S. (1967). Some effects of context on voice onset time in English stops. *Language and Speech*, 10, 1–28.

MacKain, K. S. (1982). Assessing the role of experience on infants' speech discrimination. *Journal of Child Language*, 9, 527–42.

Maddox, W. T. & Ashby, F. G. (1993). Comparing decision bound and exemplar models of categorization. *Perception & Psychophysics*, 53, 49–70.

Martin, C. S., Mullennix, J. W., Pisoni, D. B., & Summers, W. V. (1989). Effects of talker variability on recall of spoken word lists. *Journal of Experimental Psychology: Learning, Memory, and Cognition*, 15(4), 676–84.

Mattys, S. L. & Jusczyk, P. W. (2001). Phonotactic cues for segmentation of fluent speech by infants. *Cognition*, 78, 91–121.

Mattys, S. L., Jusczyk, P. W., Luce, P. A., & Morgan, J. L. (1999). Phonotactic and prosodic effects on word segmentation in infants. *Cognitive Psychology*, 38, 465–94.

Maye, J., Werker, J. F., & Gerken, L. (2002). Infant sensitivity to distributional information can affect phonetic discrimination. *Cognition*, 82, B101–B111.

McQueen, J. M., Norris, D., & Cutler, A. (1994). Competition in spoken word recognition: Spotting words in other words. *Journal of Experimental Psychology: Learning, Memory, and Cognition*, 20(3), 621–38.

Mehler, J., Jusczyk, P., Lambertz, G., Halsted, N., Bertoncini, J., & Amiel-Tison, C. (1988). A precursor of language acquisition in young infants. *Cognition*, 29(2), 143–78.

Miller, J. L. & Eimas, P. D. (1983). Studies on the categorization of speech by infants. *Cognition*, 13, 135–65.

Moffitt, A. R. (1971). Consonant cue perception by twenty-to-twenty-four-week old infants. *Child Development*, 42, 717–31.

Moog, J. S. & Geers, A. E. (1990). *Early Speech Perception Test for Profoundly Hearing-Impaired Children*. St Louis: Central Institute for the Deaf.

Moore, J. K. (2002). Maturation of human auditory cortex: Implications for speech perception. *Annals of Otology, Rhinology, and Laryngology*, supplement 189, 7–10.

Morgan, J. L. & Saffran, J. R. (1995). Emerging integration of sequential and suprasegmental information in preverbal speech segmentation. *Child Development*, 66(4), 911–36.

Morgan, J. L., Allopenna, P., & Shi, R. (1996). Perceptual bases of rudimentary grammatical categories: Toward a broader conception of bootstrapping. In J. L. Morgan & K. Demuth (eds.), *Signal to Syntax* (pp. 263–83). Hillsdale, NJ: Lawrence Erlbaum.

Morse, P. A. (1972). The discrimination of speech and nonspeech stimuli in early infancy. *Journal of Experimental Child Psychology*, 13, 477–92.

Mullennix, J. W., Pisoni, D. B., & Martin, C. S. (1989). Some effects of talker variability on spoken word recognition. *Journal of the Acoustical Society of America*, 85(1), 365–78.

Nazzi, T., Bertoncini, J., & Mehler, J. (1998). Language discrimination by newborns: toward an understanding of the role of rhythm. *Journal of Experimental Psychology: Human Perception and Performance*, 24(3), 756–66.

Nazzi, T., Dilley, L. C., Jusczyk, A. M., Shattuck-Hufnagel, S., & Jusczyk, P. W. (2003). English-learning infants' segmentation of verbs from fluent speech. Manuscript under review.

Nazzi, T., Jusczyk, P. W., & Johnson, E. K. (2000). Language discrimination by English-learning 5-month-olds: Effects of rhythm and familiarity. *Journal of Memory and Language*, 43, 1–19.

Neville, H. J. & Bruer, J. T. (2001). Language processing: How experience affects brain organization. In J. D. B. Bailey & J. T. Bruer (eds.), *Critical Thinking about Critical Periods* (pp. 151–72). Baltimore: Paul H. Brookes.

Newport, E. (1990). Maturational constraints on language learning. *Cognitive Science*, 14, 11–28.

Nittrouer, S. (2001). Challenging the notion of innate phonetic boundaries. *Journal of the Acoustical Society of America*, 110(3), 1598–605.

Nittrouer, S. (2002). A reply to "Innate phonetic boundaries revisited" [*Journal of the Acoustical Society of America*, 112, 1257–60 (2002)] (L). *Journal of the*

Acoustical Society of America, 112(4), 1261–4.

Nosofsky, R. M. (1988). Similarity, frequency, and category representations. *Journal of Experimental Psychology: Learning, Memory, and Cognition*, 14(1), 54–65.

Nygaard, L. C., Sommers, M. S., & Pisoni, D. B. (1994). Speech perception as a talker-contingent process. *Psychological Science*, 5(1), 42–6.

Palmeri, T. J., Goldinger, S. D., & Pisoni, D. B. (1993). Episodic encoding of voice attributes and recognition memory for spoken words. *Journal of Experimental Psychology: Learning, Memory, and Cognition*, 19, 309–28.

Perruchet, P. & Vinter, A. (1998). PARSER: A model for word segmentation. *Journal of Memory and Language*, 39, 246–63.

Pisoni, D. B. (1973). Auditory and phonetic memory codes in the discrimination of consonants and vowels. *Perception & Psychophysics*, 13, 253–60.

Polka, L. & Bohn, O. S. (1996). A cross-language comparison of vowel perception in English-learning and German learning infants. *Journal of the Acoustical Society of America*, 100(1), 577–92.

Polka, L. & Werker, J. F. (1994). Developmental changes in perception of non-native vowel contrasts. *Journal of Experimental Psychology: Human Perception and Performance*, 20, 421–35.

Polka, L., Colantonio, C., & Sundara, M. (2001). A cross-language comparison of /d/–/ð/ perception: Evidence for a new developmental pattern. *Journal of the Acoustical Society of America*, 109(5), 2190–201.

Ponton, C. W. & Eggermont, J. J. (2001). Of kittens and kids: Altered cortical maturation following profound deafness and cochlear implant use. *Audiology & Neuro-Otology*, 6, 363–80.

Rauschecker, J. P. & Korte, M. (1993). Auditory compensation for early blindness in cat cerebral cortex. *Journal of Neuroscience*, 13, 4538–48.

Rebscher, S. J., Snyder, R. L., & Leake, P. A. (2001). The effect of electrode configuration and duration of deafness on threshold and selectivity of responses to intracochlear electrical stimulation. *Journal of the Acoustical Society of America*, 109(5), 2035–48.

Remez, R. E., Fellowes, J. M., & Rubin, P. E. (1997). Talker identification based on phonetic information. *Journal of Experimental Psychology: Human Perception and Performance*, 23(3), 651–66.

Saffran, J. R., Aslin, R. N., & Newport, E. L. (1996). Statistical learning by 8-month-old infants. *Science*, 274, 1926–8.

Singh, L. (2002). Variability and Constancy in Infants' Formation of Lexical Categories. Doctoral dissertation, Brown University, Providence, RI.

Sommers, M. S., Nygaard, L. C., & Pisoni, D. B. (1994). Stimulus variability and spoken word recognition. I. Effects of variability in speaking rate and overall amplitude. *Journal of the Acoustical Society of America*, 96, 1314–24.

Stager, C. L. & Werker, J. F. (1997). Infants listen for more phonetic detail in speech perception than in word-learning tasks. *Nature*, 388, 381–2.

Stevens, K. N., Liberman, A. M., Studdert-Kennedy, M. G., & Ohman, S. E. G. (1969). Cross-language study of vowel perception. *Language and Speech*, 12, 1–23.

Sussman, H. M. (1984). A neuronal model for syllable representation. *Brain and Language*, 22, 167–77.

Sussman, H. M. (1986). A neuronal model of vowel normalization and representation. *Brain and Language*, 28, 12–23.

Svirsky, M. A., Robbins, A. M., Kirk, K. I., Pisoni, D. B., & Miyamoto, R. T. (2000). Language development in profoundly deaf children with cochlear implants. *Psychological Science*, 11, 153–8.

Swingley, D. (2003). Phonetic detail in the developing lexicon. *Language and Speech*, 46, 265–94.

Swingley, D. & Aslin, R. N. (2000). Spoken word recognition and lexical representation in very young children. *Cognition*, 76, 147–66.

Swingley, D. & Aslin, R. N. (2002). Lexical neighborhoods and the word-form representations of 14-month-olds. *Psychological Science*, 13(5), 480–4.

Swoboda, P., Morse, P. A., & Leavitt, L. A. (1976). Continuous vowel discrimination in normal and at-risk infants. *Child Development*, 47, 459–65.

Thiessen, E. D. & Saffran, J. R. (2003). When cues collide: Use of stress and statistical cues to word boundaries by 7- and 9-month-old infants. *Developmental Psychology*, 39, 706–16.

Tincoff, R. & Jusczyk, P. W. (1996). Are word-final sounds perceptually salient for infants? Paper presented at the Fifth Conference on Laboratory Phonology, Evanston, IL, July.

Trehub, S. E. (1973). Infants' sensitivity to vowel and tonal contrasts. *Developmental Psychology*, 9, 91–6.

Trehub, S. E. (1976). The discrimination of foreign speech contrasts by infants and adults. *Child Development*, 47, 466–72.

Tsushima, T., Takizawa, O., Sasaki, M., Siraki, S., Nishi, K., Kohno, M., Menyuk, P., & Best, C. (1994). Discrimination of English /r-l/ and /w-y/ by Japanese infants at 6–12 months: Language specific developmental changes in speech perception abilities. Paper presented at the International Conference on Spoken Language Processing, Yokohama, Japan; October.

van de Weijer, J. (1998). *Language Input for Word Discovery* (vol. 9). Nijmegen, The Netherlands: Max Planck Institute Series in Psycholinguistics.

Walley, A. C. (1993). The role of vocabulary development in children's spoken word recognition and segmentation ability. *Developmental Review*, 13, 286–350.

Walley, A. C., Smith, L. B., & Jusczyk, P. W. (1986). The role of phonemes and syllables in the perceived similarity of speech sounds for children. *Memory & Cognition*, 14(3), 220–9.

Werker, J. F. & Lalonde, C. E. (1988). Cross-language speech perception: Initial capabilities and developmental change. *Developmental Psychology*, 24, 672–83.

Werker, J. F. & Pegg, J. E. (1992). Infant speech perception and phonological acquisition. In C. A. Ferguson, L. Menn, & C. Stoel-Gammon (eds.), *Phonological Development: Models, Research, Implications* (pp. 285–311). Timonium, MD: York Press.

Werker, J. F. & Tees, R. C. (1984). Cross-language speech perception: Evidence for perceptual reorganization during the first year of life. *Infant Behavior and Development*, 7, 49–63.

Werker, J. F., Cohen, L. B., Lloyd, V. L., Casasola, M., & Stager, C. L. (1998). Acquisition of word-object associations by 14-month-old infants. *Developmental Psychology*, 34, 1289–1309.

Werker, J. F., Fennell, C. T., Corcoran, K. M., & Stager, C. L. (2002). Infants' ability to learn phonetically similar words: Effects of age and vocabulary size. *Infancy*, 3, 1–30.

Woodward, J. Z. & Aslin, R. N. (1990). Segmentation cues in maternal speech to infants. Paper presented at the 7th biennial meeting of the International Conference on Infant Studies, Montreal, Quebec, Canada; April.

18 Speech Perception in Childhood

AMANDA C. WALLEY

18.1 The Gap

There is a rather glaring gap in our knowledge about the development of speech perception. Whereas a great deal has been learned in the last 30 years regarding infant perception (since the seminal study of Eimas et al., 1971, in which young infants' categorical discrimination for an English phonemic contrast was demonstrated), much less is known about perception in the 16 years or so that intervene between infancy and adulthood. Developmental researchers' engrossment with infancy can be attributed to theoretical, methodological, and empirical factors, including the opportunity afforded to determine those abilities given by nature, the implementation of increasingly sophisticated testing procedures, and the positive findings that have obtained (Bornstein, 1992). To this we may add the recent rise of developmental neuroscience and claims about the special, even overriding importance of development within the first three years of life (cf. Bruer, 1999; Kuhl, 2000).

What we have learned about infant speech perception is indeed impressive (for reviews, see Aslin, Jusczyk, & Pisoni, 1998; Jusczyk, 1997). One fairly well-established finding is that early development entails a shift from a language-general to a language-specific pattern of perception (cf. Nittrouer, 2001; Polka, Colantonio, & Sundara, 2001). That is, infants are sensitive at the outset to a wide variety of phonological structures and so are prepared to learn any language to which they might be habitually exposed, but then sometime over the first year of life, sensitivity to many non-native sounds declines. For example, Werker and Tees (1984) showed that 6- to 8-month-olds from English-speaking homes were able to discriminate Hindi consonantal contrasts, as well as those in a Native Canadian language (Nthlakapmx), but that by 9–10 months, this sensitivity had begun to wane – and that by 11–12 months, these same infants no longer attended to these distinctions. (In contrast, older infants from these other language backgrounds could still discriminate these contrasts.) This sort of developmental loss or pruning was attributed to the advent of contrastive phonology around 9–12 months of age, when the infant begins to focus attention on those sounds in the native language that are crucial for distinguishing differences in word meaning (see also Jusczyk, 1993; Stager & Werker, 2000).

However, Kuhl et al. (1992) subsequently found that infants exhibit a "perceptual magnet" effect by 6 months of age (for a full description and critical review, see Walley & Sloane, 2001). Specifically, American infants equate (or fail to discriminate) an English vowel prototype /i/ and its variants, whereas they display better discrimination for a Swedish vowel prototype /y/ and its variants; conversely, Swedish infants equate the Swedish stimuli, but not the English ones. Thus, native language influences for vowels are evident well before 9–12 months, or the point at which it is generally thought that speech sounds first become interfaced with meaning, and infants thus gain entry to the native language proper. Kuhl and colleagues therefore maintained that the infant's initial attunement to the segmental properties of the native language occurs independently of early word learning and is the result of simple exposure to the distributional properties of sounds. Both of these theoretical stances have been challenged (to varying extents) by recent evidence about when, more precisely, infants begin to link sound and meaning (see Section 18.2.2).

Unfortunately, the overall impression that is left by much of this research is that little, if anything, of import happens in terms of perceptual development beyond 1 or 2 years of age. Yet one major theoretical reason to expect changes has been alluded to already – namely, during early and middle childhood, there is substantial vocabulary growth (e.g., increases in the size of the lexicon or the number of words that are known) (Anglin, 1993). Such growth in the child's lexical or knowledge base should necessitate changes (perhaps of a qualitative nature) in the way that speech patterns are represented and/or processed. A second reason to expect perceptual advance in childhood is that there is continued exposure to the native language, which might have more subtle (perhaps quantitative), but nevertheless important influences. This expectation is consistent with second-language learning research which has indicated that the phonological system is quite open or flexible up until about 7 years of age (see Walley & Flege, 1999). Third, the reading task with which young children in literate cultures are confronted (especially those who must master an alphabetic writing system) might be expected to have a significant impact on phonological representations and/or processing (see Goswami, 2000).

Little attention has, however, been directed toward speech perception in typically-developing children, so that this would seem to constitute the weakest link in our understanding of the growth of speech perception. In the following sections, I will selectively review what *is* known about speech perception in childhood. I will briefly outline a model of the development of spoken word recognition (the Lexical Restructuring Model; see Metsala & Walley, 1998) and then highlight the extent to which it is supported by existing data. This model focuses on the impact of spoken vocabulary growth in early and middle childhood, and also provides a framework for understanding changing interactions between phonetic and lexical levels of processing, as well as phonological awareness and early reading success. Finally, I will note some places where the model appears to fall short and identify other important gaps in what we know about speech perception in childhood.

18.2 Filling the Gap: The Lexical Restructuring Model

Largely because of the influence of infant perception studies (from Eimas et al., 1971, through Kuhl et al., 1992), there has been a substantial, ingrained theoretical bias among developmental researchers that phonetic/phonemic segments are present and functional as units of perception from early infancy. For example, according to Native Language Magnet theory (Kuhl, 1993, p. 133), "[in part because] infants exhibit a language-specific magnet effect at the level of phonetic segments," their speech representations must be "sufficiently fine-grained to allow segments to be individuated." Yet this claim about segmental perception has not been directly evaluated in most studies, including demonstrations of the perceptual magnet effect. That is, studies of the effect have typically involved the presentation of isolated vowel stimuli, and so it is unclear whether infants represent/process these stimuli as segments per se or as whole syllables.

Over the last decade, there has, in fact, been a growing consensus that infants' speech representations are not, at the outset, organized around individual phonetic/phonemic segments. Instead, these representations are initially holistic (i.e., based on larger units, such as the syllable) and only gradually, in early through middle childhood, do they become more fully specified and/or undergo segmental restructuring (for review, see Metsala & Walley, 1998; Walley, 1993b). Our Lexical Restructuring Model (LRM; Metsala & Walley, 1998) emphasizes the role of vocabulary growth in prompting such changes for the representation and/or processing of spoken words. In the model, vocabulary growth includes increases in the overall size of the mental lexicon (or the number of words that are known), as well as changes in the familiarity and phonological similarity relations of individual lexical items. Specific expectations about the impact of these factors on spoken word recognition and relevant empirical evidence will be considered below.

In addition, LRM seeks to explicate the relations between children's spoken word recognition, phonological awareness, and beginning reading ability. According to the model, phonemic segments develop gradually as implicit perceptual units for basic speech perception and spoken word recognition, and only later as explicit cognitive units that can be harnessed for the reading task (see also Fowler, 1991; Stanovich, 1988). By this emergent view, phonological awareness, especially the ability to access and manipulate phonemes, is not simply a problem of recovering existing units of speech representation, as the traditional accessibility position has maintained (e.g., Liberman, Shankweiler, & Liberman, 1989; Rozin & Gleitman, 1977); rather, such awareness, which is crucial for learning letter-sound rules, is initially limited by the very nature or developmental status of underlying speech representations (for more complete references, see Garlock, Walley, & Metsala, 2001; Metsala & Walley, 1998). Some of the more relevant data bearing on the emergent position will be discussed below.

18.2.1 *The development of phonetic perception*

Infants' discrimination of various phonetic/phonemic contrasts does not necessarily involve the detection of localized, segmental differences; rather, discrimination might be mediated by more holistic processes. One of the best demonstrations to this effect can be found in the work of Jusczyk and colleagues (see Jusczyk, 1993), who showed that when 2-month-old infants are familiarized with a stimulus set, such as /bi ba bo/, they are equally likely to dishabituate to /du/ and /bu/ – i.e., they treat /bu/ as novel, even though it shares a consonantal segment with the habituation stimuli. In contrast, young infants do seem to extract or retain some memory for a shared syllable. Sometime between 6 and 9 months of age, infants are, as we have seen, becoming attuned to the consonants and vowels of their native language. Around 9 months, they also begin to display sensitivity to subsyllabic information, such as shared initial consonants and consonant-vowel combinations (Jusczyk, Goodman, & Baumann, 1999), and to the phonotactic patterns, or sequential arrangement of phonetic segments, of their native language (Jusczyk, Luce, & Charles-Luce, 1994). However, the fact that such early sensitivity is evident under optimal testing conditions (e.g., given repeated presentations of stimuli in the clear) does not necessarily mean that the abilities revealed by these tests are robust ones or that development is complete.

In fact, a number of studies point to extant developmental differences in the perception of both vowels and consonants. For example, 3-year-olds' perception of synthetic vowels (/æ/ and /ʌ/) is more dependent on dynamic spectral change information than adults' (Murphy, Shea, & Aslin, 1989) and 5- to 11-year-olds' perception of /i/, /a/ and /u/ is more influenced by stimulus duration, as well as consonantal context (Ohde, Haley, & McMahon, 1996). The highly context-dependent nature of children's perception is better documented for consonants (see Walley & Flege, 1999). In a study by Nittrouer and Studdert-Kennedy (1987), 3- to 5-year-olds' identifications of syllable initial fricatives from a synthetic /s-ʃ/ continuum were more influenced by vocalic transitions than 7-year-olds' and adults'; these older subjects were more sensitive to the frequency information in the fricative noise. Similarly, Krause (1982) found that 3-year-olds needed a larger difference than adults in preceding vowel length to identify stimuli ending in voiced and voiceless stops, and other researchers have observed that young children pay particular attention to formant transitions in judging place of stop consonant articulation (e.g., Ohde et al., 1995; Walley & Carrell, 1983).

A corollary finding in these and other past studies is that consonant perception by children up to about 5 or 6 years of age appears less categorical than perception by adults; specifically, the slopes of children's identification functions for various stimulus continua are shallower than adults' (e.g., Burnham, Earnshaw, & Clark, 1991; for additional references, see Hazan & Barrett, 2000; Walley & Flege, 1999). More recent investigations have indicated that there are further increases in the consistency of vowel and consonant categorization, including a steepening of the slopes of identification functions, into late childhood and even early adolescence, as well as gains in the ability to make use of impoverished acoustic-phonetic information (e.g., Hazan & Barrett, 2000; Johnson, 2000). Still other studies have shown that young children (about 5 years of age) classify speech patterns on the basis of overall similarity relations, whereas older listeners use phoneme identity (e.g., Treiman & Breaux, 1982; Walley, Smith, & Jusczyk, 1986; see also Section 18.2.3).

Together, these studies suggest that children's representations for speech patterns are not yet adult-like; i.e., their representations are not as fine-grained or segmental, but are instead more holistic in nature and based to a greater extent on information distributed throughout the speech waveform. According to the Developmental Weighting Shift model (see Nittrouer et al., 2000), young children rely to a greater extent than adults on dynamic cues in making phonetic decisions because they are more focused on the recovery of syllabic structure; only with maturation and additional linguistic experience does their weighting of various acoustic properties come to resemble that of adults more closely and be more flexible. This shift is seen to be precipitated, in part, by lexical growth (see also Fowler, 1991); thus, there seems to be fairly widespread agreement that as the lexicon grows, greater attention to the details of the speech signal are required. Despite the transparent nature of this claim, definitive empirical support is lacking. In particular, there have been few developmental studies of how phonetic perception is influenced by lexical status and/or word familiarity.

One exception is a study by Walley and Flege (1999), in which American English 5-year-olds, 9-year-olds, and adults identified synthetic stimuli on a native vowel continuum ranging from /ɪ/ to /i/ and a foreign continuum ranging from /ɪ/ to a foreign vowel /ʏ/ (presented in a nonword, /C_C/ context). No marked age differences in the location of phoneme boundaries were found – a result that is consistent with the work of Kuhl and others (e.g., Kuhl et al., 1992), suggesting that the vowel space is partitioned quite early in infancy vis-à-vis the native language. However, the slopes of subjects' identification functions became progressively steeper with age, especially for the native continuum. This result is consistent with the notion that young children's perception is not as fine-grained or segmental as that of older listeners. Yet when the stimuli were presented in the context of highly familiar words (i.e., "beep" and "bib"), then young children's slopes were much more similar to those of older listeners. Thus, developmental differences in how sharply defined phonemic category boundaries are may depend, in part, on variations in lexical knowledge. More generally, there are potentially important perceptual-cognitive/linguistic interactions in childhood that remain to be examined.

18.2.2 *Beginning spoken word recognition ability*

To this point we have seen that much of the work on speech perception in infancy and childhood has tended to employ fairly simple stimuli (e.g., V or CV contrasts). There is however one conspicuous trend apparent in current research – namely, a tendency to accord greater attention to infants' perception of more complex and ecologically-relevant stimuli and/or to their perception of speech stimuli in ecologically-relevant contexts (Morgan, 2002; Walley, 2002; Werker, 2002).

Of course, one of the infant's/toddler's primary tasks in acquiring their native language is to establish a lexical knowledge base – i.e., some mental repository for sound-meaning mappings, to which they can then refer during on-line spoken language comprehension. This task is a multifaceted and demanding one that includes segmenting words from continuous speech, noting correspondences between recurring speech patterns and nonlinguistic events, discovering the relevant semantic and syntactic features of words, as well as translating sound sequences into articulatory ones (Menyuk & Menn, 1979).

Substantial empirical evidence has accrued regarding when these component abilities first appear. For example, newborn infants can perceptually distinguish between lexical vs. grammatical words (e.g., "chew" vs. "that's"), but by 6 months of age, this ability is replaced by a preference for the former (see Shi & Werker, 2001); 7.5-month-olds can segment words from fluent speech (Jusczyk & Aslin, 1995); and sometime around 9 to 12 months of age, they can map isolated words onto objects and events in the world (e.g., Thomas et al., 1981).

Let us examine more closely this estimate for when infants first begin to link sound and meaning. A conservative estimate comes from laboratory studies of recognitory comprehension. For example, Thomas et al. (1981) found that 13-month-olds, but not 11-month-olds, looked longer at the referents of words that were known vs. unknown, according to maternal report, in a four alternative forced-choice (4AFC) testing procedure where they were told to "Look at the _____!" (see also Hallé & Boysson-Bardies, 1994; Woodward, Markman, & Fitzsimmons, 1994). Yet, in naturalistic settings with heavy contextual support, infants have first been observed to understand the meanings of individual words and short phrases around 8 to 10 months (e.g., Benedict, 1979; Fenson et al., 1994).

This lower limit of about 9 months for the sound-meaning barrier has effectively been smashed in a recent study by Tincoff and Jusczyk (1999). (This event was not, however, completely unexpected; see Walley, 1993a). In Experiment 1, it was shown that 6-month-olds looked longer at videos of their own parents when told to do so – e.g., they look longer at their father, not their mother, when told "Look at Daddy!" In Experiment 2, another group of infants did not exhibit any difference in looking time for videos of unfamiliar parents. This earliest demonstration to date of infants' ability to pair spoken words with the appropriate referent or to engage in recognitory comprehension is most likely attributable to the use of salient social figures, rather than commonplace objects as in previous studies (see also Mandel, Jusczyk, & Pisoni, 1995), and perhaps to the use of a 2AFC vs. 4AFC looking procedure. Clearly these findings, which mesh with the work of Baillargeon and others on symbolic/representational abilities in early infancy (see Bjorklund, 2000, ch. 7), have important implications for the two theoretical views of native language attunement outlined earlier (see Section 18.1). In particular, these results suggest that such attunement may not occur in a strictly passive manner, independent of word learning, as NLM theory maintains (e.g., Kuhl et al., 1992).

In addition to a concern with revealing ever earlier perceptual and cognitive competencies, there has, at the same time, been more attention paid to word perception by older infants/toddlers – i.e., some of the concerns of infant research have spilled over into later developmental periods, when referential/symbolic abilities are becoming more firmly established. This trend marks a departure from past work in which higher-level cognitive factors, including linguistic knowledge, were essentially regarded as contaminating factors that muddied the perceptual picture. In any event, current work focuses more on how the perceptual abilities of infants are linked to the (changing) functional requirements of the language acquisition task – especially on their implications for the organization of the nascent mental lexicon, and for beginning spoken word recognition ability.

This work, much of it conducted by Jusczyk and colleagues, has shown that older infants are beginning to attend differentially to those speech patterns that conform to the particular prosodic and phonotactic patterns of their native language. For example, 9-month-old English-learning infants, but not 6-month-olds, prefer to listen to lists of English vs. Dutch words, and Dutch infants exhibit a similar native language bias (Jusczyk et al., 1993), and Dutch 9-month-olds prefer to listen to words in their native language with permissible vs. impermissible onset and offset clusters (Friederici & Wessels, 1993). In addition, although young infants' speech representations may be holistic, Jusczyk et al. (1999) showed that those of older, 9-month-olds are becoming more fine-grained. In particular, it was found that infants at this age are sensitive to shared features that occur at the beginnings of syllables (such as initial consonants and initial consonant-vowels), but not to those at the ends of syllables. Such growing sensitivity to the internal structure of syllables may, it was suggested, go hand-in-hand with developing a lexicon for the native language. Further, Jusczyk et al. (1994) found that 9- but not 6-month-olds prefer to listen to high-probability phonotactic patterns (e.g., /rɪs/ vs. /guʃ/). In the adult literature (see Luce & Pisoni, 1998), words with these sort of patterns, which tend to reside in "dense" neighborhoods or overlap with many words on a segmental basis, are typically more difficult to recognize than words from "sparse" neighborhoods; i.e., across a variety of tasks, sparse words are recognized more accurately and quickly than dense words (e.g., "fudge" vs. "mash") because they have fewer competitors.

With respect to development, Jusczyk et al. (1994, p. 641) suggested that "one potential drawback of building up dense neighborhoods in the lexicon first is that a more detailed representation of a particular item is necessary in order to distinguish it from its near neighbors." In support, Stager and Werker (1997) found that when listening for meaning in a word-object pairing task, 14-month-olds actually fail to detect the same phonetic detail that they (and younger infants) can easily detect in a simple syllable discrimination task. After habituating to presentations of pictures of novel objects (A and B) that were paired with similar labels (/bɪ/ and /dɪ/), these infants did not dishabituate when the object labels were switched (e.g., object A was presented with /dɪ/, rather than /bɪ/). In contrast, older infants did dishabituate or notice the switch when dissimilar labels were used (/lɪf/ vs. /nim/). Similarly, Hollich, Jusczyk and Luce (2000, cited in Jusczyk & Luce, 2002) found that 17-month-olds learned a new word from a sparse neighborhood more readily than one from a dense neighborhood (cf. Storkel, 2001). These results can be explained in terms of the greater computational demands of word learning (especially for phonetically similar items) vs. simple sound discrimination. For the more demanding task of linking words with objects, infants/toddlers may use just enough available information to avoid confusing a new word with the few words in their lexicons. Importantly, individual segments may not be needed to distinguish the small number of words that are known to the older infant/toddler – "Daddy" vs. "cat" could, for example, be distinguished on the basis of number of syllables and a variety of other non-segmental cues. Thus, there appears to be an important shift from analytic to holistic perception in early to late infancy (Stager & Werker, 2000; see also Walley, 1993b), which is followed by another shift in early to middle childhood to more analytic perception (see Section 18.2.3).

As Jusczyk and Luce (2002) point out, the view that infants' first lexical representations are underspecified has been challenged by several recent studies. For example, Houston and Jusczyk (2000) have shown that these representations may contain talker-specific information. In addition, Fernald, Swingley, and Pinto (2001) have provided evidence that 18- to 21-month-olds look at the correct visual target when presented with only partial, word-initial phonetic information. However, their conclusion regarding the fairly detailed nature of early word representations may be limited by certain methodological problems, including a lack of appropriate stimulus controls that would rule out the use of co-articulatory information in explaining infants' performance (Luce & Walley, 2005). Further, the bulk of the existing research indicates that spoken word recognition by children is still not adult-like.

18.2.3 *Spoken word recognition in childhood*

During the initial construction of the lexicon, holistic representations may suffice to support word recognition, and we have just seen evidence to this effect. Presumably, however, the nature of speech representation/processing begins to change in early childhood and there is a shift toward more analytic perception at the word level. This change might be precipitated by the "vocabulary growth spurt"; whereas the child's first 50 words are acquired slowly, around 18 months of age there is typically a large and sudden increase in the number of words that can be comprehended and produced, such that the child's vocabulary may double or even triple within the span of a few short months (e.g., Reznick & Goldfield, 1992; for more detail, see Walley, 1993b). This rapid expansion would seem to necessitate the implementation of more fully specified and/or segmental representations – some way of keeping a growing number of words distinct from one another.

In fact, several researchers have proposed that competition among items in a burgeoning lexicon – a concept that is central to many adult models of spoken word recognition (see Luce & Pisoni, 1998) – may serve as a key mechanism for development. For example, according to Nittrouer, Studdert-Kennedy, and McGowan (1989, p. 131), "[as] the number and diversity of the words in a child's lexicon increase, words with similar acoustic and articulatory patterns begin to cluster . . . ultimately [precipitating] the coherent units of sound and gesture that we know as phonetic segments" (see also Fowler, 1991; Garlock et al., 2001; Jusczyk & Luce, 2002; Walley, 1993b).[1] Fowler (1991) further suggested that for young children, as well as potentially poor readers, highly familiar lexical items gradually become more fully specified in phonemic or gestural terms than less familiar items. This shift may occur fairly slowly and extend into middle childhood, because there is still substantial vocabulary expansion after the initial growth spurt, and prior to substantial reading experience (Fowler, 1991; Metsala & Walley, 1998).

Although there is not a great deal of empirical evidence bearing directly on these proposals about the role of vocabulary growth (in terms of overall size, acoustic-phonetic overlap, and/or familiarity) in the development of spoken word recognition, that which does exist suggests that word recognition by children is still holistic in comparison to that by adults (see Walley, 1993b). First, structural analyses conducted by Charles-Luce and Luce (1990, 1995) have indicated that as late as 7 years of age, children's lexicons consist predominantly of phonetically dissimilar items (i.e., word neighborhoods are relatively sparse), the recognition of which could be accomplished by holistic vs. more segmental processes (cf. Dollaghan, 1994). However, age-related changes were also observed. For example, between 5 and 7 years, as the lexicon continues to increase in size, there is a trend toward denser similarity neighborhoods that should require more fine-grained or analytic recognition processes.

Next, we consider some of the perceptual/behavioral evidence on spoken word recognition by children (for review, see Metsala & Walley, 1998; Walley, 1993b). Several studies have shown that young children (about 5 years of age) are less sensitive to the position in a word of mispronunciations and other experimental disruptions than are older listeners (e.g., Cole & Perfetti, 1980; Walley, 1988). Also, although young children do not need to hear an entire word in order to recognize it, they need more acoustic-phonetic input than do adults (e.g., Elliott, Hammer, & Evan, 1987; Walley, Michela, & Wood, 1995). This is the case, even though children have smaller lexicons, and thus must discriminate amongst fewer words. Further, 5- and 8-year-olds are better at detecting mispronounced segments in familiar, early-acquired words than in less familiar, later-acquired words (Walley & Metsala, 1990, 1992), and 7- to 11-year-olds are better at recognizing high-frequency words from sparse, as opposed to dense, neighborhoods in the gating task, where increasing amounts of speech input from word-onset are presented (Metsala, 1997a).

Much of this work is consistent with the proposal that children's lexical representations are still quite holistic, and only gradually become more fully specified or segmental over the course of childhood. However, in many of these earlier studies, word familiarity and phonological similarity on children's recognition of spoken words have not always been systematically investigated. Especially little is known about how these lexical factors influence spoken word recognition by children below first-grade level – before they have had substantial reading experience. Therefore, Garlock et al. (2001) examined the performance of preschoolers and kindergarteners (5.5 years of age), first- and second-graders (7.5 years of age), and adults for items in two spoken word recognition tasks (gating and word repetition) for lexical items that varied orthogonally in terms of age of acquisition, frequency of occurrence, and neighborhood density. Of particular concern was whether young children would show a "competition effect" – i.e., better recognition of words from sparse vs. dense neighborhoods.

The word repetition results obtained by Garlock et al. are perhaps of greatest interest. In this task, listeners attempted to repeat spoken words that were presented in the clear or in white noise, and thus with some segments, such as fricatives, masked to a greater extent than others. As can be seen in Figure 18.1,

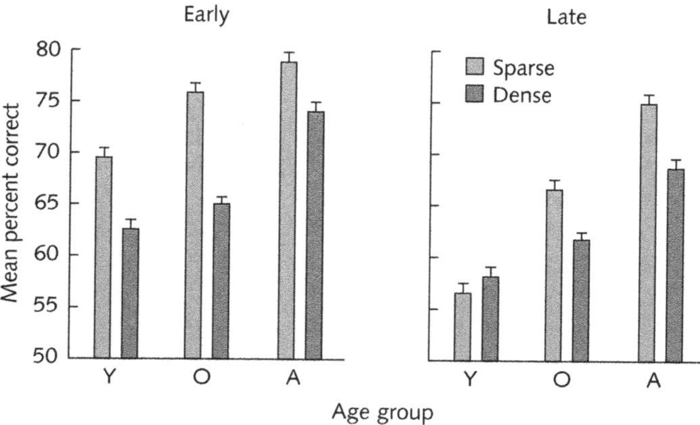

Figure 18.1 Mean percent correct scores in the word repetition task as a function of age of acquisition (AOA) and neighborhood density (ND) for young children (Y), older children (O), and adults (A) in the Garlock et al. (2001) study. (Results are collapsed across the intact and noise conditions, since separate analyses showed a similar pattern.)

competition effects for familiar, early-acquired words were larger for children than adults, but this pattern was reversed for less familiar, later-acquired words. (Notably, word frequency effects were minimal, suggesting that statistical regularities in language input, when defined only in terms of frequency of occurrence, are not all-important.) With increases in age and word familiarity then, competition effects emerge and become more widespread. Thus, by about age 5, children do display a competition effect, but one that is restricted to familiar words (cf. Hollich et al., 2000; Storkel, 2001). This effect was actually larger for children than adults, because performance was best and most similar across age for early-acquired words from sparse neighborhoods, and poorest for words from dense neighborhoods among children.

How do these findings fit with the general claim that vocabulary growth contributes to developmental changes in spoken word representation and processing (e.g., Fowler, 1991; Metsala & Walley, 1998; Nittrouer et al., 1989)? This claim does not translate simply into the expectation that children's recognition should be best for words from dense neighborhoods (although this pattern has been observed in other tasks; see Section 18.2.4). Rather, by this view, age differences should be greatest for words with very dynamic or unstable representations, and smallest for words with more robust representations and few competitors. In general, the findings described above confirm these predictions; i.e., the ability to recognize words from partial input was best and age differences were smallest for highly familiar words from sparse neighborhoods, and it improved the most between childhood and adulthood for other words. Notably however, young children's recognition of familiar, sparse words was still not as good as that of older listeners – even though there are fewer of these items in their lexicons to be distinguished from one another.

Even more recently, Storkel (2002) has provided important evidence bearing on proposals regarding lexical restructuring. In her study, preschoolers (4 years of age) classified familiar CVC test words in terms of their similarity to sparse and dense standards; the crucial test words varied in type of similarity (phonemic, manner or place of articulation) and position of overlap (in the onset + nucleus = CV or in the rime = VC) (see also Gerken, Murphy, & Aslin, 1995). The results indicated that membership in dense neighborhoods is based on phonemic similarity in either position, whereas membership for sparse neighborhoods is based on phoneme similarity in the onset + nucleus, but manner similarity in the rime – an interesting asymmetry that is consistent with the claim that words in dense vs. sparse neighborhoods tend to have more detailed, segmental representations. Further, the beginnings of words, regardless of neighborhood association, are more susceptible to segmental restructuring – a finding that supports models of word recognition which place special emphasis on the continuous, transient nature of the speech waveform, and thus the priority of partial, word-initial input (e.g., Jusczyk, 1993; Marslen-Wilson, 1989).

In interpreting her results, Storkel (2002) favors a weak version of lexical restructuring, according to which the salience of similarity relations or neighborhood membership shifts in development, rather than a strong version involving structural changes per se. While certainly presentations of LRM (e.g., Garlock et al., 2001; Metsala & Walley, 1998) and its very name suggest changes at a fundamental or underlying level, the focus of the model is on developmental changes in representation *and/or* processing (which may be inextricably linked) at the *word* level (see also Stager & Werker, 2000). Thus, I have tried to be somewhat circumspect in my use of these terms for much of the present discussion. Walley (1993b, pp. 291–2) provides a more extensive discussion of this issue and I suspect there is no major disagreement with Storkel.

Storkel favors a weak restructuring account of developmental changes in the lexicon (i.e., changes in attention) because it may be better able to handle variability in children's performance across different tasks, such as the apparent salience of onset in word perception and production, as opposed to the salience of the rime in making some similarity judgments. However, there is another potentially theoretically important task difference that merits attention. As noted previously, word learning and word recognition by children is better for words from sparse vs. dense neighborhoods (Garlock et al., 2001; Hollich et al., 2000; Metsala, 1997a, 1997b; cf. Storkel, 2001). In contrast, children's performance is better (and more segmental) for dense vs. sparse words in the classification or similarity judgment task that Storkel (2002) employed. A similar result has been found in two other studies employing tasks that tap more explicit awareness of the sound structure of speech (De Cara & Goswami, 2003; Metsala, 1999).

Thus, the effect of neighborhood density appears to differ markedly, depending on level of processing and/or the extent to which conscious awareness of sounds is involved in speech processing. That is, increased neighborhood density impedes performance in more basic speech perception tasks, whereas it facilitates performance in tasks that require the ability to manipulate or consciously access phonological structure. The latter sort of tasks have been strongly implicated in early reading success (for review, see Brady & Shankweiler, 1991). In the following section, I will discuss the relation between speech perception, phonological awareness, and beginning reading ability, and offer a possible explanation for the different effects of neighborhood density that have just been described.

18.2.4 Speech perception, phonological awareness, and beginning reading

Several decades of study point to strong links between phonological awareness and beginning reading ability (Brady & Shankweiler, 1991), but only lately has attention turned to identifying the early origins of phonological awareness skills. Many researchers now agree that developmental advances in basic speech representation and processing provide some foundation for these skills, which, in turn, are critical for reading (e.g., De Cara & Goswami, 2003; Elbro, Borstrøm, & Petersen, 1998; Fowler, 1991; Jusczyk, 1993; Stanovich, 1988; for additional references, see Garlock et al., 2001). Even so, the empirical support for such a developmental sequence is meager. Many studies have shown that basic speech processing skills (e.g., categorical perception) vary as a function of reading ability in both children and adults, and that poor readers are slower and/or less accurate at recognizing spoken words and nonwords than good readers (see Manis et al., 1997). Also, poor readers exhibit deficits in phonological awareness tasks, such as initial phoneme isolation (saying the first sound in "cat") and initial phoneme deletion (saying "cat" without the first sound), and these problems persist into adulthood (see Brady & Shankweiler, 1991). However, few studies have attempted to relate all three abilities (i.e., basic speech processing, phonological awareness, and reading ability) – with some notable exceptions.

First, in a study by Swan and Goswami (1997), poor readers, reading age (RA) matched, and chronological age (CA) matched children performed similarly well in syllable and onset-rime awareness tasks for words with representations of adequate quality (as indexed by picture naming accuracy). In contrast, poor readers' phoneme awareness was impaired relative to that of CA controls, who performed more poorly than older, RA controls. Second, McBride-Chang, Wagner, and Chang (1997) found that speech perception (identification of stimuli from a voice-onset-time continuum as either "bath" or "path"), together with verbal short-term memory (STM) and IQ, predicted 26% of the gains made in phoneme awareness by kindergarteners and 42% of their phoneme awareness in grade 1. Kindergarteners with high and low speech perception scores later differed in word reading, but not when phoneme awareness was controlled. Third, Elbro et al. (1998) showed that kindergarteners' pronunciation accuracy, a measure of the completeness of speech representations, predicted phoneme awareness in grade 2 for both normal children and those at risk for reading problems. Finally, Garlock et al. (2001) found that the recognition of familiar, early-acquired words from sparse neighborhoods contributed to phonological awareness among individual first- and second-graders; in turn, phonological awareness, receptive vocabulary, and verbal short-term memory contributed to word reading.

These results support the claim that the relation between speech representation/processing and reading ability is mediated by the development of phonological awareness, but clearly more research delineating the relations among various speech processing abilities and the precise role that each plays in early reading acquisition is needed. For example, Garlock et al.'s (2001) finding that the recognition of early-acquired words from sparse as opposed to dense neighborhoods is predictive of phonological awareness might seem anomalous, or counter to the claim that vocabulary growth prompts such awareness (e.g., Metsala & Walley, 1998). Yet, to the extent that restructuring has occurred for these familiar words – for some children more than others – their recognition predicts phonological awareness. Metsala (1997b) also found that words from sparse vs. dense neighborhoods were better recognized by normally-achieving (NA), but not reading-disabled (RD) children (9 years of age). Although the two group's performance did not differ for words from dense neighborhoods, RD children were especially poor at recognizing words from sparse neighborhoods. She therefore suggested that spoken word recognition by RD children is relatively holistic and best characterized in terms of developmental delays in the segmental restructuring of lexical representations. Further, for a subset of both NA and RD children (7 years of age), the recognition of words from sparse neighborhoods, together with phonological awareness, predicted word and pseudoword reading. Thus, two studies now implicate the recognition of these words in beginning reading and reading-related abilities.

To better understand the developmental effects of phonological similarity, an examination of the results of two other recent studies and some further consideration of task requirements might be helpful. First, Metsala (1999) found that lexical status, age of acquisition, and neighborhood density influenced young children's performance in a variety of phonological awareness tasks. In particular, 3- and 4-year-olds' phoneme blending was better for familiar words from dense as opposed to sparse neighborhoods in a picture-pointing task. Second, De Cara and Goswami (2003) showed that 5- and 6-year-old prereaders were better at making rime judgments for words from dense vs. sparse neighborhoods, indicating that the former are represented with greater segmental specificity than the latter. This effect was, however, restricted to children with larger receptive vocabularies – a finding that provides additional support for the claim that phonological awareness emerges primarily as a result of spoken vocabulary growth (e.g., Fowler, 1991; Metsala & Walley, 1998; Nittrouer et al., 1989).

There is then a noteworthy pattern that is beginning to emerge in the literature. In three studies now (Garlock et al., 2001; Metsala, 1997a, 1997b), children's recognition of familiar (early-acquired or high-frequency) words in the gating and word repetition tasks has proved better for items residing in sparse vs. dense neighborhoods. A similar result has been found for word learning (Hollich et al., 2000; but see Storkel, 2001). In three other studies (De Cara & Goswami, 2003; Metsala, 1999; Storkel, 2002), the opposite pattern has been found for phonological awareness and similarity classification. Thus, inhibitory/competition effects of neighborhood density may be primary during spoken word recognition, which involves discriminating among multiple lexical candidates. In contrast, the facilitatory influence of probabilistic phonotactics (the frequencies and sequences of phonemic segments), which is positively correlated with neighborhood density, may be primary for phonological awareness and classification tasks. In these tasks, attention is typically focused not on the word level, but rather on the sublexical structure or component sounds of various speech patterns.

This analysis is consistent with Vitevitch and Luce's (1998) work, in which the dissociable effects of probabilistic phonotactics and neighborhood density have been demonstrated for adults. That is, when a lexical level of processing is induced with the use of word stimuli in a naming task, competitive effects of neighborhood density are found (e.g., response times are slower for words from dense vs. sparse neighborhoods). In contrast, when nonword stimuli are used, and thus lexical processing is made more difficult, facilitative effects of probabilistic phonotactics are observed (response times are faster for high- vs. low-probability phonotactic patterns). This advantage, it was proposed, arises by virtue of higher activation levels that are associated with such patterns within a connectionist framework. Of course, to bolster the derivative explanation for the developmental data, it would be desirable to show that the same children's performance varies as a function of task (i.e., that recognition is better for sparse vs. dense words, and vice versa for phonological awareness).

Finally, although most reading researchers agree that phonological representations for spoken words become increasingly fine-grained over the course of childhood (see Garlock et al., 2001), there remains at least one major issue – namely, the extent to which awareness of phonemes in particular (as opposed to larger units such as onsets and rimes) arises before or only after reading experience. Metsala and Walley (1998), together with Fowler (1991), have emphasized that some *beginning* awareness of phonemes (as a result of changes in lexical representation) serves as a precursor to early reading success, while acknowledging the important influence of reading experience with an alphabetic orthography on the full-fledged development of such awareness.

Yet, according to De Cara and Goswami (2003), most theorists maintain that phoneme awareness is strictly a product of reading experience, and the bulk of the empirical evidence to date would seem to support this position. For example, Foy and Mann (2001) found that speech perception and production abilities among 4- to 6-year-old prereaders were more directly associated with rhyme, as opposed to phoneme awareness; in contrast, phoneme awareness was most closely associated with age, receptive vocabulary knowledge, and letter instruction. Also, a different pattern of perception and production errors was found for children who could read at least one word vs. children who could not read at all, but showed some phoneme awareness. It was therefore concluded that awareness of phonemes develops primarily as a result of formal reading instruction. Further, literacy experiences may contribute to variations among individual children in the nature of more basic speech representation/processing.

Still, as Foy and Mann (2001, p. 320; see also Fowler, 1991; Mann, 1991) themselves note, ". . . as parsimonious as it may be to think of reading as changing the internal representation of speech, this view begs an explanation of some other observations that phoneme awareness can arise in the absence of literary exposure . . ." This is only one of many intriguing questions regarding the relations in development between speech perception and reading that remain to be explicated. A clearer picture of these relations should emerge with more comprehensive assessments, including longitudinal studies of children's basic speech perception/ spoken word recognition ability, their phonological awareness skills and early reading ability.

18.3 Other Gaps and Future Directions

We are beginning to learn more about speech perception and spoken word recognition in childhood, and thus to fill the gap between what is known about infants and adults. Still, we have a long way to go if we are to arrive at a complete picture of the development of these abilities.

First, longitudinal studies that span late infancy, toddlerhood, and early childhood are needed. Such studies will illuminate how certain developmental achievements, such as the establishment of the mental lexicon, as well as the fast and accurate recognition of spoken words, are rooted in the perceptual and cognitive abilities of infants. In this way, we will also learn more about how various speech perception abilities interact in development, and how they are related to beginning reading and reading-related skills (especially phoneme awareness). For example, information from the same children across different tasks and over time should reveal how increases in the phonological similarity of words that are known may have differential effects on spoken word recognition and phonological awareness.

Second, a substantial body of cross-linguistic data attests to the importance of phoneme awareness in learning to read alphabetically-represented languages (e.g., Danish, English, German, Greek, Swedish; see Goswami, 2000), but we know little about the development of spoken word recognition in languages other than English. Clearly, such information is needed to establish the generalizability of current findings. To this end, Vincente, Castro, and Walley (2001, 2003) have been studying spoken word recognition by Portuguese children, because many of the words that they first acquire are polysyllabic and thus phonologically dissimilar – in contrast to English. Our question then is the extent to which neighborhood density has an impact on spoken word recognition and phonological awareness by Portuguese vs. English children.

Undoubtedly, there are additional lines of inquiry that should be pursued. In this era of increasing facility in the assessment of human brain mechanisms, detailed anatomical and functional studies during infancy and childhood could also provide a new and invaluable source of clues about the development of sensitivity to the auditory and linguistic properties of speech. Studies of this sort with infants are beginning to appear (e.g., Dehaene-Lambertz, Dehaene, & Hertz-Pannier, 2002), but we need more information as the child makes progress in the language acquisition task (see Bjorklund, 2000). The knowledge that is gained through this approach, together with further perceptual/behavioral studies, could well prove to be the missing, and thus strongest link with regard to our understanding of speech and language development.

ACKNOWLEDGMENTS

Michael Sloane provided helpful comments on an earlier version of this paper, as did Robert Remez and David Pisoni. I would also like to acknowledge Peter W. Jusczyk for the ineffable influence that he has had on my past and current thinking. Sadly, he cannot dispute any of the ideas that I have advanced here; happily, he was so prolific and his work so outstanding that it will serve to guide all who are interested in the development of speech perception and related fields for many years to come.

NOTE

1 Admittedly, this position sidesteps an important question – namely, how does the child/learner know when to assimilate novel variants to existing representations, and when to establish new representations, despite variation of equivalent subtlety? That is, in some cases, the perceiver is required to realize that similar segmental forms are nonetheless different words, but, in other cases, that similar forms are allophonic variants and not different words at all. Clearly this cannot be accomplished merely through exposure to the sound properties of language (e.g., to their statistical distribution), and some researchers have begun to tackle the issue of how phonological and lexical factors interact in acquisition (e.g., Gierut, Morrisette, & Hust Champion, 1999: Merriman & Marazita, 1995; Stager & Werker, 2000; Storkel, 2001).

REFERENCES

Anglin, J. M. (1993). Vocabulary development: A morphological analysis. *Monographs of the Society for Research in Child Development*, 58(10).

Aslin, R. N., Jusczyk, P. W., & Pisoni, D. B. (1998). Speech and auditory processing during infancy. In D. Kuhn & R. Siegler (eds.), *Handbook of Child Psychology* (5th edition, vol. 2: *Cognition, Perception, and Language*, pp. 147–98). New York: John Wiley & Sons.

Benedict, E. (1979). Early lexical development: Comprehension and production. *Journal of Child Language*, 6, 183–200.

Bjorklund, D. F. (2000). *Children's Thinking: Developmental Function and Individual Differences* (3rd edition). Belmont, CA: Wadsworth/Thomson Learning.

Bornstein, M. H. (1992). Perception across the lifespan. In M. H. Bornstein & M. E. Lamb (eds.), *Developmental Psychology* (pp.155–209). Hillsdale, NJ: Lawrence Erlbaum.

Brady, S. A. & Shankweiler, D. P. (1991). *Phonological Processes in Literacy: A Tribute to Isabelle Y. Liberman*. Hillsdale, NJ: Lawrence Erlbaum.

Bruer, J. T. (1999). *The Myth of the First Three Years*. New York: The Free Press.

Burnham, D. K., Earnshaw, L. J., & Clark, J. E. (1991). Development of categorical identification of native and non-native bilabial stops: Infants, children and adults. *Journal of Child Language*, 18, 231–60.

Charles-Luce, J. & Luce, P. A. (1990). Similarity neighborhoods of words in young children's lexicons. *Journal of Child Language*, 17, 205–15.

Charles-Luce, J. & Luce, P. A. (1995). An examination of similarity neighborhoods in young children's receptive vocabularies. *Journal of Child Language*, 22, 727–35.

Cole, R. A. & Perfetti, C. A. (1980). Listening for mispronunciations in a children's story: The use of context by children and adults. *Journal of Verbal Learning and Verbal Behavior*, 19, 297–315.

De Cara, B. & Goswami, U. (2003). Vocabulary development and phonological neighborhood density effects in 5-year-old children. *Journal of Child Language*, 30, 695–710.

Dehaene-Lambertz, G., Dehaene, S., & Hertz-Pannier, L. (2002). Functional neuroimaging of speech perception in infants. *Science*, 298, 2013–15.

Dollaghan, C. A. (1994). Children's phonological neighbourhoods: Half empty or half full? *Journal of Child Language*, 21, 257–71.

Eimas, P. D., Siqueland, E. R., Jusczyk, P. W., & Vigorito, J. (1971). Speech perception in early infancy. *Science*, 171, 304–6.

Elbro, C., Borstrøm, I., & Petersen, D. K. (1998). Predicting dyslexia from kindergarten: The importance of distinctness of phonological representations of lexical items. *Reading Research Quarterly*, 33, 36–60.

Elliott, L. L., Hammer, M. A., & Evan, K. E. (1987). Perception of gated, highly familiar spoken monosyllabic nouns by children, teenagers, and older adults. *Perception & Psychophysics*, 42, 150–7.

Fenson, L., Dale, P., Reznick, J., Bates, E., Thal, D., & Pethick, S. (1994). Variability in early communicative development. *Monographs of the Society for Research in Child Development*, 58, 1–173.

Fernald, A., Swingley, D., & Pinto, J. P. (2001). When half a word is enough: Infants can recognize spoken words using partial phonetic information. *Child Development*, 72, 1003–15.

Fowler, A. E. (1991). How early phonological development might set the stage for phoneme awareness. In S. A. Brady & D. P. Shankweiler (eds.), *Phonological Processes in Literacy: A Tribute to Isabelle Y. Liberman* (pp. 97–117). Hillsdale, NJ: Lawrence Erlbaum.

Foy, J. G. & Mann, V. (2001). Does strength of phonological representations predict phonological awareness in preschool children? *Applied Psycholinguistics*, 22, 301–25.

Friederici, A. D. & Wessels, J. (1993). Phonotactic knowledge and its use in infant speech perception. *Perception & Psychophysics*, 54, 287–95.

Garlock, V. M., Walley, A. C., & Metsala, J. L. (2001). Age-of-acquisition, word frequency and neighborhood density effects on spoken word recognition by children and adults. *Journal of Memory and Language*, 45, 468–92.

Gerken, L. A., Murphy, W. B., & Aslin, R. N. (1995). Three- and four-year-olds' perceptual confusions for spoken words. *Perception & Psychophysics*, 57, 475–86.

Gierut, J. A., Morrisette, M. L., & Hust Champion, A. (1999). Lexical constraints in phonological acquisition. *Journal of Child Language*, 26, 261–94.

Goswami, U. (2000). Phonological representations, reading development and dyslexia: Towards a cross-linguistic theoretical framework. *Dyslexia*, 6, 133–51.

Hallé, P. A. & Boysson-Bardies, B. (1994). Emergence of an early receptive lexicon: Infants' recognition of words. *Infant Behavior and Development*, 17, 119–29.

Hazan, V. & Barrett, S. (2000). The development of phonemic categorization in children aged 6–12. *Journal of Phonetics*, 28, 377–96.

Hollich, G. & Luce, P. A. (2002). Lexical neighborhood effects in 17-month-old word learning. *Proceedings of the Boston University Conference on Language Development.*

Houston, D. M. & Jusczyk, P. W. (2000). The role of talker-specific information in word segmentation by infants. *Journal of Experimental Psychology: Human Perception and Performance*, 26, 1570–82.

Johnson, C. E. (2000). Children's phoneme identification in reverberation and noise. *Journal of Speech, Language and Hearing Research*, 43, 144–57.

Jusczyk, P. W. (1993). From general to language-specific capacities: The WRAPSA model of how speech perception develops. *Journal of Phonetics*, 21, 3–28.

Jusczyk, P. W. (1997). *The Discovery of Spoken Language*. Cambridge, MA: MIT Press.

Jusczyk, P. W. & Aslin, R. N. (1995). Infants' detection of the sound patterns of words in fluent speech. *Cognitive Psychology*, 29, 1–23.

Jusczyk, P. W., Friederici, A. D., Wessels, J., Svenkerund, V. Y., & Jusczyk, A. M. (1993). Infants' sensitivity to the sound patterns of native language words. *Journal of Memory and Language*, 32, 402–20.

Jusczyk, P. W., Goodman, M. B., & Baumann, A. (1999). Nine-month-olds' attention to the sound similarities in syllables. *Journal of Memory and Language*, 40, 62–82.

Jusczyk, P. W. & Luce, P. A. (2002). Speech perception and spoken word recognition: Past and present. *Ear and Hearing*, 23, 2–40.

Jusczyk, P. W., Luce, P. A., & Charles-Luce, J. (1994). Infants' sensitivity to phonotactic patterns in the native language. *Journal of Memory and Language*, 33, 630–45.

Krause, S. E. (1982). Vowel duration as a perceptual cue to postvocalic consonant voicing in young children and adults. *Journal of the Acoustical Society of America*, 71, 990–5.

Kuhl, P. K. (1993). Early linguistic experience and phonetic perception: Implications for theories of developmental speech perception. *Journal of Phonetics*, 21, 125–39.

Kuhl, P. K. (2000). Language, mind, and brain: Experience alters perception. In M. S. Gazzaniga (ed.), *The New Cognitive Neurosciences* (2nd edition, pp. 99–115). Cambridge, MA: MIT Press.

Kuhl, P. K., Williams, K. A., Lacerda, F., Stevens, K. N., & Lindblom, B. (1992). Linguistic experience alters phonetic perception in infants by 6 months of age. *Science*, 255, 606–8.

Liberman, I. Y., Shankweiler, D., & Liberman, A. M. (1989). The alphabetic principle and learning to read. In D. Shankweiler & I. Y. Liberman (eds.), *Phonology and Reading Disability: Solving the Reading Puzzle* (pp. 1–33). Ann Arbor, MI: University of Michigan Press.

Luce, P. A. & Pisoni, D. B. (1998). Recognizing spoken words: The Neighborhood Activation Model. *Ear and Hearing*, 19, 1–36.

Luce, P. A. & Walley, A. C. (2005). A review and critique of infant word recognition studies. In preparation.

Mandel, D. R., Jusczyk, P. W., & Pisoni, D. B. (1995). Infants' recognition of the sound patterns of their own names. *Psychological Science*, 6, 315–18.

Manis, F. R., McBride-Chang, C., Seidenberg, M. S., Keating, P., Doi, L. M., Munson, B., & Petersen, A. (1997). Are speech perception deficits associated with developmental dyslexia? *Journal of Experimental Child Psychology*, 66, 211–35.

Mann, V. A. (1991). Are we taking a too narrow view of the conditions necessary for the development of phonological awareness? In S. A. Brady & D. P. Shankweiler (eds.), *Phonological Processes in Literacy: A Tribute to Isabelle Y. Liberman* (pp. 55–64). Hillsdale, NJ: Lawrence Erlbaum.

Marslen-Wilson, W. D. (1989). Access and integration: Projecting sound onto meaning. In W. D. Marslen-Wilson (ed.), *Lexical Access and Representation* (pp. 3–24). Cambridge, MA: Bradford.

McBride-Chang, C., Wagner, R. K., & Chang, L. (1997). Growth modeling of phonological awareness. *Journal of Educational Psychology*, 89, 621–30.

Menyuk, P. & Menn, L. (1979). Early strategies for the perception and production of words and sounds. In P. Fletcher & M. Garman (eds.), *Language Acquisition* (pp. 49–70). Cambridge: Cambridge University Press.

Merriman, W. E. & Marazita, J. M. (1995). The effect of hearing similar-sounding words on two-year-olds' disambiguation of novel noun reference. *Developmental Psychology*, 31, 973–84.

Metsala, J. L. (1997a). An examination of word frequency and neighborhood density in the development of spoken word recognition. *Memory & Cognition*, 25, 47–56.

Metsala, J. L. (1997b). Spoken word recognition in reading disabled children. *Journal of Educational Psychology*, 89, 159–69.

Metsala, J. L. (1999). Young children's phonological awareness and nonword repetition as a function of vocabulary development. *Journal of Educational Psychology*, 91, 3–19.

Metsala, J. L. & Walley, A. C. (1998). Spoken vocabulary growth and the segmental restructuring of lexical representations: Precursors to phonemic awareness and early reading ability. In J. L. Metsala & L. C. Ehri (eds.), *Word Recognition in Beginning Literacy* (pp. 89–120). Hillsdale, NJ: Lawrence Erlbaum.

Morgan, J. (2002). Word recognition and phonetic structure acquisition: Possible relations. *Journal of the Acoustical Society of America*, 111, 2454.

Murphy, W. D., Shea, S. L., & Aslin, R. N. (1989). Identification of vowels in "vowelless" syllables by 3-year-olds. *Perception & Psychophysics*, 46, 375–83.

Nittrouer, S. (2001). Challenging the notion of innate phonetic boundaries. *Journal of the Acoustical Society of America*, 110, 1598–605.

Nittrouer, S., Miller, M. E., Crowther, C. S., & Manhart, M. J. (2000). The effect of segmental order on fricative labeling by children and adults. *Perception & Psychophysics*, 62, 266–84.

Nittrouer, S. & Studdert-Kennedy, M. (1987). The role of coarticulatory effects in the perception of fricatives by children and adults. *Journal of Speech & Hearing Research*, 30, 319–29.

Nittrouer, S., Studdert-Kennedy, M., & McGowan, R. S. (1989). The emergence of phonetic segments: Evidence from the spectral structure of fricative-vowel syllables spoken by children and adults. *Journal of Speech & Hearing Research*, 32, 120–32.

Ohde, R. N., Haley, K. L., & McMahon, C. W. (1996). A developmental study of vowel perception from brief synthetic consonant-vowel syllables. *Journal of the Acoustical Society of America*, 100, 3813–24.

Ohde, R. N., Haley, K. L., Vorperian, H. K., & McMahon, C. W. (1995). A developmental study of the perception of onset spectra for stop consonants in different vowel environments. *Journal of the Acoustical Society of America*, 97, 3800–12.

Polka, L., Colantonio, C., & Sundara, M. (2001). A cross-language comparison of /d/-/ð/ perception: Evidence for a new developmental pattern. *Journal of the Acoustical Society of America*, 109, 2190–201.

Reznick, J. S. & Goldfield, B. A. (1992). Rapid change in lexical development in comprehension and production. *Developmental Psychology*, 28, 406–13.

Rozin, P. & Gleitman, L. R. (1977). The structure and acquisition of reading: II. The reading process and the acquisition of the alphabetic principle. In A. S. Reber & D. L. Scarborough (eds.), *Toward a Psychology of Reading* (pp. 55–141). Hillsdale, NJ: Lawrence Erlbaum.

Shi, R. & Werker, J. (2001). Six-month-old infants' preference for lexical words. *Psychological Science*, 12, 70–5.

Stager, C. L. & Werker, J. F. (1997). Infants listen for more phonetic detail in speech perception than in word-learning tasks. *Nature*, 388, 381–2.

Stager, C. L. & Werker, J. F. (2000). Developmental changes in infant speech perception and early word learning: Is there a link? In M. B. Broe & J. B. Pierrehumbert (eds.), *Papers in Laboratory Phonology V: Acquisition and the Lexicon* (pp. 181–93). Cambridge: Cambridge University Press.

Stanovich, K. E. (1988). Explaining the differences between the dyslexic and the garden-variety poor reader: The phonological-core variable-difference model. *Journal of Learning Disabilities*, 21, 590–604.

Storkel, H. L. (2001). Learning new words: Phonotactic probability in language development. *Journal of Speech, Language, and Hearing Research*, 44, 1321–37.

Storkel, H. L. (2002). Restructuring of similarity neighborhoods in the developing mental lexicon. *Journal of Child Language*, 29, 251–74.

Swan, D. & Goswami, U. (1997). Phonological awareness deficits in developmental dyslexia and the phonological representations hypothesis. *Journal of Experimental Child Psychology*, 66, 18–41.

Thomas, D., Campos, J. J., Shucard, D. W., Ramsay, D. S., & Shucard, J. (1981). Semantic comprehension in infancy:

A signal detection approach. *Child Development*, 52, 798–803.

Tincoff, R. & Jusczyk, P. W. (1999). Some beginnings of word comprehension in 6-month-olds. *Psychological Science*, 10, 172–5.

Treiman, R. & Breaux, A. M. (1982). Common phoneme and overall similarity relations among spoken syllables: Their use by children and adults. *Journal of Psycholinguistic Research*, 11, 581–610.

Vincente, S., Castro, S. L., & Walley, A. C. (2001). Similarity neighborhood analyses of Portuguese young children's lexicons. Paper presented at the 12th Conference of the European Society for Cognitive Psychology, Edinburgh, Scotland, September.

Vincente, S., Castro, S. L., & Walley, A. C. (2003). A developmental analysis of similarity neighborhoods for European Portuguese. *Journal of Portuguese Linguistics*, 2, 115–33.

Vitevitch, M. S. & Luce, P. A. (1998). When words compete: Levels of processing in perception of spoken words. *Psychological Science*, 9, 325–9.

Walley, A. C. (1988). Spoken word recognition by young children and adults. *Cognitive Development*, 3, 137–65.

Walley, A. C. (1993a). More developmental research is needed. *Journal of Phonetics*, 21, 171–6.

Walley, A. C. (1993b). The role of vocabulary growth in children's spoken word recognition and segmentation ability. *Developmental Review*, 13, 286–350.

Walley, A. C. (2002). The future of infant speech perception: Gotta wear shades. *Journal of the Acoustical Society of America*, 111, 2454.

Walley, A. C. & Carrell, T. D. (1983). The role of the CV syllable onset spectrum and formant transitions in the adult's and child's perception of place of articulation. *Journal of the Acoustical Society of America*, 73, 1011–22.

Walley, A. C. & Flege, J. E. (1999). Effects of lexical status on the perception of native and nonnative vowels: A developmental study. *Journal of Phonetics*, 27, 307–32.

Walley, A. C. & Metsala, J. L. (1990). The growth of lexical constraints on spoken word recognition. *Perception & Psychophysics*, 47, 267–80.

Walley, A. C. & Metsala, J. L. (1992). Young children's perception of spoken words varying in age-of-acquisition. *Memory & Cognition*, 20, 171–82.

Walley, A. C. & Sloane, M. E. (2001). The perceptual magnet effect: A review of empirical findings and theoretical implications. In F. Columbus (ed.), *Advances in Psychology Research* (pp. 65–92). Huntington, NY: Nova Science Publishers.

Walley, A. C., Michela, V. L., & Wood, D. R. (1995). The gating paradigm: Effects of presentation format on spoken word recognition by children and adults. *Perception & Psychophysics*, 57, 343–51.

Walley, A. C., Smith, L. B., & Jusczyk, P. W. (1986). The role of phonemes and syllables in the perceived similarity of speech sounds for children. *Memory & Cognition*, 14, 220–9.

Werker, J. F. (2002). From speech perception to word learning and beyond. *Journal of the Acoustical Society of America*, 111, 2454.

Werker, J. F. & Tees, R. C. (1984). Cross-language speech perception: Evidence for perceptual reorganization during the first year of life. *Infant Behavior and Development*, 7, 49–63.

Woodward, A. L., Markman, E. M., & Fitzsimmons, C. M. (1994). Rapid word-learning in 13- and 18-month-olds. *Developmental Psychology*, 30, 553–66.

19 Age-Related Changes in Spoken Word Recognition

MITCHELL S. SOMMERS

19.1 Overview

Aging is associated with significant declines in the ability to identify and remember spoken words (CHABA, 1988). These age-related impairments are perhaps not surprising in light of the well-documented reduction in auditory sensitivity (presbycusis) that is a hallmark of the aging auditory system (Corso, 1971; Gates et al., 1990; see Willott, 1991 for review). Considerable evidence is also available, however, to suggest that factors other than presbycusis contribute to age-related deficits in spoken word recognition (CHABA, 1988; Plomp & Mimpen, 1979; Townsend & Bess, 1980; Wingfield, Alexander, & Cavigelli, 1994; Wingfield et al., 1985). For example, older adults often exhibit poorer speech perception than younger adults even when absolute sensitivity is equated for the two age groups (CHABA, 1988; Sommers & Danielson, 1999). In addition, age differences in spoken word recognition are exaggerated under difficult listening conditions such as the presence of background noise (Plomp & Mimpen, 1979), reverberant environments (Nabelek & Robinson, 1982), and fast speaking rates (Wingfield, 1996; Wingfield, et al., 1985; Wingfield et al., 1999). Taken together, these findings suggest that age-related changes in spoken word recognition result from a combination of peripheral (auditory) and central (cognitive) factors.

The aim of the present chapter is to critically examine and evaluate the extant literature on how age-related declines in auditory and cognitive abilities may contribute to poorer speech perception in older adults. The first section of the chapter will consider studies that have examined the contribution of presbycusis and other peripheral auditory impairments as factors mediating age-related changes in spoken word recognition. Next, I will review evidence that age differences in cognitive abilities also contribute to impaired spoken language processing in older adults. As part of this latter discussion, two types of cognitive abilities will be examined. The first are specialized processing capacities that are used primarily to translate acoustic speech signals into meaningful linguistic perceptions. The second are more global mechanisms that subserve a number of generalized cognitive functions. In the final section of the chapter, I first discuss recent investigations that have examined the interaction between peripheral and cognitive abilities in accounting for age differences in speech perception and conclude with a consideration of future directions for integrating the multiple approaches that have been used to understand age-related changes in spoken language processing. The overall goals of the chapter are to provide a critical evaluation of the literature on how age-related changes in auditory and cognitive functions, both independently and in combination, contribute to the poorer speech perception abilities of older adults and to propose a more integrative framework for understanding the speech perception difficulties of older listeners.

19.2 Peripheral Auditory Function and Age-Related Changes in Spoken Word Recognition

Presbycusis refers to the systematic and progressive reduction in absolute hearing sensitivity as a function of age (Willott, 1991). In general, age-related hearing loss is greater for high frequencies than for low frequencies and results primarily from the basal-to-apical loss of hair cells that begins at approximately age 30 and continues throughout the adult lifespan (Morrell et al., 1996). Considerable evidence is now available to suggest that age-related changes in absolute sensitivity can account for a significant percentage of the variance in spoken word recognition by older adults (CHABA, 1988; Dubno, Dirks, & Morgan, 1984; Humes, 1991, 1996; Humes & Christopherson, 1991; Humes et al., 1994; Marshall, 1981; Pichora-Fuller, Schneider, & Daneman, 1995; van Rooij & Plomp, 1992). Humes et al. (1994), for example, used an individual differences approach to examine factors that contribute to age-related declines in speech perception. Fifty older adults received a battery of auditory and cognitive tests, including measures of absolute sensitivity, suprathreshold function, and intellectual ability. Performance on these measures was then used to predict identification accuracy for a range of speech stimuli that included nonsense syllables, isolated words, and words in sentence context. In addition, the speech perception measures were obtained at two different presentation levels (70 and 90 dB SPL), both in quiet and in the presence of background noise. With the exception of speech presented at 90 dB SPL in background noise, audibility was the only factor to emerge as a significant predictor of performance on the speech perception measures, accounting for approximately 70% of the variance. Van Rooij and Plomp (1992) also found that pure-tone thresholds were the single best predictor of speech perception, accounting for approximately 48% of the variance in groups of older adults ranging in age from 60 to 93. Other studies using correlational approaches (Humes & Roberts, 1990; Jerger, Jerger, & Pirozzolo, 1991) have also demonstrated that audibility is the single best predictor of overall speech perception performance in older adults.

Support for presbycusis as the principal contributor to age-related changes in speech perception has also been obtained using experimental, rather than correlational designs. In one study, Dubno et al. (1984) used an experimental approach to dissociate the effects of age and hearing loss on age-related declines in speech perception. They measured speech reception thresholds (SRTs)[1] for spondees and for words presented in SPIN sentences (Bilger et al., 1984). The four participant groups tested in the study were normal-hearing and hearing-impaired older and younger adults. The rationale for using this design was that differences between normal-hearing and hearing-impaired older adults would suggest that, independent of other age-related deficits, hearing impairment makes a significant contribution to age differences in spoken word recognition. Differences between groups of older and younger adults with similar hearing sensitivity (e.g., differences between normal-hearing young and old), on the other hand, would implicate factors other than audibility as accounting for age differences in speech perception. As expected, SRTs measured in quiet were significantly higher for the two hearing-impaired groups than for the two normal-hearing groups. Of particular importance, however, is that the interaction between age and hearing status was not significant. Younger and older adults with similar hearing thresholds also exhibited comparable SRTs. These findings suggest that hearing impairment has similar effects on speech perception in younger and older adults and implicates age-related differences in audibility as the principal factor responsible for older adults' poorer speech perception.

In addition to changes in absolute sensitivity, there is also evidence that suprathreshold functions such as frequency, intensity, and temporal discrimination may be impaired in older listeners (Cheesman et al., 1995; Dubno et al., 1984; Fitzgibbons & Gordon-Salant, 1994; Patterson et al., 1982; Schneider, 1997; Schneider et al., 1994) and that these impairments may adversely affect speech perception, especially under degraded listening conditions. Several investigators (Humes & Christopherson, 1991; Lee & Humes, 1992) have suggested that age-related deficits in frequency resolution may play a particularly important role in explaining age differences in speech perception, especially the disproportionate difficulty that older adults have perceiving speech in noise. The reasoning behind this proposal is that age-related broadening of auditory filters would increase acoustic masking, making it more difficult for older adults to extract important phonetic information from the speech signal. Consistent with this proposal, Humes and Christopherson (1991) and Lee and Humes (1992) found that in addition to audibility, frequency discrimination thresholds also accounted for a small, but significant, percentage of the variance in older adults' speech perception (3–14%). Similarly, Glasberg and Moore (1989) reported that frequency discrimination was strongly correlated with SRTs in noise but not with SRTs in quiet; SRTs in quiet were best accounted for by absolute sensitivity. Finally, Klein, Mills, & Adkins (1990) found that for older adults, masked thresholds and not absolute sensitivity accounted for a greater percentage of the variance in identifying speech in noise. Taken together, these findings indicate that age differences in frequency discrimination may be particularly important for understanding why older adults are disproportionately impaired when listening to speech in the presence of background noise compared to young adults.

Although the studies cited above suggest that age-related changes in suprathreshold functions can contribute to the speech perception difficulties of older adults, these findings must be interpreted somewhat cautiously because several other investigations have reported that hearing loss can impair suprathreshold auditory functions, including frequency and temporal resolution (Glasberg & Moore, 1986; Ryan, Dallos, & McGee, 1979; Sommers & Humes, 1993). Sommers and Humes

(1993), for example, found equivalent auditory filter widths in older adults with moderate hearing losses and a group of younger adults with simulated hearing losses that matched the average loss of the older adults. In this same study, Sommers and Humes also reported that younger and older adults with normal hearing exhibited nearly identical auditory filter widths. These findings suggest that age-related changes in frequency resolution may result from hearing impairment rather than from specific deficits in frequency resolution. Unfortunately, most studies that have examined the relationship between suprathreshold functions and speech perception in older adults have failed to dissociate the effects of hearing loss from other psychoacoustic abilities (Patterson et al., 1982). Therefore, it remains unclear whether age-related changes in psychoacoustic abilities, independent of presbycusis, make a unique contribution to the speech perception deficits observed in older adults.

In summary, age-related hearing loss is almost certainly the single most important factor affecting speech perception in older adults. Under ideal listening conditions, such as when stimuli are presented in quiet, audibility can account for over 80% of the variance in the speech perception abilities of older adults (Humes et al., 1994). Under more difficult listening conditions, such as in the presence of background noise or reverberation, the importance of audibility is reduced but can still explain approximately half of the systematic variance in speech perception. Suprathreshold functions, such as frequency and temporal resolution, may account for additional variance in spoken word recognition under these more difficult listening conditions but relatively few studies have been designed explicitly to dissociate the effects of audibility and suprathreshold functions on spoken language processing in older adults.

19.3 Cognitive Declines and Age-Related Changes in Spoken Word Recognition

Although there is strong evidence for the importance of audibility in explaining the spoken language difficulties of older adults, several lines of research suggest that age-related cognitive declines also affect speech perception in this population. First, a number of manipulations that reduce the cognitive demands of speech perception, including the addition of semantic context (Nittrouer & Boothroyd, 1990; Sommers & Danielson, 1999; Wingfield, Aberdeen, & Stine, 1991), the presence of prosodic and syntactic information (Wingfield, Lindfield, & Goodglass, 2000), and the use of slower speaking rates (Wingfield & Ducharme, 1999; Wingfield et al., 1999) all function to reduce age differences in spoken language processing. Conversely, manipulations that increase the cognitive demands of speech perception, such as using multiple, rather than single talkers (Sommers, 1997; Sommers & Danielson, 1999), increasing the difficulty of lexical selection (Sommers, 1996; Sommers & Danielson, 1999), and using unfamiliar talkers (Yonan & Sommers, 2000) all exaggerate age-related differences in spoken language processing. Second, several recent studies (Sommers & Danielson, 1999; van Rooij & Plomp, 1992) have found that age-related declines in general cognitive abilities, such as working memory capacity – the ability to maintain and manipulate information simultaneously in short-term memory – and inhibitory control – the ability to suppress activation levels on task-irrelevant information – are predictive of individual differences in spoken language processing, independent of age differences in hearing. Taken together, these results suggest that in addition to peripheral auditory impairments, age differences in speech perception and spoken language processing may result from declines in both general cognitive abilities and specialized perceptual mechanisms used for speech perception.

19.3.1 *Methodological issue*

Before discussing studies that have investigated the relationship between age-related cognitive declines and impaired speech perception, it is important to consider a critical methodological limitation of such experiments. Specifically, age-related impairments in peripheral auditory functions make it difficult to equate baseline performance across age groups and this potentially limits the generalizability of many investigations. For example, consider a hypothetical experiment designed to compare the effects of word frequency on spoken word recognition in older and younger adults. Ideally, we would want to establish listening conditions that produce equivalent performance for older and younger adults on one level of the independent variable (e.g., equate performance on high-frequency words) and then determine how manipulating this variable (e.g., switching to low-frequency words) affects younger and older adults. The difficulty is that presbycusis and other age-related peripheral auditory dysfunctions often prevent researchers from being able to equate baseline performance using the same testing conditions. Thus, if we measured identification performance for high-frequency words using the same testing parameters for older and younger adults, older adults would likely perform significantly worse than younger adults. Interpreting these results would be problematic because it would be difficult to establish the relative contributions of age-related cognitive and sensory declines to the age-related reduction in identifying high-frequency words. Moreover, any interpretation of the results regarding the change from high- to low-frequency words would be confounded by age differences in baseline performance (in this case, age differences in identification of high-frequency words).

One potential solution to this problem is to vary listening conditions to produce approximately equivalent baseline performance across age groups. As an example, we might test older and younger adults at different signal-to-noise ratios or we might increase stimulus intensity for older adults. Although such adjustments can allow researchers to equate baseline performance for different participant groups, they introduce another important limitation; any compensations made to equate baseline performance will introduce potential confounds into the experiment. Currently, there is no ideal solution to this methodological difficulty nor is there consistency in how (or if) investigators could adapt their experimental designs to minimize the effects of baseline differences between age groups. Therefore, in evaluating studies of cognitive abilities and age-related declines in speech perception, it is essential to consider limitations on possible interpretations stemming from this fundamental methodological difficulty.

19.3.2 *Age-related cognitive declines and the environmental support hypothesis*

One theoretical framework that is useful for understanding the contribution of age-related cognitive declines to spoken word recognition is the environmental support hypothesis (Craik, 1986; Humphrey & Kramer, 1999). Briefly, the environmental support framework suggests that aging is associated with declines in both global and task-specific cognitive abilities. However, the effects of such declines can be attenuated, according to the theory, by providing older adults with additional information or support from the environment. For example, within the area of memory research, the concept of environmental support has been used to explain the well-documented finding that age differences in recognition are significantly smaller than age differences in recall (Craik & McDowd, 1987). According to the environmental support hypothesis, recognition provides greater environmental support for memory retrieval than recall because recall requires individuals to self-generate potential responses. For most recognition tests, in contrast, all of the potential study items are presented by the experimenter and can serve as retrieval cues, obviating the need to self-generate potential responses. Thus, the environmental support hypothesis would argue that recognition provides greater environmental support for memory retrieval and therefore age differences are reduced when older adults are tested using recognition, compared with recall.

Within the domain of speech perception, one of the best demonstrations of the environmental support hypothesis is in understanding the effects of providing semantic context. In general, age differences in spoken word recognition can be attenuated, and in some cases eliminated, by placing words in semantically meaningful sentences (Cohen & Faulkner, 1983; Hutchinson, 1989; Nittrouer & Boothroyd, 1990; Pichora-Fuller et al., 1995; Sommers & Danielson, 1999; Wingfield et al., 1991). For example, Sommers and Danielson (1999) compared identification scores for isolated words and words in context using both low-predictability (e.g., "she was thinking about the *cat*") and high-predictability (e.g., "the dog chased the *cat*") sentences (Bilger et al., 1984) as a function of age. As shown in Figure 19.1, scores for isolated words and low-predictability (LP) sentences were approximately 10–20% greater for younger than for older adults. Identification scores for words in high-predictability (HP) sentences, however, did not differ across the two age groups. Similarly, Pichora-Fuller et al. (1995) compared identification scores for older and younger adults again using both high- and low-predictability sentence contexts. They reported that, although both older and younger adults benefited from the addition of a meaningful semantic context, older adults exhibited significantly greater differences between low-predictability and high-predictability sentences than did younger adults. Wingfield et al. (1991) used a gating procedure (Grosjean, 1980) to examine age differences in the benefits of adding semantic context. In the gating paradigm, increasing amounts of a speech signal (gates) are presented on successive trials and participants are asked to guess the word after each gate. Wingfield et al. found that older adults needed significantly greater amounts of information (more gates) than young adults to identify words presented in isolation, but

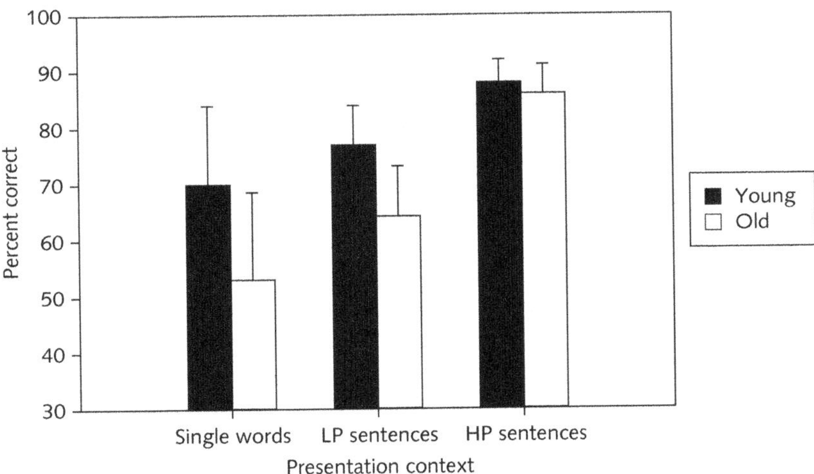

Figure 19.1 Effects of semantic context on spoken word recognition. Identification scores for words presented in isolation (single words), low-predictability sentences (LP sentences), and high-predictability sentences (HP sentences) as reported in Sommers and Danielson (1999). Young adult data are displayed in the filled bars and data from older adults are displayed in the open bars. Significant age differences were observed for the single words and low-predictability (LP) sentences but not for the high-predictability (HP) sentences, suggesting that older adults benefit more from the addition of semantic context than do younger adults.

age differences in gating were eliminated following the addition of semantic context.

Further evidence that semantic context can function as a source of environmental support for spoken word recognition comes from studies demonstrating that the benefits of context increase under more difficult listening conditions (Pichora-Fuller et al., 1995; Sommers & Danielson, 1999). If context supports word recognition by providing information external to the speech signal that listeners can use to obtain or disambiguate phonetic content, then dependence on semantic context should increase as a function of the difficulty of the listening situation. To investigate this hypothesis, Pichora-Fuller et al. compared identification performance for high-predictability and low-predictability sentences at signal-to-noise ratios ranging from −10 to +15 dB. For younger adults, the benefits of adding semantic context decreased from approximately 25% at a signal-to-noise ratio of 0 to approximately 10% at a signal-to-noise ratio of +10. For older adults, differences between identification scores for HP and LP sentences were reduced from approximately 60% at a 0 dB signal-to-noise ratio to approximately 20% at a +10 dB signal-to-noise ratio. Taken together, these findings suggest that the constraints imposed by semantic contexts can serve as a reliable source of environmental support for word recognition that is, at least in part, independent of the acoustic signal. Older adults can therefore compensate for age-related reductions in the audibility of speech signals, by greater reliance on other sources of information, including semantic context.

As noted earlier, a potential limitation of studies comparing cognitive abilities and speech perception in older and younger adults is that baseline performance measures often differ for the two groups. In the present case, conclusions regarding age-related differences in the use of semantic context are potentially compromised by the fact that older and younger adults differ on their ability to identify words in LP sentences. Several findings, however, argue against baseline differences as the primary reason that older adults generally exhibit greater benefits from the addition of semantic context. First, Nittrouer and Boothroyd (1990) developed a metric for assessing the benefits of context that is independent of overall performance levels and still found improved use of semantic context by older adults. Second, Sommers and Danielson (1999) designed their study specifically to compare age differences in the use of semantic context after equating performance in a baseline condition. In their study, performance in the low-predictability condition was equated across age groups by using different signal-to-noise ratios for older and younger participants and older adults still exhibited significantly greater benefits from the addition of semantic context. Although these findings do not completely eliminate concerns regarding differential baseline performance (the use of different signal-to-noise ratios introduces a potential confound) they do suggest that, at least under certain testing conditions, older adults can exhibit greater benefits from the addition of semantic context even when baseline performance is similar across age groups.

One question that arises from studies of age differences in the use of semantic context is what mechanisms are responsible for older adults' ability to benefit disproportionately from the addition of contextual information. One possibility is suggested by studies indicating that age-related deficits in working memory are among the most reliable findings in the cognitive aging literature (Mitchell et al., 2000; Salthouse, 1992, 1993; Salthouse, Babcock, & Shaw, 1991; Salthouse & Meinz, 1995; Salthouse & Skovronek, 1992) and that reducing working memory demands can often attenuate age differences in cognitive performance (Pichora-Fuller et al., 1995). Thus, it may be that the addition of semantic context improves speech perception by decreasing working memory demands and that older adults improve disproportionately because context functions to decrease the importance of their impaired working memory system. Indirect support for this proposal comes from a study by Wingfield, Lombardi, & Sokol (1984). In their study, Wingfield et al. compared older and younger adults' ability to benefit from contextual information that either preceded or followed a target word. The rationale for this approach was that in the case of preceding context, semantic information can be continually updated and stored in a single representation. This would minimize working memory demands by allowing listeners to maintain only the most current situation model in memory. However, in the case of following context, participants needed to maintain a more direct representation, including memory for individual lexical items until the target word could be disambiguated. Thus, Wingfield et al. predicted that older adults would benefit as much or more than younger adults from the addition of contextual information that *preceded* a target word but would not benefit as much as younger adults from the addition of context that *followed* a target word. Consistent with this prediction, Wingfield et al. reported that older adults exhibited greater benefits from the addition of preceding context than did younger adults but were less able than young listeners to benefit from contextual information that followed a target word. These findings are in good agreement with the environmental support framework because they suggest that preceding context provides additional environmental support for speech recognition by reducing working memory demands.

In summary, the findings from several studies suggest that older adults benefit to a greater extent than younger adults from the addition of semantic context. This differential benefit from top-down contextual constraints may be partially attributable to reductions in working memory demands, at least for the case of contextual information that precedes a target word. Moreover, age differences in the benefits of semantic context may be a specific example of a more general phenomenon in which older adults are disproportionately facilitated by the addition of environmental support.

A second type of environmental support that is potentially available during spoken word recognition is talker familiarity (Nygaard & Pisoni, 1998; Nygaard, Sommers, & Pisoni, 1994; Yonan & Sommers, 2000). Prior exposure to a talker's voice can facilitate speech perception because it improves listeners' ability to adjust quickly to the acoustic variability in speech signals that results from differences in the size and shape of vocal tracts. Specifically, individual variability in vocal tract configuration results in a many-to-one mapping between acoustic speech sounds and phonetic perceptions. Thus, the same word produced by a man, woman, or child will have very different acoustic characteristics.

One mechanism that has been proposed to account for listeners' ability to accommodate this high degree of variability is perceptual normalization (Johnson, 1990; Nearey, 1989). In the case of talker variability, normalization refers to a set of cognitive operations that are used to convert highly variable speech signals into canonical symbolic representations matching those stored in long-term memory. Familiarity with a talker's voice has been shown to improve speech perception by reducing the demands of talker normalization (Nygaard & Pisoni, 1998; Nygaard et al., 1994; Yonan & Sommers, 2000). That is, prior exposure to a talker's voice enables listeners to learn the procedures needed for normalizing that voice, thereby making normalization easier for subsequent productions of novel words produced by that talker. Consistent with this proposal, Nygaard et al. (1994) found that, for young adults, identification scores were approximately 10% higher for words produced by familiar voices than for words spoken by unfamiliar voices.

More recently, Yonan and Sommers (2000) extended this work to older adults. They proposed that if familiarity with a talker's voice serves as a type of environmental support for perceptual normalization, then older adults might exhibit greater benefits of talker familiarity than younger adults. This prediction was based on earlier findings that older adults have greater difficulty with talker normalization than do younger adults (Sommers, 1997). In addition, Yonan and Sommers investigated whether different types of environmental support (e.g., talker familiarity and semantic context) might combine to further reduce age differences in spoken word recognition. Using a perceptual learning paradigm adapted from Nygaard et al. (1994), Yonan and Sommers first trained older and younger adults to identify six different voices (three men and three women) and then tested them on identification of words in LP and HP sentences. The critical manipulation in this study was that half the sentences used in the speech perception tests were

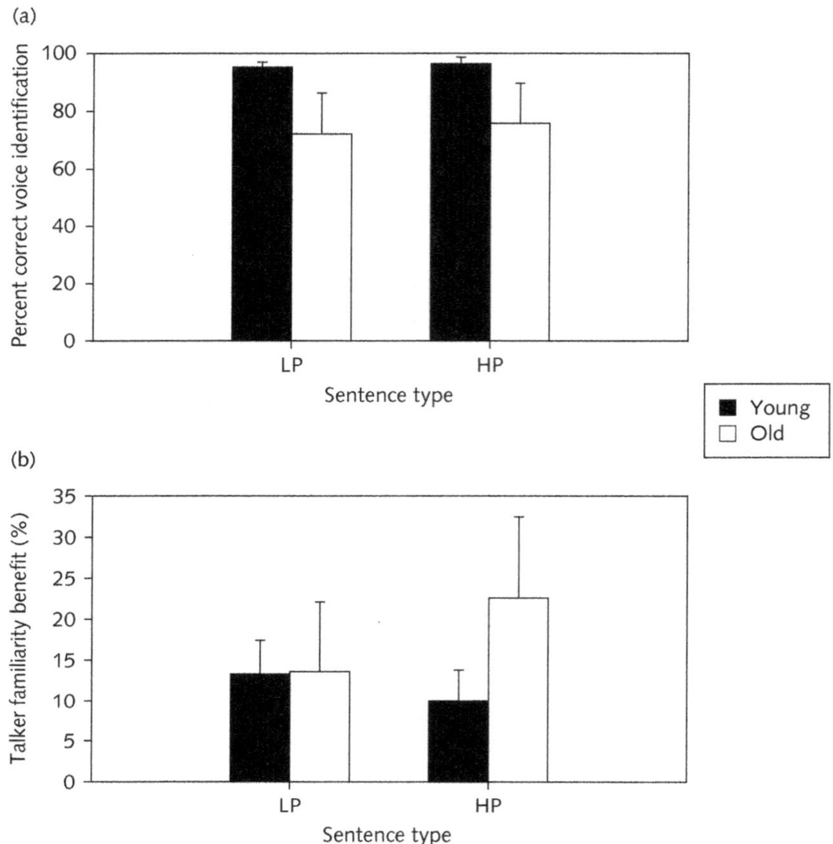

Figure 19.2 (a) Comparison of older and younger adults' ability to identify the voices of three men and three women in low-predictability (LP) and high-predictability (HP) sentences from Yonan and Sommers (2000). Older adults exhibited significantly poorer voice identification than younger adults for both types of stimulus material. (b) The effects of prior experience with a talker's voice (i.e., talker familiarity benefit) on identification of sentence-final words in LP and HP sentences. Older and younger adults exhibited similar benefits for familiar talkers in LP sentences but older adults demonstrated greater benefits from talker familiarity in the HP sentences.

spoken by familiar talkers (ones they had been trained to identify) and half were spoken by unfamiliar talkers.

The findings for voice identification and talker familiarity are displayed in Figure 19.2. Consider first age differences in the ability to identify the six talkers who produced the LP and HP sentences (Figure 19.2a). Consistent with previous studies of memory for non-linguistic features of spoken words (Kausler & Puckett, 1981; Naveh-Benjamin & Craik, 1995) older adults exhibited significantly poorer voice discrimination than did younger adults. Despite this reduced ability to identify talkers, however, as shown in Figure 19.2(b) older adults benefited as much or more than young adults from having sentences produced by familiar talkers. For example, across the three signal-to-noise ratios used in this study, young adults exhibited approximately a 10% increase in identification scores for HP sentences produced by familiar talkers, compared with sentences spoken by unfamiliar talkers. The corresponding benefit for older adults was approximately 22%. Moreover, for HP sentences produced by familiar talkers, which represented the combined effects of talker familiarity and semantic context, age differences in spoken word recognition were essentially eliminated. These findings suggest that older adults can use talker familiarity and semantic context as environmental support to compensate for peripheral hearing loss and impaired talker normalization abilities.

In addition to the effects of talker familiarity and semantic context, prosodic information has also been investigated as a source of environmental support for spoken language processing (Wingfield et al., 2000; Wingfield, Lahar, & Stine, 1989). Prosody refers to a complex set of linguistic features that includes stress, duration, and intonation contour. Prosodic information can serve many functions in the normal course of speech perception and spoken language processing including delineating lexical and syntactic boundaries, disambiguating meaning, and specifying semantic emphasis (Darwin, 1975; Norris, McQueen, & Cutler, 1995; Soto-Faraco, Sebastiàn-Gallés, & Cutler, 2001; Wales & Toner, 1975; Wingfield & Klein, 1971). Thus, although citation and monotonic speech are clearly perceptible, retention and comprehension of speech improves when natural prosodic information is available to facilitate parsing and comprehension (Wingfield et al., 1984).

Given that prosodic information is an important component of the speech signal, several investigators have examined whether older adults are able to use prosody as an aid to spoken word recognition (Stine & Wingfield, 1987; Wingfield et al., 1989; Wingfield et al., 2000). In one study, Stine and Wingfield (1987) investigated age differences in recall of spoken sentences as a function of the extent to which natural prosodic information was preserved. Both older and younger adults exhibited greater accuracy for words produced in sentences with normal prosody than for sentences spoken with equal stress on all syllables, suggesting that the presence of normal prosodic information can facilitate spoken language processing. Of particular relevance, older adults exhibited significantly greater benefits from the addition of prosodic information than did younger adults and this differential age benefit increased for more difficult listening conditions. These findings parallel the results obtained with semantic context and talker familiarity in that a source of environmental support, prosodic information in this case, differentially benefited older adults and this advantage was greater under more difficult listening conditions.

Taken together, studies of age-related differences in the use of semantic context, talker familiarity, and prosodic information suggest that older adults maintain and exploit at least some of the specialized cognitive abilities needed for speech perception. In addition, older adults increase their reliance on such abilities to compensate for peripheral auditory impairments. These findings stand in marked contrast to the extensive literature on age-related declines in more generalized cognitive abilities such as working memory capacity, processing speed, and executive control (see Craik & Salthouse, 2000). Establishing the importance of such generalized cognitive impairments in explaining the speech perception difficulties of older adults is important because age-related declines in one or more of these fundamental cognitive abilities could contribute to the observed age differences in speech perception.

One example of a general cognitive ability that declines with age and that may contribute to age-related impairments in understanding speech is speed of processing. Older adults require more time for information processing than younger adults and age-related differences in processing speed increase as a function of task complexity (Salthouse, 1996; Salthouse & Meinz, 1995). One consequence of age-related slowing is that older adults take longer to complete the component operations required to perform a given cognitive activity and performance on tasks that are dependent on such operations is often degraded. General slowing has become an important explanatory factor within the cognitive aging literature because reduced processing speed can account for a significant percentage of age-related variance across a broad range of cognitive tasks (Salthouse, 1996; Salthouse & Meinz, 1995).

Within the domain of speech perception, studies examining the role of general slowing as a factor contributing to age-related impairments in spoken language processing have produced somewhat mixed results (Gordon-Salant & Fitzgibbons, 1993; Konkle, Beasley, & Bess, 1977; Schmitt & Carroll, 1985; Tun, 1998; Wingfield & Ducharme, 1999; Wingfield et al., 1985; Wingfield & Stine, 1992). One set of findings that provides support for the importance of processing speed in accounting for age differences in speech perception is that older adults are disproportionately impaired by increasing speaking rate (Tun, 1998; Wingfield & Ducharme, 1999; Wingfield et al., 1985; Wingfield & Stine, 1992). Wingfield et al. (1985), for example, compared the performance of younger and older adults on a sentence repetition task using speaking rates that varied from 275 to 425 words per minute. Consistent with the general slowing hypothesis, older adults exhibited greater declines than younger adults in their ability to repeat sentences and this age difference increased as a function of the speaking rate used to generate the stimulus materials. An important control in their study was that participants were allowed to adjust the listening level so that age differences in audibility of the speech signal were minimized. Tun (1998) also reported a significant interaction between age and speaking rate using a sentence identification task. She found that older adults were significantly more impaired than younger adults by increasing speaking rate and this age difference was greater when stimuli were presented at lower signal-to-noise ratios. In another study, Wingfield and Stine (1992) compared speech recognition for older and younger adults as a function of both speaking rate and propositional density. Consistent with earlier findings, they reported greater effects of speaking rate on older adults and this age difference was magnified for the more difficult, propositionally dense, passages.

It is important to emphasize that the pattern of findings across these studies, greater age differences for faster speaking rates and more degraded listening conditions, is exactly what would be predicted by the cognitive slowing framework. If older adults require more time to execute the component operations underlying speech perception, then increasing speaking rate would amplify the effects of age-related slowing by reducing the time available for phonetic processing. Thus, as speaking rate increases, age-related general slowing will reduce the probability that older adults can successfully complete each of the operations required for speech perception. Moreover, greater task complexity will increase the number of component operations required for successful speech perception. Age-related declines in processing speed will therefore be exaggerated under difficult listening conditions.

A related approach that has been used to examine processing speed as a factor contributing to age differences in speech perception is to determine how time expansion of the speech signal affects older and younger adults. The rationale for this approach is straightforward; if poorer performance with faster speaking rates is a consequence of general slowing, then providing older adults with additional time for speech processing, by expanding the speech signal, should reduce age differences. Unfortunately, evaluation of this approach is complicated by differences in the methods used for signal expansion. Wingfield et al. (1999) found that older and younger adults' impaired performance with faster speaking rates could be partially reversed by inserting silent periods at natural linguistic boundaries (between phrases and clauses). In contrast, Gordon-Salant and Fitzgibbons (1997) found little benefit for normal-hearing older or younger adults from increasing inter-word interval. Schmitt and McCroskey (1981) and Schmitt (1983) also failed to find significant improvements in comprehension from proportional expansion of all speech segments.

One explanation for the differential findings with respect to speech signal expansion is that increasing signal duration may only improve performance when additional processing time is provided at natural syntactic boundaries. Consistent with this explanation, Wingfield et al. (1999) found that inserting silence at random points within the speech signal had little effect on overall performance but inserting silent periods selectively between natural phrases and clauses significantly improved speech processing. Older and younger adults may therefore use the short silent intervals at natural syntactic boundaries as periods for consolidating phonetic, lexical, and semantic information. Time expansion may only be effective at reducing age differences attributable to general slowing if the increased processing time is provided at these selective intervals to allow more time for consolidation.

The importance of age-related general slowing for speech perception has been challenged recently by findings from studies examining the relationship between individual differences in processing speed and speech perception (Sommers & Danielson, 1999; Tun, 1998). Sommers and Danielson (1999), for example, obtained a composite measure of processing speed across three tasks varying in overall complexity. This measure was then used as a predictor variable in a series of multiple regression analyses to assess the independent contribution of processing speed for spoken word identification in both single-talker and multiple-talker listening conditions. Processing speed did not account for a significant percentage of the variance in identification scores for either the single- or multiple-talker conditions. Tun (1998) also used an individual differences approach to investigate the importance of processing speed for perception of compressed speech. Similarly to Sommers and Danielson, Tun (1998) failed to find a significant contribution of processing speed even for the fastest speaking rates. This finding is particularly instructive with respect to the role of general slowing in speech perception because age-related reductions in processing speed should be especially important for identifying speech produced at fast speaking rates.

Although studies using the individual differences approach have generally failed to find a significant contribution of processing speed to speech perception, it is important to note that these studies have used relatively few (and sometimes only one) measures of processing speed. To date, there have been no systematic large-scale studies of the relationship between processing speed and speech perception in which processing speed was assessed across a continuum of tasks that produce a large range of response latencies. Such experiments are important because estimates of processing speed are more accurate as the range of response latencies increases. In addition, most of the studies that have examined processing speed and speech perception have failed to measure the reliability of the speed measures and this failure could lead to significant inaccuracies in assessing the extent of general slowing. Therefore, although correlational studies suggest a minimal role for processing speed in accounting for age-related changes in speech perception, more systematic examinations are needed to provide stronger support for this position.

In addition to general slowing, a second fundamental change in cognitive processing with age is a reduced ability to inhibit task-irrelevant information (Hasher & Zacks, 1988; May et al., 1999; McDowd, 1997; McDowd & Filion, 1992; McDowd & Oseas-Kreger, 1991; but see Burke, 1997 for criticisms of the inhibitory deficit hypothesis). Specifically, the inhibitory deficit hypothesis argues that aging impairs attentional control mechanisms such that older adults are more susceptible to interference from extraneous or task-irrelevant information. This reduction in executive control abilities can result from age-related declines in the ability to filter out task-irrelevant information or from impairments in suppressing activated, but no longer relevant, information. The inhibitory deficit hypothesis has become an important theoretical framework within the cognitive aging literature because it is able to account for age differences across disparate tasks, including increased susceptibility to Stroop interference (Spieler, Balota, & Faust, 1996), impaired language comprehension (Hasher & Zacks, 1988), and increased incidence of false memories (Balota et al., 1999; Sommers & Lewis, 1999).

With respect to spoken word recognition, both types of inhibitory failures, reduced filtering of extraneous information and impaired suppression of task-irrelevant stimuli, provide useful constructs for understanding specific age-related changes in speech perception. For example, breakdowns in the filtering component of inhibition may contribute to older adults' increased susceptibility to background masking. If older adults are less able than young adults to attenuate and exclude extraneous background stimuli, then masking noise may disproportionately impair their ability to recognize spoken words. To examine this proposal, Tun and Wingfield (1999) compared the effects of several different types of background maskers on perception and recall of speech by older and younger adults. Participants were first tested in quiet and then in the presence of: (1) one distracting voice; (2) two distracting voices; (3) a 20-talker background babble; and (4) a white noise masker. Tun and Wingfield reasoned that if increased susceptibility to masking was simply a result of age-related peripheral changes producing greater acoustic masking, then the largest age differences should occur for the white noise masker because this had the greatest amount of acoustic energy. If, however, age-related differences in susceptibility to background masking is more selective in nature and is due to an impaired ability to inhibit or filter irrelevant information, then age differences might be greatest for the background babble because the semantic content of the babble would be most difficult to ignore. Consistent with the latter prediction, older adults exhibited greater masking than young adults for all conditions except the white noise masker. As noted, this finding is difficult to reconcile with a purely peripheral-based acoustic account of masking because the white noise masker had the highest overall energy levels.

The second type of inhibitory deficit, a reduced ability to suppress activated but no-longer-relevant information, can also provide a useful framework for understanding specific age-related changes in spoken word recognition. As an example, most current models of spoken word recognition (Jusczyk & Luce, 2002; Luce & Pisoni, 1998; Marslen-Wilson, 1990; Norris, 1994; Norris et al., 1995) suggest that presentation of a spoken word first activates a set of lexical candidates and these activated representations then compete for a best match with the acoustic input. Sommers (1996) used one current model, the neighborhood activation model (NAM; Luce & Pisoni, 1998), to test the hypothesis that part of older adults' difficulty with speech perception is a reduced ability to inhibit and suppress lexical candidates that were initially activated but that are no longer consistent with the current acoustic input. To test this proposal, Sommers used a basic premise of the NAM to make predictions about which words would be most difficult for older adults to identify because they impose the greatest demands on inhibitory abilities. According to the NAM, lexically hard words are items, such as CAT, that have many similar sounding neighbors while lexically easy words are items, such as YOUNG, that have a small number of lexical neighbors (neighbors are defined operationally as any word that can be created by adding, deleting, or substituting a single phoneme in the target word). Sommers (1996) predicted that older adults should have disproportionately greater difficulty perceiving lexically hard words because identifying words with many lexical neighbors requires listeners to inhibit a greater number of competitor items that were initially activated as candidate words but are no longer viable based on the current acoustic information.

Figure 19.3 displays percent correct identification as a function of lexical difficulty for older and younger adults. Note first that performance for lexically easy words was nearly identical for older and younger adults. This result was achieved by testing the two groups at slightly different signal-to-noise ratios (younger and older adults were tested at 0 and +4 dB signal-to-noise ratios, respectively). Performance for lexically difficult words, in contrast, was significantly poorer for older than for younger adults. Thus, when older and younger adults were matched for performance on lexically easy words, as a means of minimizing differences in audibility, older adults exhibited significantly greater difficulty identifying hard words than did younger adults. In a follow-up investigation, Sommers and Danielson (1999) found that individual differences in inhibitory abilities based on other measures were the single best predictor of the ability to identify lexically hard words. These findings suggest that age-related inhibitory deficits may contribute to poorer speech perception by reducing older adults' ability to suppress activation levels on lexical candidates that are no longer consistent with current acoustic-phonetic input.

The inhibitory deficit hypothesis also provides a basis for understanding why older adults may benefit more than younger listeners from the addition of

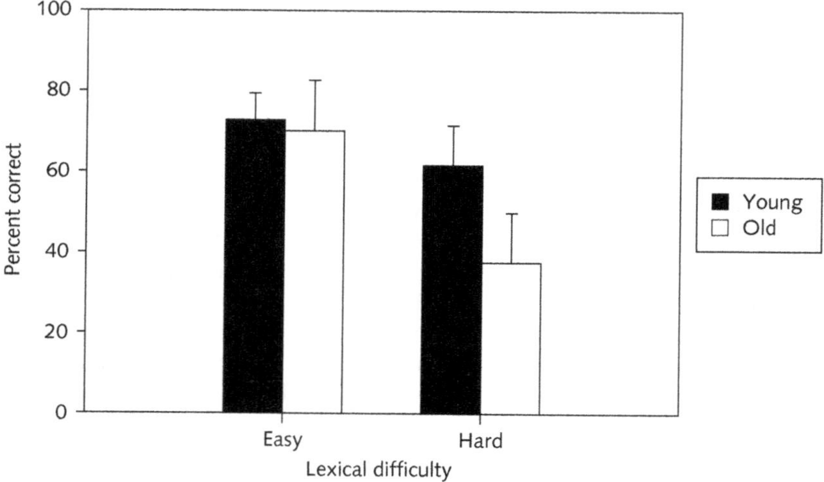

Figure 19.3 Comparison of older and younger adults' ability to identify lexically easy and hard words in a background of noise from Sommers (1996). Older adults were tested at slightly higher signal-to-noise ratios than younger adults, to equate performance for lexically easy words. Under these listening conditions, older adults exhibited significant deficits in the ability to identify lexically hard words, compared with their younger counterparts.

semantic context. Recall that a number of studies have found that age differences in spoken word recognition can be attenuated by placing words in semantically meaningful sentences (Cohen & Faulkner, 1983; Hutchinson, 1989; Nittrouer & Boothroyd, 1990; Wingfield et al., 1991). Sommers and Danielson (1999) suggested that this differential benefit of semantic information could be explained by considering the dynamics of inhibitory processes within activation-competition models of spoken word recognition. Specifically, they proposed that one way in which contextual constraints could improve spoken word recognition is by reducing the need to inhibit lexical competitors. According to this proposal, semantic contexts serve to restrict the number of lexical candidates that are activated to only those items that are consistent with the current semantic constraints. For example, within the NAM, the word CAT presented in isolation would activate items such as BAT, CUT, and FAT. However, within a semantically constrained sentence such as "the dog chased the CAT," the lexical neighbors FAT and CUT would not be activated because they would not be consistent with the preceding context. Thus, according to Sommers and Danielson, older adults may exhibit greater benefits from the addition of context because semantic information functions to reduce inhibitory demands by limiting the number of potential lexical candidates.

To test their hypothesis, Sommers and Danielson (1999) compared the effects of adding semantic contexts for older and younger adults as a function of the lexical difficulty of target items. The prediction was that the addition of semantic contexts would have greater effects on identification of lexically hard than on lexically easy words because easy words have relatively few competitors and adding semantic context would not be particularly beneficial since inhibitory demands are already low. In contrast, lexically hard words should benefit substantially from the addition of semantic context because many neighbors need to be inhibited to identify these items and semantic constraints would significantly reduce these inhibitory demands. Moreover, Sommers and Danielson suggested that older and younger adults should exhibit similar benefits from adding context when identifying lexically easy words because age-related inhibitory deficits would have few consequences for items with a small number of competitors. The increased inhibitory demands associated with identifying lexically hard words, however, should make context more important for older adults and should therefore improve identification scores more for older than for younger adults.

Consistent with these predictions, older and younger adults exhibited nearly identical improvements (approximately 15%) from the addition of semantic context when identifying easy words, but older adults displayed significantly greater improvements than young adults when identifying lexically hard words – approximately 22% for young adults and 31% for older adults. Furthermore, an error analysis indicated that for words presented in isolation, older adults were more likely than younger adults to provide a lexical neighbor of the target item as an incorrect response. This finding is exactly what would be predicted if older adults have greater difficulty inhibiting lexical competitors of the target item. In the semantically constrained condition, however, younger and older adults did not differ in the probability of providing a lexical neighbor as an incorrect response, suggesting that the change from isolated words to semantic contexts reduced the number of potential lexical competitors for older adults to a greater extent than for younger adults.

Other researchers examining the role of inhibitory deficits as a factor contributing to age differences in spoken word recognition have investigated older adults' ability to suppress activation resulting from semantic, rather than phonological, information. Stine and Wingfield (1994) used the gating paradigm to determine whether older adults were impaired in their ability to inhibit high-probability semantic competitors. In their study, listeners were presented with increasing amounts (i.e., gates) of a sentence-final word. The critical manipulation was that target items were always the second most probable response to a sentence context. For example, listeners might be presented with the context "all of the guests had a good ______________," where the blank would be filled with increasing amounts of acoustic information for a target word. In this example, the most probable completion is "time," but the target item used in the study was "dinner." Therefore, listeners needed to inhibit activation of "time" in order to produce the correct response "dinner." Stine and Wingfield found no age differences in the ability to inhibit the most probable competitor ("time") and argued that these findings were inconsistent with the inhibitory deficit hypothesis. However, their findings are entirely consistent with the results of Sommers and Danielson (1999) who argued in favor of the inhibitory deficit hypothesis. Specifically, Sommers and Danielson found age-related deficits in the ability to identify lexically hard words when they were presented in isolation but not when they were presented in a semantically meaningful context. Based on these findings, they argued that context functions to limit the number of potential lexical candidates and therefore reduces the inhibitory demands required for word recognition. In the Stine and Wingfield study, listeners were only required to inhibit a single lexical item, albeit the most probable competitor. Therefore, consistent with Sommers and Danielson, older adults in the Stine and Wingfield study may have been able to inhibit the single most probable competitor because the presence of semantic context minimized inhibitory demands. What remains unclear is whether older adults would be able to inhibit multiple candidates that were plausible within a given context.

19.3.3 *Interactions between auditory and cognitive abilities*

The approach that I have taken thus far is to consider, independently, the importance of peripheral (auditory) and central (cognitive) changes as factors contributing to age-related declines in spoken language processing. This approach has been useful for identifying individual abilities that mediate spoken word recognition, for specifying how these abilities decline with age, and in establishing the effects of such declines on spoken word recognition in older adults. Clearly, however, speech perception is a complex process requiring the integration of sensory, perceptual, and cognitive abilities. In concluding the chapter, I will therefore consider examples of recent studies that have started to address the interaction between peripheral and cognitive abilities in understanding the speech perception difficulties of older adults.

One methodology that has been particularly instructive for revealing the combined effects of peripheral and cognitive impairments is to compare the performance of normal-hearing and hearing-impaired older adults on speech perception tasks (Gordon-Salant & Fitzgibbons, 1997; Sommers, 1997). Typically, the normal-hearing older adults in these studies consist of individuals with clinically normal hearing thresholds for frequencies up to approximately 4 kHz and the hearing-impaired participants are individuals with mild-to-moderate sloping high-frequency losses typical of presbycusis. In one study, Sommers (1997) compared normal-hearing and hearing-impaired older adults' ability to accommodate acoustic-phonetic variability resulting from trial-to-trial changes in the talker producing spoken words. Listeners in this study were presented with identical lists of words but received them either in a single-talker or multiple-talker condition. The results indicated that the change from single to multiple talkers produced significantly greater declines for the hearing-impaired individuals than for age-matched normal-hearing participants. Sommers interpreted these findings as suggesting that reduced sensitivity in the hearing-impaired group not only made the speech less audible, but the impoverished input resulting from the peripheral impairments also undermined the talker normalization process. These results demonstrate a type of "triple jeopardy" facing hearing-impaired older adults; presbycusis reduces audibility but also produces an impoverished acoustic representation of the speech signal. Hearing-impaired older adults must then process these sensory degraded representations using cognitive abilities that may also be compromised with age because of slowing and attenuation of executive functions.

A second approach that has been used to examine the interaction between auditory and cognitive factors in explaining age-related speech perception difficulties is the dual-task paradigm. Pichora-Fuller et al. (1995), for example, had older and younger adults identify sentence-final words from the Speech Perception in Noise (SPIN) test and then measured listeners' memory for those items. An important manipulation in this study was that set size, or the number of words that participants had to maintain in memory, was varied from one to six items. As expected, older adults identified fewer words than younger adults and this age difference increased for lower signal-to-noise ratios. However, even at the poorest signal-to-noise ratio (0 dB) neither age group showed an effect of set size on identification performance; speech perception scores within a group were relatively constant whether listeners had to remember one item or six items. Had the dependent measure in this study been restricted to percent correct identification, the findings would have suggested that reduced audibility produced lower word recognition in older adults but that increasing cognitive demands, by manipulating set size, had little or no effect on the accuracy of spoken word recognition. An examination of the recall data, however, revealed that at less favorable signal-to-noise ratios, recall performance also dropped dramatically as a function of set size for both older and younger adults, with significantly greater declines for older participants. In accounting for these data, Pichora-Fuller et al. suggested that listeners were able to complete the operations necessary for word identification at each level of set size, but maintaining this level of performance at higher set size values came at the expense of completing the operations mediating memory storage. Their findings emphasize that degraded sensory input resulting from peripheral factors, in this case lower signal-to-noise ratios, not only affects sensory processing but can also have substantial consequences for cognitive functions such as recall.

19.4 Conclusions

The goal of this chapter was to provide a critical evaluation of studies that have examined the role of age-related changes in auditory and cognitive abilities in accounting for the speech perception deficits of older adults. One general conclusion that emerges from the review is that presbycusic hearing loss is the single most important factor in explaining age differences in spoken word recognition. Even under listening conditions that maximize cognitive processing demands, audibility accounts for approximately 50% of the variance in older adults' speech perception scores (Humes et al., 1994; van Rooij & Plomp, 1992). This finding has important clinical implications because, of all the factors that contribute to age differences in speech perception, reduced sensitivity is perhaps the most amenable to intervention and rehabilitation through the use of sensory aids such as hearing aids and/or cochlear implants.

A second conclusion that emerges from the studies reviewed here is that a number of cognitive factors also contribute to age-related declines in spoken word recognition. These cognitive changes include both global processing abilities, such as working memory deficits and impaired inhibitory control, as well as more specialized speech processing mechanisms, such as those mediating talker normalization. Although cognitive declines are less amenable to treatment than peripheral impairments, older adults are able to compensate for these losses to some extent if sufficient environmental support is available (e.g., familiar talkers and predictable contexts). Clinically, these findings suggest that in many instances age-related differences in spoken language processing can be attenuated by making relatively small changes in the listening environment.

Finally, it is encouraging to see a trend in more recent studies towards investigations that are focused on examining the interaction between the component operations required for speech perception. Experiments designed to establish how age-related declines in multiple cognitive abilities combine to affect speech perception in older adults are beginning to provide a more comprehensive picture of both normal and impaired speech perception (Pichora-Fuller et al., 1995; Sommers & Danielson, 1999; Tun, 1998). Similarly, investigations aimed at specifying the interaction between hearing loss and basic cognitive functions have demonstrated the importance of studying the mutual dependence of central and peripheral mechanisms in understanding age-related changes in speech perception (Pichora-Fuller et al., 1995; van Rooij & Plomp, 1992). The results of these and future studies will not only add to the growing literature on factors that affect speech perception in older adults but will also contribute to the development of theories and models of spoken word recognition.

NOTE

1 The speech reception threshold is generally defined as the signal-to-noise ratio required for 50% correct recognition of speech stimuli.

REFERENCES

Balota, D. A., Cortese, M. J., Duchek, J. M., Adams, D., Roediger, H. L., McDermott, K. B., & Yerys, B. E. (1999). Veridical and false memories in healthy older adults and in dementia of the Alzheimer's type. *Cognitive Neuropsychology*, 16, 361–84.

Bilger, R. C., Nuetzel, J. M., Rabinowitz, W. M., & Rzeczkowski, C. (1984). Standardization of a test of speech perception in noise. *Journal of Speech & Hearing Research*, 27, 32–48.

Burke, D. M. (1997). Language, aging, and inhibitory deficits: Evaluation of a theory. *Journals of Gerontology Series B-Psychological Sciences & Social Sciences*, 52, P254–P264.

CHABA (Committee on Hearing and Bioacoustics, Working Group on Speech Understanding and Aging) (1988). Speech understanding and aging. *Journal of the Acoustical Society of America*, 83, 859–95.

Cheesman, M. F., Hepburn, D., Armitage, J. C., & Marshall, K. (1995). Comparison of growth of masking functions and speech discrimination abilities in younger and older adults. *Audiology*, 34, 321–33.

Cohen, G. & Faulkner, D. (1983). Word recognition: Age differences in contextual facilitation effect. *British Journal of Psychology*, 74, 239–51.

Corso, J. F. (1971). Sensory processes and age effects in normal adults. *Journal of Gerontology*, 26, 90–105.

Craik, F. I. M. (1986). A functional account of age differences in memory. In F. Klix

& H. Hagendorf (eds.), *Human Memory and Cognitive Capabilities: Mechanisms and Performance* (pp. 409–22). North Holland: Elsevier.

Craik, F. I. M. & McDowd, J. M. (1987). Age differences in recall and recognition. *Journal of Experimental Psychology: Learning, Memory, and Cognition*, 13, 474–9.

Craik, F. I. M. & Salthouse, T. (2000). *The Handbook of Aging and Cognition*. Hillsdale, NJ: Lawrence Erlbaum.

Darwin, C. J. (1975). On the dynamic use of prosody in speech perception. In A. Cohen & S. G. Nooteboom (eds.), *Structure and Process in Speech Perception* (pp. 178–94). Berlin: Springer-Verlag.

Dubno, J. R., Dirks, D. D., & Morgan, D. E. (1984). Effects of age and mild hearing loss on speech recognition in noise. *Journal of the Acoustical Society of America*, 76, 87–96.

Fitzgibbons, P. J. & Gordon-Salant, S. (1994). Age effects on measures of auditory duration discrimination. *Journal of Speech & Hearing Research*, 37, 662–70.

Gates, G. A., Cooper, J., Kannel, W. B., & Miller, N. J. (1990). Hearing in the elderly: The Framingham cohort, 1983–1985. Part I: Basic audiometric test results. *Ear and Hearing*, 11, 247–56.

Glasberg, B. R. & Moore, B. C. (1986). Auditory filter shapes in subjects with unilateral and bilateral cochlear impairments. *Journal of the Acoustical Society of America*, 79, 1020–33.

Glasberg, B. R. & Moore, B. C. (1989). Psychoacoustic abilities of subjects with unilateral and bilateral cochlear hearing impairments and their relationship to the ability to understand speech. *Scandinavian Audiology Supplementum*, 32, 1–25.

Gordon-Salant, S. & Fitzgibbons, P. J. (1993). Temporal factors and speech recognition performance in young and elderly listeners. *Journal of Speech & Hearing Research*, 36, 1276–85.

Gordon-Salant, S. & Fitzgibbons, P. J. (1997). Selected cognitive factors and speech recognition performance among young and elderly listeners. *Journal of Speech, Language, and Hearing Research*, 40, 423–31.

Grosjean, F. (1980). Spoken word recognition processes and the gating paradigm. *Perception and Psychophysics*, 28, 267–83.

Hasher, L. & Zacks, R. T. (1988). Working memory, comprehension, and aging: A review and new view. *The Psychology of Learning and Motivation*, 22, 193–225.

Humes, L. E. (1991). Understanding the speech-understanding problems of the hearing impaired. *Journal of the American Academy of Audiology*, 2, 59–69.

Humes, L. E. (1996). Speech understanding in the elderly. *Journal of the American Academy of Audiology*, 7, 161–7.

Humes, L. E. & Christopherson, L. (1991). Speech identification difficulties of hearing-impaired elderly persons: The contributions of auditory processing deficits. *Journal of Speech & Hearing Research*, 34, 686–93.

Humes, L. E. & Roberts, L. (1990). Speech-recognition difficulties of the hearing-impaired elderly: The contributions of audibility. *Journal of Speech & Hearing Research*, 33, 726–35.

Humes, L. E., Watson, B. U., Christensen, L. A., Cokely, C. G., Halling, D. C., & Lee, L. (1994). Factors associated with individual differences in clinical measures of speech recognition among the elderly. *Journal of Speech & Hearing Research*, 37, 465–74.

Humphrey, D. G. & Kramer, A. F. (1999). Age-related differences in perceptual organization and selective attention: Implications for display segmentation and recall performance. *Experimental Aging Research*, 25, 1–26.

Hutchinson, K. M. (1989). Influence of sentence context on speech perception in young and older adults. *Journal of Gerontology*, 44, 36–44.

Jerger, J., Jerger, S., & Pirozzolo, F. (1991). Correlational analysis of speech audiometric scores, hearing loss, age, and cognitive abilities in the elderly. *Ear and Hearing*, 12, 103–9.

Johnson, K. (1990). The role of perceived speaker identity in F0 normalization of vowels. *Journal of the Acoustical Society of America*, 88, 642–54.

Jusczyk, P. W. & Luce, P. A. (2002). Speech perception and spoken word recognition: Past and present. *Ear and Hearing*, 23, 2–40.

Kausler, D. H. & Puckett, J. M. (1981). Adult age differences in memory for modality attributes. *Experimental Aging Research*, 7, 117–25.

Klein, A. J., Mills, J. H., & Adkins, W. Y. (1990). Upward spread of masking, hearing loss, and speech recognition in young and elderly listeners. *Journal of the Acoustical Society of America*, 87, 1266–71.

Konkle, D. F., Beasley, D. S., & Bess, F. H. (1977). Intelligibility of time-altered speech in relation to chronological aging. *Journal of Speech & Hearing Research*, 20, 108–15.

Lee, L. W. & Humes, L. E. (1992). Factors associated with speech recognition abilities of the hearing-impaired elderly. *American Speech and Hearing Association*, 34, 212.

Lindfield, K. C., Wingfield, A., & Goodglass, H. (2000). The contribution of prosody to spoken word recognition. *Applied Psycholinguistics*, 20, 395–405.

Luce, P. A. & Pisoni, D. B. (1998). Recognizing spoken words: The neighborhood activation model. *Ear and Hearing*, 19, 1–36.

Marshall, L. (1981). Auditory processing in aging listeners. *Journal of Speech and Hearing Disorders*, 46, 226–40.

Marslen-Wilson, W. (1990). Activation, competition, and frequency in lexical access. In G. T. Altamann (ed.), *Cognitive Models of Speech Processing: Psycholinguistic and Computational Perspectives* (pp. 148–72). Cambridge, MA: MIT Press.

May, C. P., Zacks, R. T., Hasher, L., & Multhaup, K. S. (1999). Inhibition in the processing of garden-path sentences. *Psychology and Aging*, 14, 304–13.

McDowd, J. M. (1997). Inhibition in attention and aging. *Journals of Gerontology Series B-Psychological Sciences & Social Sciences*, 52, P265–P273.

McDowd, J. M. & Filion, D. L. (1992). Aging, selective attention, and inhibitory processes: A psychophysiological approach. *Psychology and Aging*, 7, 65–71.

McDowd, J. M. & Oseas-Kreger, D. M. (1991). Aging, inhibitory processes, and negative priming. *Journal of Gerontology*, 46, 340–5.

Mitchell, K. J., Johnson, M. K., Raye, C. L., Mather, M., & D'Esposito, M. (2000). Aging and reflective processes of working memory: Binding and test load deficits. *Psychology and Aging*, 15, 527–41.

Morrell, C. H., Gordon-Salant, S., Pearson, J. D., Brant, L. J., & Fozard, J. L. (1996). Age- and gender-specific reference ranges for hearing level and longitudinal changes in hearing level. *Journal of the Acoustical Society of America*, 100, 1949–67.

Nabelek, A. K. & Robinson, P. K. (1982). Monaural and binaural speech perception in reverberation for listeners of various ages. *Journal of the Acoustical Society of America*, 71, 1242–8.

Naveh-Benjamin, M. & Craik, F. I. (1995). Memory for context and its use in item memory: Comparisons of younger and older persons. *Psychology and Aging*, 10, 284–93.

Nearey, T. M. (1989). Static, dynamic, and relational properties in vowel perception. *Journal of the Acoustical Society of America*, 85, 2088–113.

Nittrouer, S. & Boothroyd, A. (1990). Context effects in phoneme and word recognition by young children and older adults. *Journal of the Acoustical Society of America*, 87, 2705–15.

Norris, D. (1994). Shortlist: A connectionist model of continuous speech recognition. *Cognition*, 52, 189–234.

Norris, D., McQueen, J. M., & Cutler, A. (1995). Competition and segmentation in spoken-word recognition. *Journal of Experimental Psychology: Learning, Memory and Cognition*, 21, 1209–28.

Nygaard, L. C. & Pisoni, D. B. (1998). Talker-specific learning in speech perception. *Perception & Psychophysics*, 60, 355–76.

Nygaard, L. C., Sommers, M. S., & Pisoni, D. B. (1994). Speech perception as a talker-contingent process. *Psychological Science*, 5, 42–6.

Patterson, R. D., Nimmo-Smith, I., Weber, D. L., & Milroy, R. (1982). The deterioration of hearing with age: Frequency selectivity, the critical ratio, the audiogram, and speech threshold. *Journal of the Acoustical Society of America*, 72, 1788–1803.

Pichora-Fuller, M. K., Schneider, B. A., & Daneman, M. (1995). How young and old adults listen to and remember speech in noise. *Journal of the Acoustical Society of America*, 97, 593–608.

Plomp, R. & Mimpen, A. M. (1979). Speech-reception threshold for sentences as a function of age and noise level. *Journal of the Acoustical Society of America*, 66, 1333–42.

Ryan, A., Dallos, P., & McGee, T. (1979). Psychophysical tuning curves and auditory thresholds after hair cell damage in the chinchilla. *Journal of the Acoustical Society of America*, 66, 370–8.

Salthouse, T. A. (1992). Working-memory mediation of adult age differences in integrative reasoning. *Memory & Cognition*, 20, 413–23.

Salthouse, T. A. (1993). Influence of working memory on adult age differences in matrix reasoning. *British Journal of Psychology*, 84, 171–99.

Salthouse, T. A. (1996). The processing-speed theory of adult age differences in cognition. *Psychological Review*, 103, 403–28.

Salthouse, T. A., Babcock, R. L., & Shaw, R. J. (1991). Effects of adult age on structural and operational capacities in working memory. *Psychology and Aging*, 6, 118–27.

Salthouse, T. A. & Meinz, E. J. (1995). Aging, inhibition, working memory, and speed. *Journals of Gerontology series B-Psychological Sciences & Social Sciences*, 50, 297–306.

Salthouse, T. A. & Skovronek, E. (1992). Within-context assessment of age differences in working memory. *Journal of Gerontology*, 47, 110–20.

Schmitt, J. F. (1983). The effects of time compression and time expansion on passage comprehension by elderly listeners. *Journal of Speech & Hearing Research*, 26, 373–7.

Schmitt, J. F. & Carroll, M. R. (1985). Older listeners' ability to comprehend speaker-generated rate alteration of passages. *Journal of Speech & Hearing Research*, 28, 309–12.

Schmitt, J. F. & McCroskey, R. L. (1981). Sentence comprehension in elderly listeners: The factor of rate. *Journal of Gerontology*, 36, 441–5.

Schneider, B. (1997). Psychoacoustics and aging: Implications for everyday listening. *Journal of Speech-Language Pathology and Audiology*, 21, 111–24.

Schneider, B. A., Pichora-Fuller, M. K., Kowalchuk, D., & Lamb, M. (1994). Gap detection and the precedence effect in young and old adults. *Journal of the Acoustical Society of America*, 95, 980–91.

Sommers, M. S. (1996). The structural organization of the mental lexicon and its contribution to age-related changes in spoken word recognition. *Psychology and Aging*, 11, 333–41.

Sommers, M. S. (1997). Stimulus variability and spoken word recognition. II: The effects of age and hearing impairment. *Journal of the Acoustical Society of America*, 101, 2278–88.

Sommers, M. S. & Danielson, S. M. (1999). Inhibitory processes and spoken word recognition in young and older adults: The interaction of lexical competition and semantic context. *Psychology and Aging*, 14, 458–72.

Sommers, M. S. & Humes, L. E. (1993). Auditory filter shapes in normal-hearing, noise-masked normal, and elderly listeners. *Journal of the Acoustical Society of America*, 93, 2903–14.

Sommers, M. S. & Lewis, B. P. (1999). Who really lives next door: Creating false memories with phonological neighbors. *Journal of Memory and Language*, 40, 83–108.

Soto-Faraco, S., Sebastian-Galles, N., & Cutler, A. (2001). Segmental and suprasegmental mismatch in lexical access. *Journal of Memory and Language*, 45, 412–32.

Spieler, D. H., Balota, D. A., & Faust, M. E. (1996). Stroop performance in healthy younger and older adults and in individuals with dementia of the Alzheimer's type. *Journal of Experimental Psychology: Human Perception and Performance*, 22, 461–79.

Stine, E. A. & Wingfield, A. (1987). Process and strategy in memory for speech among younger and older adults. *Psychology and Aging*, 2, 272–9.

Stine, E. A. & Wingfield, A. (1994). Older adults can inhibit high-probability competitors in speech recognition. *Aging and Cognition*, 1, 152–7.

Townsend, T. H. & Bess, F. H. (1980). Effects of age and sensorineural hearing loss on word recognition. *Scandinavian Audiology*, 9, 245–8.

Tun, P. A. (1998). Fast noisy speech: Age differences in processing rapid speech with background noise. *Psychology and Aging*, 13, 424–34.

Tun, P. A. & Wingfield, A. (1999). One voice too many: Adult age differences in language processing with different types of distracting sounds. *Journals of Gerontology series B-Psychological Sciences & Social Sciences*, 54, 317–27.

van Rooij, J. C. & Plomp, R. (1992). Auditive and cognitive factors in speech perception by elderly listeners. III: Additional data and final discussion. *Journal of the Acoustical Society of America*, 91, 1028–33.

Wales, R. & Toner, H. (1975). Intonation and ambiguity. In W. E. Cooper & E. C. T. Walker (eds.), *Sentence Processing: Psycholinguistic Studies Presented to Merrill Garrett* (pp. 185–201). Hillsdale, NJ: Lawrence Erlbaum.

Willott, J. F. (1991). *Aging and the Auditory System: Anatomy, Physiology and Psychophysics*. San Diego: Thompson.

Wingfield, A. (1996). Cognitive factors in auditory performance: Context speed of processing and constraints on memory. *Journal of the American Academy of Audiology*, 7, 175–82.

Wingfield, A. & Ducharme, J. L. (1999). Effects of age and passage difficulty on listening-rate preferences for time-altered speech. *Journals of Gerontology Series B-Psychological Sciences & Social Sciences*, 54, P199–P202.

Wingfield, A. & Klein, J. F. (1971). Syntactic structure and acoustic pattern in speech perception. *Perception & Psychophysics*, 9, 23–5.

Wingfield, A. & Stine, E. A. (1992). Age differences in perceptual processing and memory for spoken language. In R. L. West & J. D. Sinnott (eds.), *Everyday Memory and Aging: Current Research and Methodology* (pp. 101–23). New York: Springer-Verlag.

Wingfield, A., Aberdeen, J. S., & Stine, E. A. (1991). Word onset gating and linguistic context in spoken word recognition by young and elderly adults. *Journal of Gerontology*, 46, P127–P129.

Wingfield, A., Alexander, A. H., & Cavigelli, S. (1994). Does memory constrain utilization of top-down information in spoken word recognition? Evidence from normal aging. *Language and Speech*, 37, 221–35.

Wingfield, A., Lahar, C. J., & Stine, E. A. (1989). Age and decision strategies in running memory for speech: Effects of prosody and linguistic structure. *Journal of Gerontology*, 44, 106–13.

Wingfield, A., Lindfield, K. C., & Goodglass, H. (2000). Effects of age and hearing sensitivity on the use of prosodic information in spoken word recognition. *Journal of Speech, Language and Hearing Research*, 43, 915–25.

Wingfield, A., Lombardi, L., & Sokol, S. (1984). Prosodic features and the intelligibility of accelerated speech: Syntactic versus periodic segmentation. *Journal of Speech, Language and Hearing Research*, 27, 128–34.

Wingfield, A., Poon, L. W., Lombardi, L., & Lowe, D. (1985). Speed of processing in normal aging: Effects of speech rate, linguistic structure, and processing time. *Journal of Gerontology*, 40, 579–85.

Wingfield, A., Tun, P. A., Koh, C. K., & Rosen, M. J. (1999). Regaining lost time: Adult aging and the effect of time restoration on recall of time-compressed speech. *Psychology and Aging*, 14, 380–99.

Yonan, C. A. & Sommers, M. S. (2000). The effects of talker familiarity on spoken word identification in younger and older listeners. *Psychology and Aging*, 15, 88–99.

20 Speech Perception in Deaf Children with Cochlear Implants

DAVID B. PISONI

20.1 Introduction

Each week for the last 12 years I have traveled from my home in Bloomington to Riley Hospital for Children at the IU Medical Center in Indianapolis, a distance of some 60 miles each way, to work on an unusual clinical research project. I am part of a multidisciplinary team of basic and clinical researchers who are studying the development of speech perception and language skills of profoundly deaf children who have received cochlear implants. My colleague, Dr Richard Miyamoto, a pediatric otologist and head and neck surgeon, has been providing profoundly deaf adults and children with cochlear implants since the early 1980s when the first single-channel implants were undergoing clinical trials. Since the approval of cochlear implants by the FDA as a treatment for profound deafness, over 60,000 patients have received cochlear implants at centers all over the world (Clarke, 2003).

A cochlear implant is a surgically implanted electronic device that functions as an auditory prosthesis for a patient with a severe to profound sensorineural hearing loss. It provides electrical stimulation to the surviving spiral ganglion cells of the auditory nerve, bypassing the damaged hair cells of the inner ear to restore hearing in both deaf adults and children. The device provides them with access to sound and sensory information from the auditory modality. The current generation of multichannel cochlear implants consist of an internal multiple electrode array and an external processing unit (see Figure 20.1). The external unit consists of a microphone that picks up sound energy from the environment and a signal processor that codes frequency, amplitude, and time and compresses the signal to match the narrow dynamic range of the ear. Cochlear implants provide temporal and amplitude information. Depending on the manufacturer, several different place coding techniques are used to represent and transmit frequency information in the signal.

For postlingually profoundly deaf adults, a cochlear implant provides a transformed electrical signal to an already fully developed auditory system and intact mature language processing system. These patients have already acquired spoken language under normal listening conditions so we know their central auditory system and brain are functioning normally. In the case of a congenitally deaf

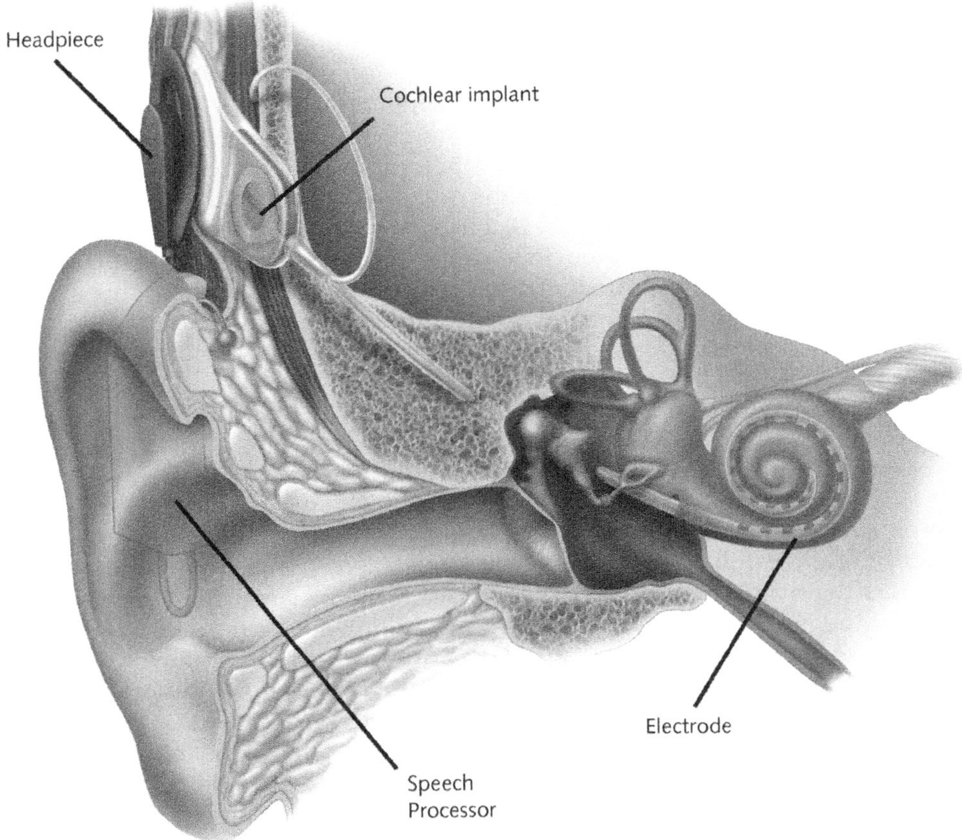

Figure 20.1 Simplified diagram of the internal and external components of a multichannel cochlear implant system. Current systems consist of a microphone that picks up sound from the environment, a speech processor that converts sound into an electrical signal, and a surgically implanted internal electrode array that transmits a pattern of amplitude-modulated pulses to each electrode in a tonotopic fashion reflecting the place-frequency coding of the cochlea. The external speech processor uses a transcutaneous radio-frequency (RF) transmitter to send electrical signals to an internal receiver which is connected directly to the implanted electrode array. *Source*: Courtesy of Cochlear Americas.

child, however, a cochlear implant provides novel electrical stimulation through the auditory sensory modality and an opportunity to perceive speech sounds and develop spoken language for the first time after a period of auditory deprivation. Congenitally deaf children have not been exposed to speech and do not develop spoken language normally. Although the brain and nervous system continue to develop in the absence of normal auditory stimulation, there is now evidence to suggest that some cortical reorganization has already taken place during the period of sensory deprivation before implantation and that several aspects of speech and language skills after implant may develop in an atypical fashion. Both peripheral and central differences in neural function are likely to be responsible for the wide range of variability observed in outcome and benefit following implantation.

This chapter is concerned with congenitally deaf children who have received cochlear implants. These children are the most interesting and theoretically important clinical population to study because they have been deprived of sound and auditory stimulation at a very early point in neural and cognitive development. After implantation their hearing is restored with electrical stimulation that is designed to simulate the response of a healthy cochlea to speech and other auditory signals. Aside from the obvious clinical benefits of cochlear implantation as a method of treating profound prelingual deafness in children, this clinical population also provides a unique opportunity to study the effects of auditory deprivation on the development of speech perception and language processing skills and to assess the effects of restoration of hearing via artificial electrical stimulation of the nervous system. In some sense, one can think of research on this clinical population as the modern-day analog of the so-called "forbidden experiment" in the field of language acquisition, except that in this case after a period of deprivation has occurred, hearing is restored via medical intervention and children receive exposure to sound and stimulation through the auditory modality. Under these conditions, it is possible to study the consequences of a period of auditory deprivation on speech and language development as well as the effects of restoring hearing using artificial electrical stimulation of the auditory nerve.

While cochlear implants work and appear to work well for many profoundly deaf adults and children, they do not always provide benefits to all patients who receive them. Compared to other behavioral data I have seen in the field of speech perception and spoken word recognition over the years, the audiological outcomes and benefits following cochlear implantation were simply enormous and hard to fully understand at first glance. Some deaf adults and children do extremely well with their cochlear implants and display what initially appear to be near-typical speech perception and language skills on a wide range of traditional clinical speech and language tests when tested under quiet listening conditions in the laboratory. In contrast, other adults and children struggle for long periods of time after they receive their cochlear implant and often never achieve comparable levels of speech and language performance or verbal fluency.

The low-performing patients are unable to talk on the telephone and frequently have a great deal of difficulty in noisy environments or situations where more than one talker is speaking at the same time. Almost all of these patients do derive some minimal benefits from their cochlear implants. They are able to recognize some nonspeech sounds and have an increased awareness of where they are in their environment in terms of space and time. But they have a great deal of difficulty perceiving speech and understanding spoken language in a robust fashion under a wide range of challenging listening conditions.

I began to wonder why this pattern of results occurred and I became curious about the underlying factors that were responsible for the enormous differences in audiological outcome. Actually seeing some of these deaf children with my own eyes and talking with them and their parents each week made a big difference in appreciating the magnitude of this problem and the consequences of the wide range of variability in outcome for the children and their families. In addition to the enormous variability observed in the speech and language outcome measures, several other findings have been consistently reported in the clinical literature on cochlear implants in deaf children. An examination of these findings provides some preliminary insights into the possible underlying cognitive and neural basis for the variability in outcome and benefit among deaf children with cochlear implants. A small handful of traditional demographic variables have been found to be associated with outcome and benefit after implantation. When these contributing factors are considered together, it is possible to begin formulating some specific hypotheses about the reasons for the variability in outcome and benefit.

Almost all of the clinical research on cochlear implants has focused on the effects of a small number of demographic variables, such as chronological age, length of deprivation, and age of implantation, using traditional outcome measures based on assessment tools developed by clinical audiologists and speech pathologists. Although rarely discussed explicitly in the literature, these behaviorally-based clinical outcome measures of performance are the final product of a large number of complex sensory, perceptual, cognitive, and linguistic processes that contribute to the observed variation among cochlear implant users. Until recently, little if any research focused on the underlying information processing mechanisms used to perceive and produce spoken language in this clinical population. Our investigations of these fundamental neurocognitive and linguistic processes have provided some new insights into the basis of individual differences in profoundly deaf children with cochlear implants.

In addition to the enormous individual differences and variation in clinical outcome measures, several other findings have been consistently reported in the literature on cochlear implants in children. Age at implantation has been shown to influence all outcome measures of performance. Children who receive an implant at a young age (less than 3 years) do much better on a whole range of outcome measures than children who are implanted at an older age (over 6 years). Length of auditory deprivation or length of deafness is also related to outcome and benefit. Children who have been deaf for shorter periods of time before implantation do much better on a variety of clinical measures than children who have been deaf for longer periods of time. Both findings demonstrate the contribution of sensitive periods in sensory, perceptual, and linguistic development and serve to emphasize the close links that exist between neural development and behavior, especially, hearing, speech and language development (Ball & Hulse, 1998; Konishi, 1985; Konishi & Nottebohm, 1969; Marler & Peters, 1988).

Early sensory and linguistic experience and language processing activities after implantation have also been shown to affect performance on a wide range of outcome measures. Implanted children who are immersed in "Oral-only" communication environments do much better on clinical tests of speech and language development than implanted children who are enrolled in "Total Communication" programs (Kirk, Pisoni, & Miyamoto, 2000). Oral communication approaches emphasize the use of speech and hearing skills and actively encourage children to produce spoken language to achieve optimal benefit from their implants. Total communication approaches employ the simultaneous use of some form of manual-coded English along with speech to help the child acquire language using both sign and spoken language inputs. The differences in performance between groups of children who are placed in oral communication and total communication education settings are observed most prominently in both receptive and expressive language tasks that involve the use of phonological coding and phonological processing skills such as open-set spoken word recognition, language comprehension, and measures of speech production, especially measures of speech intelligibility and expressive language.

Until just recently, clinicians and researchers have been unable to find reliable preimplant predictors of outcome and success with a cochlear implant (see, however, Bergeson & Pisoni, 2004). The absence of preimplant predictors is a theoretically significant finding because it suggests that many complex interactions take place between the newly acquired sensory capabilities of a child after a period of auditory deprivation, properties of the language-learning environment, and various interactions with parents and caregivers that the child is exposed to after receiving a cochlear implant. More importantly, however, the lack of preimplant predictors of outcome and benefit makes it difficult for clinicians to identify those children who are doing poorly with their cochlear implant at a time in development when changes can be made to modify and improve their language processing skills.

Finally, when all of the outcome and demographic measures are considered together, the available evidence strongly suggests that the underlying sensory and perceptual abilities for speech and language "emerge" after implantation. Performance with a cochlear implant improves over time for almost all children. Success with a cochlear implant therefore appears to be due, in part, to perceptual learning and exposure to a language model in the environment. Because outcome and benefit with a cochlear implant cannot be predicted reliably from traditional behavioral measures obtained before implantation, any improvements in performance observed after implantation must be due to sensory and cognitive processes that are linked to maturational changes in neural and cognitive development (see Sharma, Dorman, & Spahr, 2002).

Our current hypothesis about the source of individual differences in outcome following cochlear implantation is that while some proportion of the variance in performance can be attributed directly to peripheral factors related to audibility and the initial sensory encoding of the speech signal into "information-bearing" sensory channels in the auditory nerve, several additional sources of variance also come from more central cognitive and linguistic factors that are related to psychological processes such as perception, attention, learning, memory, and language. How a deaf child uses the initial sensory input from the cochlear implant and the way the environment modulates and shapes language development are fundamental research problems that deal with perceptual encoding, verbal rehearsal, storage and retrieval of phonetic and phonological codes, and the transformation and manipulation of phonological and neural representations of the initial sensory input in a range of language processing tasks.

To investigate individual differences and the sources of variation in outcome, we began by analyzing a set of data from a longitudinal project on cochlear implants in children (see Pisoni et al., 1997, 2000). Our first study was designed to study the "exceptionally" good users of cochlear implants – the so-called "Stars." These are the children who did extremely well with their cochlear implants after only two years of implant use. The "Stars" are able to acquire spoken language quickly and easily and appear to be on a developmental trajectory that parallels normal-hearing children, although delayed a little in time (see Svirsky et al., 2000). The theoretical motivation for studying the exceptionally good children was based on an extensive body of research on "expertise" and "expert systems" theory (Ericsson & Smith, 1991). Many important new insights have come from studying expert chess players, radiologists, and other individuals who have highly developed skills in specific knowledge domains.

20.2 Analysis of the "Stars"

We analyzed scores obtained from several different outcome measures over a period of six years from the time of implantation in order to examine changes in speech perception, word recognition, and comprehension over time (see Pisoni et al., 2000 for complete report). Before these results are presented, however, we describe how the "Stars" and a comparison group of lower-performing children were originally selected.

The criterion used to identify the "Stars" was based on scores obtained from one particular clinical test of speech perception, the Phonetically Balanced Kindergarten (PBK) Words test (Haskins, 1949). This PBK test is an open-set test of spoken word recognition (also see Meyer & Pisoni, 1999) and is very difficult for prelingually deaf children when compared to other closed-set speech perception tests routinely included in the standard clinical assessment battery (Zwolan et al., 1997). Children who do reasonably well on the PBK test display ceiling levels of performance on other closed-set speech perception tests that measure speech pattern discrimination skills.

Open-set tests like the PBK test measure word recognition and lexical selection processes (Luce & Pisoni, 1998). The child is required to search and retrieve the phonological representation of a test word from lexical memory and repeat it to the examiner. Open-set tests of word recognition are extremely difficult for hearing-impaired children with cochlear implants because the task demands require that the listener perceive and encode fine phonetic differences based entirely on information present in the speech signal without the aid of any external context or retrieval cues. A child must identify and then discriminate a unique phonological representation from a large number of lexical equivalence classes in memory (see Luce & Pisoni, 1998). It is important to emphasize here that although recognizing isolated spoken words in an open-set test format may seem like a simple task at first glance, it is very difficult for a hearing-impaired child who has a cochlear implant. Typically-developing children with normal hearing routinely display ceiling levels of performance under comparable testing conditions (Kluck, Pisoni, & Kirk, 1997).

To learn more about why the "Stars" do so well on open-set tests of word recognition, we analyzed outcome data from children who scored exceptionally well on the PBK test two years after implantation. For comparison, we also obtained PBK scores from a group of low-performing children. The PBK score was used as the "criterial variable" to identify and select two groups of children for subsequent analysis using an "extreme groups" design. The "Stars" were children who scored in the upper 20% of all children tested on the PBK test two years post-implant. The "Low-Performers" consisted of children who scored in the bottom 20% on the PBK test two years post-implant. After the children were sorted into two groups, we examined their performance on a range of other clinical outcome measures that were available as part of a large-scale longitudinal study at Indiana University. The speech perception data we discuss here include measures of speech feature discrimination, spoken word recognition, and comprehension.

Scores for the two groups were obtained from a longitudinal database containing a variety of demographic and outcome measures from 160 deaf children (see Pisoni et al., 2000). Other measures of vocabulary knowledge, receptive and expressive language and speech intelligibility were also obtained (see Pisoni et al., 1997, 2000 for more details). All of the children in both groups were prelingually deafened. Each child received a cochlear implant because he or she was profoundly deaf and was unable to derive any benefit from conventional hearing aids. All children had used their cochlear implant for two years at the time when these analyses were completed. Using this selection procedure, the two groups turned out to be roughly similar in age at onset of deafness and length of implant use.

20.3 Speech Feature Discrimination

Measures of speech feature discrimination for both consonants and vowels were obtained for both groups of children using the Minimal Pairs Test (Robbins et al., 1988). This clinical test uses a two-alternative forced-choice picture pointing task. The child hears a single word spoken in isolation on each trial using live voice presentation by an examiner and is required to select one of the pictures that correspond to the test item. Examples of two test plates are shown in Figure 20.2.

A summary of the consonant discrimination results for both groups of subjects is shown in Figure 20.3. Percent correct discrimination is displayed separately for manner, voicing, and place of articulation as a function of implant use in years. Chance performance on this task is 50% correct as shown by a dotted horizontal line. A second dotted horizontal line is also displayed in this figure at 70% correct corresponding to scores that were significantly above chance using the binominal distribution.

Examination of the results for the Minimal Pairs Test obtained over a period of six years of implant use reveals several findings. First, performance of the "Stars" was consistently better than the control group for every comparison across all three consonant features. Second, discrimination performance improved over time with implant use for both groups. The increases were primarily due to improvements in discrimination of manner and voicing by the "Stars." At no interval did the mean scores of the comparison group ever exceed chance performance on discrimination of voicing and place features. Although increases in minimal pair discrimination performance were observed over time for the controls, their scores never reached the levels observed with the "Stars," even for the manner contrasts that eventually exceeded chance performance in Years 4, 5, and 6.

The results of the Minimal Pairs Test demonstrate that both groups of children have difficulty perceiving, encoding, and discriminating fine phonetic details of isolated spoken words in a simple two-alternative closed-set testing format.

Figure 20.2 Examples of two test plates used to measure speech feature discrimination on the Minimal Pairs Test.
Source: A. M. Robbins, J. J. Renshaw, R. T. Miyamoto, M. J. Osberger, & M. L. Pope (1988). *Minimal Pairs Test*. Indianapolis, IN: Indiana University School of Medicine.

Although the "Stars" discriminated differences in manner of articulation after one year of implant use and showed consistent improvements in performance over time for both manner and voicing contrasts, they still had a great deal of difficulty reliably discriminating differences in place of articulation, even after five years of experience with their implants. In contrast, the "Low-Performing" children were just barely able to discriminate differences in manner of articulation above chance after four years of implant use. The lower-performing children also had a great deal of difficulty discriminating differences in voicing and place of articulation even after five or six years of use.

The pattern of speech feature discrimination results shown in Figure 20.3 suggests that both groups of children encode spoken words using "coarse" phonological representations. Their representations appear to be "underspecified" and contain much less fine-grained acoustic-phonetic detail than the lexical representations that normal-hearing children typically use. The "Stars" were able to discriminate manner and to some extent voicing much sooner after implantation than the "Low-Performers." In addition, the "Stars" also displayed consistent improvements in speech feature discrimination over time after implantation.

The speech feature discrimination data reveal several differences in the encoding of sensory information and the phonological representations that are used for subsequent word learning and lexical development. It is likely that if a child cannot reliably discriminate small phonetic differences between pairs of spoken words that are phonetically similar under these relatively easy forced-choice test

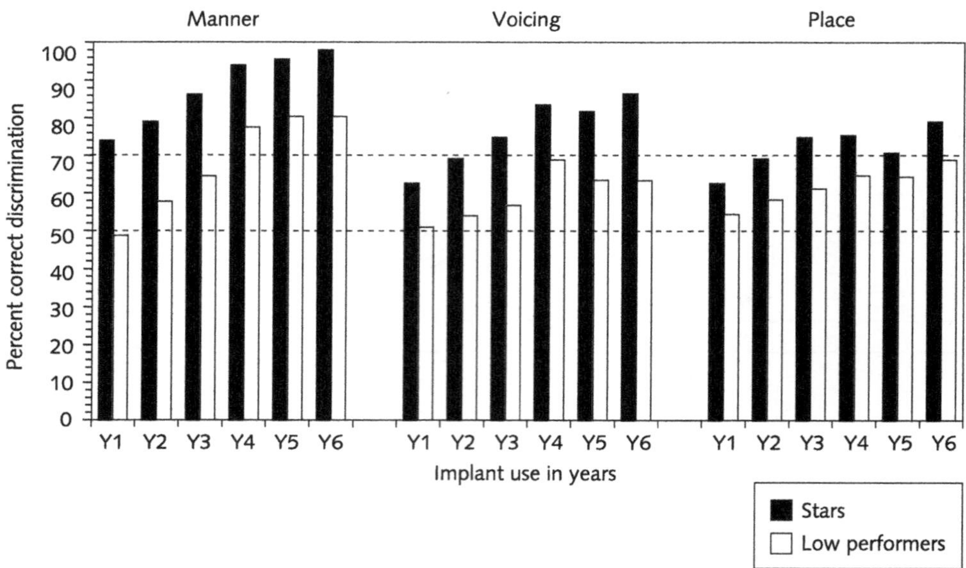

Figure 20.3 Percent correct discrimination on the Minimal Pairs Test (MPT) for manner, voicing, and place as a function of implant use.
Source: D. B. Pisoni, M. Cleary, A. E. Geers, & E. A. Tobey (2000). Individual differences in effectiveness of cochlear implants in prelingually deaf children: Some new process measures of performance. *Volta Review*, 101, 111–64. Reprinted with permission from the Alexander Graham Bell Association for the Deaf and Hard of Hearing. www.agbell.org

conditions, they will also have difficulty recognizing words in isolation with no context or retrieving the phonological representations of highly familiar words from memory for use in simple speech production tasks that require immediate repetition. We would also expect them to display a great deal of difficulty in recognizing and imitating nonwords.

20.4 Spoken Word Recognition

Two additional word recognition tests were used to measure open-set word recognition. Both tests use words that are familiar to preschool age children. The Lexical Neighborhood Test (LNT) contains monosyllabic words; the Multisyllabic Lexical Neighborhood Test (MLNT) contains multisyllabic words (Kirk, Pisoni, & Osberger, 1995). Both tests contain two different sets of words that are used to measure lexical discrimination and provide detailed information about how the lexical selection process is carried out. Half of the items in each test are lexically "easy" words and half are lexically "hard" words.

The differences in performance on the easy and hard words provide an index of how well a child is able to make fine phonetic discriminations among acoustically similar words. Differences in performance between the LNT and the MLNT provide a measure of the extent to which the child is able to make use of word length cues to recognize and access words from the lexicon. The test words are

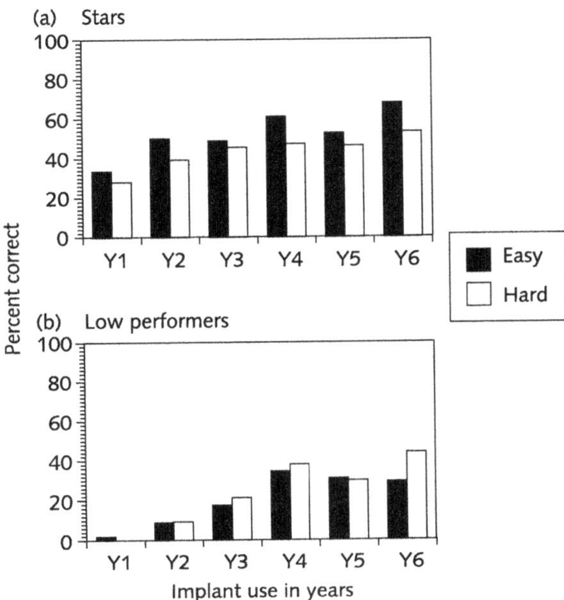

Figure 20.4 Percent correct word recognition performance for the Lexical Neighborhood Test (LNT) monosyllabic word lists as a function of implant use and lexical difficulty. *Source*: D. B. Pisoni, M. Cleary, A. E. Geers, & E. A. Tobey (2000). Individual differences in effectiveness of cochlear implants in prelingually deaf children: Some new process measures of performance. *Volta Review*, 101, 111–64. Reprinted with permission from the Alexander Graham Bell Association for the Deaf and Hard of Hearing. www.agbell.org

presented in isolation one at a time by the examiner using a live-voice auditory-only format. The child is required to imitate and immediately repeat a test word after it is presented by the examiner.

Figures 20.4 and 20.5 show percent correct word recognition obtained on the LNT and the MLNT for both groups of children as a function of implant use. Several consistent differences in performance are shown in these two figures. The pattern of these differences provides some insights into the task demands and processing operations used in open-set word recognition tests. First, the "Stars" consistently demonstrate higher levels of word recognition performance on both the LNT and the MLNT than the "Low-Performers." These differences are present across all six years but they are most prominent during the first three years after implantation. Word recognition scores for the "Low-Performers" on both the LNT and the MLNT are very low and close to the floor compared to the performance observed for the "Stars" who are doing moderately well on this test although they never reached ceiling levels of performance on either test even after six years of implant use. Normal-hearing children typically display very high levels of performance on both of these tests by age 4 (Kluck et al., 1997).

The "Stars" also displayed a word length effect at each testing interval. Recognition was always better for long words on the MLNT than for short words on the LNT. This pattern is not present for the "Low-Performers" who were unable to

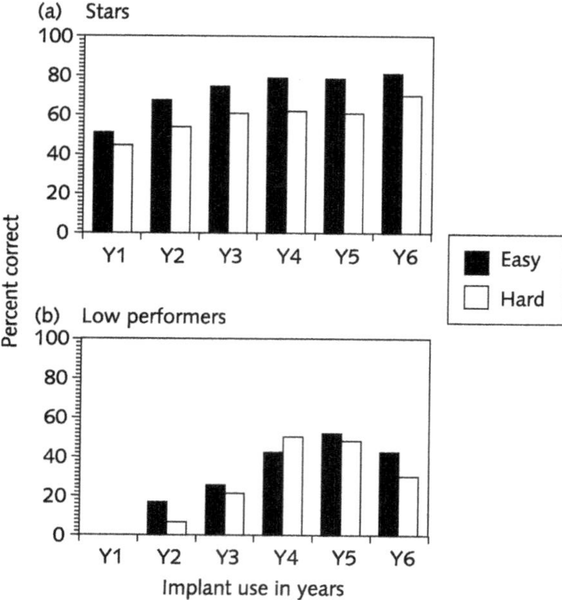

Figure 20.5 Percent correct word recognition performance for the Multisyllabic Lexical Neighborhood Test (MLNT) word lists as a function of implant use and lexical difficulty. *Source*: D. B. Pisoni, M. Cleary, A. E. Geers, & E. A. Tobey (2000). Individual differences in effectiveness of cochlear implants in prelingually deaf children: Some new process measures of performance. *Volta Review*, 101, 111–64. Reprinted with permission from the Alexander Graham Bell Association for the Deaf and Hard of Hearing. www.agbell.org

do this open-set task at all during the first three years. The existence of a word length effect for the "Stars" suggests that these children are recognizing spoken words "relationally" in the context of other words they have in their lexicon (Luce & Pisoni, 1998). If these children were just recognizing words in isolation, either holistically as global temporal patterns or segment-by-segment without reference to the representations of words they already knew, we would expect performance to be worse for longer words than shorter words because longer words contain more stimulus information. But this is not what we found.

The pattern of results for the "Stars" is exactly the opposite of this prediction and parallels earlier results obtained with normal-hearing adults and normal-hearing typically-developing children (Kirk et al., 1995; Kluck et al., 1997; Luce & Pisoni, 1998). Longer words are easier to recognize than shorter words because they are phonologically more distinctive and discriminable and therefore less confusable with other phonetically similar words. The present findings suggest that the "Stars" are recognizing words based on their knowledge of other words in the language using processing strategies that are similar to those used by normal-hearing listeners.

Additional support for role of the lexicon and the use of phonological knowledge in open-set word recognition is provided by another finding. The "Stars" also displayed a consistent effect of "lexical discrimination." As shown in Figures 20.4 and 20.5, the "Stars" recognized lexically "easy" words better than lexically "hard" words. The difference in performance between "easy" words and "hard" words is present for both the LNT and the MLNT vocabularies although it is larger and more consistent over time for the MLNT test. Once again, the lower-performing children did not display sensitivity to lexical competition among the test words.

The differences in performance observed between these two groups of children on both open-set word recognition tests were not at all surprising because the two extreme groups were initially created based on their PBK scores, another open-set word recognition test. However, the overall pattern of the results shown in Figures 20.4 and 20.5 is theoretically important because the findings demonstrate that the processes used in recognizing isolated spoken words are not specific to the particular test items on the PBK test or the experimental procedures used in open-set tests of word recognition. The differences between the two groups of children generalized to two other open-set word recognition tests that use completely different test words.

The pattern of results strongly suggests a common underlying set of linguistic processes that is employed in recognizing and imitating spoken words presented in isolation. Understanding the cognitive and linguistic processing mechanisms that are used in open-set word recognition tasks may provide new insights into the underlying basis of the individual differences observed in outcome measures in children with cochlear implants. It is probably no accident that the PBK test, which is considered the "gold standard" of performance, has had some important diagnostic utility in identifying the exceptionally good users of cochlear implants over the years (see Kirk et al., 1995; Meyer & Pisoni, 1999). The PBK test measures fundamental language processing skills that generalize well beyond the specific word recognition task used in open-set tests. The important conceptual issue is to explain why this happens and identify the underlying cognitive and linguistic processing mechanisms used in open-set word recognition tasks as well as other language processing tasks. We will return to this issue again below.

20.5 Comprehension of Common Phrases

Language comprehension performance was also measured in these two groups of children using the Common Phrases Test (Osberger et al., 1991), an open-set test with three presentation formats: auditory-only (CPA), visual-only (CPV), and combined auditory plus visual (CPAV). Children are asked questions or given directions to follow under these three conditions. The results of the Common Phrases Test are shown in Figure 20.6 for both groups of subjects as a function of implant use for the three different presentation formats.

Figure 20.6 shows that the "Stars" performed consistently better than the "Low-Performers" in all three presentation conditions and across all six years of implant use although performance begins to approach ceiling levels for both groups in the CPAV condition after five years of implant use. CPAV conditions were always better than either the CPA or CPV conditions. This pattern was observed for both groups of subjects. In addition, both groups displayed improvements in performance over time in all three presentation conditions. Not surprisingly, the largest

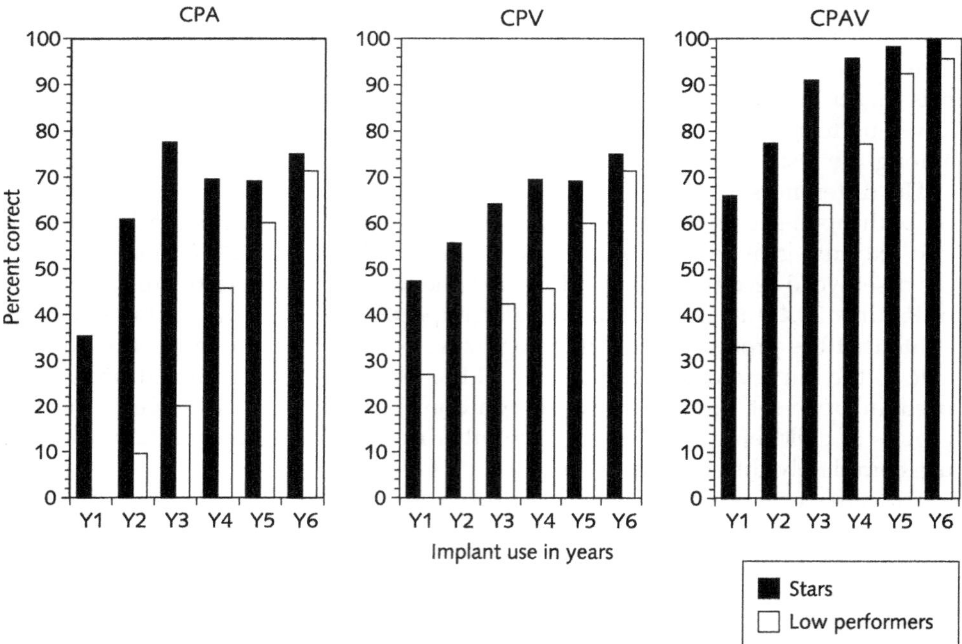

Figure 20.6 Percent correct performance on the Common Phrases Test for auditory-only (CPA), visual-only (CPV) and combined auditory plus visual (CPAV) presentation modes as a function of implant use.
Source: D. B. Pisoni, M. Cleary, A. E. Geers, & E. A. Tobey (2000). Individual differences in effectiveness of cochlear implants in prelingually deaf children: Some new process measures of performance. *Volta Review*, 101, 111–64. Reprinted with permission from the Alexander Graham Bell Association for the Deaf and Hard of Hearing. www.agbell.org

differences in performance between the two groups occurred in the CPA condition. Even after three years of implant use, the lower-performing children were barely able to perform the common phrases task above 25% correct when they had to rely entirely on auditory cues in the speech signal to carry out the task.

20.6 Correlations Among Measures of Speech Perception

These descriptive results show that the exceptionally good performers, the "Stars," do well on measures of speech feature discrimination, spoken word recognition, and language comprehension. They also do well on other tests of receptive and expressive language, vocabulary knowledge, and speech intelligibility (see Pisoni et al., 1997, 2000). This pattern of findings suggests that a common source of variance may underlie the exceptionally good performance of the "Stars" on a range of different speech and language outcome measures. Until our investigation of the exceptionally good children, no one had studied individual differences in outcome in this clinical population or the underlying perceptual, cognitive, and linguistic processes. The analyses of speech feature discrimination, spoken word recognition, and spoken language comprehension scores summarized here demonstrate that a child who displays exceptionally good performance on the PBK test also shows good scores on other speech perception tests. Analyses of the other outcome measures revealed a similar pattern of results.

To assess the relations between these different tests, we carried out a series of simple correlations on the speech perception scores and the other outcome measures. We were interested in the following questions: Does a child who performs exceptionally well on the PBK test also perform exceptionally well on other tests of speech feature discrimination, word recognition, and comprehension? Is the good performance of the "Stars" restricted only to open-set word recognition tests or is it possible to identify a common underlying variable or process that can account for the relations observed among the other outcome measures?

Simple bivariate correlations were carried out separately for the "Stars" and "Low-Performers" using the test scores obtained after one year of implant use (see Pisoni et al., 1997, 2000 for the full report). The results of the correlational analyses on the outcome measures revealed a strong and consistent pattern of intercorrelations among all of the test scores for the "Stars" (see Pisoni et al., 1997, 2000). This pattern was observed for all three of the speech perception tests described here as well as vocabulary knowledge, receptive and expressive language, and speech intelligibility. The outcome measures that correlated the most strongly and most consistently with the other tests were the open-set word recognition scores on the LNT and MLNT tests.

The finding that performance on open-set word recognition was strongly correlated with all of the other outcome measures was of special interest to us. The pattern of intercorrelations among all these dependent measures strongly suggests a common underlying source of variance. The extremely high correlations with the open-set word recognition scores on the LNT suggest that the common source of variance may be related to the processing of spoken words, specifically to the encoding, storage, retrieval, and manipulation of the phonological representations of spoken words. The fundamental cognitive and linguistic processes used to recognize (decompose) and repeat (reassemble) spoken words in open-set tests like the PBK or LNT are also used in other language processing tasks, such as comprehension and speech production, which draw on the same sources of information about spoken words in the lexicon.

The results of the correlational analyses suggest several hypotheses about the source of the differences in performance between the "Stars" and the "Low-Performers." Some proportion of the variation in outcome appears to be related to how the initial sensory information is processed and used in clinical tests that assess speech feature discrimination, word recognition, language comprehension, and speech production. Unfortunately, the data available on these children were based on traditional audiological outcome measures that were collected as part of their annual clinical assessments. All of the scores on these behavioral tests are "endpoint measures" of performance that reflect the final product of perceptual and linguistic analysis. Process measures of performance that assess what a child does with the sensory information provided by his or her cochlear implant were not part of the standard research protocol used in our longitudinal study so it was impossible to examine differences in processing capacity and speed. It is very likely that fundamental differences in both information processing capacity and speed are responsible for the individual differences observed between these two groups of children.

For a variety of theoretical reasons, we refocused our research efforts to study "working memory." One reason is that working memory plays a central role in human information processing because it serves as the primary interface between sensory input and stored knowledge in long-term memory. Another is that working memory has also been shown to be a major source of individual differences in processing capacity across a wide range of domains from perception to memory to language (Ackerman, Kyllonen, & Roberts, 1999; Baddeley, Gathercole, & Papagno, 1998; Carpenter, Miyake, & Just, 1994; Gupta & MacWhinney, 1997).

20.7 Measures of Working Memory

To obtain some new measures of working memory capacity from a large group of deaf children following cochlear implantation, we began collaborating with Dr Ann Geers and her colleagues at Central Institute for the Deaf in St Louis where there was a large-scale clinical research project underway. They collected a wide range of different outcome measures of speech, language, and reading skills from 8- and 9-year-old children who had used their cochlear implants for at least three and a half years. Thus, in this study, chronological age and length of implant use were controlled.

Using the test lists and procedures from the WISC-III (Wechsler, 1991), forward and backward auditory digit spans were obtained from 176 deaf children who were tested in separate groups during the summers of 1997, 1998, 1999, and 2000. Forward and backward digit spans were also collected from an additional group of 45 age-matched normal-hearing 8- and 9-year-old children who were tested in Bloomington, Indiana, and served as a comparison group (see Pisoni & Cleary, 2003).

The WISC-III memory span task requires the child to repeat a list of digits that is spoken live-voice by an experimenter at a rate of approximately one digit per second (WISC-III Manual, Wechsler, 1991). In the "digits-forward" condition, the child is required simply to repeat the list as heard. In the "digits-backward" condition, the child is told to "say the list backward." In both subtests, the lists begin with two items and increase in length until a child gets two lists incorrect at a given length, at which time testing stops. Points are awarded for each list correctly repeated with no partial credit.

A summary of the digit span results for all five groups of children is shown in Figure 20.7. Forward and backward digit spans are shown separately for each group. The children with cochlear implants are shown on the left by year of testing; the normal-hearing children are shown on the right. Each child's digit span in points was calculated by summing the number of lists correctly recalled at each list length.

The results shown in Figure 20.7 reveal a systematic pattern of the forward and backward digit spans for the deaf children with cochlear implants. All four groups are quite similar to each other. In each group, the forward digit span is longer

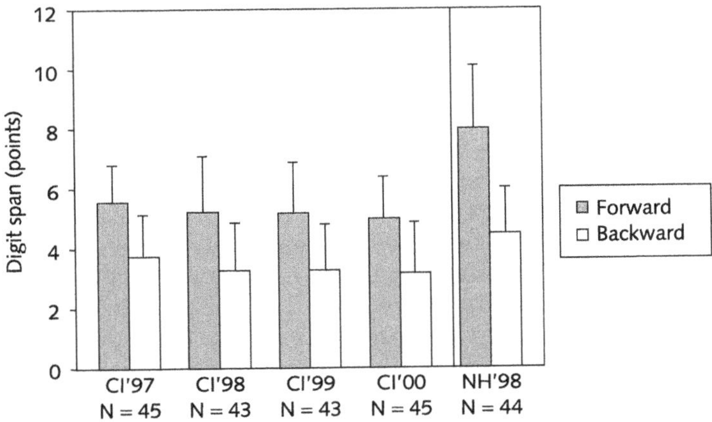

Figure 20.7 WISC digit spans scored by points for the four groups of 8- and 9-year-old children with cochlear implants and for a comparison group of 8- and 9-year-old. normal-hearing children. Error bars indicate one standard deviation from the mean
Source: D. B. Pisoni & M. Cleary (2003). Measures of working memory span and verbal rehearsal speed in deaf children after cochlear implantation. *Ear and Hearing*, 24, 106S–120S. Reprinted by permission of Lippincott Williams & Wilkins.

than the backward digit span. The pattern is quite stable over the four years of testing despite the fact that these scores were obtained from independent groups of children. The difference in span length between forward and backward report was highly significant for the entire group of 176 deaf children and for each group taken separately ($p < .001$).

The forward and backward digit spans obtained from the 44 age-matched normal-hearing children are shown in the right-hand panel of Figure 20.7. These results show that the digit spans for the normal-hearing children differ in several ways from the spans obtained from the children with cochlear implants. First, both digit spans are longer than the spans obtained from the children with cochlear implants. Second, the forward digit span for the normal-hearing children is much longer than the forward digit spans obtained from the children with cochlear implants. This latter finding is particularly important because it demonstrates atypical development of the deaf children's short-term memory capacity and suggests several possible differences in the underlying processing mechanisms that are used to encode and maintain sequences of spoken digits in immediate memory.

Numerous studies have suggested that forward digit spans reflect coding strategies related to phonological processing and verbal rehearsal mechanisms used to maintain information in short-term memory for brief periods of time before retrieval and output response. Differences in backward digit spans, on the other hand, are thought to reflect the contribution of controlled attention and operation of higher-level "executive" processes that are used to transform and manipulate verbal information for later processing operations (Rosen & Engle, 1997; Rudel & Denckla, 1974).

The digit spans for the normal-hearing children shown in Figure 20.7 are age-appropriate and fall within the published norms for the WISC-III. However, the forward digit spans obtained from the children with cochlear implants are atypical and suggest possible differences in encoding and/or verbal rehearsal processes used in immediate memory. In particular, the forward digit spans reflect differences in processing capacity of immediate memory between the two groups of children. These differences may cascade and affect other information processing tasks that make use of working memory and verbal rehearsal processes. Because all of the clinical tests that are routinely used to assess speech and language outcomes rely heavily on component processes of working memory and verbal rehearsal, it seems reasonable to assume that these tasks will also reflect variability due to basic differences in immediate memory and processing capacity.

20.8 Correlations with Digit Spans

In order to learn more about the differences in auditory digit span and the limitations in processing capacity, we examined the correlations between forward and backward digit spans and several speech and language outcome measures also obtained from these children at CID (see Pisoni & Cleary, 2003). Of the various demographic measures available, the only one that correlated strongly and significantly with digit span was the child's communication mode. This measure is used to quantify the nature of the child's early sensory and linguistic experience after receiving a cochlear implant in terms of the degree of emphasis on auditory-oral language skills by teachers and therapists in the educational environment.

We found that forward digit span was positively correlated with communication mode ($r = +.34$, $p < .001$). Children who were in language-learning environments that primarily emphasized oral skills displayed longer forward digit spans than children who were in total communication environments. However, the correlation between digit span and communication mode was highly selective in nature because it was restricted only to the forward digit span scores; the backward digit spans were not correlated with communication mode or any of the other demographic variables.

In order to examine the effects of early experience in more detail, a median split was carried out on the communication mode scores to create two subgroups. Figure 20.8 shows the digit spans plotted separately for the oral and total communication children for each of the four years of testing at CID. The oral group consistently displayed longer forward digit spans than the total communication group. While the differences in forward digit span between oral and total communication children were highly significant, the differences in backward digit span were not. This pattern suggests that the effects of early sensory and linguistic experience on immediate memory is related to coding and verbal rehearsal processes that affect only the forward digit span conditions in this task.

The difference in forward digit span between oral and total communication children is present for each of the four groups. These differences could be due to several factors such as more efficient encoding of the initial stimulus patterns into stable phonological representations in working memory, speed and efficiency

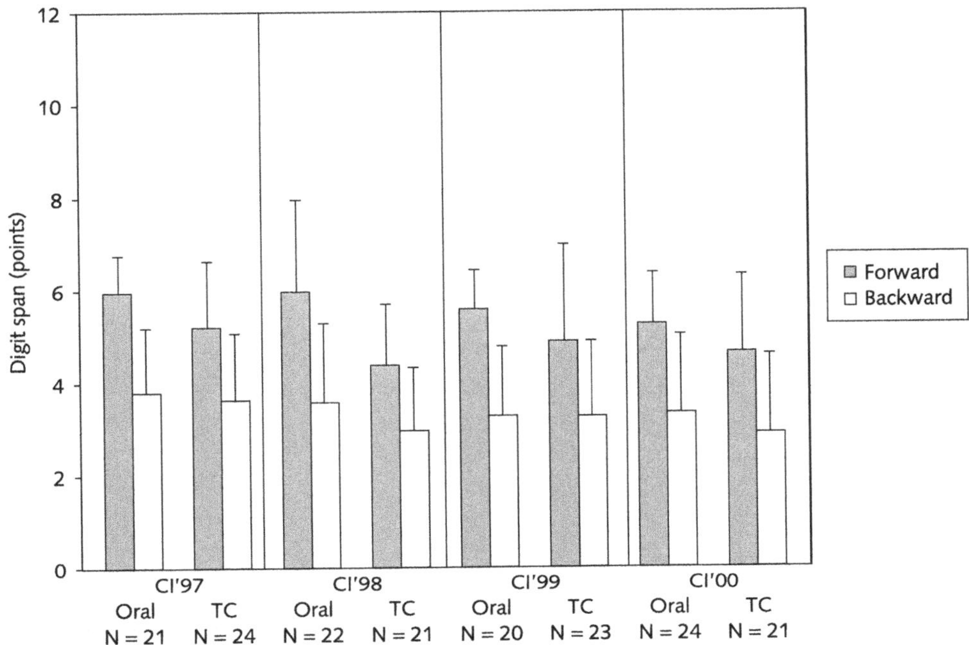

Figure 20.8 WISC digit spans scored by points for the four groups of 8- and 9-year-old children with cochlear implants, separated by communication mode. For each year, scores for the oral group are shown to the left of those for the total communication group. Error bars indicate one standard deviation from the mean. *Source*: D. B. Pisoni & M. Cleary (2003). Measures of working memory span and verbal rehearsal speed in deaf children after cochlear implantation. *Ear and Hearing*, 24, 106S–120S. Reprinted by permission of Lippincott Williams & Wilkins.

of the verbal rehearsal processes used to maintain phonological information in working memory, or possibly even speed of retrieval and scanning of information in working memory after recognition has taken place. All three factors could influence measures of processing capacity and any one of these could affect the number of digits correctly recalled from immediate memory in this task.

20.9 Digit Spans and Word Recognition

Although these results indicate that early experience in an environment that emphasizes oral language skills is associated with longer forward digit spans and increased information processing capacities of working memory, without additional converging measures of performance, it is difficult to specify precisely what elementary processes and information processing mechanisms are actually affected by early experience and which ones are responsible for the increases in forward digit spans observed in these particular children. Recent studies of normal-hearing children have demonstrated close "links" between working memory and

Table 20.1 Correlations between WISC digit span and three measures of spoken word recognition (from Pisoni & Cleary, 2003)

	Simple bivariate correlations		*Partial correlations*[a]	
	WISC forward digit span	*WISC backward digit span*	*WISC forward digit span*	*WISC backward digit span*
Closed set word recognition (WIPI)	.42***	.28***	.25**	.12
Open set word recognition (LNT-E)	.41***	.20**	.24**	.07
Open set word recognition in sentences (BKB)	.44***	.24**	.27***	.09

*** $p < 0.001$, ** $p < 0.01$

[a] Statistically controlling for: communication mode score, age at onset of deafness, duration of deafness, duration of cochlear implant use, number of active electrodes, VIDSPAC total segments correct (speech feature perception measure), age

learning to recognize and understand new words (Gathercole et al., 1997; Gupta & MacWhinney, 1997). Other research has found that vocabulary development and several important milestones in speech and language acquisition are also associated with differences in measures of working memory, specifically, measures of digit span, which can be used as estimates of processing capacity of immediate memory (Gathercole & Baddeley, 1990).

To determine if immediate memory capacity is related to spoken word recognition, we correlated the WISC forward and backward digit span scores with three different measures of word recognition. A summary of the correlations between digit span and word recognition scores based on these 176 children is shown in Table 20.1.

The WIPI test (Word Intelligibility by Picture Identification Test) is a closed-set test of word recognition in which the child selects a word from among six alternative pictures (Ross & Lerman, 1979). As described earlier, the LNT is an open-set test of word recognition and lexical discrimination that requires the child to imitate and reproduce an isolated word (Kirk et al., 1995). Finally, the BKB is an open-set word recognition test in which key words are presented in sentences (Bench, Kowal, & Bamford, 1979).

Table 20.1 displays two sets of correlations. The left-hand portion of the table shows the simple bivariate correlations of the forward and backward digit spans with the three measures of word recognition. The correlations for both the forward and backward spans reveal that children who had longer WISC digit spans also had higher word recognition scores on all three word recognition tests. This finding is present for both forward and backward digit spans. The correlations are all positive and reached statistical significance.

The right-hand portion of Table 20.1 shows a summary of the partial correlations among these same measures after we statistically controlled for differences due to communication mode, age at onset of deafness, duration of deafness, duration of device use, number of active electrodes, speech feature perception, and chronological age. When these "contributing variables" were removed from the correlational analyses, the partial correlations between digit span and word recognition scores became smaller in magnitude overall. However, the correlations of the forward digit span with the three word recognition scores were still positive and statistically significant while the correlations of the backward digit spans were weaker and no longer significant.

These results demonstrate that children who have longer forward WISC digit spans also show higher word recognition scores; this relationship was observed for all three word recognition tests even after the other sources of variance were removed. The present results suggest a common source of variance that is shared between forward digit span and measures of spoken word recognition that is independent of other mediating factors that have been found to contribute to the variation in these outcome measures.

20.10 Digit Spans and Speaking Rate

While the correlations of the digit span scores with communication mode and spoken word recognition suggest fundamental differences in encoding and rehearsal speed which are influenced by the nature of the early experience a child receives, these measures of immediate memory span and estimates of information processing capacity are not sufficient on their own to identify the underlying information processing mechanism responsible for the individual differences. Additional converging measures are needed to pinpoint the locus of these differences more precisely. Fortunately, an additional set of behavioral measures was obtained from these children for a different purpose and made available to us for several new analyses.

As part of the research project at CID, speech production samples were obtained from each child to assess speech intelligibility and measure changes in articulation and phonological development following implantation (see Tobey et al., 2000). The speech samples consisted of three sets of meaningful English sentences that were elicited using the stimulus materials and experimental procedures developed by McGarr (1983). All of the utterances produced by the children were originally recorded and stored digitally for playback to groups of naïve adult listeners who were asked to transcribe what they thought the children had said. In addition to the speech intelligibility scores, we measured the durations of the individual sentences in each set and used these to estimate each child's speaking rate.

The sentence durations provide a quantitative measure of a child's articulation speed which we knew from a large body of earlier research in the memory literature was closely related to speed of subvocal verbal rehearsal (Cowan et al., 1998). Numerous studies over the past 25 years have demonstrated strong relations between speaking rate and memory span for digits and words (for example

Baddeley, Thompson, & Buchanan, 1975). The results of these studies suggest that measures of an individual's speaking rate reflect articulation speed and this measure can be used as an index of rate of covert verbal rehearsal for phonological information in working memory. Individuals who speak more quickly have been found to have longer memory spans than individuals who speak more slowly.

The forward digit span scores for the 176 children are shown in Figure 20.9 along with estimates of their speaking rates obtained from measurements of their

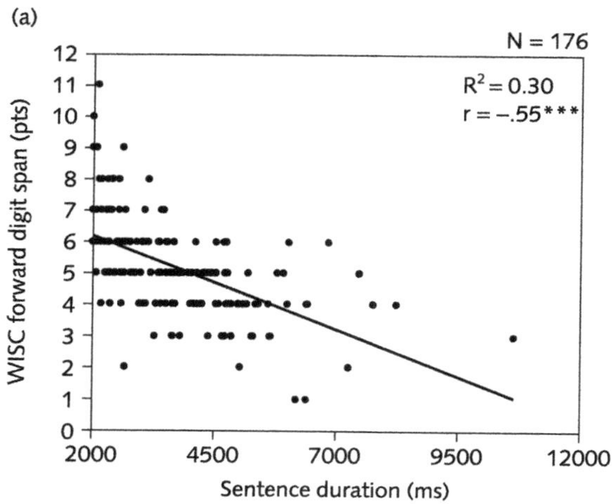

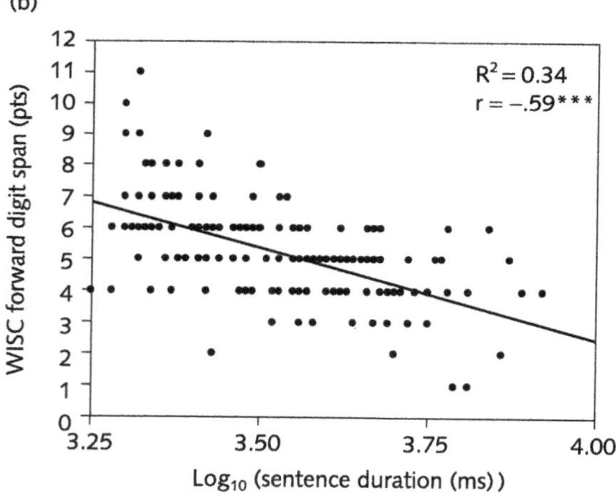

Figure 20.9 Scatterplots illustrating the relationship between average sentence duration for the seven-syllable McGarr Sentences (abscissa) and WISC forward digit span scored by points (ordinate). Each data-point represents an individual child. Non-transformed duration scores are shown in (a), log-transformed duration scores in (b). R-squared values indicate percent of variance accounted for by the linear relation.

Source: D. B. Pisoni & M. Cleary (2003). Measures of working memory span and verbal rehearsal speed in deaf children after cochlear implantation. *Ear and Hearing*, 24, 106S–120S. Reprinted by permission of Lippincott Williams & Wilkins.

productions of meaningful English sentences. The pattern of results in both figures is very clear; children who produce sentences with longer durations speak more slowly and, in turn, have shorter forward digit spans. The correlations between forward digit span and both measures of sentence duration were strongly negative and highly significant ($r = -.63$ and $r = -.70$; $p < .001$, respectively). It is important to emphasize once again, that the relations observed here between digit span and speaking rate were selective in nature and were found only for the forward digit spans. There was no correlation at all between backward digit span scores and sentence duration in any of our analyses.

The dissociation between forward and backward digit spans and the correlation of the forward spans with measures of speaking rate suggests that verbal rehearsal speed may be the primary underlying factor that is responsible for the variability and individual differences observed in deaf children with cochlear implants on a range of behavioral speech and language tasks. The common feature of each of these outcome measures is that they all make use of the storage and processing mechanisms of verbal working memory.

20.11 Speaking Rate and Word Recognition

To determine if verbal rehearsal speed is also related to individual differences in word recognition performance, we examined the correlations between sentence duration and the three different measures of spoken word recognition described earlier. All of these correlations are also positive and suggest once again that a common processing mechanism, verbal rehearsal speed, may be the factor that underlies the variability and individual differences observed in these word recognition tasks.

Our analysis of the digit span scores from these deaf children uncovered two important correlations linking forward digit span to both word recognition performance and speaking rate. Both of the correlations with forward digit span suggest a common underlying processing factor that is shared by each of these dependent measures. This factor appears to reflect the speed of verbal rehearsal processes in working memory. If this hypothesis is correct, then word recognition and speaking rate should also be correlated with each other because they make use of the same processing mechanism. This is exactly what we found. As in the earlier analyses, differences due to demographic factors and the contribution of other variables were statistically controlled for by using partial correlation techniques. In all cases, the correlations between speaking rate and word recognition were negative and highly significant. Thus, slower speaking rates are associated with poorer word recognition scores on all three word recognition tests. These findings linking speaking rate and word recognition suggest that all three measures, digit span, speaking rate, and word recognition performance are closely related because they share a common underlying source of variance.

To determine if digit span and sentence duration share a common process and the same underlying source of variance which relates them both to word recognition performance, we re-analyzed the intercorrelations between each pair of variables with the same set of the demographic and mediating variables systematically partialled out. When sentence duration was partialled out of the analysis, the correlations between digit span and each of the three measures of word recognition essentially approached zero. However, the negative correlations between sentence duration and word recognition were still present even after digit span was partialled out of the analysis, suggesting that processing speed is the common factor that is shared between these two measures.

The results of these analyses confirm that the underlying factor that is shared in common with speaking rate is related to the rate of information processing, specifically, the speed of the verbal rehearsal process in working memory. This processing component of verbal rehearsal could reflect either the articulatory speed used to maintain phonological patterns in working memory or the time to retrieve and scan phonological information already in working memory (see Cowan et al., 1998). In either case, the common factor that links word recognition and speaking rate appears to be related in some way to the speed of information processing operations used to store and maintain phonological representations in working memory (see Pisoni & Cleary, 2003).

20.12 Speech Timing and Working Memory

In addition to our recent studies on verbal rehearsal speed, we have also obtained several new measures of memory scanning during the digit recall task from a group of deaf children with cochlear implants and a group of typically-developing age-matched normal-hearing children (see Burkholder & Pisoni, 2003). Our interest in studying speech timing in these children was motivated by several recent findings reported by Cowan and his colleagues who have carefully measured response latencies and interword durations during recall tasks in children of different ages.

In one study of immediate recall, Cowan et al. (1994) found that interword pause times provided a reliable measure of the dynamics of the memory scanning and retrieval process during development. Their results showed that children's interword pauses in immediate recall increased as list length increased. This finding supports Cowan's earlier (1992) proposal that serial scanning is carried out during the pauses. Recall of longer lists requires that more items have to be scanned serially, therefore prolonging interword pause time. Additional evidence showing that items in short-term memory are scanned during interword pauses was obtained in another study by Cowan et al. (1998) who found that children with shorter interword pauses also had longer immediate memory spans.

Cowan et al. (1998) also reported that older children have shorter pause durations in immediate recall than younger children. Taken together, their results on speech timing suggest that the memory span increases observed in older children might be associated with both shorter interword pauses during serial recall and faster speaking rates. Shorter interword pauses indicate that the scanning mechanisms used to retrieve items from short-term memory are executed faster and more efficiently in the older children. Combined with increases in articulation speed, this factor may enhance the ability to engage in efficient verbal recall strategies as children develop. These findings on speech timing in immediate memory tasks led Cowan and his colleagues to propose that two processing operations – serial scanning and retrieval of items from short-term memory and subvocal verbal rehearsal of phonological information – are used by typically-developing children in recall and both of these factors affect measures of working memory capacity (Cowan, 1999; Cowan et al., 1998).

Recently, we obtained several measures of speech timing during immediate recall from a group of deaf children who use cochlear implants (see Burkholder & Pisoni, 2003). Measures of speaking rate and speech timing were also obtained from an age-matched control group of normal-hearing, typically-developing children. Articulation rate and subvocal rehearsal speed were measured from sentence durations elicited using meaningful English sentences. Relations between articulation rate and working memory in each group of children were compared to determine how verbal rehearsal processes might differ between the two populations. To assess differences in speech timing during recall, response latencies, durations of the test items, and interword pauses were measured in both groups of children.

For the analysis of the speech-timing measures during recall, we analyzed only the responses from the digit span forward condition. Analysis of the speech-timing measures obtained during recall revealed no differences in the average duration of articulation of the individual digits or response latencies at any of the list lengths. There was no correlation between the average articulations taken from digit span forward and forward digit span scores when all children were considered together or when the children were evaluated in groups according to hearing ability or communication mode.

However, we found that interword pause durations in recall differed significantly among the groups of children. The average of individual pauses that occurred during recall in the forward condition was significantly longer in the deaf children with cochlear implants than in the normal-hearing children at list lengths three and four.

The results of this study replicated our previous findings showing that profoundly deaf children with cochlear implants have shorter digit spans than their normal-hearing peers. As expected, deaf children with cochlear implants also displayed longer sentence durations than normal-hearing children. Total communication users displayed slower speaking rates and shorter forward digit spans than the oral communication users. In addition to producing longer sentence durations than normal-hearing children, the deaf children with cochlear implants also had much longer interword pause durations during recall. Longer interword pauses are assumed to reflect slower serial scanning processes which may affect the retrieval of phonological information in short-term memory (Cowan, 1992; Cowan et al., 1994). Taken together, the pattern of results indicates that both slower subvocal rehearsal and serial scanning are associated with shorter digit spans in the deaf children with cochlear implants.

The overall pattern of speech-timing results found in both groups of children is quite similar to the findings reported by Cowan et al. (1998) with normal-hearing children. Their findings suggest that covert verbal rehearsal and the speed of serial scanning of items in short-term memory are two factors that affect immediate memory span in normal-hearing children. Cowan et al. also found that children who were faster at subvocal verbal rehearsal and serial scanning displayed longer immediate memory spans than children who executed these processes more slowly. However, his findings were obtained from typically-developing normal-hearing children who differed only in chronological age.

Comparable results were observed in our study using children of similar chronological ages but with quite different developmental histories that reflect the absence of sound and early auditory experience during critical periods of perceptual and cognitive development. The effects of early auditory and linguistic experience found by Burkholder and Pisoni (2003) suggest that the development of subvocal verbal rehearsal and serial scanning processes may not only be related to maturationally-based milestones that are cognitively or metacognitively centered, such as the ability to effectively organize and utilize these two processes in tasks requiring immediate recall. Rather, efficient subvocal verbal rehearsal strategies and scanning abilities also appear to be experience- and activity-dependent reflecting the development of neural mechanisms used in speech perception and speech production.

Because the group of deaf children examined in the Burkholder and Pisoni (2003) study fell within a normal range of intelligence, the most likely developmental factor responsible for producing slower verbal rehearsal speeds, scanning rates, and shorter digit spans is an early period of auditory and linguistic deprivation prior to receiving a cochlear implant. Sensory deprivation may result in widespread developmental brain plasticity and neural reorganization, further differentiating deaf children's perceptual and cognitive development from the development of normal-hearing children (Kaas, Merzenich, & Killackey, 1983; Shepard & Hardie, 2001). Brain plasticity affects not only the development of the peripheral and central auditory systems but other higher cortical areas as well both before and after cochlear implantation (Ryugo, Limb, & Redd, 2000; Teoh, Pisoni, & Miyamoto, 2004, in press).

20.13 Discussion and Conclusions

Our recent findings on speech perception and working memory provide some new insights about the elementary information processing skills of deaf children with cochlear implants and the underlying cognitive and linguistic factors that affect the development of their speech and language skills on a range of outcome measures. These studies were specifically designed to obtain new process measures of performance that assessed the operation of verbal working memory in order to understand the nature of the capacity limitations in encoding and processing phonological information. Several important findings have emerged from our analysis of the memory span data suggesting that working memory capacity, verbal rehearsal speed, and scanning processes in short-term memory contribute additional unique sources of variance to the outcome measures obtained with deaf children following cochlear implantation. The pattern of digit span scores, measures of speaking rate, and speed of scanning of items in short-term memory demonstrate clearly the presence of atypical development of short-term working memory capacity in these deaf children and supports our initial hypothesis that cognitive processing variables contribute to the large individual differences observed in a range of outcome measures used to assess speech and language performance in these children.

The only demographic variable that was correlated with these cognitive processing measures was the child's communication mode. Deaf children who were immersed in oral-only environments displayed longer forward digit spans, faster speaking rates, and more efficient scanning of short-term memory than the children who were in total communication environments. The presence of selective effects of early sensory experience on working memory suggests that the stimulus environment and the specific kinds of activities and experiences that children have with their parents and caretakers in the language-learning environment operate in a highly selective manner on a specific information processing mechanism and subcomponent of the human memory system that is used for encoding, maintaining, and retrieving phonological information in short-term memory. We suspect there may be something unique about the oral environment and the specific experiences and activities that the child engages in on a regular basis that produces selective effects on verbal rehearsal and phonological coding of speech signals.

Because children from total communication environments may simply have less exposure to speech and spoken language in their early linguistic environment after receiving their implant than oral children, they may display problems in both processing and actively rehearsing phonological information in short-term memory. In terms of initial encoding and recognition, the reduced exposure to speech and spoken language may affect the development of automatic attention and specifically the speed with which speech signals can be identified and encoded into stable phonological representations in short term memory. Thus, total communication children may have fundamental problems in scanning and retrieving phonological information in short-term memory. In terms of verbal rehearsal, total communication children may have slower and less efficient verbal rehearsal processes once information gets into short-term memory simply because they have had less experience than oral children in producing speech and actively generating phonological patterns.

Passive exposure to speech without explicit analysis and conscious manipulation of phonological representations may not be sufficient to develop robust lexical representations of spoken words and fluency in control of speech production. Deaf children who receive cochlear implants may need to be actively engaged in processing spoken language in order to develop automaticity and automatic attention strategies that can be carried out rapidly without conscious effort or processing resources. This may be one direct benefit of auditory-oral education programs. The excellent spoken language skills acquired by children in these programs may reflect the development of highly automatized phonological analysis skills which permit the child to engage in active processing strategies in perception that involve "decomposition" of a speech pattern into a sequence of discrete phonological units and then the "reassembly" of those individual units into sequences of gestures and sensory-motor patterns for use in speech production and articulation.

The development of automatized phonological processing skills may result in increases in the speed and efficiency of constructing phonological and lexical representations of spoken words in working memory. Recovering the internal structure of an input pattern in speech perception as a result of perceptual analysis and then reconstructing the same pattern in speech production may serve to establish permanent links between speech perception and production and may lead to further development of highly efficient sensory-motor articulatory programs for verbal rehearsal and coding of words in working memory. Thus, the development of phonological processing skills may simply be a by-product of the primary emphasis on speech and oral language skills in oral-only educational environments and may account for why these children consistently display better performance on a wide range of outcome measures of speech and language.

The present set of findings permits us to identify a specific information processing mechanism, the verbal rehearsal process in working memory, that is responsible for the limitations on processing capacity. Processing limitations are present in a wide range of clinical tests that make use of verbal rehearsal and phonological processing skills to encode, store, maintain, and retrieve spoken words from working memory. These fundamental information processing operations are components of all of the current clinical outcome measures routinely used to assess receptive and expressive language functions. Our findings suggest that the variability in performance on the traditional clinical outcome measures used to assess speech and language processing skills in deaf children after cochlear implantation may simply reflect fundamental differences in the speed of information processing operations such as verbal rehearsal, scanning of items in short-term memory, and the rate of encoding phonological and lexical information in working memory.

We believe these new results are clinically and theoretically significant because they suggest a motivated theoretically-based explanation for the enormous variability and individual differences observed in a range of speech and language processing tasks that make use of the same verbal rehearsal processes. As in normal-hearing typically-developing children, the present findings suggest that differences in verbal rehearsal speed may be the primary factor that is responsible for the large individual differences in speech and language development observed in deaf children following cochlear implantation.

ACKNOWLEDGMENTS

This work was supported by NIH-NIDCD Training Grant T32DC00012 and NIH-NIDCD Research Grants R01DC00111, R01DC00064 to Indiana University and NIH-NIDCD Research Grant R01DC03100 to Central Institute for the Deaf. I would like to thank Miranda Cleary for her help and advice on all stages of the research described in this chapter. I would also like to thank Ann Geers, Chris Brenner, and Mike Strube of CID for their help and assistance. I am also grateful to Steven Chin for his editorial comments on an earlier version of this paper.

REFERENCES

Ackerman, P. L., Kyllonen, P. C., & Roberts, R. D. (1999). *Learning and Individual Differences*. Washington, DC: American Psychological Association.

Baddeley, A., Gathercole, S., & Papagno, C. (1998). The phonological loop as a language learning device. *Psychological Review*, 105, 158–73.

Baddeley, A. D., Thomson, N., & Buchanan, M. (1975). Word length and the structure of short-term memory. *Journal of Verbal Learning and Verbal Behavior*, 14, 575–89.

Ball, G. F. & Hulse, S. H. (1998). Birdsong. *American Psychologist*, 53, 37–58.

Bench, J., Kowal, A., & Bamford, J. (1979). The BKB (Bamford-Kowal-Bench) sentence lists for partially-hearing children. *British Journal of Audiology*, 13, 108–12.

Bergeson, T. & Pisoni, D. B. (2004). Audiovisual speech perception in deaf adults and children following cochlear implantation. In G. Calvert, C. Spence, & B. E. Stein (eds.), *Handbook of Multisensory Integration* (pp. 749–72). Cambridge, MA: MIT Press.

Burkholder, R. & Pisoni, D. B. (2003). Speech timing and working memory in profoundly deaf children after cochlear implantation. *Journal of Experimental Child Psychology*, 85, 63–88.

Carpenter, P. A., Miyake, A., & Just, M. A. (1994). Working memory constraints in comprehension. In M. A. Gernsbacher (ed.), *Handbook of Psycholinguistics*, (pp. 1075–122). San Diego: Academic Press.

Clarke, G. (2003). *Cochlear Implants: Fundamentals and Applications*. New York: Springer-Verlag.

Cowan, N. (1992). Verbal memory and the timing of spoken recall. *Journal of Memory and Language*, 31, 668–84.

Cowan, N. (1999). The differential maturation of two processing rates related to digit span. *Journal of Experimental Child Psychology*, 72, 193–209.

Cowan, N., Keller, T., Hulme, C., Roodenrys, S., McDougall, S., & Rack, J. (1994). Verbal memory span in children: Speech timing clues to the mechanisms underlying age and word length effects. *Journal of Memory and Language*, 33, 234–50.

Cowan, N., Wood, N. L., Wood, P. K., Keller, T. A., Nugent, L. D., & Keller, C. V. (1998). Two separate verbal processing rates contributing to short-term memory span. *Journal of Experimental Psychology: General*, 127, 141–60.

Ericsson, K. A. & Smith, J. (1991). *Toward a General Theory of Expertise: Prospects and Limits*. New York: Cambridge University Press.

Gathercole, S. & Baddeley, A. (1990). Phonological memory deficits in language disordered children: Is there a causal connection? *Journal of Memory and Language*, 29, 336–60.

Gathercole, S. E., Hitch, G. J., Service, E., & Martin, A. J. (1997). Phonological short-term memory and new word learning in children. *Developmental Psychology*, 33, 966–79.

Gupta, P. & MacWhinney, B. (1997). Vocabulary acquisition and verbal short-term memory: Computational and neural bases. *Brain and Language*, 59, 267–333.

Haskins, H. (1949). A phonetically balanced test of speech discrimination for children. Unpublished Master's Thesis, Northwestern University, Evanston, IL.

Kaas, J. H., Merzenich, M. M., & Killackey, H. P. (1983). The reorganization of somatosensory cortex following peripheral nerve damage in adult and developing mammals. *Annual Review of Neuroscience*, 6, 325–56.

Kirk, K. I., Pisoni, D. B., & Miyamoto, R. T. (2000). Lexical discrimination by children with cochlear implants: Effects of age at implantation and communication mode. In S. B. Waltzman & N. L. Cohen (eds.), *Cochlear Implants* (pp. 252–4). New York: Thieme.

Kirk, K. I., Pisoni, D. B., & Osberger, M. J. (1995). Lexical effects on spoken word recognition by pediatric cochlear implant users. *Ear and Hearing*, 16, 470–81.

Kluck, M., Pisoni, D. B., & Kirk, K. I. (1997). Performance of normal-hearing children on open-set speech perception tests. *Progress Report on Spoken Language Processing No. 21*. Bloomington, IN: Speech Research Laboratory.

Konishi, M. (1985). Birdsong: From behavior to neuron. *Annual Review of Neuroscience*, 8, 125–70.

Konishi, M. & Nottebohm, R. (1969). Experimental studies in the ontogeny of avian vocalizations. In R. A. Hinde (ed.), *Bird Vocalizations* (pp. 29–48). New York: Cambridge University Press.

Luce, P. A. & Pisoni, D. B. (1998). Recognizing spoken words: The neighborhood activation model. *Ear and Hearing*, 19, 1–36.

Marler, P. & Peters, S. (1988). Sensitive periods for song acquisition from tape recordings and live tutors in the swamp sparrow, Melospiza georgiana. *Ethology*, 77, 76–84.

McGarr, N. S. (1983). The intelligibility of deaf speech to experienced and inexperienced listeners. *Journal of Speech & Hearing Research*, 26, 451–8.

Meyer, T. A. & Pisoni, D. B. (1999). Some computational analyses of the PBK Test: Effects of frequency and lexical density on spoken word recognition. *Ear and Hearing*, 20, 363–71.

Osberger, M. J. et al. (1991). Independent evaluations of the speech perception abilities of children with the Nucleus 22-channel cochlear implant system. *Ear and Hearing*, 12, 66–80.

Pisoni, D. B. & Cleary, M. (2003). Measures of working memory span and verbal rehearsal speed in deaf children after cochlear implantation. *Ear and Hearing*, 24, 106S–120S.

Pisoni, D. B., Cleary, M., Geers, A. E., & Tobey, E. A. (2000). Individual differences in effectiveness of cochlear implants in prelingually deaf children: Some new process measures of performance. *Volta Review*, 101, 111–64.

Pisoni, D. B., Svirsky, M. A., Kirk, K. I., & Miyamoto, R. T. (1997). Looking at the "Stars": A first report on the intercorrelations among measures of speech perception, intelligibility, and language development in pediatric cochlear implant users. *Research on Spoken Language Processing Progress Report No. 21*. Bloomington, IN: Speech Research Laboratory, (pp. 51–91).

Robbins, A. M., Renshaw, J. J., Miyamoto, R. T., Osberger, M. J., & Pope, M. L. (1988). *Minimal Pairs Test*. Indianapolis, IN: Indiana University School of Medicine.

Rosen, V. M. & Engle, R. W. (1997). Forward and backward serial recall. *Intelligence*, 25, 37–47.

Ross, M. & Lerman, J. (1979). A picture identification test for hearing-impaired children. *Journal of Speech & Hearing Research*, 13, 44–53.

Rudel, R. G. & Denckla, M. B. (1974). Relation of forward and backward digit repetition to neurological impairment in children with learning disability. *Neuropsychologia*, 12, 109–18.

Ryugo, D., Limb, C., & Redd, E. (2000). Brain plasticity: The impact of the environment on the brain as it relates to hearing and deafness. In J. Niparko et al. (eds.), *Cochlear Implants: Principles and Practices* (pp. 33–56). Philadelphia: Lippincott Williams & Wilkins.

Sharma, A., Dorman, M. F., & Spahr, A. J. (2002). A sensitive period for the development of the central auditory system in children with cochlear implants: Implications for age of implantation. *Ear and Hearing*, 23, 532–9.

Shepard, R. K. & Hardie, N. (2001). Deafness-induced changes in the auditory pathway: Implications for cochlear implants. *Audiology and Neuro-Otology*, 6, 305–18.

Svirsky, M. A., Robbins, A. M., Kirk, K. I., Pisoni, D. B., & Miyamoto, R. T. (2000). Language development in profoundly deaf children with cochlear implants. *Psychological Science*, 11, 153–8.

Teoh, S. W., Pisoni, D. B., & Miyamoto, R. T. (2004). Cochlear implantation in adults with prelingual deafness: I. Clinical results. *Laryngoscope*, 114, 1536–40.

Teoh, S. W., Pisoni, D. B., & Miyamoto, R. T. (in press). Cochlear implantation in adults with prelingual deafness: II. Underlying constraints that affect audiological outcomes. *Laryngoscope*.

Tobey, E. A., Geers, A. E., Morchower, B., Perrin, J., Skellett, R., Brenner, C., & Torretta, G. (2000). Factors associated with speech intelligibility in children with cochlear implants. *Annals of Otology, Rhinology and Laryngology Supplement*, 185, 28–30.

Wechsler, D. (1991). *Wechsler Intelligence Scale for Children*, 3rd edition (WISC-III). San Antonio, TX: The Psychological Corporation.

Zwolan, T. A., Zimmerman-Phillips, S., Asbaugh, C. J., Hieber, S. J., Kileny, P. R., & Telian, S. A. (1997). Cochlear implantation of children with minimal open-set speech recognition skills. *Ear and Hearing*, 18, 240–51.

21 Speech Perception following Focal Brain Injury

WILLIAM BADECKER

Damage to specific regions of a functionally differentiated brain results in behavioral dissociations that reveal, albeit indirectly at times, the brain's specific functional organization. For this reason, acquired impairments have the potential to uncover properties of perceptual and/or cognitive mechanisms underlying speech perception. By mapping out these dissociations, for example, one can hope to clarify how speech perception is related to the perception of music or environmental sounds (e.g., enabling us to identify processing mechanisms they do or do not share). Similarly, one can attempt to exploit fractionation within the cognitive-perceptual system to discover its functional organization. Finally, functional dissociations can be related to site of injury in order to develop an anatomically situated model of the speech perception system. These goals are ambitious, and as a consequence, many of the issues discussed in this chapter remain largely unsettled and underspecified. It is instructive, though, to consider both what we have learned from cognitive neuropsychology about the mechanisms that underlie this complex ability, and also what empirical and conceptual gaps must be bridged in order to improve our understanding of the machinery for perceiving speech.

The discussion in this chapter will assume a broad conception of speech perception – that it includes all of the processes that are required in order to gain access to a representation of lexical identity when presented with a spoken word form, short of the mechanisms that disambiguate homophones on the basis of syntactic or semantic context. Since lexical identity must be understood at least in part in terms of the meaning associated with a particular word, this will include mechanisms that map auditory stimuli onto lexical meanings. However, it should be possible to distinguish among the stages of this mapping process, and our discussion of speech perception following focal brain injury will attempt to make such discriminations wherever possible. To facilitate this discussion, patient analyses will make reference to the general model of the central speech perception system sketched in Figure 21.1. Between the acoustic-phonetic level and the semantic level of representation, the model posits explicit intermediate phonological representations (both segmental and lexical). So, our model may be distinguished from direct access models (Gaskell & Marslen-Wilson, 1997), in which low-level auditory representations are mapped directly onto (distributed) representations

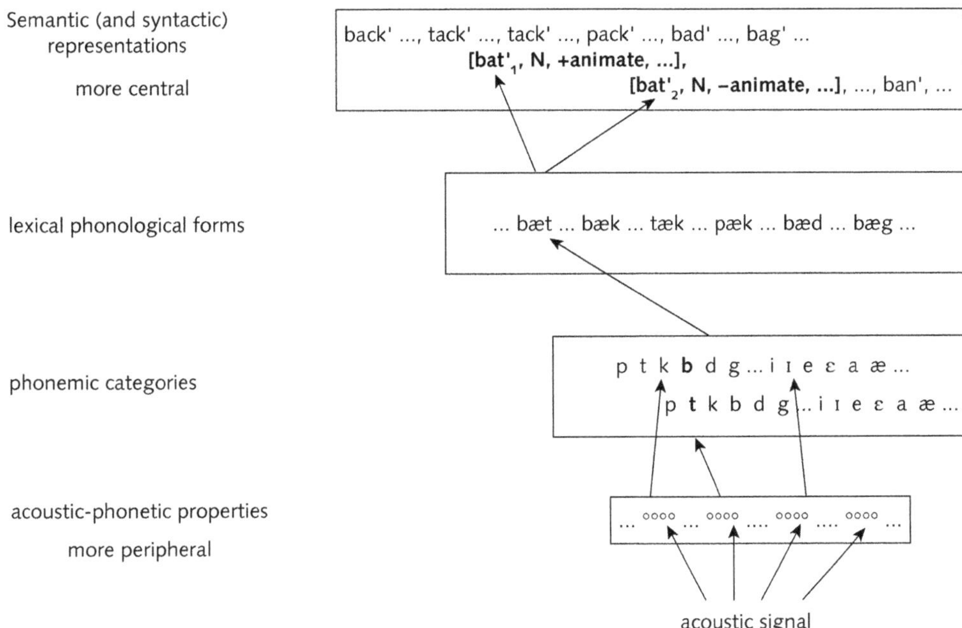

Figure 21.1 Schematic representation of the mapping from a speech signal onto representations of lexical identity.

of lexical semantics without mediating representations of lexical form, and from lexical-spectral models (Klatt, 1979), in which spectrotemporal analyses are mapped directly onto representations of lexical identities. In addition, the model maps acoustic-phonetic representations directly onto phonemic representations and does not interpose a level of perceptual analysis that would require positing autonomous distinctive feature representations (or processing units). Unlike speech perception models such as TRACE (McClelland & Elman, 1986), which posits atomic phoneme units whose activation is determined (in part) by input from independent distinctive feature units, the model proposed here follows a more traditional linguistic analysis in construing distinctive features as constituents of segmental representations at the phonemic (and lexical phonological) level.[1]

On other matters, the model is underspecified. It makes no commitment about whether segmental, lexical-phonemic, or lexical-semantic representations are encoded in a computationally localist or distributed format. Likewise, it is neutral with regard to whether tasks such as phoneme identification require positing phoneme decision units that are themselves independent of the segmental representations at the model's phonemic level (Norris, McQueen, & Cutler, 2000), or whether the phoneme representations of the present model can be accessed directly for labeling purposes. What the model does claim is that successful phoneme labeling requires relatively intact processing at the hypothesized segmental phonemic level.

Before proceeding, one point regarding the methodology of neuropsychological investigation deserves mention. It is natural to look for similarities among cases of acquired deficit, and natural as well to think of individuals with similar patterns of impairment as members of a group. However, these groups themselves have no legitimate status in our reasoning about models of cognitive or perceptual processing. In order to exploit a specific pattern of preserved vs. impaired abilities to support (or to falsify) a particular model of speech perception, one must document this reliable pattern in one or more individual patients – and not piece it together from the varied performance of separate cases, or from the average performance of members of some clinical category (Caramazza, 1984). Hence, I offer a word of caution regarding the labels employed in this chapter. Mention of the clinical labels used to refer to case studies in the literature is often unavoidable, if only because in most reports cases are presented as instances of a category that is defined in terms of a general pattern of preserved and impaired abilities (e.g., cortical deafness, pure word deafness, Wernicke's aphasia, etc.). While these labels may be taken to indicate some commonality at the gross level of behavior, what commonality exists can at best be taken as a matter of clinical definition: They do not entail that specific, individual components of the speech perception system will have the same status (intact vs. damaged) in any two members of a single clinical category. Category labels are used here largely as points of contact with the neuropsychological literature relating to speech perception.

21.1 Patterns of Disrupted Speech Perception

One of the basic facts about the mechanisms that subserve language is that they are strongly lateralized in the neuroanatomical substrate. This includes at least some of the mechanisms for auditory lexical recognition and comprehension. Language deficits (aphasias) following focal brain injury are frequently accompanied by some degree of speech perception defect (Basso, Casati, & Vignolo, 1977; Blumstein, Baker, & Goodglass, 1977; Franklin, 1989; Goldblum & Albert, 1972; Gow & Caplan, 1996; Miceli et al., 1978; Miceli et al., 1980). Notably, auditory lexical comprehension may be disrupted following lesions in the left hemisphere that leave visual (i.e., written) lexical comprehension relatively intact (Franklin, Howard, & Patterson, 1994; Gazzaniga et al., 1973). Such patterns of impairment, when considered jointly with other selective deficits, can be taken as evidence that the lexical system has modality specific pathways for accessing lexical semantic information (Ellis & Young, 1988; Hillis, 2001). For example, the patient JBN, described by Hillis et al. (1999), was able to make phoneme and word discriminations and could repeat CV syllables accurately, but was severely impaired in auditory lexical decision and could not match pictures to spoken names. In contrast, her performance on visual lexical decision and on picture-word matching with written words was error free. Other cases of left hemisphere injury described below result in selective auditory comprehension deficits that disrupt phoneme discrimination and labeling. These dissociations suggest that injury to left hemisphere structures can selectively disrupt the mechanisms that underlie speech perception at some stage of the recognition process. However, there is also evidence that both hemispheres contribute to speech perception, and that the right hemisphere may independently support some limited capacities for segmental and lexical perception. For example, patients whose speech production abilities are entirely disrupted by injection of sodium amytal to the dominant left hemisphere may be able to respond to simple verbal commands (McGlone, 1984; Wada & Rasmussen, 1960) or to discriminate between syllables with consonant voicing contrasts (Boatman et al., 1998). Further evidence that auditory cortex in both hemispheres contributes to speech perception, and that the right hemisphere exhibits limited receptive speech processing abilities, derives from the types of lesions that are found to selectively disrupt auditory and speech perception.

Although many studies of acquired speech perception deficits involve cases in which the disruption forms part of an impairment complex that includes aphasia (e.g., Baum, 2001; Boyczuk & Baum, 1999; Gow & Caplan, 1996), there are numerous interpretive complications that can arise when higher order language deficits accompany disruptions to the speech perception process. For this reason the main focus of our discussion will be on perceptual impairments that leave other aspects of language relatively intact.

Acquired auditory disorders include a variety of deficits that affect speech perception. The first that we consider is one in which more central components of the system sketched in Figure 21.1 appear to be cut off from auditory input, either through extensive damage to acoustic-phonetic processing mechanisms themselves, or through disconnection of these mechanisms from input from the peripheral hearing system. Cortical deafness is a profile that arises from a disconnection between points in the ascending auditory pathway and cortical auditory areas in *both* hemispheres (Bahls et al., 1988; Engelien et al., 2000; Mozaz Garde & Cowley, 2000; Tanaka et al., 1991; see also references from Griffiths, Rees, & Green, 1999). Despite its clinical label, cortical deafness is associated with bilateral *subcortical* lesions. On the basis of reports of persistent cases of the impairment, Tanaka et al. (1991) maintain that cortical deafness follows from damage "to the auditory radiation . . . believed to emerge from the [Medial Geniculate Body (MGB)] and project mainly to Heschl's gyrus" (p. 2394). The perceptual impairment caused by extensive bilateral injury to the MGBs is consistent with subjective hearing at most frequencies at highly elevated thresholds, but patients presenting with this rare condition typically describe themselves as deaf, and abnormal audiometric thresholds are observed in all behavioral detection tasks. However, it has been demonstrated objectively, using auditory evoked potentials, that this subjective deafness is not the result of peripheral hearing loss. When the patient reports include this test, normal brain-stem potentials, which indicate that the peripheral mechanisms are intact up to and including the cochlear nuclei, contrast with abnormal (or absent) middle and late auditory evoked potentials (Bahls et al., 1988; Engelien et al., 2000; Tanaka et al., 1991).

Cortical deafness can occur without associated lexical or other aphasic deficits. For example, spontaneous speech and written language comprehension can be relatively spared in such patients (Bahls et al., 1988; Engelien et al., 2000; Michel, Peronnet, & Schott, 1980; Tanaka et al., 1991). Furthermore, cortical deafness is not domain-specific: it disrupts the perception of environmental and musical sounds as well as speech sounds. However, the perceptual defect in turn causes impaired performance on all tasks that require phonetic or phonological processing. Despite the severe disruption of auditory recognition and awareness in both language and non-language domains, some patients with cortical deafness can localize both environmental and speech sounds. They may exhibit other varieties of auditory sensitivity – e.g., orienting to sounds, showing a startle reflex – that do not depend on conscious attention to sound (Mozaz Garde & Cowley, 2000). Startle responses may be elicited in some patients without awareness of the sound itself (Tanaka et al., 1991, patient 1), although cases of cortical deafness have also been reported in which no such reflexes are evident either for unattended sounds, or for any sounds at all (Bahls et al., 1988; Engelien et al., 2000).

Some controversy exists concerning the role of attention in cases diagnosed as cortical deafness. Because behavioral audiometric measures may reveal some sensitivity at elevated thresholds to pure tones in specific frequency ranges, there is some question of whether awareness of sub-threshold sounds may be attenuated due to an attentional deficit. However, in instances of cortical deafness where focused attention has been found to improve auditory perception, its ameliorating benefit for the perception of speech appears to be limited. Engelien et al. (2000) describe a young patient SB who suffered consecutive strokes in the area of the left and right middle cerebral arteries, leaving him with a severe auditory perceptual deficit (in addition to a severe impairment in executing the skilled movements that are required for fluent speech). SB was able to communicate by writing and reading, although he had occasional word finding difficulties and made phonemic errors in spoken production. SB showed no hearing when he was not attending to sounds, nor did he orient to unattended sounds (including someone shouting his name), although normal brain-stem auditory evoked potentials verified that peripheral hearing mechanisms were intact. He also did not show normal physiological responses to unattended sounds (e.g., no galvanic skin response), and PET showed no activity associated with unattended auditory stimulation. When he was instructed to focus his attention to sound, though, behavioral and physiological (GSR) response patterns changed. SB was able to detect sound onsets and offsets, as well as changes in intensity (though not changes in frequency). Whereas unattended pure tones below 90–120 db went undetected, focused attention brought SB's detection thresholds to near normal levels within the frequency range of speech. Even with focused attention, though, SB was poor at localizing sounds, and he was unable to discriminate or identify environmental or speech sounds.

An acquired inability to *recognize* sounds (auditory agnosia) has been observed in a variety of forms. Auditory agnosia is distinct from cortical deafness in that patients are sensitive to the presence of sounds and typically can detect changes in frequency, intensity, and duration (though not always with normal acuity). Despite being able to register sounds, the agnosic patient may complain that sounds from the affected domain are unintelligible noise. In its least selective forms, auditory agnosia diminishes the recognition of all types of auditory stimuli, causing disruptions of varying degrees to the perception of musical, environmental, and speech sounds (Auerbach et al., 1982; Godefroy et al., 1995; Miceli, 1982; Miceli et al., 1980). However, the dissociations observed in selective auditory agnosias can be striking. Processing of environmental and speech sounds can remain intact or relatively intact although music perception is severely impaired (see Peretz, 2001, for a review); whereas for other patients speech perception may be disrupted in the context of intact perception of music and of environmental sounds (Coslett, Brashear, & Heilman, 1984; Metz-Lutz & Dahl, 1984; Takahashi et al., 1992; Yaqub et al., 1988). Moreover, speech perception may be relatively intact in comparison to disrupted perception of music and environmental sounds (Fuji et al., 1990; Lambert et al., 1989; Spreen, Benton, & Fincham, 1965; Taniwaki et al., 2000). In two patients Van Lancker and Canter (1982) studied, lesions localized in the left hemisphere left them "grossly deficient in environmental sound recognition as tested by the clinical audiologist. . . . [and yet both] performed normally in familiar voice recognition" (p. 193). Such patterns of dissociation between preserved and impaired recognition provide evidence that the auditory system is organized into functionally distinguishable processing components, and that different brain regions process auditory input according to different principles (Peretz, 2001; Polster & Rose, 1998).

The speech signal carries information about phoneme identity, but also about speaker identity, speaker affect, and lexical and grammatical properties of the utterance. Case studies indicate that access to these varieties of information may dissociate.[2] However, for reasons of space the focus of discussion will be on acquired deficits affecting phonemic and lexical perception.

Patients with a perceptual deficit that impairs the recognition of speech sounds are clinically described as exhibiting pure word deafness (or auditory verbal agnosia). Such deficits affect a wide variety of language processing tasks, including the ability to comprehend and repeat spoken utterances. The clinical diagnosis of pure word deafness does not entail that the auditory agnosia is restricted to the verbal domain, however. The ability to process music or environmental sounds may or may not be preserved in cases bearing this label. Rather, the term "pure" in the clinical label is used to contrast this form of auditory agnosia with preserved (or relatively preserved) comprehension of written language along with intact spoken and written language production. This dissociation between the ability to process written versus spoken language provides an important element of support for localizing the deficit within the speech perception system. Additional dissociations show that the information that is extracted from the speech signal depends on a number of distinct processing mechanisms. For example, Yaqub et al. (1988) describe an Arabic-speaking patient who presented with pure word deafness, but who showed no evidence of agnosia for music or environmental sounds. Brain-stem auditory evoked potentials indicated intact peripheral hearing.[3] His comprehension of spoken language was significantly impaired, although he was able to read and comprehend written language and his spoken output was fluent, grammatical, and did not include paraphasias. In contrast to his poor comprehension for spoken words and sentences, the patient could discriminate male and female voices, he could tell whether the spoken language was Arabic, and he exhibited preserved abilities in processing both grammatical and affective prosody: He was able to identify questions, imperatives, and exclamations, and he made accurate judgments concerning the speaker's affect (whether the speaker was happy, sad, or emotionally neutral).

In several reported case studies, the acquired deficit to speech perception had a greater effect on the ability to identify voicing or place of articulation in stop consonants than on the perception of vowels (Auerbach et al., 1982; Miceli, 1982; Saffran, Marin, & Yeni-Komshian, 1976; Wang et al., 2000; Yaqub et al., 1988).[4] Divergent performance for place and voicing in stop consonants has also been noted. For example, Yaqub et al.'s (1988) patient could identify vowels (97% correct), but his forced-choice labeling indicated that stop-consonant perception was abnormal. In addition, the patient was worse in identifying place of articulation than voicing among stop consonants. The patient's ability to *discriminate* between two segments that differed in place (or in voicing) was not reported, though, so it is difficult to determine from the report what balance of "apperceptive" versus "associative" defect underlies the perceptual deficit. Poeppel (2001) notes that other patients show a similar dissociation in the perception of vowels and consonants, but that they differ from Yaqub et al.'s patient in that either they are worse in the perception of voicing than of place (Saffran et al., 1976), or they appear equally impaired in perceiving place and voicing among stop consonants. (See also Gow & Caplan, 1996, who found evidence for the double dissociability of voice and place perception among the aphasic patients they tested.) Based on this double dissociation, it appears that the differential effect of the perceptual deficit in discriminating consonant voicing and place of articulation may arise as a result of some functional modularity at early stages of speech perception.

Although the dissociation between (good) vowel and (poor) stop-consonant perception is frequently observed as a feature of word deafness, the basis for the processing asymmetry is still not fully understood. The opposite pattern of dissociation has not been observed. One possible explanation for the perceptual dissociation hinges on the functional selectiveness of the auditory agnosia: If the deficit that gives rise to a speech perception deficit does not also disrupt the perception of environmental sounds, it could be that the preserved capacity to discriminate and identify vowels simply reflects the recruitment of cortical auditory mechanisms that are non-specific to speech (i.e., implicating some or all of those undamaged mechanisms that subserve the preserved ability to process environmental sounds). Though plausible, there may be some problem with this as a general explanation of this consonant-vowel dissociation. For example, Kazui et al. (1990) report a patient who presented with a non-specific auditory agnosia (affecting speech, music, and environmental sounds). This patient also exhibited a strong asymmetry in identification tasks between the relatively spared perception of vowels and the impaired perception of stop consonants (indexed by poor place discrimination).

Another account is that preserved vowel identification reflects intact subcortical mechanisms that are sufficient to discriminate among vowels, whereas consonant perception requires processing in cortical structures (as well as subcortical structures). Lesion studies in animal models indicate that subcortical structures, including the auditory nerve and cochlear nucleus, can encode many of the acoustic features necessary for vowel discrimination and identification, including formant frequencies, duration, and vowel intensity (Delgutte, 1980; Sachs, Voight, & Young, 1983; Sachs & Young, 1979). Damage limited to cortical auditory areas that subserve consonant perception will not disrupt vowel perception as long as the hypothesized subcortical areas retain secondary connections to points somewhere further up along the auditory lexical route that can linguistically interpret the output of subcortical "transducers." That is, perceptual discriminations may rely on distinctions made in subcortical structures, but one lesson from cortical deafness is that completely severing the subcortical from the cortical components of the auditory pathway will extinguish conscious perception for any segment type. So, if stop-consonant perception requires elaboration and refinement of the acoustic signal in cortical auditory structures, whereas the refinements of the signal that are necessary for vowel perception are carried out largely in subcortical structures, then lesions to (or disconnections of) cortical mechanisms that mediate consonant perception will be consistent with preserved subcortical discrimination among vowels.

Yet a third interpretation of consonant-vowel dissociations is that the perceptual deficit arises from selective damage to specialized auditory mechanisms that distill information in the signal from narrow temporal processing windows about the time-varying properties of the speech sound. This account may also be interpreted as an elaboration of the preceding, anatomical account of the dissociation. Diminished temporal acuity was demonstrated in a number of patients presenting with word deafness by using nonspeech protocols such as click counting, click fusion,[5] and other discrimination tasks (Albert & Bear, 1974; Auerbach et al., 1982; Godefroy et al., 1995; Tanaka, Yamodori, & Mori, 1987; Wang et al., 2000; Yaqub et al., 1988). Other studies found abnormal discrimination and/or labeling when temporal cues for place or voicing were varied in synthetic speech stimuli (Auerbach et al., 1982; Miceli, 1982; Saffran et al., 1976). For example, the patient described by Auerbach et al. (1982) exhibited abnormal discrimination among synthetic speech stimuli when VOT was manipulated: Within-category VOT contrasts went undetected (as seen in the normal discrimination profile), but differences that straddled the category boundary failed to elicit a sharp discrimination peak. Evidence of a temporal acuity deficit has been taken to indicate that in some patients the perceptual impairment underlying word deafness is "prephonemic" in character (Auerbach et al., 1982; see also Phillips & Farmer, 1990; Poeppel, 2001). Placing the impairment at the prephonemic (acoustic-phonetic) level of the model in Figure 21.1 may find some support in the fact that, in some word-deaf patients, speech perception is reported to be significantly improved by lip reading (Albert & Bear, 1974; Auerbach et al., 1982; Buchman et al., 1986; Denes & Semenza, 1975; Kazui et al., 1990; Saffran et al., 1976; Takahashi et al., 1992; von Stockert, 1982). To the extent that the benefit depends on a capacity to map visual information onto phonemic categories, it suggests that speech based representations at the phonemic and lexical levels may be relatively preserved in these specific patients.

The focus on temporal acuity deficits in case studies of word deafness raises a number of interesting issues regarding the kinds of early auditory processes that contribute to speech perception. For example, is it possible to mark a clear boundary between early acoustic perceptual mechanisms that are specific to speech versus those that are recruited for the early processing of environmental sounds, or are the same early perceptual mechanisms recruited for processing all sounds with the appropriate acoustic properties? Although some cases of pure word deafness present without agnosia for environmental sounds, the large majority of reported cases do present with joint speech and environmental sound agnosias (Buchman et al., 1986; Griffiths et al., 1999; Phillips & Farmer, 1990). Is this merely the result of an anatomical accident (e.g., physical adjacency of domain-specific mechanisms)? Or are there more principled connections between the elements of these co-occurring deficits? As Phillips and Farmer (1990) note, the existence of patients with word deafness without apparent agnosia for environmental sounds is not alone enough to motivate early domain specific auditory mechanisms. Dissociations in the ability to discriminate or identify speech vs.

environmental sounds could instead reflect two sources of divergence between the way speech and environmental sounds are processed: (1) the different acoustic properties needed to discriminate between sounds within one or the other domain, and (2) differences in how the output of early acoustic processing gets mapped onto domain specific representations at higher associative processing levels. Two ingredients are needed to motivate an early separation in the perceptual system. One is evidence that the perception of speech sounds can dissociate from the ability to recognize environmental sounds that are comparable on the acoustic dimensions that are relevant to speech perception. The other is evidence that the defect in speech perception affects discrimination, and not just the ability to label speech sounds. As yet no case study has addressed this matter adequately.

The connection between temporal processing impairments is also in need of closer scrutiny. Whereas detecting place and voicing for stop consonants requires intact perceptual mechanisms with fine-grain temporal resolution, the ability to detect place and voicing in fricatives [f, s, ʃ, v, z, ʒ] and place in nasals [m, n, ŋ] does not, since at least some of the corresponding cues are distributed over comparatively long spans of signal. For this reason, one might expect that the perception of voicing or place of articulation would dissociate for stops and fricatives. Studies of word deafness that examine stop-consonant place and voice perception typically do not provide the relevant comparisons, but data from one study speak in part to this issue. Miceli (1982) reports a case of acquired auditory defect following bilateral temporal lobe injuries. Brain stem auditory evoked potentials indicated that peripheral hearing mechanisms remained intact. The patient, MT, was able to understand written language, but auditory recognition was defective for speech, music, and environmental sounds. In addition, Miceli reports that when MT's ability to recognize environmental sounds was tested in either simple labeling or picture-sound matching tasks, her errors were predominantly based on acoustic similarity (e.g., MT matched the sound of a drum to a picture of a hammer, and the sound of a braying donkey to a picture of a handsaw cutting wood). Lip reading improved her comprehension of spoken language, but her comprehension was also significantly altered by context: Conversational topic shifts were particularly disruptive. Testing with natural speech stimuli revealed that MT was significantly better at identifying vowels than at discriminating between stop consonants. Identification tasks with stop consonants showed a consistent pattern of misperception across syllable contexts: She was severely impaired in her ability to identify place of articulation, but only mildly so in the perception of voicing. Identification and discrimination tasks with synthetic stop consonants also revealed severe impairments in the perception of place, although her performance with VOT materials revealed abnormal perception of this voicing cue as well. However, MT had no difficulty in performing the auditory discrimination tasks with fricatives, affricates, or nasals. Unfortunately, temporal acuity tests with nonspeech tasks (e.g., click fusion) were not reported, so it remains difficult to refine the connection between impaired stop-consonant perception and temporal acuity deficits.

Deficits that implicate representations or processes further upstream from the acoustic-phonetic level (e.g., at the phonemic level) are also documented. However, it is often difficult to account for the complex pattern of a specific speech perception deficit in terms of a single processing stage. In some cases, for example, there is evidence of a deficit to both phonemic and higher-level phonological processing mechanisms in patients who meet the clinical criteria for pure word deafness. Caramazza, Berndt, and Basili (1983) report a patient, JS, who presented with a pure word deafness profile following a unilateral left-hemisphere lesion. Behavioral audiometry indicated that peripheral hearing mechanisms were intact. The patient's ability to recognize environmental sounds was intact; however, his perceptual ability for musical sounds was not reported, nor were there tests of temporal acuity with nonspeech stimuli. JS was severely impaired on all language tasks requiring phonemic processing, although his comprehension of written words was virtually intact. For example, he performed poorly on a lexical-decision task with spoken forms (57%), whereas he exhibited a relatively preserved capacity for distinguishing written words from nonwords (91%). His performance was poor on both phoneme discrimination and identification tasks using synthetic CV syllables that varied VOT: He failed to identify stop consonants from different phonetic categories (/da/ vs. /ta/) as distinct, and he consistently labeled the stimuli as /da/ in the identification task. However, his discrimination and labeling performance diverged dramatically with natural speech stimuli. The spoken stimuli were nonword syllables of the form /Ca/ (with the consonants /p, b, t, d, k, g, tʃ, dʒ, f, v, s, z/) for the consonant tasks; and monosyllabic words (*beat*, *bit*, *bet*, *bat*, *but*, and *boot*) for the vowel tasks. He performed at ceiling levels on the discrimination task for both consonants and vowels. In contrast, he was severely impaired when asked to label the natural speech sounds for both the consonant and vowel tasks. For example, JS performed poorly on a visual-auditory matching task (using reduced response sets for place discrimination: /ba, da, ga/ for one block of trials; /pa, ta, ka/ for the other), and he exhibited similarly poor performance on the vowel identification task. Caramazza et al. concluded that JS was able to process the sounds acoustically, but not phonemically.

Based on JS's intact discrimination performance with natural speech stimuli, one can infer that at least some prephonemic processing abilities required for speech perception were preserved. In contrast, the more severe deficit in phonemic labeling, along with other evidence from auditory comprehension and lexical decision, suggest that prephonemic representations could not be mapped normally onto phonological representations. One plausible analysis locates the deficit at the phonemic level of the model in Figure 21.1. Other, higher-level deficits may also be implicated in this patient, though. JS produced nonword paraphasias in his spoken output, and his comprehension of written language was impaired above the word level. Caramazza et al. (1983) conjecture that a phonological processing deficit was implicated not only in the comprehension of spoken language, but also in the comprehension of written sentences. The authors see this as a consequence of a necessary reliance on phonological recoding to perform higher-level (syntactic) processing of written sentences.

Impairments that disrupt spoken language comprehension but leave written language comprehension intact (or relatively preserved) have also been observed in patients whose acoustic and phonetic perception appear to be preserved. This pattern of comprehension deficit and intact segmental perception, when seen in combination with a preserved capacity to repeat and make accurate lexical decisions, has been described as word-meaning deafness (Bramwell, 1984 [1897];

Franklin et al., 1994; Franklin et al., 1996; Kohn & Friedman, 1986; Yamadori & Albert, 1973). For example, Franklin et al. (1996) describe a patient, DrO, who appeared to exhibit a disconnection between the lexical phonological level and the semantic level of the model in Figure 21.1. DrO performed normally (and on some measures better than controls) on tests of auditory temporal acuity (e.g., click fusion and formant frequency modulation) and on phoneme discrimination tasks with both word and nonword CVC stimuli, which provides at least some evidence that early auditory and phonemic processing mechanisms were intact. He also performed at normal levels on a lexical decision task (with both high and low imageable words and phonologically plausible nonwords), and though his lexical repetition was below ceiling, he was substantially better at repeating words than at repeating nonwords. This lexicality effect suggests that his below ceiling performance on repetition tasks may reflect the presence of a memory related deficit. His performance on these lexical tasks suggests that he was able to identify and discriminate between lexical forms fairly well. In contrast, DrO was unable to comprehend spoken words (in particular low imageability words) that he was nevertheless able to repeat accurately, and his comprehension for low imageability items presented auditorily was markedly worse than for the same words presented visually. Franklin et al. cite several such examples from a definition task. Asked to define the spoken word "slow," DrO responded "slow, slow, slow, slow, I know what it is, but I can't get it, slow, slow – you'll have to write it down for me." When the word was then written for him, DrO replied "Oh, slow, well slow is the opposite of fast." For the spoken target "mature" he replied "mature, mature, mature, what's a mature? I don't know, I missed it"; but when then shown the written word, he responded: "Oh, mature, mature – that is somebody who is very wise and usually older" (Franklin et al., 1996, p. 1150). The contrasting comprehension performance for speech and writing suggests that DrO's representations of lexical meanings were preserved, but that he was unable to *access* those meanings when words were presented auditorily. The pattern of modality-specific comprehension deficit seen in patients like DrO would appear to leave the speech perception system relatively intact up to and including the level of lexical-phonological representation, and to selectively implicate the mapping from these intact lexical-phonological representations onto associated semantic representations.

A breakdown in the mapping from representations of lexical-phonological forms to more abstract lexical-semantic representations also appears to contribute to more complicated patterns of acquired deficit, including cases of aphasia profiles that are clinically labeled transcortical sensory aphasia (TSA) and Wernicke's aphasia. Defective lexical comprehension is a clinical criterion for both of these varieties of fluent aphasia (as are impairments in naming, fluent though semantically empty spontaneous speech, and the tendency to produce lexical paraphasias). However, the lexical comprehension deficits are not by principle limited to the auditory modality and therefore may involve more abstract lexical-semantic deficits. The two aphasia categories are distinguished primarily on the basis of whether the patient can repeat spoken words or sentences: By definition, repetition is intact in transcortical sensory aphasia; it is impaired in Wernicke's aphasia. The critical matter in clarifying the nature of the auditory comprehension deficit in any individual patient, though, is just where the comprehension process breaks down. For example, a transcortical sensory aphasic may be intact in processing sublexical auditory information – as evidenced by the ability to repeat both words and nonwords – but exhibit bad auditory comprehension. It appears in at least some cases of TSA that the auditory comprehension deficit derives from a disconnection of early intact mechanisms for identifying speech sounds from more abstract, modality independent representations of meaning. For example, the patient RR was able to match spoken words to pictures with reasonable accuracy (90%) when a single distracter picture was either phonologically related or unrelated to the target name, but his performance fell to chance levels when the distracter was semantically related to the target (Berndt, Basili, & Caramazza, 1987).

Variation in performance patterns and in the location and extent of the lesions that can give rise to Wernicke's aphasia or to TSA suggest that there can be substantial functional heterogeneity among the combinations of deficits that fall under either of these clinical categories of aphasia. Nevertheless, there are data which indicate that the speech perception resources that are required for the preserved ability to repeat words or nonwords in TSA, or to perform auditory lexical decision, may draw heavily on mechanisms of the uninjured, non-dominant hemisphere (Berthier et al., 1991; Praamstra et al., 1991). Representative evidence regarding contributions to speech perception from structures in the non-dominant hemisphere can be seen in a patient described by Praamstra et al. (1991). Following an initial temporoparietal injury to the left hemisphere, the patient presented with a language deficit that was classified as Wernicke's aphasia. Auditory and written comprehension were impaired, as was repetition. The patient showed some ability to repeat individual sounds, monosyllabic Dutch words, and "foreign" words, though not at normal levels of performance. Although there may be some indication from below-normal performance on these repetition tasks that an auditory perceptual defect existed following this left-hemisphere injury, the patient's intact ability to perform auditory lexical decision suggests that auditory lexical and sublexical processing was relatively intact in comparison to the disruptions that gave rise to the lexical comprehension deficit. This pattern of preserved and impaired capacities changed abruptly, though, following a second CVA, this time to the contralateral temporal auditory cortex. The second stroke left the patient severely word deaf: His performance on auditory lexical decision fell to chance, whereas his performance on visual lexical decision was error free. Auditory comprehension and repetition were also substantially reduced, whereas naming and other central language functions not requiring auditory input remained at levels that had been observed before the second stroke. Tasks with synthetic CV stimuli revealed abnormal discrimination for place and abnormal identification for both place and voicing among stop consonants. The outcome indicates that right-hemisphere auditory mechanisms supported most (if not all) speech perception in the period between the two focal injuries. This would suggest that both hemispheres in the normal brain support speech perception. What remains to be determined is just which elements of the auditory comprehension system that is schematized in Figure 21.1 normally draw on right-hemisphere mechanisms.

21.2 Pure Word Deafness and Lateralization

Pure word deafness is particularly relevant to matters of *anatomical localization* insofar as the deficit can reveal which components of speech perception are lateralized to the left hemisphere. The data are not entirely transparent. Pure word deafness is most often seen in patients with bilateral temporal lesions (Auerbach et al., 1982; Coslett et al., 1984; Mendez & Geehan, 1988; Miceli, 1982; Motomura et al., 1986; Tanaka et al., 1987; Yaqub et al., 1988; see also Griffiths et al., 1999). In more than one of these case studies it is noted that the verbal agnosia was observed following a second, right-hemisphere lesion, but that the initial left-hemisphere lesion left no observable speech perception deficit once initial symptoms had resolved (Auerbach et al., 1982; Kazui et al., 1990; Tanaka et al., 1987). Such observations suggest that some amount of speech perception can be carried out in both hemispheres – which is consistent with the finding that some speech perception is possible following anesthetization of the left hemisphere (Boatman et al., 1998). However, there are also cases of speech perception deficit that fit the profile of pure word deafness following unilateral injury. Geschwind (1965) cites a case of pure word deafness reported by Liepmann in 1898 in which "ordinary deafness could be ruled out." At autopsy, Liepmann determined that the lesion was "located subcortically in the left temporal lobe." Other cases of pure word deafness resulting from unilateral subcortical (left-hemisphere) lesions have been verified by imaging (Saffran et al., 1976; Takahashi et al., 1992; Wang et al., 2000) or implicated by strictly clinical/behavioral measures (Caramazza et al., 1983; Denes & Semenza, 1975; Gazzaniga et al., 1973).

The contrasting lesion patterns associated with pure word deafness have been offered several interpretations. Auerbach et al. (1982) proposed that patients who exhibit pure word deafness following bilateral destruction of primary auditory cortex suffer from a "pre-phonemic temporal auditory acuity deficit" (p. 272), whereas they maintain that temporal auditory acuity is not implicated in patients who exhibit the perceptual deficit following unilateral (left) temporal lobe damage. Instead, Auerbach et al. suggest that word deafness following unilateral injury implicates a "higher disorder in phonemic discrimination" (p. 296). The connection between the laterality of lesion and the type of perceptual deficit may not be as clear cut as Auerbach et al.'s typology of word deafness predicts. For example, a unilateral (left-hemisphere) injury that produces word deafness may cause a prephonemic deficit: Saffran et al.'s (1976) patient showed substantial disruption in discriminating among stop consonants that differ in voicing, and a less severe, though notable, defect for place. Similarly, Wang et al. (2000) describe a patient with a single, left-hemisphere lesion who was able to perform accurately on discrimination tasks with pitch or amplitude differences in pure tone stimuli, but who was markedly impaired in distinguishing short rising vs. falling sinewave stimuli. The patient was also able to discriminate among vowels and diphthongs, but performed poorly on word stress contrasts (*hotdog/hot dog*), and on minimal pair discrimination and identification (auditory visual word matching) with CVC words. One complication regarding such cases is the possibility of functionally mixed origins: An agnosia for speech sounds may reflect selective damage (1) to so-called "associative" mechanisms that map auditory representations onto higher order categories of speech and language, (2) to earlier auditory mechanisms that are tuned to specific properties of the acoustic signal (Griffiths et al., 1999; Phillips & Farmer, 1990), or (3) to elements of both associative and perceptual mechanisms and representations.

Poeppel (2001) adopts much of Auerbach et al.'s (1982) proposal regarding the apparent association between auditory acuity deficits and the presence of bilateral injury, although he makes further differentiations among the expected patterns of word deafness based on whether the injury destroys primary or neighboring auditory cortex in the two hemispheres. He also argues that, even though resources in both left and right hemisphere appear to support early stages of speech perception, the two hemispheres process auditory stimuli differently, in part because they respond to acoustic properties at different temporal grains. According to Poeppel's model, primary auditory cortex (or surrounding belt structure) in the left hemisphere responds best to fast changes in the acoustic signal – changes that take place within a brief temporal window (25–40 ms) – whereas the homologous structures of the right hemisphere operate over spans up to 200–300 ms. Accordingly, it is hypothesized that left-hemisphere structures are better adapted to detect the rapid changes that are relevant to place and voicing contrasts among stop consonants, whereas right-hemisphere structures support finer spectral discriminations (Zatorre & Belin, 2001; Zatorre, Belin, & Penhune, 2002) and are better at detecting properties that unfold over longer periods. Evidence for such hemispheric asymmetries derives from a number of sources. Robin, Tranel, and Damasio (1990) had patients with unilateral temporal, parietal or temporoparietal lesions (and normal controls) perform nonspeech tasks designed to probe the processing of temporal information (click fusion; location of a shortened gap between two tones in a six-tone sequence) and spectral information (e.g., frequency discrimination; pitch matching) in the auditory signal. They report that each of the patients with left-hemisphere injury performed worse than the right-hemisphere patients and controls on the temporal perceptual tasks, whereas each of the patients in the right-hemisphere group performed more poorly than the left-hemisphere patients and controls on the spectral tasks. Zatorre et al. (2002) review several recent studies using electrophysiological recording and measures of cerebral blood flow (PET and fMRI) that provide further support for the view that the left and right hemispheres exhibit relative specialization for temporal vs. spectral properties of auditory events respectively, and that auditory cortex in the left hemisphere alone may have the capacity to reliably extract from fast temporal changes the information that is required for discriminating the place and voicing properties of some speech sounds.[6] These differences in temporal vs. spectral sensitivity can, on Poeppel's (2001) account, give rise to early deficits that selectively disrupt the perception of speech segments that are better discriminated in the left hemisphere than in the right in the intact brain.

Above the level of acoustic-phonetic processing, the speech perception system appears to be strongly lateralized.[7] Evidence for this view derives from the fact that injury to temporoparietal structures in the left hemisphere frequently impair auditory comprehension and speech perception (in addition to other language functions), whereas injury confined to homologous structures in the right hemisphere do not. However, it is the existence of pure word deafness following unilateral (left-hemisphere) lesions that provides some of the strongest evidence that representations of lexical form and meaning reside predominantly in the left hemisphere. Imaging and autopsy studies of patients with pure word deafness following a single left-hemisphere lesion indicate that the affected structures include both the auditory cortex of the left hemisphere and the subcortical fibers connecting the auditory cortex of the right hemisphere to the posterior temporal and temporoparietal auditory areas of the left hemisphere (Takahashi et al., 1992). If the representation of lexical form and meaning were *robustly* bilateral, then one could reasonably expect that intact right-hemisphere language areas would adequately support auditory lexical recognition and comprehension. Instead, a deep left-hemisphere lesion that simultaneously (1) disconnects right-hemisphere auditory cortex from left-hemisphere language areas and (2) destroys (or disconnects) the auditory cortex of the left hemisphere itself will effectively sever the auditory route for language comprehension at the acoustic-phonetic or phonemic level.

In summary, acoustic-phonetic processing appears to be carried out all along the ascending auditory pathway, up to and including the MGB and the auditory cortices of the two hemispheres. It is also somewhat clear that the lexical-phonological and lexical-semantic levels of the model in Figure 21.1 are both strongly lateralized to the left hemisphere. What is less certain is how the phonemic level of the model in Figure 21.1 is distributed anatomically. The patient JS, whose performance most suggests a deficit at this representational level, exhibited a form of word deafness following a unilateral, left-hemisphere lesion (Caramazza et al., 1983). Unlike word-deaf patients whose impairment was identified as pre-phonemic, JS's impairment affected all classes of speech sounds, and appears to implicate more abstract, phonological processing mechanisms. This could be taken as evidence that phonemic representations are strongly lateralized, since one might otherwise expect intact right-hemisphere resources to support phonemic labeling. The problem with such an argument, though, is that JS's poor performance on phoneme identification may reflect a disruption to left-hemisphere representations and/or processes that are required for phoneme labeling tasks, but that are not themselves part of the central speech perception system itself (Norris et al., 2000). Hence, whether the phonemic level of the speech perception system is strongly lateralized remains to be sorted out.

21.3 Segmental and Lexical Perception in Clinical Aphasia Groups

Studies of speech perception relating to the clinical categories of aphasia have focused on the hypothesis that impairments in lexical comprehension, especially in patients categorized as Wernicke's aphasics, might derive from speech perception deficits at either the phonemic or acoustic-phonetic levels (e.g., Basso et al., 1977; Blumstein, Baker, & Goodglass, 1977; Blumstein, Cooper et al., 1977; Boyczuk & Baum, 1999). Other studies sort patients on the basis of comprehension measures alone to determine the potential contribution of a speech perception impairment (e.g., Yeni-Komshian & Lafontaine, 1983), or into groups based on the locus of injury – left- vs. right-hemisphere – and whether there is an associated language deficit (e.g., Baum, 2002; Miceli et al., 1978; Miceli et al., 1980). For reasons of space, we will focus on the syndrome based studies of links between speech perception and auditory lexical comprehension deficits. Phonemic discrimination and labeling were the standard tools for evaluating speech perception in these studies. The general finding is that auditory lexical comprehension deficits in aphasic patients cannot in every instance be attributed to a perceptual deficit below the lexical level. For example, Blumstein, Baker, & Goodglass (1977) compared the comprehension abilities of patients from different clinical categories to their ability to perform discrimination tasks with natural word and nonword stimuli: phonemic contrasts involving differences in voicing (pear – bear), place of articulation (pin – tin), or both place and voicing (pen – den); different syllables (describe – prescribe); and different phoneme orders (tax – task). When the patients categorized as Broca's aphasics (who as a group performed best on both comprehension and discrimination) were set aside, the correlation between comprehension measures and phoneme discrimination scores was poor. The correlation among the Wernicke's patients was unreliable, albeit in the expected (i.e., positive) direction.

Studies with synthetic speech stimuli likewise failed to establish clear associations between lexical comprehension and performance on segmental discrimination and labeling tasks (Basso et al., 1977; Blumstein, Cooper et al., 1977). For example, Basso et al. had brain damaged and neurologically intact matched controls perform a /ta/ – /da/ labeling task in which VOT was varied in 10 ms steps from –150 to +150. They identified patients as having a Phonemic Identification Defect (PID) if their labeling profile was abnormal in comparison to control subjects, and they distinguished three degrees of PID based on the extent of departure from the mean control pattern for the boundary zone between the /ta/ and /da/ labeling functions. Basso et al. found that PID was almost entirely limited to patients with left-hemisphere injury, and only to those among the left-hemisphere patients who suffered some aphasic deficits. They observed a significant correlation between the degree of PID and the patient's performance on a standardized instrument for measuring auditory comprehension (Token Test). However, they also found that PID was a poor predictor of auditory lexical comprehension deficit: All but one of the patients categorized as Broca's aphasics produced a labeling profile that was taken to indicate a PID, despite the fact that these patients all exhibited good auditory comprehension; and for nearly a third of the patients in their group of fluent aphasics with poor comprehension (including 13 identified as severe Wernicke's aphasics, 2 as transcortical sensory aphasics, and 3 mixed Wernicke's transcortical sensory aphasics), the testing revealed no evidence of PID. Blumstein, Cooper et al. (1977) also failed to establish a consistent link between comprehension and segmental perception abilities in their labeling and discrimination study using the /ta/ – /da/ VOT continuum. Their study extends Basso et al.'s data in that they observed a dissociation between labeling and discrimination: Whereas every patient who failed to discriminate between synthetic stimuli from opposite sides of the voicing boundary also failed on the labeling tasks, three of their four Wernicke's patients exhibited normal performance on the discrimination task, but were unable to label the synthetic stimuli.[8] In another study of phoneme categorization, Blumstein et al. (1994) observed that the fluent aphasics in their labeling experiment (the Wernicke's and Conduction aphasics) failed to exhibit a lexicality effect of the sort Ganong

(1980) found with normal participants – i.e., the patients failed to shift the boundary between voiced and voiceless consonants when one end of the VOT continuum resulted in a word and the other in a nonword (*duke* – *tuke* and *doot* – *toot*).

Based on these and other findings (e.g., Milberg, Blumstein, & Dworetzky, 1988), Blumstein and colleagues concluded that disrupted perception of segmental types is not a reliable contributing element in the auditory lexical comprehension deficits that form part of the clinical profile for aphasic syndromes such as Wernicke's aphasia and TSA. They conjecture that the auditory comprehension defects observed with aphasic patients reflect a compromise to the interface between the lexicon and the representation of speech sounds. One should note, of course, that there is no evidence from these studies to suggest that a deficit in auditory or phonemic level processing *cannot* (or is unlikely to) co-occur with other components of the aphasic profile: Such a deficit may (and likely does) contribute to a disruption to auditory lexical comprehension in some cases. Variability between patients with regard to this potential contribution is perhaps to be expected, though, if only because a speech perception deficit is not a criterion for clinical classification in any aphasic syndrome, whereas defective auditory lexical comprehension specifically *is* one of the defining criteria for both Wernicke's aphasia and TSA. Due to the lack of details presented *on a patient-by-patient basis* about the specific pattern of preserved and impaired abilities in speech perception and auditory lexical comprehension, even tantalizing observations about (1) dissociations between phonemic discrimination vs. identification, or (2) dissociations between segmental vs. lexical recognition have been of little direct value in helping to clarify properties of the speech perception system or to understand the neurological basis of this system. What these studies have succeeded in showing, though, is that not all auditory lexical comprehension deficits seen in aphasia can be reduced to perceptual defects at phonemic or pre-phonemic processing levels.

21.4 Concluding Remarks

Examination of acquired deficits that affect speech perception and auditory lexical comprehension reveals that there is substantial structure in the speech perception system. In particular, it appears that the auditory route to lexical meaning includes multiple processing stages that can be selectively disrupted by focal brain injury, and that patient studies can help clarify the architecture of this multi-stage process. For reasons of space, the discussion in this chapter has focused on whether the model in Figure 21.1 is sufficient to capture the patterns of dissociation that have been observed in patient studies, rather than how this model compares to other potential functional architectures for the speech perception system (e.g., Franklin, 1989; Hickok & Poeppel, 2000). Certainly there are aspects of the current model that are in need of elaboration. In particular, evidence from different patterns of dissociation for vowel and consonant perception (and for stop-consonant place and voicing perception) suggest that the acoustic-phonetic stage of the perceptual process is significantly more complex than this model would suggest. In other respects, the present model may make distinctions that are not strongly supported by the patient data discussed here. For example, whether the phonemic and lexical phonological levels must be differentiated may not be supported by the neuropsychological data as strongly as are some of the model's other processing distinctions. One can hope, though, that further development of this or other models of speech perception will benefit from analyses of how the architecture of the speech perception system has been found to fracture following focal brain injury.

ACKNOWLEDGMENTS

This paper could not have been written without the insights and advice that I received from Dana Boatman. I would also like to thank Fero Kuminiak, Elliot Moreton, Rebecca Piorkowski, David Poeppel, Brenda Rapp, Carlo Semenza and the editors of this handbook for many helpful proposals for improving earlier drafts of this work. I have no doubt that this chapter would be better had I incorporated more of their suggestions. Needless to say, all faults that remain are my own invention.

NOTES

1 I leave the issue of how syllabic organization is to be incorporated into the present model as a matter that remains to be decided.

2 For a comprehensive review of research on deficits that diminish the ability to perceive (and produce) grammatical and affective prosody, see Baum & Pell (1999).

3 It is important to rule out peripheral hearing loss in cases of auditory agnosia and pure word deafness. Peripheral hearing mechanisms carry out some acoustic processing (frequency and intensity coding), and so damage to these mechanisms would vastly complicate any attempt to clarify how more central structures refine and interpret the spectrotemporal properties of the speech signal.

4 Cortical stimulation studies have also established that consonant discrimination (but not vowel discrimination) can be disrupted at specific temporal sites (Boatman et al., 1997).

5 Participants are asked to determine if they detect one or two events when the clicks are presented dichotically. Word-deaf patients have been reported to distinguish discrete clicks only when they are separated by intervals of silence ranging from approximately 16 ms to over 100 ms, whereas intact controls can perceive two clicks as independent auditory events when they are separated by as little as 3–4 ms.

6 This characterization leaves open the role of left-hemisphere structures in making the fine-grain spectral discriminations that underlie vowel and fricative perception. However, it is implausible that there could be a wholesale division of labor between the two hemispheres along the lines of having fast temporal changes processed in left-hemisphere auditory cortex and slower, spectral processing in the right-hemisphere for segmental perception. Setting aside the problem it raises for integrating coordinated spectrotemporal cues across hemispheres, the hypothetical role of hemispheric specialization defined in these terms would also appear to face difficulties explaining consonant-vowel

dissociations in pure word deafness following bilateral lesions.

7 This asymmetry appears to be the norm despite the fact mentioned above that, in at least some individuals, the right hemisphere appears to support (very) limited auditory lexical processing abilities.

8 Hickok & Poeppel (2000) have interpreted this dissociation to indicate that the ability to label phonemic segments taps into mechanisms that lie outside of the central speech perception system. (Cf. Norris et al.'s (2000) phonemic decision units in Merge.) Hickok & Poeppel argue from both lesion and imaging studies that phonemic labeling and other tasks that depend on explicit access to sub-lexical speech units draw on a processing pathway from auditory areas to "extra-auditory" left-hemisphere structures (including portions of inferior parietal cortex and Broca's area) that serve as an interface between auditory and motor processing.

REFERENCES

Albert, M. & Bear, D. (1974). Time to understand: A case study of word deafness with reference to the role of time in auditory comprehension. *Brain*, 97, 373–84.

Auerbach, S., Allard, T., Naeser, M., Alexander, M., & Albert, M. (1982). Pure word deafness: Analysis of a case with bilateral lesions and a deficit at the prephonemic level. *Brain*, 105, 271–300.

Bahls, F., Chatrain, G., Mesher, R., Sumi, S., & Ruff, R. (1988). A case of persistent cortical deafness: Clinical, neurophysiologic, and neuropathologic observations. *Neurology*, 38 1490–3.

Basso, A., Casati, G., & Vignolo, L. (1977). Phonemic identification deficit in aphasia. *Cortex*, 13, 85–95.

Baum, S. (2001). Contextual influences on phonetic identification in aphasia: The effects of speaking rate and semantic bias. *Brain and Language*, 76, 266–81.

Baum, S. (2002). Consonant and vowel discrimination by brain-damaged individuals: Effects of phonological segmentation. *Journal of Neurolinguistics*, 15, 447–61.

Baum, S. & Pell, M. (1999). The neural basis of prosody: Insights from lesion studies and neuroimaging. *Aphasiology*, 13, 581–608.

Berndt, R., Basili, A., & Caramazza, A. (1987). A dissociation of functions in a case of Transcortical Sensory Aphasia. *Cognitive Neuropsychology*, 4, 79–107.

Berthier, M., Starkstein, S., Leiguarda, R., Ruiz, A., Mayberg, H., Wagner, H., Price, T., & Robinson, R. (1991). Transcortical aphasia: Importance of the nonspeech dominant hemisphere in language repetition. *Brain*, 114, 1409–27.

Blumstein, S., Baker, E., & Goodglass, H. (1977). Phonological factors in auditory comprehension in aphasia. *Neuropsychologia*, 15, 19–30.

Blumstein, S., Burton, M., Baum, S., Waldstein, R., & Katz, D. (1994). The role of lexical status on the phonetic categorization of speech in aphasia. *Brain and Language*, 46, 181–97.

Blumstein, S., Cooper, W., Zurif, E., & Caramazza, A. (1977). The perception and production of voice-onset time in aphasia. *Neuropsychologia*, 15, 371–83.

Boatman, D., Hall, C., Goldstein, M., Lesser, R., & Gordon, B. (1997). Neuroperceptual differences in consonant and vowel discriminations: As revealed by direct cortical electrical interference. *Cortex*, 33, 83–98.

Boatman, D., Hart, J., Lesser, R., Honeycutt, N., Anderson, N., Miglioretti, D., & Gordon, B. (1998). Right hemisphere speech perception revealed by amobarbital injection and electrical interference. *Neurology*, 51, 458–64.

Boyczuk, J. & Baum, S. (1999). The influence of neighborhood density on phonetic categorization in aphasia. *Brain and Language*, 67, 46–70.

Bramwell, B. (1984). A case of word meaning deafness (1897), with introduction by A. W. Ellis, *Cognitive Neuropsychology*, 1, 245–58. (Reprinted from: Illustrative cases of aphasia. *Lancet*, 1 (1897), 1256–9.)

Buchman, A., Garron, D., Trost-Cardamone, J., Wichter, M., & Schwartz, M. (1986). Word deafness: One hundred years later. *Journal of Neurology, Neurosurgery, and Psychiatry*, 49, 489–99.

Caramazza, A. (1984). The logic of neuropsychological research and the problem of patient classification in aphasia. *Brain and Language*, 21, 9–20.

Caramazza, A., Berndt, R. S., & Basili, A. G. (1983). The selective impairment of phonological processing: A case study. *Brain and Language*, 18, 128–74.

Coslett, H., Brashear, H., & Heilman, K. (1984). Pure word deafness after bilateral primary auditory cortex infarcts. *Neurology*, 34, 347–52.

Delgutte, B. (1980). Representation of speech-like sounds in the discharge patterns of auditory-nerve fibers. *Journal of the Acoustical Society of America*, 68, 843–57.

Denes, G. & Semenza, C. (1975). Auditory modality specific anomia: Evidence from a case of pure word deafness. *Cortex*, 11, 401–11.

Ellis, A. & Young, A. (1988). *Human Cognitive Neuropsychology*. Hillsdale, NJ: Lawrence Erlbaum.

Engelien, A., Huber, W., Silbersweig, D., Stern, E., Frith, C., Döring, W., Thron, A., & Frankowiak, R. (2000). The neural correlates of "deaf-hearing" in man: Conscious sensory awareness enabled by attentional modulation. *Brain*, 123, 532–45.

Franklin, S. (1989). Dissociations in auditory word comprehension: Evidence from nine fluent aphasic patients. *Aphasiology*, 3, 189–207.

Franklin, S., Howard, D., & Patterson, K. (1994). Abstract word meaning deafness. *Cognitive Neuropsychology*, 11, 1–34.

Franklin, S., Turner, J., Lambon, R. M., Morris, J., & Bailey, P. (1996). A distinctive case of word meaning deafness? *Cognitive Neuropsychology*, 13, 1139–62.

Fuji, T., Fukatsu, R., Watabe, S., Ohnuma, A., Teramura, K., Kimura, I., Saso, S., & Kogure, K. (1990). Auditory sound agnosia without aphasia following a right temporal lobe lesion. *Cortex*, 26, 263–8.

Ganong, W. (1980). Phonetic categorization in auditory word perception. *Journal of Experimental Psychology: Human Perception and Performance*, 6, 110–25.

Gaskell, M. & Marslen-Wilson, W. (1997). Integrating form and meaning: A distributed model of speech perception. *Language and Cognitive Processes*, 12, 613–56.

Gazzaniga, M., Glass, A., Sarno, M., & Posner, J. (1973). Pure word deafness and hemispheric dynamics: Case history. *Cortex*, 9, 136–43.

Geschwind, N. (1965). Disconnection syndromes in animals and man. *Brain*, 88, 237–94, 585–644.

Godefroy, O., Leys, D., Furby, A., De Reuck, J., Daems, C., Rondpierre, P., Debachy, B., Deleume, J.-F., & Desaulty, A. (1995). Psychoacoustical deficits related to bilateral subcortical hemorages: A case with apperceptive auditory agnosia. *Cortex*, 31, 149–59.

Goldblum, M.-C. & Albert, M. (1972). Phonemic discrimination in sensory aphasia. *International Journal of Mental Health*, 1, 25–9.

Gow, D. & Caplan, D. (1996). An examination of impaired acoustic-phonetic processing in aphasia. *Brain and Language*, 52, 386–407.

Griffiths, T., Rees, A., & Green, G. (1999). Disorders of human complex sound processing. *Neurocase*, 5, 365–78.

Hickok, G. & Poeppel, D. (2000). Towards a functional neuroanatomy of speech

perception. *Trends in Cognitive Sciences*, 4, 131–8.
Hillis, A. (2001). The organization of the lexical system. In B. Rapp (ed.), *The Handbook of Cognitive Neuropsychology: What Deficits Reveal about the Human Mind* (pp. 185–210). Philadelphia, PA: Psychology Press.
Hillis, A., Boatman, D., Hart, J., & Gordon, B. (1999). Making sense out of jargon: A neurolinguistic and computational account of jargon aphasia. *Neurology*, 53, 1813–24.
Kazui, S., Naritomi, H., Swada, T., Inoue, N., & Okuda, J.-I. (1990). Subcortical auditory agnosia. *Brain and Language*, 38, 476–87.
Klatt, D. (1979). Speech perception: A model of acoustic-phonetic analysis and lexical access. *Journal of Phonetics*, 7, 279–312.
Kohn, S. & Friedman, R. (1986). Word-meaning deafness: A phonological-semantic dissociation. *Cognitive Neuropsychology*, 3, 291–308.
Lambert, J., Eustache, F., Lechevalier, B., Rossa, Y., & Viader, F. (1989). Auditory agnosia with relative sparing of speech perception. *Cortex*, 25, 71–82.
McClelland, J. & Elman, J. (1986). The TRACE model of speech perception. *Cognitive Psychology*, 18, 1–86.
McGlone, J. (1984). Speech comprehension after unilateral injection of sodium amytal. *Brain and Language*, 22, 150–7.
Mendez, M. & Geehan, G. (1988). Cortical auditory disorders: Clinical and psychoacoustic features. *Journal of Neurology, Neurosurgery, and Psychiatry*, 51, 1–9.
Metz-Lutz, M. N. & Dahl, E. (1984). Analysis of word comprehension in a case of pure word deafness. *Brain and Language*, 23, 13–25.
Miceli, G. (1982). The processing of speech sounds in a patient with cortical auditory deficit. *Neuropsychologia*, 20, 5–20.
Miceli, G., Caltagirone, C., Gainotti, G., & Payer-Rigo, P. (1978). Discrimination of voice versus place contrasts in aphasia. *Brain and Language*, 6, 47–51.
Miceli, G., Gainotti, G., Caltagirone, C., & Masullo, C. (1980). Some aspects of phonological impairment in aphasia. *Brain and Language*, 11, 159–69.
Michel, F., Peronnet, F., & Schott, B. (1980). A case of cortical deafness: clinical and electrophysiological data. *Brain and Language*, 10, 367–77.
Milberg, W., Blumstein, S., & Dworetzky, B. (1988). Phonological processing and lexical access in aphasia. *Brain and Language*, 34, 279–93.
Motomura, N., Yamadori, A., Mori, E., & Tamaru, F. (1986). Auditory aphasia: Analysis of a case with bilateral subcortical lesions. *Brain*, 109, 379–91.
Mozaz Garde, M. & Cowley, A. (2000). "Deaf Hearing": Unacknowledged detection of auditory stimuli in a patient with cerebral deafness. *Cortex*, 36, 71–80.
Norris, D., McQueen, J., & Cutler, A. (2000). Merging information in speech recognition: Feedback is never necessary. *Behavioral and Brain Sciences*, 23, 299–370.
Peretz, I. (2001). Music perception and recognition. In B. Rapp (ed.), *The Handbook of Cognitive Neuropsychology: What Deficits Reveal about the Human Mind* (pp. 519–40). Philadelphia, PA: Psychology Press.
Phillips, D. & Farmer, M. (1990). Acquired word deafness, and the temporal grain of sound representation in the primary auditory cortex. *Behavioural Brain Research*, 40, 85–94.
Poeppel, D. (2001). Pure word deafness and the bilateral processing of the speech code. *Cognitive Science*, 25, 679–93.
Polster, M. & Rose, S. (1998). Disorders of auditory processing: Evidence for modularity in audition. *Cortex*, 34, 47–65.
Praamstra, R., Hagoort, P., Maasen, B., & Crul, T. (1991). Word deafness and auditory cortical function. *Brain*, 114, 1197–225.
Robin, D., Tranel, D., & Damasio, H. (1990). Auditory perception of temporal

and spectral events in patients with focal left and right cerebral lesions. *Brain and Language*, 39, 539–55.

Sachs, M. & Young, E. (1979). Encoding of steady-state vowels in the auditory nerve: Representation in terms of discharge rate. *Journal of the Acoustical Society of America*, 66, 470–9.

Sachs, M., Voight, H., & Young, E. (1983). Auditory nerve representation of vowels in background noise. *Journal of Neurophysiology*, 50, 27–45.

Saffran, E., Marin, O., & Yeni-Komshian, G. (1976). An analysis of speech perception in a case of word deafness. *Brain and Language*, 3, 209–28.

Spreen, O., Benton, A., & Fincham, R. (1965). Auditory agnosia without aphasia. *Archives of Neurology*, 13, 84–92.

Takahashi, N., Kawamura, M., Shinotou, H., Hirayaha, K., Kalia, K., & Shindo, M. (1992). Pure word deafness due to left hemisphere damage. *Cortex*, 28, 295–303.

Tanaka, Y., Kamo, T., Yoshida, M., & Yamodori, A. (1991). So-called cortical deafness: Clinical neuropsychological and radiological observations. *Brain*, 114, 2385–401.

Tanaka, Y., Yamodori, A., & Mori, E. (1987). Pure word deafness following bilateral lesions. *Brain*, 110, 381–403.

Taniwaki, T., Tagawa, K., Sato, F., & Iino, K. (2000). Auditory agnosia restricted to environmental sounds following cortical deafness and generalized auditory agnosia. *Clinical Neurology and Neurosurgery*, 102, 156–62.

Van Lancker, D. & Canter, G. (1982). Impairment of voice and face recognition in patients with hemispheric damage. *Brain and Cognition*, 1, 185–95.

von Stockert, T. (1982). On the structure of word deafness and mechanisms underlying the fluctuations of disturbances of higher cortical functions. *Brain and Language*, 16, 133–46.

Wada, J. & Rasmussen, T. (1960). Intracarotid injection of sodium amytal for the lateralization of cerebral speech dominance. *Journal of Neurosurgery*, 17, 266–82.

Wang, E., Peach, R., Xu, Y., Schneck, M., & Manry, C. (2000). Perception of dynamic acoustic patterns by an individual with unilateral verbal auditory agnosia. *Brain and Language*, 73, 442–55.

Yamadori, A. & Albert, M. (1973). Word category aphasia. *Cortex*, 9, 83–9.

Yaqub, B., Gascon, G., Al-Nosha, M., & Whitaker, H. (1988). Pure word deafness (acquired verbal auditory agnosia) in an Arabic speaking patient. *Brain*, 111, 457–66.

Yeni-Komshian, G. & Lafontaine, L. (1983). Discrimination and identification of voicing and place contrasts in aphasic patients. *Canadian Journal of Psychology*, 37, 107–31.

Zatorre, R. & Belin, P. (2001). Spectral and temporal processing in human auditory cortex. *Cerebral Cortex*, 11, 946–53.

Zatorre, R., Belin, P., & Penhune, V. (2002). Structure and function of auditory cortex: Music and speech. *Trends in Cognitive Sciences*, 6, 37–46.

22 Cross-Language Speech Perception

NÚRIA SEBASTIÁN-GALLÉS

22.1 Introduction

It has long been known that speech perception is influenced by the phonological properties of the listener's native language. Maybe the first reference can be traced back to the Bible. In Judges 12: 5–6, a cross-language speech production task was used to decide about the origin (maternal language) of a man:

> and it was so, that when those Ephraimites which were escaped said, Let me go over; that the men of Gilead said unto him, Art thou an Ephraimite? If he said, Nay. Then said they unto him, Say now Shibboleth: and he said Sibboleth: for he could not frame to pronounce it right. Then they took him, and slew him at the passages of Jordan: and there fell at that time of the Ephraimites forty and two thousand.[1]

As this quotation shows, although the difficulties of mastering the processing of a non-native language have always attracted human attention, it has not been until quite recently that researchers have begun to understand the basic sensory, perceptual, and linguistic mechanisms that operate at its base. In fact, our knowledge is still very limited when we consider the neurological substrate underlying it. Furthermore, most studies in this field have dealt with the perception of segments (vowels and consonants). In fact, there are excellent reviews covering these topics (Strange, 1995). But there is much more to the field of speech perception that depends on the phonological properties of the native language (or first language, L1) than just the perception of phonetic segments. In this chapter we will not only discuss issues on segmental speech perception (compared with other existing reviews we will offer a short and selective summary), but also extend and cover those other aspects of cross-language speech perception usually neglected in this type of overview.

Another distinctive feature will characterize the present chapter. Whenever possible, special attention will be devoted to physiological and brain imaging techniques. Over the past few years, this type of research method has become more and more available. The availability of these techniques is opening new windows and new questions (and puzzles) are being formulated.

22.2 Phonological Deafness: What Cannot Be Heard

The process of speech perception can be described, in the most simplistic way, as what happens in between the perception of an acoustic wave and the discovery of the meaning of words. Though highly simplistic, this description points to the crucial characteristic of the processing, namely, the huge change in processing format: from physical sound waves to neural patterns representing the meaning of words. Fortunately, this chapter will only deal with the impact of cross-language differences in this processing and will leave out many peripheral questions and will focus on linguistic units.

Languages "sound" different, these differences are so evident that other mammals, like cotton-top tamarin monkeys and rats (Ramus et al., 2000; Toro, Trobalón, & Sebastián-Gallés, 2003; Toro, Trobalon, & Sebastián-Gallés, 2004) realize that Japanese and Dutch speakers talk "different." The way these animals make the distinction is not at first trivial, since they cannot distinguish backwards Japanese from backwards Dutch. Although we do not know what types of information these animals use to perceive the differences, we know that we, humans, structure the speech signal into different linguistic units and that we can use a wide range of different types of phonological knowledge to deal with the signal: segments, syllables, stress patterns, and so on.

Languages differ from each other in all these types of knowledge. For instance, the word "string" could not be a word in most languages of the world, among other reasons, simply because it starts with three consonants and this is something that only a few languages allow. Cross-language speech perception is the field that studies what happens when listeners of a particular language perceive another language differing in some aspects from their own and the perceptual consequences of the mismatch between the properties of the maternal language and the foreign one. For instance, this research tries to explain what speakers of Spanish do when listening to the word "string": because of different properties of Spanish phonology, we (native Spanish listeners) hear an "e" at the beginning of this word; that is, "string" becomes "estring." Probably the converse happened when Englishmen, many years ago went to a place named "España" and transformed it into "Spain," deleting this initial "e." In a sense, both Spanish listeners and English listeners could be said to have experienced a perceptual illusion.

Speech "illusions" are quite common when we hear foreign languages. Basically, three different types of illusions may happen (this is an adaptation of the classification proposed by Seguí, Frauenfelder, & Hallé 2001):

1 *Deafness*: we cannot hear a difference. The most popular example is the difficulty (inability) of Japanese listeners to perceive the difference between the English words "road" and "load": the listener "ignores" the contrasting information that is present in the signal.
2 *Mirage*: the listener "creates" information not present in the signal, one example is the epenthetic vowels that (e)Spanish (e)speakers add at the beginning of English words.

3 *Mutation*: the listener changes one sound into another, like the transformation of /tl/ clusters by English and French listeners (non-existing in their native language) into /tr/ or /kl/ (both clusters existing in English and French).

As we will see, these patterns of illusions occur across all phonological systems.

22.3 Segmentals

As already mentioned, the way listeners of different languages perceive the segments of foreign languages has received a lot of attention. Well-developed models exist explaining how non-native (or second language, L2) segments are perceived. One of the most influential is the Perceptual Assimilation Model (PAM) (Best, 1995; Best, McRoberts, & Goodell, 2001; Best, McRoberts, & Sithole, 1988). This model proposes that the structure of the native language plays a crucial role in the way non-native phonemic systems are perceived. Basically three possible situations can be encountered: non-native sounds can be perceived as exemplars of an existing L1 phonetic category (either as good or as bad exemplars of it), as exemplars of a sound category non-existing in the native language, or even as nonspeech sounds. What would make it difficult to perceive an L2 phonemic contrast is whether the sounds are mapped into a single L1 category, and if the L2 sounds are relatively good exemplars of this single L1 category. If both factors co-occur, it is very difficult to perceive the L2 contrast; this difficulty arises from the fact that both L2 sounds would be *assimilated* to the L1 category. Of course, this would be the most extreme case of difficulty, and a whole range of possibilities exists in between this case and very accurate discriminations, which would occur when a pair of L2 speech sounds are perceptually assimilated by two distinct L1 speech sounds.

Another very influential model in this domain is the Speech Learning Model (SLM) (Flege, 1995, 2002). The most interesting characteristic of this model is that it directly addresses the issue of L2 segment acquisition. This model incorporates mechanisms analogous to those described in the PAM, but it assumes that they are mostly effective in initial stages of second language acquisition. According to Flege, although everyday experience with L2 seems to indicate that our capacity for learning foreign languages diminishes with age, his model proposes that "the mechanisms and processes used in learning the [native language] sound system . . . remain intact over the life span" (Flege, 1995, p. 239). This provocative assumption has found support in studies with electrophysiological measures and with neural network simulations (McClelland et al., 1999).

Most empirical evidence on segmental speech perception (and in fact, on speech perception in general) has been gathered using behavioral measures where participants are required to give "yes-no" responses. For example, in identification or discrimination tasks, they are asked to report whether a particular sound belongs to a specific category, or if it sounds different from a designated category. These measures may not be sensitive to potential unconscious differences. In this way, the results of behavioral studies may have underestimated the grain of representation and processing status of cross-language phonological competence level.

Our knowledge of how linguistic experience shapes the underlying neural-sensory representations of speech is quite limited. In general, it seems that differences in the way the first language is represented across individuals are not very large, particularly when compared with the representation of second languages (Dehaene et al., 1997, although there is evidence showing that even music perception – the tritone auditory illusion – can be altered by the properties of the maternal language; Deutsch, Henthorn, & Dolson, 2000). In the past years there has been an increasing number of studies indicating that different Event Related Potential (ERP) signatures can be obtained for native and non-native phoneme perception. When segment perception is considered, most of the evidence has been gathered analyzing the differences in the Mismatch Negativity (MMN) response. The MMN evoked response is a characteristic electrophysiological response component produced when a series of identical sounds (the standard) is interrupted by a different stimulus (the deviant). It has traditionally been considered an index of pre-attentive processing, since it is obtained without active participation from subjects (who are consciously performing another task, with their attention focused on that other task). Furthermore, and importantly for the present purposes, the MMN can be elicited when the stimuli are not behaviorally discriminated. Näätänen et al. (1997) analyzed the perception of Finnish vowels by Estonian and Finnish listeners. Estonian and Finnish have very similar vowel structures; for example, the vowels /e/, /o/ and /ø/, which differ only in the second formant (F2) frequency, exist in both languages. However, only Estonian has the vowel /ɯ/, whose formant values fall approximately between /ø/ and /o/. This particular vowel distribution in Estonian would make the perception of /ɯ/ particularly difficult for Finnish listeners, since they would categorize exemplars of /ɯ/ as either /ø/ or /o/ (according to both PAM and SLM). The results of Näätänen et al.'s study showed larger MMN responses for across language phonemic category differences than for within language category. The explanation Näätänen et al. gave for this pattern of results was that Finnish participants did not have a phonetic category for the vowel /ɯ/, while Estonian participants did. The overall conclusion of this study was that the amplitude of the MMN is smaller for non-native contrasts than for native ones.

These results have been confirmed more recently with other contrasts and other populations, for instance, Phillips et al. (1995) studied the /ɹ/–/l/ contrast with Japanese speakers; Sharma & Dorman (2000) compared Hindi English listeners with the [ba]–[pa] Hindi – but not English – contrast; Winkler et al. (1999) analyzed the perception of Hungarian and Finnish vowel contrasts in speakers of these two languages; and Rivera-Gaxiola et al. (2000) explored the perception of the labial /ba/–Hindi dental/retroflex [da] contrast for English-speaking participants (although see Dehaene-Lambertz, 1997 who did not observe this pattern of results with native French participants listening to the Hindi dental/retroflex alveolar plosive [d] contrast). One conclusion of these studies investigating the processing of native and non-native phonetic categories with electrophysiological measures, is that the MMN is a useful tool to analyze how non-native sounds are perceived; indeed, the results are consistent with the notion that the MMN reflects a relatively abstract level of processing in which language-specific categories play a role.

While these studies have addressed the question of cross-language segment perception, another relevant group of studies also using this type of measures has analyzed the neuronal changes produced as a result of segment training programs. In these studies, pre- and post-training ERP signatures were compared. Tremblay et al. (1997) trained a group of native English speakers to distinguish between different bilabial plosives at a VOT boundary where no category change occurred in English. The training had the consequence of increasing the MMN response; interestingly, the increase was larger in the left hemisphere. These authors also showed that the training was not specific to the trained stimuli, but that the increase also generalized to an untrained alveolar contrast. An interesting observation was that the changes occurred very rapidly (the "first day of significant change" occurred after the first training session). Tremblay, Kraus, & McGee (1998) also noticed that for many participants changes in the MMN were obtained before any significant behavioral change was displayed.

These results indicate that the perceptual system does not lose its capacity to perceive the auditory properties of the speech sounds. In fact, they suggest that very rapid changes may occur as a consequence of exposure to new foreign sounds. These data are thus in agreement with the SLM model and suggest that even late adults can improve their non-native speech perception abilities.

Despite the evidence for a high degree of plasticity of the perceptual system, everyday experience indicates that second language learners continue to have great difficulties with particular foreign sounds. Takagi and Mann (1995) studied adult Japanese natives who had moved to the US and who had been using English daily for more than 12 years. They observed that in spite of this high degree of exposure all performed below the level of native English speakers, at least in some particular phonetic environments (85% below for consonant clusters). It could be argued that participants in this study learned their second language after puberty. However, different studies show that when early and highly skilled bilinguals are compared in their L1 and L2, there is some perceptual processing advantage for the L1 (Bosch, Costa, & Sebastian-Gallés, 2000; Mack, 1989; Pallier, Bosch, & Sebastián, 1997; Pallier, Colomé, & Sebastián-Gallés, 2001; Sebastián-Gallés & Soto-Faraco, 1999). In all these studies, individuals who had been exposed to their second language in the very first years of their lives and who had attained a very high proficiency in their second language showed statistically significant differences when compared with natives. Furthermore, other studies indicate that even those second language learners who have managed to distinguish difficult non-native contrasts do not use the same acoustic parameters that natives do. For instance, although American English natives use as the primary acoustic cue spectral differences between F2 and F3 to differentiate [ɹ] and [l], Underbakke et al. (1988) observed that Japanese listeners used temporal differences to distinguish these sounds. If native speakers use the most adaptive and efficient mechanisms to process their language, then it can be said that at least for their second language, bilinguals use less efficient procedures. Taken together, these data indicate that the fundamental processing of L1 and L2 speech sounds differs. Although it is indisputable that the capacity to acquire new sounds is not lost after the first years of life, there are no data supporting the assumption that L1 and L2 segments are processed in equivalent ways.

Recently McAllister, Flege, & Piske (2002) have suggested that the differential processing of L1 and L2 sounds could be due to the existing differences at the lexical level between both languages. A large L2 lexicon would exert pressure on the phonological system to create new phonetic categories, in order to avoid a large number of homophones. These authors base their claims on data of native English and Spanish speakers who were very fluent in Swedish (and who had lived for an extended period of time in Sweden). Contrary to Swedish listeners, neither English nor Spanish listeners use vowel duration as a primary cue to vowel contrasts. Nevertheless, both English and Spanish natives learned to use this cue to correctly perceive Swedish words. However, these data are in clear contrast with those reported by Pallier et al. (2001). Pallier et al. also analyzed how Spanish-Catalan bilinguals represented Catalan minimal pairs involving distinctions difficult for Spanish-dominant bilinguals to perceive. In different studies (Bosch et al., 2000; Pallier et al., 1997; Pallier et al., 2001; Sebastián-Gallés & Soto-Faraco, 1999) the perceptual capacities of Spanish-Catalan bilinguals born in Catalonia, exposed to their second language very early in life (usually before 4 years of age), and who had been exposed to their two languages in their everyday life were explored. In these studies it has been observed that Spanish-dominant bilinguals (those born within monolingual Spanish families, and who before 4 years of age only had occasional contact with Catalan) experienced great difficulties in perceiving Catalan-specific contrasts. Pallier et al. (2001) specifically tested the hypothesis of whether these highly skilled bilinguals stored as homophones Catalan minimal pairs. With this aim, they studied the repetition priming effect in a lexical decision task comparing Catalan-dominant and Spanish-dominant bilinguals. In this study minimal pairs involving Catalan-specific contrasts were used. If Spanish-dominant bilinguals had actually stored Catalan-specific minimal pairs as two different lexical entries, they should not show repetition effects, that is, the latencies to respond to /os/ ('bear') should not be affected by the previous presentation of /ɔs/ ('bone'), in fact, these bilinguals should perform like the Catalan-dominant ones. In contrast, if they had stored these words as homophones, they should show equivalent priming savings as actual repetitions, the previous presentation of /ɔs/ should have the same priming effect as the previous presentation of /os/ on the subsequent recognition of /os/. This is indeed what it was found. Figure 22.1 shows a summary of the results. Catalan-dominant bilinguals showed repetition priming effects only for real repetitions (when exactly the same word was repeated: /os/ preceded by /os/), no repetition effects were observed for minimal pairs (/os/ preceded by /ɔs/). Spanish-dominant bilinguals showed parallel effects for real repetitions and for Catalan-specific minimal pairs, indicating that they had stored them as homophones. Importantly, both groups of bilinguals showed equivalent command of Catalan, at least for their lexical knowledge, since no statistically significant differences were observed either in their error rates or latencies in the performed lexical decision task.

It is difficult to reconcile at the present time all of the available data. Many different factors influence the way foreign sounds are perceived. On the one hand, there are those factors related to language distance: language similarities and differences, the fundamental role of the particular relationship between L1 and L2 sounds (the major properties already captured by the PAM and SLM

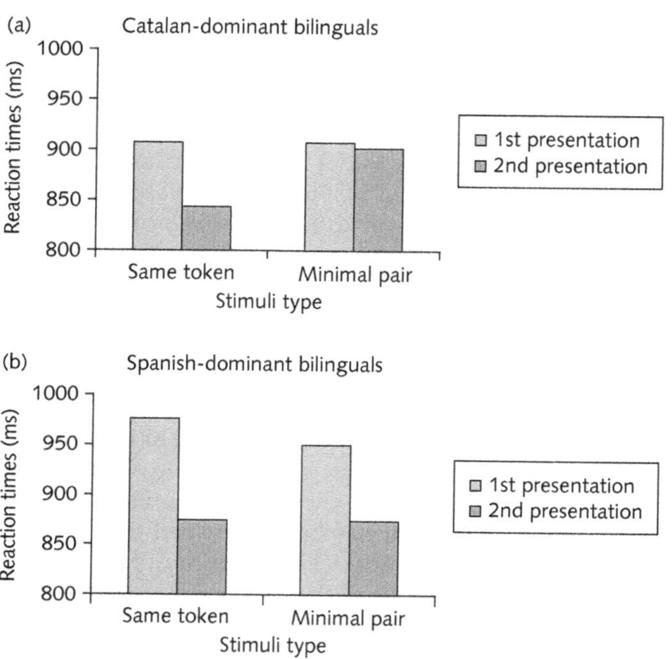

Figure 22.1 Mean reaction times of Catalan-dominant (a) and Spanish-dominant (b) bilinguals in the Pallier, Colomé, and Sebastián-Gallés (2002) study.

proposals). On the other hand, there are those factors related to individual differences in the exposure to the second language. Factors like age of acquisition, language input (language use), current use of the first language, and so on, also play fundamental roles. Because these factors not only affect how foreign phonemes are perceived but also other aspects of speech perception, we will come back to them and discuss them further at the end of this chapter.

22.4 Suprasegmentals

It has been repeatedly claimed that the phoneme cannot be the unit of analysis of the speech signal. Contextual variation (the fact that the same phoneme has different physical realizations as a function of the surrounding phonemes) and parallel transmission (that most of the time, more than just one phoneme is being uttered) just make it impossible. If the speech signal cannot be directly analyzed into phonemes, then what are the units of speech perception? Different scholars have explored the possibility that larger units might be used in perception. Interestingly, the results of some of this research have shown important cross-linguistic differences.

22.4.1 Parsing the speech signal into syllables

Syllables are universal units; all languages have syllables and although not all languages exactly agree in parsing a specific string of sounds into the same syllables, there are many similarities in the way the different languages parse the speech signal into syllables. For instance, all languages in the world would consider the sequence /ki/ as one syllable and not two /k/ + /i/: /k/ cannot be a syllable in any possible language. Also, a wide variety of languages would consider that the sequence /kanda/ is segmented into two syllables /kan/ and /da/, no language in the world would parse that string into /kand/ + /a/ or into /k/ + /anda/. So, it seemed reasonable to wonder whether the continuous speech stream is segmented into syllable-sized units. In fact, newborns are sensitive to syllable length: they are able to discriminate two- from three-syllable sequences, even when they are equated in length (Bijeljac-Babic, Bertoncini, & Mehler, 1993).

In 1981, Jacques Mehler and his colleagues (Mehler et al., 1981) ran an experiment where they measured how long it took for French listeners to decide whether a particular CV or CVC sequence appeared at the beginning of French words. Experimental stimuli consisted of word pairs sharing their three initial phonemes, but differing in their syllabic structure; that is, they used pairs of the type "carotte-carton" or "palais-palmier," for which the first member of the pairs had a CV syllable, and the second a CVC. These authors observed a significant interaction between word syllabic structure and type of target: participants were faster at detecting targets that coincided with the initial syllable structure of the words (i.e., CA in "carotte") than when it did not coincide (i.e., CA in "carton"). From these data, they concluded that the syllable was the universal unit of speech perception. However, when English listeners were tested with analogous materials by Cutler et al. (1986), there was no trace of this cross-over interaction. What was the basis for this difference?

As mentioned earlier, not all languages parse the speech stream in the same way, thus, while for a Spanish or a French speaker the sequence /lemən/ would be "naturally" parsed into the two syllables /le/ and /mən/, for a native English speaker it would be more naturally parsed into /lem/ and /ən/; in fact, many native English speakers could give different alternative responses, like /lem/ and /mən/. Analogously, when asked to segment /kanda/ into its "natural" parts, the most likely response Japanese speakers would give is /ka/, /n/, and /da/, a response that would surprise listeners of Indo-European languages (in subsequent studies, it has been observed that Japanese speakers in these syllable monitoring experiments give patterns of response in accordance with the notion that they segment the speech signal into mora-sized units, Otake et al., 1993). These important differences across languages proved to be fatal for the hypothesis of the syllable as a universal unit of speech perception, but they suggested. that languages can be sorted in terms of their rhythm and that this dimension has important consequences for the way languages are perceived.

The status of the syllable in speech perception is quite controversial. On the one hand, the experimental evidence has shown that even languages for which "syllabic" responses were expected have not yielded to univocal syllabic cross-over interactions. Sebastián-Gallés et al. (1992) failed to obtain this pattern with Spanish and the pattern with Catalan was not very clear. On the other hand, other experimental situations have been able to uncover robust syllabic effects in French, Spanish, and Portuguese (Kolinsky, Morais, & Clytens, 1995; Morais et al., 1993; Pallier et al., 1993).

22.4.2 *The rhythm of languages*

When visiting a place where there are lots of tourists, we are often consciously aware that different languages are being produced. Sometimes we may fail to notice that different languages are spoken, other times we clearly perceive that different languages are produced. We assume that we do not know these languages and therefore we have no lexical knowledge available to support recognition. While non-natives without any knowledge of Germanic languages may fail, at first, to realize the differences between German and Dutch, there do not seem to be any major confusions between French and English or between Japanese and Italian. The rhythm of languages is a major determinant in these patterns of confusion.

Language classifications in terms of their rhythm were first proposed by Pike (1945). He proposed a distinction between syllable-timed and stress-timed languages. This distinction was further accepted and developed by many different authors (Abercrombie, 1967; Bertinetto, 1989; Ladefoged, 1975; Port, Dalby, & O'Dell, 1987). In a simplistic way, what these authors have proposed is that languages differ in their temporal organization: syllable-timed languages would be those showing isochrony at the syllable level, while stress-timed languages show regular intervals between stressed syllables (a third group has been proposed, for languages like Japanese and Tamil, that would show regularity in the intervals between morae). However the reality proved to be more complex and this classification was subject to a lot of criticism (for instance, Dasher & Bolinger, 1982; Dauer, 1983). But the data of the studies reviewed in the previous section and data from early language discrimination capacities in newborns and infants gave new support to it, and recent proposals have made a more sophisticated version of it. Recently, Ramus and coworkers (Ramus, Nespor, & Mehler, 1999) have proposed that the rhythm of languages can be described as the combination of the percentage of the signal corresponding to vowels (%V) and the variation in the consonant groups/segments (ΔC).

Human newborns can discriminate some languages, but not all, from others. In particular, they can discriminate French from Russian, English from Italian, or English from Japanese but they cannot discriminate English from Dutch (Bahrick & Pickens, 1988; Bosch & Sebastián-Gallés, 1997; Christophe & Morton, 1998; Dehaene-Lambertz & Houston, 1998; Mehler et al., 1988; Moon, Cooper, & Fifer, 1993). In order to account for this pattern of discriminations, it has been proposed that infants can extract the rhythm of the languages they hear (by computing the two above-mentioned measures). These very early cross-language language discrimination capacities could be responsible, later on, for the different degrees of difficulties that listeners experience in adjusting to foreign languages (and also for the differences reviewed in the previous section).

One of the most remarkable capacities of the speech processing system of a proficient listener is its ability to compensate for poor acoustic environments. Noise and distortion are handled with little effect on comprehension. However, this adjustment does not always apply in an equally satisfactory way when we are perceiving a foreign language. When listening to a non-native language, even quite small distortions may have catastrophic consequences. One trivial source of this effect is the larger lexicon natives have for their maternal language (and also more efficient syntactic capacities), but another non-trivial source can be the influence of differences in the rhythmic properties of the languages. Holding proficiency constant at the lexical and syntactic levels, not all foreign speakers of English are equally easily understood; the difficulty is dependent on both the language of the speaker and the language of the listener (Bent & Bradlow, 2003). For instance, for Spanish listeners, Italian and Greek natives are easier to understand than German and Japanese natives, when speaking in English. But this is not the case for Dutch listeners.

Various studies have addressed the proposal that some of the differences in perception can be explained with reference to language rhythm by studying cross-linguistic adaptation to time-compressed speech (Altmann & Young, 1993; Dupoux & Green, 1997; Mehler et al., 1993; Pallier et al., 1998; Sebastián-Gallés et al., 2000). In these studies, participants were presented with time-compressed stimuli belonging to different languages and the influence of this exposure was later measured by their (re)adaptation to time-compressed samples of their maternal language. The results revealed significant effects of language rhythm: the former presentation of sentences in a language from the same rhythmic group improved the intelligibility of the test sentences (in the maternal language), while the presentation of time-compressed sentences in a language from a different rhythmic group had no effect on the intelligibility of the test sentences. Figure 22.2 shows a summary of results reported by Sebastián-Gallés et al. (2000). Participants in the control group were directly tested with the experimental sentences without any habituation. Participants in the other groups listened to time-compressed sentences in each of the reported languages (the results of the Greek group are the average of the two conditions in the original experiment 2).

These studies showed that the adaptation did not depend on semantic factors (adaptation was found with nonwords that followed the phonology of the maternal language of the listeners, and it was also found with languages with the same rhythm as the maternal language, but totally unknown to the listener) and further that it occurred at a relatively abstract level (a change of voice – male to female – had no effect on the adaptation). When considered together, these studies support the assumption that cross-linguistic speech perception differences also exist at the rhythmic level.

22.4.3 *Stress, accent, and tone*

Stress is a complex dimension. Stressed syllables may differ from unstressed ones in duration, energy, or pitch change. In most languages, differences in stress imply different meanings: stress can be an important cue to distinguish different meanings, that is, stress can have a contrastive lexical value. But in some languages

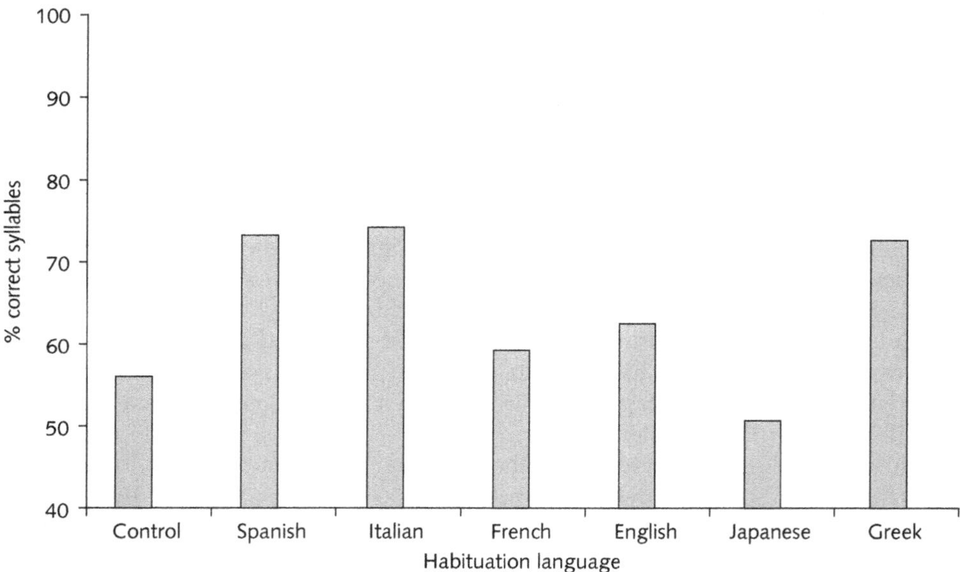

Figure 22.2 Percentage of correct syllables reported of test sentences for each induction group (adapted from Sebastián-Gallés et al., 2000).

this is not the case. For instance, in French, there are no two words just differing in the stress value of their syllables. In fact, French is a fixed-stress language: all content words bear stress on their last syllable. If stress does not need to be processed to identify lexical items (although it might be used to segment words in fluent speech), it may not have to be stored in the lexicon of speakers of fixed-stress languages. One potential implication of this fact is that French listeners should have difficulties in perceiving (contrastive) stress. This is what the comparative research carried out by Dupoux and coworkers with Spanish and French listeners has proved using different methodologies (Dupoux et al., 1997; Dupoux, Peperkamp, & Sebastián-Gallés, 2001). In the Dupoux et al. (1997) study, native French and Spanish individuals were asked to perform an ABX task with non-words (in both languages) just differing in the position of the stress. Their results showed significant differences in both populations; Spanish native listeners performed better than French natives. Interestingly, when they were asked to perform an AX task, where acoustic information could be used, French participants were able to perceive the differences between stimuli stressed at different positions. These results have been recently confirmed by Dupoux et al. (2001) using a short-term memory task (see Pepperkamp & Dupoux, 2002 for a theoretical proposal of these perceptual difficulties).

However, cross-linguistic differences in speech perception are not restricted to the stress deafness that listeners of fixed-stress languages exhibit. In English, a language with variable stress, stress information does not seem to play an important role in lexical access (Cutler, 1986). In Cutler's experiment, English listeners were asked to perform a cross-modal lexical decision task. They were presented with associated pairs and it was found that the presentation of one member of a minimal pair just differing in stress value primed not only the recognition of words associated to its meaning, but also to the other member of the pair; that is, "forbear" facilitated the recognition of words associated to itself and also to "forebear." In contrast, speakers of Dutch and Spanish (Cutler & Donselaar, 2001; Soto-Faraco, Sebastián-Gallés, & Cutler, 2001) seem to be sensitive to this type of information in the process of lexical activation. These authors, using procedures analogous to those used with the English listeners, observed that lexical activation was sensitive to stress information. If all of these languages have contrastive stress, why is it the case that English listeners do not seem to consider stress information in lexical activation? Listeners could rely on the reduced number in English of true minimal pairs involving a change in stress. Indeed, in English stress changes almost always implies a change in vowel quality; in this circumstance, the actual use of stress cues would be of little use to English speakers in lexical access, as they could rely on segmental information instead. In contrast, in Dutch and in Spanish taking into consideration stress information would really help in distinguishing between lexical candidates, since in both of these languages there is no such redundancy between stress and segmental change.[2]

22.5 Phonotactics

The last domain we consider where cross-linguistic differences have been observed in speech perception is phonotactics. Phonotactics refers to the knowledge listeners have about whether a string of segments is likely to be a word in their own language. For instance, any Japanese listener when asked if "klamp" could be a Japanese word knows that the answer is no.

Phonotactic knowledge about language is acquired quite early in life. The first evidence has been observed at 9 months of age. Friederici and Wessels (1993) compared American and Dutch 9-month-old infants and the results showed that they preferred to listen to lists of words of their own language, but only when they were not low-pass filtered. In this case, they showed no preference. This result was taken to indicate that infants were paying attention to some phonotactic properties of the stimuli. Similarly, Friederici and Wessels (1993) observed that Dutch 9-month-olds preferred to listen to legal (conforming to the phonotactics of their maternal language) versus illegal (non-conforming to the phonotactics of the maternal language) word boundary clusters. This preference would indicate not only some language-specific phonotactic knowledge at this early age, but also that this knowledge was actively used to segment the speech signal into meaningful units.

Most of the adult studies in this domain have analyzed how listeners perceive legal versus illegal consonant clusters. In the pioneering study of Massaro and Cohen (1983), native English speakers were asked to categorize ambiguous stimuli, from a /r/–/l/ continuum, when they followed another consonant (in a consonant cluster). In some cases, the cluster was a possible ("legal") sequence in English, like /tr/ or /bl/, and in others it was impossible ("illegal"), like /tl/. The results showed that listeners' responses were influenced by the "legality" of the cluster. For instance, participants were biased to perceive ambiguous stimuli as /r/ when the preceding consonant was a /t/, probably because /tl/ does not exist as a word onset consonant cluster in English, while /tr/ does. More recently, Pitt (1998) reported comparable results for English speakers when listening to initial word /tl/ and /sr/ sequences. Hallé et al. (1998) have reported analogous results with native French listeners. They found that native French speakers tend to perceive initial stimuli /dl/ and /tl/ as /gl/ and /kl/, that is, they showed a tendency to transform illegal sequences in French into phonotactically legal ones.

Few studies have analyzed how foreign language phonotactics is perceived and compared to results obtained with native listeners. While the previous studies have explored the perceptual biases produced by the native language phonotactics by comparing legal and illegal sequences, they did not compare the performances with those of natives (the illegal sequences analyzed in English and French are legal in other languages). To our knowledge, only three studies have done these comparisons. The first study was on how Chinese listeners perceive the English final-word /d/–/t/ contrast (Flege & Wang, 1989). A second one was carried out by Dupoux et al. (1999) who compared how Japanese and French listeners perceive different phonological contrasts. Let us consider this study in some detail. These authors compared the perception of long and short vowels (a phonological distinction non-existing in French) with the perception of consonant clusters (not possible in Japanese, but existing in French). When Japanese and French listeners were asked to perform a discrimination task between pairs of pseudowords differing in their vowel length (like [ebuza] versus [ebuuza]), Japanese listeners had no difficulty performing the task, while French listeners were unable to perceive the same differences reliably. They perceived both stimuli as [ebuza]. In contrast, when the same individuals were asked to discriminate between stimuli like [ebza] versus [ebuza], the opposite pattern was found. Japanese listeners perceived both stimuli as instances of [ebuza].

Dehaene-Lambertz, Dupoux, and Gout (2000) analyzed the ERP responses to these materials with another group of French and Japanese participants in an experimental paradigm involving the presentation of a deviant stimulus after four similar ones. The electrophysiological results showed weaker, or even absent, responses for Japanese participants when the deviant stimulus involved a phonotactically impossible consonant cluster in their maternal language, that is, they showed weaker or no ERP changes for stimuli like "ebzo" after the presentation of four "ebuzo" tokens. The results were in clear contrast with those of French natives who showed significant electrophysiological changes. Jacquemot et al. (2003) have further explored this issue and investigated the brain substrate of these differences by means of an fMRI study. Their study was aimed at identifying the underlying brain mechanisms involved in the detection of acoustic changes and phonological changes. Interestingly, and in agreement with the ERP study, the fMRI scans showed significant differences in the brain mechanisms for the very same stimuli as a function of the maternal language: some particular areas (specifically the left supramarginal region and the left posterior superior temporal gyrus) were only activated for stimuli conforming to the phonotactics of the maternal language.

The third study that has compared native and non-native listeners was carried out by Sebastián-Gallés and Bosch (2002). In this study, both infant and adult Spanish-Catalan bilinguals (differing in their L1) were compared in their perception of final-word consonant clusters. While Spanish does not allow for final-word consonant clusters, Catalan does. But not just any consonant cluster is possible in Catalan (in general, those following the sonority ranking are allowed – like [nf] – while those violating the sonority ranking are not – like [tl]). The results of this study showed that while 10-month-old monolingual Catalan infants and Catalan-dominant bilinguals (infants being raised in a bilingual family, but with Catalan being spoken more than Spanish) preferred to listen to lists of stimuli that were legal in Catalan, both monolingual Spanish and Spanish-dominant bilinguals did not show any preference (since any consonant cluster would be illegal in their dominant language). In contrast, the results obtained with adult bilinguals showed a different pattern. In this case, only two groups of participants were tested: those who were raised as Spanish monolinguals during the very first years of life, but who later on were exposed to both languages and who currently used them, and those who were the mirror image, but with Catalan as the only language during the first years of life. Listeners were asked to perform a phoneme monitoring task or a gating task. The results showed small, but significant differences between both populations in the direction that Catalan-dominant bilinguals were influenced more by the legality of the consonant clusters than the Spanish-dominant bilinguals.

22.6 Concluding Remarks

In this chapter, an important issue has received little attention and we do not want to finish without addressing it. This question deals with second language acquisition, both in childhood and adulthood. While in most domains, studies on language development begin analyzing children of 3–4 years of age (more or less), speech perception studies, from a developmental point of view, almost exclusively finish somewhere between 12 and 24 months of age (with some exceptions). It would seem as if after this age, little is changed in the way language is perceived. This also holds true for cross-language speech perception research, where most studies tend to use just two different populations: infants and adults. In the latter case, age of acquisition (or age of arrival) is systematically varied and it has proved to be a highly relevant variable in explaining individuals' performances. If this is the case, then it seems that a particularly interesting field of research should be how speech perception is modified during childhood (see Walley, this volume). However, this topic has received little attention and the available data point in the direction that significant changes occur during childhood in the way the native language is perceived (Baker et al., 2002; Hazan & Barrett, 1999; Johnson, 2000; Walley & Flege, 2000).

Another question is related to the debate about the extent to which a second language can be learned. Nobody questions that some aspects of a second language are particularly easily acquired, while others are particularly difficult. As the research on segmental speech perception has shown, the phonological properties of the maternal language and those of the second language play a crucial role: there are no "absolute" difficult things. While these aspects are indisputable, the degree of plasticity of the speech perception system, and therefore, of our capacity to acquire foreign sound systems, is at the focus of intense debates. Because most research has been performed in the segment perception domain, we will discuss this issue within this context.

There are many different factors that determine success or failure in acquiring a second language, like age of acquisition, amount of exposure, and motivation. The theoretical goals of the researcher are also important in determining the degree of success: if native-like performance is the ultimate goal, the results can be said to be quite poor (Takagi, 2002). If significant increases in performance in short periods of time is the goal, the results are more successful. Taken together, most training methods (many of them using Japanese listeners learning English) manage to get significant improvements in relatively short periods of time: Lively et al. (1994) about 12%, McCandliss et al. (2002) around 10%, just to mention a couple of studies. Although these results can be taken as behavioral evidence showing how the human brain manages to "solve" a particular perceptual problem, we are far from understanding the neurobiological and cognitive mechanisms that make these rapid improvements possible. On the one hand, it has already been mentioned that non-natives may not use the same acoustic cues that natives use in perceiving a particular foreign contrast. On the other hand, it is unclear what characteristics the training methods must have to be most effective. Let us consider the two particular studies just mentioned that have trained the same contrast with speakers of the same L1 (the /r–l/ to Japanese), thus avoiding problems of language and population lack of comparability.

Pisoni and his coworkers (Bradlow et al., 1997; Lively et al., 1994; Logan, Lively, & Pisoni, 1991) advocate the use of training methods that include a high variability both in speakers and stimuli. Because the same phoneme can be realized in many different ways depending not only on the phonetic environment, but also on the particular talkers, Pisoni and colleagues argue that the best way to develop robust phonetic categories is to use learning methods that emphasize exposure to most varied situations. The authors assume that although these types of stimuli may initially be more difficult to process by non-native listeners "the potential long-term benefits in terms of developing new phonetic categories outweighed these concerns" (Logan et al., 1991, p. 876). In contrast, McCandliss and coworkers (McCandliss et al., 2002) propose that the best training methods should start with stimuli that participants are able to correctly categorize (even if they do not represent good exemplars of the target categories to be learned). These authors have used a methodology based on fading techniques (see Jamieson & Morosan, 1986). Participants are presented with exaggerated, acoustically modified tokens and are gradually required to process closer and closer exemplars. One fundamental property of this procedure is that the listeners do not make any errors. McCandliss et al. claim that because of the lack of errors in categorization, feedback is not necessary.[3] It is clear that the learning mechanisms underlying both types of laboratory training methods are fundamentally different in nature; however, the final performances do not significantly differ in both studies. As mentioned earlier, the improvements in both studies were slightly above 10%.[4] It is important to mention here that while the final level of performance observed in both studies was about the same, McCandliss and his colleagues never tested generalization of their learning methodology to new stimuli using the same perceptual task or transfer of learning to a different perceptual task. Thus, it is impossible to determine whether the fading procedures they used actually promoted robust perceptual learning that extended beyond only the specific stimulus materials used in training and testing. The research studies carried out by Pisoni and his colleagues assessed both generalization and transfer of training in speech perception as well as speech production in order to demonstrate the robustness of the high-variability training methodology and the theoretical importance of exposure to multiple exemplars during perceptual learning. This particular case illustrates how far we are from a full understanding of the underlying brain mechanisms and the relative contributions of different aspects of the signal in the process of second language acquisition.

In the previous pages, a selective review of issues related to cross-language speech perception has been presented. Two main goals have been pursued. First, we tried to show that there is much more in this domain than just comparative studies of segment perception. Second, it should be clear that future research will have to use all available methodological tools – only joint efforts including both behavioral and brain-based measures (as well as computer simulations) will make it possible to fully understand the way we perceive foreign languages.

ACKNOWLEDGMENTS

Preparation of this manuscript was facilitated by a grant from the James S. McDonnell Foundation (Bridging Brain, Mind and Behavior Program), by BSO2001-3492-C04-01 grant from the Spanish Ministerio de Ciencia y Tecnología and by a grant from the Catalan Government (2001SGR00034).

NOTES

1 I want to acknowledge the origin of this reference to the Bible to Mehler & Dupoux (1994).
2 There are other aspects within suprasegmentals where important cross-linguistic differences have been reported. In particular, a great deal of research has been devoted to the perception of tone (Bluhme & Burr, 1971; Gandour, 1983; Kiriloff, 1969; Lee & Nusbaum, 1993; Wang, Spence, & Sereno, 1999). Jack Gandour and coworkers have reported very interesting studies about cross-linguistic differences in pitch perception using imaging techniques (Gandour et al., 2000, 2002a, 2002b, in press). Because of length constraints, these studies will not be reviewed here.
3 Although their results are in clear conflict with this basic assumption: participants with feedback performed better than participants without it.
4 This was so even if in the McCandliss et al. study tokens were artificially modified, while in the Pisoni and coworkers' studies, naturally produced stimuli were used. Also, the Pisoni et al. studies particularly stressed the capacity of participants to generalize to new materials, while this was not the case in the McCandliss et al. one.

REFERENCES

Abercrombie, D. (1967). *Elements of General Phonetics*. Edinburgh: Edinburgh University Press.

Altmann, G. T. M. & Young, D. (1993). Factors affecting adaptation to time-compressed speech. Paper presented at Eurospeech '93, Madrid (Spain).

Bahrick, L. E. & Pickens, J. N. (1988). Classification of bimodal English and Spanish language passages by infants. *Infant Behavior and Development*, 11, 277–96.

Baker, W., Trofimovich, P., Mack, M., & Flege, J. E. (2002). The effect of perceived phonetic similarity on non-native sound learning by children and adults. *Proceedings of the 26th Annual Boston University Conference on Language Development* (pp. 36–47). Boston, MA.

Bent, T. & Bradlow, A. R. (2003). The interlanguage speech intelligibility benefit. *Journal of the Acoustical Society of America*, 114, 1600–10.

Bertinetto, P. (1989). Reflections on the dichotomy "stress" vs. "syllable-timing." *Revue de Phonetique Appliquée*, 91–3, 99–130.

Best, C. T. (1995). A direct realist view of cross-language speech perception. In W. Strange (ed.), *Speech Perception and Linguistic Experience* (pp. 171–206). Baltimore, MD: York Press.

Best, C., McRoberts, G., & Goodell, R. (2001). Discrimination of non-native consonant contrasts varying in perceptual assimilation to the listener's native phonological system. *Journal of the Acoustical Society of America*, 109, 775–94.

Best, C. T., McRoberts, G. W., & Sithole, N. N. (1988). The phonological basis of perceptual loss for non-native contrasts: Maintenance of discrimination among Zulu clicks by English-speaking adults and infants. *Journal of Experimental Psychology: Human Perception and Performance*, 14, 345–60.

Bijeljac-Babic, R., Bertoncini, J., & Mehler, J. (1993). How do four-day-olds categorize multisyllabic utterances? *Developmental Psychology*, 29, 711–21.

Bluhme, S. & Burr, R. (1971). An audio-visual display of pitch for teaching Chinese tones. *Studies in Linguistics*, 22, 51–7.

Bosch, L. & Sebastián-Gallés, N. (1997). Native-language recognition abilities in four-month-old infants from monolingual and bilingual environments. *Cognition*, 65, 33–69.

Bosch, L., Costa, A., & Sebastián-Gallés, N. (2000). First and second language vowel perception in early bilinguals. *European Journal of Cognitive Psychology*, 12(2), 189–222.

Bradlow, A. R., Pisoni, D. B., Yamada, R. A., & Tohkura, Y. (1997). Training Japanese listeners to identify English /r/ and /l/ IV: Some effects of perceptual learning on speech production. *Journal of the Acoustical Society of America*, 101, 2299–310.

Christophe, A. & Morton, J. (1998). Is Dutch native English? Linguistic analysis by two-month-olds. *Developmental Science*, 1, 215–19.

Cutler, A. (1986). Forbear is a homophone: Lexical prosody does not constrain lexical access. *Language and Speech*, 29, 201–20.

Cutler, A. & Donselaar, W. van (2001). Voornaam is not a homophone: Lexical prosody and lexical access in Dutch. *Language and Speech*, 44, 171–95.

Cutler, A., Mehler, J., Norris, D., & Segui, J. (1986). The syllable's differing role in the segmentation of French and English. *Journal of Memory and Language*, 25, 385–400.

Dasher, R. & Bolinger, D. (1982). On pre-accentual lengthening. *Journal of the International Phonetic Association*, 12, 58–69.

Dauer, R. M. (1983). Stress-timing and syllable-timing reanalyzed. *Journal of Phonetics*, 11, 51–62.

Dehaene, S., Dupoux, E., Mehler, J., Cohen, L., Paulesu, E., Perani, D., van de Moortele, P.-F., Lehericy, S., & Le Bihan, D. (1997). Anatomical variability in the cortical representation of first and second language. *Neuroreport*, 17, 3809–15.

Dehaene-Lambertz, G. (1997). Electrophysiological correlates of categorical phoneme perception in adults. *NeuroReport*, 8, 919–24.

Dehaene-Lambertz, G., Dupoux, E., & Gout, A. (2000). Electrophysiological correlates of phonological processing: A cross-linguistic study. *Journal of Cognitive Neuroscience*, 12, 635–47.

Dehaene-Lambertz, G. & Houston, D. (1998). Faster orientation latencies toward native language in two-month old infants. *Language and Speech*, 41, 21–43.

Deutsch, D., Henthorn, T., & Dolson, M. (2000). Bilingual speakers perceive a musical illusion in accordance with their first language. *Journal of the Acoustical Society of America*, 108, 2591.

Dupoux, E. & Green, K. (1997). Perceptual adjustment to highly compressed speech: Effects of talker and rate changes. *Journal of Experimental Psychology: Human Perception and Performance*, 23, 914–27.

Dupoux, E., Christophe, P., Sebastiàn-Gallés, N., & Mehler, J. (1997). A distressing deafness in French. *Journal of Memory and Language*, 36, 406–21.

Dupoux, E., Kakehi, K., Hirose, Y., Pallier, C., & Mehler, J. (1999). Epenthetic vowels in Japanese: A perceptual illusion? *Journal of Experimental Psychology: Human Perception and Performance*, 25, 1568–78.

Dupoux, E., Peperkamp, S., & Sebastián-Gallés, N. (2001). A robust method to study stress "deafness." *Journal of the Acoustical Society of America*, 110, 1606–18.

Flege, J. E. (1995). Second language speech learning: Theory, findings and problems. In W. Strange (ed.), *Speech Perception and Linguistic Experience* (pp. 233–72). Baltimore, MD: York Press.

Flege, J. E. (2002). Interactions between the native and second-language phonetic systems. In T. P. P. Burmeister & A. Rohde (eds.), *An Integrated View of Language Development: Papers in Honor of Henning Wode* (pp. 217–24). Trier: Wissenschaftlicher Verlag.

Flege, J. E. & Wang. (1989). Native-language phonotactic constraints affect how well Chinese subjects perceive the word-final /t/-/d/ contrast. *Journal of Phonetics*, 17, 299–315.

Friederici, A. D. & Wessels, J. M. I. (1993). Phonotactic knowledge and its use in infant speech perception. *Perception & Psychophysics*, 54, 287–95.

Gandour, J. (1983). Tone perception in Far Eastern languages. *Journal of Phonetics*, 11, 149–75.

Gandour, J., Dzemidzic, M., Wong, D., Lowe, M., Tong, Y., Hsieh, L., Satthamnuwong, N., & Lurito, J. (in press). Temporal integration of speech prosody is shaped by language experience: An fMRI study. *Brain and Language*.

Gandour, J., Wong, D., Hsieh, L., Weinzapfel, B., Van Lancker, D., & Hutchins, G. (2000). A crosslinguistic PET study of tone perception. *Journal of Cognitive Neuroscience*, 12, 207–22.

Gandour, J., Wong, D., Lowe, M., Dzemidzic, M., Satthamnuwong, N., Tong, Y., & Li, X. (2002a). A crosslinguistic fMRI study of spectral and temporal cues underlying phonological processing. *Journal of Cognitive Neuroscience*, 14, 1076–87.

Gandour, J., Wong, D., Lowe, M., Dzemidzic, M., Satthamnuwong, N., Tong, Y., & Lurito, J. (2002b). Neural circuitry underlying perception of duration depends on language experience. *Brain and Language*, 83, 268–90.

Hallé, P. A., Seguí, J., Frauenfelder, U., & Meunier, C. (1998). Processing of illegal consonant clusters: A case of perceptual assimilation? *Journal of Experimental Psychology: Human Perception and Performance*, 24, 592–608.

Hazan, V. & Barrett, S. (1999). The development of phoneme categorisation in children aged 6 to 12 years. *Proceedings of the 14th International Congress of Phonetics Sciences* (pp. 2493–6), Berkeley, CA.

Jacquemot, C., Pallier, C., LeBihan, D., Dehaene, S., & Dupoux, E. (2003). Phonological grammar shapes the auditory cortex: A functional magnetic resonance imaging study. *Journal of Neuroscience*, 23, 9541–6.

Jamieson, D. G. & Morosan, D. E. (1986). Training non-native speech contrasts in adults: Acquisition of English /ð/-/d/ contrast by francophones. *Perception & Psychophysics*, 40, 205–15.

Johnson, C. (2000). Children's phoneme identification in reverberation and noise. *Journal of Speech, Language, and Hearing Research*, 43, 129–43.

Kiriloff, C. (1969). On the auditory perception of tones in Mandarin. *Phonetica*, 20, 63–7.

Kolinsky, R., Morais, J., & Clytens, M. (1995). Intermediate representations in spoken word recognition: Evidence from word illusions. *Journal of Memory and Language*, 34, 19–40.

Ladefoged, P. (1975). *A Course in Phonetics*. New York: Harcourt Brace Jovanovich.

Lee, L. & Nusbaum, H. (1993). Processing interactions between segmental and suprasegmental information in native speakers of English and Mandarin Chinese. *Perception & Psychophysics*, 53, 157–65.

Lively, S. E., Pisoni, D. B., Yamada, R. A., Tohkura, Y., & Yamada, T. (1994). Training Japanese listeners to identify English /r/ and /l/ III: Long-term retention of new phonetic categories. *Journal of the Acoustical Society of America*, 96, 2076–87.

Logan, J. S., Lively, S. E., & Pisoni, D. B. (1991). Training Japanese listeners to identify English /r/ and /l/: A first report. *Journal of the Acoustical Society of America*, 89, 874–86.

Mack, M. (1989). Consonant and vowel perception and production: Early English-French bilinguals and English monolinguals. *Perception & Psychophysics*, 46, 189–200.

Massaro, D. W. & Cohen, M. M. (1983). Phonological context in speech perception. *Perception & Psychophysics*, 34, 338–48.

McAllister, R., Flege, J. E., & Piske, T. (2002). The influence of the L1 on the acquisition of Swedish vowel quantity by native speakers of Spanish, English and Estonian. *Journal of Phonetics*, 30, 229–58.

McCandliss, B. D., Fiez, J. A., Protopapas, A., Conway, M., & McClelland, J. L. (2002). Success and failure in teaching the r-l contrast to Japanese adults: Predictions of a Hebbian model of plasticity and stabilization in spoken language perception. *Cognitive, Affective, and Behavioral Neuroscience*, 2, 89–108.

McClelland, J. L., Thomas, A., McCandliss, B. D., & Fiez, J. A. (1999). Understanding failures of learning: Hebbian learning, competition for representational space, and some preliminary experimental data. In J. Reggia, E. Ruppin, & D. Glanzman (eds.), *Brain, Behavioral and Cognitive Disorders: The Neurocomputational Perspective* (pp. 77–80). Oxford: Elsevier.

Mehler, J. & Dupoux, E. (1994). *What the Infants Know*. Oxford: Blackwell.

Mehler, J., Dommergues, J. Y., Frauenfelder, U., & Segui, J. (1981). The syllable's role in speech segmentation. *Journal of Verbal Learning and Verbal Behavior*, 20, 298–305.

Mehler, J., Jusczyk, P. W., Lambertz, G., Halsted, G., Bertoncini, J., & Amiel-Tison, C. (1988). A precursor of language acquisition in young infants. *Cognition*, 29, 143–78.

Mehler, J., Sebastián-Gallés, N., Altmann, G., Dupoux, E., Christophe, A., & Pallier, P. (eds.) (1993). *Understanding Compressed Sentences: The Role of Rhythm and Meaning* (vol. 682). New York: Annals of the New York Academy of Sciences.

Moon, C., Cooper, R., & Fifer, W. (1993). Two-day-olds prefer their native language. *Infant Behavior and Development*, 16, 495–500.

Morais, J., Kolinsky, R., Cluytens, M., & Pasdeloup, V. (1993). *Unidades no reconhecimento de fala em Portugues* [Speech recognition units in Portuguese]. *Actas do Primero encontro de processamento da lingua portuguesa.* Lisbon, Portugal: Fundaçao Calouste Gulbenkian.

Näätänen, R., Lehtokoski, A., Lennes, M., Cheour, M., Huotilainen, M., Livonen, A., Vainio, M., Alku, P., Ilmoniemi, R. J., Luuk, A., Allik, J., Sinkkonen, J., & Alho, K. (1997). Language-specific phoneme representations revealed by electric and magnetic brain responses. *Nature*, 385, 432–4.

Otake, T., Hatano, G., Cutler, A., & Mehler, J. (1993). Mora or syllable? Speech segmentation in Japanese. *Journal of Memory and Language*, 32, 258–78.

Pallier, C., Bosch, L., & Sebastián, N. (1997). A limit on behavioral plasticity in vowel acquisition. *Cognition*, 64, B9–B17.

Pallier, C., Colomé, A., & Sebastián-Gallés, N. (2001). The influence of native-language phonology on lexical access: Exemplar-based vs. abstract lexical entries. *Psychological Science*, 12, 445–9.

Pallier, C., Sebastián-Gallés, N., Dupoux, E., Christophe, A., & Mehler, J. (1998). Perceptual adjustment to time-compressed speech: A cross-linguistic study. *Memory & Cognition*, 26, 844–51.

Pallier, C., Sebastián, N., Felguera, T., Christophe, A., & Mehler, J. (1993). Attentional allocation within syllabic structure of spoken words. *Journal of Memory and Language*, 32, 373–89.

Pepperkamp, S. & Dupoux, E. (2002). A typological study of stress "deafness." In C. Gussenhoven & N. Warner (eds.), *Papers in Laboratory Phonology 7* (pp. 203–40). Berlin: Mouton de Gruyter.

Phillips, C., Marantz, A., McGinnis, M., Pesetsky, D., Wexler, K., Yellin, A., Poeppel, D., Roberts, T., & Rowley, H. (1995). Brain mechanisms of speech perception: A preliminary report. *MIT Working Papers in Linguistics*, 26, 125–63.

Pike, K. L. (1945). *The Intonation of American English*. Ann Arbor, Michigan: University of Michigan Press.

Pitt, M. A. (1998). Phonological processes and the perception of phonotactically illegal consonant clusters. *Perception & Psychophysics*, 60, 941–51.

Port, R. F., Dalby, J., & O'Dell, M. (1987). Evidence for mora-timing in Japanese. *Journal of the Acoustical Society of America*, 81, 1574–85.

Ramus, F., Hauser, M. D., Miller, C., Morris, D., & Mehler, J. (2000). Language discrimination by human newborns and by cotton-top tamarin monkeys. *Science*, 288, 349–51.

Ramus, F., Nespor, M., & Mehler, J. (1999). Correlates of linguistic rhythm in the speech signal. *Cognition*, 73, 265–92.

Rivera-Gaxiola, M., Csibra, G., Johnson, M., & Karmiloff-Smith, A. (2000). Electrophysiological correlates of cross-linguistic speech perception in native English speakers. *Behavioural Brain Research*, 111, 13–23.

Sebastián-Gallés, N. & Bosch, L. (2002). The building of phonotactic knowledge in bilinguals: The role of early exposure. *Journal of Experimental Psychology: Human Perception and Performance*, 28, 974–89.

Sebastián-Gallés, N. & Soto-Faraco, S. (1999). On-line processing of native and non-native phonemic contrasts in early bilinguals. *Cognition*, 72, 112–23.

Sebastián-Gallés, N., Dupoux, E., Costa, A., & Mehler, J. (2000). Adaptation to time-compressed speech: Phonological determinants. *Perception & Psychophysics*, 62, 834–42.

Sebastián-Gallés, N., Dupoux, E., Segui, J., & Mehler, J. (1992). Contrasting syllabic effects in Catalan and Spanish. *Journal of Memory and Language*, 31, 18–32.

Seguí, J., Frauenfelder, U., & Hallé, P. (2001). Phonotactic constraints shape speech perception: Implications for sublexical and lexical processing. In E. Dupoux (ed.), *Language, Brain and Cognitive Development* (pp. 195–208). Cambridge, MA: MIT Press.

Sharma, A. & Dorman, M. F. (2000). Neurophysiologic correlates of cross-language phonetic perception. *Journal of the Acoustical Society of America*, 107, 2697–703.

Soto-Faraco, S., Sebastián-Gallés, N., & Cutler, A. (2001). Segmental and suprasegmental cues for lexical access. *Journal of Memory and Language*, 45, 412–32.

Strange, W. (ed.) (1995). *Speech Perception and Linguistic Experience: Issues in Cross-Language Research*. Baltimore: York Press.

Takagi, N. (2002). The limits of training Japanese listeners to identify English /r/ and /l/: Eight case studies. *Journal of the Acoustical Society of America*, 111, 2887–96.

Takagi, N. & Mann, V. (1995). The limits of extended naturalistic exposure on the perceptual mastery of English /r/ and /l/ by adult Japanese learners of English. *Applied Psycholinguistics*, 16, 379–405.

Toro, J. M., Trobalón, J. B., & Sebastián-Gallés, N. (2003). The use of prosodic cues in language discrimination tasks by rats. *Animal Cognition*, 6, 131–6.

Toro, J. M., Trobalón, J. B., & Sebastián Gallés, N. (2004). Sentence discrimination and generalization by rats. *Cognitiva*, 16, 3–11.

Tremblay, K., Kraus, N., Carrell, T., & McGee, T. (1997). Central auditory system plasticity: Generalization to novel stimuli following listening training. *Journal of the Acoustical Society of America*, 6, 3762–73.

Tremblay, K., Kraus, N., & McGee, T. (1998). The time course of auditory perceptual learning: Neurophysiological changes during speech-sound training. *Neuroreport*, 9, 3557–60.

Underbakke, M., Polka, L., Gottfried, T. L., & Strange, W. (1988). Trading relations in the perception of /r/-/l/ by Japanese learners of English. *Journal of the Acoustical Society of America*, 84, 90–100.

Walley, A. & Flege, J. E. (2000). Effects of lexical status on children's and adults' perception of native and non-native vowels. *Journal of Phonetics*, 27, 307–32.

Wang, Y., Spence, M., & Sereno, J. (1999). Training American listeners to perceive Mandarin tones. *Journal of the Acoustical Society of America*, 106, 3649–58.

Winkler, I., Lehtoksoki, A., Alku, P., Vainio, M., Czugler, I., Csepe, V., Aaltonen, O., Raimo, I., Alho, K., Lang, H., Iivonen, A., & Nätäänen, R. (1999). Pre-attentive detection of vowel constrasts utilizes both phonetic and auditory memory representations. *Cognitive Brain Research*, 7, 357–69.

23 Speech Perception in Specific Language Impairment

SUSAN ELLIS WEISMER

Children with specific language impairment (SLI) present an intriguing puzzle since they display a significant language disorder in the absence of any clearly identifiable etiology. Unlike children with neuropathological disorders such as Down syndrome or autism, there are no associated conditions that might readily explain why these children should experience delayed onset and acquisition of language. Key characteristics of SLI include normal range nonverbal intelligence, normal hearing, absence of emotional disturbance (no evidence of pervasive developmental disorder), and absence of frank neurological deficits. There is considerable heterogeneity among children with SLI with respect to profiles of language deficits across various linguistic domains and processes. Although morphosyntactic deficits are often considered to be a hallmark of SLI, these children may also exhibit semantic and pragmatic difficulties. Some children have difficulties with perceptual/comprehension processes as well as production processes, whereas other children only exhibit expressive language deficits.

Current theoretical accounts of SLI can be broadly grouped into competence-based grammatical deficit models versus performance-based processing limitation models (see Joanisse & Seidenberg, 1998; Leonard, 1998). Competence-based accounts of the disorder stem from a nativist, generative grammar framework in which linguistic knowledge is viewed as a modular facility that is encapsulated and largely independent of other cognitive domains. According to this perspective, language impairments are thought to be reflective of problems in the child's underlying grammar, with specific theories differing as to which aspects of the child's grammar are posited to be impaired (Gopnik & Crago, 1991; Rice, Wexler, & Redmond, 1999). Alternately, SLI is viewed as a manifestation of a broader cognitive/information processing deficit within various performance-based, processing limitation accounts; this is the point of view represented in the present chapter. The different iterations of processing limitation accounts of SLI range from claims about specific constraints in temporal processing or phonological working memory to claims that linguistic deficits are secondary to more generalized information processing limitations.

A broad view of speech perception will be adopted in this chapter, which entails not only traditional investigations of phoneme perception, but recognition of spoken words and comprehension of connected speech in more naturalistic contexts (see Cleary & Pisoni, 2001). In exploring the issue of speech perception in children with SLI, this chapter will examine a diverse array of cognitive functions from auditory/temporal processing to understanding spoken language and will relate findings in these areas to varying limited processing accounts of specific language impairment.

23.1 Auditory/Temporal Processing Abilities of Children with SLI

There is evidence to support the claim that children with SLI exhibit auditory processing deficits based on findings from a variety of psychophysical tasks involving presentation of rapid nonverbal auditory information, including rapid perception, same-different discrimination, auditory tracking, and backward masking tasks (Tallal, 1976; Tallal & Piercy, 1973; Tallal et al., 1981; Visto, Cranford, & Scudder, 1996; Wright et al., 1997). Research has also shown that children with SLI are significantly poorer than their normal language peers in phoneme perception of synthesized speech stimuli; this finding stems from performance on a number of tasks including those tapping rapid perception, same-different discrimination, phonetic identification, and just-noticeable-differences (JND) involved in fine-grained discrimination (Elliott, Hammer, & Scholl, 1989; Leonard, McGregor, & Allen, 1992; Sussman, 1993, 2001; Tallal & Piercy, 1975; Tallal, Stark, & Mellits, 1985).

Attempts to trace language impairment to auditory perceptual deficits have a long history (see Leonard, 1998). The bulk of the contemporary research supporting the claim that auditory processing deficits underlie SLI has been conducted by Tallal and colleagues. She and her associates have carried out numerous studies to examine the processing of linguistic and nonlinguistic stimuli by children with language impairment (see review by Leonard, 1998). Findings from this line of research have led to the conclusion that children with SLI exhibit a pervasive temporal processing impairment that impedes their ability to perceive or produce rapidly convergent sensory and motor information (Tallal et al., 1998; Tallal, Miller, & Fitch, 1993). Although the temporal processing deficit in SLI is not thought to be specific to the auditory modality or verbal stimuli, it is posited to have an impact on specific aspects of speech perception (and production) involving rapid processing, within the time frame of tens of ms. Difficulties that children with SLI experience in temporal processing of the speech signal have been characterized by Tallal as involving problems processing brief formant transitions, brief intervals between segments, and brief steady-state segments that are embedded within the speech stream (Stark & Heinz, 1996b). According to the temporal processing deficit account of SLI, a basic temporal integration deficit disrupting the processing of rapidly changing auditory information leads to impairments in speech perception, producing cascading developmental effects on phonological representation and higher levels of spoken language processing, as well as on phonological-orthographic associations involved in reading (Clark et al., 2000; Tallal et al., 1998; Tallal et al., 1993).

The relation between auditory temporal processing skills and language abilities/disabilities has been examined in various studies. The performance of infants and toddlers on temporal processing measures has been reported to predict later language abilities (Benasich & Tallal, 1996, 2002; Trehub & Henderson, 1996). Benasich and Tallal (2002) reported that rapid auditory processing abilities of 6- to 9-month-old infants from families with and without a history of language disorder predicted language outcomes at 24 and 36 months. Tallal and colleagues also found a relation between degree of temporal processing impairment and degree of receptive language impairment in children with SLI (Tallal et al., 1985). Claims regarding the link between generalized temporal processing deficits and language skills have also been made based on intervention results. Tallal and her associates have developed a computer-based intervention program, referred to as Fast ForWord, which has been reported to result in substantial language gains within a short time span (Merzenich et al., 1996; Tallal et al., 1996; Tallal et al., 1998). Earlier work had shown that speech discrimination by children with SLI could be significantly improved by extending critical temporal/spectral cues within synthesized speech syllables (Tallal & Piercy, 1975). The Fast ForWord intervention program utilizes acoustically modified speech that is designed to retrain underlying neural mechanisms responsible for processing temporal aspects of speech. This approach is based on the assumption that improving temporal processing skills should result in improvements in language abilities.

Recent findings by Marler, Champlin, and Gillam (2001), however, question whether this program actually results in improved temporal processing abilities that are responsible for the language gains in children with SLI. Marler et al. found that over the course of training, signal thresholds for children with and without language impairment decreased by similar amounts in backward and simultaneous masking. When improvement occurred in backward masking for children with temporal processing deficits, it was abrupt, occurred early in the training regime, and was also observed for a different computer-based language intervention program that was not designed to improve auditory perceptual skills.

Challenges to Tallal's claim that temporal processing deficits underlie language and/or reading problems have been made on theoretical grounds by other researchers who argue that the perceptual substrate for processing nonlinguistic input is not the same as that for speech; these investigators view the primary impairment as specifically linguistic in nature (e.g., Mody, Studdert-Kennedy, & Brady, 1997; Nittrouer, 1999). Although differing interpretations have been offered to account for speech perception problems displayed by children with SLI (see discussion below), much of the empirical evidence can be accommodated within the temporal processing hypothesis. This hypothesis predicts that these children should have particular difficulty discriminating brief formant transitions within stop consonant/vowel syllables, but that they should have no problems discriminating steady-state acoustic spectra characterizing vowels. There are, however, speech perception findings for children with SLI that are not consistent with these predictions. For example, children with SLI have been shown to display significant difficulty in identifying [sa]-[ʃa] contrasts, which involve spectral rather than temporal differences (see Stark & Heinz, 1996b), and replications of Tallal's tasks have revealed problems in areas other than rapid temporal processing (Bishop, Bishop et al., 1999). Sussman (1993) found that children with SLI were significantly poorer than controls at identifying [ba]-[da] contrasts, but were not poorer in discriminating between these syllables. Finally, other studies have revealed that children with SLI exhibit difficulties with vowel perception that are inconsistent with Tallal's claims (Stark & Heinz, 1996b; Sussman, 2001).

Counter-evidence also exists regarding nonverbal auditory processing deficits in children with SLI based on their performance on psychophysical tasks. McArthur and Hogben (2001) found that only a subset of children with SLI who had concomitant reading impairments had poor auditory backward masking thresholds. The SLI group without reading problems did not perform significantly worse than controls on the backward masking task, though they did display poor intensity discrimination thresholds. Other researchers have failed to find significant differences between children with SLI and normal language controls on auditory processing tasks. For example, Bishop, Carlyon et al. (1999) found no evidence of auditory processing deficits in school-age children with SLI compared to controls matched on age and nonverbal cognitive abilities across three tasks, including backward masking, frequency modulation, and pitch discrimination using temporal cues. Based on their findings, Bishop and colleagues conclude that auditory temporal processing deficits are neither necessary nor sufficient to cause language disorders; however, they suggest that such deficits may be a moderating influence on language development for children who are at genetic risk for language disorder.

Numerous questions have also been raised about how to interpret poor performance on auditory psychophysical tasks. Research with adults has shown that individual differences on these tasks are not related to speech discrimination or language abilities (Hirsh & Watson, 1996). Children's performance on these measures clearly changes as a function of the amount of practice with the stimuli (Bishop, Carlyon et al., 1999; Marler et al., 2001). Furthermore, several researchers have suggested that poor performance by children with SLI may reflect difficulties with other cognitive demands of the task such as memory or attention rather than isolating a specific perceptual deficit (Bishop, Carlyon et al., 1999; Marler et al., 2001; McArthur & Hogben, 2001). Based on a combination of psychoacoustic and electrophysiological data, Marler, Champlin, and Gillam (2002) concluded that an impairment in auditory memory for complex, nonlinguistic sounds contributes to auditory processing deficits observed in children with SLI.

23.2 Speech Perception and Processing of Low-Phonetic Substance Morphemes in SLI

Clark et al. (2000) quote Leonard (1998) as commenting on the enduring findings of rapid auditory processing deficits in SLI; however, they fail to note that Leonard offers a different interpretation of these findings than the account proposed by Tallal and colleagues. Leonard contends that children with SLI have a general processing capacity limitation, rather than a basic temporal integration deficit. Within this view, it is the combined effect of relative stimulus duration and additional cognitive demands of the task that lead to the results. That is, difficulties with /ba/-/da/ contrasts exhibited by children with SLI are thought to be due to the brevity of contrastive portions of the stimuli paired with demands of the task (that involve not only perceiving the difference between the two stimuli, but remembering the target stimulus associated with the button press). Leonard has attempted to link the pattern of perceptual problems in SLI that has been reported by Tallal with particular grammatical deficits that these children display; this view is referred to as the "surface hypothesis" due to its focus on the physical (acoustic-phonetic) properties of English grammatical morphology.

According to the surface hypothesis account proposed by Leonard and colleagues (Leonard, 1989, 1998; Leonard et al., 1992; Montgomery & Leonard, 1998), the morphological deficits exhibited by children with SLI are tied to their difficulties in processing/acquiring morphemes with "low phonetic substance." These include nonsyllabic consonant segments and unstressed syllables with shorter duration than adjacent morphemes (although fundamental frequency and intensity typically interact with duration, these variables have not been explicitly incorporated into the surface hypothesis). According to this perspective, it is not assumed that there is a basic perceptual deficit or problem with the underlying grammar in SLI. It is assumed that children with SLI have a general processing capacity limitation, involving reduced speed of processing, which negatively influences their ability to process relatively brief duration grammatical morphemes. Limitations in processing capacity are thought to impede the combined operations of perceiving low phonetic substance morphemes and hypothesizing their grammatical function. Drawing on Pinker's (1984) learnability theory, Leonard proposed that inflected (or modulated) forms require additional processing compared to bare stems; these added information processing operations involve relating the inflected form to the stem, hypothesizing its grammatical function, and placing it in the appropriate cell of a morphological paradigm (Leonard, 1998). Thus, it would be expected that processing of inflected forms would require more time in working memory than would bare stems. Several possible explanations for processing breakdowns of low phonetic substance morphemes have been offered by Leonard and colleagues (e.g., Montgomery & Leonard, 1998). They suggest that processing of the inflected word may be terminated before the inflection so that resources can be devoted to the next word in the utterance. Alternately, it is suggested that the inflected word is perceived adequately but that the division of resources leads to decay of the inflection before the morphological analysis is finished or that the partial decay of the inflected word means that there is confusion between the inflected and bare stem form. Although the surface account has not been specified in terms of traditional working memory components, it appears that reduced scanning speed would primarily be involved in the first explanation, whereas rehearsal limitations would be implicated more heavily in the latter two explanations.

Evidence in support of the surface hypothesis comes from patterns of morphological deficits observed in spoken language samples, as well as from several behavioral tasks. Based on a review of prior research, Leonard (1989) demonstrated that closed-class morphemes that typically distinguish English-speaking children with SLI from controls matched on mean length of utterance (MLU) were of short relative duration. Leonard and colleagues have also provided cross-linguistic support for the surface hypothesis for children with SLI who are learning languages such as Italian, Hebrew, and French (see review by Leonard, 1998).

In an early experimental investigation of the surface hypothesis, Leonard et al. (1992) examined minimal pair discrimination of synthetic speech stimuli in children with productive deficits in grammatical morphology. The specific pattern of deficits that these children with SLI demonstrated in the perception of syllable-final and weak syllable contrasts (characteristic of many English grammatical morphemes) was consistent with the predictions of the surface hypothesis. Despite the fact that there is evidence that children with SLI are sensitive to the presence of grammatical morphemes (McNamara et al., 1998), they appear to be relatively less adept at processing morphemes with low perceptual salience. Montgomery and Leonard (1998) found that children with SLI had greater difficulty processing and making judgments about low-phonetic substance morphemes than higher-substance morphemes. On a word recognition task, the response times of children with SLI indicated that they were sensitive to a higher-phonetic substance inflection (-ing) immediately preceding a target word, but not to lower-phonetic substance inflections (-s, -ed). In contrast, age-matched and language-matched controls were sensitive to both high- and low-phonetic substance inflections. On the grammaticality judgment task, children with SLI only scored below age-matched controls on sentences in which low-phonetic substance inflections were omitted in obligatory contexts. In a related investigation, Criddle and Durkin (2001) have found that children with SLI were significantly poorer at detecting phonemic changes in target novel morphemes than language-matched controls when the morphemes were presented in nonfinal utterance position. They concluded that children with SLI demonstrated underspecified phonological representations of morphemes in low perceptual salience contexts.

Certain findings have challenged the surface hypothesis account. A recent study by Evans and colleagues (Evans et al., 2002) provided mixed support for this view. These investigators replicated the findings of Leonard et al. (1992) for the same synthetic speech tokens, using an alternate data analysis (signal detection) method. However, the pattern of deficits was not the same for natural speech versions of these contrast pairs; children with SLI differed from the controls only on a single contrast ([das]-[daʃ]) for natural speech stimuli. Furthermore, Evans et al. reported that use of inflectional morphology in spontaneous language samples was not significantly correlated with perception of either the synthetic or natural contrast pairs for this sample of school-age children.

The most critical challenges to the surface hypothesis have come primarily from researchers who support a linguistic deficit account of SLI. These include cases in which the account appears incomplete based on cross-linguistic evidence and others that question the accuracy of certain key assumptions for English (e.g., Oetting & Rice, 1993). The surface hypothesis is one of few accounts of SLI that has undergone such extensive scrutiny with respect to cross-linguistic evidence. Future studies contrasting characteristics of SLI across languages varying in morphological richness will help to determine the extent to which children with purported limitations in processing capacity devote their cognitive resources to dominant properties of that particular language at the expense of other features.

23.3 Generalized Processing Capacity Limitations and Speed of Information Processing in SLI

The generalized slowing hypothesis represents an account of SLI that is compatible with the surface hypothesis, but extends to areas beyond grammatical morphology.

According to this view, SLI is thought to be characterized by deficient speed of information processing that is not restricted to speech or the auditory modality. A number of studies have shown that children with SLI respond more slowly than typically-developing children on various linguistic tasks such as word recognition (Montgomery & Leonard, 1998), as well as on nonlinguistic tasks such as mental rotation (Johnston & Ellis Weismer, 1983). According to the generalized slowing hypothesis proposed by Kail and colleagues (Kail, 1994; Leonard, 1998; Miller et al., 2001), a proportional slowing effect is posited in SLI; speed of processing is viewed as an index of processing capacity in that speed determines the amount of work that can be completed per unit of time. Thus, children with SLI are thought to have a general processing capacity limitation, involving reduced processing speed, which cuts across both linguistic and nonlinguistic information. The motivation for positing a more broadly defined limited processing capacity framework is to account for the range of deficits observed in this population. Even though these children are classified as having "specific" language impairment and they perform within normal range on standardized measures of nonverbal intelligence, it is well established that they demonstrate certain cognitive limitations in addition to their deficits in linguistic skills (see Leonard, 1998). In order to account for these children's relatively greater problems in the verbal domain, it has been argued that cognitive processes involved in language learning, such as parsing the speech stream and extracting linguistic information from acoustic material, are more time-dependent than many other types of nonlinguistic processing; further, it has been suggested that uneven effects of this slowing might be expected across the language, since processing of certain grammatical morphemes is more time-dependent than other aspects of the language and is therefore more likely to be vulnerable to subtle reductions of processing speed (Miller et al., 2001).

Kail (1994) conducted a meta-analysis of reaction time (RT) data from several previously published studies to assess the proportional model of slowing in SLI. As predicted, Kail found a proportional and linear relationship between the mean RTs for the SLI and control groups. The SLI group was about 30% slower in their responses than the age-matched controls regardless of the specific task or condition. Thus, the children with SLI appeared to be slower than children with normal language in completing each component of processing by a constant factor. Recently, Miller et al. (2001) examined speed of responding across ten different linguistic and nonlinguistic tasks in a group of school-aged children with SLI and controls matched on nonverbal IQ. Mean RT for the SLI group increased as a function of mean RTs of the controls under three different regression models (proportional, linear, power function). Since all three models offered good fits for the data, Miller et al. focused their interpretations on the proportional model, which they viewed as most parsimonious. Results revealed that children with SLI responded more slowly than controls across all tasks combined, as well as for linguistic and nonlinguistic tasks analyzed separately. These results provide support for Kail's hypothesis, though the degree of slowing for children with SLI was not as great as that found previously.

Although there is growing support for the slowing hypothesis of SLI, several findings challenge this account. There is evidence to suggest that children with SLI do not necessarily demonstrate deficits in processing speed compared to age-matched controls on tasks that entail relatively low levels of cognitive processing, such as auditory detection (Edwards & Lahey, 1996; Ellis Weismer & Hesketh, 1996, 1998; Windsor & Hwang, 1999a). It may be the case that some minimum level of task complexity/cognitive load is required before generalized slowing is apparent in children with SLI. For example, choice reaction time tasks (depending on the dimension of choice and number of alternatives) may reveal slowing effects that are not apparent in simple detection tasks. There is also some question about how to best model the pattern of slowing that is observed in the responses of children with SLI. Based on research in normal development and aging, various linear and nonlinear models of processing speed/slowing have been proposed. Windsor and colleagues have explored several mathematical models for capturing the type of slowing exhibited in SLI (Windsor & Hwang, 1999b; Windsor et al., 2001). In their initial study, Windsor and Hwang (1999b) found similar results across several models and focused their interpretations on the proportional model. The results indicated that the mean RT of the SLI group was approximately one-fifth slower than that of the controls. However, in a subsequent study that involved a more extensive corpus of RT data (25 studies examining 20 different tasks), Windsor et al. (2001) reported that different models yielded quite different results. Findings using the standard proportional model were consistent with prior results; however, when a hierarchical linear model (HLM) was used, the data indicated study-specific slowing rather than generalized slowing and the increased degree of variability resulted in a lack of statistically significant differences across groups. Lahey and colleagues (Lahey, Edwards, & Munson, 2001) found evidence for linear slowing in SLI based on their meta-analysis; however, they failed to find significant correlations between degree of slowing and severity of language impairment as measured by standardized test scores. This result is consistent with the earlier findings of Edwards and Lahey (1996) who reported that SLI children's word recognition speed was not significantly correlated with language test scores. Lahey et al. propose several plausible explanations for the lack of association between processing speed and language abilities relating to: (1) the lack of sensitivity of standardized tests compared to other measures of language processing, (2) age-dependent relationships at different stages of language learning, (3) threshold effects of slowing upon relative levels of language facility, or (4) the possibility that RT is not an optimal index of processing speed.

23.4 Spoken Word Recognition and Lexical Access in SLI

Deficits in lexical access have been inferred from findings that children with SLI demonstrate difficulties with word naming and recall (see Leonard, 1998). Studies have also examined spoken word recognition abilities of school-age children with SLI, utilizing paradigms involving word monitoring in sentence contexts (Montgomery, 2000; Stark & Montgomery, 1995), lexical decision tasks (Edwards & Lahey, 1996; Windsor & Hwang, 1999a), and gating tasks (Dollaghan, 1998; Montgomery, 1999). These studies provide additional insights into claims regarding perceptual deficits, slowed processing, or limitations in working memory capacity in children with SLI. Various models of spoken word recognition have postulated interactions between perceptual processes involved in processing acoustic-phonetic information in the speech waveform and the listener's use of other types of contextual information, including phonological, semantic, syntactic, and pragmatic/discourse information (Luce & Pisoni, 1998; Marslen-Wilson & Tyler, 1980; Salasoo & Pisoni, 1985). The interplay between variables such as frequency, neighborhood density, and phonotactic probability has been demonstrated in research on adult language processing (Vitevitch & Luce, 1998; Vitevitch et al., 1999), as well as in developmental studies (see review by Storkel & Morrisette, 2002). Studies of word recognition and nonword processing in children with SLI have just begun to explore these interconnections.

Stark and Montgomery (1995) examined how processing of temporal/spectral aspects of speech interact with semantic and syntactic processes. Specifically, they investigated effects of time compression and low-pass filtering on word recognition in sentence contexts for children with and without language impairment. Group differences favoring the normal language controls were found for both accuracy and latency measures. These differences were attributed to less efficient lexical retrieval operations rather than processing of acoustic-phonetic information. Children with SLI and children with normal language abilities responded similarly to adjustments in the temporal/spectral features of the stimuli. Both groups showed slower word recognition under the filtered condition, but not under time compression. Stark and Montgomery concluded that reduction of high frequency acoustic-phonetic cues and rate of presentation of acoustic-phonetic cues have independent effects on children's word recognition, with reduced access to acoustic-phonetic cues being more problematic than altered temporal cues. However, they noted that one cannot infer from these results that presentation rate will not adversely affect children with SLI on other tasks involving less familiar words in more demanding tasks (see discussion below regarding speaking rate effects reported by Ellis Weismer & Hesketh, 1996).

Findings from auditory lexical decision tasks have also provided some evidence that children with SLI are less proficient than normal language peers at recognizing both uninflected and inflected words presented in isolation. Edwards and Lahey (1996) found that children with SLI were significantly slower than age-matched peers in making lexical decisions on a task using familiar nouns and nonsense words. An analysis of subgroups of SLI revealed that it was the children with receptive-expressive profiles, rather than those with expressive-only deficits, who were significantly slower than age-mates. Speed of word recognition was not significantly correlated with the SLI group's performance (accuracy levels) on standardized tests of vocabulary and morphosyntactic knowledge. However, these measures might not provide a sensitive index of spoken language processing that would be expected to be closely linked to inefficient word recognition skills. Windsor and Hwang (1999a) examined the effects of phonological opacity – stress and vowel changes that base words undergo to form derivatives – on word recognition by children with and without language impairment in two auditory lexical decision tasks. The pattern of results was interpreted as supporting a limited processing capacity account of SLI, since children with language impairment demonstrated disproportionate difficulty only with phonologically opaque derivatives that involve using additional processing operations to ascertain base-suffix relations. These findings are consistent with the general limited capacity view of SLI, but do not distinguish between speed of processing or working memory explanations.

In an effort to investigate the initial stages of spoken word recognition in children with SLI, researchers have employed gating tasks in which segments of words are presented successively. Typical listeners use temporal and/or spectral cues in prior segments, especially word-onset information, to predict upcoming segments (Lahiri & Marslen-Wilson, 1991). The question is whether children with SLI display specific deficits in the early acoustic-phonetic analysis phase of word recognition compared to children with normal language abilities. In a study by Montgomery (1999), a forward gating task was employed in which children were presented successive segments of familiar monosyllabic (CVC) nouns; children were then asked to identify/produce the target words and rate their confidence in the word identification following each gate. The children with SLI performed similarly to controls on seven different measures of "lexical mapping"; this term is used by Montgomery to refer collectively to the first two stages of word recognition – lexical contact and lexical activation – proposed by the revised cohort theory (Frauenfelder & Tyler, 1987; Marslen-Wilson & Zwiterslood, 1989). These results were interpreted as indicating that children with SLI do not demonstrate deficits in the acoustic-phonetic analysis phase of spoken word recognition for highly familiar words.

Dollaghan (1998) also examined spoken word recognition by children with and without language impairment using a successive, forward gating paradigm. Stimuli included unfamiliar (recently learned) words, familiar, phonologically related words (differing only in the final consonant), and familiar, phonologically unrelated words. Results indicated that children with SLI were similar to age-matched controls with respect to the point at which they recognized familiar monosyllabic words; however, they required significantly more acoustic-phonetic information to recognize unfamiliar words. Additionally, the children with SLI were significantly poorer than controls at guessing the initial consonant of both familiar and unfamiliar words at the earliest gated interval and were much less likely to initiate a lexical search in the expected phonological neighborhood. Dollaghan interpreted her results as implicating both lower-level speech perception processes (identification of initial consonants in familiar words) and limitations in representing phonological information in memory (familiarity effect).

23.5 Nonword Processing/Novel Word Learning and Working Memory Capacity in SLI

Some researchers have viewed processing limitations in SLI from the standpoint of restrictions in available resources within working memory. Research on the role of working memory in language disorders has stemmed from limited capacity models of language processing (Baddeley, 1986, 1998; Gathercole & Baddeley, 1993; Just & Carpenter, 1992; Just, Carpenter, & Keller, 1996). These models differ in their conception of working memory and the paradigms used to evaluate this construct (see Ellis Weismer, Evans, & Hesketh, 1999; Montgomery, 2000);

nevertheless, a common premise is that there is a limited pool of processing resources available to perform computations and when demands exceed available resources, the processing and storage of linguistic information is degraded. According to these models, success in comprehending and/or producing language is dependent upon the ability to actively maintain and integrate linguistic material in working memory. Numerous investigations have demonstrated associations between working memory capacity and language abilities for both adults (e.g., Carpenter, Miyake, & Just, 1994; King & Just, 1991) and children (e.g., Adams & Gathercole, 2000; Gathercole & Baddeley, 1993; Swanson, 1996). Constraints in working memory capacity have been hypothesized to be a factor in atypical language functioning based on differing theoretical frameworks (Gathercole & Baddeley, 1993; Just & Carpenter, 1992). Much of the research on SLI has focused on restrictions in storing and processing verbal information within the phonological loop as conceptualized by Baddeley's (1986, 1998) model of working memory (also see his more recent notions of language processing within a multicomponent working memory system, Baddeley, 2003).

A particularly robust finding regarding developmental language impairment is that children with SLI exhibit deficits in nonword repetition (Bishop, North, & Donlan, 1996; Briscoe, Bishop, & Norbury, 2001; Dollaghan & Campbell, 1998; Edwards & Lahey, 1998; Ellis Weismer et al., 2000; Gathercole & Baddeley, 1990; Montgomery, 1995). Nonword repetition has been used extensively by Baddeley and colleagues, among others, as a measure of phonological working memory (Baddeley, 1986, 1998). In an initial investigation of nonword processing in SLI, Gathercole and Baddeley (1990) concluded that children with SLI have significantly poorer phonological working memory than controls matched on nonverbal cognitive abilities or language level. A study by van der Lely and Howard (1993) disputed these findings and a debate ensued regarding the reasons for the conflicting results (see Gathercole & Baddeley, 1995; Howard & van der Lely, 1995). Montgomery (1995) replicated the original findings of Gathercole and Baddeley and interpreted his results as evidence that children with SLI display reduced phonological memory capacity. A number of subsequent studies have confirmed that children with SLI have deficits in nonword repetition and research has continued to explore the basis for these difficulties.

Several investigations have revealed a genetic component in reduced nonword repetition performance by children with language disorders (Bishop et al., 1996; Bishop, Bishop et al., 1999). Based on their findings from a study of twins with language impairment, Bishop et al. (1996) suggested that deficits in nonword repetition provide a phenotypic marker of developmental language disorder. Bishop, Bishop and colleagues (1999) replicated their earlier findings showing that nonword repetition yielded high estimates of group heritability. They also found that nonword repetition was a better predictor of low language scores than a measure of auditory processing abilities as indexed by Tallal's repetition task.

There has been considerable debate regarding the underlying cognitive processes involved in nonword repetition, especially as related to children's language development (Adams & Gathercole, 2000; Bowey, 1996; Gathercole, 1995; Gathercole et al., 1999; Metsala, 1999). One of the issues under investigation pertains to the extent to which long-term memory (prior lexical knowledge) influences performance on nonword tasks (Dollaghan, Biber, & Campbell, 1995; Gathercole,

1995; Snowling, Chiat, & Hulme, 1991). In studies with adults, research has demonstrated that nonwords with high-probability constituents are given higher ratings of "wordlikeness" and show an advantage in terms of recognition memory (Frisch, Large, & Pisoni, 2000). That is, listeners' knowledge of frequently occurring sound patterns in words is recruited to facilitate processing of nonwords. Gathercole (1995) has argued that repetition of "low-wordlike" stimuli is primarily dependent upon phonological working memory, whereas repetition of "high-wordlike" nonwords is additionally mediated by long-term memory.

Several recent investigations have examined the influence of phonotactic probabilities on nonword recall by typically-developing children; these studies have demonstrated that children perform better on high phonotactic probability nonwords than low-probability nonwords and that these sequence frequency effects are most evident for children with relatively smaller vocabularies (Edwards, Beckman, & Munson, in press; Gathercole et al., 1999). Although the precise nature of the relationship between nonword processing, wordlikeness, and vocabulary knowledge has not been firmly established, studies have demonstrated that children with language impairment perform significantly worse than their normal language peers even when features of the nonwords are adjusted to reduce wordlikeless (Dollaghan & Campbell, 1998; Edwards & Lahey, 1998). Therefore, it does not appear to be the case that their poor extant language skills alone can account for the difficulties that children with SLI have in processing nonwords.

Various researchers have explored other possible explanations for nonword repetition deficits in SLI. Several investigations have sought to rule out the contribution of speech production difficulties to poor nonword repetition by children with language impairment (Dollaghan & Campbell, 1998; Edwards & Lahey, 1998; Ellis Weismer et al., 2000). For example, Ellis Weismer and colleagues (2000) conducted an individual error analysis on the nonword items for each of the 581 children in their sample to determine whether there was any evidence that children could produce the sounds constituting the nonwords in other contexts. Such evidence was found for all but 22 children (14 with language impairment and 8 with typical language) and overall findings were the same regardless of whether or not these cases were included in the analyses. Based on their pattern of findings and detailed error analyses, Edwards and Lahey (1998) concluded that the problems children with SLI exhibited in nonword repetition could not be accounted for by response processes (motor planning or execution) or auditory discrimination; rather, they proposed that the deficits were attributable to problems in the formation of phonological representations or the storage of phonological representations in working memory.

Several studies of SLI have specifically focused on perceptual components of nonword processing. Various investigations have utilized discrimination tasks in order to examine the role of auditory perceptual deficits in nonword processing by children with SLI independent of output processes (Gathercole & Baddeley, 1990; Marton & Schwartz, 2003; Montgomery, 1995). There is little support for the proposal that perceptual deficits can explain these children's poor performance on nonword repetition tasks. Montgomery (1995) found evidence for differences between children with SLI and controls in their ability to discriminate between 4-syllable nonwords that differed in a single phoneme, but failed to find any group differences in discrimination abilities at shorter syllable lengths. Gathercole and Baddeley (1990) reported that young children with SLI had no difficulty with discrimination of monosyllabic real words or nonwords. Although Marton and Schwartz (2003) found that school-age children with SLI performed significantly worse than age-matched controls on working memory tasks involving production of real and nonwords, there was no difference between the groups on a nonword discrimination task consisting of minimal pairs differing in stress pattern and associated vowel neutralization. Notably, the children with SLI performed similarly to the controls at all lengths of nonwords (2-, 3-, and 4-syllables), demonstrating the ability to perceive relatively subtle distinctions between these nonwords. Taking a somewhat different approach to exploring this issue, Briscoe et al. (2001) compared nonword repetition abilities in children with SLI to those with identified auditory perceptual deficits (mild to moderate hearing loss). Both groups exhibited similar difficulty with longer rather than shorter nonwords, but the children with SLI also displayed deficits on digit recall and were more negatively impacted by increased phonological complexity of nonwords. Based on these findings, Briscoe and colleagues concluded that auditory perceptual deficits alone could not sufficiently account for the pattern of difficulties observed in children with SLI.

Evidence that children with SLI have difficulty in novel word learning comes from fast mapping, quick incidental learning, and extended novel word learning paradigms (Dollaghan, 1987; Ellis Weismer & Hesketh, 1996, 1998; Rice, Buhr, & Oetting, 1992; Rice et al., 1994). "Novel" words in these studies have included both nonwords and unfamiliar real words. In examining factors related to lexical learning difficulties in SLI, Rice and colleagues have concluded that their findings do not support a processing limitation explanation. For example, Rice et al. (1992) reported that the insertion of a pause prior to novel (unfamiliar) words did not significantly affect passage comprehension by children with SLI. However, other research that has explored novel word learning in SLI has provided support for the role of processing capacity limitations.

Ellis Weismer and colleagues (Ellis Weismer, 2000; Ellis Weismer & Hesketh, 1996, 1998) investigated effects of prosodic manipulations of the speech signal (natural speech) on lexical learning by children with SLI within a limited processing capacity framework (based on Just and Carpenter's, 1992, capacity theory). Factors assumed to influence the cognitive load of the linguistic processing task were manipulated, including speaking rate and vocal (emphatic) stress. We hypothesized that embedding novel words (such as "koob") in sentences presented at fast speaking rates would exceed children's capacity limitations and result in restricted word learning, whereas the added processing time afforded by slower speaking rates would facilitate computation and storage of representational elements. Limitations in processing capacity might be posited to entail restrictions in the rate at which information can be processed such that elements within the speech stream are not fully processed before upcoming material appears, resulting in partial representations. Use of emphatic stress on novel words within sentences was hypothesized to reduce processing demands by cueing listeners as to important new information to which they should allocate their attentional resources. That is, it was assumed that acoustic changes associated with the emphatically stressed word (in addition to acoustic changes in the preceding linguistic context) might affect the way that total resources were allocated such that higher

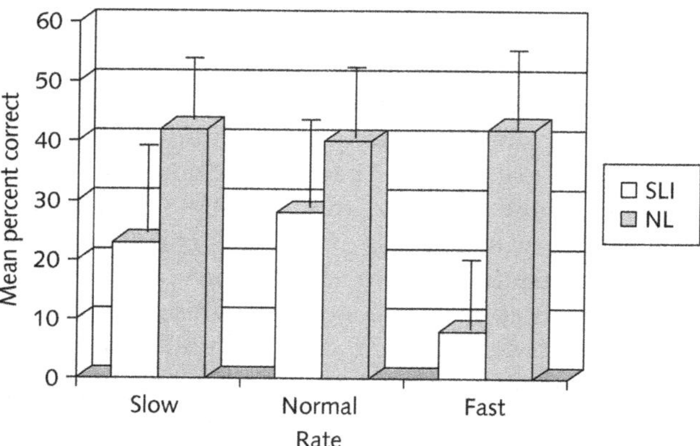

Figure 23.1 Mean percent correct novel word production for items presented at slow, normal, and fast rate for the group with specific language impairment (SLI) and the normal language (NL) control group (error bars denote 1 SD above the mean).

activation levels would be associated with stressed than unstressed elements. Accordingly, we expected that the words receiving special emphasis within utterances would undergo increased computational activity, resulting in storage of more complete computational products for later recall.

Findings from our studies (Ellis Weismer & Hesketh, 1996, 1998) supported a limited capacity model of language processing and demonstrated that children with SLI were less proficient overall than their normal language peers in novel word learning. We found that variations in speaking rate had the most effect on the tasks requiring the greatest processing demands (Ellis Weismer & Hesketh, 1996). There was no significant rate effect for comprehension of novel words, with all children performing at relatively high levels of accuracy. However, words that had been presented at a fast rate during the exposure trials were produced correctly significantly less often by children with SLI than by the controls (see Figure 23.1). Furthermore, the group with SLI demonstrated the same recognition accuracy pattern as the controls (for target labels versus phonetically similar/dissimilar foils) only for words trained at slow rate. Thus, speaking rate variations had a disproportionate impact upon novel word learning for children with SLI, which was most apparent for processes requiring more complete phonetic detail (production and recognition). An error analysis of children's production of the fast rate targets (summarized in Table 23.1) suggested that capacity limitations affected phonological representations. Children with SLI made significantly more vowel errors, changes in syllable shape, and substitution of real words for novel words than did the controls. Children with SLI also mislabeled the objects more often than controls (recalling the phonological form of a particular novel word but associating it with the wrong object). Errors of this type were thought to implicate additional difficulties with deriving semantic properties of a word and/or relating the referent for the semantic properties via lexical access; these difficulties appear to extend beyond just deficits in phonological memory.

Ellis Weismer and Hesketh (1998) found that variations in the stress patterns of stimulus sentences modeled during training influenced children's word learning.

Table 23.1 Error pattern analysis summary of children's production of fast rate novel words. Comparisons between the group with specific language impairment (SLI) and the normal language control group are denoted as non-significant (NS) or significant

Error pattern	*Fast rate group differences*
No response	NS
Consonant error	NS
Vowel error	*
Syllable shape change	*
Substitution of real word	*
Use of other object label	*

* $p < .05$, based on Wilcoxon-Mann-Whitney tests

Novel words presented with emphatic stress were correctly produced by both groups significantly more often than those presented with neutral stress. The fact that the groups did not respond differentially to the stress manipulations might be viewed as failing to support the claim that children with SLI have special restrictions in language processing capacity. On the other hand, the relatively small boost in performance afforded by emphatic stress on this particular task may not have provided an adequate test of differential processing abilities across groups under varying cognitive loads. It is possible that certain cognitive processes that contribute to efficiency or total capacity for language processing (Just & Carpenter, 1992) are more vulnerable than other processes in children with SLI. Taken together, findings from these studies suggest that constraints in rate of processing may play a greater role in these children's capacity limitations than do inefficiencies in the allocation of cognitive resources.

Restrictions in the processing capacity of working memory have been implicated in poor performance by children with SLI on various measures that extend beyond nonword processing and novel word learning (for a brief overview, see Ellis Weismer, 2004). For instance, restrictions have been demonstrated on listening span and dual-processing sentence comprehension tasks (Ellis Weismer et al., 1999; Ellis Weismer & Thordardottir, 2002; Montgomery, 2000). Although Montgomery (2000) concluded that inefficient lexical retrieval operations accounted for slow real-time sentence processing of children with SLI, he argued that difficulties with off-line sentence comprehension tasks reflected limitations in working memory capacity related to problems coordinating requisite processing and storage functions.

23.6 Conclusions and Future Directions

Based on the earlier review of findings, it is apparent that children with SLI exhibit deficits in a number of cognitive functions that underlie normal spoken language processing. It is also the case that there is considerable debate about how to interpret the existing data and there is little support among researchers for one processing-based account of SLI over other possible contenders. It is likely that an attempt to isolate a single cognitive operation as the explanation for SLI will not be the most productive approach. Research directed at identifying individual components as the causal factor in language disorder appear to stem, at least implicitly, from earlier serial information processing models in which relatively discrete levels of processing were designated. Parallel distributed models of information processing would lead us to consider multiple, integrated cognitive operations within patterns of typical and atypical functioning; that is, one would expect perception, recognition, learning, and memory to be integrally related processes (see Pisoni, 2000). Therefore, it is not surprising to see evidence demonstrating that children with SLI display deficits in each of these areas. Nevertheless, it is possible that a given cognitive operation is relatively more problematic for a particular child.

Numerous investigators have discussed the heterogeneity of SLI and possibility of different underlying factors for various subgroups of children (e.g., Bishop, Carlyon et al., 1999; Ellis Weismer, 2004). For example, a subgroup of children with SLI who had both receptive and expressive deficits was found to display poor speech perception skills, whereas those with only expressive deficits were not (Stark & Heinz, 1996a). Similarly, evidence of slowed processing speed is more apparent for children with receptive-expressive deficits than for those with only expressive deficits (Miller et al., 2001; Windsor & Hwang, 1999b). There are several dimensions along which subgroups of SLI might be delineated in addition to receptive/expressive deficit profiles, and continued investigation into meaningful patterns of impairment within this general condition is warranted. It is also possible that restrictions in certain cognitive operations have differential impacts at various points in development. For instance, Tallal et al. (1981) have suggested that temporal processing deficits in SLI may be linked to particular developmental time points. This suggestion was based on their findings that younger children with SLI (5- and 6-year-olds) were equally impaired regardless of sensory modality, whereas older children with SLI (7- and 8-year-olds) made nearly twice as many errors in the auditory modality than they did in the visual modality. There is a need for more longitudinal research exploring directionality issues and possible shifts in the role of different cognitive functions in language deficits in SLI across the developmental span. In order to establish causal developmental chains, it will be especially important to conduct large prospective studies spanning infancy through the preschool period in order to examine the constellation of factors that contribute to typical and delayed trajectories of early spoken language development.

Future directions of research focused on elucidating the nature of spoken language deficits in SLI are likely to entail cross-disciplinary collaborations that draw on new conceptual frameworks and methodological paradigms. Theories linking perception/comprehension with production (Fowler & Galantucci, this volume) and linguistic processing with acquisition (e.g., Seidenberg & MacDonald, 1999) may provide a more complete picture of SLI and help to sort out issues such as age of acquisition versus frequency/familiarity effects. Emerging methodological and technological advances will also be critical in amassing converging sources of evidence regarding the nature of underlying linguistic and cognitive deficits in SLI.

For instance, eye tracking procedures have been used to establish that typically-developing infants can recognize spoken words using word-initial phonetic information, and to examine speed and accuracy of word recognition in relation to vocabulary abilities (Fernald, Swingley, & Pinto, 2001); these techniques might be profitably applied to the study of word recognition in SLI. Further work is needed that integrates findings from off-line and on-line processing measures, capitalizes on computational modeling techniques, and combines behavioral measures with electrophysiological or neuroimaging techniques. Leonard, Weber-Fox, and their colleagues are currently exploring speed of processing in SLI using event-related potentials in addition to response times from behavioral tasks. Similarly, Ellis Weismer, Plante, and their colleagues are combining performance on behavioral measures with activation patterns from functional magnetic resonance imaging (fMRI) to explore the proposal that limitations in working memory capacity affect language processing abilities in children with SLI. In investigations of the neural basis of spoken language comprehension, research with adults has examined interactions and mutual constraints among different types of linguistic processing (Keller, Carpenter, & Just, 2001). In future studies it will be important to explore constellations of factors, which may shift dynamically over development, that are assumed to contribute to the difficulties that children with SLI experience in processing spoken language.

ACKNOWLEDGMENTS

Preparation of this manuscript was supported by NIDCD grant R01 DC03731, "Linguistic Processing in Specific Language Delay" and NIDCD grant P50 DC02746, "Midwest Collaboration on Specific Language Impairment."

REFERENCES

Adams, A. & Gathercole, S. (2000). Limitations in working memory: Implication for language development. *International Journal of Language and Communication Disorders*, 35, 95–116.

Baddeley, A. (1986). *Working Memory*. Oxford: Claredon Press.

Baddeley, A. (1998). *Human Memory: Theory and Practice* (revised edition). Boston, MA: Allyn & Bacon.

Baddeley, A. (2003). Working memory and language: An overview. *Journal of Communication Disorders*, 36, 189–208.

Benasich, A. & Tallal, P. (1996). Auditory temporal processing thresholds, habituation, and recognition memory over the first year. *Infant Behavior Development*, 19, 339–57.

Benasich, A. & Tallal, P. (2002). Infant discrimination of rapid auditory cues predicts later language impairment. *Behavioral Brain Research*, 136, 31–49.

Bishop, D., Bishop, S., Bright, P., James, C., Delaney, T., & Tallal, P. (1999). Different origin of auditory and phonological processing problems in children with language impairment: Evidence from a twin study. *Journal of Speech, Language, and Hearing Research*, 42, 155–68.

Bishop, D., Carlyon, R., Deeks, J., & Bishop, S. (1999). Auditory temporal processing impairment: Neither necessary nor sufficient for causing language impairment in children. *Journal of Speech, Language, and Hearing Research*, 42, 1295–310.

Bishop, D., North, T., & Donlan, C. (1996). Nonword repetition as a behavioral marker for inherited language impairment: Evidence from a twin study. *Journal of Child Psychology and Psychiatry*, 36, 1–13.

Bowey, J. (1996). On the association between phonological memory and receptive vocabulary in five-year-olds. *Journal of Experimental Child Psychology*, 63, 44–78.

Briscoe, J., Bishop, D., & Norbury, C. (2001). Phonological processing, language, and literacy: A comparison of children with mild-to-moderate sensorineural hearing loss and those with specific language impairment. *Journal of Child Psychology and Psychiatry*, 42, 329–40.

Carpenter, P., Miyake, A., & Just, M. (1994). Working memory constraints in comprehension: Evidence from individual differences, aphasia, and aging. In M. Gernsbacher (ed.), *Handbook of Psycholinguistics* (pp. 1075–122). San Diego, CA: Academic Press.

Clark, M., Rosen, G., Tallal, P., & Fitch, R. (2000). Impaired processing of complex auditory stimuli in rats with induced cerebrocortical microgyria: An animal model of developmental language disabilities. *Journal of Cognitive Neuroscience*, 12, 828–39.

Cleary, M. & Pisoni, D. (2001). Speech perception and spoken word recognition: Research and theory. In E. Goldstein (ed.), *Blackwell Handbook of Perception* (pp. 499–534), Handbook of Experimental Psychology Series. Malden, MA: Blackwell.

Criddle, M. & Durkin, K. (2001). Phonological representation of novel morphemes in children with SLI and typically developing children. *Applied Psycholinguistics*, 22, 363–82.

Dollaghan, C. (1987), Fast mapping in normal and language-impaired children. *Journal of Speech and Hearing Disorders*, 52, 218–22.

Dollaghan, C. (1998). Spoken word recognition in children with and without specific language impairment. *Applied Psycholinguistics*, 19, 193–207.

Dollaghan, C. & Campbell, T. (1998). Nonword repetition and child language impairment. *Journal of Speech, Language, and Hearing Research*, 41, 1136–46.

Dollaghan, C. A., Biber, M. E., & Campbell, T. F. (1995). Lexical influences on nonword repetitions. *Applied Psycholinguistics*, 16, 211–22.

Edwards, J. & Lahey, M. (1996). Auditory lexical decisions of children with specific language impairment. *Journal of Speech & Hearing Research*, 39, 1263–73.

Edwards, J. & Lahey, M. (1998). Nonword repetitions of children with specific language impairment: Exploration of some explanations for their inaccuracies. *Applied Psycholinguistics*, 19, 279–309.

Edwards, J., Beckman, M., & Munson, B. (in press). The interaction between vocabulary size and phonotactic probability effects on children's production accuracy and fluency in novel word repetition. *Journal of Memory and Language*.

Elliott, L., Hammer, M., & Scholl, M. (1989). Fine-grained auditory discrimination in normal children and children with language-learning problems. *Journal of Speech & Hearing Research*, 32, 112–19.

Ellis Weismer, S. (2000). Intervention for children with developmental language delay. In D. Bishop & L. Leonard (eds.), *Speech and Language Impairments in Children: Causes, Characteristics, Intervention and Outcome* (pp. 157–76). Philadelphia, PA: Psychology Press/ Taylor.

Ellis Weismer, S. (2004). Memory and processing capacity. In R. Kent (ed.), *MIT Encyclopedia of Communication Disorders* (pp. 349–52). Cambridge, MA: MIT Press.

Ellis Weismer, S. & Hesketh, L. (1996). Lexical learning by children with specific language impairment: Effects of linguistic input presented at varying speaking rates. *Journal of Speech & Hearing Research*, 39, 177–90.

Ellis Weismer, S. & Hesketh, L. (1998). The impact of emphatic stress on novel word learning by children with specific language impairment. *Journal of Speech, Language, and Hearing Research*, 41, 1444–58.

Ellis Weismer, S. & Thordardottir, E. (2002). Cognition and language. In P. J. Accardo, B. T. Rogers, & A. J. Capute (eds.), *Disorders of Language Development* (pp. 21–37). Baltimore, MD:York Press.

Ellis Weismer, S., Evans, J., & Hesketh, L. (1999). An examination of verbal working memory capacity in children with specific language impairment. *Journal of Speech, Language, and Hearing Research*, 42, 1249–60.

Ellis Weismer, S., Tomblin, J., Zhang, X., Buckwalter, P., Chynoweth, G., & Jones, M. (2000). Nonword repetition performance in school-age children with and without language impairment. *Journal of Speech, Language, and Hearing Research*, 43, 865–78.

Evans, J., Viele, K., Kass, R., & Tang, F. (2002). Use of grammatical morphology and perception of synthetic and natural speech in children with specific language impairments. *Journal of Speech, Language, and Hearing Research*, 45, 494–504.

Fernald, A., Swingley, D., & Pinto, J. (2001). When half a word is enough: Infants can recognize spoken words using partial phonetic information. *Child Development*, 72, 1003–15.

Frauenfelder, U. & Tyler, L. (1987). The process of spoken word recognition: An introduction. *Cognition*, 25, 150–7.

Frisch, S., Large, N., & Pisoni, D. (2000). Perception of wordlikeness: Effects of segment probability and length on the processing of nonwords. *Journal of Memory and Language*, 42, 481–96.

Gathercole, S. (1995). Is nonword repetition a test of phonological memory or long-term knowledge? It all depends on the nonwords. *Memory & Cognition*, 23, 83–94.

Gathercole, S. & Baddeley, A. (1990). Phonological memory deficits in language disordered children: Is there a causal connection? *Journal of Memory and Language*, 29, 336–60.

Gathercole, S. & Baddeley, A. (1993). *Working Memory and Language Processing*. Hove, UK: Lawrence Erlbaum.

Gathercole, S. & Baddeley, A. (1995). Short-term memory may yet be deficient in children with language impairments: A comment on van der Lely & Howard (1993). *Journal of Speech & Hearing Research*, 38, 463–72.

Gathercole, S., Frankish, C., Pickering, S., & Peaker, S. (1999). Phonotactic influences on short-term memory. *Journal of Experimental Psychology: Learning, Memory, and Cognition*, 25, 84–95.

Gopnik, M. & Crago, M. (1991). Familial aggregation of a developmental language disorder. *Cognition*, 39, 1–50.

Hirsh, I. & Watson, C. (1996). Auditory psychophysics and perception. *Annual Review of Psychology*, 47, 461–84.

Howard, D. & van der Lely, H. (1995). Specific language impairment in children is not due to a short-term memory deficit: Response to Gathercole and Baddeley. *Journal of Speech & Hearing Research*, 38, 466–72.

Joanisse, M. & Seidenberg, M. (1998). Specific language impairment: A deficit in grammar or processing? *Trends in Cognitive Sciences*, 2, 240–7.

Johnston, J. & Ellis Weismer, S. (1983). Mental rotation abilities in language-disordered children. *Journal of Speech & Hearing Research*, 26, 397–403.

Just, M. & Carpenter, P. (1992). A capacity theory of comprehension: Individual differences in working memory. *Psychological Review*, 99, 122–49.

Just, M., Carpenter, P., & Keller, T. (1996). The capacity theory of comprehension: New frontiers of evidence and arguments. *Psychological Review*, 103, 773–80.

Kail, R. (1994). A method for studying the generalized slowing hypothesis in children with specific language impairment. *Journal of Speech & Hearing Research*, 37, 418–21.

Keller, T., Carpenter, P., & Just, M. (2001). The neural bases of sentence comprehension: A fMRI examination of syntactic and lexical processing. *Cerebral Cortex*, 11, 223–37.

King, J. & Just, M. (1991). Individual differences in syntactic processing: The role of working memory. *Journal of Memory and Language*, 30, 580–602.

Lahey, M., Edwards, J., & Munson, B. (2001). Is processing speed related to severity of language impairment? *Journal of Speech, Language, and Hearing Research*, 44, 1354–61.

Lahiri, A. & Marslen-Wilson, W. (1991). The mental representation of lexical form: A phonological approach to the recognition lexicon. *Cognition*, 38, 245–94.

Leonard, L. (1989). Language learnability and specific language impairment in children. *Applied Psycholinguistics*, 10, 179–202.

Leonard, L. (1998). *Children with Specific Language Impairment*. Cambridge, MA: MIT Press.

Leonard, L., McGregor, K., & Allen, G. (1992). Grammatical morphology and speech perception in children with specific language impairment. *Journal of Speech & Hearing Research*, 35, 1076–85.

Luce, P. & Pisoni, D. (1998). Recognizing spoken words: The Neighborhood Activation Model. *Ear and Hearing*, 19, 1–36.

Marler, J., Champlin, C., & Gillam, R. (2001). Backward and simultaneous masking measured in children with language-learning impairments who received intervention with Fast ForWord or Laureate Learning Systems software. *American Journal of Speech-Language Pathology*, 10, 258–68.

Marler, J., Champlin, C., & Gillam, R. (2002). Auditory memory for backward masking signals in children with language impairment. *Psychophysiology*, 39, 767–80.

Marslen-Wilson, W. & Tyler, L. (1980). The temporal structure of spoken language understanding. *Cognition*, 8, 1–71.

Marslen-Wilson, W. & Zwiterslood, P. (1989). Accessing spoken words: The importance of word onsets. *Journal of Experimental Psychology: Human Perception and Performance*, 15, 576–85.

Marton, K. & Schwartz, R. (2003). Working memory capacity limitations and language processes in children with specific language impairment. *Journal of Speech, Language, and Hearing Research*, 46, 1138–53.

McArthur, G. & Hogben, J. (2001). Auditory backward recognition masking in children with specific language impairment and children with a specific reading disability. *Journal of the Acoustical Society of America*, 109, 1092–100.

McNamara, M., Carter, A., McIntosh, B., & Gerken, L. (1998). Sensitivity to grammatical morphemes in children with specific language impairment. *Journal of Speech, Language, and Hearing Research*, 41, 1147–57.

Metsala, J. (1999). Young children's phonological awareness and nonword repetition as a function of vocabulary development. *Journal of Educational Psychology*, 91, 3–19.

Merzenich, M., Jenkins, W., Johnston, P., Schreiner, C., Miller, S., & Tallal, P. (1996). Temporal processing deficits of language-learning impaired children ameliorated by training. *Science*, 271, 77–81.

Miller, C., Kail, R., Leonard, L., & Tomblin, J. (2001). Speed of processing in children with specific language impairment. *Journal of Speech, Language, and Hearing Research*, 44, 416–33.

Mody, M., Studdert-Kennedy, M., & Brady, S. (1997). Speech perception deficits in poor readers: Auditory processing or phonological coding?

Journal of Experimental Child Psychology, 64, 199–231.

Montgomery, J. (1995). Examination of phonological working memory in specifically language-impaired children. *Applied Psycholinguistics*, 16, 355–78.

Montgomery, J. (1999). Recognition of gated words by children with specific language impairment: An examination of lexical mapping. *Journal of Speech, Language, and Hearing Research*, 42, 735–43.

Montgomery, J. (2000). Relation of working memory to off-line and real-time sentence processing in children with specific language impairment. *Applied Psycholinguistics*, 21, 117–48.

Montgomery, J. & Leonard, L. (1998). Real-time inflectional processing by children with specific language impairment: Effects of phonetic substance. *Journal of Speech, Language, and Hearing Research*, 41, 1432–43.

Nittrouer, S. (1999). Do temporal processing deficits cause phonological processing problems? *Journal of Speech, Language, and Hearing Research*, 42, 925–42.

Oetting, J. & Rice, M. (1993). Plural acquisition in children with specific language impairment. *Journal of Speech & Hearing Research*, 36, 1236–48.

Pinker, S. (1984). *Language Learnability and Language Development*. Cambridge, MA: Harvard University Press.

Pisoni, D. (2000). Cognitive factors and cochlear implants: Some thoughts on perception, learning, and memory in speech perception. *Ear and Hearing*, 21, 70–8.

Rice, M., Buhr, J., & Oetting, J. (1992). Specific-language-impaired children's quick incidental learning of words: The effect of a pause. *Journal of Speech & Hearing Research*, 35, 1040–8.

Rice, M., Oetting, J., Marquis, J., Bode, J., & Pae, S. (1994). Frequency of input effects on word comprehension of children with specific language impairment. *Journal of Speech & Hearing Research*, 37, 106–22.

Rice, M., Wexler, K., & Redmond, S. (1999). Grammaticality judgments of an extended optional infinitive grammar: Evidence from English-speaking children with specific language impairment. *Journal of Speech, Language, and Hearing Research*, 42, 943–61.

Salasoo, A. & Pisoni, D. (1985). Interaction of knowledge sources in spoken word identification. *Journal of Memory and Language*, 24, 210–31.

Seidenberg, M. & MacDonald, M. (1999). A probabilistic constraints approach to language acquisition and processing. *Cognitive Science*, 23, 569–88.

Snowling, M., Chiat, S., & Hulme, C. (1991). Words, nonwords, and phonological processes: Some comments on Gathercole, Willis, Emslie, and Baddeley. *Applied Psycholinguistics*, 12, 369–73.

Stark, R. & Heinz, J. (1996a). Perception of stop consonants in children with expressive and receptive-expressive language impairment. *Journal of Speech & Hearing Research*, 39, 676–86.

Stark, R. & Heinz, J. (1996b). Vowel perception in children with and without language impairment. *Journal of Speech & Hearing Research*, 39, 860–9.

Stark, R. & Montgomery, J. (1995). Sentence processing in language-impaired children under conditions of filtering and time compression. *Applied Psycholinguistics*, 16, 137–54.

Storkel, H. & Morrisette, M. (2002). The lexicon and phonology: Interactions in language acquisition. *Language, Speech, and Hearing Services in Schools*, 33, 24–37.

Sussman, J. (1993). Perception of formant transition cues to place of articulation in children with language impairments. *Journal of Speech & Hearing Research*, 36, 1286–99.

Sussman, J. (2001). Vowel perception by adults and children with normal language and specific language impairment: Based on steady states or transitions? *Journal of the Acoustical Society of America*, 109, 1173–80.

Swanson, H. (1996). Individual and age-related differences in children's working memory. *Memory & Cognition*, 24, 70–82.

Tallal, P. (1976). Rapid auditory processing in normal and disordered language development. *Journal of Speech & Hearing Research*, 19, 561–71.

Tallal, P. & Piercy, M. (1973). Developmental aphasia: Impaired rate of nonverbal processing as a function of sensory modality. *Neuropsychologia*, 11, 389–98.

Tallal, P. & Piercy, M. (1975). Developmental aphasia: The perception of brief vowels and extended stop consonants. *Nature*, 13, 69–74.

Tallal, P., Merzenich, M., Miller, S., & Jenkins, W. (1998). Language learning impairments: Integrating basic science, technology, and remediation. *Experimental Brain Research*, 123, 210–19.

Tallal, P., Miller, S., Bedi, G., Byma, G., Wang, X., Nagarajan, S., Schreiner, C., Jenkins, W., & Merzenich, M. (1996). Language comprehension in language-learning impaired children improved with acoustically modified speech. *Science*, 271, 81–4.

Tallal, P., Miller, S., & Fitch, R. (1993). Neurobiological basis of speech: A case for the preeminence of temporal processing. *Annals of the New York Academy of Science*, 682, 27–47.

Tallal, P., Stark, R., Kallman, C., & Mellits, D. (1981). A reexamination of some nonverbal perceptual abilities of language-impaired and normal children as a function of age and sensory modality. *Journal of Speech & Hearing Research*, 24, 351–7.

Tallal, P., Stark, R., & Mellits, D. (1985). Relationship between auditory temporal analysis and receptive language development: Evidence from studies of developmental language disorders. *Neuropsychologia*, 23, 527–36.

Trehub, S. & Henderson, J. (1996). Temporal resolution in infancy and subsequent language development. *Journal of Speech & Hearing Research*, 39, 1315–20.

van der Lely, H. & Howard, D. (1993). Children with specific language impairment: Linguistic impairment or short-term memory deficit? *Journal of Speech & Hearing Research*, 36, 1193–207.

Visto, J., Cranford, J., & Scudder, R. (1996). Dynamic temporal processing of nonspeech acoustic information by children with specific language impairment. *Journal of Speech & Hearing Research*, 39, 510–17.

Vitevitch, M. & Luce, P. (1998). When words compete: Levels of processing in perception of spoken words. *Psychological Science*, 9, 325–9.

Vitevitch, M., Luce, P., Pisoni, D., & Auer, E. (1999). Phonotactics, neighborhood activation, and lexical access for spoken words. *Brain and Language*, 68, 306–11.

Windsor, J. & Hwang, M. (1999a). Children's auditory lexical decisions: A limited processing capacity account of language impairment. *Journal of Speech, Language, and Hearing Research*, 42, 990–1002.

Windsor, J. & Hwang, M. (1999b). Testing the generalized slowing hypothesis in specific language impairment. *Journal of Speech, Language, and Hearing Research*, 42, 1205–18.

Windsor, J., Milbrath, R., Carney, E., & Rakowski, S. (2001). General slowing in language impairment: Methodological considerations in testing the hypothesis. *Journal of Speech, Language, and Hearing Research*, 44, 446–61.

Wright, B., Lombardino, L., King, W., Puranik, C., Leonard, C., & Merzenich, M. (1997). Deficits in auditory temporal and spectral resolution in language-impaired children. *Nature*, 387, 176–8.

Part V Recognition of Spoken Words

24 Spoken Word Recognition: The Challenge of Variation

PAUL A. LUCE AND CONOR T. MCLENNAN

24.1 Introduction

We are entering the fourth decade of research and theory devoted to understanding how listeners perceive spoken words. Although much has been learned, solutions to fundamental problems elude us (Jusczyk & Luce, 2002), and even when consensus has been reached on answers to some of the basic questions, considerable effort continues on further demonstrations of well-established phenomena that are accounted for by well-worn models or their variants (see, for example, Allopena, Magnuson, & Tanenhaus, 1998; Gaskell & Marslen-Wilson, 2002). Certainly, theoretical refinement signals a mature science; stasis – be it in the form of apparently intractable problems or minimal progress on new research and theoretical foci – signals a paradigm in need of new challenges.

Consider the Trace model of spoken word recognition. Introduced in 1986, Trace (McClelland & Elman, 1986) has been enormously influential, in part because it was the first connectionist model to attempt to account for spoken word processing. (As a measure of the model's influence, yearly average citation counts exceed most other widely cited theoretical papers in the field, including Marslen-Wilson & Welsh, 1978; Marslen-Wilson & Tyler, 1980; and Norris, 1994). Moreover, the model was instantiated in a computer simulation that has been widely available. One could either conduct simulations of the model to evaluate its predictions (Frauenfelder & Peeters, 1990) or simply speculate about how it might account for data. Whatever the case, owing to its computational specificity, as well as its apparent ability to simulate a wide range of phenomena, Trace has dominated the theoretical landscape for years.

Despite its dominance, Trace has had its share of detractors. In fact, a number of competing models have been proposed. For example, Shortlist (Norris, 1994), PARSYN (Luce et al., 2000) and the Distributed Cohort Model (Gaskell & Marslen-Wilson, 1997, 1999, 2002) attempt to overcome some of Trace's more glaring inadequacies. Nonetheless, all of these models for the most part attempt to account for the same basic empirical phenomena (although they may differ, sometimes subtly, in how they go about doing so; see Norris, McQueen, & Cutler, 2000).

In short, 18 years after its introduction, the Trace model and its descendants still monopolize the theoretical discussion. However, a number of compelling issues have arisen over the years that suggest that a new theoretical paradigm is in order. These issues – concerning both allophonic and indexical variation – are for the most part ignored by the dominant computational models, in part because their architectures are not easily amenable to the modifications required to account for these phenomena. In what follows, we focus on a selected subset of recent findings that suggest that we need to reconsider the way in which we think about representation and process in spoken word recognition. While we note our indebtedness to Trace and its ancestors for the insights they have provided us, we attempt to highlight new challenges to the theoretical zeitgeist.

To understand the emerging challenges to the dominant paradigm, we must, of course, understand the paradigm itself. Thus, we begin with a short tutorial on current computational models of recognition, after which we turn our focus to a selective discussion of some of the issues that have occupied our attention for the past few years, paying particular attention to those empirical issues that have direct bearing on the current batch of computational models. Having set the stage, we then consider some recent, still evolving theoretical and empirical issues that we suggest may provide new challenges, and hence new insights, into the nature of spoken word perception.

24.2 Recent Models of Spoken Word Recognition

24.2.1 *Trace*

The Trace model (McClelland & Elman, 1986) is an interactive-activation, localist connectionist model of spoken word recognition that consists of three levels of primitive processing units – or nodes – that correspond to features, phonemes, and words. (In *localist* models of word recognition, individual processing units correspond to entities such as allophones, phonemes, or words.) Trace's processing units have excitatory connections between levels and inhibitory connections among levels, with the connections serving to raise and lower activation levels of the units depending on the stimulus input and the activity of the overall system. By passing activation between levels, the model serves to confirm and accentuate evidence in the input corresponding to a given feature, phoneme, and word. Moreover, lateral inhibition among units within a level enables winning units to suppress the activity of their competitors.[1]

Although Trace has had considerable influence, the model incorporates a decidedly questionable architecture. Its system of nodes and connections are duplicated over successive time slices of the input, a rather inelegant (and probably psychologically implausible) means of dealing with the temporal dynamics of spoken word recognition.

24.2.2 *Shortlist*

Norris' (1994) Shortlist model, a descendant of Trace, is also a localist connectionist model of spoken word recognition. In the first stage of the model, a "shortlist" of word candidates is activated that consists of lexical items that match the bottom-up speech input. In the second stage of processing, the shortlist of lexical items enters into a network of word units, much like the lexical level of Trace. Lexical units at this second level of processing compete with one another via lateral inhibitory links for recognition.

Shortlist simulates the temporal dynamics of spoken word recognition without resorting to the unrealistic architecture of Trace, in which single words are represented by a plethora of identical nodes across time. In addition, Shortlist attempts to provide an explicit account of segmentation of words from fluent speech via mechanisms of lexical competition. Finally, Shortlist is the current example of an autonomous model of recognition. Unlike Trace, Shortlist does not allow for top-down lexical influences on its phoneme units; flow of information between phoneme and word is unidirectional and bottom-up. Thus, the Shortlist model embodies the notion, which has received some empirical support (Burton, Baum, & Blumstein, 1989; Cutler, Norris, & Williams, 1987; McQueen, 1991), that the processing of phonemes in the input is autonomous of top-down, lexical influences (see Norris et al., 2000, and the accompanying responses).

24.2.3 *PARSYN*

PARSYN (Luce et al., 2000) is a localist connectionist model with three levels of interconnected units: (1) an input allophone level, (2) a pattern allophone level, and (3) a word level. Connections between units within a level are mutually inhibitory. However, links among allophone units at the pattern level are also *facilitative* across temporal positions. Connections between levels are facilitative, also with one exception: The word level sends inhibitory information back to the pattern level, quelling activation in the system once a single word has gained a marked advantage over its competitors. The first, or *input*, layer consists of position-specific allophonic units arranged into banks of receptors corresponding to the temporal sequence of the input. The second, or *pattern*, layer of units exactly duplicates the input layer, with units at the pattern level receiving direct facilitative input from the allophone input units. However, the input and pattern layers differ in the interconnections between the units. Whereas banks of units at the input level do not directly interact over time, units at the pattern level receive facilitative input from other pattern layer units in preceding and/or following temporal positions. The weights on these within-level connections correspond to forward and backward position-specific transitional probabilities. In addition, resting levels of the pattern-layer nodes correspond to the position-specific probability of occurrence. The transitional probabilities and activation levels of allophone units are designed to represent the (first order) probabilistic phonotactic constraints of the words in English. The third layer consists of *word* units. Word level units receive facilitative input from their constituent position-specific allophones at the pattern level. Each word level unit is capable of inhibiting all the other word units.

PARSYN is aimed at simultaneously accounting for effects of lexical competition and probabilistic phonotactics (see below; also see Auer & Luce, this volume). Moreover, unlike Trace and Shortlist, PARSYN proposes an intermediate allophonic – as opposed to phonemic – level of representation.

24.2.4 *Distributed cohort model*

In Gaskell and Marslen-Wilson's (1997, 1999, 2002) distributed cohort model (DCM), activation corresponding to a word is *distributed* over a set of simple processing units (i.e., the DCM is not a localist model). In particular, featural input based on speech input is projected onto simple semantic and phonological units. Because the DCM is distributed, there are no intermediate or sublexical units of representations. Moreover, lexical competition is expressed as a blending of multiply consistent lexical items based on bottom-up input, in contrast to the mechanism of lateral inhibition employed by the localist models.

24.2.5 *Some comparisons*

Trace, Shortlist, PARSYN, and DCM all assume that multiple form-based representations of words compete for recognition. The localist models each propose that word units are connected via lateral inhibitory links, enabling a unit to suppress or inhibit the activation of its competitors (see McQueen, Norris, & Cutler, 1994). The degree to which a unit inhibits its competitors is proportional to the activation level of the unit itself, which is determined in large part by its similarity to the input. The DCM, on the other hand, proposes a blending model of lexical competition, in which increases in the number of phonologically similar words consistent with the input result in more diffusely activated distributed representations. Nonetheless, in all models, competitor activation is assumed to be a function of the degree of similarity of the competing words to the input.

Trace, Shortlist, and PARSYN posit sublexical levels of representation. In contrast, DCM explicitly eschews intermediate units (although, as is often the case in distributed models, these units may be emergent). However, each model to varying degrees suffers from a significant weakness in terms of how they map input onto their form-based representations, be they lexical or sublexical. In particular, the models rely on coding the acoustic-phonetic signal into either abstract phonetic features (in Trace or DCM) or phonemes (in Trace and Shortlist) that vary *neither* as a function of time, rate, phonological context, or talker. That is, the models ignore much of the contextual and temporal detail encoded in the signal. Although Trace allows for overlapping features in an attempt to capture effects of coarticulation, the features themselves remain unchanged by the context in which they occur. Whereas Shortlist holds out promise for more realistic input based on the output of a simple recurrent network, the model as implemented makes no use of context-dependent, sub-phonemic information in lexical processing. Although PARSYN's use of allophonic representations attempts to capture some context-dependency at the sublexical level, it too fails to make full use of the rich source of information embodied in the speech signal itself. Moreover, PARSYN's allophonic representational scheme may make it incapable of representing more abstract (perhaps phonemic) units (see below).

24.3 Core Issues: Activation and Competition

Much to its credit, the research on the core issues in spoken word recognition has gone hand-in-hand with theory and model development. Indeed, one can see an intimate link between the theories we just discussed and the core empirical issues of activation and competition. Virtually all current models of spoken word recognition share the assumption that the perception of spoken words involves two fundamental processes: activation and competition (see Gaskell & Marslen-Wilson, 2002; Luce & Pisoni, 1998; Marslen-Wilson, 1989; McClelland & Elman, 1986; Norris, 1994). Although there is some consensus that input activates a set of candidates in memory that are subsequently discriminated among, details of the activation and competition processes are still in dispute.

24.3.1 *Activation*

Current computational models of spoken word recognition all ascribe, to varying degrees, to the notion of *radical activation*. These models (e.g., Trace, Shortlist, PARSYN, and – at least in principle – DCM) propose that form-based representations consistent with stimulus input may be activated at any point in the speech stream. The notion of radical activation differs from various earlier proposals that initial activation of lexical items is restricted to word onsets (as in the earliest version of cohort theory: Marslen-Wilson & Welsh, 1978) or stressed syllables (Cutler & Norris, 1988). According to radical activation models, spoken input corresponding to *dog* may activate *bog* based on the overlapping vowel and final consonant, despite the fact that the two words differ initially. Of course, most radical activation models afford priority to *dog* in recognition process, primarily because of the relative temporal positions of the mismatch and overlap. Furthermore, in the localist models, lateral inhibition at the lexical (and sometimes sublexical) levels typically grants considerable advantage to representations overlapping at the beginnings of words. Nevertheless, radical activation models propose that any consistency between input and representation may result in some degree of activation.

Evidence for radical activation abounds. For example, Connine, Blasko, and Titone (1993) found facilitative priming effects between rhyming nonword primes and real word targets, suggesting that activation of competitors is *not* limited to overlapping word-initial information. The conclusion that competitor activation depends on initial overlap is also contradicted by a series of intra-modal form-based priming studies (Goldinger, Luce, & Pisoni, 1989; Goldinger et al., 1992; Luce et al., 2000). In one of these studies, Luce et al. presented participants with primes and targets that were phonetically similar but shared no position-specific segments (e.g., *shun-gong*). The participants' task was to shadow the target word.

Luce et al. found that shadowing times were significantly slower for targets following phonetically related primes than to ones following unrelated primes. This result is consistent with the radical activation account, given that none of the prime-target pairs shared word-initial segments. Moreover, the finding that phonetically related primes actually slowed, rather than facilitated, response times provides direct support for the activation-competition framework, which states that similar form-based representations compete for recognition.

Allopena et al. (1998) provide additional support for radical activation models. Using a head-mounted eye tracker with which participants' eye movements could be monitored as they followed spoken instructions to manipulate objects on a computer screen, Allopena et al. found that rhyming competitors are activated early in the recognition process. When asked to use a mouse to click on a picture of a *beaker*, participants' fixation probabilities indicated that they also considered a picture of a *speaker* to be a likely candidate. These findings indicate that shared word-initial information is *not* necessary to activate competitors.

The preponderance of the evidence has led to a general consensus that spoken word recognition is best modeled as a process of activation of multiple word forms that are consistent with the input. Moreover, this activation process appears to be radical, in that consistencies between input and representation at any point in time may – at least in principle – result in activation of lexical items in memory.

24.3.2 *Competition*

In activation-competition models, the hallmark of the lexical recognition process is competition among multiple representations of words activated in memory. As a result, the role of competition has been a primary focus of research and theory on spoken word recognition in the last few years (e.g., Cluff & Luce, 1990; Gaskell & Marslen-Wilson, 2002; Goldinger et al., 1989; Marslen-Wilson, 1989; McQueen et al., 1994; Norris, McQueen, & Cutler, 1995; Vitevitch & Luce, 1998, 1999).

Evidence for competition among form-based lexical representations activated in memory has come from a variety of experimental paradigms. For example, Luce and colleagues (Cluff & Luce, 1990; Luce & Pisoni, 1998) have shown that *similarity neighborhood density* and *frequency*, both indices of lexical competition, have demonstrable effects on processing time and accuracy in speeded single-word shadowing, auditory lexical decision, and perceptual identification. A similarity neighborhood is defined as a collection of words that are similar to a given target word. Neighborhoods may vary on both the density and frequency of the words that comprise them. Luce and colleagues have shown that words residing in densely populated similarity neighborhoods, in which lexical competition is predicted to be strong, are processed less quickly and less accurately than words residing in sparsely populated neighborhoods. Moreover, in similarity neighborhoods composed of high-frequency words, competition is more severe than in neighborhoods of low frequency words, resulting in slower and less accurate processing.

Although there is now considerable evidence for competitive effects in spoken word recognition, some debate remains over the precise mechanisms underlying lexical competition. As noted above, in models of recognition such as Trace,

Shortlist, and PARSYN, lateral inhibition among lexical representations is a fundamental feature of the competitive process. The DCM, on the other hand, eschews the notion of lateral inhibition in favor of a competitive process that results from the blending of multiple distributed representations (Gaskell & Marslen-Wilson, 1997, 1999, 2002). At present, there is no definitive evidence to help distinguish between these accounts of lexical competition (see, however, Gaskell & Marslen-Wilson, 2002).

24.3.3 *Activation-competition models*

When considered within a larger context, the differences among the current batch of activation-competition models appear to be rather minor. Indeed, the less jaundiced eye might see remarkable unanimity among the models. For example, all agree that spoken word recognition is characterized by multiple activation of and competition among form-based lexical items. Although details may vary, the basic facts appear to have been established. Admittedly, there are other phenomena addressed by the models, for example, segmentation, lexical embeddedness, the nature of lexical feedback, and the role of context, to name a few. However, given the fundamental similarity of the current models, it is doubtful that any of these issues will prove to be determinative in deciding which model should prevail, especially given that fixes and additions are always in the offing (see, for example, the Merge model, Norris et al., 2000).

We should view the current state of theoretical affairs as an indication that we are converging on some basic truths and that the science aimed at understanding spoken word perception is maturing. However, new insights tend not to spring from consensus but from challenges. We now turn to two exciting areas of research that have emerged over the past few years that pose just such challenges to the current theoretical status quo: processing and representation of indexical and allophonic variation. We argue that these recent research foci, which are largely ignored by the current models, demand our attention. Indeed, each of these areas of research may lead us to a new conceptualization of spoken word process and representation.

24.4 Challenges: Variation in Spoken Word Recognition

24.4.1 *Indexical variation*

Each of the theories of spoken word recognition we have discussed assumes that lexical items are represented in memory by abstract phonological codes that only preserve information relevant for lexical discrimination. Indexical variation – arising from differences in speaking rate, differences among talkers, differences in affective states, and so on – is treated as irrelevant information that is discarded early in the encoding process (i.e., the input is normalized). Trace, Shortlist, PARSYN, and DCM propose that input is mapped onto abstract features, allophones, phonemes, or some combination of the three, which are then used to contact form-based lexical representations. However, spoken words may differ on many physical dimensions not captured by these abstract units, and these dimensions may have demonstrable consequences for lexical representation and process.

Recent research has suggested that putatively irrelevant surface details of words – such as information specific to a given talker – are preserved in some form in memory (see Goldinger, 1996, 1998; Pisoni, 1997, for reviews). The findings regarding *specificity effects* have led to the proposal that lexical items are represented in memory by representations that preserve, rather than discard, much of the physical detail of the stimulus (Goldinger, 1996, 1998). Specifically, this research has examined the effects of indexical variation on spoken word processing and representation.

24.4.1.1 Indexical variation and processing

Variation in the surface details of spoken stimuli has pronounced implications for spoken word processing. According to Pisoni (1992a), the earliest research to investigate processing costs due to talker variability (one form of indexical variation) was carried out by Peters (1955) and Creelman (1957). Peters compared the intelligibility of single-talker and multiple-talker messages in noise. He found that single-talker messages were reliably more intelligible than multiple-talker messages. Creelman compared the intelligibility of words spoken by either a single talker or by multiple talkers and found an inverse relationship between identification performance and the number of talkers: As the number of talkers increased, identification performance decreased.

In the late 1980s, Pisoni and his colleagues revisited the effects of talker variability on spoken word perception. Mullennix, Pisoni, and Martin (1989) examined participants' identification performance for English words spoken by either a single talker or by multiple talkers. Replicating the earlier work by Peters and Creelman, they found that participants' identification performance was more accurate in the single-talker than in the multiple-talker condition. Likewise, Mullennix et al. also found that participants were not only less accurate but also slower to repeat words in lists containing multiple talkers compared to lists produced by a single talker.

A number of other studies have demonstrated performance costs (measured in terms of decreased accuracy, increased reaction times, or both) associated with processing words spoken by multiple talkers, relative to a single-talker (see Goldinger, Pisoni, & Logan, 1991; Martin, Mullennix, Pisoni, & Summers, 1989; Palmeri, Goldinger, & Pisoni, 1993; also see Pisoni, 1990, 1992b). For example, similar findings have been obtained in preschool children (Ryalls & Pisoni, 1997) and hearing-impaired adults (Kirk, Pisoni, & Miyamoto, 1997). Research has also demonstrated that changes in talkers affect the perception not only of words but of speech segments themselves. For example, identification of vowels (Verbrugge et al., 1976) and consonants (Fourcin, 1968) is more accurate when they are produced by a single talker than when they are produced by multiple talkers.

Clearly, perception of both segments and words is directly affected by indexical variation. However, this important observation has yet to be acknowledged in current models of recognition. In fairness, these models have restricted their domain of focus to issues such as activation, competition, and segmentation. Nonetheless, the pervasive effects of indexical variability on spoken word perception suggest that an adequate model of recognition must have some mechanism for accounting for the sensitivity of the perceptual system to lexically irrelevant variation. Of course, the answer may simply be that prelexical normalization processes – which are *not* within the explanatory domain of current computational models of word recognition – reduce resources available for encoding, rehearsal, or both, thus producing processing deficits in the face of indexical variation. That is, a front-end model of normalization in speech perception interfaced to Trace, Shortlist, PARSYN, or DCM may be sufficient for explaining specificity effects on processing.[2]

On the other hand, processing effects on indexical variation may require that the representational schemes embodied in current models be re-examined (see, for example, Remez, Fellowes, & Rubin, 1997). In particular, do specificity effects indicate that lexical and sublexical representations themselves are highly specific, or – more likely – that these representations adapt or retune themselves to each encounter with the speech stimulus? If those representations responsible for spoken word processing are plausibly implicated in effects of indexical variation, our current models are inadequate. In short, the implications of indexical variation effects may be deep and may force us to rethink computational models consisting of abstract sublexical and lexical nodes.

24.4.1.2 *Indexical variation and representation*

A more serious challenge to current models comes from research on the *representation* of indexical variation, in particular from research using the long-term repetition priming paradigm (Church & Schacter, 1994; Goldinger, 1996; Luce & Lyons, 1998; Schacter & Church, 1992; Sheffert, 1998). This paradigm has enabled investigators to examine the degree of specificity and abstractness of form-based representations, which has in turn provided new insights into the architecture of the word recognition system. Investigators have used the phenomenon of long-term, form-based repetition priming to determine the degree to which lexical representations encode the variability inherent in spoken words.

The logic of the repetition paradigm is simple: Processing of a spoken word (as measured by accuracy, processing time, or both) is facilitated when the word is repeated exactly. However, if the first and second presentations (*prime* and *target*, respectively) mismatch on some dimension, the priming effect is often attenuated. We can infer from a reduction in priming that the prime and target activate somewhat different *specific* form-based lexical representations. If, on the other hand, the priming effect is unaffected by any differences between the prime and target, we can conclude that the prime and target activate the same underlying representations.

Church and Schacter (1994) and Schacter and Church (1992) observed effects of talker variation in implicit tasks such as fragment completion and identification of low-pass filtered stimuli. Participants were more likely to complete a fragment of a word if it was repeated in the same voice. Participants were also more accurate at identifying low-pass filtered words that were repetitions of previously presented items if the repetition preserved surface characteristics of the stimulus. Goldinger (1996) presented words in recognition and perceptual identification tasks with varying delays between prime and target and found significant effects of voice in both recognition and identification. In another experiment, he demonstrated that effects of voice varied with level of processing, such that strongest effects of stimulus specificity were observed in the shallower processing conditions, especially for recognition memory.

Luce and Lyons (1998) examined the effects of changing voice on stimulus repetition in both auditory lexical decision and recognition memory tasks (Biederman & Cooper, 1992; Cooper et al., 1992). They first presented participants with a list of stimuli spoken by two talkers in a lexical decision task. They followed this first block of lexical decision trials with either (1) another block of lexical decision trials (implicit task) or (2) a block of old/new recognition trials (explicit task). The stimuli in the second block of the experiment were either repeated in the same voice, a new voice, or were new items that had not appeared in the first block.

Luce and Lyons demonstrated that repetition priming for spoken words might not always be sensitive to changes in the surface characteristics of the stimuli. When participants were required to make lexical decisions to spoken words in the second block of trials, response times to repetitions in the same voice were not statistically different from response times to repetitions in the different voice, although overall effects of repetition priming were robust. However, in the explicit old/new recognition memory experiment, they obtained significant effects of voice: Participants responded *old* more quickly to words repeated in the same voice than to words repeated in the different voice. The results of Luce and Lyons' explicit old/new recognition task are consistent with the previous demonstrations that voice matters in recognition memory. However, the failure to observe specificity effects in the implicit priming task does *not* replicate previous work.

Luce, McLennan, and Charles-Luce (2003) have proposed that the failure of Luce and Lyons to observe specificity effects in lexical decision lay in the rapidity of the response, a proposal they dubbed the *time course hypothesis*. Compared to off-line identification, responses in the lexical decision task may be so rapid as to precede potentially slower acting effects of stimulus specificity in processing (Hintzman & Caulton, 1997; Hintzman & Curran, 1997).

Evidence for the time course hypothesis comes from a number of sources. For example, Goldinger (1996) reports one of the few spoken word recognition studies that has examined response latencies in which voice was manipulated. Response latencies to classify stimuli in his fastest condition were almost 100 ms longer than the latencies in Luce and Lyons' priming task. Thus, it may be that if participants are capable of making an identification decision quickly enough, effects of stimulus specificity will be small. Conversely, when responses are slower, as in Luce and Lyons' old/new recognition experiment or in Church and Schacter's and Goldinger's studies, effects of voice emerge. (See also Mullennix et al., 1989, and Goldinger et al., 1991).

Further support for this hypothesis comes from a study by McLennan, Luce, and Charles-Luce (2003). In contrast to the stimuli used by Luce and Lyons, which were short consonant-vowel-consonant words with a fairly high average frequency, McLennan et al. examined specificity effects for longer, lower-frequency bisyllabic spoken words (again presented in the clear for a speeded response). All things considered, Luce and Lyons' short, higher frequency stimuli should be recognized faster than McLennan et al.'s longer, lower-frequency stimuli. If the time course hypothesis is viable, specificity effects should emerge for those stimuli requiring longer processing times. Indeed, the average processing times to target stimuli in McLennan et al.'s study was 65 ms longer than the average lexical decision times reported by Luce and Lyons and, as predicted, large effects of specificity were observed.

Taken together, the Luce and Lyons and McLennan et al. results suggest that specificity effects may take time to develop. If we are able to tap into the perceptual process early, by examining processing of short, high-frequency words in a speeded task, no effects of indexical variability are observed. However, specificity effects on long-term priming are clearly in evidence when perception is slowed, even in a speeded perceptual task.

24.4.1.3 *Summary*

Although somewhat varied, the overall results of studies examining the effects of voice on identification and memory are consistent with exemplar-based (e.g., Hintzman, 1986) or distributed representations that encode lexically irrelevant information. According to these models, variation is encoded directly as changes in representations – taking the form of new exemplars or subtle changes in connection weights in distributed representations. An advantage of these types of models is that they have the potential for solving the long-standing problem of perceptual normalization in speech perception by dispelling the notion that the ultimate goal of the perceptual process is to map acoustic-phonetic information onto *abstract* form-based representations of words in memory. In exemplar-based and certain distributed models, the representational currency of the perceptual encoding process is more-or-less true to the details of the stimulus itself. If correct, current computational models fail in their representational assumptions.

The time course of specificity effects also poses a significant challenge to current computational models. If current models cannot account for effects of indexical information on both processing and representation, they are certainly inadequate as models of the time course of specificity effects. The results we have just discussed suggest a system in which rapid recognition may proceed based on abstract codes untainted by surface variation. However, slight delays in processing – as encountered when attempting to identify bisyllabic words – may afford the opportunity for indexical information to exert its influence.

The consequences of encoding lexically irrelevant information directly into sublexical and lexical representations may lead us toward new models with substantially different architectures. For example, the work on long-term repetition priming (and, to a lesser extent, that on processing of indexical information) demonstrates that the perceptual system is highly adaptive, constantly tuning itself to changing environment stimulation: Under the appropriate circumstances, representations may reflect the details of words last encountered. If adaptation is indeed fundamental to word perception, the current cadre of computational models may fail not only to account for the adaptive nature of the system, these models also may be substantially in error in their proposed representations and architecture: Systems of interconnected nodes corresponding to abstract sublexical and lexical representations may be poor approximations to reality.

24.4.2 *Allophonic variation*

Our thesis in this chapter is that accounting for variability in spoken word recognition poses a specific challenge to our current models. We believe that this case is amply supported by the research on representation and process of indexical variation in spoken word recognition. However, recent work on *allophonic variation* suggests further inadequacies in the current models. Whereas indexical variability refers to variations in a spoken word that arise from differences among talkers, speaking rates, affective states, and so on (Abercrombie, 1967; Pisoni, 1997), *allophonic variation* refers to articulatory and acoustic differences among speech sounds belonging to the same phonemic category (Ladefoged, 2000).[3] For example, the stop consonant /p/ is articulated somewhat differently before a vowel (as in *pot*), after a vowel (as in *top*), and in a consonant cluster (as in *spot*). Each of these different versions are referred to as allophones of the phoneme /p/. Recent research on allophonic variation has led to further insights into the potential inadequacies of current modeling approaches.

Traditionally, spoken word perception has been characterized as being comprised of a series of linguistic stages of analysis, with form-based representations becoming successively more abstract at each stage of processing. This view of mediated lexical access finds its expression in Trace, Shortlist, and PARSYN. Recently, these mediated access models have been challenged by direct access models, which state that after the initial recoding of sensory data, information is mapped directly onto form-based lexical representations. For example, the DCM proposes that lexical representations are accessed directly from phonetic features. In short, although both mediated and direct access theories assume that sensory information is initially recoded in some manner, they differ as to whether additional levels of representation intervene between sensory recoding and lexical representation.

Evidence in support of direct access models comes from a series of experiments reported by Marslen-Wilson and Warren (1994; see also Whalen, 1984, 1991, and Streeter & Nigro, 1979). Marslen-Wilson and Warren examined processing for a set of cross-spliced words and nonwords containing subcategorical mismatches. They observed processing costs only when mismatching coarticulatory information involved words. However, nonwords cross-spliced with other nonwords failed to exhibit processing costs associated with subcategorical mismatch. Marslen-Wilson and Warren concluded that the failure to find effects of subcategorical mismatch for nonwords is due to the absence of intermediate representations that could detect the subcategorical mismatch.

Recently, McQueen, Norris, and Cutler (1999) challenged Marslen-Wilson and Warren's finding. They found that the crucial distinction between words cross-spliced with other words and nonwords cross-spliced with other nonwords could be made to come and go as a function of task demands. Moreover, they found that models with a phonemic level of representation could simulate the data pattern obtained by Marslen-Wilson and Warren, thus calling into question the claim that mediated models should always show effects of conflicting information at a sublexical level. Nonetheless, a lack of positive evidence for sublexical representations persists. As a result, the debate between mediated and direct access theories remains unresolved.

We recently examined the status of intermediate representations in more detail by exploring the perceptual consequences of allophonic variation (McLennan et al., 2003). More specifically, we examined flapping in American English. A flap (/ɾ/) is a neutralized version and allophone of intervocalic /t/ and /d/. In casually produced American English, when a /t/ or a /d/ is produced between two vowels, as in *greater* or *Adam*, it is often realized as a flap, a segment that is neither exactly a /t/ nor exactly a /d/ (see Patterson & Connine, 2001). We attempted to determine if flaps map onto their underlying, abstract phonemic counterparts, /t/ and /d/. Mediated access theories predict that allophonic variation occurring on the surface should map onto more abstract, underlying phonological representations (see e.g., Pisoni & Luce, 1987). However, according to direct access theories, allophonic variation occurring on the surface should map directly onto lexical representations. Therefore, examining the perceptual consequences of allophonic variation may help to distinguish between these competing theories.

We used the long-term repetition priming paradigm to determine if flapped segments are mapped onto underlying intermediate form-based representations of /t/s, /d/s, or both, or if flaps are represented veridically as they appear in casual speech as /ɾ/. In particular, we attempted to determine if the surface allophonic representation, /ɾ/, is recoded into the underlying phonological representations, /t/ or /d/, as predicted by mediated access theories of spoken word recognition.

In this set of experiments, two blocks of stimuli containing carefully and casually articulated versions of words were presented. Casually articulated (hypoarticulated) words are produced in a relaxed manner, whereas carefully articulated words are more clearly articulated. Intervocalic /t/s and /d/s are flapped in casually articulated words but not in carefully articulated words. We hypothesized that priming of casually articulated stimuli by carefully articulated stimuli (or vice versa) would indicate the presence of a mediating underlying representation in memory. The presence of specificity effects – in which flaps fail to prime carefully articulated segments, and vice versa – indicates the absence of intermediate representations, consistent with direct access theories. Conversely, lack of specificity effects indicates the presence of intermediate representations, consistent with mediated access theories.

To review, Trace, Shortlist, and PARSYN all assume that access to the lexicon is mediated by intervening representations. Direct access theories, such as the DCM, assume that following initial sensory registration, access to the lexicon is direct. Thus, these classes of theories make opposite predictions regarding the perceptual consequences of allophonic variation.

The results of a series of repetition priming experiments were not entirely consistent with either mediated or direct access models, suggesting that the dichotomy represented by Trace, Shortlist, and PARSYN on the one hand and the DCM on the other may fail to capture the underlying nature of the representational and processing system devoted to spoken word perception. In our initial experiments, we found that flapped words primed carefully articulated words as much as carefully articulated words primed themselves, a result consistent with mediated access models. However, much like the effects of indexical variation discussed above, degree of priming from flapped to carefully articulated words varied as a function of the time course of processing. In general, when participants responded relatively slowly, we found evidence for the activation of underlying representations. However, when we manipulated the experimental conditions in such a way as to encourage more rapid responding, we observed no evidence for the activation of mediating representations.[4]

Overall, we demonstrated that *underlying* representations appear to dominate processing when spoken input is phonologically ambiguous (i.e., when flaps are present) and when enough time is allowed for the underlying representations to have an effect on recognition. Alternatively, *surface* representations appear to dominate processing when spoken input is unambiguous and when there is little time for the underlying representations to have an effect on recognition.

No current computational model of spoken word recognition is capable of capturing this pattern of results. For example, Trace and Shortlist both lack an allophonic layer of representation, a minimal requirement dictated by the finding that under appropriate circumstances flaps activate their phonemic counterparts. Only PARSYN incorporates an explicit allophonic level. However, PARSYN lacks phonemic representations, which may prove problematic in accounting for the activation of underlying forms (although PARSYN's lexical representations are phonemically coded). In addition, although certain of the mediated access models may account for the finding that underlying representations are activated, they appear incapable of providing an account of the time course of processing, namely that when responses are rapid, effects of underlying representations are absent. Finally, although the DCM can account for those situations in which underlying representations are *not* activated, the model will probably be hard pressed to simulate activation of underlying representations when processing is slowed. Once again, the current cadre of models fails to meet the challenge posed by variation.

Noting the apparent inability of the current computational models to account adequately for the findings on the representation and processing of allophonic variation, we proposed an account of these findings based on Grossberg's ARTPHONE model (Grossberg, Boardman, & Cohen, 1997; see also Vitevitch & Luce, 1999). According to this model, acoustic-phonetic input comprised of relatively veridical surface representations resonate with chunks corresponding to more abstract phonological representations, as well as to chunks corresponding to less abstract, allophonic representations. In the absence of ambiguity in the input, the resonances between surface forms and chunks corresponding to underlying representations preserve detail (see Grossberg & Myers, 2000). However, underlying representations (or chunks) activated by *ambiguous* input (i.e., flaps) may result in a restoration of surface representations not actually in the input (i.e., underlying /t/ and /d/). Furthermore, the restoration of surface representations by the underlying chunks requires time. Thus, tasks that tap into the recognition process prior to restoration of the surface representation should fail to show effects of underlying abstract representations, presumably because the underlying representations have not had sufficient time to establish resonance with a restored surface form. In short, the adaptive resonance framework is able to account for both the coexistence of specific and abstract representations *and* the relative speed with which they influence processing.

24.5 Conclusion

We began our discussion with the observation that the scientific endeavor aimed at understanding how listeners perceive spoken words appears to have reached a plateau, concerning itself with refinements and extensions of well-worn models that account for many of the major phenomena in the field. We have argued that challenges to the existing theoretical paradigm already exist, in the form of research on indexical and allophonic variation, and that these challenges may lead to the next generation of models of spoken language perception.

The challenges posed by variation are fundamental: We need to rethink the representational schemes of our models. The emerging evidence suggests the coexistence of representations that encode both the specific and the abstract. Moreover, we must conceive of systems in which processing of the specific and abstract follows a predictable time course, a time course that reflects the underlying architecture of the processing system itself. Finally, our next generation of models must appreciate the adaptive nature of perception. Even adult brains appear to tune, finely and frequently, to environmental stimulation. Adequate models of recognition must incorporate representational systems that can account for the adaptive nature of perception, and such an account will certainly have deep implications for the nature and architecture of the representational system itself.

Our belief is that the adaptive resonance framework outlined above is a good starting point: It does not propose a rigid hierarchy of abstract sublexical and lexical nodes, it explicitly incorporates a learning component that leads to constant tuning of representations to input, and it has the capability (although largely unexplored) of addressing the challenge of variation.

ACKNOWLEDGMENTS

This work was supported (in part) by research grant number R01 DC 0265801 from the National Institute on Deafness and Other Communication Disorders, National Institutes of Health. We thank Jan Charles-Luce for her assistance and helpful advice.

NOTES

1 This version of Trace as well as the other computational models discussed here use various coding schemes to abstractly represent the phonetic input to the models.

2 Specifying the precise nature of this initial prelexical process – which must somehow discard irrelevant variation by mapping specific information on to more abstract, canonical features or

segments – may be itself prove to be an enterprise equal in scope to the lexical processing models themselves. See Mullennix et al. (1989) for discussion.

3 Allophonic variation may arise from the predictable interaction of the articulators, and thus may be systematic across languages, or may be dictated or allowed by the phonology, thus being dialect- or language-specific.

4 It may appear that we are making contradictory proposals about the time course of specificity, in particular, that processing of indexical specificity lags behind activation of more abstract representations, whereas processing of allophonic specificity precedes activation of underlying representations. We point out that in our framework, allophonic information is only specific relative to underlying abstract phonemic representations; allophonic variation itself constitutes fairly abstract information, especially compared to indexical variability (see, however, Remez, Fellowes, & Rubin, 1997). Thus, not all sources of variability (i.e., indexical and allophonic) are created equal and may indeed follow distinct courses of temporal processing.

REFERENCES

Abercrombie, D. (1967). *Elements of General Phonetics*. Chicago: Aldine.

Allopenna, P. D., Magnuson, J. S., & Tanenhaus, M. K. (1998). Tracking the time course of spoken word recognition using eye movements: Evidence for continuous mapping models. *Journal of Memory and Language*, 38, 419–39.

Biederman, I. & Cooper, E. E. (1992). Size invariance in visual object priming. *Journal of Experimental Psychology: Human Perception and Performance*, 18, 122–33.

Burton, M. W., Baum, S. R., & Blumstein, S. E. (1989). Lexical effects on the phonetic categorization of speech: the role of acoustic structure. *Journal of Experimental Psychology: Human Perception and Performance*, 15, 567–75.

Church, B. A. & Schacter, D. L. (1994). Perceptual specificity of auditory priming: Implicit memory for voice intonation and fundamental frequency. *Journal of Experimental Psychology: Learning, Memory, and Cognition*, 20, 521–33.

Cluff, M. S. & Luce, P. A. (1990). Similarity neighborhoods of spoken bisyllabic words. *Journal of Experimental Psychology: Human Perception and Performance*, 16, 551–63.

Connine, C. M., Blasko, D. G., & Titone, D. (1993). Do the beginnings of words have a special status in auditory word recognition? *Journal of Memory and Language*, 32, 193–210.

Cooper, L. A., Schacter, D. L., Ballesteros, S., & Moore, C. (1992). Priming and recognition of transformed three-dimensional objects: Effects of size and reflection. *Journal of Experimental Psychology: Learning, Memory, and Cognition*, 18, 43–57.

Creelman, C. D. (1957). The case of the unknown talker. *Journal of the Acoustical Society of America*, 29, 655.

Cutler, A. & Norris, D. G. (1988). The role of strong syllables in segmentation for lexical access. *Journal of Experimental Psychology: Human Perception and Performance*, 14, 113–21.

Cutler, A., Norris, D., & Williams, J. N. (1987). A note on the role of phonological expectation in speech segmentation. *Journal of Memory and Language*, 26, 480–7.

Fourcin, A. J. (1968). Speech-source interference. *IEEE Trans. Audio Electroacoustics*, ACC-16, 65–7.

Frauenfelder, U. & Peeters, G. (1990). Lexical segmentation in TRACE: An exercise in simulation. In G. T. Altmann (ed.), *Cognitive Models of Speech Processing* (pp. 50–86). Cambridge, MA: MIT Press.

Gaskell, M. G. & Marslen-Wilson, W. D. (1997). Integrating form and meaning: A distributed model of speech perception. *Language and Cognitive Processes*, 12, 613–56.

Gaskell, M. G. & Marslen-Wilson, W. D. (1999). Ambiguity, competition, and blending in spoken word recognition. *Cognitive Science*, 23, 439–62.

Gaskell, M. G. & Marslen-Wilson, W. D. (2002). Representation and competition in the perception of spoken words. *Cognitive Psychology*, 45, 220–66.

Goldinger, S. D. (1996). Words and voices: Episodic traces in spoken word identification and recognition memory. *Journal of Experimental Psychology: Learning, Memory, and Cognition*, 22, 1166–83.

Goldinger, S. D. (1998). Echoes of echoes? An episodic theory of lexical access. *Psychological Review*, 105(2), 251–79.

Goldinger, S. D., Luce, P. A., & Pisoni, D. B. (1989). Priming lexical neighbors of spoken words: Effects of competition and inhibition. *Journal of Memory and Language*, 28, 501–18.

Goldinger, S. D., Luce, P. A., Pisoni, D. B., & Marcario, J. K. (1992). Form-based priming in spoken word recognition: The roles of competitive activation and response biases. *Journal of Experimental Psychology: Learning, Memory, and Cognition*, 18, 1210–37.

Goldinger, S. D., Pisoni, D. B., & Logan, J. S. (1991). On the nature of talker variability effects on recall of spoken word lists. *Journal of Experimental Psychology: Learning, Memory, and Cognition*, 17(1), 152–62.

Grossberg, S. & Myers, C. W. (2000). The resonant dynamics of speech perception: Interword integration and duration-dependent backward effects. *Psychological Review*, 107, 735–67.

Grossberg, S., Boardman, I., & Cohen, M. (1997). Neural dynamics of variable-rate speech categorization. *Journal of Experimental Psychology: Human Perception and Performance*, 23, 483–503.

Hintzman, D. L. (1986). "Schema abstraction" in a multiple-trace memory model. *Psychological Review*, 93, 411–28.

Hintzman, D. L. & Caulton, D. A. (1997). Recognition memory and modality judgments: A comparison of retrieval dynamics. *Journal of Memory and Language*, 37, 1–23.

Hintzman, D. L. & Curran, T. (1997). Comparing retrieval dynamics in recognition memory and lexical decision. *Journal of Experimental Psychology: General*, 126, 228.

Jusczyk, P. W. & Luce, P. A. (2002). Speech perception and spoken word recognition: Past and present. *Ear and Hearing*, 23, 1–40.

Kirk, K. I., Pisoni, D. B., & Miyamoto, R. C. (1997). Effects of stimulus variability on speech perception in listeners with hearing impairment. *Journal of Speech, Language, and Hearing Research*, 40, 1395–405.

Ladefoged, P. (2000). *A Course in Phonetics* (5th edition). San Diego: Harcourt Brace Jovanovich.

Luce, P. A. & Lyons, E. A. (1998). Specificity of memory representations for spoken words. *Memory & Cognition*, 26, 708–15.

Luce, P. A. & Pisoni, D. B. (1998). Recognizing spoken words: The neighborhood activation model. *Ear and Hearing*, 19, 1–36.

Luce, P. A., Goldinger, S. D., Auer, E. T., & Vitevitch, M. S. (2000). Phonetic priming, neighborhood activation, and PARSYN. *Perception & Psychophysics*, 62, 615–25.

Luce, P. A., McLennan, C., & Charles-Luce, J. (2003). Abstractness and specificity in spoken word recognition: Indexical and allophonic variability in long-term repetition priming. In

J. Bowers & C. Marsolek (eds.), *Rethinking Implicit Memory* (pp. 197–214). Oxford: Oxford University Press.

Marslen-Wilson, W. D. (1989). Access and integration: Projecting sound onto meaning. In W. D. Marslen-Wilson (ed.), *Lexical Access and Representation* (pp. 3–24). Cambridge, MA: Bradford.

Marslen-Wilson, W. D. & Tyler, L. K. (1980). The temporal structure of spoken language understanding. *Cognition*, 8, 1–71.

Marslen-Wilson, W. D. & Warren, P. (1994). Levels of perceptual representation and process in lexical access: Words, phonemes, and features. *Psychological Review*, 101, 653–75.

Marslen-Wilson, W. D. & Welsh, A. (1978). Processing interactions and lexical access during word recognition in continuous speech. *Cognitive Psychology*, 10, 29–63.

Martin, C. S., Mullennix, J. W., Pisoni, D. B., & Summers, W. V. (1989). Effects of talker variability on recall of spoken word lists. *Journal of Experimental Psychology: Learning, Memory, and Cognition*, 15(4), 676–84.

McClelland, J. L. & Elman, J. L. (1986). The TRACE model of speech perception. *Cognitive Psychology*, 18, 1–86.

McLennan, C., Luce, P. A., & Charles-Luce, J. (2003) Representation of lexical form. *Journal of Experimental Psychology: Learning, Memory, & Cognition*, 29, 52–53.

McQueen, J. M. (1991). The influence of the lexicon on phonetic categorization: Stimulus quality and word-final ambiguity. *Journal of Experimental Psychology: Human Perception and Performance*, 17, 433–43.

McQueen, J. M., Norris, D., & Cutler, A. (1994). Competition in spoken word recognition – spotting words in other words. *Journal of Experimental Psychology: Learning, Memory, and Cognition*, 20, 621–38.

McQueen, J. M., Norris, D., & Cutler, A. (1999). Lexical influence in phonetic decision making: Evidence from subcategorical mismatches. *Journal of Experimental Psychology: Human Perception and Performance*, 25, 1363–89.

Mullennix, J. W., Pisoni, D. B., & Martin, C. S. (1989). Some effects of talker variability on spoken word recognition. *Journal of the Acoustical Society of America*, 85, 365–78.

Norris, D. (1994). Shortlist: A connectionist model of continuous speech recognition. *Cognition*, 52, 189–234.

Norris, D., McQueen, J., & Cutler, A. (1995). Competition and segmentation in spoken word recognition. *Journal of Experimental Psychology: Learning, Memory, and Cognition*, 21, 1209–28.

Norris, D., McQueen, J., & Cutler, A. (2000). Merging information in speech recognition: Feedback is never necessary. *Brain and Behavioral Sciences*, 23, 299–325.

Palmeri, T. J., Goldinger, S. D., & Pisoni, D. B. (1993). Episodic encoding of voice attributes and recognition memory for spoken words. *Journal of Experimental Psychology: Learning, Memory, and Cognition*, 19(2), 309–28.

Patterson, D. & Connine, C. M. (2001). Variant frequency in flap production: A corpus analysis of variant frequency in American English flap production. *Phonetica*, 58, 254–75.

Peters, R. W. (1955). The relative intelligibility of single-voice and multiple-voice messages under various conditions of noise. *Joint Project Report*, 56 (pp. 1–9). US Naval School of Aviation Medicine, Pensacola, Florida.

Pisoni, D. B. (1990). Effects of talker variability on speech perception: Implications for current research and theory. In H. Fujisaki (ed.), *Proceedings of the 1990 International Conference on Spoken Language Processing* (pp. 1399–407). Kobe, Japan, November 18–22.

Pisoni, D. B. (1992a). Some comments on invariance, variability, and perceptual normalization in speech perception. *Proceedings of the International Conference on Spoken Language Processing* (pp. 587–90). Banff, Canada.

Pisoni, D. B. (1992b). Talker normalization in speech perception. In Y. Tohkura, E. Vatikiotis-Bateson, & Y. Sagisaka (eds.), *Speech Perception, Production, and Linguistic Structure* (pp. 143–51). Tokyo, Japan: Ohmsha Press.

Pisoni, D. B. (1997). Some thoughts on "normalizaton" in speech perception. In K. Johnson & J. W. Mullennix (eds.), *Talker Variability in Speech Processing* (pp. 9–32). San Diego, CA: Academic Press.

Pisoni, D. B. & Luce, P. A. (1987). Acoustic-phonetic representations in word recognition. *Cognition*, 25, 1–52.

Remez, R. E., Fellowes, J., & Rubin, P. E. (1997). Talker identification based on phonetic information. *Journal of Experimental Psychology: Human Perception and Performance*, 23, 651–66.

Ryalls, B. O. & Pisoni, D. B. (1997). The effect of talker variability on word recognition in preschool children. *Developmental Psychology*, 33, 441–52.

Schacter, D. L. & Church, B. A. (1992). Auditory priming: Implicit and explicit memory for words and voices. *Journal of Experimental Psychology: Learning, Memory, and Cognition*, 18, 915–30.

Sheffert, S. M. (1998). Voice-specificity effects on auditory word priming. *Memory & Cognition*, 26, 591–8.

Streeter, L. A. & Nigro, G. N. (1979). The role of medial consonant transitions in word perception. *Journal of the Acoustical Society of America*, 65, 1533–41.

Verbrugge, R. R., Strange, W., Shankweiler, D. P., & Edman, T. R. (1976). What information enables a listener to map a talker's vowel space? *Journal of the Acoustical Society of America*, 60, 198–212.

Vitevitch, M. S. & Luce, P. A. (1998). When words compete: Levels of processing in spoken word perception. *Psychological Science*, 9, 325–329.

Vitevitch, M. S. & Luce, P. A. (1999). Probabilistic phonotactics and neighborhood activation in spoken word recognition. *Journal of Memory and Language*, 40, 374–408.

Whalen, D. H. (1984). Subcategorical phonetic mismatches slow phonetic judgments. *Perception & Psychophysics*, 35, 49–64.

Whalen, D. H. (1991). Subcategorical phonetic mismatches and lexical access. *Perception & Psychophysics*, 50, 351–60.

25 Probabilistic Phonotactics in Spoken Word Recognition

EDWARD T. AUER, JR. AND
PAUL A. LUCE

25.1 Introduction

The distributional properties of the perceiver's linguistic environment have demonstrable effects on almost all aspects of spoken language processing, and representation. From the perception of segment to sentence, the likelihood of linguistic constituents determines, in large part, the accuracy and efficiency of processing, the nature of the encoded representation, and even the course of acquisition. For example, research on lexical processing has demonstrated that words occurring frequently in the language are recognized more quickly and accurately than infrequently occurring words (Howes, 1957; Luce & Pisoni, 1998; Savin, 1963). More recently, work focusing on sublexical, or segmental, processing has demonstrated that perceivers are sensitive to the distribution of phonotactic patterns occurring in spoken words. Within linguistics, *phonotactics* typically refers to a system of rules or constraints that govern the legality of the occurrence of segments and sequences of segments within the syllables and words of a given language (cf. Coleman & Pierrehumbert, 1997; Pierrehumbert, 2003). For example, in English, /tra/ may legally occur at the beginning of a syllable, whereas /tba/ may not. Within the category of phonotactically legal configurations, segments and their sequences occur in the linguistic environment with varying frequencies. For example /kæ/ occurs very frequently in English, whereas /kɔɪ/ occurs less frequently. We use the term *probabilistic* phonotactics to refer to the distribution of relative frequencies, or likelihoods of segments and segment sequences occurring in a perceiver's linguistic environment. In this chapter, we focus on the current state of knowledge regarding the sensitivity of perceivers to probabilistic phonotactics.

From infancy to adulthood, probabilistic phonotactics plays a determining role in the processing, representation, and acquisition of spoken language. The probability of segments and segmental sequences has been shown to affect the speed and ease of recognizing individual words (Auer, 1992; Luce & Large, 2001; Vitevitch & Luce, 1999), provide a signal to word boundaries in fluently articulated speech (Gaygen, 1997; Mattys & Jusczyk, 2001; Mattys et al., 1999; McQueen,

1998), and influence listeners' subjective metalinguistic judgments of wordlikeness (Bailey & Hahn, 2001; Frisch, Large, & Pisoni, 2000; Treiman et al., 2000; Vitevitch et al., 1997). Sensitivity to probabilistic phonotactics has been shown to be a major factor in lexical acquisition and, concomitantly, learners' ability to hold words in memory for analysis (Gathercole et al., 1999; Goh & Pisoni, 2003; Saffran, Newport, & Aslin, 1996; Storkel, 2001; Storkel & Rogers, 2000).

Theoretical accounts of perceivers' sensitivity to and knowledge of probabilistic phonotactics vary. In some computational models of spoken word recognition, segment and sequence probabilities are encoded directly into the activation levels of and connections among sublexical units (Auer, 1992; Luce et al., 2000). Other approaches model effects of probabilistic phonotactics as emerging from the interactions among lexical units, with no explicit representation or storage of segment or segment sequence frequency (McClelland & Elman, 1986). Finally, probabilistic phonotactics may be – in whole or part – a reflection of the allophonic variation within a given language, with likelihoods of segments being determined to some extent by the language-specific phonology or the more universal constraints on the behavior of the articulators. Although it is at present unclear which of these accounts are correct, recent behavioral research (Vitevitch & Luce, 1999) and neurophysiological evidence (Pylkkanen, Stringfellow, & Marantz, 2001) suggest that phonotactic effects arise at an early stage of processing, prior to any significant lexical involvement in the perceptual process.

The ubiquity of probability/frequency effects suggests the existence of a processing principle that may be common to all levels of language processing and, in fact, perceptual systems in general. In particular, regardless of the level of linguistic description (feature, segment, word, sentence), increased probability of occurrence of units and patterns of units facilitates processing. Thus, the same type of processing mechanism responsible for word frequency effects may be responsible for segmental frequency and segment sequence frequency (probabilistic phonotactic) effects. Furthermore, the pervasiveness of probabilistic effects underscores the *adaptive* nature of a processing system that is constantly tuning itself to its environment.

In this chapter, we present the evidence supporting the critical roles of the perceiver's sensitivity to probabilistic phonotactics in lexical processing, segmentation, and acquisition as well as the theoretical accounts of these effects and their implications for contemporary models of spoken word recognition. We also consider recent evidence regarding the neural substrate for probabilistic phonotactics effects that has accrued to date. Despite substantial progress in our understanding of the role of probabilistic phonotactics in spoken word recognition, much remains to be learned. Thus, the chapter concludes with a discussion of some possible future directions for research on probabilistic phonotactics.

25.2 Probabilistic Phonotactics in Infancy

Between the ages of 6 and 9 months infants begin to acquire knowledge of the sounds and sequences of sounds used in the native language. Jusczyk, Friederici et al. (1993) investigated infants' sensitivity to the segments and sequences of segments (i.e., *phonotactics*) within their language. In particular, Jusczyk et al.

compared 6- and 9-month-old English and Dutch infants' responses to lists of English and Dutch words. The researchers chose English and Dutch because of their similarity in prosodic characteristics and dissimilarities in segmental composition and phonotactics. At 6 months, English infants demonstrated no preference for listening to words from their native language over words from the non-native language. However when the same lists were presented to 9-month-old infants, English infants exhibited longer listening times for words spoken in English, whereas Dutch infants exhibited longer listening times for words spoken in Dutch. Jusczyk et al. interpreted their results as evidence that by 9 months, infants have acquired knowledge regarding the typical segments and segment sequences (i.e., *phonotactic* patterns) definitive of words in their native language.

In a subsequent study, Jusczyk, Luce, & Charles-Luce (1994) investigated whether infants were also sensitive to differences in the *relative* frequencies of segmental sequences, or *probabilistic phonotactics*, within their native language. In this study, sets of nonword stimuli were generated that were either common or uncommon in terms of both positional segment frequency (i.e., the frequency with which a phoneme occurs within a word) and biphone frequency (i.e., the probability of two sequential phonemes co-occurring). At 6 months, infants exhibited no preference for listening to nonwords of either frequently or infrequently occurring phonotactic configurations. In contrast, 9-month-old infants showed longer listening times for nonwords of high phonotactic probability. Thus, between 6 and 9 months of age, infants develop sensitivities to the distribution of phonotactic patterns within their language. Jusczyk et al. (1994), suggested that this preference for frequently occurring patterns may play a role in the development of the lexicon and word recognition skills. One specific implication is that phonotactic knowledge could serve as a signal to the segmentation of words in continuous speech.

Not only are infants sensitive to segment and sequence frequency, they are also able to register co-occurrences of larger patterns, a skill that may be crucial for learning which syllables combine to form words in the native language. Saffran et al. (1996) demonstrated that 8-month-old infants are able to track novel recurring patterns in connected speech. Saffran et al. presented 8-month-olds with a 2.5-minute stream of continuous speech consisting of consonant-vowel nonsense syllables. They manipulated the transitional probabilities between syllables in connected speech to test the hypothesis that syllables may cohere into words simply based on the statistical likelihood of their co-occurrence. Saffran et al. found that following a brief exposure to the connected speech stimuli, infants responded more favorably to high-probability sequences of syllables, supporting the hypothesis that with only minimal exposure, infants can make use of differences in transitional probabilities between syllables to identify likely words and segment them from the speech stream.

Johnson and Jusczyk (2001) replicated the Saffran et al. demonstration of 8-month-old infants' sensitivity to the distributional structure of segmental sequences. However, when transitional probabilities were pitted against stress and allophonic cues to juncture, 8-month-olds relied on the phonetic cues and not syllable-to-syllable transitional probabilities. These results suggest that by 8 months of age, infants exploit all available information, both distributional and phonetic, for segmenting words from the incoming speech stream. (Strictly speaking, of course, the phonetic cues are themselves *distributional*, given that they are events that correlate with juncture and hence may signal boundaries by their higher frequencies of occurrence at junctures.)

Recent findings have shown that infants are sensitive to the probabilistic phonotactics associated with word boundaries in their native language (Mattys et al., 1999). Mattys et al. examined infants' sensitivity to two possible cues to word boundaries: (1) phonotactic probability of sequences of medial consonants in bisyllabic CVC-CVC nonwords and (2) metrical stress pattern (strong-weak versus weak-strong). Research has demonstrated that in adult perceivers, strong-weak prosodic patterns (e.g., *baby*), which are much more frequent in English than weak-strong patterns (e.g., *alert*; see Cutler & Carter, 1987), facilitate extraction of words from fluent speech for both infants and adults (Cutler & Butterfield, 1992; Cutler and Norris, 1988; Jusczyk, Cutler, & Redanz, 1993). Specifically, strong syllables act as cues to word onsets.

Mattys et al. pitted this important prosodic cue to word boundaries against phonotactic probability. To do this, they generated sequences of medial consonants (the C-C in the CVC-CVC stimuli) that were either frequent word internally and infrequent across word boundaries or were infrequent word internally and frequent across word boundaries. (Sequence frequency was computed using a corpus of child-directed speech.) All of the consonant pairs were matched for total frequency of occurrence in the corpus. Thus, any differences in preference for these consonant pairs in word internal position would be related to the infants' knowledge of *position-specific* phonotactic probabilities.

Mattys et al. presented the nonwords varying in medial consonant sequence and metrical stress pattern to 9-month-old infants in the head-turn preference procedure. Infants listened longer to frequent than infrequent within-word medial clusters in strong-weak nonwords. Because a strong-weak pattern favors interpretation of the CVC-CVC stimuli as a single word, infants preferred those nonwords with the consistent, word internal consonant sequence. When Mattys et al. inserted a pause between the CVC syllables, which clearly signaled the presence of two separate words, infants' preference shifted to stimuli containing cross-word consonant sequences. Thus, when the stimuli were perceived as two monosyllabic nonwords, infants preferred the stimuli containing medial clusters that occurred frequently across word boundaries. Mattys et al. concluded that by 9 months of age, infants are sensitive to both the distribution of phonotactic patterns within and across words and the relationship between phonotactics and stress patterns in signaling word boundaries. They interpreted their results as evidence that prosody and probabilistic phonotactics work together in facilitating segmentation of words from the speech stream.

Although the Mattys et al. study demonstrated that infants are indeed sensitive to the probabilistic phonotactics within and between words, their results do not provide direct evidence that infants use this information to segment words from the speech stream. In a follow-up study, Mattys and Jusczyk (2001) investigated whether English-learning 9-month-olds could segment words from utterance contexts in which phonotactic cues suggest a likely word boundary. In this study, infants listened to familiarization passages containing nonwords. Within a passage, phonotactic probabilities either did or did not signal a word boundary. After familiarization, Mattys and Jusczyk assessed infants' preference for nonwords whose boundaries had been marked by phonotactic cues. Their results demonstrated that infants listened longer to nonwords marked by phonotactic cues to word boundaries. This result was obtained regardless of whether the cues marked both the onset and offset of a word, the onset alone, or the offset alone. Mattys and Jusczyk interpreted their results as evidence that the infants had used phonotactic cues to guide their segmentation of words from the passages of connected speech.

Research suggests that between the ages of 6 and 9 months, infants acquire substantial knowledge about the probabilistic phonotactics of their native language, including position-specific segmental and biphone frequency. Moreover, infants appear to use this information to determine patterns that constitute well-formed words in their language and to segment words from the continuous stream of speech, both necessary prerequisites to the acquisition of a full-fledged adult form-based lexicon.

25.3 Probabilistic Phonotactics in Early Childhood

Recent research has demonstrated that the young child's remarkable ability to acquire novel words during early development may be facilitated by sensitivity to probabilistic phonotactics. Storkel (2001) and Storkel and Rogers (2000) investigated the influence of phonotactic probability on the acquisition of consonant-vowel-consonant nonwords in children ranging from age 3 to 13 years of age. The children were exposed to nonwords varying in position-specific segmental frequency and biphone frequency (high or low). The researchers paired the nonwords with unfamiliar object referents during the exposure phase of the experiments, after which they tested recognition of the nonwords to assess acquisition during exposure. The results demonstrated that nonwords composed of more frequent segments and biphones were acquired more easily.

The analyses of error patterns in the recognition tests assessing nonword acquisition provided evidence that phonotactic probability affected more than phonological pattern acquisition. Specifically, the error patterns suggested that the quality of memories for the acquired referent was also affected by the probabilistic phonotactics of the nonwords. Memory for referents of nonwords with high-probability phonotactics tended to be more holistic, giving rise to semantic confusions in a referent identification task, whereas memory for referents of nonwords with low-probability phonotactics appeared to be impoverished, giving rise to semantically unrelated errors.

Storkel (2001) interpreted these results as consistent with a theory of lexical development in which children become sensitive to the regularities in the speech input through experience. This tuning to the statistical structure of the language results in processing advantages for frequently occurring patterns. According to Storkel, because language processing occurs within a system that has a limited amount of processing capacity, when perceptual processing is more difficult, fewer resources are available to support other processes involved in language comprehension. Storkel reasoned that nonwords with high-probability phonotactics are easier to perceive and thus less taxing of limited capacity resources, thereby enabling rapid development of new lexical and semantic representations. In short, the perceptual advantage associated with high-probability form-based patterns creates advantages at all levels of language processing, especially when acquiring new lexical items.

Gathercole et al. (1999) have also demonstrated advantages in the recall of high phonotactic frequency nonwords by children. However, their interpretation of the source of the advantage contrasts with that of Storkel (2001). Gathercole et al., examined 7- and 8-year-olds' immediate memory for words and nonwords that were high, low, or very low in their phonotactic probability. Children's recall was greater for high than low phonotactic frequency nonwords. The advantage was a result of a larger number of totally correct than partially correct responses for the high-frequency items. Gathercole et al. interpreted this result as evidence that the phonotactic effects were a result of syllable frequency and not the frequencies of the components of the syllable. Gathercole et al. also obtained evidence for a recall advantage for real words over nonwords matched for phonotactic pattern frequency, suggesting different sources for the effects of the phonotactic pattern frequency and lexicality.

In contrast to Storkel, who ascribed effects of phonotactic probability to perceptual processing, Gathercole et al. suggested that phonotactic frequency and lexical effects on immediate recall arise at a later stage of processing. In particular, they argued, based on distributions of incorrect, partially correct, and correct responses, that the observed effects of lexicality and phonotactic frequency occurred at the storage and/or recall stage and not during perceptual processing. They also argued that phonotactic and lexical information affect storage and recall differently in the reconstruction of incomplete memory traces. The lexical effect arises from the use of stored phonological representations of words, whereas the phonotactic frequency effect arises from the use of stored information regarding syllable frequencies to "provide a probability based reconstruction of incomplete memory traces" (Gathercole et al., 1999, p. 92).

It is currently difficult to definitively reconcile the conflicting claims of Storkel and Gathercole given the pronounced differences in experimental paradigms and stimuli used by the researchers. However, it is highly unlikely that memory traces representing probabilistic phonotactics only play a role in reconstruction. Both the adult work and that of Jusczyk and colleagues strongly suggest a perceptual locus of probabilistic effects. Moreover, given the findings of Jusczyk et al. (1994), which demonstrated infants' sensitivity to phonotactic patterns even when segmental composition was controlled, it is unlikely that effects of phonotactics are based on syllable frequency alone. Indeed, attempts to match segments while manipulating phonotactics (as in the Gathercole et al. work) all but ensure that differences in positional *segmental* probabilities will either be eliminated or so minimized as to be undetectable by standard behavioral techniques. Taken together, there are compelling reasons to attribute effects of sublexical and subsyllabic probabilistic phonotactics to both perceptual processes and representations. This latter view corresponds to many current theoretical accounts of spoken language recognition that characterize perception as the integral interaction of memory and input (e.g., Grossberg, Boardman, & Cohen, 1997). To the extent that memory representations encode probabilistic phonotactics, the effects of segmental likelihood may be inescapable during perception.

The evidence to date suggests that probabilistic phonotactics influences vocabulary acquisition in children. Taken together, the current research on probabilistic phonotactic effects in young children suggests a highly adaptive system that is tuned to distributional properties of the segments and segment sequences in the linguistic environment. Moreover, the evidence strongly suggests that probabilistic phonotactics has its impact at several stages of analysis, including on-line perceptual processing and the relatively late stage of storage and recall of newly learned patterns.

25.4 Probabilistic Phonotactics in Adults

25.4.1 Spoken word recognition

Effects of probabilistic phonotactics are not restricted to the young language learner. Indeed, some of the most compelling evidence for the role of the statistical properties of phonological patterns comes from research on adult perceivers. Treiman et al. (2000) observed that adult participants' performance on rating and blending tasks was sensitive to probabilistic differences among phonetic sequences. In the rating task, participants were asked to judge the degree to which nonsense words sounded like they could be real English words. High-probability patterns were rated to be more "English-like" than low-probability patterns (see also, Bailey & Hahn, 2001; Frisch et al., 2000; Vitevitch et al., 1997). In the blending task, participants were asked to combine two segment sequences into a single sequence. For example, participants were presented with /kap/ and /pit/, to which they were to respond with /pap/. In this task, high-probability sequences remained intact more often than low-probability sequences. (See also Brown & Hildum, 1956; Eukel, 1980.)

Vitevitch et al. (1997) investigated whether probabilistic phonotactic information influenced *processing times* for spoken stimuli. Using a speeded single-word repetition task, participants were presented with spoken bisyllabic nonwords composed of phonotactically legal phonetic sequences that varied in segmental and sequential probabilities. Repetition latencies were *faster* for nonwords composed of frequently occurring segments and segment sequences compared to nonwords composed of infrequently occurring segments and sequences. The finding that adult perceivers process high phonotactic probability stimuli more rapidly appears to contradict the predictions of – and evidence for – activation and competition models of spoken word recognition, in particular, the Neighborhood Activation Model (NAM; Luce & Pisoni, 1998). According to NAM, spoken words that sound like many other words (i.e., words in dense similarity neighborhoods) should be recognized more slowly and less accurately than words with few similar sounding words (i.e., words in sparse similarity neighborhoods) because of increased competition among form-based representations. Indeed, much evidence has accrued to support the claim that increased similarity neighborhood density slows processing time (see Luce & Pisoni, 1998, for a review).

Neighborhood density effects provide a clear example of a second fundamental property of adaptive systems, namely, that phonetically similar items compete. Although evidence to date has demonstrated competition only at the lexical level, we suspect that competition – like probability effects – is manifest at every level of processing.

A contradiction arises when we note that words residing in high density neighborhoods are typically also high in phonotactic probability, whereas words in low density neighborhoods consist of less probable segments and sequences. Thus, in contrast to the findings of Vitevitch et al., NAM, which includes no mechanism to simulate phonotactic frequency effects and focuses instead on lexical competition, predicts that high-probability phonotactic stimuli should be processed *more slowly* than low-probability phonotactic stimuli.

Vitevitch and Luce (1998; see also Vitevitch & Luce, 1999) tested the hypothesis that the apparently divergent effects of phonotactics and similarity neighborhood density could be reconciled by taking the lexicality of the stimulus into account. They hypothesized that processing of nonword stimuli would expose the effects of phonotactic frequency, whereas with word stimuli, the lexical competition effects would predominate. They presented participants with monosyllabic words and nonwords that covaried in lexical neighborhood density and phonotactic probability. Vitevitch and Luce generated two sets of words and nonwords: (1) high phonotactic probability/high neighborhood density stimuli and (2) low phonotactic probability/low neighborhood density stimuli. Using a speeded single-word auditory repetition task, Vitevitch and Luce replicated the pattern of results obtained in the Vitevitch et al. study for *nonwords*: High-probability/density nonwords were repeated more quickly than low-probability/density nonwords. However, the *words* followed the pattern of results predicted by NAM. That is, high-probability/density words were repeated *more slowly* than low-probability/density words.

Vitevitch and Luce (1998) proposed that two levels of representation and processing – one lexical and one sublexical – are responsible for the differential effects of phonotactics and neighborhoods. In particular, they suggested that facilitative effects of probabilistic phonotactics reflect differences among activation levels of *sublexical* units, whereas effects of similarity neighborhoods arise from competition among *lexical* representations (see Cluff & Luce, 1990; Goldinger, Luce, & Pisoni, 1989; Marslen-Wilson, 1989; McQueen, Norris, & Cutler, 1994; Norris, McQueen, & Cutler, 1995). Thus, intra-word competition is greater for words occurring in dense similarity neighborhoods, resulting in slower processing. Apparently, lexical competition effects overshadow any benefit high density words may accrue by virtue of their high-probability phonotactic patterns. On the other hand, effects of segmental and sequential probabilities emerge for *nonwords* because they fail to make direct contact with a single lexical unit, and thus do not result in large-scale lexical competition. In the absence of strong lexical competition effects, sublexical facilitation results in advantages for nonwords that have more frequent segmental sequences (i.e., with high phonotactic likelihood).

Although the research examining neighborhood density and phonotactics strongly suggests the operation of two levels of representation, Vitevitch and Luce (1998) did not demonstrate effects of probabilistic phonotactics on real words. Thus, it is possible that the effect of phonotactics is restricted to nonwords. To reconcile these lines of research, additional measures were needed that were differentially sensitive to the distributional differences in segments and to lexical identification. Subsequent research by Luce and Large (2001; see also Auer, 1992) indicates that facilitative effects of probabilistic phonotactics are not restricted to nonwords. By orthogonally manipulating density and phonotactics, thereby unconfounding their effects, Luce and Large demonstrated simultaneous competitive effects of neighborhood density and facilitative effects of probabilistic phonotactics for *both* words and nonwords. Again, this line of research illustrates the basic principles of an adaptive neural information processing system, namely, pervasive probability and competition effects at all representational levels. (See Section 25.5.3 for a more detailed description of adaptive processing.)

25.4.2 Segmentation

In fluent connected speech, acoustic-phonetic events are rarely reliable signals for junctures, or the boundaries between words (e.g., Lehiste, 1972; Nakatani & Dukes, 1977), giving rise to the well-worn problem of segmentation. In addition to research on allophonic, prosodic, and lexical solutions to the segmentation problem, recent research has focused on the role of phonotactics (Gaygen & Luce, 2002; McQueen, 1998; Norris et al., 1997). If listeners are sensitive to variations in the frequencies of segments and their sequences, probabilistic phonotactics may provide useful information for segmentation. Norris et al. (1997) demonstrated that participants were able to detect words embedded in nonsense words faster and more accurately when the additional segments of the nonsense words formed phonotactically legal syllables (or possible words) than when the additional segments did not constitute well-formed syllables in English. That is, subjects were faster and more accurate at detecting "apple" in "vuffapple," where "vuff" is itself a phonotactically legal syllable, than "apple" in "fapple," in which the additional segment "f" does not constitute a legal syllable. These results suggest that listeners are able to use phonotactic properties as information about juncture in the real-time segmention of fluent speech.

McQueen (1998) conducted a series of studies on the role of phonotactics in segmentation in Dutch. As in Norris et al. (1997), words were embedded in multisyllabic words and the participants' task was to detect the presence of the real word as quickly and accurately as possible. The real words were embedded either at the onset or offset of the bisyllablic nonword. In addition, the phonotactic legality of the consonant sequences at the syllable boundary either favored segmentation of the real word or hindered its detection. Phonotactic legality of the consonant sequences influenced the speed of word detection. McQueen interpreted his results as further evidence that phonotactic information aids in the segmentation of spoken words. Gaygen and Luce (2002) have provided further evidence that English listeners use their knowledge of phonotactic probabilities in segmentation. However, their results suggest that phonotactic probabilities primarily influence identification of word onsets, with detection of offsets being subserved by lexical processes.

If probabilistic phonotactics effects reflect the operation of a fundamental principle of adaptive systems – namely the marked sensitivity of the system to the distributional properties of the spoken input – facilitative influences of high-frequency sequences (i.e., probability effects) should be widespread, affecting acquisition, recognition, and even segmentation. Clearly, the evidence accrued thus far supports the hypothesis that sublexical probability effects are implicated in almost every aspect of spoken language processing. Moreover, the evidence from research on segmentation strongly suggests an independent, exclusively sublexical locus for the effects of probabilistic phonotactics.

25.5 Probabilistic Phonotactics and Models of Spoken Word Recognition

Current models of spoken word recognition are generally consistent with the two general processing principles of adaptive systems, pervasive frequency/likelihood and competition effects at all representational levels, although they may differ in their specific implementation of these principles. However, models of adult spoken word recognition vary both in the extent and the manner in which they account for the effects of probabilistic phonotactics (see Luce & McLennan, this volume). Research on probabilistic phonotactics and lexical competition in adult perceivers supports the existence of at least two levels of representation and process in spoken word recognition (Bailey & Hahn, 2001; Pitt & McQueen, 1998; Vitevitch & Luce, 1999): a facilitative sublexical level and a competitive lexical level. Thus, models of spoken word recognition that lack a sublexical level of representation, such as NAM (Luce & Pisoni, 1998) and Cohort theory (Marslen-Wilson, 1989), cannot readily account for the divergent effects of phonotactics and lexical competition. Other contemporary models having multiple levels of representation, such as Trace, Shortlist, and PARSYN, may more accurately account for spoken word recognition effects as a function of neighborhood activation and probabilistic phonotactics. However, these models differ in the proposed mechanisms and representations responsible for accounting for effects of probabilistic phonotactics (see Figure 25.1). One main difference among the models involves the way in which phonotactic knowledge is stored. In some models (e.g., PARSYN), segment and sequence frequencies are stored explicitly, whereas in other models (e.g., Trace), effects of phonotactics are emergent, arising from interactions among lexical units.

25.5.1 *Trace*

McClelland and Elman's (1986) Trace is a connectionist model of spoken word recognition, owing many of its processing assumptions to its predecessor, McClelland and Rumelhart's (1981) interactive activation model of visual word recognition. Trace consists of a set of highly interconnected simple processing units arranged into three levels, corresponding to feature, phoneme, and word units. Encoding the temporal nature of speech is accomplished by reduplicating all of the units at each level at each time point over a spatial left-to-right coding of time. The inter-level connections are excitatory, whereas the intra-level connections are inhibitory. The excitatory connections between the phoneme and lexical level are bi-directional. Thus, not only do words benefit from the activation of their component phonemes, but the component phonemes benefit from the activation of the word units. Phonotactic effects are modeled in Trace via top-down feedback from the lexical layer. Hence, Trace incorporates no explicit storage of phonotactic information.

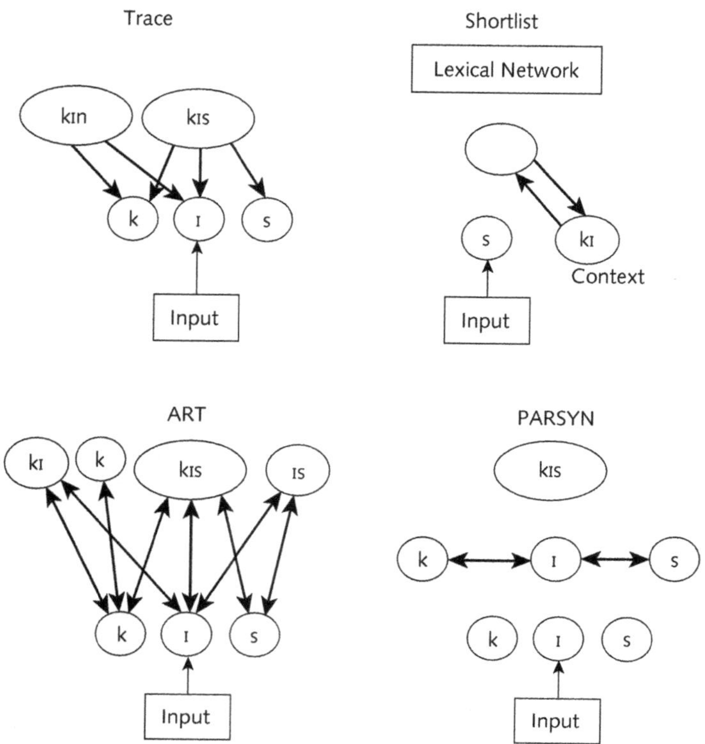

Figure 25.1 Schematic depiction of the components and connections most relevant to simulating effects of probabilistic phonotactics in four models of spoken word recognition.

As words become activated via the bottom-up input during recognition, they send facilitation back to their component phonemes. Lexical feedback creates an advantage in the network for input containing sequences of segments that occur in many words (i.e., a dense neighborhood). Pitt and McQueen (1998) obtained evidence that is particularly problematic for Trace's implementation of phonotactic knowledge. Because both lexical and phonotactic effects are modeled by lexical feedback in Trace, Pitt and McQueen reasoned that it should not be possible to observe effects of phonotactics in the absence of lexical effects. However, in a series of experiments, they demonstrated effects of transitional probabilities on phoneme perception that were independent of lexical influences. Based on this finding, the authors argued for a model in which phonotactic effects arise from a level of processing distinct from the lexical level. In addition, as mentioned above, Vitevitch and Luce (1999) argued for separable effects of phonotactics and lexical competition. Finally, Bailey and Hahn (2001) investigated the independent variance accounted for by lexical and phonotactic variables in wordlikeness judgments of nonwords. They obtained evidence for independent contributions of both phonotactic and lexical information. Taken together, the evidence to date does not support the hypothesis that phonotactic effects are merely the result of lexical level feedback.

25.5.2 *Shortlist*

In contrast to Trace, Shortlist is strictly a feedforward model of spoken word recognition (Norris, 1994), with no feedback from lexical to segmental levels. As segmental sized representations are input to the system, a search is performed through a lexical database to find those candidates consistent with the current segmental input; the resulting candidates form the *shortlist*. Words are chosen for the shortlist based on their bottom-up score, computed as a function of their match and mismatch with the input, as well as limitations on the number of words allowed to compete. After each segment, an interactive-activation network is created containing nodes for all the words in the shortlist, with word nodes interconnected via inhibitory connections.

As implemented by Norris (1994), Shortlist does not include phonotactic knowledge. However, a predecessor – the dynamic net model (Norris, 1990) – provides a mechanism through which phonotactic knowledge could be implemented in the form of a recurrent network at the segment level. In this recurrent network, activity from a previous point in time is presented as context for the current input. Because recurrent networks are particularly useful in modeling sequential dependencies, such as phonotactics (Norris, 1994; Stoianov & Nerbonne, 1998), a modified Shortlist could plausibly model separate effects of phonotactics and lexical competition during the recognition of words.

Recent versions of Shortlist have incorporated an explicit phonotactic constraint – dubbed the Possible Word Constraint (PWC) – to model the role of one type of phonotactics in segmentation of words in fluent speech. The PWC refers to the finding that listeners prefer to parse spoken input into a sequence of phonotactically permissible words. That is, a segmentation of the input that results in words comprising zero probability segment sequences should be disfavored over segmentation that results in words comprising segmental sequences with probabilities of occurrence greater than zero. Thus, Norris et al. (1997) reasoned that the spoken word *tea* should be easier to spot in *teaglant* than *teag* because the segmentation *tea* from *teag* results in the phonotactically illegal word *g*. This constraint was implemented within Shortlist as a penalty on the activation of words when their boundaries will result in a violation of the PWC. Specifically, "if there are only consonants between the segment at the boundary of the current candidate word and the next boundary in the input (working forward and backward) then the current segment is not a possible boundary" (Norris et al., 1997, p. 210). In order to apply this constraint, Shortlist must have information about the location of possible word boundaries in the input stream. That is, phonotactic, metrical, and other physical cues (e.g., silence) must still be used to mark the location of possible syllable boundaries in the input stream. The PWC arbitrates possible boundary placement. Thus, with the addition of the PWC, Shortlist attempts to simulate perceivers' sensitivity to syllable boundaries signaled by phonotactic constraints (see McQueen, 1998).

25.5.3 *Adaptive Resonance Theory (ART)*

Vitevitch and Luce (1999) proposed an account for the effects of probabilistic phonotactics and lexical competition within the framework of Grossberg's (1986) adaptive resonance theory (ART) of speech perception (Grossberg et al., 1997). In Vitevitch and Luce's model, the speech percept results from the resonant state that develops between items and list chunks active in a short-term memory. Items correspond to feature clusters, whereas list chunks in working memory correspond to groupings of feature clusters of various sizes including segments, sequences of segments, and words. Two properties of the processing in ART are particularly relevant to the explanation of the contradictory effects of probabilistic phonotactics and lexical competition (Vitevitch & Luce, 1998). First, active list chunks compete via lateral inhibition. Second, longer list chunks will inhibit shorter list chunks (Grossberg et al., 1997). The inhibitory influence of dense lexical neighborhoods arises naturally from the first property. Perceptually similar words compete with one another due to the lateral inhibitory links. Furthermore, the activation of chunks corresponding to segments and sequences of segments are inhibited by the existence of strong activation of longer word chunks. In contrast, when nonwords are presented to the system, because the activation of chunks is a function of frequency of experience, high phonotactic probability sequences/chunks will achieve stronger resonant states than low-probability phonotactic sequences/chunks. Thus, the contradictory effects of phonotactic probability and neighborhood density can be modeled within the framework proposed by Grossberg et al. (1997).

The adaptive resonance framework is well suited to account for probability effects. An adaptive system that constantly (albeit subtly) tunes itself to properties of the linguistic environment provides a straightforward and flexible mechanism for accounting for the effects of variations in phonotactic probability on word perception. Unlike traditional connectionist models in which the probabilities of word and segment may be hard-wired in unit thresholds or activation functions, an adaptive system learns and changes with each exposure to respond more quickly and robustly to common events, instead of reacting to the environment based on a static database of expectations.

25.5.4 *PARSYN*

The PARSYN model (Auer, 1992; Luce et al., 2000) is a connectionist implementation of the NAM. It extends NAM by simulating the dynamics of the spoken word recognition process as well as adding an explicit processing level at which probabilistic phonotactics influences spoken word recognition. The speed and ease of recognition are hypothesized to be influenced by both *PARadigmatic* and *SYNtagmatic* states of the model (hence the name, PARSYN, see Figure 25.2). The paradigmatic state refers to the number of active alternatives, or neighborhood density, at a given point in time during the recognition process. Phonetic patterns that are similar to many other patterns have more active paradigmatic states than phonetic patterns that are fairly unique. The syntagmatic state refers to the

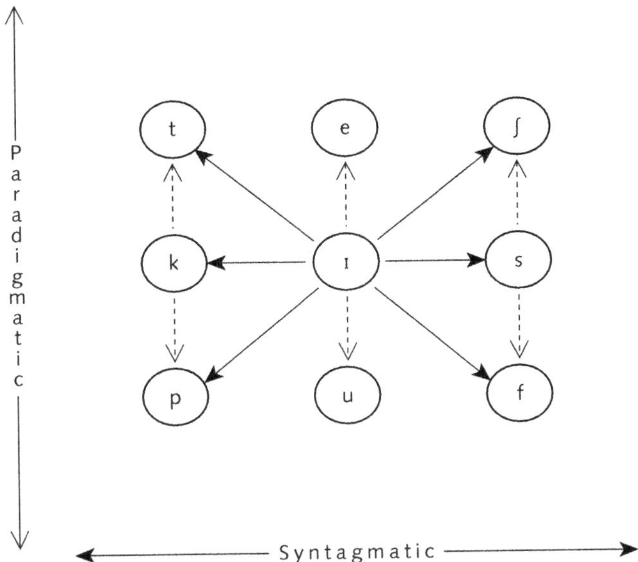

Figure 25.2 Schematic depiction of the paradigmatic and syntagmatic dimensions that reflect the two general processing principles of competition (paradigmatic) and frequency of occurrence (syntagmatic) as implemented in the PARSYN model.

probabilistic phonotactics associated with the segments being processed. Put simply, a commonly encountered phonetic pattern will have a more highly activated syntagmatic state than a rarely encountered pattern. Thus, the paradigmatic state reflects the implementation of the general processing principle of competition among active items. Whereas the syntagmatic state reflects the implementation of the general processing principle of a preference or bias for more frequently experienced items.

PARSYN is distinct from other models of spoken word recognition because it explicitly encodes probabilistic phonotactic information in the network (see below). Furthermore, it includes the possibility of both forward, or predictive, transitional probabilities, as well as backward, or postdictive, transitional probabilities. Investigations of probabilistic phonotactics to date have focused on either predictive phonotactic probabilities or have ignored the directionality of the phonotactic probability altogether by using simple biphone probabilities. However, several researchers (Cluff & Luce, 1990; Cutler et al., 1987; Ganong, 1980; Salasoo & Pisoni, 1985) have demonstrated that *later* occurring information affects the processing of previously presented information. Therefore, previously activated segments may be enhanced or inhibited via postdiction from segments currently being processed. PARSYN has three levels of units: (1) an input level, (2) a pattern level, and (3) a word level. Connections between units within a level are mutually inhibitory, with one exception: Links among segments at the pattern level are facilitative across temporal positions in the model and explicitly implement probabilistic phonotactics in the model. Connections between levels are facilitative. The equations governing the processing dynamics of PARSYN are the same as those of McClelland and Elman's (1986) Trace and McClelland and Rumelhart's interactive activation model (1981).

The input layer consists of position-specific segmental units arranged into banks of receptors corresponding to the temporal sequence of the input. In the first temporal position, segments correspond to the pre-vocalic consonants and vowels. In the next three temporal positions, duplicate sets of nodes correspond to pre-vocalic consonants, vowels, post-vocalic consonants, and a word boundary marker. In the input layer, the units receive facilitative input from an external input vector encoding perceptual similarity amongst segments (see below). The pattern layer of units exactly duplicates the input layer. However, the input and pattern layers differ in the interconnections between the units. Whereas units at the input level do not directly interact over time, units at the pattern level receive facilitative input from pattern layer units in preceding and/or following temporal positions. The weights on these within-level connections correspond to log frequency-weighted forward and backward position-specific transitional probabilities. In addition, resting levels of the pattern layer nodes are set to correspond to the log frequency-weighted position-specific probability of a segment's occurrence. Thus, segments that commonly occur in a given temporal position will begin processing with higher resting activation levels than less commonly occurring segments. In the pattern layer, all of the units within a temporal position are capable of mutual inhibition. Finally, at the word level, each unit may also inhibit all other word units as a function of its activity level.

Input to the model is based on a position-specific allophonic transcription of the input word. The transcription is translated into a sequence of input vectors that correspond to the cycle of processing and the temporal position of the input. The input values used for any given segment encode an estimate of the perceptual similarity of that segment and all other segments. Thus, given the acoustic-phonetic input for /t/, the entry in the vector corresponding to /t/ will have the highest value. However, entries in the vector corresponding to other segments that are perceptually similar to /t/ (e.g., /p/ or /k/) will also have values ranging between 0 and the value entered for /t/, isomorphic with the degree of their similarity with /t/ (see Auer, 1992).

Auer (1992) evaluated the predictions based on the output of specific simulations of PARSYN. Three specific issues were addressed with three separate simulations. First, lexical competition effects in the absence of explicit probabilistic phonotactics were modeled by a simulation in which no cross-temporal activation at the pattern level (corresponding to phonotactic transitional probability) was permitted. Second, lexical competition in the presence of forward phonotactics was simulated by only allowing the activity to flow forward in time at the pattern level. Third, lexical competition in the presence of backward phonotactics was simulated by only allowing information to flow backward in time.

A clear pattern of results emerged across six behavioral processing time studies: First, the inhibitory effect of lexical competition (i.e., similarity neighborhood density) was replicated even when phonotactic probability was controlled. Second, forward phonotactics influenced the speed of lexical processing in the presence of controlled lexical competition effects. Specifically, high-frequency phonotactic patterns were processed more quickly than low frequency patterns. Finally, no evidence was obtained for an influence of backward phonotactic frequency. The results of lexical competition and forward phonotactic probabilities are consistent with more recent evidence in the literature on word recognition (Luce & Large, 2001).

The absence of an effect of backward transitional probabilities may have arisen because backward phonotactic influences did not have sufficient time to develop. In these studies, the stimulus words were all short consonant-vowel-consonant words. Thus, given that the earliest point at which backward constraints may be active is at the onset of vowel information, the recognition of the word may be completed well before the backward constraints have had sufficient time to influence processing. This interpretation suggests the possibility that backward phonotactic effects may be more evident in longer words. In addition, backward phonotactic effects may be detectable in words that have high *forward* probabilities. If forward predictability raises activation levels of later occurring segments, these same segments may have increased opportunity to project their influence backward, thus affording sufficient time for the emergence of demonstrable effects of backward probabilities, even in short words.

Several contemporary models provide mechanistic accounts for the influence of probabilistic phonotactics on both the process of word recognition and the segmentation of words from connected speech. However, none of the implementations of contemporary spoken word recognition models provides a complete account of the influences of probabilistic phonotactics. The research demonstrating separable influences of lexical density and probabilistic phonotactics has provided valuable new knowledge about the constraints on the structure of models of spoken word recognition. Specifically, models of spoken word recognition must accommodate opposing effects of facilitation of frequent sublexical elements and inhibitory effects of lexical neighborhoods.

25.6 Neural Evidence of Probabilistic Phonotactics

Relatively little evidence exists regarding the cortical processes that support a perceiver's sensitivity to probabilistic phonotactics. Furthermore, virtually no *developmental* cognitive neuroscience research has directly investigated the neural underpinnings of effects of probabilistic phonotactics on word recognition, lexical acquisition, or speech segmentation. However, recent structural anatomic findings on the development of thalamocortical connections in the human auditory system (Moore, 2002; Moore & Guan, 2001) provide some insights into the gross localization of the neural substrate for probabilistic phonotactic effects. Specifically, Moore (2002) has provided anatomical evidence that suggests that efficient conduction of auditory input to cortex begins between the ages of 4.5 months and 1 year. This onset of cortical processing of auditory inputs from the brainstem appears to parallel the time course of the onset of several language-specific functions in human infant studies, including those of sensitivity to and use of probabilistic phonotactics. One interpretation of these structural results is that cortical, and not lower (i.e., brainstem), sites are responsible for the processing of probabilistic phonotactics. Although the identity of the exact cortical substrate(s) responsible for effects of probabilistic phonotactics requires further research, recent functional brain imaging studies have suggested that Wernicke's area is sensitive to probabilistic sequential dependencies in novel stimulus streams

(Bischoff-Grethe et al., 2000). However, the areas observed in this study may or may not be relevant to the on-line processing of spoken words and effects of probabilistic phonotactics. More recent fMRI evidence (Jacquemot, Pallier, LeBihan, Dehaene, & Dupoux, 2003) suggests that processing of phonotactic constraints may be performed within the left superior temporal and the left anterior supramarginal gyri.

Pylkkanen et al. (2001) have investigated the influence of probabilistic phonotactics effects using magnetoencephalography (MEG). Magnetic activity of the brain was recorded synchronous with the presentation of words that covaried in phonotactic probability and neighborhood density (Vitevitch & Luce, 1999). Vitevitch and Luce (1999) interpreted their results as evidence that phonotactic effects are prelexical and similarity neighborhood density effects are lexical. Pylkkanen et al. sought evidence supporting the M350 response as a neural correlate of initial lexical activation. Specifically, they reasoned that if the latency of the M350 component paralleled the phonotactic frequencies (i.e., earlier latency for higher frequencies), then this component reflects initial lexical activation. In contrast, if the latency of the M350 component paralleled lexical density (i.e., later latency for high density), then this component reflects a later decision stage in lexical processing. Pylkkanen et al. obtained results consistent with the hypothesis that the M350 component is sensitive to initial lexical activation. Earlier M350 latencies were obtained for both words and nonwords with higher phonotactic frequencies. However, the generality of the Pylkkanen et al. results must be interpreted with some caution. The stimuli in the Pylkkanen study were visually presented in print and not as spoken words. Although Pylkkanen et al. replicated the behavioral results of Vitevitch and Luce (1999), it is unclear whether a similar pattern of MEG results would be obtained for spoken stimuli.

25.7 Some Future Directions

Research to date has demonstrated that human listeners – from infancy through adulthood – are sensitive to and use probabilistic phonotactics during spoken word recognition. However, several important empirical questions remain regarding the precise role of probabilistic phonotactics in spoken word recognition.

First, more refined metrics for computing probabilistic phonotactics are needed. To date, the majority of studies have focused on segment-to-segment or, biphone co-occurrence probabilities. These probabilities are computed on the basis of frequency counts derived from large corpora of text or dialogue that serve as ideal samples of the language environment. However, perceivers may not be perfect recorders of word incidence in their linguistic environment. Further, investigation into the relationship between theories of familiarity and incidence in the linguistic environment is needed to provide the underpinnings for computing more accurate probabilities. Furthermore, phonotactic constraints occur over even longer stretches of contiguous segments. For example, /r/ is the only consonant in English that follows /st/ in word initial position. It is possible that the frequencies of sublexical sequences larger than biphones play a role in spoken word recognition. Along with frequencies of longer sublexical sequences, additional research is needed that investigates the sensitivity of perceivers to sequential dependencies across non-contiguous segments, such as pre- and post-vocalic consonants. Such a finding could potentially rule out models such as simple recurrent networks, which are incapable of capturing non-contiguous dependencies in natural languages. Finally, most studies of phonotactics to date have largely ignored the directionality of the probabilities. An alternative that has only begun to be investigated is the role of backward, or postdictive, phonotactics. These probabilities would likely have more influence in the recognition of longer words where sufficient time exists for later occurring segments to influence the perception of earlier segments.

A second area of needed research focuses on the neural underpinnings of spoken word recognition. The investigation of the neural substrate supporting speech perception is still in its infancy and substantial work remains to be done (see Bernstein, this volume). Virtually nothing is known about the neural structures and processing mechanisms specifically responsible for probabilistic phonotactic effects. The dissociation of probabilistic phonotactics and lexical effects provides a powerful contrast for investigating the neural substrate supporting spoken word recognition (e.g., Pylkkanen et al., 2001). Furthermore, since probabilistic phonotactic effects are likely related to the general processing principle that favors frequently occurring patterns, elucidating our understanding of the neural mechanisms supporting probabilistic phonotactics should also provide insights into more general cortical mechanisms used in perception, memory, and learning.

25.8 Summary and Conclusions

Between the ages of 6 and 9 months infants begin to acquire very detailed knowledge of the probabilistic phonotactics of their language. Infants appear to use this information to determine patterns that constitute possible well-formed words and to segment words from the continuous stream of speech, both necessary prerequisites to the acquisition of full-fledged adult form-based lexicon. The evidence from research with children demonstrates the influence of probabilistic phonotactics on the acquisition of new vocabulary. This body of evidence is consistent with the proposal that probabilistic phonotactics has its impact at several stages of information processing, including on-line perceptual processing and the relatively late stage of storage and recall of newly learned patterns.

In adult perceivers, probabilistic phonotactics has been found to influence on-line spoken word recognition by serving as a cue for word segmentation and as a source of information that affects the speed and efficiency of isolated word recognition. The research on adults demonstrating separable influences of lexical density and probabilistic phonotactics has provided valuable new knowledge about the constraints on the structure of models of spoken word recognition and provides a useful contrast for investigating the cortical substrate for spoken word recognition. However, no contemporary spoken word recognition models, as implemented, provide an account for the influences of probabilistic phonotactics on both word recognition and segmentation.

We have proposed two general processing principles of the spoken language processing system. First, frequently occurring units and patterns of units are favored during recognition. Second, active units compete with one another for recognition. Probabilistic phonotactics effects are the result of the first principle operating on sublexical patterns. In contrast, neighborhood effects are the result of the second principle operating on lexical units. Both principles arise from the operation of an adaptive processing system that continually tunes and modifies itself to the changing properties of the linguistic environment of the perceiver.

ACKNOWLEDGMENTS

This work was supported (in part) by research grant numbers R01 DC 0265801 and R01 DC 04856 from the National Institute on Deafness and Other Communication Disorders, National Institutes of Health.

REFERENCES

Auer, E. T., Jr. (1992). Dynamic processing in spoken word recognition. Doctoral Dissertation, State University of New York at Buffalo, Buffalo, NY.

Bailey, T. M. & Hahn, U. (2001). Determinants of wordlikeness: Phonotactics or lexical neighborhoods? *Journal of Memory and Language*, 44, 568–91.

Bischoff-Grethe, A., Propoer, S. M., Mao, H., Daniels, K. A., & Berns, G. S. (2000). Conscious and unconscious processing of nonverbal predictability in Wernicke's area. *The Journal of Neuroscience*, 20(5), 1975–81.

Brown, R. W. & Hildum, D. C. (1956). Expectancy and the perception of syllables. *Language*, 32, 411–19.

Cluff, M. S. & Luce, P. A. (1990). Similarity neighborhoods of spoken bisyllabic words. *Journal of Experimental Psychology: Human Perception and Performance*, 16, 551–63.

Coleman, J. S. & Pierrehumbert (1997). Stochastic phonological grammars and acceptability. In *Computational Phonology. Third Meeting of the ACL Special Interest Group in Computational Phonology* (pp. 49–56). Somerset, NJ: Association for Computational Linguistics.

Cutler, A. & Butterfield, S. (1992). Rythmic cues to speech perception: Evidence from juncture misperception. *Journal of Memory and Language*, 31, 218–36.

Cutler, A. & Carter, D. M. (1987). The predominance of strong initial syllables in the English vocabulary. *Computer Speech and Language*, 2, 122–42.

Cutler, A., Mehler, J., Norris, D., & Segui, J. (1987). Phoneme identification and the lexicon. *Cognitive Psychology*, 19, 141–77.

Cutler, A. & Norris, D. G. (1988). The role of strong syllables in segmentation for lexical access. *Journal of Experimental Psychology: Human Perception and Performance*, 14, 113–21.

Eukel, B. (1980). Phonotactic basis for word frequency effects: Implications for lexical distance metrics. *Journal of the Acoustical Society of America*, 68, S33.

Frisch, S. A., Large, N. R., & Pisoni, D. B. (2000). Perception of wordlikeness: Effects of segment probability and length on the processing of nonwords. *Journal of Memory and Language*, 42, 481–96.

Ganong, W. F. (1980). Phonetic categorization in auditory word perception. *Journal of Experimental Psychology: Human Perception and Performance*, 6, 110–25.

Gathercole, S. E., Frankish, C. R., Pickering, S. J., & Peaker, S. (1999). Phonotactic influences on short-term memory. *Journal of Experimental Psychology: Learning Memory and Cognition*, 25, 84–95.

Gaygen, D. (1997). The effects of probabilistic phonotactics on the segmentation of continuous speech. Doctoral Dissertation, State University of New York at Buffalo, Buffalo, NY.

Gaygen, D. E. & Luce, P. A. (2002). Troughs and bursts: Probabilistic phonotactics and lexical activation in the segmentation of spoken words in fluent speech. (Manuscript submitted for publication.)

Goh, W. D. & Pisoni, D. B. (2003). Effects of lexical neighborhoods on immediate memory span for spoken words. *Quarterly Journal of Experimental Psychology*, 56A, 929–54.

Goldinger, S. D., Luce, P. A., & Pisoni, D. B. (1989). Priming lexical neighbors of spoken words: Effects of competition and inhibition. *Journal of Memory and Language*, 28, 501–18.

Grossberg, S. (1986). The adaptive self-organization of serial order in behavior: Speech, language, and motor control. In E. C. Schwab & H. C. Nusbaum (eds.), *Pattern Recognition by Humans and Machines: Vol. 1. Speech Perception* (pp. 187–294). New York: Academic Press.

Grossberg, S., Boardman, I., & Cohen, M. (1997). Neural dynamics of variable-rate speech categorization. *Journal of Experimental Psychology: Human Perception and Performance*, 23, 483–503.

Howes, D. H. (1957). On the relation between the intelligibility and frequency of occurrence of English words. *Journal of the Acoustical Society of America*, 29, 296–305.

Jacquemot, C., Pallier, C., LeBihan, D., Dehaene, S., & Dupoux, E. (2003). Phonological grammar shapes the auditory cortex: A functional Magnetic Resonance Imaging study. *Journal of Neuroscience*, 23(29), 9541–646.

Johnson, E. K. & Jusczyk, P. W. (2001). Word segmentation by 8-month-olds: When speech cues count more than statistics. *Journal of Memory and Language*, 44, 1–20.

Jusczyk, P. W., Friederici, A. D., Wessels, J., Svenkerud, V. Y., & Jusczyk, A. M. (1993). Infants' sensitivity to sound patterns of native language words. *Journal of Memory and Language*, 32, 402–20.

Jusczyk, P. W., Cutler, A., & Redanz, N. (1993). Preference for predominant stress patterns of English words. *Child Development*, 64, 675–87.

Jusczyk, P. W., Luce, P. A., & Charles-Luce, J. (1994). Infants' sensitivity to phonotactic patterns in the native language. *Journal of Memory and Language*, 33, 630–45.

Lehiste, I. (1972). The timing of utterances and linguistic boundaries. *Journal of the Acoustical Society of America*, 51, 2018–24.

Luce, P. A., Goldinger, S. D., Auer, E. T., & Vitevitch, M. S. (2000). Phonetic priming, neighborhood activation, and PARSYN. *Perception & Psychophysics*, 62, 615–25.

Luce, P. A. & Large, N. (2001). Phonotactics, neighborhood density, and entropy in spoken word recognition. *Language and Cognitive Processes*, 16, 565–81.

Luce, P. A. & Pisoni, D. B. (1998). Recognizing spoken words: The neighborhood activation model. *Ear and Hearing*, 19, 1–36.

Marslen-Wilson, W. D. (1989). Access and integration: Projecting sound onto meaning. In W. D. Marslen-Wilson (ed.), *Lexical Access and Representation* (pp. 3–24). Cambridge, MA: Bradford.

Mattys, S. L. & Jusczyk, P. W. (2001). Phonotactic cues for segmentation of fluent speech by infants. *Cognition*, 78, 91–121.

Mattys, S. L., Jusczyk, P. W., Luce, P. A., & Morgan, J. L. (1999). Word segmentation in infants: How phonotactics and prosody combine. *Cognitive Psychology*, 38, 465–94.

McClelland, J. L. & Elman, J. L. (1986). The Trace model of speech perception. *Cognitive Psychology*, 18, 1–86.

McClelland, J. L. & Rumelhart, D. E. (1981). An interactive activation model of the effect of context in perception: Part 1. An account of basic findings. *Psychological Review*, 88, 375–407.

McQueen, J. M. (1998). Segmentation of continuous speech using phonotactics. *Journal of Memory and Language*, 39, 21–46.

McQueen, J. M., Norris, D., & Cutler, A. (1994). Lexical influence in phonetic decision making: Evidence from subcategorical mismatches. *Journal of Experimental Psychology: Human Perception and Performance*, 25, 1363–89.

Moore, J. K. (2002). Maturation of human auditory cortex: Implications for speech perception. *Annals of Otology Rhinology & Laryngology*, 111(5), supplement 189(2), 7–10.

Moore, J. K. & Guan, Y. L. (2001). Cytoarchitectural and axonal maturation in human auditory cortex. *Journal of the Association for Research on Otolaryngology*, 2, 297–311.

Nakatani, L. H. & Dukes, K. D. (1977). Locus of segmental cues for word juncture. *Journal of the Acoustical Society of America*, 62, 714–19.

Norris, D. (1990). A dynamic-net model of human speech recognition. In G. T. M. Altmann (ed.), *Cognitive Models of Speech Processing: Psycholinguistic and Computational Perspectives* (pp. 87–105). Cambridge, MA: MIT Press.

Norris, D. (1994). Shortlist: A connectionist model of continuous speech recognition. *Cognition*, 52, 189–234.

Norris, D., McQueen, J. M., & Cutler, A. (1995). Competition and segmentation in spoken word recognition. *Journal of Experimental Psychology: Learning, Memory, and Cognition*, 21, 1209–28.

Norris, D., McQueen, J. M., Cutler, A., & Butterfield, S. (1997). The possible-word constraint in the segmentation of continuous speech. *Cognitive Psychology*, 34, 191–243.

Pierrehumbert, J. (2003). Probabilistic phonology: Discrimination and robustness. In R. Bod, J. Hay, & S. Jannedy (eds.), *Probabilistic Linguistics* (pp. 177–228). Cambridge, MA: MIT Press.

Pitt, M. A. & McQueen, J. M. (1998). Is compensation for coarticulation mediated by the lexicon? *Journal of Memory and Language*, 39, 347–70.

Pylkkanen, L., Stringfellow, A., & Marantz, A. (2001). Neuromagnetic evidence for the timing of lexical activation: An MEG component sensitive to phonotactic probability but not to neighborhood density. *Brain and Language*, 81, 666–78.

Saffran, J. R., Newport, E. L., & Aslin, R. N. (1996). Word segmentation: The role of distributional cues. *Journal of Memory and Language*, 35, 606–21.

Salasoo, A. & Pisoni, D. B. (1985). Interaction of knowledge sources in spoken word identification. *Journal of Memory and Language*, 24, 210–31.

Savin, H. B. (1963). Word-frequency effect and errors in the perception of speech. *Journal of the Acoustical Society of America*, 35, 200–6.

Stoianov, I. & Nerbonne, J. (1998). Exploring phonotactics with simple recurrent networks. In F. van Eynde, I. Schaurman, & N. Schel Kens (eds.), *Proceedings of Computational Linguistics in the Netherlands, 2000* (pp. 51–67).

Storkel, H. L. (2001). Learning new words: Phonotactic probability in language development. *Journal of Speech & Hearing Research*, 44, 1321–37.

Storkel, H. L. & Rogers, M. A. (2000). The effect of probabilistic phonotactics on lexical acquisition. *Clinical Linguistics and Phonetics*, 14(6), 407–25.

Treiman, R., Kessler, B., Knewasser, S., Tincoff, R., & Bowman, M. (2000). English speakers' sensitivity to phonotactic patterns. In M. B. Broe & J. Pierrehumbert (eds.), *Papers in Laboratory Phonology V: Acquisition and the Lexicon* (pp. 269–82). Cambridge: Cambridge University Press.

Vitevitch, M. S. & Luce, P. A. (1998). When words compete: Levels of processing in spoken word perception. *Psychological Science*, 9, 325–9.

Vitevitch, M. S. & Luce, P. A. (1999). Probabilistic phonotactics and neighborhood activation in spoken word recognition. *Journal of Memory and Language*, 40, 374–408.

Vitevitch, M. S., Luce, P. A., Charles-Luce, J., & Kemmerer, D. (1997). Phonotactics and syllable stress: Implications for the processing of spoken nonsense words. *Language and Speech*, 40, 47–62.

Part VI Theoretical Perspectives

26 The Relation of Speech Perception and Speech Production

CAROL A. FOWLER AND
BRUNO GALANTUCCI

26.1 Introduction

For the most part, speech perception and speech production have been investigated independently. Accordingly, the closeness of the fit between the activities of speaking and of perceiving speech has not been frequently addressed. However, the issue is important, because speakers speak intending to be understood by listeners.

We will focus on two central domains in which it is appropriate to explore the relation of speech production to speech perception: the public domain in which speakers talk, and listeners perceive what they say; and the private domain in which articulatory mechanisms support talking, and perceptual mechanisms support listening to speech.

In the public domain, we will suggest that the fit between the activities of talking and listening must be close and that, in fact, languages could not have arisen and could not serve their functions if the fit were not close. In respect to the private domain, we will focus specifically on a proposal identified with the motor theory of speech perception (e.g., Liberman, 1996; Liberman & Mattingly, 1985) that articulatory mechanisms are brought to bear on speech perception.

The public and private domains of speech are not unrelated. Speech is an evolutionary achievement of our species, and it is likely that the required tight coupling of the public activities of talking and of perceiving talk that shaped the evolution of language involve the evolution of the mechanisms that serve language use.

As for evidence for our claim that, in the public domain, the fit between talking and listening is close, we will sample research findings suggesting that primitive objects of speech perception are gestures. If this is the case, then gestures constitute a public currency of both perceiving and producing speech.

As for evidence relating to the motor theory's claim that, in the private domain, there is coupling of mechanisms that support talking and listening, research findings are limited; however, the evidence is buttressed by numerous findings of couplings between mechanisms supporting action and mechanisms supporting its perception. We review some of that evidence in a later section.

26.2 The Relation between Production and Perception in Public Language Use

26.2.1 *Theoretical context*

Language exhibits duality of patterning (Hockett, 1960). That is, it has syntactic structuring of words in sentences and phonological structuring of consonants and vowels in words. Although the meaningful utterances that the first level of structuring yields surely are the main foci of language users' attention, our focus here will be on the phonological level. This is because, at this level, languages provide the forms that speakers use to make their linguistic messages public.

Underlying the effectiveness of public language is a "bottom-line" requirement, namely that listeners must, in the main, accurately perceive the language forms that talkers produce. We will refer to this as achievement of "parity" (cf. Liberman & Whalen, 2000) here, a relation of sufficient equivalence between phonological messages sent and received. Because achievement of parity is essential to communicative efficacy, we expect properties of languages to be shaped by this requirement. We propose two such properties.

First, the forms should be the public actions of speakers, or they should be isomorphic with those actions. That is, if language forms are the very parts of our language system that permit its public use, and if, in public use of language, talkers intend to convey these forms to listeners by some kind of public action, successful communication would be fostered if the public actions were the forms themselves or were isomorphic with them. The second parity-fostering property is related to the first. It is that language forms should be preserved throughout a communicative exchange. That is, talkers should intend to convey a message composed of a sequence of phonological forms, their public actions should count as producing those forms for members of the language community, and the forms should be conveyed to listeners by acoustic signals that constitute information about them. In turn, listeners should perceive and recognize those language forms.

In general, linguists and psycholinguists do not agree that languages have these parity-fostering properties. In particular, they do not identify activities of the vocal tract as phonological forms. Rather, forms are components of linguistic competence in the mind of the language user. For example:

> Phonological representation is concerned with speakers' implicit knowledge, that is with information in the mind. (Pierrehumbert, 1990, p. 376)

> [Phonetic segments] are *abstractions*. They are the end result of complex perceptual and cognitive processes in the listener's brain . . . They have no physical properties. (Repp, 1981, p. 1462)

> Auditory coding of the signal is followed by processes that map the auditory representation onto linguistic units such as phonetic features, phonemes, syllables or words. (Sawusch & Gagnon, 1995, p. 635)

Nor are language forms considered isomorphic with vocal tract activities. For example, MacNeilage and Ladefoged (1976, p. 90) remark that:

> there has been . . . an increasing realization of the inappropriateness of conceptualizing the dynamic processes of articulation itself in terms of discrete, static, context-free linguistic categories such as "phoneme" or "distinctive feature." This development does not mean that these linguistic categories should be abandoned – as there is considerable evidence for their behavioral reality (Fromkin, 1971). Instead it seems to require that they be recognized . . . as too abstract to characterize the actual behavior of the articulators themselves. They are, therefore, at present better confined to primarily characterizing earlier premotor stages of the production process . . . and to reflecting regularities at the message level.

This dichotomy between message level forms and physical implementations of speech remains today, a quarter century after publication of MacNeilage and Ladefoged's paper. For example, it is apparent in the comprehensive model of language production of Levelt, Roelofs, & Meyer (1999). There, phonological forms are abstract and featurally underspecified representations,[1] whereas the phonetic forms that drive articulation are the articulatory gestures of Browman and Goldstein (e.g., 1992; also see below Section 26.2.2.1).

The apparent mismatch between properties of phonological segments (or phonemes) and articulatory actions occurs in part because talkers coarticulate when they speak; that is, they overlap vocal tract activities for consonants and vowels temporally and spatially. Coarticulation is identified, for the most part, as destructive of some essential properties of phonological segments, in particular, their discreteness, their static nature and their context-invariance. Coarticulated consonants and vowels are analogous to smashed Easter eggs in Hockett's (1955) famous metaphor, they are distortions of phonetic segments according to Ohala (e.g., 1981), and they eliminate the possibility of articulatory or acoustic invariants corresponding to consonants and vowels according to Liberman and Mattingly (1985; see also Liberman, 1996).

These characterizations signify not only that the public actions that count as speaking are not language forms and are not isomorphic with them, but also, therefore, that language forms are not preserved throughout a communicative exchange. They are present as components of the talker's plan to produce an utterance, and, if the listener recovers the phonological message, they are known to the listener as well. However, they are not preserved in the talker's public actions. This means that the acoustic signal cannot provide certain information about the forms. Accordingly, the listener has to reconstruct the forms from such things as "auditory cues" (Sawusch & Gagnon, 1995) or acoustic and optical cues (e.g., Massaro, 1998). In this perspective, language forms reside in the minds of language users, not in the intermediate media – vocal tract, air, ear – that support communication.

We ask whether this perspective is realistic in effectively characterizing the fit between talking and listening as poor. We think that it is not. Rather, because research in speech production and perception is generally undertaken independently, researchers have not confronted the issue of their mutual fit. Here we begin with the hypothesis that languages do have the parity-fostering characteristics listed above and ask whether we can eliminate the barriers that current thinking about speaking and listening has erected in the way of this hypothesis.

26.2.2 Evidence

26.2.2.1 The nature of phonological forms

By most accounts, phonological forms are collections of featural attributes. They are essentially timeless; they are discrete one from the other, and they are context-free. In all of these respects, they appear quite different from the articulatory actions of speaking and from the consequent acoustic signals. Articulatory actions are dynamic and overlapping, and the specific movements that constitute production of a consonant or a vowel are context-sensitive due to coarticulation. The acoustic speech signal likewise undergoes constant change, there are no phone-sized segments apparent in it, and the acoustic structure specifying a given consonant or vowel is highly context-sensitive.

By one account, however, atoms of phonological competence are not different in these ways from actions of the vocal tract during speech. This is the account provided by articulatory phonology (e.g., Browman & Goldstein, 1992, 1995).

Eliminating the differences between descriptions in the two domains requires adjustments in how we think about both the elements of phonological competence and articulatory actions. A crucial move in this direction is to assume that elements of phonological competence have their primary home in the vocal tract, not in the mind. They are linguistically significant actions of the vocal tract, called *gestures*. Gestures are not movements of individual articulators, but rather are coordinated actions usually of two or more articulators. The actions create and release constrictions. An example is the bilabial closure that occurs in production of English /b/, /p/, and /m/. Gestures are atoms of phonological competence as well (Browman & Goldstein, 1992).

Making this move necessarily eliminates the discrepancies between the language forms of phonological competence and the actions that implement them in speaking. Gestures are dynamic as they are produced and as they are perceived and known. Moreover, although they are produced in overlapping time frames, they are discrete. That is, in the syllable /bi/, for example, a constriction is made at the lips. Overlapping with that, temporally, the tongue body forms a constriction at the palate for /i/. Both constrictions are made; they are discrete in the sense of being distinct one from the other. Moreover, at a coarse-grained level of description, the two gestures are context-free. The lips always make contact for /b/; a palatal constriction is always made for /i/, regardless of the coarticulatory context. The synergistic relations among the articulators that contribute to a gesture allow the coarse-grained gestural action to be invariantly achieved, even though, at a finer-grained level of description, due to coarticulation, the movements that achieve the gesture are context-sensitive (cf. Abbs & Gracco, 1984; Kelso et al., 1984). Thus the jaw may contribute more to lip closure in the context of a coarticulating close vowel such as /i/ than in the context of an open vowel such as /a/.

For present purposes, the important achievement of articulatory phonology is in showing that languages can have the parity-fostering properties suggested above. According to articulatory phonology, phonological forms are in fact the public actions in which speakers engage when they talk, and consequently, they may be preserved throughout a communicative exchange. They are the atoms of talkers' plans to speak and of their vocal tract activity. Moreover, because they are the immediate causes of structure in the acoustic speech signal, and because distinctive gestures structure the signal distinctively, the signal can provide information for the gestures. If listeners use this information as such and track gestures (Fowler, 1986, 1996), then phonological language forms are preserved throughout a communicative exchange.

Identifying phonological atoms as public gestures does not preclude their serving the roles that features have served in more traditional phonologies. For example, whether a speaker produces the word *big* or the word *dig* depends on the oral constriction gesture for the initial consonant of the word. Gestures minimally distinguish words (Browman & Goldstein, 1992).

We now consider evidence that the primitives of listeners' perceptions of speech are language forms like those proposed by articulatory phonologists. We consider four kinds of evidence.

26.2.2.2 *Evidence that listeners perceive phonological gestures*

The earliest findings that listeners perceive articulatory gestures was obtained by Liberman and his colleagues at Haskins Laboratories. Two findings provide complementary evidence. One (Liberman et al., 1954) is that, in two-formant synthetic syllables, /di/ and /du/, the critical information specifying that the initial consonant of each syllable is /d/ is physically quite different. It is a high rise in the frequency of the second formant transition in /di/ and a low fall in frequency in /du/. Separated from the remainder of the syllables, the transitions sound quite distinct, and neither sounds like /d/. In context, they sound alike. There is something alike about /di/ and /du/ when they are naturally produced. Both /d/ gestures are achieved by a constriction of the tongue tip against the alveolar ridge of the palate. The transitions, produced after release of the constrictions, are acoustically dissimilar because of coarticulation by the following vowel. In this instance, the same gesture, which has two distinct acoustic consequences (i.e., the distinct second formant transitions), is perceived as the same consonant. Perception tracks articulation.

The second finding (Liberman, Delattre, & Cooper, 1952) was obtained when voiceless stop consonants were cued by stop bursts rather than by formant transitions. In this case, an invariant burst, centered at 1440 Hz was identified predominantly as /p/ before /i/ and /u/ but as /k/ before /a/. Due to coarticulation, to produce the same stop burst in the different contexts requires a labial constriction before /i/ and /u/, but a velar constriction before /a/. Here, different gestures, giving rise because of coarticulation to the same bit of acoustic structure, are perceived as different.

Both findings appear to show that "when articulation and the sound wave go their separate ways" (Liberman, 1957, p. 121), perception tracks articulation.

There is another kind of finding showing that speech perception tracks articulation. This finding concerns how listeners parse the acoustic speech signal to recover phonological forms. They parse the signal along gestural lines.

Due to coarticulation, different gestures can have converging effects on common acoustic dimensions. For example, production of an unvoiced consonant may cause a high falling fundamental frequency (F0) pattern on a following vowel (e.g., Silverman, 1987). This may occur because the vocal folds are tensed to keep them apart during consonant production (e.g., Löfqvist et al., 1989). When they are adducted for the following vowel, the tension will raise F0 at vowel onset. (For other accounts, see Kingston & Diehl, 1994.) Likewise, a high vowel is associated with a higher F0 than a low vowel, an outcome that also is likely to have a cause in production constraints (Whalen & Levitt, 1995; Whalen et al., 1995). These segmental effects are superimposed on the intonation contour of the larger utterance in which they are produced. However, neither is heard as part of the intonation contour or even as pitch (e.g., Fowler & Brown, 1997; Pardo & Fowler, 1997; Silverman, 1987). Rather, the F0 contour caused by the voiceless consonant contributes to the perception of voicelessness (e.g., Pardo & Fowler, 1997; Silverman, 1986); that caused by vowel height contributes to the perception of vowel height (e.g., Reinholt Peterson, 1986). Listeners parse acoustic speech signals along gestural lines.

The sight of a human face mouthing one syllable dubbed onto a different, acoustically presented, syllable can lead listeners to hear something different than they hear in the absence of the video display. For example, acoustic /ma/ dubbed onto a face mouthing /da/ will be reported most frequently as /na/, a percept that integrates the visible alveolar gesture with the acoustically specified voicing and nasality (McGurk & MacDonald, 1976).

An analogous effect occurs when the haptic feel of consonantal gestures is substituted for the visible face (Fowler & Dekle, 1991). Although explanations for the original McGurk effect have been proposed that do not invoke perception of gestures as the common currency allowing audio-visual integration of phonetic information (e.g., Massaro, 1998), we believe that the haptic findings do require a gestural account. This interpretation leads to the prediction that, when print replaces the visible or felt facial gestures, the McGurk effect should disappear because print is not immediately caused by vocal tract gestures. Under conditions like those of the haptic experiment, Fowler and Dekle found no effect of print on acoustic speech perception. Given this set of findings, and the fact that visually and haptically perceived faces provide information about the same gestural events, we interpret these data sets as converging evidence in favor of the claim that listeners perceive gestures.

Another source of evidence that listeners perceive gestures concerns the rapidity of imitation. Canonically, choice response times exceed simple response times by 100 to 150 ms (Luce, 1986). In a characteristic choice task, participants might push one button when a green light flashes and a different button if a blue light flashes. In the simple task, they hit the same response button whenever any light flashes, whether it is green or blue.

When stimuli and responses are spoken utterances, the difference between choice and simple response latencies can become quite small, with both sets of latencies near those of rather fast simple response times (Porter & Castellanos, 1980; Porter & Lubker, 1980). This suggests that the element of choice in the choice task has been reduced. In the choice task as implemented by Porter and colleagues, a model speaker produced extended /a/ and then, after an unpredictable interval, shifted to something else, say, /ba/, /da/, or /ga/. Participants shadowed the model's disyllable. In the simple task, participants were assigned a syllable (say, /ba/): as in the choice task, they shadowed the model's extended /a/, but when the model shifted to /ba/, /da/, or /ga/, the participants produced their designated syllable, no matter what the model uttered. Porter and Castellanos (1980) found a 50 ms difference between simple and choice response times; Porter and Lubker (1980) found an even smaller difference. These results suggest that the participant's production of syllables in the choice task benefits from hearing the same syllable as the signal that prompts responding as if the signal serves as instructions for the required response. We have recently replicated Porter and Castellanos' experiment (Fowler et al., 2003), and we found a 26 ms difference between choice and simple response times with average simple responses times around 160 ms.

If listeners perceive gestures, these results are easy to understand. In the choice task, perceiving the model's speech is perceiving instructions for the required phonetic gestural response. We obtained two additional outcomes consistent with this interpretation. First, in the simple task, on one-third of the trials, the syllable that the participant produced was the same as the model's syllable. In our task, the responses were /pa/, /ta/, and /ka/. For a participant whose designated syllable was /pa/, the response matched the model's on trials when the model said /pa/. If listeners perceive gestures and the percept serves as a goad for an imitative response, responses should be faster on trials in which the model produced the participant's designated syllable than on other trials. We found that they were. Second, in a subsequent experiment, in which only choice responses were collected, we nearly doubled the voice onset times (VOTs) of half the model's syllables by manipulating the speech samples, and we asked whether our participants produced longer VOTs on those trials than on trials with original model VOTs. They did, and we concluded that our participants were, in fact, perceiving the model's speech gestures (specifically, the particular phasing between oral constriction and laryngeal devoicing), which served as a goad for an imitative response.

26.2.3 Conclusion regarding the fit between the public actions of talking and listening to speech

We find no convincing barriers to the idea that phonological forms are public actions, and we find evidence in its favor. If phonological forms are the public actions of speakers when they talk – that is, if phonological forms are gestures, and if, as the evidence suggests, listeners perceive gestures – then languages do meet the requirements of parity. Language forms are the public actions of the vocal tract during speech, and they are preserved throughout a communicative exchange.

We next consider the relations between the mechanisms that support talking and listening to speech.

26.3 The Relation between Mechanisms for Talking and Listening

26.3.1 The motor theory

In Liberman and Mattingly's theory (1985) there is another way in which speech perception and speech production are related, aside from their sharing public language forms. Parity in communication may also be fostered if the mechanisms for producing and perceiving speech are related. Liberman and Mattingly (1985, 1989) suggested that such a relation is realized in a speech module, that is, a dedicated piece of neural circuitry that evolved as a specialization for producing and perceiving speech.

However, the existence of such a module was not inferred solely on the basis of the theoretical constraints imposed by the requirements of parity. Its existence was suggested by empirical observations and by the flood of research findings that accompanied the development of speech technology.

A first step along the path that led to the proposal of the speech module was the realization that speech is not an acoustic alphabet. This conclusion was based on findings that, when a linguistic message is produced as a sequence of discrete acoustic units, it cannot be perceived at practically useful rates (Liberman et al., 1967). Notably, such a conclusion does not hold in general. In the visual modality, for example, speech can be rendered alphabetically, both in production (i.e., writing) and in perception (reading). The essence of the discovery by Liberman and colleagues was that an acoustic analog of an orthographic alphabet was not workable (cf. also Harris, 1953), even with carefully designed alphabets and extensive training of alphabet learners.

This conclusion suggested that a dedicated mechanism to handle speech may exist: If speech cannot be replaced by an acoustic alphabet, then its perception may require machinery different from the kind of machinery that handles print and perhaps different from the machinery that handles other acoustic sequences, such as Morse code.

The second step occurred when a more thorough understanding of the speech signal became available due to the advent of spectrograms. One of the earliest discoveries was that, in real speech, acoustic information about phonemes is not temporally discrete. A given bit of acoustic signal can contain information about several phonemes and, conversely, one phoneme can influence the acoustic signal for a period of time longer than its length as conventionally measured (that is, as a discrete acoustic interval). These discoveries deepened the puzzle of the relation between the physical instantiation of speech and its linguistic units. The speech signal is continuous, and it codes phonetic information in a highly parallel fashion, yet the phonetic percept is discrete and sequential. However, what appears to be a complicated puzzle for the scientist may be an optimal solution for nature. On one side, if the physical instantiation of speech were a sequential signal made of discrete units, then speech would be a highly inefficient communication bearer in the acoustic medium.[2] On the other side, if linguistic units, specified in parallel in the signal, were to blend in perception, then listeners would not perceive the particulate units that are the atoms of open and productive phonological systems

(Studdert-Kennedy, 2000). A transformation from continuous-parallel information to discrete, sequential units in perception and a transformation going the other way in production seemed to be central to the design of human languages. But, how are these transformations achieved?

This was another indication that a dedicated mechanism exists to handle speech: the perceptual system for speech must be capable of transforming continuous-parallel acoustic structure into discrete-sequential phonological entities rapidly and accurately. No other acoustic percept imposes such requirements on the auditory system; this peculiarity calls for a specialized module.

The third step was closely related to the second. Speech is a physically continuous-parallel signal because, when it is produced, the vocal tract massively coarticulates the discrete phonetic units. In the view of Liberman and colleagues (e.g., Liberman et al., 1967), coarticulation is necessary to evade limits on the temporal resolving power of the ear. The capacity to coarticulate must have coevolved with that of decoding the effects of coarticulation in the acoustic signal, because neither capability would be useful without the other. Perhaps, then, these capabilities are both grounded in a common mechanism, identified by Liberman and Mattingly (1985) as a phonetic module.

The module evolved as a cortical structure shared between speech perception and production; its primary goal is to make motor knowledge about the effects of coarticulation available to the perceptual system. It is a compact evolutionary solution to the problem of coding discrete-sequential messages in a continuous-parallel acoustic signal, and it provides a rationale for the observation that perception tracks articulation.

In a later development, Liberman and Mattingly (1985) adopted as perceptual objects the phonetic gestures of Browman and Goldstein's (1986) articulatory phonology (see Section 26.2.2.1 above). That is, Liberman and Mattingly (1985) proposed that listeners perceive gestures, not individual movements of individual articulators. However, they preserved their earlier idea that coarticulation in speech destroys the discrete character of phonetic units in the acoustic signal, gestures no less than classical consonants and vowels (contrary to our earlier proposal). Accordingly, the gestures that listeners perceive, in the theory, are intended, not actual, gestures. The phonetic module enabled recovery of intended gestures from highly encoded speech signals.

Still later, Liberman and Mattingly (1989) explored the consequences of having postulated a phonetic module. Specifically, they attempted to locate the module within the architecture of the auditory system. To this end, they distinguished open and closed modules. Open modules (also called horizontal systems) are all-purpose devices that provide information about the energy distribution patterns detected by sensory systems. They are open in the sense that they can adaptively adjust to new environmental situations. The percepts they render are *homomorphic* with (that is, have the same form as) the proximal stimulation that causes them. In the case of the auditory system, for example, pitch is the homomorphic percept for frequency, and loudness is the homomorphic percept for intensity. Closed modules (also called vertical systems) are special-purpose devices that provide information about the distal structure that is behind the proximal energy distribution patterns detected by the sensory systems. They are closed in the sense that, being highly specialized for a particular kind of stimulation, they cannot adapt to new environmental situations. The percepts they render are *heteromorphic* with respect to proximal stimulation in that they have the same form as the distal events that cause the proximal stimulation. For example, speech perception and sound localization yield heteromorphic percepts (phonetic gestures and the location of a sounding source, respectively).

If speech percepts are attributed to a closed module, the question arises about their relationship with other auditory percepts, those coming from the open module as well as those coming from other closed modules. Liberman and Mattingly proposed that closed modules serially precede open modules, preempting the information that is relevant for their purposes and passing along whatever information is left to open modules.[3] This particular architectural design leads to the possibility of *duplex perception*, that is, the phenomenon that occurs when information left after preemption by the closed modules gives rise to homomorphic percepts: Homomorphic and heteromorphic percepts are simultaneously produced in response to the same stimulus.

26.3.2 Evidence especially favoring a motor theory of speech perception

The motor theory makes three closely related claims. It claims that listeners perceive intended gestures, that perception is achieved by a module of the nervous system dedicated to speech production and perception, and that speech perception recruits the speech motor system.

We have reviewed some of the evidence suggesting that gestures are perceived. Here we review evidence relating to the other two claims, focusing largely on the third.

The strongest behavioral evidence for a dedicated speech processing system is provided by findings of duplex perception. In one version of this finding, listeners are presented with a synthetic /da/ or /ga/ syllable, where /da/ and /ga/ were synthesized to be identical except for the third formant transition, which falls for /da/ and rises for /ga/. If the part of the syllable that is the same for /da/ and /ga/ (called the "base") is presented to one ear and the distinguishing transition is presented to the other, listeners integrate the information across the ears and hear /da/ or /ga/, depending on the transition. However, at the same time, they also hear the transition as a pitch rise or fall (e.g., Mann & Liberman, 1983). The finding that part of the signal is heard in two different ways at the same time suggests that two different perceptual systems are responsible for the two percepts. One, a phonetic processor, integrates the base and the transition and yields a phonetic percept, /da/ or /ga/. The other yields a homomorphic percept. Presumably this is an auditory processor, an open module.

This interpretation has been challenged on a variety of grounds (e.g., Fowler & Rosenblum, 1990; Pastore et al., 1983). We will not review those challenges here. Rather, we note that the motor theoretical interpretation of duplex perception would be buttressed by evidence favoring the third claim of the theory, that there is motor system or motor competence involvement in perceiving speech. This is because, generally, theorists do not claim motor involvement in auditory perception.

In fact, evidence for motor involvement in speech perception is weak. However, apparently this is because such evidence has rarely been sought, not because many tests have yielded negative outcomes. We have found three sets of supportive behavioral data and some suggestive neuropsychological data.

Following a seminal study by Eimas and Corbit (1973), there were many investigations of "selective adaptation" in speech perception. Listeners heard repeated presentations of a syllable at one end of an acoustic continuum, say /pa/, and then identified members of, say, a /pa/ to /ba/ continuum. After hearing repeated /pa/ syllables, listeners reported fewer /pa/s in the ambiguous region of the continuum. Eimas and Corbit suggested that phonetic feature detectors (a detector for voicelessness in the example) were being fatigued by the repetitions, making the consonant with that feature less likely to be perceived than before adaptation. Although this account was challenged (e.g., by Diehl, Kluender, & Parker, 1985), for our purposes, the interpretation is less important than the finding by Cooper (1979) that repeated presentations of a syllable such as /pi/ had weak but consistent effects on *production* of the same syllable or another syllable sharing one or more of its features. For example, VOTs of produced /pi/s and /ti/s were reduced after adaptation by acoustic /pi/. This finding implies a perception-production link of the sort proposed by the motor theory.

Bell-Berti et al. (1978) provided further behavioral evidence for a motor theory. The vowels /i/, /ɪ/, /e/, and /ɛ/ of English can be described as differing in either of two ways. They decrease in height in the series as listed above. Alternatively, /i/ and /e/ are described as tense vowels; /ɪ/ and /ɛ/ are their lax counterparts. Within the tense vowel pair and the lax pair, vowels differ in height. Bell-Berti et al. found that speakers differed in how they produced the vowels in the series in ways consistent with each type of description. Four of their ten speakers showed activity of the genioglossus muscle (a muscle of the tongue affecting tongue height) that gradually decreased in the series of four vowels as listed above suggesting progressively lower tongue heights. The remaining six speakers showed comparable levels of activity for /i/ and /e/ that were much higher than activity levels for the two lax vowels. This suggested use of a tense-lax differentiation of the vowels.

In a perception test, the ten participants partitioned into the same two groups. Listeners identified vowels along an /i/ to /ɪ/ continuum under two conditions. In one, the vowels along the continuum were equally likely to occur. In the other condition, an anchoring condition, the vowel at the /i/ end of the continuum occurred four times as frequently as the other continuum members, a manipulation that decreases /i/ responses. The magnitude of this anchoring effect differed in the two groups of talkers; across the ten participants, the effect magnitude had a bimodal distribution. Participants who had shown progressively decreasing levels of genioglossus activity in their production of the four vowels showed considerably larger effects of anchoring than the six speakers who produced /e/ with more genioglossus activity than /ɪ/. The authors speculated that the difference occurred because, for the second group of listeners, /i/ and /ɪ/ are not adjacent vowels, whereas they are for members of the first group. Whether or not this is the appropriate account, it is remarkable that the participants grouped in the same way as listeners as they had as talkers. This provides evidence suggesting that speech percepts include information about motor production of speech.

Kerzel and Bekkering (2000) provide additional behavioral findings that they interpret as consistent with the motor theory. They looked for compatibility effects in speech production. On each trial, participants saw a face mouthing /bʌ/ or /dʌ/. At a variable interval after that, they saw either of two symbol pairs (in one experiment, ## or &&) that they had learned to associate with the spoken responses /ba/ and /da/. Kerzel and Bekkering found an effect of the irrelevant visible speech gesture on latencies to produce the syllables cued by the symbols such that /ba/ responses were faster when the face mouthed /bʌ/ than when it mouthed /dʌ/. Likewise /da/ responses were facilitated by visible /dʌ/. Kerzel and Bekkering argued that these effects had to be due to stimulus (visible gesture)-response compatibility, not stimulus-stimulus (that is, visible gesture-visible symbol) compatibility, because the symbols (## and &&) bear an arbitrary relation to the visible gestures whereas the responses do not. Their interpretation was that the visible gestures activated the speech production system and facilitated compatible speech actions, an account consistent with the motor theory. It has yet to be shown that acoustic speech syllables, rather than visible speech gestures, have the same effect.

There is some recent neuropsychological evidence providing support for a motor theory of speech perception. Calvert and colleagues (1997) reported that auditory cortical areas activate when individuals view silent speech or speech-like movements. Moreover, the region of auditory cortex that activated for silent lipreading and for acoustic speech perception was the same. More recently, they (MacSweeney et al., 2000) replicated the findings using procedures meant to ensure that fMRI scanner noise was not the source of the auditory cortical activation.

Using transcranial magnetic stimulation of the motor cortex, Fadiga et al. (2002) found enhanced muscle activity in the tongue just when listeners heard utterances that included lingual consonants. Conversely, using PET, Paus et al. (1996) found activation of secondary auditory cortex, among other brain regions, when participants whispered nonsense syllables with masking noise to prevent their hearing what they produced.

26.3.3 *The larger context in which the motor theory can be evaluated and supported*

The motor theory's claim that a linkage exists in speech mechanisms supporting speech production and perception receives additional support when it is considered in a larger context of research. Liberman (e.g., 1996) proposed that a production-perception link was a special solution to a special problem: the necessity of parity achievement in human spoken communication. We propose to deny that the link is special to the mechanisms used to implement speech (Fowler & Rosenblum, 1990). Rather, we suggest that linkages between motor and perceptual systems are blueprints of the architecture of cognition, above and beyond speech, and even above and beyond communication devices. Let us consider the evidence.

26.3.3.1 *Above and beyond speech*

Some species that use acoustic signals to recognize mates have linkages between the systems underlying the production of sounds in one animal and those underlying their perception by its mate. For example, evidence has been reported for a genetic coupling in crickets and frogs of the mechanisms for sound production by males and for sound perception by females (Doherty & Gerhardt, 1983; Hoy, Hahn, & Paul, 1997). Although the exact nature of the genetic mechanisms that support the linkages is still debated (Boake, 1991; Butlin & Ritchie, 1989; Jarvis & Nottebohm, 1997), there is agreement that the production and perception systems have coevolved (Blows, 1999). The motor system of the sender and the perceptual system of the receiver have shaped one another, permitting mate recognition and thus, the possibility of preserving the species or, when the parity constraint is significantly violated, of differentiating them by speciation (Ryan & Wilczynski, 1988).

The existence of linkages between production and perception of mating signals is confirmed also, at an anatomo-physiological level, for songbirds such as zebra finches (Williams & Nottebohm, 1985), canaries (Nottebohm, Stokes, & Leonard, 1976), and white-sparrows (Whaling et al., 1997), and for other birds such as parrots (Plummer & Striedter, 2000). In these animals, the neural motor centers that underlie song or sound production are sensitive to acoustic stimulation. The neural centers that support sound production in parrots are different from those that support song production for the songbirds. However, for all of these birds, there is an increase in auditory responsivity of the motor nuclei as the similarity between the acoustic stimulation and the song or sound produced by the bird itself or its conspecifics increases. The fact that over very different taxa, and through different mechanisms, a linkage is present between perception and production of acoustic communication signals is a first strong suggestion that motor-perceptual interactions may be more general than the special adaptation proposed by the motor theory of speech perception.

26.3.3.2 *Above and beyond communication systems*

Although it is suggestive, the evidence we summarized above is limited in its scope, because the production-perception linkages in crickets, frogs, and birds are all in the domain of animal communication. The emergence of these perception-action linkages might be considered a special solution to a common special problem, that of achieving parity in communication systems. But other evidence suggests that linkages between motor and perceptual systems are ubiquitous and are not specific to the requirements of communication.

Viviani and colleagues (see Viviani & Stucchi, 1992 for a review) have demonstrated experimentally that the motor system is brought to bear on visual and haptic perception of movements (Kandel, Orliaguet, & Viviani, 2000; Viviani, Baud-Bovy & Redolfi, 1997; Viviani & Mounod, 1990; Viviani & Stucchi, 1989, 1992). They infer that motor competence is brought to bear on perception whenever the two-thirds power law, a law that they consider a signature of biological motion, manifests itself as a constraint shaping perception of motion.[4]

For example, Viviani and Stucchi (1992) presented observers with a light spot moving along various continuous trajectories on a computer screen. Participants were asked to adjust the velocity profile of the motion to make it look uniform. In line with previous observations by Runeson (1974), Viviani and Stucchi found that participants judged as uniform motions that were, by objective measurement, highly variable.[5] This occurred even when observers were shown examples of uniform motion. The velocity profiles of the motions chosen as uniform all closely fit the two-thirds power law; thus, viewers perceive as uniform motions that are uniform only in their close obedience to the laws that govern biological movements. Similar effects of adherence to the two-thirds power law in perceptual performance are shown in visual judgments of motion trajectories (Viviani & Stucchi, 1989), pursuit tracking of two-dimensional movements (Viviani & Mounod, 1990), and motoric reproductions of haptically felt motions (Viviani, et al., 1997).

Other evidence for linkages between the motor and perceptual systems comes from experiments that manipulate stimulus-response compatibility and show facilitation or inhibition of motor performance due, respectively, to a compatible or incompatible perceptual stimulus that signals the initiation of the response movement (for a review, see Hommel et al., 2001).

In particular, Stürmer, Aschersleben & Prinz (2000), extended to the domain of hand gestures results like those obtained in the speech domain by Kerzel and Bekkering (2000). Their participants had the task of producing either a grasping gesture (first close the hand from a half-open position then return to half-open) or a spreading gesture (first open from a half-open position then return to half-open). The go signal for the movement was presented on a video, and it consisted of a color change on a model's hand, with different colors signaling the different gestures to be performed. Initially the hand was skin-colored; then it changed to red or blue. Along with the go signal, at varying latencies relative to the go signal, the model's hand produced either of two gestures that the participants were performing. Although participants were told to ignore the irrelevant information, they were faster to produce their responses when the movement matched the one presented on the computer screen. This finding is consistent with studies of speech reviewed earlier (Fowler, et al., 2003; Porter & Castellanos, 1980; Porter & Lubker, 1980) showing that responses are facilitated when stimuli cuing them provide instructions for their production. It is interesting that the same effect occurs for nonspeech (hand gestures in the research of Stürmer et al.) as well as for speech gestures.

26.3.3.3 Neuroimaging

Following Rizzolatti and colleagues' discovery of "mirror neurons"[6] in the premotor cortex of monkeys (see for example, Rizzolatti, 1998; Rizzolatti & Arbib, 1998; Rizzolatti et al., 1996) evidence has accumulated that a neural system exists in primates, including humans, for matching observed and executed actions (for a review see Decety & Grezes, 1999).

For example, using fMRI, Iacoboni et al. (1999) found that two cortical regions selectively engaged in finger-movement production – the left frontal operculum (area 44) and the right anterior parietal cortex – showed a significant increase in activity when the movements were imitations of movements performed by another individual compared to when the movements were produced following non-imitative spatial or symbolic cues. Remarkably, one of the two regions – area 44 – includes Broca's area, one of the important cortical regions for the production of speech.

Strafella & Paus (2000), used transcranial magnetic stimulation to demonstrate that perceiving handwriting is accompanied by an increase in the activity of the muscles of the hand (first dorsal interosseus); perceiving arm movements is accompanied by an increase in activity of muscles of the arm (biceps).

The foregoing is just a sampling of the evidence for perception-production linkages either in behavior or in the mechanisms supporting perception and action. In the context of these findings, the specific claim of the motor theory of motor recruitment in speech perception accrues considerable credibility.

26.4 Conclusions

For speech to serve its public communication function, listeners must characteristically perceive the language forms that talkers produce. We call this a requirement for achieving parity, following Liberman and colleagues (cf. Liberman & Whalen, 2000). We suggested that properties of language have been shaped by the parity requirement, and a significant example of this shaping is language's use of phonetic gestures as atoms of phonological competence, of speech production, and of speech perception. We provided evidence that gestures are perceived.

A review of behavioral and neuropsychological evidence within the speech domain, within the study of communication systems more generally, and in the larger domain of perception as well, uncovers evidence for linkages between mechanisms that support motor performance and those that support perception. This body of evidence is in favor of one claim of the motor theory while disfavoring another one. It favors the motor theory's claim of a link between speech production and perception mechanisms. Although within the speech domain there is weak evidence for this claim, its plausibility increases significantly when we consider the ubiquity of evidence for perception-production links across the board in cognition. This ubiquity, in turn, disfavors the motor theory's claim that a linkage is special to speech in providing a special solution to a special perceptual problem.

A next question to be addressed by future research is why perception-production linkages are so pervasive. Do these links reflect a general solution to a general problem? Rizzolatti and Arbib (1998) suggest that the perception-action links that mirror neurons support in primates provide an empathic way of recognizing the actions of others, possibly another kind of parity achievement. Perhaps achieving parity between the world as perceived and the world as acted upon is the main function of cognitive systems (Gibson, 1966), whether or not mirror neurons underlie them.

We began this chapter by remarking that the closeness of the fit between the activities of speaking and perceiving speech has not been frequently addressed. We now conclude by asking why, given the ubiquity of such linkages, cognitive science generally continues to investigate perception and action as if they were independent, especially in the domain of speech. We do not know the answer to this question. However, we do know that, when the assumption of logical independence between perception and action is made, then the *problem* of their relation arises. We have tried to show that there is another possible approach, in which the apparent problem becomes a resource. We assumed logical dependence between perception and action, and we found that this assumption forced us to sharpen our understanding of language as a unitary phenomenon, significantly eroding the barriers that have been erected between its physical instantiations and its abstract nature.

ACKNOWLEDGMENTS

Preparation of the manuscript was supported by NIH grants HD-01994 and DC-03782 to Haskins Laboratories.

NOTES

1 That is, phonological forms are represented as bundles of features, but the forms are underspecified in that their predictable features are not represented.
2 According to Liberman et al. (1967), it would have a rate of transmission equivalent to that of Morse code, approximately ten times slower than normal speech.
3 Notice that this architecture does not specify the relationship between two or more closed modules. Liberman and Mattingly suggested that closed modules are not arranged in parallel because that would make preemption cumbersome, but they left to empirical investigation the question of the relations among them.
4 In brief, the law states that when humans make curved movements, the angular velocity of their movements is proportional to the two-thirds power of the curvature.
5 The difference between minima and maxima was above 200%.
6 These are neurons that respond both when an action such as grasping an object is performed and when the same action by another animal is perceived.

REFERENCES

Abbs, J. & Gracco, V. (1984). Control of complex gestures: Orofacial muscle responses to load perturbations of the lip during speech. *Journal of Neurophysiology*, 51, 705–23.

Bell-Berti, F., Raphael, L. R., Pisoni, D. B., & Sawusch, J. R. (1978). Some relationships between speech production and perception. *Phonetica*, 36, 373–83.

Blows, M. W. (1999). Evolution of the genetic covariance between male and female components of mate recognition: An experimental test. *Proceedings of the Royal Society of London Series B-Biological Sciences*, 266, 2169–74.

Boake, C. R. B. (1991). Coevolution of senders and receivers of sexual signals: Genetic coupling and genetic correlations. *Trends in Ecology & Evolution*, 6, 225–7.

Browman, C. & Goldstein, L. (1986). Towards an articulatory phonology. *Phonology Yearbook*, 3, 219–52.

Browman, C. & Goldstein, L. (1992). Articulatory phonology: An overview. *Phonetica*, 49, 155–80.

Browman, C. & Goldstein, L. (1995). Dynamics and articulatory phonology. In R. Port & T. van Gelder (eds.), *Mind as Motion: Explorations in the Dynamics of Cognition* (pp. 175–93). Cambridge, MA: MIT Press.

Butlin, R. K. & Ritchie, M. G. (1989). Genetic coupling in mate recognition systems: What is the evidence? *Biological Journal of the Linnean Society*, 37, 237–46.

Calvert, G., Bullmore, E. T., Brammer, M. J., Campbell, R., Williams, S. C. R., McGuire, P., Woodruff, P. W. R., Iverson, S., D., & David, A. S. (1997). Activation of auditory cortex during silent lipreading. *Science*, 276, 593–6.

Cooper, W. E. (1979). *Speech Perception and Production: Studies in Selective Adaptation*. Norwood, NJ: Ablex Publishing Company.

Decety, J. & Grezes, J. (1999). Neural mechanisms subserving the perception of human actions. *Trends in Cognitive Sciences*, 3, 172–8.

Diehl, R., Kluender, K., & Parker, E. (1985). Are selective adaptation effects and contrast effects really distinct? *Journal of Experimental Psychology: Human Perception and Performance*, 11, 209–20.

Doherty, J. A. & Gerhardt, H. C. (1983). Hybrid tree frogs: Vocalizations of males and selective phonotaxis of females. *Science*, 220, 1078–80.

Eimas, P. & Corbit, J. (1973). Selective adaptation of feature detectors. *Cognitive Psychology*, 4, 99–109.

Fadiga, L., Craighero, L., Buccino, G., & Rizzolatti, G. (2002). Speech listening specifically modulates the excitability of tongue muscles: A TMS study. *European Journal of Neuroscience*, 15, 399–402.

Fowler, C. A. (1986). An event approach to the study of speech perception from a direct realist perspective. *Journal of Phonetics*, 14, 3–28.

Fowler, C. A. (1996). Listeners do hear sounds not tongues. *Journal of the Acoustical Society of America*, 99, 1730–41.

Fowler, C. A. & Brown, J. (1997). Intrinsic F0 differences in spoken and sung vowels and their perception by listeners. *Perception & Psychophysics*, 59, 729–38.

Fowler, C. A. & Dekle, D. J. (1991). Listening with eye and hand: Crossmodal contributions to speech perception. *Journal of Experimental Psychology: Human Perception and Performance*, 17, 816–28.

Fowler, C. A. & Rosenblum, L. D. (1990). Duplex perception: A comparison of monosyllables and slamming doors. *Journal of Experimental Psychology: Human Perception and Performance*, 16, 742–54.

Fowler, C., Brown, J., Sabadini, L., & Weihing, J. (2003). Rapid access to speech gestures in perception: Evidence from choice and simple response time tasks. *Journal of Memory and Language*, 49, 396–413.

Fromkin, V. (1971). The nonanomalous nature of anomalous utterances. *Language*, 47, 27–52.

Gibson, J. J. (1966). *The Senses Considered as Perceptual Systems*. Boston, MA: Houghton-Mifflin.

Harris, C. (1953). A study of the building blocks in speech. *Journal of the Acoustical Society of America*, 25, 962–9.

Hockett, C. (1955). *A Manual of Phonetics*. Bloomington, IN: Indiana University Press.

Hockett, C. (1960). The origin of speech. *Science*, 203, 89–96.

Hommel, B., Müsseler, J., Aschersleben, G., & Prinz, W. (2001). The theory of event coding (TEC): A framework for perception and action planning. *Behavioral and Brain Sciences*, 24, 849–78.

Hoy, R. R., Hahn, J., & Paul, R. C. (1977). Hybrid cricket auditory-behavior: Evidence for genetic coupling in animal communication. *Science*, 195, 82–4.

Iacoboni, M., Woods, R. P., Brass, M., Bekkering, H., Mazziotta, J. C., & Rizzolatti, G. (1999). Cortical mechanisms of human imitation. *Science*, 286, 2526–8.

Jarvis, E. D. & Nottebohm, F. (1997). Motor-driven gene expression. *Proceedings of the National Academy of*

Sciences of the United States of America, 94, 4097–102.

Kandel, S., Orliaguet, J.-P., & Viviani, P. (2000). Perceptual anticipation in handwriting: The role of implicit motor competence. *Perception & Psychophysics*, 62, 706–16.

Kelso, J. A. S., Tuller, B., Vatikiotis-Bateson, E., & Fowler, C. A. (1984). Functionally-specific articulatory cooperation following jaw perturbation during speech: Evidence for coordinative structures. *Journal of Experimental Psychology: Human Perception and Performance*, 10, 812–32.

Kerzel, D. & Bekkering, H. (2000). Motor activation from visible speech: Evidence from stimulus-response compatibility. *Journal of Experimental Psychology: Human Perception and Performance*, 26, 634–47.

Kingston, J. & Diehl, R. (1994). Phonetic knowledge. *Language*, 70, 419–54.

Levelt, W. J. M., Roelofs, A., & Meyer, A. (1999). A theory of lexical access in speech production. *Behavioral and Brain Sciences*, 22, 1–38.

Liberman, A. M. (1957). Some results of research on speech perception. *Journal of the Acoustical Society of America*, 29, 117–23.

Liberman, A. M. (1996). *Speech: A Special Code*. Cambridge, MA: Bradford Books.

Liberman, A. M. & Mattingly, I. (1985). The motor theory revised. *Cognition*, 21, 1–36.

Liberman, A. M. & Mattingly, I. (1989). A specialization for speech perception. *Science*, 243, 489–94.

Liberman, A. M. & Whalen, D. H. (2000). On the relation of speech to language. *Trends in Cognitive Sciences*, 4, 187–96.

Liberman, A. M., Cooper, F., Shankweiler, D., & Studdert-Kennedy, M. (1967). Perception of the speech code. *Psychological Review*, 74, 431–61.

Liberman, A. M., Delattre, P., & Cooper, F. (1952). The role of selected stimulus variables in the perception of the unvoiced-stop consonants. *American Journal of Psychology*, 65, 497–516.

Liberman, A. M., Delattre, P., Cooper, F. S., & Gerstman, L. (1954). The role of consonant-vowel transitions in the perception of the stop and nasal consonants. *Psychological Monographs: General and Applied*, 68, 1–13.

Löfqvist, A., Baer, T., McGarr, N., & Seider Story, R. (1989). The cricothyroid muscle in voicing control. *Journal of the Acoustical Society of America*, 85, 1314–21.

Luce, R. D. (1986). *Response Times*. New York: Oxford University Press.

MacNeilage, P. & Ladefoged, P. (1976). The production of speech and language. In E. C. Carterette & M. P. Friedman (eds.), *Handbook of Perception: Language and Speech* (pp. 75–120). New York: Academic Press.

MacSweeney, M., Amaro, E., Calvert, G., Campbell, R., David, A. S., McGuire, P., Williams, S. C. R., Woll, B., & Brammer, M. J. (2000). Silent speechreading in the absence of scanner noise: An event-related fMRI study. *Neuroreport*, 11, 1729–33.

Mann, V. & Liberman, A. M. (1983). Some differences between phonetic and auditory modes of perception. *Perception & Psychophysics*, 14, 211–35.

Massaro, D. (1998). *Perceiving Talking Faces*. Cambridge, MA: MIT Press.

McGurk, H. & MacDonald, J. (1976). Hearing lips and seeing voices. *Nature*, 264, 747–8.

Nottebohm, F., Stokes, T. M., & Leonard, C. M. (1976). Central control of song in canary, serinus-Canarius. *Journal of Comparative Neurology*, 165, 457–86.

Ohala, J. (1981). The listener as a source of sound change. In C. Masek, R. Hendrick, R. Miller, & M. Miller (eds.), *Papers from the Parasession on Language and Behavior* (pp. 178–203). Chicago: Chicago Linguistics Society.

Pardo, J. & Fowler, C. A. (1997). Perceiving the causes of coarticulatory acoustic variation: Consonant voicing and vowel pitch. *Perception & Psychophysics*, 59, 1141–52.

Pastore, R., Schmuckler, M., Rosenblum, L., & Szczesiul, R. (1983). Duplex perception for musical stimuli. *Perception & Psychophysics*, 33, 469–74.

Paus, T., Perry, D., Zatorre, R., Worsley, K. & Evans, A. (1996). Modulation of cerebral blood flow in the human auditory cortex during speech: Role of motor-to-sensory discharges. *European Journal of Neuroscience*, 8, 2236–46.

Pierrehumbert, J. (1990). Phonological and phonetic representations. *Journal of Phonetics*, 18, 375–94.

Plummer, T. K. & Striedter, G. F. (2000). Auditory responses in the vocal motor system of budgerigars. *Journal of Neurobiology*, 42, 79–94.

Porter, R. & Castellanos, F. X. (1980). Speech production measures of speech perception: Rapid shadowing of VCV syllables. *Journal of the Acoustical Society of America*, 67, 1349–56.

Porter, R. & Lubker, J. (1980). Rapid reproduction of vowel-vowel sequences: Evidence for a fast and direct acoustic-motoric linkage. *Journal of Speech & Hearing Research*, 23, 593–602.

Reinholt Peterson, N. (1986). Perceptual compensation for segmentally-conditioned fundamental-frequency perturbations. *Phonetica*, 43, 31–42.

Repp, B. (1981). On levels of description in speech research. *Journal of the Acoustical Society of America*, 69, 1462–4.

Rizzolatti, G. (1998). Recognizing and understanding motor events. *International Journal of Psychophysiology*, 30, 6.

Rizzolatti, G. & Arbib, M. A. (1998). Language within our grasp. *Trends in Neurosciences*, 21, 188–94.

Rizzolatti, G., Fadiga, L., Gallese, V., & Fogassi, L. (1996). Premotor cortex and the recognition of motor actions. *Cognitive Brain Research*, 3, 131–41.

Runeson, S. (1974). Constant velocity: Not perceived as such. *Psychological Research-Psychologische Forschung*, 37, 3–23.

Ryan, M. J. & Wilczynski, W. (1988). Coevolution of sender and receiver: Effect on local mate preference in cricket frogs. *Science*, 240, 1786–8.

Sawusch, J. & Gagnon, D. (1995). Auditory coding, cues and coherence in phonetic perception. *Journal of Experimental Psychology: Human Perception and Performance*, 21, 635–52.

Silverman, K. (1986). F0 cues depend on intonation: The case of the rise after voiced stops. *Phonetica*, 43, 76–92.

Silverman, K. (1987). The structure and processing of fundamental frequency contours. Unpublished PhD dissertation, Cambridge University.

Strafella, A. P. & Paus, T. (2000). Modulation of cortical excitability during action observation: A transcranial magnetic stimulation study. *Neuroreport*, 11, 2289–92.

Studdert-Kennedy, M. (2000). Evolutionary implications of the particulate principle: Imitation and the dissociation of phonetic form from semantic function. In C. Knight, M. Studdert-Kennedy, & J. Hurford (eds.), *The Evolutionary Emergence of Language* (pp. 161–76). Cambridge: Cambridge University Press.

Stürmer, B., Aschersleben, G., & Prinz, W. (2000). Correspondence effect with manual gestures and postures: A study of imitation. *Journal of Experimental Psychology: Human Perception and Performance*, 26, 1746–59.

Viviani, P. & Mounoud, P. (1990). Perceptuomotor compatibility in pursuit tracking of two-dimensional movements. *Journal of Motor Behavior*, 22, 407–43.

Viviani, P. & Stucchi, N. (1989). The effect of movement velocity on form perception: Geometric illusions in dynamic displays. *Perception & Psychophysics*, 46, 266–74.

Viviani, P. & Stucchi, N. (1992). Biological movements look uniform: Evidence of motor-perceptual interactions. *Journal of Experimental Psychology: Human Perception and Performance*, 18, 603–23.

Viviani, P., Baud-Bovy, G., & Redolfi, M. (1997). Perceiving and tracking kinesthetic stimuli: Further evidence of motor-perceptual interactions. *Journal of Experimental Psychology: Human Perception and Performance*, 23, 1232–52.

Whalen, D. & Levitt, A. (1995). The universality of intrinsic F0 of vowels. *Journal of Phonetics*, 23, 349–66.

Whalen, D., Levitt, A., Hsaio, P., & Smorodinsky, I. (1995). Intrinsic F0 of vowels in the babbling of 6-, 9-, and 12-month old French- and English-learning infants. *Journal of the Acoustical Society of America*, 97, 2533–9.

Whaling, C. S., Solis, M. M., Doupe, A. J., Soha, J. A., & Marler, P. (1997). Acoustic and neural bases for innate recognition of song. *Proceedings of the National Academy of Sciences*, 94, 12694–8.

Williams, H. & Nottebohm, F. (1985). Auditory responses in avian vocal motor neurons: A motor theory for song perception in birds. *Science*, 229, 279–82.

27 A Neuroethological Perspective on the Perception of Vocal Communication Signals

TIMOTHY Q. GENTNER AND GREGORY F. BALL

27.1 Introduction: Relations between Human and Nonhuman Animal Studies of Vocal Behavior

One path-breaking observation made about speech in the latter half of the twentieth century is that it is "special" (Liberman, 1982). An important step taken by the cognitive revolution initiated in the 1950s was to take speech and language out of the realm of general psychological processes such as learning and perception (e.g., Skinner, 1957) by claiming that unique neural and behavioral mechanisms needed to be postulated to explain the acquisition, production, and perception of human speech and language (Chomsky, 1959). When the plurality of human language behaviors are conceptualized as species-typical biological adaptations (e.g., Lenneberg, 1967; Pinker, 1994), however, the strong claim of uniqueness appears less universally tenable. To say that human language behaviors have evolved, is to say that the neural and behavioral specializations that mediate speech and language abilities are a result of natural (and/or sexual) selection pressures in humans. Given that no extant species of primates, including the closely related great apes, share with *Homo sapiens* comparable faculties of language and speech, it would be surprising if humans did not show any anatomical and physiological specializations for language production and processing. At the same time, comparative studies (Kleunder, Diehl, & Killeen, 1987; Kuhl & Miller, 1975, 1978) also demonstrate that at least some of the behaviors associated with speech perception (e.g. categorical perception, perceptual constancy) are not restricted to humans (but see Trout, 2001). As such, it would be equally surprising to find that some anatomical structures and physiological mechanisms for vocalization and vocal signal perception are *not* conserved across taxa.

There are at least two views concerning the value of comparative studies of nonhuman animals to our understanding of human speech and language. One perspective in the cognitive science community is that studies of nonhuman animals are simply irrelevant to the study of human speech (e.g., Chomsky, 2000). Chomsky has championed the notion that the "language faculty" of humans is a natural biological phenomenon and should be studied as such. In its strongest form, this argument claims that very few of the behavioral or cognitive phenomena associated with communication in nonhuman animals have attributes that even approach human speech. Accordingly, studies of nonhuman animals can only claim relevance to human language by asserting that something that is *not* language (i.e., nonhuman animal communication systems) *is* language. In contrast, others in the human language community (e.g. Liberman, 1996), while completely embracing the notion that language is a specialized human trait, have argued that comparative studies of nonhuman animals have much to teach students of human language about how a species-typical trait like speech might develop and how it is produced and perceived in adulthood. In a trivial sense, animal studies must, by necessity, inform the cellular basis of human language, because the central nervous systems of humans and many nonhuman animals share certain cell types such as neurons and glia. Although no one is likely to object to such a broad claim, commonalities of this sort hardly make a good case for considering nonhuman animal studies. Yet, as we have already noted, commonalities between humans and nonhumans go far beyond the cellular level.

Recently, Hauser, Chomsky, and Fitch (2002) have proposed that human language abilities can be divided into faculties in the "broad sense" and faculties in the "narrow sense." Broad faculties include sensory-motor processes underlying language production, and the conceptual-intentional abilities to formulate communication content. For example, some of the perceptual attributes that facilitate speech comprehension in humans and are observed in nonhuman animals can be considered examples of broad language faculties. Narrow faculties include such skills as the recursive properties exhibited in grammar and syntax. For example, humans can easily take a finite number of forms and recombine them infinitely. This combinatorial skill is obvious in human language but can also be observed in nonlinguistic domains such as numerical competence. Hauser et al. (2002) argue that comparative studies can illuminate broad language faculties by identifying developmental and neural mechanisms of processes common to human and nonhuman animals, and narrow faculties by identifying constraints that limit the occurrence of these human-specific traits in nonhuman animals. In other words, comparative studies can inform our understanding of human language by pointing out important similarities *and differences* in underlying processes and mechanisms.

Perhaps the strongest case for considering comparative data from nonhuman animals in understanding human language acquisition and production is illustrated empirically by neuroethological studies of birdsong. Given the differences in semantics and syntax between the two communication systems, no one would claim that birdsong is a language. However, to learn and to produce songs birds must solve the problem of how the auditory system regulates the development and production of complex vocal behaviors. More so than any other known animal behavior, vocal learning in songbirds presents the most direct analogy to the problems solved by the human central nervous system in learning to produce speech after exposure to a model and in maintaining vocal production over time

(Ball & Hulse, 1998; Doupe & Kuhl, 1999; Marler, 1970). Although birds do not have language, components of their vocal behaviors show a striking resemblance to important fundamental components of human speech and language.

The evolved sensory-motor processes that mediate vocal learning in songbirds are almost certainly not homologous in all aspects to the evolved processes that mediate language in humans. Yet, our knowledge of the neural and behavioral mechanisms of birdsong has already yielded insight to analogous processes in the human central nervous system (Margoliash, 2003). The goal of the current essay is to extend this analogy to include neurobiological mechanisms that underlie the perceptual processing of human speech and birdsong. We point to commonalities in the pre-semantic processing of species-typical vocal signals, and explore how studies of one can inform our understanding of the other.

27.2 Neuroethology: Neuroscience of Natural Behavior

Until very recently, the study of behavior and the study of the brain proceeded on independent tracks. In contrast, it is now understandable that molecular biologists studying the function of brain-specific gene expression collaborate with neuroscientists who study the behavioral expression of the action of neural circuits. Cognitive psychologists and systems-level neuroscientists are now working together on problems such as the neural basis of memory, perception, and language in a way that would have been unthinkable even 15 years ago (e.g. Gazzaniga, 1995). Emerging disciplines that involve cross-fertilization among the fields of behavior and neurobiology are given new names such as "Cognitive Neuroscience." Another hybrid discipline that straddles the behavioral and neural sciences is "Neuroethology." Investigators working in this field are interested in the neural and physiological mechanisms of behavior and perception, as are many systems-level neuroscientists. The focus of neuroethology, however, is on natural (i.e., ethological) behaviors.

27.2.1 *The ethological perspective*

Ethology can be broadly defined as the biological study of animal behavior (Immelmann & Beer, 1989). It generally involves the study of naturally occurring behaviors (i.e., species-typical behaviors) in the context of the animal's ecology. Ethological investigations can be conducted in a field setting or in the laboratory but the importance of relating findings to naturally occurring behaviors is paramount (Tinbergen, 1963).

In the 1960s, Brown and Hunsperger (1963) coined the term "neuroethology" to describe their studies of the neural basis of species-typical behaviors. Early neuroethology was dominated by studies of invertebrates (see Camhi, 1984). Contemporary work on vertebrate neuroethology is best known to most neuroscientists because of its success in elucidating the neural circuits mediating such behaviors as echolocation in bats, sound localization in owls, electroreception and perception in weakly electric fish, and the learning, production, and perception of birdsong.

Modern ethology emerged from a debate between ethologists and comparative psychologists that was carried out in the 1950s (see Grasse, 1956). From this debate a consensus of sorts emerged that was articulated by Tinbergen (1963), and later given more detail by Hinde (1970). Tinbergen pointed out that at least some of the disagreements between the ethologists and the comparative psychologists were due to the fact that they were unknowingly asking different questions about behavior. He argued that there are four basic causal questions one can ask about a particular behavior. These are:

1 Immediate causation: What stimulus and/or physiological factors cause this behavior to be produced at this time rather than another time?
2 Behavioral development: What ontogenetic processes mediate the emergence of a given behavior in the adult animal?
3 Adaptive significance: What is the functional significance of engaging in this behavior in terms of reproductive success or survival?
4 Evolutionary history: How did this behavior evolve over taxonomic history?

Questions (1) and (2) are often considered together under the rubric of "proximate" cause, and questions (3) and (4) are referred to collectively as "ultimate" causes. These so-called "levels of analysis" (Sherman, 1988) provide a very useful heuristic in organizing multiple explanations of the causes and significance of observed behaviors.

27.2.2 Neuroethology

Following the scheme originally developed by Tinbergen (1963), *neuro*ethologists ask questions related to the physiological mechanisms mediating immediate (i.e., proximate) causation and development. They focus on how the nervous system and related physiological systems such as the endocrine system and the immune system function to regulate the occurrence of species-typical behavior. Although they usually work in laboratory settings, they often investigate wild species and pose questions in terms of the organism's natural history.

One of the earliest intersection points between classical ethology and behavioral neuroscience concerns the selectivity of perception. Although it is obvious that perception requires an active selection process of some sort, ethologists discovered that an extraordinarily limited range of stimuli often lead an animal to exhibit a behavioral response. Indeed, based on experiments in a variety of taxa, it became clear that animals often respond to only one special part of the array of complex stimuli presented to them. Stimuli that are especially potent in eliciting behavioral responses are referred to as "sign stimuli" by ethologists (Tinbergen, 1951). These sorts of relationships between a stimulus and response underscore the notion, first articulated by von Uexküll, that one must consider an animal's functional environment based on its perceptual abilities to understand the organization of the mechanisms controlling its behavior (von Uexküll, 1957[1934]). The concept of a sign-stimulus has since guided neuroethologists in research on the physiological basis of perception in different species.

27.3 Bird Song: Behavior and Perception

Birdsong has long been viewed as an excellent example of the value in applying all four of Tinbergen's (1963) questions to the study of behavior (e.g., Hinde, 1982). Although we will not try to review both the proximate and ultimate aspects of birdsong in depth here, a good summary of the adaptive significance and evolution of birdsong can be found in Catchpole and Slater (1995).

27.3.1 Definition and function of song

Vocalizations in birds and other animals are often divided into two general categories: calls and songs. Calls usually refer to simpler vocalizations, produced by both sexes, that are used in contexts such as signaling alarm, maintaining flock cohesion, facilitating parent–young contact, and providing information about food sources. The term "song" refers to vocalizations that are generally more elaborate and used in the context of courtship and mating. The term "birdsong" is limited to such vocalizations produced by species in the songbird order (e.g., Catchpole & Slater, 1995; Thorpe, 1961). For most of these species, "song" is usually the most complex vocalization produced; it is usually sung loudly from a prominent perch, and is often associated with stereotyped courtship behaviors.

The decision to classify a vocalization as a song or a call is also related to the perceived function of the vocalization. The main functions ascribed to song behavior are territory defense (or spacing behavior) and mate attraction (Kroodsma & Byers, 1991). In many songbird species, especially among species that live in the temperate zone, there are marked sex differences in song behavior, with male song being more complex and more frequently sung than female song (Nottebohm, 1975). In evolutionary terms, the greater use of song by males is likely related to the effects of sexual selection, with both intrasexual (i.e., song is used to repel competing males from the territory) and intersexual selection (i.e., females choose males based on their songs) mechanisms operating differentially on males and females (e.g., Searcy & Andersson, 1986). In the tropics, avian social systems differ to some extent from those in the temperate zone, and female territorial defense along with female song is much more common than among temperate zone species (e.g., Levin, 1996).

27.3.2 The study of song perception

One often stated similarity between birdsong and human speech is the shared dependence of these two vocal communication signals on developmental learning. To produce functional species-typical vocalizations, both birds and humans must be exposed to "model" vocalizations early in life. The so-called "critical period" for song learning has been the topic of much research. Like any communication signal, however, the function of birdsong (in the adaptive sense) relies on accurate production *and* perception. Here we focus on the songbirds' capacity to perceive and make sense of incoming natural acoustic information, i.e., song.

What are the basic sensory capacities of the avian hearing system? What higher-level capacities exist in songbirds to process sounds as complex signals? Do songbirds have the capacity to form abstract relations among auditory stimuli? Do they form perceptual categories for their own species' song as compared with the songs of other species? How is song processed as a functional signal? Given the range of adaptive functions served by song production, how are these different "meanings" coded in the acoustics of song? And what are the neural mechanisms that underlie song processing?

27.3.3 *Song perception and the problem of vocal recognition*

In general, songbirds respond to sounds according to psychophysical principles familiar to humans. Virtually all species tested have an audiogram with a lower limit of frequency sensitivity in the region of 100–200 Hz and a higher limit in the region from 8–10 kHz, with maximum sensitivity in the range of 1–3.5 kHz, depending on the species (Fay, 1988). Likewise, the temporal resolution of hearing is similar to that observed in humans, with gap detection (between sine tones) at around 2.5 ms (Klump & Maier, 1989; Okanoya & Dooling, 1990b). Interestingly, while little is known about the information coded in birdsongs at the millisecond timescale, recent data indicate that for birds the sensitivity to fine temporal structure in complex waveforms may exceed that for humans (Dooling, Leek, Gleich, & Dent, 2002). Like speech for humans, conspecific song for birds holds functional (i.e., adaptive) significance. Because selection pressures are likely to shape the physiological mechanisms that regulate song perception, the manner in which these acoustically complex signals are processed deserves special attention.

Variation in communication signals (i.e., songs) can occur in the spectro-temporal properties of the signal itself and also in the spatial-temporal distribution of signal sources. Together, this variation leads to at least two general classes of receiver behavior. First, because not all acoustic events are of equal interest, animals must be able to dissociate appropriate target signals from irrelevant/background noise, including non-target conspecific vocalizations. This problem has been studied in the context of the so-called cocktail party effect (Cherry & Taylor, 1954) and more generally in terms of auditory stream segregation (Bregman, 1990). Despite its obvious importance, relatively few studies have addressed this phenomenon in nonhumans (e.g. Fay, 1988; MacDougall-Shackleton et al., 1998). It may be that the acoustic parameters governing stream segregation of acoustic communication signals vary dramatically from those involved in the segregation of pure tone sequences (c.f. Hulse, MacDougall-Shakleton, & Wisniewski, 1997). In any case, the basic ability is likely to be widespread. Recent reviews cover both stream segregation and the closely related topic of auditory spatial localization in nonhuman animals (Feng & Ratnam, 2000; Klump, 2000). Most research using conspecific communication signals assumes that the test subject has successfully extracted the target signal by presenting stimuli in isolation, or over a coincidently recorded low-noise background. This assumption implies an independence of localization/segregation processes and the subsequent classification behaviors that may not prove biologically realistic.

Once an auditory object is formed, a second general class of behavior emerges as these objects or events are organized into behaviorally relevant classes. For example, females might use male vocalizations to help choose a mate and therefore are likely, under appropriate conditions, to discriminate between heterospecific and conspecific songs or even the songs of different conspecific males. The presence of such distinctions, or class boundaries, implies the detection of and discrimination among multiple auditory objects along with an association between the object representations and a behavioral response. At the behavioral level, these processes are collectively referred to as perceptual recognition.

According to this definition, recognition can take many forms, depending on the specific boundaries between classes of vocalizations. Often these acoustic boundaries correspond to other behaviorally relevant distinctions (e.g., species, sex, kin, and individual). That is, they are not arbitrary but rather reflect the ecology of the particular animal under consideration. Although not all forms of recognition behavior are likely to be mediated by the same neural mechanisms, there are likely to be shared features across species, particularly when relevant classification requires discrimination among subsets of conspecific vocalizations. The recognition of communication signals based on intraspecific acoustic variation is widespread and taxonomically diverse. For example, penguin chicks can recognize the calls of their parents (Jouventin, Aubin, & Lengagne, 1999; Aubin, Jouventin, & Hildebrand, 2000). Bottlenose dolphins have individually distinctive whistles that mothers and independent offspring can use to recognize one another (Sayigh et al., 1999). Female African elephants appear able to recognize the infrasonic calls of female family, bond group, and even more distant kin (McComb et al., 2000), and female spotted hyenas can recognize specific vocalizations of their own pups (Holekamp et al., 1999).

27.3.4 *Categorization*

From a cognitive standpoint, the common ability to associate sets of vocalizations with external referents raises the possibility that such animals are able to categorize the acoustic information in vocal signals in a more formal sense. For our purposes, categorization can take two forms.

27.3.4.1 *Phonetic categorization*

First, we can ask if songbirds are capable of perceiving any features of their song categorically in the sense that humans perceive certain speech sounds categorically (Liberman et al., 1967). For example, in human speech perception there is an abrupt switch from perceiving the phoneme "ba" to perceiving it as "pa" as voice onset time (VOT) increases gradually. On either side of the critical phoneme boundary, changes in VOT have little or no effect on perception of the phoneme ("ba" remains "ba"), but across the boundary, the effect of a small change in VOT is sudden and profound as "ba" suddenly switches perceptually to "pa" (Abramson & Lisker, 1967). Phonetic categorization as described has been found in a variety of mammals (Harnad, 1987), and is strongly suggested in at least one species of songbird. Nelson and Marler (1989) found in a playback study that territorial swamp sparrows were relatively indifferent to initial swamp sparrow song syllables differing in duration until a certain critical duration was reached. At that critical duration, the song duration switched to that characteristic of a syllable with a different natural function, and the birds responded to it accordingly.

27.3.4.2 Categorization as concept formation

Apart from categorical perception in the unit-boundary sense just discussed, researchers have also asked whether songbirds are capable of assigning broad classes of natural birdsong stimuli to categories, based on same-species versus other-species song criteria, for example (Emlen, 1972; Falls, 1982; Marler, 1982). In this case, we are using the term category to define a case in which animals must place stimuli into different discriminable groups based on presumed common features, prototypes, or functions among exemplars within a group. The ability to form such categories is important for many reasons (Estes, 1994; Murphy, 2002). For example, if information can be sorted and stored in distinctive categories, there is a gain both in the efficiency with which old information can be retrieved for later use, and in the facility with which new information can be acquired and stored in memory. In fact, Dooling et al. (1992) found that budgerigars, canaries, starlings, and zebra finches classified together song exemplars according to species, but distinguished song exemplars of their own species much better than exemplars of other species. The results provide evidence for special processing of ones' own species' song, a process akin to the special processing that is involved in human speech perception as compared with processing arbitrary acoustic stimuli (e.g., Kuhl, 1989; Liberman, 1982; Mullennix & Pisoni, 1990). Similarly, budgerigars discriminate and classify human vowel sounds much as humans do (Brown, Dooling, & O'Grady, 1988; Dooling et al., 1987). Taken together, these experiments suggest that certain aspects of human speech perception are not unique to humans and may reflect more general principles of perception and categorization common to many species.

Whether or not such principles are hardwired remains somewhat of an open question. Several subtypes of the Japanese macaque "coo" vocalizations can be defined on the basis of acoustic variation (Green, 1975). Much of this work has focused on two particular subtypes of coo vocalizations, the smooth-early-high (SEH) and smooth-late-high (SLH), so-called because of the relative position of the peak of one frequency component that sweeps up and then down over the time course of the call. Although Japanese macaque mothers can discriminate the coos of their young from others (Pereira, 1986), the role of individual recognition cues in the coo vocalizations has not been investigated. Nevertheless, the SEH and SLH call types function in different behavioral contexts (Green, 1975), and Japanese macaques appear to possess a species-specific bias for discriminations involving these coos when the relevant variation is in the relative timing of the FM peak (Zoloth et al., 1979).

Although initial data suggested that the SEH and SLH calls can be perceived categorically (May, Moody, & Stebbins, 1989), more recent data from the field indicate that many adult female coo vocalizations have FM peaks within the ambiguous region between "early" and "late" prototypes (Owren & Casale, 1994). The category boundaries determined in laboratory tests do not coincide with natural variation in the distribution of calls in the field. Nonetheless, all of the results to date show clear evidence that the coo calls are perceived as perceptually distinct classes (if not categorically), and several studies provide support for the proposal that the relative position of the FM peak within the coo is the most salient cue to discrimination among different coos (Le Prell & Moody, 2000; May, Moody, & Stebbins, 1988). Amplitude cues also appear to function in call discrimination (Le Prell & Moody, 1997). Thus, the stimulus dimensions involved in "real-world" classification and/or categorization of coo calls may involve a more dynamic stimulus space than the findings suggested by the original studies.

27.4 The Songbird Model for Individual Vocal Recognition

Whether or not songbirds categorize conspecific vocalizations in the strict sense, the occurrence of basic vocal recognition is common, and its evolutionary functions are well described, having been examined more extensively here than in any other group of animals. Various forms of intraspecific vocal recognition have been observed in nearly every species of songbird studied to date (see Falls, 1982; Stoddard, 1996). In general, vocal recognition in songbirds provides for the association of specific songs with specific singers or locations, serving as a basis for decisions in more elaborate social behaviors such as female choice (Lind, Dabelsteen, & McGregor, 1997; Wiley, Hatchwell, & Davies, 1991), female preference (O'Loghlen & Beecher, 1997), and communal kin recognition (Beecher, 1991). Another complex social behavior in which individual vocal recognition plays an important role is territoriality, where it functions in both the manipulation and maintenance of territorial boundaries (e.g., Godard, 1991) and thus may have indirect effects on reproductive success (Hiebert, Stoddard, & Arcese, 1989).

27.4.1 *Song recognition in males*

27.4.1.1 *Field studies*

The function of male song in maintaining and establishing songbird territories is well established. For example, abolishing a male songbird's ability to sing has dramatic effects on his success at holding a territory (e.g., Peek, 1972), and simply broadcasting a conspecific song from an unoccupied territory leads to significantly lower rates of settlement in that territory compared to controls (Krebs, Ashcroft, & Webber, 1978). Moreover, territory residents often respond weakly, or not at all, to a neighbor singing from a familiar location but more strongly to a stranger singing from that same location. Using these facts along with a variety of clever song-playback techniques in the field, a large number of studies have demonstrated that males in many (at least 23) songbird species are capable of discriminating among neighbors and strangers on the basis of song alone. In several species, listeners are capable of recognizing individual singers on the basis of their songs (see Stoddard, 1996).

27.4.1.2 Signal variation

There are several ways that singer identity could be represented in the acoustic variation of male birdsong. In the simplest case, individual males might sing a unique song or sets of songs (i.e., repertoires), and recognition would follow by the association of specific songs with specific singers. This strategy appears to be used by song sparrows (Beecher, Campbell, & Burt, 1994), and European starlings (Gentner & Hulse, 2000). One feature of this strategy is that recognition is constrained by memory capacity. Although recognition memory capacity deserves further study, initial results suggest that the capacity of these systems is, in fact, quite high (see Gentner et al., 2000) and, at least for song sparrows, exceeds the number of exemplars that an individual is likely to face at a single time in the wild (Stoddard et al., 1992).

A second recognition strategy relies on morphological differences in the acoustics of shared song types. In both white-throated sparrows and field sparrows, the songs of neighboring territorial males share several acoustic features but vary slightly in frequency. Neighbors rely on these subtle frequency differences to recognize one another (Brooks & Falls, 1975; Nelson, 1989). Related to this is a third possible strategy for recognition. If the morphology of the vocal-production apparatus varies slightly between individuals, then this variation might impart unique spectral features, or so-called "voice characteristics," to all of an individual's vocalizations. A potential role for voice characteristics has been suggested for great tits (Weary & Krebs, 1992), but vocal recognition in song sparrows (Beecher et al., 1994) and starlings (Gentner & Hulse, 2000) is not affected by these putative cues. Finally, vocal recognition might also rely on the sequence in which multiple song types are sung. That is, different males may share song types but sing them in individually distinctive temporal patterns. The role of this final cue has not been extensively studied in songbirds, but there is some evidence to suggest that European starlings are sensitive to the sequence of motifs within familiar song bouts (Gentner & Hulse, 1998).

For species in which males sing multiple songs, the four mechanisms outlined above may not be mutually exclusive. There is no a priori reason to believe that individual vocal recognition in a single species relies on acoustic variation coded in only a single dimension, nor is there any reason to suspect that all species of songbirds use the same recognition strategies. Given the approximately 4,500 different species of songbirds – each singing acoustically distinct songs – and the occurrence of vocal recognition in a wide range of behavioral contexts, it is likely that vocal-recognition information is coded at multiple levels throughout a songbird's repertoire.

27.4.1.3 Laboratory studies

Given the likely diversity of vocal-recognition behaviors across songbird species, it is reasonable to consider whether there are corresponding peripheral perceptual specializations among songbirds that in theory might provide an "open channel" of communication within a species while limiting confusion across species. For instance, different species might concentrate the acoustic energy of their songs in defined spectral bands. This hypothesis is supported by several observations of species-specific advantages during operant discriminations of multiple conspecific and heterospecific songs in several different species (Cynx & Nottebohm, 1992; Dooling et al., 1992; Okanoya & Dooling, 1990a; Sinnott, 1980). As mentioned earlier, however, the overwhelming data from psychophysical studies of hearing in birds indicate that most basic sensory processing capabilities (e.g., frequency sensitivity) are conserved across songbird species (Dooling et al., 2000). Thus, it appears that biases for the discrimination of species-specific vocalizations, and hence mechanisms for vocal recognition, result from evolutionary or ontogenic changes in the (presumably) central processing mechanisms that underlie pattern perception. This is consistent with the more general assumption that the perceptual (and cognitive) processes underlying individual vocal recognition take the neural representation of acoustically complex signals (i.e., song) as their input. Recent laboratory studies of European starlings have addressed these questions directly by determining more precisely the form of the acoustic signal controlling recognition in this species.

27.4.1.4 *Song recognition in starlings*

Male starlings present their songs in long episodes of continuous singing referred to as bouts (see Figure 27.1 for an excerpt of male starling song). Song bouts, in turn, are composed of much smaller acoustic units referred to as motifs (Adret-Hausberger & Jenkins, 1988; Eens, Pinxten, & Verheyen, 1991), which in turn are composed of still smaller units called notes (Figure 27.1). Notes can be broadly classified by the presence of continuous energy in their spectrographic representations, and although several notes may occur in a given motif, their pattern is usually highly stereotyped between successive renditions of the same motif. One can thus consider starling song as a sequence of motifs, where each motif is an acoustically complex event. The number of unique motifs that a male starling can sing (i.e., his repertoire size) can be quite large, and consequently different song bouts from the same male are not necessarily composed of the same set of motifs. This broad acoustical variation in their song provides several potential cues that

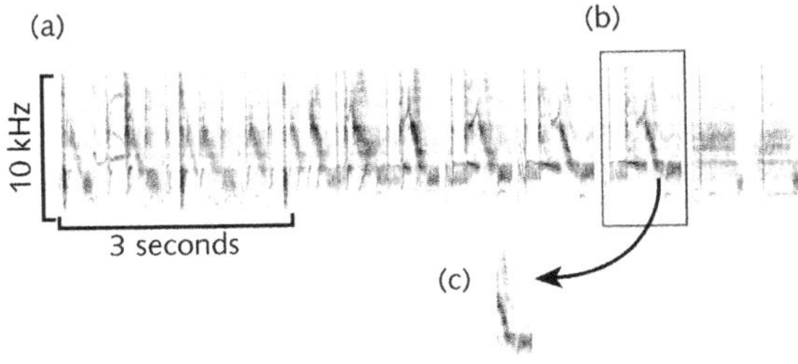

Figure 27.1 Sonogram of starling song segment. Power across the frequency spectrum is shown as a function of time. Darker regions show higher power. Starling song bouts are organized hierarchically. Normal bouts of song can last over a minute, and are comprised of series of repeated motifs. (a) Shows a short sequence of motifs as they might appear in a much longer song bout. A single motif is outlined in (b). Complete song bouts contain many different motifs. Motifs are comprised of stereotyped note patterns. An example of one note is shown in (c).

starlings might use when learning to recognize the songs of an individual conspecific and while maintaining that recognition over time. One straightforward recognition mechanism is the association of specific motifs with specific singers. Although some sharing of motifs does occur among captive males (Hausberger, 1997; Hausberger & Cousillas, 1995), the motif repertoires of different males living in the wild are generally unique (e.g., Chaiken, Böhner, & Marler, 1993; Eens, Pinxten, & Verheyen, 1989). Thus, learning which males sing which motifs can provide discriminative cues for song classification.

As shown in Figure 27.2, data from operant studies in starlings indicate that song recognition is based at the level of the motif. Starlings trained operantly to recognize individual conspecifics by one set of songs can readily generalize correct recognition to novel songs from the same singers (Gentner & Hulse, 1998). However, recognition falls to chance when these novel song bouts have no motifs in common with the training songs (Gentner et al., 2000). Likewise, starlings trained to discriminate among pairs of motifs will reverse the discrimination when transferred to the same motif sung by the opposite individual and perform at chance when transferred to novel motifs sung by the training singers. This failure to generalize correct recognition to songs composed of novel motifs, or to single novel motifs, is inconsistent with the use of individually invariant source and/or filter properties (voice characteristics) for vocal recognition. Instead, the data suggest that starlings learn to recognize the songs of individual conspecifics by attending to information contained at (or below) the level of the motif. Starlings appear to associate distinct sets of motifs (or variant motif features) with individual singers.

If starlings learn to recognize individuals by the sets of unique motifs that they sing, then once learned, it should be possible to control recognition systematically by varying the proportions of motifs in a given bout that come from two "vocally familiar" males. That is, recognition behavior ought to follow the proportional distribution of motifs from two vocally familiar males rather than the presence or absence of single diagnostic motifs from either male. The behavioral data confirm this prediction by showing that when starlings are compelled to classify conspecific songs, they do so by memorizing large numbers of unique song components (i.e., motifs) and then organizing subsets of these motifs into separate classes (Gentner & Hulse, 2000). As a cognitive recognition strategy, classifying songs according to their component (motif) structure represents a straightforward method of dealing with these complex acoustic signals. Because individual starlings tend to possess unique motif repertoires, disjoint sets of motifs will generally correspond to individual identity. Therefore, attending to the motif structure captures a significant portion of the individual variation in the signal, albeit at the expense of a large memory capacity.

The behavioral data suggest several hypotheses regarding the neural mechanisms underlying the recognition of natural (i.e., high-dimensional) acoustic events. First, the functionality of motifs as auditory objects in recognition behavior implies their explicit representation in the central nervous system. That is, the response functions of single neurons or of populations of neurons in appropriate forebrain auditory regions should reflect the segmentation of song at the level of the motif. Second, because recognition behavior requires the *learned* association between sets of motifs and singers, motif representations (or the representations

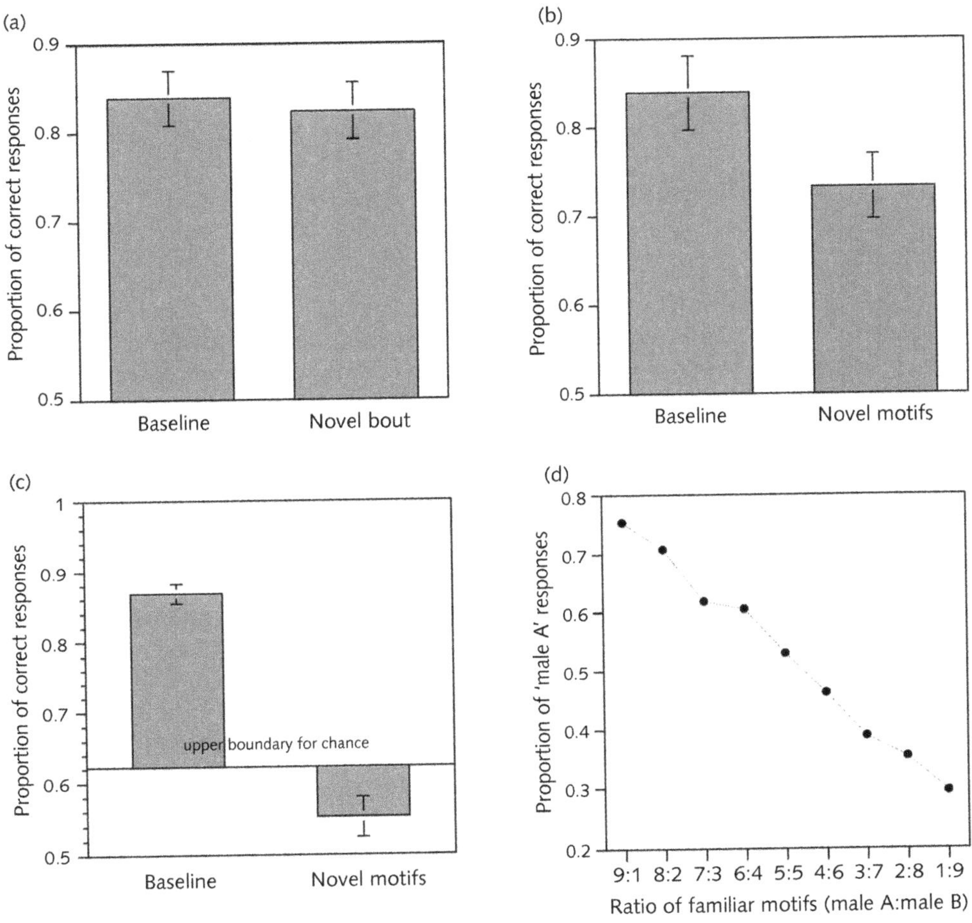

Figure 27.2 Vocal recognition behavior in European starlings. (a) Mean (±SEM) proportion of correct responses given during asymptotic performance on an operant recognition task ("Baseline"), and during initial transfer to novel songs containing familiar motifs ("Novel bout"). (b) and (c) Mean (±SEM) proportion of correct responses during transfer from the baseline training to novel songs from the same singers composed of "Novel motifs". Data in (b) show the transfer when the subjects were exposed to the training and test songs outside of the operant apparatus, whereas the data in (c) show the results for the same transfer after controlling for this experience. Note that in (c) recognition of the novel motifs falls below chance. (d) Data showing the close (and approximately linear) relationship between the statistical distribution of familiar motifs from two different singers and song recognition.

of sub-motif features that correspond to unique motifs) should reflect the behavioral relevance of specific motifs. That is, there should be a bias for representations of familiar motifs. Third, the representational mechanisms and capacity (i.e., memory) of the system should permit the acquisition of very large numbers of acoustically complex, natural objects (motifs). The nature of object representation, representational plasticity, and memory capacity are central questions for any researcher interested in the neural coding of natural vocal stimuli, including human speech and language. Below, we consider these questions in the context of the neural representation of birdsong.

27.4.2 *Neural representations of birdsong*

27.4.2.1 *Bird's own song*

Research on the neural mechanisms of birdsong has followed the ethological studies in emphasizing strongly male song learning and production. All songbirds possess a network of cytoarchitectonically distinct brain regions, referred to collectively as the "song system" (see Figure 27.3). Together, the various regions of the song system are thought to function primarily in the production and juvenile acquisition of song. The song system itself is composed of two subsystems: the vocal-motor pathway (VMP), which plays a direct role in the adult song production; and the anterior-forebrain pathway (AFP), which is thought to function primarily in vocal acquisition among juveniles, and in subsequent maintenance of song in adults. A number of comprehensive reviews on song-system neurobiology are available (e.g., Brainard & Doupe, 2002; Brenowitz, Margoliash, & Nordeen, 1997; Nottebohm, 1996). One hallmark of cells within many of the song system nuclei is their selective response to a "bird's own song," or BOS (see Margoliash, 1987). That is, one readily finds neurons throughout the song system whose firing rates and/or temporal response properties are "tuned" to

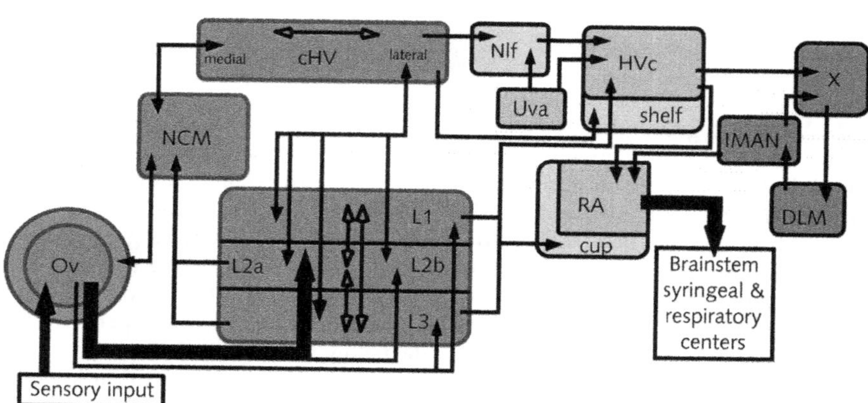

Figure 27.3 Schematic of the songbird primary auditory pathways (light gray), vocal motor pathway (VMP, gray), and anterior forebrain pathway (AFP, dark gray). Ov = nucleus ovoidalis; L1–L3 = field L complex; NCM = caudomedial neostriatum; cHV = caudoventral hyperstriatum; NIf = nucleus interfacialis; Uva = nucleus uvaeformis; RA = robust nucleus of the archistriatum; lMAN = lateral magnocellular nucleus of the anterior neostriatum; DLM = dorsolateral region of the medial thalamus; X = area X; HVc is used as the proper name. Ov comprises a core and a surround. HVc and RA have subjacent regions, the "shelf" and "cup," respectively.

the acoustics of the song that the bird sings. In the nucleus HVc (see Figure 27.3), the stimulus specificity observed for BOS has both spectral and temporal components, with responses contingent upon the presence (and absence) of acoustic energy in specific frequency bands or upon specific temporal combinations of sounds (Margoliash, 1983; Margoliash & Fortune, 1992). In addition, these so-called "BOS responses" are strongly modulated by behavioral state (Dave, Yu, & Margoliash, 1998; Schmidt & Konishi, 1998), and are, in at least some cases, observed in cells that also show strongly coupled pre-motor activity during song production (Dave & Margoliash, 2000; Yu & Margoliash, 1996). The sensory-motor integration at both the cellular- and system-level which gives rise to the BOS response is an active area of research among birdsong neuroethologists. Understanding these physiological mechanisms will likely impact the broader study of sensorimotor learning in other systems, and may be of value in understanding the perceptual role of self-generated sounds in human speech processing (see Margoliash, 2003).

Despite early suggestions that BOS selective responses in song system nuclei, specifically the VMP, might reflect a "motor theory" of song perception (*sensu* Liberman et al., 1967), recent data suggest a somewhat different interpretation. The state dependent nature of these responses, and the absence of auditory responses altogether in many VMP neurons in the awake animal (Dave et al., 1998), argue against the notion that the pathways controlling vocal output also contribute to sensory representations of song. Instead, BOS selectivity more likely reflects the involvement of acoustic feedback circuits in ongoing regulation of song production mechanisms. It now appears that only very specific sorts of auditory information, namely BOS, are admitted to the song system so that the bird can detect, and thus correct, any deviations between the intended song and that actually produced. Nonetheless, there are data that suggest a production-independent role for both HVC and the AFP in adult song perception. Lesions to lMAN in canaries affect auditory, but not visual discrimination (Burt et al., 2000); lesions to HVc in female canaries abolish female behavioral preferences for conspecific over heterospecific song (Brenowitz, 1991) and for sexually attractive song phrases over other phrases of conspecific song (Del Negro et al., 1998; but see MacDougall-Shackleton et al., 1998). In both male and female starlings, HVc lesions affect the ability to form new associations with familiar songs while leaving retention of learned conspecific song discriminations intact (Gentner et al., 2000). Clearly the role of these structures, and by extension the general role of vocal-motor systems in sensory perception and cognition, requires further study ideally through electrophysiology in awake animals.

27.4.2.2 Auditory system

Within the auditory system proper (See Figure 27.3) the links between physiological responses and vocal perception are more direct. Auditory signals impinging on the bird's ear (following the general vertebrate pathway) are coded tonotopically in the cochlea, continue through the thalamus, and into Field L2 – the avian analog to mammalian primary auditory cortex. As one moves "higher" into the central structures, away from the primary cortex, increasing selectivity for complex stimuli and species-specific vocalizations emerges (e.g., Leppelsack & Vogt, 1976; Theunissen & Doupe, 1998). The pattern of increasing response selectivity from Field L2 to the higher-order areas continues into NCM and cHV (Müller &

Leppelsack, 1985; Sen, Theunissen, & Doupe, 2001), suggesting that these regions are involved in the extraction of complex features common to song.

Neurons in NCM (see Figure 27.3) are broadly tuned to conspecific songs (Grace et al., 2003) and respond to repeated presentations of a single conspecific song in a stimulus-specific manner. The repeated presentation of a single conspecific song elicits a rapid modulation in the initial firing rate of NCM neurons (Chew et al., 1995; Stripling, Volman, & Clayton, 1997). If the same song is repeated on the order of 200 times, this initial modulation of the firing rate is no longer observed when that same song is presented on subsequent trials, even though the initial response modulation can still be observed for other conspecific songs. These stimulus-specific changes in the response properties of NCM neurons have led to the hypothesis that NCM may play an important role in individual vocal recognition. The putative role in song memory processes is supported by the fact that many neurons in NCM (and cHV) show a rapid and selective up-regulation of the immediate early gene (IEG) *zenk* in response to the presentation of conspecific songs (Mello, Vicario, & Clayton, 1992), in a manner that is sensitive to the acoustics of particular song syllables (Ribeiro et al., 1998). Interestingly, these IEG responses also habituate to the repeated presentation of the same conspecific song (Mello, Nottebohm, & Clayton, 1995) and are elevated during specific components of vocal-recognition in starlings (Gentner et al., 2001). In mammals, the homolog to *zenk* is required for expression of certain forms of long-term potentiation (LTP – a common model for learning and memory at the cellular level, in which neuronal responses, usually in hippocampal cells, remain elevated for long periods after an initial tetanic stimulation) and the consolidation of long-term memories in mice (Jones et al., 2001). This suggests that *zenk* expression in NCM and cHV may be related to learning about conspecific songs.

Recent data demonstrate directly the role of cmHV in learned recognition of song. After training starlings to recognize two sets of conspecific songs, Gentner and Margoliash (2003) observed that single neurons and populations of neurons in the medial cHV respond selectively to acoustic features contained in those songs that the birds had learned to recognize. In contrast, no neurons were selective for similar features in songs that were novel to the birds. This finding argues very strongly that the response functions of cmHV, at both the single unit and the population level, are a direct product of each bird's unique sensory experience. Mechanisms of experience-dependent plasticity act to modify the responses of cmHV neurons based on the functional demands of song recognition. Several additional results from this study are consistent with this proposal. First, the spectro-temporal tuning properties of cmHV cells correspond closely to song features correlated with individual motifs. That is, the same auditory objects that control recognition behavior also predict the responses of selective cells in cmHV. Second, the variation in neuronal response strength among the familiar songs was dependent upon the reinforcement contingencies used for recognition training. For animals trained with a go/no-go procedure to discriminate between two sets of songs, the S+ songs elicited the significantly stronger responses than S– songs, which in turn elicited significantly stronger responses than novel songs. When positive reinforcement is available for both sets of songs, the response strengths associated with each set of familiar songs are similar, but still greater than those associated with novel songs. Thus, the response profiles of neurons in cmHV are shaped not only by task relevant acoustic features of conspecific songs in a "bottom-up" fashion, but also by so-called "top-down" mechanisms presumably through reward systems (Gentner & Margoliash, 2003).

27.5 Conclusions

In the absence of an efficient coding scheme, the high-dimensionality and range of natural stimuli could easily overwhelm the capacity and fidelity of any representational system. In songbirds coding efficiency is improved by two mechanisms. First, the song is parsed into perceptual objects (i.e., motifs) that capture the behaviorally relevant variation among very complex signals (songs). Second, the representation of these complex auditory objects is dynamic, and is closely dependent upon the functional demands of the task at hand. At the present time, it unclear whether or not these dynamic, functional object representations arise from the convergence of more static representations of embedded, simpler song features, or more general representations of the input signal. Regardless, the songbird data raise the interesting hypothesis that similarly well-defined dynamic representations of functional speech units may exist in humans, corresponding perhaps to the articulatory gestures that underlie single phonemes or high-probability phonological patterns relevant in specific contexts.

It is clear that human language processing, and thus by necessity the processing of speech, displays innumerable aspects that far exceed the perceptual and cognitive abilities of any other species. Human language is inarguably special in many ways. Still, like any other behavior it is highly constrained, and many of the constraints on speech perception and production are shared with other organisms that rely on vocal communication. We have tried to point out some of those constraints. While the underlying neural mechanisms that regulate any one biological system should never be expected to map one-to-one onto another system, we gain fundamental new knowledge by understanding both the differences and the similarities between systems.

REFERENCES

Abramson, A. & Lisker, L. (1967). Discriminability along the voice continuum: Cross-language tests. *Proceedings of the Sixth International Congress of Phonetic Sciences* (pp. 569–73). Prague, Czech Republic.

Adret-Hausberger, M. & Jenkins, P. F. (1988). Complex organization of the warbling song in starlings. *Behaviour*, 107, 138–56.

Aubin, T., Jouventin, P., & Hildebrand, C. (2000). Penguins use the two-voice system to recognize each other. *Proceedings of the Royal Society of London B Biological Sciences*, 267, 1081–7.

Ball, G. F. & Hulse, S. H. (1998). Bird song. *American Psychologist*, 53, 37–58.

Beecher, M. D. (1991). Successes and failures of parent–offspring recognition in animals. In P. G. Hepper (ed.), *Kin Recognition* (pp. 94–124). Cambridge: Cambridge University Press.

Beecher, M. D., Campbell, S. E., & Burt, J. (1994). Song perception in the song sparrow: Birds classify by song type but not by singer. *Animal Behaviour*, 47, 1343–51.

Brainard, M. S. & Doupe, A. J. (2002). Auditory feedback in learning and maintenance of vocal behaviour. *Nature Reviews Neuroscience*, 1, 31–40.

Bregman, A. S. (1990). The auditory scene. In *Auditory Scene Analysis: The Perceptual Organization of Sound*. Cambridge, MA: MIT Press.

Brenowitz, E. A. (1991). Altered perception of species-specific song by female birds after lesions of a forebrain nucleus. *Science*, 251, 303–5.

Brenowitz, E. A., Margoliash, D., & Nordeen, K. W. (1997). An introduction to birdsong and the avian song system. *Journal of Neurobiology*, 33, 495–500.

Brooks, R. J. & Falls, J. B. (1975). Individual recognition by song in white-throated sparrows. III: Song features used in individual recognition. *Canadian Journal of Zoology*, 53, 1749–61.

Brown, J. L. & Hunsperger, R. W. (1963). Neuroethology and the motivation of agonistic behavior. *Animal Behavior*, 11, 439–48.

Brown, S. D., Dooling, R. J., & O'Grady, K. (1988). Perceptual organization of acoustic stimuli by budgerigars (*Melopsittacus undulatus*). III: Contact calls. *Journal of Comparative Psychology*, 102, 236–47.

Burt, J. M., Lent, K. L., Beecher, M. D., & Brenowitz, E. A. (2000). Lesions of the anterior forebrain song control pathway in female canaries affect song perception in an operant task. *Journal of Neurobiology*, 42, 1–13.

Camhi, J. M. (1984). *Neuroethology: Nerve Cells and the Natural Behavior of Animals*. Sunderland, MA: Sinauer Associates.

Catchpole, C. K. & Slater, P. J. B. (1995). *Bird Song: Biological Themes and Variations* (1st edition). Cambridge: Cambridge University Press.

Chaiken, M., Böhner, J., & Marler, P. (1993). Song acquisition in European starlings, Sturnus vulgaris: A comparison of the songs of live-tutored, tape-tutored, untutored, and wild-caught males. *Animal Behaviour*, 46, 1079–90.

Cherry, E. & Taylor, W. (1954). Some further experiments upon the recognition of speech, with one and with two ears. *Journal of the Acoustical Society of America*, 26, 554–9.

Chew, S. J., Mello, C., Nottebohm, F., Jarvis, E. D., & Vicario, D. S. (1995). Decrements in auditory responses to a repeated conspecific song are long-lasting and require two periods of protein synthesis in the songbird forebrain. *Proceedings of the National Academy of Science*, 92, 3406–10.

Chomsky, N. (1959). A review of B. F. Skinner's *Verbal Behavior*. *Language*, 35, 26–58.

Chomsky, N. (2000). *New Horizons in the Study of Language and Mind*. New York: Cambridge University Press.

Cynx, J. & Nottebohm, F. (1992). Role of gender, season, and familiarity in discrimination of conspecific song by zebra finches (Taeniopygia guttata). *Proceedings of the National Academy of Science*, 89, 1368–71.

Dave, A. S. & Margoliash, D. (2000). Song replay during sleep and computational rules for sensorimotor vocal learning. *Science*, 290, 812–16.

Dave, A. S., Yu, A. C., & Margoliash, D. (1998). Behavioral state modulation of auditory activity in a vocal motor system. *Science*, 282, 2250–4.

Del Negro, C., Gahr, M., Leboucher, G., & Kreutzer, M. (1998). The selectivity of sexual responses to song displays: Effects of partial chemical lesion of the HVC in female canaries. *Behavioural Brain Research*, 96, 151–9.

Dooling, R. J., Brown, S. D., Klump, G. M., & Okanoya, K. (1992). Auditory perception of conspecific and heterospecific vocalizations in birds: Evidence for special processes. *Journal of Comparative Psychology*, 106, 20–8.

Dooling, R. J., Leek, M. R., Gleich, O., & Dent, M. L. (2002). Auditory temporal resolution in birds: Discrimination of harmonic complexes. *Journal of the Acoustical Society of America*, 112, 748–59.

Dooling, R. J., Lohr, B., & Dent, M. L. (2000). Hearing in birds and reptiles. In R. J. Dooling, R. R. Fay, & A. N. Popper (eds.), *Comparative Hearing: Birds and Reptiles* (pp. 308–59). New York: Springer.

Dooling, R. J., Park, T. J., Brown, S. D., & Okanoya, K. (1987). Perceptual organization of acoustic stimuli by budgerigars (Melopsittacus undulatus). II: Vocal signals. *Journal of Comparative Psychology*, 101, 367–81.

Doupe, A. J. & Kuhl, P. K. (1999). Birdsong and human speech: Common themes and mechanisms. *Annual Review of Neuroscience*, 22, 567–31.

Eens, M., Pinxten, M., & Verheyen, R. F. (1989). Temporal and sequential organization of song bouts in the European starling. *Ardea*, 77, 75–86.

Eens, M., Pinxten, R., & Verheyen, R. F. (1991). Organization of song in the European starling: Species-specificity and individual differences. *Belgian Journal of Zoology*, 121, 257–78.

Emlen, S. T. (1972). An experimental analysis of the parameters of bird song eliciting species recognition. *Behaviour*, 41, 130–71.

Estes, W. K. (1994). *Classification and Cognition*. New York: Oxford University Press.

Falls, J. B. (1982). Individual recognition by sound in birds. In D. E. Kroodsma & E. H. Miller (eds.), *Acoustic Communication in Birds* (pp. 237–78). New York: Academic Press.

Fay, R. R. (1988). *Hearing in Vertebrates: A Psychophysics Databook*. Winnetka, IL: Hill-Fay Associates.

Feng, A. S. & Ratnam, R. (2000). Neural basis of hearing in real-world situations. *Annual Review of Psychology*, 51, 699–725.

Gazzaniga, M. S. (ed.) (1995). *The Cognitive Neurosciences*. Cambridge, MA: MIT Press.

Gentner, T. Q. & Hulse, S. H. (1998). Perceptual mechanisms for individual vocal recognition in European starlings, Sturnus vulgaris. *Animal Behaviour*, 56, 579–94.

Gentner, T. Q. & Hulse, S. H. (2000). Perceptual classification based on the component structure of song in European starlings. *Journal of the Acoustical Society of America*, 107, 3369–81.

Gentner, T. Q. & Margoliash, D. (2003). Neuronal populations and single cells representing learned auditory objects. *Nature*, 424, 669–74.

Gentner, T. Q., Hulse, S. H., Bentley, G. E., & Ball, G. F. (2000). Individual vocal recognition and the effect of partial lesions to HVc on discrimination, learning, and categorization of conspecific song in adult songbirds. *Journal of Neurobiology*, 42, 117–33.

Gentner, T. Q., Hulse, S. H., Duffy, D., & Ball, G. F. (2001). Response biases in auditory forebrain regions of female songbirds following exposure to sexually relevant variation in male song. *Journal of Neurobiology*, 46, 48–58.

Godard, R. (1991). Long-term memory for individual neighbors in a migratory songbird. *Nature*, 350, 228–9.

Grace, J. A., Amin, N., Singh, N. C., & Theunissen, F. E. (2003). Selectivity for conspecific song in the zebra finch auditory forebrain. *Journal of Neurophysiology*, 89, 472–87.

Grasse, P. (ed.) (1956). *L'Instinct dans le compartement des animaux et de l'homme*. Paris: Masson.

Green, S. (1975). Variation of vocal pattern with social situation in the Japanese monkey (*Macaca fuscata*): A field study. In L. A. Rosenblum (ed.), *Primate Behavior* (pp. 1–102). New York: Academic Press.

Harnad, S. (1987). *Categorical Perceptions: The Groundwork of Cognition*. Cambridge: Cambridge University Press.

Hausberger, M. (1997). Social influences on song acquisition and sharing in the European starling (*Sturnus vulgaris*). In C. Snowden & M. Hausberger (eds.), *Social Influences on Vocal Development* (pp. 128–56). Cambridge: Cambridge University Press.

Hausberger, M. & Cousillas, H. (1995). Categorization in birdsong: From behavioural to neuronal responses. *Behavioural Processes*, 35, 83–91.

Hauser, M. D., Chomsky, N., & Fitch, W. T. (2002). The faculty of language: What is it, who has it, and how did it evolve? *Science*, 298, 1569–79.

Hiebert, S. M., Stoddard, P. K., & Arcese, P. (1989). Repertoire size, territory acquisition and reproductive success in the song sparrow. *Animal Behaviour*, 37, 266–73.

Hinde, R. A. (1970). *Animal Behaviour* (2nd edition). New York: McGraw-Hill.

Hinde, R. A. (1982). *Ethology: Its Nature and Relations with Other Sciences.* New York: Oxford University Press.

Holekamp, K. E., Boydston, E. E., Szkman, M., Graham, I., Nutt, K. J., Birch, S., & Piskiel, A. (1999). Vocal recognition in the spotted hyena and its possible implications regarding the evolution of intelligence. *Animal Behaviour*, 58, 383–95.

Hulse, S. H., MacDougall-Shackleton, S. A., & Wisniewski, A. B. (1997). Auditory scene analysis by song birds: Stream segregation of birdsong by European starlings (*Sturnus vulgaris*). *Journal of Comparative Psychology*, 111, 3–13.

Immelmann, K. & Beer, C. G. (1989). *A Dictionary of Ethology*. Cambridge, MA: Harvard University Press.

Jones, M. W., Errington, M. L., French, P. J., Fine, A., Bliss, T. V., Garel, S., Charnay, P., Bozon, B., Laroche, S., & Davis, S. (2001). A requirement for the immediate early gene Zif268 in the expression of late LTP and long-term memories. *Nature Neuroscience*, 4, 289–96.

Jouventin, P., Aubin, T., & Lengagne, T. (1999). Finding a parent in a king penguin colony: The acoustic system of individual recognition. *Animal Behaviour*, 57, 1175–83.

Kluender, K. R., Diehl, R. L., & Killeen, P. R. (1987). Japanese quail can learn phonetic categories. *Science*, 237, 1195–7.

Klump, G. M. (2000). Sound localization in birds. In R. J. Dooling, R. R. Fay, & A. N. Popper (eds.), *Comparative Hearing: Birds and Reptiles* (pp. 249–307). New York: Springer.

Klump, G. M. & Maier, E. H. (1989). Gap detection in the starling (*Sturnus vulgaris*). I: Psychophysical thresholds. *Journal of Comparative Physiology*, A 164, 531–8.

Krebs, J., Ashcroft, R., & Webber, M. (1978). Song repertoires and territory defense in the great tit. *Nature*, 271, 539–42.

Kroodsma, D. E. & Byers, B. E. (1991). The functions of bird song. *American Zoologist*, 31, 318–28.

Kuhl, P. K. (1989). On babies, birds, modules, and mechanisms: A comparative approach to acquisition of vocal communication. In R. J. Dooling & S. H. Hulse (eds.), *The Comparative Psychology of Audition: Perceiving Complex Sounds* (pp. 379–419). Hillsdale, NJ: Lawrence Erlbaum.

Kuhl, P. K. & Miller, J. D. (1975). Speech perception by the chinchilla: Voiced-voiceless distinction in alveolar plosive consonants. *Science*, 190, 69–72.

Kuhl, P. K. & Miller, J. D. (1978). Speech perception by the chinchilla: Identification function for synthetic VOT stimuli. *Journal of the Acoustical Society of America*, 63, 905–17.

Le Prell, C. G. & Moody, D. B. (1997). Perceptual salience of acoustic features of Japanese monkey coo calls. *Journal of Comparative Psychology*, 111, 261–74.

Le Prell, C. G. & Moody, D. B. (2000). Factors influencing the salience of temporal cues in the discrimination of synthetic Japanese monkey (*Macaca fuscata*) coo calls. *Journal of Experimental Psychology: Animal Behavior Processes*, 26, 261–73.

Lenneberg, E. (1967). *Biological Foundations of Language*. New York: John Wiley & Sons.

Leppelsack, H. J. & Vogt, M. (1976). Response to auditory neurons in the forebrain of a song bird to stimulation with species-specific sounds. *Journal of Comparative Physiology*, 107, 263–74.

Levin, R. (1996). Song behavior and reproductive strategies in a duetting wren, Thryothorus nigricapillus. II: Playback studies. *Animal Behaviour*, 52, 1107–17.

Liberman, A. M. (1982). On finding that speech is special. *American Psychologist*, 37, 148–67.

Liberman, A. M. (1996). *Speech: A Special Code*. Cambridge, MA: Bradford Books/ MIT Press.

Liberman, A. M., Cooper, F. S., Shankweiler, D. P., & Studdert-Kennedy, M. (1967). Perception of the speech code. *Psychological Review*, 74, 431–61.

Lind, H., Dabelsteen, T., & McGregor, P. K. (1997). Female great tits can identify mates by song. *Animal Behaviour*, 52, 667–71.

MacDougall-Shackleton, S. A., Hulse, S. H., Gentner, T. Q., & White, W. (1998). Auditory scene analysis by European starlings (Sturnus vulgaris): Perceptual segregation of tone sequences. *Journal of the Acoustical Society of America*, 103, 3581–7.

Margoliash, D. (1983). Acoustic parameters underlying the responses of song-specific neurons in the white-crowned sparrow. *Journal of Neuroscience*, 3, 1039–57.

Margoliash, D. (1987). Neural plasticity in birdsong learning. In J. P. Rauschecker & P. Marler (eds.), *Imprinting and Cortical Plasticity* (pp. 23–54). New York: Plenum.

Margoliash, D. (2003). Offline learning and the role of autogenous speech: New suggestions from birdsong research. *Speech Communication*, 41, 165–78.

Margoliash, D. & Fortune, E. (1992). Temporal and harmonic combination-sensitive neurons in the zebra finch's HVc. *Journal of Neuroscience*, 12, 4309–26.

Marler, P. R. (1970). Birdsong and speech development: Could there be parallels? *American Scientist*, 58, 669–73.

Marler, P. R. (1982). Avian and primate communication: The problem of natural categories. *Neuroscience and Biobehavioral Reviews*, 6, 87–94.

May, B., Moody, D. B., & Stebbins, W. C. (1988). The significant features of Japanese macaque coo sounds: A psychophysical study. *Animal Behaviour*, 36, 1432–44.

May, B., Moody, D. B., & Stebbins, W. C. (1989). Categorical perception of conspecific communication sounds by Japanese macaques, *Macaca fuscata*. *Journal of the Acoustical Society of America*, 85, 837–47.

McComb, R., Moss, C. F., Sayialel, S., & Baker, L. (2000). Unusually extensive networks of vocal recognition in African elephants. *Animal Behaviour*, 59, 1103–9.

Mello, C., Nottebohm, F., & Clayton, D. F. (1995). Repeated exposure to one song leads to a rapid and persistent decline in an immediate early gene's response to that song in zebra finch telencephalon. *Journal of Neuroscience*, 15, 6919–25.

Mello, C., Vicario, D. S., & Clayton, D. F. (1992). Song presentation induces gene expression in the songbird forebrain. *Proceedings of the National Academy of Science*, 89, 6818–22.

Mullennix, J. W. & Pisoni, D. B. (1990). Stimulus variability and processing dependencies in speech perception. In R. J. Dooling & S. H. Hulse (eds.), *The Comparative Psychology of Audition: Perceiving Complex Sounds* (pp. 97–128). Hillsdale, NJ: Lawrence Erlbaum.

Müller, C. M. & Leppelsack, H. J. (1985). Feature extraction and tonotopic organization in the avian forebrain. *Experimental Brain Research*, 59, 587–99.

Murphy, G. L. (2002). *The Big Book of Concepts*. Cambridge, MA: MIT Press.

Nelson, D. A. (1989). Song frequency as a cue for recognition of species and individuals in the field sparrow (Spizella pusilla). *Journal of Comparative Psychology*, 103, 171–6.

Nelson, D. A. & Marler, P. (1989). Categorical perception of a natural stimulus continuum: birdsong. *Science*, 244, 976–8.

Nottebohm, F. (1975). Vocal behavior in birds. In D. S. Farner & J. R. King (eds.), *Avian Biology*, vol. 5 (pp. 287–332). New York: Academic Press.

Nottebohm, F. (1996). The King Solomon lectures in neuroethology: A white canary on Mount Acropolis. *Journal of Comparative Physiology*, A 179, 149–56.

Okanoya, K. & Dooling, R. J. (1990a). Song-syllable perception in song sparrows (*melospiza melodia*) and swamp sparrows (*melospiza georgiana*): An approach from animal psychophysics. *Bulletin of the Psychonomic Society*, 28, 221–4.

Okanoya, K. & Dooling, R. J. (1990b). Detection of gaps in noise by budgerigars (*Melopsittacus undulatus*) and zebra finches (*Poephila guttata*). *Hearing Research*, 50, 185–92.

O'Loghlen, A. L. & Beecher, M. D. (1997). Sexual preferences for mate song types in female song sparrows. *Animal Behaviour*, 53, 835–41.

Owren, M. J. & Casale, T. M. (1994). Variations in fundamental frequency peak position in Japanese macaque (*Macaca fuscata*) coo calls. *Journal of Comparative Psychology*, 108, 291–7.

Peek, F. W. (1972). An experimental study of the territorial function of vocal and visual display in the male red-winged blackbird (*Agelaius phoeniceus*). *Animal Behaviour*, 20, 112–18.

Pereira, M. R. (1986). Maternal recognition of juvenile offspring coo vocalizations in Japanese macaques. *Animal Behaviour*, 34, 935–7.

Pinker, S. (1994). *The Language Instinct*. New York: William Morrow & Co.

Ribeiro, S., Cecchi, G. A., Magnasco, M. O., & Mello, C. (1998). Toward a song code: Evidence for a syllabic representation in the canary brain. *Neuron*, 21, 359–71.

Sayigh, L. S., Tyack, P. L., Wells, R. S., Solow, A. R., Scott, M. D., & Irvine, A. B. (1999). Individual recognition in wild bottlenose dolphins: A field test using playback experiments. *Animal Behaviour*, 57, 41–50.

Schmidt, M. F. & Konishi, M. (1998). Gating of auditory responses in the vocal control system of awake songbirds. *Nature Neuroscience*, 1, 513–18.

Searcy, W. A. & Andersson, M. (1986). Sexual selection and the evolution of song. *Annual Review of Ecology and Systematics*, 17, 507–33.

Sen, K., Theunissen, F. E., & Doupe, A. J. (2001). Feature analysis of natural sounds in the songbird auditory forebrain. *Journal of Neurophysiology*, 86, 1445–58.

Sherman, P. W. (1988). The levels of analysis. *Animal Behaviour*, 36, 616–19.

Sinnott, J. M. (1980). Species-specific coding in bird song. *Journal of the Acoustical Society of America*, 68, 494–7.

Skinner, B. F. (1957). *Verbal Behavior*. New York: Appleton-Century-Crofts.

Stoddard, P. K. (1996). Vocal recognition of neighbors by territorial passerines. In D. E. Kroodsma & E. H. Miller (eds.), *Ecology and Evolution of Acoustic Communication in Birds* (pp. 356–74). Ithaca, NY: Cornell University Press.

Stoddard, P. K., Beecher, M. D., Loesche, P., & Campbell, S. E. (1992). Memory does not constrain individual recognition in a bird with song repertoires. *Behaviour*, 122, 274–87.

Stripling, R., Volman, S. F., & Clayton, D. F. (1997). Response modulation in the zebra finch neostriatum: Relationship to nuclear gene regulation. *Journal of Neuroscience*, 17, 3883–93.

Theunissen, F. E. & Doupe, A. J. (1998). Temporal and spectral sensitivity of complex auditory neurons in the nucleus HVc of male zebra finches. *Journal of Neuroscience*, 18, 3786–802.

Thorpe, W. H. (1961). *The Biology of Vocal Communication and Expression in Birds*. London: Cambridge University Press.

Tinbergen, N. (1951). *The Study of Instinct*. Oxford: Clarendon Press.

Tinbergen, N. (1963). On aims and methods of ethology. *Zeitschrift für Tierpsychologie*, 20, 410–33.

Trout, J. D. (2001). The biological basis of speech: What to infer from talking to the animals. *Psychological Review*, 108, 523–49.

von Uexküll, J. (1957[1934]). A stroll through the worlds of animals and men. In Claire H. Schiller (ed. and trans.), *Instinctive Behavior: The Development of a Modern Concept*, (pp. 5–80). New York: International Universities Press.

Weary, D. M. & Krebs, J. R. (1992). Great tits classify songs by individual voice characteristics. *Animal Behaviour*, 43, 283–7.

Wiley, R. H., Hatchwell, B. J., & Davies, N. B. (1991). Recognition of individual male song by female dunnocks: a mechanism increasing the number of copulatory partners and reproductive success. *Ethology*, 88, 145–53.

Yu, A. & Margoliash, D. (1996). Temporal hierarchical control of singing in birds. *Science*, 273, 1871–5.

Zoloth, S. R., Peterson, M. R., Beecher, M. D., Green, S. G., Marler, P., Moody, D. B., & Stebbins, W. C. (1979). Species-specific perceptual processing of vocal sounds by monkeys. *Science*, 204, 870–3.

Index

Lightning Source UK Ltd.
Milton Keynes UK
UKOW05f0404150416

272275UK00001B/2/P